CREATING INCLUSIVE CLASSROOMS
Effective and Reflective Practices for All Students

Fifth Edition

Spencer J. Salend
State University of New York at New Paltz

Upper Saddle River, New Jersey
Columbus, Ohio

Library of Congress Cataloging in Publication Data

Salend, Spencer J.
  Creating inclusive classrooms : effective and reflective practices for all students / Spencer J. Salend.—
5th ed.
    p. cm.
  Includes bibliographical references and indexes.
  ISBN 0-13-140813-5 (pbk.)
  1. Inclusive education—United States. 2. Maintstreaming in education—United States. 3.
Curriculum planning—United States. 4. Classroom management—United States. 5.
Children with disabilities—Education.—United States. I. Title.

LC1201.S24 2005
371.9'046—dc22   2004044556

Vice President and Executive Publisher: Jeffery W. Johnston
Acquisitions Editor: Allyson Sharp
Development Editor: Heather Doyle Fraser
Editorial Assistant: Kathleen S. Burk
Production Editor: Sheryl Glicker Langner
Design Coordinator: Diane C. Lorenzo
Photo Coordinator: Cynthia Cassidy
Cover Design: Kristi Holmes
Cover Image: Laura DeSantis
Production Manager: Laura Messerly
Director of Marketing: Ann Castel Davis
Marketing Manager: Autumn Purdy
Marketing Coordinator: Tyra Poole

This book was set in New Caledonia by Carlisle Communications, Ltd. It was printed and bound by
Courier Kendallville, Inc. The cover was printed by The Lehigh Press Inc.

PHOTO CREDITS: Richard Hutchings/Photo Researchers, Inc., p. 1; Anthony Magnacca/Merrill, pp. 8, 17, 108, 120, 124, 155, 162, 254, 286, 302, 317, 353, 372, 395, 427, 438, 441, 457, 468, 475, 518; Scott Cunningham/Merrill, pp. 2, 46, 70, 223, 225, 238, 248, 273, 282, 334, 346, 349, 452, 494, 508; Paul Conklin/PhotoEdit, p. 12; Michael Newman/PhotoEdit, pp. 21, 265; Larry Hamill/Merrill, pp. 23, 312, 378, 402; Richard Hutchings/PhotoEdit, p. 36; Laura Dwight/Laura Dwight Photography, p. 60; Andy Crawford/Dorling Kindersley Media Library, p. 86; David Young-Wolff/Photo Edit, pp. 89, 404, 483; Tom Watson/Merrill, pp. 101, 324, 333, 389; Richard Abarno/Corbis/Stock Market, p. 111; U. S. Census Bureau, pp. 135, 161, 257; John Paul Endress/Silver Burdett Ginn, p. 143; Todd Yarrington/Merrill, pp. 156, 229, 414; David Mager/Pearson Learning, p. 173; Robin L. Sachs/PhotoEdit, p. 186; Nancy Acevedo, p. 195; Mary Kate Denny/PhotoEdit, p. 208; PH School, p. 231; Karen Mancinelli/Pearson Learning, p. 292; Bill Aron/PhotoEdit, p. 358; KS Studios/Merrill, p. 384; Silver Burdett Ginn, p. 418; Jonathan Nourok/PhotoEdit, p. 422 ; SuperStock, Inc., p. 489; Grantpix/Photo Researchers, Inc., p. 493; Robin Sachs/PhotoEdit, p. 499; Peggy Greb/Agricultural Research Service/USDA, p. 502; Laima Druskis/PH College, p. 522; Gabe Palmer/Corbis, p. 533.

Pearson Education Ltd.
Pearson Education Singapore Pte. Ltd.
Pearson Education Canada, Ltd.
Pearson Education–Japan

Pearson Education Australia Pty. Limited
Pearson Education North Asia Ltd.
Pearson Educación de Mexico, S.A. de C.V.
Pearson Education Malaysia Pte. Ltd.

10 9 8 7 6 5 4 3
ISBN: 0-13-140813-5

Preface

As reflections of society, our nation's schools have historically been challenged to respond to various societal changes and mandates. The movement toward inclusion has developed as a dynamic way to meet these educational challenges. However, there is still a considerable gap between theory and practice. This book is intended to fill that gap by keeping the perspectives of teachers, students, and families in mind, and translating current research on inclusion into effective and reflective classroom practices that address and expand the realities of the classroom setting. Within each chapter are numerous text-based and CD-ROM video-based classroom examples and case studies of real situations that educators, students, and family members encounter in inclusive classrooms as well as guidelines, strategies, technology, and procedures that have been used to address these situations to educate *all students* successfully in inclusive classrooms.

The book is designed to serve as a text for undergraduate, graduate, and in-service courses for teachers, ancillary support personnel, and administrators interested in acquiring the knowledge, skills, and dispositions to educate *all learners*. Because of its focus on instructional procedures and collaboration, the book also can serve as a supplementary text for a course on instructional methods or consultation.

ORGANIZATION AND APPROACH

The book is organized into four parts. Part I includes Chapters 1, 2, and 3 and introduces you to the foundations and fundamentals of inclusion and the challenges of its implementation. Part II includes Chapters 4, 5, 6, and 7 and provides you with strategies for creating an inclusive environment that supports learning for *all students*. Part III includes Chapters 8, 9, 10, and 11 and offers you strategies to differentiate instruction to promote the learning of *all students* within inclusive educational settings. Part IV consists of Chapter 12, which offers a framework and specific strategies and resources for evaluating inclusion programs in terms of individual and programmatic progress.

A Principled Philosophy

The following principles of effective inclusion also provide a framework for this book. These four principles—*all learners and equal access, individual strengths and needs and diversity, reflective practices and differentiated instruction,* and *community and collaboration*—are integrated into each chapter of the book and demonstrate that inclusion is not just a government mandate but a principled philosophy of reflective, effective teaching for individualizing the educational system for *all students*.

These four principles, along with the incorporation of diversity and instructional technology into each chapter, make the book consistent with the professional standards for preparing teachers to work in today's diverse classrooms established by the Council for Exceptional Children (CEC), Educational Testing Service (PRAXIS), and the Interstate New Teacher Assessment and Support Consortium (INTASC). The summary questions at the end of each chapter provide you with the alignment of these standards to the content in the book. The principles, content, and innovative pedagogical and technological features also are designed to help you become an effective and reflective practitioner who is able to think critically about your values, beliefs, and practices and to refine your professional practices to facilitate the learning of *all students*.

A Non-Categorical Approach

The book is also organized to serve as a model for creating inclusive classrooms for *all students*. It is meant to facilitate your development of a holistic approach to educating students while focusing on individual strengths and needs rather than on global disability characteristics. Thus, it is not separated into chapters by disability category or cultural and linguistic background that imply and focus on the differences that have been used to segregate students from one another. Rather, the book approaches inclusion as an ongoing, dynamic process for *all students*. Chapter titles and content relate to and address the key factors that contribute to effective and reflective practices for educating *all students* in inclusive settings. Instead of separate chapters on students with various disabilities or students from culturally and linguistically diverse backgrounds, information and classroom-based examples related to these students as well as other students are integrated and embedded in each chapter. It is also important to note that strategies appropriate for one group of students also can be used with other groups of students.

NEW ADDITIONS AND SPECIAL FEATURES

Content Coverage

Each chapter has been significantly revised to reflect not only current research on what is happening in the field but also how these changes are affecting educators, students, and families, and the delivery of effective instructional programs to *all students*. Among the changes you will see are:

◇ A section on IDEA (immediately following the Preface) that contains the latest information on the Individuals with Disabilities Education Act (IDEA) and how this law will affect classroom teachers.

◇ More elementary and secondary classroom examples presented in each chapter.

◇ New content related to *diversity, collaboration,* and *technology* integrated into each chapter.

◇ New figures in Chapter 1—the first *contrasts inclusion and mainstreaming* and the second *compares the IDEA and Section 504* and *information on the No Child Left Behind Act.*

◇ A broader and more detailed discussion of *the special education identification process,* and *guidelines for developing IEPs and implementing them in inclusive settings* in Chapter 2. Chapter 2 also includes current information about *students with high-incidence and low-incidence disabilities,* and *strategies for helping them access and succeed in the general education curriculum.*

◇ In Chapter 3, additional information related to educating *students who are gifted and talented* as well as the latest research and programs on *differentiating cultural and language differences from learning problems* and teaching *students from culturally and linguistically diverse backgrounds.*

◈ An expanded discussion of effective communication and teaming skills, person-centered planning, cooperative teaching, professional development, advocating for students and their families, and communicating with families in Chapter 4.

◈ Expanded coverage on strategies and resources for *facilitating an acceptance of individual differences and friendships* between your students, including *ways you can instill inclusive values in students*, and specific activities to *foster religious diversity and a global perspective, and to deal with issues of fairness and insensitive acts* in Chapter 5.

◈ Chapter 6 now contains additional and updated coverage on *generalization, self-advocacy, postsecondary options, and self-determination* to help students make the transition to inclusive settings.

◈ New and expanded sections on *building relationships with and among students, teaching social skills, positive behavioral supports, and bullying prevention strategies and programs* in Chapter 7.

◈ Revisions and updates to Chapters 8, 9, 10, and 11 include the latest on differentiating instruction, motivating students (see Chapter 9), using technology to support student learning, and using research-based strategies for teaching various content areas and fostering students' literacy development (see Chapter 10).

◈ Updated sections in Chapter 12 that offer you *information and sample assessment devices to evaluate the success of your inclusion program.* In addition, this chapter also provides you with new information on *grading students, using instructional rubrics, testing accommodations, diploma options,* and *test-taking skills* which can assist you in helping students perform at their optimal levels on standardized and high-stakes testing.

Pedagogical Elements and Special Features

Within each chapter are innovative features designed to help you understand, personalize, and reflect upon the content presented in the book, and promote your use of effective practices and instructional technology. These features include:

◈ *Chapter-opening focus questions* that serve as advance organizers and provide a structure for the chapter content;

◈ *Chapter-opening vignettes* of a student or teacher, or both, that depict the issues discussed within the chapter;

◈ *Classroom-based examples and case studies* of teachers implementing effective inclusive educational practices in their classrooms;

◈ *Ideas for Implementation* that offer practical examples of the application of techniques in the book that are effective for *all students* educated in inclusive classrooms; and

◈ *Examples of effective elementary and secondary teaching practices* within the text of each chapter.

◈ *Resource margin notes* that provide you with additional information and resources related to the material in the book;

◈ *Summaries* at the end of each chapter that address the chapter heading questions are designed to help you review the main points of each chapter, and provide links to the CEC, PRAXIS, and INTASC professional standards (a complete listing of the CEC, PRAXIS, and INTASC standards referred to in the text can be found on the Companion Website);

This textbook also contains several new and updated features designed to introduce you to content about technology and foster your use of technology, including:

◇ *CD-ROM video cases, an innovative and new feature in all chapters,* that provide examples of teachers and students engaged in activities that depict strategies presented in the book and reflective follow-up questions;

◇ *Using Technology to Promote Inclusion,* a new feature that appears in all chapters, uses a variety of formats to present issues, strategies, and resources for using technology to help your students access and succeed in inclusive classrooms;

◇ *Set Your Sites margin notes* in every chapter that link you to websites offering additional information and resources related to specific topics in the book. These sites can be accessed via hot links from the Companion Website, located at *http://www.prenhall.com/salend.*

Each chapter also contains several features designed to prompt you to reflect upon and interact with the material presented in the book, including:

◇ *Reflecting on Professional Practices*—vignettes describing a classroom experience from the teacher's point of view followed by reflective questions

◇ *Reflecting on Your Practices*—checklists designed to assist you in examining your practices, behaviors, and beliefs

◇ *CD-ROM Follow-up Questions*—questions that ask you to reflect on CD-ROM video cases of teachers and students in inclusive classrooms

◇ *What Would You Do in Today's Diverse Classroom?*—descriptions of classroom situations followed by a set of reflective questions

◇ *Reflective Margin Notes*—questions that ask you to reflect on your personal experiences related to the material in the book

◇ *Reflective Photo Captions*—photo-linked questions that ask you to reflect on information and strategies in the book

ANCILLARIES

The ancillaries and supplements package for the fifth edition has been expanded considerably. Several updated, exciting supplements are now available for students and instructors, and the high-quality supplements that have always been offered with the text have been thoroughly revised and expanded.

◇ *Instructor's Manual*—The fifth edition includes an Instructor's Manual to assist students and instructors in using the text. Chapters in the manual parallel the organization and content of the text. Each chapter of the manual includes chapter objectives, chapter overview, transparency masters and PowerPoint presentations (*NEW!*), learning activities, as well as a comprehensive test bank containing both short-answer and essay questions.

◇ *Computerized Testbank Software*—The computerized testbank software gives instructors electronic access to the test questions printed in the Instructor's Manual, allowing them to create and customize exams on their computer. The software can help professors manage their courses and gain insight into their students' progress and performance. Computerized testbank software is available in both Macintosh and PC/Windows versions.

◇ *Companion Website*—Located at *http://www. prenhall.com/salend*, the Companion Website for this text includes a wealth of resources for both students and professors. The *Syllabus Manager* enables professors to create and maintain the class syllabus online while also allowing the student access to the syllabus at any time from any computer on the Internet. In addition, on a passcode-protected portion of the site, professors can access instructor resources for the text. The student portion of the website helps students guage their understanding of chapter content through the use of online chapter reviews and interactive multiple choice and essay quizzes. The *Set Your Sites* feature contains links to all the websites mentioned in the margins of the text and assists students in using the Web to do additional research on chapter topics and key issues. In addition, in the *Video Cases* module, students have access to in-depth activities that connect the *Inclusive Classrooms Video Cases on CD-ROM* to chapter content. The *Standards* module gives a complete listing of all of the CEC, PRAXIS, and INTASC professional standards referred to in the text. Finally, the *Message Board* feature encourages student interaction outside of the classroom.

◆ *Inclusive Classrooms: Video Cases on CD-ROM*—The CD-ROM that accompanies the fifth edition of the text provides immediate access to living classroom examples of teaching and learning strategies for inclusion. These examples are video clips, grouped by topic and classroom, which give the pre-service teacher a good picture of what inclusion looks like in a preschool, an elementary school, a middle school, and a secondary school. In each classroom, you will see a lesson that clearly shows the impact of inclusion on supporting students with challenging behaviors (preschool), classroom climate (elementary), assesment and planning (middle), and partial participation and cooperative learning (secondary).

Each classroom case contains 9 video clips. In each case, you will see how children with learning disabilities, attention deficit disorders, and mild/moderate disabilities are successfully engaged in the classroom community and in learning. Because of the natural support and inclusive stance of the teachers and schools, it may be difficult to identify which children are indeed identified as having disabilities or in need of other accommodations.

An activity and user guide is available on the Companion Website for both instructors and students.

◆ *Videos to accompany the text*—Course instructors receive a complimentary set of two videos that can be used to supplement and extend information and issues introduced in the text. These two videos are new to this edition: *Heather's Story* chronicles the experiences of a fourth grade child with Down syndrome and her family and teachers as she joins an inclusive classroom for the first time; *Video Cases in Inclusive Classrooms* show four different cases of students in inclusive settings—a preschool classroom, an elementary school classroom, a middle school team meeting, and a high school physics class.

ACKNOWLEDGMENTS

This book is a result of the collaborative efforts of my students, colleagues, friends, and relatives. The book is an outgrowth of many ideas I learned from students at Woodlawn Junior High School (Buffalo, New York) and Public School 76 (Bronx, New York), colleagues from PS 76—George Bonnici, Nydia Figueroa-Torres, Jean Gee, and Jean Barber—and colleagues at the University of Kentucky, and the State University of New York at New Paltz. Much of the information in this book was learned through interactions with teachers, administrators, and students in the Easton (Pennsylvania) Area School District and other school districts, who both welcomed me and shared their experiences. Many of the examples and vignettes are based on the experiences of my students at the State University of New York at New Paltz. I truly value my colleagues and students, who continue to educate me and add to my appreciation of the remarkable dedication and skill of teachers.

I also want to acknowledge my students, colleagues, and friends who provided support and guidance throughout all stages of the book. I especially want to recognize Deborah Anderson, Lee Bell, John Boyd, Pauline Bynoe, Devon Duhaney, Hala Elhoweris, Meenakshi Gajria, Luis Garrido, Charleen Gottschalk, Margaret Gutierrez, Karen Giek, Mark Metzger, Bob Michael, Winifred Montgomery, Jean Mumper, Helen Musumeci, Kathy Pike, Sarah Ryan, Altagracia Salinas, Robin Smith, Shawna Sylvestre, Lorraine Taylor, Margaret Wade-Lewis, Delinda van Garderen, Halee Vang, and Catharine Whittaker for supporting and inspiring me throughout the process. My deepest appreciation also goes to Laurel Garrick Duhaney for preparing the innovative instructor's manual that accompanies this book and to Lenore Schulte for her invaluable assistance in coordinating various aspects of the book.

This book would not have been possible without the efforts and skills of Heather Doyle Fraser, who provided me with the professional support needed to create a more readable, practically-oriented, and pedagogically sound book. I also appreciate the work of Allyson Sharp, Key Metts, and Sheryl Langner. I also am grateful to the following reviewers: Kathleen Cooter, Texas Christian University; Frank Kohler, University of Northern Iowa; Regina Foley, Southern Illinois University at Carbondale; and Joyce Williams Bergin, Armstrong Atlantic State University. Their thoughtful and professional comments helped to shape and improve the book.

Dedication

I want to dedicate this book to Suzanne Salend, my collaborator in life, Jack Salend, my son, and Madison Salend, my granddaughter, in recognition of their love, spirit, intelligence, encouragement, strength, and passion. They have taught me how to accept and grow from a challenge. I hope that this book will help you accept and grow from the challenge of creating inclusive classrooms for *all students*.

Contents

PART I
Understanding the Foundations and Fundamentals of Inclusion   1

CHAPTER 1

Understanding Inclusion   2

What Is Special Education?   5
  Special Education   5
What Is Inclusion?   6
  Inclusion   6
  Mainstreaming   6
Principles of Effective Inclusion   7
What Is the Least Restrictive Environment?   12
  Least Restrictive Environment   12
What Factors Contributed to the Movement to Educate Students in Inclusive Classrooms?   15
  Normalization   16
  Deinstitutionalization   16
  Early Intervention and Early Childhood Programs   16
  Technological Advances   17
  Civil Rights Movement and Resulting Litigation   18
  Advocacy Groups   20
  Segregated Nature of Special Schools and Classes   21
  Disproportionate Representation   21
  Standards-Based Reform and No Child Left Behind Act   23
What Are the Laws That Affect Special Education?   25
  The Individuals with Disabilities Education Act (IDEA)   25
  Other Laws Affecting Special Education   28
What Is the Impact of Inclusion?   32
  Impact of Inclusion on Students with Disabilities   32
  Impact of Inclusion on Students Without Disabilities   36
  Impact of Inclusion on Educators   38
  Impact of Inclusion on Families   40
Summary   43

CHAPTER 2

Understanding the Diverse Educational Strengths and Needs of Students with Disabilities   46

How Does the Special Education Identification Process Work?   49
  Comprehensive Planning Team   49
  Prereferral System   50
  Eligibility Determination   51
  Individualized Education Program   51
  Student Involvement   60
How Can IEPs Be Implemented in General Education Settings?   64
  Involve Teachers in the IEP Process   64
  Align the IEP to the General Education Curriculum   65
  Differentiate Instruction to Address IEP Goals   66
  Establish an Implementation Plan   67
  Engage in Curriculum Mapping   69
What Are the Educational Strengths and Needs of Students with High-Incidence Disabilities?   69
  Students with Learning Disabilities   70
  Students with Emotional and Behavioral Disorders   72
  Students with Attention Deficit Disorders   76
  Types of ADD   77
  Students with Mental Retardation   78
  Students with Speech and Language Disorders   80
What Are the Educational Strengths and Needs of Students with Low-Incidence Disabilities?   82
  Help Students Access the General Education Curriculum   83
  Collaborate with Related Service Providers, Paraeducators, and Peers   83
  Use Assistive and Instructional Technology   84
  Adopt a Competency-Oriented Approach   84
  Understand and Address Students' Unique Abilities and Needs   85

Medication Monitoring   98
Students with Sensory Disabilities   100
Summary   104

CHAPTER 3

Understanding the Diverse Educational Strengths and Needs of Learners Who Challenge Schools   108

How Have Economic Changes Affected Students and Schools?   110
A Nation of Visible Rich and Invisible Poor   110
Poverty   111
How Have Demographic Shifts Affected Students and Schools?   117
Immigration   118
What Are the Educational Strengths and Needs of Students from Culturally and Linguistically Diverse Backgrounds?   121
Cultural Considerations   121
Linguistic Considerations   122
How Can I Differentiate Cultural and Language Differences from Learning Difficulties?   122
Diversify the Comprehensive Planning Team and Offer Training   123
Compare Student Performance in Both Primary and Secondary Languages   123
Consider the Processes and Factors Associated with Second Language Acquisition   124
Employ Alternatives and Traditional Standardized Testing   126
Identify Diverse Life and Home Experiences That Might Affect Learning and Language Development   126
Analyze the Data and Develop an Appropriate Educational Plan   126
What Are the Educational Strengths and Needs of Students Who Are Gifted and Talented?   129
Students with Special Needs Who Are Gifted and Talented   132
What Is the Effect of Discrimination and Bias on Schools and Students?   133
Racial Discrimination   133
Gender Bias   135
Gay, Lesbian, Bisexual, and Transgendered (GLBT) Youth   138
Students with HIV/AIDS   139

How Have Family Changes Affected Students and Schools?   141
Changing Definition of Family   141
Child Abuse   145
Substance Abuse   148
What Are Some Alternative Philosophies for Structuring Schools to Address Societal Changes?   148
Multicultural Education   150
Multicultural Education and Inclusion   150
Summary   151

PART II

Creating an Inclusive Environment That Supports Learning for All Students   155

CHAPTER 4

Creating Collaborative Relationships and Fostering Communication   156

Who Are Members of the Comprehensive Planning Team?   158
Family Members   158
School Administrators   158
General Educators   159
Special Educators   159
Paraeducators   159
School Psychologists   161
Speech and Language Clinicians   161
Social Workers   161
School Counselors   162
Vocational Educators   162
School Physicians and Nurses   162
Physical and Occupational Therapists   163
Staff from Community Agencies   163
Professionals for Students Who Are Second Language Learners   163
How Can Members of the Comprehensive Planning Team Work Collaboratively?   164
Employ Collaborative and Interactive Teaming   164
Use Person-Centered Planning   167
Work in Cooperative Teaching Arrangements   168
Employ Collaborative Consultation   175
Promote Congruence   179
Engage in Professional Development   181

How Can I Foster Communication and Collaboration
    with Families? 185
  Gain the Trust of Families 186
  Advocate for Students and Their Families 187
  Ensure Confidentiality 188
  Meet Regularly with Families 189
  Resolve Conflicts Constructively 192
  Address the Diverse Needs, Backgrounds, and
      Experiences of Families 192
  Use Written Communication 197
  Employ Technology-Based Communications 200
  Encourage and Facilitate Family Observations 200
  Offer Educational Programs to Families 203
Summary 205

CHAPTER 5

Creating an Environment That Fosters
Acceptance and Friendship 208

How Do Attitudes Toward Individual Differences
    Develop? 210
How Can I Assess Attitudes Toward Individual
    Differences? 211
  Attitude Assessment Instruments 211
  Knowledge of Individual Differences Probes 212
  Student Drawings 212
  Observational Techniques 212
  Sociometric Techniques 214
How Can I Teach Acceptance of Individual
    Differences Related to Disability? 214
  Attitude Change and Information-Sharing
      Strategies 214
  Use Disability Simulations 218
How Can I Teach Acceptance of Individual Differences
    Related to Culture, Language, Gender, Religion,
    and Socioeconomic Status? 226
  Reflect on Your Knowledge, Experiences, and Beliefs
      Related to Diversity 226
  Promote Acceptance of Cultural Diversity 226
  Teach Others to Respond to Stereotyping and
      Discrimination 236
How Can I Facilitate Friendships? 238
  Teach About Friendships 238
  Offer Social Skills Instruction 240
  Foster Communication Among Students 241
  Use Circles of Friends 243

Create a Friendly Classroom Environment 243
Use Peer-Based Strategies 244
Encourage Participation in Extracurricular and
    Community-Based Activities 245
Involve Family Members 246
Summary 246

CHAPTER 6

Creating Successful Transitions to
Inclusive Settings 248

How Can I Help Students Make the Transition to
    General Education Classrooms? 250
  Understand Students' Unique Abilities and
      Challenges 250
  Use Transenvironmental Programming 251
How Can I Help Students from Specialized Schools
    and Preschool Programs Make the Transition to
    Inclusive Settings? 260
  Plan the Transitional Program 260
  Adapt Transitional Models 262
How Can I Help Students from Linguistically and
    Culturally Diverse Backgrounds Make the
    Transition to Inclusive Settings? 264
  Teach Cultural Norms 264
  Orient Students to the School 264
  Teach Basic and Interpersonal Communication
      Skills 265
  Teach Cognitive Academic Language Proficiency
      Skills 266
  Offer Newcomer Programs 267
How Can I Help Students Make the Transition from
    School to Adulthood? 267
  Develop an Individualized Transition Plan 267
  Prepare Students for Employment 270
  Foster Independent Living Arrangements 272
  Promote Students' Participation in Leisure
      Activities 273
  Explore Postsecondary Opportunities 273
How Can I Help Students Develop Self-
    Determination? 274
  Teach Goal Setting and Attainment 274
  Offer Choices 277
  Foster Self-Awareness 278
  Develop Self-Advocacy and Leadership Skills 278
  Promote Self-Esteem 279

Provide Attribution Training   279

Provide Access to Positive Role Models   281

Use Self-Determination Curricula   283

Summary   284

CHAPTER 7

Creating a Classroom Environment That Promotes Positive Behavior   286

Schoolwide Positive Behavioral Support System   288

How Can I Collaborate with Others to Conduct a Functional Behavioral Assessment?   289

Create a Diverse Multidisciplinary Team   289

Identify the Problematic Behavior   290

Define the Behavior   290

Observe and Record the Behavior   290

Obtain Additional Information About the Student and the Behavior   293

Perform and Antecedents-Behavior-Consequences (A-B-C) Analysis   293

Analyze the Data   293

Develop Hypothesis Statements   294

Consider Sociocultural Factors   295

Develop a Behavioral Intervention Plan   297

Evaluate the Plan   297

How Can I Promote Positive Classroom Behavior in Students?   297

Relationship Building Strategies   297

Develop Students' Self-Esteem   299

Social-Skills Instruction   302

Antecedent-Based Interventions   304

Follow Routines   305

Consequence-Based Interventions   307

Self-Management Interventions   310

Group-Oriented Management Systems   313

Behavior Reduction Interventions   318

How Can I Prevent Student from Harming Others?   320

Students Who Are Bullies   320

Students with Aggressive and Violent Behaviors   322

How Can I Adapt the Classroom Design to Accommodate Students' Learning, Social, and Physical Needs?   323

Seating Arrangements   323

Teacher's Desk   324

Bulletin Boards and Walls   324

Learning Centers and Specialized Areas   325

Classroom Design Adaptations   325

Summary   330

PART III

Differentiating Instruction for All Students   333

CHAPTER 8

Differentiating Instruction for Diverse Learners   334

How Can I Differentiate Instruction for Students?   337

Tailor Curricular Goals and Strategies for Your Students and Your Learning Environment   337

Individualize and Personalize Your Curriculum   338

Use Curricular Accommodations   339

Use Universally Designed Curriculum and Teaching Materials   340

Use Individualized Teaching Accommodations   342

Use Instructional Materials Accommodations   342

Provide Personal Supports   343

Address Students' Learning Styles and Preferences   344

Address Students' Sensory Abilities   345

Consider Treatment Acceptability   347

How Can I Differentiate Instruction for Students Who Have Difficulty Reading and Gaining Information from Print Materials?   347

Use Teacher-Directed Text Comprehension Strategies   347

Teach Student-Directed Text Comprehension Strategies   350

Enhance the Readability of Materials   353

How Can I Differentiate Instruction for Students from Diverse Cultural and Language Backgrounds?   356

Use a Multicultural Curriculum   356

Use Multicultural Teaching Materials   358

Use Culturally Relevant and Responsive Teaching Strategies   359

Use Reciprocal Interaction Teaching Approaches   360

Use Effective ESL Approaches   361

Encourage Students to Respond   363

How Can I Use Instructional Technology and Assistive Devices to Differentiate Instruction for Students?   363

Instructional Technology   364

Assistive Devices   370

Summary   375

CHAPTER 9

Differentiating Large- and Small-Group Instruction   378

How Can I Adapt Large-Group Instruction for Students?   480

Have Students Work Collaboratively   380

Encourage Students to Ask Questions   381

Help Students Take Notes   382

Teach Note-Taking Skills and Strategies   385

Foster Students' Listening Skills   385

Gain and Maintain Students' Attention   386

Give Clear and Detailed Directions   387

Motivate Students   389

How Can I Use Effective Teacher-Centered Instruction?   391

Elements of Effective Teacher-Centered Instruction   391

How Can I Successfully Use Cooperative Learning Arrangements with Students?   402

Select an Appropriate Cooperative Learning Format   404

Establish Guidelines for Working Cooperatively   406

Form Heterogeneous Cooperative Groups   407

Arrange the Classroom for Cooperative Learning   407

Develop Students' Cooperative Skills   407

Evaluate Cooperative Learning   409

Summary   412

CHAPTER 10

Differentiating Reading, Writing, and Spelling Instruction   414

How Can I Help Students Learn to Read?   416

Offer Early Identification   416

Promote Phonological Awareness   416

Promote Reading Fluency   418

Enhance Students' Text Comprehension   422

Use a Balanced Approach   426

Use Remedial Reading Programs, Strategies, and Materials   428

How Can I Help Students Learn to Write?   429

Make Writing Meaningful and an Integral Part of the Curriculum   429

Use Journals   431

Use a Process-Oriented Approach to Writing Instruction   431

Provide Feedback   438

Teach Students to Use Learning Strategies   439

Use Computer-Supported Writing Applications   440

How Can I Help Students Learn to Spell?   444

Use a Combination of Approaches   444

Adapt Spelling Instruction   445

Summary   450

CHAPTER 11

Differentiating Mathematics, Science, and Social Studies Instruction   452

How Can I Differentiate Mathematics Instruction?   454

Use a Problem-Solving Approach   454

Present Mathematics Appropriately   455

Use Teaching Aids   456

Use a Variety of Instructional Approaches   459

Help Students Develop Their Math Facts and Computation Skills   464

Provide Feedback and Use Assessment to Guide Future Teaching   466

How Can I Differentiate Science and Social Studies Instruction?   467

Choose and Use Appropriate Instructional Materials   467

Use Content Enhancements   474

Use a Variety of Instructional Approaches and Practices   480

Address the Needs of Diverse Learners   490

Summary   491

PART IV
Evaluating Individual and Programmatic Progress   493

CHAPTER 12

Evaluating Student Progress and the Effectiveness of Your Inclusion Program   494

How Can I Evaluate the Academic Performance of Students?   496

Standardized Testing   496

Alternatives to Standardized Testing   502

Gathering Additional Information About the Academic Progress of Diverse Learners   519

Reporting Information About the Academic Progress of Diverse Learners   522

How Can I Grade Students in Inclusive Settings?   523

Report Card Grading   523

How Can I Evaluate the Social and Behavioral Performance of Students?   530

Observational and Sociometric Techniques   530

Self-Concept Measures   531

How Can I Measure Perceptions of My Inclusion Program?   531

Students' Perceptions   532

Teachers' Perceptions   532

Family Members' Perceptions   537

How Can I Improve the Effectiveness of My Inclusion Program?   539

Examine the Impact of Student Performance   539

Determine Program Strengths, Concerns, and Possible Solutions   539

Summary   542

References   545

Name Index   589

Subject Index   607

Note: Every effort has been made to provide accurate and current Internet information in this book. However, the Internet and information posted on it are constantly changing, and it is inevitable that some of the Internet addresses listed in this textbook will change.

Special Features

REFLECTING ON PROFESSIONAL PRACTICES

Implementing Inclusion   9
Supporting Students on Medications   100
Assessing Second Language Learners   130
Working as a Cooperative Teaching Team   176
Empowering Language   219
Teaching Students to Use Learning Strategies   256
Using Self-Management Strategies   314
Using Instructional Technology and Assistive
    Devices to Differentiate Instruction   374
Using Cooperative Learning   411
Using a Process Approach to Teaching Writing   439
Using Semantic Webs   479
Using Student Portfolios   512

REFLECTING ON YOUR PRACTICES

Examining Disproportionate Representation   24
Implementing a Prereferral System   53
Examining Equity in the Classroom   139
Evaluating Meetings with Families   191
Selecting Books and Other Materials About
    Individual Differences   224
Promoting Students' Self-Determination   283
Examining Rules   308
Examining the Readability and Legibility of
    Your Materials   357
Delivering Oral Presentations to Students   381
Creating a Balanced and Literacy-Rich
    Learning Environment   430

Selecting Textbooks   470
Using Teacher-Made Tests   520

USING TECHNOLOGY TO PROMOTE INCLUSION

Fostering Inclusion and Independence   19
Conducting an Individualized Technology
    Assessment   63
Bridging the Digital Divide   134
Creating and Implementing a Homework
    Website   202
Fostering Acceptance and Friendships   239
Supporting Successful Transitions   276
Supporting Student Learning and Behavior   327
Preparing Readable and Legible Materials   355
Making Large- and Small-Group Instruction
    Accessible to All Students   410
Making Literacy Instruction Accessible to All
    Students   448
Making Mathematics, Science, and Social
    Studies Instruction Accessible to All
    Students   487
Using Technology-Based Testing   505

IDEAS FOR IMPLEMENTATION

Explaining Your Inclusion Program
    to Families   42
Preparing for and Participating in the IEP
    Meeting   65
Helping Students Who Exhibit Oppositional and
    Defiant Behaviors Succeed in Inclusive
    Classrooms   74

XV

Helping Students with ADD Succeed in Inclusive
    Classrooms   79
Helping Students with Expressive Language
    Disorders Succeed in Inclusive Classrooms   82
Helping Students with Cerebral Palsy Succeed in
    Inclusive Classrooms   87
Helping Students with TS Succeed in Inclusive
    Classrooms   90
Helping Homeless Students and Students from
    Lower Socioeconomic Backgrounds
    Succeed in Inclusive Classrooms   115
Supporting GLBT Students   140
Teaching Students Who Have AIDS   141
Working with Students Whose Families Are
    Undergoing Changes   145
Promoting Congruence   182
Facing the Challenges of Being a Beginning
    Teacher   183
Attending Professional Conferences   184
Overcoming Economic Barriers to Family
    Participation   197
Affirming Acceptance of Linguistic Diversity   230
Promoting Gender Equity   233

Facilitating Friendship Skills   241
Teaching Organizational Skills   260
Promoting Generalization   263
Promoting Leisure Skills   275
Promoting Students' Self-Esteem   300
Using Learning Centers   325
Transferring Students Who Use Wheelchairs   330
Adjusting the Complexity of Text Language   354
Differentiating Instruction for Second
    Language Learners   362
Motivating Students   393
Adapting Independent Assignments   401
Helping Students Complete Homework   403
Teaching Handwriting   443
Teaching Spelling   446
Developing Students' Word Problem-Solving
    Skills   462
Ensuring Safety in Laboratory Settings   481
Promoting Students' Memory   485
Promoting Math and Science Education for All
    Students   490

A Changing IDEA

HOW THE INDIVIDUALS WITH DISABILITIES EDUCATION IMPROVEMENT ACT OF 2004 MAY AFFECT YOUR INCLUSIVE CLASSROOM

More than any other law, the *Individuals with Disabilities Education Act (IDEA)* has affected the educational system for learners with disabilities in this country. Before it was enacted into law in 1975, more than one million students with disabilities were denied a public education, and those who attended public schools were segregated from their peers without disabilities. Since its enactment, students with disabilities have gained greater access to inclusive classrooms and the general education curriculum. The *IDEA* has been amended and reauthorized numerous times since its passage in 1975 (The highlights of these amendments are presented in Figure 1.4, and discussed chapter 1).

With the passage of the *Individuals with Disabilities Education Improvement Act of 2004,* the Congress reauthorized the IDEA again. This reauthorization includes important changes related to IEPs, family involvement, the special education identification, prereferral, and discipline processes, and paperwork and administrative requirements. Some of the new provisions that may affect your inclusive classroom, and your students and their families are discussed next.

Changes to the IEP and Family Involvement

An important hallmark of special education programs is the delivery of an individually tailored education for students with disabilities specified in an Individualized Education Plan (IEP). As we will discuss and learn more about in chapter 2, the IEP is a written individualized plan that lists the special education and related services students with disabilities will receive and includes a listing of the important annual academic and non-academic goals. In the new reauthorization, the Congress eliminated short-term objectives and benchmarks from student IEPs so that annual goals relate to the accountability and testing provisions of the No Child Left Behind Act as well as each state's learning standards. However, IEPs for students with disabilities who take alternate assessments rather than participating in state and federal testing programs still must include benchmarks and short-term objectives. In addition, other revisions to the IEP and family involvement include:

- Offering families the option of developing three-year IEPs that address and coincide with the student's natural transition points, such as moving to elementary school from a preschool or participating in post-secondary activities after graduating from high school.
- Allowing families and school districts to agree to exempt any member of the IEP team from attending all or part of an IEP meeting when the team member's area of expertise or related service is not being discussed. When a team member's areas of expertise or related service is being considered by the IEP team, families and school districts also can agree to excuse the team member and obtain written input from the individual prior to the meeting.
- Permitting school districts and families to change the IEP after the annual meeting using written documents rather than reconvening the team, and to agree to meet using alternative means such as video and phone conferences.
- Requiring a description in the IEP of how and when progress in meeting annual goals will be assessed and shared with family members. These descriptions of student progress may be provided via quarterly or periodic communications with families such as report cards.
- Raising the age for all transition requirements including developing transition plans to 16 (previously it was age 14), and requiring the IEP to include "postsecondary goals addressing training, education, employment and, where appropriate, living skills."
- Ensuring that IEPs include a summary of a student's academic and functional achievement upon graduation or at age 21.
- Expanding the use of mediation to resolve differences between school districts and families related to the IEP and other procedural disagreements.

These changes make it important for you to work with others, including students and their families, to create high quality IEPs that are aligned to an engaging and challenging curriculum and implemented in your inclusive classroom. It also means that you need to understand your students' strengths, challenges, experiences, and cultural and linguistic backgrounds (see chapters 2 and 3) and use innovative, motivating and differentiated instructional practices so your students can succeed in the general education curriculum (see chapters 8, 9, 10, and 11). In addition, these changes emphasize the need for you to work collaboratively and communicate with family members and other professionals to implement inclusive practices (see chapter 4), and help your students make successful transitions (see chapter 6). Finally, these changes highlight the importance of you and your colleagues evaluating the success of your inclusive classroom for *all students, their families, and professionals* (see chapter 12). *Changes in the Special Education Identification, Prereferral and Disciplinary Processes.*

Since the initial passage of the IDEA, the number of students with learning disabilities has increased dramatically, which has raised concerns about how these students are identified. Therefore, the current reauthorization of the IDEA provides for the development and use of new ways to identify students with learning disabilities. Prior to the current reauthorization, school districts used an IQ-Achievement Discrepancy Model, which seeks to identify students as having a learning disability if there is a gap between their learning potential and actual achievement. An alternative to the IQ-Achievement Discrepancy Model allowed under the latest reauthorization is the Response to Intervention (RTI) method, whereby only students who do not respond to intensive research-based interventions would be identified as having a learning disability. To address the overidentification of students with learning and other types of disabilities, the Congress also is allowing school districts to use IDEA funds to support the establishment of preferral services for students not identified as needing special education but who need additional academic or behavioral support to succeed in general education classrooms. The new reauthorization also requires school districts to implement prereferral programs to reduce high rates of special education placements for their students from culturally and linguistically diverse backgrounds.

The IDEA amendments of 1997 contained provisions that had a significant impact on disciplinary actions for students with disabilities. Under these provisions, school personnel cannot remove students with disabilities from school for more than 10 days unless the disciplinary action is related to carrying a weapon to school or knowingly possessing, using, or selling illegal drugs at school. In these cases, the IEP team can unilaterally place a student in an interim alternative setting for up to 45 school days. The 2004 reauthorization adds *"inflicted serious bodily injury on another person while at school, on school premises, or at a school function"* to the list of disciplinary actions that can result in students with disabilities being removed from school for up to 45 calendar days (under the IDEA of 1997, it was 45 school days).

In making the disciplinary decisions, the IDEA of 1997 mandated that the IEP team conduct a *manifestation determination,* an examination to determine if the student's disability made it difficult for the student to control the behavior and understand its impact and consequences. If the team determined that the misbehaviors of students with disabilities are not related to their disability, they can be disciplined in the same ways as students without disabilities. Whereas the IDEA of 1997 required *school districts* to show that a student's behavior was not related to the student's disability, the latest reauthorization has revised the manifest determination process so that *families* must demonstrate that their child's misbehaviors are the result of their child's disability. Under the recent reauthorization, the Congress also took actions that prohibit school districts from requiring students to take medications in order to attend school, receive services or be evaluated for special education.

These changes underscore the importance of *all students* developing the academic, social, and behavioral skills that allow them to become valued members of their class, their school, and their community. Therefore, you need to collaborate with others to help your students engage in positive behaviors that support their learning and socializing with others (see chapter 7), and create a welcoming and safe learning environment that fosters your students' acceptance of each other and friendships (see chapter 5).

Changes to Paperwork Requirements

One of the criticisms of the IDEA over the years has been its paperwork and administrative requirements. In recognition of these concerns, the recent reauthorization includes several initiatives such as developing and disseminating model IEP, IFSP and family notice forms and conducting pilot programs in 15 states to examine ways to reduce paperwork and administrative requirements.

Part I

Understanding the Foundations and Fundamentals of Inclusion

Part 1 of this book, which includes Chapters 1, 2, and 3, introduces the concept of inclusion and the challenges of its implementation. The information presented in part 1 also is designed to provide a framework for creating learning environments that support the learning and socialization of *all students;* differentiating your instruction to accommodate *all students* and provide them with access to and help them succeed in the general education curriculum; and evaluating the success of your inclusion program for *all students, their families, and professionals.* Chapter 1 introduces you to the concepts of special education, inclusion, and the least restrictive environment, the philosophical principles that guide this book, the factors that contributed to the growth of inclusion, and the current research on the impact of inclusion on students, teachers, and families. Chapter 2 introduces you to the prereferral and placement system for students with disabilities, the Individualized Education Program, and the various special education categories. Chapter 3 introduces you to various societal changes and their impact on students and schools, and explains alternative philosophies for structuring schools to address these changes.

Chapter 1

Understanding Inclusion

Marie and Mary

Marie was born in 1949. By the time she turned 3, her parents were sensing that she was developing slowly—speaking little and walking late. Marie's pediatrician told them not to worry; Marie would grow out of it. After another year of no noticeable progress, Marie's parents took her to other doctors. One said she had an iron deficiency, and another thought she had a tumor.

By the time Marie was old enough to start school, she was diagnosed as having mental retardation and was placed in a separate school for children with disabilities. She was doing well at the school when the school district informed her family that the school was being closed and that the district had no place for Marie and the other students. Marie's family protested to school officials and their state legislator, but the school district was not required by law to educate children like Marie.

Concerned about her future, Marie's family sent her to a large state-run program about 200 miles from their home. During visits, they found that Marie was often disheveled, disoriented, and uncommunicative. Once she even had bruises on her arms and legs. After much debate, Marie's family decided to bring her home to live with them. Although now an adult, Marie cannot perform activities of daily living, and her parents are worried about what will happen to her when they are no longer able to care for her.

Mary, born in 1991, also was diagnosed as having mental retardation. Soon after birth, Mary and her parents enrolled in an early intervention program that included family education sessions and home visits by a professional. Mary's parents joined a group of families that was advocating for services. When Mary was 3, she attended a preschool program with other children from her neighborhood. The school worked with Mary's family to develop an Individualized Family Service Plan to meet Mary's educational needs, coordinate the delivery of services to Mary and her family, and assist her family in planning for the transition to public school. After preschool, Mary moved with the other children to the local elementary school. At that time, her family met with the school district's comprehensive planning team to develop an Individualized Education Program (IEP) for Mary. The team recommended that Mary be educated in a self-contained special education class and mainstreamed for special classes like art, music, and physical education. However, Mary's family thought she should be in a setting that fostered her language and literacy skills and allowed her to interact with her peers who were not disabled. As a result, Mary was placed in a general education setting and received the services of a collaboration teacher and a speech/language therapist, who worked with Mary and her teacher in an inclusive classroom. Over the years, Mary had some teachers who understood her needs and others who did not, but she and her family persevered. Occasionally, other students made fun of Mary, but she learned to ignore them and participated in many after school programs.

When Mary was ready to move to junior high school, the teachers and her family worked together to help Mary make the transition. She was taught to change classes, use a combination lock and locker, and use different textbooks. Her IEP was revised to include instructional and testing accommodations, as well as the use of word processing to help her develop written communication skills. Mary participated in the science club and volunteer activities after school and went to the movies with her friends on Saturdays.

Mary graduated from junior high school and entered high school, where her favorite subjects are social studies and science. She also enjoys socializing with her friends during lunch. A peer helps Mary by sharing notes with her, and Mary's teachers have modified the curriculum for her. She uses a laptop computer with large print, a talking word processor, and a word prediction program. She is also taking a course called "Introduction to Occupations" and participates in a work-study program. Mary hopes to work in a store or office in town when she graduates.

What factors and events led Marie and Mary and their families to have such different experiences in school and society? After reading this chapter, you should have the knowledge, skills, and dispositions to answer that as well as the following questions.

★ **What is special education?**
★ **What is inclusion?**
★ **What is the least restrictive environment?**
★ **What factors contributed to the movement to educate students in inclusive classrooms?**
★ **What are the laws that affect special education?**
★ **What is the impact of inclusion?**

As the stories of Marie and Mary indicate, the education and treatment of individuals with disabilities has undergone a change (Best, 2001; Shapiro, 1999). Prior to 1800, individuals with disabilities were feared, ridiculed, abandoned, or simply ignored. As educational methods were developed in the late 1700s that showed the success of various teaching methods, society began to adopt a more accepting and humane view of individuals with disabilities. However, the nineteenth century saw the rise of institutions for individuals with disabilities, like the one Marie experienced, that isolated them from society. Although institutional settings played an important role until the 1970s, the early twentieth century also saw the rise of special schools and special classes for students with disabilities. The 1960s and 1970s also fostered a period of advocacy and acceptance, which resulted in legislative and judicial actions that provided individuals like Mary and her family with access to society, early intervention programs, and the public schools. In the late 1980s and mid-1990s, individuals with disabilities and their families formed advocacy groups that fostered public policies that allowed individuals with disabilities to become full and equal members of society.

Today, these factors, aided by the technological advances of the 1990s and early 2000s, are transforming our notions of disability and providing individuals with disabilities with full access to the educational, economic, social, cultural, and political mainstream. Thus, whereas Marie's life was characterized by frustration, isolation, and lack of understanding, Mary's experiences were much more positive and inclusive. Although Marie was initially placed in a separate school for students with disabilities, no laws existed that required states to educate children with special needs. When the school closed, Marie's family had few options, and Marie was forced into an even more segregated environment, a state-run institution. Conditioned to live a life fully dependent on others, Marie was limited at the time by society's restrictive perceptions of individuals with disabilities.

Mary, on the other hand, benefited from early diagnosis and intervention. She was educated with her peers without disabilities in preschool and included in classes with students from her neighborhood throughout her educational career. Mary's full rights of citizenship, including the right to a free and appropriate education, were ensured by special laws that help protect and empower individuals with disabilities; these laws also recognized that *all students* can learn and granted Mary's family the right to advocate for her when they disagreed with the school's decisions. Mary's teachers had high expectations of what she could accomplish, and they worked together to individualize her instruction and capitalize on her strengths. Upon her graduation from high school, Mary is being prepared to act on her own choices, lead a more independent life, and make positive contributions to her community. Born more than four decades later than Marie, Mary benefited from a totally changed societal perception of what individuals with disabilities can learn and accomplish when supported by their families, peers, teachers, and community.

Resource

Polloway (2000) offers a listing of influential individuals in special education and their contributions, and Shapiro (1999), and the July–August issue of *Remedial and Special Education, 19*(4) (1998) present a history of the treatment and education of children and adults with disabilities.

Set Your Sites

For more information related to the history of individuals with disabilities in the United States, go to the Web Links module in Chapter 1 of the Companion Website.

What Is Special Education?

Special Education

While Mary benefited from receiving special education services to address her unique needs, unfortunately these services were not available for Marie. *Special education* involves delivering and monitoring a specially designed and coordinated set of comprehensive, research-based instructional and assessment practices and related services to students with learning, behavioral, emotional, physical, health, or sensory disabilities. These instructional practices and services are tailored to identify and address the individual needs and strengths of students; to enhance their educational, social, behavioral and physical development; and to foster equity and access to all aspects of society. Special education is characterized by the following features:

- *Individualized assessment and planning:* Learning goals and instructional practices are based on individualized assessment data.
- *Specialized instruction:* Instructional pratices and materials, curricula, related services, and assistive technology are tailored to the unique needs and strengths of students.
- *Intensive instruction:* Instructional practices are precisely designed and systematically implemented for a sufficient period of time.
- *Goal-directed instruction:* Instructional practices are guided by learning goals that promote independence and success in current and future settings.
- *Research-based instructional practices:* Instructional practices are chosen based on their research support.
- *Collaborative partnerships:* Professionals, students, family and community members work collaboratively to coordinate their goals and efforts.
- *Student performance evaluation:* Instructional practices are evaluated frequently in terms of outcomes on student performance and revised accordingly (Crockett, 2002; Heward, 2003).

What Is Inclusion?

Inclusion

While Marie attended schools and institutional settings that segregated students with disabilities, Mary's educational experiences were based on *inclusion,* an important and essential feature of special education. Inclusion is a philosophy that brings diverse students, families, educators, and community members together to create schools and other social institutions based on acceptance, belonging, and community (Bloom, Perlmutter, & Burrell, 1999). Inclusion recognizes that *all students* are learners who benefit from a meaningful, challenging, and appropriate curriculum, and differentiated instruction techniques that address their unique strengths and needs. Inclusion seeks to establish collaborative, supportive, and nurturing communities of learners that are based on giving *all learners*° the services and accommodations they need to succeed, as well as respecting and learning from each other's individual differences (Jackson, Ryndak & Billingsley, 2000). Rather than segregating students, as in the school Marie briefly attended before being placed in an institution, advocates of inclusion work collaboratively to create a unified educational system like Mary's (Hunt, Hirose-Hatae, Doering, Karasoff, & Goetz, 2000). While inclusion has focused on individuals with disabilities, it is designed to alter the educational system so that it is more able to accommodate and respond to the diverse strengths, needs, and experiences of *all students* (Voltz, Brazil, & Ford, 2001).

Inclusion programs also provide *all students* with access to a challenging, engaging, and flexible curriculum that helps them to be successful in society (Fisher & Frey, 2001; Roach, Salisbury, & McGregor, 2002). To achieve this, educators establish individualized expectations for all students that are based on the general education curriculum (Matlock, Fielder & Walsh (2001), and offer differentiated teaching practices to accommodate students' individual differences and to help all students succeed (Ford, Davern, & Schnorr, 2001; Tomlinson, 2000). (We will learn more about how to use differentiated instruction to help all students access and succeed in the general education curriculum in part 3 and other chapters of this book).

The following interrelated principles, on pages 8 and 9, which provide a framework for this textbook, summarize the philosophies on which inclusive practices are based.

Mainstreaming

Because the concept of inclusion grew out of mainstreaming and shares many of its philosophical goals and implementation strategies, the terms *mainstreaming* and *inclusion* mean different things to different people (Hines, 2001; Snyder, Garriott, & Aylor, 2001). Therefore, you may hear some people use them interchangeably, while others see them as very different concepts (See Figure 1.1).

Following the passage of PL 94-142 (an important law we'll discuss later in this chapter), the term *mainstreaming* referred to the partial or full-time programs that educated students with disabilities with their general education peers. Thus, the definition and scope of mainstreaming varied greatly, from any interactions between students who

---

° *All learners/students* refers to the full range of students who are educated in general education classrooms and includes learners with individual differences related to "ethnicity, race, socioeconomic status, gender, disability, language, religion, sexual orientation and geographical area" (National Council for the Accreditation of Teacher Education (NCATE), 2001, p. 53).

Reflective

Why is access to the general education curriculum important? Which settings provide students with disabilities the best access to the general education curriculum? Inclusive classroooms? Special education classrooms? A combination of the two?

Resource

Villa and Thousand (2000) and Kavale and Forness (2000) outline and discuss the history of inclusive schooling, and Smith-Davis (2002) and Booth and Ainscow (1998) provide a international perspective on inclusion.

Set Your Sites

For more information on inclusion, go to the Web Links module in Chapter 1 of the Companion Website.

cd-rom

To view examples of preschool, elementary, and secondary inclusion programs, go to Cases 1, 2, and 4 on the CD-ROM, and view all the video clips. How are the four principles of inclusion reflected in the different classrooms? What additional strategies, resources, and supports could the educators employ to make their classrooms encompass the principles of inclusion and foster the success of their inclusion programs?

REFLECTING ON PROFESSIONAL PRACTICES

Implementing Inclusion

7:45 a.m.: Ms. Williams enters the school's office, greets the school secretary, and reviews her mail, which includes a message from one of her student's parents that her son will be late because he has a doctor's appointment.

7:52 a.m.: Ms. Williams enters her classroom. While she sips some tea, she boots up one of the computers in the room and checks her e-mail. She reads a message from a parent whose child will be absent and would like her to send today's homework assignment via e-mail. She starts to review a children's book about the school experiences of a student who does not speak English.

8:01 a.m.: As Ms. Silver enters her classroom, she greets Ms. Williams and thanks her for making tea. She sees Ms. Williams reviewing the book. "What do you think of it?" she asks. "I think it will be a good book to use. We can tie it in to our social studies unit on immigration and our community meetings on friendships." Ms. Williams nods and says, "How's your Spanish? Maybe we can have students work in math by using numbers in Spanish."

8:45 a.m.: Ms. Williams' and Ms. Silver's 23 students start entering the classroom. Amid the chatter, the students organize themselves for the day. While the students socialize, several students perform class jobs. They take the attendance, water the plants, perform the lunch count, and boot up the computers. The class is made up of 12 girls and 11 boys and includes 7 students with disabilities: 4 students with learning disabilities, 1 student with an emotional/behavioral disorder, 1 student with multiple disabilities, and 1 student who has a health impairment. The class also includes 3 African American students, 2 Hispanic students, and 1 who recently arrived in the United States from Eastern Europe.

9:00 a.m.: Ms. Silver rings a bell and the students go to their desks, which are arranged in groups of five or six. Each group contains a mixture of students by gender, ability, and cultural and linguistic background. One student from each group serves as a homework checker, verifying which students have completed their homework and what help students need. Half of the homework checkers report to Ms. Williams and half report to Ms. Silver, who record their findings. Before the reading groups assemble, a group of students selects a song and leads the class in singing it.

9:10 a.m.: The students go to their reading groups. Ms. Williams works with one group, while Ms. Silver works with another. As Ms. Williams starts to read a story to her group, several students remind her that Nicole needs her positioning board so that she can see the book. Several students also work independently. James works with Mr. Thomas, the paraeducator. First, James listens to and reads along with an audiocassette of a passage from a book; then he reads the section without the audiocassette and answers questions about what he has read and heard. Felicia is using the Internet to find another book written by her favorite author, which her teachers said she could read next.

After each student has had a chance to read, the teachers give them a choice of activities concerning the book. Some students choose to design a book cover reflecting important elements of the book; others choose to write about what they think will happen next; several students work together to role play the part of the story they just read; and some create a Venn diagram comparing themselves with a character in the book.

9:55 a.m.: While Ms. Williams prepares the materials for science class, Ms. Silver and Mr. Thomas remind the students that they have 5 minutes to finish their work and get ready for science. They show the students some rocks they will be working with in science class. Ms. Silver asks Lewis to help Sandy clean up and get ready for the next activity.

10:05 a.m.: The students go back to their desks and get ready for science class. While Ms. Williams reviews the concepts covered in the previous science class, Ms. Silver moves around the room to make sure that all of the students are ready for science and paying attention. Ms. Williams tells the students, "Today, we are going to learn more about different types of rocks." She shows them the flowchart that they had previously developed to identify and classify rocks. After Ms. Williams reviews the flowchart with the students and demonstrates how to use it to categorize a rock, the teachers place the students in groups. Each group is given six rocks and told to use the flowchart to identify the types of rocks they have and the reasons for their classifications. Ms. Williams, Ms. Silver, and Mr. Thomas circulate to

(Continued on page 10)

Principles of
Effective Inclusion

All Learners and Equal Access

Effective inclusion *improves the educational system for* all learners *by placing them together in general education classrooms—regardless of their learning ability, race, linguistic ability, economic status, gender, learning style, ethnicity, cultural and religious background, religion, family structure, and sexual orientation.* Inclusion programs also provide *all students* with equal access to a challenging, engaging, and flexible general education curriculum and the appropriate services that help them to be successful in society (Fisher & Frey, 2001; Roach, Salisbury, & McGregor, 2002). Students are given a multilevel and multimodality curriculum, as well as challenging educational and social experiences that are consistent with their abilities and needs. Inclusionary schools welcome, acknowledge, affirm, and celebrate the value of *all learners* by educating them together in high-quality, age-appropriate general education classrooms in their neighborhood schools (Bloom, Perlmutter, & Burrell, 1999; Kluth, Villa, Thousand, 2002). *All students* have opportunities to learn and play together, and participate in educational, social, and recreational activities (Edmiaston & Fitzgerald, 2000).

Individual Strengths and Needs and Diversity

Principle 2

Effective inclusion *involves sensitivity to and acceptance of individual strengths and needs and diversity.* Educators cannot teach students without taking into account the diverse factors that shape their students and make them unique (Tomlinson, 2003). Forces such as disability, race, linguistic background, gender, and economic status interact and affect academic performance and socialization; therefore, educators, students, and family members must be sensitive to inclusionary practices, which promote acceptance, equity, collaboration, and are responsive to individual strengths and needs and embrace diversity (Voltz, Brazil, & Ford, 2001; Sapon-Shevin, 2003). In inclusive classrooms, *all students* are valued as individuals capable of learning and contributing to society. They are taught to appreciate diversity and to value and learn from each other's similarities and differences (Hunt et al., 2000).

Reflective Practices and Differentiated Instruction

Principle 3

Effective inclusion *requires reflective educators to examine their attitudes, and differentiate their assessment, teaching, and classroom management practices, to accommodate individual needs and provide all learners with meaningful access to and progress in the general education curriculum.* In inclusive classrooms, teachers are reflective practitioners who are flexible, responsive, and aware of students' strengths and needs. They think critically about their values and beliefs and routinely examine their own practices for self-improvement and to ensure that *all students'* needs are met (Costa & Kallick, 2000). Educators individualize education and differentiate instruction for *all students* in terms of assessment techniques, general education curriculum accessibility, teaching strategies, technology, universal and physical design accommodations, classroom management techniques and a wide array of resources and related services based on their needs (Ford, Davern, & Schnorr, 2001; Hitchcock, Meyer, Rose, & Jackson, 2002; Tomlinson, 2003).

Community and Collaboration

Principle 4

Effective inclusion *is a group effort; it involves establishing community based on collaboration among educators, other professionals, students, families, and community agencies* (Hunt, Soto, Maier, & Doering, 2003; Jackson, Ryndak, & Billingsley, 2000). Inclusion seeks to establish a nurturing community of learners that is based on acceptance and belonging and the delivery of the support and services that students need in the general education classroom (Sapon-Shevin, 2003). People work cooperatively and reflectively, establishing community, communicating regularly, and sharing resources, responsibilities, skills, decisions, and advocacy for the students' benefit (Hunt et al., 2000; Ruder, 2000). School districts provide support, training, time, and resources to restructure their programs to support individuals in working collaboratively and reflectively to address students' needs.

Implementing Inclusion (Continued)

assist the groups, monitor their cooperative skills, and make sure that each group member is participating. Near the end of the time period, each group shares its findings. James and Nicole identify the colors of each rock for their groups. The teachers note the different ways the rocks can be categorized and tell the students that they will continue to work on other rocks tomorrow.

11:10 a.m.: Mr. Thomas announces that it is free time. He shows the students a board game, and several students start playing it. Several other students have brought their yo-yos to school and show each other different tricks they can perform. Other students play with various toys, musical instruments, and computers.

11:30 a.m.: Ms. Williams tells the students that they have 5 minutes left and should start thinking about mathematics.

11:35 a.m.: Ms. Silver asks the students to go to their desks and get ready for math. Several students are still on the floor by the cabinet near the teachers' desks. One student yells, "Geneviere's pen is under the cabinet, and we can't reach it." Ms. Silver again tells the students to go to their desks as Ms. Williams tries to help Geneviere retrieve her pen.

11:38 a.m.: The pen has been retrieved, and the teachers and Mr. Thomas work with the students in math groups. Some students are using Base Ten Blocks to understand place value and count, while others are using them to work on multidigit addition, subtraction, and multiplication. Near the end of the period, the groups come together to play a math game. Throughout the game, students are rotated from team to team, the questions are individualized based on students' skills levels, and the answers to the game's math questions require the input of more than one member of each team.

12:20 p.m.: Ms. Williams asks the students to get ready for lunch, and Ms. Silver takes them to lunch.

12:40 p.m.: The students finish lunch and go outside to play. Milton is playing with a group of students and gets a little too rough. Several of the students call Milton a name.

1:01 p.m.: The students return to class, and Mr. Thomas tells Ms. Williams and Ms. Silver about the name-calling that occurred during recess. The teachers take turns reading aloud while students go to the bathroom or for a drink of water.

1:15 p.m.: Ms. Williams and Ms. Silver announce, "We are going to have a community meeting." Without mentioning names, Mr. Thomas describes the name-calling incident. Ms. Williams and Ms. Silver then ask a series of questions. "What does it mean to call someone a name?" "Why does one person call another person a name?" "How does it feel when someone calls you a name?" and "What can be done to prevent name-calling?" Students share their responses and brainstorm solutions to the problem. The teachers summarize the students' responses and end the community meeting by role-playing a conflict between students and asking the students to identify ways in which the conflict could be handled without name-calling.

1:58 p.m.: Ms. Silver asks the students to line up, and Mr. Thomas takes them to music class. Meanwhile, the educators begin assembling a bulletin board. They start discussing the students' reactions to the community meeting, as well as additional activities they could use to counter name-calling and to foster a cooperative spirit in the group. They also discuss potential items related to the unit on rocks that students could include in their portfolios, and they put notes to families in students' homework folders.

2:22 p.m.: Ms. Cameron, the speech and language teacher, stops by to talk with the teachers about tomorrow's Writers' Workshop activity. She talks about how she plans to work on expanding sentences with her Writers' Workshop group and says that she will need to use the overhead projector in the classroom. The teachers also discuss the roles family volunteers will play during the Writers' Workshop.

2:40 p.m.: The students return from music class. While one student reads the homework assignment from the chalkboard, Ms. Williams, Ms. Silver, and Mr. Thomas move around the room to make sure that all the students have their colored homework folders and notebooks. The students perform end-of-the-day jobs such as shutting down the computers, washing the chalkboard, and organizing materials.

3:05 p.m.: The teachers praise the students for their good work and remind them of the discussion in the community meeting. While Ms. Silver walks the students to their buses, Ms. Williams sends the day's homework assignment by e-mail to the family that had requested it in the morning.

3:15 p.m.: Ms. Silver and Ms. Williams meet to copy and prepare materials, plan activities, and discuss report grades and testing accommodations for individual students.

4:30 p.m.: Ms. Silver and Ms. Williams wish each other good night and leave the school.

- What aspects of their school day and program make you believe that Ms. Silver, Mr. Thomas, and Ms. Williams work in an inclusion classroom?
- What roles did Ms. Silver, Mr. Thomas, Ms. Williams, and their students play in their classroom?
- How did Ms. Silver, Mr. Thomas, and Ms. Williams address the educational, social, and behavioral needs of their students?

- What types of support services do Ms. Silver and Ms. Williams receive to help them implement their program?
- What types of support do educators need to implement an inclusion program?
- How does their classroom reflect the four principles of inclusion?

To learn about how to implement inclusion in secondary-level content-area classrooms, read the chapter 8 opening vignette.

- How are the four principles of inclusion implemented in secondary-level classrooms?

Companion Website

To answer these questions online and share your responses with others, go to the Reflection module in Chapter 1 of the Companion Website.

A comparison of inclusion and mainstreaming

FIGURE 1.1

INCLUSION	MAINSTREAMING
Who	
• All learners have the right to be educated in general education classrooms.	• Selected learners earn their way into general education classes based on their readiness as determined by educators.
What	
• Full access to the general education curriculum and all instructional and social activities	• Selected access to the general education curriculum and instructional and social activities
Where and When	
• Full-time placement in general education classrooms	• Part-time to full-time placement in general education classrooms
How	
• A full range of services is integrated into the general education setting (e.g., cooperative teaching).	• A full range of services is delivered inside and outside the general education setting (e.g., resource room).
• General and special education are merged into a unified service delivery system.	• General and special education are maintained as separate service delivery systems.
Why	
• To foster the academic, social-emotional, behavioral, and physical development of students and to prepare them to be contributing members of society	• To foster the academic, social-emotional, behavioral, and physical development of students and to prepare them to be contributing members of society

The least restrictive environment (LRE) requires educational agencies to educate students with disabilities as much as possible with their peers who do not have disabilities. How does the least restrictive environment principle work in your school district?

did and did not have disabilities to more specific integration of students with disabilities into the social and instructional activities of the general education classroom. Often, the decision to place a student in a mainstreamed setting was based on educators' assessment of his or her readiness; thus, it was implied that students had to earn the right to be educated full-time in an age-appropriate general education classroom. Because the concept of mainstreaming was broadly interpreted and implemented, the practice of mainstreaming involved many different service delivery models, including pull-out programs in which students left the general education setting for supportive services such as resource room programs and speech and language services.

What Is the Least Restrictive Environment?

Least Restrictive Environment

Both inclusion and mainstreaming are rooted in the concept of the *least restrictive environment (LRE)*. The LRE requires schools to educate students with disabilities as much as possible with their peers who do not have disabilities. The LRE is determined individually, based on the student's educational needs rather than the student's disability. The LRE concept promotes the placement of students with disabilities in general education classrooms (Kluth, Villa, & Thousand, 2002). It also means that students can be shifted to self-contained special education classes, specialized schools, and residential programs only when their school performance indicates that even with supplementary aids and services, they cannot be educated satisfactorily in a general education classroom.

The LRE also prefers to allow students to attend school as close as possible to their homes and to interact with other students from the neighborhood. The participation of

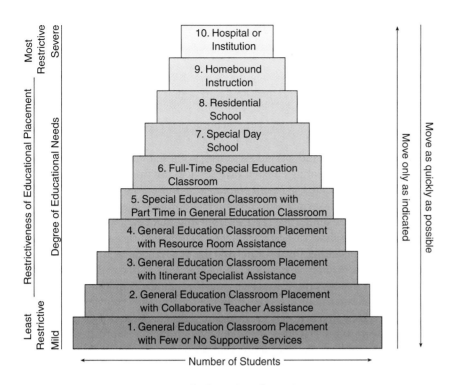

FIGURE 1.2   **Continuum of educational services**

students with disabilities in all parts of the school program, including extracurricular activities, also is an important aspect of the LRE (Mills, 1998). The LRE also relates to the principle of natural proportions, according to which the ratio of students with and without disabilities in a classroom reflects the ratio of the larger population.

Continuum of Educational Placements

To implement the LRE and organize the delivery of special education services, school districts use a continuum of educational placements ranging from the highly *integrated* setting of the general education classroom to the highly *segregated* setting where instruction is delivered in hospitals and institutions (Deno, 1970; Thomas & Rapport, 1998). Figure 1.2 presents the range from most to least restrictive educational placements for students, although variation exists within and among schools and agencies. A student is placed in the LRE based on his or her needs, skills, abilities, and motivation. A student moves to a less restrictive environment as quickly as possible and moves to a more segregated one only when necessary. The placement options, which vary in the extent to which students have access to the general education curriculum and peers, presented in Figure 1.2, will now be described.

> *Option 1. General education classroom placement with few or no supportive services.* The LRE is the general education classroom with few or no supportive services. The student is educated in the general education classroom, with the general education classroom teacher having the primary responsibility for designing and teaching the instructional program. The instructional program is individualized to the needs of the student, who may use assistive technology and

alternative learning strategies. Indirect services such as teacher inservice education to individualize the instructional program for students with disabilities may be offered.

Option 2. General education classroom placement with collaborative teacher assistance. This placement option is similar to option 1. However, the general education classroom teacher and the student receive collaborative services from ancillary support personnel in the general education classroom. We refer to this as a *push-in program.* The collaborative services will vary, depending on the nature and level of the student's needs as well as those of the teacher. Guidelines for implementing collaborative services are provided in chapter 4.

Option 3. General education classroom placement with itinerant specialist assistance. Teaching takes place in the general education classroom, and the student also receives supportive services from itinerant teachers (Sadler, 2001). Depending on the school district's arrangement, itinerant teachers may deliver services to students either inside or outside the general education classroom.

Option 4. General education classroom placement with resource room assistance. Resource room teachers offer direct services to students with disabilities, usually in a separate resource room within the school. They provide individualized remedial instruction in specific skills (such as note-taking, study skills, and so on) to small groups of students. In addition, resource teachers often provide supplemental instruction that supports and parallels the instruction given in the general education classroom. Since these teachers typically work in a location outside of the general education classroom, we refer to this as a *pull-out program.* The resource room teacher also can help general classroom teachers plan and implement instructional accommodations for students. For example, a science teacher and a resource room teacher might meet to identify the vocabulary words that support the key concepts in units of instruction. They would then coordinate their instruction, with the resource room teacher providing supplementary instruction to help students master the key vocabulary terms they identified.

Option 5. Special education classroom placement with part time in the general education classroom. In this option, the student's primary placement is in a special education classroom within the same school building as peers who are not disabled. The student's academic program is supervised by a special educator. The amount of time spent in the general education setting for academic instruction and socialization varies.

Option 6. Full-time special education classroom. This placement alternative is similar to option 5. However, contact with peers who are not disabled typically is exclusively social; teaching takes place in a separate classroom. Students in option 6 share common experiences with other students on school buses, at lunch or recess, and during schoolwide activities (assemblies, plays, dances, sporting events, and so on).

Option 7. Special day school. Students in this placement alternative attend a school different from that of their neighborhood peers. Placement in a special school allows school districts to centralize services. This option is highly restrictive and is sometimes used with students with more severe emotional, physical, and cognitive disabilities.

Option 8. Residential school. Residential programs also are designed to serve students with more severe needs. Students attending residential schools live at the school and participate in a 24-hour program. In addition to providing education, these programs offer the comprehensive medical and psychological services that students may need.

Option 9. Homebound instruction. Some students, such as those who are recovering from surgery or an illness or who have been suspended from school, may require homebound instruction. In this alternative, a teacher teaches the student at home. Technological advances now allow students who are homebound to interact and take classes with their peers at school.

Option 10. Hospital or institution. Placing individuals with disabilities in hospitals and institutions has been reduced by the deinstitutionalization movement, but it still exists. As with the other placement options, education must be part of any hospital or institutional program. These placements should be viewed as short term, and an emphasis should be placed on moving these individuals to a less restrictive environment.

Reflective

Some advocates of inclusion see these options as a deterrent to educating students in general education classrooms because they maintain a dual system of general and special education. Others think that these placements recognize the diverse needs of students and the different ways of addressing these needs. What is your view?

Judicial decisions in *Daniel R.R. v. State Board of Education* (1989), *Greer v. Rome City School District* (1991), *Oberti v. Board of Education of the Borough of Clementon School District* (1993), *Sacramento City Unified School District, Board of Education v. Holland* (1994), *Clyde K. and Sheila K. v. Puyallup School District* (1994), *Poolaw v. Bishop* (1995), and *Seattle School District No. 1 v. B.S.* (1996) have established guidelines that you must consider when implementing the LRE concept for your students (Kluth, Villa, & Thousand, 2002; Thomas & Rapport, 1998; Yell, 1998). Taken together, these cases suggest that *all* students have a right to be educated in general education settings, and that in placing a student in the LRE, your school district should consider:

- the anticipated educational benefits in the general education setting with appropriate supplementary aids and services compared with the benefits of the special education classroom.
- the noneducational, social, and self-concept benefits that are likely to occur in the general education setting, including interactions with classmates.
- the impact of the student with a disability on the education of classmates without disabilities.
- the effect of the student with a disability on teachers and their instructional time.
- the cost of educating the student in the general education setting with supplementary aids and services, and the effect of these costs on the district's resources for educating other students.

What Factors Contributed to the Movement to Educate Learners in Inclusive Classrooms?

The number of school districts implementing inclusion for their students with disabilities has increased significantly. Data from the U.S. Department of Education indicate the number of students with disabilities in general education classrooms has climbed steadily (McLeskey, Henry, & Hodges, 1999), and the movement toward educating *all learners* in general education classes continues to be an ongoing direction for the field of education (Voltz, Brazil, & Ford, 2001). In the following sections, we will look at several factors contributing to this movement. (Societal changes have also occurred, and inclusion has proved to be effective for educating diverse learners in general education classrooms. These societal changes are discussed in greater detail in Chapter 3.)

Normalization

Reflective

In what ways has the normalization principle been implemented in your community?

Inclusion is rooted in the principle of *normalization*, which originated in Scandinavia and was later brought to the United States (Wolfensberger, 1972). Normalization seeks to provide opportunities, social interactions, and experiences that parallel those of society to adults and children with disabilities. Thus the philosophy of educating students with disabilities in inclusive settings rests on the principle that educational, housing, employment, social, and leisure opportunities for individuals with disabilities should resemble as closely as possible the opportunities and activities enjoyed by their peers who are not disabled.

Deinstitutionalization

Up to very recently, individuals with disabilities were placed in institutions that isolated them from the public. Think back to the chapter-opening vignette: Whereas Marie spent some time in an institution, this option was never considered for Mary, in part, because of the movement toward deinstitutionalization (Katsiyannis, Zhang, & Archwamety, 2002). Because of the terrible conditions found in many institutions, as well as a growing awareness of the negative effects of institutionalization, institutions for individuals with disabilities were closed and smaller, community-based independent living arrangements were developed. Unfortunately, few funds have been earmarked for services to support these arrangements, limiting the impact of the deinstitutionalization movement.

Early Intervention and Early Childhood Programs

The effectiveness of early intervention and early childhood programs (like the one Mary attended) has promoted the placement of students with disabilities in general education settings (Barnett & Hustedt, 2003; Lieber et al., 2002). Effective early intervention and early childhood programs offer *all students* and families access to:

cd-rom

To view examples of preschool inclusion programs, go to Case 1: Difficult Behavior on the CD-ROM, and view all the video clips. What roles do the teachers and paraeducators perform to implement the principles of early childhood inclusion programs?

Set Your Sites

For more information on early intervention and early childhood programs, go to the Web Links module in Chapter 1 of the Companion Website.

- developmentally, individually, and culturally appropriate practices: the instructional practices and the curriculum are designed to address the individual, developmental, and cultural needs of students.
- natural environments: the settings where young children commonly learn everyday skills.
- family-centered service coordination: the process of forming partnerships with families to assist them in identifying and obtaining the services, supports, and resources they need to foster learning and development.
- transition practices: the planning and delivery of practices that help young children make the transition to general education classrooms (Dunst & Bruder, 2002; La Paro, Pianta, & Cox, 2000).

These programs have increased the physical, motor, cognitive, language, speech, socialization, and self-help skills of many children from birth through age 6. They have also reduced the likelihood that secondary disabilities will occur, empowered families to promote their child's development, and decreased the probability that children with disabilities will be socially dependent and institutionalized as adults. In a follow-up study comparing adults who received early childhood services with adults who did not, Schweinhart and Weikart (1993) found that those who received early childhood services made more money, attained a higher level of education, and used fewer social services than those who did not.

Technological Advances

Freedom. That's what assistive technology means to me. (Matt Boyer, a teen who uses assistive technology)

Mary's placement in inclusive settings also was fostered by technology that was not available when Marie was growing up. These technological advances have changed the quality of life for many individuals, empowering them by fostering their access, independence, and achievement (Goldberg & O'Neill, 2000). Assistive and instructional technology allows individuals with communication, physical, learning, and sensory disabilities to gain more control over their lives and environment, as well as greater access to society and general education classrooms (Bryant, Bryant, & Raskind, 1998). While these devices were developed for individuals with disabilities, they have consequences and benefits for *all members of society.*

The Technology-Related Assistance for Individuals with Disabilities Act of 1988 and the Assistive Technology Act of 1998 acknowledge the use of assistive technology as a tool for improving the lives of individuals with disabilities and their inclusion in society (Bryant & Seay, 1998). These acts and the IDEA delineate two aspects of assistive technology: devices and services. An *assistive technology device* is defined as any item, piece of equipment, or product system—whether bought, modified, or customized—that is used to increase, maintain, or improve the functional capabilities of an individual with a disability.

Assistive technology is often categorized as being high or low technology. Whereas *high technology* devices tend to be electronic and commercially produced, low technology devices are usually nonelectric and homemade. High technology devices that are used in classrooms include electronic communication, speech recognition, and reading systems, motorized wheelchairs, long canes, adapted keyboards, touch screens, and magnification aids (Parette & McMahan, 2002). *Low technology* assistive devices that students may use in the classroom include pencil holders, and strings attached to objects to retrieve them if they fall on the floor. An *assistive technology service* is defined as any

Resource

Edmiaston and Fitzgerald (2000), Fox, Dunlap, and Cushing (2002), and Udell, Peters, and Templeman (1998) offer guidelines for designing and implementing inclusive early childhood programs.

Medical and assistive technology devices have promoted the inclusion movement. How have you and your family benefited from medical and assistive technology?

Set Your Sites

For more information on helping individuals with disabilities obtain the assistive technology they need, go to the Web Links module in Chapter 1 of the Companion Website.

Reflective

Technological and medical advances have affected *all members of society.* For example, Alexander Graham Bell's attempts to amplify his voice to communicate more effectively with his wife, who had a hearing impairment, led to the invention of the telephone. What high and low technological devices do you use?

service that directly assists an individual with a disability to select, acquire, or use an assistive technology device, including physical, occupational, and speech therapy. These acts also addressed the principle of universal design, a concept or philosophy that guides the design and delivery of products and services so that they are usable by individuals with a wide range of functional capabilities (Hitchcock et al., 2002) (We will learn more about universal design in chapter 8).

As a result of these acts, many state education departments have established programs to link individuals with the devices they need. For example, the Trace R & D Center at the University of Wisconsin at Madison (*www.trace.wisc.edu*) has developed a CD-ROM that contains descriptions and ordering information on more than 20,000 assistive devices. Additional information on assistive and instructional technology is presented in chapters 2 and 8.

Civil Rights Movement and Resulting Litigation

Separate educational facilities are inherently unequal. This inherent inequality stems from the stigma created by purposeful segregation which generates a feeling of inferiority that may affect their hearts and minds in a way unlikely ever to be undone. (Earl Warren, Chief Justice of the Supreme Court, *Brown v. Board of Education*)

There was no equality of treatment merely by providing students with the same facilities, textbooks, teachers, and curriculum, for students who do not understand English are effectively foreclosed from any meaningful education. (The Supreme Court in *Lau v. Nichols*, 1974)

The impetus toward educating students like Mary in inclusive, general education settings was also aided by the civil rights movement. The precedent for much special education-related litigation was established by *Brown* v. *Topeka Board of Education* (1954). The decision in this landmark civil rights case determined that segregating students in schools based on race, even if other educational variables appear to be equal, is unconstitutional. This refutation of the doctrine of "separate but equal" served as the underlying argument in court actions brought by families to ensure that their children with disabilities received a free, appropriate public education.

One example of such a court action is *Pennsylvania Association for Retarded Children* v. *Commonwealth of Pennsylvania* (1972). The families of children like Marie questioned the Pennsylvania School Code that was being used to justify the education of students with disabilities in environments that segregated them from their peers without disabilities. In a consent agreement approved by the court, the Commonwealth of Pennsylvania agreed that all students with mental retardation had a right to a free public education. The agreement further stated that placement in a general education public school classroom is preferable to more segregated placements and that families have the right to be informed of any changes in their children's educational program. A second case, *Mills* v. *Board of Education of the District of Columbia* (1972), extended the right to a free public education for students with disabilities. The judge also ruled that the cost of educational services was not a justifiable reason for denying special education services to students who needed them. Both of these cases were catalysts for change in the way individuals with disabilities were educated in the public school system. Figure 1.3 summarizes other cases that influenced the education of children with disabilities, as well as children with culturally and linguistically diverse backgrounds.

USING TECHNOLOGY TO PROMOTE INCLUSION

Fostering Inclusion and Independence

My name is Robin Smith. I always wanted to be a teacher and was excited when my goal became a reality. I enjoyed my job and looked forward to going to school every day. After several years of teaching, I started to feel exhausted and have recurring body aches. When I wasn't teaching or eating, I was sleeping. After two years, I was finally diagnosed as having adult-onset severe rheumatoid arthritis.

My condition got worse and I had to leave teaching. My fingers were like clay as they seemed to take a different shape every day. Eventually, I moved back home with my family. I could barely move my arms and legs and entered a hospital for several months. Upon leaving the hospital my life revolved around sleeping, eating, and going to physical therapy five times a week.

I took arthritis and anti-inflammatory medications, which over time helped me to regain limited use of my hands and feet. With the help of a motorized wheelchair, I started to get involved in the community. I also became active in several groups advocating for individuals with disabilities. I used a tape recorder with dictation and a 1-pound portable computer to write grants for these groups and to prepare materials to lobby legislators.

While I was feeling better physically and emotionally, I missed teaching. I wanted to combine my love of teaching and my advocacy work and decided to pursue a doctorate in special education. My state's Office of Vocational Rehabilitation helped me in several ways. I needed a vehicle to get to and from my home to school and to participate in other required off-campus activities. After I purchased a vehicle, the Vocational Rehabilitation Office paid to retrofit it so that I could drive it and transport my motorized chair. This involved raising the roof and installing a lift, zero-effort steering, automatic gear shifting, toggle switches, and an electronic seat. While these adaptations helped, I used some home-made materials to more efficiently use the vehicle. I used a long and short dressing stick to reach the radio, fan, temperature controls, and gear-shift buttons, and to pick up things from the floor. I also tied a string to the directional signal to make it easier for me to use. I used to use a "reacher" to pull tickets out of machines when entering a toll booth. Now that most toll booths have an electronic system, I use the "reacher" only to enter parking areas.

My success in school was aided by use of a small computer that was like a personal digital assistant with a keyboard. I used it to take notes, and as a word processor, calendar, and address book. After school, I transferred the information to a desktop computer. I also tried voice-recognition software, but I found it inconsistent. I completed my doctorate, and was pleased to be hired as a special education professor. I continue to use many of the same things I did as a student to do the different aspects of my job.

The university I work for is about 200 miles from my family, so I live alone, which is a challenge. However, I use several everyday things to make my life a little easier. I place long sticks with hooks throughout my home so that I can reach things and put my clothes on. I tie strings to the doors to help me open and close them, and clip key rings and other small important objects to my clothes so I don't drop them. I tie loops on light objects so that I can pick them up from the floor with my sticks, and use a dust pan with a handle to pick up heavier items. I use an anti-skid mat to get up from chairs and electronic gadgets in the kitchen.

As with many other people, it has been a challenge for me to meet my goals. However, my personal strength, the support of others, and access to technology has helped me reach my goals.

- What high and low technology assistive devices were helpful to Robin Smith?
- How did these assistive devices foster Robin Smith's independence and inclusion in society?
- How was Robin Smith able to obtain these assistive devices?
- How would Robin Smith's life be different if she did not have access to these assistive devices?
- What high and low technology assistive devices might benefit your students?
- How can you help your students obtain these devices?

Court cases related to special and inclusive educational practices.

FIGURE 1.3

Since the *Brown* v. *Topeka Board of Education* case (1954), several cases have dealt with the educational rights of students with disabilities and students from diverse cultural and linguistic backgrounds, as well as the schools' responsibility to educate them. These cases also helped establish the importance of giving students a general education in an inclusive setting.

Hobson v. *Hansen* (1967). The federal district court for the District of Columbia ruled that tracking was unconstitutional and should be abolished, as it segregated students on the basis of race and/or economic status.

Diana v. *California State Board of Education* (1970). The California State Board of Education agreed to modify its assessment practices for identifying Mexican American students referred to special education, including testing students in their primary language, eliminating culturally biased test items, using nonverbal tests, and creating alternative intelligence tests (Baca, 1998).

Lau v. *Nichols* (1974). The U.S. Supreme Court extended the concept of equal educational opportunity to include special language programs for students who speak languages other than English. The *Lau* decision, coupled with PL 94-142, also mandated bilingual special education services and set the precedent for other laws and lawsuits relating to meeting the educational needs of students who speak languages other than English (Baca, 1998).

Larry P. v. *Riles* (1979). The federal district court in California ruled that the intelligence tests used to determine whether African American students were eligible for special education classes for students with mental retardation were racially and culturally biased, and ordered California to develop nondiscriminatory procedures for placing students in special education classes. In 1986, the *Larry P.* ruling was extended to question the use of intelligence testing to place African American students in all types of special education categories (Yell, 1998).

Board of Education of the Hendrick Hudson School District v. *Rowley* (1982). The Supreme Court ruled that PL 94-142 was designed to provide students with disabilities reasonable opportunities to learn but that it did not require school districts to help them reach their maximum potential.

Irving Independent School District v. *Tatro* (1984). The Supreme Court stated that whether a medical service is a related service depends on who provides it, rather than on the service itself. This decision also depends on the extent to which the procedure or service must be delivered during the school day for the student to participate in the educational program (Rapport, 1996).

Timothy W. v. *Rochester, N.H. School District* (1989). The Supreme Court let stand a U.S. Court of Appeals ruling that no matter how severe a student's disability is or how little a student may benefit, the school must educate the student.

Agostini v. *Felton* (1997). The Supreme Court ruled that school districts may provide on-site special education and related services to students attending religious schools (Osborne, Dimattia, & Russo, 1998).

Cedar Rapids Community School District v. *Garret F.* (1999). The Supreme Court ruled that the IDEA entitles students with disabilities to medical services performed by nonphysicians, regardless of their cost to the school district, or their complexity.

Set Your Sites

For more information on special education case law, go to the Web Links module in Chapter 1 of the Companion Website.

(For the purposes of this text, culturally and linguistically diverse students are defined as those who are not native members of the Euro-Caucasian culture base currently dominant in the United States and/or those whose native or primary language is not English.)

Reflective

Think of a relative, friend, or neighbor who has a disability. How has that individual affected you and others in your family and neighborhood? How have you advocated for that individual?

Set Your Sites

For more information on disability rights groups, go to the Web Links module in Chapter 1 of the Companion Website.

Set Your Sites

For more information related to the largest professional organization addressing issues related to individuals with disabilities, go to the Web Links module in Chapter 1 of the Companion Website.

Advocacy Groups

Fueled by the momentum of civil rights campaigns, advocacy groups of family members like Mary's and Marie's parents, professionals, and individuals with disabilities banded together to seek civil rights and greater societal acceptance for individuals with disabilities. Besides alerting the public to issues related to individuals with disabilities, advocacy groups lobbied state and federal legislators, brought lawsuits, and protested polices of exclusion and segregation (Katsiyannis, Yell, & Bradley, 2001). The result was greater societal acceptance and rights for individuals with disabilities like Mary.

Various economic, political, and environmental factors have increased the number of individuals with disabilities, adding to the growth of the disability rights movement. Individuals with disabilities have transformed themselves from invisible and passive recipients of sympathy to visible and active advocates of their rights as full members of society. These advocacy groups also have created a disability culture that celebrates and affirms disability, fosters community among individuals with disabilities, promotes disability awareness, and challenges society's conventional notions of disability (Martin, 1997). In chapter 4, we will discuss ways you can be an effective advocate for your students, their families, and important educational issues.

Many individuals become disabled after birth, and anyone can join this group at any time. How are your family members, friends, and neighbors with disabilities included in society?

Set Your Sites

For more information on programs to help students graduate, go to the Web Links module in Chapter 1 of the Companion Website.

Resource

Martin, Tobin, and Sugai (2002); Benz, Lindsrom, and Yovanoff (2000); Collet-Klingenberg (1998); Kortering & Braziel (1999); and Sinclair, Christenson, Evelo, and Hurley (1998) provide information, strategies, and models to help you work with others to help students complete school.

Segregated Nature of Special Schools and Classes

As the institutionalization of individuals with disabilities declined, the number of special schools and special classes within public schools for students with disabilities rose. However, educators, families and advocacy groups eventually questioned the segregation of these students. In 1968, Lloyd Dunn argued that special education classes for students with mild disabilities were unjustifiable because they served as a form of homogeneous grouping and tracking. He cited studies showing that students labeled as mildly disabled "made as much or more progress in the regular grades as they do in special classes" (p. 8), as well as studies showing that labeling reduces the student's self-concept and the teacher's expectations for success in school.

Studies on the effectiveness of special education programs also revealed that, progress aside, students with disabilities still have high dropout and incarceration rates and low employment rates (Martin, Tobin, & Sugai, 2002; Scanlon & Mellard, 2002). Graduation and promotion tests also are contributing to many students leaving school without a diploma (Heubert, 2003). Attending schools with few resources and programs for motivating students and encouraging family participation is another major contributor to school dropout.

Resource

Levine and Nourse (1998) summarize the research on postschool outcomes, postsecondary education, and employment for males and females with learning disabilities; and Heal, Khoju, and Rusch (1997) examine quality-of-life issues for students after they leave special education high school programs.

Disproportionate Representation

Dunn (1968) also raised concerns about the *disproportionate representation* of students from culturally and linguistically diverse backgrounds in special education classes that segregated these students, and saw inclusive placements as a way to counter this segregation. Disproportionate representation, also referred to as *disproportionality*, is the presence of students from a specific group in an educational program that is higher or

Reflective

How will the learning standards and testing in your state affect the dropout rate in your school district? Which types of students will be most affected?

lower than one would expect based on their representation in the general population of students (Salend, Garrick Duhaney, & Montgomery, 2002). It also includes the overrepresentation and underrepresentation of students from culturally and linguistically diverse backgrounds in terms of educational classification and placement, and access to programs, services, resources, curriculum, instruction, and classroom management techniques (Artiles & Zamora-Duran, 1997).

Unfortunately, Losen and Orfield (2002), and the National Research Council at the Academy of Science's (2002) report found that Dunn's concerns 35 years earlier about disproportionate representation are now a reality for some groups. African American and Native American students, particularly males, are overrepresented in terms of their classification as students with three types of disabilities: learning disabilities, mental retardation, and emotional disturbance. This overrepresentation in special education has raised concerns about students being placed in a separate program that hinders their educational and social performance by limiting their access to the general education curriculum (Patton & Townsend, 1999).

Conversely, when a specific group of students participate at lower rates than their prevalence in the general population of students, underrepresentation is occurring. For example, Hispanic, Native Indian, and African American students are underrepresented in programs designed for gifted and talented students (Ford, 1998) and tend to have less access to prereferral and ancillary services (Ochoa, Robles-Pina, Garcia, & Bruenig, 1999). Underrepresentation also can have a negative impact on students' academic and social performance since it denies them access to services, programs, and resources tailored to address their educational needs (Poon-McBrayer & Garcia, 2000).

A variety of educational and sociocultural factors interact to contribute to the disproportionate representation of students from culturally and linguistically diverse backgrounds (Obiakor & Ford, 2002; Zhang & Katsiyannis, 2002). While having a lower socioeconomic status increases the likelihood that students will be placed in special education (Macmillan & Reschly, 1998), the race and ethnicity of students and the unequal funding of schools appear to be major variables that contribute to the disproportionate representation of students from culturally and linguistically diverse backgrounds (Biddle & Berliner, 2002; Coutinho, Oswald, & Best, 2002).

Since issues of disproportionality are multifaceted and shaped by the cultural experiences of students and professionals (Gollnick & Chinn, 2002; Knotek, 2003), educators need to examine whether their policies, practices, attitudes, and behaviors result in disparate treatment of and disparate impact on students from culturally and linguistically diverse backgrounds (Voltz, 1998). *Disparate treatment* refers to treating students differently because of their characteristics and membership in a group such as their racial and linguistic background. An example would be disciplining such students differently from other students for the same offense (Townsend, 2000). Even when all students are treated similarly, this similar treatment can still have different outcomes, or a *disparate impact* on, members of different groups. For example, sending a letter written in English inviting families to attend a meeting may result in few families who do not speak English attending the meeting.

You can help minimize disproportionate representation by delivering a wide range of effective culturally sensitive educational strategies and services within the general education program that support student learning and family involvement (We will learn about these strategies and services in subsequent chapters of this book). These varied services should address students' and their families' unique needs and strengths as well as their experiential, cultural, and linguistic backgrounds, and therefore help minimize the need for placement in special education.

Reflective

Can you think of other examples of disparate treatment and disparate impact in schools? In society?

Resource

Salend, Garrick Duhaney, and Montgomery (2002) offer guidelines for examining and addressing issues related to disproportionate representation, and Montgomery (2001) provides suggestions for creating culturally responsive, inclusive classrooms.

Set Your Sites

For more information on disproportionate representation, go to the Web Links module in Chapter 1 of the Companion Website.

Students from culturally and linguistically diverse backgrounds, particularly African American males, tend to be overrepresented in special education programs and underrepresented in programs for gifted and talented students. Why do you think this is the case?

Standards-Based Reform and No Child Left Behind Act

The challenge to reform our educational system means that schools must restructure and coordinate their efforts and programs to help *all learners*—including those with disabilities—have access to and succeed in the general education curriculum to meet specific learning standards and the legislative provisions of the No Child Left Behind Act (NCLB) (Fisher & Frey, 2001; Roach, Salisbury, & McGregor, 2002). Learning standards establish curricular expectations that identify the things that learners should know and be able to do at the various grade levels. They also provide a framework that guides what is taught and how student learning is facilitated and assessed.

Standards-based reform efforts and the No Child Left Behind Act also have established that *all learners* should be included in high-stakes assessments aligned with statewide learning standards (Allbritten, Mainzer, & Ziegler, 2004). For example, the No Child Left Behind Act contains provisions mandating that school districts show they are making adequate yearly progress on state tests for *all their students* including subgroups of students identified in terms of their disability, socioeconomic status, language background, race, and ethnicity. These efforts seek to make schools accountable for educating *all learners* and translating assessment results into instructional accommodations that support learning (Thurlow, 2002; Walsh, 2001). Thus, rather than segregating students with disabilities based on their performance on standardized achievement tests, many schools are implementing inclusion programs to unify general and special education into one service delivery system to provide *all learners* with a general education (Matlock, Fielder, & Walsh, 2001).

Resource

Allbritten et al. (2004) discuss ways the No Child Left Behind Act may affect students with disabilities.

REFLECTING ON YOUR PRACTICES

Examining Disproportionate Representation

As specified in the Individuals with Disabilities Education Act (IDEA), school districts and state departments of education must determine whether the problems of overrepresentation and underrepresentation exist, as well as the nature of these problems. You can evaluate the extent to which students in your school district are disproportionately represented by addressing the following questions:

- Are students from culturally and linguistically diverse backgrounds disproportionately referred for and placed in special education? Gifted and talented programs?
- Do the reasons for referrals for special education differ based on the cultural and linguistic background of the students?
- Do patterns of identification by disability category differ by race or ethnicity?
- Do placements within the general education setting vary based on the cultural and linguistic backgrounds of students?
- Do members of the multidisciplinary teams reflect the diversity of the student population they serve and have the training and experience to properly and accurately assess the needs of students from diverse backgrounds?
- Do students from culturally and linguistically diverse backgrounds have equal access to the school district's prereferral, supportive, and transitional services, and extracurricular and community activities?
- Do placement teams consider the impact of cultural, linguistic, and experiential backgrounds and account for assessment bias when assessing students and their educational needs?

- Do the curriculum, teaching and classroom management strategies, and instructional materials address the experiences and needs of students from culturally and linguistically diverse backgrounds?
- Are students from culturally and linguistically diverse backgrounds disciplined or treated differently than other students for comparable behaviors?
- Do educators assess the extent to which student behavior is related to cultural, experiential, and linguistic factors?
- Do educators create respectful classrooms that promote acceptance of diversity?
- Are families and community members from culturally and linguistically diverse backgrounds involved in all aspects of the school?
- Do educators employ strategies to interact with family and community members in culturally sensitive ways and adjust their services to the diverse backgrounds of students' families?
- Does the school district maintain a complete database on issues related to disproportionate representation?

How would you rate the extent to which disproportionate representation exists in your school district?

( ) Doesn't Exist
( ) Exists to Some Extent
( ) Exists Extensively

What are some goals and steps your school district can adopt to address disproportionate representation?

Another aspect of standards-based reform is providing families with school choice as a means of prompting all schools to promote the performance of *all their students*. The No Child Left Behind Act requires school districts to offer families alternatives (i.e., school choice, extra tutoring) if their children attend schools where students do not perform well on state tests. School choice has led to the use of school vouchers and the development of charter schools, which have had a varied impact on student performance (Cosmos, 2000). Howe and Welner (2002) caution that school choice may conflict with the goal of inclusion because school choice and charter schools may either exclude students with special needs as not a good fit for their school, or practice the principle of nonexclusion and enroll these students but fail to provide them with the curricula and instructional accommodations they need to master the learning standards.

What Are the Laws That Affect Special Education?

The factors just discussed helped shape several education and civil rights laws designed primarily to include individuals with disabilities like Marie and Mary in *all* aspects of society. The most important of these laws is the Individuals with Disabilities Education Act, also known as the IDEA.

The Individuals with Disabilities Education Act (IDEA)

Initially known as the Education for All Handicapped Children Act (PL 94-142), it has been amended numerous times since its passage in 1975 and was renamed the Individuals with Disabilities Education Act in 1990. Highlights of these amendments are presented in Figure 1.4, and discussed next. The IDEA mandates that a *free and appropriate education* be provided to all students with disabilities, regardless of the nature and severity of their disability. It affirms that disability is "a natural part of the human experience" and acknowledges the normalization principle by asserting that individuals with disabilities have the right to "enjoy full inclusion and integration into the economic, political, social, cultural, and educational mainstream of society." The IDEA is the culmination of many efforts to ensure the rights of full citizenship and equal access for individuals with disabilities.

According to Turnbull, Turnbull, Shank, and Smith (2004), the IDEA is based on six fundamental principles that govern the education of students with disabilities. Under the first principle, *zero reject,* schools cannot exclude any student with a disability and each state must locate children who may be entitled to special education services. Under the second principle, *nondiscriminatory evaluation,* schools must evaluate students fairly to see whether they have a disability and provide guidelines for identifying the special education and related services they will receive if they do have a disability. The principle of a *free and appropriate education* requires schools to follow individually tailored education for each student defined in an Individualized Education Plan (IEP). The principle of the *least restrictive environment* (LRE) requires schools to educate students with disabilities with their peers who are not disabled to the maximum extent appropriate. The *procedural due process* principle provides safeguards against schools' actions, including the right to sue if schools do not carry out the other principles. The final principle requires *family and student participation* in designing and delivering special education programs and IEPs, which are explained in greater detail in chapter 2.

Reflective

How will the standards-based movement and No Child Left Behind Act provisions affect students with special needs? Your curriculum? Your teaching practices? Your work environment?

Resource

Seif (2004); Ford, Davern, and Schnorr (2001); Matlock, Fielder, and Walsh (2001); Nolet and McLaughlin (2000); Roach, Salisbury, and McGregor (2002); and Townsend (2002) offer frameworks and guidelines for incorporating standards-based reform into inclusion programs.

Resource

Katsiyannis, Yell, and Bradley (2001) outline and reflect on the history and impact of the Individuals with Disabilities Education Act, and Osborne, Russo, and DiMattia (2000) examine the provisions of the IDEA that apply to students in private schools.

An Overview of IDEA from 1975 to the Present: A Changing IDEA

Since IDEA was first passed in 1975, it has been amended and changed numerous times (see Figure 1.4). This section will outline the key concepts and changes of each law, as well as introduce several other laws affecting special education.

A changing IDEA

FIGURE 1.4

PL 94-142:   Education of All Handicapped Children Act of 1975

- Required the public schools to locate and educate school-age students with disabilities according to the following principles:
  - zero reject
  - nondiscrimination evaluation
  - free and appropriate education
  - least restrictive environment
  - procedural due process
  - family and student involvement
- Mandated the development of an Individualized Education Program (IEP) for school-age students with disabilities.

PL 99-457:   The Infants and Toddlers with Disabilities Act of 1986

- Provided financial incentives to encourage states to create early intervention and early childhood programs for children with disabilities from birth to age 5.
- Extended the rights of PL94-142 to infants, toddlers, and preschoolers with disabilities from birth to age 5.
- Mandated the development of an Individualized Family Service Plan (IFSP) for eligible children with disabilities.

PL 101-476:   The Individuals with Disabilities Education Act of 1990

- Changed the name of the law to reflect "individuals first" language.
- Expanded the categories of disability to include autism and traumatic brain injury.
- Added two related services: rehabilitation counseling and social work services.
- Increased the commitment to address the needs of culturally and linguistically diverse students with disabilities.
- Included transitional services as a requirement for the IEPs of students age 16 and older.

PL 105-17:   The Individuals with Disabilities Education Act Amendments of 1997

- Enhanced the role of families by ensuring their involvement in any group that makes decisions about their child's educational placement and requiring the IEP to include a statement of how often the student's family will be regularly informed of their child's progress.
- Modified components of the IEP to provide greater access to the general education curriculum and nonacademic activities in schools (see chapter 2 for additional information); to address students' unique needs with respect to behavioral interventions, assistive technology, instruction in Braille, and communication and language; and to include a statement of transition needs for students beginning at age 14, and transition services, including interagency responsibilities or linkages, at age 16 or younger (see chapters 2 and 6 for additional information).
- Expanded the composition of the IEP team to include both the student's general education and special education teachers, and professionals who are knowledgeable about the general education curriculum, district resources, and the instructional implications of the evaluation data (see chapter 2 for additional information).
- Added the inclusion of a statement on the IFSP relating to the delivery of early intervention services in natural environments with same-age peers without disabilities, including a justification of the use of other environments.
- Required the inclusion of students with disabilities in state and district assessments.
- Added provisions related to disciplining students with disabilities, conducting functional behavioral assessments, and using positive behavioral interventions and supports.
- Revised the eligibility requirements so that students may not be identified as having disability if their classification is based on lack of instruction in reading or mathematics or limited proficiency in English.
- Mandated that states and school districts collect and examine data related to disproportionate representation.
- Required states to offer mediation services for families and school districts to resolve their differences voluntarily.
- Established that students without disabilities can receive incidental benefits from the special education and related services that are provided to their classmates with disabilities.

PL 94-142: Education for All Handicapped Children Act.   Passed in 1975, this act mandates that a free and appropriate education be provided to all students with disabilities, regardless of the nature and severity of their disability. It outlines the IEP and states that students with disabilities will be educated in the LRE with their peers who are not disabled to the maximum extent appropriate. It also guarantees that students with disabilities and their families have the right to nondiscriminatory testing, confidentiality, and due process.

PL 99-457: Infants and Toddlers with Disabilities Act of 1986.   PL 99-457 extended many of the rights and safeguards of PL 94-142 to children with disabilities from birth to 5 years of age and encouraged early intervention services and special assistance to students who are at risk. It also included provisions for developing an Individualized Family Service Plan (IFSP) for each child. The components of an IFSP are presented in Figure 1.5.

Reflective

By replacing the term *handicapped* with the term *disabilities* in the IDEA, Congress recognized the importance of language. What do the terms *regular, normal,* and *special* imply? How do these terms affect the ways we view students with disabilities and the programs designed to meet their needs? Do these terms foster inclusion or segregation?

PL 101-476: Individuals with Disabilities Education Act of 1990.   In 1990, PL 101-476 changed the title of PL 94-142 from the Education for All Handicapped Children Act to the Individuals with Disabilities Education Act (IDEA), reflecting "individuals first" language. Additionally, all uses of the term *handicapped* were replaced by the term *disabilities*. IDEA continued the basic provisions outlined in PL 94-142 and made the following changes: the category of children with disabilities was expanded to include autism and brain injury; related services were expanded to include rehabilitation counseling and social work services; and the commitment to address the needs of linguistically and culturally diverse youth with disabilities was increased.

PL 105-17: The IDEA Amendments of 1997.   PL 105-17 included several provisions to improve the educational performance of students with disabilities by having high expectations for them, giving them greater access to general education and including them in local and state assessments, and making general and special educators and administrators members of the team that writes students' IEPs. PL 105-17 also sought to strengthen the role of families in their children's education and to prevent the disproportionate representation of students from diverse backgrounds in special education programs. The major provisions of PL 105-17 are presented in Figure 1.4.

Components of the IFSP

FIGURE 1.5

- ◈ A statement of the infant's or toddler's present level of development
- ◈ An assessment of the family's strengths and needs for enhancing the child's development, including the resources, priorities, and concerns of the family
- ◈ A statement of the outcomes to be achieved for the child and family
- ◈ A list of the criteria, techniques, and timelines for evaluating progress
- ◈ A statement of the early education services that will be delivered to meet the child's and family's unique needs, including their intensity and frequency
- ◈ A statement of the natural environments where the early education services will be delivered, as well as why other environments will be used if necessary
- ◈ The dates for starting services and their duration
- ◈ The name of the family's service coordinator, who will supervise the implementation of the program
- ◈ The procedures for moving the child from early intervention to preschool
- ◈ Annual evaluation of the IFSP, with a review every 6 months or more often if necessary

PL 108-446 Individuals with Disabilities Education Improvement Act:
With the passage of the Individuals with Disabilities Education Improvement Act of
2004, the Congress authorized the IDEA again. Information on the current reauthorization is presented in the IDEA supplement located at the beginning of this book. For an
update on the reauthorization of the IDEA and other topics discussed in this chapter, go
to the Legal Update module in chapter 1 of the Companion Website.

Other Laws Affecting Special Education

While your class will include many students who have unique needs, many of these students may not be eligible for special education services under the IDEA. However, they
may qualify for special and general education services under two civil rights laws, whose
goal is to prevent discrimination against individuals with disabilities: Section 504 of the
Rehabilitation Act (Section 504) and the Americans with Disabilities Act (ADA). Under
these acts, individuals qualify for services as having a disability if they:

1. have a physical or mental impairment which substantially limits one or more major
   life activities.
2. have a record of such an impairment.
3. are regarded as having such an impairment by others.

   Major life activities are broadly identified to include walking, seeing, hearing, speaking, breathing, learning, working, caring for self, and performing manual tasks. To be covered against discrimination under these acts, an individual must be *otherwise qualified,*
which means the individual must be qualified to do something (e.g, perform a job, sing in
the choir, have the entry level scores to be in the honors classes), regardless of the presence of a disability (Smith, 2002). Compliance with the provisions of Section 504 and the
ADA is monitored by the Office of Civil Rights (OCR) according to the principles of disparate treatment and disparate impact, terms we learned about earlier in this chapter.

Section 504 of the Rehabilitation Act

Some of your students may receive special education services under Section 504 of the
Rehabilitation Act (PL 93-112). While Section 504 was passed by Congress in 1973, its
role in schools has increased significantly in the last 10 years. Section 504 serves as a civil
rights law for individuals with disabilities and forbids all institutions receiving federal
funds from discriminating against individuals with disabilities in education, employment,
housing, and access to public programs and facilities. It also requires these institutions to
make their buildings physically accessible to individuals with disabilities. Section 504 provides students with the right to a general education, extracurricular activities in their local schools, instructional and curriculum accommodations, and equal access to services
and programs available to students without disabilities. Students who qualify for services
under the IDEA are also entitled to the protections of Section 504.

   Section 504 has both similarities to and differences from the IDEA (deBettencourt,
2002) (see Figure 1.6). Like the IDEA, Section 504 requires schools to provide eligible
students with a free, appropriate public education, which is defined as general or special education that includes related services and reasonable accommodations. Both the
IDEA and Section 504 also require that families be notified of the identification, evaluation, and placement of their children, and that students be educated with their peers

A comparison of the Individuals with Disabilities Education Act (IDEA) and Section 504

IDEA	SECTION 504
Type/Purpose/Funding/Enforcement	
• A federal law guaranteeing and guiding the delivery of special education services to eligible children with disabilities. • Monitored and enforced by the Office of Special Education Programs of the U.S. Department of Education. • Provides some federal monies to states and school districts.	• A civil rights law forbidding discrimination against individuals with disabilities who are otherwise qualified by programs that receive federal funds. • Monitored and enforced by the Office of Civil Rights of the U.S. Department of Education. • Provides no additional federal monies to states and local school districts, and does not allow IDEA funds to be used to provide service to individuals covered only by 504.
Eligibility	
• Covers individuals up to age 21. • Defines *disability* categorically as having one or more of the 13 disability classifications that have an adverse effect on educational performance.	• Covers individuals throughout their lives. • Defines *disability* functionally as having a physiological or mental impairment that substantially limits one or more major life activities.
Evaluation	
• A multifactored and nondiscriminatory evaluation in all areas related to suspected disability must be conducted to determine eligibility. • Eligibility decision is made by a multidisciplinary team of professionals, family members, and the child when appropriate.	• A multiple source and nondiscriminatory evaluation in the area(s) of suspected need(s) must be conducted to determine eligibility. • Eligibility decision is made by a group of individuals who are knowledgeable with respect to the child, the assessment procedures, and the placement options.
Free Appropriate Public Education	
• Defines appropriate education in terms of its educational benefits. • An individualized education program (IEP) is required. • Related aids and services are required to be delivered to help students benefit from special education. • Requires that students be educated in the least restrictive environment.	• Defines an appropriate education in terms of its comparability to the education offered to students without disabilities. • An individualized accommodation plan (often called a 504 accommodation plan) is required. • Related aids and services are delivered if they are needed to help students access appropriate educational programs. • Requires that students be educated in the least restrictive environment including having equal access to nonacademic and extracurricular activities.
Due Process Procedure	
• Informed and written consent from parents/guardian is required. • Establishes specific due process procedures for notification and impartial hearings. • Families who disagree with the identification, education or placement of their child have a right to an impartial hearing. • Families have the right to participate in the hearing and to be represented by counsel.	• Notice must be given, but consent is not required. • Leaves due process procedures up to the discretion of school districts. • Families who disagree with the identification, education or placement of their child have a right to an impartial hearing. • Families have the right to participate in the hearing and to be represented by counsel.

Note: de Bettencourt (2002); Henderson (2001); Katsiyannis, Landrum, and Reid (2002); Smith (2002).

without disabilities to the maximum extent possible (Katsiyannis, Landrum, & Reid, 2002). However, because Section 504 is based on a broader functional definition of disabilities than the IDEA and covers one's lifespan, far more individuals qualify for special education services under Section 504 than under the IDEA. As a result, potential recipients of services under Section 504 include students with attention deficit disorders, social maladjustments, temporary and long-term health conditions (e.g., arthritis, asthma, diabetes, epilepsy, heart conditions), communicable diseases, AIDS, and eating disorders. Individuals who abuse substances are eligible for services under Section 504 as long as they are in rehabilitation or recovery programs. However, if they begin to abuse substances again, they are no longer eligible until they return to a rehabilitation or recovery program. It also covers individuals with disabilities who are not eligible to receive services under the IDEA because they are now older than 21 or because their learning difficulties are not severe enough to warrant classification as an individual with learning disabilities or mental retardation.

Section 504 has fewer specific procedural requirements to guide its implementation than does the IDEA; however, it is suggested that schools employ best practices and follow the policies and procedures that they use to implement the IDEA. While Section 504 does not require the development of an IEP, educators must make accommodations to meet the learning needs of all students with disabilities covered under Section 504 (deBettencourt, 2002). If a student needs special or related services or reasonable accommodations, a planning team that knows the student, the assessment data, and the available services, placements, and accommodations develops a written accommodation plan. A sample Section 504 accommodation plan is presented in Figure 1.7.

Because Section 504 addresses discrimination that denies students equal access to academic, nonacademic, and extracurricular activities, it also covers some situations not addressed in the IDEA that you will probably encounter in your school. For example, under 504, you must make sure that all your field trips and after-school programs (e.g., recreational activities, athletic teams) are accessible to *all your students*. However, if an activity is open only to students with certain qualifications, the *otherwise qualified* principle applies. Here, students with disabilities may not be selected to participate in a specific activity as long as they are given the same opportunity as other students to demonstrate whether they have the qualifications. For example, students with disabilities should be provided with an equal opportunity to try out for the school's soccer team and the decision regarding their selection for the team should be based on their ability to demonstrate their skills at playing soccer. Section 504 also affects the grading of students and their access to honors and awards (Salend & Garrick Duhaney, 2002), which we will learn more about in chapter 12.

Americans with Disabilities Act

In 1990, Congress enacted PL 101-336, the Americans with Disabilities Act (ADA), a civil rights act designed to integrate individuals with disabilities into the social and economic mainstream of society. Whereas Section 504 applies to programs that receive federal funds, the ADA extends the civil rights of individuals with disabilities by providing them with access to public facilities including schools, restaurants, shops, state and local government activities and programs, telecommunications, and transportation. Employers and service providers in the public and private sectors cannot discriminate against them. The ADA requires employers to make reasonable accommodations for individuals with disabilities to allow them to perform essential job functions unless the accommodations would present an undue hardship. Under Title III of the ADA, concerning the educational implications of the ADA, schools must make their facilities accessible to students with disabilities.

Resource

Blazer (1999) offers tips for developing Section 504 classroom accommodation plans.

Reflective

While the IDEA provides funding to schools for eligible students, money for students eligible under Section 504 comes from the school district's general education funds. As a school administrator, would you prefer a student to be eligible under the IDEA or Section 504? As a parent of a child with special needs, what would you prefer?

Reflective

Despite passage of the ADA, individuals with disabilities may conceal their disabilities from their employers (Dickinson & Verbeek, 2002). Why do you think this occurs?

Reflective

Testing services have traditionally flagged the scores of students with disabilities who receive testing accommodations on such tests as the SAT and the GRE. Do you think this is appropriate? Is it a violation of Section 504 or the ADA?

Set Your Sites

For more information on Section 504 and the ADA, go to the Web Links module in Chapter 1 of the Companion Website.

FIGURE 17

Sample Section 504 accommodation plan

Name: John Jones

School: Porter High School

Date: 10/6/05

Grade: 10th

Age: 15

Follow-up Date(s): John's plan will be reviewed and evaluated at the end of each semester.

Teachers: Mr. J. McKenzie (Social Studies), Mr. W. Dumont (English), Ms. M. Tinsley (Biology), Mr. S. Labiosa (Spanish), Ms. R. Shankar (Mathematics)

1. **General Strengths:** Individualized standardized testing indicates that John is a capable student who is performing at or near grade level. His favorite subjects in school are mathematics and science. He wants to succeed in school and is very interested in going to college.

2. **General Concerns:** John's performance in school is erratic. He completes approximately 40% of his assignments and does poorly on tests. Observation of John in his classes shows that he often calls out and frequently fidgets in his seat or leaves it without permission. His teachers also report that he rarely pays attention to directions and is often distracted by events in the classroom. They also note that John rarely interacts with his peers.

3. **Nature and Impact of Disability:** John has been diagnosed as having a Attention Deficit Disorder with Hyperactivity (ADHD) by his family physician. Behavior rating scales and observations by educators and family members suggest that John's activity level is significant and interferes with his educational and social performance in school and at home.

Goal	Accommodations	Person(s) responsible for accommodations
1. To increase John's work completion	A. Step-by-step written and verbal directions for assignments, including examples, will be given to John. B. Assignments will be broken into several shorter parts and John will receive a break of 5 minutes between assignments. C. A daily homework notebook system will be implemented. D. Learning strategy instruction will be provided to John.	A. John's teachers B. John's teachers C. John, John's family, and John's teachers D. Special education teacher
2. To increase John's performance on tests	A. Study and test-taking skills instruction will be provided to John. B. John will receive the following testing accommodations: extended time, breaks, and testing in a separate location.	A. Special education teacher B. John's teachers
3. To increase John's on-task behavior	A. A self-monitoring system will be used by John to keep track of his on-task behavior. B. A daily behavior report card system will be implemented C. John's work area will be located at front of the room.	A. John and John's teachers B. John, John's teachers, and John's family C. John's teachers
4. To increase John's socialization with peers	A. Social skills and attribution training instruction will be provided to John. B. John will be taught about and encouraged to participate in extracurricular and community-based activities.	A. Special education teacher B. John, John's family, John's teachers, and John's school counselor

Participants:

Mr. John Jones, Student
Ms. Janice Jones, Parent
Ms. Roberta Shankar, Mathematics teacher
Mr. Jose Garcia, Special education teacher

Mr. William Dumont, English teacher
Ms. Freda Hargrove, School Counselor
Mr. Carl Rogan, District 504 Coordinator
Dr. Loren Phillips, Family physician

_____
(Parent/guardian)
I agree with the 504 accommodation plan
outlined above

_____
(Parent/guardian)
I do not agree with the 504 accommodation plan
outlined above

What Is the Impact of Inclusion?

In the following sections, we will review the research on the impact of inclusion on students, families, and educators. This research allows us to assess the extent to which inclusion is achieving its intended benefits and to identify issues that need to be addressed to improve inclusion programs for *all learners.* Because inclusion is a relatively recent movement, these studies are not longitudinal, and studies that examine the long-term impact on a wide range of students, families, and educators are needed to help us learn more about inclusion. It also is important to keep in mind that inclusion programs are mulitifaceted and varied in their implementation and the services provided, which can explain the differing results reported in studies.

Impact of Inclusion on Students with Disabilities

Several studies have examined the effect of general education placement on students with disabilities. Their findings reveal a varied impact on students' academic and social performance and on their reactions to and attitudes toward inclusion. Note that like many other educational programs, inclusion may impact students in different ways as they age and based on their nature of their disability. Thus, the impact of inclusion on elementary-level students and secondary-level students and students with varying disability conditions may differ as well as their reactions to inclusion.

Academic Performance

Resource

Salend and Duhaney (1999) summarize the research on inclusion programs, on students with and without disabilities, and on their teachers.

Several studies and school reports on the impact of inclusion on the academic performance of elementary- and secondary-level students with disabilities are discussed next. In general, the findings suggest that the academic performance of students with disabilities can be enhanced when they receive appropriate curricular and instructional accommodations within the general education setting.

Elementary-Level Students.   Some studies show that for elementary-level students with mild disabilities, inclusion results in better outcomes, including improved standardized test scores, mathematics and reading performance, grades, on-task behavior, motivation to learn, and more positive and attitudes toward school and learning as well as mastery of IEP goals (Hunt et al., 2000; Peetsma, 2001; Shinn, Powell-Smith, Good, & Baker, 1997; Waldron & McLeskey, 1998 a, b). Research also reveals that elementary students with mental retardation and more severe disabilities in inclusion programs learned targeted skills, had more engaged and instructional time, and had greater exposure to academic activities than students with severe disabilities educated in special education settings (Freeman, & Alkin, 2000; Helmstetter, Curry, Brennan, & Sampson-Saul, 1998; Hunt et al., 2003). Observational studies of inclusive classrooms also indicate that elementary students with severe disabilities received more academic instruction and appropriate levels of individualized instruction within the general education settings that supported their learning (Logan & Malone, 1998; McDonnell, Thorson, and McQuivey, 2000).

Resource

Freeman and Alkin (2000) provide a review of the studies that have examined the impact of inclusive educational placements on the academic and social performance of students with mental retardation, and Rafferty, Piscitelli, and Boettcher (2003) examine the impact of inclusion on preschoolers with disabilities.

However, some research also questions the effectiveness of inclusion on the academic performance of elementary students with disabilities. Some studies indicate that certain students with mild disabilities are not given "specially designed instruction" to meet their academic needs in inclusion programs (Baker & Zigmond, 1995; Fuchs, Deshler, & Zigmond, 1994; Lloyd, Wilton, & Townsend, 2000) and perform better academically in pull-out resource programs (Manset & Semmel, 1997; Marston, 1996; Zigmond et al., 1995). Some studies also suggest that higher-functioning preschoolers and elementary students with disabilities benefit more from placement in inclusion programs than their lower-functioning counterparts (Klingner, Vaughn, Hughes, Schumm, & Elbaum, 1998b; Mills, Cole, Jenkins, & Dale, 1998).

Secondary-Level Students.   Studies show that secondary students with mild disabilities educated in inclusive settings can make academic gains and transitions, and achieve academic engagement and passing rates that are comparable to those of their peers without disabilities (Cawley, Hayden, Cade, Baker-Kroczynski, 2002; Forgan & Vaughn, 2000; Wallace, Anderson, Bartholomay, & Hupp, 2002). Rea, McLaughlin, and Walther-Thomas (2002) found that secondary students with learning disabilities educated in inclusive settings received higher grades in all content areas, earned higher or comparable standardized test scores, and attended school more frequently than their peers who were served in pull-out programs. Secondary students with moderate and severe disabilities also improved in reading and classroom work skills when they received instruction in inclusive settings (Dore, Dion, Wagner, & Brunet, 2002; McDonnell, Johnson, Polychronis, & Risen, 2002).

Data from some states indicate that inclusive placements are resulting in more students with disabilities taking and passing statewide assessments (Wyatt, 2000). Research with students in grades 7 through 12 reveals that time spent in general education classes may improve students' chances of completing high school, going to college, getting a job, earning a higher salary, and living independently (Malian & Love, 1998; SRI International, 1993; U.S. Department of Education, 1995). However, Katsiyannis, Zhang, and Archwamety (2002) found that while there has been an upward trend to educate students with mental retardation in general education classrooms, there also has been a decrease in the graduation rates with a diploma or certificate of these students. Billingsley and Albertson (1999) reported that general education placements may not be providing students with severe disabilities with the functional skills they need for success in school and community settings

Social and Behavioral Performance and Attitudes Toward Placement

> Like most people, I don't remember much about my first years in school. Most of my memories are from the last 2 years in special education. I remember becoming unhappy about school then. I think I was at the age when I began to realize I was separated from the "regular kids." I can remember that during lunch the special ed kids and the "regular" kids ate at separate tables, and all the special ed kids were herded onto the G-12 bus. The incident that sticks out in my mind involved a kid named Jimmy, who was in another special education classroom but lived in my neighborhood. One morning at the bus stop, Jimmy told me that he was going to start going to the neighborhood school with the "regular" kids. I can remember the sadness I felt that it was not me. (Stussman, 1996, p. 15)

Certain studies have examined the social, behavioral, and self-concept outcomes for students with disabilities educated in inclusive settings. In general, the social, behavioral, and self-concept outcomes for students with disabilities educated in inclusive settings are better than those of students educated in noninclusive settings. However, these outcomes tend to lag behind those of their classmates without disabilities.

The personal accounts of students with disabilities about their experiences in general education settings present a mixed picture (Ferri, Keefe, & Gregg, 2001). Some students reported that life in the general education classroom was characterized by fear, frustration, ridicule, and isolation (Eisenman & Tascione, 2002), while others saw placement in general education as the defining moment in their lives in terms of friendships, intellectual challenges, self-esteem, and success in their careers. Some students felt that they benefited from receiving special education services, while others noted that receiving these services in separate locations placed them at risk for disclosure, stigma, shame, dependence, and lowered expectations (Eisenman & Tascione, 2002; Ferri, Keefe, & Gregg, 2001). Students with mobility related disabilities reported that the barriers they encountered in inclusive settings included difficulties with the physical environment of their schools, isolation and bullying from their classmates, and a lack of understanding from their teachers (Pivik, McComas, & Laflamme, 2002). Several studies have observed students in inclusive settings or surveyed and interviewed students with disabilities about their educational placement preferences, as well as their experiences in general and special education settings.

Elementary-Level Students.   Elementary students with mild disabilities in inclusion classes develop friendships with other students, have self-concept scores similar to those of their classmates without disabilities, and are rated as equal to their general education peers in terms of disruptive behavior (Banerji & Dailey, 1995; Lee, Yoo & Bak, 2003). While research suggests that students with learning disabilities feel a part of their classes' social networks, they also report that they experience school-related loneliness (Pavri & Monda-Amaya, 2001). They are less often accepted and more often rejected by those without disabilities, and they have lower self-perceptions and self-concepts than their general education peers (Lloyd, Wilton, & Townsend, 2000; Pavri & Luftig, 2000; Wigle & DeMoulin, 1999).

Research reveals that students with mental retardation in inclusive classrooms achieve social acceptance ratings that are higher than those of their counterparts who are educated in noninclusive settings and lower than their classmates without disabilities (Freeman & Alkin, 2000). Studies suggest that elementary students with moderate or severe disabilities in inclusion programs interact with others more often, receive and offer increased social support, and develop more long-lasting and richer friendships with their general education peers (Hall & McGregor, 2000; Hunt, Farron-Davis, Beckstead, Curtis, & Goetz, 1994; Hunt et al., 2003). However, interactions between these students and those without disabilities are often initiated by the latter, are often assistive, and tend to decline over the school year (Hall & McGregor, 2000; Evans, Salisbury, Palombaro, Berryman, & Hollowood, 1992; Lee et al., 2003). With respect to behavioral skills, research indicates that elementary students with severe disabilities educated in inclusive settings engage in behaviors that are similar to their classmates without disabilities (McDonnell, Thorson, McQuivey, & Kiefer-O'Donnell, 1997).

Some studies indicate that although many elementary students with disabilities prefer to leave the general education classroom to receive individualized services that help them academically, they also believe that the general education classroom is best for meeting their academic and social needs (Elbaum, 2002). They also worry about the recreational and academic activities they are missing when they are being pulled out of their general education classrooms (Ferri, Keefe, & Gregg, 2001; Klingner, Vaughn, Schumm, Cohen, & Forgan, 1998a; Padeliadu & Zigmond, 1996; Vaughn & Klingner, 1998). Elementary students also reported that leaving the general education classroom for specialized services was embarrassing, and provoked name-calling and ridicule from their peers (Reid & Button, 1995).

Secondary Students.   Studies show that secondary students with learning disabilities or emotional disorders educated in general education classrooms had higher levels of social acceptance, and comparable levels of behavioral incidents as their peers educated in pull-out programs, which suggests that the demands of the general education setting did not result in increased acting-out behavior (Cawley et al., 2002; Rea, McLaughlin, & Walther-Thomas, 2002). Research also shows that middle school students with learning disabilities had friendship ratings and self-concept scores that were comparable to those of their classmates without disabilities (Forgan & Vaughn, 2000). Hughes, Carter, Hughes, Bradford, and Copeland (2002) found that when high school students with and without disabilities interact in noninstructional roles they have more high quality interactions and discuss a greater variety of conversational topics than when they interact in instructional roles.

However, while high school students with moderate or severe disabilities have increased social interactions in inclusive educational placements (Hughes, 2002; Kennedy, Shukla, & Fryxell, 1997), compared with their peers without disabilities, they engage in fewer social interactions with classmates, and spend more time as passive participants in interactions (Mu, Siegel, & Allinder, 2000). Research also indicates that while some students with moderate or severe disabilities received average social status ratings from their peers without disabilities (Mu, Siegel, & Allinder, 2000), others have minimal, brief, and superficial social interactions with their classmates without disabilities (Dore et al., 2002).

Behaviorally, research indicates that while high school students with learning and emotional disabilities taught in general education classrooms are more likely to be the focus of teacher attention than their peers without disabilities, they engage in low levels of inappropriate behavior and their behavior resembles that of their classmates (Wallace et al., 2002). However, Zhang (2001) reported that secondary-level students with mild mental retardation demonstrated more self-determined behaviors in resource room programs than in general education classrooms.

> I hated high school. Whether I was in the regular or special education class, it was bad. I was often lost in the regular class, and sometimes other kids would tease me. It was terrible for me when I had to read out loud. Sometimes, I made like I was sick or had to go to the bathroom. Anything to avoid having to read in front of my classmates. I blamed the teachers. If they spent more time with me, I could have learned more. But they didn't have the time, and it was embarrassing to be helped by the teacher in front of the other kids. Nobody wanted that.
>
> Then, it got worse. I was placed in a special education class. I didn't want anyone to know I was in that class. I knew eventually they would find out, and my friends would not like me anymore, and think I was stupid. No one would date me. Even the kids in the special education class avoided each other and made a special effort to be seen with their friends in the regular classes.
>
> I know I was supposed to learn more in the special education class and I think I did. But I still didn't learn anything important. We kept learning this easy, boring stuff over and over again. You just sit there and get bored, and angry. (A high school student with a learning disability)

As this student's comments indicate, some secondary students with disabilities report having mixed and mostly negative experiences in both general and special education (Eisenman & Tascione, 2002; Guterman, 1995; Lovitt, Plavins, & Cushing, 1999). In terms of social development, despite some name-calling, students tended to prefer placement in general education because their friends were in those classes and they were treated like other students. Students also worried that their special education placement would cause them to lose their friends and to feel stigmatized and deficient. Academically, while some students preferred special education classes because they received more help, liked the smaller class size, and believed the work was easier, other students viewed special education as low-level, irrelevant, and repetitive, and not helping them learn very much. Although some students preferred the general education setting because it was more challenging and "cooler" and resulted in more learning, others reported that it was not reasonable for their general education teachers to accommodate their learning needs and that such accommodations would lead to increased academic stigma. However, Gibb, Allred, Ingram, Young, and Egan (1999) found that the majority of junior high school students with emotional and behavioral disorders enjoyed being educated with all other students in the school, and felt that inclusion helped them socially and academically.

Reflective

If you were a student with a disability, would you prefer a general or a special education setting?

Impact of Inclusion on Students Without Disabilities

Academic Performance

Studies have also examined the impact of inclusion on the academic performance of students without disabilities. In general, these findings suggest that placement in an inclusive classroom does not interfere with, and may enhance, the academic performance of students without disabilities.

Elementary Students.   The impact of inclusive education on the academic performance of elementary students without disabilities has also been studied. The findings

Research indicates that inclusion results in general education students developing positive attitudes toward, meaningful friendships with, and sensitivity to the needs of students with disabilities. Have you observed these benefits in your students?

indicated that their academic performance was equal to or better than that of general education students educated in noninclusive classrooms (Saint-Laurent et al., 1998; Sharpe, York, & Knight, 1994); these positive academic outcomes were usually reported for high-achieving students (Klingner et al., 1998b). Also, inclusion of students with severe disabilities did not significantly reduce the teaching time for their peers without disabilities or cause many interruptions in teaching (Hollowood, Salisbury, Rainforth, & Palombaro, 1994; McDonnell, 2002).

Secondary Students.   Similar results have been found with respect to the academic impact on secondary students without disabilities. Cawley et al. (2002) noted that the presence of learners with disabilities did not have a negative effect on the educational performance of their general education peers without disabilities. Wallace et al. (2002) found that although students with disabilities received more attention from general education teachers, their classmates without disabilities demonstrated high levels of academic engagement. Copeland et al. (2002) and Cushing and Kennedy (1997) reported that the academic performance of students without disabilities was enhanced when they were provided with opportunities to provide peer support to students with moderate or severe disabilities.

Social Performance

Research has also addressed the social impact of inclusion programs on students without disabilities. These studies reveal that students without disabilities have positive views of inclusion and benefit socially in several ways from being educated in inclusive settings.

> Maybe (inclusive education) serves much more the other children rather than the disabled child. I know that it serves both; but in fact the lesson learned by the rest of the school population is so important, and it is this sort of respect for everybody, for all people, no matter what (A teacher working in an inclusive school) (Hunt et al., 2000, p. 315).

Elementary Students.   Hunt et al. (2000) noted that inclusion programs benefited *all students* by making them more accepting of each other and helping them to be familiar with and adjust to individual differences. Elementary students without disabilities have reported that inclusion programs helped them to understand individual differences in physical appearance and behavior, the connection between their experiences and the feelings of students with disabilities, and the worth of their peers (Biklen, Corrigan, & Quick, 1989). Friendships between elementary students without disabilities and students with moderate and severe disabilities did develop in inclusive classrooms (Staub, 1998). However, these friendships began during noninstructional activities, and as the friendships developed, the majority of the students without disabilities assumed a caretaking role (Staub, Schwartz, Gallucci, & Peck, 1994).

Secondary Students.   Research suggests that the attitudes of teenagers toward individuals with disabilities has been positively influenced by inclusion (Krajewski & Hyde, 2000). Middle school students educated in an inclusive setting showed reduced fear of human differences and greater understanding and tolerance of others, including their peers with disabilities. Those who attended a noninclusive school were more prone to stereotyping and held more negative characterizations of peers with disabilities and diverse backgrounds (Capper & Pickett, 1994). Furthermore, middle and high school students in inclusive classrooms had positive views of inclusion and believed that it helped them understand individual differences, the needs of others, their ability to deal with disability in their own lives, and their ability to make friends with students with disabilities (Cook-Sather, 2003; Helmstetter, Peck, & Giangreco, 1994; Hendrickson, Shokoohi-Yekta, Hamre-Nietupski, & Gable, 1996; Hughes et al., 2002).

Impact of Inclusion on Educators

Because the cooperation of educators is critical to the success of inclusion programs, studies have investigated the attitudes of general and special educators toward inclusive education, their experiences, and their concerns about program implementation. These studies and their findings, which are summarized below, reveal that teachers have complex and varying attitudes and reactions to and experiences with inclusion. More information on the experiences of general and special education teachers working collaboratively to implement inclusion is presented in chapter 4.

Attitudes Toward Inclusion

> I'm a fourth-grade "Regular Ed" teacher who was very reluctantly drafted to have a child with severe disabilities in my room. It didn't take me long to be genuinely glad to have Sandy in my class. I can support inclusion. But please tell me who is going to watch out for people like me? Who will make sure administrators give us smaller class loads to compensate? Who will keep the curriculum people off my back when I don't cover the already overwhelming amount the state expects us to cover? After all, to properly achieve inclusion my time will now be more pressed than ever. Who will ensure that I receive the time I need to meet with the rest of the team (special educator, physical therapist, occupational therapist, etc.)? Who will watch over us? (Giangreco, Baumgart, & Doyle, 1995, p. 23)

Educators tend to agree with the principle of placing students with disabilities in general education classrooms, although some controversy still exists (McLeskey, Waldron, So, Swanson, & Loveland, 2001). Although some teachers and administrators support the inclusion (Waldron, McLeskey, & Pacchiano, 1999), some support it only when it requires them to make minimal accommodations (Dore et al., 2002). Others are satisfied with a pull-out system for delivering special education services and believe that full-time inclusion of students with mild disabilities would not be academically or socially beneficial.

Educators working in inclusive classrooms tend to have more positive views of inclusion than those who teach in noninclusive settings (McLeskey et al., 2001). In general, elementary teachers appear to favor inclusion more than secondary teachers (Balboni & Pedrabissi, 2000; Cole & McLeskey, 1997). Educators also tend to support inclusion for students who demonstrate the academic and behavioral skills to fit into the general education setting (Praisner, 2003). The factors affecting their attitudes include the effectiveness of the program for students with disabilities and their general education classmates, the development of a school community, the availability of administrative and family support, and the adequacy of the support services and training they receive (Austin, 2001; Hunt et al., 2000; McLeskey & Waldron, 2002; Praisner, 2003; Roll-Pettersson, 2001).

Soodak, Podell, and Lehman (1998) found that teachers' responses to inclusion are related to their teaching effectiveness, teaching experience, use of differentiated teaching practices, perceptions of the various student disability categories, and school-based conditions such as the use of teacher collaboration and the size of classes. Cook, Tanker-

Reflective

Why do you think there are differences in the attitudes of elementary and secondary teachers toward inclusion? Teachers who work in inclusive settings and those who do not? What factors affect your attitude toward inclusion?

sley, Cook, and Landrum (2000) reported that general education teachers working in inclusion programs were more likely to identify their students with disabilities in the categories of teacher concern and rejection, and less likely to view them in the category of teacher attachment. Cook (2001) found that teachers were more likely to reject students with mild disabilities than students with severe disabilities.

Outcomes for General Educators

Positive outcomes for general educators included increased confidence in their teaching efficacy, more favorable attitudes toward students with disabilities, greater awareness of themselves as positive role models for *all students*, more skill in meeting the needs of *all students* with and without disabilities, and acquaintance with new colleagues (Boudah et al., 2000; Giangreco, Dennis et al., 1993; Siegel-Causey, McMorris, McGowen, & Sands-Buss, 1998; Snyder, Garriott, & Aylor, 2001; Stanovich, 1999). Concerns included the negative attitudes of others; insufficient support, training, and time to collaborate with others; the large size of their classes; and the difficulty in meeting the medical needs and behavioral challenges of students with disabilities, and in designing and implementing appropriate instructional accommodations (Coots, Bishop, & Grenot-Scheyer, 1998; D'Alonzo, Giordano, & Vanleeuwen, 1997; Downing, Eichinger, & Williams, 1997; Serry, Davis, & Johnson, 2000; Snyder, Garriott, & Aylor, 2001; Weiss & Lloyd, 2002). In light of these concerns, educators frequently have questions regarding the implementation of inclusion (see Figure 1.8).

FIGURE 1.8

Questions educators have about inclusion

Based on research, the following are some questions that you and other teachers may have about inclusion. As you read this book, you will be able to answer these questions.

◆ What is inclusion? What are the goals of the inclusion program?

◆ Is inclusion for all students with disabilities or just for certain ones?

◆ Do students with disabilities want to be in my class? Do they have the skills to be successful?

◆ What instructional and ancillary support services will students with disabilities receive? Can these services be used to help other students?

◆ Will my class size be adjusted?

◆ Will the education of my students without disabilities suffer?

◆ What do I tell the students without disabilities about the students with disabilities?

◆ How do I handle name calling?

◆ What do I tell families about the inclusion program? What do I do if families complain about the program or don't want their child to be in my class?

◆ What roles will families play to assist me and their child?

◆ Do I decide whether I work in an inclusion program?

◆ Am I expected to teach the general education curriculum to everyone? How can I do that?

◆ What instructional modifications and classroom management strategies do I need to use?

◆ How am I supposed to evaluate and grade my students with disabilities?

◆ What instructional and ancillary support services will I receive?

◆ How can I address the health, medical, and behavioral needs of students with disabilities?

◆ What does it mean to work collaboratively with other professionals in my classroom? Will I be able to work collaboratively with others?

◆ Will I receive enough time to collaborate and communicate with others?

◆ What type of training and administrative support will I receive to help me implement inclusion successfully?

◆ Who will monitor the program? How do I know if the inclusion program is working? How will I be evaluated?

Outcomes for Special Educators

Special educators working in inclusion programs reported having a greater sense of being an important part of the school community, an enriched view of education, greater knowledge of the general education system, and greater enjoyment of teaching that was related to working with students without disabilities and observing the successful functioning of their students with disabilities (Cawley et al., 2002). For example, Cawley and his colleagues (2002) reported that being an integral part of general education program increased the status of special education teachers with respect to students without disabilities; these students viewed the special educators as their teachers and introduced them to their families in that way.

Their concerns were related to their fear that inclusion would result in the loss of specialized services to students with disabilities and their jobs (Cook, Semmel, & Gerber, 1999; Downing et al., 1997). Teachers working in cooperative teaching arrangements also report disagreements related to delineating responsibilities for instructing and disciplining students with disabilities (Fennick & Liddy, 2001), which can result in inequitable responsibilities that limit the instructional roles of special educators in the classroom (Austin, 2001; Weiss & Lloyd, 2003). This lack of parity may particularly occur at the secondary level, where the general educator is trained in the content area and therefore may assume the major responsibilities for teaching (Fisher, Frey, & Thousand, 2003). Some special education teachers also were worried that their subordinate role in the general education classroom would cause students to view them as a teacher's aide or visitor rather than a teacher.

Reflective

Some educators propose that teachers should be allowed to decide whether to work in a setting that includes students with disabilities. Do you think teachers should have this choice? Should they be allowed to choose the students in terms of the academic levels, ethnic, linguistic, and religious backgrounds, socioeconomic status, gender, and sexual orientation they want to teach? If you were given such a choice, what types of students would you include? Exclude?

Impact of Inclusion on Families

Like students and their teachers, family members have different views of and experiences with inclusion. These reactions can affect the important roles that family members perform in the implementation of successful inclusion programs and the establishment of meaningful and reciprocal family–school collaborations.

In general, studies suggest that while the attitudes and reactions of families of children with and without disabilities appear to be generally positive, family members also have important concerns that need to be addressed. Their varied perspectives seem to complex and multidimensional and affected by a variety of interacting variables related to the impact of the inclusion program on their children (Garrick Duhaney & Salend, 2000).

Families of Children with Disabilities

I wanted my child to have the same experiences as other kids and to learn to live in the real world with its joys and frustrations, and the inclusion program has allowed her to do that. She has learned to be more independent which will be helpful for preparation for later life. I don't believe that isolating her from other children is better for her or for her classmates. I want my child to learn from other kids and they can learn from her.

Inclusion has been an emotionally exhausting struggle for me. I ask for something for my child. It's denied by the school district, and I have to fight for it. Everything always seems to fall on me even if it should not be my responsibility. It's taking its toll on our family in terms of time, resources, and energy. I wish things could happen without me.

My child has done well in the special education class. He receives special attention from a trained teacher who understands his needs, and I don't have to worry about other kids making fun of him. Some students can be included, but many of our students need special attention and individualized instruction, which only special education teachers can provide.

Some families of children with disabilities believe that inclusive education benefited their children, providing them with increased friendships and access to positive role models, a more challenging curriculum, higher expectations and academic achievement, and better preparation for the real world, as well as an improved self-concept and better language and motor skills (Bennett, Deluca, & Bruns, 1997; Davern, 1999; Freeman, Alkin, & Kasari, 1999; Gallagher et al., 2000; Gibb et al., 1997; Grove & Fisher, 1999; Hanson et al., 2001; Palmer, Fuller, Arora, & Nelson, 2001; Seery et al., 2000). Family members also noted that inclusive placements benefit students without disabilities by helping them be sensitive to individual with disabilities, and allowing them to experience firsthand how others deal with adversity, and appreciate their own abilities (Palmer et al., 2001). As a result, many families often advocate for inclusive settings for their children until they encounter barriers from schools (Hanson et al., 2001).

Family members also have concerns about inclusive education, including the loss of individualized special education services, a functional curriculum, instructional accommodations, and community-based instruction delivered by specially trained professionals (Gallagher et al., 2000; Palmer et al., 2001; Pivik, McComas, & Laflamme, 2002; Pumpian, & Sax, 1998; Seery et al., 2000), as well as the fear that their children will be targets of verbal abuse and ridicule, which will lower their self-esteem (Freeman et al., 1999; Hanson et al., 2001; Lovitt & Cushing, 1999; Pivik, McComas, & Laflamme, 2002; Palmer et al., 2001). Some family members of children with severe disabilities are concerned that their children's significant needs, size, or behavior may preclude them from benefiting from inclusive educational placements (Palmer et al., 2001).

Resource

Zinkil and Gilbert (2000) offer guidelines that you can share with families to assist them in examining inclusion programs.

Reflective

Some family members of children with disabilities report that they encountered difficulties finding inclusive classrooms for their children, which required a significant amount of their time and energy (Gallagher et al., 2000; Jackson, Ryndak, & Billingsley, 2000; Soodak & Ervin, 2000). Why do you think this is the case?

Reflective

Gallagher et al. (2000) found that siblings of individuals with disabilities had attitudes toward inclusion that were similar to their parents' attitudes. What factors contribute to this similarity?

Families of Children Without Disabilities

I'm all for having a variety of students in the class, but won't these students take time away from the other kids and slow things down? We don't have enough money in the district to implement it. Classes are too big as it is and the teachers are not trained to teach those students. And the regular students will make fun of the special education students.

While I didn't know much about the inclusion program when I was notified that my child would be in it, it has had a positive impact on my child. He has grown academically and has become more sensitive to others. I am very pleased and hope that he will be in a similar program next year.

Several studies have also explored the reactions and experiences of families of children without disabilities in inclusive and integrated educational programs. Family members said an inclusive classroom did not prevent their children from receiving a good education, appropriate services, and teacher attention. It also led to improved feelings of self-worth related to helping others, an increased sense of personal development, and a greater tolerance of human differences (Giangreco, Edelman, Cloninger, & Dennis, 1993; Hanson et al., 2001; Hunt et al., 2000; Staub, 1998). Family members also felt that inclusion benefits children with disabilities; it promotes their acceptance, improves their self-concept, and exposes them to the real world (Hunt et al., 2000; Staub et al., 1994).

Some family members initially had doubts about inclusion. They worried about the effectiveness of the instruction, whether their children would receive less teacher attention, and whether their children would pick up the inappropriate behaviors of children with disabilities (Reichart et al., 1989). However, they found that their fears of inappropriate behaviors were groundless (Peck, Carlson, & Helmstetter, 1992). Some families of

IDEAS FOR IMPLEMENTATION

Explaining Your Inclusion Program to Families

Ms. Carr, a general education teacher, and Ms. Stevens, a special education teacher, had worked as a cooperative teaching team in an inclusion program for several years. Things had gone well over the years, and they tried to make improvements to their program each year. This year they decided to focus on family involvement. Because many families in the past did not know much about inclusion, they devoted the first open school night to explaining their inclusion program to families.

There was a good turnout of family members. Ms. Carr and Ms. Stevens started talking about their program. They discussed the philosophy and goals of the program, the day's schedule, communications with families, and various other aspects of the program. They also introduced the paraeducators who would be working in the classroom and noted how fortunate the class was to have their assistance for all the learners in the class. They briefly explained the research on inclusion in language that families could understand, and cited examples of how their students had grown academically and socially. They invited family members of former students with and without disabilities to speak about the program and its impact on their children.

Next, the teachers solicited questions from family members. Family members asked questions like, "Does the class have computers?" and "How does the teaming work?" One family member asked, "If there are two teachers in a class, which one is my son's 'real' teacher?" Ms. Carr and Ms. Stevens explained that they both teach all the students. Sometimes one of them leads a lesson while the other helps students to participate, and sometimes they both work with small groups at the same time. They concluded the meeting by thanking families for attending and participating, inviting them to visit and volunteer in the class, and discussing future activities for collaborating with families.

Here are some other ideas you can use to create an inclusive classroom that has the support of your learners' families:

- Conduct a needs assessment to identify and recognize the diverse experiences and perceptions of family members with respect to inclusion, and what aspects of the program they would like to know more about.
- Anticipate the questions family members may have about the program, and use positive language to describe the program.
- Highlight that the program is designed to benefit and meet the individual needs of all learners (e.g., adopted children, children experiencing divorce or illness, second language learners, learners who are gifted and talented, students who are shy) by discussing the range of needs that all learners have and how they might be met under this instructional arrangement.
- Emphasize the value of learning about individual differences as important features of an education in our diverse and ever changing society, and employ activities that introduce families to individual differences.
- Invite former students, family members of former students, and other professionals to talk about the inclusion program.
- Encourage families to ask questions. Respond to each question with empathy, understanding and sensitivity, and offer positive ways in which that issue or situation will be addressed.
- Provide families with access to additional information about inclusion (e.g., websites, videos, articles, books).

Reflective

If your child had a disability, would you prefer a general or special education setting? If your child did not have a disability, which class would you prefer?

children with and without disabilities felt that their children would receive less teacher attention, harming their children's education (Peck et al., 1992; Reichart et al., 1989). In general, family members expressed less concern about their children being educated with children with physical and sensory disabilities than about children with severe disabilities and children with behavior disorders (Green & Stoneman, 1989).

In summary, research indicates that inclusion is a complex undertaking that can have a positive impact on students, their teachers, and their families. However, this impact appears to be related to educators' willingness to accommodate the diverse needs of students and their families. This, in turn, depends on the administrative support, resources, and training that educators receive to implement effective inclusion programs. Given these findings, and the continued commitment to educating students with disabilities in general education classrooms, this book is intended to provide you with the knowledge, skills, and dispositions to develop and implement effective inclusion programs and create learning environments that promote the academic and behavioral/social performance of *all of your learners*. Toward these ends, the book offers you strategies to aid you in providing all your learners with access to the general education curriculum; to promote the sensitivity to and acceptance of your students' individual needs and differences; to help you work collaboratively with your colleagues, families, students, and community agencies; and to assist you in reflecting on and differentiating your teaching and curriculum to so that *all your learners* benefit academically, behaviorally, and socially.

Summary

This chapter has presented some of the foundations of inclusion as a philosophy for educating students with disabilities in general education settings. Some of the challenges associated with inclusion and its implementation have also been discussed. As you review the chapter, consider the following questions and remember the following points.

What Is Special Education?
CEC 1, PRAXIS 1

Special education involves delivering and monitoring a specially designed and coordinated set of comprehensive, research-based instructional and assessment practices and related services. These instructional practices and services are tailored to identify and address the individual needs and strengths of students, to enhance their educational, social, behavioral, and physical development, and to foster equity and access to all aspects of society.

What Is Inclusion?
CEC 1, 9, PRAXIS 1, 3, INTASC 3, 5, 9

Inclusion is a philosophy that brings students, families, educators, and community members together to create schools based on acceptance, belonging, and community. Inclusionary schools welcome, acknowledge, affirm, and celebrate the value of all learners by educating them together in high-quality, age-appropriate general education classrooms in their neighborhood schools. Whereas mainstreaming can be viewed as either part-time or full-time placement based on a student's readiness for placement in the general education setting, inclusion is thought of as full-time placement in the general education setting based on the belief that all students have the right to be educated in general education classrooms.

What Is the Least Restrictive Environment (LRE)?
CEC 1, 9, PRAXIS 1, 2, 3, INTASC 3, 9, 10

The LRE requires that students with disabilities be educated as much as possible with their peers without disabilities. The LRE tells us to look at and consider the general education setting as the first option, not the last, and to move to a more restrictive setting cautiously and only as needed.

What Factors Contributed to the Movement to Educate Students in Inclusive Classrooms?

CEC 1, 2, 3, 9, PRAXIS 2, 3, INTASC 3, 9, 10

Contributing factors include normalization, deinstitutionalization, early intervention and early childhood programs, technological advances, the civil rights movement and its resulting litigation, advocacy groups, the segregated nature of special schools and classes, disproportionate representation, and standards-based reform.

What Are the Laws that Affect Special Education?

CEC 1, 9, PRAXIS 2, INSTASC 2, 9, 10

Several laws have had a broad impact on students with disabilities, including PL 94-142, the Education for All Handicapped Children Act; PL 99-457, the Education for All Handicapped Children Act Amendments of 1986; PL 101-476, the Individuals with Disabilities Education Act; PL 105-17, the IDEA Amendments of 1997; PL 93-112, the Rehabilitation Act and Section 504; and PL 101-336, the Americans with Disabilities Act. These laws contain a variety of provisions that promote the inclusion of individuals with disabilities in schools and all aspects of society.

What Is the Impact of Inclusion?

CEC 1, 9, 10, PRAXIS 1, 3, INTASC 3, 9, 10

Research on the impact of inclusion is inconclusive and offers a variety of perspectives. Some studies suggest that inclusion often results in positive academic and social outcomes for students with disabilities; other studies indicate that some students with disabilities do not receive the instructional accommodations they need to benefit from inclusion. Studies suggest that students without disabilities are not harmed academically by an inclusive education and that they benefit socially.

General and special educators have mixed reactions to inclusion. Their attitudes are related to their efficacy in implementing inclusion, which in turn depends on the administrative support, resources, time, and training they receive to implement effective inclusion programs. The attitudes and reactions of families of children with and without disabilities to inclusion are complex, multidimensional, and affected by many interacting variables.

What Would You Do in Today's Diverse Classroom?

1. ★   Marcus, a high school student, experiences some significant challenges in learning. Because he reads at a fifth-grade level, he struggles with many assignments and does poorly on many exams. Marcus is well-liked by peers, and participates in several after-school activities. His family expects him to go to college, just like his siblings, and wants him to take all general education classes.

    ★   Melissa uses a laptop to communicate with others and complete her work. Her classmates and teachers recognize that she is academically capable, but are put off by her flapping hands, vocal outbursts, and limited eye contact. Melissa's family and her special education teacher believe that she has done well in school because she receives special attention and services from a trained teacher who understands her needs, and they are worried about other students making fun of her. Therefore, they are not sure that the school's inclusion program is the best educational setting for Melissa.

★ Melvin has always been one of the best students in his class. His family members are very proud of his success, and spend a great deal of time working with him. They are very active in school, and think that Melvin needs to be in smaller classes, have more time with his teachers, and receive more challenging assignments. Therefore, they are concerned about his placement in an inclusion program.

★ Marsha breathes oxygen-enriched air through a tracheoctomy tube and requires the services of a licensed nurse. She is able to complete her schoolwork like her peers so her parents want her to be placed full-time in a general education setting.

★ Maria moved to the United States last year. She is well-behaved and is starting to learn English. In class, she keeps mostly to herself and has difficulty completing tasks and participating in class discussions. Her favorite time of the school day is recess, when she plays games with her classmates and attempts to communicate with them. Her family believes that school is very important and is happy she is in an inclusion program in her school.

★ What legal, philosophical, historical and social factors impact the educational placement for these learners?

★ Why do you think these families feel the way they do about inclusion?

★ How do you think inclusion might affect these students? Their families? Their peers? Their teachers?

★ What challenges do these students and their families, peers, and teachers face in making inclusion a successful experience for all?

★ What knowledge, skills, dispositions, resources, and supports do you need to address these feelings and challenges?

2. You have been asked by your principal to be part of a committee to develop a program to explain your school's inclusion programs to students, families, and educators.

★ What would you like to be the goals of the program?

★ How would you define and describe your school's inclusion program?

★ What types of information about inclusion and the school's inclusion programs would you like the committee to share with others?

★ What strategies for sharing information about inclusion with others would you like the committee to recommend?

 To answer these questions online and share your responses with others, go to the Reflection module in chapter 1 of the Companion Website.

Chapter 2

Understanding the Diverse Educational Strengths and Needs of Students with Disabilities

Marty

Ms. Tupper was concerned about Marty's inconsistent performance in school. He knew a lot about many topics and liked to share his knowledge with others. He picked things up quickly when he heard them explained or watched them demonstrated. He loved it when the class did science activities and experiments. However, Marty's performance in reading and math was poor. Despite having highly developed verbal skills, he also had difficulties with writing assignments.

Ms. Tupper noticed that Marty had trouble starting and completing his assignments. Sometimes he began a task before receiving all the directions; at other times, he ignored the directions and played with objects in the room or at his desk. He frequently worked on an assignment for only a short period of time and then switched to another assignment. When he completed assignments, his work was usually of high quality. Marty's parents were concerned. They thought he was smart but lazy and capable of doing better work.

Marty also worried about his difficulties in school. He wondered why he was not like others. He thought he was "not smart" and that reading, writing, and math would always be hard. Sometimes, out of frustration, he acted like the class clown. At other times, he was quiet and withdrawn to avoid drawing attention to his difficulties. Marty loved to talk and joke with others. He was fun to be with but sometimes he got carried away, which bothered some of his friends. Marty was the best student in the class at fixing things. When other students needed assistance with mechanical things, they came to Marty. Marty enjoyed taking things apart and putting them back together. In his neighborhood, he was famous for fixing bicycles and other toys.

Ms. Tupper liked Marty and felt frustrated by her inability to help him learn. She decided that she needed assistance to help address Marty's needs and contacted the school's Student Study Team. The team met with Ms. Tupper and Marty's family to discuss Marty, including his strengths, challenges, interests, and hobbies, as well as effective instructional techniques to use. They also gathered information by observing Marty in several school settings and talking with him. The team then met with Ms. Tupper and Marty's parents to plan some interventions to address Marty's needs. They talked about and agreed to try several environmental and curricular accommodations. To improve Marty's on-task behavior and the communication between Ms. Tupper and Marty's parents, a daily report card system was used. Ms. Tupper also moved Marty's seat closer to the front of the room to improve her monitoring of his ability to pay attention and understand directions. To help Marty with reading and writing, Ms. Tupper tried graphic organizers and peer tutoring. In math, she attempted to increase her use of manipulatives and cooperative learning groups.

Members of the Student Study Team worked with Ms. Tupper to implement and evaluate the effectiveness of these interventions. The team met periodically to review

Marty's progress through observations, interviews, and an analysis of work samples. While the interventions improved Marty's ability to complete his work, Marty failed to make significant progress in reading, writing, and math.

As a result, the Student Study Team referred Marty to the school district's Comprehensive Planning Team to determine whether he would benefit from special education and related services. With the consent of Marty's family, the Comprehensive Planning Team conducted a comprehensive assessment of Marty's performance in a variety of areas. The school psychologist gave him an intelligence test and concluded that Marty had above-average intelligence and strong verbal skills. Tests of fine motor and gross motor abilities as part of a physical exam conducted by the school physician also revealed Marty's strengths in these areas. An interview with Marty and the observations of his family also led the team to believe that Marty's learning difficulties were lowering his self-esteem.

The special education teacher assessed Marty's skills in reading and math using several achievement and criterion-referenced tests. Marty's reading showed weaknesses in word recognition, oral reading, and reading comprehension. In decoding, he had trouble sounding out words and relied on contextual cues. In reading comprehension, Marty had trouble responding to questions related to large amounts of information and interpreting abstractions.

Marty's math performance revealed both strengths and weaknesses. He performed well in the areas of geometry, measurement, time, and money. However, he had difficulty in solving word problems, and performing multistep computations.

After all the data were collected, the team met to determine Marty's eligibility for special education. They reviewed the data and listened to the views of the various team members. Some members thought Marty had a learning disability. Others thought he had an attention deficit disorder and should be served under Section 504. Several members also believed that Marty needed a program for gifted and talented students. After some discussion and debate, the team concluded that Marty's inability to perform academic tasks at a level in line with his potential showed that he had a learning disability. The team also decided that Marty should remain in Ms. Tupper's class and that an Individualized Educational Program to meet his needs there should be developed. They also agreed to recommend Marty for inclusion in the district's gifted and talented program.

What factors should educators consider in designing an appropriate educational program for Marty? Does Marty qualify for special education services? After reading this chapter, you should have the knowledge, skills, and dispositions to answer these as well as the following questions.

★ **How does the special education identification process work?**
★ **How can IEPs be implemented in general education settings?**
★ **What are the educational strengths and needs of students with high-incidence disabilities?**
★ **What are the educational strengths and needs of students with low-incidence disabilities?**

How Does the Special Education Identification Process Work?

Comprehensive Planning Team

A comprehensive team of professionals and family members, with the student when appropriate, makes important decisions concerning the education of students like Marty. The special education identification process that the comprehensive team follows for students who are experiencing difficulties in school is outlined in Figure 2.1. As we saw in the chapter-opening vignette, the team initially provided prereferral assistance to work with Ms. Tupper to address Marty's needs in her class. Once it was determined that he needed additional services, the team assessed his eligibility for special education via the IDEA or Section 504 and developed an IEP based on his strengths and needs, current assessment data, and the concerns of Marty's family. While Marty's family actively participated in the decision-making process and agreed with the team's recommendations, when disagreements between families and schools arise, mediation services are offered to resolve differences voluntarily (Mills & Duff-Mallams, 2000). If an agreement still cannot be reached after mediation, a due process hearing conducted by an impartial hearing officer is scheduled (Getty & Summy, 2004).

As the student's teacher, you can be an important member of the team. The other members of the team are:

- the family members of the child (we will learn more about communicating and collaborating with families in chapter 4).
- a representative of the school district who is knowledgeable about the general education curriculum and the availability of resources.
- an individual who can determine the instructional implications of the evaluation results.
- other individuals selected at the discretion of the family or the school district who have knowledge or special expertise regarding the child.
- the student when appropriate.

The diverse perspectives and experiences of the members of the team and the ways in which the team functions to make decisions collaboratively are described in chapter 4.

When students from culturally and linguistically diverse backgrounds are referred to the comprehensive planning team, the team frequently faces many challenges such as differentiating linguistic and cultural differences from learning difficulties, and developing an appropriate educational program that addresses students' linguistic, cultural, and experiential backgrounds (we will learn more about these issues in chapter 3 and other chapters in the book). Therefore, it is recommended, although not mandated, that the planning team include individuals who are fluent in the student's native language, understand the student and the family's culture, and can help collect and interpret the data in culturally and linguistically appropriate ways (Ortiz, 1997; Salend & Salinas, 2003). The inclusion of these individuals allows the team to learn about the family's and the student's cultural perspective and experiential and linguistic background, and to assist in the determination of the origins of the student's learning difficulties.

Resource

Getty and Summy (2004) offer information about due process procedures

Reflective

In chapter 1, we learned about the differences between the IDEA and Section 504. How are they different?

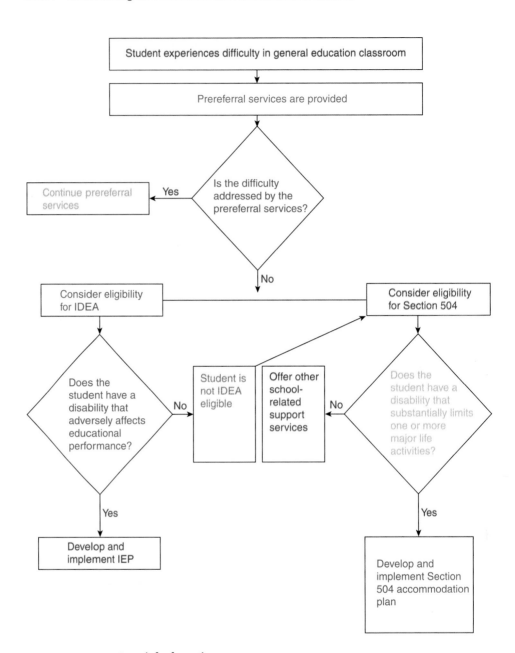

FIGURE 2.1   Special education process

Prereferral System

Like many school districts, Marty's school district employed a *prereferral system,* sometimes referred to as a *teacher assistance team, instructional support team,* or *child or student study team.* Prereferral is a preventive problem-solving process assisting classroom teachers like Ms. Tupper before referral for a special education placement is considered (Buck, Polloway, Smith-Thomas, & Cook, 2003; Ormsbee, 2001). The team helps teachers gather information about students and develop and use methods to successfully educate students like Marty in the general education classroom. Prereferral interventions are determined based on the individual student's strengths and challenges; educational, social, and medical history; and language and cultural background, as well as the teacher's concerns and the nature of the learning environment. The team works collaboratively with teachers and family members to develop a plan that includes a range of methods for addressing the student's strengths and challenges (a sample prereferral planning form is presented in Figure 2.2). The implementation and the effectiveness of these methods is then assessed for a sufficient period of time before formally evaluating the student for placement in special education (Lane, Mahdavi, & Borthwick-Duffy, 2003). **To view examples of a group of professionals engaged in the prereferral process, go to Case 3: Assess Plan on the CD-ROM, and view all the video clips. What steps does the prereferral team follow to create a plan to help the student succeed in general education?**

Prereferral strategies are especially important in addressing the disproportionate representation of students from diverse backgrounds (Knotek, 2003). In addition to identifying the source of students' difficulties in school, effective prereferral interventions with students from diverse backgrounds include embedding students' culture and language in the curriculum, establishing collaborative school and community relationships, offering meaningful and relevant academic programs, understanding how cultural and linguistic backgrounds affect learning, and involving families in all school and classroom activities (Craig et al., 2000; Ortiz, 2001; Watson & Houtz, 2002).

Ormsbee (2001) offers guidelines and forms that can foster the success of the prereferral process, and Craig, Hull, Haggart and Perez-Selles (2000), Baca and de Valenzuela (1998), and Ortiz and Wilkinson (1991) describe effective prereferral models for use with students from culturally and linguistically diverse backgrounds.

Eligibility Determination

When prereferral strategies are not effective, as in the case of Marty, the planning team, with the consent of the student's family, determines whether a student is eligible for special education. To determine eligibility for special education services under the IDEA, the team uses standardized and informal assessment procedures including interviews and observations to determine if the student has a disability that adversely affects educational performance. If the student is not IDEA eligible, the team may consider the student for special education services under Section 504. As we saw in chapter 1, if a student is eligible for 504, an accommodation plan must be developed.

Although problems with labeling students have been noted, state and federal funding formulas require the use of labels and definitions. However, no two students are alike; therefore, each educational program must be based on individual needs rather than on a label.

Individualized Education Program

If the comprehensive planning team determines that a student's needs require special education services, an IEP is developed for the student (Drasgow, Yell, & Robinson, 2001). The IEP is a written, individualized plan listing the special education and related services students with disabilities will receive to address their unique academic, social, behavioral, communication, and physical strengths and needs. It contains several components that seek to provide students with disabilities with greater access to the general education curriculum (Huefner, 2000), which are outlined next. (Later in this chapter, you will learn about specific disabilities and the educational strengths and needs of students with these disabilities.)

IEP Components

The IEP developed by the team must include the following components:

1. A statement of the student's current levels of educational performance in terms of academic, socialization, behavioral, and communication skills. This statement also

FIGURE 2.2

Sample prereferral planning form

Student: _____   Grade: _____

Teacher: _____

Intervention Goal
What observable, measurable changes do we want to see in the student? _____
_____
_____
_____

Academic Modifications | **Details of Intervention Plan** | **Behavioral Strategies**

What strategy/method is to be used?
How is it to be done? Where? When?
Who will do it?

Family/Home Activities | **Motivational/Incentives System**

Data Collection Activities
How will effectiveness be assessed? _____
_____
Who will collect the data? _____
_____
How often will data be collected? _____
_____

Follow Up Plans/Procedures
How often will the team meet to monitor the plan? _____
_____
What are our criteria for success? _____
_____
Who will help the teacher implement the plan? _____
_____

General Comments

Source: From "Effective Preassessment Team Procedures: Making the Process Work for Teachers and Student," by C.K. Ormsbee, 2001, *Intervention in School and Clinic, 36,* p. 151. Copyright 2001 by PRO-ED, Inc. Reprinted with permission.

should address how the disability affects the student's involvement and progress in the general education curriculum. In developing the IEP, the team also should assess and address the strengths of the child and the child's family's concerns for enhancing their child's education.

REFLECTING ON YOUR PRACTICES

Implementing a Prereferral System

Prereferral interventions have reduced the number of students placed in special education. You can evaluate your school's prereferral system by addressing the following questions:

- Are administrators, educators, and family members committed to implementing and promoting a prereferral system?
- Are there criteria for the selection of educators to serve on the prereferral support team?
- Does the prereferral support team include educators who have a range of backgrounds, experiences, expertise, and training and who perform a variety of functions?
- Are family members and community agencies involved in the prereferral process?
- Does the prereferral support team have the resources and time to perform its activities?
- Is there a system to help teachers access the services of the prereferral team?
- Do the forms and procedures employed in the prereferral system facilitate the process?
- Do prereferral support teams have adequate and reasonable procedures for determining the goals and types of prereferral systems based on students' strengths; challenges; educational, social, and medical history; and language and cultural background, as well as the teacher's concerns and the learning environment?

- Does the prereferral support team consider and suggest a range of reasonable instructional and family involvement strategies, curricular and classroom design accommodations, alternative assessment procedures, testing accommodations, culturally relevant instructional and classroom management techniques, adaptive devices, teacher training and collaboration activities, and school-based and community-based supportive services to address the referral problems?
- Are prereferral interventions suggested by the prereferral support team implemented as intended and for a sufficient period of time?
- Does the prereferral support team collect data to examine the effectiveness of the prereferral interventions and the prereferral process and to make revisions based on these data?

How would you rate your school's prereferral system?

( ) Excellent
( ) Good
( ) Needs Improvement
( ) Needs Much Improvement

What are some goals and steps to improve your school's prereferral system?

2. A list of annual goals relating to the students' progress in the general education curriculum, as well as other education needs. Keep in mind that IEPs for students who take alternate assessments rather than participating in state and federal testing programs still must include benchmarks and short-term objectives.

3. A statement of the special education and related services, as well as supplementary aids and services and other supports, to help the student reach the annual goals, be involved and progress in the general education curriculum, and participate in extracurricular and nonacademic activities with other students. These services and aids include transportation, speech and language therapy, psychological services, counseling, school health and social work services, physical and occupational training, interpreters, hearing and vision services, and family education as well as others that help students benefit from a special education program. This statement also should address the program modifications and support for school personnel, such as general educators receiving consultation services or training related to specific issues.

4. An explanation of the extent, if any, to which the student will *not* participate in the general education classroom and in other activities with students without disabilities.

5. A statement of any testing accommodations that the student will need to participate in state or districtwide assessments. If the IEP team determines that a student will not participate in a particular assessment, the IEP must include an explanation of why the test is not appropriate and state what alternative methods will be used to assess the student's learning and progress. (See chapter 12 for specific information about testing accommodations and alternative assessment techniques.)

6. A description of how and when progress in meeting annual goals in the IEP will be assessed and when reports on the student's progress toward achieving annual goals will be shared with family members.

7. A projected date for the initiation of services and modifications, as well as their anticipated frequency, location, and duration.

A sample IEP for Marty, the student we met at the beginning of this chapter, is presented in Figure 2.3, and a sample IEP meeting agenda is presented in Figure 2.4 (page 59). For an update on legal issues related to IEPs and other topics discussed in this chapter, go to the Legal Update module in chapter 2 of the Companion Website.

Resource

Clark (2000), Etscheidt and Bartlett (1999) and Roberts and Baumberger (1999) offer guidelines for developing and evaluating IEPs, including selecting goals and objectives and determining supplementary aids and services.

Special Considerations in Developing IEPs

In addition to the components of the IEP just outlined, the IEP team also can consider several special factors related to the unique needs of students, which are outlined next:

- For a student whose behavior interferes with his or her learning or that of others, the IEP team should consider behavioral strategies, including positive behavior interventions, strategies, and supports. To address behaviors that interfere with learning and socialization, some teams perform a functional behavioral assessment and develop an individualized behavioral plan (see chapter 7). (Under the latest reauthorization, the Congress is considering eliminating requirements for functional behavioral assessments and behavior plans.)
- For a student who is developing English proficiency, the IEP team should consider the student's language needs as they relate to the IEP (see chapter 3).
- For a student who is blind or visually impaired, the IEP should provide for instruction in Braille and the use of Braille unless the IEP team determines otherwise.
- For a student who is deaf or hard of hearing, the IEP team should consider the language and communication needs of the student, the student's academic level, the full range of needs (including the student's social, emotional, and cultural needs), and the student's opportunities for direct communication with peers and professionals in his or her language and communication mode.

Recommendations for designing IEPs for students with medical needs, with sensory impairments, and from diverse backgrounds are presented in Figure 2.5 on page 61.

Assistive Technology

The IEP team also should determine whether the student needs assistive technology devices and services. This decision is based on an individualized technology assessment that usually includes: (a) identification of the student's strengths, challenges, preferences, age, gender, cultural perspectives, level of and desire for independence, educational, social,

FIGURE 2.3

Sample IEP

Unified School District
Individualized Education Program

Student: Marty Glick

School: Hudson Elementary

Placement: General Education Classroom

Date of IEP Meeting: 12/17/2005

Date of Initiation of Services: 1/3/2006

Dominant Language of Student: English

DOB: 8/5/95

Grade: 5

Disability Classification: LD

Notification to Family: 11/28/2005

Review date: 1/3/2007

CURRENT LEVEL OF PERFORMANCE IN THE GENERAL EDUCATION CURRICULUM ACADEMIC/EDUCATIONAL ACHIEVEMENT

Mathematics

Marty's strongest areas include geometry, measurement, time, and money. He has difficulty with multiplication, division, fractions, and word problems. He especially had difficulty solving problems that contained nonessential information.

Reading

Marty's reading is characterized by weaknesses in word recognition, oral reading, and comprehension. Marty had difficulty with the passages that were written at a third-grade level. His oral reading of the passages revealed difficulties sounding out words and a reliance on contextual cues. He had particular problems with comprehension questions related to large amounts of information and interpreting abstractions.

Written Language

Marty's writing portfolio reveals that he has many ideas to write about in a broad range of genres. However, Marty avoids using prewriting tools such as semantic webs or outlines to organize his thoughts. Consequently, his stories don't usually follow a chronological sequence, and his reports do not fully develop the topic. He uses a variety of sentence patterns but frequently ignores the need for punctuation. Marty has difficulty editing his own work but will make mechanical changes pointed out by the teacher. He rarely revises the content or organization of his writing in a substantial manner. Marty's teacher has observed that Marty enjoys working on the computer and performs better on writing tasks when he uses a talking work processor.

SOCIAL DEVELOPMENT

Level of Social Development

Marty shows attention difficulties when attempting some academic tasks. He has a good sense of humor and seems to relate fairly well to his peers.

Interest Inventory

Marty likes working with peers and using computers. He prefers projects to tests. He likes working with his hands and fixing things.

PHYSICAL DEVELOPMENT

Marty is physically healthy and has no difficulties with his hearing and vision. He has had no major illnesses or surgeries, and he is not taking any medications.

BEHAVIORAL DEVELOPMENT

A functional assessment of Marty's classroom behavior indicates that Marty is frequently off-task and has difficulty completing his assignments. He often works on assignments for a short period of time and then works on another assignment, engages in an off-task activity such as playing with objects, leaves his work area, or seeks attention from his teacher or his peers. His behavior also appears to be affected by other activities in the classroom, the placement of his work area near certain students, and the type and difficulty of the activity.

(continued)

Figure 2.3 (Continued)

RELATED SERVICES

Service	Frequency	Location
Group counseling	Once/week	Social worker's office

SUPPLEMENTARY AIDS AND SERVICES

Service	Frequency	Location
Collaboration teacher	2 hours/day	General education classroom
Paraprofessional	3 hours/day	General education classroom

PROGRAM MODIFICATION AND SUPPORT FOR SCHOOL PERSONNEL

Marty and his teacher will receive the services of a collaborative teacher and a paraeducator. Marty's teacher will be given time to meet with the collaboration teacher, who also will modify materials, locate resources, administer assessments, and coteach lessons. Marty's teacher also will receive training related to differentiated instruction, classroom management, and assessment alternatives and accommodations.

EXTENT OF PARTICIPATION IN GENERAL EDUCATION PROGRAMS AND WITH PEERS WITHOUT DISABILITIES

Marty will remain in his fifth-grade classroom full-time. The collaboration teacher and the paraeducator will provide direct service to Marty in the general education classroom.

RATIONALE FOR PLACEMENT

It is anticipated that Marty's educational needs can best be met in the general education classroom. He will benefit from being exposed to the general education curriculum with the additional assistance of the collaboration teacher and the paraeducator. The use of testing modifications and computers with talking word processors also should help Marty benefit from his general education program. Marty's social skills and self-concept also will be improved by exposure to his general education peers. Counseling will provide him with the prosocial skills necessary to interact with his peers and complete his work.

INSTRUCTIONAL PROGRAM

Annual Goal: Marty will read, write, listen, and speak for information and understanding. (State Learning Standard 1 for English Language Arts)

Evaluation Procedures

1. Given the choice of a narrative trade book at his instructional level, Marty will be able to retell the story, including major characters, the setting, and major events of the plot sequence.

   Teacher-made story grammar checklist

2. Given a passage from his social studies or science textbook, Marty will develop three questions that require inferential or critical thinking.

   Teacher evaluation of student response

3. Using a prewriting structure to organize his ideas, Marty will write a paragraph describing a process that shows logical development and has a minimum of five sentences.

   Writing rubric

Annual Goal: Marty will read, write, listen, and speak for literary response and expression. (State Learning Standard 2 for English Language Arts)

Evaluation Procedures

1. After choosing a favorite poem to read to his peers, Marty will memorize it and recite it with fluency and intonation.

   Peer and teacher feedback

2. Given the choice of texts with multi-syllabic words, Marty will read with 90% accuracy.

   Teacher analysis of running record

3. Given a choice of biographies, Marty will reflect upon the events and experiences which relate to his own life.

   Teacher evaluation of dialogue journal

Annual Goal: Marty will understand mathematics and become mathematically confident by communicating and reasoning mathematically. (State Learning Standard 3 for Mathematics, Science, and Technology)

Evaluation Procedures

1. Given a one-step word problem with a distractor, Marty will write the relevant information and operation needed to solve it 90 percent of the time.

   Teacher-made worksheet

2. Given the task of writing five one-step word problems with a distractor, Marty will write four that are clear enough for his classmates to solve.

   Teacher evaluation of student response

Annual Goal: Marty will demonstrate mastery of the foundation skills and competencies essential for success in the workplace. (State Learning Standard 3a for Career Development and Occupational Studies)

Evaluation Procedures

1. When working independently on an academic task, Marty will improve his time on task by 100 percent.

   Self-recording

2. When working in small groups, Marty will listen to peers and take turns speaking 80 percent of the time.

   Teacher observation or group evaluation

TRANSITION PROGRAM

Marty is very interested in and skilled at working with his hands to make and fix things. In addition to using these skills as part of the educational program, Marty will participate in a career awareness program designed to explore his career interests.

This program will expose Marty to a variety of careers and allow him to experience work settings and meet professionals who are involved in careers related to Marty's interests. This program also will aid Marty in understanding his learning style, strengths and weaknesses, interests, and preferences.

Annual Goal: Marty will be knowledgeable about the world of work, explore career options, and relate personal skills, aptitudes, and abilities to future career decisions. (State Learning Standard 1 for Career Development and Occupational Studies)

Evaluation Procedures

1. Marty will identify three careers in which he may be interested and explain why he is interested in each one.

   Self-report

2. Marty will research and explain the training and experiential requirements for the three careers he has identified.

   Interview

3. Marty will evaluate his skills and characteristics with respect to these careers by identifying his related strengths and needs.

   Self-report

4. Marty will follow and observe individuals involved in these three careers as they perform their jobs.

   Student-maintained log

ASSISTIVE TECHNOLOGY AND COMMUNICATION NEEDS

Marty will be given a computer and talking word processing system with word prediction capabilities and a talking calculator to assist him with classroom activities and tests.

PARTICIPATION IN STATEWIDE AND DISTRICTWIDE ASSESSMENTS, AS WELL AS TESTING ACCOMMODATIONS AND ALTERNATIVES

Marty will participate in all statewide and districtwide assessments. He will take these tests individually in a separate location, with extended time and breaks every 30 minutes. Tests that last for more than 2 hours will be administered over several days, with no more than 2 hours of testing each day. Marty will be allowed to use a computer with a talking word processing program and word prediction capabilities. For math tests that do not involve mental computation, he will be allowed to use a talking calculator.

When possible and appropriate, Marty will demonstrate his mastery of classroom content through projects and cooperative learning activities rather than teacher-made tests. When Marty must take teacher-made tests, they will be administered in a separate location by his collaboration teacher with extended time limits. A mastery level grading system will be employed.

(continued)

Figure 2.3 (Continued)

METHOD AND FREQUENCY OF COMMUNICATION WITH FAMILY

Marty's family will be regularly informed through IEP progress reports, curriculum-based assessments, and Marty's general education report cards. In addition, feedback on Marty's performance and progress will be shared with his family through quarterly scheduled family-teacher meetings, results of state and district assessments, and portfolio reviews.

Committee Participants	**Relationship/Role**
Ms. Rachel Tupper	5th grade teacher
Mr. Terry Feaster	Special Ed. teacher
Mr. Kris Brady	Sp. Ed. administrator
Ms. Jessica Amatura	Educational evaluator

Signature(s)

If family members were not members of the committee, please indicate:

I agree with the Individualized Education Program   _____
I disagree with the Individualized Education Program   _____

Harry Glick, Agnes Glick

Parent/Guardian Signature

I participated in this meeting. I agree with the goals and services of the Individualized Educational Program.

Marty Glick

Student's Signature

---

and community-based goals, and ability, willingness, and training needed to use the device; (b) the strengths, challenges, and cultural values of the family, including the sociocultural factors that affect the family as well as the impact of the device on the family; (c) the needs of the student in his or her customary environments, such as the classroom, school, home, and work setting; (d) the nature of the technology, including its potential effectiveness, ease of use, features, obtrusiveness, effect on peers, noticeability, comfort level, dependability, adaptability, durability, transportability, safety, cost, and comparability to other devices; and (e) a statement addressing the advantages and disadvantages of the alternative strategies and technologies for meeting the student's identified technology needs and the training students and families need to use the device (Parette & McMahan, 2002). For example, while a device may be very effective in helping a student communicate, the student and the family may not use it in social settings in order to avoid attention from others. In addition, the IEP team should consider whether the device allows the student to function at a higher level and/or more efficiently as well as the training needed to ensure that the device has maximum benefit for the student.

Additional guidelines for determining appropriate technology to meet the needs of students and their families are presented in Figure 2.6 (page 62) . Information on assistive technology is also presented in chapters 1 and 8.

Resource

Parette, Huer, and Hourcade (2003) and Parette and McMahan (2002) offer guidelines that IEP teams can use to identify and address the assistive technology goals, expectations, cultural values, and commitments of families.

FIGURE 2.4

Sample IEP meeting agenda

- Welcome IEP team members and thank them for coming to the meeting
- Introduce all IEP team members and briefly explain each team member's role
- Explain the purpose of the meeting:
     Describe reasons that the meeting is being held
     Preview what will happen in the meeting
     Focus comments on the student
     Describe specific focus if applicable (e.g., eligibility or transition)
- Accentuate the positive: Review achievement/progress with current IEP goods and objectives
- Discuss strengths and areas of need or improvement. Review assessment results.
- Write current levels of educational performance:
     List strengths and ability levels
     List areas of need/improvement
- Write goals and objectives or benchmarks: (Reference general curriculum)
     How will the goals and objectives/benchmarks be met?
     How will the goals and objectives/benchmarks be evaluated?
     Who will monitor the goals and objectives/benchmarks?
     Who will report progress toward goals and objectives/benchmarks? How? How often?
- Determine services needed to achieve annual goals and advance in general curriculum:
     What special education services are needed?
     What related services are required for student to benefit from special education?
     What program modifications, supports, or supplementary aids and services are needed in general education programs?
- Discuss participation in general curriculum, extracurricular, and nonacademic activities
- Discuss participation in state and district assessment activities
- Consider appropriate special factors: Behavioral strategies   Assistive technology
                                                Braille instruction   Extended School Year (ESY)
                                                Language needs for limited-English-proficient students
                                                Communication and language needs
- Review student placement
- Provide parents with prior notice for free and appropriate public education
- Summarize discussion and decisions made in the IEP meeting
- Sign the IEP
- Provide copies of the IEP to IEP team participants as appropriate
- Thank IEP team members for coming

Note: This agenda proposes a potential format for an individualized education program (IEP) meeting. The agenda should be modified to meet the specific IEP meeting discussion for the individual student.

Source: From "A Field of IEP Dreams: Increasing General Education Teacher Participation in the IEP Development Process," by R. R. Menlove, P. J. Hudson, and D. Suter, 2001, *Teaching Exceptional Children, 33*(5), pp. 28–33. Copyright 2001 by The Council for Exceptional Children. Reprinted with permission.

Transition Services

The transition services component of the IEP can address natural transition points and a variety of areas related to transition (Steere & Cavaiuolo, 2002). For example, for students who will go to college after graduation, the transition services component may relate to learning study skills and advocating for one's needs. For students who will go to work, the transition services component may focus on assessing employment interests and preferences, developing important job-seeking and job performance skills, finding recreational opportunities, and preparing for independent living. Some schools meet the

Resource

Wood, Karvonen, Test, Browder, and Algozzine (2004) identify ways to include self-determination and self-advocacy goals in IEPs. Chapter 6 contains strategies for promoting self-determination and self-advocacy.

The comprehensive planning team works with family members to design a student's IEP. What have been your experiences in collaborating with others to develop IEPs?

 Resource

Steere and Cavaiuolo (2002) offer guidelines and strategies for identifying and addressing transition planning in the IEP process.

transition services requirement by developing an Individualized Transition Plan (ITP) as part of the IEP. Issues related to transitional planning and a sample ITP are presented in chapter 6.

Student Involvement

> When I started working on the student-led IEP, I was very excited because I could tell the teachers what I needed instead of them telling me what I need (Hapner & Imel, 2002, p. 123).

> I made note cards to read during my IEP. I looked in books to find examples of what we can say during the meeting. I filled out papers that asked how I was benefiting from my IEP and what I was learning. I felt really ready to do my IEP (Hapner & Imel, 2002, p. 123).

> I catch on really fast with math. I don't like to use the calculator much—just to check the answers. I can do real long problems in my head. My teacher tripped out about that (Hapner & Imel, 2002, p.126).

The IDEA supports the involvement of students with disabilities in the IEP process, which can in turn promote the implementation and success of the instructional program and the planning and delivery of transition services (Mason, McGahee-Kovac, & Johnson, 2004; Torgerson, Miner, & Shen, 2004). As the previous comments indicate, students can offer a unique perspective on their own strengths and challenges, preferences, interests, hobbies, talents, and career goals, as well as successful teaching strategies and materials. Involving students in the team and the IEP process can help the team focus on positive aspects of the student's performance and ensure that practical, functional, and meaningful goals are included in the IEP. Because student involvement in instructional planning can be empowering, it also can foster students' motivation, self-reflection, independence, self-advocacy, and self-determination (Nevin, Malian, & Williams, 2002) (We will learn more about motivating students in chapter 9, and promoting their self-advocacy and self-determination in chapter 6).

 Resource

Van Dycke and Peterson (2003) offer a process for helping students develop their IEP goals.

FIGURE 2.5

Special considerations in designing IEPs

SPECIAL CONSIDERATIONS FOR STUDENTS WITH MEDICAL NEEDS

The IEPs for students with medical needs should identify and address their unique needs and be developed collaboratively with medical professionals. Therefore, IEPs for these students should contain a health plan and include:

- the findings of medical and therapy evaluations
- appropriate health-related goals
- suggestions for placement, related services and supports, scheduling, and classroom adaptations
- medical treatments and medication requirements, including potential side effects
- equipment requirements
- vocational, social, and psychosocial needs
- training for students so that they can perform or direct others to perform or direct others to perform specialized health care procedures
- training for professionals and families
- procedures for dealing with emergencies (American Federation of Teachers, 1993; Heller, et al., 2000; Hill, 1999; Phelps, 1995; Prendergast, 1995)

SPECIAL CONSIDERATIONS FOR STUDENTS WITH SENSORY IMPAIRMENTS

The IEPs for students with sensory impairments can address their unique needs and focus on helping them succeed in the LRE. Therefore, IEPs for these students should address:

- the skills and instructional strategies necessary to develop reading and writing
- the skills and technological devices needed to access information
- orientation and mobility instruction
- socialization skills
- transitional, recreational, and career education needs (Heumann & Hehir, 1995)

SPECIAL CONSIDERATIONS FOR STUDENTS FROM LINGUISTICALLY AND CULTURALLY DIVERSE BACKGROUNDS

The IEPs for students from diverse backgrounds should give teachers additional information to guide the educational program for these students. IEPs for these students should include:

- a summary of assessment results, including the student's language skills in her or his native language and English and in social and academic interactions, as well as information about the student's life outside of school
- the language(s) of instruction matched to specific goals and objectives
- the goals and objectives related to maintaining the student's native language and cultural identity and learning English
- teaching strategies relating to the student's linguistic ability, academic skill, cultural and socioeconomic background, and learning style
- teaching materials and curricula that address the student's linguistic and cultural background
- motivation strategies and reinforcers that are compatible with the student's cultural and experiential background
- related services that reflect the student's educational, medical, psychological, linguistic, and cultural needs
- bilingual and culturally sensitive educators, paraeducators, community volunteers, and other district resources available to meet the student's needs (Garcia & Malkin, 1993; Ortiz, 1997)

The involvement of students will vary based on their age and their ability level (Barrie & McDonald, 2002). Younger students can be involved by asking them to discuss what they like about school and how their school experience can be improved. Older students can share information about their educational strengths and challenges and plans for the future.

You and your colleagues and family members can use various strategies to help students participate in the team process (Barrie & McDonald, 2002; Conderman, Ikan, & Hatcher, 2000; Hapner & Imel, 2002; Kroeger, Leibold, & Ryan, 1999; Mason et al., 2004; Snyder, 2002; Thoma, Rogan, & Baker, 2001). (These strategies also can

Resource

Dabkowski (2004) and Rock (2000) provide guidelines for facilitating the involvement of family members in the IEP process, and Browder and Lohrmann-O'Rourke (2001) offer strategies for helping nonverbal students participate in IEP meetings.

Technology
Is the AT functional and appropriate for the child?
Does the device provide for greater opportunities for choice and control?
Does it match the needs of the child?
Does the device physically fit into the child's environments?

Service System
What is the most appropriate AT needed by the child and family?
How can we provide case coordination to secure services for you and your child?
How can we support you in meeting your priority AT goals?

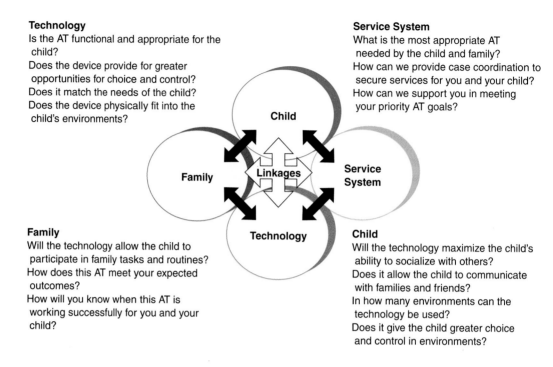

Family
Will the technology allow the child to participate in family tasks and routines?
How does this AT meet your expected outcomes?
How will you know when this AT is working successfully for you and your child?

Child
Will the technology maximize the child's ability to socialize with others?
Does it allow the child to communicate with families and friends?
In how many environments can the technology be used?
Does it give the child greater choice and control in environments?

FIGURE 2.6   **A comprehensive approach to selecting assistive technology (AT) for students**

Source: From H. P. Parrette and M. J. Brotherson, *Education and Training in Mental Retardation and Developmental Disabilities,* vol. 31, 1996, p. 32. Copyright 1996 by The Council for Exceptional Children. Reprinted by permission.

be modified to assist family members in learning about and participating in the IEP process. We will learn more collaborating with families and person-centered planning in chapter 4).

Before the meeting you can discuss with students the purpose of the meeting, including who will attend, what will go on, and how to participate. You can provide students with an overview of appropriate aspects of special education laws, the components of the IEP, and copies of their current IEPs. It also is helpful to review current assessment data and IEPs and relevant vocabulary with students, conduct simulated meetings, and help students develop and rehearse their comments before the meeting. You also can give students inventories and checklists to help them identify their strengths, challenges, goals, learning styles, study skills, transition and career goals, interests, preferences, concerns, and feelings about the issues to be discussed including the need for and effectiveness of various instructional and testing accommodations. (See Figure 2.7 for a listing of questions for students.) Student involvement in the IEP process also can be facilitated by providing students with opportunities to talk with other students who have successfully participated in the IEP process, and view videos of simulated student-led IEP meetings. You also can teach students the social and communication skills they need to participate in IEP meetings (Torgerson et al., 2004).

At the meeting, you can help students participate by asking them to introduce the participants; explain their disabilities, strengths, and challenges; describe effective in-

Resource

Mason et al. (2004), Torgerson et al. (2004), Hapner and Imel (2002), Zickel and Arnold (2001), and Martin, Marshall, Maxson, and Jerman (1996a; 1996b) developed objectives, lesson plans, strategies, and instructional materials to teach students how to be actively involved in the IEP process.

USING TECHNOLOGY TO PROMOTE INCLUSION

Conducting an Individualized Technology Assessment

As part of the IEP for Elisa Sanchez, a student with a significant communication disorder, the IEP team met with her family to discuss her needs in terms of assistive technology devices and services. Because of Elisa's expressive language difficulties, the team was considering recommending that Elisa use some type of augmentative or alternative communication system. While some members proposed that Elisa continue to use a communication board, others thought that her ability to communicate with others in a variety of environments would be enhanced by her use of an electronic device with digitized speech.

Recognizing the importance of Elisa and her family's feelings regarding these choices, the team solicited information from them regarding their perspectives on these technologies. Convinced that Elisa had the skills to effectively use either system, they spoke with her and her family about their preferences. Elisa indicated that she was eager to use the electronic system as "it would make communicating with others easier, and faster for everyone, and allow me to say more." Since the system was programmed in English and Spanish, she liked that she could select the language in which she needed to communicate depending on the person with whom she was speaking.

While her family agreed with Elisa, they also had some concerns. They worried about paying for the device, and using, transporting, and maintaining it. They also were concerned that it would draw attention to Elisa in public settings and make them feel different.

The team found this information very helpful and used it to determine the assistive technology devices and services that would be incorporated into Elisa's IEP. The team decided that Elisa could benefit from using both types of communication systems and that she and her family could determine when to use each system. They discussed the need for tailoring the system to Elisa and her family so that the symbols, photographs, and voices used matched those of the family's culture. They also agreed that the school district would purchase a light-weight system, and work with Elisa and her family to help them learn how to use and care for and transport it. It also was arranged that the company that sold the system would provide technical support to Elisa's family in Spanish.

- How would Elisa's use of technology affect her access to your inclusive classroom and to society?
- Why are the preferences and goals of students and their families important in determining assistive technology devices and services?
- How would you solicit information from students and families about their perspectives on assistive technology devices and services?
- What preferences and perspectives toward the technology did the IEP team need to consider for Elisa and her family?
- How were these preferences and perspectives addressed by the IEP team?
- What other factors should the IEP team consider when conducting an individualized technology assessment?

structional accommodations; discuss their past and future goals; and ask and answer questions regarding their strengths, challenges, aspirations, and opinions. You should also limit your use of professional jargon and acronyms, speak directly to students rather than speaking about students to others, give them time to formulate and present their responses, listen and pay attention to their comments, ask them for input and opinions, and incorporate their comments into the educational program. Students also can collaborate with other team members to develop important components of the IEP such as identifying instructional objectives and accommodations, and related services. Following the meeting, you can give students a copy of their IEP and encourage them to review it periodically and to work toward meeting the goals and objectives listed there.

 Set Your Sites

For more information on the special education and IEP process and involving students in the development of their IEPs, go to the Web Links module in Chapter 2 of the Companion Website.

FIGURE 2.7

Sample student questions

- How do you feel about school?
- What do you like about school?
- How could school be improved for you?
- What are your greatest strengths and talents in school? What do you do well in school?
- In what areas do you think you need to improve at school?
- How would you describe your behavior in school?
- How do you get along with other students in your class/school?
- Who are you? How would you describe yourself?
- What are your strengths? What are your needs/challenges?
- What are your successes? Dreams/hopes for the future?
- What things would you like to learn about yourself?
- What things would you like to learn in school?
- In what ways do you learn best?
- What things could your teacher(s) do to help you learn or be more successful in school?
- Are you completing your classwork, homework, and assigned projects? If not, why not?
- Briefly describe your study skills and work habits.
- In what school and community activities do you participate? If none, why?
- What do you like to do after school? What are your hobbies?
- What careers interest you?
- What are your goals after you graduate from this school?

How Can IEPs Be Implemented in General Education Settings?

The IEP can provide students with disabilities with access to the general education curriculum (Pugach & Warger, 2001). This section provides you with ways you can work with others to implement the IEP in the general education classroom.

Resource

Menlove, Hudson, and Suter (2001) outline the factors that limit the involvement of general education teachers in the IEP process and strategies for increasing their participation, including a survey to evaluate the IEP meeting.

Reflective

Have you participated in the development of an IEP? What factors hindered and fostered your involvement and involvement of others? How could the IEP process be improved?

Involve Teachers in the IEP Process

The inclusion of general educators in the IEP planning process can foster the link between the IEP and the general education setting (Werts, Mamlin, & Pogoloff, 2002). The involvement of general educators provides the team with important information about the general education curriculum as well as their perceptions of the student's progress within it. Their direct involvement in the IEP process also provides a basis for general educators receiving the supportive services to help students access and succeed in the general education curriculum.

Similarly, the involvement of special educators also provides the team with relevant information about the student's academic, behavioral, and social strengths and needs, which is essential to determining and implementing the instructional and testing accommodations that also help students access and succeed in the general education curriculum. The inclusion of special educators also can help insure that instructional goals and strategies address student needs related to a functional or specialized curriculum (Huefner, 2000).

IDEAS FOR IMPLEMENTATION

Preparing for and Participating in the IEP Meeting

Although he had participated in his school's open house and several family–teacher meetings during his brief time as a teacher, Mr. Myers was nervous about attending his first IEP meeting. While he had learned about IEPs when he was studying to be a teacher, he had never participated in developing one. He spoke to his mentor teacher about his uncertainty, who suggested that he talk to Ms. Gonzalez, the special education teacher. When Mr. Myers approached her, Ms. Gonzalez was not surprised, as even many experienced teachers were intimidated initially by the IEP process. Ms. Gonzalez began by explaining to Mr. Myers that his input was extremely important. She showed him a sample IEP, and explained the different components and how they were developed. She also previewed who would be at the meeting; the agenda of the meeting, including the issues to be discussed; and what team members would be asked to address. She told him that he would be asked to talk about the student's progress in the general education curriculum, how the student's disability affected his performance in class, and what services the student and he would need to achieve the goals in the IEP. She noted that other teachers had found it helpful to bring samples of student work to illustrate their comments regarding their students' strengths and challenges. She also gave him a handout from the state that summarized laws and information related to special education and the IEP process and a list of relevant websites. At the meeting, Mr. Myers, although still nervous, actively participated and benefited from hearing the perspectives of others. As a group, they developed an IEP that addressed the student's varied needs and offered the supports that Mr. Myers needed to implement it.

Here are some other strategies that you can use to participate in IEP meetings:

*   Prepare for the meeting by learning about the issues to be discussed and their relationship to the information you have to share, reviewing current information regarding the student (e.g., current assessment data and IEP), and obtaining an agenda for the meeting.
*   Identify and share with other team members your goals for the meeting and the issues you would like to be addressed so those items can be part of the meeting agenda.
*   Outline the services you provide to the student and the family and their responses to these services.
*   Discuss positive aspects of the student's performance first, including the best ways in which the student learns.
*   Describe in clear and observable terms the student's strengths and needs as well as the services and supports you will need to implement the student's IEP.
*   Support your statements by citing examples and sharing work samples and anecdotal records.
*   Avoid using professional jargon, and seek clarification when you don't understand terms or information presented by others.
*   Ask questions to obtain more information, and to clarify and reflect on the impact and feasibility of major decisions, responsibilities, and dates.
*   Be prepared to compromise and mend fences when you disagree with families or other participants.

Note: Lytle and Bordin (2001); Menlove, Hudson, and Suter (2001).

Align the IEP to the General Education Curriculum

General and special education teachers also can assist the team in aligning the IEP to the general education curriculum by converting the curriculum into measurable learning objectives that can be addressed instructionally (Walsh, 2001). In the case of Marty, the involvement of Ms. Tupper helped the IEP team to translate the state standards into more specific objectives that Ms. Tupper could teach in her classroom. As seen in Figure 2.8, this process begins with collecting assessment data to determine students' current levels of performance within the curriculum (Matlock, Fielder, & Walsh, 2001). Curriculum-related measurable short-term objectives and annual goals are then identified.

Resource

Lingugaris/Kraft, Marchand-Martella, and Martella (2001), Walsh (2001), and Matlock, Fielder, and Walsh (2001) offer guidelines, strategies, and forms to help you write IEP goals and align them to the general education curriculum.

FIGURE 2.8

Developing standards-based goals and objectives aligned with district standards

Phase 1: Assessment

1.1 Select the curricular area to be addressed. Review the students' current assessments and present levels of performance. Examine work samples, curriculum-based measures, CRTs, classroom assignments, and unit tests.

1.2 Study the district's standards in the specific curricular area thoroughly to become familiar with the content and skills at each grade level.

1.3 Identify the standards that the student has already mastered. There may be skills mastered at two or three different grade levels. Note the standards mastered in some way (i.e., highlight, date, initial, underline). Identify the grade level where the majority of mastered standards are clustered. Use this information to develop a description of the student's present level of performance.

1.4 A summary of the standards mastered should be included in the present levels of performance in the student's IEP as it demonstrates how the student is working in the district's core curriculum.

Phase 2: Selection of Short-Term Objectives/Benchmarks

2.1 Select the standards for instruction using the following criteria:
- Degree of importance (i.e., Is this skill a critical element of instruction?)
- Sequence of instruction (i.e., Is this the next logical step in the sequence of instruction?)
- Learning rate and past progress of the student (i.e., Are the student's cognitive level and rate of learning adequate for mastering this skill?)

2.2 A standard may be too broad. It may be necessary to break it down into smaller increments of learning (i.e., task analyze the standard).

2.3 Identify those standards that will be included in the IEP as short-term objectives or benchmarks.

2.4 The instructional sequence for the standard can be based on whether it is designated to be taught during the first trimester (T1), second trimester (T2), or third trimester (T3).

2.5 Consider the level of accuracy to demonstrate mastery, materials and instructional methodologies, and how progress will be measured (work samples, curriculum-based measures, unit tests, running records, fluency measures, criterion-referenced tests).

Phase 3: Develop the Measurable Annual Goal

3.1 Based on the standards selected for instruction in Phase 2, use the following format for the development of the measurable annual goal:

Given daily instruction in _____ , the student will master _____/_____ standards at
                          (curricular area)   ratio

the _____ grade level with _____% accuracy as measured by _____ by
       grade   methods of measurement

_____ .
    (date)

3.2 The measurable annual goal may target mastery of more standards than are included as short-term objectives or benchmarks in the IEP.

Note: IEP = individualized education program. CRT = criterion-referenced test.

Source: From "Building the Foundation for Standards-Based Instruction for All Students," by L. Matlock, K. Fielder, and D. Walsh, 2001, *Teaching Exceptional Children, 33*(5), p. 71.

Differentiate Instruction to Address IEP Goals

The successful implementation of the IEP in the general education setting is related to the use of differentiated instruction to address IEP goals. Therefore, you and the team can work collaboratively to identify and employ a range of curricular, instructional, technological, and testing accommodations and supports to provide *all learners* with access

FIGURE 2.9

Sample IEP matrix

MATRIX OF DAVID'S IEP OBJECTIVES AND THE SCHEDULE

Name *David Sebastian*   Grade/Age *Sophomore/15*   School Year *2005/2006*

IEP Objectives	World Civics	Geometry	English	P.E.	Biology	Counseling	Lunch	Assemblies	Club Mtgs.	Passing Periods	Peer Support Groups	After School
1. Self-regulate impulsive behaviors	X	X	X	X	X	X	X	X	X	X	X	X
2. Type out a message for emotional support						X						X
3. Self-regulate to make changes	X	X	X	X	X	X	X	X	X	X	X	X
4. Eye contact with persons	X	X	X		X	X	X		X		X	X
5. Functional math	X	X	X	X	X	X	X	X	X	X	X	X
6. Initiate conversation	X		X	X		X	X		X	X	X	
7. Vocational awareness exploration	X	X	X	X		X	X				X	X
8. Active member of class discussions	X	X	X	X	X							
9. Participate in a peer support group											X	
10. Public transportation skills												X

Source: From "The Evolution of Secondary Inclusion," by J. Thousand, R. L. Rosenberg, K. D. Bishop, and R. A. Villa, 1997, *Remedial and Special Education, 18,* p. 281. Copyright 1997 by PRO-ED, Inc. Reprinted by permission.

to the general education curriculum (Hitchcock et al., 2002; Watson & Houtz, 2002). We will learn more about how to differentiate instruction in subsequent chapters.

Set Your Sites

For more information related to helping your students access the general education curriculum, go to the Web Links module in Chapter 2 of the Companion Website.

Establish an Implementation Plan

Once the IEP has been developed, a plan to implement it in the general setting can be established. You can work with the IEP team to create a matrix that links the student's IEP goals and services with the student's general education program (see Figure 2.9). In creating the matrix, you need to integrate the objectives, related services, technology, and instructional accommodations outlined in the student's IEP with the critical components of the classroom schedule, curriculum, and routines. The goals and objectives of the IEP

FIGURE 2.10

Sample program-at-a-glance

Student's Name: *David Sebastian*

Age __17__   Disability   Down Syndrome, Communication Support

	Staff	Rm.
1	Coppes	SC 123
2	Hubbard	A 206
3	Eshilian	Study Skills
4	Bove	L 123
5	Lablin	Vocational Skills
6	Miller	Study Skills

Lives with: Mother and father. (Sister and brother have moved out)

Positive Student Profile:	IEP Objectives:
Friendly	Self-regulate for behaviors
Stays with a task	Type or say messages/communication
Good sense of humor	Deal with change
Very motivated	Eye contact with students and adults
Very artistic	Functional math
	Initiate conversations
	Vocational awareness
	Class participation
	Attend and participate in support group
	Self-advocacy
	Utilization of mass transportation

Management Needs:

Needs support to maintain attention

Needs support to maintain behaviors in class

If it is necessary, have David leave class and not interrupt others while he goes to the Study Skills room or the Guidance Office

Medical Needs: Has had 1 to 2 seizures per year. Knows when they are coming.

Grading Accommodations: May need more time, large print, support from other students for note taking, or support at times from staff and students.

Other Comments:

Service Coordinator   Ellen North   Extension   123
Parent/Guardian   Adele and Robert   Phone   888-555-1234

Source: From "The Evolution of Secondary Inclusion," by J. Thousand, R. L. Rosenberg, K. D. Bishop, and R. A. Villa, 1997, *Remedial and Special Education, 18*, p. 281. Copyright 1997 by PRO-ED, Inc. Reprinted by permission.

are then implemented by all professionals in the general education classroom as part of the class's ongoing instructional activities.

The success of the plan can be fostered by highlighting and communicating meaningful IEP information to those who will be responsible for implementing it. This is particularly important at the secondary level when students have several teachers. One way to do this is through use of forms that provide a brief and quick visual summary of important IEP information (Saint-Laurent, 2001; Thousand et al., 1997). For example, you can develop a program-at-a-glance form that gives the student's teachers and supportive service personnel essential aspects of the student's IEP (see Figure 2.10). Finally, an inclusive IEP needs-and-accommodation checklist, a list of the student's educational needs and instructional accommodations for addressing them, can be shared with those who work with the student.

Engage in Curriculum Mapping

You can engage in *curriculum mapping*, a process for examining what you teach, to foster and evaluate your success at implementing students' IEPs (Koppang, 2004). In curriculum mapping, you examine what you teach by creating a map listing: (a) the content covered in class; (b) the key skills taught; and (c) the assessment strategies used to document student learning. You can then periodically examine your curriculum maps with your colleagues to validate successful teaching practices that foster student learning and determine revisions that need to be made to your instructional program.

Resource

Koppang (2004) offers guidelines for conducting curriculum mapping.

What Are the Educational Strengths and Needs of Students with High-Incidence Disabilities?

Students like Marty are referred to as having *high-incidence* disabilities or mild disabilities that include such disability categories as learning disabilities, mild mental retardation, mild emotional/behavioral disorders, and speech/language impairments. Students with high-incidence disabilities make up 94 percent of the students with disabilities, and have many things in common. (Later in the chapter, we will meet and learn about students with low-incidence disabilities, which include students with physical, sensory, and more significant disabilities.)

The factors that contribute to the development of high-incidence disability categories appear to be multifaceted and are the focus of ongoing research. Several biological and sociocultural factors appear to interact to affect an individual's learning and behavioral abilities and styles. Biological factors such as one's temperament, and neurological development are thought to play an important role in making individuals more predisposed to certain behaviors (Tannock & Martinussen, 2001). Environmental factors also may make some individuals more likely to engage in specific behaviors (Amen, 2000). Experiential factors such as the nature of an individual's interactions with family members and educators, family life, cultural, linguistic, and economic background also influence students' behaviors.

The developmental nature of the high-incidence disability categories affect individuals in different ways as they age. In early childhood, while children with these conditions may exhibit learning difficulties and high levels of activity, they may not be viewed as different from other young children who typically engage in similar behaviors, albeit at lower rates. However, as they enter elementary school and the academic and behavioral demands increase, their learning and behavioral difficulties impact their school performance and may start to cause frustration, social rejection, low self-esteem, and a dislike of school. Some learners may outgrow their condition or some of the symptoms associated with it when they reach adolescence. However, many do not, and the interaction with the typical adolescent desire for independence, peer acceptance, and conformity intensifies their academic, organizational, and social difficulties.

As we saw in the case of Marty, educators often have trouble differentiating among students with these disability categories because their behaviors tend to interfere with their learning and academic performance, their social interactions and friendships with others, and their emotional development (Farmer, 2000). As a result, the teaching strategies you will use to promote their learning also overlap. Because the vast majority of students with high-incidence disabilities are educated in inclusive classrooms, you will need

Students with disabilities have a variety of strengths and challenges, and no two students are alike. How are your students similar and different from each other?

to differentiate your curriculum and your teaching strategies to help them access and succeed in the general education curriculum. (Strategies for accomplishing this are presented in this chapter and throughout this book.) These students also challenge you to be knowledgeable of their unique characteristics so that an educational program that addresses their strengths and needs is planned and implemented.

Students with Learning Disabilities

Your class will include students like Marty, whose school performance and behavior may not live up to their potential and your expectations. While they may do some things well, they lag behind their classmates in many areas. You may view them as unmotivated or not trying hard enough, however, like Marty, they may have some type of learning disability.

Students with *learning disabilities* make up 5 percent of the total school population. Slightly more than half of the students receiving special education services have *learning disabilities,* making them the largest and fastest-growing group of students with disabilities (Blair & Scott, 2002; Fuchs & Fuchs, 1998). This growing prevalence rate is due to several factors, including the social acceptability of the learning disabilities label. In most cases, the cause of a student's learning disability is not known (Mercer, 1997).

A *specific learning disability* is a disorder in one or more of the basic psychological processes involved in understanding or using spoken or written language, which may appear as an impaired ability to listen, think, speak, read, write, spell, or do mathematical calculations. The term *learning disability* includes such conditions as perceptual handicaps, brain injury, minimal brain dysfunction, dyslexia, and developmental aphasia. It does not include learning problems that are primarily the result of visual, hearing, or motor handicaps, mental retardation, emotional disturbance, or environmental, cultural, or economic disadvantage.

Like Marty, many students with learning disabilities have average or above-average intelligence, although they often fail to perform academically in line with their potential as well as their peers (Boudah & Weiss, 2002). Therefore, many of these students often show a discrepancy between their ability and their actual performance in your classroom. The characteristics and behaviors of these students vary; some have difficulties in only one area, while others have difficulties in a variety of areas, such as learning, language, perceptual, motor, social, and behavioral difficulties. Because of the wide range of characteristics associated with learning disabilities, these students present many challenges for educators.

Learning and Academic Difficulties

Many students with learning disabilities have memory, attention, and organizational difficulties that hinder their ability to learn and master academic content (Boudah & Weiss, 2002; McNamara & Wong, 2003). Students with learning disabilities experience difficulties perceiving, processing, remembering, and expressing information (Bergert, 2000). Their learning profiles also are characterized by their tendency to use inefficient and ineffective learning strategies. As a result, they often exhibit difficulties in reading, writing, and mathematics.

Many of these students also experience reading difficulties (Fuchs, Fuchs, Mathes, Lipsey, & Eaton, 2000; Miller & Felton, 2001). These difficulties appear as the failure to recall letters, their sounds, and words; overreliance on whole-word, phonological, and contextual reading strategies; a slow reading rate; and poor listening and reading comprehension ability. When reading, they may lose their place, and/or read in a choppy way. As they enter the secondary grades, these reading difficulties may result in misreading of directions, an avoidance of reading and writing, and trouble accessing and comprehending information in content area textbooks (Bergert, 2000).

Many students with learning disabilities who have reading difficulties also may have trouble writing. An examination of their writing may reveal problems in the areas of idea generation, text organization, sentence structure, vocabulary usage, spelling, and grammar. These writing difficulties can affect their performance across the curriculum.

Although most students with learning disabilities have reading problems, they may be proficient in some content areas and below-average in others. However, large numbers of students with learning disabilities also experience difficulty with mathematics. You may observe this in their lack of knowledge of basic facts and difficulties in discriminating numbers, symbols, and signs; understanding math terms and vocabulary; solving problems; making comparisons; and performing more complex procedures.

Language and Communication Difficulties

Language difficulties are a common characteristic of many students with learning disabilities (Bergert, 2000). As a result, some of these students may use immature speech patterns, experience language comprehension difficulties, and have trouble expressing themselves. In the classroom, they may have difficulty learning new vocabulary, following directions, understanding questions, pronouncing and rhyming words, and expressing their needs.

Increased attention has focused on the needs of students with nonverbal learning disabilities who have a hard time processing nonverbal, visual-spatial information and communications such as body language, gestures, and the context of linguistic interactions (Telzrow & Bonar, 2002). While these students may talk a lot, their language tends to be repetitive, which results in a communication style and word selection that is narrow and rigid (Foss, 2001). They rely on spoken language to communicate, speaking in a flat tone of voice and often interpreting language literally (Vacca, 2001). When interacting with others, they frequently fail to identify and understand nonverbal social cues, and assess

Resource

Telzrow and Bonar (2002), Morris (2002) and Vacca (2001) offer information and guidelines that can assist you in identifying and addressing the learning strengths and challenges of students with nonverbal learning disabilities.

Set Your Sites

For more information on students with nonverbal learning disabilities, go to the Web Links module in Chapter 2 of the Companion Website.

Set Your Sites

For more information on teaching students with learning disabilities, go to the Web Links module in Chapter 2 of the Companion Website.

Reflective

It has been noted that more than 80 percent of the nation's students could be considered learning disabled under the current definition of the term. How many of the students you work with could qualify using this definition? Why does the definition allow so many students to be identified as having a learning disability?

the reactions of others (Morris, 2002). Because students with nonverbal learning disabilities tend to focus on details rather than the whole, they often experience difficulties understanding information that is presented visually, completing novel and complex tasks, establishing priorities, identifying main ideas, taking notes, and organizing and connecting their written products (Telzrow & Bonar, 2002). You can aid these students by helping them to understand part–whole relationships, establishing and following routines, giving specific sequenced verbal directions that help them set priorities for completing multitask activities, beginning lessons with familiar content prior to introducing more novel and complex material, and providing them with social skills instruction (Foss, 2001). You also can aid them in developing accurate and flexible interpretations of words, verbal analogies, body language, and facial expressions; by fostering their verbal expressive and reasoning skills; and by teaching them to decrease their use of irrelevant verbiage.

Perceptual and Motor Difficulties

Even though it appears that their senses are not impaired, many students with learning disabilities may have difficulty recognizing, discriminating, and interpreting visual and auditory stimuli. For example, some of these students may have trouble discriminating shapes and letters, copying from the blackboard, following multiple-step directions, associating sounds with letters, paying attention to relevant stimuli, and working on a task for a sustained period of time.

Students with learning disabilities also may have gross and fine motor difficulties. Gross motor deficits include awkward gaits, clumsiness, poor balance, and an inability to catch or kick balls, skip, and follow a rhythmic sequence of movements. Fine motor problems include difficulty cutting, pasting, drawing, tracing, holding a pencil, writing, and copying and aligning columns. Another motor problem found in some students with learning disabilities is hyperactivity, which results in constant movement and difficulty staying seated.

Social-Emotional and Behavioral Difficulties

Students with learning disabilities may have social and behavioral difficulties and may show signs of a poor self-concept, task avoidance, social withdrawal, loneliness, frustration, and anxiety (Elbaum, 2002; Pavri & Monda-Amaya, 2000). They may engage in classroom behaviors that interfere with their learning and fail to predict the consequences of their behaviors. Because of their poor social skills, they may fail to interpret social cues and adjust their behaviors accordingly, which can result in difficulties relating to and being accepted by their peers (Fuchs, Fuchs, Mathes, & Martinez, 2002; Pavri & Monda-Amaya, 2001). For example, some students with learning disabilities may have difficulties understanding the subtle cues that guide social relationships, which can hinder their development of friendships. As students age, their lack of social skill can result in difficulties accepting feedback, advocating for oneself, understanding the perspectives of others, and resisting peer pressure (Bergert, 2000).

Students with Emotional and Behavioral Disorders

Several terms are used to refer to students with emotional and behavior disorders. Although an estimated 3 percent to 5 percent of students have emotional and behavioral disorders, only 1 percent are identified as such, with boys significantly outnumbering girls. Like students with learning disabilities, many of these students experience learning and motivational difficulties that cause them to underachieve in reading, writing, mathematics, and other content area courses (Anderson, Kutash, & Duchnowski, 2001). Their classroom behaviors also may interfere with learning for themselves and their classmates. While their classroom behavior is often the focus of their educational programs, these students often have language difficulties that you will need to address in your classroom (Benner, Nelson, & Epstein, 2002).

Students with emotional disturbance exhibit one or more of the following characteristics over a long period of time and to a marked degree, which adversely affects their educational performance:

1. Inability to learn that cannot be explained by intellectual, sensory, or health factors
2. Inability to build or maintain good relationships with peers and teachers
3. Inappropriate behaviors or feelings under normal circumstances
4. A general, pervasive mood of unhappiness or depression
5. A tendency to develop physical symptoms or fears associated with personal or school problems

The term *emotional and behavior disorders* includes children who have schizophrenia. It does not include children who are socially maladjusted unless they are emotionally disturbed.

Some of these students as well as those with attention deficit disorders also may display oppositional and defiant behaviors (Forness, Walker, & Kavale, 2003). These students engage in a variety of behaviors designed to resist the requests of authority figures, which often interfere with their school performance. As a result, they tend to seek attention, bother, blame or argue with others, or express their anger and frustration indirectly by engaging in manipulative, vindictive, and/or noncompliant behavior.

Students with emotional and behavior disorders also include those with obsessions, compulsions, and anxiety disorders (Forness et al., 2003). You can help students with obsessions and anxiety disorders by working with their families and mental health professionals in your school, helping students avoid situations that trigger their conditions, and giving them choices. You also can support them by being aware of their conditions and empathetic and sensitive to their unique needs.

Resource

Forness, Walker, and Kavale (2003) offer information on psychiatric conditions and guidelines for addressing these conditions.

While many of us exhibit some type of compulsive behavior, students with obsessive-compulsive disorders (OCD) feel compelled to think about or perform repeatedly an action that appears to be meaningless and irrational and is against their own will. Students with anxiety disorders include those with generalized anxiety disorder, separation anxiety disorder, social phobia, panic disorders, or a combination of these conditions (Schlozman, 2002a). Students with generalized anxiety disorder chronically worry, have difficulty relaxing, and frequently complain of stomachaches and headaches. Students whose anxiety is triggered by their separation from their primary caregivers also may complain of physical ailments when they are expected to be away from their caregivers. Students with social phobias experience anxiety related to interactions in public settings and therefore they may avoid speaking in front of the class, trying out for clubs or teams, and establishing close friendships. When confronted with specific types of events, students with panic disorders may experience emotional discomfort and a variety of physical symptoms such as shortness of breath, heart palpitations, and excessive sweating and fainting.

As part of their adjustment to a new culture, many immigrants also may show signs of anxiety, fears, and depression. However, their conditions may not be identified because they may show up via culture-bound syndromes such as a fear of wind and cold, or an uncontrollable mimicking of others (Kershaw, 2003). Because these culture-bound syndromes are often not recognized by many mental health professionals, and immigrants

Ideas for Implementation

Helping Students Who Exhibit Oppositional and Defiant Behaviors Succeed in Inclusive Classrooms

Justin seemed to delight in irritating Mr. Howe, and it was working. Even the simplest request from Mr. Howe resulted in resistance from Justin. While Mr. Howe initially dealt with Justin's resistance by trying to cajole, convince, or bribe him to comply, he had started to lose his patience with Justin. Now, when Justin refused to do something, Mr. Howe got angry and quickly threatened him in front of the class, which Justin seemed to enjoy even more.

Mr. Howe realized he was playing into Justin's hands and contacted the school's prereferral team, which included Ms. Douglas, a special educator who had worked with Justin and his family. The team collected information about Justin and his behavior. They analyzed several recent incidents to identify the actions of Justin and Mr. Howe that precipitated and maintained their power struggles. Justin's family also discussed how they use routines and structure transitions to avoid these confrontations with him at home. Based on this information, the team concluded that Justin enjoyed his confrontations with Mr. Howe. The team then collaborated with Mr. Howe to create a plan to try to reduce Justin's power struggles. They determined which classroom rules were nonnegotiable and what the consequences would be for violating them. They used these rules to establish a home–school contract with Justin's family. They also discussed instructional changes Mr. Howe could make to motivate Justin and involve him in the learning process and in monitoring his own behavior.

Mr. Howe also tried to change his demeanor and facial expressions with Justin, and made sure that he calmly gave brief, easy-to-follow directions and provided Justin with some choices. If Justin resisted, Mr. Howe briefly listened to Justin's explanation, and either discussed it privately with him or quickly exited the situation. When Justin complied with Mr. Howe's request, Mr. Howe occasionally and privately acknowledged it by employing a quick walk-by reinforcement such as a gesture, whisper, or a pat on the back, or leaving a note for Justin to find later in the day.

Here are some other strategies you can use to help students who exhibit oppositional and defiant behaviors succeed in your inclusive classroom:

- Minimize resistance behaviors that are related to learning difficulties by implementing appropriate instructional accommodations and curricular enhancements and adjustments.
- Identify and try to minimize the events that trigger students' oppositional and defiant behaviors.
- Establish and follow routines, help students make transitions, and structure activities so that students work with their classmates.
- Use learning activities that are motivating and instructionally appropriate for students.
- Build relationships with students inside and outside the classroom. For example, you can attend an extracurricular activity in which your students participate, and connect classroom activities to students' interests and hobbies.
- Provide students with opportunities to make choices.
- Look for opportunities to enhance students' self-esteem.
- Try to avoid escalating the situation, making threats, using body language that communicates disapproval, and responding emotionally during confrontations.
- Solicit student input into the rules for the classroom and the consequences for following and not following them.
- Offer social skills and learning strategies instruction and teach students to use self-management.

Additional guidelines for implementing these and other recommendations are presented in subsequent chapters.

Note: Jensen (2001); Shukla-Mehta and Albin (2003); Woolsey-Terrazas and Chavez (2002).

may not feel comfortable seeking help from others, these conditions often go untreated. Therefore, it is important for you to collaborate with culturally sensitive professionals who can help you and your students and their families understand and address these conditions.

Students with emotional and behavioral disorders are often categorized as mildly or severely disturbed, depending on their behaviors and the nature of their condition. Students who are *mildly emotionally disturbed* may resemble students with learning disabilities and mild retardation in terms of their academic and social needs. Although the intellectual and cognitive abilities of students with mild behavior disorders vary, in the classroom they often have learning and behavior difficulties that result in poor academic performance and self-control, little on-task behavior, reduced frustration tolerance, poor self-concept, and low social skills (Cullinan, Evans, Epstein, & Ryser, 2003; Sutherland & Wehby, 2001). While inappropriate behaviors may mark all students to some degree, those with emotional disturbances may often use inappropriate and noncompliant behavior. They thus run the risk of performing poorly in all academic areas, being rejected by their teachers and classmates, and having high dropout, absenteeism, and suspension rates (Kauffman, 2001; Lago-Dellelo, 1998). Consequently, their rates of success in graduating, enrolling in postsecondary education, obtaining competitive employment, and living independently are lower than other students with high-incidence disabilities (Anderson, Kutash, & Duchnowski, 2001).

However, with teaching strategies tailored to their strengths and challenges, their academic work and behavior can improve significantly through use of positive behavioral supports, social skills instruction, behaviorally based interventions, and differentiated instruction (we will learn how to implement these strategies in your classroom in subsequent chapters of this book) (Gunter, Coutinho & Cade, 2002). They also can benefit from *wraparound planning*, a multidisciplinary process for collaboratively designing and delivering student- and family-centered educational, counseling, medical, and vocational services to address their unique needs and behaviors (Anderson & Matthews, 2001; Eber, Smith, Sugai, & Scott, 2002).

 Resource

Gunter, Coutinho, and Cade (2002) present effective classroom practices that support the academic and behavioral performance of students with emotional and behavioral disorders, and Anderson and Matthews (2001) describe a model program for linking schools and community agencies to address the unique needs of students with emotional and behavioral disorders and their families.

Depression and Suicide

Unfortunately, a significant percentage of all adolescents experience symptoms of depression and consider committing suicide (Forness et al., 2003; Marcotte, Fortin, Potvin, & Papillon, 2002). Students with emotional and behavioral disorders may be particularly vulnerable to depression and suicide as are other students who suffer a significant loss via death or divorce, are victims of abuse, or witness violent acts.

Although most individuals who are depressed do not attempt or commit suicide, there is a high correlation between depression and suicide (Bostic, Rustuccia, & Schlozman, 2001). Therefore, you should be aware of the following warning signs of depression:

- overwhelming sadness, apathy, irritability, and hopelessness, along with a persistent loss of interest and enjoyment in everyday pleasurable activities
- a change in appetite, weight, sleep pattern, body movements, or participation and energy levels
- pervasive difficulty in concentrating, remembering, or making decisions
- anger, rage, and overreaction to criticism
- a sense of inappropriate guilt, worthlessness, or helplessness and a decrease in self-esteem
- recurrent thoughts of death or suicide
- inability to get over the death of a relative or friend and the breakup of friendships
- noticeable neglect of personal hygiene, dress, and health care and/or self-mutilation
- an increase in giving valued items to others or engaging in risky behaviors
- a dramatic change in school performance characterized by a drop in grades and an increase in inappropriate behaviors
- a radical change in personality or increased use of drugs or alcohol

Resource

Schlozman (2002b) offers information and resources to assist you in teaching students with bipolar disorders.

Reflective

While elementary-level girls and boys experience depression at the same rate, adolescent females are twice as likely to be depressed than their male classmates (Bostic, Rustuccia, & Schlozman, 2001). Girls and boys also experience different depressive symptoms (Marcotte et al., 2002), with boys being four times more likely to succeed at committing suicide (Schlozman, 2001). Why do you think this is the case?

Resource

Jensen (2001), Schlozman (2001), Stough and Baker (1999), and Wright Strawderman, Lindsey, Navarrete, and Flippo (1996) provide information and strategies that can help you identify and treat depression in students.

Resource

Anderegg and Vergason (1992) outline the legal decisions that define a teacher's responsibilities when dealing with suicidal students. Bostic, Rustuccia, and Scholzman (2001), McIntosh and Guest (2000), Poland (1995), and Guetzloe (1989) provide guidelines that can help educators develop programs to counter suicide, including assessing a student's suicide potential, counseling suicidal students, working with families, and dealing with the aftermath of suicide.

Set Your Sites

For more information on depression, suicide, students with emotional and behavioral disorders, and other mental health issues, go to the Web Links module in Chapter 2 of the Companion Website.

Some students also may have a *bipolar disorder*, which results in them having fluctuating moods that vary from depression to a mania that may be characterized by grandiose thoughts and actions, recklessness, and a reduced need for sleep (Schlozman, 2002b).

You take several actions to help students who you suspect are depressed or suicidal (Bostic, Rustuccia, & Schlozman, 2001; Schlozman, 2001). First, you need to be aware of important events in students' lives such as break-ups, family conflicts, excessive drinking or alcohol consumption, and impending legal or disciplinary actions. You also can speak to and collaborate with family members and other professionals such as guidance counselors, social workers, and school psychologists to help the student receive the services of mental health professionals. It is also important that you work extra hard to establish and maintain a personal connection with the student and facilitate the student's interactions with peers. Since some students may be reluctant to share their feelings with others, reading about literary and historical figures who triumphed over depression can be used as a way to prompt them to discuss their feelings.

You also should be aware of school policies dealing with depressed and suicidal students, make appropriate referrals, provide adequate supervision, and document and report your specific observations and changes in students' behavior. If you encounter a student who is threatening suicide, you can respond in the following manner:

- Introduce yourself to the student (if you are not known) and tell the student that you are there to help.
- Stay with the student, remaining calm and speaking in a clear, gentle, and nonthreatening manner.
- Show concern for the student.
- Ask the student to give up any objects or substances that can cause harm.
- Encourage the student to talk and acknowledge the student's comments.
- Help the student clarify the problem(s).
- Avoid being judgmental and pressuring the student.
- Help the student identify options to suicide and reinforce positive statements and comments on alternatives to suicide.
- Remind the student that there are others who care and are available to help (Guetzloe, 1989; McIntosh & Guest, 2000).

Students with Attention Deficit Disorders

Steven has difficulty completing assignments. Sometimes he starts an assignment before his teachers finish giving the directions. At other times, he squirms in his seat, and calls out answers to questions. Observations of Steven in his classes reveal that he often leaves his seat without permission to interact with his peers, or to hang out by the window. When he works on an assignment, he focuses on it for a short time period and then switches to another activity.

Nicole, a quiet student, is described by her teachers as disorganized, unmotivated, and a bit lazy. Her teachers notice that she spends a lot of time in her own world and frequently seems to daydream. As a result, Nicole often asks them to repeat directions. However, even after they explained the assignment to her, she dawdles at her desk, stares into space, and fails to complete her work.

While Steven and Nicole differ in many ways, they both exhibit behavioral patterns that are characterized by difficulty identifying and maintaining attention to relevant classroom directions, information, and stimuli, which affect their school performance and indicate that they may have some type of *attention deficit disorder* (*ADD*). ADD is the most common childhood psychiatric condition, affecting between 3 percent and 5 percent of the students in the United States. There is no definitive cause of ADD (Dowdy, Patton, Smith, & Polloway, 1998). While the factors that contribute to the development of attention difficulties appear to be multifaceted and are the focus of ongoing research, there is a growing recognition of it as a neurological condition (Tannock & Martinussen, 2001). Although ADD tends to occur at the same rate in all types of student groups regardless of socioeconomic status and ethnicity, boys like Steven are three to nine times more likely to be diagnosed than girls like Nicole, in part because ADD is more likely not to be detected or treated in female students (Bender, 1997).

Because ADD is a psychiatric diagnosis rather than a separate disability category recognized in the Individuals with Disabilities Education Act, it is defined by the American Psychiatric Association (1994) as "a persistent pattern of inattention, impulsivity, and/or hyperactivity-impulsivity that is more frequent and severe than is typically observed in individuals at a comparable level of development" (p. 78). The persistent pattern must:

1. occur for at least six months.
2. be evident before age 7.
3. interfere with the individual's social, educational, and occupational performance in two or more settings (e.g., home, school, work).
4. not be related to other medical or psychiatric conditions such as schizophrenia, or anxiety and mood disorders.

Types of ADD

There are three types of students with ADD based on the unique characteristics that accompany their high levels of inattention (Tannock & Martinussen, 2001). The first type includes students like Steven, whose attention deficit disorder is associated with constant motion. These students are referred to as students whose inattentiveness is accompanied by hyperactivity (ADHD-HI or ADDH), impulsivity, distractibility, and disorganization (Carbone, 2001). In the classroom, their high level of activity and impulsivity may lead them to engage in such high activity behaviors as fidgeting with hands and feet and objects, squirming, calling out, being out of seat, talking excessively, and interrupting others. Socially, these students often engage in aggressive, intrusive, immature, impulsive, uncooperative, and bossy behaviors that may lead them to be rejected by their peers and adults (Henker & Whalen, 1999). For example, they may fail to wait their turn during social activities or share with others, which can result in their classmates avoiding or rejecting them.

Nicole is an example of the second type of students with attention deficit disorders. These students are referred to as having an attention deficit disorder that is predominately of the inattentive type (ADD/IA), without hyperactivity (ADD/WO), or undifferentiated attention deficit disorder (UADD). Like students with ADD with hyperactivity and impulsivity, these students engage in a variety of behaviors that reveal their inattention, distractibilty, and disorganization. However, their inattentiveness appears to be related to their distractibility and preference for internal events rather than their frequent movements. While these students tend not to be viewed as behavior problems, their classroom behavior may be characterized by their paying attention to extraneous information and stimuli; daydreaming; and appearing to be lethargic, shy, disorganized, and forgetful (Barkley, 1998; Carbone, 2001). Socially, while these students are less likely to exhibit behaviors that alienate their peers, they are often neglected and overlooked by peers. Students with the third type of attention deficit disorder exhibit multiple behaviors that are similar to both Steven and Nicole. These students, who make up the largest group of students with ADD, are referred to as students with a combination of hyperactivity and distractibility (ADHD-C).

All three types of students with ADD have several things in common. Their inattentiveness, disorganization, and poor motivation interferes with their learning and academic performance, their social interactions and friendships with others, and their emotional development (Bender, 1997; Carlson, Booth, Shin, & Canu, 2002). Because students with all three types of ADD also exhibit learning, behavioral, and social-emotional profiles that resemble other students with high-incidence disabilities and other health impairments, it is very difficult to differentiate the presence of ADD from one of these other conditions. Students who are gifted and talented also may exhibit behaviors that are similar to students with ADD (Flint, 2001; Zentall, Moon, Hall, & Grskovic (2001). Educators also encounter difficulty in distinguishing the existence of ADD from the behavioral patterns found in children suffering from depression, residing in chaotic living conditions, and experiencing health and nutrition problems and auditory processing problems. Because of the differing cultural values and expectations of teachers and students, and because of acculturation issues, many students from culturally and linguistically diverse backgrounds are overidentified or underidentified as having ADD (Salend & Rohena, 2003).

While ADD is a psychiatric diagnosis and is not recognized as a separate disability under the IDEA, school districts must provide special education and related services to students with ADD under the IDEA if these students are otherwise health impaired, learning disabled, or emotionally disturbed. As we saw in chapter 1, students with ADD who do not qualify for services under the IDEA can be eligible for services under Section 504. Whether students with ADD qualify for services under Section 504 or the IDEA, they will probably be educated in the general education classroom, requiring you to use a variety of effective educational interventions (Miranda, Presentacion, & Soriano, 2002). Because these students may be taking medication, you must also collaborate with family members, the student's physician, and the school nurse to manage, monitor, and evaluate their response to these medications (Austin, 2003). (Later, we will discuss how you can monitor students who are taking medications.)

Resource

A special issue of *Intervention in School and Clinic* 38(5) presents information about and strategies for teaching students with ADD.

Set Your Sites

For more information on students with ADD, go to the Web Links module in Chapter 2 of the Companion Website.

Students with Mental Retardation

The significant increase in students with learning disabilities has been paralleled by a decrease in students with mental retardation to approximately 1 percent (U.S. Department of Education, 1997). Students with mental retardation demonstrate "significantly subaverage general intellectual functioning, existing concurrently with deficits in adaptive behavior and manifested during the developmental period, which adversely affects a child's educational performance."

Learners with mental retardation have traditionally been classified as having mild, moderate, or severe/profound mental retardation. There also has been a movement to classify them in terms of the intensities of the supports they need: intermittent, limited, extensive, and pervasive (Wehmeyer, 2003).

Students with *mild retardation* have IQs that range from above 50 to below 75, and need intermittent and/or limited supports to foster their learning. Like their counterparts with other high-incidence disabilities, these students exhibit similar behaviors, are often

IDEAS FOR IMPLEMENTATION

Helping Students with ADD Succeed in Inclusive Classrooms

Ms. Postell liked Lewis but found him difficult to teach. No matter how hard Lewis tried, he was never able to pay attention and complete his work. He was frequently out of his seat asking her for help, looking out of the window, or bothering another student.

To help Lewis, Ms. Postell varied the types of activities, as well as the locations where students performed them. She followed a teacher-directed activity with a learning game or instructional activity that involved movement. She also adapted assignments by breaking them into smaller chunks, having students work for shorter periods of time, and providing short breaks between activities so that they could move around. When she noticed that Lewis was getting restless, she gave him an excuse to leave his seat for a short time, such as taking a message to the office or sharpening a pencil for her. Here are some other strategies you can use to help students with ADD succeed in your inclusive classroom:

- Vary the types of learning activities, minimize schedule changes, and limit distractions.
- Establish the right learning environment by placing students in work areas with no distracting features and clutter; away from stimulating areas such as doors, bulletin boards, and windows; and near positive role models and the teacher.
- Offer a structured program; set reasonable limits and boundaries; establish, post, and review schedules and rules; follow classroom routines; help students make transitions; and inform students in advance of deviations from the classroom routines and schedule.
- Give clear, concise, step-by-step written and verbal directions for assignments that include examples. Provide students with daily assignment sheets and notebooks, and encourage students to show all their work when completing assignments.
- Use visuals such as graphic organizers and lists, provide note-takers or copies of notes to support oral instruction and directions, and adjust the presentation rate of material according to the students' needs.
- Increase the motivational aspects of the curriculum and lessons and the attentional value of the materials as part of the lesson. For example, you can add novelty to lessons and tasks by using color, variation in size, movement, and games. You can also structure learning activities so that students are active and learn by doing.

- Break lessons into parts, allow students extra time to work on assignments, and give students one assignment at a time.
- Use a multimodality approach to learning that provides opportunities for active responding and prompt, frequent feedback. Employ self-paced instruction such as peer tutoring and computer-assisted instruction.
- Give students choices concerning instructional activities. For example, offer students two or three activities and allow them to select one of them.
- Offer students outlets for their energy such as hands-on learning activities, active instructional games, class jobs, or the opportunity to squeeze a ball. Employ technology (such as computers and calculators) and media (such as CDs/DVDs and videos) to help students learn and to maintain their interest.
- Teach learning strategies, self-management techniques, meditation, and organizational and study skills. Help students to organize their classwork and homework assignments. For example, you can encourage and prompt students to use daily assignment notebooks, different-colored notebooks for each class, and daily and weekly schedules. You can also suggest that they wear a hip- or backpack to carry important information and items.
- Monitor students' performance frequently, individualize homework assignments, and offer students alternative ways to show their mastery of content.
- Pay attention to the students' self-esteem and social-emotional development. Recognize and use students' strengths, special interests, and talents, and involve students in afterschool activities.
- Teach students with ADD and their classmates about ADD. For example, you can introduce students to ADD by bringing in books such as *First Star I See* (Caffrey, 1997), *Zipper: The Kid with ADHD* (Janover, 1997), and *Joey Pigza Loses Control* (Gantos, 2000).

Additional guidelines for implementing these and other recommendations are presented in subsequent chapters.

Note: Brown, Ilderton, and Taylor (2001); Carbone (2001); DuPaul and Eckert (1998); Garrick Duhaney (2003); Miranda, Presentacion, and Soriano (2002); Salend, Elhoweris, and Van Garderen (2003); Zentall et al. (2001)

now taught in general education classrooms, and benefit from your use of many of the same teaching practices.

However, while students with other high-incidence disabilities may have an uneven learning profile, with strengths and challenges in different areas, students with mild retardation typically show a steady learning profile in all areas. In addition to memory, attention and motivational difficulties, their learning profile also is characterized by a slow rate of learning and generalizing and applying their learning to other situations (Heward, 2003). These cognitive difficulties can result in the frustration of repeated school failure, which in turn may lead to low self-esteem, an inability to work independently, a mistrust of their own judgments, and an expectancy of failure. Many students with mild retardation may also have poor social and behavioral skills, making it hard to interact with their peers (Leffert, Siperstein, & Millikan, 2000).

Students with *moderate retardation* have IQ scores that range from 30 to 50, and often need consistent and long-term supports to support their learning (Hamill & Everington, 2002). Learners with moderate mental retardation also include several genetically based syndromes:

- *Down syndrome:* a condition associated with difficulties in learning and expressive and receptive language development and relative strengths in visual short-term memory
- *Fragile X syndrome:* a condition associated with learning, speech, and language difficulties, and autisticlike behaviors
- *Prader-Willi syndrome:* a condition associated with cognitive and sequential processing difficulties, obsessive-compulsive behaviors, and relative strengths in integrating stimuli into a unified whole
- *Williams syndrome:* a condition associated with anxieties and fears; heart and health problems; hypersensitivity to sound; difficulty with visual-spatial tasks; and relative strengths and talents in terms of language, sociability, verbal processing, and music (Fidler, Hodapp, & Dykens, 2002; Reis, Schader, Milne, & Stephens, 2003; Symons, Clark, Roberts, & Bailey, 2001).

Resource

Hamill and Everington (2002) offer information, strategies, and resources for teaching students with moderate and severe disabilities in inclusive learning environments.

Set Your Sites

For more information on students with mental retardation, go to the Web Links module in Chapter 2 of the Companion Website.

These students also have adaptive behavior needs that affect their daily functioning (Turnbull et al., 2004). Therefore, educational programs for these students often focus on the development of communication and on vocational, daily living, leisure, work, health and safety and functional academic skills.

Students with *severe and profound retardation* have IQ scores below 30 and may have significant cognitive, communication, behavioral, physical, speech/language, perceptual, and medical needs. Educational programs for these students help them to live independently, contribute to and participate in society, and develop functional living and communication skills. While these students have traditionally been educated in self-contained classrooms or specialized schools, successful programs and instructional methods exist to integrate them into the mainstream of the school (Wolery & Schuster, 1997). Later in this chapter, we will learn more about students with significant cognitive disabilities such as students with severe and profound retardation.

Students with Speech and Language Disorders

Your class also will include students with speech and language disorders, who have difficulties receiving or sending information, ideas, and feelings (Heward, 2003). In the classroom they may experience difficulty following your directions, understanding and responding to your questions, expressing their thoughts, pronouncing words, learning new vocabulary, and being understood by others (Brice, 2001). While the impact of speech and language disorders on students' behaviors varies, these communication difficulties can interfere with their learning and their interactions with their classmates.

A student with a speech/language impairment has "a communication disorder such as stuttering, impaired articulation, a language impairment, or a voice impairment, that adversely affects a child's educational performance." Although the cause of most communication disorders is difficult to identify, environmental factors such as vocal misuse, inappropriate language models, lack of language stimulation, and emotional trauma may contribute to a speech or language impairment. Also, students from various ethnic backgrounds and geographic regions may have limited experience with English or speak with a different dialect, so you should be careful in identifying these students as having a communication disorder (Salend & Salinas, 2003). (We will learn more about distinguishing cultural and language differences from learning difficulties in Chapter 3.)

Students with speech and language disorders have receptive and expressive language difficulties that affect their communication and make it difficult for them to receive, understand, and express verbal messages in the classroom. Whereas speech-related disorders refer to the verbal aspects of communicating and conveying meaning, language-related disorders address one's ability to understand and communicate meaning (Owens, 2001).

Speech and language disorders fall into two different types: receptive and expressive. *Receptive language* refers to the ability to understand spoken language. Students with receptive language problems may have difficulty following directions and understanding content presented orally.

Expressive language refers to the ability to express one's ideas in words and sentences (Sunderland, 2004). Students with expressive language disorders may be reluctant to join in verbal activities. This can impair both their academic performance and their social-emotional development. Expressive language problems may be due to speech disorders that include articulation, voice, and fluency disorders. Articulation problems include omissions (e.g., the student says *ird* instead of *bird*), substitutions (the student says *wove* instead of *love*), distortions (the student may distort a sound so that it sounds like another sound), and additions (the student says *ruhace* for *race*).

Voice disorders relate to deviations in the pitch, volume, and quality of sounds produced. Breathiness, hoarseness, and harshness, as well as problems in resonation, are all indications of possible voice quality disorders. Fluency disorders relate to the rate and rhythm of an individual's speech (Ramig & Shames, 2002). Stuttering is the most prevalent fluency disorder.

Some students with language disorders also may have *pragmatic* difficulties, which cause them to have problems understanding and following the rules that guide communication and language usage. As a result, they may have difficulty adjusting to different conversational contexts. For example, they may interrupt others or give the impression that they are not listening, which can affect their ability to initiate and maintain social relationships with others (Benner, Nelson, & Epstein, 2002).

You can help students with speech and language disorders by creating a classroom that fosters language learning (Schoenbrodt et al., 1997; Wegner & Edmister, 2004). You can create this type of environment by giving students opportunities to hear language and to speak; creating functional situations that encourage students to communicate; using concrete materials and hands-on learning activities that promote language; offering students academic and social activities that allow them to work, interact, and communicate with other students; asking students to relate classroom material to their lives; and designing the classroom to promote interactions and language (e.g., posting photographs and other visuals that promote discussion, and placing students' desks in groups rather than in rows).

Set Your Sites

For more information on students with speech and language disorders, go to the Web Links module in Chapter 2 of the Companion Website.

IDEAS FOR IMPLEMENTATION

Helping Students with Expressive Language Disorders Succeed in Inclusive Classrooms

Mr. Lombardi's class includes Jessie, a student who stutters. Mr. Lombardi finds it uncomfortable to watch Jessie struggle to express his thoughts, and he avoids asking him to respond. When Jessie does speak, Mr. Lombardi occasionally interrupts him and completes his sentences.

Mr. Lombardi approached Ms. Goldsmith, the speech and language teacher who works with Jessie in his class, for some suggestions. Ms. Goldsmith said, "Why don't you start by asking Jessie to respond to questions that can be answered with relatively few words, such as 'yes' or 'no' questions? Once he adjusts to that, you can ask him to respond to questions that require a more in-depth response. This way, you control the difficulty of the response, and you can help Jessie succeed and develop his confidence.

"If he struggles with a word or a sentence, telling him to relax, slow down, or to take a deep breath is not going to help him and he may even find comments like that demeaning. Be patient, and don't speak for him or interrupt him. In this way, you will serve as a model for the other students, who also will benefit from your teaching them how to respond to Jessie and other students who have difficulty expressing themselves. Let's make some time to talk about how we can teach the other students how to respond to Jessie."

Here are some other strategies you can use to help students who have difficulty responding orally succeed in your inclusive classroom:

- Respond to what the students say rather than how they say it. For example, you can use your body language and facial expressions to show students that you are focused on the content of the communication.
- Make typical eye contact with students, and pause a few seconds before responding to show them how to relax, and to slow down the pace of the conversation.
- Stay calm, do not hurry students when they speak, criticize or correct their speech, or force them to speak in front of others.
- Establish a learning environment that encourages all students to take their time in responding and answering questions.
- Teach all students to monitor and think positively about their speech, and how to respond to classmates who have expressive language difficulties.
- Have students read in unison with their classmates if they tend to stutter when reading aloud.
- Serve as a good speech model by using a slow and relaxed speech rate, pausing at appropriate times when speaking, and using simplified language and grammatical structures.
- Collaborate with students and their families and speech/language professionals to learn about their concerns and expectations and to get their suggestions.

Note: Shapiro (1999); Trautman (2000); Wegner and Edmister (2004)

What Are the Educational Strengths and Needs of Students with Low-Incidence Disabilities?

Students with physical, sensory, and multiple and significant disabilities are sometimes referred to as having *low-incidence disabilities* because they make up only 6 percent of the students with disabilities. These students demonstrate a wide range of behaviors, and are sometimes categorized based on the functional impact of their disabilities and the level of support that they need: mild, moderate, and severe (Best & Bigge, 2001). Because there is a great deal of variation in the characteristics of students with low-incidence disabilities, designing and implementing programs to meet the needs of these students is a challenge. However, you will find that teaching these students can be a rewarding, enjoyable, and fulfilling experience, and that they can succeed in your classroom.

Help Students Access the General Education Curriculum

Students with low-incidence disabilities can learn and participate in the general education curriculum. Hunt et al. (2003), Wehmeyer, Lance, and Bashinski (2002), King-Sears (2001) and Sailor, Gee, and Karasoff (2000) offer models for helping *all learners,* including those with low-incidence disabilities, gain access to the general education curriculum. The steps in these models include:

1. analyzing the general education curriculum to identify the goals of the lesson/activity/assignment and to determine the extent to which students can participate in the lesson/activity/assignment without the use of instructional accommodations.
2. delineating the rationale for the instructional goals and format(s), and the teaching strategies to be employed.
3. enhancing the general education curriculum by incorporating IEP goals into the curriculum, adding content to the curriculum to foster success (e.g., learning strategies instruction), and identifying ways in which the content can be taught to students with a range of learning abilities and styles.
4. making the general education curriculum more accessible by using universal design and instructional and assistive technology; adjusting the presentation and response modes, the instructional objectives, arrangement, and materials, and the pace, complexity, or size of the activity or assignment; and providing additional supports from peers and other adults.
5. assessing student performance within the general education curriculum via use of formal and informal assessment strategies, and revising or continuing the educational program based on these data.

Specific strategies for differentiating instruction to help *all students* access and succeed in the general education curriculum are presented in this chapter as well as other chapters of this book.

Some learners with low-incidence disabilities also may benefit from access to a functional curriculum that teaches them the skills they need to function independently in inclusive schools, their homes, and community settings, and provides them with the social and communication skills to access the general education curriculum (Agran, Alper, & Wehmeyer, 2002; Hamill & Everington, 2002). Since these skills are best taught in natural and community-based settings, you can teach them to your students in real-life and inclusive environments such as your classroom or community settings (Westling & Fox, 2000).

Collaborate with Related Service Providers, Paraeducators, and Peers

Because of their unique needs and chronic conditions, some students with low-incidence disabilities may need the services of related service providers such as physical therapists; vision, hearing, orientation, and mobility specialists; speech and language professionals;

paraeducators; and peers to access and succeed in inclusive settings (Fisher & Frey, 2001; Snell & Janney, 2000; Trautman, 2004). You can also increase the effectiveness of the services these individuals provide by collaborating with them to establish goals, integrate these services throughout the school day, plan instruction, share responsibilities, reinforce and support each other's efforts, and evaluate student progress (Hamill & Everington, 2002; Hunt et al., 2003). Additional information to assist you in collaborating with other professionals is provided in chapters 4 and 8.

Use Assistive and Instructional Technology

The educational, social, and behavioral performance of these students also can be fostered by providing them with the assistive and instructional technology they need to succeed in the general education classroom. These technologies, which can assist students with low-incidence disabilities in learning; accessing information; communicating; performing daily living skills; supporting, stabilizing, and protecting body parts; moving from one location to another; and participating in leisure activities (Hamill & Everington, 2002), are discussed in subsequent chapters of this book.

Adopt a Competency-Oriented Approach

Learners with low-incidence disabilities are often thought of in terms of what they cannot do, and their relatively visible disabilities may affect how others perceive and interact with them (Best, 2001a). However, like their classmates, these learners display a full range of individual characteristics that include many positive traits that affect and enhance their learning, motivation, and ability to get along with others, and have a positive impact on their classmates (Smith, 2000). **To view an example of educators identifying and using student strengths, go to Case 3: Assess Plan on the CD-ROM and click on the identify strengths video clip. How does initially focusing on a student's strengths assist the instructional planning process?**

 cd-rom

In teaching these students, it is important for you to adopt a competency-oriented approach (Smith, 2002). Rather than seeing students in terms of what they cannot do, educators with a competency-oriented approach focus on what students can do, and use these strengths to create a learning environment that supports their integration, participation, and growth, and maximizes their abilities (Smith, Salend, & Ryan, 2001).

You can implement a competency-oriented approach in your classroom by:

* learning about students and what they can do.
* being patient and taking the time to establish trusting relationships.
* building community in your classroom.
* having challenging expectations for them.
* treating them fairly and in age-appropriate ways.
* providing them with the same opportunities and choices as your other students.
* offering instructional activities that focus on their strengths and preferred methods of learning.
* referring to students in terms of their strengths.
* using a variety of ways to assess their progress.
* meeting regularly with and coordinating your activities with their families.
* taking risks and learning from them (Merritt, 2001; Smith et al., 2001; Smith, 2002; Williard-Holt, 1999).

Understand and Address Students' Unique Abilities and Needs

Learners with low-incidence disabilities vary greatly in terms of their abilities and learning needs and preferences. Some students with low-incidence disabilities will need access accommodations such as the use of Braille to succeed in your classroom, while others will have more significant cognitive needs, which will mean that you have to make significant adjustments in what and how you teach them (Ford, Davern, & Schnorr, 2001). Therefore, you also can support their learning and access to appropriate general education and functional curricula by understanding their unique abilities and needs and using effective teaching practices that address these characteristics, which are discussed in the following sections.

Students with Physical and Health Needs

Students with physical disabilities are identified as students with orthopedic impairments or students with other health impairments. Students with *orthopedic impairments* are defined as having a

> severe orthopedic impairment which adversely affects a child's educational performance. The term includes impairments caused by congenital anomaly (e.g., clubfoot, absence of some member, etc.), impairments caused by disease (e.g., poliomyelitis, bone tuberculosis, etc.), and impairments from other causes (e.g., cerebral palsy, amputations, and fractures or burns which cause contractures).

Students with *other health impairments* are defined as having

> limited strength, vitality, or alertness, including a heightened alertness to environmental stimuli, that results in limited alertness with respect to the educational environment, that is due to chronic or acute health problems such as attention deficit disorder, a heart condition, tuberculosis, rheumatic fever, nephritis, asthma, sickle-cell anemia, epilepsy, lead poisoning, leukemia, or diabetes, which adversely affects a child's educational performance.

The term *other health impaired* can also include students who are medically fragile or those who may be dependent on technological devices for ventilation, oxygen, and tube feeding (Heller, Fredrick, Dykes, Best, & Cohen, 1999).

Because of the many conditions included in this category, its specific characteristics are hard to define and vary greatly from student to student (Wadsworth & Knight, 1999). Students with physical and health conditions tend to have IQ scores within the normal range, and have numerous educational, social, technological, and health-care needs.

When developing inclusive education programs for these students, you need to be aware of several factors (Heller, Fredrick, Best, Dykes, & Cohen, 2000; Hill, 1999; Pivik, McComas, & Laflamme, 2002). While many of these conditions are stable, some are progressive, and others are terminal (Best, 2001a). Some of these conditions are congenital, which means they are present at birth, and others are acquired, which means they are due to an illness or accident. Because of their conditions, these students may be absent frequently or may have limited exposure to certain experiences that we take for granted. It also is important to remember that these students and their families have mobility, physical, medical, and social-emotional needs that you should address. Be aware of the importance of your communication and collaboration with the student's family and medical providers, as well as the educational rights of students with special health-care needs

Students with special physical and health needs can learn to perform their routine health-care procedures independently, like this student with diabetes who is giving herself an insulin injection. How can you and your colleagues support students in developing their independence?

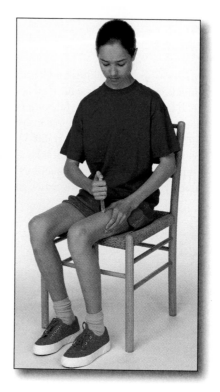

Resource

Wadsworth and Knight (1999) developed the Classroom Ecological Preparation Inventory (CEPI) to help comprehensive planning teams collect information to provide students with physical and health needs with access to general education classrooms.

(Bartlett, 2000; Thomas & Hawke, 1999). Finally, professional organizations can provide information and resources, and can offer support groups for students and their families.

The progress of some students, particularly those with physical and sensory disabilities, also depends on the use of adaptive and prosthetic devices. The failure of these devices to work properly can limit the likelihood of success for students who need them; therefore, you will need to monitor their working condition. If there are problems, you should contact students' families or appropriate medical personnel.

Students with Cerebral Palsy

Cerebral palsy, which affects voluntary motor functions and muscle tension or tone, is caused by damage to the central nervous system before birth or during one's early years. It is not hereditary, contagious, progressive, or curable (Hill, 1999). Although there is no typical student with cerebral palsy, students with cerebral palsy may have seizures; perceptual difficulties; and motor, sensory, and speech impairments (Best & Bigge, 2001). There are four primary types of cerebral palsy: hypertonia, hypotonia, athetosis, and ataxia and some students have a combination of these conditions.

- *Hypertonia*: movements that are jerky, exaggerated, and poorly coordinated
- *Hypotonia*: loose, flaccid musculature and sometimes difficulty maintaining balance
- *Athetosis* (also referred to as *dyskinetic*): uncontrolled and irregular movements usually occurring in the arms, hands, or face
- *Ataxia*: difficulties in balancing and using the hands

IDEAS FOR IMPLEMENTATION

Helping Students with Cerebral Palsy Succeed in Inclusive Classrooms

As the school year was coming to an end, Mr. Lewis thought about his first interactions with Linda, a student with cerebral palsy. At first he was too protective; he underestimated her abilities and limited her participation in certain activities. He remembered that the turning point for him was seeing Linda during recess playing with the other students. Although her movements were limited, she was every bit as playful as the other students. From that moment on, he began to treat Linda like other students. He assigned her classroom jobs, reprimanded her when she misbehaved, and encouraged her to participate in all classroom and school activities. Rather than excusing her from assignments, he gave her more time to complete them, reduced the amount of boardwork and textbook copying she had to do, placed rubber bands or plastic tubing around the shaft of her writing utensil, and gave her felt-tipped pens and soft lead pencils so that she could write with less pressure.

Here are some other strategies you can use to help students with cerebral palsy succeed in your inclusive classroom:

- Understand that students may need more time to complete a task, and give them more time to respond verbally.
- Do not hesitate to ask students to repeat themselves if others do not understand their comments.
- Learn how to position, reposition, and transfer students who use wheelchairs; teach students to reposition themselves; and learn how to push wheelchairs (see Parette and Hourcade, 1986; Ricci-Balich & Behm, 1996; and Summers et al., 1997).
- Provide students with assistive technology and let them use computers, calculators, talking books, and audiocassettes.
- Give students two copies of books: one set for use in school and the other set for use at home.
- Give students easy access to personal and classroom supplies.
- Give students copies of class notes and assignments.
- Plan students' schedules so that they move from class to class when the hallways are less crowded.

Because their educational program will need to address their motor and physical needs, you will need to collaborate with physical and occupational therapists, medical personnel, and family members to foster their learning, socialization, independence, and physical, communication, and emotional development (Dormans, Pellegrino, & Batshaw, 1998).

Students with Spina Bifida (Myelomeningocele)

Another group of students with unique physical and medical needs are those with *spina bifida (myelomeningocele)*. Spina bifida is caused by the failure of the vertebrae of the spinal cord to close properly, which usually results in paralysis of the lower limbs, as well as loss of control over bladder function. Students with spina bifida often have good control over the upper body but may need to use a prosthetic device for mobility such as a walker, braces, or crutches. They also may need a catheter or bag to minimize bladder control difficulty and a shunt for hydrocephalus. Spina bifida can affect students' cognitive, physical, social-emotional, and language development.

In addition to designing and implementing programs that meet their academic and social needs, you can help these students by working with the school nurse to (a) monitor shunts for blockages (some of the signs of blockage are headaches, fatigue, visual or coordination difficulties, repetitive vomiting, and seizures); (b) ensure that the student's bladder, bowel, and catheterization needs are being addressed properly and privately;

Resource

Best and Bigge (2001), Hill (1999), and Dormans, Pellegrino & Batshaw (1998) offer information, strategies, and resources that can help you create an inclusive classroom that addresses the needs of students with cerebral palsy.

Set Your Sites

For more information on students with cerebral palsy, go to the Web Links module in Chapter 2 of the Companion Website.

Resource

Rowley-Kelley and Reigel (1993) offer guidelines for preventing skin breakdown in students who use wheelchairs, including making sure that students are positioned properly and moved periodically so that they shift their body weight; giving students opportunities to leave their wheelchairs and use prone standers, braces, and crutches; and examining students' skin for redness and swelling.

Resource

Robinson and Toporek (1999) and Lutkenhoff (1999) provide information and resources about spina bifida.

Set Your Sites

For additional information and resources about students with spina bifida and other spinal cord injuries, go to the Web Links module in Chapter 2 of the Companion Website.

Resource

Let's Face It (2000) has produced a list of resources about individuals with facial differences that includes books, videos, resources, and organizations.

Set Your Sites

For more information on students with respiratory conditions, go to the Web Links module in Chapter 2 of the Companion Website.

Resource

Getch and Neuharth-Pritchett (1999), Hill (1999), and McLoughlin and Nall (1995) offer guidelines and strategies that can be used when working with students who have asthma and allergies.

(c) be aware of the signs of urinary infections (the indicators of bladder infections include a change in urine color or odor, increased frequency of urination with a reduction in urine volume, and fever or chills; (d) prevent sores and other forms of skin breakdown; and (e) determine the extent to which students should participate in physical activities (Hill, 1999; Rowley-Kelley & Reigel, 1993). Because students with spina bifida may be dependent on others to assist them with their physical needs, it is very important for you to foster their independence and socialization with others (Best, 2001b).

Students with Asthma and Allergies

Asthma is an incurable and treatable respiratory ailment causing difficulty in breathing due to constriction and inflammation of the airways. It is the most common childhood chronic illness and the leading cause of absence from school (Madden, 2000). The symptoms of asthma, which can occur at any age, vary and include repeated episodes of wheezing, sneezing, coughing, shortness of breath, and tightness in the chest. The conditions that trigger an asthma attack also vary and include stress; respiratory viruses; exertion and exercise; certain weather conditions; strong emotions; pollens; pet dander; and airborne irritants such as smoke, strong odors, and chemical sprays.

By being aware of the stimuli that trigger students' asthma and allergies, you can create learning conditions and activities that minimize the likelihood of an attack. In working with these students, you may need to observe their unique reactions and warning signs, and learn about each student's asthma and allergy management plan and your school's policies for dealing with asthma and emergency medical treatments (Best, 2001c). You also may need to deal with frequent absences; collaborate with families and medical personnel; help make sure that students who use inhalers carry them at all times; and understand the side effects of medications on behavior and learning. Also, keep the classroom free of dust, plants, perfumes, strong smells, cold or dry air, and other materials and situations that trigger reactions; and understand the students' capacity for physical activities (Getch & Neuharth-Pritchett, 1999; McLoughlin & Nall, 1995). You also can teach *all your students* about asthma and allergies using the American Lung Association's Open Airways for Schools curriculum (Madden, 2000), and children's books such as *So You Have Asthma Too!* (Sander, 1993), *All About Asthma* (Ostrow & Ostrow, 1989), *Taking Asthma to School* (Gosselin, 1998a), and *ZooAllergy* (Gosselin, 1996a).

Some of your students may have food allergies, which can affect their well being. While the types and severity of food allergies vary, you need to be aware of the foods that your students must avoid, and ways to keep them safe. Therefore, it is important for you to collaborate with your students' families and medical and nutritional personnel to learn about your students' conditions and the foods they must avoid. When necessary, it is also important for you to:

- be especially vigilant during holidays, special events. and birthday celebrations.
- establish policies that prevent food sharing.
- refrain from reusing food containers.
- maintain jars of family-provided foods that are safe for students.
- use and label eating and serving utensils for use with different foods.
- clean tables using different rags.
- share information about food allergies with other professionals including substitute teachers.
- understand and follow procedures in case of an emergency.

Asthma is the most common childhood chronic illness. How do you minimize the likelihood that students with asthma and allergies will experience an attack?

Students with Tourette Syndrome

Your classroom also may include students with Tourette syndrome (TS), an inherited neurological disorder whose symptoms appear in childhood (Ottinger, 2003). These symptoms include involuntary multiple muscle movements and tics, and uncontrolled, repeated verbal responses such as noises (laughing, coughing, throat clearing), words, or phrases. The symptoms, which are affected by stress and environmental factors, appear and disappear at various times, change over time, and may result in others being scared, annoyed, or amused (Chamberlain, 2003a; Jacobs, 2001). While many students with TS perform well academically, others may have learning disabilities, language disorders, obsessive-compulsive behaviors, and difficulty paying attention and controlling impulses, which may result in academic and social difficulties (Prestia, 2003).

Resource

Chamberlain (2003a) and Ottinger and Prestia (2003) offer information, resources, and interventions for understanding and addressing the unique characteristics of students with TS.

Set Your Sites

For more information on students with TS, go to the Web Links module in Chapter 2 of the Companion Website.

Students with Diabetes

At some point, you will have a student with *diabetes*. These students lack enough insulin and therefore have trouble gaining energy from food. Be aware of the symptoms of diabetes, including frequent requests for liquids, repeated trips to the bathroom, unhealthy skin color, headaches, vomiting and nausea, failure of cuts and sores to heal, loss of weight despite adequate food intake, poor circulation as indicated by complaints about cold hands and feet, and abdominal pain. When a student has some of these symptoms, contact the student's family, the school nurse, or another medical professional (Hirsch, 2000).

For diabetic students, be aware of the signs of *hyperglycemia* (high blood sugar) and *hypoglycemia* (low blood sugar) and be able to act in an emergency (Rosenthal-Malek & Greenspan, 1999). Students with hyperglycemia are thirsty, tired, and lethargic and have dry, hot skin, loss of appetite, difficulty breathing, and breath that has a sweet, fruity odor. Those with hypoglycemia are confused, drowsy, inattentive, irritable and dizzy, perspiring, shaking, and hungry, with headaches and a pale complexion. When these conditions occur, you must be prepared to act and contact medical personnel immediately. In the case of hyperglycemia, it may be appropriate to have the student drink water or diet soda.

IDEAS FOR IMPLEMENTATION

Helping Students with TS Succeed in Inclusive Classrooms

You could see the signs of anguish on Ms. Dean's face as her principal told her that Frank, a student with Tourette syndrome (TS), would be joining her class next week. Ms. Dean prided herself on how well-behaved her students were, and as she read about Frank's periodic episodes of uncontrolled verbal responses, she was worried about how they would affect her students and her ability to manage their behavior.

Ms. Dean's principal suggested that she talk to Mr. Lopez, a special education teacher who had worked with Frank in the past. Mr. Lopez told her, "Frank is really a neat kid. He works hard, and he's got a wonderful sense of humor. You're going to like him."

Ms. Dean said, "I'm sure he's a nice kid. But what do you do when he starts having his episodes?"

Mr. Lopez said, "I spoke to Frank and his family about my concerns. They were worried about it as well. We came up with the following system. Before Frank's verbalizations became uncontrollable and distracting, we created a situation that allowed him to leave the room for short periods of time. I would ask him to take a message to the office or return a book to the library and he would go to a private location like the nurse's office. Sometimes, when Frank sensed an episode coming on, he signaled me and he left the room. It worked pretty well.

I also helped the other students learn about and understand the needs of students with TS. I showed the class the video *Stop It! I Can't,* which showed several students

with TS achieving in school and dealing with ridicule from their peers. The students were very supportive and understanding of Frank."

Here are some other strategies you can use to help students with TS succeed in your inclusive classroom:

- Be patient, and react to students' involuntary inappropriate behavior with tolerance rather than anger.
- Seat students near the front of the class and the teacher's desk so that they can be subtly redirected to pay attention.
- Offer students with vocal tics the opportunity to drink water throughout the day to avoid throat dryness.
- Provide students with a quiet location to take tests.
- Use alternative assignments to minimize the stress on students with TS.
- Offer activities to develop students' social and friendship making skills.
- Praise students and take advantage of opportunities to enhance their self-esteem.
- Seek assistance from others such as counselors, school nurses, occupational and physical therapists, school psychologists, and families.

Note: Bronheim (n.d.); Ottinger (2003); Prestia (2003)

For hypoglycemia, it may be appropriate to give the student a source of sugar immediately, such as a half cup of fruit juice, two large sugar cubes, or a can of regular soda. Therefore, you should keep these supplies in your classroom so that they are readily available in case of an emergency.

You can take certain actions to help students with diabetes succeed in school (Rosenthal-Malek & Greenspan, 1999). You can limit hyperglycemia or hypoglycemia by making sure that students eat at the right times. Observe students after physical education class and recess and make sure that their blood sugar levels are measured. You also may need to modify your rules so that students with diabetes can eat snacks and leave the classroom as needed, as well as refrain from penalizing them for frequent absences and lateness. It also may be necessary to reschedule tests or other high-stakes activities for students with diabetes if their performance is affected by their condition. Finally, you can work with the school nurse, family members, certified diabetes educators, and students with diabetes, if they are willing, to educate *all students* about diabetes. For example, you can conduct health science lessons about diabetes and introduce diabetes to students via books such as *Taking Diabetes to School* (Gosselin,

Set your Sites

For more information on students with diabetes, go to the Web Links module in Chapter 2 of the Companion Website.

1998b), *Sugar Was My Best Food: Diabetes and Me* (Peacock & Gregory, 1998), and *Sweet Invisible Body: Reflections on a Life with Diabetes* (Roney, 1999).

Students with Seizure Disorders

Many students, including those with physical disabilities and other health impairments, may have seizures (Brown, 1997). When these seizures occur on a regular basis, the individual is said to be suffering from a *convulsive disorder* or *epilepsy* (Hill, 1999). There are several types of seizures: tonic-clonic, tonic, absence, and complex and simple partial seizures (Michael, 1995; Spiegel, Cutler, & Yetter, 1996).

Tonic-Clonic Seizure.   Also referred to as *grand mal*, this type of seizure is marked by loss of consciousness and bladder control, stiff muscles, saliva drooling out of the mouth, and violent body shaking. After a brief period, the individual may fall asleep or regain consciousness and experience confusion.

Tonic Seizure.   A tonic seizure involves sudden stiffening of the muscles. Because the individual becomes rigid and may fall to the ground, these seizures often cause injuries.

Absence Seizure.   Also referred to as *petit mal*, this type of seizure is characterized by a brief period in which the individual loses consciousness, appears to be daydreaming, looks pale, and drops any objects he or she is holding.

Complex and Simple Partial Seizures.   When a seizure affects only a limited part of the brain, it is called a *partial seizure*. Also referred to as a *psychomotor seizure*, a complex partial seizure is characterized by a short period in which the individual remains conscious but engages in inappropriate and bizarre behaviors. After 2 to 5 minutes, the individual regains control and often does not remember what happened. During a partial seizure, the individual also remains conscious and may twitch and experience a feeling of deja vu. Prior to these seizures, students may experience an *aura* or a *prodrome*, a sensation and a symptom indicating that a seizure is imminent.

Guidelines for dealing with seizures in your classroom are presented in Figure 2.11.

Resource

Michael (1995) and Spiegel et al. (1996) offer guidelines for working with students who have seizure disorders.

Set Your Sites

For more information on students with seizure disorders, go to the Web Links module in Chapter 2 of the Companion Website.

Students Treated for Cancer

A growing number of students treated for cancer are attending school, which can provide a normalizing experience for them and enhance their quality of life (Bessell, 2001). The type and length of cancer therapy vary. However, while many treatments are effective in treating the cancer, they are toxic and can affect the student's cognitive, gross and fine motor, language, sensory, and social-emotional development, as well as resulting in life-threatening chronic health problems (Duenwald & Grady, 2003; Ladd, 2002). Frequent or lengthy hospitalizations resulting in erratic school attendance also can hinder learning, self-esteem, and socialization. On returning to school, students with cancer may experience many physical and psychological challenges including dealing with depression, social anxiety, poor self-concepts, and school phobia (Bessell, 2001; Hill, 1999).

Students with cancer may also be embarrassed by their appearance and worried about losing their friends and being teased by their peers. Therefore, while you need to be sensitive to their unique needs, it is also important for you to treat them in ways that acknowledge what they can do and make them feel like their classmates (Bessell, 2001). You also can collaborate with the student, family members, other educators, and medical professionals to address these concerns by using interactive activities that help the

FIGURE 2.11

Guidelines for dealing with seizures

Students who have seizures need few modifications in the general education setting, but you can minimize the potentially harmful effects of a seizure by carefully structuring the classroom environment and considering the following guidelines before, during, and after a seizure occurs.

BEFORE THE SEIZURE

◆ Be aware of the warning signs that indicate an impending seizure, and encourage the student to speak to you immediately if he or she is able to recognize the aura or prodrome. In these cases, if time allows, remove the student to a private and safe location.

◆ Encourage the student with epilepsy to wear a Medic-Alert bracelet or necklace or carry a wallet card.

◆ Teach students about epilepsy and what to do when a classmate has a seizure. With the student's permission, you, the school nurse, the student, and family members can talk with the class about epilepsy and how to respond to seizures. Children's books such as *Taking Seizure Disorders to School* (Gosselin, 1996b) can be used to introduce students to these issues.

DURING THE SEIZURE

◆ Prevent the student from being injured during a seizure by staying composed and keeping the other students calm (it often helps to remind the class that the seizure is painless).

◆ Do not restrain the student, place fingers or objects in the student's mouth, or give the student anything to eat or drink.

◆ Make the student as comfortable as possible by helping him or her to lie down and loosening tight clothing.

◆ Protect the student by placing a soft, cushioned object under the head, ensuring that the space around the student's work area is large enough to thrash around in, and keeping the area around the student's desk free of objects that could harm the student during the seizure.

AFTER THE SEIZURE

◆ Help the student by positioning the student's head to one side to allow the discharge of saliva that may have built up in the mouth; briefly discussing the seizure with the class, encouraging acceptance rather than fear or pity; providing the student with a rest area in which to sleep; and documenting the seizure.

◆ Contact other necessary school and medical personnel and the student's family.

◆ Document and share with others relevant information regarding a student's seizure. Kuhn, Allen, and Shriver (1995) and Michael (1992) have developed a Seizure Observation Form that can help you record the student's behavior before the seizure, initial seizure behavior, behavior during the seizure, behavior after the seizure, actions taken by you, the student's reaction to the seizure, peer reactions to the seizure, and your comments.

Notes: Hill (1999); Michael (1995); Spiegel et al. (1996)

Set Your Sites

For more information on students treated for cancer, go to the Web Links module in Chapter 2 of the Companion Website.

Set Your Sites

For more information on the grieving process, go to the Web Links module in Chapter 2 of the Companion Website.

Resource

Peckham (1993) developed a sample lesson plan and guidelines for teaching students about cancer that can be adapted for other chronic and serious conditions.

student's peers understand the student's illness, including the fact that cancer is not contagious and that radiation treatments don't make the individual "radioactive" (Ladd, 2002). Peers also may benefit from understanding the side effects of chemotherapy. In addition, you may need to handle issues related to dying and death (Winter, 2002). Guidelines to help you deal with these issues with students and families and to understand the grieving process are available (Hill, 1999; Kelker, Hecimovic, & LeRoy, 1994; Macciomei, 1996; Peckham, 1993).

Medically Fragile Students

School districts are serving an increasing number of students who are *medically fragile* (Sewall & Balkman, 2002). While not all students who are medically fragile require special education services, these students do require the use of specialized technological health-care procedures to maintain their health and/or provide life support.

Medically fragile students have a variety of chronic and progressive conditions, including congenital malformations; loss of limbs; and neurological, infectious or muscular diseases such as cystic fibrosis and muscular dystrophy (Best, 2001b, c; Prendergast,

1995). While the developmental needs of these students and the extent and nature of their disabilities may vary, these students have comprehensive medical needs and important socialization needs (Strong & Sandoval, 1999). In classroom situations, these students may have limited vitality and mobility, fatigue, and attention problems.

Decisions on their educational program and placement should be based on their medical and educational needs and should be made in conjunction with families and support personnel such as physical, occupational, and respiratory therapists, doctors, and nurses who can work with you to develop health-care plans for these students and make instructional accommodations to address their needs (Best, 2001c; Summers et al., 1997). The health plan may need to address such issues as giving students rest periods, help in the lunchroom (e.g., carrying their trays, special dietary considerations), assistive technology, electric devices (e.g., electric pencil sharpener), locker assistance, modified physical activity, early release to help them move from class to class, and schedule adjustments (e.g., shortened day, periods, and bus routes). You can help these students by allowing them to use assistive and instructional technology to obtain, retain, and present information and have an extra set of books for use at home. They may benefit from use of a desk podium to raise their papers or use of a marker instead of a pencil. You can also minimize their fatigue by limiting the number of motor responses you ask them to make. For example, you can limit boardwork and textbook copying by providing them with peer note-takers, as well as written copies of directions and other important information.

The social and emotional needs of the student must also be considered. Their needs include embarrassment related to the symptoms associated with their conditions, the side effects of treatment on their appearance and behavior, dependence on medical devices, difficulty in accepting their illness, withdrawal and depression, and the need for friendships. Create opportunities for these students to participate in social activities with peers. For example, you can encourage social interactions with others by teaching adults and other students to talk directly to the student rather than to the student's aide or nurse.

When working with these students, become familiar with their equipment, ventilation management, cardiopulmonary resuscitation, universal precautions, and other necessary procedures. It is necessary to understand the warning signs indicating that equipment needs repair; make sure that replacement equipment is readily available; and establish procedures for dealing with health emergencies, equipment problems, and power failures, as well as minimizing interruptions due to medical interventions that the student may need.

Resource

Hill (1999) offers sample forms that school districts can use to identify and plan for students' special physical and health-care needs, including information checklists; health-care plans; transportation, treatment, and emergency-care plans; activity participation forms; communication logs; and entry/reentry checklists.

Set Your Sites

For more information on students who are medically fragile, go to the Web Links module in Chapter 2 of the Companion Website.

Resource

Katsiyannis and Yell (2000) and Sewall and Balkman (2002) offer a summary of legal guidelines and recommendations for providing health services to medically fragile students.

Students with Traumatic Brain Injury

Another group of students who have diverse learning, physical and medical needs are those with traumatic brain injury (TBI) (Best, 2001b; Witte, 1998). More than 1 child in the United States sustain some type of TBI each year, which is the most common cause of death or disability (Keyser-Marcus, Briel, Sherron-Target, Yasuda, Johnson, & Wehman, 2002). TBI is defined as "an acquired injury to the brain caused by an external physical force, resulting in total or partial functional disability or psychosocial impairment, or both, that adversely affects a child's educational performance. The term applies to open or closed head injuries resulting in impairments in one or more areas, such as cognition; language; memory; attention; reasoning; abstract thinking; judgment; problem-solving; sensory, perceptual, and motor abilities; psychosocial behavior; physical functions; information processing; and speech. The term does not apply to brain injuries that are congenital or degenerative, or brain injuries induced by birth trauma."

TBI may be categorized as mild, moderate, or severe, depending on how long one loses consciousness, whether there is a skull fracture, and the extent and nature of the aftereffects (D'Amato & Rothlisberg, 1996). The characteristics of students with TBI depend on their level of functioning prior to the injury, the nature and location of the injury, their recovery time, and the age at which it occurred (Keyser-Marcus et al., 2002). Table 2.1 describes the effects of TBI on students and strategies for helping them in your classroom. For example, because students with TBI may have trouble concentrating and remembering and organizing things, you can show them how to use memory and organization aids such as paging systems, electronic watches and organizers, memory notebooks, checklists, and daily logs (Keyser-Marcus et al., 2002). In addition, you can help students recognize what they can do rather than only what they are no longer able to do. It also is helpful to remain calm and redirect students when their behavior is inappropriate.

It is important to be aware of the differences between students with TBI and those with learning and behavioral problems (Doelling, Bryde, & Parette, 1997). The per-

Characteristics of and strategies for accommodating students with TBI

TABLE 2.1

Effects of TBI:	Provide Student With:	Teach By:
Cognitive and Academic Skill Impacts • Memory • Problem-solving and planning • Attention and concentration • Reading recognition and comprehension • Mathematics calculation and reasoning	• Diagrams, maps, charts, or other graphic cues • Cognitive organizers • Opportunities for problem-solving in functional settings • Preferential seating, proximity to visual or auditory aids and instructional assistance • Personal work space free from distracting stimuli • Individual peer tutor or opportunities to participate in structured collaborative groups	• Using strategies for problem-solving and coping (self-talk, verbal rehearsal, self-questioning, reflection) • Memory aids (visualization, mnemonic devices, paraphrasing, and retelling) • Using survey and preview techniques • Providing practice in guided reading activities • Task analyzing academic requirements • Using a variety of prompts and fading as self-regulation improves
Language Impacts • Expressive • Receptive • Written language	• Support from related services personnel • Assistive technology to communicate and process information and to accommodate motor and sensory deficits • Age-appropriate language models • Opportunities for structured and unstructured communication exchange • Visual aids in conjunction with auditory input • Functional materials and experiential learning opportunities	• Modeling questioning techniques • Providing appropriate wait time to formulate and respond to questions • Teaching note-taking formats and practicing during guided lectures • Stressing previewing, active listening, brainstorming, and reviewing from notes and graphic aids • Checking comprehension regularly • Conducting frequent cumulative review • Teaching specific spelling and production strategies • Matching complexity of instructional language to student's PLP (Present Level of Performance) • Modifying writing requirements based on PLP

Effects of TBI:	Provide Student With:	Teach By:
Social Impacts		
• Peer/adult interactions • Labile mood • Self-concept • Verbal outbursts or aggressive episodes • Response to stress/demands • Pragmatic language	• Support from related services personnel having expertise in social communication skill development • Support from peer, buddy, and cooperative learning partners • Strategies and skills for dealing with anger and frustration • Systems for self-monitoring behavior and charting progress • Varied schedules of reinforcement • Structured environment • External cues (charts, contracts, graphs, posted rules, timers, etc.) • Opportunity to remove self and place to go when overwhelmed by stimuli and demands of environment • Opportunities for success with activities appropriate to PLP • System to alert student to problems and cues for redirection to desired target behaviors	• Conducting ecological analysis prior to programming • Identifying TBI-related behaviors and collaboratively developing consistent, positive support plans • Conducting an analysis of the communicative intent of behaviors and teaching skills appropriate to individual needs • Targeting behaviors of greatest concern and implementing behavioral changes gradually • Using direct instruction, modeling, role playing, and scripting to teach specific social and communication skills • Encouraging practice across natural environments • Teaching skills in small group & structured settings • Generalizing skills to larger, less structured contexts
Organizational Skill Impacts		
• Assignment completion • Arrangement and retrieval of materials • Organization of personal work space • Time management • Orientation and direction	• Group, class, or individual schedule • Daily or weekly calendar and materials checklist corresponding to schedule demands • Individual work area with provision for materials and completed tasks • Notebooks with dividers, colored folders, plastic bins, or portfolio containers • Reduced assignments and/or additional time • Opportunities to practice transition routes (e.g., classroom to cafeteria)	• Using consistent routine, introducing gradual changes in routine • Teaching organizational skills directly related to planning, material organization, and schedule completion • Implementing schedule systems and other organizational cues that transfer across settings and individuals (e.g., resource room to general education settings) • Clearly delineating areas of the classroom by purpose (personal space, leisure areas, centers for instruction) • Collaborating with personnel to consistently provide organizational cues

Source: From "What are multidisciplinary and ecobehavioral approaches?" by J. Doelling, S. Bryde, and H.P. Parette, 1997, *Teaching Exceptional Children, 30,* pp. 58–59. Copyright 1997 by The Council for Exceptional Children. Reprinted by permission.

formance and behavior of students with TBI tend to be more variable than those of students with learning and behavioral disabilities. Thus, they may be able to perform algebra and fail to remember monetary values. In the six months to a year following their injury, students with TBI also may make accelerated gains in their academic skills, which can be followed by subsequent plateaus and advances in learning.

Students with TBI also are more likely to tire easily, have headaches, and feel overwhelmed and frustrated. Therefore, you may need to provide them with periodic breaks, schedule important classes when students are most alert, adjust their workloads and deadlines, and divide assignments into smaller units (Keyser-Marcus et al., 2002). It also is important to keep in mind that students with TBI and their family members, friends,

Resource

Keyser-Marcus et al. (2002) offer information, resources and strategies for identifying and addressing the educational needs of students with traumatic brain injury and Stuart and Goodsitt (1996), Doelling and Bryde (1995), Phelps (1995), and Clark (1996) offer guidelines for helping students who have been hospitalized make the transition to school.

Set Your Sites

For more information on students with brain injuries, go to the Web Links module in Chapter 2 of the Companion Website.

Resource

Katsiyannssis, Ellenburg, Acton, and Torrey (2001) offer information and teaching strategies addressing the needs of students with Rett Syndrome.

and teachers remember successful experiences before the trauma occurred, which can cause psychosocial problems for everyone involved. In particular, adolescents with a brain injury may have trouble coping with the reality of their new condition (Hill, 1999). Because these students have probably been treated in hospitals, they also may need help in making the transition back to school.

It also is important to (a) establish and maintain communication with families, (b) obtain information about the student's injuries and their consequences from families and medical personnel, and (c) be sensitive to families and understand the pressures associated with having a child with TBI. Conoley and Sheridan (1996) provide strategies for helping families of children with TBI, including education, family support and advocacy, family counseling, and home–school collaboration.

Students with Autism Spectrum Disorder

Your classroom also will include students with *autism spectrum disorder* (ASD), a broad continuum of cognitive and neuro-behavioral conditions that typically include impairments in socialization and communication coupled with repetitive patterns of behavior. While some students with ASD may have severe mental retardation, others may be selected for participation in programs for students who are gifted and talented.

In addition to students with autism, and Asperger syndrome (which are discussed next), ASD also includes students with:

- *Childhood Disintegrative Disorder:* a condition associated with a loss of speech and other previously learned skills and the presence of other autisticlike behaviors following an initial period of normal development.
- *Rett Syndrome:* a progressive genetic disorder affecting girls which affects one's neurological development and often includes a loss of previously learned skills, repetitive hand movements and a loss of functional use of one's hands (Katsiyannis, Ellenburg, Action, & Torrey, 2001).
- *Pervasive Developmental Disorder-Not Otherwise Specified (PDD-NOS) or atypical autism:* a condition that resembles autism but is usually not as severe or extensive (Dunlap & Bunton-Pierce, 1999; Lord & McGee, 2001).

Autism, also referred to as *Pervasive Developmental Disorder (PDD)*, usually involves a severe disorder in communication, socialization, and behavior that typically occurs at birth or within the first three years of life. Students with autism may have trouble staying engaged, responding to verbal cues and interacting with others, and showing affection. They also may engage in repetitive and perseverative movements and stereotypical behavior, exhibit various inappropriate behaviors, and have challenges learning and understanding and using language (Dunlap & Bunton-Pierce, 1999). They also may be resistant to playing with others or to changes in routines, and be over- or under-sensitive to some types of sensory experiences (Westling & Fox, 2000).

One form of ASD is known as *Asperger syndrome* (Safran, 2001). While their academic performance and I.Q. usually varies from average to exceptional, students with Asperger syndrome tend to be very literal and fact-oriented, have good but rigid verbal skills, and adhere strictly to routines (Safran, 2002a). These individuals also tend to have a narrow range of interests, resulting in their displaying great interest in and talking a lot about esoteric subjects (e.g., train schedules, ceiling fans), which weakens their social functioning (Williams, 2001). As a result, they may have difficulty completing assignments, paying attention, processing information, following classroom routines, and making transitions (Marks et al., 2003). Because these students also have difficulties reading and understanding social, facial, and nonverbal cues, they may be socially awkward or intrusive and therefore may not make friends of the same age or may appear to be rude (Barnhill, 2001; Carrington, Templeton, & Papinczak, 2003).

Because they display a wide range of characteristics depending on the nature and severity of their ASD, these students also vary greatly in ability and personality. While some may have severe cognitive disabilities, others may benefit from participation in your school's program for students who are identified as gifted and talented. Socially, some may prefer to be alone and others may develop an enjoyment in socializing with others.

Many teaching and classroom management strategies can be used to promote the learning and prosocial behaviors of students with ASD in general education classrooms. You can:

- recognize students' individualized strengths, interests, and talents and use them to motivate and help them learn.
- provide students with alternative ways to complete assignments.
- help students to maintain their self-esteem, and find mentors, heroes, and friends with and without disabilities.
- establish and follow routines and make instructions and expectations clear.
- use positive behavioral supports and structure the classroom to increase their appropriate behaviors and decrease their inappropriate behaviors.
- create a learning environment that is respectful of individual differences and does not tolerate teasing and bullying.
- highlight key concepts; use graphic organizers; and post word and symbol cards, posters, photographs, and visual activity schedules that prompt these students to understand language and the sequence of activities, and to use prosocial behaviors.
- familiarize students with new activities, information, routines, and materials prior to introducing them in class.
- provide students with alternatives to stressful situations or overstimulating environments (e.g., noisy lunchroom) such as a home base where they can go to escape stress, prevent behavioral incidents, regain control of their behavior, and organize themselves.
- teach students to use learning strategies that guide them in performing academic tasks and remembering important information.
- use social skill training programs to help them learn to read social cues, take turns, initiate interactions with others, ask for help from others, and work and play cooperatively with others.
- work with families and related service providers to learn more about the students' strengths, skills, interests, and communication patterns and to make sure that students continue to use prosocial behaviors in a variety of situations (Bullard, 2004; Donnelly, 2002; Marks et al., 2003; Safran, 2002a; Williams, 2001).

You can also encourage your students to support and interact with each other and to serve as good role models by teaching them about autism, the importance and value of making friends with all types of students, and other ways to communicate (Williams, 2001). For example, videos, children's books, and/or guest speakers can be used to teach students about communicating in different ways, responding to attention seeking and unusual behaviors, beginning and maintaining interactions, including others in play and learning activities, and using appropriate behaviors (English, Goldstein, Kaczmarek, & Shafer, 1996).

Set Your Sites

For more information on students with autism spectrum disorders, go to the Web Links module in Chapter 2 of the Companion Website.

Resource

Bullard (2004), Marks et al. (2003), and Safran (2002b) provide resources and strategies for teaching students with Asperger Syndrome, and a special 2001 issue of *Intervention in School and Clinic 36*(5) is devoted to information about and teaching strategies for use with students with Asperger syndrome.

Students with Severe, Significant, or Multiple Disabilities

The terms *individuals with severe, significant, or multiple disabilities* often refer to individuals with profound mental retardation and sensory, communication, medical, motor, behavioral, and emotional disabilities. Because of the significant medical, cognitive, language, physical, and social needs of students with severe and multiple disabilities, there is no one set of traits that characterizes this group of individuals (Westling & Fox, 2000). As a result, they also need many different levels of ongoing support to perform life activities and to participate in integrated educational and community settings (Turnbull et al., 2004). However, students with severe and multiple disabilities may have some of the following: (a) impaired cognitive functioning and memory, which causes them to learn at a slower rate, and have difficulty maintaining new skills and using them in other situations; (b) delayed use of receptive and expressive language; (c) impaired physical and motor abilities; and (d) limited repertoire of socialization, daily living, vocational, and behavioral skills. These students also can be a joy to have in your classroom, as many of them display and model warmth, self-determination, humor, and other positive traits (Heward, 2003).

Inclusive educational programs for students with severe and multiple disabilities have increased their cognitive functioning and social interaction skills (Kennedy et al., 1997; Salisbury, Evans, & Palombaro, 1997). You can help them learn in your inclusive classroom by providing them with an educational program tailored to their unique needs by:

- giving them a developmentally appropriate, community-based curriculum that teaches them in natural settings the functional and academic skills they need to be more independent and socialize and succeed in inclusive settings. For example, you can include functional skills such as coin identification and making purchases in your mathematics curriculum.
- embedding instructional goals for students within the general education curriculum.
- task analyzing instructional goals to break them into discrete and multiple-stepped skills.
- using positive behavioral supports.
- using age-appropriate activities and materials with them.
- giving them opportunities to socialize with others and to work in cooperative learning groups.
- encouraging them to make choices and to develop their self-determination.
- giving them useful technology and assistive devices.
- working collaboratively with families and other professionals.
- using gestural, physical, pictorial, model, and oral prompts as necessary.
- making sure that you promote the maintenance and generalization of skills taught to students.
- monitoring their progress in learning and socializing with others (Heward, 2003; Westling & Fox, 2000; Wolfe & Hall, 2003).

Specific strategies for implementing these suggestions are discussed in subsequent chapters of this book.

Medication Monitoring

A growing number of students, particularly those with medical and mental health needs, epilepsy, or ADD, are taking prescription drugs to improve their school experience and performance (Goode, 2003). The use of drugs with students is very controversial. Some

Resource

Wolfe and Hall (2003), Westling and Fox (2000), and Snell and Brown (2000) offer information, guidelines, strategies, and resources for teaching students with severe and multiple disabilities in inclusive educational settings.

Resource

Giangreco, Cloninger, and Iverson (1998) have developed *Choosing Options and Accommodations for Children (C.O.A.C.H.)*. It offers assessment, a curriculum, and teaching and communication strategies for use with students with severe disabilities in inclusive settings.

Set Your Sites

For more information on students with multiple and severe disabilities, go to the Web Links module in Chapter 2 of the Companion Website.

Resource

Engleman, Griffin, Griffin, and Maddox (1999) and Haring and Romer (1995) provide guidelines for helping students who are deaf-blind in inclusive classrooms.

believe that drugs can improve academic, behavioral, and social performance; others believe that they are ineffective or have only short-term benefits and can have adverse side effects. Recently, there have been concerns about the long-term impact of medications that have not been tested on children, including their impact on subsequent substance abuse problems, and the pressures on students who use medications to sell or trade them to others (Scholzman & Scholzman, 2000).

Some educators suggest that the decision to use drugs should be based on the student's behavior and other symptoms rather than the student's label or diagnosis. Further, they believe, drug use should be considered only after appropriate teaching and classroom management techniques have been used correctly, for a reasonable amount of time, and proved ineffective (Austin, 2003; Howell, Evans, & Gardiner, 1997). Questions that can guide families and professionals in making decisions regarding the use of medications are provided in Figure 2.12.

Ultimately, the decision to use drugs is made by the families and physicians of students. Once that decision is made, it is important for you to (a) know the school district's policies on drug management; (b) learn about and help others learn about the type of medication: dosage, frequency, schedule, and duration; benefits, symptoms, and side effects (e.g., changes in appetite and energy level, aches and pains, irritability, repetitive movements or sounds); (c) use a multimodal approach that includes academic, behavioral/social, and family-based methods; and (d) work collaboratively with families, medical personnel, and other professionals to develop a plan to monitor students' progress and behavior while taking the drug and maintain communication with families and medical professionals (Katisyannis et al., 1997; Snider, Busch, & Arrowood, 2003). Because many medications have side effects, you should keep a record of students' behavior in school, including their academic performance, social skills, notable changes in behavior, and possible drug symptoms (Schulz & Edwards, 1997). This record should be shared with families and medical personnel to assist them in evaluating the efficacy of and need for continued use of the medication.

Resource

Austin (2003), Pancheri and Prater (1999), Sweeney et al. (1997), and Schulz and Edwards (1997) provide overviews and summaries of the potentially positive effects and negative side effects of the most commonly prescribed drugs for students.

FIGURE 2.12

Questions to guide decisions regarding the use of pharmacological interventions

- Have educational, social/behavioral, and family-based interventions proven to be ineffective after having been implemented as intended and for an appropriate period of time? If so, why were they ineffective? What other accommodations can be implemented?
- In what ways do the behaviors interfere with the child's learning behavior, socialization, and the learning of others? Is the student's behavior severe enough to warrant use of medication?
- Does the student have other conditions such as tics or mental illness?
- How does the student feel about taking the medication?
- What does the student know about the medication and its effects?
- Will the medication be detected as a controlled substance via urinalysis and therefore prevent the student from participating in competitive sports and other after-school activities or from entering the military?
- What are the attitudes and cultural perspectives of family members and peers regarding the use of medication?
- Can the family afford to pay for the medication?
- What support do the family members need to supervise the use of medication and prevent abuse by the student or by others?
- Do the medical and school district professionals have a plan for appropriate administration, follow-up, monitoring, and communication?

Note: Austin (2003); Kollins, Barkley, & DuPaul (2001).

REFLECTING ON PROFESSIONAL PRACTICES

Supporting Students on Medications

Ms. Cheng is proud of her ability to work with challenging students, so it was a blow when Ms. White, a student's mother, called to tell her that the family had decided to place Shaun on medication. Ms. Cheng had tried several teaching and classroom management strategies with Shaun, but they had not been very effective. She knew that the White family was considering the use of drugs. She gave them information about drugs but expressed her concerns about their potential side effects and their effectiveness. However, the Whites decided to try them.

Ms. Cheng realized that regardless of her beliefs, it was now her job to work with the family and the medical staff to manage and evaluate the use of drugs with Shaun. Ms. Cheng researched her district's policies, which included a statement on who can give drugs to students; forms for obtaining the physician's approval, including the name of the drug, dosage, frequency, duration, and possible side effects; a format for maintaining records of drugs given to students; procedures for receiving, labeling, storing, dispensing, and disposing of drugs; and guidelines for students administering drugs to themselves.

Next, Ms. Cheng met with the Whites, their physician, and the school nurse. First, they discussed the potential benefits and adverse side effects of the medication, and the school nurse gave everyone information and a list of references about the medication. They also reviewed procedures on who would administer the drug, when, how, and where. It was agreed that Mr. Schubert, the school nurse, would be the only one to handle the drug, and would give it to Shaun in his office.

Mr. Schubert explained that he stored all medications together in a secured location, clearly labeled each student's medication, and maintained a record of the medications dispensed. He also discussed the importance of maintaining confidentiality, and of not attributing the student's good or bad behavior to the drug, such as asking "Have you taken your medication yet?" after a student misbehaves. He also planned to talk with Shaun about the drug's possible side effects, and how Shaun could handle comments from other students about taking it.

Finally, the group developed a plan for monitoring the drug's effect on Shaun. They agreed that Ms. Cheng and the other professionals would use observations and checklists, and interview Shaun to collect data on the drug's effects and side effects on Shaun's academic skills, classroom behavior, and social interactions. The family also agreed to talk with him and keep a diary on Shaun at home and on their feelings about his behavior, friendships, and schoolwork. Ms. Cheng was happy that they also talked about the importance of individualized teaching and classroom management techniques for Shaun, as well as a plan and criteria for phasing out the use of the drug. They ended the meeting by setting up procedures for communicating with each other and setting a date and a time for their next meeting. While still concerned, Ms. Cheng left the meeting feeling somewhat better.

- Why was Ms. Cheng concerned about the decision to place Shaun on a drug?
- As a teacher, how do you feel about this issue?
- How do you think the White family felt about their decision? What do you think about the school district's response to their decision?
- What are the roles of families, teachers, doctors, school nurses, and students in drug use with students?
- Why did Ms. Cheng feel better at the end of the meeting?

 To answer these questions online and share your responses with others, go to the Reflection module in chapter 2 of the Companion Website.

Students with Sensory Disabilities

Students with Hearing Impairments

Students with hearing impairments include students who are deaf and hearing impaired (Schirmer, 2004). Students are considered *deaf* when they have "a hearing impairment that is so severe that the child is impaired in processing linguistic information through hearing, with or without amplification, which adversely affects educational perform-

Students with hearing loss may have difficulty following directions or remaining engaged in activities requiring listening. How do you help your students with hearing loss follow directions?

ance." *Hearing impairment* is defined as "an impairment in hearing, whether permanent or fluctuating, that adversely affects a child's educational performance but that is not included under the definition of deafness."

The degree of hearing loss is assessed by giving the student an audiometric test, which measures the intensity and frequency of sound that the student can hear. The intensity of the sound is defined in terms of decibel (db) levels; the frequency is measured in hertz (Hz). Based on the audiometric evaluation, the hearing loss is classified as ranging from mild to profound.

Some hearing losses may not be detected before the student goes to school. Many students with hearing losses are identified by teachers. Figure 2.13 presents some of the warning signs of a possible hearing loss. If you suspect that a student may have a hearing loss, refer the student to the school nurse or physician for an audiometric evaluation and contact the family.

The intellectual abilities of students with hearing impairments parallel those of students with hearing (Williams & Finnegan, 2003). However, the student with a hearing impairment experiences communication problems in learning an oral language system. These problems can create difficulties in gaining experience and information that hinder the academic and literacy performance and social-emotional development of these students (Goldin-Meadow & Mayberry, 2001; Pakulski & Kaderavek, 2002). Depending on their hearing levels, students with hearing impairments may use assistive technology and the following methods to communicate:

- *oral/aural:* use of speaking, speech reading, and residual hearing to communicate with others
- *manual:* use of some form of visual-gestural language to communicate with others

FIGURE 2.13

Warning signs of a possible hearing loss

Students with a hearing loss may do some or all of the following:

◇ Have trouble following directions and paying attention to messages presented orally
◇ Speak poorly and have a limited vocabulary
◇ Ask the speaker or peers to repeat statements or instructions
◇ Avoid oral activities and withdraw from those that require listening
◇ Respond inconsistently and inappropriately to verbal statements from others
◇ Mimic the behavior of others
◇ Rely heavily on gestures and appear to be confused
◇ Turn up the volume when listening to audiovisual aids such as televisions, radios, and cassette recorders
◇ Speak with a loud voice
◇ Cock the head to one side
◇ Complain of earaches, head noise, and stuffiness in the ears

Resource

Pittman and Huefner (2001) offer a historical overview of the controversies regarding the approaches to educating students with hearing impairments, and Goldin-Meadow and Mayberry (2001) provide a summary of the literature on how students with hearing impairments learn to read.

Resource

Easterbrooks and Baker (2001) developed a matrix of questions that educators and IEP teams can use to identify and address the communication and learning needs of students with hearing impairments.

Set Your Sites

For more information on teaching students with hearing disabilities, go to the Web Links module in Chapter 2 of the Companion Website.

- *bilingual-bicultural:* use of some form of visual-gestural language such as American Sign Language (which is not based on English) and the written form of English, with no use of spoken English
- *total communication:* use of a combination of approaches, including manual and oral/aural methods (Schirmer, 2004)

Some individuals also use cued speech, which involves dividing words into syllables and then communicating them via hand movements and lip reading (Heward, 2002).

An estimated 80 percent of the students with hearing impairments are served in public schools, with more than a third of them in general education classrooms. As their teacher, you can collaborate with other professionals to develop and implement an educational program that addresses their unique communication, learning, and socialization needs (Litchfield & Lartz, 2002). To minimize their auditory difficulties, you can create a visually rich learning environment and use written materials, visual aids such as graphic organizers, and cues to support instruction (Williams & Finnegan, 2003). You can use experiential and hands-on learning that allows these students to experience a concept; provide a context for understanding language, reading, and writing; and act out and role-play important principles, concepts, and information (Schirmer, 2004). You also can promote learning by linking words with pictures or graphics that students will recognize, using gestures and facial expressions, restating and paraphrasing statements, speaking in shorter sentences, teaching new vocabulary, checking for understanding, connecting new learning to students' prior knowledge about the topic, using cooperative learning, and adapting the classroom environment for them (Marlatt, 2004; Pakulski & Kaderavek, 2002). Socially, these students should be encouraged to take part in all school and community activities, and these activities should be adapted to help them participate (Fiedler, 2001). Specific teaching, technological, and classroom design factors in differentiating instruction for students with hearing impairments to help them access and succeed in the general education curriculum are presented in chapters 7 and 8.

In designing educational programs for students with hearing impairments, you should also be aware of the deaf culture movement. These groups view individuals with hearing impairments as a distinct cultural group whose language, needs, values, behaviors, customs, social interaction patterns, folklore, and arts are quite different from those of hearing individuals who communicate through spoken language (Humphries, 1993). Thus, students with hearing impairments need to be exposed to the deaf culture, and you should view deafness as a cultural issue and explore ways of promoting the bilingual and bicultural abilities of these students.

Students with Visual Impairments

Your classroom also may include students with visual impairments. A student with a *visual disability* has "an impairment in vision that, even with correction, adversely affects a child's educational performance. The term includes both partial sight and blindness."

Students with visual impairments are classified into three types based on their ability to use their vision: low vision, functionally blind, and totally blind (Lewis, 2004). Students who have *low vision* can see nearby objects but have trouble seeing them at a distance. While they may work slowly with visual stimuli, they usually can read print using some type of optical aid or by having access to enlarged and or contrast enhanced print. Students who are *functionally blind* usually need Braille for effective reading and writing; they can use their vision to move through the classroom and classify objects by color. Students who are *totally blind* have no vision or limited light perception and do not respond to visual input. Like students who are functionally blind, these students need tactile and auditory teaching activities.

Since visual impairments can hinder a student's cognitive, language, motor, and social development, early detection is important. Figure 2.14 presents some of the warning signs that a student may be experiencing visual problems. If you suspect that a student may have a visual problem, refer the student to the school nurse or physician for an evaluation and contact the family.

Students with visual impairments are a varied group. Most of these students have IQ scores within the normal range. However, their cognitive, language, and social development may be affected because of their limited ability to obtain, experience, and understand visual information, move around their environment, and learn by observing others (Heward, 2003; Lewis, 2004). For example, these students may have problems learning spatial concepts or vocabulary that describes objects. Their language may rely on verbalisms, or words or phrases that are inconsistent with sensory experiences. Also, because of limited mobility, some students with visual impairments may have delayed motor development.

FIGURE 2.14

Warning signs of a possible visual difficulty

Visual problems are indicated when the student does any or all of the following:

- ◇ Holds reading material close to the eyes
- ◇ Has trouble seeing things from a distance and/or performing close-up tasks
- ◇ Reads slowly and has immature handwriting
- ◇ Rests the head on the desk when writing or coloring
- ◇ Has poorly organized notebooks
- ◇ Frequently skips lines, loses place, needs breaks, uses a finger as a guide, and uses head movements when reading
- ◇ Blinks, squints, rubs the eyes, or tilts the head frequently
- ◇ Covers or closes one eye
- ◇ Frequently has swollen eyelids and inflamed or watery eyes
- ◇ Complains of seeing double or seeing halos around lights and having headaches
- ◇ Exhibits irregular eye movements
- ◇ Appears clumsy, trips over and bumps into things, walks hesitantly, and has difficulty negotiating stairs and drop-offs

Approximately 85 percent of the students with visual impairments are served in public schools, and about two-thirds of them are taught in general education classrooms. As their teacher, you can work with vision specialists to learn about appropriate instructional and curricular accommodations, materials, assistive technology, and resources (Cox & Dykes, 2001; Griffin, Williams, Davis, & Engelman, 2002). You also will need to adapt your teaching materials by pairing visually presented information with tactile/kinesthetic- and auditory-based learning activities, using Braille, audiocassettes, and digitized materials, as well as an enlarging machine to prepare large-print materials (Downing & Chen, 2003). For example, outlining a chart with string can help students with visual impairments to tactilely access visual information. You also can foster learning by letting students work with real objects and manipulatives, linking new material to students' prior knowledge, providing students with opportunities to use materials prior to beginning the lesson, checking for comprehension regularly, using cooperative learning arrangements, and giving students many activities to practice new skills in natural environments.

In addition to the general education curriculum, you may need to work with an orientation and mobility specialist to help these students learn how to move around your classroom and school (Griffin et al., 2002; Tolla, 2000). They and their classmates also need to be taught how to interact with each other. They also should be encouraged to participate in all school and community activities, and these activities should be adapted to help them take part. Specific teaching, technological, and classroom design factors in differentiating instruction for students with visual impairments to help them access and succeed in the general education curriculum are presented in chapters 7 and 8.

Set Your Sites

For more information on teaching students with visual disabilities, go to the Web Links module in Chapter 2 of the Companion Website.

Resource

"Sources of Braille Reading Materials," a list of organizations that offer Braille reading materials, is available from the National Library Service for the Blind and Physically Handicapped.

Summary

This chapter has provided information to help you understand the educational strengths and needs of students with disabilities and how you can effectively educate them in inclusive classrooms. Other strategies to address these needs are presented in later chapters. As you review the questions asked in this chapter, consider the following questions and remember the following points.

How Does the Special Education Identification Process Work?
CEC 1, 2, 3, 9, 10, PRAXIS 1, 2, 3, INTASC 2, 3, 9, 10

A planning team composed of professionals and family members, and the student when appropriate, makes important decisions about the education of the student with disabilities. Before considering a referral for special education placement, the planning team uses a *prereferral system*. That is, a team of educators works together to help classroom teachers develop and use methods to keep students in the general education classroom. If the prereferral system is not successful, the planning team determines if a student needs special education and related services. If the team determines that a student is eligible for special education, an IEP is developed.

How Can IEPs Be Implemented in General Education Settings?
CEC 1, 4, 5, 6, 7, 9, 10, PRAXIS 2, 3, INTASC 2, 3, 4, 5, 6, 7, 9, 10

The IEP serves as a tool for providing students with disabilities with access to the general education curriculum. The implementation of the IEP in the general education setting can be facilitated by involving teachers in the IEP process,

Council for Exceptional Children

PRAXIS

inTASC

aligning the IEP goals to the general education curriculum, differentiating instruction to address IEP goals, establishing an implementation plan, and engaging in curriculum mapping.

What Are the Educational Strengths and Needs of Students With High-Incidence Disabilities?

CEC 1, 2, 3, 4, 5, 6, 7, 9, PRAXIS 1, 3, INTASC 2, 3, 4, 5, 6, 7, 9, 10

Students with high-incidence, or mild disabilities include those with learning disabilities, mild emotional and behavioral disorders, mild mental retardation, speech/language impairments, and ADD. The characteristics, behaviors, strengths and needs of these students vary; some have difficulties in only one area, others in several areas. These challenges may occur as learning, language and communication, perceptual, motor, social, and behavioral difficulties.

What Are the Educational Strengths and Needs of Students With Low-Incidence Disabilities?

CEC 1, 2, 3, 4, 5, 6, 7, 9, PRAXIS 1, 3, INTASC 2, 3, 4, 5, 6, 7, 9, 10

Students with physical, sensory, and significant disabilities are sometimes referred to as having low-incidence disabilities. These students have a range of characteristics. No two students are alike, and each educational program must be based on individual strengths and needs rather than disability categories.

What Would You Do in Today's Diverse Classroom?

As a member of your school district's comprehensive planning team, you are asked to address the educational needs of the following students:

★ Samuel is not working up to his potential. He rarely does his work, and when he does, it is either incomplete or incorrect. He shows little self-control, is frequently off-task, gets angry easily, and often seems withdrawn. He annoys other students and has trouble making friends. He frequently calls out, leaves his seat, and refuses to comply with his teacher's requests. He needs more and more of his teacher's time.

★ Ethel was recently in a serious car accident. Although she was wearing a seat belt, her skull was cracked and there was considerable swelling of her brain. She lapsed into a coma for several days and had surgery to repair the damage to her skull. She has had several seizures since the accident and is taking medication to control them. Since she returned to school several months ago, her academic performance has slipped and she seems to be a different person. She has trouble controlling her impulses, organizing her work, socializing with others, and maintaining attention.

★ Tony is uneasy with visual tasks and usually performs poorly on them. When reading, he holds the book close to his eyes and frequently skips lines, loses his place, needs breaks, and uses his finger as a guide. He often rests his head on the desk when working, and his notebook is poorly organized. He appears clumsy, trips over and bumps into things, and walks hesitantly.

★ Sadie has significant learning and communication difficulties. She knows her name, basic colors, and some functional words, and she can follow simple commands. Although she can say single words, only a few of her words are understandable. She likes being with others and attempts to participate in all activities.

1. What prereferral strategies might be appropriate for Samuel, Ethel, Tony, and Sadie?

2. Do you think that these students qualify for special education services? If so, under which disability category do they qualify? If not, why not?

3. What goals should their IEPs address, and what services should they receive to meet those goals?

4. How might placement in a general education classroom benefit these students?

5. How would you feel about having Samuel, Ethel, Tony, and Sadie in your class?

6. What knowledge, skills, dispositions, resources and supports do you need to address their strengths and needs?

To answer these questions online and share your responses with others, go to the Reflection module in Chapter 2 of the Companion Website.

Chapter 3

Understanding the Diverse Educational Strengths and Needs of Learners Who Challenge Schools

Halee

My mother told me that I was born during the war, which continued for the first 10 years of my life. Between ages 2 and 10, I lived on and off with my grandmother so that I could provide her with some companionship. No matter where I lived, the bombing seemed to follow me. Several times a week, the bombing would start and we would have to leave our homes and hide in the forest.

Finally, when I was 10, the bombing stopped and the war ended. My family was airlifted to an internment camp in a neighboring country, but I was left behind with my grandmother. Three months later, my father returned to get me and smuggled me into the camp. While I was happy to be reunited with my family, I missed my grandmother, who did not come with us.

Although we moved several times from one camp to another, each of the camps was the same. We lived in a small area surrounded by barbed wire, and we had no privacy or toilet facilities. Our camp was frequently raided by the locals, and we were often targets of burglary, rape, and murder.

I didn't get to go to school because I was a girl. My responsibilities were to help my mother take care of my brothers and sisters. However, I did hear about how life would be wonderful and full of riches for us if we could get to the United States. After living in the camps for 3 years, we came to the United States. When our plane landed at the airport, I saw a man putting garbage in a clean and shiny plastic bag and thought that the United States really was a wealthy country. However, this view was short-lived, as we were placed in a small apartment in the poorest section of the city. Soon after settling in, I started school. When I got off the bus with my sister, the teachers were pointing here and there, and I went wherever they pointed. Although I was old enough to be in a higher grade class, I was assigned to a lower grade class. I was scared and very cautious.

I really felt confused by the social interactions and the behaviors of my classmates. At home, I was supposed to be passive and obedient. However, in school, all the other kids were very verbal and physically expressive. One time, we went to a swimming pool and I didn't know that I was supposed to bring a bathing suit. In fact, I didn't know what a bathing suit was. When we arrived at the pool, someone gave me a bathing suit. I put it on over my underwear and was very embarrassed when everyone laughed at me.

I struggled academically and my teachers thought I had a learning problem, and referred me for special education or something. However, I knew my academic struggles were due to the fact that I didn't understand or speak much English. When teachers and students spoke to me, I looked around to see what my classmates were doing and then mimicked them. I felt overwhelmed, as I didn't understand what they were saying. They would repeat themselves over and over again or talk very slowly, as if that would make me understand them. I wanted to run away to escape their bombarding me, but there was no forest to run to for safety.

What factors led to some of the difficulties that Halee had in school? Should Halee have been placed in special education classes? How does inclusion affect students like Halee? After reading this chapter, you should have the knowledge, skills, and dispositions to answer these as well as the following questions.

★ **How have economic changes affected students and schools?**
★ **How have demographic shifts affected students and schools?**
★ **What are the educational strengths and needs of students from culturally and linguistically diverse backgrounds?**
★ **How can I differentiate cultural and language differences from learning difficulties?**
★ **What are the educational strengths and needs of students who are gifted and talented?**
★ **What is the effect of discrimination and bias on students and schools?**
★ **How have family changes affected students and schools?**
★ **What are some alternative philosophies for structuring schools to address societal changes?**

The United States continues to undergo major changes that have a tremendous effect on schools and the students they seek to educate. Society has been re-shaped as a result of changing economic conditions, demographic shifts, racism and sexism, changes in the structure of families, and increases in substance abuse and child abuse. These factors have contributed to a society that jeopardizes the physical and mental health of its children. These factors also make it more likely that students like Halee and the other students you will meet in this chapter—who are not disabled—may experience difficulties in school, be referred to and placed in special education settings, and drop out of school. For students with identified disabilities, these factors often interact with their disability to place students in double jeopardy.

Schools must now respond to these societal changes and meet the needs of increasingly diverse groups of students who challenge the school structure. Inclusive educational practices have focused on the needs of students with disabilities, but it is important to remember that inclusion programs seek to restructure schools so that they address the needs of *all learners*. Like students with disabilities, *all students* benefit from educators who modify their attitudes, teaching techniques, curricula, and family involvement strategies to reflect and accommodate students and their families; promote sensitivity to and acceptance of individual differences; and work collaboratively with other professionals, families, students, and community agencies.

How Have Economic Changes Affected Students and Schools?

A Nation of Visible Rich and Invisible Poor

In the United States today, there is a growing disparity between the highly visible wealthy and the invisible poor, old and young, and a shrinking middle class (Hodgkinson, 2001).

Children represent the fastest growing poverty group in the United States. Why do you think this is occurring?

As a result, the United States is becoming a rich nation with poor children who are more invisible and worse off than their poor counterparts in other Western industrialized nations (Madrick, 2002). The gap between rich and poor keeps widening, helping to make the United States an economically stratified nation rather than an egalitarian one (Fallows, 2000). These economic changes have had a profound effect on children, who represent the fastest-growing poverty group in the United States. The majority of children from lower socioeconomic backgrounds in the United States are white, although African American, Hispanic American, Native American, and Asian American children are more likely to live in poverty than are their white counterparts. Children from lower socioeconomic backgrounds are more likely to attend underfunded schools, which, in turn, affects their academic performance (Biddle & Berliner, 2002).

Poverty

Poverty in the United States continues to affect a wide range of children and adults (Clemetson, 2003a). While nearly 20 percent of U.S. children live in poverty, these percentages are higher for African American children (30 percent), Hispanic children (38 percent), and children with disabilities (28 percent) (Madrick, 2002; Park, Turnbull & Turnbull, 2002). When families are both poor and members of nondominant linguistic and ethnic groups, the harmful effects of poverty tend to be greater and long-lasting.

As Figure 3.1 indicates, the harmful effects of poverty often interact to affect all aspects of a child's life, including cognitive development and school performance. The mothers of children from lower socioeconomic backgrounds often do not receive early prenatal care. From birth through adolescence, these children also are more likely to suffer from illnesses and diseases and less likely to receive appropriate medical care. Children from lower socioeconomic backgrounds often live in substandard housing; lack health insurance; are more likely to be victims of hunger, poor diets, lead poisoning, child abuse, and neglect; usually enter school with fewer skills than their peers; and often attend schools that have limited funds and high teacher turnover rates (Holloway, 2000; Slavin, 1998). As a result,

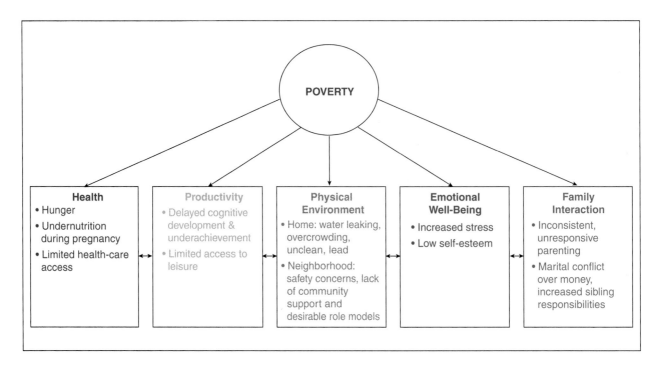

FIGURE 3.1 **Effects of poverty on five family life domains**
Source: From "Impacts of Poverty on Quality of Life in Families of Children with Disabilities," by J. Park, A. P. Turnbull, and H. R. Turnbull, 2002, *Exceptional Children*, 68, pp. 151–172. Copyright 2002 by The Council for Exceptional Children. Reprinted with permission.

they are more likely to be absent, to move during the school year, to fail in school, to be recommended for and placed in remedial and special education programs, and to drop out of school than their middle- and upper-income peers (Warger, 2002).

The effects of the depth, timing, and duration of poverty on students are also important factors (Brooks-Gunn & Duncan, 1997). Students who live in extreme poverty for a long time and students with disabilities are particularly likely to suffer. Students who experience poverty earlier in their lives are more likely to be harmed than students who experience poverty only in their later years.

One approach to addressing the multifacted needs of students and families who experience poverty, including students with disabilities, is the full-service school (Warger, 2002). Full-service schools are school-family-community partnerships that offer a range of integrated, comprehensive services addressing the holistic needs of students and families at school buildings or within community settings (Park, Turnbull, & Turnbull, 2002). The services include child and after-school care, health care, tutoring, transportation, drop-out prevention, job training and adult education, and assistance with social services and employment.

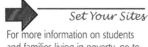

Set Your Sites

For more information on students and families living in poverty, go to the Web Links module in Chapter 3 of the Companion Website.

Set Your Sites

For more information on working in urban schools, go to the Web Links module in Chapter 3 of the Companion Website.

Urban Poverty

Poverty is prevalent in U.S. cities, where about 30 percent of all students live in poverty (U.S. Department of Education, 1996). Urban children from lower socioeconomic backgrounds often live in crowded, rundown apartments; are more likely to have lead poisoning, which can cause learning and behavioral difficulties, stunted growth, and hearing loss;

encounter violence and crime; have limited access to health care; suffer malnutrition; and attend underfunded, dilapidated schools. Children from lower socioeconomic backgrounds in our nation's cities are also less likely to receive immunization against diseases.

Homelessness.   The growing gap between rich and poor has led to a dramatic increase in homelessness in urban and rural areas, particularly among families with children (Egan, 2002). Homeless children do not have a regular and adequate residence and may be living with others, in cars, motels, bus/train stations, campgrounds, or shelters (Council for Exceptional Children, 2003). Sadly, approximately 1.4 million children or 2 percent of the students in the United States are likely to become homeless during the school year (Bernstein, 2000). This group of students also includes adolescents who leave their homes for a variety of reasons.

The McKinney-Vento Homeless Assistance Act is a federal law that guarantees homeless children the right to a free, appropriate public education in a mainstream school environment, and seeks to eliminate barriers to their school attendance. For example, it requires school districts to employ a homeless-education liaison and to provide students who are homeless with transportation to attend the same school even if they change residences. But in spite of this law, many homeless students in this country are not attending school. Many of these students do not attend school because of transportation needs, inappropriate class placement, lack of school supplies and clothes, poor health, hunger, and residency and immunization requirements. In addition, many of them cannot produce birth certificates, school files, and other important records and forms. Homeless students also may have few recreational opportunities; little privacy; and limited access to meals, books, school materials, and toys.

Homeless students are more vulnerable to the deleterious effects of poverty than other students from lower socioeconomic backgrounds (Egan, 2002). Consequently, students who are homeless may perform poorly in school and be in need of special education services; may be separated from their families for extended periods of time; and are often held over (Egan, 2002; Rafferty, 1998). Because they may lack washing facilities and adequate clothing, homeless students may have health care needs and may be ridiculed by peers (Janofsky, 2001). However, because of their frequent movement from place to place and their high absenteeism rates, many homeless students who are eligible for supportive services do not receive them. Some students also may be embarrassed by their homelessness or fearful that they will be separated from their families, and may attempt to hide it from their teachers and peers (Egan, 2002).

Several school districts have developed strategies for educating homeless students (Rafferty, 1998; Holloway, 2003). These strategies include providing transportation to frequently changing residences, specialized instruction, and tutoring; meals, showers, school materials, and clothes; medical care, counseling, and other supportive services; and after-school and full-year programs to meet these students' basic and recreational needs. These school districts also have employed an interagency approach, and have designed and implemented their services in collaboration with shelters and other community agencies.

Set Your Sites
For more information on homeless students and families, go to the Web Links module in Chapter 3 of the Companion Website .

Rural Poverty

Rural school districts serve more students living in poverty than do nonrural school districts and for longer periods of time (U.S. Department of Education, 1995). Rural school districts also serve more students with disabilities in general education classrooms than do nonrural school districts, as well as a growing number of students who are learning English.

Set Your Sites
For more information on working in rural schools, go to the Web Links module in Chapter 3 of the Companion Website.

Children of Migrant Workers

My name is Erika Garcia. My parents work very hard in the pickles. Sometimes my sister and I go to help my parents. We have seen my parents work many times, and just by looking, we see it is hard. First, you have to wake up at 5:45 A.M. because everyone goes to the field at 6:00 A.M. Picking pickles is like cracking your back. Some people hang the basket on their waist, and some drag it along.

After work we go home, and my mom and dad take a shower and my mom makes a lot of tortillas. Then we take a nap, and then we go back to the fields at 6:00 P.M. and do more rows of pickles to get a good start in the morning. My parents sent me to summer school but then they needed some help, and so I only went to school for 3 weeks because I needed to help them by working in the fields or watching my brothers and sisters. When I work picking pickles, my back hurts, and my fingers bleed and sting from the pesticides.

Then when the pickles finished, my mom and dad worked in the tomatoes. When the tomatoes are done, my dad works in the sugarbeets. My mom stays home, and my sisters and I go to school. My dad works at 5:00 A.M. and comes home at 1:00 A.M. Sometimes I don't get to see him for up to 4 days. Then when the sugarbeets finish, we go back to Texas and return to Ohio around May 1, and start the season all over again. It's very hard work.

Students like Erika, whose family members travel from state to state to pick the ripening crops, make up one group of culturally and linguistically diverse students who live in rural areas—the children of migrant workers (Greenhouse, 2002; Shafer, 2001). Because of the migrant lifestyle, these students experience many challenges in school. Entering new schools, learning a new language, making new friends, adjusting to new cultural and school expectations, being taught with different instructional techniques and materials, and meeting different graduation requirements are some of these difficulties. As they move from location to location, migrant students and their families face isolation and economic, cultural, and social discrimination (Thompson & Wiggins, 2002). Poor sanitation in the fields and work camp facilities; overcrowded, substandard housing and poor diets; exposure to pesticides and other hazards of agricultural work (particularly harmful to pregnant women and young children); limited health care; and low wages make migrant youth particularly vulnerable to health conditions and poor performance in schools (Fuentes, 2001; Strong & Maralani, 1998). As we saw in the case of Erika, migrant students often work in the fields to help support their families, watch their younger siblings while their parents are working, and serve as the link between their families and societal institutions such as schools (Davis, 1997; Greenhouse, 2002).

You can help improve the school adjustment and performance of migrant students in a variety of ways (These strategies also can be used with other mobile families such as children of military personnel and children whose families are undergoing changes). You can welcome and orient them to your class, and assign classroom buddies and mentors to help them. You can also acknowledge their strengths and unique experiences, promote their self-esteem, reach out to their families, and involve them in extracurricular activities. When they are getting ready to move, you can provide their families with a portfolio of their children's work and a checklist of school-related documents they should bring with them so that they can facilitate their child's adjustment to their new school. Educationally, you can assess their academic, health, and social adjustment needs; collaborate with migrant and bilingual educators to address these needs; and in-

IDEAS FOR IMPLEMENTATION

Helping Homeless Students and Students from Lower Socioeconomic Backgrounds Succeed in Inclusive Classrooms

Ms. Charles has several students in her classroom from households with limited financial resources, including one student, Thomas, who is homeless. She started a supply closet to help Thomas, but it has helped other students as well.

Ms. Charles persuaded several groups to donate to the supply closet. The local grocery store contributed snacks, the local social service agency gave her clothes, and the Student Association at the local college provided school supplies. Ms. Charles keeps these items in a closet, and when students like Thomas don't have something they need, she supplies it quickly and quietly.

"I think it's really working," she notes. "I've noticed that Thomas is coming to school more, feeling better about himself, and interacting with others more, particularly at snack time." Ms. Charles shared these insights with her principal, who said that the school district would pay for Thomas to go on field trips.

Here are some other ideas you can use to create an inclusive and supportive classroom for homeless students and students from lower socioeconomic backgrounds:

- Learn about your students' home lives, and school and community resources addressing students and families living in poverty.
- Be aware of signs of economic difficulties such wearing the same clothes, being late to school, wanting to stay in school rather than go home, not having school supplies, not completing homework, and not having notes signed by family members.
- Encourage and foster resiliency in students by providing them with opportunities to perform activities that allow them to display their abilities, work with and assist others, and interact with mentors.

- Give students some control over their learning. For example, allow students to choose the order in which they complete assignments.
- Create a positive, safe, accepting, caring, and structured learning environment.
- Help students and their families to complete forms, such as those necessary for the student to receive school breakfast and school lunch.
- Collaborate and communicate with administrators, social workers, and personnel from shelters and local agencies.
- Use school resources to address students' needs. For example, showers in the school's gymnasium can be made discreetly available to students whose homes lack such facilities.
- Provide students with a personal study space in the classroom that is labeled with the student's name, decorated by the student, or personalized by a special symbol selected by the student.
- Give students a feeling of accomplishment by breaking assignments into smaller, more manageable segments.
- Understand that students may have particular difficulties completing homework and assignments that require economic resources and offer help and alternatives such as borrowing a laptop computer, or doing the work in school with a peer or under your supervision.
- Encourage students to be involved in extracurricular activities.

Note: Holloway (2003); Park, Turnbull, & Turnbull (2002).

clude their experiences and cultural backgrounds in the curriculum (Kindler, 1995; Menchaca & Ruiz-Escalante, 1995; Quinn, 2001). For example, some teachers incorporate the experiences of migrant workers into their math and English classes by using word problems that ask students to calculate the miles traveled by migrant families or to estimate a fair wage based on the number of buckets of produce they have picked (Johanneson, 1999), and reading and writing assignments about their lives and family members (Shafer, 2001). Additional strategies and resources for bringing the experiences of migrant students into your classroom and helping others learn about the migrant lifestyle are presented in Chapter 5.

Resource

A national migrant hotline (800-234-8848) is available to help migrant families and Martinez and Velazquez (2000) offer suggestions for involving migrant families in the educational process.

It is also important for you to work with others to overcome the barriers that prevent family members of migrant children from being involved in their children's education (Martinez & Velazquez, 2000). Some successful ways that schools have involved migrant families include working with migrant educators, holding events that are culturally appealing, using interpreters and translators, providing a welcoming environment, acknowledging family involvement and its impact on their children's education, and offering educational and vocational services for families and community members (e.g., informational sessions and courses on learning English, obtaining citizenship and a high school diploma, applying for college, employment opportunities and training, and family education) (Lopez, Scribner, Mahitivanichcha, 2001). We will learn about other ways to collaborate and communicate with families in Chapter 4.

Set Your Sites

For more information on migrant students and their families, go to the Web Links module in Chapter 3 of the Companion Website.

Because migrant families travel within and between states, you also need to be aware of the programs available to address the needs of migrant students and their families and promote cooperation among teachers (Lopez, Scribner, & Mahitivanichcha, 2001). For example, migrant High School Equivalency Programs (HEP) provide a variety of services to help migrant teenagers graduate from high school. The Portable Assisted Study Sequence (PASS) addresses the high dropout rate among migrant students related to the loss of credits because of frequent travel and high absenteeism; it allows them to complete self-directed courses with teacher monitoring as they travel with their families. Once migrant students graduate, they also may participate in a College Assistance Migrant Program (CAMP), which offers a comprehensive array of services to help them succeed in college. You can obtain more information about these and other programs for migrant students by contacting your local migrant education center or your state director of migrant education.

Native Americans.   Many of the more than 1.5 million Native Americans reside in remote rural areas. Because of their high unemployment and poverty rates, language differences and limited access to health care, Native American youth often experience challenges that affect their educational performance and school completion (Belluck, 2000; Garrett, Bellon-Harn, Torres-Rivera, Garrett, & Roberts, 2003).

As with other students, you can promote their school success by holding high expectations for them, and using culturally sensitive strategies to collaborate and communicate with their families (Belluck, 2000; Brownell & Walther-Thomas, 2000). Diversifying your curriculum to address their cultural, experiential, and linguistic backgrounds and to counter negative and stereotypical portrayals of Native Americans can help them succeed in your classroom and enhance the education of *all students* (Sparks, 2000a). You can also assist these students by learning about and respecting their cultural, historical, and language backgrounds and understanding how they affect their learning and your educational goals for them. For example, you can:

Resources

Garrett et al. (2003), Sparks (2000a, 2000b) and Swisher and Tippiconnic (1999) offer guidelines for learning about Native American learners, teaching them, and involving their elders in the classroom and school.

- use modeling, demonstration, and hands-on learning techniques.
- supplement oral instruction with use of visuals including Native American images.
- employ flexible timing for completing assignments.
- offer activities that ask students to work cooperatively.
- understand that some students may not feel comfortable being "spotlighted" in front of the class.
- provide real-life examples to explain key points.
- allow students time to practice a task, skill, or activity.
- involve family, elders, and community groups.
- offer a range of ways for students to demonstrate mastery (Garrett et al., 2003; Sparks, 2000a; Swisher & Tippiconnic, 1999).

Set Your Sites

For more information on Native American students, go to the Web Links module in Chapter 3 of the Companion Website.

Suburban Poverty

Even though we often think that the suburbs are affluent, many people from lower socioeconomic backgrounds also live there (Hodgkinson, 2001). Therefore, as a teacher in the suburbs, you also are likely to teach students struggling to deal with poverty. You also will have many students from culturally and linguistically diverse backgrounds in your classroom, and encounter communities that are dealing with increased poverty, crime, segregation, racial divisions, acquired immunodeficiency syndrome, homelessness, and unemployment.

Wealthy Children.   Affluence also has an impact on the educational, social, and behavioral development of children. Brown (2000) notes that wealth can produce psychological and emotional challenges such as a sense of entitlement, a perception of one's self-esteem in terms of wealth, and a desire to have the newest and the best of everything. Baldwin (1989) uses the term *cornucopia kids* to describe wealthy children "who grow up with expectations (based on years of experience in the home) that the good life will always be available for the asking whether they develop personal accountability and achievement motivation or not" (p. 31). Baldwin notes that these children expect the best and the most expensive, demand constant stimulation, have difficulty completing projects, often form superficial relationships, fail to develop a sense of compassion for others, take little responsibility for personal property, mislead others when confronted with a demanding situation, and are present- and pleasure-oriented. As a result of being insulated from challenge, risk, and consequence, these youth may be underachievers in school; may suffer from boredom, low self-esteem, and a lack of motivation; and may be susceptible to poor school performance, teenage sex, and substance abuse.

How Have Demographic Shifts Affected Students and Schools?

There have been dramatic changes in the population of the United States, which has become a far more culturally and linguistically diverse country (Hodgkinson, 2001). Since 1980, the U.S. population has grown at the rate of approximately 9 percent per year, with a significant increase in the Asian and Pacific Islander, Hispanic, and Native American populations (Holmes, 1998; Schmitt, 2001a).

While many of these groups share common traits, variety characterizes the U.S. population. For instance, there are more than 300 independent Native American groups, with different beliefs, customs, traditions, and languages. Similarly, although some Asian and Pacific Islander groups may hold some common beliefs, they come from more than 25 different countries with unique languages, religions, and customs. Hispanic groups speak different dialects of a common language, and each group's identity is based on separate beliefs, traditions, histories, and social institutions.

Population projections suggest that school-age children of color and native speakers of languages other than English now constitute 36 percent of U.S. students, with 46 percent in 2020 (Banks & Banks, 2001). Currently, these students either make up or approach the majority of students in many urban school districts, and students whose first language is not English make up the fastest growing group of students in schools (Collier & Thomas, 2002). Culturally and linguistically diverse students are likely to experience conflicts because schools are not sensitive to their culture, language, family background, and learning styles (Baca & Cervantes, 1998).

Resources

Hodgkinson (2001) offers educational demographic information and suggestions for using this information to support student learning.

Set Your Sites

For more information on demographic changes, go to the Web Links module in Chapter 3 of the Companion Website.

Immigration

A significant factor in the U.S. population changes and the makeup of schools is immigration, with foreign-born adults and children being at an all time high (Clemetson, 2003b; Scott, 2002). Children of immigrants make up approximately 20 percent of the children in the United States. Many immigrants go through a series of stages as they struggle to adjust to their new country (Collier, 1996; Igoa, 1995). Initially, they may be curious as they encounter a new language and culture. Afterward, however, many immigrants may experience shock, depression, and confusion. They also may show signs of anxiety, withdrawal, fatigue, distractibility, and disorientation, which may reveal itself through culture-bound syndromes (Kershaw, 2003). In the final stage, they either assimilate and give up the cultural values of their homeland to become part of the mainstream culture or they become part of the dominant culture while maintaining their own cultural values and traditions.

Students Who Are Immigrants

Resource

McBrien (2003) offers strategies for supporting and teaching students who are refugees.

A growing number of immigrant students are refugees like Halee, the student we met at the beginning of this chapter, who left their countries to escape political, religious, or racial repression, or to have better economic opportunities (McBrien, 2003). Like Halee, to reach their new country, many of these students endure a long, difficult, and life-threatening journey characterized by malnutrition, disease, torture, and fear (LeDuff, 2001), and it is important for you to learn about and try to understand their immigration experiences. Once they arrive, they must cope with a type of post-traumatic stress disorder as a result of witnessing atrocities and torture, experiencing losses, and attempting to adjust to a new society. In school, they often encounter racial tension and rejection from peers that takes the form of physical attacks (fights, robberies, and so on), mimicking, and verbal harassment. Immigrant youth also may fear authority figures such as the principal because the child or a family member has an undocumented status. As a result, these youth may be reluctant to make friends with others, to seek help from and interactions with professionals, to attempt to gain recognition or excel in programs, or to draw attention to themselves.

Students who are immigrants face many difficulties as they enter and progress through school (see Figure 3.2). As a result, they are often placed in special education by mistake or not promoted. You can promote the education of students who are immigrants in a variety of ways. You can try to learn some vocabulary from their native language so that you can communicate with them and show them that you value them and their language. You also can bring their culture and experiences into your classroom by giving them opportunities to tell their stories through narratives, role playing, and bibliotherapy, using media in their native language, and encouraging them to do projects using materials in their native language. You can also help these students adjust to their new culture and language by offering them language enrichment programs, using nonverbal teaching methods such as music, dance, and art, and teaching them about their new culture.

Socially, you can assist these students by using peers and community members as a resource, encouraging these students to participate in culturally sensitive in-school and extracurricular activities, and inviting them to join peer discussion and support groups related to their interests and experiences. It is also important to involve parents, extended family members, and knowledgeable community members in the student's educational program. Finally, you can provide students and their families with materials containing information about the school and about their rights written in their own language.

FIGURE 3.2

Difficulties facing students who are immigrants

Students who are immigrants are likely to encounter several problems, including the following:

- ◈ Learning a new language that differs from their native language in terms of articulation, syntax, and graphic features
- ◈ Adjusting to a new culture that values and interprets behavior in different ways
- ◈ Obtaining access to health care that addresses their needs, such as mental health services to help them deal with their experiences of being tortured or seeing their relatives and friends tortured, raped, and executed
- ◈ Experiencing guilt as a result of their survival and concern about leaving others behind
- ◈ Facing economic pressures to work to support their family in the United States and family members in their native country
- ◈ Coping with sociocultural and peer expectations, such as self-hatred and youth gangs
- ◈ Dealing with cross-cultural and intergenerational conflicts and post-traumatic stress disorder
- ◈ Being targets of racism, violence, and harassment
- ◈ Developing a positive identity and self-concept
- ◈ Entering school with little, occasional, or no schooling in their native countries
- ◈ Being unfamiliar with schools in America
- ◈ Lacking school records and hiding relevant facts in order to avoid embarrassment, seek peer acceptance, and promote self-esteem
- ◈ Having to serve as cultural and language interpreters for their families

Note: Harris (1991).

Educational Rights of Students Who Are Immigrants

It is also important for you to be aware of the educational rights of students who are immigrants. As a result of the Supreme Court decision in *Plyler* v. *Doe* (1982), all undocumented students have the same right as U.S. citizens to attend public schools. School personnel cannot take actions or establish policies that deny students access to public schools, and they have no legal obligation to implement immigration laws. Schools cannot prevent these students from attending school based on their undocumented status, nor can they treat these students in a different way when identifying their residency. School personnel cannot engage in activities that may intimidate or threaten students and their families based on their immigration status, such as allowing Immigration and Naturalization Service (INS) personnel to enter or remain near the school or requiring students or their families to identify their immigration status. They may not inquire about the immigration status of students or their families; ask students to provide Social Security numbers, which may indicate their immigration status; or give the immigration status information contained in a student's school file to outside agencies without the families' permission. **For an update on legal issues related to immigrant students and other topics discussed in this chapter, go to the Legal Update module in Chapter 3 of the Companion Website.**

Reflective

Rosibel and her family arrived in the United States several months ago. After Rosibel applied to participate in the free lunch program, the principal asked you to obtain her Social Security number. As Rosibel's teacher, what would you do? (Developed by Elizabeth Sealey.)

Set Your Sites

For more information on the needs of immigrant students and their families, go to the Web Links module in Chapter 3 of the Companion Website.

Bilingual Education

Effective bilingual education programs employ both the native and the new language and culture of students to teach them. As students acquire English language skills, more and more of the curriculum is taught in English. In addition to teaching English, bilingual education programs help students maintain their first language, and pride in their cultural backgrounds. Many students who are immigrants may be eligible for bilingual education services under the Bilingual Education Act. This act established guidelines and funding to encourage school districts to employ bilingual education practices to teach students who speak languages other than English.

Research indicates that many second language learners improve their cognitive and sociocultural development, academic progress, self-esteem, and learning of English in bilingual education programs (Collier & Thomas, 2002; Portes, 2002). When students are taught in their first language, they develop essential background knowledge. This makes it easier for them to learn a second language and read, write, and perform academically in English. In comprehensive longitudinal studies, Thomas and Collier (1997) and Ramirez (1992) found that bilingual education does not prevent students from learning English language skills, and it helps students catch up to and/or outperform their English-speaking counterparts in English and other areas of the curriculum. Bilingual education also allows second language learners to keep up with their English-speaking peers in learning the content of the general education curriculum (science, social studies, mathematics, and so on). Studies also show that students who received English-only instruction lag behind their peers who attend a bilingual education program (Portes, 2002). Finally, with bilingual education, these students have higher levels of self-esteem and academic aspirations and can continue to communicate with their family and community members in their native language (Portes, 2002).

Second language learning also has personal, cognitive, cultural, and societal benefits (Met, 2001; Portes, 2002). Personally, second language learning offers students greater access to other individuals, resources, and employment opportunities, as well as a greater understanding of their heritage and cultural diversity. It also can promote greater family cohesion as children still retain their first language and use it to communicate with their families. Cognitively, learning a second language helps students improve their reading and problem-solving skills and promotes their creativity. In terms of societal benefits, individuals who speak more than one language can increase the economic competitiveness of the United States.

Two-Way Bilingual Education Programs.   One integrated example of a bilingual education program is a *two-way program* that mixes students who speak languages other than English with students who speak English (Calderon & Minaya-Rowe, 2003; Thomas & Collier, 2003). These dual language programs seek to help *all students* develop proficiency in both languages, as well as an understanding of different cultures. One language at a time is used to deliver instruction, but content is taught in each language approximately 50 percent of the time.

Resource

Calderon and Minaya-Rowe (2003) offer information and resources for designing and implementing two-way bilingual education programs.

Reflective

If you moved to another country that had a different language and culture when you were in fourth grade, what aspects of school would be difficult for you? Would you want to receive your academic instruction in English or the language of your new country?

Set Your Sites

For more information on second language learners, go to the Web Links module in Chapter 3 of the Companion Website.

Research indicates that many second language learners will benefit in terms of academic progress and acquisition of English skills from bilingual education programs. How could all students benefit from a bilingual education?

English as a Second Language.   A program that can be a component of or an alternative to a bilingual education program is instruction in English as a second language (ESL), sometimes referred to as English to Speakers of Other Languages (ESOL). ESL is usually a pull-out program that uses the students' native culture and language to develop their skills in understanding, speaking, reading, and writing English. In ESL programs, content instruction and communication occur only in English. Additional information about ESL professionals and techniques is provided in Chapters 4 and 8.

Resource

Collier and Thomas (2002) provide a summary of the research on ESL and bilingual education programs.

What Are the Educational Strengths and Needs of Students from Culturally and Linguistically Diverse Backgrounds?

A growing number of students attending schools in the United States are students from culturally and linguistically diverse backgrounds. Data on the educational performance of these students indicate that they are achieving below their potential and at a level that is not commensurate with their white peers (ERIC Clearinghouse on Urban Education, 2001; Rolon, 2003). These data interact with a variety of other factors to result in a disproportionate number of these students being inappropriately served in special education programs, and failing to complete school and attend postsecondary education (Alson, 2003; Chubb & Loveless, 2002).

Assessment materials and procedures should be selected and used so that they do not discriminate racially and culturally and so that a student is not found to have a disability due to language difficulties. However, research indicates that standardized tests *are* culturally and socially biased (Hilliard, 2000). As a result, a disproportionate number of students from culturally and linguistically diverse backgrounds are misclassified as having disabilities. Because of having had this problem in the past, some school districts are now underidentifying these students in terms of their needs for special education. Therefore, when designing programs targeting the academic and behavioral needs of students, educators need to build upon students' strengths and be aware of the cultural, linguistic, and economic factors that affect both themselves and their students.

Cultural Considerations

Our schools—and therefore the academic and social expectations for our students—are based on mainstream, middle-class culture. It is important to be aware of this potential cultural mismatch and bias and its effects on your students' academic performance and cultural identities. It also is important for you to understand your students' different backgrounds, and respect and accommodate their similarities and differences. You can do this by using culturally relevant teaching so that your instructional strategies and curricula reflect the different cultures, experiences, and languages of your students. You also need to reflect upon how cultural assumptions and values influence your own expectations, beliefs, and behaviors, as well as those of your students, other professionals, families, and community members (Edgar, Patton, & Day-Vines, 2002). It is also important for you to develop cultural competence and intercultural communication skills so that you can support your students' cultural identities, and establish collaborative partnerships with them and with family and community members (Yeh & Drost, 2002). (We will learn more about culturally relevant teaching and ways to develop your cultural competence and your students' cultural identities in subsequent chapters of this book.)

Reflective

How have your cultural, linguistic, and ethnic identities affected you? Advantaged and disadvantaged you in society?

Resource

Edgar, Patton, and Day-Vines (2002) offer suggestions for developing cultural competence.

Learning Style

Because cultural differences also affect the way individuals process, organize, and learn material, you need to observe students and adjust your teaching behaviors to identify and match the diverse learning styles of your students. Irvine (1991) notes that many students from nondominant cultures use a learning style based on variation, movement, divergent thinking, inductive reasoning, and an emphasis on people. Gilbert and Gay (1989) provide the following example to show how the stage-setting behaviors of some African American students may be misinterpreted by teachers:

> Stage setting behaviors may include such activities as looking over the assignment in its entirety; rearranging posture; elaborately checking pencils, paper, and writing space; asking teachers to repeat directions that have just been given; and checking perceptions of neighboring students. To the black student these are necessary maneuvers in preparing for performance; to the teacher they may appear to be avoidance tactics, inattentiveness, disruptions, or evidence of not being prepared to do the assigned task. (p. 277)

Another factor that affects how classrooms are structured and how students function is the way activities and classroom interactions are ordered (Cloud & Landurand, n.d.). In polychronic cultures, individuals engage in many different activities at the same time. For example, students from polychronic cultures may talk with others while doing seatwork, whereas those from monochronic cultures may prefer to work without talking.

Researchers also have found cross-cultural differences in movement (Cloud & Landurand, n.d.). Students who are used to being active may have difficulties in classrooms where movement is limited. These differences also can influence the teacher's perception of a student's academic and behavioral performance. Other cultural factors that may affect classroom behavior are discussed in Chapter 7.

Reflective

How has your cultural background affected your learning style? Your teaching and communication style?

Linguistic Considerations

Students' ability to use language has a great effect on their educational performance. The number of students who are learning English is growing much faster than the overall student population, nearly doubling in the last twenty years (Lewin, 2001). Because these students often have the usual difficulties associated with learning a second language, such as poor understanding, limited vocabulary, grammatical and syntactical mistakes, and articulation difficulties, they tend to be over-referred for special education. If they are placed in special education classes, these students often receive little support in their native language, which can hurt their linguistic and academic development. Therefore, since students should not be identified as having a disability based on limited English proficiency, you and other members of the comprehensive planning team must be able to understand the behaviors of second language learners that resemble those of students with learning, speech, and language disabilities so that second language learners are not inappropriately placed in special education. These behaviors are presented in Table 3.1.

How Can I Differentiate Cultural and Language Differences from Learning Difficulties?

As we discussed earlier in this chapter, students like Halee who are learning a second language and students with high incidence disabilities often exhibit similar learning, attention,

TABLE 3.1 | Characteristics of second language learners resembling those of students with learning disabilities

Characteristics of Students with Learning Disabilities	Characteristics of Second Language Learners
Significant difference between the student's performance on verbal and nonverbal tasks and test items	May have more success in completing nonverbal tasks than verbal tasks
Difficulty mastering academic material	May have difficulty learning academic material that is abstract or taken out of context
Language difficulties	May have language difficulties that are a normal part of second language learning, such as poor comprehension, limited vocabulary, articulation problems, and grammatical and syntactical errors
Perceptual difficulties	May have perceptual difficulties related to learning a new language and adjusting to a new culture
Social, behavioral, and emotional difficulties	May experience social, behavioral, and emotional difficulties as part of the frustration of learning a new language and adjusting to a new culture
Attention and memory difficulties	May have attention and memory problems because it is difficult to concentrate for long periods of time when teaching is done in a new language.

Note: Fradd & Weismantel (1989); Mercer (1987).

social, behavioral, and emotional difficulties. As a result, educators are being challenged to work with comprehensive planning teams to conduct meaningful assessments and determine appropriate educational programs for students whose primary language is not English (Salend & Salinas, 2003). In assessing second language learners, it is also important for the team to recognize that students should not be identified as having a disability if their eligibility and school-related difficulties are based on their proficiency in English or their lack of opportunity to receive instruction in reading or mathematics. The following sections offer guidelines for more accurately and fairly assessing second language learners to differentiate learning difficulties from language differences.

Diversify the Comprehensive Planning Team and Offer Training

The composition and training of the comprehensive planning team are critical factors in determining the educational strengths and needs of second language learners (Ochoa, Robles-Pina, Garcia, & Breunig 1999). Therefore, the team should include family and community members, as well as professionals who are fluent in the student's native language (e.g., bilingual educators), understand the student and the family's culture, and can help collect and interpret the data in culturally and linguistically appropriate ways. The inclusion of these individuals allows the team to learn about the family's and the student's cultural perspective and experiential and linguistic background, and to assist in the determination of the origins of the student's learning difficulties. They can help determine whether students' learning difficulties can be explained by cultural perspectives, experiential factors, and linguistic variables.

Compare Student Performance in Both the Primary and Secondary Languages

The assessment plan for second language learners should collect data to compare student performance in both the primary and secondary languages (Salend & Salinas, 2003). Data relating to students' performance in both languages can be collected through the use of informal and standardized tests, language samples, observations, questionnaires, and interviews. These methods can be employed to examine students' language proficiency, language dominance, language preference, and code switching (Goh, 2004). *Language proficiency* relates to the degree of skill in speaking the language(s) and includes receptive and expressive language skills. While proficiency in one language does not necessarily mean lack of proficiency in another language, *language dominance* refers to the language in which the student is most fluent and implies a comparison of the student's abilities in two or more languages. *Language preference* identifies the language in which the student prefers to communicate, which can vary depending on the setting. *Code switching*, a phenomena commonly observed in individuals learning a second language, relates to using words, phrases, expressions and sentences from one language while speaking another language (Brice & Roseberry-McKibbin, 2001).

Consider the Processes and Factors Associated with Second Language Acquisition

The assessment process for second language learners like Halee should recognize that learning a second language is a long-term, complex, and dynamic process that involves different types of language skills and various stages of development. Therefore, when assessing second language learners, the team needs to consider the factors that affect second language acquisition, and understand the stages students go through in learning a second language.

Gaining proficiency in a second language involves the acquisition of two distinct types of language skills. *Basic interpersonal communication skills* (BICS) are the social language skills that guide students in developing of social relationships and engaging in casual face-to-face conversations (e.g., Good morning. How are you?). Even though they are relatively repetitive, occur within a specific and clearly defined context, and are not cognitively demanding, research indicates that they typically take up to 2 years to develop in a second language (Cummins, 1989). *Cognitive/academic language proficiency* (CALP) refers to the

Why is it important for you to understand the stages students go through in learning a second language and adjusting to a new culture?

Stages of second language learning

FIGURE 3.3

In learning a second language, some students may go through the following stages:

◇ *Preproduction or Silent period.* Students focus on processing and understanding what they hear but avoid verbal responses. They often rely on modeling, visual stimuli, context clues, and key words, and use listening strategies to understand meaning. They often communicate by pointing and physical gestures. They may benefit from classroom activities that allow them to respond by imitating, drawing, pointing, and matching.

◇ *Telegraphic or Early Production period.* Students begin to use two- or three-word sentences and show limited comprehension. They usually have a receptive vocabulary of approximately 1,000 words and an expressive vocabulary of approximately 100 words. They may benefit from classroom activities that employ language they can understand; require them to name, label, and group objects; ask them to respond to simple questions and use vocabulary they already understand; and offer praise and encouragement for their attempts to use their new language.

◇ *Interlanguage and Intermediate Fluency period.* Students use longer phrases and start to use complete sentences. They often mix basic phrases and sentences in both languages. They may benefit from classroom activities that encourage them to experiment with language and develop and expand their vocabulary.

◇ *Extensions and Expansions period.* Students expand on their basic sentences and extend their language abilities to synonyms and synonymous expressions. At this stage, they are developing good comprehension skills, using more complex sentence structures, and making fewer errors when speaking. They may benefit from classroom reading and writing activities, as well as from instruction that expands on their vocabulary and knowledge of grammar.

◇ *Enrichment period.* Students are taught learning strategies to assist them in making the transition to the new language.

◇ *Independent Learning period.* Students begin to work on activities at various levels of difficulty with different groups.

Note: Maldonado-Colon (1995).

language skills that relate to literacy, cognitive development, and academic development in the classroom. It includes understanding such complex academic terms as photosynthesis, onomatopoeia, and least common denominator. Because CALP does not have an easily understood context, and tends to be cognitively demanding, it often takes up to 7 years to develop and use these language skills. Since CALP skills developed in one's first language foster the development of CALP in one's second language, it is important to gather information on students' proficiency and educational training in their native language.

In learning a second language, students also go through developmental stages (see Figure 3.3) that should be considered when evaluating their learning. Initially, second language learners' understanding of the new language is usually greater than their production. Many second language learners go through a *silent period* in which they process what they hear but refrain from verbalizing. This is often misinterpreted as indicating a lack of cognitive abilities, disinterest in school, or shyness.

When students are ready to attempt to speak a new language, their verbalizations are usually single words such as "yes" or "no" or recurring phrases such as "How are you?" and "Thank you." Once students are ready to speak their new language, their verbalizations gradually increase in terms of their semantic and syntactic complexity. You can help students who are ready to speak by creating a risk-free environment, focusing on communication rather than grammar, providing visual cues and physical gestures that offer students a context for understanding verbal comments, and acknowledging and responding to their attempts to communicate (Fueyo, 1997).

It also is important for the team to be aware of other factors that may affect students and their developmental progress in maintaining their native language and learning their new language such as age, educational background, and language exposure. Therefore, keep the following in mind:

• Students who have been educated in their native language often progress faster in learning a new language that those who have not had a formal education (Collier & Thomas, 2002).

- It also is very common for students to attempt to apply the rules of their first language to their second language, which can affect students' pronunciation (e.g., students say *share* for *chair*), syntax (e.g., in Spanish, adjectives follow the noun and agree with the gender and number of the noun), and spelling (Tiedt & Tiedt, 2002).
- As some students learn a second language, they may experience language loss in their native language (Schiff-Myers, Djukic, McGovern-Lawler, & Perez, 1993).
- Children who simultaneously learn two languages from birth may initially experience some temporary language delays in achieving developmental language milestones and some language mixing, which tends to disappear over time (Fierro-Cobas & Chan, 2001).

Employ Alternatives to Traditional Standardized Testing

Rather than relying solely on potentially biased, standardized tests, the team can employ a variety of alternative assessment procedures to assess students from culturally and linguistically diverse backgrounds accurately (Langdon, 2002). Such assessment alternatives, which we will learn about in Chapter 12, include performance-based and portfolio assessment, curriculum-based measurements, instructional rubrics, dynamic assessment, student journals and learning logs, and self-evaluation techniques. These assessment alternatives can provide the team with more complete profiles of students like Halee including their academic strengths and needs, learning styles, and the impact of the school environment on their learning.

Identify Diverse Life and Home Experiences That Might Affect Learning and Language Development

Many second language learners have diverse life experiences that can have a significant impact on their learning and language development, such as being separated from family members for extended periods of time (Abrams, Ferguson, & Laud, 2001). Students' home environments also can affect their language acquisition including the language(s) that students are exposed to in their homes and communities (Langdon, 2002). Identifying these experiences and factors can help determine if students' learning and language difficulties are related to the existence of a disability or other experiential factors. Therefore, you and other professionals can use the guidelines in Figure 3.4 to collect information to determine if a student's difficulties in learning are due to language, cultural, and experiential factors or lack of exposure to effective instruction. They team also should consider the effect of the student's motivation, personality, and social skills on school performance.

Analyze the Data and Develop an Appropriate Educational Plan

After the data have been collected, the team analyzes the information and makes decisions about students' educational programs (Salend & Salinas, 2003). For second language learners, the analysis should focus on examining the factors that affect learning and lan-

FIGURE 3.4

Life experience factors and questions to consider in assessing second language learners

LENGTH OF RESIDENCE IN THE UNITED STATES

- How long and for what periods of time has the student lived in the United States?
- What were the conditions and events associated with the student's migration?
- If the student was born in the United States, what has been the student's exposure to English?

Students may have limited or interrupted exposure to English, resulting in poor vocabulary, slow naming speed, and minimal verbal participation. Being born and raised in the United States does not guarantee that students have developed English skills and have had significant exposure to English and the U.S. culture.

SCHOOL ATTENDANCE PATTERNS

- How long has the student been in school?
- What is the student's attendance pattern? Have there been any disruptions in school?

Students may fail to learn language skills because they do not attend school.

SCHOOL INSTRUCTIONAL HISTORY

- How many years of schooling did the student complete in the native country?
- What language(s) were used to guide teaching in the native country?
- What types of classrooms has the student attended (bilingual education, English as a second language, general education, speech/language therapy services, special education)?
- What has been the language of instruction in these classes?
- How proficient is the student in reading, writing, and speaking in the native language?
- What strategies and teaching materials have been successful?
- What were the outcomes of these educational placements?
- What language does the student prefer to use in informal situations with adults? In formal situations with adults?

Students may not have had access to appropriate instruction and curricula, resulting in problems in language learning, reading, and mathematics.

CULTURAL BACKGROUND

- How does the student's cultural background affect second language learning?
- Has the student had enough time to adjust to the new culture?
- What is the student's acculturation level?
- Does the student want to learn English?

Since culture and language are closely linked, lack of progress in learning a second language can be due to cultural and communication differences and/or lack of exposure to the new culture. For example, some cultures rely on body language as a substitute for verbal communication. Various cultures also have different perspectives on color, time, gender, distance, and space, which can affect language.

PERFORMANCE IN COMPARISON WITH PEERS

- Does the student's language skill, learning rate, and learning style differ from those of other students from similar experiential, cultural, and language backgrounds?
- Does the student interact with peers in the primary language and/or English?
- Does the student have difficulty following directions, understanding language, and expressing thoughts in the primary language? In the second language?

The student's performance can be compared with that of students who have similar traits rather than with that of students whose experiences in learning a second language are very different.

(continued)

127

Figure 3.4 (continued)

HOME LIFE

◆ What language(s) or dialect(s) are spoken at home by each of the family members?

◆ What language(s) are spoken by the student's siblings?

◆ When did the student start to speak?

◆ Is the student's performance at home different from that of siblings?

◆ What language(s) or dialect(s) are spoken in the family's community?

◆ Is a distinction made among the uses of the primary language or dialect and English? If so, how is that distinction made? (For example, the non-English language is used at home, but children speak English when playing with peers.)

◆ What are the attitudes of the family and the community toward schooling, learning English, and bilingual education?

◆ In what language(s) does the family watch television, listen to the radio, and read newspapers, books, and magazines?

◆ What language does the student prefer to use at home and in the community?

◆ To what extent does the family interact with the dominant culture and in what ways?

◆ How comfortable are the student and the family in interacting with the dominant culture?

Important information on the student's language proficiency, dominance, and preference can be obtained by getting data from family members. The student's language learning can be improved by involving family members in the educational program.

HEALTH AND DEVELOPMENTAL HISTORY

◆ What health, medical, sensory, and developmental factors have affected the student's learning and language development?

A student's difficulty in learning language may be related to various health and developmental problems.

Note: Langdon, (1989).

guage development, determining whether learning and language difficulties occur in both languages, and developing an educational plan to promote learning and language acquisition. Damico (1991) offers questions that can guide you and others in examining the data to assess the extent to which students' diverse life experiences and cultural and linguistic backgrounds serve as explanations for the difficulties they may be experiencing in schools. These questions include the following:

1. What factors and conditions may explain the student's learning and/or language difficulties (e.g., stressful life events, lack of opportunity to learn, racism, acculturation, and experiential background)?

2. To what extent does the student demonstrate the same learning and/or language difficulties in community settings as in school and/or in the primary language?

3. To what extent are the student's learning and/or language difficulties due to normal second language acquisition, dialectical differences, or cultural factors?

4. Did bias occur prior to, during, and after assessment such as in the reliability, validity, and standardization of the test as well as with the skills and learning styles assessed?

5. To what extent were the student's cultural, linguistic, dialectic and experiential backgrounds considered in collecting and analyzing the assessment data (e.g., selection, administration, and interpretation of the test's results; prereferral strategies; learning styles; family involvement)?

These questions also can guide the team in differentiating between two types of second language learners, and planning appropriate educational programs for these students (Rice & Ortiz, 1994). One type of second language learner is like Halee. These students tend to have some proficiency in their native language. However, their skills in and difficulty in learning their new language are consistent with the typical stages of second language acquisition, and they need help to develop their skills in their new language. These students may benefit from an academically rich curriculum and appropriate instructional

FIGURE 3.5

Student behaviors to observe when distinguishing a language difference from a learning difficulty

Teachers can tell when a student from a linguistically and culturally diverse background might need special education services for a language-learning disability when some of the following behaviors are manifested in comparison with similar peers:

1. Nonverbal aspects of language are culturally inappropriate.
2. Student does not express basic needs adequately.
3. Student rarely initiates verbal interaction with peers.
4. When peers initiate interaction, student responds sporadically/inappropriately.
5. Student replaces speech with gestures, communicates nonverbally when talking would be appropriate and expected.
6. Peers give indications that they have difficulty understanding the student.
7. Student often gives inappropriate responses.
8. Student has difficulty conveying thoughts in an organized, sequential manner that is understandable to listeners.
9. Student shows poor topic maintenance ("skips around").
10. Student has word-finding difficulties that go beyond normal second language acquisition patterns.
11. Student fails to provide significant information to the listener, leaving the listener confused.
12. Student has difficulty with conversational turn-taking skills (may be too passive or may interrupt inappropriately).
13. Student perseverates (remains too long) on a topic even after the topic has changed.
14. Student fails to ask and answer questions appropriately.
15. Student needs to hear things repeated, even when they are stated simply and comprehensibly.
16. Student often echoes what she or he hears.

Source: From C. Roseberry-McKibbin, *Multicultural Education,* Summer 1995, p. 14. Reprinted by permission.

strategies that recognize and support their primary and secondary languages and cultural identity (Ortiz, 2001; Watson & Houtz, 2002).

The other type of second language learner has language, academic, and social behaviors in the first and second languages that are significantly below those of peers who have similar linguistic, cultural, and experiential backgrounds (Ortiz, 1997). In addition, these students may show some of the behaviors listed in Figure 3.5 both in school and at home. Further, assessment may show that they have not made satisfactory progress even with an appropriate curriculum and teaching provided by qualified educators for a long period of time. These students may have a disability and may benefit from a special education program and IEP that addresses their unique linguistic, cultural, experiential backgrounds, and learning strengths and needs. Strategies for differentiating instruction to support the learning of both types of second language learners are presented in Chapter 8.

What Are the Educational Strengths and Needs of Students Who Are Gifted and Talented?

Another group of students whose special needs are often overlooked are those who are gifted and talented (Stephens & Karnes, 2000). According to the Gifted and Talented Students Act of 1988, the federal government defines gifted and talented children as those "who give evidence of high performance capability in areas such as intellectual, creative, artistic, or leadership capacity, or in specific academic fields, and who require special services or activities not ordinarily provided by the school." These students may differ from their peers in terms of the speed at which they learn new material, the

REFLECTING ON PROFESSIONAL PRACTICES

Assessing Second Language Learners

Blanca moved to the United States from Chile and was placed in Ms. Ruger's class. She sat quietly in the back of the room and kept to herself. Whenever directions were given, she seemed lost and had difficulty completing tasks and participating in class discussions. During teacher-directed activities, Blanca often looked around at other students or played with materials at her desk.

Ms. Ruger was concerned about Blanca's inability to pay attention and complete her work. She would watch Blanca talk "a lot" (for Blanca) at recess with the other students but be quiet in class during academic instruction. Ms. Ruger felt that as a teacher she was doing something wrong, that she was intimidating Blanca.

She thought Blanca might have a learning problem and referred Blanca to the school's prereferral team. The prereferral team, which included Ms. Nilo, a bilingual special educator, began to work with other members of the team to gather information about Blanca. Although Blanca's school records were minimal and dated, Ms. Nilo was able to interpret them for the team and Ms. Ruger.

Ms. Nilo assessed Blanca's skills in Spanish. She reported that Blanca grasped concepts quickly when they were explained in Spanish and figured out grammatical patterns in English exercises when directions were explained to her. Blanca told Ms. Nilo that she hadn't read in Spanish for a long time. When she read in Spanish with Ms. Nilo, she was able to decode and comprehend what she read. Blanca could retell stories in her own words, predict sequences in stories, and answer comprehension questions accurately.

Ms. Nilo was also able to obtain information about Blanca's past by speaking to Blanca's mother in Spanish. Ms. Nilo reported that Blanca had not had an easy life. Her mother had come to the United States 10 years before and left Blanca as an infant with her grandmother. Ten years later, Blanca was finally reunited with her mother. Blanca joined her mother and a family of strangers, as Blanca's mother had remarried and had a second daughter, who was now 6 years old. Because she doesn't speak English, did not attend school, and works long hours to make ends meet, Blanca's mother finds it difficult to help Blanca with her schoolwork and relies on Blanca to help take care of the younger sister, and to cook and clean. Blanca's mother also told Ms. Nilo that although her children watch cartoons in English, the interactions in the home are in Spanish. Interactions with the family also revealed that the family has few links to and interactions with the community, and that their lifestyle parallels the traditions of her native country.

Other members of the prereferral team collected data on Blanca's English skills. One team member observed Blanca in her classroom, in the cafeteria, and during recess. The team met to share their findings and concluded that Blanca was beginning to learn English. They noted that Blanca was a capable student who was having many of the difficulties second language learners experience in learning a new language and adjusting to a new culture.

The team also discussed and identified ways to assist Ms. Ruger in understanding and meeting Blanca's needs. They helped Ms. Ruger understand that it is not uncommon for students like Blanca to appear to lose their concentration after about 10 minutes of instruction. They explained to Ms. Ruger that instruction delivered in the student's second language requires intense concentration, which is difficult for a second language learner to sustain for long periods of time. They said that Blanca's behavior was not a disability but rather an indication that her "system was shutting down" and that she needed a break. They also talked about learning a second language and how social language develops first, as well as the difficulties in learning the academic language used in the classroom.

Ms. Ruger seemed to understand and to feel better. Knowledge of Blanca's past gave her insights into the emotional side of Blanca. She worked with Ms. Nilo and others on the prereferral team to make instructional, content, and testing accommodations to address Blanca's strengths and needs.

- Why did Ms. Ruger refer Blanca for assessment?
- What strategies did the prereferral team use to collect information about Blanca?
- Why did the team conclude that Blanca did not qualify for special education services?
- What role did Ms. Nilo play?
- Why was it important for the prereferral team to include her?
- If you had a student like Blanca, what services do you think she would need to succeed in your class?
- What services would you need to help Blanca?

 To answer these questions online and share your responses with others, go to the Reflection module in Chapter 3 of the Companion Website.

depth of their mastery, and the topics that interest them (Johnson, 2000). Like all students, students who are gifted and talented differ in their strengths, interests, motivation, learning styles, and needs (Callahan, 2001). Some of them might be advanced in all academic areas, while others might excel in only one area, or struggle in some areas.

Traditional methods used to identify students who are gifted and talented have relied primarily on intelligence testing; however, many educators are now broadening the concepts of intelligence and talent (Stanford, 2003). For example, Gardner (1993) uses the framework of *multiple intelligences* to outline at least eight areas in which individuals may exhibit their intelligence and talent (Campbell, 1997). These areas are as follows:

Resource

Stanford (2003) offers instructional techniques, curricular accommodations and assessment strategies for use in inclusive classrooms that are based on the principles of multiple intelligences.

> *Verbal-linguistic.* Sensitivity to the sounds and functions of language and an ability to use language and express oneself verbally or in writing.
> *Logical-mathematical.* Ability to organize and solve numerical patterns, use logic, understand the principles of causal systems, and deal with the abstract.
> *Visual-spatial.* Ability to perceive the visual-spatial world accurately and to create and interpret visual experiences.
> *Musical.* Ability to produce, recognize, remember, and appreciate various forms of musical expression and a sense of rhythm, pitch, and melody.
> *Bodily-kinesthetic.* Ability to control one's physical movements and work skillfully with objects to solve problems, make something, or participate in a production.
> *Interpersonal.* Ability to understand and respond to the feelings, moods, and behaviors of others and to get along and work with others.
> *Intrapersonal.* Ability to understand one's own feelings, reactions, needs, and motivations, as well as one's strengths and weaknesses.
> *Naturalistic.* Ability to understand the environment and other parts of the natural environment.

Educators also are examining the concept of emotional intelligence, which involves understanding one's feelings and the feelings of others as well as the ability to use one's social and collaborative skills to establish and maintain relationships with others (Goleman, 1995; Shelton, 2000).

Resource

Obiakor (2001a) and Shelton (2000) offer guidelines, strategies, and resources for developing emotional intelligence in students.

Although educators tend to focus more often on the academic needs of students who are gifted and talented, these students often have unique social and emotional needs that should be addressed. Some of these students experience difficulties such as uneven development, resentment from peers, perfectionism and self-criticism, pressure to conform, avoidance of risks, and difficulty making friends or finding peers who have similar interests and abilities. Currently, the vast majority of students identified as gifted and talented are educated in general education classrooms. Like *all students*, these students can benefit from the use of the strategies and principles for creating inclusive classrooms presented in this book.

You can accommodate gifted and talented students in your classroom by providing all students with varied learning activities and multiple ways of demonstrating their understanding and mastery (Callahan, 2001; Willard-Holt, 2003). You can adapt your teaching program for them by presenting activities that actively engage students in directing their learning (Winebrenner, 2001). To do this, give students opportunities to select what they want to learn, the ways in which they want to learn it, and how they will demonstrate their learning. For example, students can be asked to select their own topics for cooperative learning groups, papers, presentations, and independent study assignments. You also can employ curriculum compacting, which involves allowing students who demonstrate mastery at the beginning of a unit of study to work on new and more challenging

Resource

Winebrenner (2001) and Callahan (2001) offer guidelines, strategies, and resources for teaching students identified as gifted and talented in inclusive classrooms, and Higgins and Boone (2003) offer suggestions for helping these students make transitions.

cd-rom

To view examples of a group of professionals addressing the inclusion of a student identified as gifted and talented, go to Case 3: Assess Plan on the CD-ROM, and view all of the video clips. What are the challenges that educators encounter in educating some students who are gifted and talented and what are some ways to address these challenges?

material or student-selected topics via alternate learning activities. They also can be given choices about whether to present their learning by telling a story; participating in a debate; writing a poem, story, or play; creating a video, song, artwork, or photo album; teaching another student; or reporting on a community-based project.

In addition, you can create a learning environment that encourages students to be creative, develop their strengths, take risks, and extend their learning (Johnson, 2000). For example, when learning to solve word problems, you can ask students to create their own word problems, and to explain their reasoning. In social studies, students can write journal entries from individuals who have opposite points of view on a specific issue or event. You also can ask students to respond to higher-level questions that allow them to justify and discuss their responses. Problem-based and discovery learning approaches can allow students to work on complex open-ended problems and issues that have multifaceted solutions. Participation in leadership, mentoring and service learning programs can also be used to motivate students and extend their learning and leadership skills (Higgins & Boone, 2003). It also is important for you to work with students and their families to help them to understand and commit to talent development, to set challenging learning goals, and to access school and community resources that foster students' talents and interests (Feldhusen, 2001). Additional ways to differentiate instruction to support the learning of students who are identified as gifted and talented are presented in subsequent chapters.

Resource

Sternberg (1996) offers strategies to promote creativity in the classroom.

Students with Special Needs Who Are Gifted and Talented

Resource

Willard-Holt (1999) offers guidelines in recognizing giftedness in students with disabilities.

Although we often think of students with disabilities as having learning difficulties, students with special needs, like Marty, the student we met at the beginning of Chapter 2, may also be identified as being gifted and talented (Willard-Holt, 1999; Winebrenner, 2003). Unfortunately, like other students who are gifted and talented, students with special needs who are gifted and talented are often overlooked and underserved (Flint, 2001).

The traditional method of identifying students who are gifted and talented underidentifies and underserves gifted and talented students who are from culturally and linguistically diverse or lower socioeconomic backgrounds, disabled, and female (Ford, 1998). To counter this potential bias, you can work with others in your school district to adopt an inclusive and culturally relevant concept of giftedness, use many different forms of assessment, and consider multiple perspectives when identifying the unique talents and learning needs of *all students* (Belcher & Fletcher-Carter, 1999; Sarouphim, 1999). For example, indicators of giftedness can be expanded to include coping with living in poverty, assuming adult roles in one's home, having a strong sense of self, speaking more than one language, and understanding one's cultural identity. The process for identifying students as gifted and talented also can be expanded by involving family and community members and peers in the assessment process, and using observations, interviews, self-identification, and portfolios (Schwartz, 1997).

In addition to broadening the identification process, educators can use a variety of strategies to differentiate instruction for students with special needs who are also gifted and talented (Robinson, 1999; Winebrenner, 2003). These strategies include the following:

Resource

Ford (2000) offers guidelines for infusing multicultural content into the curriculum for students identified as gifted and talented.

- employing assistive and instructional technology to allow students to perform based on their strengths
- infusing multicultural content into the curriculum

- providing tutorial support and mentors
- offering instruction in the use of learning strategies and self-management skills
- using flexible learning arrangements that allow *all students* to work in different groups
- collaborating with students to develop learning contracts that specify individualized learning goals, activities, timelines, and evaluation criteria
- providing students with choices and opportunities to work on assignments that require different learning styles

Set Your Sites

For more information on students who are gifted and talented, go to the Web Links module in Chapter 3 of the Companion Website.

What Is the Effect of Discrimination and Bias on Students and Schools?

Racial Discrimination

Students from specific racial, linguistic, and religious backgrounds face discrimination in society and school (Nieto, 2000). While this discrimination is displayed openly in verbal harassment and physical violence in society, it is more subtle in institutions such as schools, which are becoming more segregated. Orfield, Frankenberg, and Lee (2003) found that the segregation of white, African American, and Latino/a students from one another is growing at a significant rate. They found that:

- The typical white student attends a school that is 80 percent white.
- The typical African American student attends a school where students from culturally and linguistically diverse backgrounds make up 66 percent.
- The typical Latino/a student attends a school where more than half of the students are Latino/a.

Kozol (1991) and the Harvard Civil Rights Project (2001) compared schools that serve students who are from lower socioeconomic backgrounds and predominantly African American and Hispanic with schools that serve students who are wealthy and predominantly white. In addition to almost complete segregation, they found severe inequalities in funding, preschool opportunities, class sizes, physical facilities, resources, remedial services, instructional materials, textbooks, licensed teachers, technology, and expectations of student performance. These inequalities are the basis for different treatment and expectations in the classroom based on race and language background (Nieto, 2000).

Through subtle experiences at school, students internalize perceptions of themselves held by educators and other members of society (Taylor, 2003). Positive perceptions about an individual's race and identity can promote increased self-esteem and success in school, whereas negative attitudes can achieve the opposite results. Unfortunately, school curricula, teacher behaviors, assessment instruments, teaching materials and textbooks, family involvement procedures, and peer relationships usually address the academic and socialization needs of white middle-class students only (Nieto, 2003). As a result, students from lower socioeconomic backgrounds and students from nondominant groups suffer both hidden and overt discrimination in schools. This can cause underachievement and loss of cultural identity, leading eventually to placement in special education classes. Schools and teachers need to challenge racism and offer education programs that promote the identity and academic performance of *all students*.

Reflective

Because mainstream schools do not educate African American students effectively, several urban school districts have proposed separate schools for African American boys. Do you think this separation by gender and race is appropriate?

Using Technology to Promote Inclusion

Bridging the Digital Divide

Technology has become an essential tool for accessing information and the general education curriculum, and an important teaching tool for differentiating instruction to support student learning. However, despite the growing availability of computers, a *digital divide* still exists. The digital divide means that your students from culturally and linguistically diverse backgrounds, students living in poverty, students with disabilities, and female students may encounter barriers that affect their access to and use of technology in their homes and schools (Brown, Higgins, & Hartley, 2001). The existence of the digital divide can limit your goal of providing access to excellence for *all your students*, and extend some of the inequities that already exist in classrooms, schools, and society. While providing *all learners* with access to technology and the training they need to use it effectively is a challenge, here are some strategies that others have used to bridge the digital divide:

- Collect information to determine which students have access to and use technology, and which students do not.
- Identify and make others aware of the barriers to use of and access to technology.
- Teach *all students* the skills they need to access information via technology, and offer technology courses, workshops, and camps at times that are convenient for students and their families.
- Establish partnerships with businesses and community based organizations such as libraries, colleges, and community centers to make technology available to students and their families after school. For example, you can contact the Connect/Net/Connectado Campaign (*www.connectnet.org*), a coalition of businesses and community groups that assists in bridging the digital divide.
- Provide students and their families with a list of free or low-cost resources that can help them get online (e.g., local libraries, community centers).
- Create a technology lending library so that students and their families can borrow laptop computers and other technological devices.

- Integrate technology throughout the school via computer labs and roving computer stations, and make computer labs attractive, desirable, and enjoyable places for *all students*.
- Conduct technology events that relate to students' interests and special themes, and activities (e.g., speakers, films, mentors) that counter stereotypical views associated with technology use.
- Encourage *all students* to join technology clubs.
- Keep classrooms and computer labs open to students after school hours.
- Incorporate a range of technologies into classrooms by using them to deliver instruction, placing them in high visibility/desirability areas of the room, and regularly scheduling time for *all students* to work with them individually or in groups.
- Motivate students to use technology by providing them with opportunities to use a wide range of hardware, applications, educational games, and simulations, and to apply their technology skills to benefit and connect with their families, communities, and other students.
- Use a multifaceted approach to instruction and grading so that students are not penalized for their lack of access to technology. For example, provide students with alternatives when giving them assignments that require them to use technology to which they do not have access.
- Communicate with students and their families so that hard copies of products available online are also available for students and families who cannot access the material online.
- Choose software programs and digital materials that are challenging, interactive, and motivating, allow choices in terms of levels of difficulty, are sensitive to diversity, avoid negative stereotypes, and can be used in several languages.

Note: Brown, Higgins, and Hartley (2001); Education Commission of the States (2000).

Multiracial/Ethnic Students

Because of the changing demographics in the United States, teachers will be serving an increasing number of students from multiracial/ethnic families (Schmitt, 2001a). Multiracial/ethnic students who grow up appreciating their rich multiracial/ethnic identity are able to function well in many cultures, and to understand and adjust to a variety of perspectives (Leyva, 1998). However, these students and their families face racial discrimination and many challenges, such as being forced to choose one racial identity over the other, describing themselves to others, and making friends and participating in social groups that are generally based on racial and ethnic similarities (Chiong, 1998). The result can be cultural and racial identification problems, self-concept difficulties, the feeling of being an outsider in two or more cultures, and pressures to cope with conflicting cultural perspectives and demands (Yeh & Drost, 2002).

Resource

Kerwin and Ponterotto (1994) offer a list of resources for multiracial/ethnic students and their families and educators, including support groups, correspondence clubs, publications, recommended readings, and books.

Set Your Sites

For more information on multiracial/ethnic students, go to the Web Links module in Chapter 3 of the Companion Website.

Gender Bias

Teachers also have been exploring differences in the way schools respond to female and male students and the outcomes of this different treatment (Jobe, 2003). Schools tend to treat girls differently from boys and inadvertently reinforce stereotyped views of girls in terms of behavior, personality, aspirations, and achievement, which may stunt their academic and social development (American Association of University Women, 1998; Sadker & Sadker, 1994). Boys and girls generally enter school with equal academic abilities and self-concepts, but girls usually lag behind boys in both areas when they graduate from high school (ERIC Clearinghouse on Urban Education, 2001). Although the gap has narrowed in most areas in recent years, girls' access to technology and training in computer sciences and underrepresentation in high-paying and high-status careers are still troubling issues (American Association of University Women, 2000; Nelson & Smith, 2001).

In mainly white, middle-class schools, many elementary and secondary classrooms have been found to be structured unequally:

- Boys talk and are called upon more, are listened to more carefully, and are interrupted less than girls.

Because girls generally don't act out and attract as much attention as boys, their unique and special needs are sometimes overlooked. What are some of the unique needs of your female students?

- Boys are given more feedback, asked to respond to higher-level questions, and take more intellectual risks than girls.
- Boys are more likely to believe that their poor academic performance is due to lack of effort and can be corrected by greater effort, whereas girls tend to believe that their poor performance is an indication of their inability.
- Boys and other male characters are more likely to be portrayed in basal readers and children's literature than girls and female characters, who are often presented in stereotypical ways.
- Boys who are enrolled in programs for the gifted and talented in elementary school are more likely than girls to continue in these programs in secondary school (American Association of University Women, 1998; Sadker & Sadker, 1994; Zittleman & Sadker, 2003).

These studies were conducted mainly in white, middle-class classrooms. However, gender and race interact, making African American and Hispanic girls even more susceptible to bias in society and in school. In addition, many female students from nondominant cultural backgrounds face conflicts between the cultural values of mainstream U.S. society, which emphasize independence and ambition, and their own culture, which may promote traditional roles for women. Females from culturally and linguistically diverse and from lower socioeconomic backgrounds also may have to assume responsibilities at home or work to help support their families.

There also appears to be a self-esteem gap in the ways society and schools respond to girls and boys (Jobe, 2003). Girls are taught by society to base their self-esteem on physical appearance and popularity, while boys are encouraged to do so in relation to school and sports. Girls, particularly in adolescence, may be vulnerable to peer pressure that encourages social success at the expense of high marks. This fear of rejection and of being smart but not popular can cause girls to underachieve, to attempt to hide their success, to not enroll in advanced and challenging courses, and to select careers that are not commensurate with their skills. Frequently, when girls do achieve at high levels or show an interest in a math or science career, they are counseled by advisors who ask them questions that they would not ask boys, such as, "How will you handle your family if you're a doctor?" (Smithson, 1990, p. 2). Because girls generally don't act out and attract as much attention as boys, their unique and specialized needs are often overlooked, and therefore programs to address these needs are not funded. Biased tests, curricula, and textbooks also hinder the school performance and reduce the self-esteem of female students. As these students leave school and start to work, they continue to encounter different treatment. As a result, they become overrepresented in low-paying and low-status occupations that offer fewer benefits and training opportunities and less job security (U.S. Department of Education, 1998).

Gender stereotypes also affect boys, albeit in different ways. For example, data indicate that:

- Girls score higher on reading and writing standardized tests than boys.
- Girls are less likely to be placed in special education than boys.
- Girls complete school, take advance placement courses, and go on to college in higher rates than boys (Taylor & Lorimer, 2003).

Resource

Jobe (2003) and Taylor and Lorimer (2003) offer strategies and resources for helping female and male students succeed in school.

Like girls, the education of boys can be enhanced by providing them with positive role models, helping them learn to identify and challenge stereotypes, offering them a challenging and motivating curriculum that addresses their needs and interests, and using cooperative and active learning strategies (Taylor & Lorimer, 2003).

Eating Disorders

The pressures placed on girls in terms of their appearance via advertising, fashion, and entertainment that promote an idealized view of the female body and the need to be the "perfect girl" contribute to the likelihood that some of your female students may have eating disorders such as bulimia and anorexia (Schlozman, 2002c). Students who participate in your school's sports programs, who are perfectionists, and who experience loss of personal relationships (e.g. family deaths or breakups) are particularly susceptible to developing some type of eating disorder (Manley, Rickson, & Standeven, 2000). Bulimia involves binging on food followed by attempts to purge oneself of the excess calories by vomiting, taking medications or laxatives, fasting, or exercising. Anorexia, which is less prevalent than bulimia, involves refusal to eat and a disturbed sense of one's body shape or size, which results in a skeletal thinness and loss of weight that is denied by the individual. Both conditions affect one's health, emotional development, and school performance, and can be life-threatening. You can help these students by being aware of the warning signs of these conditions which you may observe via their frequent requests to go to the bathroom, and dental problems, bad breath, and hair loss (see Table 3.2). You also can collaborate with medical and psychological professionals (e.g., family physician, dietitian, school counselors, nurse, social worker, etc.), and family members to implement a comprehensive program to address related issues and support healthy eating habits, and observe and document student behaviors. You also can reflect on your com-

Set Your Sites

For more on female students, go to the Web Links module in Chapter 3 of the Companion Website.

TABLE 3.2	Behavioral, cognitive, and affective characteristics of individuals with anorexia nervosa and bulimia nervosa		
		Anorexia nervosa	**Bulimia nervosa**
	Behavioral	May set very high goals for themselves	May set very high goals for themselves
		Significant weight loss	Possible weight fluctuations
		Restrictive eating pattern (dieting)	Restrictive eating pattern (dieting)
		Possible binge eating/purging	Binge eating/purging
		Excessive exercise	Possible excessive exercise
		Increased social isolation	Often more socially outgoing
		Avoidance of eating situations	
		Easily fatigued	
	Cognitive	Difficulty concentrating due to preoccupation with food, calories, weight, or shape	Difficulty concentrating due to preoccupation with food, calories, weight, or shape
		Seeing things in an all-or-none, black-and-white fashion	Seeing things in an all-or-none, black-and-white fashion
		Difficulty retaining information	
		Indecisive	
	Affective	May feel like a failure if anything is less than "perfect"	May feel like a failure if anything is less than "perfect"
		Depression	Depression
		Anxiety	Anxiety
		Mood swings	Mood swings
		Irritability	Irritability
		Poor self-esteem	Poor self-esteem
		Sense of shame or guilt about the eating disorder	Sense of shame or guilt about the eating disorder

Source: From "Children and Adolescents with Eating Disorders: Strategies for Teachers and School Counselors," by R. S. Manley, H. Rickson, and B. Standeven, 2000, *Intervention in School and Clinic, 35*, pp. 228–231. Copyright 2000 by PRO-ED, Inc. Reprinted with permission.

Resource

Manley, Rickson, and Standeven (2000) and Schlozman (2002c) provide information and strategies for understanding and addressing the needs of students with eating disorders. Aronson (1997) provides resources for teaching your students about individual differences in body size and type.

Set Your Sites

For more information on students with eating disorders, go to the Web Links module in Chapter 3 of the Companion Website.

Set Your Sites

For more information on students who are overweight, go to the Web Links module in Chapter 3 of the Companion Website.

ments, behaviors, and attitudes regarding body image; model healthy attitudes and behaviors; teach students how to critique messages from the society and the media; and make sure that students are not ridiculed because of their appearance (Manley, Rickson, & Standeven, 2000; Schlozman, 2002c).

Unfortunately, a growing number of children in the United States are overweight. These children may experience a variety of health problems, including a lack of energy, and discrimination, which can affect their learning, socialization, and self-esteem. While some of these children have medical conditions that make them prone to being overweight, diet and a sedentary lifestyle also are culprits (i.e., spending significant amounts of time watching TV or on a computer). Rather than focusing on a student's size, losing weight, or diets, you can promote the acceptance of different body types, and emphasize and model healthful lifestyles, eating, and exercise as ways to feel better and have more energy (Wolfe, Burkman, & Streng, 2000).

Gay, Lesbian, Bisexual, and Transgendered (GLBT) Youth

> *Late last semester, I walked into the boys' locker room after gym, and my eyes fell upon a new sign. On the side of a blue locker, somebody had scribbled, "KILL THE FAGGOT" in deodorant. I stopped dead in my tracks, and stared at the sign in anger and disappointment. But what I noticed next was even worse. My friends, my classmates, walked by the sign barely noticing. Nobody noticed, and nobody reacted, because nobody cared. I felt like I would explode, like I would cry, but I didn't say anything. I went on with my day. I went on pretending. . . . I'm sick of it. I'm sick of hearing my friends, my classmates, my teachers say faggot, fairy, and dyke. I'm sick of hearing homophobic jokes in the cafeteria, and being forced to either laugh along, or get looked at funny for speaking up against them. I'm sick of living the fear that if I were discovered, I would be ostracized, tormented, and probably beaten up. I can't stand watching students and teachers snicker, say "Eww," or turn away every time they hear about a gay person. And it isn't only cafeteria jokes that contribute to the homophobia. It seems that homosexuals have been crossed out of history. (Students for Social Justice, n.d., p. 3)*

Set Your Sites

For more information on GLBT students, go to the Web Links module in Chapter 3 of the Companion Website.

Resource

GLSEN (2002a,2002b) and Goldstein (2001) offer guidelines, strategies, and resources for designing and implementing classroom lessons on GLBT issues.

As this student's comments indicate, gay, lesbian, bisexual, and transgendered (i.e., individuals who do not identify themselves as either of the two sexes) (GLBT) youth and youth who are questioning and exploring their sexual identity face homophobia and discrimination in schools and society. This discrimination often takes the form of ridicule or bias-related physical assaults, which hinder the students' educational performance, emotional development, and participation in school-related programs (Guetzloe, Hirschfield, Kosciw, & Schwartz, 2002). Furthermore, when these events occur, very few teachers intervene. As a result, many GLBT youth attempt to hide their sexual orientation, while others are disciplined and referred for placement in special education programs for students with emotional and behavioral disorders (Raymond, 1997).

Because of the pressure to grow up "differently" and because of the homophobia in society, GLBT youth are at greater risk for poor school performance, substance abuse, leaving school, and suicide (Edwards, 1997). They also frequently encounter rejection and abuse from their families, which affects their decision to reveal their sexual preference to others and results in high rates of homelessness. As a result of their isolation and victimization,

REFLECTING ON YOUR PRACTICES

Examining Equity in the Classroom

You can evaluate how well your own classroom practices promote equity for *all students* by addressing the following questions:

- Do I avoid grouping students based on gender and race, such as by forming separate lines, separate teams, separate seating arrangements, and separate academic learning groups, and comparing students across gender and racial variables?
- Do I know about the beliefs, traditions, customs, and experiences of all students in my classroom?
- Do I assign students of both sexes and *all races* to class and school jobs on a rotating basis?
- Do I use textbooks and teaching materials that include the contributions of both sexes and *all races and groups*?
- Do I use gender/race-inclusive and gender-neutral language?
- Do I provide male and female students with same-sex and same-race models and mentors who represent a variety of perspectives and professions?
- Do I encourage *all students* to explore various careers, as well as academic, extracurricular, and recreational activities?
- Do I decorate the classroom with pictures of males and females from *all races, religions, sexual orientations, and economic backgrounds* and performing a variety of activities?
- Do I use cooperative learning groups and cross-sex and cross-race seating arrangements?
- Do I encourage and teach students to examine and discuss books, stories, movies, and other materials in terms of stereotypes and perspectives across race, religion, sexual orientation, socioeconomic status, and gender?
- Do I identify and eliminate gender, racial, and other forms of bias in my assessment strategies and my curriculum?
- Do I encourage female and male students of *all races* to take risks, make decisions, assume leadership positions, and seek challenges?
- Do I affirm efforts and attributes that contribute to success in *all students*?

How would you rate how well you create a classroom environment that promotes equity for *all your students*? ( ) Excellent ( ) Good ( ) Needs Improvement ( ) Needs Much Improvement

What are some goals and steps you could adopt to promote equity in your classroom?

GLBT youth are particularly susceptible to suicide and have an attempted suicide rate that is three times higher than that of their heterosexual peers.

Students with HIV/AIDS

Another group of students who have encountered bias are those with acquired immune deficiency syndrome (AIDS), a viral condition that destroys an individual's defenses against infections. Human immunodeficiency virus (HIV), which causes AIDS, is passed from one person to another through the exchange of infected body fluids. Most children with HIV acquire the disease at birth. It is growing most rapidly among heterosexual men and women, infants, and teenagers (Stolberg, 1998). Some of the characteristics associated with adolescents make teenagers, especially those with disabilities, particularly susceptible to being exposed to HIV/AIDS (Blanchett, 2000).

While there are no known incidents of the transmission of AIDS in school, the idea of teaching students with AIDS continues to be debated. In *School Board of Nassau County, Florida et al.* v. *Arline* (1987), the Supreme Court ruled that individuals with infectious diseases, including AIDS, are covered under Section 504 of the Rehabilitation Act. Similarly, while special education is not required for all students with AIDS, such

Set Your Sites

For more information on HIV/AIDS, go to the Web Links module in Chapter 3 of the Companion Website.

Supporting GLBT Students

Mr. Rivers read the flier inviting him to attend a meeting of the Gay, Lesbian, Bisexual, Transgendered, and Straight Teachers Network. As a junior high school teacher for 5 years, Mr. Rivers had witnessed his share of homophobic comments and actions from students and colleagues, and it bothered him that he had not confronted these biased individuals. At the meeting, the group viewed *It's Elementary: Talking About Gay Issues in School*, a video that shows elementary and middle school students learning and talking about homophobia. Mr. Rivers thought the video was informative; it gave him some ideas on how to include antihomophobia education in his classroom and school. However, he was still not convinced that it was the school's role to do this. He was concerned that others would view providing support for GLBT youth as promoting sexuality and homosexuality.

At the next meeting, he heard others talk about how they implemented antibias activities in their schools. One educator noted that "invisibility was a major issue" for their school. "We all assume everyone is heterosexual, and it's as if these kids don't exist. We decided to make GLBT issues visible and used our language, the school environment, and the curriculum to achieve that goal. We started by using the terms *gay, lesbian, transgendered,* and *bisexual* in school and in positive ways. We also tried to use gender-neutral language such as *partner* or *significant other* rather than *boyfriend* or *girlfriend*. We sought to promote visibility and support by displaying books, posters, and stickers that are sensitive to GLBT issues and by wearing GLBT-positive symbols. We got other teachers to put a pink or rainbow triangle on their classroom doors to indicate that everyone is safe in their rooms. We also placed books, magazines, and newspapers dealing with issues of sexual orientation on our bookshelves, offices, and common areas. We used the curriculum to make GLBT issues more visible. To counter the bias and exclusion in the curriculum regarding GLBT issues and individuals, we expanded the curriculum to include these issues and individuals in positive ways. For instance, some teachers mention the sexual orientation of famous GLBT historical figures, authors, musicians, scientists, and poets, which helps establish positive role models for students. We also promoted a discussion of GLBT issues by inviting speakers to talk to classes, assemblies, and faculty and family meetings and by structuring class projects around these issues. It has really helped."

Another group of teachers spoke about their efforts to respond immediately and sincerely to incidents of homophobia, heterosexism, and stereotyping in school. They talked about the legal requirement and need to establish and enforce sexual harassment, antiviolence, and antidiscrimination policies in the schools. They told the audience that "you need to make it clear that language has power, and that abusive language has harmful effects and will not be tolerated. Persons who make derogatory comments, and jokes, and use harassment focusing on an individual's sexuality or other personal characteristics, should be quickly informed that the school community considers their behavior inappropriate and that it will not be tolerated."

Mr. Rivers left the meeting determined to counter homophobic behavior in his school. He spoke to his principal, and to several teachers and students, and shared some materials and resources with them. Together they formed the GLBT/Straight School Alliance, an afterschool club that welcomed all members of the school and the local community who were interested in learning more about issues of sexual orientation in a safe environment. The group used various activities that promoted an accepting, safe, nondiscriminatory, and supportive environment in which all students are valued.

Here are some other ideas you can use to create an inclusive and supportive classroom for GLBT youth and youth who are questioning and exploring their sexual identity:

- Deal with harassment by swiftly and consistently enforcing the school's antidiscrimination policy.
- Use teaching materials that address issues related to sexual orientation and provide accurate information.
- Learn more about GLBT issues and speak to students about the terms they prefer to use to define and describe themselves.
- Include a discussion of issues related to individuals who are GLBT in the school district's plan to address student diversity.
- Provide *all students* with role models and confidential access to you and materials that address their unique needs and concerns.
- Refrain from advising students to reveal their sexual orientation to others, and help them understand the factors they should consider in sharing their sexuality with others.
- Help students and their families obtain appropriate services from agencies and professionals who are sensitive and trained to deal with GLBT issues. For example, you can work with others to develop and distribute a list of resources available in the community, regionally, and nationally.
- Acknowledge the achievements and concerns of GLBT students publicly. For example, you and your students can write an article for the school or community newspaper or the PTA newsletter.

Note: Edwards (1997); GLSEN (2002a, 2002b); Goldstein (2001); Lamme & Lamme (2002); Raymond (1997).

IDEAS FOR IMPLEMENTATION

Teaching Students Who Have AIDS

Mr. Ball was recently informed that Mary, one of his students, had AIDS. Not knowing much about AIDS, Mr. Ball decided that he needed to learn more. He used the Internet and found websites that provided information about students with AIDS. Through the Internet, he "spoke" with other teachers who had taught students like Mary. They told him that he needed to follow and maintain the legal guidelines for confidentiality contained in the Family Educational Rights and Privacy Act, which meant that he could not share information about Mary's medical condition with others. They also encouraged him to remember that Mary's social needs might be greater than her academic needs. With that advice, Mr. Ball was determined to encourage and assist Mary in participating in as many classroom and extracurricular activities as possible. Only if necessary would he limit Mary's participation in sports or other activities.

Here are some other ideas you can use to create an inclusive and supportive classroom for students with AIDS:

- Collaborate with others to deliver sensitive, nonjudgmental, and compassionate services to students and their families.
- Work closely with medical personnel. Because of their condition, students with AIDS may be more susceptible to common childhood infections and serious contagious diseases (e.g., hepatitis or tuberculosis).

- Pay attention to quality-of-life issues including relationships with friends and families, enjoying learning, broadening perspectives, and achieving independence and self-determination.
- Take universal precautions to protect one's health and safety, as well as the health and safety of the student with AIDS and other students. Methods include using protective barriers such as disposable surgical gloves, masks, aprons and eyewear when providing personal or health care to the student, covering wounds, using puncture-proof containers, cleaning surfaces with blood spills using a disinfectant, washing hands, and having access to facilities for washing and properly disposing of all items (e.g. gloves, bandages) that may be exposed (Edens, Murdick, & Gartin, 2003).
- Educate *all students* and families about the school district's policies and procedures regarding HIV/AIDS, and about the use of universal precautions that protect *all students*.
- Use diverse ways to include information about HIV/AIDS and its prevention as an important part of the curriculum. Guidelines and resources to introduce students to these issues are presented in Chapter 5.

Note: Johnson, Johnson, & Jefferson-Aker (2001); Kelker, Hecimovic, & LeRoy (1994); Prater & Sileo (2001).

---

students who also have special educational needs may be eligible for services under the IDEA. Thus, students with AIDS should have the same rights, privileges, and services as other students and should not be excluded from school unless they represent a direct health danger to others (e.g., engage in biting or scratching others, practice self-abuse, have open sores). Decisions on how to educate students with AIDS should be made by an interdisciplinary team based on the students' educational needs and social behaviors, as well as the judgments of medical personnel. Teachers must also obtain written, informed consent before disclosing HIV-related information.

Resource

Edens, Murdick, and Gartin (2003) offer resources and guidelines for using universal precautions in classrooms.

How Have Family Changes Affected Students and Schools?

Changing Definition of Family

During the last two decades, the structure of the U.S. family has undergone compelling changes. High divorce rates, economic pressures requiring both parents to work, and welfare reform have brought dramatic changes in the composition, structure, and function

Set Your Sites

For more information on two-parent and single-parent families, go to the Web Links module in Chapter 3 of the Companion Website.

of families (Bernstein, 2000, 2002; Schmitt, 2001b). As a result, the definition of *family* in the United States has changed dramatically, and you are likely to have students who live with both parents, one parent, other family members, friends, two mothers, two fathers, or foster families. Regardless of the family's composition, it is important for you to recognize that while these families may have unique needs, they also share the same strengths, joys, frustrations, and needs as other families. These different configurations also mean that you will need to employ different strategies to encourage them to be partners with you in their children's education (Varied strategies for collaborating and communicating with families are presented in Chapter 4).

Single-Parent Families

One result of the changes in families is the growing number of children living in single-parent homes (Lewin, 2001). Currently, fewer than 50 percent of the children in the United States live with both biological parents, and it is estimated that 59 percent of all children will live in a single-parent household before they reach the age of 18. The growing number of children born to single mothers also has increased the number of single-parent families; 27 percent of children younger than 18 live with a single parent who has never married (Holmes, 1994; Lewin, 2000).

Divorce

I was 4 at the time. I was not aware of the divorce exactly, but I was aware that something was out of the ordinary and I didn't like it. Dad was gone. There was a lot of anger, and I had to listen to my mom constantly try to get me to agree with her that he was rotten to leave us. I didn't know what to think. I knew that I wanted him to come back. I'd ask her, "Where is Dad?" and she'd say, "Go ask him!" If I saw him, I'd say, "How come you don't live with us anymore?" and he'd say, "Go ask your mother." I couldn't bring my folks back together no matter how hard I tried. I just didn't know how. I thought if I just wished it, that wishing would be enough. (Michael, age 19)

Divorce has increased the number of children living in single-parent homes, which means that you, as a teacher, are likely to have many students like Michael in your class (Frieman, 1997). Approximately 90 percent of these children live with their mothers, who face many burdens as they assume many of the economic and social roles necessary to sustain the family. Divorce also can be hard for nonresidential parents, frequently fathers, who may find that their role in the child's life is decreased.

The effects of divorce tend to vary from child to child; however, the effects on boys seem to be more profound and persistent. Initially, children whose parents have divorced may exhibit anger, anxiety, depression, loneliness, noncompliance, confusion, behavior and health problems, difficulty establishing close relationships, and poor school performance (Wallerstein, Lewis, & Blakeslee, 2000). Children who experience divorce, particularly girls, frequently assume roles of caretakers for other family members, and may feel pressured to grow up too fast (Duenwald, 2002). While some researchers note that the negative effects of divorce are short-lived (Hetherington & Kelly, 2000), others believe that they are long-lasting (Wallerstein, Lewis, & Blakeslee, 2000). For some children, divorce may have positive effects. Children raised in two-parent families where the parents are in conflict have more difficulty adjusting than chil-

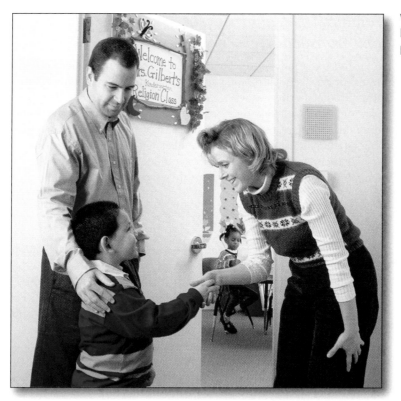

What can teachers do to help students from single-parent households?

dren raised in supportive, conflict-free, single-parent homes. The effects of a single divorce or multiple divorces on children depend on several factors, including the amount and nature of the conflict between the parents, the continuity parents provide for their children after the divorce, how much help parents can give their children, and the need to move (Chira, 1995).

As a result of conflicts between divorced parents, you may be put in a difficult situation. Some teachers deal with these conflicts by sending copies of all communications and assignments to both parents, as well as giving both parents the opportunity to attend conferences, either jointly or separately, depending on their preferences (Frieman, 1997). School districts may have different policies regarding communication with family members, and the legal situations between family members may be complex, so consult your principal regarding contacts with both parents. For example, at the beginning of the school year, you can request a list of adults who may interact with your students at school. Since many children live in blended families, in which one of their parents has married someone who also has children, you should also seek clarification regarding the roles of these parents.

Extended Families

There also has been a dramatic increase in the number of children who live in extended families or in households headed by family members other than their parents. Since 4.5 million children live with their grandparents (Hodgkinson, 2001; Reese, 2003), you will probably also have children in your class who live in such a family. In addition to adapting your family involvement strategies to address their needs (see Chapter 4), you can help grandparent-headed households by linking them to groups that offer services to them.

Set Your Sites

For more information on families led by grandparents, go to the Web Links module in Chapter 3 of the Companion Website.

Resource

Lamme and Lamme (2002) offer information, strategies, and resources for collaborating and supporting families headed by gay, lesbian, bisexual, and transgendered parents.

Families Headed by Gay, Lesbian, Bisexual, and Transgendered Parents

An estimated 6 million to 12 million children live in families headed by gay, lesbian, bisexual or transgendered family members (Lamme & Lamme, 2002). These families are structured in a variety of ways, including two-adult families, single-parent families, joint parenting arrangements, and extended families. Although some studies suggest that children raised by gay and lesbian parents are well adjusted, these children also may have unique difficulties. Because their families may attract prejudice, these children may try to hide their family relationships from others. You can work with these families by learning more about them and the issues they face, and create a friendly and welcoming environment for *all families*.

Adopted Children

Between 1 percent and 2 percent of the children in the United States have been adopted. Some of these adoptions are referred to as special-needs adoptions because they involve children who are difficult to place with a family, such as those exposed prenatally to drugs or those with emotional or developmental disabilities (Ganzel, Peterson, & Snyder, 2002). Whether children are adopted soon after birth or later, they and their families may face numerous adjustments and challenges (Meese, 1999). Early on, children must adjust to their new family and environment and deal with the separation from former caregivers, relatives, and friends, which can result in difficulties making emotional attachments with others, or feeling pressure to be perfect in order to stay with their new family. They may believe that they caused others to "give them away because they are bad," which can make them depressed or afraid that they may be abandoned again. As they reach adolescence, adopted children may again experience grief as they seek to develop their identities and try to understand their biological past. Their behavior also may be shaped by the extent to which they were victims of abuse and neglect, and by whether they have lived with many families (Kirby, 1997).

It is important to be sensitive to the unique needs of the child and the child's family (Meese, 1999; Stroud, Stroud, & Staley, 1997). You can help *all children* appreciate the various ways families are formed and model positive attitudes toward adoption. For example, rather than using the terms *real* or *natural* parent and *adoptive* parent, you can use the terms *birth* or *biological* parent and parent, respectively. You also can give students alternatives to assignments that assume that students live with their biological parents or family members, and incorporate representations of adoptive families in classroom activities and discussions. For instance, rather than asking students to create a family tree or share baby pictures with the class, you can allow students to chronicle an important time in their lives or share a favorite picture of themselves. When working with students who were adopted after infancy, be aware of anniversaries (e.g., birthdays of relatives and the date they were removed from their birth home) that may cause unexplained or unusual behaviors. In addition, be sensitive to the feelings of adoptive parents, understand your role in the telling process, and become aware of adoption services and agencies that can assist you in working with students and their families.

Set Your Sites

For more information on adopted children and their families, go to the Web Links module in Chapter 3 of the Companion Website.

Resource

Ganzel et al. (2002) and Stroud et al. (1997) offer guidelines for working with adoptive parents and their children.

Foster Families

Resource

Emerson and Lovitt (2003) offer guidelines for working with foster children and their families.

An estimated 600,000 children and youth live with foster families (Emerson & Lovitt, 2003). For a variety of reasons, many of these students experience school- and postschool-related difficulties. They might blame themselves for their removal from

IDEAS FOR IMPLEMENTATION

Working with Students Whose Families Are Undergoing Changes

As Ms. Doney's students were writing in their journals, Felicia started to cry and Ms. Doney took her aside and asked, "What's the matter?"

Felicia said, "Last night, my parents told me that my father was going to move."

Ms. Doney asked, "How does it make you feel?" "Sad." :Felicia said. "I miss my dad. I want him back."

Ms. Doney said, "I know it's hard for you. Would you like to talk more with me about this?"

"No, not now," Felicia said. "Can I work on the computer now and do my work later? I just want to be alone." Ms. Doney agreed and reminded Felicia that she was available to talk with her.

As she had done with many of her other students who were having family difficulties, Ms. Doney also referred Felicia to the school's counseling service, which offered students an opportunity to talk with a counselor and peers about their feelings.

Here are some other ideas you can use to create an inclusive and supportive classroom for students whose families are undergoing changes:

• Encourage students to attend and participate in counseling.

• Teach students how to express their feelings in appropriate ways.
• Communicate with the student's family concerning the child's social and academic adjustment.
• Lessen sources of stress in school and make exceptions where possible.
• Encourage students to differentiate between events that they can control (e.g., working hard in school, performing a class job) and events that are beyond their control.
• Provide alternatives to projects that are based on traditional assumptions of families.
• Use books and teaching materials that deal with children in a wider range of family arrangements. For example, the book *Who's in the Family?* (Skutch, 1995) uses a lighthearted approach to introduce students to all types of family arrangements in the human and animal worlds.

Note: Frieman (1997); Noble (1997).

their families and might move from one household to another. Thus they might be secretive about their home life, be picked on by other students, and need special services. To help these students, you can obtain background information about them, establish a good relationship with their foster families, and set reasonable social, behavioral, and academic goal. You also can encourage them to participate in after-school activities, and implement strategies for enhancing self-esteem. It also is important to work collaboratively with other professionals such as the social worker and guidance counselor and with community agencies, and help these students feel a part of your classroom and your school.

 *Resource*
Bryde (1998) and McCarty and Chalmers (1997) have compiled a list of children's literature on differences in family structures.

Child Abuse

A growing number of families are unfortunately engaging in child abuse. Your female students and your students with disabilities are particularly prone to being victims of abuse. Abuse can affect all aspects of a child's life including their psychological, behavioral, social, educational and neurological development (Teicher, 2002).

Because of the rise of child abuse and its harmful effects on children, states have passed laws that require you and other professionals who work with children to identify (see Figure 3.6 for the physical and behavioral indicators of child abuse) and report

Physical and behavioral signs of child abuse

FIGURE 3.6

PHYSICAL ABUSE

Physical Signs

- Bruises, welts, and bite marks
- Lacerations and abrasions
- Burns
- Fractures
- Head injuries
- Parentally induced or fabricated illnesses
- Unexplained injuries

Behavioral Signs

- Avoidance of interactions with parents and other adults
- Anxiety when other children are injured or crying
- Aggressiveness, shyness, and mood changes
- Frequent attempts to run away from home
- Fear of parents or of going home
- Talking about excessive parental punishment
- Blaming self for reactions of parents
- Habit disorders such as self-injurious behavior, phobias, and obsessions
- Wearing inappropriate clothing to conceal injuries
- Low self-image
- Suicide attempts

NEGLECT

Physical Signs

- Physical and emotional needs
- Symptoms of substance withdrawal
- Delayed physical, cognitive, and emotional development
- Attending school hungry or fatigued
- Poor hygiene and inappropriate dress
- Speech/language problems
- Limited supervision
- Medical needs that go unattended for extended periods of time
- Frequent absence from school

Behavioral Signs

- Begging and stealing
- Early arrival to and late departure from school
- Frequent fatigue and falling asleep in class
- Substance abuse
- Thefts and other delinquent acts
- Wearing dirty clothing, wearing clothing that is not appropriate for the weather, wearing the same clothing several days in a row
- Talk about lack of supervision
- Frequent attempts to run away from home
- Stereotypical behaviors such as sucking, biting, and rocking
- Antisocial behavior
- Habit disorders such as phobias, obsession, and hypochondria
- Extreme changes in behavior
- Suicide attempts

(continued)

SEXUAL ABUSE

Physical Signs

- ◇ Problems in walking or sitting
- ◇ Bloody, stained, or ripped clothing
- ◇ Pain in or scratching of genital area
- ◇ Bruises or bleeding in genital area
- ◇ Evidence of sexually transmitted diseases
- ◇ Pregnancy
- ◇ Painful discharges
- ◇ Frequent urinary infections
- ◇ Foreign materials in body parts

Behavioral Signs

- ◇ Avoiding changing clothes for or engaging in activities during physical education class
- ◇ Engaging in withdrawn, fantasy, or infantile actions
- ◇ Talking about bizarre, sophisticated, or unusual sexual acts
- ◇ Difficulty making friends
- ◇ Delinquent behavior
- ◇ Running away from home
- ◇ Forcing other students to engage in sexual acts
- ◇ Engaging in seductive behaviors with others
- ◇ Fear of being touched by others
- ◇ Absent from school frequently
- ◇ Expressing negative feelings about self
- ◇ Frequent self-injurious acts and suicide attempts

Source: From New York State Department of Education, *The Identification and Reporting of Child Abuse and Maltreatment* (n.d.).

suspected cases of child abuse (Lowenthal, 2001). When reporting child abuse, familiarize yourself with your school's policies and document the data that led you to suspect child abuse. It may be helpful to talk with other professionals concerning their views and knowledge of the child and the family, and with your principal to discuss the components of a complete report, how to deal with the family's reactions to the report, and the administrative support you will receive. Since it is an emotionally upsetting experience, you should also seek out educators, family members, and community members who can provide emotional support.

In cases of suspected abuse of children from culturally and linguistically diverse backgrounds, you also may need to consider the family's cultural background. In many cultures, medical and spiritual cures may require marking the child's body, leaving bruises, and leaving other marks that may be considered abuse. In some cases, confronting family members with information or concerns about their treatment of their child can lead to further difficulties for the child. While it is important to understand the family's cultural perspective and select the most beneficial outcomes for students, your course of action must comply with laws on child abuse.

In addition to reporting suspected cases of abuse, you can give students choices and other opportunities that allow them to experience some sense of control, and provide them with a safe and supportive learning environment. You also can use positive techniques to help them learn to manage their behavior and understand their emotional responses.

Resource

Lowenthal (2001) offers information, guidelines, and resources to assist you in identifying and preventing child abuse. Bryde (1998) has compiled a list of children's books that deal with child abuse.

Reflective

Kevin has been misbehaving. Your principal tells you to talk to his family. You are concerned about their reaction, as they frequently use physical punishment to discipline Kevin. What would you do? What professionals might assist you?

Set Your Sites

For more information on child abuse and prevention efforts, go to the Web Links module in Chapter 3 of the Companion Website.

Substance Abuse

Although alcohol and drug use among students has declined slightly, many families from all economic backgrounds, ethnic backgrounds, and geographic regions are dealing with the problem of substance abuse by children or other family members (Finn, Willert, & Marable, 2003). While substance abuse rates are roughly equal for boys and girls, it is more widespread among whites than among African Americans or Hispanics and more widespread among suburban and rural students than among urban students. Students with disabilities also may have significant substance abuse problems (Cosden, 2001). Substance abuse can hinder student learning and can result in high rates of inappropriate and aggressive behavior and attendance problems.

Resource

Adair (2000) and Drug Strategies (1999) identify and evaluate popular substance abuse prevention programs.

Set Your Sites

For more information on substance abuse, go to the Web Links module in Chapter 3 of the Companion Website.

Because of the harmful effects of substance abuse, you should be aware of some of the signs of possible substance abuse (see Figure 3.7). You also can help prevent problems by learning more about substance abuse, including its effects, prevention strategies, and treatment programs. You also can work to increase your students' attachment to school by interacting with them in a respectful and caring manner and encouraging them to be involved in extracurricular activities and schoolwide programs (Finn, Willert, & Marable, 2003). It also is important to work collaboratively with family and community members, agencies, students, and other professionals to design and implement substance abuse prevention programs (Adair, 2000).

Substance-Abused Newborns

Substance abuse among all socioeconomic groups has increased the number of substance-abused newborns (Watson & Westby, 2003). Many of these infants are small and underweight, are born prematurely, have birth defects, show neurological damage, exhibit irritability, and have trouble relating to and forming attachments to others. In classrooms, they may have difficulty learning and socializing with others, can be easily frustrated or overwhelmed by the many sights and sounds, and may withdraw or become aggressive and difficult to manage. They also may have communication and motor delays, organizational and processing problems, and difficulties in socializing and playing with others. Programs that offer medical care, nutritional counseling, and instruction in parenting skills and in obtaining community services are needed for these children and their families. In your classroom, you can provide them with a structured and supportive learning environment, which may involve:

- following a predictable schedule and routines.
- providing advance warning of changes in schedules or events.
- establishing a few simple rules.
- giving step-by-step directions.
- using repetition, prompts, modeling, peer tutors, checklists, concrete teaching aids, and shorter lessons and assignments.
- being positive and patient (Jensen, 2001).

What Are Some Alternative Philosophies for Structuring Schools to Address Societal Changes?

Changes in the society in the United States have significantly increased the number of students like those discussed in this chapter, whose needs challenge schools and whose

Signs of alcohol and other drug use

FIGURE 3.7

Signs of alcohol and other drug (AOD) use vary, but there are some common indicators of AOD problems. Look for changes in performance, appearance, and behavior. These signs may indicate AOD use, but they may also reflect normal teenage growing pains. Therefore, look for a series of changes, not isolated single behaviors. Several changes together indicate a pattern associated with use.

CHANGES IN PERFORMANCE
- Distinct downward turn in grades—not just from Cs to Fs, but from As to Bs and Cs
- Assignments not completed
- A loss of interest in school; in extracurricular activities
- Poor classroom behavior such as inattentiveness, sleeping in class, hostility
- Missing school for unknown reasons
- In trouble with school, at work, or with the police
- Increased discipline problems
- Memory loss

CHANGES IN BEHAVIOR
- Decrease in energy and endurance
- Changes in friends (secrecy about new friends, new friends with different lifestyles)
- Secrecy about activities (lies or avoids talking about activities)
- Borrows lots of money, or has too much cash
- Mood swings; excessive anger, irritability
- Preferred style of music changes (pop rock to heavy metal)
- Starts pulling away from the family, old friends, and school
- Chronic lying, stealing, or dishonesty
- Hostile or argumentative attitude; extremely negative, unmotivated, defensive
- Refusal or hostility when asked to talk about possible alcohol or other drug use

CHANGES IN APPEARANCE AND PHYSICAL CHANGES
- Weight loss or gain
- Uncoordinated
- Poor physical appearance or unusually neat. A striking change in personal habits
- New interest in the drug culture (drug-related posters, clothes, magazines)
- Smells of alcohol, tobacco, marijuana
- Frequent use of eye drops and breath mints
- Bloodshot eyes
- Persistent cough or cold symptoms (e.g., runny nose)
- Always thirsty, increased or decreased appetite, rapid speech
- AOD paraphernalia (empty alcohol containers, cigarettes, pipes, rolling papers, plastic bags, paper packets, roach clips, razor blades, straws, glass or plastic vials, pill bottles, tablets and capsules, colored stoppers, syringes, spoons, matches or lighters, needles, medicine droppers, toy balloons, tin foil, cleaning rags, spray cans, glue containers, household products)

Source: From "School-Based Alcohol and Other Drug Prevention Programs: Guidelines for the Special Educator," by D. L. Elmquist, 1991, *Intervention in School and Clinic, 27*, pp. 10–19. Copyright 1991 by PRO-ED. Reprinted by permission.

academic profiles resemble those of students with high-incidence disabilities; however, these students frequently do not have disabilities. Unfortunately, the vague definitions of disabilities, imprecise and discriminatory identification methods, and limited funding resulting in a lack of appropriate services, all increase the chances that these students will be identified incorrectly as needing special education. Several alternative viewpoints, such as multicultural education and inclusion, have been proposed for structuring schools to meet the needs of *all students* without labeling and separating them (Obiakor, 2001b).

These philosophies challenge schools to reorganize their curricula, teaching, staff allocation, and resources into a unified system that pursues both equity and excellence by asserting that *all students* have strengths and can learn at high levels in general education programs. They also seek to transform schooling for *all students* by celebrating diversity, offering differentiated instruction to address students' strengths and needs, acknowledging the importance of social relationships, establishing a sense of community in schools and classrooms, and fostering the involvement of families, community members, and groups in schools.

Multicultural Education

Reflective

We refer to students who have needs that challenge the school system as *at risk, handicapped, culturally disadvantaged,* or *linguistically limited*. How might things be different if we referred to schools as *risky, disabling, disadvantaging,* and *limiting*?

Set Your Sites

For more information on multicultural education, go to the Web Links module in Chapter 3 of the Companion Website.

One important educational philosophy for restructuring schools is *multicultural education* (Banks & Banks, 2001). This term originated in the post–civil rights efforts of various ethnic and language groups to have their previously neglected experiences included in the structures and curricula of schools (Nieto, 2003). Multicultural education seeks to help teachers acknowledge and understand the increasing diversity in society and in the classroom, and to see their students' diverse backgrounds as assets that can support student learning and the learning of others. For many, multicultural education has expanded to include concerns about socioeconomic status, disability, gender, national origin, language background, religion, and sexual orientation (National Council for the Accreditation of Teacher Education, 2001).

Definitions of *multicultural education* range from an emphasis on human relations and harmony to a focus on social democracy, justice, and empowerment for *all learners*. These definitions focus on the development of students' academic skills, and help students understand their backgrounds and perspectives as well as those of other groups that make up society. Multicultural education also includes students taking actions that transform society and make it more democratic and equitable for *all*.

Proponents of multicultural education also try to change the language of schools. Terms such as *culturally disadvantaged, linguistically limited, at risk, slow learners, handicapped,* and *dropouts* locate problems within students rather than within the educational system (Freire, 1970). These labels present a view of students that often contradicts the way these students view themselves. These conflicting views can disable students academically and prevent the development of self-esteem.

Multicultural Education and Inclusion

Multicultural education and inclusion are inextricably linked (Nieto, 2003; Scott, 2002). Many of the challenges confronting advocates for multicultural education are also faced by those who support inclusion. As seekers of educational reform, the multicultural education and inclusion movements share many of the same principles. Both movements:

1. seek to provide access, equity, and excellence for *all learners*.
2. focus on students' individual strengths and needs and diversity.
3. involve the use of reflective practices and differentiated instruction to support student learning.
4. recognize the importance of community and collaboration.

Both movements also have common academic and affective goals for *all learners*. These goals include promoting challenging learning environments that focus on students' strengths, needs, and experiences; developing positive attitudes toward oneself, one's culture, and the cultures and experiences of others; understanding and accepting individual differences and multiple identities; working collaboratively with families and other professionals; and appreciating the interdependence among various groups and individuals (Hunt et al., 2000).

Many of the key elements of multicultural education are also those of inclusion (Nieto, 2003; Sapon-Shevin, 2001). The best practices in terms of assessment, teaching accommodations, culturally responsive teaching, curriculum reform, and an appreciation of individual differences are common to both movements. The empowerment and support of families and communities, and the collaborative efforts of teachers, are other important components of both philosophies. By recognizing their common aims, those who support inclusion and multicultural education seek to create a unified school system in which *all students* are welcomed and affirmed in their classrooms. The inclusion and multicultural education movements mean that increasing numbers of these students will be educated in general education settings. Therefore, educators must be trained and willing to create inclusive classrooms that address their students' diverse educational, cultural, and linguistic strengths and needs, and reflect upon their efforts to support the learning of *all* their students.

Summary

This chapter offered information on how societal changes have helped to make inclusive education necessary to meet the strengths and needs of increasingly diverse groups of students who challenge the existing school structure. As you review the chapter, consider the following questions and remember the following points:

How Have Economic Changes Affected Students and Schools?
CEC 2, 3, 9, PRAXIS 2, INTASC 2, 9, 10
The United States has experienced dramatic economic changes marked by a growing gulf between wealthy and poor and old and young, as well as a shrinking middle class. As a result of these changes, schools are being challenged to meet the educational strengths and needs of a growing number of students who live in urban, rural, and suburban poverty.

How Have Demographic Shifts Affected Students and Schools?
CEC 1, 2, 3, 6, 9, PRAXIS 2, INTASC 2, 3, 9, 10
The makeup of the U.S. population has also changed dramatically, making the United States a more linguistically and culturally diverse country. As a result, schools will need to structure their programs and services to address a more diverse student population.

What Are the Educational Strengths and Needs of Students from Culturally and Linguistically Diverse Backgrounds?
CEC 1, 2, 3, 5, 6, 9, PRAXIS 2, INTASC 2, 3, 6, 9, 10
In addressing the educational strengths and needs of your students from culturally and linguistically diverse backgrounds, be sensitive to and adapt your

services to take into account the cultural, linguistic, and economic factors that affect you, your students, and their families. It is important to develop cultural competence and intercultural communication skills, and to support your students' cultural identities. You must also adjust your teaching behaviors and curricula to reflect your students' differing cultural backgrounds, learning styles, economic and experiential backgrounds, and linguistic abilities.

How Can I Differentiate Cultural and Language Differences from Learning Difficulties?

CEC 1, 2, 3, 6, 8, 9, 10, PRAXIS 1, 3, INTASC 2, 3, 6, 8, 9, 10

You can work with a diverse team of professionals and family members to assess your students' performance in both their primary and secondary languages, understand the processes and factors associated with learning a second language, employ alternatives to traditional testing and identify your students' diverse life and home experiences. You and the team can then analyze this information to try to differentiate cultural and language differences from learning difficulties, and develop an appropriate educational plan. Students whose linguistic, academic, and social behaviors in both languages are well below those of peers who have similar linguistic, cultural, and experiential backgrounds may have a learning difficulty.

What Are the Educational Strengths and Needs of Students Who Are Gifted and Talented?

CEC 7, PRAXIS 3, INTASC 2, 3

In addition to focusing on the academic strengths of students who are gifted and talented, you also need to recognize that these students often have unique social and emotional needs as well. You can address these needs by using Gardner's framework of multiple intelligences and by creating a learning environment that encourages students to be creative, develop their strengths, take risks, and direct their learning.

What Is the Effect of Discrimination and Bias on Students and Schools?

CEC 1, 2, 3, 5, 9, PRAXIS 2, INTASC 2, 3, 6, 9, 10

Students from specific racial, linguistic, and religious backgrounds, female students, gay and lesbian students, and students with HIV/AIDS can be victims of discrimination in society and schools. This discrimination harms their school performance, socialization, self-esteem, and outcome in later life. You must use a variety of strategies to foster the academic performance and self-esteem of these students.

How Have Family Changes Affected Students and Schools?

CEC 1, 2, 3, 9, 10, PRAXIS 2, INTASC 2, 3, 9, 10

Because of the dramatic changes in the composition, structure, and function of families, you will probably have students who live with both parents, one parent, family members, friends, two mothers, two fathers, or foster parents. You also may be called on to help families deal with child abuse or substance abuse. Regardless of the family's composition, it is important to recognize that while these families may have unique needs, they also have many of the same joys, frustrations, and strengths and needs as other families.

What Are Some Alternative Philosophies for Structuring Schools to Address Societal Changes?

CEC 1, 5, 9, PRAXIS 3, INTASC 3

Inclusion and multicultural education are philosophical movements that challenge schools to restructure their services and resources into a unified system that addresses societal changes. Multicultural education and inclusion share similar goals and principles and seek to provide access, equity and excellence for *all students.*

What Would You Do in Today's Diverse Classroom?

It is August, and you read the following reports about your students:

★ Carl's family is homeless. He is absent frequently and often comes to school tired and hungry. The other students avoid Carl, and he appears to be a loner. He loses school materials whenever he takes things home and rarely completes his homework.

★ Erica has good skills, and her family gives her everything she needs. However, she has trouble completing projects, lacks motivation, needs constant attention, and has few friends.

★ Zoltan arrived in the United States last year after escaping his war-torn country with his uncle's family. He lives with his uncle's family, and misses and worries about his parents and family members who still live in their country. He speaks and understands very little English and often gets into trouble because he doesn't understand and follow the rules.

★ Julia's parents recently separated and it was a surprise to everyone. Her parents had been very active in school and in other aspects of Julia's life. Her behavior is now very erratic. Sometimes she withdraws, and at other times she gets angry for no apparent reason. She often complains of headaches that prevent her from completing her work.

1. How would placement in a general education class benefit Carl, Erica, Zoltan, and Julia?

2. What concerns would you have about having these students in your class?

3. What are the educational strengths and needs of Carl, Erica, Zoltan, and Julia? What would be your goals for them?

4. What strategies could you use to address their educational strengths and needs?

5. What knowledge, skills, dispositions, resources and supports do you need to address their strengths and needs?

 To answer these questions online and share your responses with others, go to the Reflection module in Chapter 3 of the Companion Website.

Part II

Creating an Inclusive Environment That Supports Learning for All Students

Part 2 of the book, which includes chapters 4, 5, 6, and 7, provides strategies for creating an inclusive environment that supports learning for *all students*. Chapter 4 introduces the members of the comprehensive planning team and provides strategies for establishing collaborative relationships and fostering communication with professionals and family members. Chapter 5 offers strategies that support learning by fostering acceptance of individual differences related to disability, culture, language, gender, religion, and socioeconomic status and promoting friendships among your students. Chapter 6 provides a framework for helping students make the transition to inclusive learning environments and from school to adulthood. It also offers strategies for helping your students develop self-determination. Chapter 7 discusses ways in which you can plan and implement strategies to promote positive behaviors that foster learning and prevent students from harming each other. It also provides guidelines for designing your classroom to accommodate students' learning, social, and physical needs.

Chapter 4

Creating Collaborative Relationships and Fostering Communication

The Smith Family

We knew it would be another rough year. Last year, Paul's teacher told us that he wasn't doing as well as the other students. Now after only 2 months, Paul's new teacher, Mr. Rodl, called and said, "Paul is falling behind, and we need to do something." Mr. Rodl asked us to come to a meeting with a team of professionals to discuss Paul's progress. He said we could schedule the meeting at a time that was convenient for us.

Going into the meeting was scary. There sat Paul's teacher, the principal, the school psychologist, and several other people we didn't know. Mr. Rodl started the meeting by introducing us to the others in the room. Then he said, "Since I work closely with Paul, I'll lead the meeting and coordinate the decisions we'll make about Paul's program. We call that being the service coordinator."

He asked each person in the room to talk about Paul. As different people spoke, others asked questions. When several people used words we didn't understand, Mr. Rodl asked them to explain the words to us. When our turn came, Mr. Rodl asked us to talk about what was happening with Paul at home, what we thought was happening with him at school, and what we would like to see happen at school.

At first, we felt very nervous. As people in the room listened to and discussed our comments, we became more relaxed. The group discussed several ways to help Paul. In the end, we all came up with a plan to help Paul learn better. Mr. Rodl summarized the plan and the roles each person would play to make it successful. We also discussed how we would continue to communicate and collaborate to help Paul, and agreed to set up a home-school contract to share information about and support Paul's progress. We left the meeting feeling really good about being part of a team that was trying to help our son.

What factors made this meeting successful? What strategies could professionals and families employ to collaborate and communicate to help students such as Paul learn better? After reading this chapter, you should have the knowledge, skills, and dispositions to answer these as well as the following questions:

★ **Who are the members of the comprehensive planning team?**
★ **How can members of the comprehensive planning team work collaboratively?**
★ **How can I foster communication and collaboration with families?**

An essential principle of effective inclusion programs is good collaboration and communication among teachers, other professionals, families, and community members and resources (McLeskey & Waldron, 2002). Good collaboration and communication can strengthen the connection between school and home and create a shared commitment to learning. This chapter offers strategies for creating collaborative relationships and fostering communication with other professionals, families, and community members to support the learning of *all students*.

Who Are the Members of the Comprehensive Planning Team?

As we saw in chapter 2, the comprehensive planning team, including students and their families, makes collaborative decisions about the strengths and challenges of students, and provides appropriate services to students and their families (Ogletree, Bull, Drew, & Lunnen, 2001). Effective teams engage in a *wraparound process,* a multidisciplinary, interagency, strength-based process for collaboratively designing and delivering individualized, culturally sensitive, school- and community-based educational, counseling, medical, and vocational services to address the unique strengths, challenges and behaviors of students and their families (Anderson & Matthews, 2001; Eber, Smith, Sugai, & Scott, 2002). The wraparound process guides the team in solving problems, coordinating a full-range of services available to students, families, educators, and schools, and sharing the responsibility for implementing inclusion.

In addition to students (see chapter 2 for guidelines for involving students in the educational planning process), the team may consist of general and special educators, administrators, support personnel, family members, peers, local community resources, and professional and family-based organizations, as shown in Figure 4.1. The members of the team and their roles vary, depending on the needs of students, families, and educators. The roles and responsibilities of the different team members are described in the following sections.

Family Members

Family members are key members of the planning team, and communication and collaboration with them are essential (Ryan, Kay, Fitzgerald, & Paquette, 2001). They can provide various types of information on the student's adaptive behavior and medical, social, and psychological history. Family members also can help the team design and implement educational programs and determine appropriate related services.

School Administrators

A school administrator who supervises the districtwide services usually serves as the chairperson of the team. The chairperson is responsible for coordinating meetings and delivering services to students and their families. The chairperson also ensures that all legal guidelines for due process, family involvement, assessment, and confidentiality have been followed. Through their leadership and support, school administrators also can foster acceptance of and commitment to the concept of inclusion and encourage educators and families to collaborate (Salisbury & McGregor, 2002).

FIGURE 4.1   **Members of the comprehensive planning team**

General Educators

The team should include a general education teacher who has worked with the student and who can offer information on the student's strengths and weaknesses, as well as data on the effectiveness of specific teaching methods. General educators can provide a perspective on the academic and social rigors of the general education curriculum and classroom. As we discussed in chapter 2, involving general educators in the process also can allay their fears and promote their commitment to helping the student succeed in an inclusive setting.

Special Educators

The special educator provides information on the student's academic and social skills and the student's responses to different teaching techniques and materials. When a student is to be placed in an inclusive setting, the special educator can collaborate with general education classroom teachers on curricular and teaching accommodations, classroom management strategies, testing accommodations, grading alternatives, assistive devices, and peer acceptance (Fisher, Frey, & Thousand, 2003).

Resource

Conderman and Katsiyannis (2002) offer information about the roles of secondary level special educators.

Paraeducators

Paraeducators perform many important roles to help you promote the educational performance of *all students* in inclusive settings (Doyle, 2002; Giangreco, Edelman, & Broer, 2003). Therefore, it is important for them to be part of the planning team and have

cd-rom

Resource

Mueller and Murphy (2001) offer guidelines for determining when a student needs the services of paraeducators.

a shared vision for the inclusion of students. Including paraeducators on the planning team also can help them understand students' strengths and challenges, effective instructional strategies, and the goals of students' educational programs (Riggs, 2001). Their participation in the planning process also can clarify their roles and responsibilities in supporting you—and not replacing you—in implementing and assessing students' educational programs effectively. See Figure 4.2 for a delineation the roles of paraeducators so that they are not asked to assume responsibilities that teachers should perform. **To view examples of teachers and paraeducators collaborating in classrooms, go to Case 1: Difficult Behavior on the CD-ROM, and view all the video clips. What roles do the teachers and paraeducators perform?**

Since paraeducators often reside in the community, they may also provide valuable information regarding links to community-based services. In particular, paraeducators who are educated in or have experience with students' languages and cultures can play an important role in educating students who are second language learners. Therefore, it is important that you and other members of the team treat them with respect, and appreciate and acknowledge them for the meaningful contributions they make (Giangreco, Edelman & Broer, 2001). It is also important to share information with them, solicit their perspectives, address their concerns and suggestions, and offer them support, training and feedback to improve their performance (French, 2002). We will discuss in chapter 8

FIGURE 4.2

Delineating the roles and responsibilities of paraeducators in inclusive settings

Roles and Responsibilities of Paraeducators

Paraeducators can support teachers and students by:
- ☐ assisting students with daily living skills and health and physical needs (e.g., toileting and feeding).
- ☐ performing clerical duties and custodial tasks (e.g., insuring proper positioning).
- ☐ supervising students during activities outside the classroom.
- ☐ recording behavior and helping manage students' behavior.
- ☐ reading to students and playing educational games with them.
- ☐ serving as a translator.
- ☐ preparing, individualizing, and adapting materials.
- ☐ providing individualized and small-group instruction and reinforcing concepts/skills taught previously.
- ☐ helping students with motor and mobility difficulties, and providing emotional support.
- ☐ observing students.
- ☐ facilitating social interactions with peers.
- ☐ modeling appropriate skills.
- ☐ ensuring student safety.
- ☐ prompting students.

Roles and Responsibilities Outside the Scope of Paraeducators

Paraeducators should not be asked to replace professionals by:
- ☐ being solely responsible for delivering instruction to specific students.
- ☐ administering and interpreting formal and informal assessment instruments unless trained to do so or monitored by a trained professional.
- ☐ signing formal documents such as IEPs.
- ☐ assigning grades.
- ☐ disclosing confidential information.

Note: Carroll (2001); Riggs & Mueller (2001).

Paraeducators serve important roles in inclusive classrooms. What roles do paraeducators perform to promote the success of students in inclusive classrooms?

how you can collaborate and communicate with them to differentiate instruction and deliver appropriate services to support the academic, social, and behavioral performance of your students.

School Psychologists

The school psychologist is trained in the administration and interpretation of standardized tests. In addition to testing, school psychologists collect data on students by observing them in their classrooms and by interviewing other professionals who work with the students. School psychologists also sometimes counsel students and family members and assist classroom teachers in designing teaching and classroom management strategies (Habel & Bernard, 1999).

Set Your Sites

For more information on school psychology, go to the Web Links module in Chapter 4 of the Companion Website.

Speech and Language Clinicians

Information on students' communication abilities can be provided by the speech and language clinician. To rule out or confirm a language disability, these clinicians are often the first persons to whom students learning English are referred. They can also help you improve the communication skills and academic success of students in the classroom (Sunderland, 2004).

Social Workers

The social worker serves as a liaison between the home and the school and community agencies. The social worker counsels students and families, assesses the effect of the student's home life on school performance, and assists families during emergencies. In addition, the social worker can help families obtain services from community agencies,

Speech and language clinicians develop students' communication skills. How do you collaborate with them?

contact agencies concerning the needs of students and their families, and evaluate the impact of services on the family. Social workers also may offer counseling and support groups for students and their families.

School Counselors

Set Your Sites

For more information on school counseling, go to the Web Links module in Chapter 4 of the Companion Website.

The school counselor can provide information on the student's social and emotional development, including self-concept, attitude toward school, and social interactions with others (Deck, Scarborough, Sferrazza, & Estill, 1999). In schools that don't have a social worker, the counselor may assume that role. Frequently, counselors coordinate, assess, and monitor the student's program, as well as report the student's progress to members of the team. The counselor also may counsel students and their families. For example, during the transition period, the student may need counseling to adjust socially and emotionally to the general education classroom.

Vocational Educators

Vocational educators offer valuable information on the student's work experiences and career goals. They can help the team develop the transitional services component of students' IEPs. Vocational educators also provide students with vocational and career education experiences. This involves collaboration with families and employers in the community.

School Physicians and Nurses

School physicians and nurses can aid the team by performing diagnostic tests to assess the student's physical development, sensory abilities, medical problems, and central nervous system functioning. They can provide information on nutrition, allergies, chronic illnesses, and somatic symptoms. In addition, they can plan and monitor medical interventions and discuss the potential side effects of any drugs used. Since physicians' services are costly, many medically related services may be provided by school nurses (Bigby, 2004).

Physical and Occupational Therapists

Students with fine and gross motor needs may need the direct or indirect services of physical and occupational therapists (Shapiro & Sayers, 2003). These therapists can recommend various types of adaptive equipment and suggest how to adapt teaching materials and classroom environments. The physical therapist usually focuses on the assessment and training of the lower extremities and large muscles; the occupational therapist deals with the upper extremities and fine motor abilities. The physical therapist helps students strengthen muscles, improve posture, and increase motor function and range. The occupational therapist works with students to prevent, restore, or adapt to impaired or lost motor functions. This therapist also helps students develop the necessary fine motor skills to perform everyday actions independently.

Staff from Community Agencies

For many students, the team will need to work collaboratively with staff from community agencies. For example, if a student with a visual impairment must have an assistive device, a community agency can be contacted to help purchase it. In working with community organizations, the team should consider the unique medical, behavioral, and social needs of each student, as well as the financial resources of the student's family. Since many students may require similar services from agencies, teams can maintain a file of community agencies and the services they provide.

Professionals for Students Who Are Second Language Learners

In addition to the professionals described above, teams for students who are learning English and who are referred for special education services should include personnel who are fluent in the student's native language and bicultural in the student's home culture. Therefore, planning teams working with these students should include such professionals as ESL teachers, bilingual educators, and migrant educators.

ESL Teachers

As we discussed in chapter 3, ESL teachers instruct students in English. They build on students' existing language skills and experiences to enhance their learning of English, and can help the team address the language and learning strengths and needs of students. They also can offer many effective strategies for teaching second language learners (see Chapter 8).

Bilingual Educators

As we saw in chapter 3, many students come from backgrounds where English is not spoken and need the help of a bilingual educator. This educator performs a variety of roles. These include assessing and teaching students in their native language and in English, involving

Resource

Shapiro and Sayers (2003) and Neal, Bigby, and Nicholson (2004) offer guidelines and strategies for collaborating with occupational and physical therapists, adapted physical educators, and therapeutic recreation specialists in inclusive settings.

Set Your Sites

For more on occupational and physical therapy, go to the Web Links module in Chapter 4 of the Companion Website.

Set Your Sites

For more on ESL, go to the Web Links module in Chapter 4 of the Companion Website.

Resource

Salend, Dorney, and Mazo (1997) describe the roles of bilingual special educators in creating inclusive classrooms.

families and community members in the educational program, helping students maintain their native culture and adjust to their new culture, and working with general educators.

Migrant Educators

To help educate migrant students, the federal government funds migrant education programs through the states. Typically, when a migrant family moves to a new area, it is certified as being eligible for migrant status and services by a recruiter from a local migrant education agency. Then a migrant educator helps the family enroll the children in school. The migrant educator also contacts local agencies, organizations, businesses, and other community resources that can assist migrant families. Once the migrant students are in school, the migrant educator often gives them supplementary individualized instruction in small groups.

How Can Members of the Comprehensive Planning Team Work Collaboratively?

Employ Collaborative and Interactive Teaming

Successful comprehensive planning teams are collaborative and interactive, and are structured around the keys to team effectiveness presented in Table 4.1. All members work together to achieve a common goal, are accountable to the team, and share their diverse expertise and perceptions with others. They are interdependent and understand their roles and roles of others. A key member of the team is the case manager, service coordinator, or support facilitator. This person promotes the team process, coordinates the services for students and their families, and provides follow-up to ensure that goals are being met (Thomas et al., 2001).

Critical variables affecting team effectiveness

TABLE 4.1

Team Goals

Purpose of the team is clear.

Team goals are understood by all members.

Team goals are regularly reviewed.

Team goals are established by team members.

Team goals are clearly stated.

Team goals are modified by team members.

Team goals are supported by the family.

Team goals are attainable.

Team goals are prioritized.

Members anticipate both positive and negative outcomes.

Members are statisfied with goals that have been selected.

Team Roles and Team Membership

Team members are committed to the team process.

The team has a leader.

Members are accountable to the team.

Team roles are clearly understood.

Team roles are perceived by members as being important.

New team members are added when practical.

The team leader is unbiased.

Team Communication

Decisions are made for the good of the student.

Team members have adequate listening time.

Decisions are alterable.

Team members have equal opportunities to speak.

Decisions are reached by consensus.

Team Cohesion

Members feel safe sharing ideas.

The team has trust among members.

Members (especially parents) feel equally empowered.

The team has a unified goal.

The team has time to celebrate.

The team has support from superiors.

Members have respect for each other.

The team has recognition for efforts.

The team has autonomy for decision making.

The team has a healthy regard for disagreement.

Team Logistics

Progress is evaluated internally, by members.

Team procedures are clearly understood.

Team Outcomes

Team makes modifications to the plan as needed.

Members are clear about their reposibilities for the plan.

Members are committed to implementing the plan.

Solutions are practical.

A plan was implemented.

Team reviews the impact of the plan.

A plan was developed.

Parent satisfaction is part of the evaluation.

Outcomes are evaluated internally, by members.

The family is generally feeling better.

A plan was agreed on.

A decision was made.

Outcomes are evaluated at regularly scheduled times.

Members are satisfied with the plan.

Source: From "Process Variables Critical for Team Effectiveness," by J. L. Fleming and L. E. Monda-Amaya, 2001, *Remedial and Special Education, 22,* pp. 158–171. Copyright 2001 by PRO-ED, Inc. Reprinted with permission.

In addition, effective collaborative and interactive teams have the following characteristics:

1. *Reflective inquiry.* Effective teams use dynamic processes to reflect on and problem solve solutions to a range of issues and problems.

2. *Legitimacy and autonomy.* Effective teams have a recognized and supported function and are free to operate independently.

3. *Purposes and objectives.* Effective teams have identified goals and work together, sharing information and expertise to achieve these goals. The team members have a common set of norms and values that guides the team's functioning.

4. *Competencies of team members and clarity of their roles.* The members of effective teams are skilled not only in their own disciplines but also in collaborative problem solving, communication, and cultural diversity.

5. *Role release and role transitions.* Effective teams consist of members who can share their expertise with others, implement programs, use strategies from other disciplines, learn from others, and seek assistance and feedback.

6. *Awareness of the individuality of others.* Effective teams consist of members who recognize and accept the perspectives, skills, and experiences of others.

7. *Process of team building.* Effective teams are committed to the process of working together and functioning as a team. Conflicts between team members are resolved through problem solving, communication, and negotiation.

8. *Attention to factors that affect team functioning.* Effective teams use cooperative goal structures, create a supportive communication climate, share roles, and reach decisions through consensus.

9. *Leadership styles.* Effective teams rotate leadership responsibilities. Leaders are expected to solicit all points of view and involve all members in the decision-making process.

10. *Implementation procedures.* Effective teams consider a variety of factors when designing and implementing interventions.

11. *Commitment to common goals.* Effective teams are committed to collaborative goals and problem-solving techniques.

12. *Resources and support to be successful.* Effective teams have the resources, training, support, and time to be successful. (Thomas et al., 2001; Ogletree et al., 2001; Salisbury & McGregor, 2002).

Successful teams also develop good interpersonal and communication skills. Fleming and Monda-Amaya (2001) and Garmston and Wellman (1998) summarized the roles that team members can perform to help the team function efficiently and establish a caring, positive, trusting working environment:

1. *Initiating.* All members identify problems and issues to be considered by the team.

2. *Information gathering and sharing.* All members collect and share relevant information.

3. *Clarifying and elaborating.* All members seek clarification, probe for specific facts and details, and provide elaboration.

4. *Summarizing.* All members review and paraphrase key points discussed by the team.

5. *Consensus building.* All members participate in decision making.

6. *Encouraging.* All members encourage others to participate in the process and pay attention to the contributions of others.

7. *Harmonizing and compromising.* All members assume that others have good intentions, and seek to resolve conflict and compromise.

8. *Reflecting.* All members reflect on their own feelings, comments, and behaviors, as well as those of others.

9. *Balancing.* All members try to balance advocacy and inquiry.

To help the team develop these skills, the team can establish ground rules to guide their interactions and the decision-making process. Individual team members can also be assigned roles such as facilitator, recorder, timekeeper, observer, and summarizer. You can use effective communication skills to support success of the team by: (a) listening carefully to others as they express their ideas, perspectives, concerns and solutions; (b) being tolerant of differing points of view; (c) presenting your positions, feelings, and perspectives using "I" statements, examples to support your statements and graphics when appropriate; (d) understanding culturally based differences in verbal and nonverbal communication; (e) respecting the confidentiality of others; (f) disagreeing respectfully; and (g) being willing to compromise. **To view examples of a group of professionals functioning as a team, go to Case 3: Assess Plan on the CD-ROM, and view all the video clips. What interpersonal, communication, and professional skills do the team leader and members demonstrate that establish a collaborative, positive, and trusting working relationship?**

Resource

Ogletree et al. (2001) and Lytle and Bordin (2001) offer guidelines for working as a collaborative and interactive team.

Reflective

How would you describe your communication style? What communication skills do you use that support the success of teams? What communication skills would you like to improve?

cd-rom

Use Person-Centered Planning

Effective teams use *person-centered planning* to guide the delivery of services to students and their families (Kelly, Siegel, & Allinder, 2001). Person-centered planning recognizes the importance of the roles that students and their families play as advocates in identifying meaningful goals and appropriate strategies and services for meeting them. Person-centered planning also employs a variety of assessment procedures to identify the strengths, preferences, personal characteristics, cultural, linguistic, and experiential backgrounds and needs of students and their families (Keyes & Owens-Johnson, 2003). These variables are then examined to develop a comprehensive and holistic plan to coordinate the students' inclusion programs. Additional information and resources on using person-centered planning to develop individualized transition plans is presented in chapter 6.

Resource

Bui and Turnbull (2003) provide suggestions for making the person-centered planning process culturally sensitive.

Map Action Planning System

One person-centered planning strategy that many teams use is the Map Action Planning System (MAPS) (Ryan et al., 2001). MAPS also can be used to help the team develop IEPs (Keyes & Owens-Johnson, 2003). In MAPS, team members, including students with disabilities, their families, and peers, meet to develop an inclusion plan by first answering the following questions:

1. *What is a map?* This question allows participants to think about the characteristics of a map.

2. *What is (the student's name) history?* This question helps the team understand the events that have shaped the student's life and family.

3. *What is your (our) dream for (the student's name)?* This question allows team members to share their visions and goals for the student's future.

4. *What is your (our) nightmare?* This question helps the team understand the student's and family's fears.

5. *Who is (the student's name)?* This question gives all team members the opportunity to describe their perceptions of the student.

6. *What are (the student's name) strengths, gifts, and talents?* This question helps the team focus on and identify the student's positive attributes.

7. *What are (the student's name) needs? What can we do to meet these needs?* These questions help the team define the student's needs in a variety of areas.

8. *What would be an ideal day for (the student's name)? What do we need to do to make this ideal real?* These questions help the team plan the student's program by listing the goals and activities for the student, services and accommodations needed to achieve the goals and foster participation in these activities, and individuals responsible for delivering the services and accommodations.

Resource

Keyes and Owens-Johnson (2003) provide guidelines on implementing *Essential Lifestyle Planning,* a strategy that teams can use to engage in person-centered planning.

Work in Cooperative Teaching Arrangements

Many school districts are using *cooperative teaching* to educate *all students* in general education classrooms. In cooperative teaching, general education teachers and supportive service personnel such as special educators and speech/language therapists collaborate to teach students in inclusive settings (Friend & Cook, 2000; Hunt et al., 2003). Teachers involved in cooperative teaching share responsibility and accountability for planning and delivering instruction, evaluating, grading, and disciplining students. Students are not removed from the classroom for supportive services. Instead, academic instruction and supportive services are provided where the need exists: in the general education classroom.

Cooperative teaching teams can use many different instructional arrangements based on the purpose of the lesson, the nature of the material covered, and the needs of students. Examples of these instructional arrangements are described here and in Figure 4.3.

- *One teaching/one helping:* One teacher instructs the whole class while the other teacher circulates to collect information on students' performance or to offer help to students (see Figure 4.3a). This arrangement is also used to take advantage of the expertise of one teacher in a specific subject area.
- *Parallel teaching:* When it is necessary to lower the student–teacher ratio to teach new material or to review and practice material previously taught, both teachers can teach the same material at the same time to two equal groups of students (see Figure 4.3b).
- *Station teaching:* When teaching material that is difficult but not sequential or when several different topics are important, both teachers can teach different content at the same time to two equal groups of students, and then switch groups and repeat the lesson (see Figure 4.3c).
- *Alternative teaching:* When teachers need to individualize instruction, remediate skills, promote mastery, or offer enrichment based on students' needs, one teacher can work with a smaller group or individual students while the other teacher works with a larger group (see Figure 4.3d).
- *Team-teaching:* When it is important to blend the talents and expertise of teachers, both teachers can plan and teach a lesson together (see Figure 4.3e).

There are moments when things happen in the classroom that the kids do that are really funny. And you want to share that. And when she's in here, we just laugh hysterically. It's really more enjoyable because you've got another person there to share that with. If you try to save it until you get home to your spouse, you nearly forget it with everything else going on. But we'll just hoot at some of the things that happen. Like, I don't think I'll ever forget one of our little boys, he calls us Ms. McSmith. He combined the beginning of her name with the end of mine—and so we're both Ms. McSmith. It doesn't matter which one of us he tries to talk to, that's what he'll call us. (From a member of a cooperative teaching team) (Phillips, Sapona, & Lubic, 1995, pp. 266–267)

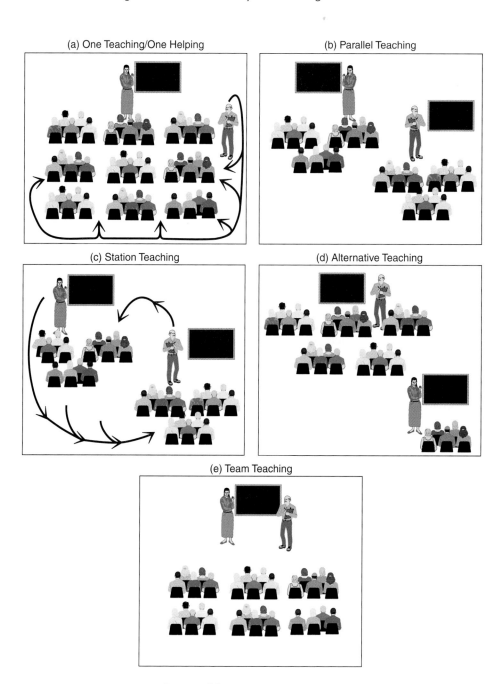

FIGURE 4.3   Cooperative teaching arrangements

Cooperative teaching is designed to minimize some of the problems of pull-out programs, such as students missing academic instruction, insufficient communication and coordination between professionals, scheduling problems, and fragmentation of the curriculum. It also allows supportive services and modified teaching for students with academic difficulties without labeling them. In addition to helping students with disabilities, cooperative teaching gives *all students* the assistance and expertise of at least two professionals rather than just one (Austin, 2001). Teachers working in cooperative teams also note that these programs help make teaching more enjoyable and stimulating, give them new insights and experiences regarding teaching strategies, and prevent the isolation that sometimes occurs when teachers work alone (Brownell, Yeager, Rennells, & Riley, 1997; Fennick & Liddy, 2001).

> At first, I was nervous, because you're not used to having another teacher in the classroom and all of a sudden you've got another person. I'm like, "Am I doing this right? Does she think this is okay?" Even though I knew her and I really liked her personally, I still thought, "What if she doesn't like my style of teaching? What if she thinks I'm lazy? What if she doesn't like this or that?" That sounds terrible, but the most difficult adjustment wasn't really pointed towards the kids, it was what she thought of me. (From a member of a cooperative teaching team) (Phillips et al., 1995, pp. 266–267)

Cooperative teaching teams may encounter several problems that can limit their effectiveness (McLeskey & Waldron, 2002). Lack of time to plan and implement programs, no administrative support, resistance from colleagues, concerns about grading, increased workloads, and increased responsibilities are major obstacles to successful cooperative teaching (Rice & Zigmond, 2000; Walther-Thomas, Korinek, McLaughlin, & Williams, 2000). Teachers also report that they need to learn to work and teach together so that both members of the team assume responsibility for *all students* and perform relevant and meaningful tasks that promote student learning (Weiss & Lloyd, 2003). For instance, if one teacher is always the instructional leader and the other teacher is relegated to the role of assistant or aide for a few students, the team may not be effective. This lack of parity may particularly occur at the secondary level, where the general educator is trained in the content area and therefore may assume the major responsibilities for teaching (Fisher, Frey, & Thousand, 2003). Team teaching takes time and requires teachers to deal with philosophical, pedagogical, historical, logistical, and territorial issues, as well as concerns about working with and being observed by another professional. You can address these issues by considering the following:

- Discuss why you want to work together and agree on the goals you have for your classroom. It is also important to establish ground rules for your collaboration and discuss what you expect of each other, as well as your concerns and fears about working cooperatively.
- Learn about each other's abilities, beliefs, routines, teaching styles classroom management, family involvement approaches, and assessment strategies. Noonan, McCormick, and Heck (2003), Kennedy, Higgins, and Pierce (2002), and Walther-Thomas, Korinek, McLaughlin, & Williams (2000) present forms, surveys and questions that cooperative teaching teams can use to become familiar with each other's skills, interests, teaching styles, and educational philosophies.
- Understand and coordinate each other's responsibilities and areas of expertise, as well as the roles of others. Frederico, Herrold, and Venn (1999) developed a checklist to use in coordinating the roles and responsibilities of teachers, support service personnel, administrators, family and community members, and the school district (see Figure 4.4).
- Be sensitive to cross-cultural perspectives and interactions. Understand and accept multiple perspectives, and work toward accepting and responding appropriately to each other's cultural beliefs and communication styles (Jairrels, 1999).
- Arrange the classroom to support collaboration. Agree on the placement of your work areas, students, and materials, and the scheduling of routines and activities. Make sure both teacher's work areas are in prominent locations in the room, and that both of you share materials and classroom spaces and have easy access to them (Gately & Gately, 2001).

FIGURE 4.4

Checklist for planning inclusive cooperative teaching arrangements

RESPONSIBILITIES	General Education Teacher	Special Education Teacher	Principal	Support Services	Parents & Community	School District
General Responsibilities						
Describe the school's position on inclusion						
Prepare the teaching staff for inclusion						
Offer teachers a choice of inclusion teaching						
Describe the inclusion program to parents						
Provide full support services in the general class						
Establish an inclusion support group						
Explain the inclusion program to school personnel						
Specific Professional Responsibilities						
Ensure compliance with state and federal guidelines						
Provide student information to the inclusion team						
Supervise the teaching assistant(s)						
Serve as the student case manager						
Monitor individualized education program (IEP) standards						
Maintain cumulative folders						
Participate in parent conferences						
Assign grades on report cards each semester						
Learning to Be an Inclusion Team Teacher						
Attend inclusion inservice						
Function as part of the inclusion team						
Respect the role of each school inclusion team member						
Teacher-Student Interaction						
Adapt curricular activities for students with disabilities						
Teach student peers to assist students with disabilities						
Use adaptations in classroom activities						
Develop daily lesson plans						
Work one-on-one with students as needed						
Design interaction activities for students						
Assign "buddies" to students with disabilities						

(continued)

Figure 4.4 (continued)

RESPONSIBILITIES	General Education Teacher	Special Education Teacher	Principal	Support Services	Parents & Community	School District
Beliefs About Teaching Inclusion						
Maintain a sense of humor						
Treat the inclusion class as "Our Class," not "My Class"						
Become a community of inclusion learners						
Avoid labeling children in the inclusion program						
Treat all students as equals						
Use appropriate behavior management						
End-of-Year Responsibilities						
Administer end-of-year standardized testing						
Assign final grades on report cards						
Determine student promotions						
Determine inclusion program successes						
Identify inclusion program failures						
Invite others to join the inclusion team						
Select teachers for the next year's inclusion classroom(s)						

Source: From "Helpful Tips for Successful Inclusion: A Checklist for Educators," by M. A. Frederico, W. G. Herrold, and J. Venn, 1999, *Teaching Exceptional Children, 32*(1), pp. 76–82. Copyright 1999 by The Council for Exceptional Children. Reprinted with permission.

- Establish and agree on a common set of expectations for judging and grading students' academic, behavioral, and social performance (Rice & Zigmond, 2000) (We will learn about grading students in inclusive settings in chapter 12.)
- Develop communication, problem-solving, and team-building skills. Work toward honestly, respectfully, and reflectively talking to and listening to others, expressing opinions without taking a value position, and understanding each other's verbal and nonverbal communication styles (McCormick, Noonan, Ogata, & Heck, 2001). It is also important to use self-disclosure and perspective taking, to think and communicate in terms of "we" and "our" rather than "I" and "my," and to make decisions by consensus.
- Understand that cooperative teaching is a developmental process, and be prepared to encounter problems at first. Successful cooperative teaching goes through stages and therefore involves taking time to adjust to working with another person to resolve logistical and territorial issues, to determine roles and responsibilities, and to blend skills (Gately & Gately, 2001).

- Work toward establishing an equal status relationship. Share the workload, vary responsibilities, and don't relegate one person to a lesser role. Make sure that the contributions of all team members are recognized and valued by students, students' families, and other professionals.
- Vary the arrangements used to teach students based on the purpose of the lesson, the nature of the content covered, and the strengths and needs of students. Use a range of activities that allows both team members to take a leadership role and to feel comfortable. A format for planning cooperative teaching lessons is presented in Figure 4.5.
- Meet periodically with families to explain the program and to share information on students' progress.
- Communicate regularly to reevaluate goals, solve problems, plan instruction, divide responsibilities, share instructional roles and administrative tasks, brainstorm new ideas and approaches, and talk about students' progress (Fennick, 2001).
- Seek support and feedback from families and other professionals. Solicit the support of your administrator, who can be instrumental in providing the time, professional development opportunities, and resources to facilitate the success of your collaborative efforts.
- Address philosophical, pedagogical, logistical, and interpersonal differences directly and immediately. Don't let differences escalate, and be willing to listen to the other person's perspective, discuss the situation and possible solutions from your perspective, and compromise (Langerock, 2000).
- Assess the impact of the program on *all students,* and revise the program based on these data. A variety of formal and informal measures can be used to examine the impact of your collaboration on your students' educational, behavioral, and social progress (see chapter 12).
- Engage in self-evaluation and reflection to examine the team's success and the ways the team can improve. Continually examine shared values and goals, as well as concerns, problems, misunderstandings, expectations, and plans for the future. Interviews (see Figure 4.6) and surveys (see Figure 4.7) can be used to help you

Resource:

Weiss and Lloyd (2002) and Rice and Zigmond (2000) provide information and descriptions of cooperative teaching arrangements at the secondary level, and Fennick (2001) outlines the ways teaching teams can collaborate to help students make a successful transition from high school.

How can cooperative teaching teams make sure both teachers perform meaningful roles that facilitate student learning?

FIGURE 4.5

Cooperative teaching lesson plan format

General Educator _____   Special Educator _____

Date	What are we going to teach?	Which co-teaching technique will we use?	What are the specific tasks of both teachers?	What materials are needed?	How will we evaluate learning?	Information about students who need follow-up work

Source: From "The ABCDEs of Co-Teaching," by S. Vaughn, J. S. Schumm, and M. E. Arguelles, 1997, *Teaching Exceptional Children, 30*(2), pp. 4–10.

FIGURE 4.6

Sample cooperative teaching interview

◈ How is cooperative teaching working in your class?

◈ What components and practices of your cooperative teaching team appear to be effective?

◈ What difficulties have you encountered working as a cooperative teaching team?

◈ What do you enjoy the most about working in a cooperative teaching team?

◈ What are your biggest concerns about working in a cooperative teaching team?

◈ What support from others, resources, and training have you received to work successfully as a cooperative teaching team? What support from others, resources, and training have been most helpful? Least helpful? What additional support from others, resources, and training would be helpful?

◈ How has your cooperative teaching team affected the academic, social, and behavioral development of your students, and your interactions with their families? Describe the positive and negative benefits you have observed in your students and their families.

◈ How do your students' families and other professionals feel about your cooperative teaching team?

◈ How has working in a cooperative teaching team affected you as a professional and a person? Describe the positive and negative effects for you.

◈ In what ways have your roles changed as a result of working in a cooperative teaching team? How do you feel about your new roles?

◈ How did the collaboration process change throughout the school year?

◈ What did you learn from working as a cooperative teaching team?

◈ How do you work through conflicts?

◈ What suggestions would you have for others interested in working in cooperative teaching teams?

◈ What schoolwide and districtwide practices have supported your efforts to work as a cooperative teaching team? Hindered your efforts? In what ways should these practices be revised?

FIGURE 4.7

Sample cooperative teaching survey

Directions: Please indicate your feeling about the following statements using this scale:

Strongly Disagree (1)	Disagree (2)	Neutral (3)	Agree (4)	Strongly Agree (5)

1. I like working in a cooperative teaching team.	1 2 3 4 5
2. Students benefit from being taught by a cooperative teaching team.	1 2 3 4 5
3. I feel like this is our classroom.	1 2 3 4 5
4. Students with disabilities receive fewer specialized services as a result of cooperative teaching.	1 2 3 4 5
5. My students' families are satisfied with our cooperative teaching arrangement.	1 2 3 4 5
6. Other professionals are supportive of our cooperative teaching arrangement.	1 2 3 4 5
7. Our cooperative teaching team has sufficient time to communicate effectively.	1 2 3 4 5
8. Our cooperative teaching team shares responsibility for all instructional and noninstructional activities.	1 2 3 4 5
9. Our cooperative teaching team blends the teaching styles, philosophies, talents, and expertise of both teachers.	1 2 3 4 5
10. Working in a cooperative teaching team has encouraged me to try new instructional strategies.	1 2 3 4 5
11. Our school district provides the necessary support from others, resources, and training to implement cooperative teaching effectively.	1 2 3 4 5
12. I enjoy teaching more because I work in a cooperative teaching team.	1 2 3 4 5
13. I like having another adult in the classroom.	1 2 3 4 5
14. It is easy to communicate with my cooperative teaching partner.	1 2 3 4 5
15. I perform a subordinate role in our cooperative teaching team.	1 2 3 4 5
16. I have benefited professionally and personally from working as a cooperative teaching team.	1 2 3 4 5
17. My workload has increased as a result of working in a cooperative teaching team.	1 2 3 4 5
18. I am satisfied with the schoolwide and districtwide policies regarding cooperative teaching teams.	1 2 3 4 5
19. I would like to continue to work in a cooperative teaching team.	1 2 3 4 5

reflect upon aspects of your cooperative teaching team (Austin, 2001; Gately & Gately, 2001; Noonan et al., 2003; Salend, Gordon, & Lopez-Vona, 2002).

- Acknowledge and celebrate success. Enjoy, share, attribute, and reflect on your accomplishments as a team.

Employ Collaborative Consultation

Teachers may also use *collaborative consultation* to facilitate the success of their inclusion programs (Logan & Stein, 2001; Voltz, Brazil, & Ford, 2001). This involves working together to implement mutually agreed-on solutions to prevent and address learning and behavioral difficulties and to coordinate instructional programs for *all students*. Collaborative consultation is designed to address students' strengths and needs and to give general education teachers improved knowledge and skills to deal with similar situations in the future.

The "consultant," usually a special, bilingual, or multicultural educator or an ancillary staff member (a school psychologist, speech and language therapist, or physical therapist),

Reflective

Think about a situation in which you worked collaboratively with a team. How was the outcome affected by the collaboration? What problems and successes did the team have in working collaboratively? How did the team resolve the problems?

REFLECTING ON PROFESSIONAL PRACTICES

Working as a Cooperative Teaching Team

Cathy, a general education teacher, and Sarah, a special educator, were asked by their principal to work together as a cooperative teaching team. Their class, located in Cathy's former classroom, included 24 students, 7 of whom had been identified as having a disability. Although they had worked together before to reintegrate students with disabilities into the general education classroom for specific subject areas and activities, they were both anxious and excited about working as a cooperative teaching team. Initially, Cathy and Sarah experienced some difficulties. Sarah felt out of place in Cathy's classroom. She was frustrated because she didn't know where the supplies and materials were located and frequently had to ask Cathy. She also worried that Cathy would have all the responsibilities and be the "real" teacher and that she would function as a teacher's aide.

Cathy sensed Sarah's concern and was also worried about their differences in terms of roles, teaching style, and philosophy. Sometimes she wondered whether Sarah thought she was too controlling, and disapproved of her concern about getting students ready for the statewide tests. Both Cathy and Sarah were also concerned that the students and their families viewed one of them as the teacher and the other one as a teacher's assistant.

At first, Sarah and Cathy had some difficulty determining their responsibilities and blending their skills. They struggled as they attempted to teach lessons together and coordinate their instructional activities. Sometimes, while Cathy led a lesson, Sarah seemed lost and felt like a helper rather than a teacher. They also had different opinions about the abilities of the students with disabilities. Sarah worried that "her" students would not be able to keep up with Cathy's plans for all the students, and that they were not receiving the services they needed. At the first family meeting their roles were clearly delineated, with Sarah speaking to the classified students' families separately. They quickly realized that this was a mistake and were determined to work on blending their skills.

As they worked together, they began to notice and respect each other's skills, perspectives, experiences, and areas of expertise. Cathy was impressed with Sarah's effectiveness in dealing with behavior problems, and Sarah was excited about the way Cathy made whole language activities come alive. They both wanted to learn from each other. They also started to improve in planning and teaching lessons together and performing administrative tasks. In teaching together, they began to anticipate each other's styles. Their principal observed them teaching a lesson and noticed that they were starting to teach together in a natural way even though their perspectives were different. When they completed the students' report cards together, they were amazed at how close they were in assessing students' needs and progress.

As they got to know each other, Cathy and Sarah began to experiment with new teaching methods, and both seemed to have a renewed enjoyment of teaching. They used role plays, puppets, and sometimes spontaneously acted out stories and lessons. Both teachers were surprised by how much more fun they and their students were having in class.

Although things were going well, Cathy and Sarah's concerns about teaming and their philosophical differences surfaced periodically. Sarah, who was trained in a skills-based approach, was concerned that Cathy's whole language approach was not effective with some of the students. Sarah discussed this with Cathy, who was very understanding, and they decided to do skills work, too.

Their commitment to teaming was sustained by the positive changes they saw in their students. Sarah and Cathy were pleased that all the students had progressed developmentally, academically, and socially. They were particularly surprised and motivated by the influence of their collaboration on the sense of community in the classroom, which was seen in the students' unusual sensitivity to their peers.

Cathy and Sarah also were pleased with the support they received from their principal. The principal met periodically with them to discuss problems and solutions, to acknowledge their efforts and growth, and to offer assistance, support, and resources. The principal also rearranged their schedules to give them planning time together and encouraged them to visit schools with model programs.

Looking back on their experiences as a cooperative teaching team, Sarah and Cathy agreed that it was a successful year. Sarah noted, "What an incredible year! After so many years as a special education teacher, it was refreshing to interact with a greater variety of children. It was a great learning year for me. I don't think teachers know how enjoyable teaching can be when you share it." Cathy said, "This is the end of a wonderful year. The children and we as teachers became a close-knit community of learners. We all did learn and grow this year. It was like dancing with someone; sometimes you lead and sometimes

(continued)

you follow. We began with a lot of apprehension and ended with much enthusiasm."

- Why do you think Cathy and Sarah were initially both anxious and excited about working together as a co-operative teaching team?
- What problems and concerns did they have?
- How did working together benefit Cathy and Sarah and their students?
- What factors helped to make this a successful school year?

- How would you feel if you were asked to be part of a cooperative teaching team?
- What resources, knowledge, skills, and dispositions do you need to teach effectvely in a cooperative teaching team?

 To answer these questions online and share your responses with others, go to the Reflection module in Chapter 4 of the Companion Website.

works collaboratively with the general education teacher, who has primary responsibility (Kampwirth, 1999). Figure 4.8, a diary of the experiences of a collaborative consultation teacher, presents some of the services provided.

Steps in Collaborative Consultation

The steps in effective collaborative consultation are (a) goal and problem clarification and identification, (b) goal and problem analysis, (c) plan implementation, and (d) plan evaluation (Wilkinson, 2003), which can be recorded by teams using Figure 4.9.

Goal and Problem Clarification and Identification.   The first step in the consultation process is to identify goals and problems, using who, what, and where questions that help teachers clarify and agree on their goals and concerns. For example, consultation teams can address such questions as: What are students' strengths? What challenges will students have in this class? What goals do we have for students? What can we do to address these challenges and help students achieve our goals? (Vargo, 1998). Goals and problems also can be identified by examining students' IEPs and observing students in their classrooms.

Often it is best for the consultation to focus on one situation at a time. If several problem areas must be handled simultaneously, it is advisable to set priorities and deal with the most important ones first. A consultation assistance request form that can be used to identify goals and problems is presented in Figure 4.10.

Goal and Problem Analysis.   In the second phase of the consultation process, educators analyze the features that appear to be related to the identified goals and problems (Logan & Stein, 2001). These may include the curriculum, the physical environment of the room, teaching strategies, grouping arrangements, teaching and learning styles, peer relationships, student ability levels, family, and the school's policies and procedures. This analysis helps educators to plan appropriate intervention strategies.

Plan Implementation.   During this phase, educators plan which interventions to use to address the identified goals and difficulties (Appl, Troha, & Rowell, 2001). They brainstorm and share their expertise, considering factors such as practicality, effectiveness, resources needed, and effects on others. Once the preferred interventions have been selected, they can be outlined in detail, and responsibilities and timelines can be determined.

FIGURE 4.8

Diary of a collaborative consultation teacher

September 7: *I can only be in one place at a time! Juggling teacher schedules and getting to students for assistance in their academic areas of need will be a feat worthy of a gold medal. And on top of that, time has to be set aside to conference with classroom teachers. I'm frustrated!!*

September 8: *I've worried about how junior high students would accept my presence in the classroom. . . . I discussed this with Mr. T, the building principal. During the grade level orientations, Mr. T introduced me as a teacher who would be in several different classes to assist students.*

September 13: *I did it! Schedules typed, all academic areas covered. I even managed to schedule time to conference with teachers (and it's not during lunch!). Mrs. C is not too keen on meeting with me on a regular basis and voiced a great concern about how much work this would add to her already overloaded schedule. Copies of all schedules have been sent to teachers, administrators, and parents. I have contacted every parent by phone and explained the service.*

September 14: *Mrs. M came to see me. She blurted out to me that she didn't know if she could go through with having me work in her room. She indicated to me that she felt extremely intimidated and was worried about what I would think. My first reaction was, "Don't be silly." Thank goodness I didn't say that. It really wasn't silly, because, I, too, was very nervous. I told Mrs. M that I understood what she meant, and explained my own nervousness.*

September 18: *A pleasant surprise. Mr. K introduced me as a co-teacher. He told his students that if they had any questions they could ask either himself or me. . . . I was wondering exactly how this would work out, when several different students raised their hands for assistance. In the end, I put together a small group of children to work with at the back table. How nice to see that the students I expected to work with, along with other students, accepted my presence and wanted my help.*

September 20: *I met with Mrs. E today. Together we worked on J's IEP, reviewed her entire curriculum, and decided on goals which should be included. It was wonderful having her input.*

October 12: *Mrs. C asked me if I would be willing to take a group of students for the social studies lesson and work on latitude and longitude. . . . We discussed the format and objectives of the lesson. During the class, we divided the room into groups and each taught a group. After the lesson, we were able to meet and discuss the results.*

November 16: *Ms. D, a first grade teacher, approached me and asked if I could speak with her about one of her students. I do not have a student in her room. We met after school and discussed the difficulties this child was having. Ms. D then asked if I would sit in on a parent conference. I guess there is a lot more to this job than just working with my assigned students.*

November 20: *Today's consultation with Mrs. K centered on getting her feedback on a study guide I created. We went over all the points, and at the end of the conversation she asked me if I would mind if she duplicated the guide and gave it to all her students.*

December 5: *Mrs. M indicated that the whole class was having difficulty getting the concept of contractions. We discussed some strategies, and she asked if I would like to teach the lesson the following morning. At the end of the consultation session, she turned to me and said, "You know, I am still a little nervous, but I really do like this collaborative consultation."*

Source: From "Diary of a Consulting Teacher," by K. Giek, 1990, *The Forum, 16*(1) pp. 5–6. Copyright 1990 by New York State Federation of Chapters of the Council for Exceptional Children. Reprinted by permission.

Plan Evaluation. Once the intervention has been implemented, its effectiveness should be checked periodically. This can be done by direct observation, curriculum-based assessments, analysis of student work samples, and other techniques that assess student progress (see chapter 12).

Follow-up evaluation can also examine how the intervention has been implemented, whether it needs to be revised, and what additional problem areas need to be solved. Feedback should be an ongoing, interactive process focused on the intervention plan rather than on the individuals involved.

FIGURE 4.9

Collaborative consultation planning form

Child: _____ Teachers: _____ Date: _____

Team members present: _____

Child's strengths and interests:

Concerns about the child's learning:

Problem statement:

Brainstorming ideas:

Idea(s) selected:

Implementation of the idea:

How/what?	When?	Who?

Timeline for implementation:

Evaluation of the intervention:

      Outcomes:

      Future plans:

Source: From "Reflections of a First-Year Team: The Growth of a Collaborative Partnership," by D. J. Appl, C. Troha, and J. Rowell, 2001, *Teaching Exceptional Children, 33*(3), pp. 4–8.

Even though consultation is effective, professionals may resist its use. This attitude is often associated with frustration, professional pride, and different views of the process. Other major barriers include insufficient time for team members to meet and overwhelming caseloads. Successful consultation programs give classroom teachers and support staff time to consult with one another, and offer educators reasonable caseloads and schedules.

 *Resource*

Wilkinson (2003), Logan and Stein (2001), and Appl, Troha, and Rowell (2001) offer examples of the use of collaborative consultation to support students' learning and appropriate behavior in inclusive classrooms.

Promote Congruence

Successful collaboration and communication requires *congruence,* a logical relationship among the curriculum, learning goals, teaching materials, strategies used in the general education classroom, and supportive services programs. A congruent program is one based on common assessment results, goals and objectives, teaching strategies, and materials.

Ideally, supplemental and remedial teaching should parallel the general education curriculum. Unfortunately, many of these programs are fragmented, based on different—and conflicting—curricula and teaching approaches. These incompatible and conflicting programs can confuse students rather than help them learn. For instance, confusion can occur when students receive reading instruction using a phonetic approach in the resource room and a whole language approach in the general education classroom.

You can use two models for coordinating teaching so that the ancillary program supplements learning in the general education classroom: an a priori model and a post hoc model. In the *a priori* model, supportive services educators teach content that supports the content to be learned in the general education classroom. This instruction lays the

ASSISTANCE NEEDED

Teacher _____   Today's Date

Student _____

Other _____   _____

☐ There's a problem. Let's put our heads together.
☐ I need your help in the classroom.
☐ Develop alternative assignment or activity.
☐ Arrange cooperative learning groups & activities.
☐ Implement peer tutoring or peer partners.
☐ Produce alternative materials or locate resources.
☐ Develop a modified grading system.
☐ Create a study guide.   ☐ Plan a lesson.
☐ Modify materials.   ☐ Team teaching.
☐ Modify a test.   ☐ Classroom management.
☐ Develop guided notes.   ☐ Instructional strategies.

When? _____

Additional information:
_____
_____
_____
_____

FIGURE 4.10   Consultation assistance request form

Source: From "Collaborative Teaching in the Secondary School," by E.A. Knackendoffel, 1996, in D. D. Deshler, E. S. Ellis, & B. K. Lenz (Eds.), *Teaching Adolescents with Learning Disabilities* (2nd ed.), p. 585. Copyright 1996 by Love. Reprinted with permission.

foundation for instruction in the general education classroom. For example, the ESL educator might introduce on Monday the spelling words that will be introduced on Friday in the general education classroom.

In the *post hoc* model, supportive instruction reinforces skills previously introduced in the general education classroom. Thus, rather than introducing new content, the supportive services educator reviews and reteaches content previously covered in the general education classroom. For example, while a student is learning how to add fractions in the general educating classroom, the resource teacher helps the student understand the process and develop automatic methods of responding to similar items.

Meetings

Meetings such as IEP conferences also can be used to establish congruence by involving general and supportive services educators in planning and implementing teaching programs. They can agree on common objectives, teaching methods and materials, and evaluation procedures to assess student learning. As students master the objectives, additional meetings can be held to revise the instructional program and evaluate congruence.

Student Interviews

You also can use student interviews to ensure and evaluate congruence. Specifically, you can ask students, "What things are you learning in (class)?" "What type of activities do you do in (class)?" "What materials do you use in (class)?" and "Does (class) help you in other classes?" (Johnston, Allington, & Afflerbach, 1985).

Note Card Systems

Congruence and communication between professionals can be fostered by the use of a note card system. Each professional working with the student completes a note card that serves as an ongoing record of the student's performance in that class for a specified period of time. The information on the card could include a rating of the student's progress, a list of the skills mastered and not mastered, upcoming assignments and tests, successful strategies, teaching materials being used, and skills other teachers can attempt to foster. One educator can be asked to categorize the information and share it with others to ensure the continuity of instruction. A sample note card is presented in Figure 4.11.

Engage in Professional Development

Your ability to collaborate and communicate with others and create inclusive classrooms also can be enhanced by engaging in professional development activities to improve your teaching. These professional development activities include attending workshops, faculty meetings, and professional conferences, reading journal articles and books, viewing videos, joining professional organizations and study groups, and taking classes (Hollingsworth, 2001). For example, many teachers work in collaborative groups to reflect on teaching strategies and programs designed to enhance student learning (Buysse, Sparkman, & Wesley, 2003).

Many school districts are asking teachers to create their own individualized professional development plans. These plans include one's professional development goals, the

Resource

Buysse, Sparkman, and Wesley (2003), Hollingsworth (2001), Watanabe (2002), Routman (2002), and Herner and Higgins (2000) offer guidelines and forms that help educators engage in study groups and small group dialogues to foster student learning, and Guskey (2002) provides suggestions for evaluating professional development activities.

FIGURE 4.11

Sample note card

Student's Name: Time Period:
Class/Supportive Service: Educator:
Skills taught:
Instructional strategies and materials used:
Upcoming assignments/tests:

Assignment/Test Date Due

Skills to be reinforced in other settings:
Suggested activities to reinforce skills:
Comments:

IDEAS FOR IMPLEMENTATION

Promoting Congruence

Ms. Rivera is concerned about Elisa, a migrant student, who leaves her classroom several times a day for supplemental education. To alleviate her concerns, Ms. Rivera meets with Mr. D'Alessandro, Elisa's ESL teacher, to coordinate their activities. They discuss how to plan their programs so that Mr. D'Alessandro's sessions will reinforce what Ms. Rivera is teaching in the classroom.

They decide that Mr. D'Alessandro will preview stories with Elisa before they are read in Ms. Rivera's classroom. Also, Mr. D'Alessandro will review new words from the story and read the story again with Elisa. To coordinate these activities and check on Elisa's progress, Ms. Rivera and Mr. D'Alessandro meet weekly. With this planning, Ms. Rivera feels better and Elisa is better able to participate in class.

Here are some other strategies you can use to establish congruence:

- Work with supportive services educators so that their assessment procedures, curricula, and teaching strategies are aligned with those used in the general education classroom.
- Find time for general education and supportive service teachers to share lesson plans and materials and observe each other's classrooms.

- Schedule time for teachers to collaborate in planning the student's instructional program.
- Use flexible scheduling that gives educators planning time to collaborate and coordinate their teaching.
- Have supportive services personnel such as special and bilingual education teachers give presentations at faculty meetings or on inservice days, and conduct a faculty meeting in the classrooms of these personnel.
- Maintain a file in which staff members list the areas of expertise they would be willing to share with others.
- Encourage all staff members to visit and observe each other's teaching activities. Ask faculty members to switch roles for a day.
- Designate an area of the teachers' lounge as a "materials table" where teachers leave certain materials that they think would be of value to others, or set up a lending library.
- Teach study skills and learning strategies using the textbooks of the general education program.

Set Your Sites

For more on professional development activities, go to the Web Links module in Chapter 4 of the Companion Website.

Resource

Daresh (2003), Whitaker (2000), Conderman and Stephens (2000), Maroney (2000), and Lloyd, Wood, and Moreno (2000) provide information about the challenges faced by beginning teachers and strategies and resources for addressing them.

learning activities one will engage in to achieve these goals, and the products that will be developed and their effect on the teaching and learning process.

One form of professional development that is particularly helpful for beginning teachers is teacher mentoring (Conderman & Stephens, 2000; Daresh, 2003). Mentoring programs involve frequent collaborative interactions between experienced, effective teachers and new teachers to address the challenges that new teachers encounter. Mentoring dyads observe each other's classrooms, discuss their teaching, assessment, and classroom management practices, curricula, and instructional materials, and develop plans to facilitate the teaching, learning, and collaboration process. Mentors also provide information related to the field and the school district, as well as emotional support. In addition to helping mentees adjust to the profession and their jobs, mentoring programs also benefit mentors (Whitaker, 2000).

For many experienced educators, professional development activities are important aspects of their efforts to obtain certification from the National Board for Professional Teaching Standards (NBPTS) (Helms, 2000). Educators apply for NBPTS certification based on their preparation of a portfolio and their responses to exercises, interviews, and exams. The portfolio and responses are then evaluated in terms of their commitment to student learning, their knowledge of their subject matter, and their ability to foster a positive learning environment, assess student progress, reflect on their practices, and collaborate with and learn from others.

IDEAS FOR IMPLEMENTATION

Facing the Challenges of Being a Beginning Teacher

Ms. Salinas had always wanted to be a teacher and was looking forward to her first teaching position in an inclusion program. Before the school year began, she went into her classroom to get it ready, and worked on reviewing student records, preparing lessons, and creating a newsletter for families. When school began, she was confident that she could apply what she had learned in her teacher education program. While things got off to a good start, Ms. Salinas started feeling stressed out. Even though she arrived early and stayed late, she found herself overwhelmed by the paperwork and her unfamiliarity with the district policies. When some lessons didn't go as planned, and when she had conflicts with one of the paraeducators and a family member, Ms. Salinas started questioning her decision to be a teacher. Sensing Ms. Salinas' frustration, her principal spoke to her about being mentored by Mr. O'Connor, an experienced teacher with an excellent reputation in the school district. Ms. Salinas was reluctant but her principal explained that what she was experiencing was typical, and that mentoring is provided to all beginning teachers.

A week later Ms. Salinas and Mr. O'Connor met after school. They talked about the challenges facing a beginning teacher, and Mr. O'Connor shared some of his first-year teaching experiences, which were very similar to what Ms. Salinas was experiencing. He also told her that he wished he had the help of someone when he started teaching, and that she should try not to be too hard on herself.

They made a plan to observe each other's classrooms so that they could both learn from one another. After Mr. O'Connor's first observation, he told her that she was doing fine and made some suggestions about teaching strategies she might want to try, which he modeled for her when she came to see his classroom. They also spent time talking about the district's policies, inclusion programs, the curriculum and discipline, and how to handle conflicts with other professionals and family members. Mr. O'Connor liked being helpful to Ms. Salinas, and also learned some things from her. Ms. Salinas appreciated the support and felt better about her decision to be a teacher.

Here are some other strategies for facing the challenges of being a beginning teacher:

- Recognize that teaching is a difficult and challenging job and give yourself permission to experiment and learn from your experiences.

- Take care of your emotional and physical health. Remember your personal and family needs. Find time to do things you like to do and to keep your life as balanced as possible.
- Learn about your students and their families. It will help you understand them and gain their support and trust.
- Get to know the other professionals (e.g., other teachers and service providers, paraeducators, school secretaries, janitors, cafeteria workers, and administrators) in your school and school district and establish a good working relationship with them. Ask them about schoolwide policies and procedures, and about ways to help you and your students and their families.
- Reflect on your teaching practices. For example, maintain a journal where you can respond to the following: (a) What happened? (Briefly describe the situation/experience); (b) What was the outcome of this situation/experience? Was it successful? Why or why not?; (c) What did you learn from this situation/experience?; (d) What would you do differently?; and (e) What does this show about your growth as a teacher?
- Take advantage of whatever professional development activities you can fit into your schedule.
- Use materials and resources (e.g., lesson plans, assessment activities, classroom management plans) that you developed or acquired as part of your participation in your teacher education program.
- Keep in touch with your former classmates and even your professors. Use them as a resource and as a sounding board.

 For more on teacher mentoring and information helpful to beginning teachers, go to the Web Links module in Chapter 4 of the Companion Website.

Note: Conderman & Stephens (2000), Lloyd, Wood, & Moreno (2000); Maroney (2000); Whitaker (2000).

IDEAS FOR IMPLEMENTATION

Attending Professional Conferences

Ms. Roman, a teacher education candidate, was excited about the opportunity to attend her first professional conference. Her friends and professors had told her about the opportunities she would have to attend sessions that offered current information, teaching strategies, resources, and research that would assist her in teaching and doing assignments for her courses. She was also looking forward to spending time with her peers and meeting other professionals.

At the first session Ms. Roman attended she met Ms. Stevens, who had been teaching for 7 years. Ms. Stevens told her that she tried to attend as many conferences as she could because they made her more knowledgeable regarding the profession, and gave her ideas to implement in her classroom and share with her colleagues, administrators, and students' families. Ms. Stevens gave Ms. Roman several tips for making the most of the conference. "Right after I register, I sit down with the program, highlight the sessions I want to attend, and plan my schedule. If I'm with others, we split up and share information and handouts later in the day. I try to arrive at sessions early to get a seat, and I take a notebook, pencils, and highlighters to help me take notes during sessions. I also take sticky labels with my contact information and business cards in case the presenters run out of handouts. Don't be afraid to ask questions. It helps you learn, and the presenters like it because it shows you are interested in what they have to say. I take breaks when I'm tired and always plan several trips to see the exhibits, and to network and socialize with others. I've made many good contacts and new friends attending conferences and I look forward to seeing them every year." Here are some other strategies you can use to make conferences more productive and enjoyable:

- Prepare in advance by reviewing conference programs, and checking on registration, hotel, and travel information and the weather.
- Dress professionally and comfortably. Bring a variety of clothes that are appropriate for the range of situations you may encounter such as attending professional sessions, networking and socializing with others, and interviewing for jobs.
- Place water and snacks and other conference related materials in an easy-to-carry bag, and take breaks when you need them.
- Choose sessions that will help you in your classroom or your college courses, extend your learning in new areas, and share information with others.
- Attend a range of sessions including regular sessions, poster sessions, and opening and closing sessions.
- Act professionally by attending and actively listening and participating in sessions. Take notes, ask questions, participate in activities, share your knowledge, and acknowledge presenters for a job well done. If you must leave a session, do so without distracting others.
- Network and socialize with others in sessions and hospitality rooms, during breaks, at meals, social events and special interest group meetings. Wear nametags, initiate conversations with others, accept invitations from others, and invite others to join you and your group.
- Bring copies of your resumes, samples of your work, and your professional portfolio if you plan on interviewing for jobs at the conference.
- Complete evaluation forms for each session you attend and for the whole conference. Let conference planners know about aspects of the conference that were effective as well as those that could be improved.
- Make sure that you have the funds to cover your costs and keep records of your expenses, especially if you want to be reimbursed in a timely manner. Inquire about how you can reduce your costs by being part of a group, or volunteering to work at the conference.
- Share information and handouts from the conference with others when you return home.

Note: Mullins, McKnab, & Dempsey (2002).

Online Services

You and other members of the team can engage in professional development, obtain information and communicate with others via online services such as electronic mail (E-mail) and the Internet. E-mail allows individuals to "talk to" and distribute communications to others. It can be used to share ideas and concerns, develop lessons, and brainstorm solutions to problems. Online services give professionals, families, and students access to a wide range of resources (e.g., databases, documents, reports, and materials) from around the world and opportunities to exchange information and ideas with colleagues. Online discussion groups offer interactions with others who are working in model programs and are interested in similar issues. For example, you can be part of a listserv, an E-mail list that lets you correspond with others on common interests. For students, online services offer exciting, challenging, and novel learning experiences (see chapter 8 for more information on using online services for teaching purposes).

Most professional organizations or clearinghouses offer professional development and maintain a list of online computer networks and resources, including discussion and support groups. For example, the Educational Resources Information Center (ERIC), through its *AskERIC* service (*www.ericir/syr.edu*), offers electronic lists and databases with information on curricula, professional development, pedagogy, and teaching materials. Special education sites on the World Wide Web can be located through the use of *SERI—Special Education Resources on the Internet* (*www.hood.edu/seri*).

Set Your Sites

For more on using the Internet for lesson planning, go to the Web Links module in Chapter 4 of the Companion Website.

Set Your Sites

For more on listservs, go to the Web Links module in Chapter 4 of the Companion Website.

How Can I Foster Communication and Collaboration with Families?

A key component of effective inclusion programs is communication and collaboration with the student's family. As well as being educationally sound, involving family members in the education of their children can help you build support for your inclusion program. You can view them as a valuable resource and partner in the educational process by (a) using a variety of ways to share information with them; (b) engaging families in curriculum planning; (c) holding meetings with them to develop students' IEPs; (d) inviting them to attend school and classroom events; (e) providing them with information and resources so that they can help their children learn and complete their homework; and (f) soliciting information from them about their children's strengths, needs, and progress. You also can encourage families to support the educational program by asking them to (a) talk frequently with their children about school and its importance; (b) read with and to their children on a regular basis; (c) volunteer in your classroom; and (d) establish routines in the home that support learning. For example, some teachers involve families in the learning process by sending home active and enjoyable learning activities that family members can do with their children (Stephens & Jairrels, 2003).

Unfortunately, the practices used in some school districts reduce family involvement and empowerment (U.S. Department of Education, 2001). Harry, Allen, and McLaughlin (1995) examined the experiences of family members after their children were placed in special education. They found that the attitudes and involvement of family members changed over time. At first, family members supported their children's schooling and acted as advocates on behalf of their children. Later, they became disillusioned with the special

Reflective

Research indicates that family involvement in school declines significantly as students age (U.S. Department of Education, 2001). Why do you think this is the case? What could you and schools do to counter this pattern?

education program and the lack of opportunities for family advocacy. The authors concluded that these changes were related to five practices used by the professionals at the school:

1. Late notices and inflexible scheduling of conferences.
2. Limited time for conferences.
3. Emphasis on compliance and completion of paperwork rather than family participation, information sharing, and problem solving.
4. The use of professional jargon that was not explained to family members.
5. The emphasis on professionals' power and authority over family members. The authority of professionals was established through the following powers:
   a. *Power of structure.* Professionals reported and family members listened.
   b. *Power of need.* Family members' need for professional help and services made it difficult for them to disagree or express dissatisfaction.
   c. *Power of kindness.* The apparent kindness of professionals made it hard for family members to disagree.
   d. *Power of group.* The opinions and consensus of professionals overpowered the family's perspectives and disagreement.
   e. *Power of manipulation.* Experiences and expertise of professionals were used to gain agreement from family members.

Gain the Trust of Families

Resource

Dennis and Giangreco (1996) offer suggestions for interacting with families in culturally sensitive ways.

Family involvement and empowerment are based largely on the trust established between families and educators (Davern, 1999). If families and school personnel distrust or feel uncomfortable with each other, the family's involvement and therefore the student's performance may be harmed. You can involve and empower families by working with them using methods that are based on collaboration, mutual trust, and respect and that

How do you promote mutual trust with and gain the respect of your students' families?

recognize the strengths of each family. Trust also can be established when schools collaborate with families to offer and coordinate a broad range of flexible, usable, and understandable services that address the many changing needs of families.

When the experiences and expertise of family and community members are incorporated into school programs, the result is mutual respect and trust among schools, families, and the community. Students see their families and community actively engaged in schools and classrooms. In the process, families and the community become empowered, positive partners in the educational process. Families and community members can be part of an ongoing program that allows them to share their experiences and knowledge in schools.

You also can gain the trust of families by learning about the strengths, experiences, cultures, and attitudes of families and students and then interacting with them in ways that acknowledge their strengths and respect their cultural values (Bui & Turnbull, 2003; Al-Hassan & Gardner, 2002). For example, some families may have cultural beliefs that view the teacher as a highly respected person, and that it is not their role to disagree with you or to interfere in their children's education, or ask questions. Therefore, rather than viewing them as disinterested in their children's education, it is important for you to understand their positive beliefs about education and adjust your interactions with them accordingly.

In addition to understanding the cultural perspectives of your students' families, you can examine your own viewpoints, attitudes, and behaviors related to your cultural background and diversity. It is important to recognize how your cultural beliefs may conflict with those of your students and their families and to interact with students and families in culturally sensitive ways (Harry, Kalyanpur, & Day, 1999; Obiakor, 1999). Figure 4.12 presents some activities you can use to increase your cultural awareness.

Set Your Sites

For more on school-community partnerships, go to the Web Links module in Chapter 4 of the Companion Website.

Advocate for Students and Their Families

You can gain the trust of families by advocating for them and their children, which is part of your professional responsibility (Scheuermann & Johns, 2002). Advocacy can help you establish a strong bond with your students and their families, which can foster

---

FIGURE 4.12

Activities to promote cultural awareness

- Talk to your students and their families about their experiences and culture.
- Learn about your students' communities.
- Read books, articles, poetry, short stories, and magazine articles about different cultures.
- View films, videocassettes, DVDs, and television shows, and listen to radio shows about different cultures.
- Attend classes and workshops on different cultures, and visit museums focused on different cultures.
- Use the Internet to obtain information about and interact with others from different cultures.
- Travel to places inside and outside the United States that reflect cultural diversity.
- Learn from knowledgeable community members from different cultures.
- Work with colleagues, students, and community members from different cultures.
- Socialize with friends and neighbors from different cultures.
- Volunteer to work in a community agency that serves individuals from different cultures.
- Participate in community events, celebrations, and festivals of different cultures.
- Join professional organizations that are committed to meeting the needs of individuals from different cultures.

communication and collaboration. In school, you can engage in advocacy informally via conversations with others and formally via your participation in comprehensive planning team meetings and other committees that influence decision making (Gartin, Murdick, Thompson, & Dyches, 2002). You also can post articles or relevant materials in prominent locations in your school or community, and lead discussions about the issues discussed. Outside of school, you can advocate by:

- joining professional organizations, and other groups that offer support for advocacy efforts.
- keeping abreast of current issues and practices by subscribing to publications and listservs, and attending professional conferences and workshops.
- contacting legislators and policy makers and writing letters to the editor regarding issues that affect your students and families and your profession.
- challenging myths and inaccurate and stereotypical statements made by others.
- making presentations to community groups and school boards.
- inviting community members and influential decision makers to visit your classroom and other effective programs in your school and community (Scheuermann & Johns, 2002; Zionts & Callicott, 2002).

You can enhance the success of your advocacy efforts by being aware of the law and related issues, developing your communication, collaboration, and conflict resolution skills, and helping students and their families learn to be effective advocates for themselves. For example, you can help families develop advocacy skills by encouraging them to network with others and build coalitions around issues that affect their child's education, services, or legal rights, and to access resources available within the school and community (Mathur & Smith, 2003). You can also offer activities to educate them about conferencing skills, special education procedures and terminology, family rights, and available services and advocacy.

When advocating for students and families, you also need to be aware of the personal and professional risks. At times, your views and positions on issues affecting your students and their families may put you in the difficult position of opposing your school district or others with whom you work. Thus, you need to be able to deal with indirect and direct pressure to conform with school district requests, and possible reprisals (Gartin et al., 2002).

Ensure Confidentiality

Ensuring students and families their right to *confidentiality*, which is specified in the Family Educational Rights and Privacy Act (FERPA) and the IDEA, is essential to establishing a trusting and collaborative relationship with families and students. Educators directly involved in teaching a student may have access to his or her records, but before a school district can allow other persons to review these records, it must obtain consent from the family.

Confidentiality also guarantees the family the opportunity to obtain, review, and challenge their child's educational records. The family can obtain their child's records by requesting a copy, which the school district must provide. However, the family may have to pay the expenses incurred in duplicating the records. If the family disagrees with these records, the family can challenge them by asking school officials to correct or delete the information or by writing a response to be included in the records.

In addition to addressing protecting records, confidentiality means that professionals should refrain from:

Resource

Scheuermann and Johns (2002), Zionts and Callicott (2002), and Gartin, Murdick, Thompson, and Dyches (2002) offer information, suggestions, and resources that can help you be an effective advocate and understand the challenges you might encounter in assuming this role.

Set Your Sites

For more on family advocacy, go to the Web Links module in Chapter 4 of the Companion Website.

Reflective

What are some issues for which you would advocate for students and families? How could you advocate for your students and their families? What factors would affect your ability to advocate for them?

Set Your Sites

For an update on legal issues related to confidentiality and other topics discussed in this chapter, go to the Legal Update module in chapter 4 of the Companion Website.

- revealing personally identifying information about students (e.g., their disability or immigration status, medical conditions and needs, test scores, etc.) and families to others.
- speaking about students in public ways and places (e.g., teacher's room, meetings with other families, college classes and in-service sessions, etc.) that allow specific students to be identified.

Meet Regularly with Families

As we saw in the chapter-opening vignette with the Smith family, you can foster collaboration and communication with families and increase their involvement by improving the quality of family–educators conferences (Valle & Aponte, 2002). These steps and strategies are discussed here.

Plan the Meeting

Plan carefully for the meeting by identifying the reasons for the meeting and developing an appropriate agenda. The agenda should allow enough time to discuss and resolve issues and address concerns of families and other educators. These issues and concerns can be determined by contacting others *before* the meeting so that they understand what will be discussed at the meeting. Share the agenda with families and other participants, encourage them to bring useful records and materials to the meeting, and give them the necessary background information to take part in the meeting. Important documents and materials such as copies of legal rights, IEPs, work samples, test results, and other teachers' comments related to agenda items and student performance can be organized and sent to participants beforehand. Some families may appreciate it if you give them a list of questions or suggestions to help them participate in the meeting, and tell them which school personnel will also be there. For example, before the meeting, you can ask family members to be prepared to discuss their goals for their child's educational programs, their perceptions of their child's feelings about school, interests, hobbies, strengths and needs, their suggestions for effective strategies, and any questions and concerns they have. You also may want to invite family members to observe in the classroom as a way to prepare for the meeting.

Good planning also ensures that the meeting time is convenient for families and professionals. Families can be contacted early to determine what times and dates are best for them, to encourage them to invite persons who are important to them, and to determine whether they need help with transportation or child care. Once the meeting has been scheduled, you can contact families and professionals in advance to give them the time, place, purpose, and duration of the meeting and to confirm that they will be there. Follow-up reminders to families via mail, E-mail, or telephone will make them more likely to attend.

Structure the Environment to Promote Communication

The setting for the conference can be organized for sharing information. Comfortable, same-size furniture can be arranged to promote communication among all participants. Barriers such as desks and chairs should not be placed between families and teachers. Chairs can be placed around a table or positioned so that all persons can see each other. Some teachers find it helpful to use video and the Internet to access and share information and to use easels or chalkboards to record ideas and important points (Rock, 2000).

Resource

Fleury (2000) offers guidelines for protecting the confidentiality of your students when working with paraeducators and substitutes.

Set Your Sites

For more on confidentiality and the Family Educational Rights and Privacy Act (FERPA), go to the Web Links module in Chapter 4 of the Companion Website.

Reflective

Given families' and students' right to confidentiality, what would you do in the following situations? Teachers are discussing students and their families during lunch in the teachers' lounge. You notice that the students' records in your school are kept in an unsupervised area.

Welcome family members and other participants, engage in pleasant, informal conversation before the meeting starts, and offer refreshments. This will help participants feel comfortable and establish rapport. To improve participation and follow-up, you can ask the participants if they would like pads and pencils to take notes and give them name tags.

To make sure that the meeting is not interrupted, post a note on the door indicating that a conference is in session. Distractions caused by the telephone can be minimized by taking the phone off the hook, asking the office to hold all calls, or using a room that does not have a phone.

Conduct the Conference

As Mr. Rodl did in the chapter-opening vignette, you should conduct the conference in a way that encourages understanding, participation, and collaboration. Introduce participants or ask them to introduce themselves, and review the agenda and the purpose of the meeting. The meeting can start on a positive note, with participants discussing the strong points of the student's performance. Next, participants can review any concerns they have about the student. They should present information in a way that is understandable to all and share materials such as work samples, test results, and anecdotal records to support and illustrate their comments.

You can ask families to discuss the issues or situations from their perspective or to respond to open-ended questions. Family sharing at meetings can be increased by listening attentively; by being empathetic; by acknowledging and reinforcing participation ("That's a good point"; "I'll try to incorporate that"); by avoiding asking questions that have yes/no or implied answers; by asking questions that encourage family members to respond rather than waiting for them to ask questions or spontaneously speak their minds; by informing them that there may be several solutions to a problem; by not criticizing family members; by using language that is understandable but not condescending; by checking periodically for understanding; by paraphrasing and summarizing the comments of family members; and by showing respect for families and their feelings.

You can adjust the structure of the meeting, depending on how the family prefers to communicate. For families that value personal relationships, you can create a friendly, open, and personal environment by demonstrating concern for family members, sitting close by, and using self-disclosure, humor, and casual conversation. Other families may be goal-oriented and respond to professionals they perceive as competent and organized. These families may expect you to structure the meeting, set goals, define roles, and ask questions of family members.

End the meeting on a positive note by summarizing the issues discussed, points of agreement and disagreement, strategies to be used to resolve problems, and roles to be played by family members and educators. At the end of the meeting, participants can agree on a plan of action, establish ongoing communications systems, and set a date for the next meeting. A sample schedule of activities for a family–educators conference is presented in Figure 4.13.

Teleconferencing

Recent technological advances now allow school districts to conduct meetings via telecommunications that allow families to participate without leaving work or their homes. When using telecommunications, you should ensure that the technology gives all participants immediate access to all the information presented and allows them to interact directly and actively throughout the meeting. Before the meeting, all participants should receive copies of the materials that will be discussed and referred to at the meeting.

Sample schedule for a family-educators conference

FIGURE 4.13

1. Welcome participants.
2. Introduce family members and professionals, including an explanation of the roles of each professional and the services they provide to the student.
3. Discuss the purpose of the meeting and review the agenda.
4. Review relevant information from prior meetings.
5. Give family members the opportunity to discuss their view of their child's strengths and needs.
6. Discuss student's strengths and needs and performance from the perspective of the professionals. Educators support their statements with work samples, test results, and anecdotal records.
7. Discuss comments of family members and professionals attempting to achieve a consensus.
8. Determine a plan of action.
9. Summarize and review the results of the meeting.
10. Determine an appropriate date for the next meeting.
11. Adjourn the meeting.
12. Evaluate the meeting.

REFLECTING ON YOUR PRACTICES

Evaluating Meetings with Families

You can evaluate your meetings with families by considering the following questions:

- Was I prepared, and did I help others prepare for the meeting?
- Did I schedule the meeting at a time and place that was convenient for the family members and other participants?
- Did I ask for suggestions from the family and other participants about the agenda?
- Was the purpose of the meeting clear to all?
- Did I allow enough time for the meeting?
- Did I create a welcoming, respectful, and comfortable environment that encouraged participants to share their perspectives and work collaboratively?
- Did the meeting occur without interruptions?
- Did the meeting address the issues participants wanted to discuss?
- Did all participants have enough opportunities and time to present their opinions and receive feedback from others?
- Did participants discuss the strong points of the student's performance?
- Did I use student work samples to support my comments?
- Did I listen attentively, and acknowledge and encourage participation from others?
- Did I communicate in a clear, nonthreatening manner using language that others could understand?
- Did I adjust the content, structure, tone, and interaction patterns of the meeting to be consistent with the family's cultural, linguistic, and experiential background?
- Did I end the meeting effectively?
- Was the family's confidentiality protected?
- Which aspects of the meeting did I like the best? Which did I like the least?
- Was every participant satisfied with the outcome(s) of the meeting?

How would you rate the quality of your meetings with families? ( ) Excellent ( ) Good ( ) Needs Improvement ( ) Needs Much Improvement

What steps could you take to improve your meetings with families?

Resolve Conflicts Constructively

Your ability to establish a trusting and collaborative relationship with families also will be affected by how you and your students' families resolve the conflicts that may occur during the school year (Mathur & Smith, 2003). These disputes often are the result of miscommunication and different views concerning academic performance and grades, student behavior and disciplinary actions, educational placement, and the availability and delivery of educational and related services. It is important that you also recognize that these conflicts may also be related to families' past experiences with schools.

In addition to regularly communicating and collaborating with families using the strategies presented in this chapter, you can do several things to limit the potential negative consequences of conflicts with families and develop constructive solutions that address the concerns and issues that are at the center of conflicts. Recognize that families are knowledgeable about their children and show that you care about and respect them and their children. Rather than viewing family members negatively as "overprotective," "troublemakers," "uncaring," or "uncooperative," try to identify the factors that might explain their perspectives and behavior. It also is important to understand the family's emotional reactions to their child's difficulties, which may include a combination of disappointment, fear, anger and avoidance.

When interacting with the family, maintain an attitude of communication, collaboration, and conciliation, and a commitment to what is best for the student (Lake & Billingsley, 2000; Valle & Aponte, 2002). Listen carefully and reflectively as family members share their concerns and perspectives without interrupting them, seeking clarification only when necessary. Avoid acting emotionally, making assumptions or promises that you cannot keep, and the tendency to rebut each point brought up by the family. While you don't have to agree with families, it is important that you refrain from dismissing or diminishing their comments, recognize their role in making decisions about their children, and avoid using language that might escalate the situation. Be constructive by calmly, directly, and honestly discussing your viewpoint and the reasons for it, and citing and displaying documentation to support your statements. Convey your message with a respectful tone of voice and appropriate body language. Emphasize points of agreement, propose choices and options, and seek solutions that are acceptable to all parties. If conflicts cannot be resolved constructively by you and the family, seek the assistance of others who can help mediate disputes. Ultimately, it is important for you to mend fences with families.

Set Your Sites

For more information on mediation of disputes, go to the Web Links module in Chapter 4 of the Companion Website.

Address the Diverse Needs, Backgrounds, and Experiences of Families

Families, like students, have diverse strengths, needs, backgrounds, perspectives, resources, and experiences, and are structured in different ways. In communicating and collaborating with families, be aware of these factors and how they affect families, and adjust your style and services accordingly to promote family involvement.

Resource

Parette and Petch-Hogan (2000) offer questions that can guide you in enhancing and reflecting upon your efforts to involve families from culturally and linguistically diverse backgrounds in the educational process, and Al-Hassan and Gardner (2002) provide suggestions and resources for involving families of immigrant students in the educational process.

Cultural Factors

Families are interested in their children's education, but different cultural perspectives can make it hard to establish traditional school–family interactions (Bui & Turnbull, 2003; Harry, 2002). In designing culturally sensitive programs to involve and empower families, you should adjust to the family's level of acculturation, beliefs about schooling, prior experience with discrimination, structure, child-rearing practices, developmental expectations, perceptions of disability, emotional responses, and communication patterns. These factors will now be discussed.

Level of Acculturation.   The level of *acculturation*, the extent to which members of one culture adapt to a new culture, will affect a family's cultural perspective (Harry, 2002). Because children tend to acculturate faster than adults, children may perform some roles in the new culture that adults assumed in their native country, such as interacting with social institutions like schools. These roles involve time and stress and the dependence of adult family members on children. This can have a significant impact on adult–child relationships and the student's academic performance.

Beliefs About and Knowledge of Educational System.   Family members' beliefs about and knowledge of the educational system and their prior experiences with schools also can affect their involvement in school (Al-Hassan & Gardner, 2002; Thorp, 1997). Family members with limited knowledge of the educational system or negative experiences as students may not feel comfortable participating in family–school activities. These understandings, beliefs and experiences also can influence what they expect of you and the schools their children attend. Family members of children who are immigrants may also have different perceptions of schooling.

Prior Experience with Discrimination.   Many families may have suffered discrimination, which can influence their behavior and attitudes (Davis, Brown, Bantz, & Manno, 2002). These families may not want to attend meetings at the school if they or others have been discriminated against or treated with disrespect there. You can increase the family's comfort in attending school-related events and establish trust and a welcoming environment by doing the following:

- Invite important extended family members to school events.
- Address elders first.
- Refer to family members by their titles, such as Mr., Mrs., Ms., Dr., or Reverend (or ask them how they like to be addressed).
- Make school facilities available for community activities.
- Speak to families in a respectful and sincere manner.
- Respond in a warm and caring way.
- Decorate the school and classrooms with icons from various cultures.

Family Structure.   Most school-based strategies for involving families focus on the needs of the nuclear family. However, many cultures emphasize the value of the extended family (Cartledge, Kea, & Ida, 2000; Davis et al., 2002). For example, many families live in a framework of collective interdependence and kinship interactions. They share resources and services, and offer emotional and social support (Lue & Green, 2000). Rather than asking for help from schools in dealing with educational issues, these families may feel more comfortable relying on community members or agencies. Therefore, you need to identify and involve the informal systems that support families.

In many families, roles are hierarchical, and elders may play an important role in decision making and child care (Bui & Turnbull, 2003; Mathews, 2000). When working with families that value and rely on extended family members, you can involve all family members in the school program. For example, in writing to families, you could say that all family members are welcome at educational meetings.

Resource

Sparks (2000b) offers strategies for involving elders in schools.

Child-Rearing Practices, Developmental Expectations, and Perceptions of Disability.   Families also have different perspectives on child rearing, appropriate behavior, disability, and developmental milestones, which can affect how they view their children's educational program (Bui & Turnbull, 2003; Harry, 2002). For example, many white, middle-class families may stress the importance of children reaching developmental milestones at appropriate ages, but other families may not. Similarly, for some families, independence is a goal for their child, but others may view it as interfering with their preference that their child remain a part of the family. Since the behavioral and developmental expectations of schools and families may conflict, you must work cooperatively with families to develop a culturally sensitive and relevant teaching program. The program should include agreed-on bicultural behaviors, appropriate cultural settings for these behaviors, and cross-cultural criteria for measuring progress.

Families also may have different attitudes toward the meaning of *disability* and its impact on the family (Garcia, Mendez Perez, & Ortiz, 2000; Lamorey, 2002). For example, some use a broader idea of disability that is often related to the child's ability to function at home and the family's beliefs about the child's future. As a result, they may also resist, resent, or misunderstand the labeling of their child as having a disability, which can cause them to not trust the school.

The family's feelings about the causes of their child's difficulties may also have a cultural and religious basis (Bui & Turnbull, 2003; Lamorey, 2002). They may believe that the child's difficulties are caused by reprisals for rule violations by family members, spirits, failure to avoid taboos, fate, choice, and lifestyle imbalances (Harry, 2002). Families also may have perspectives that cause them to prefer home remedies and alternative practices, and to reject Western views of medicine and technology. Therefore, you may have to address these issues before families accept and respond to traditional educational strategies.

Resource

Lamorey (2002) provides information on various cultural beliefs about disability and suggestions for adjusting educational services to address these diverse beliefs.

Emotional Responses.

Because families also have different emotional responses to having a child with a disability, you need to understand these responses and adjust your services accordingly (Bailey & Smith, 2000; Ulrich & Bauer, 2003). Families may go through several transformative stages as they learn to adjust to and accept their child's disability (Healey, 1996; Singer, 2002). These stages, which vary from family to family based on experience, culture, socioeconomic level, the nature of the child's disability, and the support they receive from others, may include the following:

Stage 1: Families may be shocked and dejected, and experience grief and fear.

Stage 2: Families may be confused, deny their child's disability, reject their child, or avoid dealing with the issue/situation by looking for other explanations.

Stage 3: Families may experience anger, self-pity, disappointment, guilt, and a sense of powerlessness that may be expressed as rage or withdrawal.

Stage 4: Families may start to understand and accept their child's disability and its impact on the family.

Stage 5: Families may accept, love, and appreciate their child unconditionally.

Stage 6: Families may begin to focus on living, on the benefits accrued, on the future, and on working with others to teach and provide support services to their child.

How does having a child with a disability affect the whole family?

In addition to helping families as they go through these stages, be aware of the varied and culturally appropriate coping strategies that families use and consider these strategies when designing and delivering services (Harry, 2002; Lustig 2002). You also can aid families by being honest with them, showing genuine care and compassion, being empathetic rather than sympathetic, and encouraging them to obtain supportive services. You can also encourage them to communicate with other family members and other important persons in their lives, join family-support groups, ask questions, and express their emotions.

It also is important for you to understand and help others recognize that many families report experiencing positive effects as a result of raising a child with a disability (Ferguson, 2002; Taunt & Hastings, 2002). These benefits for parents and siblings include developing coping skills and family cohesiveness, facilitating shared values and parenting, increasing one's perspective on life, sense of purpose/responsibility, and sensitivity to others and assertiveness, improving communication within the family, and expanding the family's social network.

Cross-Cultural Communication Patterns.

Communication patterns that differ from one culture to another can make it hard to develop trusting relationships between you and your students' families (Bruns & Fowler, 1999; Quinn, 2001). Be sensitive to differences in communication styles, and interpret verbal and nonverbal behaviors within a social and cultural context. For example, eye contact, wait time, word meanings, facial and physical gestures, voice quality, personal space, and physical contact have different meanings in various cultures. You also need to understand that communications between cultures are affected by turn taking, by physical closeness or distance, and by spoken and unspoken rules of conversation. For example, in some cultures "yes" connotes "I heard you" rather than agreement. Similarly,

Reflective

Research indicates that families of children with low-incidence disabilities are more involved in school than families of children with high-incidence disabilities (U.S. Department of Education, 2001). Why do you think this is the case?

Resource

Harry (2002) discusses trends and issues that can help you understand and collaborate with families from culturally and linguistically diverse backgrounds.

Reflective

Think about several people you talk to regularly. How do their communication styles differ in terms of eye contact, wait time, word meanings, facial and physical gestures, voice quality, personal space, and physical contact? How do these differences affect you? How do you adjust your communication style to accommodate these differences?

individuals from some cultures may interpret laughter as a sign of embarrassment rather than enjoyment.

Cultural differences also may affect communication, the discussion of certain issues, and the ways in which families view, seek, and receive assistance (Thorp, 1997). Some families may not feel comfortable discussing personal problems and concerns, viewing that behavior as being self-centered or disgracing the family, while others may be reluctant to disagree in order to maintain harmony (Mathews, 2000). Some families may not want to interact with the school staff because they believe that teachers know what is best for their children and that it is not appropriate for them to question the authority of teachers. Community members who understand the family's needs, emotional responses, and culture can help break down these communication barriers by helping you to understand and interpret the family's communication behaviors; serving as liaisons among schools, families, and communities; and orienting new families to the school (Park & Turnbull, 2001).

Linguistic Factors

Set Your Sites

For online access to dictionaries and communication in many languages, go to the Web Links module in Chapter 4 of the Companion Website.

Language factors also may block communication between schools and families (Park & Turnbull, 2001). Communication difficulties may be compounded by problems in understanding educational jargon and practices that may not exist in the families' language and culture. For example, some families from different cultural and language backgrounds believe that special education implies a program that is better than general education. You can correct this misconception by giving these families forms, lists of key educational terms, and information about their rights in their native languages. Learning greetings and words in the family's native language also can create a positive environment that promotes communication and respect.

Interpreters and translators can be used to promote communication between English-speaking educators and families who speak other languages (Al-Hassan & Gardner, 2002; Santos, Lee, Validivia, & Zhang, 2001). Whereas intrepreters foster oral communications during face-to-face meetings, translators focus on rewriting correspondence and documents in the family's primary language. (We will discuss the roles of translators later in this chapter.) Interpreters should speak the same dialect as the family; maintain confidentiality; avoid giving personal opinions; seek clarification from families and professionals when they have problems communicating certain information; use reverse translation when exact translations are not possible; and show respect for families and professionals. The interpreter will be more effective if you discuss the topics and terminology with the interpreter before the meeting, use nonverbal communication as well as speech, are aware of the nonverbal behaviors of family members, and ask for the interpreter's feedback about the meeting. It is also important that family members and professionals speak to each other rather than directing their comments to interpreters.

While many families may rely on their child to interpret for them in general, the child or other students should not interpret during meetings. Children serving as an interpreter for their family can have a negative impact on the family, as this situation reverses the traditional adult–child relationship. For children, interpreting places them in the adult role in the family, which can make them anxious and frightened. For adults, being dependent on their child as their interpreter can be considered demeaning. It also may be awkward for family members to share information about their child when the child is interpreting.

Set Your Sites

For more information on collaborating with translators and interpreters, go to the Web Links module in Chapter 4 of the Companion Website.

Socioeconomic Factors

Many socioeconomic factors also can affect the family's participation in their child's education (Lopez, Scribner, & Mahitivanichcha, 2001). Long work schedules, time conflicts, transportation problems, and child-care needs can be serious barriers that you and your colleagues need to address. These barriers can be reduced by the use of home visits. However, many families may consider a home visit intrusive, so you should ask for the family's permission before visiting their home.

Use Written Communication

You can use written communication such as letters and notes and other documents such as orientation manuals and homework guidelines to establish ongoing communication with families (Boone, Wolfe, & Schaufler, 1999; Williams & Cartledge, 1997). Written communication is often used to share information on students, schedule meetings, and obtain informed consent from families. It is important that you evaluate written documents sent to families in terms of readability, legibility, and use of jargon. Look at Figure 4.14, and note how the letters to family members are different. Which letter is more likely to result in family members attending the meeting? Letter A is impersonal, uses technical terms, places the school's needs above the needs of family members, can intimidate the family, and does little to encourage family participation. Letter B is welcoming and less formal, tries to establish rapport, and respects the family, their scheduling needs, and their contributions to the education of their child. It also avoids professional jargon, encourages participation and collaboration, and gives the family suggestions for preparing for the meeting. You also can increase the effectiveness of your written communication with families by sharing affective and factual information; examining its readability; emphasizing positive aspects of students and their families; using examples, visuals, icons, and cultural referents; and monitoring the response rate from family members. Since some family members may have difficulty accessing written information, find alternatives to written communication, and offer some form of oral communication to clarify written communications and documents.

Resource

Boone et al. (1999) provide guidelines for preparing written communications to families.

IDEAS FOR IMPLEMENTATION

Overcoming Economic Barriers to Family Participation

Ms. Saavedra was concerned that several of her students' families were not able to attend open school night. She contacted several of the families and found that some had transportation problems and others couldn't find a sitter to watch their children. For the next meeting, Ms. Saavedra contacted families in advance to determine whether they needed a ride to school. She then organized carpools so that all family members could attend. She also notified families that they could bring their children with them; child care would be provided by students from the high school.

Here are some other strategies you can use to overcome economic barriers to family participation:

- Conduct activities and meetings at locations in the community.

- Make sure activities don't require families to spend money. For example, if a fee must be charged, provide families with options that allow them to volunteer to perform a task in lieu of paying a fee.
- Ask for the support and assistance of persons, groups, and agencies from the community.
- Structure sessions so that adults and their children are not separated.
- Schedule meetings at times that are convenient for family members.
- Use community organizations to share information with families.

Note: Lopez, Scribner, & Mahitivanichcha (2001); Rhodes (1996).

FIGURE 4.14

Samples of written correspondence to families

LETTER A

To Whom It May Concern:

The school district has scheduled a meeting to review your child's educational program. The meeting will be held on March 15, 2005, in the conference room at the administrative offices.

The following members of the school district will be in attendance:

Mrs. Lorraine Hamilton	School Social Worker
Mrs. Constance Franks	Special Education Teacher
Mr. Patrick Hardees	General Education Teacher
Mr. Donald Fein	School Psychologist
Mrs. Joanne Frederick	Principal

If you would like the school physician to be at the meeting, please contact my office at least three days prior to the meeting.

Please contact my office if you plan to attend the meeting. My office will be able to tell you approximately what time your child will be discussed. If you are unable to attend the meeting in person, you may participate by telephone.

The meeting will take place as scheduled unless you request otherwise. I will send the results in writing after the meeting is over. Feel free to contact me with any questions or concerns related to your child's education.

Yours truly,

Donald Smith,

Director of Pupil Personnel Services

LETTER B

Dear Truman Family:

Hello. My name is Donald Smith, and I am the Director of Pupil Personnel Services for the Bellville School District. It is my job to assist you in understanding the educational system and to work with you in creating an educational program that meets the needs of your child.

Your child's teachers would like to schedule a meeting with you to discuss your child's educational program. It is important that you attend this meeting. You know your child better than anyone and can provide important information concerning your child's school performance. You may also wish to bring others with you to attend the meeting. It is also possible for you to request that the school physician attend this meeting.

If you have time, you can do several things to prepare for the meeting. You can talk to your child and his/her teachers about his/her performance in school and the ways to improve his/her learning. You also can visit your child's classroom. It also will be helpful if you bring materials to the meeting such as your child's schoolwork, school records, and reports, as well as medical information. At the meeting, we will talk about the goals for your child's education, the way your child learns best, and his/her favorite activities and interests.

I will be calling you to schedule the meeting at a time that is most convenient for your family and to answer any questions you may have. We also can assist you in attending the meeting by providing you with transportation, child care, and the services of an interpreter. I look forward to speaking with you and working with you to meet the educational needs of your child.

Yours truly,

Donald Smith,

Director of Pupil Personnel Services

Resource

Santos et al. (2001) offer guidelines and resources for translating materials and working with translators.

Translators who help to prepare written communications and community members can help you develop culturally relevant and sensitively written documents that are rewritten into the native languages of your families (Santos et al., 2001). You can collaborate with translators to produce quality translated materials by using examples and activities that are culturally appropriate, including visuals and photographs that appeal to and depict the intended audience, and avoiding technical terms and jargon or including an explanation when you must use them. While software and web-based translation programs are available to provide quick translation of material, you should exercise caution in using them because they often fail to capture the cultural, syntactical, and linguistic meanings of the communication and address dialectical and word differences, which can result in confusing or offensive communications.

Informative Notice

You can share information with families by using an informative notice. This is a brief written communication that alerts families to various school and classroom activities, student progress, and the materials students will need to complete their assignments. At the beginning of the school year, the informative notice can take two forms: (a) postcards to students welcoming them to your class, and (b) letters to families to introduce yourself and various aspects of your classroom, to explain your expectations, and to ask for their support and collaboration (Williams & Cartledge, 1997).

Newsletters

Another form of written communication with families is a *newsletter,* which can tell them about school and classroom events, extracurricular activities, meetings, school policies, and menus, and offer family education. Consider the following when creating newsletters:

- Make them brief (no more than three pages) and attractive (use colored paper and graphics).
- Present information in bulleted or numbered lists.
- Involve students in creating them.
- Post them on the Internet.
- Focus them on information and topics that are useful to students and their families.
- Solicit feedback on their value and suggestions for future issues (Hollingsworth, 2001).

Daily Note

The *daily note* is a brief note that alerts families to the accomplishments and improvements in their children and other issues of interest or concern. The value of daily notes can be increased by providing a space for family members to write their messages to you. Daily notes can be made more effective by pairing them with praise from family members. Therefore, when family members receive these positive notes from you, they should be encouraged to read the notes promptly; praise their child in the presence of others; put the note in a prominent location (such as on the refrigerator door) where their child and others are likely to see it; and share their desire to receive additional notes of praise.

Two-Way Notebooks

You also can communicate with families by using *two-way notebooks* and assignment folders (Hall, Wolfe, & Bollig, 2003). Two-way notebooks, carried to and from school by students, allow you and family members to exchange comments and information and ask questions. The notebook can have the student's name on it, as well as a place for family members' signatures, the date, and the number of assignments included.

Daily/Weekly Report Cards

The daily/weekly report card, a written record of the student's performance in school, is effective in communicating with families. Its content and format will vary, depending on the needs of students, and could include information on academic performance, preparedness for class, effort, behavior, peer relationships, and homework completion. The

Resource

Hall, Wolfe, and Bollig (2003) offer guidelines for communicating with families via home-to-school notebooks.

format should be easy for you to complete and easy for families to interpret. As students demonstrate success over a period of time, the report card can be shared with families weekly, biweekly, and then monthly. A sample daily report card is presented in Figure 4.15. **To hear educators discussing their strategies for communicating with families, go to Case 3: Assess Plan on the CD-ROM and click on the adapt modify video clip. How does communication with families foster students' positive behavior and learning?**

Home-School Contracts

The daily report system also has been used as part of a home-school contract. *Home-school contracts* allow families like the Smiths to learn about their children's progress in school and reinforce their children's improved academic performance or behavior in school. You observe students in school and report your observations to families, who then deliver reinforcers to their children. These reinforcers take many forms. Tangible reinforcers include making special foods; buying clothes, music, or software programs; providing money toward the purchase of a desired item; or getting a pet. Families can also use activity reinforcers such as fewer chores, a family activity, trips, a party at the house, a rented video/DVD, or a special privilege. Before using a home-school contract, you can discuss the specifics of the program with the family. This discussion gives both parties an understanding of the behavior to be changed, details of the communication system between home and school, potential reinforcers, and when and how to deliver the reinforcers. Once the system is in place, follow-up communication is critical to talk about the implementation and impact of the system.

Employ Technology-Based Communications

Reflective

Have you used e-mail, the Internet, a weblog, or a telephone answering machine to communicate with others? What were the advantages and disadvantages? How do these systems affect the communications and the information shared? What skills do teachers and family members need to use these systems effectively and efficiently?

Set Your Sites

For more information on giving family members access to information related to their children's needs, go to the Web Links module in Chapter 4 of the Companion Website.

Technological innovations are changing the ways in which schools, students and families interact and communicate (Hutinger & Clark, 2000). Many schools and families use websites, e-mail, multilingual hotlines, and telephone answering machines to receive and send messages. For example, families can use these systems to view their children's work and grades online, see what the school is serving for lunch, check on their child's attendance record, or find out what homework has been assigned. You and your students can communicate with families by maintaining a *weblog*, a journal of the class's activities that is posted on the Internet. You can also use technology to provide families with suggestions for teaching specific skills to their children; report on student performance in school; give families information on their rights and specific programs; offer information on local events of interest to students and their families; encourage family members to attend conferences; and recommend books and other learning materials to families. If family members cannot attend a meeting, an e-conference can be conducted with the professional(s). When using technology-based communication systems, you need to protect the confidentiality of students and their families.

Encourage and Facilitate Family Observations

Communication between the home and the school can be improved by encouraging family members to observe in the classroom. This experience allows family members to see and understand different aspects of the school environment and student behavior. It

Sample daily report card

FIGURE 4.15

Student _____   *Date _____

Teacher _____   Class _____

*Please return report on the next school day

Behaviors		Rating					
1. Follows instructions cooperatively.	0	1	2	3	4	5
2. Stays on task.	0	1	2	3	4	5
3. Works quietly.	0	1	2	3	4	5
4. Completes assignments.	0	1	2	3	4	5
5. Remains in assigned area.	0	1	2	3	4	5

Rating Keys:
          0 = very poor
          1 = poor
          2 = fair
          3 = good
          4 = very good
          5 = EXCELLENT!

Teacher Comments   Signature _____   Date _____

_____
_____
_____
_____

Student Comments   Signature _____   Date _____

_____
_____
_____
_____

Parent Comments   Signature _____   Date _____

_____
_____
_____
_____

Source: From "How to Empower Adolescents: Guidelines for Effective Self-Advocacy," by D. A. Battle, L. L. Dickens-Wright, and S. Murphy, 1998, *Teaching Exceptional Children, 30*(3), pp. 28–32.

gives families the background information needed to discuss school-related concerns with you.

Family members can be prepared for the observation if you review ways to enter the room unobtrusively; locations in the room to sit; suitable times to observe; appropriate reactions to their child and other students; and the need to maintain confidentiality. Before the observation, you can discuss with family members the purpose of the observation and the unique aspects of the educational setting, such as behavior management systems and reading programs. After the observation, you can meet with family members again to discuss what they saw.

USING TECHNOLOGY TO PROMOTE INCLUSION

Creating and Implementing a Homework Website

As part of her efforts to prepare her students for the state tests, Ms. Harrison increased her use of homework assignments. However, despite frequent reminders to her students, she was disappointed by their inconsistency in completing their homework. To remedy the situation, she decided to send a letter to her students' families explaining the importance of homework and asking them to make sure that their children completed their homework.

Several family members responded and one parent suggested that Ms. Harrison E-mail the assignments to families. Ms. Harrison mentioned this request to Ms. Taylor, the school's instructional technology (IT) specialist, who told Ms. Harrison that it was a good idea and that she would work with her to create a homework website. Sensing Ms. Harrison's concerns about her technology skills and the time demands of creating and maintaining the site, Ms. Taylor told her that they would start slowly. They began by creating a website called the Homework Assistance Center (HAC) that contained a welcome, an index, and a menu of the content of the site. It also included homework policies, homework assistance recommendations, and ways to contact Ms. Harrison.

When the website was created, Ms. Harrison sent home a note to families introducing them to the site and explaining how to access it. The teachers also invited families to attend a meeting where Ms. Taylor and Ms. Harrison explained the website and showed the families how to use it, which they also did with Ms. Harrison's students. They also provided students and their families with guidelines for evaluating web-based information. At the meeting, the students and their families asked numerous questions, which the teachers answered. The teachers also posted some of these questions and their answers on the Frequently Asked Questions section of the website.

As students and families felt comfortable using the site, Ms. Harrison added homework assignments and models and rubrics. Although she noted an improvement in her students' homework completion and an increase in her communication with families, Ms. Harrison also had some concerns. She worried about her students who did not have access to the Internet, which put them at a disadvantage. In addition, she observed that some students and families were misusing the system and inundating her with E-mail. Ms. Taylor suggested that they establish rules regarding the nature of the messages to be sent, the approximate time period within which a response to an E-mail may be expected,

and the type of assistance that Ms. Harrison would be providing to families or students to complete assignments.

Ms. Taylor also suggested that Ms. Harrison add a digital suggestion box so that students and families could provide feedback, and make recommendations about how to improve the site. The feedback was very positive and discussed the possibilities of adding new features including links to online resources for specific assignments and homework assistance sites.

Here are some other ways you can gradually use the Internet to improve homework communication and completion:

- View the web-based system as a supplement to a multifaceted approach to communicating with families, which includes face-to-face interactions.
- Set up the site so that when users access it, they are welcomed and provided with an overview of the site.
- Offer users an index of the items and content available in each of the site's menus, and a listing of guidelines for using the site effectively and efficiently, or answers to frequently asked questions and their answers.
- Offer families suggestions for helping their children with homework, and solicit feedback from families regarding these policies and practices.
- Create an electronic assignment log (e-log) that lists the assignment(s), directions, and guidelines for completing and evaluating the assignment.
- Provide families with an electronic calendar or planner that lists and provides relevant information about assignments.
- Individualize assignments by giving students a menu of homework assignments, and allow them to select the assignment that best accommodates their learning styles, resources, interests, special skills, and methods of displaying their learning.
- Create authentic and innovative homework assignments that make homework a more enjoyable, motivating, and meaningful experience for students and their families. For example, Internet-based homework assignments can be structured so that students and their families take "virtual field trips" to museums and scientific and

(continued)

- historical sites, or play online academically integrated games.
- Form online cooperative homework groups to provide *all* group members with access to peer tutoring and peer checking, homework discussions, and information sharing.
- Provide family members with online access to materials and resources that they can employ to assist their children with specific assignments. For example, families can be assigned a PIN number that provides them with access to a password-protected answer key that includes explanations for arriving at the correct answers, or guidelines for explaining how to solve problems.

- Guide students and their families in assessing and directing their progress on assignments by posting rubrics, self-evaluation checklists, and exemplary models of assignments.
- Allow students to submit their homework assignments online.
- Examine the impact of the web-based system on students, educators, family members and other relevant individuals, and revise it accordingly. For example, create an online survey that users complete to evaluate various aspects of the website, and a digital suggestion box that allows users to E-mail their comments about the website and their suggestions for improving it.

If family members cannot arrange to come to school, you can use video to introduce them to various aspects of your inclusive classroom, and to increase their awareness of their children's progress (Hundt, 2002). In using video observations, you need to determine what will be recorded, as well as when, how often, and by whom will it be recorded. You also must obtain permission from your students' families to record them and share the recordings with others. It is also helpful to provide families with a format to guide them in viewing the videos. For example, you can provide families with an introduction to the activities recorded, a summary of the video, and questions they can answer as they view the video.

Offer Educational Programs to Families

Because family members may need education to perform various roles in the educational process, many schools offer family education as part of their delivery of services to students and their families (Lopez, Scribner, & Mahitivanichcha, 2001). Some schools have family education committees that offer schoolwide programs and activities including open houses, orientation sessions, and workshops/courses on specific issues. Other schools collaborate with national and local family-based organizations such as the Parent Teacher Association (PTA) and the National Parent Information Network (NPIN) to conduct a range of family education sessions and programs. When setting up and evaluating family education programs, you, your colleagues, and your students' families can consider the following issues.

Offer Educational Programs to All Family Members

Although most programs educate mothers, education should be available to all family members, including fathers, grandparents, and siblings. For example, education and support can address the special needs of siblings and help them understand inclusion and the nature of their brother's or sister's disability and deal with the impact of having a brother or sister with special needs (Cramer et al., 1997; Gallagher et al., 2000). Education for siblings can focus on helping them understand the causes of various disabilities; fostering the learning of their siblings; dispelling myths and misconceptions about disabilities; discussing ways of interacting with and assisting their sibling; dealing with

Set Your Sites

For more on family education programs and school/home partnerships, go to the Web Links module in Chapter 4 of the Companion Website.

Reflective

Do you have a family member with a disability? How has this individual affected other family members? What types of educational programs would benefit the family?

Resource

Dyches and Burrow (2003) offer a list of children's literature that can be used to help siblings learn about disabilities and family issues related to having a sibling with a disability.

Set Your Sites

For more information on siblings of children with special needs, go to the Web Links module in Chapter 4 of the Companion Website.

unequal treatment and excessive demands; responding to the reactions and questions of their friends and other persons; and understanding human differences (Meyer, Vadasy, & Fewell, 1996; Tekin & Kirgaali-Iftar, 2002). Education also can address the pressure to take on the role of parents for their sibling, the long-term needs and future of their sibling and concerns siblings may have about their own children being born with a disability (Berlinger, 2001).

Focus the Content of the Educational Program on Families' Needs

The education program should focus on the needs of family members (Lopez, Scribner, & Mahitivanichcha, 2001). Generally, education should give family members the skills to teach their child at home; the ability to communicate and collaborate with professionals serving their child; information on how the child will be taught; the ability to serve as advocates for their child; the counseling and emotional support they need; the information they need to obtain services for their child; and ways to plan for their child's future. Families of younger children may want information about child care and development, early intervention, discipline, the school's expectations, legal rights of families and children, and how to find community resources. Families of adolescents may prefer information on services and agencies that can help them and their children make the transition to the adult world and find employment. Family members who speak languages other than English may benefit from family-based ESL and literacy programs, as well as instruction in the policies and practices of the school district.

Conduct the Educational Program in a Range of Settings

Education can occur in the home or in the school. Home-based education, which occurs in the family's and child's natural environment, can promote the ability to maintain the skills learned and to use them in many different settings. Home-based education programs are especially appropriate for families who have trouble attending school meetings because of transportation problems or work schedules. School-based education allows many families to be educated as a group, making it easy to share information and experiences. School-based programs also give families the opportunity to meet and interact with many different professionals and families. In some cases, it may be important to conduct the educational programs in nonintimidating, community-based locations such as religious establishments, social clubs, community centers, restaurants, and shopping malls.

Schools are also offering family education programs online. Online delivery of educational programs allows family members to access the information at their convenience and to select the material that is most useful to them. It also provides families with opportunities to share their questions and concerns with others and to access other materials and websites.

Use a Variety of Strategies to Educate Families

Set Your Sites

For more on helping to educate families with children with special needs, go to the Web Links module in Chapter 4 of the Companion Website.

You can use a variety of strategies to educate families, including lectures, group discussion, role playing, simulations, presentations by service providers and other family members, and demonstrations. Videos such as DVDs are excellent because they provide a visual image and a model; allow family members and educators to stop the video at any time to discuss, review, or replay the content; and can be viewed in school or at home. Print materials and education programs for families are also available from state education departments, as well as from local groups serving families and professional organizations. Family education programs and materials can be previewed by contacting various family-based organizations.

Experienced, skilled, and highly respected family members can be a valuable resource for educating other families (Singer, 2002). These individuals can share their knowledge and real-life experiences with other family members, and provide emotional support and information on the services available in the community.

Summary

This chapter provided guidelines for establishing an inclusive environment that supports the learning of *all students* by creating collaborative relationships and fostering communication among professionals, families, and community members. As you review the questions posed in this chapter, remember the following points:

Who Are the Members of the Comprehensive Planning Team?
CEC 1, 7, 9, 10, PRAXIS 2, 3, INTASC 10
The comprehensive planning team may consist of students, general and special educators, administrators, support personnel such as speech and language therapists, bilingual educators, paraeducators, family members, peers, local community resources, and professional and family-based organizations. The members of the team vary, depending on the strengths and needs of students, families, and educators.

How Can Members of the Comprehensive Planning Team Work Collaboratively?
CEC 1, 7, 9, 10, PRAXIS 2, 3, INTASC 1, 3, 9, 10
Members of the comprehensive planning team can work collaboratively by using collaborative and interactive teaming, person-centered planning, cooperative teaching, and collaborative consultation, as well as by promoting congruence and engaging in professional development.

How Can I Foster Communication and Collaboration with Families?
CEC 1, 2, 3, 7, 9, 10, PRAXIS 2, 3, INTASC 3, 10
You can foster communication and collaboration with families by gaining their trust, advocating for them and their children, ensuring confidentiality, meeting regularly with families, resolving conflicts constructively, using written and technology-based communication, encouraging and facilitating observations at the school or via technology, and offering educational programs to families. Families, like students, have diverse strengths, needs, backgrounds, perspectives, resources, and experiences, and are structured in different ways. In communicating and collaborating with families, be aware of these factors and adjust your style and services accordingly to promote family involvement.

What Would You Do in Today's Diverse Classroom?

As a teacher in an inclusion classroom, you encounter the following situations:

★   You and other members of the comprehensive planning team believe that a student would benefit from the services from a physical therapist. However, your Pupil Personnel Director suggests that it not be included on the IEP because of concerns about the cost and availability of these services.

★   When you volunteered to work in a cooperative teaching team, you and your partner were excited about the possibility of using a variety of teaching arrangements. However, you find that your team is using the same format, with the same teacher taking the lead while the other teacher monitors individual students.

★   Your school's PTA is sponsoring a family night and dinner and is charging families $10 to attend. While some your students' families in your school are interested in attending, the cost is preventing them from attending.

★   One of your students has been acting as the class clown and fails to complete his schoolwork. His family is concerned and believes that he should receive special education services. Although you are also concerned about the student, you do not believe he needs special education services.

1.   What challenges(s) are you encountering in each situation?

2.   What factors do you need to consider in addressing them?

3.   How would you address these situations?

4.   What knowledge, skills, dispositions, resources, and support do you need to address these situations?

To answer these questions online and share your responses with others, go to the Reflection module in chapter 4 of the Companion Website.

Chapter 5

Creating an Environment That Fosters Acceptance and Friendship

Mr. Monroig

One of Mr. Monroig's goals is to teach his students how to interact with, understand, and accept others. Mr. Monroig asks students to identify aloud two things they think are easy and two things that are hard to do. He notes the similarities and differences between the students' responses and records them on a "same/different" chart. He then discusses with the class some of the factors that affect the ease with which one can perform a task. He asks them to identify things that would be easy or hard to do if they:

> *had difficulty reading.*
> *used a wheelchair.*
> *didn't understand English.*
> *couldn't hold a pencil.*
> *had difficulty seeing.*
> *had difficulty hearing.*

Mr. Monroig then has the students perform various tasks with and without a simulated difficulty. He has students watch a television show in Spanish, attempt to go to the bathroom using a wheelchair, and walk around the classroom blindfolded. He videos them performing these activities and as students view the video, he asks, "What was easy and hard for you?" and "How did it feel?"

He asks the students to think about something they would like to improve that is hard for them. He also asks his students to respond to the question, "If you knew someone who found something hard to do in our class, what could you do to show that person that you understand that some things are hard?" He then presents classroom scenarios related to some of the difficulties that the students have mentioned, and leads the students in brainstorming the ways students can help each other. He guides the class in examining each suggestion by asking students to evaluate it in terms of its impact on the student and the class.

Mr. Monroig concludes the activity by having students complete a contract that lists their goals for improving their area of difficulty, the ways that they will work to improve it, and the things that their classmates could do to assist them. He then asks each student to share their contract with the class and to maintain a reflective journal of their experiences. At the end of each week, he selects different students to discuss their journal, their progress, and what others have done to assist them.

What other strategies can Mr. Monroig use to help his students understand and accept individual differences and develop friendships? After reading this chapter, you will have the knowledge, skills and dispositions to answer these as well as the following questions:

★ **How do attitudes toward individual differences develop?**
★ **How can I assess attitudes toward individual differences?**

★ **How can I teach acceptance of individual differences related to disability?**
★ **How can I teach acceptance of individual differences related to culture, language, gender, religion, and socioeconomic status?**
★ **How can I facilitate friendships?**

Like Mr. Monroig's classroom, today's classrooms include students with a variety of individual differences. These differences can be a rich source of learning for *all students,* but they also can create divisions and conflicts among students that you will need to address. Therefore, rather than assuming that your students respect and accept one another, an important goal of your inclusive classroom is to teach *all students* to appreciate diversity and to value and learn from each other's similarities and differences. Teaching students to accept and appreciate the value of individual differences can be integrated into your curriculum, and reinforced by making your classroom reflect *all your students.* This will facilitate the acceptance of *all students* and establish a sense of community in the classroom (Sapon-Shevin, 2003; Obenchain & Abernathy, 2003). It can also help your students understand that they are more similar to each other than different and can identify their unique strengths and challenges, likes, and dislikes. Finally, it can help reduce name-calling, staring, and the formation of exclusive cliques and make it easier for students to develop friendships.

How Do Attitudes Toward Individual Differences Develop?

Although young children are aware of and curious about cultural and physical differences, they do not have set ideas about normalcy. Unfortunately, because of observational learning, societal influences, and the environment in which they are raised, many students enter school holding misconceptions and stereotypical views about persons they perceive as different (Shapiro, 1999). While students are inquisitive about individual differences, the behaviors of adults teach them not to talk about these differences (Tatum, 2000).

Many studies show that students who do not have disabilities have negative attitudes toward their peers who do, and this often can cause them to reject students with disabilities (Farmer, 2000; Shapiro, 1999). This peer rejection often results in loneliness and lowered self-esteem, which can hinder one's school success and self-identity (Geisthardt, Brotherson, & Cook, 2002; Pavri & Monda-Amaya, 2001;). For example, Reid and Button (1995) studied narratives written by students with disabilities. At school these students experienced isolation ("I [had] nobody to play with. . . . I had almost no friends. . . . I mean nobody really cared about how I felt." [p. 609]) and victimization ("They always called me names. . . . People call us retarded . . . or tell lies about you [and] it makes you feel mad" [p. 608]).

Factors such as cultural background, gender, age, socioeconomic status, and experiences in inclusive classrooms may interact with disability to influence the acceptance of students (Favazza, Phillipsen, & Kumar, 2000; Krajewski & Hyde, 2000). Students taught in inclusion programs appear to have more favorable attitudes toward their classmates

Reflective

When you were growing up, did you have opportunities to interact with children and adults with disabilities? How did these experiences help you understand and accept individual differences?

Resource

Pavri (2001) presents strategies for assessing and addressing loneliness in students.

with disabilities. General education students tend to be more accepting of students with sensory and physical disabilities and less accepting of students with learning and emotional problems. Wealthy students with disabilities are viewed more positively by their classmates than those who are poor, and girls with learning disabilities are more likely than boys with learning disabilities to be rejected by their peers. However, female and younger students tend to have more favorable attitudes toward students with disabilities.

Many factors lead to the development of negative attitudes toward students with individual differences, which can affect students' self-identities (Eisenman & Tascione, 2002; Tatum, 2000). The way children are raised limits interactions between them based on disability, race, and language abilities. Attitudes toward persons who have disabilities, speak different languages, and have different cultures also are shaped by the media, literature, and visual images and representations in society, which unfortunately tend to portray these groups negatively and in stereotypical ways. For example, Shapiro (1999) noted that fairy tales, comic books and cartoons, which are used to introduce children to the culture, often present persons with individual differences as bumbling (e.g., Mr. Magoo), evil (e.g., Captain Hook), deformed (e.g., Rumpelstiltskin), and comical (e.g. Porky Pig and Elmer Fudd). As a result, many children learn that individual differences have low-status and negative connotations and they often react to these individuals with disabilities with fear, pity, fascination, and ridicule.

Reflective

How are persons with disabilities and those from various cultural and linguistic backgrounds presented in books, television shows, movies, and cartoons? How do these portrayals affect you and your students' understanding and acceptance of individual differences?

How Can I Assess Attitudes Toward Individual Differences?

It is important to understand your students' attitudes toward and knowledge of individual differences as well as their social interactions and friendships as a starting point to help you plan appropriate activities. You can use the techniques described below to do this.

Attitude Assessment Instruments

Several instruments have been developed to assess attitudes toward individuals with disabilities (Favazza et al., 2000; Shapiro, 1999). One of them is the *Acceptance Scale,* which includes elementary and secondary versions (Antonak & Livneh, 1988). Students indicate their agreement with ("Yes, I agree"), disagreement with ("No, I disagree"), or uncertainty about ("Maybe; I'm not sure") items that are phrased either negatively ("I wouldn't spend my recess with a kid with a disability") or positively ("I believe I could become close friends with a special education student"). The *Personal Attribute Inventory for Children (PAIC)* (Parish, Ohlsen, & Parish, 1978) is an alphabetically arranged checklist consisting of 24 negative and 24 positive adjectives that asks students to select 15 adjectives that best describe a particular student or group of students.

These instruments can be adapted to assess attitudes toward persons with other types of individual differences by modifying the directions. For example, the Acceptance Scale can be adapted by asking students to complete each item with respect to individuals who speak a language other than English. You also can adapt these instruments by simplifying the language, phrasing items in a true-false format, and using pictorials. Picture-oriented attitude scales are especially appropriate for measuring the attitudes of young students.

Knowledge of Individual Differences Probes

You also can use individual differences probes to assess your students' feelings about differences and factual knowledge about various groups ("What does it mean to have a learning disability?"); stereotypical views of others (True or false: "Homeless people are adults who don't work and choose to be homeless"); needs of other individuals ("What are three things that you would have difficulty doing in this classroom if you didn't speak English?"); ways to interact with others ("If you had a hearing impairment, how would you want others to interact with you?"); and devices and aids designed to help individuals ("What is a device that a student with one arm could use?"). A sample probe on disabilities is presented in Figure 5.1.

You also can assess your students' knowledge of and feelings about individual differences by using sentence completion items (Shapiro, 1999). For example, you can ask your students to respond to the following:

If I used a wheelchair, I would want others to:
When I hear someone speak another language, I feel:

Student Drawings

Having students draw a picture of a scene depicting other individuals can be a valuable way of assessing their attitudes (Favazza et al., 2000; Shapiro, 1999). To assess students' feelings accurately, you can also ask them to write a story explaining their picture. For example, examine the picture in Figure 5.2. How would you rate the attitude toward individuals with disabilities of the student who drew this picture? At first, the drawing may suggest that the student has a negative attitude. However, the accompanying story shows the student's attitude much more clearly. The student explained the picture by stating, "People with disabilities are almost always made fun of. This picture shows a person with a disability crying because of the way other people laugh at him. Put yourself in his position."

Observational Techniques

Through direct observations of interactions between students, you can gain insights into their attitudes towards others and their interaction patterns, as well as the factors that can foster their friendships (Hall & Strickett, 2002). You can examine the interactions of your students by observing them during various learning and social activities. This information can then be analyzed by considering the following questions:

- How often are students with and without disabilities interacting with each other?
- How long do these interactions last?
- What is the nature of these interactions (e.g., spontaneous, assistive, reciprocal, instructional, disciplinary, attention-seeking, playful)?
- Who is beginning and ending the interactions?
- How many students without disabilities are interacting with their peers with disabilities?
- What events, activities, individuals, objects, and other stimuli seem to promote interactions?
- What events, activities, individuals, objects, and other stimuli seem to limit interactions?

Sample probe on disabilities

YES	☐	
NO	☐	1. Is a person with a disability usually ill?
NOT SURE	☐	
YES	☐	
NO	☐	2. Can people who are blind go to the store by themselves?
NOT SURE	☐	
YES	☐	
NO	☐	3. Were people with disabilities born that way?
NOT SURE	☐	
YES	☐	
NO	☐	4. Do you feel sorry for someone who has a disability?
NOT SURE	☐	
YES	☐	
NO	☐	5. Are all deaf people alike?
NOT SURE	☐	
YES	☐	
NO	☐	6. Do all children have a right to go to your school?
NOT SURE	☐	

Source: From *What's the Difference? Teaching Positive Attitudes Toward People with Disabilities,* (p. 5), by E. Barnes, C. Berrigan, and D. Biklen, 1978. Copyright 1978 by Human Policy Press. Reprinted by permission of the publisher.

FIGURE 5.2   **Student drawing depicting an individual with a disability**

213

- What roles, if any, do race, gender, language, religion, sexual orientation, and socioeconomic factors play in the interactions among students?
- Do the students with and without disabilities have the skills needed to interact with their peers?
- What are the outcomes of these interactions?
- Do these interactions change over time?

Resource

Carrington et al. (2003) developed a series of questions for interviewing students about their friendships and friendship-making skills.

cd - rom

Resource

The *Educational Assessment of Social Interaction (EASI)* (Hunt, Alwell, Farron-Davis, & Goetz, 1996), the *Interactive Partnership Scale (IPS)* (Hunt et al., 1996), the *Social Interaction Checklist (SIC)* (Kennedy et al., 1997), the *Social Contact Assessment Form* (Kennedy et al., 1997), and the *School-Based Social Network Form* (Kennedy et al., 1997) can help you record and categorize your observations of student interactions.

These observations can be supplemented by interviews with students, peers, family members, and other professionals to learn about student interactions and the social skills they use effectively (Hall & McGregor, 2000; Lee, Yoo, & Bak, 2003). **To view an example of student interactions, go to Case 1: Difficult Behavior on the CD-ROM and click on the natural supports video clip. What does your observation of these student interactions indicate about their acceptance of individual differences and friendships?**

Sociometric Techniques

Data on the social relationships students prefer and their friendships can be collected using sociometric techniques (Hall & Strickett, 2002; Lee et al., 2003). A peer-nomination sociogram involves asking students to respond confidentially to a series of questions that reveal classmates with whom they would like to perform a social or classroom activity. Because it is important to obtain information on both popular and unpopular students in the class, sociograms should include both acceptance (i.e., "Which 5 students from this class would you most like to invite to your birthday party?") and rejection ("Which 5 students from this class would you least like to sit next to during lunch?") questions. In addition to providing data on the acceptance or rejection of students, sociograms can help you identify students who need to improve their socialization skills.

Several structured sociometric rating procedures have been developed for teachers. They provide specific questions to ask students and standardized procedures to follow when administering the rating scale. For example, *Reciprocal Friendships Nomination* asks students to identify those classmates who are friends as well as those who are not friends (Tur-Kaspa, 2002). You can also gather information on the quality and reciprocity of and satisfaction with your students' friendships by using surveys and interviews such as the *Playmates and Friends Questionnaire for Teachers* (Buysse, Goldman, & Skinner, 2002), or *Friendship Quality Questionnaire* (Parker & Asher, 1993).

How Can I Teach Acceptance of Individual Differences Related to Disability?

Attitude Change and Information-Sharing Strategies

When students have negative attitudes toward individuals they view as different, you can foster positive attitudes by using a variety of *attitude-change* and *information-sharing strategies*. Key factors in the success of these strategies are:

- viewing *all* persons as capable individuals with unique personalities, qualities, likes, dislikes, strengths, and challenges.

- promoting the view that similarities and differences are natural and positive and that we *all* benefit from diversity and appreciating individual differences.
- fostering sensitivity rather than sympathy.
- emphasizing that we *all* have more similarities and than differences and that our differences make us unique and our similarities unite us.
- establishing frequent collaborative interactions and ongoing *equal-status relationships,* in which both parties view each other as equal in social, educational, or vocational status.
- sharing meaningful and credible information and addressing issues and questions openly, honestly, accurately, and objectively.
- fostering an understanding of the importance of one's individuality, independence, dignity, and self-determination, and avoiding pitying and protective responses.
- providing information, direct contact, and experiences that share important information about and counter stereotyped views of others perceived as different.
- engaging in actions that support others (Shapiro, 1999).

Many different strategies to change attitudes, share information, and teach students about individual differences are described in this chapter. Figure 5.3 is a checklist for selecting a strategy that works in your own classroom situation. You also can get help from students, their families, and other educators in planning and implementing these strategies. For example, your school's nurse and occupational and physical therapists can collaborate with you to teach your students about physical disabilities and the assistive devices these individuals use. You also can collaborate with school counselors, who can use their training to lead role-plays and group discussions. Other professionals also can help you identify resources such as curriculum materials, guest speakers, and community organizations that can be used to educate your students about individual differences. In collaborating with families and other professionals, you may need to discuss and resolve different perspectives toward individual differences and attitude-change strategies.

Many of the guidelines and strategies used to teach acceptance of individual differences related to disability can be adapted to teach students about individual differences related to culture, language, gender, religion, family structure, and socioeconomic status as well. They also can be used to address issues related to sexual orientation, which we discussed in chapter 3.

Reflective

What are your attitudes and behaviors in regard to individual differences? Are there individual differences with which you feel comfortable? Uncomfortable? How do you reveal these attitudes to others? How did you develop these attitudes and behaviors?

FIGURE 5.3

Attitude change strategy checklist

Several attitude change strategies exist. You can determine which strategy to use in your classroom by answering the following questions:

- Is the strategy appropriate for my students?
- What skills do I need to implement the strategy? Do I have these skills?
- What resources do I need to implement the strategy? Do I have these resources?
- Does the strategy teach critical information about the group and the acceptance of individual differences?
- Does the strategy present positive, nonstereotypical examples of the group?
- Does the strategy establish an equal-status relationship?
- Does the strategy offer students activities in which to learn about the group and individual similarities and differences?
- Does the strategy promote follow-up activities?

Reflect On Your Attitudes, Behaviors, and Language

Because students look up to and are influenced by their teachers, you can serve as a role model by reflecting on your attitudes and behaviors. You also can interact with your students in ways that show you are comfortable with individual differences and respect and care about *all of them* (Davern, 1999; Pivik et al., 2002; Tomlinson, 2001). It is especially important for you to watch your language because it communicates how you think, feel, and act regarding individual differences and the inclusion of various types of learners. Here are some ways your language and interactions can focus on students' competence, strengths, and similarities rather than their deficits and differences, and create a classroom environment that models your acceptance of diversity and *all your students.*

Focus on the individual and acknowledge individual differences when they are relevant to the situation: Use individuals-first language, which focuses on the person rather than on their individual differences, and refer to your students by their names. For example, saying, "the inclusion kids will work with Mr. Josephs, and everyone else will work with me" sets students apart and objectifies them. Similarly, using nicknames for students with unusual names also can make students feel different.

Resource

Shapiro (1999) provides a review of language and terminology related to individual differences and their effect on attitudes toward individuals with disabilities.

Reflective

What individual differences do you have? How do they define you and your experiences?

While you should focus on the individual, it is also important to acknowledge the individual differences of your students when these differences are relevant to the situation. Ignoring individual differences may mean not acknowledging important aspects of who students are, how they define themselves, and how they experience the world. For example, rather than ignoring students' use of a wheelchair or cultural or racial identity, it is important to acknowledge them as an aspect of how they experience the world.

View students as multidimensional.   Learn about *all your students'* backgrounds, strengths, interests, hobbies, and talents. Share this information with others, and incorporate it into your classroom in varied ways.

Note the similarities among students.   Take opportunities to acknowledge the ways in which *all your students* are similar.

Describe students in positive and meaningful ways.   Offer positive descriptions of *all your students* related to their abilities and progress. For example, describe students in terms of what they can do or who they are (e.g., a speaker of Spanish who is also learning English), rather than what they cannot do (e.g., limited English proficient), or who they are not (e.g., non-English speaking). Avoid referring to students using terms such as *dropouts* or *disadvantaged*, which focus on their difficulties.

Establish high and appropriate expectations for students.   Articulate challenging and reasonable expectations for *all your students*, and expect all of them to participate academically and socially and to complete their work.

Affirm students and their achievements.   Use verbal and nonverbal communication to acknowledge *all your students* and their contributions, and note how the presence of *all your students* benefits the class. **To view an example of a teacher acknowledging a student's contribution, go to Case 4: Support Participation on the CD-ROM and click on the recognize efforts video clip. How does affirming students help create an environment that supports learning, acceptance and friendships?**

cd-rom

Deliver feedback to support learning and effort.   Use informational feedback to foster the learning and effort of *all your students* such as, "You're really working hard," "You have the skill to do this," and "Try another way of doing this."

Listen to students, give them choices, and solicit their preferences.   Show *all your students* that you view them as active and competent learners by offering them choices, and asking them about their preferences.

Provide opportunities for students to assume leadership positions.   Allow *all your students* to perform important class positions and jobs, and to assume roles that offer them opportunities to show their strengths and assist others. For example, develop a chart of class jobs and a system for rotating them among all students, and introduce it by telling the class, "These are important jobs, and everyone can do them and will have a chance to do them."

Use language and talk about topics that are age-appropriate.   Speak to *all your students* in age-appropriate language and about age-appropriate topics.

Speak directly to students.   Discourage talking about students as if they were not there, and talk to *all your students*, even those who benefit from the services of interpreters and paraeducators.

Foster academic and social interactions with peers.   Structure academic and social activities so that *all your students* interact with each other, and comment positively when students interact appropriately (strategies for doing this are discussed later in this chapter and in chapter 9).

Respect your students and their independence.   Demonstrate respect for *all your students*, offer them assistance only when necessary, and refrain from placing them in embarrassing situations.

Act promptly and decisively when students behave inappropriately and hurt others.   Respond quickly so that *all your students* understand that hurtful comments and actions are not acceptable (strategies for doing this are discussed later in this chapter). (Smith, Salend, & Ryan, 2001; Sapon-Shevin, 2003).

Address Issues of Fairness

You also may need to address your students' concerns about issues of fairness. Through your language and actions you can help your students understand that it is not necessarily fair to treat everyone in the same way, as it does not acknowledge and respect individual differences. You can address fairness issues in your classroom by:

- helping your students understand the complexities associated with fairness, the differences between equality and equity, and that treating everyone in the same way is not always fair. For example, you can ask students to role-play and discuss various scenarios that depict situations when it is fair and appropriate to treat everyone in similar ways and situations when it is fair and appropriate to treat individuals differently.
- making your use of differentiated instruction to provide *all students* with varied learning activities and multiple ways of demonstrating their understanding and mastery of learning standards explicit to *all students and their families*.

- teaching *all your students* to understand how they are unique and to view themselves in terms of their own strengths, challenges, performance, and progress rather than defining themselves in relation to others.
- using classroom meetings to explain and discuss issues of fairness.
- asking *all your students* to identify the things that are difficult for them and the special things that they need to help them succeed (as Mr. Monroig did in the chapter-opening vignette).
- explaining that *all students* in your classroom get what they need to succeed, and the reasons for treating students in different ways (without violating confidentiality or placing students in awkward situations) (Singh, 2001; Tomlinson, 2001b, Welch, 2000).

Set Your Sites

For more information on promoting equity in classrooms and schools, go to the Web Links module in Chapter 5 of the Companion Website.

Use Disability Simulations

An effective method that Mr. Monroig used to teach his students about individuals with disabilities was the use of *disability simulations,* in which students experience how it feels to have a disability (Hartwell, 2001; Pearl, 2004). In addition to demonstrating the difficulties encountered by individuals with disabilities, simulations expose students to the accommodations that individuals with disabilities find helpful. Simulations of varying disabilities and sample follow-up questions are presented in Figure 5.4.

Resource

Pearl (2004), Hartwell (2001), Shapiro (1999), Freedman-Harvey and Johnson (1998), and Horne (1998) offer additional simulation activities and guidelines and suggestions for using them.

When using simulations, you need to be aware of some limitations (Smart, 2001). Attitude changes related to simulations tend to be brief and may result in a feeling of sympathy. You also need to make sure that students don't trivialize the experience and think that having a disability is fun and games (e.g., wheeling around in a wheelchair). You can counter these limited reactions and make the simulations more effective by using several guidelines. You can select simulations that are as realistic as possible and tell the students that they must take the activities seriously and not quit until they are complete. During the simulations, you can assign an observer to watch and, if necessary, help students who are participating in the activities. You also may want to make video recordings of them, which can be used to have students reflect on the simulations by conducting group discussions and by asking students to write about their experiences. A participant reaction form that can be used to help students reflect on their experiences is presented in Figure 5.5.

Reflective

Simulate several disabilities for part or all of a day. How did the simulations make you feel? How did others treat you? What problems did you experience? What did you learn? How did you adapt to the various disabilities?

As Mr. Monroig did in his class, you can follow up simulations by having students identify and work on something that is difficult for them. They also can maintain a journal of their progress, the barriers they encounter, and their reflections on what they have learned about themselves and others.

Study About Disabilities and Successful Individuals with Disabilities

Many famous individuals have some type of disability. Lessons and assignments on the achievements of highly successful individuals with disabilities, and how they dealt with and compensated for their disability, can help present disabilities in a more positive light (Hartwell, 2001; Jairrels, Brazil, & Patton, 1999). You can have students write about a friend or relative who has a disability, complete a research report on the topics related to disability, or search Internet sites addressing disability (Eisenman & Tascione, 2002).

REFLECTING ON PROFESSIONAL PRACTICES

Empowering Language

Ms. Ryan, a teacher education student, realized that her field placement in the FDR School gave her a lot of "food for thought." While she was learning about assessment, curriculum, teaching, and working with students and their families, several incidents forced her to reflect on the issues of teacher behavior as well as the language used in special education and its effects on students, families, and professionals.

The first incident occurred during an informal conversation with a teacher while the students were working nearby. The teacher nodded toward a student who was struggling with his work and said, "Can you believe he was supposed to be mainstreamed?" The second incident occurred later that same day. As the teacher prepared materials for a math assessment, the paraeducator approached her and asked, "They get to use calculators?" In front of the whole class, the teacher responded, "Well, they are special education students."

During the third incident, Ms. Ryan observed another teacher who approached her students' differences in a very different way. One student asked the teacher why another student received extra time to complete an assignment, saying, "That's not fair." The teacher responded, "Just like you, all the students in the class are learning new things in their own ways. In this class, we do not expect everyone to learn, look, sound, and act the same." Later, the teacher told the students, "In your lives, you are going to meet a lot of people who are different from you, and it is these differences that make life special. Think about how boring it would be if we were all the same."

The final incident occurred when Ms. Ryan attended a planning team meeting that included a student and the student's family. The team discussed the student's strengths and needs and strategies to enhance learning, rather than the student's disability category. Team members and the student noted that "he was good at some things and had difficulty with other things." The educators listened carefully to the comments made by the student and the family and said that they believed that the student could succeed in their classroom. They told the student that "trying is one of the stepping stones to learning."

- How did the behaviors and language of the teachers in the first two incidents differ from the behaviors and language of the teachers in the second two incidents?
- How were the students, teachers, and family members affected by the language associated with special education and individual differences?
- How would you categorize your language and interactions with students, family members, and other professionals?
- How can you use language and behaviors that show your acceptance of individual differences?
- How can you help students discuss their individual differences in empowering ways?

 To answer these questions online and share your responses with others, go to the Reflection module in Chapter 5 of the Companion Website.

Invite Guest Speakers

You can expose students directly to individuals with disabilities by inviting guest speakers who have disabilities (Calloway, 1999; Hartwell, 2001). When using guest speakers, it is important that you carefully identify, select, and prepare them, and determine whether you want to have several speakers at the same time (Shapiro, 1999). You can find potential guest speakers by contacting local community agencies, professional and advocacy organizations, and special education teachers. Meet with any potential speakers to determine how relevant and appropriate it would be to invite them. Determine whether speakers can speak in an open and honest way and in language that your students can understand. It is also important to consider whether they can use short anecdotes and humorous and meaningful stories and examples that present their independent lives in a positive light and foster positive attitudes.

FIGURE 5.4

Sample disability simulations and follow-up questions.

VISUAL IMPAIRMENT SIMULATIONS

Activity

Have students wear blindfolds during part of the school day. Blindfold one student and assign another student as a helper to follow the blindfolded student around the room and building. Periodically, have the helper and the blindfolded student change roles. Structure the activity so that students must move around in the classroom, eat a meal, go to the bathroom, and move to other classes. Have the blindfolded student complete a form, with the helper providing verbal assistance only.

Follow-up Questions

1. What difficulties did you have during the activity? What difficulties did you observe as a helper?
2. What did you do that helped you perform the activities without seeing?
3. What did the helper do to help you perform the activities?
4. What changes could be made in school to assist students who can't see? At home?

HEARING IMPAIRMENT SIMULATIONS

Activity

Show a movie or video without the sound. Ask students questions that can be answered only after having heard the sound. Show the same film or video again with the sound and have students respond to the same questions.

Follow-up Questions

1. How did your answers differ?
2. What information did you use to answer the questions after the first viewing?

PHYSICAL DISABILITIES SIMULATIONS

Activity

Put a dowel rod in the joints of the students' elbows while their arms are positioned behind their backs. Ask students to try to comb their hair, tie their shoes, write a story, draw, and eat.

Follow-up Questions

1. Were you successful at combing your hair? Tying your shoes? Writing the story? Drawing? Eating?
2. What other activities would you have difficulty doing if you had limited use of your hands?
3. Are there any strategies or devices that you could use to perform the tasks?

Activity

Place students in wheelchairs and have them maneuver around the classroom and the school. Structure the activity so that students attempt to drink from a water fountain, write on the blackboard, make a phone call, go to the bathroom, and transfer themselves onto a toilet. Because of the potential architectural barriers in the school, have a same-sex peer assist and observe the student in the wheelchair.

Follow-up Questions

1. What difficulties did you encounter in maneuvering around the school?
2. What were the reactions of other students who saw you in the wheelchair? How did their reactions make you feel?
3. What are some barriers that would make it hard for a person who uses a wheelchair to move around on a street? In a store?
4. What modifications can make it easier for individuals who use wheelchairs to maneuver in schools? In streets, stores, or homes?

SPEECH IMPAIRMENT SIMULATIONS

Activity

Assign students in pairs. Have one student try to communicate messages to the other by using physical gestures only, by talking without moving the tongue, and by using a communication board.

Follow-up Questions

1. What strategies did you use to communicate the message?
2. How did you understand your partner's message?
3. If you had difficulty talking, how would you want others to talk to you?

LEARNING DISABILITIES SIMULATIONS

Activity

Place a mirror and a sheet of paper on the students' desks so that students can see the reflection of the paper in the mirror. Have the students write a sentence and read a paragraph while looking in the mirror. Then have the students do the same tasks without looking in the mirror. Compare their ability to do the tasks under the two different conditions.

Follow-up Questions

1. What difficulties did you experience in writing and reading while looking in the mirror?
2. How did it feel to have difficulty writing and reading?
3. What other tasks would be hard if you saw this way all the time?

Note: Horne (1998); Shapiro (1999).

Once a speaker has been selected, you can meet with this individual to discuss the goals of the presentation and possible topics to be covered. Speakers may want to address such topics as the difficulties they encounter now, as well as those they experienced when they were the students' age; school and childhood experiences; hobbies and interests; family; jobs; a typical day; future plans; causes of their disability; ways to prevent their disability (if possible); accommodations they need; ways of interacting with others; and assistive devices they use. It is also essential that you discuss with speakers the materials they may need and the accommodations and assistive devices they require, so that your school and classroom are accessible and set up appropriately. It is also important for you to confirm dates and times and to ensure that speakers have appropriate parking and transportation to and from your school.

To help speakers tailor their remarks to students, you can provide background information about the class (age level, grade level, exposure to and understanding of disabilities) and possible questions students may ask. Before the speaker comes to class, you can have students identify the questions they have about the disability to be discussed. You also can prepare students by providing them with information about disabilities and the speaker beforehand. Schedule time during the presentation to welcome and introduce speakers and to allow students to ask questions and share their feelings and experiences. Because some students may hesitate to ask questions, you can help overcome their reluctance by initially asking the speaker some of the questions the students previously identified. As a follow-up activity, have students write thank you notes or create projects that express their appreciation.

Students with disabilities and their family members (with the permission of the student) can also share information about the characteristics of the disability and the child's needs (Pivik et al., 2002). They can use home videos, photographs, and items that reveal

Resource

Pearl (2004) offers guidelines about involving students with disabilities in teaching their peers about disabilities.

FIGURE 5.5

Simulation participant reaction form

PARTICIPANT REACTION FORM

Participant's Name _____

Activity_____   Date _____

I. Describe your reactions to this activity by completing the following:
   1. Describe your behaviors during the activity. What did you do?
   2. Describe your emotions during the activity. How did you feel after the activity?
   3. How were your reactions to this experience different than what you expected? Explain.

II. Rate your reactions to the activity on the scale provided.
   SD = strongly disagree   D = disagree   A = agree   SA = strongly agree

1. This activity made me feel incompetent.	SD	D	A	SA
2. This activity was easier to do than expected.	SD	D	A	SA
3. One of the worst things in the world would be to do this activity every day for the rest of my life.	SD	D	A	SA
4. This activity made me feel dumb.	SD	D	A	SA
5. This activity was fun to do.	SD	D	A	SA
6. This activity made me think a long time about this disability.	SD	D	A	SA
7. This activity made me feel helpless.	SD	D	A	SA

III. Rate your reactions to persons with this disability by completing the following.
   SD = strongly disagree   D = disagree   A = agree   SA = strongly agree

1. A person with this disability would have a hard time having a boyfriend or girlfriend.	SD	D	A	SA
2. A person with this disability could never have a professional occupation.	SD	D	A	SA
3. A person with this disability would have a very hard time being a parent.	SD	D	A	SA
4. A person with this disability would have a hard time liking him or herself.	SD	D	A	SA
5. A person with this disability needs a lot of assistance keeping house.	SD	D	A	SA
6. A person with this disability has few friends.	SD	D	A	SA
7. A person with this disability would probably never be able to vote in national elections.	SD	D	A	SA
8. A person with this disability cannot keep track of his or her own finances.	SD	D	A	SA
9. A person with this disability has few leisure activities he or she really enjoys.	SD	D	A	SA
10. A person with this disability would enjoy coming to visit me at my house.	SD	D	A	SA

Source: From "Simulations Promote Understanding of Handicapping Conditions," by C. Wesson and C. Mandell, 1989, *Teaching Exceptional Children, 21,* p. 34. Copyright 1989 by The Council for Exceptional Children. Reprinted with permission.

important information about one's strengths, interests, hobbies, and challenges. They also can address the accommodations and assistive devices used, as well as questions and concerns raised by classmates. For example, students who use a wheelchair can explain to the class that they will ask others to push them if they need assistance, how the chair works, and how to push someone in the chair (Shapiro, 1999). If the student or a family member is not able to address the class, a professional who works with the student can serve as a guest speaker.

Use Films/Videos and Books

Many films and videos depict the lives of persons with individual differences and disabilities (Safran, 2000). Movies and videos such as *A Beautiful Mind, Forrest Gump, The Tic Code, Shine, King Gimp, Nell, Philadelphia, My Left Foot, The Color of Paradise,*

Children of a Lesser God, Awakenings, and *Rain Man* can be viewed and discussed. Audiovisual materials such as DVDs and videos of news segments and documentaries from professional organizations and television stations are available to introduce students to various disabilities and individual differences (Shapiro, 1999). For example, the Alexander Graham Bell Association for the Deaf provides a video that simulates different types of hearing losses, and public television produces many shows that deal with individuals with disabilities.

Books about individuals with disabilities and related issues can counter stereotypical views and can teach students about individual differences and disabilities (Morrison & Rude, 2002; Rohner & Rosberg, 2003). They also serve as a springboard for helping students reflect on their beliefs about individual differences and disabilities, and what strategies they can employ to support persons with individual differences (Prater, 2000). They also can be used to help your students with disabilities understand their own disabilities more clearly and relate to others (Dyches & Burrow, 2003). You can increase the effectiveness of these books with guided discussions and activities related to the story's plot, information about disabilities, the characteristics and abilities of the characters, the stereotypes that are depicted and challenged, and the similarities between the characters and your students (Favazza & Odom, 1997).

Older students can be introduced to individuals with disabilities via literature and first-person accounts of exceptionality (Kluth, 2004; Morrison & Rude, 2002; Smead, 1999). For example, *Learning Disabilities and Life Stories* (Rodis, Garrod, & Boscardin, 2001) is a collection of autobiographical essays written by a range of adolescents that provides accounts of growing up with learning disabilities. Compilations of selections from famous authors around the theme of individuals with disabilities can include follow-up discussion questions to give students insights into the experiences and feelings of persons with disabilities (Bowers, 1980; Landau, Epstein, & Stone, 1978). Folktales also can be used and analyzed to promote a greater understanding of individuals with disabilities.

Set Your Sites

For more information on films about individuals with disabilities, go to the Web Links module in Chapter 5 of the Companion Website.

Resource

Rohner and Rosberg (2003), Dyches and Burrow (2003), Shapiro (1999), Bryde (1998), Prater (1998; 2000), and Winsor (1998) have compiled helpful lists of books about disabilities and giftedness that teachers can use with their students across a range of age and grade levels.

Set Your Sites

For more information on books about individuals with disabilities for use with your students, go to the Web Links module in Chapter 5 of the Companion Website.

Resource

Smead (1999), offers an annotated bibliography of books presenting personal accounts of exceptionality.

Teachers can use books to teach students about individual differences. What books have helped you learn about individual differences?

REFLECTING ON YOUR PRACTICES

Selecting Books and Other Materials About Individual Differences

You can examine the appropriateness of the books and materials you use to teach students about individual differences by considering the following:

- Does the author have the background to accurately depict and present information about the group(s) discussed?
- Are the language, plot, and style of the book or material appropriate for your students and free of bias?
- Is the book or material factually correct, realistic, and presented in a culturally appropriate manner?
- Is the book or material written using accurate and appropriate language and terminology?
- Are individuals with differences depicted in a variety of situations and settings that represent their own cultural norms?
- Are individuals with differences portrayed in a positive, well-rounded, independent, complex, and nonstereotypical way?
- Does the book or material address important issues and recognize and include the contributions of individuals from diverse groups?

- Does the book or material introduce students to the accommodations and devices that individuals with differences find helpful?
- Does the book or material allow the students to develop an equal-status relationship with others and learn about the things they share with others?
- Does the book or material help students understand subtle stereotypes and present diversity within and across groups?
- In what proportion are individuals from different groups shown in the illustrations?
- Are the illustrations accurate, current, and nonstereotypical?
- Will the book or material and the illustrations stimulate questions and discussions about individuals with differences?

How would you rate your selection of books and materials about individual differences? ( ) Excellent ( ) Good ( ) Needs Improvement ( ) Needs Much Improvement

What are some goals and steps you could adopt to improve your selection of books and materials about individual differences?

Use Curriculum Guides and Instructional Materials

Many curriculum guides and instructional materials to teach students about individual differences are available (National Information Center for Children and Youth with Disabilities, 2000; Shapiro, 1999). These curricular and teaching materials can be used to infuse content about individual differences related to disability into your classroom or as part of a separate unit of study. These usually include a variety of goals, learning activities, materials to implement the activities, multimedia materials, and a teacher's guide.

You also can promote acceptance by creating a classroom environment that supports the acceptance of individual differences through the use of teaching materials and games (Shapiro, 1999). For example, you can introduce materials that stimulate discussions, such as photographs and posters of individuals with disabilities, multiracial dolls, dolls with differing abilities and assistive devices, and stuffed animals that depict individuals with disabilities. You also can use games such as Empathy, where students work in teams to travel through Multicappia with various disability conditions. Winning teams gain empathy points by demonstrating their understanding of a wide range of disability conditions.

Kids on the Block (www.kotb.com) offers a variety of awareness programs for teaching sensitivity, awareness, and understanding related to educational differences and social/

Resource

The National Information Center for Children and Youth with Disabilities (2000) offers an annotated listing of curriculum materials and other resources related to disability awareness.

Teachers can use a variety of instructional materials to teach children about disabilities and individual differences. How do you teach your students about individual differences?

NOTE: The Kids on the Block is an educational company that uses puppets to teach children about disabilities, differences, and social concerns. Created in 1977, the educational puppet curriculums are in use worldwide by more than 1,700 community-based troupes. For information call 1-800-368-KIDS.

safety issues. For example, it offers puppet shows involving life-size puppets representing students with disabilities in real-life situations. The vignettes encourage the audience to explore their feelings toward individuals with disabilities and to ask questions about persons with specific disabilities. In addition, Kids on the Block offers programs on medical conditions (AIDS, diabetes) and on such topics as aging, divorce, teen pregnancy, child abuse, substance abuse, and cultural differences.

Teach About Assistive Devices

Since many students with disabilities may use assistive devices, teaching others about these devices can be beneficial. Wherever possible, it is best for the students with disabilities to introduce and explain the aids and devices they use. It is also important to help students learn that these devices are important tools that help people and not toys and to refrain from touching or playing with them without permission. If students do not feel comfortable showing and explaining the aids they use, a professional or family member can do so.

Use Collaborative Problem-Solving

Collaborative problem-solving can sensitize students about when and how to assist classmates by presenting scenarios on classroom and interpersonal situations that students are likely to encounter in the inclusive classroom (Salisbury et al., 1997). As Mr. Monroig did in the chapter-opening vignette, scenarios related to some of the classroom difficulties that students are experiencing can be presented. Afterward, students can discuss it collaboratively and brainstorm possible solutions. You can promote the discussion by helping students identify the issues, providing additional information when necessary, and sharing your own beliefs about fairness. Once potential solutions are generated, the class

Resource

Shapiro (1999) offers information, assessment and intervention strategies, curriculum guides, programs, and resources on attitudes toward individuals with disabilities.

Resource

Pavri & Monda-Amaya (2001) developed vignettes that can teach students about classroom-based social situations that involve peer support, including dealing with rejection, jealousy, peer conflicts, different personality traits, and different physical appearances.

Reflective

Think about how to use collaborative problem-solving in the following situation: In the social studies class, students are required to take notes. Some of the students have trouble doing this. What solutions do you think other students would suggest?

can evaluate their completeness; fairness; feasibility; ability to solve the problem; and impact on peers, teachers, and the targeted student(s). Following this discussion, the class can select a solution, which is then implemented and evaluated.

How Can I Teach Acceptance of Individual Differences Related to Culture, Language, Gender, Religion, and Socioeconomic Status?

Learning activities can teach students to accept individual differences related to culture, language, gender, religion, and socioeconomic status. These activities can be integrated into your curriculum to create a classroom that welcomes, acknowledges, and celebrates the value and experiences of *all students*.

Reflect On Your Knowledge, Experiences, and Beliefs Related to Diversity

As we discussed earlier in this chapter, your attitudes, behaviors, and language related to diversity will affect your students' views and behaviors with respect to diversity (Edgar, Patton, & Day-Vines, 2002). Therefore, it is important for you to reflect on your knowledge, experiences, and beliefs related to your students' diversity and use your reflections to take actions to create an inclusive learning environment that fosters an understanding and acceptance of diversity (Montgomery, 2001). Questions that can be used or adapted to help you reflect on your students' diversity are presented in Figure 5.6.

Promote Acceptance of Cultural Diversity

Many students may view peers who come from other cultures and speak other languages as different, and may seldom interact with them because of their unique language, clothes, and customs. You can help students overcome these attitudes by teaching them about different cultures and the value of cultural diversity. With these activities, students gain a multicultural perspective that allows them to identify underlying and obvious similarities and differences among various groups. An environment that accepts other cultures can enhance the self-esteem and learning performance of *all students* by affirming their cultures, languages, religions, and experiences. Additional guidelines on creating and using a multicultural curriculum in different content areas are presented in chapter 8.

You can use antibias curricula to foster your students' understanding and appreciation of differences related to race, language, gender, religion, socioeconomic status, and disability. Antibias curricula often include a variety of activities to teach students to be sensitive to the needs of others, think critically, interact with others, and develop a positive self-identity based on one's own strengths rather than on the weaknesses of others. When teaching students about cultural diversity, you can consider the following guidelines:

• Examine cultural diversity with the belief that *all students* have a culture that is to be valued and affirmed.

FIGURE 5.6

Diversity self-assessment

❖ What is my definition of diversity?

❖ Do the children in my classroom and school come from diverse cultural backgrounds?

❖ What are my perceptions of students from different racial or ethnic groups? With language or dialects different from mine? With special needs?

❖ What are the sources of these perceptions (e.g., friends, relatives, television, movies)?

❖ How do I respond to my students, based on these perceptions?

❖ Have I experienced others' making assumptions about me based on my membership in a specific group? How did I feel?

❖ What steps do I need to take to learn about the students from diverse backgrounds in my school and classroom?

❖ How often do social relationships develop among students from different racial or ethnic backgrounds in my classroom and in the school? What is the nature of these relationships?

❖ In what ways do I make my instructional program responsive to the needs of the diverse groups in my classroom?

❖ What kinds of information, skills, and resources do I need to acquire to effectively teach from a multicultural perspective?

❖ In what ways do I collaborate with other educators, family members, and community groups to address the needs of all my students?

Source: From "Creating Culturally Responsive, Inclusive Classrooms," by W. Montgomery, 2001, *Teaching Exceptional Children, 33*(4), pp. 4–9. Copyright 2001 by The Council for Exceptional Children. Reprinted with permission.

- Teach initially about cultural diversity by noting the variety of students and adults in the classroom and then extending the discussion beyond the classroom.
- Collect information about your students' cultural backgrounds.
- Help students view the similarities among groups through their differences.
- Tailor the curriculum and activities to the developmental levels and interests of your students.
- Make cultural diversity activities an ongoing and integral part of the curriculum rather than a one-day "visit" to a culture during holidays or other special occasions.
- Relate experiences of cultural diversity to real life and give students hands-on experiences that address their interests.
- Teach students about the various types of individual behavior within all cultures, and emphasize the idea that families and individuals experience and live their culture in personal ways and have multiple identities (Derman-Sparks, 1989; Montgomery, 2001; Yeh & Drost, 2002).

Resource

Irvine and Armento (2001) offer guidelines and examples for integrating cultural diversity into all aspects of the curriculum.

Resource

Menkart (1999) offers guidelines on enhancing the effectiveness of heritage month celebrations.

Incorporate Cultural Diversity into the Classroom

You can incorporate acceptance of cultural diversity into your curriculum and classroom in a variety of ways (Gay, 2004) (see Figure 5.7). Use multicultural literature, poems, and folktales, and incorporate films, periodicals, and magazines on multicultural issues into the curriculum (Jairrels et al., 1999; Taylor, 2000). For example, in literature discussion groups, students can read and discuss books such as Alma Flor Ada's *My Name Is Maria Isabel* (1993), which uses the theme of a student losing her name to show the importance of respecting the unique traits of all persons. Students can then respond to questions that help them discuss and review the plot and identify the issues presented from multiple perspectives. They also can work in cross-cultural literature circles and develop character study journals in which they think about, write about, and maintain connections with the characters' feelings and situations, as well as their similarities to and differences from the

Resource

Reviews and lists of literature about various cultures and religions across many grade levels are available (Braus & Geidel, 2000; Montgomery, 2000; Office of Diversity Concerns, 1999; Schon, 2000; Taylor, 2000).

FIGURE 5.7

Activities to promote acceptance of cultural diversity

◇ Share information about your own cultural background, and ask students and their family members to do likewise.

◇ Discuss the similarities and differences among cultures including music, foods, customs, holidays, and languages.

◇ Make artifacts from different cultures.

◇ Read ethnic stories to and with students.

◇ Listen to music from different cultures and learn ethnic songs. A variety of music examples, lesson plans, audiocassettes, videocassettes, and practical strategies for teaching music from a multicultural perspective are available from the Music Educators National Conference Publication Sales (www.menc.org).

◇ Decorate the room, bulletin boards, and hallways with artwork, symbols, and murals that reflect a multicultural perspective.

◇ Make a class calendar that recognizes the holidays and customs of all cultures, and celebrate holidays that are common to several cultures in a way that recognizes each culture's customs.

◇ Plan multicultural lunches in which students and their families work together to cook multiethnic dishes. Have students interview family members about their dishes and write about their findings, which can be posted next to each dish.

◇ Take field trips that introduce students to the lifestyles of persons from different cultures.

◇ Show DVDs that highlight aspects of different cultures.

◇ Teach students ethnic games, and encourage them to use cross-cultural and cross-gender toys and other objects.

◇ Give students multicolored paints, paper, other art materials, and skin-tone crayons.

◇ Have students maintain an ethnic feelings book that summarizes their reactions to multicultural awareness activities and their experiences with their culture and other cultures.

Note: Derman-Sparks and Phillips, (1997); Nieto (2000); Schniedewind and Davidson (1998).

characters and conflict resolutions depicted (Blum, Lipsett, & Yocum, 2002; Montgomery, 2001). You can enhance the effectiveness of these books and stories by helping your students clarify the issues, concepts, and events depicted, make connections to them, and identify and engage in behaviors that are supportive of diversity (Cartledge & Kiarie, 2001). In addition to collaborating with your school librarian to identify and obtain appropriate books, your students can read multicultural books online via the International Children's Digital Library (www.icdlbook.org). In selecting these materials, you can examine them for inclusion of *all groups* and the roles they play in the specific content area.

You also can organize your classroom environment so that it acknowledges cultural diversity (Montgomery, 2001). You can use literature, arts, music, centers, or classroom displays that contain materials that are reflective of diversity. For example, you can create bulletin boards that showcase newspaper events and/or photographs of diverse community members, or you can display student work around the theme of cultural diversity.

You also can incorporate cultural diversity into your classroom by using folklore and recognizing that your students and their families can be resources for helping their peers learn about cultural diversity (Quinn, 2001). For example, you can structure classroom activities and assignments so that students share information about their cultural and experiential backgrounds. Similarly, you can diversify your students' learning by inviting family members and community members to share culturally relevant information about topics your class is studying, or by taking students on field trips to interact with diverse members of the community.

You also can use multicultural teaching and audiovisual materials and include the contributions of members of different groups in the content areas. For example, discussing the work of African American and Russian scientists in science classes or His-

Resource

Forgan (2002) developed *I SOLVE*, a learning strategy that can help your students problem-solve solutions to issues and conflicts depicted in books that are related to individual differences, so that they can take actions to address them in their classrooms.

Resource

Morroco and Hindin (2002) and Montgomery (2000) offer guidelines for using literature discussion groups to develop students' cultural understanding and acceptance.

Set Your Sites

For more information on multicultural books for use with your students, go to the Web Links module in Chapter 5 of the Companion Website.

Students can be resources for helping their peers learn about cultural diversity. How do you use your students' diversity as a resource?

panic and Irish poets in English classes can teach students about the contributions of those ethnic groups. Students can also be assigned to read books about different cultures and biographies of women who have made significant contributions to society.

Teach About Language Diversity

Acceptance of language diversity can increase the self-esteem and school performance of students who are learning English and students who speak dialects of English (Shafer, 2001). Acceptance also demonstrates a positive attitude toward students' language abilities and cultural backgrounds. Rather than viewing language diversity as a barrier to success in school, schools need to view it as an educational resource. This diversity offers teachers and students many opportunities to learn about the nature and power of language and to function successfully in the multicultural world in which they live. Therefore, schools need to support, maintain, and strengthen students' linguistic varieties and promote a view of bilingualism as an asset.

Many strategies can be used to promote acceptance of language diversity. When teaching, you can use diverse cultural and language referents, teach and offer support in students' native languages, encourage and teach students to use bilingual dictionaries, allow students to ask and answer questions in their native languages, and use peers to tutor and help students in their native languages. You can also establish social and work areas in the classroom and give students opportunities to work and interact with peers from diverse backgrounds (Hagiwara, 1998).

 Set Your Sites

For more information on incorporating folklore into the classroom, go to the Web Links module in Chapter 5 of the Companion Website.

Resource

Tiedt and Tiedt (2002) describe activities that you can use to help students learn about and value language diversity.

Teach About Dialect Differences

You know, it's funny. I speak English and Black English. Outside of school I hear a lot of white kids trying to speak like I do. They listen to rap music and try to speak like they are black. But when I'm in school, the same students make faces when I sometimes use Black English in class. It's like they don't respect our language or are afraid of it.

IDEAS FOR IMPLEMENTATION

Affirming Acceptance of Linguistic Diversity

Ms. White's school has had an increase in the number of students who are learning English. Several of these students were ridiculed because of their accents and their difficulties in understanding and talking with others. Ms. White was asked to serve on a schoolwide committee to counter this teasing and help all students feel comfortable in their new school. At the first meeting, she suggested that community members who speak the students' native languages should be invited to join the committee.

The committee decided to start by creating a school environment that welcomed students and their families and reflected the different languages spoken in the community. They posted signs, bulletin board notices, and greetings in several languages throughout the school. They also displayed books and materials written in several languages in classrooms, in the school's office, and in the school library and posted students' work in several languages. Occasionally, the school played music in different languages over the loudspeaker and invited speakers and storytellers who spoke various languages to address different classes. The changes appeared to work. Several teachers noted that the new students seemed to feel more comfortable in school and that many of the English-speaking students were attempting to speak to them by using the new students' native language.

Here are some other strategies you can use to create a school environment that accepts diversity in language:

- Encourage students to use their native language in school, and teach some words from their language to others.
- Teach lessons about languages other than English. For example, you can teach lessons that compare the English alphabet with the alphabets of other languages.

- Stock the classroom with bilingual books.
- Ask students to explain customs, games, folktales, songs, or objects from their culture in their native language, and show videos and play music in various languages.
- Use various languages in school newsletters and other written communications.
- Have students write journal entries and poems, contribute pieces to school publications, sing songs, and perform plays in their native languages.
- Use simulation activities. For example, BARNGA: A Simulation Game on Cultural Clashes can help secondary school students learn about the difficulties and isolation that immigrants experience when they arrive in a new country.
- Learn to pronounce students' names correctly, and learn greetings and words in the students' languages. When students speak to you in their native language, ask them the meaning of words and phrases you don't understand.
- Give students opportunities to communicate with pen pals from other regions of the United States and other countries via the Internet.
- Tell students that being bilingual and bicultural can enhance their opportunities for success and employment.
- Give awards and recognition for excellence in speaking languages that may not be part of typical foreign language courses offered at the school.

Note: Gullingsrud (1998); Hagiwara (1998); Nieto (2000); Shafer (2001).

Since all English-speaking students speak a dialect, you also will work with students who speak various dialects of English (Washington, 2001). Rather than making students who speak other dialects of English feel deficient and dysfunctional by interrupting and correcting them in midsentence, you can create a classroom that acknowledges and affirms the use of standard and other dialects of English as appropriate in various school and societal contexts (Day, 1998; Schorr, 1997). One effective approach for creating such a classroom is the *bridge system,* which encourages students to be bidialectical and to understand that different dialects are used in different situations. In this approach, you help students understand when to use standard English and when it is appropriate to use other dialects. For example, when you need to prompt students to

African American English is one dialect that some students use. What are other dialects that your students use? What dialects do you speak?

use standard English, you can ask, "How can you say that in school language?" In addition, you can help students become bidialectal by showing respect for students' dialects and the cultures they reflect; acknowledging the oral traditions of some students' cultures; exposing students to and discussing with them other English dialects through literature, books, songs, poetry, and films; and discussing and role-playing situations in which standard English and other dialects of English would be appropriate.

You also can help students discover and understand the connections among different languages and dialects, as well as the differences among languages (Tiedt & Tiedt, 2002). Students can study various aspects of languages and dialects and examine how words, sayings, riddles, and stories in different languages may share the same derivations. For example, students can experiment with Spanish words ending in *cia* (e.g., *distancia*) and English words ending in *ce* (e.g., *distance*) to begin to understand the commonalities of Spanish and English. Students and teachers can learn and use parallel sayings in English and other languages, and attempt to create their own sayings in many languages and dialects.

Help Your Students Develop a Global Perspective

Your students' cross-cultural understanding also can be fostered by helping them develop a global perspective. An understanding of other cultures and global issues can provide *all your students* with cross-cultural learning experiences that teach them about the similarities, differences and interdependence among people and countries from throughout the world (Skelton, Wigford, Harper, & Reeves, 2002). You can do this by:

- incorporating literature, films, history, cultural experiences, news, and other resources from around the world into your classroom and curriculum.
- using your immigrant students and their families as well as community members and international visitors as resources for helping students learn about other cultures.
- providing students with accurate information related to global cultures, conflicts, and issues that allows them to understand their complexity and challenge stereotypes and misconceptions (Bacon & Kischner, 2002; Merryfield, 2002).

You also can use technology to identify international resources, and to collaborate with others from around the world. Such technology also can provide your students with cross-cultural, equal-status experiences and opportunities to practice a foreign language and learn about other cultures (Smith, 2002). For example, they can interact with students from different parts of the world by working on collaborative online projects, communicating via videoconferencing, or using e-mail to establish electronic pen pals.

Teach Gender Equity

An effective program to teach students about cultural diversity should include activities that promote an understanding of gender equity. These activities can be integrated into all content areas to help female and male students expand their options in terms of behaviors, feelings, interests, career aspirations, and abilities. Gender equity activities also make *all students* aware of the negative effects of gender bias and of ways to combat sexism. For example, as part of your math class, you can have students graph the number of male and female athletes mentioned in their local newspaper. A variety of curriculum activities, media, books for children and adults, photographs, posters, toys, games, and professional organizations are available to use as resources for teaching students about gender equity and sexual harassment (Jobe, 2003; Sapon-Shevin, 1999; Schniedewind & Davidson, 1998; Zittleman & Sadker, 2003).

Foster Acceptance of Religious Diversity

Although many educators are worried about violating the Establishment Clause of the Constitution related to the separation of church and state, or offending students and their families, fostering religious diversity can help your students understand and respect each other (Eckman, 2001). Therefore, it is important for educators to be aware of the legal mandates and legislative policies regarding religious diversity and activity in schools, and to implement consistent policies and practices (Haynes, Chaltain, Ferguson, Hudson, & Thomas, 2003). For an update on legal issues related to religion in public schools and other topics discussed in this chapter, go to the Legal Update module in chapter 5 of the Companion Website.

Teaching about religion is an important aspect of fostering religious diversity (Eckman, 2001). In doing this, educators need to teach respect for *all* religions and religious figures by presenting them in a factual, respectful, neutral, and balanced manner and establishing a context that does not endorse, promote, distort, or denigrate any religion (Haynes & Thomas, 2001). You also need to be aware of the impact of these activities on your students, and be sensitive to and prepared to address the misinterpretations, disagreements, and discomfort that might occur.

Resource

Stanford and Siders (2001) and McGoogan (2002) offer guidelines and resources for using electronic pen pals, and using videoconferencing to promote international face-to-face interactions, respectively.

Set Your Sites

For more information on helping students develop a global perspective, go to the Web Links module in Chapter 5 of the Companion Website.

Set Your Sites

For more information on promoting gender equity, go to the Web Links module in Chapter 5 of the Companion Website.

IDEAS FOR IMPLEMENTATION

Promoting Gender Equity

After taking a workshop on gender bias in the classroom, Ms. Stillwell tried to assess its extent in her classroom. She observed that her students appeared to segregate themselves during recess and lunch. Boys sat and played with boys, and girls sat and played with girls. She also noted that she and her students frequently used male-based metaphors such as telling the class that "you guys can tackle that problem."

Ms. Stillwell decided to change her behavior and the behavior of her students. She used self-recording to keep track of her interactions with her male and female students. She also introduced several vignettes showing positive and negative interactions in schools between male and female students. Students acted out these vignettes and then discussed them in small mixed-sex groups. Each group then shared its reactions to the vignettes with the class. Ms. Stillwell continued to observe her own and her students' behaviors and noticed many improvements that made her feel better. However, she knew that she needed to continue to confront this issue and other issues in her classroom.

Here are some other strategies you can use to create an inclusive classroom that promotes gender equity:

- Help students recognize when they are responding in a sexist manner, and teach them how to challenge sex-role stereotyping in school and society.
- Model a commitment to gender equity by challenging students' stereotypical behavior and by using language that includes both genders.

- Teach students how their attitudes and behavior relating to sex roles are affected by television, movies, music, books, advertisements, and the behavior of others.
- Avoid grouping students on the basis of gender, such as by forming separate lines, teams, seating arrangements, and academic learning groups and by comparing students by gender.
- Assign students of both sexes to class and school jobs on a rotating basis.
- Establish a classroom and school environment that encourages female and male students to play and work together. For example, decorate the classroom with pictures of males and females performing a variety of activities and use cooperative learning.
- Use nonsexist teaching materials that challenge stereotypical roles and, when possible, modify sexist teaching materials.
- Provide all students access to same-sex mentors.
- Encourage male and female students to participate in a variety of physical education and extracurricular activities.

Note: Jobe (2003); Sapon-Shevin (1999); Schniedewind and Davidson (1998); Zittleman and Sadker (2003).

One of the best ways to teach about religious diversity is through the curriculum (Nord & Haynes, 1998). While many state standards include instruction about religion as part of the social studies curriculum, literature, and fine arts (Douglass, 2002), the study of various religions can be incorporated into other subject areas as well. For instance, science, physical education, health, and home economics teachers can teach about the different religious dietary regulations. In math classes, teachers can teach about the geometrical designs of the various houses of worship such as the Islamic mosque, Jewish synagogue, and Christian church. In geography and cultural studies, teachers can teach students about how religious beliefs are manifested in everyday life of people around the world.

Acknowledging religious holidays can provide schools with an effective opportunity to teach about religious diversity. However, since schools cannot celebrate holidays as religious events or take actions to encourage or discourage observance by students, educators need to address religious holidays carefully. Therefore, when making the decision to celebrate religious holidays and display religious or seasonal symbols, educators should make sure that they are used for a variety of religious groups, are employed as teaching aids and for academic purposes, and are temporary in nature (McDowell, 2002).

 Resource

Myers and Myers (2002), Dever, Whitaker and Byrnes (2001), and Bisson (1997) offer lists of literature that can be used to foster knowledge about religious diversity, and strategies for celebrating religious holidays.

In celebrating religious holidays, you need to identify the academic and social goals and roles of holidays in the educational program, determine which holidays will be celebrated, and plan how they will be celebrated (Bisson, 1997). You need to acknowledge religious holidays in a balanced and inclusive manner so that they reflect the traditions of students' families, and introduce students to traditions of others. Holidays should be celebrated in culturally relevant, nonstereotypical, respectful, and factual ways so that none of the students' religious backgrounds are excluded, trivialized, or portrayed as exotic (Myers & Myers, 2002). Therefore, it is important to research and solicit information from families and community-based religious leaders to understand the authentic and different ways that families celebrate holidays (Bisson, 1997). As part of these celebrations, you can include lessons that address the origin and religious and social meaning of various religious holidays, and avoid role-plays and other activities that may be viewed as stereotyping a group or violating or trivializing the sacred nature of rituals. The celebration of holidays should include plans for students whose families do not want them to participate in these activities (Bisson, 1997).

One inclusive way to celebrate holidays is to organize them across a range of religions and around common themes. For instance, you can use the theme of light to teach students about different religious holidays that are related to light such as Hanukkah (Jewish), Christmas (Christian), and Diwali (Hindu) (Dever, Whitaker & Byrnes, 2001). Other possible common themes for holiday celebrations could include the life cycle, liberation, cooperation, fasting, seasons, harvests, and planting. You also can use themes to refer to holidays and schoolwide activities in an inclusive manner. For example, rather than referring to events or activities by linking them to a specific holiday (e.g., Christmas break, cards, music, parties), you can refer to them by using themes (e.g., winter/holiday break, cards, music, parties) (Bisson, 1997).

You also need to be aware and respectful of aspects of your students' religions that may affect their school performance and require you to make accommodations (McDowell, 2002). These aspects include medical and dietary restrictions, clothing, rituals and observances, and absences during holidays. For example, during some holidays, students from some religious backgrounds may be required to fast or pray during school hours or miss school for extended periods of time. Similarly, some students may not be able to participate in certain school activities because of their religious beliefs.

Resource

Douglass (2002) and Haynes and Thomas (2001) offer guidelines and resources for fostering religious diversity and McDowell (2002) provides information about aspects of various religions that may require school-related accommodations.

Set Your Sites

For more information on fostering religious diversity, go to the Web Links module in Chapter 5 of the Companion Website.

Teach About Family Differences

In light of the different kinds of families that students live in, accepting cultural diversity also can include teaching about family differences (Sapon-Shevin, 1999). By teaching about family differences, you can acknowledge the different family arrangements of your students. You also can use the stories of students' families as the basis for interdisciplinary lessons (Nieto, 2000). Since students have a variety of family arrangements, it is important to be careful when assigning projects (e.g., family trees) or holding events (e.g., mother–daughter activities) that relate to or assume that students live in traditional nuclear families; instead, frame these assignments in a more inclusive manner. Other suggestions and resources for teaching about family differences were presented in chapter 3.

Teach About Homelessness, the Migrant Lifestyle, and AIDS

Homeless and migrant students and students with HIV/AIDS may be targets of ridicule by peers. To counteract this problem, you can teach about these students. This should be done carefully to avoid stigmatizing these students.

The homeless and migrant lifestyles can be presented by guest speakers and through multimedia materials and books. For example, Carger (2002), Shafer, (2001), Johanneson (1999), and Whittaker, Salend, and Gutierrez (1997) offer suggestions and resources for integrating into the curriculum reading and writing activities that reflect the experiences of migrant students and their families. Included is an annotated bibliography of monolingual and bilingual children's literature about the migrant experience. These resources and activities can be used to sensitize *all students* to the unique experiences of migrant students, as well as the importance of migrant workers to society. Photographs and videocassettes depicting the migrant lifestyle or homelessness can give students direct, real-life experiences with issues related to these individuals.

Students often learn about conditions such as AIDS through television and other media. As a result, they often have misconceptions about AIDS and are afraid to be in classrooms with students who have AIDS. Several culturally appropriate instructional strategies can be used to overcome these negative attitudes and misconceptions (Johnson, Johnson, & Jefferson-Aker, 2001). A trained professional or an individual with AIDS can be invited to speak about the social and medical aspects of the disease (Blanchett, 2000). Many curriculum materials and resources for teachers are available (Prater & Sileo, 2001). In using these materials, educators need to be sure that they present current and accurate information. Educators also need to make sure that use of the materials is consistent with school district policy.

Resources

Prater and Sileo (2001) and Bryde (1998) have compiled lists of resources and juvenile literature for educating students about HIV/AIDS.

Teach About Stereotyping

Many students gain negative perceptions of others through stereotypes. It is important to help students understand and challenge the process of stereotyping, in addition to learning about a group's experiences and history (Yeh & Drost, 2002). You can counter the harmful effects of stereotyping by doing the following:

- Invite individuals who challenge stereotypes to speak to the class.
- Have students read books and view videos that challenge stereotypes and address discrimination.
- Display pictures and materials that challenge stereotypes.
- Discuss and critique how language, books, television shows, commercials, cartoons, jokes, toys, and common everyday items (such as lunch boxes) create and foster stereotypes.
- Compare items, images, and words and expressions that portray various groups.
- List and discuss stereotypes that students have about others, as well as the stereotypes that others have about them (Derman-Sparks & Phillips, 1997; Yeh & Drost, 2002).

Reflective

Think about a situation in which you were stereotyped. What factors contributed to that stereotype? How did it make you feel? How did it affect the outcome of the situation? Think about a situation in which you stereotyped someone. What factors contributed to that stereotype? How did it make you feel? What would you do differently?

Teach About Discrimination

Issues of cultural diversity are related to issues of power in schools and society. Therefore, it is important to teach your students to recognize and confront discrimination and its harmful effects. Case studies and short stories on various cultures and instances of discrimination can be used to stimulate group discussions that introduce students to a variety of perspectives, experiences, and ideas. The purpose of such discussions is to help them reach conclusions, as well as question and affirm their own viewpoints. You can facilitate the discussion of these issues by engaging in the following:

- Respond to all questions and comments respectfully and seriously.
- Ask students, when necessary, to clarify comments and questions.

- Address students' questions and comments and confront their misrepresentations honestly using age-appropriate language and examples.
- Seek additional information for questions you cannot answer, or to correct inaccurate responses, or incomplete answers.
- Be aware of students' emotional responses (Anti-Defamation League, 2000).

Resource

Banks (2003) and Tiedt and Tiedt (2002) offer resources and activities for teaching students about discrimination.

Students can learn about these issues by experiencing them. For example, you can group students according to some arbitrary trait (e.g., hair color, eye color, type of clothing) and then treat the groups in different ways in terms of rules, assignments, compliments, grading procedures, privileges, homework, and class jobs. You can also show students what it means to be discriminated against by assigning several groups the same task while varying the resources each group is given to complete the task, so that the different performance of the groups is related to resources rather than ability. After these activities, you and your students can discuss their reactions and the effects of discrimination. You also can discuss with them how they treat others and would like to be treated by others.

Teach Others to Respond to Stereotyping and Discrimination

Once students learn about the negative effects of prejudice, they can be taught how to respond to stereotyping and discrimination. Learning how to respond appropriately is especially important for students who are the targets of stereotyping and discrimination. In doing this, it is important for you to help your students learn to differentiate legitimate dislikes (e.g., disliking foods) from discrimination and stereotyping (e.g., disliking individuals with differences) (Shapiro, 1999).

Resource

Aronson (1997) provides resources for teaching your students about individual differences in body size and type.

You can establish an inclusive classroom environment by modeling acceptance of all students and by establishing the rule that gender, race, ethnicity, language skills, ability, religion, physical appearance, sexual orientation, or socioeconomic status is not a reason for excluding or teasing someone. If someone breaks the rule, you should act immediately to support the student who has been discriminated against and to help the student describe his or her reaction to the student(s) who engaged in the exclusionary behavior. It is also important to help the excluding student(s) understand the harmful effects of prejudice (Derman-Sparks & Phillips, 1997). Books and films depicting individuals and communities confronting prejudice also can be used to help students learn how to take positive actions to challenge acts of intolerance. For example, Scholastic (2002) has developed the *Hip Kid Hop* series, which uses books and read-along CDs with hip-hop music and rhymes to teach students how to confront and resolve bigoted attitudes.

Role-playing and group discussions also can help students learn how to respond to discrimination and stereotyping (Shapiro, 1999). For example, you can present a bias-related incident and ask students to role-play their responses. Afterward, the students can discuss their experiences and reactions.

You can also form a media watch to teach your students how to act and unite to challenge discrimination and stereotyping (Shapiro, 1999). *All members* of your class can be asked to identify and share examples of bias and unbiased presentations in the media. Students can then work to take actions that:

- acknowledge constructive and complex presentations of individual differences.
- counter negative, inaccurate, and stereotypical portrayals of persons with individual differences and related issues, and the use of incorrect terminology.

- call for more presentations addressing persons with individual differences and related issues.

Sometimes students express a desire to change their physical appearance or identity. When this happens, tell students immediately that they are fine; assure them that others like them the way they are; explain to them that others who do not like them that way are wrong; point out that there are many people who have the same traits; and confront others who made negative statements that triggered the students' reactions (Derman-Sparks, 1989).

Address Insensitive and Intolerant Acts

Just as with any learning experience, students will come to school with gaps and inaccuracies in their knowledge of individual differences. As a result, sometimes students will, intentionally or unintentionally, engage in insensitive and intolerant acts toward others. Responses to such acts will vary depending on the school's policies; the nature of the act and its time and place; and the history, age, and intent of the individuals involved (Goldstein, 2001). For example, if the intent of the act was not to hurt others, you might want to deal with students privately or present the situation confidentially at a class meeting to discuss ways to avoid similar insensitive acts. You also can use class meetings and peer mediation to address and discuss misunderstandings and answer students' questions.

However, you also are likely to encounter students being intentionally intolerant of others. When this occurs, you can act promptly and decisively to help students learn that discriminatory and hurtful behaviors are unacceptable (Garbarino & deLara, 2003; Sapon-Shevin, 2003). Prompt, consistent, and firm responses to all acts of intolerance, harassment, and exclusion can minimize their negative effects and serve as a model for how students can react to them (Kinnell, 2003; Wessler, 2001). (We will discuss additional strategies for responding to bullying in chapter 7.) In addition to using the strategies presented in this chapter to establish a learning community that is respectful of all its members, you can respond decisively when intolerant behaviors occur in your school by:

- establishing and communicating policies and rules against all acts of intolerance and exclusion, and procedures for making complaints about their occurrence.
- identifying the act of intolerance and why it is unacceptable. (*You just insulted a religious group and our school. Why was it hurtful?*)
- making it clear to students that these behaviors will not be tolerated and making sure that all individuals in the area are aware of your comments and actions. (*That was a stereotype. What you did was wrong and hurtful. We respect everyone in this school, and comments like that are not welcome here.*)
- responding immediately to all incidents of intolerance by addressing impact on the community, providing direct consequences, and informing students that they must change their behavior in the future. (*This school is a community and we do not say hurtful things. We want everyone in school to feel welcome and safe. In the future, you need to think before you speak or act. What are you going to do to make sure it doesn't happen again?*)
- following up incidents by checking with the target of the intolerance. (*I'm sorry this happened to you and our school. It was wrong and unfair. You and everyone else in this school should feel welcome and safe. I will speak to the student(s) who said (did) this. If this happens again, please let me know and I will take additional action.*)
- reporting incidents to school administrators and other professionals and enlisting their support in addressing these issues (Froschl & Gropper, 1999; Wood, 2002).

Set Your Sites

For more information on establishing a media watch, go to the Web Links module in Chapter 5 of the Companion Website.

Resource

Wood (2002) offers guidelines and resources for establishing and implementing antiharassment policies.

Reflective

Think about how you would respond to your students teasing a male student who likes to sew.

Set Your Sites

For more information on teaching students diversity, fairness, equity, and tolerance, go to the Web Links module in Chapter 5 of the Companion Website.

How Can I Facilitate Friendships?

Friendships in and outside of school are important for everyone and are one of the desired benefits of inclusion programs for *all students* (Geishardt et al., 2002; Lee et al., 2003). In addition to promoting students' self-esteem, friendships also can foster students' learning, language development, and acceptance of individual differences (Buysse, Goldman, & Skinner, 2002). However, because some of your students may have few friends and limited peer support, you may need to use a variety of strategies to promote the development of friendships and peer support systems. When using these strategies, be careful that they don't inadvertently reinforce caregiving and "parenting" actions rather than reciprocal friendships. **To hear educators discussing the importance of friendships, go to Case 3: Assess Plan on the CD-ROM and click on the social setting video clip. How could the educators foster the student's friendship making skills?**

cd-rom

Teach About Friendships

Resource

Maroney (2003) and Staub (1998) offer strategies and resources for developing friendships in inclusive settings.

You can help promote friendships by integrating teaching about friendships into the curriculum (Maroney, 2003). This can include exploring the meaning and importance of friendship, the qualities of good friendship, and the problems that some students have in trying to make friends. Students can then explore their own friendships by developing a friendship chart that includes the names of several of their friends, the activities they do with their friends, the qualities they like in their friends, and how they met each friend; writing a friendship poem; or creating a wall with each block indicating a barrier to friendships (Froschl & Gropper, 1999).

Mutual friendships in and outside of school are important for all students and are one of the benefits of inclusion. How would you describe your students' friendships?

USING TECHNOLOGY TO PROMOTE INCLUSION

Fostering Acceptance and Friendships

The Internet and technology are often used as tools for fostering instruction and independence. However, they also can be good resources for fostering acceptance and friendships. Via the Internet, you can provide students with opportunities to engage in online and technology-based disability awareness activities. For example, Pivik, McComas, Macfarlane, & Laflamme (2002) have developed Barriers—The Awareness Challenge (www.health. uottawa.ca/vrlab), an online experience that allows students to experience attitudinal and physical barriers, out-of-reach objects, and inappropriate comments from others as they use a virtual wheelchair to go through a virtual school. The American Foundation for the Blind has created Braille Bug (www.afb.org/braillebug), a website that offers a variety of online activities to teach sighted students about Braille. Your students also can learn some key words in sign language by visiting websites such as www.americansignlanguage.com and www.library. thinkquest.org/10202 (Williams & Finnegan, 2003).

Here are some other ways you can use technology to teach students about individual differences, and promote interactions and friendships among students.

- Have your students learn about a variety of disabilities by visiting such online disability awareness sites as CeDIR's Disability Awareness site for youth (www.iidc.indiana.edu/cedir/kidsweb), Bandaids and Blackboards (www.irsc.org:8080/irsc/irscmain.nsf/outweb?readform&site=http://funrsc. fairfield.edu/~jfleitas/contents.html), and Special Needs ~ Special Kids (members.tripod.com/ ~imaware)
- Have your students perform online simulations by visiting the following websites: Misunderstood Minds (www.pbs.org/wgbh/misunderstoodminds/ attention.html), Pediatric Neurology.Com (pediatricneurology.com/adhd2.htm), Tourette Syndrome Plus (www.tourettesyndrome.net), National Coalition of Auditory Processing Disorders (www.ncapd.org), and Mrs. Karen Lake's Home Page (www.nacs.k12.in.us/staff/lake/lake.html).
- Obtain curriculum guides and learning materials related to individual differences and friendships online. For example, *Special Olympics Get Into It* (www.specialolympics.org/getintoit) is a series of free curriculum materials that you can obtain online with

lessons designed to help preschool, elementary, and secondary students learn about developmental disabilities and understand and accept individual differences. Information about additional disability awareness resources for use with your students is available via the websites of the National Information Center for Children and Youth with Disabilities (www.nichcy.org), the Disability Resources website (www.disabilityresources.com/DIS-AWARE), and All Kids Can (www.allkidscan.org).

- Teach students about individual differences related to disability via use of the Disability Awareness game (www.parentsinc.org/game.html), which can be played on a screen or LCD projector.
- Use e-mail, videoconferencing, and other online technologies to provide students with ongoing opportunities to communicate and work on projects with others throughout the world (McGoogan, 2002; Stanford & Siders, 2001). Sites such as E-pals (www.epals.com) and KIDLINK (www.Kidlink.org) can assist you in setting up cross-cultural, online interactions and E-buddies (www.ebuddies.org) can facilitate e-mail communications between individuals with and without developmental disabilities. The Global SchoolNet Foundation (www.gsn.org), the International Education Resource Network (www.iearn.org), and the Rome's Global Junior Challenge (www.gjc.it) can provide your students with opportunities to work with their international peers on collaborative projects in all content areas.
- Use software programs that teach about individual differences and friendships. For example, Hodgin, Levin and Matthews (1996) have developed a CD-ROM for teaching students about gender equity and Tom Snyder Productions has developed a series of computer simulation programs about making friends (www.teachtsp.com).
- Use collaborative, technology-based academic and social activities (Hobbs, Bruch, Sanko, & Astolfi, 2001; Male, 2003). For example, students can work in groups to use computers to produce newsletters, fliers, invitations, banners, and illustrations for the classroom. Students also can

(continued)

work in cooperative learning groups to use the Internet to gather information about acts of tolerance or intolerance and then create a web page to disseminate their findings to others.

- Have students work together on a WebQuest, an inquiry-oriented, cooperatively structured group activity in which some or all of the information that students use comes from resources on the Internet or videoconferencing (March, 2004). (We will learn more about WebQuests in chapter 8.) For example, you can have students work in collaborative groups to complete WebQuests that ask them to use teacher-approved websites to gather and present information on various religions, disabilities, or cultural groups. Each group can study a different religion/disability/culture and each group's project can be used to explore the similarities and differences among the various religions/disabilities/cultures studied.

- Use videos, films, and DVDs related to individual differences and friendships. For example, *KidAbility* and *A VideoGuide to (Dis)Ability Awareness* (www.pdassoc.com) are disability awareness videos that can be used to introduce your students to the lifestyles of individuals with various disability conditions and assistance technology. *What Do You Do When You See a Blind Person?* (www.afb.org) and *The Ten Commandments of Communicating with People with Disabilities* (www.pdassoc.com) provide visual models that can teach your students how to communicate with individuals with disabilities. You can obtain information about films about individuals with disabilities by visiting the website Films Involving Disabilities (www.disabilityfilms.co.uk).

- Provide students with access to adapted play materials such as toys with velcro, magnets, handles or switches, and aids to operate electronic devices.

Offer Social Skills Instruction

Teaching about friendships also should include teaching social skills, the cognitive, verbal, and nonverbal skills that guide interactions with others (Church, Gottschalk, & Leddy, 2003; Schoen & Bullard, 2002). *All students* can learn how to initiate, respond to, and maintain positive, equal-status social interactions with their peers, and also how to show empathy, and deal with frustration, conflict, rejection, and refusal (Morris, 2002; Pavri, 2001). For example, you can model and have students role-play responses to various friendship-making situations.

You can also use learning strategies and social skills curricula that teach students friendship skills such as sharing and turn-taking, listening and talking to friends, and complimenting, encouraging, respecting, and helping others (Bock, 2003; Kamps et al., 2002). Bock (2003) developed SODA, a learning strategy that guides social interactions by prompting students to:

> **S**top: Determine the room arrangement, activity, schedule, or routine and where to observe.
> **O**bserve: Note what people are doing and saying as well as how long they speak and what they do after interacting.
> **D**eliberate: Think about what to do and say and how long others would like to interact.
> **A**ct: Approach others, greet them with "Hello," and "How are you?", listen to others and ask appropriate questions, and look for cues related to whether to continue or end the interaction.

Resource

Church, Gottschalk, and Leddy (2003) and Morris (2002) offer strategies for enhancing the social and friendship skills of students, and Kuoch and Mirenda (2003) offer guidelines for using social stories to teach friendship and social skills.

Students also can be asked to reflect on their social skills by responding to the following: (a) What did you do to get along with others? (b) How well did it work? (c) How do you think the others felt about what you did? and (d) What did you learn from this experience? (Church, Gottschalk, & Leddy, 2003). More information on teaching social skills is presented in chapters 6 and 7.

IDEAS FOR IMPLEMENTATION

Facilitating Friendship Skills

Ms. Rollings and Ms. Kieck noticed that their students were having many disagreements. These disagreements frequently escalated, causing one of the teachers to intervene. Frustrated by their students' inability to work through these situations, they decided to implement a series of activities to help their students learn how to compromise. They began by having their students observe them as they role-played a situation of two people disagreeing about where to go to dinner, and then compromising on their choice of a restaurant. Following the role-play, the teachers asked:

- What did we do?
- What steps did we follow?
- What was the purpose of compromising?
- Were we satisfied with our compromise?

As the class responded to these questions, the teachers discussed how they compromised, highlighted the steps they followed to achieve their compromise, and discussed why they were satisfied with their compromise.

Next, the teachers told the class, "We demonstrated how to compromise, and now you are going to work in pairs to learn how to compromise when you have a disagreement." They reviewed the steps the students needed to perform to arrive at their compromises, and the guidelines they should follow to achieve a compromise that both parties felt good about. The teachers then gave each pair a situation that had resulted in a disagreement in their class and required a compromise. They also gave each pair a sheet that asked them to list their disagreement and possible choices as well as their compromise, how they reached it, and their level of satisfaction with it. When the students finished, the teachers asked the pairs to share their situations and explain their compromises. At the end of the activity, the teachers reminded the students to use the skills they had learned to compromise with their classmates when they had a disagreement. Later that day, the teachers were pleased when two students negotiated a compromise to a disagreement that occurred in the hallway.

Here are some other strategies you can use to create a school environment that facilitates friendships:

- Model appropriate ways of interacting with others.
- Discuss how it is important to treat everyone in a respectful way and what that means.
- Provide students with opportunities to interact in a variety of settings.
- Offer students insights about friendships by talking about the importance of your friendships and the things you like to do with friends.
- Structure activities so that students work and socialize in groups or pairs.
- Highlight the strengths, interests, and hobbies of *all your students*.
- Share information about after-school and community-based activities and encourage *all your students* to participate in them.
- Help students and other adults understand the differences between supporting others and helping them too much.

Note: Staub (1998); Turnbull, Pereira, and Blue-Banning (2000).

Foster Communication Among Students

Since students' sensory, speech, and cognitive abilities can affect their social interactions, you also may need to teach your students how to interact and communicate with classmates with disabilities (Lee et al., 2003; Staub, 1998). You can help students understand the communication needs of others by teaching and modeling appropriate terminology and ways of interacting with others. For example, you can teach them not to use such terms as *cripple, invalid, victim of, confined to a wheelchair, normal,* or *able-bodied,* as these terms are associated with sympathy and suffering or being or having bodies that are abnormal. Guidelines for communicating with individuals with disabilities that can be shared with your students are presented in Figure 5.8.

Alternative communication systems that students with disabilities use, such as Braille and sign language, can be introduced in a variety of ways that also promote academic skills.

Guidelines for communication with individuals with disabilities

FIGURE 5.8

Communicating with Individuals with Disabilities

☐ View the individual as a person, not as a disability.

☐ Refrain from "talking down" or speaking in a condescending way.

☐ Be yourself, relax, be considerate, and treat the individual with respect.

☐ Talk using language and about topics that are age appropriate.

☐ Don't apologize for using common expressions that may relate to the individual's disability such as "I've got to run" or "Have you seen Mary?"

☐ Greet the individual as you would others. If the individual cannot shake your hand, he or she will make you aware of that.

☐ Understand that the environment can affect communication. An overly noisy or dark room can make communication difficult for individuals with speech and sensory disabilities.

☐ Don't assume that the individual needs your assistance; ask.

Communicating with Individuals Who Use Wheelchairs

☐ Respect the individual's space by refraining from hanging on the wheelchair.

☐ Sit or kneel at the individual's eye level when the conversation is going to continue for a long period of time.

☐ Don't assume that the individual wants you to push the wheelchair.

Communicating with Individuals with Speech/Language Difficulties

☐ Focus your attention on the individual.

☐ Avoid correcting or speaking for the individual.

☐ Be encouraging and patient.

☐ Seek clarification when you don't understand by repeating what you did understand.

Communicating with Individuals with Visual Disabilities

☐ Introduce and identify yourself and any companions when encountering the individual.

☐ Speak directly to the individual in a normal voice.

☐ Direct communications to the individual by using the individual's name.

☐ Provide an explanation of visual events, cues, or body language, when they are important aspects of the conversation or interaction.

☐ Remember that a guide dog is responsible for the individual's safety and should not be distracted. Therefore, walk on the opposite side of the dog, and ask for permission before interacting with the dog.

☐ Tell the individual when you are leaving or ending the conversation.

Communicating with Individuals with Hearing Disabilities

☐ Make sure that you have the individual's attention before speaking.

☐ Speak clearly and in short sentences.

☐ Avoid raising your voice or exaggerating your mouth movements.

☐ Use appropriate facial expressions, physical gestures, and body movements.

☐ Refrain from repeating yourself. If the individual doesn't understand, rephrase your message, use synonyms to convey it, or write it out.

☐ Talk directly to the individual even if the individual uses an interpreter.

☐ Remember that it is harder to understand when walking and talking at the same time.

Note: Access Resources (n.d.); Mid-Hudson Library System (1990); Shapiro (1999).

You can teach students the manual alphabet and then have them practice their spelling by spelling the words manually. Similarly, rather than writing the numbers for a math problem on the chalkboard, you can present them using numerical hand signs. Basic signs can be introduced to students and used for assignments. Students who have learned Braille can be asked to read and write in Braille.

Interactions between students also can be fostered by teaching them to use a communication book (Hughes et al., 2000). Communication books contain pictorial representations of socially and culturally appropriate topics that serve to initiate interactions between students. Students need to be taught to use the communication book so that they can use it to initiate, engage in, respond to, and maintain interactions.

Use Circles of Friends

You also can use circles of friends to help *all your students* understand support systems and friendships and expand their social networks (Frederickson & Turner, 2003; Turnbull, Pereria, & Blue-Banning, 2000). To do this, give students a sheet with four concentric circles, each larger and farther away from the center of the sheet, which contains a drawing of a stick figure representing a student. First, ask students to fill in the first circle (the one closest to the stick figure) by listing the people whom they love and who are closest to them. The second circle contains a list of the people they like, such as their best friends. The third circle contains a list of groups that they like and do things with, like members of their teams or community organizations. Finally, the fourth circle contains a list of individuals who are paid to be part of their lives, such as a doctor or teacher. Students' circles are then shared with their peers, and the meaning and importance of friendships are discussed, including strategies for helping students make friends and expand their circle of friends.

Resource

Frederickson and Turner (2003) offer guidelines for implementing and evaluating circles of friends.

Reflective

Make a circle of friends for yourself. How have your friends and support group assisted you during stressful times?

You may need to address several potential concerns associated with using circles of friends (Frederickson & Turner, 2003). These issues include the perception that the targeted student is in need of help, the participation of classmates who are not part of the circle, and the importance of teaching social skills. You can address these issues by using this technique with *all your students,* and ensuring that *all your students* are included in the process and that they develop the social skills they need to support friendships with others and expand their own social networks.

Create a Friendly Classroom Environment

You also can support the development of friendships by creating a friendly classroom environment that promotes social interactions among students (Pavri, 2001). To do this, you can use friendship activities including books, cooperative academic and nonacademic games, and learning centers to establish an environment that supports friendships. For example, your students can play *In My Shoes: Friendmaking,* a game that focuses on the importance of friends and how to establish friendships (Shapiro, 1999). Have students do art activities such as creating friendship murals, bulletin boards, posters, and books with illustrations, and teach them songs with the theme of friendship. An environment that supports friendships also can be created by providing your students with access to culturally diverse, age-appropriate materials, toys, and games that they like to use with others.

Set Your Sites

For more information on toys and play-related interactions for students with disabilities, go to the Web links section in chapter 5 of the Companion Website.

Set Your Sites

For more information on multicultural games, toys, dolls, and other materials, go to the Web links section in chapter 5 of the Companion Website.

You also can create a friendly school environment by using cooperative grouping so that students work and play together in groups (Calloway, 1999). For example, you can teach students simple, noncompetitive, and enjoyable games that don't require a lot of skill or language abilities. When using these games, consider how they can be adapted by modifying the rules, using assistive devices, and employing personal assistance strategies such as playing as a team. Specific guidelines for using cooperative learning groups are presented in chapter 9.

A friendly and caring classroom environment can be fostered by activities that promote a sense of community and class cohesiveness (Obenchain & Abernathy, 2003;

Resource

Obenchain and Abernathy (2003) offer a variety of community-building strategies and activities.

Set Your Sites

For more information on promoting caring and trusting learning environments, go to the Web links section in chapter 5 of the Companion Website.

Schaps, 2003). Such community building group activities promote friendships and acceptance by creating a class identity that recognizes the similarities among students and the unique contributions of each class member. For example, students can create a class book, mural, newsletter, or tree that includes and recognizes the work and participation of everyone in the class. Throughout the school year, students can use many different getting-acquainted activities such as playing name-recognition games, developing a class directory, and interviewing each other. Schaps (2003), Sapon-Shevin (1999), Schniedewind and Davidson (1998), Jones and Jones (2001), Chuoke and Eyman (1997), and Canfield and Wells (1976) outlined activities and games that teachers can use to introduce new students to the group and promote class cohesiveness, giving all students a common experience on which to build future interactions and friendships (see Figure 5.9). Group cohesiveness and trust also can be established by using adventure-based experiential learning activities that foster the teamwork, social, and conflict-resolution skills (Forgan & Jones, 2002).

Use Peer-Based Strategies

Increasing the social and academic interactions between your students also can foster friendships and acceptance (Fuchs, Fuchs, Mathes, & Martinez, 2002; Pavri & Monda-Amaya, 2001). Academic interactions can be promoted through use of peer-mediated instruction and cooperative learning groups, which allow *all students* to learn together. (We will learn more about these strategies in chapter 9.) Socially, you can offer *all students* numerous opportunities to interact, including playing cooperative games, and provide them with the skills they need to initiate and maintain social and academic relationships. **To view an example of students working collaboratively, go to Case 4: Support Participation on the CD-ROM and click on the peer supports video clip. How does working collaboratively support student learning, acceptance of individual differences and friendships?**

cd - rom

FIGURE 5.9

Activities to promote a sense of class cohesiveness

Create a class history or class photo album that is updated periodically and includes a summary of the year's activities, as well as work produced by and information about each student.

Create special class days, such as T-Shirt Day, when all students wear their favorite T-shirts.

Create a class web page.

Publish a class newspaper/newsletter, to which each student contributes a piece or drawing during the school year.

Have students work in groups to complete a "Classmates Scavenger Hunt" by giving each group a list of feelings (e.g., "A classmate who makes others feel good"), interests (e.g., "A classmate who likes to draw"), and skills (e.g., "A classmate who is good at math") that is completed by placing the names of classmates who have those feelings, interests, or skills on a poster.

Make a class mural and have each student complete part of it.

Construct a class tree. Each branch of the tree can contain a picture of a student or a work produced by that student.

Compile a *Who's Who* book of the class, with each student having a page devoted to his or her interests, achievements, and so on.

Have a "class applause" in which the whole class acknowledges the accomplishments of classmates.

Peer Support Committees and Class Meetings

Peer support committees and class meetings can be used to address classroom social interaction problems, promote friendships and community, and ensure that *all students* are valued members of the class (Carpenter, Bloom, & Boat, 1999; Simone, 2001). The peer support committee identifies problems that students or the class as a whole are experiencing and creates strategies to address them, such as establishing buddy systems, peer helpers, and study partners. The committee also brainstorms strategies for promoting friendships in the classroom and involving students in all academic and social aspects of the school, including extracurricular activities. Typically, membership on the committee is rotated so that each member of the class has an opportunity to serve.

Some teachers also have a positive-comment box in the classroom. Class members who see another student performing a kind act that supports others record the action on a slip of paper that is placed in the comment box. At the end of the day, positive actions are shared with the class.

Peer Buddy and Partner Systems

Friendships also can be promoted through the use of peer buddy or partner systems (Kamps et al., 2002). Because peer buddy systems during noninstructional activities lead to more high quality interactions between dyads of students with and without disabilities (Hughes et al., 2002), you can try to structure classroom activities so that students have numerous opportunities to interact with their peer partners in social settings. Peers, particularly those who are valued and respected, also can interact by introducing their classmates to various academic and social features of the school, and classroom routines (Copeland et al., 2002). For example, peer buddies can help students learn the school's locker system, and encourage classmates to attend extracurricular activities. Three to five students also can be paired to be buddy groups to facilitate interactions during lunch or recess or to work on community-based projects (Hughes et al., 2001; Kamps et al., 2002). You can support the success of these peer-based systems by meeting periodically with peer partners to examine their success in supporting each other, offering education about individual differences, and rotating partners.

Resource

Copeland et al. (2002) and Hughes et al. (1999) provide guidelines for creating a high school peer buddy system.

Set Your Sites

For more information on cooperative games, go to the Web links section of chapter 5 of the Companion Website.

Encourage Participation in Extracurricular and Community-Based Activities

Many friendships begin outside of the classroom and school, so students should be encouraged to meet and make new friends through extracurricular and community-based activities (Agran, Alper, & Wehmeyer, 2002). Because these activities provide opportunities to share mutually enjoyable activities, similarities among students are highlighted. You can work with other professionals, family members, students, and community groups to offer and adapt after-school activities that allow various groups of students to participate and interact socially. More information on involving students in these activities is presented in chapter 6.

Involve Family Members

Family members can work with you to support budding friendships, develop friendship goals and plans, and problem-solve ways to facilitate friendships (Favazza et al., 2000; Geishardt et al., 2002). Family members can create opportunities for interactions outside of school (e.g., encourage their children to invite friends home or to attend a community event with the family), get to know other families with children, encourage and assist their children and others in attending extracurricular activities (e.g., learn about after-school and community activities and provide transportation), and volunteer to lead or attend these activities. They also can make their home a safe, accessible, and enjoyable place for children to gather, and supervise peer interactions when appropriate and necessary. To help family members do these things, you can offer them information and resources, and can suggest games and activities that promote friendships among children.

Summary

This chapter offered many strategies for teaching students to accept individual differences and develop friendships. As you review the chapter, consider the following questions and remember the following points.

How Do Attitudes Toward Individual Differences Develop?

CEC 1, 2, 5, 9, PRAXIS 3, INTASC 9

Many students have misconceptions about and stereotypical views of individual differences. Also, several factors appear to interact to influence attitudes toward individual differences, including cultural background, gender, age, socioeconomic status, child-rearing practices, and exposure to the media, literature, and visual images and representations in society.

How Can I Assess Attitudes Toward Individual Differences?

CEC 2, 3, 5, 8, 9, PRAXIS 3, INTASC 2, 5, 8, 9

You can assess attitudes toward individual differences by using attitude-change assessment instruments, knowledge of individual differences probes, observations, sociograms, and student drawings.

How Can I Teach Acceptance of Individual Differences Related to Disability?

CEC 2, 3, 5, 9, PRAXIS 3, INTASC 2, 3, 5, 9, 10

You can teach students about individual differences by reflecting on and modeling desired attitudes, language, and behaviors, addressing concerns about fairness, and using simulations. You can also have your students study about disabilities and the lives of successful individuals with disabilities; invite guest speakers; and use films, videos, literature, and curriculum guides and teaching materials about disabilities. Other methods include teaching about assistive devices, and using collaborative problem solving.

How Can I Teach Acceptance of Individual Differences Related to Culture, Language, Gender, Religion, and Socioeconomic Status?

CEC 1, 2, 3, 5, 6, 7, 9, PRAXIS 3, INTASC 2, 3, 5, 6, 9, 10

You can reflect on your knowledge, experiences, and beliefs related to diversity, and integrate into your curriculum and classroom learning activities and materials that promote acceptance of cultural, linguistic, and religious diversity and gender equity. These activities and materials can also be used to teach students about global perspectives, family differences, homelessness, the migrant lifestyle, AIDS, stereotyping, and discrimination, and help you and your students respond to acts of insensitivity and intolerance.

How Can I Facilitate Friendships?

CEC 2, 3, 5, 9, PRAXIS 3, INTASC 2, 3, 5, 9, 10

You can facilitate friendships among students by teaching about friendships, teaching social skills, using activities that develop social skills and encourage communication among students, using circles of friends, creating a friendly classroom environment, and using peer-based strategies. Other methods include encouraging students to participate in extracurricular and community-based activities, and involving families.

What Would You Do in Today's Diverse Classroom?

You are concerned about your students' social interaction patterns. You observe your students' interactions inside and outside the class and notice that they are:

★   telling anti-Semitic jokes.

★   using terms such as *Indian giver.*

★   mimicking a student's accent.

★   making fun of others because of their racial or ethnic identities.

★   segregating themselves by gender.

★   teasing others for being slow.

★   making fun of classmates because they wear old clothes.

1.   What are some of the factors that might cause your students to have difficulty accepting and interacting with one another?

2.   What are some other ways you could identify your students' attitudes toward each other?

3.   What are some strategies you could use to encourage your students to accept each other's individual differences, and develop friendships?

4.   How would you react if you observed these behaviors occurring in your school?

5.   What knowledge, skills, dispositions, resources, and support do you need to address situations like these?

   To answer these questions online and share your responses with others, go to the Reflection Module in chapter 5 of the Companion Website.

Chapter 6

Creating Successful Transitions to Inclusive Settings

Nick

Nick is about to be placed full-time in general education classes. Nick's special education teacher, Ms. Thomas, collaborates with Nick's new teachers to plan a program to help Nick make a successful transition. She shares information about Nick with them. They also discuss and compare the essential components that students need to succeed in their respective classrooms. Based on these similarities and differences, they identify skills and information that Nick will need to make a smooth adjustment to these classes.

Although Nick will not enter these classes for several weeks, the teachers agree that they should begin the transition program immediately. Ms. Thomas introduces Nick to the textbooks, note-taking, and assignments he will encounter in his new classes, and teaches him some learning strategies that can help him succeed with these materials and tasks. She also begins to give Nick homework assignments and tests that parallel those given by his new teachers.

Nick also visits his new classes, and Ms. Thomas videos several class sessions. She reviews these visits and videos with him to discuss classroom procedures and other critical elements of the classroom environment. In addition to introducing Nick to the routines and expectations of these classrooms, Ms. Thomas uses the video to encourage Nick to discuss any questions and concerns he has about the new settings.

Ms. Thomas also uses the video to teach Nick appropriate note-taking skills. At first, Nick and Ms. Thomas watch the video together while Ms. Thomas shows how to take notes. To make sure Nick understands the different note-taking techniques and when to apply them, Ms. Thomas stops the video and reviews with Nick why certain information is or is not recorded and why a specific format is used.

Upon entering his new classes, Nick's teachers meet with him to discuss his transition. They ask Nick to discuss how things are going for him and what they can do to assist him. They also share their feelings about Nick's progress and make suggestions that can help him. They agree that Ms. Thomas should work with Nick move on his note-taking and organizational skills.

What other factors should you consider when planning a transitional program to prepare students such as Nick for success in a general education classroom? What other transitions do students make? How can you help them make these transitions? After reading this chapter, you should have the knowledge, skills, and dispositions to answer these as well as the following questions:

★ **How can I help students make the transition to general education classrooms?**
★ **How can I help students from specialized schools and preschool programs make the transition to inclusive settings?**

★ **How can I help students from linguistically and culturally diverse backgrounds make the transition to inclusive settings?**

★ **How can I help students make the transition from school to adulthood?**

★ **How can I help students develop self-determination?**

Beginnings and transitions are difficult. Placement in inclusive settings involves many beginnings and transitions for students like Nick. Moving from one setting to another, students must learn to adjust to different curriculum demands, teaching styles, behavioral expectations, classroom designs, and student socialization patterns. Students moving from elementary to secondary settings, a special day school to an integrated program within the community's public school system, or leaving school to search for work or to enter a postsecondary program, will encounter new expectations, rules, extracurricular activities, and personnel.

It is essential to work collaboratively with other professionals, family members, and students to prepare students for the many transitions they face (Doyle, 2000). It is also crucial to teach students the skills that will help them succeed in inclusive settings (Monda-Amaya, Dieker, & Reed, 1998). This chapter offers a variety of strategies for helping students make the transition to inclusive settings. These strategies are appropriate for students with disabilities, but they also can be used to help *all students* function in inclusive settings and make transitions to new environments.

How Can I Help Students Make the Transition to General Education Classrooms?

Understand Students' Unique Abilities and Challenges

As Ms. Thomas did in the chapter-opening vignette, general education teachers can be given information about students before they are placed in inclusive settings (Doyle, 2000; Prater, 2003). This information can include the students' challenges and ability levels, as well as background information to help teachers develop a program that will help students make the transition to inclusive settings (Demchak & Greenfield, 2000; Lassman, Jolivette, & Wehby, 1999). Figure 6.1 presents questions that can guide the information-sharing process.

Additional information regarding students can supplement the information-sharing process. For students with sensory disabilities, their general education teachers can receive information on the nature of the sensory loss, as well as the amount of residual hearing or vision. For students with hearing impairments and significant cognitive disabilities, teachers also can be informed of the students' communication abilities, and the ways in which they communicate. For students who are learning English as a second language,

Resource

Demchak and Greenfield (2000) and Doyle (2000) provide guidelines for developing transition portfolios to help students make the transition to inclusive classrooms.

Sample information-sharing questions

FIGURE 6.1

What language(s) does the student speak? What language(s) does the family speak?

How does the student communicate?

What are the student's academic strengths? Academic challenges?

What instructional approaches, arrangements, and materials have been effective with the student? Which have not been effective?

What adaptive devices and technology does the student require?

What instructional and testing accommodations does the student require?

What type and amount of adult and peer support does the student need?

What factors and variables motivate the student?

What instructional activities are appropriate for use with the student?

What cultural factors should be considered in designing an educational program for the student? For involving the family in the educational program?

What social and behavioral skills does the student possess and need to develop?

What are the student's hobbies and interests?

Who are the student's friends?

In what school clubs or extracurricular activities does/could the student participate?

How does the student get along with her or his peers?

How does the student feel about her or his disability?

What school personnel and community agencies will be working with the student? What services will they provide?

To what extent will the student's family be involved in the planning process?

What communication system will be used to communicate between professionals? With family members?

What are the student's medical and medication needs?

Has the student been prepared to enter the inclusive setting?

What are the student's educational, social, cultural, linguistic, medical, and physical strengths and needs?

What classroom management strategies and classroom design adaptations have been successful?

What alternative assessment strategies, procedures, and test modifications have been used with the student?

What school-based supportive and community-based services have been used with the student? What are the outcomes of these services?

What cultural and linguistic factors have been considered in designing an educational program for the student? For involving the family in the educational program?

teachers should be apprised of their language abilities and the best approaches for helping them learn English. Finally, for students with special physical and health needs, teachers need information about health and medical issues and concerns, assistive devices, social skill development, and teaching and physical design accommodations (Wadsworth & Knight, 1999).

Use Transenvironmental Programming

A four-step transenvironmental programming model can serve as a framework for developing a program to prepare students for success in inclusive settings. The four steps in the model are (a) environmental assessment, (b) intervention and preparation, (c) generalization to the new setting, and (d) evaluation in the new environment. *Environmental assessment* involves determining what the orientation program should include by identifying the key skills that promote success in inclusive settings. In the *intervention and preparation* phase, the skills identified in the environmental assessment are taught to students using a variety of strategies. The next two steps are to *promote* and *evaluate* use of

TABLE 6.1

Sample transenvironmental programming model

General Education Class	Special Education Class
Ms. G. uses textbooks, computers, and other instructional media.	Mr. K. can teach the student to use textbooks and other instructional media.
Students interact with each other during recess.	Mr. K. can teach the student to initiate and engage in play with others.
Ms. G. expects students to raise their hands before speaking.	Mr. K. can teach the student to follow the rules of the general education classroom.
Ms. G. gives an hour of homework three times per week.	Mr. K. can give the student an hour of homework three times per week.
Ms. G. presents information through lectures and expects students to take notes.	Mr. K. can teach the student listening and note-taking skills.

the skills in inclusive settings. A sample transenvironmental programming model for a student is presented in table 6.1.

Environmental Assessment

Resource

Monda-Amaya et al. (1998), the Institute on Community Integration (n.d.), Fuchs et al. (1994), Welch (1994), and George and Lewis (1991) offer checklists, inventories, and interview protocols that can help you plan the transition to general education settings.

Reflective

Think about your transition from high school to college. What problems did you experience? How did peers help?

The content and goals of the transitional program are developed from an environmental assessment. This assessment involves analyzing the critical features of the new learning environment that affect student performance (see figure 6.2) and interviewing teachers and students (Campbell, Campbell, & Brady, 1998; Monda-Amaya et al., 1998). For students with different languages and cultures, you also should consider the language used to teach, as well as the cultural factors that affect performance. In addition, you can assess other features of the general education program, such as routines in the cafeteria and at assemblies; movement between classes; and expectations in physical education, art, and music classes. After information on the inclusive settings is collected, you and your colleagues can meet to analyze the differences between the two settings, identify areas where teaching will be needed to help students succeed in the inclusive setting, and plan strategies to address these areas (Prater, 2003). In planning the transitional program, you also may need to determine the order in which skills will be taught, as well as which skills will be taught before and after students have been placed in inclusive settings.

Some schools include a classmate on the placement team to help identify the content of the transitional program. The student can provide input in such areas as books and materials needed, social interaction patterns, class routines, and student dress. Peers also can help to welcome and orient students to their new environment and teach them about classroom- and school-related routines (Copeland et al., 2002).

Intervention and Preparation

In the intervention and preparation phase of the transenvironmental model, a variety of teaching strategies are used to prepare students to succeed in the new learning environment. These strategies and procedures are described next.

Teach Classroom and School Procedures and Successful Behaviors.

As students move to inclusive classrooms or make the transition from elementary to secondary educational settings, they need to be taught the procedures and routines of the

FIGURE 6.2

Sample environmental assessment form

Teacher: **Subject:**

Grade: **Date:**   **Teacher Completing the Observation:**

A. TEACHING MATERIALS AND SUPPORT PERSONNEL
1. What textbooks and teaching materials are used in the class? How difficult are these texts and teaching materials?
2. What supplementary materials are used in the class? How difficult are these materials? What are their unique features?
3. What types of media and technology are often used in the classroom?
4. What type(s) of support personnel are available in the classroom? How often are they available?
5. What teaching adaptations does the teacher employ?

B. PRESENTATION OF SUBJECT MATTER
1. How does the teacher present information to students (e.g., lecture, small groups, cooperative learning groups, learning centers)?
2. What is the language and vocabulary level used by the teacher?

C. LEARNER RESPONSE VARIABLES
1. How do students respond in the class (e.g., take notes, read aloud, participate in class, copy from the board)?
2. In what ways can a student request help in the classroom?
3. How are directions given to students? How many directions are given at one time?

D. STUDENT EVALUATION
1. How often and in what ways does the teacher evaluate student progress?
2. How are grades determined?
3. What types of tests are given?
4. What test modifications does the teacher use for students?
5. Does the teacher assign homework? (What type? How much? How often?)
6. Does the teacher assign special projects or extra-credit work? Please explain.

E. CLASSROOM MANAGEMENT
1. What is the teacher's management system?
2. What are the stated rules in the classroom?
3. What are the unstated rules in the classroom?
4. What are the consequences of following the rules? What are the consequences of not following the rules?
5. In what ways and how often does the teacher reinforce the students?
6. Does the teacher follow any special routines? What are they?

F. SOCIAL INTERACTIONS
1. How would you describe the social interactions inside and outside the classroom (e.g., individualistic, cooperative, competitive)?
2. What are the student norms in this class concerning dress, appearance, and interests?
3. What are the students' attitudes toward individual differences?
4. What is the language and vocabulary level of the students?
5. In what locations and ways do students interact in the classroom and the school?
6. What strategies does the teacher employ to promote friendships among students?
7. What personality variables does the teacher exhibit that seem to affect the class?

G. PHYSICAL DESIGN
1. What, if any, architectural barriers exist in the classroom?
2. How does the classroom's design affect the students' academic performance and social interactions?

Source: Adapted from "Preparing Secondary Students for the Mainstream," by S. J. Salend and D. Viglianti, 1982, *Teaching Exceptional Children, 14,* pp. 138–139. Copyright 1982 by The Council for Exceptional Children. Reprinted by permission.

Teachers can help students adapt to inclusive settings by teaching them about their surroundings. What aspect of your classroom and school would help students adapt to their surroundings?

 Resource

Allen (2001) and Adreon and Stella (2001) offer information and programs for helping students make the transition from elementary to secondary level classrooms.

new setting, as well as the skills that will help them succeed (Allen, 2001; Monda-Amaya et al., 1998). They can be introduced to several aspects of the new classroom setting such as the teacher's style, class rules, class jobs, and special events, as well as schoolwide routines such as lunch count, changing classes, using combination locks, homework, attendance, and the like. The class schedule can be reviewed, and necessary materials and supplies for specific classes can be identified. You can explain procedures for storing materials; using learning centers, media, materials, and other equipment; working on seatwork activities and in small groups; getting help; handing in completed assignments; seeking permission to leave the room; and making transitions to activities and classes. You can also tour the classroom to show students the design of the room and the layout of the school, the behaviors that they will need to succeed, and the location of teaching materials (Adreon & Stella, 2001). Once new students move into inclusive classrooms, classmates can be peer helpers to assist them in learning about the class and school routines.

Use Preteaching.   *Preteaching* can be used to prepare students like Nick for the academic, behavioral, and social expectations of the inclusive setting (Babkie & Provost, 2002). In preteaching, the special educator uses the curriculum, teaching style, and instructional format of the teacher in the general education classroom. For example, Ms. Thomas used preteaching to introduce Nick to the textbooks, note-taking requirements, assignments, homework, and tests he will encounter in his new classes.

Teach Learning Strategies.   As part of the transitional program, Ms. Thomas also taught Nick to use learning strategies that can help him to succeed in inclusive settings. *Learning strategies* are techniques that teach students how to learn, behave, and succeed in academic and social situations (Lenz, Deshler, & Kissam, 2004; Scanlon, 2002). Learning strategy instruction teaches students ways to effectively and efficiently organize, remember and retrieve important content, solve problems, and complete tasks independently (Boudah & O'Neill, 1999). In determining if a specific learning strategy should be included in the transitional program, you can address the following questions:

- Is the strategy critical for success in inclusive settings?
- Is the strategy required in many settings?
- Is the strategy age-appropriate?
- Does the student have the prerequisite skills to learn and apply the strategy?
- Does the strategy enable the student to solve problems independently? (Babkie & Provost, 2002; Lebzelter & Nowacek, 1999)

Swanson and Deshler (2003), Babkie and Provost (2002), and Baker, Gersten, and Scanlon (2002) provide steps for teaching learning strategies that you can use to help students succeed in inclusive settings. The steps include the following:

1. Select a strategy that is appropriate for the tasks or the setting and that will improve students' performance.
2. Allow students to perform a task to determine what strategy they now use and how effectively they use it.
3. Help students understand the problems caused by their current strategy, and get them interested in learning the new strategy.
4. Explain and describe the new strategy, its application, and its advantages compared with those of the old strategy.
5. Obtain a commitment from students to learn the new strategy.
6. Describe and model the new strategy for students, including a description of each step as you demonstrate it.
7. Teach students to rehearse the strategy verbally.
8. Give students opportunities to practice the strategy with materials written at their level and then with materials used in the general education classroom.
9. Develop an understanding of when to use the strategy.
10. Offer feedback on the student's use of the strategy.
11. Assess students' mastery of the strategy.
12. Develop systems to help students remember the steps of the strategy, such as self-monitoring checklists.

Once students learn the strategy, it is important for you to promote independent use and generalization of the strategy across many different situations and settings (Babkie & Provost, 2002; Jackson, 2002). Visually, you can prompt students to use the strategy by posting it in your classroom or by giving students strategy cue cards that they can use in their work areas. You also can verbally prompt students to use the strategy by asking them to use it, and encourage your students to verbalize the steps they are taking in performing a task. Collaborating with others so that they are aware of the strategy, and model, prompt, and reinforce its use also is important in helping students apply the strategy in different settings.

In later chapters, we will discuss other learning strategies that students can be taught as part of your efforts to differentiate instruction to promote their learning abilities and mastery of particular types of material.

Design Learning Strategies.   You also can design learning strategies for students (Babkie & Provost, 2002; Lombardi, 1995). First, identify and sequence the key parts of

Resource

Lebzelter and Nowacek (1999) and Montague (1997) offer guidelines for evaluating learning strategies and assessing their usefulness. Robertson, Priest, and Fullwood (2001) provide suggestions for helping students use learning strategies more efficiently.

Resource

Lenz, Deshler and Kissam (2004), Babkie and Provost (2002), and Strichart and Mangrum (2002) offer a variety of learning strategies for helping students succeed in elementary and secondary inclusive settings.

Reflective

What learning strategies do you use? Are they successful? How did you learn them? What other learning strategies might be helpful to you?

Set Your Sites

For more information on learning strategy, go to the Web Links module in Chapter 6 of the Companion Website.

Teaching Students to Use Learning Strategies

Ms. Washington has noticed that several of her students are not prepared for class physically and mentally. She observes the students closely for several days to determine which skills and strategies they use successfully and which ones they seem to lack. She then meets with the students to talk about her concerns and how their current approaches are affecting their performance. Though initially reluctant, the students indicate that they aren't pleased with their classroom performance and would like to do better. She discusses a learning strategy called PREP and explains how it might help them. PREP involves four stages:

Prepare materials
- Get the notebook, study guide, pencil, and textbook ready for class.
- Mark difficult-to-understand parts of notes, the study guide, and textbook.

Review what you know
- Read notes, study guide, and textbook cues.
- Relate cues to what you already know about the topic.
- List at least three things you already know about the topic.

Establish a positive mind set
- Tell yourself to learn.
- Suppress put-downs.
- Make a positive statement.

Pinpoint goals
- Decide what you want to find out.
- Note participation goals. (Ellis, 1989, p. 36)

After reviewing the strategy and briefly explaining each step, Ms. Washington asks the students to decide if they are willing to make a commitment to learning this strategy. One student says, "No," and Ms. Washington tells her that she does not have to learn it, but if she changes her mind, she can learn it at another time. The other students indicate that they are willing to try to learn the strategy. To increase their motivation and reinforce their commitment, Ms. Washington has the students set goals.

Ms. Washington begins by modeling and demonstrating the strategy by verbalizing and "thinking out loud" so that students can experience the thinking processes they will need when using the strategy. She models the procedure several times, using a variety of materials from the class, and reviews how she uses the PREP acronym to remember the steps in the strategy. Students discuss how the PREP strategy compares with their current approaches to learning, as well as the overt and covert behaviors necessary to implement the strategy.

Next, Ms. Washington has the students attempt to learn the steps of the strategy. She divides them into teams and has each team rehearse and memorize the strategy and its proper sequence. To help some students learn the strategy, she gives them cue cards. As students memorize the steps, Ms. Washington gives them cue cards containing less information. When the students can give the steps in the correct sequence, Ms. Washington has them apply the strategy with materials from the classroom. Students work in cooperative learning groups to practice the strategy and receive feedback from their peers. Ms. Washington circulates around the room, observes students using the strategy, and provides feedback. She encourages the students to concentrate on becoming skilled in using the strategy and not to be concerned about the accuracy of the content. As students become adept in using the strategy, Ms. Washington gives them other materials so that they can apply the strategy in many different situations. When students are able to do this, Ms. Washington gives them a test to check their mastery of the material.

Once students master the strategy, Ms. Washington encourages them to use it in her class. She observes them to see if they are employing the strategy and keeps records of their academic performance. Periodically, Ms. Washington reviews the strategy procedures. She cues students to use the strategy through verbal reminders, cue cards, listing the strategy on the board, and reviewing its components. Because the strategy has greatly improved the students' performance, Ms. Washington is working with some of the other teachers to help students use it in their classrooms.

- Why did Ms. Washington decide to teach her students to use learning strategies?
- What methods did she use to teach her students to use learning strategies?
- What did Ms. Washington do to involve her students in mastering learning strategies?
- What did she do to help her students use the learning strategies in her class and in their other classes?
- How would you teach your students to use learning strategies?

 To answer these questions online and share your responses with others, go to the Reflection module in Chapter 6 of the Companion Website.

the task or process. To make it easier for students to remember and use the strategy, try to limit the number of steps to no more than seven. Each step should be briefly stated and should begin with a verb. Next, find a word relating to each part of the task or process that will trigger a memory of that part. The words are then used to create a mnemonic that will help students remember the steps, such as an acronym using the first letter of each word. As students develop skill in using learning strategies, they can be taught to develop their own learning strategies.

Teach Students to Take on Independent Assignments.   Since students also have to complete many assignments on their own, a *job card* can help them learn to function independently. Using the job card, students determine what materials they need to do the assignment, the best ways to obtain the materials, where to complete the assignment, the amount of time needed to finish it, and the procedures for handing in their work and finishing assignments early.

Develop Students' Organization Skills.   You also can help students work independently by helping them develop their organizational skills. Following are two strategies that can help students become more organized.

Assignment Notebooks.   In many general education classrooms, students take notes and record information in their notebooks according to the specifications of their teacher(s). Students can be taught to color code their notebooks by content area, listing assignments in the notebook including page numbers, dates when the assignments are due, and relevant information needed to complete the task. You can periodically check students' notebooks for neatness, organization, completeness, and currency, and you can remind them to use the notebooks for important assignments, projects, and tests. You also can have students use a homework buddy, a peer who can be contacted for missed assignments and further clarification. To help prevent the loss of notebooks, encourage students to use folders to carry assignments and other relevant materials and information. Finally, remind students to put their names in all textbooks and cover them (Williamson, 1997).

Assignment Logs.   Your students can be taught to use an assignment log to keep track of assignments. The log consists of two pocket folders with built-in space to store

Resource

Ellis and Lenz (1996) offer guidelines and Heaton and O'Shea (1995) offer a mnemonic strategy called STRATEGY that can help you develop mnemonic learning strategies.

Reflective

With which tasks and processes do your students have trouble? Can you develop a learning strategy to help them?

An important transitional skill for success in inclusive settings is the ability to work independently. How do you help your students learn to work independently?

Sample assignment log

FIGURE 6.3

Date	Date Due	Class/ Subject	Materials Needed	Assignment	Date Completed

assignment sheets that contain the name of the assignment, a description of it, the dates the assignment was given and is due, and a place for a family member's signature. When assignments are given, students complete the information on the assignment sheet and place the sheet in the pocket folder labeled "To Be Completed." When the assignment is completed, the assignment sheet is updated (signed by a family member) and put in the "Completed Work" pocket folder. A sample assignment log is presented in Figure 6.3.

Help Students Develop Daily and Weekly Schedules.   A transitional program also can help students learn how to keep track of the many activities that occur in inclusive settings (Downing & Peckham-Hardin, 2001). Students can become more productive by developing a schedule charting their daily activities, including the time of day and the activity that should and did occur during that time period. At the beginning, you can help students plan their schedules. Later on, as they develop skill in planning and following their schedules, they can plan their own schedules and record the obstacles they encounter in following them. In developing their schedules, students can be taught to do the following:

- Identify specific goals to be accomplished.
- Consider and allot time for all types of activities, including studying, social activities, relaxation, and personal responsibilities.
- Consider the times of the day at which they are most alert and least likely to be interrupted.
- Avoid studying material from one class for long periods of time.
- Divide study time into several short periods rather than one long period.
- Be aware of their attention span when planning study periods.
- Arrange school tasks based on due dates, importance of tasks, and time demands.
- Group similar tasks together.
- Schedule time for relaxation.
- Reward studying by planning other activities.

A sample schedule is presented in Figure 6.4.

TIME MANAGEMENT CALENDAR, THE UNCALENDAR

WHAT NEEDS TO BE DONE THIS WEEK?

SCHOOL TASK	DUE	TIME TO DO IT
Book report	Friday	6 hrs.
Math Homework	Monday & Wednesday	2 hrs.
Social Studies	Tuesday & Thursday	2 hrs.

HOME

TASK	DUE	TIME
Clean Car	Sat	1 hr.

WORK

TASK		TIME
McDonalds		4-8 M-F

WEEKEND	MONDAY	DATE	TUESDAY	DATE	WEDNESDAY	DATE	THURSDAY	DATE	FRIDAY	DATE
SCHEDULE	**SCHEDULE**		**SCHEDULE**		**SCHEDULE**		**SCHEDULE**		**SCHEDULE**	
	7-8am bus ride (Homework) 8-3pm School 4-8pm Work 8:30-10:00 Homework								→	
Tasks: Time:	**Tasks: Time:**		**Tasks: Time:**		**Tasks: Time:**		**Tasks: Time:**		**Tasks: Time:**	
Book 2 hr. Report	Math 1 hr. Book 1 hr. Report (w/Patty)		Soc St. 1 hr. Book 1 hr. Report		Math 1 hr. Book 1 hr. Report (w/Patty)		Soc St. 1 hr. Book 1 hr. Report		Clean 1 hr. Car	
Comments:	**Comments:**		**Comments:**		**Comments:**		**Comments:**		**Comments:**	
Need help outlining Book Report- See Patty			Have Patty proofread book report							

FIGURE 6.4   **Sample weekly log**

Source: From "Teaching Organizational Skills to Students with Learning Disabilities," by J. M. Shields & T. E. Heron, 1989, *Teaching Exceptional Children, 21,* p. 11. Copyright 1989 by The Council for Exceptional Children. Reprinted by permission.

Generalization

Once a transitional skill has been learned in one setting, you can take steps to promote *generalization*, the transfer of training to the inclusive setting (Smith & Gilles, 2003). In planning for generalization, you must consider the student's abilities, as well as the nature of the general education classroom, including academic content, activities, and teaching style. Since transfer of training to other settings does not occur spontaneously, you must have a systematic plan to promote it.

You can promote generalization by offering students many models so that they see how the skill or strategy is used appropriately in many different settings and conditions. Generalization also can be fostered by establishing high expectations for students and providing them with multiple opportunities to perform under the different conditions and expectations they will encounter in general education classrooms. This can be done by giving students the opportunity to experience various aspects of the general education classroom and providing them with immediate and specific feedback regarding their performance. Students also can be encouraged to reflect on their own performance and to assume greater control over their learning, through your use of student-directed and peer-mediated instructional formats. You also can teach for generalization

IDEAS FOR IMPLEMENTATION

Teaching Organizational Skills

Josh is having a tough time adjusting to high school. When he does an assignment, he usually receives a good grade. However, far too often, his notebook is messy and incomplete, and he forgets to do his assignments and to study for tests. In addition to his classes, Josh participates in extracurricular activities and occasionally works at a local restaurant.

His family and teachers, frustrated by his erratic performance, decide that a weekly schedule will help Josh organize his activities and complete his schoolwork. At first, each Monday, Josh meets with one of his teachers, Ms. Gates, to plan his schedule. They divide each day into hourly time slots, list class assignments and tests, and outline after-school and home activities as well as job-related commitments. They then determine which activities have specific time commitments and record them in the schedule. Next, they list Josh's weekly assignments and due dates and estimate the amount of time needed to complete them. Josh and Ms. Gates then establish priorities and enter the items in the schedule. Finally, they review the schedule to ensure that all activities have been given sufficient time and that there is a balance among activities. Throughout the week, Ms. Gates checks Josh's progress in following the schedule. As Josh masters the steps in planning and implementing his schedule, Ms. Gates encourages him to develop his own schedule and monitor his own performance.

Here are some other strategies you can use to create an inclusive and supportive classroom that helps students develop their organizational skills:

- Teach students to maintain calendars on which they list their homework, exams, long-term assignments, and classroom and school activities, and encourage them to look at the calendar every day to determine daily activities and plan for long-term projects.
- Use class time to review schedules, notebooks, folders, and desks to reorganize them and throw out unnecessary materials.
- Give students space and materials in which to store items. For example, give them cartons to organize their desk materials or have them make simple desk organizers (see Williamson, 1997).
- Teach students to use sticky pads to record self-reminders.
- Mark a notebook page that is 20 pages from the last sheet to remind students to purchase a new notebook.
- Conduct a scavenger hunt using students' desks and lockers that causes students to clean these areas up.
- Teach students to provide feedback to peers on organizing their materials and desks.

Note: Archer and Gleason (1996); Gajria (1995); Williamson (1997).

by using several strategies to prepare students for the demands of the general education classroom, including changing reinforcement, cues, materials, response modes, and dimensions of the stimuli, settings, and teachers (see Figure 6.5).

How Can I Help Students from Specialized Schools and Preschool Programs Make the Transition to Inclusive Settings?

Plan the Transitional Program

Resource

Keefe and Spence (2003), Hanson (1999) and Fowler et al. (2000) offer guidelines for helping students and families make transitions to and from preschool programs.

Students moving from special day schools and preschool programs also need transitional programs to prepare them to enter inclusive settings (Fox, Dunlap, & Cushing, 2002; La Paro, Pianta, & Cox, 2000). In planning and using a transitional program for these

FIGURE 6.5

Generalization techniques

CHANGE REINFORCEMENT

Description/Methods

Vary amount, power, and type of reinforcers.

⬧ Fade amount of reinforcement.

⬧ Decrease power of reinforcer from tangible reinforcers to verbal praise.

⬧ Increase power of reinforcer when changing to mainstreamed setting.

⬧ Use same reinforcers in different settings.

Examples

⬧ Reduce frequency of reinforcement from completion of each assignment to completion of day's assignments.

⬧ Limit use of stars/stickers and add more specific statements, e.g., "Hey, you did a really good job in your math book today."

⬧ Give points in regular classroom although not needed in the resource room.

⬧ Encourage all teachers working with student to use the same reinforcement program.

CHANGE CUES

Description/Methods

Vary instructions systematically.

⬧ Use alternate/parallel directions.

⬧ Change directions.

⬧ Use photograph.
⬧ Use picture to represent object.
⬧ Use line drawing or symbol representation.

⬧ Use varying print forms.

Examples

⬧ Use variations of cue, e.g., "Find the . . ."; "Give me the . . ."; "Point to the . . ."

⬧ Change length and vocabulary of directions to better represent the directions given in the regular classroom, e.g., "Open your book to page 42 and do the problems in set A."

⬧ Move from real objects to miniature objects.
⬧ Use actual photograph of object or situation.
⬧ Move from object/photograph to picture of object or situation.
⬧ Use drawings from workbooks to represent objects or situations.

⬧ Vary lower and upper case letters; vary print by using manuscript, boldface, primary type.

⬧ Move from manuscript to cursive.

CHANGE MATERIALS

Description/Methods

Vary materials within task.

⬧ Change medium.

⬧ Change media.

Examples

⬧ Use unlined paper, lined paper; change size of lines; change color of paper.

⬧ Use various writing instruments such as markers, pencil, pen, typewriter.

⬧ Use materials such as films, microcomputers, filmstrips to present skills/concepts.

⬧ Provide opportunity for student to phase into mainstream.

CHANGE RESPONSE SET

Description/Methods

Vary mode of responding.

⬧ Change how student is to respond.

⬧ Change time allowed for responding.

Examples

⬧ Ask student to write answers rather than always responding orally.

⬧ Teach student to respond to a variety of question types such as multiple choice, true/false, short answer.

⬧ Decrease time allowed to complete math facts.

(continued)

Figure 6.5 (continued)

CHANGE SOME DIMENSION(S) OF THE STIMULUS

Description/Methods	Examples
Vary the stimulus systematically.	
◆ Use single stimulus and change size, color, shape.	◆ Teach colors by changing the size, shape, and shade of "orange" objects.
◆ Add to number of distractors.	◆ Teach sight words by increasing number of words from which student is to choose.
◆ Use concrete (real) object.	◆ Introduce rhyming words by using real objects.
◆ Use toy or miniature representation.	◆ Use miniature objects when real objects are impractical.

CHANGE SETTING(S)

Description/Methods	Examples
Vary instructional work space.	
◆ Move from more structured to less structured work arrangements.	◆ Move one-to-one teaching to different areas within classroom.
	◆ Provide opportunity for independent work.
	◆ Move from one-to-one instruction to small-group format.
	◆ Provide opportunity for student to interact in large group.

CHANGE TEACHERS

Description/Methods	Examples
Vary instructors.	
◆ Assign student to work with different teacher.	◆ Select tasks so that student has opportunities to work with instructional aide, peer tutor, volunteer, regular classroom teacher, and parents.

Source: From "But They Can Do It in My Room: Strategies for Promoting Generalization," by S. Vaughn, C. S. Bos, and K. A. Lund, 1986, *Teaching Exceptional Children, 18,* pp. 177–178. Copyright 1986 by The Council for Exceptional Children. Reprinted with permission.

students, you need to collaborate with other educators and with students' families to help students develop the skills they will need to be successful in their new placements (Keefe & Spence, 2003). This means you and others can work together to develop a transition timeline, prepare students for the transition, collect data on students' performance, establish communication procedures, and evaluate the transition process (Fowler, Donegan, Lueke, Hadden, & Phillips, 2000; Mhoon, 2003). Such a transitional program can introduce students to the new school's personnel and describe their roles; to the school's physical design, including the location of the cafeteria, gymnasium, and auditorium; and to important rules, procedures, and extracurricular activities. You can orient students to the new setting by giving them a map of the school with key areas and suggested routes highlighted, assigning a reliable student to help the new students learn how to get around the school, and color coding students' schedules.

Adapt Transitional Models

George, Valore, Quinn, and Varisco (1997) and Goodman (1979) have developed models for integrating students from specialized schools into schools within their community. These models also can be adapted to plan transitions from preschool programs or from hospital and institutional settings to school. The models involve:

1. *Deciding on placement.* At first, teachers, determine which community school is appropriate based on location, attitudes of school personnel, availability of services, and

IDEAS FOR IMPLEMENTATION

Promoting Generalization

Diana is having difficulty in her science and social studies classes, which present information through textbooks. Her social studies, science, and resource room teachers meet to discuss Diana's performance and agree that she would benefit from learning SQ3R, a text comprehension strategy. Diana's resource room teacher introduces the strategy and helps her learn it in that setting. However, her other teachers notice that Diana often fails to apply the strategy in their classrooms. To help her do so, they give her the following self-monitoring checklist, which presents the skills Diana should demonstrate when using the strategy in social studies and science:

Steps	Yes	No
1. Did I survey the chapter?		
(a) Headings and titles		
(b) First paragraph		
(c) Visual aids		
(d) Summary paragraphs		
2. Have I asked questions?		
3. Did I read the selection?		

4. Did I recite the main points?
5. Did I produce a summary of the main points?

Diana's use of the strategy increases, and her performance in science and social studies improves. Here are some other strategies you can use to promote generalization:

- Discuss with students other settings in which they could use the strategies and skills.
- Work with students to identify similarities and differences among settings.
- Role-play the use of the strategies and skills in other situations.
- Ask other teachers to help and prompt students to use the strategies and skills.
- Help students understand the link between the strategies and skills and improved performance in inclusive settings.
- Provide opportunities to practice the strategies and skills in inclusive settings.

needs of the students. They identify key personnel in the sending and receiving schools and programs, and they gather and share information about the students who will be moving from one setting to another.

2. *Approximating the new environment.* Teachers in the sending school help students adjust to the new school by trying to duplicate the demands, conditions, and teaching methods of the new setting.

3. *Leveling of academic skills.* Students are prepared for the academic requirements of the new setting and start using the new school's textbooks, teaching materials, and assignments.

4. *Building skills in the new school.* Staff from the sending school meet with teachers, administrators, and support staff from the new school to discuss strategies that have been used successfully with the students. Educational goals are developed and shared with teachers at the new school. The support needs of students and their teachers at the new school are identified, and appropriate strategies are instituted.

5. *Visiting the school.* Students visit and tour the new school to get a picture of the important aspects of the school and its physical design.

6. *Starting with small units of time.* At first, students may attend the new school for a brief period to help them adjust gradually. As students become comfortable in the new school, the attendance period increases until the students spend the whole school day in the new setting.

7. *Accompanying and advocating for the student.* At first, a staff member from the sending school may accompany the students to the new school to serve as a resource for the students and the staff. At the same time, a staff member from the receiving school serves as an advocate to assist the students in the new setting.

8. *Promoting social acceptance and academic success.* Teachers in the new school promote the social acceptance of the new students by locating their work area near class leaders or assigning them an important class job. Teachers also teach peers about individual differences and friendships. In addition, they use appropriate teaching adaptations and monitor their effectiveness.

9. *Opening lines of communication.* Ongoing communication systems between personnel from the sending and receiving schools and between the receiving school and the home are established.

10. *Scheduling follow-up.* As part of the communication system, follow-up meetings are held to discuss the students' progress and to resolve conflicts.

Resource

Stuart and Goodsitt (1996), Doelling and Bryde (1995), and Phelps (1995) offer guidelines for helping students and their families make the transition from hospitals and rehabilitation centers to school and home.

How Can I Help Students from Linguistically and Culturally Diverse Backgrounds Make the Transition to Inclusive Settings?

Resource

Romero and Parrino (1994) developed the *Planned Alternation of Languages (PAL)* approach to help prepare second language learners to make the transition to general education classes.

Many of the transitional strategies previously discussed are appropriate for students from linguistically and culturally diverse backgrounds. However, a transitional program for these students can also include teaching cultural norms, language, and socialization skills, as well as the terminology related to each content area (Langdon, 2002). A good transitional program for these students also will help them master the language skills necessary for academic learning, such as listening, reading, speaking, and writing (Haver, 2002). It will also teach students *pragmatics,* the functional and cultural aspects of language.

Teach Cultural Norms

A transitional program for students with various languages and cultures can teach them the cultural norms and communication skills that guide social and academic classroom life (Yeh & Drost, 2002). For example, some teachers may expect students to raise their hands to ask for help. However, some students, because of their cultural backgrounds, may hesitate to seek assistance in that way because they are taught not to draw attention to themselves. A transitional program should also help make students aware of the culture of the school, including routines, language, and customs. You can help students learn these different cultural behaviors by (a) respecting and understanding their cultural perspectives; (b) explaining to the students the new perspectives and the environmental conditions associated with them; (c) using modeling, role-playing, prompting, and scripting to teach new behaviors; and (d) understanding that it may take some time for these students to develop competence in the new culture. You also can help students make the transition to your class and school by assigning them class jobs, giving them peer helpers, and labeling objects in the classroom in their native language.

Resource

Haver (2002) provides suggestions for helping second language learners transition to general education classrooms and Bruns and Fowler (1999) offer guidelines for designing culturally sensitive transition plans.

Orient Students to the School

Several activities can be used to orient students to their new school. When students arrive, you can give them a list of common school vocabulary words and concepts. You also can pair these students with a peer who can serve as a host until they are acclimated. In

Why is it important that a transitional program for students from linguistically and culturally diverse backgrounds help students develop an awareness of routines, language, and customs?

addition, you can give students a tour of the school and photos labeled with the names of important locations and school personnel.

Teach Basic Interpersonal Communication Skills

As we discussed in chapter 3, many second language learners also need help in developing the *basic interpersonal communication skills (BICS)* needed to be successful in general education settings. BICS and other social skills can be taught using many strategies that give students valuable experiences. Some of these strategies, which you can use to teach social skills to *all your students,* are described here. They are most effective when you use them in some combination, in natural settings, and on a frequent basis (Gresham, Sugai, & Horner, 2001; Smith & Gilles, 2003). These strategies also can be used to help students develop the social interaction skills that support friendships (see chapter 5), and promote positive behavior (see chapter 7).

Modeling

Modeling allows students to view language and social interaction patterns. For example, students can observe peers in the inclusive classroom during a social interaction activity or view a video of such an activity (Buggey, 1999). You can then review these observations with students, emphasizing language, behaviors, and cues that promote social interactions—specifically, strategies and language for beginning and maintaining social interactions. You also can use video self-modeling, where students view themselves successfully performing a social or academic skill (Hitchcock, Dowrick, & Prater, 2003).

Role-Playing

Students can develop BICS and social skills by role-playing social interaction situations (Lo, Loe, & Cartledge, 2002). Where possible, the role-play should take place in the environment in which the behavior is to be used. After the role play, you can give students feedback on their performance.

Prompting

You can use prompting to help students learn relevant cues for using appropriate interpersonal skills. In prompting, students are taught to use the environment to learn new skills. For example, students and teachers can visit the playground, identify stimuli, and discuss how these stimuli can be used to promote socialization. Specifically, playground equipment, such as the slide, can serve as a prompt to elicit questions and statements such as "Do you want to play?" "This is fun!" and "Is it my turn?"

Scripting

Since much of the dialogue in social conversation is predictable and often redundant, you can show students the language and structure of social interactions via scripts that outline conversations that might occur in a specific setting (Cartledge, Wang, Blake, & Lambert, 2001). For example, a typical conversation at lunchtime can be scripted to include questions and responses relating to the day's events ("How are you doing today?"), menus ("Are you buying lunch today?"), and school or class events ("Are you going to the game after school?").

Teach Cognitive Academic Language Proficiency Skills

The strategies for teaching BICS also can be used to teach *cognitive academic language proficiency (CALP)* skills (we discussed CALP in chapter 3). CALP can be taught by giving students techniques for understanding the important vocabulary and concepts that guide instruction in inclusive settings. You can help students learn them by preteaching them prior to using them in lessons and reading activities, and using visuals and gestures to introduce, explain and reinforce their meaning (Gersten & Baker, 2000).

Students can be encouraged to list words and concepts used in the classroom discussions, textbooks, and assignments in a word file for retrieval as needed. For quick retrieval, the file can be organized alphabetically or by content area. As students master specific terms, those terms can be deleted or moved to an inactive section of the file. Students can also keep a record of key words and concepts by using the *divided page* method. Students divide a page into three columns. In column one, they list the term, phrase, or concept. The context in which it is used is given in column two, and the word is defined briefly in column three. Students can then keep a separate list for each new chapter or by subject area. These methods of listing difficult terms can be adapted for students who are learning English by recording information in their dominant language. For example, the primary language equivalent of words and phrases can be included in a word list or as separate sections of the divided page.

You also can post in your classroom a glossary of content-area terms that are important for students to know in order to learn (Palinscar, Magnusson, Cutter, & Vincent, 2002). The glossary can include technical vocabulary that is related to the topic your class is studying, synonyms and common terms for these vocabulary words, and examples of these terms.

You can help your students who are second language learners develop their BICS and CALP skills by providing them with numerous opportunities to interact with their peers in social and academic situations (Langdon, 2002). You can structure the learning environment so that your students actively use their new language in social situations, and work in cooperative learning groups (we will learn more about cooperative learning groups in

Resource

Saunders, O'Brien, Lennon, and McLean (1998) offer guidelines for developing and implementing collaborative transitional programs for second language learners.

chapter 9). Additional strategies for differentiating instruction to support the learning of students from culturally and linguistically diverse backgrounds are presented in chapter 8.

Cognitive Academic Language Learning Approach

Chamot and O'Malley (1996) have developed the *Cognitive Academic Language Learning Approach (CALLA)* to help students develop the cognitive academic language proficiency skills necessary for success in inclusive classrooms. CALLA was designed for students who speak primary languages other than English, but it can also be used to plan a transitional program for *all students.* CALLA has three components: (a) content-based curriculum, (b) academic language development, and (c) learning strategy instruction.

Content-Based Curriculum. In the content-based curriculum component of CALLA, students are gradually introduced to the curriculum of the general education classroom in the bilingual education or ESL program using the materials used in the inclusive setting. It is recommended that students be introduced to the content areas in the following sequence: science, mathematics, social studies, and language arts.

Academic Language Development. In this component, students practice using English as the language of instruction while their teachers support them through the use of concrete objects, visual aids, and gestures. Possible activities include learning academic vocabulary in different content areas, understanding oral presentations accompanied by visuals, and participating in activities by using hands-on materials such as manipulatives and models.

Learning Strategy Instruction. In the third component, students master techniques that make it easier to learn language and subject matter content

Offer Newcomer Programs

To help immigrant students adjust, many school districts have developed *newcomer programs,* which offer students academic and support services to help them make the transition to and succeed in inclusive classrooms (Schnur, 1999). The services offered include (a) activities and classes to orient students to the school and society; (b) a special curriculum that promotes the learning of English, multicultural awareness, academic content, and students' native languages; (c) support services such as counseling, tutoring, family training, information, medical and referral services, career education, and transportation; and (d) individualized and innovative teaching by specially trained teachers. After spending up to a year in a newcomer program, students transfer to bilingual/ESL or general education classrooms within the school district.

How Can I Help Students Make the Transition from School to Adulthood?

Develop an Individualized Transition Plan

As students age, comprehensive planning teams need to develop and implement Individualized Transition Plans (ITPs) to help them prepare for and make the transition from school to adult life. ITPs outline the coordinated transition services and activities and the interagency agreements and linkages that foster the transition to postschool activities.

Postschool activities include postsecondary education, vocational training, integrated employment, continuing and adult education, adult services, independent living, daily living skills, and community participation. The ITP should be based on the individual student's needs, preferences, and interests.

In designing ITPs, planning teams should use person-centered planning (Kohler & Field, 2003) and actively involve students in the process (Thoma, Rogan, & Baker, 2001) (see the guidelines for student involvement in the planning process and using person-centered planning in chapters 2 and 4). Person-centered planning involves students, family members, educators, and community-agency personnel in developing transition plans that focus on a person's strengths and preferences to create a plan to improve the person's quality of life and life satisfaction (Menchetti & Garcia, 2003). The process should include the following:

Resource

Schwartz et al. (2000) outline features and indicators of person-centered plans, teams, and organizations; and Thoma (1999) offers guidelines for involving students in the transition planning process.

- An assessment of students' career goals and interests, strengths, dreams, independence, social skills, hobbies, interpersonal relations, self-determination, decision-making skills, self-advocacy, and communication levels. Sax and Thoma (2002) and Neubert and Moon (2000) provide an overview of procedures that you can use to assess the transitional planning needs of students, and plan and evaluate transitional programs.
- An assessment of students' current and desired skill levels, interests, and challenges in making the transition to postsecondary education, employment, community participation, and/or adult living.
- An identification of transition placements and programs that match assessment data.
- An assessment of the new environment(s) to identify the physical, social, emotional, and cognitive skills necessary to perform effectively in the new setting.
- A list of the related services, functional supports, accommodations and assistive devices that can affect success in the new environment(s), as well as any potential barriers such as transportation problems.
- A statement of and timelines for the goals and objectives of the transitional program, including those related to student empowerment, self-determination, self-evaluation, and decision-making skills.
- A list of the academic, vocational, social, and adult living skills necessary to achieve the transition goals.

Resource

Johnson et al. (2003) identified barriers to and ways to facilitate successful interagency collaborations.

- A list of teaching strategies, approaches, materials, accommodations, and experiences, as well as the supportive and community-based services and supports necessary to achieve the stated goals of the transitional program.
- A statement of each individual's and participating agency's role and responsibilities, including interagency collaborations.
- A description of the communication systems that will be used to share information among professionals, among community agencies, and between school and family members.

Resource

Higgins and Boone (2003) offer guidelines for helping students who are gifted and talented make the transition from school, and Garay (2003) provides suggestions for planning and implementing transition programs for students with hearing impairments.

- A system for evaluating the success of the transition program on a regular basis (Benz, Lindstrom, & Yovanoff, 2000; Johnson, Stodden, Emanuel, Luecking, & Mack, 2002; Johnson, Zorn, Kai Yung Tam, Lamontagne & Johnson, 2003; Schwartz, Jacobson, & Holburn, 2000; Steere & Cavaiuolo, 2002).

A component of a sample transitional plan is presented in Figure 6.6. Transitional programming for students who are leaving school is designed to prepare them to participate actively in their communities and to become self-sufficient and independent. It also is designed to address the poor postschool outcomes that students with disabilities experience, including low participation in postsecondary education programs, low employment rates,

Sample component of an ITP

FIGURE 6.6

INDIVIDUALIZED TRANSITION PLAN

Name of Student Alan

Planning Meeting Date _____

Date of Birth 16 years old at time of meeting

Planning Team Alan, Alan's mother, Mrs. Thomas (classroom teacher), Jeff R.

(job coach), Mr. Jones (school administrator) and John M. (paraprofessional)

Transition Options	Goal	School Representatives and Responsibilities	Parent/Family Responsibilities	Agencies Involved Responsibilities and Contact Person	Supportive IEP Goal(s)/Objective(s)
Vocational Placements		1. Teacher will increase from 2 hrs. weekly to 5 hrs. weekly the time Alan spends working at the nursery.	1. Alan's mother will begin to give Alan a regular, weekly allowance.	1. Job coach/teacher will arrange Alan's schedule next year to include more community-based vocational experiences.	—communication
Competitive	X				—identify job(s) he likes
Supportive	X		2. Mother will begin to explore vocational options/interests by: a) checking with friends who own businesses to see if any have training opportunities for Alan; and b) spending time with Alan visiting different places and talking with Alan about the different jobs observed on these "exploration trips."	2. School administrator will initiate canvass of local businesses to explore potential vocational training sites for Alan including:	—behavior relaxation, identification of feelings
Sheltered	—	2. Job coach will expand the types of jobs Alan performs from maintenance tasks to more nursery trade related tasks.			—money management
Specify the above or other	X			a) local automotive parts refurbishing site	—skill mastery in designated tasks/jobs
It is unclear whether Alan will be better able to perform in a competitive or supportive work environment 5 years from now, but both options are being explored.		3. Job coach will introduce two additional vocational experiences for Alan each of the next 3 years so that Alan can, in his last 2 years of school, choose a vocational area of preference and refine his skills in these.		b) local shipping company	—rooming via uniform care and laundry, etc.
Identify current and past vocational experiences. Alan currently spends 2 hours each week working at a local nursery.			3. Mother will assign Alan some household "jobs" so Alan has the opportunity to be responsible for chores.	c) local supermarket chain	—functional time telling
				d) local restaurant	—learning how to use staff lounge for break/meal times
				3. Contact at local VESID office will visit school to provide overview training to staff re: job-related skills development.	—social skills training (co-workers)
				4. Job coach/teacher will perform functional assessment at each worksite to identify areas in which Alan needs support.	

Source: From *Supplement for Transition Coordinators: A Curricular Approach to Support the Transition to Adulthood of Adolescents with Visual or Dual Sensory Impairments and Coghitive Disabilities,* by J. O'Neill, G. Gothelf, S. Cohen, L. Lehman, and S. B. Woolf, 1990, New York: Hunter College of the City University of New York and the Jewish Guild for the Blind; ERIC Documentation Reproduction Service No. EC 300 449–453.

Set Your Sites

For more information on transition planning, go to the Web Links module in Chapter 6 of the Companion Website.

and low satisfaction with their adult lives (Conderman & Katsiyannis, 2002). Therefore, transitional programming often addresses four areas related to one's quality of life: employment, living arrangements, leisure, and postsecondary education (Johnson et al., 2002; Steere & Cavaiuolo, 2002; Turnbull, Turnbull, Wehmeyer, & Park, 2003). For an update on legal issues related to transitional planning and other topics discussed in this chapter, go to the Legal Update module in chapter 6 of the Companion Website.

Prepare Students for Employment

An important outcome for many young people leaving high school is employment so that they can earn money, interact with others, and advance in their careers. Working allows one to move toward financial independence, contribute to the community, and develop self-confidence (Brady & Rosenberg, 2002). Unfortunately, the unemployment rate for non-college-bound young people and those with disabilities is still quite high, and these groups are less likely to aspire to high-status occupations (Benz, Linstrom, & Yovanoff, 2000; Murray, 2003). Most students with disabilities who find employment often work in part-time, unskilled positions that pay at or below the minimum wage and offer few opportunities for advancement. These low-wage positions limit the opportunities for self-sufficiency and a reasonable quality of life.

Resource

Hutchins and Renzaglia (1998) developed a family vocational interview for involving families in the transition planning process.

The employment outcomes of students with disabilities are also related to gender and ethnicity (McNally, 2003; Murray, 2003). Although females with disabilities are less likely to find employment than males, they are more likely to live independently. White students with disabilities are more likely to find employment and receive higher wages than students of color and those who speak languages other than English.

Students with diverse languages and cultures and female students are often channeled into less challenging careers (Stuart, 2003). You can begin to address these disparities by showing *all students* the importance of work inside and outside the home, the range of jobs that people perform, the preparation for these jobs, the fear-of-success syndrome, and sex-role and cultural stereotyping and their impact on career choices.

Several models are available to address the difficulties that students with disabilities and other special needs experience in finding a job. These models are outlined here.

Resource

Ryan (2000) offers guidelines for helping students with disabilities conduct job searches, apply and interview for jobs, and be successful on the job, and Doyel (2000) provides information and resources on self-employment strategies for individuals with disabilities.

Competitive Employment

Young people who are leaving school need help in making the transition to competitive and supported employment. *Competitive employment* involves working as a regular employee in an integrated setting with co-workers who do not have disabilities and being paid at least the minimum wage (Office of Vocational and Educational Services for Individuals with Disabilites (VESID), 2000). Individuals usually find competitive employment through a job training program, with the help of family and friends, or through a rehabilitation agency.

Resource

Carter and Wehby (2003) offer a questionnaire for identifying the work-related skills that are important for job success, and Patton, de la Garza, and Harmon (1997) developed assessment and learning activities to prepare students for success in competitive and supported employment settings.

Supported Employment

While some individuals with disabilities may find competitive employment, many others, particularly those with significant disabilities, benefit from supported employment (Wehman & Targett, 2002). *Supported employment* provides ongoing assistance and services as individuals learn how to obtain competitive employment, perform and hold a job, travel to and from work, interact with co-workers, work successfully in integrated community settings, and receive a salary that reflects the prevailing wage rate.

Job Coach

Because a key component of all supportive employment models is a *job coach* or a supported employment specialist, you may be asked to work collaboratively with these professionals, families, and employers (Wehman & Targett, 2002). While the functions of the job coach depend on the supported employment model, this person may perform many different functions (VESID, 2000; Wehman & Targett, 2002).

Career Education Programs

A good career education program should begin in elementary school and occur throughout schooling to help *all students* make the transition to work (Hoyt, 2001; Sadao & Walker, 2002). Career education should include career awareness, orientation, exploration, preparation, and placement.

Elementary School Years.   In elementary school, career education programs usually focus on *career awareness,* an understanding of the various occupations and jobs available, the importance of work, and an initial self-awareness of career interests. These programs also introduce students to daily living and social skills, attitudes, values, and concepts related to work through classroom jobs, homework, chores at home, money, and hobbies.

Middle School/Junior High Years.   In middle school/junior high school, career education programs usually focus on *career orientation,* an identification of career interests through practical experience and exposure to a variety of occupations. Through field trips, speakers, special vocational classes, small job tryouts, and integrated curricula, students become familiar with work settings, attitudes, and job-related and interpersonal skills. They also develop an appreciation of the values associated with working.

High School Years.   In high school, career education programs often focus on career exploration, preparation, and placement. *Career exploration* activities give students simulated and direct experiences with many occupations to help them determine their career goals and interests. For example, students can visit work settings and observe workers as they perform their jobs. Vocational guidance and counseling also help students obtain information about a variety of jobs. *Career preparation* helps students adjust to work by offering teaching, support, and work experiences through vocational education programs. A career preparation program includes training in specific job-related skills and the opportunity to use these skills in simulated or real work settings. *Career placement,* the placement of students in jobs or other postsecondary settings, often occurs around the time of graduation from high school.

Community-Based Learning

Career education and other transitional and functional skills can be fostered via use of *community-based learning programs* such as cooperative work education or work-study programs (Burcroff, Radogna, & Wright, 2003; Kluth, 2000). In community-based learning programs, students are taught together in their communities. They also may attend school

Set Your Sites

For more on fostering the employment of students with disabilities, go to the Web Links module in Chapter 6 of the Companion Website.

Set Your Sites

For more on job accommodations for individuals with disabilities, go to the Web Links module of Chapter 6 of the Companion Website.

Set Your Sites

For more on career education for individuals with disabilities, go to the Web Links module of Chapter 6 of the Companion Website.

Resource

Burcroff, Radogna, and Wright (2003), Browder and Bambara (2000), and Beakley and Yoder (1998) offer guidelines for establishing and implementing community-based learning programs.

Resource

Allen (2003), Abernathy and Obenchain (2001), Frey (2003), Muscott (2001), and Rockwell (2001) offer guidelines and resources for designing, implementing, and evaluating service learning programs.

Set Your Sites

For more on service learning programs, go to the Web Links module in Chapter 6 of the Companion Website.

Reflective

How did you become interested in teaching? What career education programs helped you to make that decision? What job-related and interpersonal skills do you need to be an effective teacher? What career education experiences helped you develop those skills? How did your cultural background and gender affect your career choice?

Set Your Sites

For more on independent living, go to the Web Links module in Chapter 6 of the Companion Website.

and work part-time to blend their academic and vocational development. Through an agreement between schools and employers, students' educational and work experiences are coordinated. Students are encouraged to complete school while getting the training and experiences needed for future employment. Community-based learning programs give students financial aid and the opportunity to learn job-related skills and experiences.

Service Learning Programs

One type of community-based learning program is *service learning*, where students perform and reflect on experiential activities that foster their learning and benefit the community (Higgins & Boone, 2003; Frey, 2003). These programs provide real-life experiences that teach students about their communities, civic responsibility, and the world of work and career choices (Allen, 2003). They also help students develop academic, communication, social, problem-solving, and self-determination skills. Service learning activities that connect the curriculum to important activities, concerns, and actions in the community can motivate and teach students about themselves, others, and society. For example, such programs can involve creating a play area, or working in a homeless shelter or in a program for elderly persons or preschoolers.

Functional Curriculum and Career Education Models

An important part of transitional programming for students is a *functional curriculum*. In this curriculum, goals and methods tailored to individual students prepare them for a successful transition to adult living, including living, working, and socializing in their communities. When determining the individualized goals of a functional curriculum, teachers examine the importance of each goal to students' current and future needs. They also consider the relevance of each goal to the student's age and current level of performance.

Many functional curriculum and career education models are available. The *Life-Centered Career Education (LCCE)* model targets life-centered competencies involving daily living skills, personal-social skills, and occupational guidance and preparation to be integrated into the general education curriculum (Brolin, 1997). Clark and Kolstoe (1990) have developed the *School-Based Career Education Model.* This model provides career education services and functional activities from preschool through adulthood, including values, attitudes, habits, human relationships, occupational information, and job and daily living skills. Cronin and Patton's (1993) *Domains of Adulthood* model gives teachers guidelines for providing students with experiences in employment/education, home and family, leisure pursuits, community involvement, physical/emotional health, and personal responsibility and relationships.

Foster Independent Living Arrangements

As students leave school, they also may need help in learning to live in community-based living arrangements. To make a successful transition, students need training to overcome negative attitudes, environmental constraints (such as the availability of transportation, shopping, and leisure activities), and socioeconomic barriers. In addition, students can learn how to be self-sufficient and take care of their needs, maintain the property, and seek help from others when necessary.

Promote Students' Participation in Leisure Activities

Although often overlooked, leisure is an important quality-of-life issue and a key component for students who are leaving school (Modell & Valdez, 2002; Murray, 2003). Through leisure and recreational activities, individuals can develop a satisfying social life. This increases their psychological and personal well-being, their development of self-determination, and their integration into inclusive settings (Dattilo & Hoge, 1999; Johnson, Bullock, & Ashton-Shaeffer, 1999). Unfortunately, studies of the leisure activities of individuals with disabilities reveal that they are less likely to belong to school or community groups and participate in recreational activities than their peers who are not disabled.

Leisure Education

Because leisure is important for everyone, more and more leisure education services are being provided to students so that they can interact with others in community-based leisure activities throughout life. Leisure education teaches students to function independently during free-time activities at school, at home, and in the community; decide which leisure activities they enjoy; participate in leisure and recreational activities with others; and engage in useful free-time activities (Modell & Valdez, 2002).

Resource

Modell and Valdez (2002) and Collins, Epstein, Reiss, and Lowe (2001) offer guidelines for supporting the participation of students with disabilities in community-based sports, recreation, religious, and leisure activities.

Explore Postsecondary Opportunities

A growing number of students with disabilities are thinking of going to college (Janiga & Costenbader, 2002). These students will benefit from transitional and support programs that help them assess their readiness for and succeed in postsecondary education (Babbitt & White, 2002; Murray & Wren, 2003). A postsecondary transition program also

Resource

Johnson et al. (1999) provide information about recreational and leisure resources for individuals with disabilities..

All students should be encouraged to participate in leisure and afterschool activities. What leisure and afterschool activities are available for your students?

Set Your Sites

For more on leisure activities for individuals with disabilities, go to the Web Links module in Chapter 6 of the Companion Website.

Set Your Sites

For more on adapting leisure and physical activities for individuals with disabilities, go to the Web Links module in Chapter 6 of the Companion Website.

Set Your Sites

For more on fostering the inclusion of individuals with disabilities in the fine, performing, and literary arts, go to the Web Links module in Chapter 6 of the Companion Website.

should help them select and apply to appropriate colleges, which often entails frequent contacts and visits to identify and understand the available academic, financial aid, and support programs as well as the admission requirements (Lehman, Davies, & Laurin, 2000; Skinner & Lindstrom, 2003). It also should help students and their families complete the application procedures, provide required documentation, and check eligibility for supportive services and financial support (Rogers & Rogers, 2001). Another important component of the transition plan is understanding the disability-related laws that impact admissions, accommodations, and dismissals.

The postsecondary education transition program also should help students develop the skills necessary to succeed there, including engaging in self-advocacy and understanding and informing others of their disability, their strengths, challenges and goals, and the accommodations, support services, and assistive technology they will need (Skinner & Lindstrom, 2003; Taymans & West, 2001). A transitional program also can address students' attitudes and help them develop their strategies for dealing with large classes, as well as reading, note-taking, writing, test-taking, time-management, and course load demands. The transition plan also can involve teaching college-bound students with disabilities the goal-setting, social and self-advocacy skills they need to be successful, including how to communicate with professors (Lock & Layton, 2001).

How Can I Help Students Develop Self-Determination?

Resource

Thomas (2000) provides an overview of the laws that affect college students with disabilities-Madaus (2003) provides information about college foreign-language requirements for students with disabilities.

Set Your Sites

For more information on students with disabilities attending postsecondary education, go to the Web Links module in Chapter 6 of the Companion Website.

Resource

Rogers and Rogers (2001) offer a transition checklist; Mull, Sitlington, and Alper (2001) and Lock and Layton (2001) identify campus resources that can help students with disabilities succeed in postsecondary settings.

An important quality-of-life issue and an aspect of success in inclusive settings is the development of self-determination, "knowing what one wants in life and having the mechanisms to achieve these goals" (Whitney-Thomas & Moloney, 2001, p. 376). Whether moving to a general education setting or to adulthood, self-determination skills can help students control their lives and adjust to the independence and choices associated with inclusive settings and adulthood (Wehmeyer & Palmer, 2003). Since self-determination involves lifelong experiences and opportunities, you can collaborate with other teachers and family members to include goals related to self-determination on students' IEPs and ITPs, and use the strategies described below to help students develop self-determination (Steere & Cavaiuolo, 2002). It also is important for you to adjust your goals and strategies related to teaching self-determination to accommodate the cultural perspectives of your students and their families. For example, some families may view independence from the family as conflicting with their cultural values that emphasize family solidarity.

Teach Goal Setting and Attainment

Because self-determined individuals establish goals and work to achieve them, teaching students to become actively involved in setting and attaining their educational, social-emotional, and transitional goals is an important aspect of helping them become self-determined individuals (Margolis & McCabe, 2003; Palmer & Wehmeyer, 2003). To do this, you can help students address the following questions about themselves:

• Who am I?
• What are my goals?

IDEAS FOR IMPLEMENTATION

Promoting Leisure Skills

On Mondays, Ms. Whatley asked her students to describe the things they did over the weekend. Since many students said they watched television or were bored and did nothing, Ms. Whatley decided to teach them about the leisure and recreation activities available in the community. She began by discussing her own leisure activities and how much she enjoyed playing soccer and going to concerts with her friends. She also gave the class materials about community leisure activities such as newspaper articles, fliers from parks and museums, newspaper and magazine reviews of movies, music, and dance, and newspaper sports pages. As a follow-up activity, she invited members of leisure groups in the community to speak to students about their groups' activities. Three weeks later, Mondays seemed brighter to Ms. Whatley, as many of her students spoke about their participation in and enjoyment of leisure activities.

Here are some other strategies you can use to promote students' leisure skills:

- Allow and encourage students to select their own free-time activities.

- Encourage students to write and talk about their leisure activities and to participate in after-school activities.
- Give students opportunities and teach them skills to try new activities and toys.
- Teach students how to initiate play with others and role-play leisure situations.
- Take students on field trips to leisure facilities in the community.
- Teach students about social and recreational opportunities. For example, *I Belong Out There* (Program Development Associates, 1995) is a video with an accompanying booklet, including checklists and resources, that introduces individuals with disabilities to recreational opportunities and describes how to find them.
- Provide students and families with information about and access to adaptive sporting equipment.
- Teach scoring for a variety of recreational games.
- Seek the help of others, such as a therapeutic recreation specialist, physical educator, community recreation personnel, and families.

- What are the best ways to achieve my goals?
- Who can help me achieve my goals? (Imada, Doyle, Brock, & Goddard, 2002).

You also can use your students' responses to these questions to develop self-determination contracts with them (Martin et al., 2003).

Students will need to receive instruction in how to set and prioritize reasonable, concrete, and specific goals, and establish strategies and timelines for achieving them. This often involves teaching them to:

- develop goal statements including desired behaviors and levels of performance (e.g., "What are my goals?").
- identify possible steps for and barriers to achieving their goals (e.g., "What can I do to achieve my goals?" and "What things serve as barriers to achieving my goals?").
- create, implement and evaluate a plan for attaining their goals (e.g., "How can I best achieve my goals?" "Did I follow my plan?" and "Did my actions help me achieve my goals?") (Copeland & Hughes, 2002; Wehmeyer et al., 2000).

You can teach students how to use learning strategies to set and accomplish their goals and prompt them to use these strategies. For example, Mithaug (2002) taught students to set and achieve goals by teaching them to use a choice-card that assisted them in setting goals and examining their success in achieving them (see Figure 6.7 on page 278). When students encounter difficulty in achieving their goals, you also can prompt them by asking them to state their goals, and identify what they can do to achieve this goal (Price, Wolensky, & Mulligan, 2002).

 Resource

Grigal, Neubert, and Moon (2002) and Hall, Kleinert and Kearns (2000) offer guidelines for designing and implementing programs to help students with significant cognitive disabilities learn transition and employment skills in postsecondary settings.

 Resource

Browder and Lohrmann-O'Rourke (2001) developed checklists of self-determination skills that can be used to plan IEP and instructional activities, and Wehmeyer, Palmer, Agran, Mithaug and Martin (2000) offer an instructional model for teaching self-determination skills.

USING TECHNOLOGY TO PROMOTE INCLUSION

Supporting Successful Transitions

As we saw in the chapter-opening vignette, videos of inclusive settings can help introduce students to the important factors that affect academic performance and social interactions in inclusive settings and promote the use of already-learned skills in the new setting. You can also use videos of the new setting to help students identify and discuss key factors of the classroom, such as stated and unstated rules, teacher expectations, classroom routines, and the ways in which students ask for assistance.

Videos also can be used to prepare students to function in the general education setting. Like Nick, your students can learn and practice note-taking skills by viewing videos of teacher-directed activities in inclusive settings. Students also can practice appropriate responses to many general education classroom situations. Videos can be used to create a tour of the new school and the new classroom that students can view before they enter the new setting. Finally, videos made by special educators or supportive service personnel showing good behavior management techniques and teaching adaptations, physical handling, and the use of assistive technology can be viewed by general educators (Phelps, 1995).

Here are some other ways you can use technology to help students make successful transitions:

- Teach students to use a personal digital assistant (PDA) to foster their organizational and self-determination skills (Bauer & Ulrich, 2002). Students can use PDAs to electronically create and access specific features of assignments; a "to do" list; and daily, weekly, and monthly calendars. PDAs also can be programmed to remind students of due dates for assignments, and to prompt and guide students to use learning strategies and engage in certain behaviors (Davies, Stock, & Wehmeyer, 2002). For example, they can be programmed to remind students to use a specific learning strategy or perform a vocational task by periodically presenting the steps involved in using the strategy or performing the task.
- Use technology to involve students in the transitional process. Morgan, Ellerd, Gerity, and Blair (2000) have developed a CD-ROM series that uses motion video to help students identify their job preferences and introduces them to the world of work.

- Use a self-operated auditory prompt system. Students can be given an audiocassette with headphones to listen to (a) a prerecorded script that contains step-by-step instructions using understandable language and in a familiar voice; (b) individualized prompts spaced at appropriate intervals that remind students to engage in specific behaviors; and (c) statements of encouragement ("Keep focused on your work"), praise ("You are doing a good job"), and evaluation ("Did you finish the job?") (Post, Storey, & Karabin, 2002).
- Provide students with electronic mentors. Students and mentors can be matched and communicate electronically (Duff, 2000; Milstein, 2002). Thus, rather than committing to a specific time and place, mentors and mentees can interact at their convenience via E-mail. Guidelines and etiquette for communicating online can be established such as the time commitment required, the nature of the messages to be sent, the approximate time period within which a response to an E-mail may be expected, and the type of mentoring. The following websites can assist you in arranging electronic mentors for your students: *The Virtual Volunteering Project* (www.serviceleader.org/vv), the *Education Development Center's Center for Children and Technology* (www.edc.org/CCT/telementoring), *World Volunteer Web* (www.worldvolunteerweb.org), and *VolunteerMatch* (www.volunteermatch.org).
- Use virtual reality and multimedia to provide students with opportunities to learn and practice transitional skills (Davies & Hastings, 2003). Virtual reality systems can allow students to experience a variety of transitional situations and offer them a safe environment in which to practice and develop their skills. For example, via virtual reality students can take a virtual ride on public transportation, go shopping at a virtual supermarket, perform a virtual job, interact socially with others in a virtual park, or respond to a virtual job or postsecondary education-related interview (Council for Exceptional Children, 2001). Multimedia coupled with computer- and video-based technology also can provide students with opportunities to practice transition skills in

simulated community-based settings (Mechling & Gast, 2003).

- Use the Internet to provide students with access to mainstream media and communications that focus on their issues, interests, and experiences. For example, introduce and provide students with access to the following websites:

  Access to Print Materials: *The National Library Service for the Blind and Physically Handicapped* (www.loc.gov/nls) makes printed materials, including those that address disability-related issues, available on audiocassette, in Braille, and in other specialized formats. *Choice Magazine Listening* (www.choicemagazinelistening.org) offers free audio versions of articles, short stories, and poetry from popular publications.

  Disability-Related Magazines: Periodicals such as *Ability Magazine* (www.abilitymagazine.com), *The Ragged Edge Magazine* Online (www.raggededgemagazine.com), *Disability*

World (www.disabilityworld.org), *Mainstream, Magazine of the Able-Disabled* (www.mainstream-mag.com) and *Kaleidoscope: International Magazine of Literature, Fine Arts, and Disability* (www.udsakron.org/kaleidoscope.htm) publish articles, reviews, fiction, essays, and photographs on various issues affecting individuals with disabilities.

  Radio Programs: *Disability Radio Worldwide* (www.independentliving.org/radio/index.html) and *On a Roll* (ww.ican.com/channels/on_a_roll/index.cfm) are online radio programs focused on lifestyle issues for individuals with disabilities.

  Affinity Support Groups: The *Institute on Independent Living* (www.independentliving.org), *iCan* (www.iCan.com), and *The Ability Online Support Network* (www.ablelink.org) offer individuals with disabilities online support and interactions with peers.

Offer Choices

Goal setting is related to allowing students to make choices, which also can promote self-determination (Mithaug, 2002; Whitney-Thomas & Moloney, 2001). You can foster choice-making by teaching students how to make and express their choices and helping them understand the consequences of their choices (Cook-Sather, 2003; Stafford, Alberto, Fredrick, Heflin, & Heller, 2002). Because the school day involves a series of choices, you also can integrate activities involving choices into both teaching and nonteaching parts of the daily schedule (Price, Wolensky, & Mulligan, 2002). During academic tasks, students can be given choices regarding the assignments they complete, the order in which they begin and complete tasks, the learning materials they will use, the location in the room in which they prefer to work, and the individuals with whom they would like to collaborate (Jolivette, Stichter, & McCormick, 2002). If students have difficulty making choices, you can start by providing them with options, giving them yes/no or sticky-note prompts, or allowing them to make some choices during nonacademic activities. Cooperative learning arrangements, student-selected projects and rewards, self-management and metacognitive techniques, and learning strategies also allow students to assume more responsibility and control over their own learning. Additional guidelines for giving students' choices are provided in chapter 9. **To view an example of a teacher giving students' instructional choices, go to Case 2: Classroom Climate on the CD-ROM and click on the increasing interests and clear expectations video clips. How did the teacher facilitate the choice-making process for her students?**

Resource

Martin et al. (2003) and Palmer and Wehmeyer (2003) provide guidelines for teaching students to set their goals.

Resource

Jolivette et al. (2002) Stafford et al. (2002), and Smith (2002) offer guidelines for infusing student choices into classrooms.

cd-rom

Name _____

Date _____

	Set Goal? (Goal Setting)	Assign Work? (Goal Setting)	Complete Work? (Self-Recording)	Meet Goal? (Self-Evaluation)
Science		What I Will Do # _____	What I Did # _____	MATCH? Yes/No
Reading		What I Will Do # _____	What I Did # _____	MATCH? Yes/No
Math		What I Will Do # _____	What I Did # _____	MATCH? Yes/No
Social Studies		What I Will Do # _____	What I Did # _____	MATCH? Yes/No
Writing		What I Will Do # _____	What I Did # _____	MATCH? Yes/No

Number of "Yes" Responses Circled? _____

Points Earned? _____

FIGURE 6.7   Choice card

Source: From " 'Yes' Means Success: Teaching Children with Multiple Disabilities to Self-Regulate During Independent Work," by D. K. Mithaug, 2002, *Teaching Exceptional Children, 35*(1), pp. 22–27. Copyright 2002 by The Council for Exceptional Children. Reprinted with permission.

Foster Self-Awareness

Resource

Lohrmann-O'Rourke, Browder, and Brown (2000) and Hughes, Pitkin, & Lorden (1998) offer suggestions to assess the preferences and choices of students with severe disabilities.

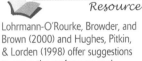

Set Your Sites

For more on teaching self-determination skills, go to the Web Links module in Chapter 6 of the Companion Website.

Self-determined individuals are also self-aware individuals, who can identify and express their preferences, strengths, and challenges. They, in turn, use their self-awareness to plan strategies to advocate for themselves, overcome their challenges, and, achieve their desires (Hitchings et al., 2001). A variety of strategies can help you involve students in understanding and assessing their learning preferences, strengths, challenges, and styles (see chapters 5 and 12). For example, Eisenman and Tascione (2002) fostered the self-awareness and self-realization of students by teaching them about special education and having them identify what they know about their individual differences and challenges, how their individual differences and challenges affect them and their views of themselves, and how they could use this information in the future.

Develop Self-Advocacy and Leadership Skills

In chapter 4, we learned about your role as an advocate for your students and their families. However, it is also important for your students to develop their self-advocacy and leadership skills (Higgins & Boone, 2003; Nevin, Malian, & Williams, 2002). Self-advocacy and leadership skills that can be taught to students to help them be successful in school and in life.

An important aspect of self-advocacy and leadership is understanding one's strengths and challenges, and establishing and implementing a plan for achieving one's goals (Garay, 2003; Kohler & Field, 2003). You can collaborate with others to help students understand their abilities, disabilities, needs, preferences, interests, and legal rights, as well as show them how to communicate this information to others and how to achieve their goals (Kling, 2000; Pocock et al., 2002). **To view an example of how self-advocacy can help students become better learners, go to Case 4: Support Participation on the CD-ROM and click on the self-advocacy video clip. How does the students' self-advocacy support their learning?**

As we saw in chapter 2, you also can help your students develop their self-advocacy and leadership skills by fostering their active participation in the IEP process and other decisions that affect them. For example, you can teach them to use I-PLAN, a self-advocacy strategy, that involves:

Inventory your strengths, areas to improve, goals, needed accommodations, and choices for learning.
Provide your inventory information.
Listen and respond.
Ask questions.
Name your goals (Van Reusen & Bos, 1994).

You can also use peer mentors, guest speakers, and books and videos about the lives of individuals with special needs to help students learn about their conditions, and accommodations that would be helpful to them (Waters, 2001).

Resource
Higgins and Boone (2003), Schnapp and Olsen (2003), Imada et al. (2002), Pocock (2002), and Raskind, Goldberg, Higgins, and Herman (2002) offer guidelines and activities for teaching advocacy and leadership skills to students with disabilities.

Resource
PROACT (Ellis, 1998) and ASSERT (Kling, 2000) are learning strategies that can help students develop effective self-advocacy skills.

Promote Self-Esteem

Promoting self-esteem in students and their own sense of self can improve their ability to advocate for themselves (Whitney-Thomas & Moloney, 2001). Students with low self-esteem often make negative statements about themselves that hinder their performance, such as "I'm not good at this and I'll never complete it." You can promote self-esteem by helping students understand the harmful effects of low self-esteem, and by structuring academic and social situations so that students succeed (Gajria, 1995). Other methods include recognizing students' achievements and talents, teaching them to use self-management techniques, asking them to perform meaningful classroom and school-based jobs, and posting their work in the classroom and throughout the school (Pavri, 2001). Additional suggestions for promoting students' self-esteem are presented in chapter 7.

Provide Attribution Training

Students' self-determination and self-esteem can be fostered by helping students develop an internal locus of control, the belief that their actions affect their success (Margolis & McCabe, 2003; Murray, 2003). An internal locus of control can be fostered via *attribution training*, which involves teaching students to analyze the events and actions that lead to success and failure. Students who understand positive attributions recognize and acknowledge that their successful performance is due to effort ("I spent a lot of time studying for this test"), ability ("I'm good at social studies"), and other factors within themselves. Students who fail to understand attribution often attribute their poor performance to bad luck ("I got the hardest test"), teacher error ("The teacher didn't teach that"), lack of ability ("I'm not good at math"), or other external factors. A sample attribution self-report and an attribution dialogue page that you can use to assess and improve your students' attributions are presented in Figures 6.8 and 6.9, respectively.

You can work with others to help students learn to use positive attributions by teaching them to (a) understand how attributions and effort affect performance, (b) view failure as the first part of learning and a sign of the need to work harder, (c) focus on improvement and analyze past successes, and (d) talk about mistakes and assume responsibility for successful outcomes (Kozminsky & Kozminsky, 2002). You also can encourage students to use positive attributions by modeling them, having students self-record them, responding to students' correct responses with effort feedback ("You're really working hard") or ability feedback ("You have the skill to do this"), and by responding to students' incorrect responses with a strategy or informational feedback ("Try another way of doing this") (Corral & Antia, 1997; Yasutake, Bryan, & Dohrn, 1996). You also can foster a learning environment that allows and encourages students to take risks

Resource

Duchardt, Deshler, and Schumaker (1995) developed a learning strategy called BELIEF and accompanying graphic devices to help students identify and change their ineffective attributions.

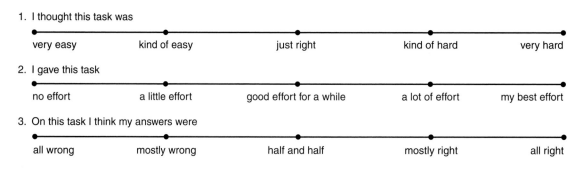

FIGURE 6.8   Sample attribution self-report

Source: From "Self-Task: Strategies for Success in Math," by N. Corral and S. D. Antia, 1997, *Teaching Exceptional Children, 29,* pp. 42–45. Copyright 1997 by The Council for Exceptional Children. Reprinted with permission.

FIGURE 6.9

Sample attribution dialogue page

Student Name: *Liat*   Date: *December 17*

Class: *Ninth grade*   School: *(Junior High)*

1. What did I succeed at this week?
    Nothing went well for me. Maybe a bit. It was hard to get through the day today, because I didn't want to look back much, and I was in a bad mood, too.

2. Why did I succeed?
    Nothing went well for me. I'm so sorry about it and I hope against hope that I'll do better and get what I want.

3. What did I not succeed at this week?
    What I didn't do well at this week is not too clear to me. But I think: to be a bit cheerful and happy. Do what I want and a little in school, but I don't feel much like studying like before.

4. Why didn't I succeed?
    I didn't succeed because I didn't feel like studying.

5. How could you make this week even more successful?
    Perhaps a little encouragement from the teacher, or maybe I'll find me a real good girlfriend like I had before and not one who takes advantage of me like the girls in my class.

6. Teacher's comments:
    This week you scored 100 on the math exam. This is a great success. I would like to know what you did to achieve such a high grade.

7. Student's reply:
    I learned the material and that's very, very easy for me. Usually, I know that material but don't do so well on tests. I don't know why.

Source: From "The Dialogue Page: Teacher and Student Dialogues to Improve Learning Motivation," by E. Kozminsky and L. Kozminsky, 2002, *Intervention in School and Clinic, 38,* pp. 88–95. Copyright 2002 by PRO-ED, Inc. Reprinted with permission.

and greater control over their learning. When possible, it is also a good idea to use intrinsic motivation rather than external motivation and rewards. (We will learn more about motivating your students in chapter 9.) **To view an example of a teacher encouraging a student to take risks, go to Case 4: Support Participation on the CD-ROM and click on the multilevel assignments video clip. How did the teacher help the student try to gain greater control over her learning?**

cd-rom

Provide Access to Positive Role Models

Access to positive role models can promote self-determination in students. These role models can be found in affinity support groups, mentors, and communications that focus on the needs, interests, and experiences of students.

Affinity Support Groups

You can foster self-determination by promoting positive group and individual identities in students. This can be done by introducing students to affinity support groups of peers with common traits (Stainback, Stainback, East, & Sapon-Shevin, 1994). For example, you and your colleagues at school can establish an affinity support group of students with

Resource

Stainback et al. (1994) offer suggestions for helping students form affinity support groups that are managed by the students themselves rather than by adults and that are inclusive rather than exclusive.

Resource

Ryan et al. (2002), Burrell et al. (2001), and Campbell-Whatley (2001) offer guidelines for developing, implementing and evaluating mentoring programs for students.

Reflective

Have you mentored others? Have you been mentored by others? Were these arrangements formal or informal? What roles did the mentor perform? What outcomes and barriers were associated with these experiences? Was it easier to be a mentor or a protégé?

Set Your Sites

For more on mentoring programs, go to the Web Links module in Chapter 6 of the Companion Website.

disabilities. Like other school groups made up of individuals with similar characteristics (e.g., sports teams, performing arts groups, academic clubs), this affinity support group can help students understand and value the skills and qualities they bring to school and learn to respect the individuality of others. The group can define their goals and activities: sharing experiences, expressing needs and interests, planning school activities, performing community service, and serving as an advocacy group to support each other.

Mentors

Mentors, self-determined, successful adults who guide and assist younger individuals, can be valuable in helping students make the transition to adulthood and develop self-determination (Burrell, Wood, Pikes, & Holliday, 2001; Higgins & Boone, 2003). Mentoring programs match mentors and protégés on the basis of shared strengths, interests, needs, goals, and personalities and provide them with opportunities to have an ongoing, reciprocal one-to-one relationship and shared experiences (Campbell-Whatley, 2001). Mentors serve as models of appropriate qualities and behaviors; teach and share knowledge; listen to the thoughts and feelings of protégés; offer advice, support, and encouragement; and promote protégés to others (Ryan, Whittaker, & Pinckney, 2002). For example, by sharing their experiences and meeting regularly with protégés, mentors serve as role models for students attending colleges and universities, working in competitive employment situations, living independently, participating in community recreation activities, and having a family life. Mentors also can help protégés understand their talents and develop confidence in their abilities.

Same-race and same-language mentors, and personnel who understand the students' language and culture, also can help students from different cultural and language backgrounds make the many school- and society-based transitions they face (Campbell-Whatley, Algozzine, & Obiakor, 1997). Mentors from the community can help culturally and linguistically diverse students with various aspects of schooling, as well as helping them continue to value their cultural and linguistic identities. For example, same-language mentors can share their past and current experiences as second language learners. This allows them to relate to students and their experiences in learning a new language, and helps students to make school- and society-based transitions.

Mentors can help students make transitions to adulthood and can help them develop self-determination. How have mentors helped you develop self-determination?

Use Self-Determination Curricula

Curricula to help students develop the attitudes, knowledge, and skills to act with self-determination also are available (Malian & Nevin, 2002; Thoma, Nathanson, Baker, & Tamura, 2002). *Steps to Self-Determination* (Field & Hoffman, 1996) is an experience-based curriculum that teaches students many skills related to self-determination that can be used in inclusive settings. Serna and Lau-Smith (1995) developed the *Learning with PURPOSE* curriculum for students and the *PURPOSE-PLANNING* curriculum for families, which can be used in inclusive settings to help students develop a range of self-determination skills. *Whose Future Is It Anyway?* (Wehmeyer & Lawrence, 1997) is a self-determination curriculum for secondary level students that includes a student manual and a coach's guide. Ludi and Martin's (1995) *Self-Determination: The Road to Personal Freedom* curriculum is designed for students from culturally and linguistically diverse backgrounds. It includes units on communication, self-understanding, rights, responsibilities, and self-advocacy. *Project Take Charge* (Powers, 1998) is a curriculum including videos that offer strategies to promote adolescent independence and self-determination, and *Take Action* (Marshall et al., 1999) offers a range of materials and activities for teaching students how to identify and attain their goals. Halpern et al. (1997) developed *Next STEP (Student Transition and Educational Planning)*, a set of learning activities, forms, vignettes, and videos designed to help students develop the self-determination skills they need to plan their lives as they exit school.

Resource

Test, Browder, Karvonen, Wood, and Algozzine (2002) offer guidelines for writing lesson plans for promoting self-determination.

REFLECTING ON YOUR PRACTICES

Promoting Students' Self-Determination

You can evaluate the extent to which you promote your students' self-determination by addressing the following questions:

- Do I integrate into the daily schedule activities that encourage students to make choices?
- Am I aware of students' preferences?
- Do I respect students' choices and decisions?
- Do I include students in planning and evaluating instructional activities?
- Do I encourage students to take responsibility for their decisions and learning?
- Do I encourage IEP teams to consider students' self-determination skills?
- Have I made it easy for students to attend and participate in IEP meetings?
- Have I taught students to advocate for themselves?
- Do I create a learning environment that helps students feel good about themselves?
- Do I encourage students to analyze how their actions contribute to success and failure?

- Do I give students opportunities to have positive role models, and to participate in service learning and community-based programs?
- Do I give students access to resources that focus on their strengths, needs, interests, and experiences?
- Do I use curricula and teaching materials and activities to promote students' self-determination?
- Do I encourage students to assume leadership positions?
- Do I understand the impact of students' cultural backgrounds on their self-determination?
- Do I model self-determination for students?

How would you rate the extent to which you promote self-determination in your students? ( ) Excellent ( ) Good ( ) Needs Improvement ( ) Needs Much Improvement

What are some goals and steps you could take to improve your students' self-determination?

Summary

This chapter offered guidelines for planning and using transitional programs to prepare students for success in inclusive settings. As you review the questions posed in this chapter, remember the following points.

How Can I Help Students Make the Transition to General Education Classrooms?

CEC 4, 5, 8, 9, 10, PRAXIS 3, INTASC 8, 9

You can help students make this transition by understanding their unique abilities and challenges, using transenvironmental programming, identifying and teaching essential classroom procedures and behaviors, and helping students to use their skills in different settings. You can help students succeed by teaching them to use learning strategies that can improve their independent work and organizational skills.

How Can I Help Students from Specialized Schools and Preschool Programs Make the Transition to Inclusive Settings?

CEC 4, 5, 7, 9, 10, PRAXIS 3, INTASC 9

You can work with others to develop a transitional plan and adapt a variety of transitional models.

How Can I Help Students from Linguistically and Culturally Diverse Backgrounds Make the Transition to Inclusive Settings?

CEC 2, 3, 4, 5, 6, 9, 10, PRAXIS 2, 3, INTASC 3, 9

You can teach students the accepted cultural norms, orient them to the new school, help them develop basic communication and cognitive academic language proficiency skills, and offer newcomer programs.

How Can I Help Students Make the Transition from School to Adulthood?

CEC 2, 4, 5, 7, 9, 10, PRAXIS 2, 3, INTASC 4, 9

You can develop an ITP that addresses students' needs in the areas of employment, independent living arrangements, leisure, and postsecondary education.

How Can I Help Students Develop Self-Determination?

CEC 2, 4, 5, 7, 9, 10, PRAXIS 2, 3, INTASC 4, 5, 9

You can teach students to set and attain their goals, offer students choices, foster their self-awareness, help them develop self-advocacy and leadership skills and self-esteem, provide attribution training and access to positive role models, and use self-determination curricula.

What Would You Do in Today's Diverse Classroom?

It is the middle of the school year, and your principal tells you that you will be receiving three new students next week: Carolina, Henry, and Alexis.

★ Carolina recently arrived in this country to be reunited with her family. Her records indicate that she attended school sporadically in her native country. She is now developing her English skills and has already learned some basic conversational skills. Carolina enjoys being with others, and they enjoy being with her.

★ Henry has been in a self-contained class for students with disabilities for the past 3 years. During that time his learning and behavior improved, and the multidisciplinary team believes that he is ready to learn in a general education class. His special education teacher reports that he needs help organizing himself and working independently. After two weeks in your class, you note that his materials are in disarray with papers shoved everywhere. His notes are written on loose-leaf paper, ripped out of his notebook, and then put back with the other papers at the end of class or thrown into his desk.

★ Alexis, a student with a disability, has recently expressed an interest in attending college. She would be the first one in her family to attend college, and knows little about colleges and applying to them.

1. What additional information would you like to have about Carolina, Henry, Alexis in order to plan transitional programs for them?

2. What goals would you have for their transitional programs?

3. What teaching and generalization strategies would you use to help Carolina, Henry, and Alexis succeed?

4. How could you promote Carolina's, Henry's, and Alexis' self-determination skills?

5. What knowledge, skills, dispositions, resources, and supports do you need to develop and implement successful transitional programs for them?

To answer these questions online and share your responses with others, go to the Reflection module in Chapter 6 of the Companion Website.

Chapter 7

Creating a Classroom Environment That Promotes Positive Behavior

Matthew

Just as Ms. McLeod is beginning a lesson, Matthew approaches her with a question. Ms. McLeod tells Matthew that she cannot answer it now and asks him to return to his seat. On the way to his seat, Matthew stops to joke around with his classmates and Ms. McLeod again asks him to sit in his seat. Matthew walks halfway to his desk, and turns to ask one of his classmates if he can borrow a piece of paper. Again, Ms. McLeod asks him to find his seat, and he finally complies.

The class begins the lesson, with Ms. McLeod asking the students various questions. Matthew calls out the answers to several questions and Ms. McLeod reminds him to raise his hand. As the lesson continues, Matthew touches another student, and the student swats Matthew's hand away. He then makes faces at Maria, who is sitting next to him. Maria laughs and starts sticking her tongue out at Matthew. Matthew raises his hand to respond to a question but cannot remember what he wants to say when Ms. McLeod calls on him, and starts making up a story and telling jokes. The class laughs, and Ms. McLeod tells Matthew to pay attention.

As Ms. McLeod begins to give directions for independent work, Matthew stares out the window. Ms. McLeod asks him to stop and get to work. He works on the assignment for 2 minutes and then "trips" on his way to the wastepaper basket. The class laughs, and Ms. McLeod tells Matthew to return to his seat and get to work. When he reaches his desk, he begins to search for a book, and makes a joke about himself. His classmates laugh, and Ms. McLeod reminds Matthew to work on the assignment. At the end of the period, Ms. McLeod collects the students' work, and notes that Matthew and many of his classmates have only completed a small part of the assignment.

What strategies could Ms. McLeod use to help Matthew improve his learning and behavior? After reading this chapter, you should have the knowledge, skills, and dispositions to answer that as well as the following questions:

- ★ **How can I collaborate with others to conduct a functional behavioral assessment?**
- ★ **How can I promote positive classroom behavior in students?**
- ★ **How can I prevent students from harming others?**
- ★ **How can I adapt the classroom design to accommodate students' learning, social and physical needs?**

F or students to be successful in inclusive settings, their classroom behavior must be consistent with teachers' demands and academic expectations and must promote their learning and socialization with peers. Appropriate academic and behavioral skills allow students to become part of the class, the school, and the community. Unfortunately, for reasons both inside and outside the classroom, the behavior of some students like Matthew may interfere with their learning and socialization as well as that of their classmates. Therefore, you may need to have a comprehensive and balanced classroom management plan. This involves the use of many of the different strategies and physical design changes discussed in this chapter to help your students engage in behaviors that support their learning and socializing with others. A good classroom management system also includes understanding students' learning and social needs; providing students with access to an engaging and appropriate curriculum; and using innovative, motivating, differentiated teaching practices and instructional accommodations, which are discussed in greater detail in other chapters. As we learned in chapters 4 and 5, it is also important to foster communication and collaboration with other professionals and families and to create a welcoming and comfortable learning environment, as well as to communicate with students, respect them, care for them, and build relationships with them (Jones, 2002).

Reflective

What social and behavioral skills are important for success in your classroom?

If students are classified as having a disability, your schoolwide and classroom policies and practices need to be consistent with certain rules and guidelines for disciplining them. Etscheidt (2002), Katsiyannis and Maag (2001), Hartwig and Ruesch (2000), and Smith (2000) offer overviews of the legal provisions related to disciplining students with disabilities, and Yell (1997) reviews the law concerning teacher liability for student injury and misbehavior. For an update on legal issues related to disciplining students and other topics discussed in this chapter, go to the Legal Update module in Chapter 7 of the Companion Website.

Schoolwide Positive Behavioral Support System

Resource

George, Harrower, and Knoster (2003), Rosenberg and Jackman (2003), Fox, Dunlap, and Cushing (2002), Turnbull et al. (2002), Sugai and Horner (2001) and White et al. (2001) describe the design and implementation of a schoolwide approach to promoting a safe and supportive learning environment.

Your classroom management plan should be consistent with and include the services available in your school's positive behavioral support system (Nelson, Martella, & Marchand-Martella, 2002; Sugai & Horner, 2001). A schoolwide approach to supporting the learning and positive behavior of *all students* involves the collaboration of educators, students, and family and community members to:

- Agree on unified expectations, rules, and procedures.
- Use wrap-around school- and community-based services and interventions.
- Create a caring, warm, and safe learning environment and community of support.
- Understand and address diversity.
- Offer a meaningful and interactive curriculum and a range of individualized instructional strategies.
- Teach social skills and self-control.
- Evaluate the impact of the system on students, educators, families, and the community and revise it based on these data (Duckworth et al., 2001; Jones, 2002; Lewis, 2001; Rosenberg & Jackman, 2003; Sugai & Horner, 2001; White, Algozzine, Audette, Marr, & Ellis, 2001).

Set Your Sites

For more on schoolwide positive behavioral support systems, go to the Web Links module in Chapter 7 of the Companion Website.

Positive behavioral interventions and supports are proactive in nature and seek to prevent students from engaging in problem behaviors by changing the environment in which the behaviors occur or teaching prosocial behaviors (Safran & Oswald, 2003). This also may include a functional behavioral assessment and a behavioral intervention plan. In the following sections, you will learn how to collaborate with others to conduct a functional behavioral assessment and how to implement specific positive behavioral interventions.

Resource

Safran and Oswald (2003) offer a review of the effectiveness of individual and schoolwide positive behavioral support strategies and systems.

How Can I Collaborate with Others to Conduct a Functional Behavioral Assessment?

A *functional behavioral assessment (FBA)* is a person-centered, problem-solving process that involves gathering information to:

- Measure student behaviors.
- Determine why, where, and when a student uses these behaviors.
- Identify the instructional, social, affective, cultural, environmental and contextual variables that appear to lead to and maintain the behavior (Knoster, 2000; Sugai, Horner, & Sprague, 1999).

While an FBA is only one aspect of a comprehensive behavior support planning process (e.g., medical, and vocational factors and systems of care and wrap-around processes should also be identified and considered) (Sugai & Horner, 1999–2000), it helps educators and family members develop a plan to change student behavior by:

- examining the causes and functions of the student's behavior.
- identifying strategies that address the conditions in which the behavior is most likely and least likely to occur (Reid & Nelson, 2002; Sugai, Horner, & Sprague, 1999).

Guidelines for conducting an FBA and examples relating to the chapter-opening vignette of Matthew and Ms. McLeod are presented here.

Create a Diverse Multidisciplinary Team

In conducting an FBA, you will collaborate with a diverse team that includes educators, and family and community members (Gable et al., 2003). The team typically includes the student's teacher(s), professionals who have expertise in the FBA process, and administrators who can ensure that the recommendations outlined in the behavioral intervention plan are implemented (Sugai, Lewis-Palmer, & Hagan-Burke, 1999–2000). The inclusion of family members also can provide the team with important information about the student's history and home-based events that may affect the student and the family (Fox, Vaughn, Wyatte, & Dunlap, 2002). Expanding the team to include community members as well as professionals who will be culturally sensitive to the student's background allows the team to learn about the student's cultural perspective and experiential and linguistic background, and to determine whether the student's behavior has a sociocultural explanation. In the case of

Resource

Scott, Liaupsin, Nelson, and Jolivette (2003) offer guidelines for conducting a team-based functional behavioral assessment and Fox and Dunlap (2002) provide suggestions for involving families in the FBA process.

Matthew, the team was composed of two of his teachers, his mother and brother, a school psychologist who had experience with the FBA process, the principal at his school, and a representative from a community group.

Identify the Problematic Behavior

First, the team identifies the behavior that will be examined by the FBA by considering the following questions: (a) What does the student do or fail to do that causes a problem? (b) How do the student's cognitive, language, physical, and sensory abilities affect the behavior? and (c) How does the behavior affect the student's learning, socialization, and self-concept, as well as classmates and adults? For example, in the chapter-opening vignette, Matthew's poor on-task behavior seems to be undermining both his learning and the classroom environment. When several behaviors are identified as problematic, it is recommended that they be prioritized based on their level of interference (Murdick, Gartin, & Stockall, 2003).

The team also needs to examine the relationship, if any, between the behavior and the student's cultural and language background. Some students from diverse backgrounds may have different cultural perspectives than their teachers, and communication problems between students and teachers often are interpreted by teachers as behavioral problems. For example, a student may appear passive in class, which may be interpreted as evidence of immaturity and lack of interest. However, in the student's culture, the behavior may be considered a mark of respect for the teacher as an authority figure.

Reflective

How would you define, in observable and measurable terms, and what recording strategies would you use to assess out-of-seat, inattentive, aggressive, tardy, noisy, and disruptive behavior?

Define the Behavior

Next, the behavior is defined in observable and measurable terms by listing its characteristics (Ryan, Halsey, & Matthews, 2003). For example, Matthew's off-task behavior can be defined in terms of his calling out and extraneous comments, his extensive comments related to teacher questions, his ability to remain in his work area, his interactions with classmates, and the amount of work he completed.

Observe and Record the Behavior

After the behavior has been defined, the team selects an appropriate observational recording method and uses it during times that are representative of typical classroom activities (Alberto & Troutman, 2003). Examples of different observational recording systems are presented in Figure 7.1.

Event Recording

If the behavior to be observed has a definite beginning and end and occurs for brief time periods, event recording is a good choice. In *event recording*, the observer counts the number of behaviors that occur during the observation period, as shown in Figure 7.1a. For example, event recording can be used to count the number of times Matthew was on task during a typical 30-minute teacher-directed activity. Data collected using event recording are displayed as either a frequency (number of times the behavior occurred) or a rate (number of times it occurred per length of observation).

Date	Length of Sessions	Number of Events
9/11	30 minutes	卌
9/15	30 minutes	卌 卌 丨
9/20	30 minutes	丨丨丨

(a) Event Recording of Call-outs

Date	Occurrence Number	Time Start	End	Total Duration
5/8	1	9:20	9:25	5 minutes
	2	9:27	9:30	3 minutes
5/9	1	10:01	10:03	2 minutes
	2	10:05	10:06	1 minute
	3	10:10	10:14	4 minutes

(b) Duration Recording of Out-of-seat Behavior

15 Sec	15 Sec	15 Sec	15 Sec
+	−	−	+
+	+	−	−
+	−	−	−
−	+	+	+
+	+	−	+

(c) Interval Recording of On-task Behavior

FIGURE 7.1   Example of observational recording strategies

You can use an inexpensive grocery, stitch, or golf counter for event recording. If a mechanical counter is not available, marks can be made on a pad, an index card, a chalkboard, or a piece of paper taped to the wrist. You also can use a transfer system in which you place small objects (e.g., poker chips, paper clips) in one pocket and transfer an object to another pocket each time the behavior occurs. The number of objects transferred to the second pocket gives an accurate measure of the behavior.

Duration and Latency Recording

If time is an important factor in the observed behavior, a good recording strategy would be either duration or latency recording. In *duration recording,* shown in Figure 7.1b, the observer records how long a behavior lasts. *Latency recording,* on the other hand, is used to determine the delay between receiving instructions and beginning a task. For example, duration recording can be used to find out how much time Matthew spends on task. Latency recording would be used to assess how long it took Matthew to begin an assignment after the directions were given. The findings of both recording systems can be presented as the total length of time or as an average. Duration recording data also can be summarized as the percentage of time the student engaged in the behavior by dividing the amount of time the behavior lasts by the length of the observation period and multiplying by 100.

Observing students and recording their behavior can provide valuable information. What types of information can observations give you about your students?

Interval Recording or Time Sampling

With *interval recording* and *time sampling,* the observation period is divided into equal intervals, and the observer notes whether the behavior occurred during each interval; a plus (+) indicates occurrence and a minus (-) indicates nonoccurrence. A + does not indicate how many times the behavior occurred in that interval, only that it did occur. Therefore, this system shows the percentage of intervals in which the behavior occurred rather than how often it occurred.

The interval percentage is calculated by dividing the number of intervals in which the behavior occurred by the total number of intervals in the observation period and then multiplying by 100. For example, you might use interval recording to record Matthew's on-task behavior. After defining the behavior, you would divide the observation period into intervals and construct a corresponding interval score sheet, as shown in Figure 7.1c. You would then record whether or not Matthew was on task during each interval. The number of intervals in which the behavior occurred would be divided by the total number of intervals to determine the percentage of intervals in which he was on task.

Anecdotal Records

An anecdotal record, also known as a *narrative log* or *continuous recording,* is often useful in reporting the results of the observation (Rao, Hoyer, Meehan, Young, & Guerrera, 2003). An *anecdotal record* is a narrative of the events that took place during the observation, and helps you to understand the academic context in which student behavior occurs, and the environmental factors that influence student behavior. Use the following suggestions to write narrative anecdotal reports:

- Give the date, time and length of the observation.
- Describe the activities, design, individuals, and their relationships to the setting in which the observation occurred.
- Report in observable terms all of the student's verbal and nonverbal behaviors, as well as the responses of others to these behaviors.

- Avoid interpretations.
- Indicate the sequence and duration of events.

A sample anecdotal relating to an observation of Matthew is presented in the chapter-opening vignette.

Obtain Additional Information About the Student and the Behavior

An important part of an FBA is obtaining information regarding the student and the behavior. Using multiple sources and methods, the team gathers information to determine the student's skills, strengths, challenges, interests, hobbies, preferences, self-concept, attitudes, health, culture, language, and experiences. Data regarding successful and ineffective interventions used in the past with the student also can be collected. Often this information is obtained by reviewing student records and by interviewing the student, teachers, family members, ancillary support personnel, and peers or having these individuals complete a checklist or rating scale concerning the behavior (Fox, Conroy, & Heckaman, 1998; Larson & Maag, 1998). For example, Ms. McLeod asked Matthew to respond to the following questions: (a) What do I expect you to do during class time? (b) How did the activities and assignments make you feel? (c) Can you tell me why you didn't complete your work? and (d) What usually happens when you disturb other students? Additional information about Matthew and the data collection strategies used by the team as part of the functional behavioral assessment process are summarized in Table 7.1.

Perform an Antecedents-Behavior-Consequences (A-B-C) Analysis

While recording behavior, an A-B-C analysis also is used to collect data to identify the possible antecedents and consequences associated with the student's behavior (Mueller, Jenson, Reavis, & Andrews, 2002). *Antecedents* and *consequences* are the events, stimuli, objects, actions, and activities that precede and trigger the behavior, and follow and maintain the behavior, respectively. A sample functional behavioral assessment for Matthew that contains an A-B-C analysis of his off-task behavior is presented in Table 7.1.

Analyze the Data

The A-B-C data are then analyzed and summarized to identify when, where, with whom, and under what conditions the behavior is most likely and least likely to occur (see Figure 7.2 for questions that can guide you in analyzing the behavior's antecedents and consequences). The A-B-C analysis data are also analyzed to try to determine why the student uses the behavior, also referred to as the *perceived function* of the behavior. The team can attempt to identify the perceived function of the behavior by considering the following:

1. What does the student appear to be communicating via the behavior?
2. How does the behavior benefit the student (e.g., getting attention or help from others; avoiding a difficult or unappealing activity; gaining access to a desired activity or peers; receiving increased status and self-concept, affiliation with others, sense of power and control, sensory stimulation or feedback, satisfaction)?

Resource

Rao et al. (2003) offer guidelines and self-evaluation rubrics for conducting observations of students.

Resource

Kern, Dunlap, Clarke, and Childs (1994), Lawry, Storey, and Danko (1993), Lewis, Scott, and Sugai (1994), O'Neill et al. (1997), and Reid & Maag (1998) offer interviews and survey questions to identify the perspectives of teachers, students, and family members on student behavior.

Resource

Mueller et al. (2002) and Knoster (2000) provide guidelines and forms for conducting an A-B-C analysis.

Sample Functional Behavioral Assessment for Matthew

TABLE 7.1

BEHAVIOR:	Off-task		
What are the antecedents of the behavior?	**What is the behavior?**	**What are the consequences of the behavior?**	**What are the functions of the behavior?**
• Teacher-directed activity • Content of the activity • Individualized nature of the activity • Duration of the activity • Location of Matthew's work area • Placement of peers' work areas • Proximity of the teacher • Teacher comment or question • Availability of other activities	Matthew calls out, makes extraneous comments in response to teacher questions or comments, distracts others, leaves his work area, and completes a limited amount of work.	• Receives teacher attention • Receives peer attention • Avoids unmotivating activity • Performs a pleasant activity (e.g., interacting with peers) • Receives reprimand • Leaves seat	• To avoid or express his disappointment with the instructional activity • To receive attention from adults and peers

DATA COLLECTION STRATEGIES: Observations, student, family and teacher interviews, behavior checklists, and standardized testing.

ADDITIONAL INFORMATION

ACADEMIC:
  • Mathew has scored significantly above grade level on standardized tests in reading and mathematics.

SOCIAL/PEER:
  • Matthew spends time alone after school because there are few activities available for him.
  • Matthew's peers describe him as the class clown.
  • Matthew likes to talk with and work with others.

FAMILY:
  • Mathew likes to interact with others in social situations and community events.
  • Matthew does his homework while interacting with others.

3. What setting events contribute to the problem behavior (e.g., the student being tired, hungry, ill, or on medication; the occurrence of social conflicts, schedule changes, or academic difficulties; the staffing patterns and interactions)?
4. How does the behavior relate to the student's culture and experiential and language background?

Possible antecedents for Matthew's behavior include the content, type, duration, and level of difficulty of the instructional activity, the extent to which the activity allows him to work with others, and the location of the teacher. Possible consequences for Matthew's behavior may include teacher and peer attention, and avoiding an unmotivating task.

Develop Hypothesis Statements

Next, the prior information collected and the A-B-C analysis data are used to develop specific and global statements, also referred to as summary statements, concerning the student and the behavior hypotheses about the student and the behavior, which are ver-

FIGURE 7.2

A-B-C analysis questions

In analyzing the antecedents of student behavior, consider if the behavior is related to the following:

◇ Physiological factors such as medications, allergies, hunger/thirst, odors, or temperature levels
◇ Home factors or the student's cultural perspective
◇ Student's learning, motivation, communication, and physical abilities
◇ The physical design of the classroom, such as the seating arrangement, the student's proximity to the teacher and peers, classroom areas, transitions, scheduling changes, and noise levels
◇ The behavior of peers
◇ Certain days, the time of day, the length of the activity, the activities or events preceding or following the behavior or events outside the classroom
◇ The way the material is presented or the way the student responds
◇ The curriculum and the teaching activities, such as certain content areas and instructional activities, or the task's directions, difficulty and staff support
◇ Group size and/or composition or the presence and behavior of peers and adults

In analyzing the consequences of student behavior, consider the following:

◇ What are the behaviors and reactions of specific peers and/or adults?
◇ What is the effect of the behavior on the classroom atmosphere?
◇ How does the behavior affect progress on the activity or the assigned task?
◇ How does the behavior relate to and affect the student's cultural perspective?
◇ What encourages or discourages the behavior?

ified (Shippen, Simpson, & Crites, 2003). Specific hypotheses address the reasons why the behavior occurs and the conditions related to the behavior including the possible antecedents and consequences. For example, a specific hypothesis related to Matthew's behavior would be that when Matthew is given a teacher-directed or independent academic activity, Matthew will use many off-task behaviors to gain attention from peers and the teacher. Global hypotheses address how factors in the student's life in school, at home, and in the community impact upon the behavior. In the case of Matthew, a possible global hypothesis can address the possibility that his seeking attention is related to his limited opportunities to interact with peers after school. After hypothesis statements are developed, direct observation is used to validate their accuracy (Sugai, Lewis-Palmer, & Hagan-Burke, 1999–2000).

Consider Sociocultural Factors

When analyzing the A-B-C information to determine hypotheses, the team should consider the impact of cultural perspectives and language background on the student's behavior and communication (Schwartz, 2001). Behavioral differences in students related to their learning histories and behaviors, preference for working on several tasks at once, listening and responding styles, peer interaction patterns, responses to authority, verbal and nonverbal communication, turn-taking sequences, physical space, eye-contact, and student/teacher interactions can be attributed to their cultural backgrounds (Cartledge et al., 2000; Townsend, 2000).

To do this, behavior and communication must be examined in a social/cultural context (Cartledge, Tillman, & Johnson, 2001). For example, four cultural factors that may affect students' behavior in school are outlined below: time, movement, respect for elders, and individual versus group performance. However, although this framework for comparing students may be useful in understanding certain cognitive, movement, and interaction styles and associated behaviors, you should be careful in generalizing a specific behavior to any cultural group. Thus, rather than considering these behaviors as characteristic of the group as a whole, you should view them as attitudes or behaviors that an individual may consider in learning and interacting with others.

Time

Different cultural groups have different concepts of time. The Euro-American culture views timeliness as essential and as a key characteristic in judging competence. Students are expected to be on time and to complete assignments on time. Other cultures may also view time as important, but as secondary to relationships and performance (Cloud & Landurand, n.d.). For some students, helping a friend with a problem may be considered more important than completing an assignment by the deadline. Students who have different concepts of time may also have difficulties on timed tests or assignments.

Movement

Different cultural groups also have different movement styles, which can affect how others perceive them and interpret their behaviors (Neal, McCray, Webb-Johnson, & Bridgest, 2003). Different movement styles can affect the ways students walk, talk, and learn. For example, some students may prefer to get ready to perform an activity by moving around to organize themselves. Other students may need periodic movement breaks to support their learning.

Respect for Elders

Cultures, and therefore individuals, have different ways to show respect for elders and authority figures such as teachers (Quinn, 2001). In many cultures, teachers and other school personnel are viewed as prestigious and valued individuals who are worthy of respect. Respect may be demonstrated in many different ways, such as not making eye contact with adults, not speaking to adults unless spoken to first, not asking questions, and using formal titles. Mainstream culture in the United States does not always show respect for elders and teachers in these ways. Therefore, the behaviors mentioned above may be interpreted as communication or behavior problems rather than as cultural marks of respect.

Individual versus Group Performance

Resource

Cartledge, Kea, and Ida (2000) and Craig et al. (2000) offer reviews of culturally based student behaviors that may be misinterpreted by teachers.

Reflective

African American and Hispanic males and poor students tend to receive harsher discipline for all types of behavioral offenses than their white peers and are more often suspended and physically punished (Townsend, 2000). Why do you think this is the case?

The Euro-U.S. culture is founded on such notions as rugged individualism. By contrast, many other cultures view group cooperation as more important (Sparks, 2000a). For students from these cultures, responsibility to society is seen as an essential aspect of competence, and their classroom performance is shaped by their commitment to the group and the community rather than to individual success. As a result, for some African American, Native American, and Hispanic American students who are brought up to believe in a group solidarity orientation, their behavior may be designed to avoid being viewed as "acting white" or "acting Anglo" (Fordham & Ogbu, 1986; Ramirez, 1989).

Humility is important in cultures that value group solidarity. By contrast, cultures that emphasize individuality award status based on individual achievement. Students from cultures that view achievement as contributing to the success of the group may perform better on tasks perceived as benefiting a group. They may avoid situations that bring attention to themselves, such as reading out loud, answering questions, gaining the teacher's praise, disclosing themselves, revealing problems, or demonstrating expertise (Bui & Turnbull, 2003).

Develop a Behavioral Intervention Plan

Based on its information and hypotheses, the team collaboratively develops a behavioral intervention plan focusing on how the learning environment will change to address the student's behavior, characteristics, strengths, and challenges (Curtiss, Mathur, & Rutherford, 2002). The plan should identify specific measurable goals for appropriate behaviors, and the individuals and services responsible for helping the student achieve these goals. It also should outline the positive, culturally appropriate teaching and behavioral supports and strategies and school and community resources that change the antecedent events and consequences by addressing the following issues: (a) What antecedents and consequences can be changed to increase appropriate behavior and decrease inappropriate behavior? (b) What teaching strategies, curricular adaptations, classroom management strategies, motivational techniques, social-skills and learning-strategy instruction, physical design modifications, and schoolwide and community-based services can be used to increase appropriate behavior and decrease inappropriate behavior? (c) Which of these changes are most likely to be effective, acceptable, easy to use, culturally sensitive, least intrusive, and beneficial to others and the learning environment? A sample behavioral intervention plan for Matthew is presented in Table 7.2 . Additional strategies for increasing appropriate behavior and decreasing inappropriate behavior and modifying the physical environment that Ms. McLeod can use are discussed later in this chapter.

Evaluate the Plan

Once the plan has been implemented, the team continues to collect data to examine how effectively the plan is influencing the student's behavior, learning, and socialization (Ryan, Halsey, & Matthews, 2003). Students from various cultural and language backgrounds also may respond differently to their teachers' behavior management strategies, so the team also needs to be aware of how the plan influences students' cultural perspectives (Ewing & Duhaney, 1996). The extent to which the plan was implemented as intended and the impact of the plan on the classroom environment and the student's peers, teachers, and family also should be assessed. Based on these data and feedback from others, the team revises the plan, changes the interventions, and collects additional data if necessary.

How Can I Promote Positive Classroom Behavior in Students?

Many supports and strategies to promote good classroom behavior exist. They include relationship-building strategies, social-skills instruction, antecedents-based interventions, consequences-based interventions, self-management techniques, group-oriented management systems, and behavior-reduction techniques. These methods are described below.

Relationship Building Strategies

Building meaningful and genuine relationships with and among your students is an essential aspect of creating a learning environment that supports their learning and promotes their positive classroom behavior (McAdams & Lambie, 2003; Schaps, 2003). You

Resource
Curtiss et al. (2002) and Buck et al. (2000) offer guidelines for developing behavioral intervention plans.

Resource
Murdick, Gartin, and Stockall (2003), Ryan, Halsey, and Matthews (2003), Shippen, Simpson and Crites (2003) and Conroy, Brown, and Davis (2001) offer guidelines for implementing functional behavioral assessments and behavioral intervention plans.

Reflective
Perform an FBA on one of your behaviors, such as studying or eating. How could you use the results to change your behavior?

Resource
Reid and Nelson (2002) and Heckaman, Conroy, Fox, and Chait (2000) summarize the research on functional behavioral assessment process.

Set Your Sites
For more on functional behavioral assessment and behavioral intervention plans, go to the Web Links module in Chapter 7 of the Companion Website.

Behavioral intervention plan for Matthew

TABLE 7.2

Goals	Interventions	Individuals	Evaluation
1. To decrease Matthew's call outs and extraneous comments.	1. Teach Matthew to use a self-management system that employs culturally appropriate reinforcers selected by Matthew.	1. Matthew • Teachers • Family members • School psychologist	1. Data on Matthew's call outs and extraneous comments. • Teachers, student, and family interview data.
2. To increase Matthew's work completion.	2. Relate the content of the instructional activity to Matthew's experiential background and interests. • Use cooperative learning groups. • Promote active student responding via response cards and group physical responses. • Provide Matthew with choices in terms of the content and process of the instructional activities. • Solicit feedback from students concerning the ways to demonstrate mastery. • Use culturally relevant materials. • Personalize instruction by using students' names, interests, and experiences. • Use suspense, games, technology, role-plays, and simulations. • Teach learning strategies.	2. Matthew • Teachers • Family members • Principal	2. Data on Matthew's work completion and accuracy. • Teacher, student, and family interview data.
3. To increase Matthew's in-seat behavior.	3. Use cooperative learning groups. • Use group-oriented response-cost system. • Establish a classwide peer-mediation system. • Place Matthew's desk near the teacher's work area.	3. Matthew • Teachers • Peers • Family members • School psychologist • Principal	3. Data on Matthew's in-seat behavior. • Teacher, student, and family interview data.
4. To increase Matthew's involvement in after-school activities.	4. Teach social skills. • Pair Matthew with peers who participate in after-school activities. • Invite community groups and school-based groups to talk to the class about their after-school activities. • Share and read in class materials about community and leisure activities. • Take field trips to community facilities and after-school activities in the community. • Work with school and community groups to increase the availability of after-school activities.	4. Matthew • Teachers • Peers • Family members • Community members • Counselor • Principal	4. Data on after-school activities attended by Matthew. • Teachers, student, family, counselor, and community member interview data.

can do this by collaborating and communicating with others (see chapter 4), fostering an acceptance of individual differences and friendships (see chapter 5), and employing cooperative learning (see chapter 9). You also can establish a classroom environment that is based on mutual respect and show your students that you are an open, caring, respectful, culturally sensitive, and honest person whom they can trust by using the strategies described here.

Reflective

What strategies did your teachers use to build relationships with you? What strategies do you use to build relationships with your students? What were the outcomes of these strategies?

Demonstrate a Personal Interest in Students

An essential aspect of building relationships with students is demonstrating a personal interest in them (Marzano & Marzano, 2003). To do this, you need to learn about what is important to them, which can be accomplished by interacting with them informally, observing them in various situations and settings, and using instructional activities to solicit information from them. You can ask students to write about their interests, hobbies, and extracurricular activities. You can then use this information to plan instructional activities, interact with them, and comment on important achievements and events in their lives. For example, you can include students' skills, achievements, and contributions in your instructional presentations and examples. You can also show your interest in students by attending extracurricular events, greeting them in the hallways, and welcoming them to your class.

Your personal interest in students also can be demonstrated by establishing and maintaining rapport with them. Rapport can be established by:

- listening actively.
- talking to students about topics that interest them.
- showing an interest in students' personal lives.
- sharing your own interests and stories.
- displaying empathy and giving emotional support.
- letting them perform activities in which they excel.
- greeting students by name.
- participating in after-school activities with them.
- recognizing special events in students' lives such as birthdays.
- displaying kindness.
- spending informal time with students.
- complimenting them (McAdams & Lambie, 2003; Owens & Dieker, 2003; Oxer & Klevit, 1995).

Develop Students' Self-Esteem

You can build relationships with students and establish a good learning environment by helping them develop their self-esteem. This can be done by providing students with opportunities to show their competence to others and to perform skills, roles, and jobs that are valued by others (Jones, 2002). You also can foster their self-esteem by listening to them and showing them that you value their ideas, opinions, interests, and skills by involving them in the decision-making process and giving them choices (Leachman & Victor, 2003). For example, you can periodically solicit students' preferences in selecting the order in which they complete a series of assignments; the location in the room where they would like to work; and the strategies, methods, materials, and breaks needed to complete assignments (Jolivette, Stichter, & McCormick, 2002). **To view an example of a teacher incorporating a student's contribution into the instructional process, go to Case 4: Support**

Set Your Sites

For more on self-esteem, go to the Web Links module in Chapter 7 of the Companion Website.

cd-rom

Participation on the CD-ROM and click on the Recognize Efforts video clip. How does recognizing students' efforts help create an environment that supports learning? Additional suggestions for promoting students' self-esteem are presented in chapter 6.

Use Humor

In addition to defusing difficult classroom situations, humor can help you and your students develop a good relationship and a positive classroom atmosphere (Allen, 2001; Richardson & Shupe, 2003). Your effective use of humor can help you put students at ease, gain their attention, and help them see you as a person. When using humor, make sure that it is not directed toward students as ridicule or sarcasm; is not misinterpreted; and is free of racial, ethnic, religious, sexual, and gender bias and connotations. You also need to be aware of events in the students' lives, your school, and the world when using humor appropriately and strategically.

Acknowledge and Praise Students

Acknowledging positive aspects of your students' behavior can promote self-esteem in students, and strengthen the bond between you and your students. Since negative responses to student behavior can escalate the misbehavior and limit interactions between students and teachers (Nelson & Roberts, 2000), it is recommended that you focus on positive aspects of student behavior (Bacon & Bloom, 2000; Hester, 2002).

Resource

Richardson and Shupe (2003) and Allen (2001) provide guidelines for using humor in the classroom.

One effective way of acknowledging students' strengths, skills, efforts, and interests is to praise them, which can create a positive environment in your classroom and encourage prosocial behavior (Hester, 2002; Sutherland, Wehby, & Yoder, 2002). You can follow several guidelines to make your praise more effective. Your praise statements should describe the specific behavior that is being praised (rather than saying, "This is a good paper," say,

---

IDEAS FOR IMPLEMENTATION

Promoting Students' Self-Esteem

Ms. Vang noticed that several of her students often made derogatory comments about themselves and seemed reluctant to volunteer and participate in classroom activities. Concerned about their attitude, Ms. Vang decided to develop some activities to help her students feel better about themselves and her classroom. To make students aware of their strengths, she posted their work on bulletin boards and acknowledged their contributions. She also set up a rotating system so that all students could act as classroom leaders.

Here are some other strategies you can use to create an inclusive and supportive classroom that promotes students' self-esteem:

- Build students' confidence by praising them, focusing on improvement, showing faith in their abilities, and acknowledging the difficulty of tasks.

- Give students learning activities that they can succeed at and enjoy.
- Relate mistakes to effort and learning and remind students of past successes.
- Encourage students to help each other and give them choices.
- Recognize and show appreciation for students' interests, hobbies, and cultural and language backgrounds.
- Make teaching personal by relating it to students' experiences.
- Use facial expressions and eye contact to show interest, concern, and warmth.

Note: Oxer & Klevit (1995); Tiedt & Tiedt (2002).

"You did a really good job of using topic sentences to begin your paragraphs in this paper") and should be tailored to the age, skill level, and cultural background of the students. It also is important to use praise to acknowledge effort as well as specific outcomes, and to individualize praise so that the students' achievements are evaluated in comparison with their own performance rather than the performance of others. You can increase the credibility of the praise by using diverse and spontaneous statements. Additional information and guidelines for using praise to acknowledge your students' academic performance are presented in chapter 9. **To view an example of a teacher using praise, go to Case 2: Classroom Climate on the CD-ROM and click on the Careful Reprimand video clip. What aspects of the teacher's use of praise made it effective?**

You also can acknowledge students by using *praise notes* (Mitchem, Young, & West, 2000). Praise notes are written statements that acknowledge what students did and why it was important. In addition to giving them to students, these notes can then be shared with others or posted in your classroom.

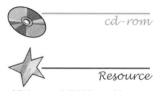

cd-rom

Resource

Mitchem et al. (2000) provide guidelines and resources for teaching students to acknowledge and praise their classmates.

Conduct Class Meetings and Use Dialoguing

Class meetings are designed to help students understand the perspectives of others, an essential ingredient of building relationships and resolving classroom-related conflicts (Bullock & Foegen, 2002). With you, students as a group can share their opinions and brainstorm solutions to classroom conflicts, class behavior problems, concerns about schoolwork, and general topics that concern students during *class meetings* (Jones & Jones, 2001; Leachman & Victor, 2003). You can promote discussion by presenting open-ended topics using *defining* questions (What does it mean to interrupt the class?), *personalizing* questions (How do you feel when someone interrupts the class?), and *creative thinking* questions (How can we stop others from interrupting the class?). In class discussions, all students have a right to share their opinions without being criticized by others, and only positive, constructive suggestions should be presented.

Classroom problems and tensions between students can be identified and handled by placing a box in the classroom where students and adults submit compliments and descriptions of problems and situations that made them feel upset, sad, annoyed, or angry (Bloom et al., 1999). Compliments and concerns can be shared with the class, and *all students* can brainstorm possible solutions to concerns.

Resource

Leachman and Victor (2003) offer guidelines for using student-led classroom meetings, and Bacon and Bloom (2000) offer suggestions for creating student advisory boards to solicit information from students.

You can also use dialoguing to build relationships with students and help them understand their behavior and work out alternatives to inappropriate behaviors. This process involves (a) meeting with students to discover their view of a situation or issue, (b) helping students identify the real issues and difficulties, (c) phrasing the issues in the students' words, (d) helping them to identify solutions to the issues and difficulties, and (e) discussing their solutions.

Be Aware of Nonverbal Communication

Your relationship with your students also will be affected by nonverbal communication, which includes physical distance and personal space, eye contact and facial expressions, and gestures and body movements. When nonverbal communication is not understood, the result can be miscommunication and conflicts between students and teachers. Therefore, your nonverbal messages should promote positive interactions, be consistent with students' behavioral expectations, and communicate attitudes.

Nonverbal behaviors also should be consistent with students' cultural backgrounds. For example, individuals from some cultures may feel comfortable standing close to persons they are talking to, while those from other cultures may view such closeness as

Building meaningful relationships with and among your students is an essential aspect of supporting their learning and promoting their positive classroom behavior. How do you establish meaningful relationships with your students?

Reflective

Observe several individuals with whom you deal regularly. How do they interact nonverbally with others? Are their nonverbal and verbal behaviors congruent? When these behaviors are incongruent, on which type of behavior do you rely?

Set Your Sites

For more information on nonverbal communication, go to the Web Links module in Chapter 7 of the Companion Website.

Resource

Bullock and Foegen (2002), Nelson, Martella, and Marchand-Martella (2002), and Daunic et al. (2000) provide guidelines for teaching conflict-resolution skills to students, and Johnson and Johnson (1996) developed a peer mediation and conflict-resolution program called the *Teaching Students to be Peacemakers Program.*

Set Your Sites

For more on conflict-resolution and peer-mediation programs, go to the Web Links module in Chapter 7 of the Companion Website.

a sign of aggressiveness. Physical gestures may also have different meanings in different cultures. For example, to some Southeast Asian groups, crossing the fingers to indicate good luck is viewed as obscene. Hand gestures are considered rude, as they are used with animals or to challenge others to a fight.

You should be sensitive to the nonverbal behaviors of your students and respond to them with congruent nonverbal and verbal messages. Examples of nonverbal and verbal messages that you can use to promote positive classroom behaviors are presented in Table 7.3.

Use Affective Education Techniques

Affective education strategies and programs help build relationships with and among students and assist them in understanding their feelings, attitudes, and values. These strategies and programs involve students in resolving conflicts. They also try to promote students' emotional, behavioral, and social development by increasing their self-esteem and their ability to express emotions effectively. Students who feel good about themselves and know how to express their feelings build positive relationships with others and tend not to have behavior problems.

Use Conflict Resolution and Peer Mediation Programs

Because conflicts often serve as a barrier to building relationships, classroom and school-related conflicts, particularly those based on age and cultural differences, can be handled through use of conflict resolution programs such as *peer mediation* (Bullock & Foegen, 2002). Peer mediation involves students trained to serve as peer mediators using communication, problem solving, and critical thinking to help students who have conflicts meet face to face to discuss and resolve disagreements (Daunic, Smith, Robinson, Miller, & Landry, 2000).

Social-Skills Instruction

An important component of an effective classroom management plan is social-skills instruction (Smith & Gilles, 2003). With social-skills teaching, students like Matthew can

TABLE 7.3

Congruency of verbal and nonverbal messages

	Approving/ Accepting	Disapproving/ Critical	Assertive/ Confident	Passive/ Indifferent
Verbal message	"I like what you are doing."	"I don't like what you are doing."	"I mean what I say."	"I don't care."
Physical distance	Sit or stand in close proximity to other person.	Distance self from other person; encroach uninvited into other's personal space.	Physically elevate self; move slowly into personal space of other person.	Distance self from other person.
Facial expressions	Engage in frequent eye contact; open eyes wide; raise brows; smile.	Engage in too much or too little eye contact; open eyes wide in fixed, frozen expression; squint or glare; turn corners of eyebrows down; purse or tightly close lips; frown; tighten jaw muscle.	Engage in prolonged, neutral eye contact; lift eyebrows; drop head and raise eyebrow.	Avert gaze; stare blankly; cast eyes down or let them wander; let eyes droop.
Body movements	Nod affirmatively; "open" posture; uncross arms/legs; place arms at sides; show palms; lean forward; lean head and trunk to one side; orient body toward other person; grasp or pat shoulder or arm; place hand to chest.	Shake head slowly; "close" posture; fold arms across chest; lean away from person; hold head/trunk straight; square shoulders; thrust chin out; use gestures of negation, e.g., finger shaking, hand held up like a stop signal.	Place hands on hips; lean forward; touch shoulder; tap on desk; drop hand on desk; join fingers at tips and make a steeple.	Lean away from other person; place head in palm of hand; fold hands behind back or upward in front; drum fingers on table; tap with feet; swing crossed leg or foot; sit with leg over chair.

Source: From "Do You See What I Mean?" by M. M. Banbury and C. R. Hebert, 1992, *Teaching Exceptional Children, 24*(2), p. 36. Copyright 1992 by The Council for Exceptional Children. Reprinted by permission.

discover how to learn and socialize with others. Social-skills instruction also can help students learn how to work in groups, make friends, recognize and respond appropriately to the feelings of others, resolve conflicts, understand their strengths, challenges and emotions, and deal with frustration and anger (Kolb & Hanley-Maxwell, 2003; Morris, 2002).

You can help students develop their social skills by clearly explaining the behavior, its importance, and when it should be used. You also can demonstrate, explain, role-play, and practice using the behavior, as well as provide students with numerous opportunities to use it in natural settings with peers (Lo, Loe, & Cartledge, 2002). Finally, you can provide feedback and use cues to promote use of the behavior in various settings. Presley and Hughes (2000) used peer modeling and role playing to teach students the social skills to express anger appropriately. Additional strategies and resources for teaching social skills are also presented in chapters 5 and 6.

You also can use social-skills programs. Williams and Reisberg (2003) and Elksnin and Elksnin (1998) provide a list of programs to teach social skills to students. You also can integrate social-skills instruction across your curriculum. You can do this by:

- embedding social skills into academic learning activities.
- using vignettes and videos that address social skills.
- having students maintain reflective journals of their social skills.
- helping students identify natural cues and consequences for prosocial behaviors.

Resource

Glaeser, Pierson, and Fritschmann (2003) offer guidelines for using comic-strip conversations to teach social skills.

Resource

Gut and Safran (2002), Forgan (2002), and Cartledge and Kiarie (2001) provide a listing of literature for children and adolescents addressing social skills, and Anderson (2000) offers a strategy for using literature to teach social skills to students.

- teaching students to use learning strategies that prompt them to engage in prosocial behaviors.
- employing cooperative learning arrangements (Herron & Barnes, 2001; Smith & Gilles, 2003; Williams and Reisberg, 2003).

You also can use literature that presents social skills (Cartledge & Kiarie, 2001). Students also can work in groups to read, discuss, and role-play the use of social skills in juvenile literature (Gut & Safran, 2002).

Antecedent-Based Interventions

Antecedent-based interventions are changes in classroom events and stimuli that precede behavior (Conroy & Stichter, 2003). They also include curricular and teaching accommodations (see chapters 8–11) and classroom design changes (discussed later in this chapter). Antecedent-based interventions will now be discussed.

Give Clear and Direct Directions

Your verbal communications with your students play an important role in helping them behave appropriately. Compliance with your requests can be fostered by speaking to students in a respectful, firm, and calm voice and manner. You also can phrase your commands to them so that they are:

- stated in positive terms and focus on what students should do rather than what they should not do.
- presented to students in an appropriate sequence when giving multiple commands.
- phrased directly rather than indirectly and tell students what to do rather than asking them to do something (Herschell, Greco, Filcheck, & McNeil, 2002).

Use Teacher Proximity and Movement

Your proximity and movement can promote good behavior (Taylor & Baker, 2002). This can be done by (a) standing near students who have behavior problems; (b) placing students' desks near you; (c) talking briefly with students while walking around the room; (d) delivering praise, reprimands, and consequences while standing close to students; and (e) monitoring your movement patterns to ensure that *all students* receive attention and interact with you (Gunter, Shores, Jack, Rasmussen, & Flowers, 1995). When using proximity, you should be aware of its effects on students. For example, Ewing and Duhaney (1996) noted that African American students may view it as lack of trust in students. **To view an example of a teacher using teacher proximity and movement, go to Case 2: Classroom Climate on the CD-ROM and click on the Careful Reprimand video clip. How did the teacher use proximity and movement to promote the students' positive behavior and learning?**

cd-rom

Use Cues

Cues can be used to promote good classroom behavior. For example, color cues can indicate acceptable noise levels in the classroom. Red can signal that the noise is too high, yellow that moderate noise is appropriate, and green that there are normal restrictions on the noise level.

Verbal and nonverbal cues such as physical gestures can be used to prompt group or individual responses (Marks et al., 2003; Taylor & Baker, 2002). These cues also can establish routines, or signal to students that their behavior is unacceptable and should be changed. For example, individualized eye contact, hand signals and head movements can be used to indicate affirmation, correction, or the need to refocus on appropriate behavior. When working with students from different cultural and language backgrounds, you should use culturally appropriate cues.

Resource

Chalmers, Olson, and Zurkowski (1999) offer guidelines for using music to foster positive classroom behavior.

Follow Routines

Since unexpected changes in classroom routines can cause students like Matthew to act out and respond in defiant ways, it is important to follow consistent and predictable routines and foster transitions from one activity to another. When students know what routines and activities to expect in the classroom each day, they are more likely to feel that they are in control of their environment, which can reduce instances of misbehavior in the classroom. **To view an example of following routines, go to Case 1: Difficult Behavior on the CD-ROM and click on the Structure Routines video clip. What purposes do routines serve for students and teachers?**

cd-rom

Consider Scheduling Alternatives

Establishing and maintaining a regular schedule is an important way to follow ongoing classroom routines. Good scheduling (see Figure 7.3) also can improve student learning and behavior (Downing & Peckham-Hardin, 2001; Hester, 2002). A regular schedule with ongoing classroom routines helps students understand the day's events. Since many students with disabilities also receive instruction and services from support personnel, you may need to coordinate their schedules with other professionals. Also, since these students may miss work and assignments while outside the room, you need to establish procedures for making up these assignments. Important factors in scheduling and ways to help your students learn the schedule are presented in Figure 7.3.

Resource

Downing and Eichinger (2003) and Downing and Peckham-Hardin (2001) offer guidelines for designing and using schedules with students with moderate and severe disabilities.

Resource

Santos and Rettig (1999) offer guidelines for meeting the needs of students with disabilities in schools that use block scheduling.

Help Students Make Transitions

Transitions from one period to the next, and from one activity to the next within a class period, are a significant part of the school day. These transitions can lead to behaviors that interfere with student learning. You can minimize problems with transitions by allowing students to practice making transitions and by making adaptations in the classroom routine (Marks et al., 2003; Buck, 1999). You can use verbal, musical, or physical cues to signal students that it is time to get ready for a new activity and that they need to complete their work (Gibson & Govendo, 1999). In addition, you can use pictorial cue cards that prompt students to (a) listen to directions, (b) put their materials away, and (c) get ready for the next activity. You also can reward groups or individual students for making an orderly and smooth transition, pair students to help each other finish an activity, and review several motivating aspects of the next activity.

Resource

Marks et al. (2003) offer examples of visual cues that can help students make classroom transitions.

Having clear expectations and giving students specific directions on moving to the next activity can help them make the transition (Hester, 2002). For example, rather than telling students, "Get ready for physical education class," you can say, "Finish working on your assignment, put all your materials away, and line up quietly." When students come from a less structured social activity like lunch or recess to a set-

Resource

Babkie and Provost (2002) offer mnemonic-based learning strategies for helping students make transitions in hallways and behave in school cafeterias.

FIGURE 7.3

Classroom scheduling guidelines

CONSIDER STUDENT CHARACTERISTICS AND CHALLENGES

◆ Consider students' physical, sensory, and cognitive abilities and chronological ages.

◆ Examine the objectives, activities, and priorities in students' IEPs.

◆ Adapt the schedule and the length of activities based on students' ages and attention spans.

◆ Involve students in planning the schedule for negotiable events such as free-time activities.

◆ Begin with a lesson or activity that is motivating and interesting to students.

◆ Plan activities so that less popular activities are followed by activities that students enjoy.

◆ Teach difficult material and concepts when students are most alert.

◆ Alternate movement and discussion activities with passive and quiet activities, and alternate small-group and large-group activities.

◆ Work with individual students during activities that require limited supervision.

◆ Give students breaks that allow them to move around and interact socially.

◆ Give students several alternatives when they complete an assigned activity early.

HELP STUDENTS LEARN THE SCHEDULE

◆ Post the schedule in a prominent location using an appropriate format for the students' ages.

◆ Review the schedule periodically with students.

◆ Record the schedule on loop tapes that automatically rewind and then repeat the same message.

◆ Avoid frequently changing the schedule.

◆ Share the schedule with families and other professionals.

Note: Keyser-Marcus et al. (2002); Murdick & Petch-Hogan (1996); Ruef, Higgins, Glaeser, & Patnode (1998).

ting that requires quiet and attention, a transitional activity is important. For example, following recess, have students write in a journal one thing that was discussed in class the previous day. This can help prepare them for the day's lesson and smooth the transition.

Establish, Teach, and Enforce Rules

To create an effective, efficient, and pleasant learning environment, it is important to establish, teach, and enforce culturally sensitive and developmentally appropriate classroom rules that promote your students' learning, socialization, and safety (Rosenberg & Jackman, 2003). It is desirable for students to be involved in developing the rules, as it communicates to students that they are also responsible for their actions. Students also are more likely to follow rules that they help create. Therefore, you can work with students to develop reasonable rules that address cooperative and productive learning behaviors, guide classroom interactions, and are acceptable both to them and to you. You can ask students what rules they think the class needs, present classroom problems and ask students to brainstorm solutions and rules to address these problems, or have students create a classroom constitution or mission statement (Bloom et al., 1999). Students also can help determine the consequences for following rules and the violations for breaking them. This process should have some flexibility based on students' individual differences and circumstances.

You can follow several guidelines to make the rules meaningful to students (Hardman & Smith, 1999). Phrase rules so that they are concise, stated in the students' language, easily understood, and usable in many situations and settings. Each rule should begin with an action verb. It should include a behavioral expectation that is defined in observable terms and the benefits of following the rule. When exceptions to rules exist, identify the exceptions and discuss them in advance. Similarly, when allowances need to be made for students, particularly those with disabilities in order to accommodate their unique needs and behaviors, the rationales for these allowances can be discussed and explained to the class.

Whenever possible, state rules in positive terms. For example, a rule for in-seat behavior can be stated as "Work at your desk" rather than "Don't get out of your seat." Rules also can be stated in terms of students' responsibilities such as "Show respect for yourself by doing your best." Rules also may be needed and phrased to help students respect *all students.* For example, you may want to introduce rules related to teasing and name-calling such as "Be polite, show respect for others, and treat others fairly."

It also is important that you help students learn the rules (Herron & Barnes, 2001; Hester, 2002). You can do this by describing and demonstrating the observable behaviors that make up the rules, giving examples of rule violations and behaviors related to the rules, and role-playing rule-following and rule-violating behaviors. You can also discuss the rationale for the rules, the contexts in which rules apply, and the benefits of each rule. At the beginning, you can review the rules frequently with the class, asking students periodically to recite them or practice one of them. It also is important to praise students for following the rules and to offer positive and corrective feedback to students who initially fail to comply so that they can succeed in the future. For example, when a student breaks a rule, you can state the rule, request compliance, and offer options for complying with it (Colvin, Ainge, & Nelson, 1997).

Posting the rules on a neat, colorful sign in an easy-to-see location in the room also can help students remember them. Some students with disabilities and younger students may have difficulty reading, so pictures representing the rules are often helpful. You also can personalize this method by taking and posting photographs of students acting out the rules, labeling the photos, and using them as prompts for appropriate behavior (Lazarus, 1998). Additionally, you can help students understand the rules and commit to following them by enforcing the rules immediately and consistently and by reminding students of the rules when a class member complies with them.

Consequence-Based Interventions

Consequence-based interventions are changes in the classroom events and stimuli that follow a behavior (Alberto & Troutman, 2003). Several consequence-based interventions will now be described.

Use Positive Reinforcement

A widely used, highly effective method for motivating students to engage in positive behaviors is *positive reinforcement.* With this method, a stimulus is given after a behavior occurs. The stimulus increases the rate of the behavior or makes it more likely that the behavior will occur again. Stimuli that increase the probability of a repeated behavior are called *positive reinforcers.* For example, you can use verbal and physical (e.g., smiling, signaling OK, thumbs up) praise as a positive reinforcer to increase a variety of classroom behaviors such as Matthew's on-task behavior.

When using positive reinforcement, you need to consider several things. First, it is critical to be consistent and make sure that reinforcers desired by students are delivered after the behavior occurs, especially when the behavior is being learned. As the student

Reflecting on Your Practices

Examining Rules

You can examine your classroom rules by considering the following:

- Are your rules necessary to prevent harm to others or their property?
- Do your rules promote the personal comfort of others?
- Do your rules promote learning?
- Do your rules encourage students to make friends?
- Do your rules address respectful behavior directed at peers, the teacher, the teacher's aide, or others in school?
- Are your rules logical and reasonable?
- How do your rules affect the class?
- Are your rules consistent with the school's rules and procedures?

- Do you involve your students in creating rules?
- Are your rules consistent with students' ages, maturity levels, cultural backgrounds, and learning and physical and behavioral needs?
- Do you have enough rules?
- Are your rules stated in positive terms and in language students can understand?
- Are your rules stated in observable terms?
- Are your consequences for following and not following the rules appropriate and fair?
- Are your rules easily enforceable?

How would you rate your rules? ( ) Excellent ( ) Good ( ) Need Improvement ( ) Need Much Improvement

What steps could you adopt to improve your classroom rules?

becomes successful, gradually deliver the reinforcement less often and less quickly and raise the standards that students must meet to receive reinforcement.

One type of positive reinforcement used by many classroom teachers is the *Premack Principle* (Premack, 1959). According to this principle, students can do something they like if they complete a less popular task first. For example, a student who works on an assignment for a while can earn an opportunity to work on the computer.

Classroom Lottery.   A positive reinforcement system that can promote good behavior is the *classroom lottery,* in which you write students' names on "lottery" tickets and place the tickets in a jar in full view of the class. At the end of the class or at various times during the day, you or a designated student draws names from the jar, and those selected receive reinforcement. The lottery system can be modified by having the class earn a group reward when the number of tickets accumulated exceeds a preestablished number.

Select Appropriate Reinforcers

Resource

Witzel and Mercer (2003) provide a summary of the research on the use of rewards including the arguments for and against use of rewards.

A key component of positive reinforcement is the reinforcers or rewards that students receive. You can use a variety of culturally relevant edible, tangible, activity, social, and group reinforcers. However, you should be careful in using reinforcers because they can have negative effects on student motivation and performance (Kohn, 2003; Witzel & Mercer, 2003). You can solve this problem by using reinforcers only when necessary, and carefully examining their impact on your students. You also can embed rewards in the activity, make rewards more subtle, use rewards equitably and for improved performance, combine rewards with praise, fade out the use of rewards, and encourage students to reinforce themselves via self-statements. Other guidelines for motivating students are presented in chapter 9.

Many food reinforcers have little nutritional value and can cause health problems, so you should work with family members and health professionals to evaluate them with respect to students' health needs and allergic reactions. Activity reinforcers, which allow students to perform an enjoyable task or activity, are highly motivating alternatives. One flexible activity reinforcer is free time. It can be varied to allow students to work alone, with a peer, or with adults.

Class jobs also can motivate students. At first, you may assign class jobs. When students perform these jobs well, they can be given jobs that require more responsibility.

Administer Reinforcement Surveys

Many behavior management systems fail because the reinforcers are not appropriate and effective. One way to solve this problem is to ask for students' preferences via a reinforcement survey (Alberto & Troutman, 2003).

Teachers typically use three formats for reinforcement surveys: open-ended, multiple-choice, and rank order. The *open-ended* format asks students to identify reinforcers by completing statements about their preferences ("If I could choose the game we will play the next time we go to recess, it would be . . ."). The *multiple-choice* format allows students to select one or more choices from a list of potential reinforcers ("If I had 15 minutes of free time in class, I'd like to (a) work on the computer, (b) play a game with a friend, or (c) listen to music on the headphones"). For the *rank order* format, students grade their preferences from strong to weak using a number system.

You can consider several factors when developing reinforcement surveys. Items can be phrased using student language rather than professional jargon (*reward* rather than *reinforcer*) and can reflect a range of reinforcement. In addition, the effectiveness ("Do students like the reinforcers and engage in the activities?"), availability ("Will I be able to give the reinforcer at the appropriate times?"), practicality ("Is the reinforcer consistent with the class and school rules?"), cultural relevance ("Is the reinforcer consistent with the students' cultural backgrounds?"), and cost ("Will the reinforcer prove too expensive to maintain?") of reinforcers on the survey can be examined. Finally, since students may have reading and/or writing difficulties, you may need to read items for students as well as record their responses.

Resource

Alberto and Troutman (2003) and Raschke (1981) provide examples of many types of reinforcement surveys, and Mason and Egel (1995) offer guidelines for using reinforcement surveys with students with developmental disabilities.

Use Contracting

You and your students may work together to develop a *contract,* a written agreement that outlines the behaviors and results of a specific behavior management system (Downing, 2002; Lassman et al., 1999). Contracts should give immediate and frequent reinforcement. They should be structured for success by calling at first for small changes in behavior. Both parties must consider the contract fair, and it must be stated in language that the students can read and understand.

A contract should be developed by you with your students. Family members and other professionals also can be involved in formulating the contract when they have specific roles in implementing it. Generally, contracts include the following elements:

- A statement of the specific behavior(s) the student is to increase/decrease in observable terms
- A statement of the environment in which the contract will be used
- A list of the types and amounts of reinforcers and who will provide them
- A schedule for the delivery of reinforcers

Resource

Downing (2002) provides sample contract forms and a contract planning worksheet.

- A list of the things the teacher and student(s) can do to increase the success of the system
- A time frame for the contract, including a date for renegotiation
- Signatures of the student(s) and teacher

Figure 7.4 presents an outline of a sample contract.

Self-Management Interventions

Resource

Johnson and Johnson (1999), King-Sears and Bonfils (2000) and McConnell (1999) developed guidelines for teaching students to use self-management strategies.

Resource

Firman, Beare, and Loyd (2002) and Levendoski and Cartledge (2000) provide examples of auditory and visual cues that can prompt students to use self-management strategies.

Self-management intervention strategies, also called *cognitive behavioral interventions,* actively involve students like Matthew in monitoring and changing their behaviors. Several of these strategies that have been used in many different inclusive settings are described here (Hutchinson, Murdock, Williamson, & Cronin, 2000; King-Sears, 1999). You may want to use combinations of these strategies. Students can be taught to use them by introducing the target behavior(s) and the self-management strategies and opportunities to practice and master them.

Self-Monitoring

In *self-monitoring,* often paired with *self-recording,* students measure their behaviors by using a data-collection system (Hughes et al., 2002b; Callahan & Rademacher, 1999). For example, Matthew can be taught to increase his on-task behavior during class by placing a 1 in a box when he pays attention for several minutes and a 2 if he does not. Matthew

---

FIGURE 7.4

Sample contract outline

This is a contract between _____ and
                                                    Student's or class's name

_____ . The contract starts on _____ and ends
Teacher's name

on _____ . We will renegotiate it on _____ .

During _____
                          Environmental conditions (times, classes, activities)

I (we) agree to _____ .
                                    Behavior student(s) will demonstrate

If I (we) do, I (we) will _____ .
                                        Reinforcer to be delivered

The teacher will help by _____ .

I (we) will help by _____ .

                                                            _____
                                                                         Teacher's Signature

                                                            _____
                                                              Student or Class Representative's Signature

                                                            _____
                                                                           Date

also can be given self-monitoring cards to prompt him to record his behavior. Sample self-recording systems are presented in Figure 7.5.

You can increase your students' ability to record their own behavior by using a *countoon*, a recording sheet with a picture of the behavior and space for students to record each occurrence (Daly and Ranalli, 2003). A countoon for in-seat behavior, for example, would include a drawing of a student sitting in a chair with a box under the chair for recording.

Self-Evaluation.   In *self-evaluation* or *self-assessment*, students are taught to evaluate their in-class behavior according to some standard or scale. For example, students like Matthew can rate their on-task and disruptive behavior using a 0 to 5 point (unacceptable to excellent) rating scale. Students then earn points, which they exchange for reinforcers, based on both their behavior and the accuracy of their rating.

You can use several strategies to assist your students in evaluating their behavior. Students can be given a listing of behaviors, which they can use to assess their behavior

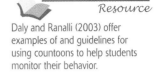

Resource

Daly and Ranalli (2003) offer examples of and guidelines for using countoons to help students monitor their behavior.

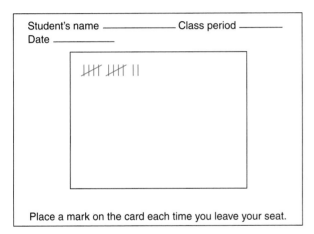

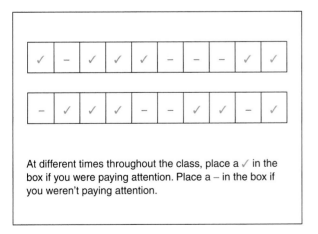

FIGURE 7.5   **Examples of self-recording systems**
Source: Adapted from M. Broden, R. V. Hall, and B. Mitts, 1971, *Journal of Applied Behavior Analysis, 4* (pp. 193, 496). Copyright 1971 by the Society for the Experimental Analysis of Behavior, Inc.

Students can use self-management strategies to monitor and change their behavior. How could you help your students use self-management?

(Hutchinson et al., 2000). For example, students like Matthew can be given a handout with the following behaviors:

- I raised my hand to answer questions.
- I paid attention to the teacher.
- I stayed in my seat.
- I began my work on time.
- I finished my work.

Students also can be asked to respond to a series of questions that prompt them to evaluate their behavior. For example, they can respond to the following:

- How would you describe your behavior in class today?
- What positive behaviors did you use? What happened as a result of these behaviors?
- Which of your behaviors were problems? Why were these behaviors a problem?
- What are some things you could do to continue to use positive behaviors? To improve your behavior?

Self-Reinforcement.   In *self-reinforcement*, students are taught to evaluate their behavior and then deliver self-selected rewards if appropriate. For example, after showing the correct behavior, students reinforce themselves by working for 15 minutes on the computer.

Self-Managed Free-Token Response-Cost.   One system that has been used successfully by students with disabilities in inclusive settings is a *student-managed free-*

token response-cost system. In this system, you give the student an index card with a certain number of symbols. The symbols represent the number of inappropriate behaviors the student may exhibit before losing the agreed-on reinforcement. After each inappropriate behavior, the student crosses out one of the symbols on the index card. If any symbols remain at the end of the class time, the student receives the agreed-on reinforcement.

Self-Instruction.   *Self-instruction* teaches students to regulate their behaviors by verbalizing to themselves the questions and responses necessary to (a) identify problems ("What am I being asked to do?"), (b) generate potential solutions ("What are the ways to do it?"), (c) evaluate solutions ("What is the best way?"), (d) use appropriate solutions ("Did I do it?"), and (e) determine if the solutions were effective ("Did it work?"). To help them do this, you can use *cueing cards,* index cards with pictures of the self-teaching steps for following directions ("stop, look, listen" and "think") that are placed on the students' desks to guide them (Swaggart, 1998).

Self-Managing Peer Interactions.   A self-management system that students can use to deal with the inappropriate behavior of their peers is 3-Steps (Schmid, 1998). When students are being bothered by peers, they use 3-Steps by (a) telling peers "Stop! I don't like that," (b) ignoring or walking away from peers if they do not stop, and (c) informing the teacher that they told them to stop, tried to ignore them, and are now seeking the teacher's help.

Reflective

Choose a behavior you would like to increase or decrease. Select one of the self-management strategies and keep track of your progress. Were you successful? If so, why? If not, why?

Group-Oriented Management Systems

Group influence can be used to promote good behavior and decrease misbehavior by using *group-oriented systems.* Group-oriented management systems have several advantages over traditional methods: They foster cooperation among members; they teach responsibility to the group and enlist the class in solving classroom problems; they are adaptable to a variety of behaviors and classrooms; and they give students a positive method of dealing with the problems of peers (Mitchem & Young, 2001).

You can increase the likelihood that group-oriented systems will be successful by:

- teaching students how the system works.
- clarifying the behavior so everyone understands it.
- setting reasonable goals and increasing them gradually.
- monitoring the system and providing students with ongoing feedback (Babyak, Luze, & Kamps, 2000).

When using group-oriented management systems, there are several possible problems. Because the success of these systems depends on the behavior of the whole group or class, a single disruptive individual can prevent the class from achieving its goals. If this happens, the offender can be removed and dealt with individually. Group-oriented management systems also can result in peer pressure and scapegoating, so you must carefully observe the impact of these systems on your students. You can attempt to minimize problems by establishing behavioral levels that *all students and groups* can achieve. You can choose target behaviors that benefit *all students,* allowing those who do not want to participate in a group to opt out. You also can use heterogeneous groups and limit the competition between groups so that groups compete against a criterion level rather than against other groups.

REFLECTING ON PROFESSIONAL PRACTICES

Using Self-Management Strategies

Kris is having difficulty completing assignments because she is frequently off task—leaving her seat, talking to classmates, playing with objects, and looking around the room. Kris's teacher, Mr. Bevier, is concerned about this behavior and decides that Kris could benefit from a strategy that increases her awareness of it. Mr. Bevier meets with Kris. They discuss her behavior and the use of a self-management strategy, which Kris agrees to try. Before starting, they meet again to discuss the system and the behavior. At first, they talk about the importance of Kris paying attention. Mr. Bevier explains that on-task behavior means eyes on the materials and/or on the teacher. Next, he demonstrates specific, observable examples of on-task and off-task behaviors, emphasizing the features of each. Afterward, he asks Kris to show examples and nonexamples of on-task behavior.

Mr. Bevier and Kris then discuss the self-management system and its benefit. Next, Mr. Bevier demonstrates the system for Kris and thinks out loud as he uses it, which prompts a discussion about the actual conditions in which the system will be used. Before using the system in class, they role-play it. Mr. Bevier assesses Kris's use of the system and gives her feedback.

Mr. Bevier and Kris meet again, and this time he asks her to complete a reinforcement survey. The survey includes the following completion items:

> The things I like to do at school are
> I am proudest in this class when I
> When I have free time in class, I like to
> The best reward the teacher could give me is
> Something that I would work hard for is

Mr. Bevier is surprised by Kris's responses. Rather than wanting tangible items, Kris states that she would prefer a class job and extra time to spend with the teacher or her friends. Mr. Bevier and Kris agree that if she succeeds in changing her behavior, she may choose a reward from among a class job, free time with a friend or Mr. Bevier, and the opportunity to work with a friend.

Next, they try the system in class. It involves placing on Kris's desk a 4- by 6-inch index card that contains 10 drawings of eyes. When Kris fails to engage in on-task behavior, she crosses out one of the eyes. If any eyes remain at the end of the class period, Kris can choose one of the activities they discussed. With this system, Kris is able to increase her on-task behavior, and Mr. Bevier notices that Kris is doing more assignments and completing them more accurately.

- Why did Mr. Bevier use a self-management system with Kris?
- What did he do to promote the success of the system? What steps did Mr. Bevier use to teach Kris to use the system?
- How could you use self-management strategies in your class? What benefits would they have for you and your students?

 To answer these questions online and share your responses with others, go to the Reflection module in Chapter 7 of the Companion Website.

Use Interdependent Group Systems

When several students in a class have a behavior problem, a good strategy is an *interdependent* group system. The system is applied to the entire group, and its success depends on the behavior of the group. Popular reinforcers for groups of students are free time, a class trip, a party for the class, time to play a group game, or a special privilege.

Group Free-Token Response-Cost System. One effective interdependent group system is a *group response-cost* system with free tokens (Salend & Allen, 1985). The group is given a certain number of tokens, which are placed in full view of the students and in easy reach of the teacher (such as paper strips on an easel or marks on the chalkboard). A token is removed each time a class member misbehaves. If any to-

A. Illustration of group
   response-cost system. The
   class is given free tokens
   (chalkboard 1), which are
   removed when a disruptive
   behavior occurs (chalkboard
   2). If any tokens remain at
   the end of the class, the
   group receives reinforcement
   (chalkboard 3).

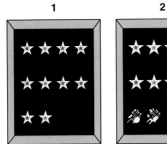

B. The Good Behavior Game

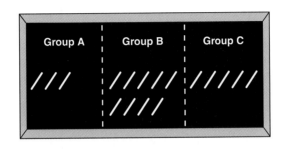

FIGURE 7.6 **Illustrations of group-oriented management strategies**
Source: From "Group Oriented Behavioral Contingencies," by S. J. Salend, 1987, *Teaching Exceptional Children, 20,* pp. 54.
Copyright 1987 by The Council for Exceptional Children. Reprinted with permission.

kens remain at the end of the time period, the agreed-on reinforcement is given to the whole group. As the group becomes successful, the number of tokens given can gradually be decreased. Adaptations of this system include allowing students to be responsible for removing the tokens (Salend & Lamb, 1986) and making each token worth a set amount. An illustration of the group response-cost system is presented in Figure 7.6a.

Good Behavior Game. The *Good Behavior Game* is an interdependent group system whereby the class is divided into two or more groups. Each group's inappropriate behaviors are recorded by a slash on the blackboard (see Figure 7.6b). If the total number of slashes is less than the number specified by the teacher, the groups earn special privileges.

You can modify the Good Behavior Game to account for different types and frequencies of misbehaviors. The system can be tailored to the students by having different groups work on different target behaviors and with different criterion levels. To minimize the competition between groups, each group can earn the reinforcement if the number of misbehaviors is less than the group's own frequency level. For example, one group may work on decreasing calling out and have a criterion level of 25, and another group may work on reducing cursing and have a criterion level of 8. Rather than competing, each group earns reinforcement if its number of slashes is less than its own criterion level. You also can modify the Good Behavior Game by giving groups merit cards for positive behaviors of the group or of individual members. These merit cards are then used to remove slashes that the group has previously earned (Tankersley, 1995).

Resource

Babyak, Luze, and Kamps (2000) provide guidelines for using the Good Behavior Game in inclusive settings.

Group Evaluation.   You also can use a variety of group-evaluation systems to promote good classroom behavior. Two examples are the group average group-evaluation system and the consensus-based interdependent group-evaluation system. In the *group average system,* you give an evaluation form to each student in the group and ask each student to rate the group's behavior. You then determine a group rating by computing an average of the students' ratings. You also rate the group's behavior using the same form, and the group rating is compared with your rating. The group earns points, which are exchanged for reinforcers, based on its behavior and accuracy in rating its behavior.

The *consensus-based system* consists of (a) dividing the class into teams and giving each team an evaluation form; (b) having each team use a consensus method for determining the team's ratings of the class's behavior; (c) having the teacher rate the class's behavior using the same evaluation form; (d) comparing each team's ratings with the teacher's rating; and (e) giving reinforcement to each team based on the behavior of the class and the team's accuracy in rating that behavior.

Group evaluation also can be adapted so that one student's evaluation of the behavior of the whole group determines the reinforcement for the whole class. In this system, you and your students rate the class's behavior using the same evaluation form. You then randomly select a student whose rating represents the class's rating. Your rating is compared with this student's rating, and the group receives reinforcement based on the class's behavior and the student's agreement with your rating.

Use Dependent Group Systems

In a *dependent group system,* a student's behavior problem is reinforced by his or her peers. In this system, the contingency is applied to the whole class, depending on the behavior of one member.

Use Independent Group Systems

In an *independent group system,* individual students are reinforced based on their own performance or behavior. Thus, reinforcement is available to each student, depending on that student's behavior.

Token Economy Systems.   One independent group system that works well in both general and special education classes is a *token economy system* (Cruz & Cullinan, 2001; Gunter, Coutinho, & Cade, 2002). Students earn tokens for showing appropriate behavior and can redeem these tokens for social, activity, tangible, and edible reinforcers. The steps of token economy systems are as follows:

> *Step 1. Collaborate with students and their families to determine the rules and behaviors that students must use to receive tokens.*
>
> *Step 2. Choose tokens that are safe, attractive, durable, inexpensive, easy to handle and dispense, and controllable by the teacher.* In selecting tokens, consider the age and cognitive abilities of students and the number of tokens needed per student.
>
> *Step 3. Identify the reinforcers that students want and determine how many tokens each item is worth.* You can establish a store where students may go to buy items with their tokens and allow students to work in the store on a rotating basis. Keep a record of what items students buy and stock the store with those items. Consider using an auction system in which students bid for available items.

Some teachers find that token systems are effective. Do you think a token system would be effective in your classroom?

Step 4. Collect other materials needed for the token economy system, such as a container for students to store their tokens and a chart to keep a tally of students' tokens. You also can establish a bank where students can store their tokens, earn interest when saving them for a period of time, and invest in stocks, commodity futures, certificates of deposit, and Treasury bills (Cook, 1999).

Step 5. Arrange the room for effective and efficient use of the system. For example, desks can be arranged so that you have easy access to all students when dispensing tokens.

Step 6. Introduce and explain the token system to students.

Step 7. Use the token system. At first, give large numbers of tokens to students by catching students behaving appropriately, and allow students to exchange their tokens for reinforcers on a regular basis to show that the tokens have real value. Pair the delivery of tokens with praise and tell the students exactly which appropriate behavior(s) was exhibited. Use a timer to remind you to dispense tokens.

Step 8. Determine how to handle incorrect behavior. You can use a timeout card, which is placed on students' desks for a brief period to indicate that no tokens can be earned. When students behave appropriately for a brief, specified time period, the timeout card is removed and students can earn tokens. Avoid taking away tokens when students do not have enough tokens.

Step 9. Revise the system to correct any problems. For example, if a student is suspected of stealing tokens from others, give the student tokens that are unique in shape or color.

Step 10. Begin to phase out the token system. You can do this by increasing the number of appropriate responses necessary to earn a token, increasing the number of tokens needed for a specific reinforcer, giving tokens on an intermittent schedule, using fewer verbal prompts, giving students fewer chances to exchange tokens for reinforcers, and using a graduated reinforcement system that moves toward the use of naturally occurring reinforcers.

Resource

Cruz and Cullinan (2001) provide guidelines for implementing a token economy system using levels.

Behavior Reduction Interventions

Teachers also are concerned about misbehavior and its impact on the learning environment and other students. There are many ways of decreasing misbehavior. In using one of these strategies, it is important to make sure that your response to student behavior doesn't escalate it (Shukla-Mehta & Albin, 2003). Therefore, when selecting a procedure, carefully consider the following questions:

Resource

Shukla-Mehta and Albin (2003) offer suggestions for preventing behavioral escalation in classrooms.

- Is the strategy aversive?
- Does it produce bad side effects?
- Is it effective?
- Does it allow me to teach another behavior to replace the undesirable one?

Another issue to consider is the *least restrictive alternative* principle, also referred to as the *least intrusive alternative*. Use this principle as a guide in selecting methods that reduce the problem behavior without limiting a student's freedom more than necessary and without being physically or psychologically unappealing. Several methods for decreasing misbehavior are presented here.

Use Redirection, Choice Statements, and Corrective Teaching

Redirection involves making comments or using behaviors designed to interrupt the misbehavior and prompt students to use appropriate behavior and work on the activity at hand (Colvin et al., 1997; Herschell et al., 2002). Redirection is most effective when it is done unobtrusively and early in the behavioral sequence. Typically, this involves removing the individuals, objects, or stimuli that appear to be causing the misbehavior, and stating clearly what you want students to do (Duckworth et al., 2001). Other redirection strategies include:

- introducing a new stimulus to recapture the student's attention.
- signaling the student verbally and nonverbally to stop a behavior.
- offering to help the student with a task.
- engaging the student in conversation.
- reminding the student to focus on the assignment.
- changing the activity or some aspect of it.
- giving the student a choice between good behavior and a minor punishment such as a loss of recess.
- modeling calm and controlled behavior, and using humor (Duckworth et al., 2001).

You also can redirect students by using *choice statements*, which prompt students to choose between engaging in positive behavior and accepting the consequences associated with continued misbehavior. Based on the age of your students and the nature of the behavior, you can use the following choice statements:

- When–then (When you _____, then you can _____)
- If–then (If you _____, then I will/you can _____)
- Either–or (Either you _____, or you will _____)
- Here are your choices (We need to _____, here are your choices:) (Herschell et al., 2002).

Corrective teaching is used to redirect and prompt students to behave well. Each time students misbehave, use corrective teaching by (a) approaching students individually with a positive or empathetic comment, (b) briefly describing the misbehavior, (c) briefly describing the desired behavior, (d) explaining why the desired behavior is important, (e) having students practice and role-play or repeat the steps in the desired behavior, and (f) delivering feedback, praise, or points (West et al., 1995). **To view examples of a teacher redirecting students, go to Case 1: Difficult Behavior on the CD-ROM and click on the Anticipate and Redirect, and Keystone Behaviors video clips. How does the teacher use anticipation and redirection to promote positive behavior?**

cd-rom

Employ Interspersed Requests

Interspersed requests, also known as *pretask requests* and *behavioral momentum,* can be used to decrease students' avoidance and challenging behaviors and to help students make transitions, and avoid a series of escalating misbehaviors (Maag, 2000). Interspersed requests motivate students to do a difficult or unpleasant task by first asking them to perform several easier tasks that they can complete successfully in a short period of time. You do this by asking students to do two to five easy tasks before giving them a task that they might resist or refuse to perform.

Use Positive Reductive Procedures/ Differential Reinforcement Techniques

In using *positive reductive procedures*, also called *differential reinforcement techniques,* you reinforce and increase a positive behavior that cannot coexist with the misbehavior that you want to decrease; this reduces the incidence of misbehavior (Hester, 2002). For example, to decrease Matthew's off-task behaviors, you could reinforce him when he is on-task.

Reflective

What are some behaviors that may serve as positive, incompatible alternatives to misbehaviors such as calling out, being off-task, being out of one's seat, and swearing?

Use Planned Ignoring

In *planned ignoring*, also called *extinction*, the positive reinforcers of a behavior are withheld or ended. When this happens, the behavior decreases. For example, Matthew's teachers might be inadvertently maintaining his habit of calling out by reminding him to raise his hand and by responding to his off-task comments. Rather than giving him attention through these reminders, you could decrease the behavior by ignoring his calling out.

Planned ignoring takes time to be effective and often initially increases the rate and/or intensity of misbehavior (Herschell et al., 2002). Therefore, you should use it only for behaviors that can be changed gradually and when you can identify and withhold all reinforcers that are maintaining these behaviors. You can speed up the effectiveness of planned ignoring by combining it with reinforcement of appropriate alternative behaviors. Planned ignoring should not be used for behaviors maintained by reinforcers that cannot be withdrawn, such as peer attention. Finally, planned ignoring might increase aggressive behavior.

Consider Careful Reprimands

Occasionally, you may need to use reprimands to deal with misbehavior. You can make these reprimands more effective by using them carefully and infrequently, by making them brief, firm, and matter-of-fact, and by delivering them immediately after the misbehavior occurs and in close contact to the student. Reprimands should be specific statements that direct students to engage in an appropriate alternative behavior ("Stop now, and do your work.") rather than questions ("Why aren't you doing your work?"). You also should combine reprimands with nonverbal behaviors such as eye contact, and avoid the use of sarcasm and judgmental language, which can harm students' self-esteem and cause

cd-rom

negative comments from peers. **To view an example of a teacher using a reprimand, go to Case 2: Classroom Climate on the CD-ROM and click on the Careful Reprimand video clip. What aspects of the reprimand made it effective?**

Rather than use a public verbal reprimand, you can speak to students privately about behavior problems. In these meetings, you can briefly and succinctly tell them what you think, ask probing questions such as, "Are you having problems with the assignment?", and discuss a plan for acting appropriately (Johns & Carr, 1995).

How Can I Prevent Students from Harming Others?

As reflections of society, schools, unfortunately, are dealing with a growing number of incidents where students are harming each other. Therefore, your school will need to establish schoolwide programs and strategies for situations that involve bullying and other violent acts (Heinrichs, 2003). You also can work with students and their families and professionals to create a safe, caring school environment that does not tolerate bullying, harassment, or violent acts and that fosters and acknowledges acceptance of individual differences and the development of friendships (see chapter 5).

Students Who Are Bullies

You may need to deal with bullying or peer harassment in your classroom or school (Olweus, 2003). Bullying reflects a power imbalance in social relationships that results in repeated instances of peer harassment that cause harm (Chamberlain, 2003b). Bullying and peer harassment may take different forms:

- *Verbal and written:* name-calling, taunting, and negative and threatening comments, phone calls, or e-mails
- *Physical:* hitting; pushing; scratching; unwanted sexual touching; damaging personal property; extorting money; and gestures that imply disapproval, intimidation, or derogatory comments
- *Social:* spreading false rumors, excluding from a group, or sharing personal information
- *Sexual:* sexually harassing and/or abusing others, and engaging in exhibitionism or voyeurism (McNamara, 1996; Trautman, 2003)

Male bullies are more likely to engage in physical bullying, while female students are more likely to bully by exclusion, manipulation of friendships, and other forms of social bullying (Chamberlain, 2003b; Olweus, 2003). While all students may be targeted by bullies, as Table 7.4 suggests, some students are particularly likely to be victimized by bullies, including students with disabilities and other individual differences.

You can collaborate with students, families, professionals, and other interested parties to develop, implement, and evaluate your school's bullying prevention program (Garbarino & deLara, 2003). Such a program should provide information to educators and families about the warning signs that a student is being bullied, which may include:

- an avoidance of school.
- a sudden decrease in academic performance.

Possible characteristics of bullies and their targets

TABLE 7.4

Passive targets	Provocative targets	Bullies
Physically weaker than peers	Physically weaker than peers	Physically stronger than peers (especially their targets)
"Body anxiety"	Typically boys	Physically effective in play, sports, and fights
Physically ineffective in play, sports, and fights	"Body anxiety"	Aggressive
Lack physical coordination	Negative view of themselves	"Want their own way"
Cautious	Unhappy	Brag
Quiet, withdrawn, or passive	Anxious	Hot-tempered
Easily upset, emotional	Insecure	Impulsive
Anxious	Hot-tempered	Easily frustrated
Insecure	Lack focus	Oppositional
Poor self-esteem	Attempt to fight or talk back when bullied but ineffective	Defiant
Viewed as "easy targets"	Hyperactive, restless	Good at talking themselves out of difficult situations
Difficulty asserting themselves	Viewed as offensive and rude	Show little empathy for targets
Don't tease, not aggressive	"High-mainteneance"	Not typically anxious or insecure
Relate better to adults than peers	Clumsy	Better than average self-esteem
Poor to good academic performance	Immature	Average to above average popularity
	Irritating habits	Average to above average academic performance
	Highly disliked by peers	Both popularity and school performance tend to decline in middle and high school
	Disliked by some adults, including teachers	
	May bully weaker students	

Source: From "A Whole-School Approach to Bullying: Special Considerations for Children with Exceptionalities," by R. R. Heinrichs, 2003, *Intervention in School and Clinic, 38,* pp. 195–204. Copyright 2003 by PRO-ED, Inc. Reprinted with permission.

- an increase in being late to class without a pausible explanation.
- a difficulty sleeping and frequent nightmares.
- a nervousness around specific class/school mates.
- a withdrawal from others.
- a reluctance to try new things (Sheras & Tippins, 2002).

Educators and families also should receive information to help them identify bullies (Heinrichs, 2003). As Table 7.4 also indicates, bullies tend to be physically stronger and more aggressive, impulsive, and defiant than their classmates.

The school's bullying prevention program also should help students, professionals, and family members understand their roles and responsibilities in addressing peer harassment, and provide them with preventive and proactive strategies and policies to deal with bullying (Mishna, 2003). Bullying prevention strategies and policies include:

- conducting a survey to determine the nature and extent of bullying problems.
- establishing school rules that prevent bullying, such as students in this school will not bully others, will treat everyone with respect, and will help others who are bullied; and consequences when these rules are not followed.
- using a confidential message box that allows students to report incidents of bullying.
- holding meetings with students to discuss bullying incidents.

- identifying locations where bullying is most likely to occur and increasing supervision of those places.
- modeling respectful behaviors toward others.
- creating a school environment that does not tolerate bullying by forming friendship groups and having students make No Bullying Zone posters.
- confronting and disciplining bullies quickly and firmly by addressing their inappropriate behavior and using the situation as an opportunity to teach prosocial behaviors (e.g., "What you did to Juan was wrong, mean, and hurtful." "I don't know where you learned that type of behavior, but we don't act that way in this school." "Is there anything you wish to say to me?" and "What are we going to do to make sure it doesn't happen again?")
- addressing victims of bullying by being supportive, refuting the actions of bullies, and informing them that you will take action to address the situation (e.g., "I'm sorry that John did that to you. He was wrong and it was not fair to you. I don't know where he learned that but I am going to talk with him about this").
- referring bullies and their victims for counseling and other appropriate services.
- fostering communication among and between teachers and families (Heinrichs, 2003; Kinnell, 2003; Migliore, 2003).

You also can prevent bullying by offering social-skills instruction to your students (Heinrichs, 2003). For bullies, you can help them develop empathy for others and teach them self-management and anger-management skills. You also can have them engage in acts that benefit and show respect for others. For example, students who have used bullying can be asked to apologize and do something nice for their victims, clean up part of the school, reflect on how harassment makes their victims feel, or keep a journal of their acts of kindness (Garrity, Jens, Porter, Sager, & Short-Camilli, 1997). Victims of bullying need to learn how to understand social cues to avoid being a victim and to respond in an assertive way that does not make the situation worse (Migliore, 2003). They must also understand when and how to get help from adults. Students who are neither bullies nor victims need to learn how to actively support victims and how to counteract bullies and their harassing acts.

Students with Aggressive and Violent Behaviors

As we have seen in our nation's schools, all segments of society and all parts of the country are encountering violence. By being aware of the warning signs, you may be able to prevent aggressive violence from occurring. The early warning signs include social withdrawal, feelings of isolation, persecution or rejection, low motivation, poor school performance, anger, frequent discipline problems, fights with others, intolerance of individual differences, substance abuse, and membership in gangs (Dwyer, Osher, & Hoffman, 2000). While the signs vary, some of the common indicators of an escalating situation are verbal abuse (e.g., cursing and threats), shouting, body tenseness, destruction of property, self-injurious actions, threatening verbal statements and physical gestures, and possession of weapons.

If you encounter a violent incident, you should attempt to follow the school policies for dealing with such situations. These policies often include assessing the situation, evacuating the classroom as soon as possible, getting help, and trying to defuse the situation. Some strategies that you use to defuse a crisis include the following:

- Remain calm and controlled.
- Allow the student to vent anger and feelings verbally.

Resource

Rigby (2002), Olweus, Limber, and Mihalic (1999), Stein and Cappello (1999), Beane (1999), Mullin-Rindler, Froschl, Sprung, Stein, and Gropper (1998), and Garrity et al. (1997) offer bullying prevention curriculum guides that can be used with elementary- and secondary-level students.

Reflective

Does your school have policies for dealing with bullying, intolerant behaviors, and derogatory language? What procedures and practices are addressed in the policy? How effective is the policy?

Set Your Sites

For more information on bullying, go to the Web Links module in Chapter 7 of the Companion Website.

Resource

Yell and Rozalski (2000) offer a review of legal issues in the prevention of school violence and Ehlenberger (2002) offers information on the right to search students.

Resource

Kellner, Bry, and Colleti (2002) provide guidelines for teaching anger-management skills to students, and Williams and Reisberg (2003) offer CALM, a mnemonic-based learning strategy that prompts students to manage their anger.

- Ignore irrelevant comments and have the student focus on the relevant issues.
- Listen to the student without interrupting or denying the student's feelings.
- Use the student's name, and speak in a clear, moderate voice and in a slow, empathetic manner.
- Establish limits that clearly and concisely inform the student of the choices and consequences.
- Maintain a positive body posture, with the hands open and in view and eye contact without staring.
- Consider the cultural and experiential background of the student.
- Remain close to the student while respecting the student's personal space.
- Persuade the student to leave the room.
- Ask the student to carefully lay down any weapon carried.

After the incident, you may need to continue to calm the student down, give support, send for medical assistance (if necessary), notify administrators and/or the police, file a report, counsel students, contact family members, and seek counseling.

How Can I Adapt the Classroom Design to Accommodate Students' Learning, Social, and Physical Needs?

The design of the classroom environment can complement your teaching style and help students learn, behave well, and develop social skills. You can affirm students and the value of education by creating an aesthetically pleasing, cheerful, and inviting classroom that is clean, well-lit, odor free, colorful, and respectful of your students' unique identities and needs. Your classroom can also be designed to ensure student safety if you check to make sure that electrical wires are anchored and covered, dangerous materials and equipment are locked in cabinets, sharp edges and broken furniture are removed, and walls, floors, and equipment are in good condition. **To view an example of effective use of classroom space, go to Case 1: Difficult Behavior on the CD-ROM and click on the Materials and Space video clip. How does the design of this classroom foster learning, positive behavior, friendships, and independence?**

Seating Arrangements

Generally, students are seated in areas that allow them to see clearly all presentations and displays. These locations also allow you to see and reach your students. When small-group teacher-directed instruction is used, students can be seated in a semicircle facing you. In a larger-group teacher-directed activity, it may be better for *all students* to face you sitting in a row, circular, or horseshoe arrangement. When students work in groups, they can arrange their desks so that they face each other, allowing them to share information efficiently and quietly. You also can encourage students to personalize their work area.

Each student's desk should be of the right size and should be placed so as to include the student in all classroom activities and maintain good posture and body alignment. The space around students' desks should be large enough to give you easy access to students in order to monitor performance and distribute papers. Students also need a place to store their materials. If students' desks are not large enough, tote trays can be used to store their supplies.

Bender and McLaughlin (1997), Webber (1997), Walker and Gresham (1997), and Embry (1997) offer suggestions and resources for making schools safer and dealing with violence, including preventing violence and managing weapons violations and hostage situations.

Resource

Bender, Shubert, and McLaughlin (2001) and Sprague and Walker (2000) offer characteristics of students who may commit violent acts and strategies for identifying these behaviors in students.

Resource

Meese (1997) offers strategies for preventing and reacting to student fights.

Resource

Murdick, Gartin, and Yalowitz (1995) offer teachers precrisis, crisis, and postcrisis guidelines for dealing with violent behaviors.

cd-rom

Teacher's Desk

The location of your desk allows you to monitor behavior and progress and to move quickly if a problem occurs (Carbone, 2001). For monitoring students, your desk can be placed in an area that provides a view of the whole classroom. Any obstacles that prevent you from scanning different parts of the room can be removed. When you are working with students in other parts of the room, you can sit facing the other students in the class.

Bulletin Boards and Walls

Bulletin boards can help you create a pleasant, attractive environment that promotes learning and class pride. *Decorative* bulletin boards make the room attractive and interesting and often relate to a theme. *Motivational* bulletin boards encourage students by showing progress and publicly displaying their work. *Instructional* bulletin boards, or *teaching walls,* often include an acquisition wall, which introduces new concepts and material, and a maintenance wall, which reviews previously learned concepts. *Manipulative* bulletin boards use materials that students can manipulate to learn new skills.

Displays should be planned so that they are at the students' eye level. Whenever possible, involve students in decorating areas of the room so that the walls and ceiling of the classroom colorful and attractive.

You also can include a space for displaying student assignments, as well as pictures, posters, and art forms that reflect the students' families, homes, neighborhoods, and other cultural groups that may not be represented in the classroom. Posting the daily assignment schedule and examples of products on part of the bulletin board or wall can help students remember to perform all assigned tasks. Wall displays can include a clock, a list of class rules, and calendar large enough to be seen from all parts of the classroom.

Posting students' work can make the classroom more attractive and can motivate students. How do your students feel when you post their work?

IDEAS FOR IMPLEMENTATION

Using Learning Centers

Ms. Carty's classroom has four centers, and groups of students rotate among them every 30 minutes. As the students work at the different centers, Ms. Carty circulates around the room to monitor the groups and offer help and directions.

At the reading center, six students are making puppets and writing dialogue for a puppet show they are going to present to the whole class on a story they have been reading. At the measurement center, students are learning about centimeters and inches by measuring the length of each other's arms, legs, fingers, and bodies. Students then record their findings, compare their measurements, and write word problems based on their measurements. At the art center, students are creating murals that show the different characteristics of the students in their group. When students complete their murals, Ms. Carty plans to place them on a bulletin board in the hallway outside the room.

Here are some other strategies you can use to create learning centers:

- Teach students how to use the centers independently and how to work in small groups. Explain the appropriate times for using the centers and the number of students that each center can accommodate.
- Use a variety of centers that allow students to explore new skills and practice those they have learned. *Skill centers* let students practice skills such as math facts, spelling words, alphabetizing, and defining vocabulary. *Discovery/enrichment centers* use many different learning activities (science experiments, math applications) that require students to increase their knowledge. A *listening center* offers instruction or recreation through listening. Arts and crafts, music, creative writing, and poetry are often the focus of activities in a *creativity center.*
- Include activities at each center geared to a range of student academic levels, interests, and needs.
- Develop and organize materials in the center so that students can work on them independently and can easily locate, select, and return them.
- Consider the equipment and furniture needs of students with physical and sensory disabilities when creating learning centers.
- Make self-correction an integral part of centers. For example, you can include a checkout center, where students can check their assignments or have their work checked by others. Typically, checkout centers include answer keys, audiocassettes of correct answers, and reference materials to help students check and revise their work and that of others.
- Observe how students work and socialize in learning centers, evaluate their products, and change materials and activities as they master new skills.

Learning Centers and Specialized Areas

Learning centers provide variety in the classroom and help you individualize instruction (Stephens & Jairrels, 2003). They also can help students develop independent and problem-solving skills and learn to work collaboratively. You also may want to establish special areas of the room for specific functions.

Classroom Design Adaptations

Many students, especially those with disabilities, need specific classroom design modifications in order to perform as well as possible. Guidelines for physical adaptations of general education classrooms are outlined here. (Also see chapter 2 for further discussion of the educational needs of these students.)

Students from Diverse Cultural and Language Backgrounds

You can arrange the classroom environment to help second language learners learn English by making language part of all classroom routines. For instance, you can label work

Set Your Sites

For more on designing safe, accessible, comfortable, and developmentally and culturally appropriate school, classroom, and playground spaces, go to the Web Links module in Chapter 7 of the Companion Website.

areas and objects in the classroom. You also can give students access to materials and learning activities, set up social and work areas, listening areas, and meeting areas, and allow students to sit and work with peer models.

Students with Hearing Impairments

Classroom design adaptations should help students with hearing impairments gain information from teachers and interact with peers (Kaderavek & Pakulski, 2002; Williams & Finnegan, 2003). To make it easier to use lip reading and residual hearing, the desks of students with hearing impairments can be placed in a central location, about two rows from the front, where students can see the teacher's and other students' lips. Hearing and lip reading also can be fostered by having the students sit in swivel chairs on casters. This makes it easy for them to move and to follow conversations. If students with hearing impairments cannot see the speaker's lips, they can be allowed to change their seats. During teacher-directed activities, these students can be seated near the teacher and to one side of the room, where they have a direct line of sight to the lips of peers and teachers. A staggered seating arrangement also can help students have a direct view of speakers (Dodd-Murphy & Mamlin, 2002). A semicircular seating arrangement can promote lip reading during small-group instruction, and it is recommended that you position yourself in front of the student when delivering one-on-one instruction.

Lighting and noise levels should also be considered in setting up work areas for students with hearing impairments (Kaderavek & Pakulski, 2002). Glaring light can hinder lip reading; therefore, the source of information should not be in a poorly lighted area or one where the light is behind the speaker. Structural noises such as those of heating and cooling units; furniture movements; and external airborne noises, such as cars or construction outside the school, can be reduced by using carpets and acoustic tiles on the floor, drapes on windows, and sound-absorbent room dividers. Also, classes containing students with hearing impairments can be placed in rooms in quiet locations and away from noise centers such as gymnasiums, cafeterias, and busy hallways and corridors. The acoustical environment and the noise level in the classroom also can be improved by placing fabrics on desks and tables, cork protectors on the edges of desks to reduce the sounds of desks closing, rubber tips on the ends of the legs of chairs and desks, and absorbent materials on the walls (Dodd-Murphy & Mamlin, 2002).

Students with hearing impairments may benefit from sitting next to an alert and competent peer who can help them follow along during verbal conversations by indicating changes in the speaker (Dodd-Murphy & Mamlin, 2002). A peer also can be assigned to give these students information conveyed on the intercom system. Peers also can be responsible for helping students with hearing impairments react to fire drills (flashing lights for fire alarms also can be located throughout the school). However, as students with hearing impairments adjust to the general education classroom, the help they receive from peers should be phased out if possible.

Students with Visual Impairments

Several classroom design adaptations can help students with visual impairments function successfully in inclusive settings (Cox & Dykes, 2001; Griffin et al., 2002). You can encourage them to use their residual vision by providing a glare-free and well-lighted work area, and having adjustable lighting. You also can reduce problems associated with glare by painting mild colors on walls, using a gray-green chalkboard, placing translucent shades on windows, installing furniture and equipment with matte finishes, and posi-

Set Your Sites

For more information on acoustics in educational settings, go to the Web Links module in Chapter 7 of the Companion Website.

Set Your Sites

For more information on amplification systems, go to the Web Links module in Chapter 7 of the Companion Website.

Supporting Student Learning and Behavior

Many classrooms contain background noises from the street, the hallways, and the ventilation and lighting systems. These background noises can interfere with student learning and behavior, especially for students with learning, attention, and hearing difficulties (Anderson, 2001). While you can improve the acoustics in your classroom by adding carpets and drapes, you also can use technology such as sound-field amplification systems (DiSarno, Schowalter, & Grassa, 2002; Dodd-Murphy & Mamlin, 2002). Without having to raise your voice, sound-field amplification systems use FM and wireless technology to increase the sound of your voice and focus student attention on verbal information. They serve to decrease the distance between you and your students and lessen the background noises that prevent students from hearing you.

There are two types of sound-field amplification systems: sound-field and personal FM (Pakulski & Kaderavek, 2002). In both systems, you wear a small and lightweight, wireless microphone, which allows you to move around the classroom. In the sound-amplification system, your speech is amplified for all of your students via a loudspeaker installed in your classroom. In the personal FM system, selected students wear headphones with a receiver that allows them to hear you more clearly.

While these systems improve the performance of *all* students who use them, you need to remember to turn off the systems when you are directing comments to specific students or other professionals. You also should be aware that sound-field systems have several advantages over personal FM systems (DiSarno, Schowalter, & Grassa, 2002). They are less costly and are used by all students. Because individual students do not have to wear headsets, there is no stigma associated with their use.

Here are some other ways you can use technology to create inclusive classroom environments that support student learning and behavior:

- Allow students to earn opportunities to use technology by demonstrating appropriate behavior (Fabiano & Pelham, 2003).
- Use an electronic system to provide students with feedback on their behavior (Condon & Tobin, 2001). For example, Condon and Tobin increased

students' prosocial behaviors by using an electronic digit-display device, which was activated remotely by a teacher to provide feedback on behavior.
- Use handheld computers or personal digital assistants to record and graph observations of student behavior and to send text messages to students about their behavior (Bauer & Ulrich, 2002).
- Teach students to use software packages to record, graph, store, access, and reflect on data regarding their learning and behavior (Gunter, Miller, Venn, Thomas, & House, 2002).
- Foster students' use of self-management techniques by teaching them to use personal digital assistants and auditory-based technology systems to visually and auditorially prompt them to demonstrate, self-record, self-evaluate, and self-reinforce their prosocial behaviors (Bauer & Ulrich, 2002; Post, Storey & Karabin, 2002).
- Use computer-based activity schedules, which employ combinations of pictures, graphics, symbols, words, sounds, and voices to help students make transitions from one scheduled activity to another (Kimball, Kinney, Taylor, & Stromer, 2003).
- Use virtual reality to help students develop their wheelchair driving and mobility skills. For example, the Oregon Research Initiative (*www.ori.org/~vr/projects/vrmobility.html*) has developed an online program that students can log onto to practice their wheelchair mobility in various environments.
- Provide students with visual impairments with illuminated magnifiers that allow them to coordinate the distance from the light source to the text, and the magnification of the print, and specially designed high-wattage, low-glare light bulbs (Griffin, Williams, Davis, & Engleman, 2002).
- Incorporate the principles of universal design by having motion sensors, automatic buttons, keypad entry, and voice recognition to activate doors, lights, lockers, elevators, sinks, and toilets; using keypad entry of finger print; and installing Braille and audible buttons in important school locations, and on signs, maps, and elevators (Pivik, McComas, & Laflamme, 2002).

tioning desks so that the light comes over the shoulder of the student's nondominant hand. During teacher-directed activities, the student should not have to look directly into the light to see the teacher. To reduce the fatigue associated with bending over, desks should have adjustable tops.

The work area for students with visual impairments should offer an unobstructed view of instructional activities, and a direct trail to the major parts of the room (Voltz, Brazil, & Ford, 2001). When these students first come to your classroom, they can be taught how to move around the room and from their desk to the major classroom locations. These students can be taught to navigate the classroom and the school by using *trace trailing*, directing them to the routes between their desks and major classroom and school landmarks by having them touch the surfaces of objects on the path (Tolla, 2000). Visual descriptions of the room and routes can supplement trace trailing and help students develop a mental picture of the room. When the room is rearranged, provide time so that these students can learn to adjust to the new arrangement. Students with visual disabilities also may benefit from tactile symbols and signs in Braille placed in important locations in the classroom.

These students' work areas should be in a quiet place, away from potentially harmful objects such as hot radiators, half-open doors, and paper cutters. Pathways throughout the room should be free of objects, and all students should be reminded not to leave things in pathways (Cox & Dykes, 2001). To help all students compensate for their visual impairment by increased attention to verbal information, they should be seated where they can hear others well. Masking-tape markers on the floor can help students with visual impairments keep their desks properly aligned. Since students with visual impairments may need prosthetic devices and optical aids, you also should consider providing them with a sufficient, convenient, safe space to store this equipment. For example, a music stand or drafting table can be placed next to the students' work areas to reduce the problems of using large-print books.

Resources

Cox and Dykes (2001) offer a checklist for developing an orientation and mobility program for students with visual impairments.

Students with Health and Physical Disabilities

Students with health and physical disabilities may encounter a variety of environmental barriers that limit their access to inclusive settings (Pivik, McComas, & Laflamme, 2002). These barriers include doors, hallways, stairs, steep or unusable ramps, and inaccessible bathrooms, lockers, water fountains, recreation areas, and elevators. You can help students avoid these barriers by placing signs around your school to direct individuals to the most accessible routes to important locations in your school (Shapiro, 1999).

Resource

Pivik, McComas, and Laflamme (2002) offer suggestions from students with physical disabilities that could be implemented to foster their physical access to schools.

Students who use wheelchairs or prostheses will need aisles and doorways at least 32 inches wide so that they can maneuver easily and safely in the classroom (Voltz, Brazil, & Ford, 2001). If possible, arrange desks and classroom furniture with aisles that can accommodate crutches and canes, and have turning space for wheelchairs. Some students may also need space to recline during the school day.

For students who use wheelchairs, the floor coverings in the classroom are important. Floors should have a nonslip surface; deep pile, shag, or sculptured rugs can limit mobility. Floors should be covered with tightly looped, commercial-grade carpet smooth enough to allow wheelchairs to move easily and strong enough to withstand frequent use. To keep the rug from fraying or rippling, tape it down from wall to wall without placing padding underneath it.

Ergonomic furniture that is rounded, with padding on the edges and with no protrusions, is appropriate for many students with physical disabilities. Work areas should be at least 28 inches high to allow students who use wheelchairs to get close to them.

Because the reach of students who use wheelchairs is restricted, work tables should not be wider than 42 inches. For comfortable seating, chairs can be curvilinear, have seat heights at least 16 inches above the ground, and be strong enough to support students who wish to pull up on and out of the chairs. Work areas for students with physical disabilities can include space for computers or other adaptive devices that they may need.

Although students with physical disabilities should have the same type of furniture as their peers, some students may need specialized chairs to help them sit independently and maintain an upright position (Best & Bigge, 2001). For example some students may need corner chairs, floor sitters, or chairs with arm and foot rests (Best, Bigge, & Reed, 2001). The chairs of some students also may be adapted by inserting foam, towels, wood, and cushions or installing shoulder and chest straps. Some students also may use special chairs with abductors or adductors to support them in aligning their legs.

Students with physical disabilities also may need the height and slant of their work areas to be adjusted to accommodate their needs and wheelchairs or prostheses (Best, Bigge, & Reed, 2001). Therefore, you may want to request that your classroom include desks with adjustable-slant boards and adjustable-height work stations. Some students may need stand-up desks; others may use a desk top or lap board placed on their wheelchairs. These desks can have a cork surface to hold students' work with push pins.

Since students with physical disabilities will have to work at the chalkboard, at least one chalkboard in the classroom can be lowered to 24 inches from the floor. To help students work at the chalkboard, attach a sturdy vertical bar as a handrail, and provide them with a sit/stand stool.

Teachers must understand the importance of body positioning and know how to reposition students and move and transfer students who use wheelchairs (Best, Bigge, & Reed, 2001). To prevent pressure sores and help students maintain proper positioning, their position should be changed every 20 to 30 minutes. Posting photographs and descriptions of suggested positions for students with physical disabilities can remind you and others to use the right positioning and transferring techniques. Equipment such as side-lying frames, walkers, crawling assists, floor sitters, chair inserts, straps, standing aids, and beanbag chairs also can help students maintain or change positions.

Several classroom adaptations can help students whose movements are limited. Buddies can be assigned to bring assignments and materials to the students' desks. Boxes or containers can be attached to students' work areas to provide them with access to and storage for their work materials. You can allow these students to leave class early to get to their next class and avoid the rush in the hallway. Securing papers by taping them to the students' desks, and using clipboards or metal cookie sheets and magnets, can help with writing assignments. Similarly, connecting writing utensils to strings taped to students' desks can help students retrieve them when dropped. Desks with textured surfaces or with a barrier around the edge also can help prevent papers, books, and writing utensils from falling. Built-up utensils, velcro fasteners, cut-out cups, switches, and non-slip placemats can be used for students with physical disabilities.

Resource

Best, Bigge, and Reed (2001) offer suggestions and equipment that can help students access objects and materials.

Resource

Best, Bigge, and Reed (2001), Best and Bigge (2001) and Kolar (1996) offers suggestions to help teachers to meet the seating, positioning, and transferring needs of students with physical disabilities and to select seating, standing, positioning and wheeled mobility aids.

Students with Behavior and Attention Disorders

You can organize your classroom to support the positive behavior of students with behavior and attention disorders (Carbone, 2001; Garrick Duhaney, 2003). Since it is easier for you to observe students, monitor performance, and deliver cues and nonverbal feedback when students are sitting nearby, you may want to locate the work areas of stu-

IDEAS FOR IMPLEMENTATION

Transferring Students Who Use Wheelchairs

When Ms. Wade felt a twinge in her back as she helped transfer Mickey from his wheelchair to his seat, she knew she had to talk with Mr. Roman, the occupational therapist. When she caught up with Mr. Roman, he smiled and said, "Welcome to the club. Luckily, there are some things that you can do so that you won't hurt your back. Before you move Mickey, loosen up so that your muscles are ready to be exerted, tell Mickey what is going to happen, and encourage him to help you in the transfer. Then, approach him directly so that you can square up, lift him with your legs, not your back, and keep your back straight. Try to maintain a smooth, steady movement and a wide base of support by placing one foot in front of the other and getting as close as possible to Mickey. As you move, take short steps and avoid becoming twisted when changing directions." The next time Ms. Wade saw Mr. Roman, she thanked him and said, "It's a piece of cake."

Here are some other strategies you can use when transferring students who use wheelchairs:

- Wear comfortable footwear that minimizes the likelihood of slipping.
- Encourage students who are able to bear some weight by standing to wear slip-resistant footwear and sturdy belts.
- Use walls or sturdy objects to assist in maintaining balance.
- Ask for assistance from others when necessary as it is easier for two people to transfer students who are difficult to lift.
- Consult with a physical or occupational therapist (Best and Bigge, 2001).

dents with behavior and attention disorders near you (Marks et al., 2003). Placing these students near good peer models can also help them learn the right classroom behaviors. To make peer models more effective, you can praise them.

You also can give students personalized spaces in the classroom and examine the movement patterns in the classroom when determining the work areas for students with behavior and attention disorders. Avoid putting the desks of these students in parts of the room that have a lot of activity or visually loaded areas of the room (Voltz, Brazil, & Ford, 2001). You also can decrease visual distractions by placing a cloth over them when they are not important for learning (Evans, Tickle, Toppel, & Nichols, 1997), and decrease auditory distractions by giving students earplugs (Marks et al., 2003).

Some teachers use a study carrel for students with attention problems. However, study carrels should not be used often because they may isolate or stigmatize these students. You can reduce the potential problems of study carrels by discussing how individuals learn and function best in different ways, allowing *all students* to use the study carrel, referring to it in a positive way, and using it for several purposes, such as a relaxation area and a computer or media center.

Resource

Garrick Duhaney (2003) and Carbone (2001) offer guidelines for designing learning environments that foster the positive behaviors of students with behavior and attention disorders.

Summary

This chapter offered guidelines for helping students learn in inclusive classrooms by promoting good classroom behavior and modifying the classroom design for various types of students. As you review the chapter, consider the following questions and remember the following points.

How Can I Collaborate with Others to Conduct a Functional Behavioral Assessment?

CEC 1, 2, 3, 5, 6, 7, 8, 9, 10, PRAXIS 3, INTASC 8, 9, 10

An FBA involves collaborating with others to identify and define the problem behavior, record the behavior using an observational recording system, obtain more information about the student and the behavior, perform an A-B-C analysis, analyze the data and develop hypothesis statements, consider sociocultural factors, and develop and evaluate a behavioral intervention plan.

How Can I Promote Positive Classroom Behavior in Students?

CEC 1, 2, 3, 4, 5, 6, 9, PRAXIS 3, INTASC 5, 6, 9

You can use relationship-building strategies, social-skills instruction, antecedents-based interventions, consequences-based interventions, self-management techniques, group-oriented management systems, and behavior-reduction techniques.

How Can I Prevent Students from Harming Others?

CEC 5, 9, PRAXIS 3, INTASC 9

You can work with students and their families and professionals to create a safe, caring school environment that does not tolerate bullying, harassment, or violence of any kind. This collaboration should also foster and acknowledge acceptance of individual differences and the development of friendships. You should be aware of the warning signs of violence and of the steps to take when violence occurs.

How Can I Adapt the Classroom Design to Accommodate Students' Learning, Social, and Physical Needs?

CEC 2, 3, 5, 9, PRAXIS 3, INTASC 5, 9

You can consider such factors as seating arrangements; positioning the teacher's desk; designing bulletin boards, walls, specialized areas, and learning centers; and using classroom design adaptations.

What Would You Do in Today's Diverse Classroom?

It is 2 months into the semester and one of your students, Victor, is misbehaving. During teaching activities, he often calls out answers without your permission, talks to other students, and makes inappropriate comments. When this happens, you reprimand Victor and remind him to raise his hand. He rarely completes his assignments, and several of your students have complained that he bothers them.

1. How would you assess Victor's behavior and the environmental events that seem to be associated with it?

2. What environmental factors might be antecedents and consequences of Victor's behavior?

3. What should be the goals of Victor's behavioral intervention plan?

4. What antecedents- and consequence-based strategies, curricular accommodations and physical design changes could be included in Victor's behavioral intervention plan?

5. What knowledge, skills, dispositions, resources, and supports do you need to implement Victor's behavioral intervention plan?

6. How would you evaluate the effectiveness of Victor's behavioral intervention plan?

It is August, and your principal has given you the list for your class. Your class of 23 students will include 1 student with a hearing disability, 1 student with a visual disability, 3 students with learning disabilities, 1 student with a behavior disorder, and 2 students who are learning English. Sketch a classroom plan including seating arrangements, the teacher's and students' desks, teaching materials, bulletin boards and walls, specialized areas, and learning centers.

1. What factors did you consider in designing your classroom?

2. How does the design relate to your educational philosophy and teaching style?

3. How has it been adapted for students with disabilities and students from diverse cultural and language backgrounds?

4. What knowledge, skills, dispositions, resources, and supports do you need to design and implement your classroom?

To answer these questions online and share your responses with others, go to the Reflection module in chapter 7 of the Companion Website.

Part III

Differentiating Instruction for All Students

Part 3 of the book, which includes chapters 8, 9, 10 and 11, is designed to help you vary your teaching to promote the learning of *all students* by accommodating their individual strengths and challenges in inclusive classrooms. It offers information, strategies, and resources to help *all learners* access and succeed in the general education curriculum.

Chapter 8 introduces the concept of differentiating instruction for *all students*, as well as how to use a variety of curricular and instructional accommodations and instructional technology and assistive devices for this purpose. Chapter 9 provides strategies for fostering learning when using large- and small-group instruction for *all students,* including how to use the principles of effective teaching and cooperative learning. Chapter 10 offers guidelines for teaching and differentiating instruction so that you can help *all students* learn to read, write, and spell. Chapter 11 presents ways to vary content area instruction to help *all students* learn by providing guidelines for differentiating mathematics, science, and social studies instruction.

Chapter 8

Differentiating Instruction for Diverse Learners

Julia and Tom

In addition to several students with learning disabilities, Ms. Taravella's inclusion class included Julia, a student with a visual disability, and Tom, a student with significant cognitive disabilities. To assist Ms. Taravella in teaching her students, her teaching team included Ms. Stoudamire, a special education teacher, and Mr. Howry, a paraeducator. Ms. Steckler, a vision specialist, also was available periodically to help the team teach Julia.

As part of the districtwide curriculum related to the study of the solar system, the class was working on a unit about the sun, the moon, and the planets. Before implementing the unit, Ms. Taravella and her teaching team collaborated to plan it. They began by discussing the essential information they wanted their students to learn and agreeing on their curricular goals. They consulted assessment information and IEPs, and determined individualized goals for their students. Whereas all of their students' curricular goals were aligned to the districtwide curriculum, Tom's goals also reflected several of the functional goals in his IEP. Because of their prior knowledge and level of mastery, the goals for Julia and several other students were enhanced to include learning about the derivation and meaning of the planets' names.

The team then used these curricular goals to create a menu of student products that varied in both difficulty and learning style to assess student mastery. The activities included creating a new planet; making visual displays and dioramas; giving oral or PowerPoint presentations; writing papers highlighting the unique characteristics of the sun, the moon, or a planet; and acting out a story about life on the sun, the moon, or a planet. The team then outlined their learning activities and the teaching strategies, student groupings, and resources they needed to use to support the participation and learning of their students.

Ms. Taravella and Ms. Stoudamire led the students in performing a variety of individualized large- and small-group learning activities. The teachers used a series of DVDs on the solar system to show colorful and animated video segments of the sun, the moon, and the different planets. Occasionally, they repeated segments or paused the presentation to highlight different features. Ms. Steckler obtained a wireless headphone system that was linked to the DVD player so that Julia could hear a running description of the visual material being presented. To help students identify, organize, and remember the important points of the DVD presentation, the teachers led the class in creating a graphic organizer comparing the planets.

The team also implemented instructional accommodations and arrangements for the students, including Julia and Tom, which were consistent with their IEPs. To support the learning of Julia and several of her classmates, the teachers and their colleagues paired visually presented information with tactile/kinesthetic- and auditory-

based learning activities. They gave these students opportunities to learn by using hands-on replicas of the sun, the moon, and the different planets. Ms. Steckler used the photocopier to prepare enlarged handouts for Julia and collaborated with Mr. Howry to create charts of the sun, the moon, and the planets with string so that Julia and her classmates could access visual information through tactile experiences.

Ms. Taravella and Ms. Stoudamire used many of the same materials in different ways to support Tom's learning. While Ms. Taravella worked with students classifying and comparing the planets, Tom worked with Ms. Stoudamire sorting replicas of the planets by size and color. Tom also used the tactile planet chart to compare the sizes of the planets and to count the number of planets. Under the guidance of Ms. Taravella, Tom, Julia, and their classmates who have difficulty accessing text used digital teaching materials to have text highlighted, defined, enlarged, or read aloud by the computer. These materials also allowed the students to record their responses by typing text, drawing, speaking, or entering words from a list.

The educators also created a WebQuest designed to guide the students in learning about the early study of and beliefs about the solar system by cultures around the world. Students worked in collaborative groups to access web-based information related to early explorations of the sun, the moon, and the planets and the different cultural meanings regarding them. They learned about the different early observatories that had been set up throughout the world, and the various tools that the early astronomers used to observe and calculate the movements in the solar system. They also learned how different calendars and rituals were established based on these movement patterns. The groups then shared their findings with their classmates and others by postings on the class's website.

After completing the unit of instruction, the students chose a strategy for sharing their learning from the list of activities that the teachers had created. To make sure that students selected appropriate activities, Ms. Taravella and Ms. Stoudamire focused their choices. They also kept a record of students' choices and encouraged them to try new activities. Julia and Tom chose to work with several other students to create a Web page about Saturn. Julia volunteered to design and create the web page, and Tom worked with Mr. Howry to draw pictures and reproduce pictures of Saturn, which were then added to the group's web page via use of a digital camera. The group's web page and the other products students completed were then posted on the class's website.

What other accommodations could Ms. Taravella and Ms. Stoudamire and their colleagues use to differentiate instruction for Julia, Tom, and the other students? After reading this chapter, you have the knowledge, skills, and dispositions to answer this as well as the following questions:

★ **How can I differentiate instruction for students?**
★ **How can I differentiate instruction for students who have difficulty reading and gaining information from print materials?**
★ **How can I differentiate instruction for students from diverse cultural and language backgrounds?**
★ **How can I use instructional technology and assistive devices to differentiate instruction for students?**

Julia, Tom, and the other students were successful learners because Ms. Taravella and her colleagues used a variety of curricular and teaching accommodations to differentiate instruction for their students. To accommodate the diverse learners in their classrooms, educators differentiate:

- *content* (what they teach).
- *process* (how they teach).
- *product* (how students demonstrate content mastery).
- *affect* (how students connect their thinking and feelings).
- *learning environment* (how the classroom is designed and what instructional groupings they use) (Tomlinson & Eidson, 2003).

They use varied curricula and instructional arrangements, strategies, resources, materials, and technology to address the individual learning strengths and challenges, preferences, and styles of their students, as well as their developmental levels, interests, and experiential, cultural, and language backgrounds. Educators also teach students to respect each other (see chapter 5), use appropriate learning strategies (see chapter 6), and use varied assessment techniques (see chapter 12) and classroom management strategies (see chapter 7) to evaluate and support student learning. This chapter describes proven accommodations for differentiating instruction to address the many unique learning strengths and challenges of students. While these accommodations can be used to help various types of students learn, they also can be used to differentiate instruction for *all students*. For example, while Ms. Taravella and her colleagues used instructional accommodations to differentiate instruction for Julia and Tom, they also used them to ensure the learning of *all* of their students.

How Can I Differentiate Instruction for Students?

Like Ms. Taravella and Ms. Stoudamire, you can engage in a variety of professional practices to differentiate instruction for your students so that they can succeed in the general education curriculum (see Figure 8.1). These practices are discussed in the following sections and in other chapters of this book. In reflecting on their use, consider their potential impact; prior effectiveness; and the skills, resources, support, and time requirements you need to implement them.

Tailor Curricular Goals and Teaching Strategies to Your Students and Your Learning Environment

As we saw in the chapter-opening vignette, the types of curricular goals and teaching strategies used to differentiate your instruction should be tailored to your students and your learning environment (Wolfe & Hall, 2003). Therefore, you need to consider your students' strengths and challenges and the variables you control in your classroom (Tomlinson, 2003). In planning lessons and units of instruction that are tailored to your students and your classroom, you and your colleagues can consider the following issues:

- What are the themes, goals, and objectives of the lesson/activity?
- What teaching materials and arrangements will be used in the lesson/activity?
- When, where, and how long will this lesson/activity occur?

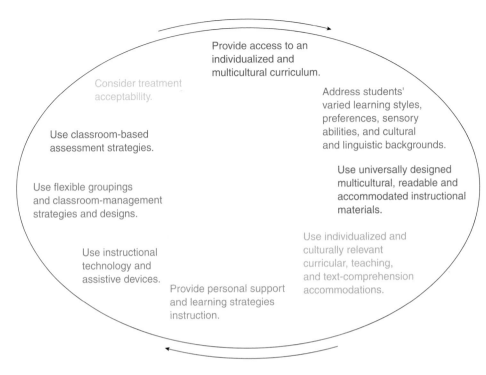

FIGURE 8.1   Differentiated instruction practices

- Will students be able to participate in this lesson/activity in the same ways as their classmates?
- What supports, learning strategies, instructional accommodations and/or instructional technology/assistive devices are needed to help students participate fully?
- How can the curriculum be supplemented or changed to address the different learning needs of students?
- How can the lesson/activity be differentiated to reflect students' learning styles, language, culture, experiences, behavioral needs, interests, talents, strengths, challenges, and IEPs?
- How can the lesson/activity be differentiated in terms of the type and amount of work, teaching materials used, grouping patterns, assistance needed, pace and time, and the products produced?
- Can the student participate in the activity but work on other skills or work with others on an activity that has different goals?
- How can the lesson/activity be differentiated to motivate and engage students and provide them with choices?
- What materials will be needed to engage students in the lesson/activity?
- How can the classroom environment be differentiated to engage students in the lesson/activity?
- How can student mastery of the content of the lesson/activity be assessed?

Resource

Wolfe and Hall (2003), Hunt, Soto, Maier, and Doering (2003), and Wehmeyer, Lance, and Bashinski (2002) offer models for designing curricular supports for students with developmental disabilities.

Individualize and Personalize Your Curriculum

An initial step in differentiating instruction is individualizing your curriculum by identifying the concepts, principles and skills you want to teach (Ford, Davern, & Schnorr, 2001; Watson & Houtz, 2002). While most students will not require accommodations in curricular goals, the curriculum for other students may need to be personalized by supplementing or changing it to address their different learning strengths, challenges, and styles. You can individualize your curricular goals by adding or reducing the material and skills to be learned, varying the levels of difficulty of the content addressed, and having students demonstrate their mastery in different ways (Jitendra, Edwards, Choutka, & Treadway, 2002). You also can personalize it by making it more multicultural, which we will discuss later in this chapter.

In addition to aligning your curricular goals to national, statewide, and district standards, your goals also should be linked to big ideas, essential questions, and critical learning outcomes (Seif, 2004). You also can personalize your curricular goals by making sure they are meaningful, appropriate, challenging, interdisciplinary, and culturally relevant for *all* your students (Voltz, 2003). Your curricular goals for students who have IEPs or 504 accommodation plans also should be consistent with these documents and individualized so that they are provided with the skills they need to access the general education curriculum (see chapter 2). For example, based on his IEP, Tom was provided with a developmentally appropriate, community-based curriculum designed to teach him in natural settings the functional and academic skills he needs to be more independent and socialize and succeed in inclusive settings. Many of your students also will benefit from curricular goals that focus on teaching them to use learning strategies (See chapter 6 and the learning strategies discussed throughout this book).

Resource

Walsh (2001), Ford, Davern, and Schnorr (2001), Matlock, Fielder, and Walsh (2001), and Seif (2004) offer guidelines and formats for aligning curriculum standards, IEPs, and teaching strategies.

Curriculum goals for your students also should relate to your assessment of their existing levels of mastery. Therefore, at the beginning of a lesson or unit of instruction you can use a variety of classroom-based assessment techniques to assess your students' prior knowledge and various levels of mastery (see chapter 12 for information about classroom-based assessment techniques). This assessment information, combined with your examination of your curriculum, can help you individualize your curricular goals for your students by determining the following:

- What levels of content mastery and skills do my students have?
- What content and skills do I expect *all* my students to learn?
- What content and skills do I expect *most* of my students to learn?
- What content and skills do I expect *some* students to learn? (Lenz, Bulgren, Kissam, and Taymans, 2004).

Use Curricular Accommodations

Once the curricular goals are individualized, curricular accommodations can be used to help a diverse group of students access and master them (Ford, Davern, & Schnorr, 2001). Some individualized curricular accommodations that you may consider include:

- giving students choices about what they learn and how they learn it.
- collaborating with students to create learning contracts that specify learning goals, activities, and products.
- altering the pace of instruction.
- enhancing the multicultural aspects of the content.
- designing alternative projects to allow students to demonstrate mastery.
- focusing on fewer objectives.
- modifying students' requirements and assessments.

Resource

Jitendra et al. (2002) offer a collaborative approach to planning content area instruction to help students access the general education curriculum.

Your lessons and curricular areas can be differentiated for academically diverse students by using accommodations such as *multilevel teaching, curriculum overlapping*, and *tiered assignments* (Villa & Thousand, 2003). In *multilevel teaching*, students are given lessons in the same curricular areas as their peers but at varying levels of difficulty

(Downing & Eichinger, 2003). For example, while other students were classifying and comparing the planets, Tom was sorting replicas of the planets by size and color. Similarly, because of her advanced level of mastery, Julia's instructional program was supplemented so that she was learning about the derivation and meaning of the planets' names.

Collicott (1991) described a four-step process for designing multilevel lessons:

Step 1. Identify the underlying concepts. Identify and examine the objectives and materials of the lesson, and determine the content and skill level differences.

Step 2. Consider the various possible teaching methods. Consider the different learning styles, and the cognitive and participation levels of students, as well as the different modes that can be used to present the lesson.

Step 3. Consider the ways in which students practice and perform. Consider the different ways students can practice and show mastery of skills and concepts. In addition, teach students to accept different modes for demonstrating skill mastery and understanding of concepts.

Step 4. Consider methods of evaluation. Consider a variety of ways to assess students' mastery.

Curriculum overlapping involves teaching a diverse group of students individualized skills from different curricular areas (Fisher & Frey, 2001). In this method, teaching of a practical, functional, specific skill related to the student's academic program is embedded in learning activities across the curriculum. For example, when the class was working on science, Tom also worked on counting the planets.

Tiered assignments allow you to tailor assignments to meet the needs of individual students. In this method, you identify concepts that need to be learned and allow students to respond in alternative ways that differ in complexity and learning style. For example, at the end of the unit, Ms. Taravella and Ms. Stoudamire gave their students a menu of choices about how they could demonstrate their learning. They also made sure that students selected appropriate activities, and tried new activities. **To view examples of a teacher using tiered assignments, go to Case 2: Classroom Climate on the CD-ROM and click on the Increasing Interests and Clear Expectations video clips. What do the students' comments and choices reveal about the impact of tiered assignments on their learning?**

Use Universally Designed Curriculum and Teaching Materials

An essential aspect of differentiating instruction for your students is the use of *universal design for learning*, which refers to designing flexible curriculum and teaching materials and activities so that they can be easily used to promote the learning of *all* (Scott, McGuire, & Shaw, 2003). While universal design originated in the field of architecture, its principles (see Figure 8.2) have been applied to educational settings to provide *all learners* with opportunities to access and succeed in the general education curriculum (Hitchcock, Meyer, Rose, & Jackson, 2002).

You can individualize your lessons and activities by using curriculum and teaching materials that incorporate *universal design for learning (UDL)* (Wehmeyer, Lance, & Bashinski, 2002). UDL allows you to tailor your curriculum and teaching materials to optimize learning for students who have a wide range of ability levels. This provides you with ways to individualize them based on students' learning styles and cognitive, physical, sensory, motivational, cultural, and language needs. Universally designed curriculum and teaching materials offer options that allow learners to receive and respond to infor-

cd-rom

Reflective

Think about a lesson you recently taught or are planning to teach. How did/could you use multilevel teaching to adapt the lesson to the needs of a student with a significant disability? A student with a mild disability? A student who is gifted and talented? A second language learner?

FIGURE 8.2

Principles of universal design

Principle 1: Equitable Use: Curriculum and teaching materials are designed so that they are useful, appealing, and safe for *all* to use. They are respectful of individual differences and are used by *all* learners in similar or equivalent ways and in different contexts.

Principle 2: Flexible Use: Curriculum and teaching materials are designed so that they accommodate individual preferences and abilities. They are flexible in terms of providing choices about the methods and pace of use.

Principle 3: Simple and Intuitive Use: Curriculum and teaching materials are designed so that they are easy for *all* to use. Their use is not dependent on one's experience, prior knowledge, language and literacy skills, or other learning preferences or abilities.

Principle 4: Perceptible Information: Curriculum and teaching materials are designed so that they communicate essential information to *all*. They present critical information to *all* using multiple formats (e.g., graphic, verbal, tactile), backgrounds with sufficient contrasts, legible text guidelines, and compatible teaching techniques and assistive technology devices.

Principle 5: Tolerance for Error: Curriculum and teaching materials are designed to minimize errors, adverse consequences, and unintentional actions. They provide safeguards and warnings to assist *all* in using them safely and efficiently.

Principle 6: Low Physical Effort: Curriculum and teaching materials are designed to be used comfortably and without much physical effort by *all*. They allow all to use them with a range of reasonable physical actions and do not require repetitive actions or sustained physical effort.

Principle 7: Size and Space for Approach and Use: Curriculum and teaching materials are designed for use by *all* regardless of one's body size, posture, and mobility. They allow all users to see, reach, and activate important features and information and offer sufficient space for assistive technology devices and personal assistance.

Note: Center for Universal Design (1997); Thompson, Johnstone, & Thurlow (2002).

mation of varying levels of difficulty in a variety of formats. Directions, content, and learning activities are clearly presented in multiple formats and learners choose the appropriate formats that fit their learning styles and preferences. Assessment, motivation, prompting, and feedback are available throughout the learning experience.

One example of UDL that Ms. Taravella and her colleagues used involved providing their students with digitally presented, interactive teaching activities (Pisha & Coyne, 2001). Electronically presented learning activities such as electronic books foster text comprehension for a broad range of students through help menus that connect them to:

- *text-to-speech capabilities and translation resources* that offer help through the use of digitized pronunciations in multiple languages and definitions of words or video clips of sign language translations.
- *teaching resources and/or strategy prompts* that are embedded in the selection to allow students to review material, understand context cues, look ahead to preview material, respond to questions, ask questions about the material, engage in games and simulations, pay attention to underlined or highlighted information, receive corrective feedback, and construct mental pictures.
- *reader-friendly resources* that allow readers to select the text size, the language read, and the page display, add color highlights, and note where the reader last read.
- *illustrative resources* that offer students access to examples; comparisons; and visuals of concepts through the use of graphics, animation, and sound.
- *informational or supplementary resources* that provide additional information and enrichment via access to multimedia presentations, electronic encyclopedias, dictionaries, and databases.

- *summarizing resources* that offer students graphics, outlines, and overviews of the structure, content, and major features of the text.
- *collaborative resources* that allow students to work together.
- *notational resources* that allow students to take notes, construct sticky notes, summarize main points, add color, and highlight text electronically as they read.
- *assessment resources* that record ongoing data on student performance and make it readily available to students and teachers (Cavanaugh, 2002; Horney & Anderson-Inman, 1999).

Additional applications of universal design for learning are discussed in this chapter and other chapters of this book.

Use Individualized Teaching Accommodations

Individualized teaching accommodations—changes in the ways information is presented or the ways students respond—are essential aspects of differentiated instruction. Stough (2002) offers a continuum for delineating accommodations based on their impact on the individual profiles of students and the level of curriculum mastery expected of students. (We will discuss this continuum again in chapter 12 when we learn about grading students in inclusive classrooms.) The first level of the continuum refers to *access accommodations*. These accommodations provide students with access to the curriculum and instruction, and do not affect the level of mastery expected of students. They help students like Julia participate at the same level as others and do not require adjustments in the structure or content of the curriculum. Examples of *access accommodations* include Braille, sign language, bilingual dictionaries, and instructional and assistive technology.

The second level of the continuum relates to *low impact* accommodations. While these accommodations involve adjustments in teaching methods, they have minimal to no impact on the level of curricular mastery expected of students. These instructional accommodations alter the ways students are taught, but do not require significant adjustments in the structure or content of the curriculum. Examples of this type of accommodation include content enhancements, word processing and spell checkers, learning strategies instruction, peer-mediated instruction.

The third level of the continuum addresses *high impact accommodations* that affect curricular expectations. These instructional accommodations, sometimes referred to as *modifications,* alter the content of the curriculum, as well as the ways students are taught, and require adjustments in the structure and content of the educational program that affect the level of curricular mastery expected of students. Examples of this level of the continuum include some of the accommodations used to teach Tom, such as the use of multilevel teaching and curriculum overlapping.

Use Instructional Materials Accommodations

Varying the instructional materials to accommodate your students is another way you can differentiate instruction. In addition to many of the strategies presented in this book, you can use the following instructional materials accommodations:

- Vary the amount of the material that students are exposed to and asked to complete (e.g., students read half the assignment and complete only the first three questions).

- Vary the format of the materials (e.g., have Julie, Tom, and other students access the materials digitally and via other forms of technology).
- Supplement the materials (e.g., provide Julia, Tom, and other students with manipulatives, replicas, visuals, graphic organizers, cues and prompts).
- Use materials that present similar content at lower readability levels.
- Use alternative materials (e.g., create a chart with string so that Julia, Tom, and their classmates could tactilely access visual information). **To view an example of a teacher adapting materials for students, go to Case 2: Classroom Climate on the CD-ROM and click on the Mutual Support video clip. How did the teacher adapt the materials to make them more accessible for students?**

Resource
Ormsbee and Finson (2000) offer guidelines for preparing and adapting written and printed materials to enhance student learning.

cd-rom

Provide Personal Supports

As was evident in the chapter-opening vignette, you can differentiate your instruction for students by providing them with personal supports from other professionals, paraeducators, and peers (Hunt et al., 2003). In addition to using a variety of cooperative-teaching instructional formats and consultation with specialists like Ms. Steckler (see chapter 4), personal supports can be provided by using paraeducators like Mr. Howry and grouping arrangements where students learn in cooperative learning groups (see chapter 9). Paraeducators also may be asked to provide physical supports so students with physical, sensory, or cognitive disabilities can access all aspects of the learning environment.

Resource
Collins, Hendricks, Fetko, and Land (2002) offer guidelines for using peers to foster learning in inclusive classrooms.

Paraeducators can be invaluable in helping you and your students, but if used improperly, they can hinder the school performance of students with disabilities (Marks, Schrader, & Levine, 1999). Giangreco, Edelman, Luiselli, and MacFarland (1997) found that when paraeducators work too closely with specific students, they can impede effective inclusion programs by:

- allowing general educators to avoid assuming responsibility for educating students with disabilities (e.g., saying, "She is so good with Mitchell that I just let her handle it").
- fostering the separation of students with disabilities from the rest of the class (e.g., working with a student with disabilities in a separate location).
- creating dependence on adults (e.g., prompting and assisting students when it is not necessary).
- limiting interactions with peers (e.g., being near the student can intimidate peers and reduce socialization).
- teaching ineffectively (e.g., not adjusting an unsuccessful activity).
- causing the loss of personal control (e.g., making decisions for students with significant communication, physical, and/or sensory difficulties).
- causing the loss of gender identity (e.g., taking students to the bathroom based on the gender of the paraeducator, not the student).
- interfering with the teaching of other students (e.g., using behaviors that distract other students).

Resource
Fleury (2000) offers guidelines for helping paraeducators and substitute teachers protect confidentiality.

To prevent these situations from occurring, it is important for you to collaborate and communicate with paraeducators to differentiate instruction and deliver appropriate services to support the learning of your students. It also is important for you to take actions to help them perform the job and address their concerns (Trautman, 2004). You can orient them by clarifying their roles, sharing your teaching philosophy, providing a tour

Resource
Giangreco, Edelman, & Broer (2003), Doyle (2002), French (2003), Riggs (2001), Mueller & Murphy (2001), Morgan and Ashbaker (2001), and Trautman (2004) provide guidelines and activities that you and your paraeducators can use to work collaboratively in inclusive settings.

of the school, introducing them to key school personnel, describing relevant programs and daily routines, and reviewing the dress code and other standards of decorum. In the orientation program, you can also explain the need for and rules on confidentiality, and discuss scheduling, handling emergencies, and other school procedures.

In addition, you can offer paraeducators an education program so that they understand and have the skills to perform their roles (Carroll, 2001; Giangreco, Edelman, & Broer, 2001). Such a program includes many types of information. It explains the roles of paraeducators inside and outside the classroom, as well as their legal and ethical responsibilities. It identifies the special medical, social, and academic strengths and challenges of students and the equipment they use. It provides an overview of the curriculum, teaching, and behavior management techniques and reviews the communication system you will be using.

While it is your job to make curriculum decisions and to supervise paraeducators when they provide instruction, it is important to communicate regularly with them (Riggs, 2001), and you can collaborate with them to jointly plan and coordinate activities, monitor student performance, and deal with problems and conflicts (French, 2002). It is also important to treat them respectfully, give them feedback on their performance and acknowledge their contributions (Giangreco, Edelman, & Broer, 2001). You can also ask paraeducators for their point of view about their roles in the school, and you can acknowledge their contributions.

Address Students' Learning Styles and Preferences

When choosing methods to differentiate instruction, you should address students' learning styles and preferences (Shelton, 2000). Note the situations and conditions that appear to influence individual students, and adjust learning and assessment activities to accommodate students' learning styles and preferences (Garrick Duhaney & Whittington-Couse, 1998; Kubina & Cooper, 2000). You can use different types of reinforcement and feedback to increase students' motivation and acknowledge their performance. As we discussed in chapter 7, you also can structure the classroom so that noise levels, students' nearness to others, distractions, movement, and desk arrangements are acceptable to students and consistent with their preferences. Whenever possible, you can adjust the lighting, temperature, ventilation, and students' work locations. For example, you can let students choose whether to work at their desks, on the floor, or in some other place (e.g., a soft lounge chair). Finally, when planning the length and nature of learning activities and daily and weekly schedules, you can think about the various learning style and preferences of students such as attention span, ability to move while learning, time of day, and grouping considerations such as learning alone or in groups and with or without adults present.

Learning and teaching styles also are classified as either *field independent* or *field sensitive*. Field-independent students appear to work best on individual tasks such as independent projects and relate formally to teachers; field-sensitive students prefer to work in groups and establish personal relationships with others, including teachers. Field-independent teachers foster learning through competition and independent assignments; field-sensitive teachers use personal and conversational teaching techniques.

Learning styles can be affected in other ways by cultural factors. For example, some cultures emphasize learning through verbal rather than visual descriptions; other cultures emphasize physical modeling over pictorials. Students' socioeconomic status can also influence their learning and cognitive styles.

Reflective

Your paraeducator has developed a close working relationship with Billy, one of your students. It's become so comfortable that your paraeducator anticipates Billy's needs before he expresses himself, and they are both reluctant to work with others. How would you address this situation?

Set Your Sites

For more information on collaborating with paraeducators, go to the Web Links module in Chapter 8 of the Companion Website.

Resource

Carbo (1994), Dunn (1996), and Johnston (1998) offer guidelines for identifying students' learning styles and designing teaching strategies and environments accordingly.

Resource

Dunn, Griggs, Olson, Beasley, and Gorman (1995) and Kavale, Hirshoren, and Forness (1998) debate the research and merits of teaching based on learning styles.

Reflective

How do you prefer to learn and teach? How do you adapt when the teaching strategy and environment are different from the way you prefer to learn? Should teachers match students' learning styles all the time? Should students be taught to adapt their learning styles to the various teaching styles they will encounter in schools?

Set Your Sites

For more information on learning styles, go to the Web Links module in Chapter 8 of the Companion Website.

Address Students' Sensory Abilities

Students with sensory disabilities have unique challenges, which you need to address when differentiating your instruction for them. For students like Julia, who have visual disabilities, you must present information orally; for students with hearing disabilities, you should use visual forms. At all times, you should encourage independence. Because the sensory functioning of students with sensory disabilities varies tremendously, you need to consider their unique needs and abilities when modifying your teaching methods.

Differentiating Instruction for Students with Visual Disabilities

As the teachers did in the chapter-opening vignette, you can collaborate with vision and mobility specialists to design and implement many different strategies to differentiate instruction for students with visual disabilities (Cox & Dykes, 2001; Griffin, Williams, Davis, & Engelman, 2002). Many of these strategies also can be used for students who are visual learners. However, understand that as students grow older, they may be reluctant to use special materials in the presence of their peers. First, you can help them follow along in class by giving important directions verbally or recording them, phrasing questions and comments so that they include students' names, and using peers to read directions and materials, describe events in the classroom, and take notes.

You also can help these students learn by giving them opportunities to learn by doing, and by providing them with large-print books, photo-enlarged handouts and tests, tactile books, Braille reference books and dictionaries, adaptive computer software, and audiocassettes (Lewis & Tolla, 2003). When providing students with tactile learning experiences, it is important to give students sufficient time to interact with all aspects of the learning materials, and provide the supports students need to benefit from the tactile representations (Downing & Chen, 2003). You also might find it helpful to experiment with the materials yourself by using them with your eyes closed.

Resource

Downing and Chen (2003) offer guidelines for using tactile strategies to differentiate instruction for students with visual disabilities.

As the educators did in the chapter-opening vignette, you can use larger letters and numerals, tactile illustrations, raised-line drawings, and graphics that avoid clutter and emphasize contrast when developing materials for students to use or when writing at the chalkboard. Use computers to produce large, clear typewritten materials. Tracing over the letters, numerals, and pictorials with a black felt-tip marker or black ballpoint pen makes it easier to see them, and placing a piece of yellow acetate over a page of print enhances the contrast and darkens the print. Students with visual impairments may suffer from visual fatigue during activities that require continuous use of visual skills. In these situations, it may be helpful to give students additional time to complete assignments and tests or to reduce the number and length of activities that call for visual concentration.

Student learning can also be promoted by using several strategies to help students locate learning materials and move around the classroom and the school. You can use *o'clock* directions to describe the location of an object on a flat surface (e.g., "Your book is at three o'clock and your pencil is at nine o'clock"). If an object is nearby and in danger of being knocked over, guide the student's hand to the object or hand the student the object by gently touching his or her hand with the object. When giving directions to specific places in the classroom or school, use nonvisual statements and remember that directions for going left and right should be in relation to the student's body rather than yours.

Differentiating Instruction for Students with Hearing Disabilities

Many strategies are available for differentiating instruction for students with hearing impairments, which also can be used for students who are auditory learners (Marlatt, 2004; Pakulski & Kaderavek, 2002; Williams & Finnegan, 2003). These strategies include (a) using good communication techniques, which include standing still and facing the person when speaking; (b) speaking clearly, at a moderate pace, and using short sentences; (c) speaking in a normal voice; (d) maintaining a proper speaking distance; (e) keeping the mouth area clear; (f) using facial and body gestures; (g) speaking in an area where the light is on your lips and face; and (h) providing transitions to indicate a change in the subject. Try to limit movement and unnecessary gestures, and present all spelling and vocabulary words in sentences (context), as many words presented in isolation look alike to lip readers. In addition, you can use visual signals to gain the student's attention, and use media such as an overhead projector or PowerPoint presentation to present material so that the student can view the material and your lips simultaneously. If necessary, rephrase, repeat, summarize, or simplify your comments and questions, as well as those of other students, to make them more understandable, and ask questions to check understanding of orally presented directions and content. When using media, shine a light on the speaker's face when the room is darkened for films or slides, and give the student the script of a video, or a record to help the student follow along.

You also can use visually oriented techniques to help students learn (Luckner, Bowen, & Carter, 2001; Schirmer, 2004). Offer demonstrations and provide examples. Supplement information presented orally with real objects, manipulatives, and concrete visual aids (e.g., maps, globes). Write daily assignments, the schedule, important directions and information, technical terms, and new vocabulary on the board, and give students test directions, assignments, vocabulary lists, models, feedback, and lecture outlines in writing. Teach students to look up difficult-to-pronounce words in the dictionary.

Resource

Luckner, Bowen, and Carter (2001) provide guidelines for using visual strategies to promote the learning of students with hearing impairments.

Students with hearing impairments may need the service of an educational interpreter. What have been your experiences working with educational interpreters?

Using Educational Interpreters Effectively.   An *educational interpreter,* a professional who helps to transfer information between individuals who do not communicate in the same way, can assist you in differentiating instruction for students with hearing impairments (Williams & Finnegan, 2003). Depending on the student's preference, many educational interpreting methods exist. Early in the school year, you and the interpreter can meet to agree on the responsibilities of both persons. Generally, the teacher has primary responsibility and the interpreter aids communication. To help teachers and interpreters communicate, planning meetings can be scheduled on a regular basis.

Since interpreters may not know the content and teaching strategies used in the classroom, it is helpful to orient them to the curriculum and to give them copies of textbooks and other relevant materials. A knowledge of class routines, projects, and long-term assignments can assist interpreters in helping students understand assignments. With a difficult unit, including technical vocabulary and other content that may be hard to explain by alternative means, you and the interpreter can meet to discuss key terms. For example, when teaching about the geological history of the earth, you could give the interpreter a list of key terms and copies of lesson plans so that the interpreter can plan in advance how to translate and explain terms such as *Paleozoic era, Oligocene epoch,* and *Jurassic period.*

To maximize the effectiveness of the interpreter in your classroom, you can:

- be sensitive to the time delays caused by interpreting.
- talk to the students, not to the interpreter.
- avoid directing comments to the interpreter during class time. Signals can be used to indicate the need for discussion after class.
- encourage the interpreter to seek help when communication problems arise during class that affect the translation process.
- avoid involving the interpreter in disciplining the student for misbehavior unless this misbehavior is directed at the interpreter. When the interpreter is involved in disciplinary actions, help students understand the roles and perspectives of the persons involved.
- place the interpreter in a position that makes interpretation easy.

Resource

The New York State Education Department (n.d.) offers guidelines for using educational interpreters in schools and classrooms.

Set Your Sites

For more information on collaborating with educational interpreters, go to the Web Links module in Chapter 8 of the Companion Website.

How Can I Differentiate Instruction for Students Who Have Difficulty Reading and Gaining Information from Print Materials?

You probably present a lot of content to your students using print materials. However, since many students have difficulty reading and gaining information from print materials, you may need to use alternative teacher- and student-directed strategies instead as well as the strategies presented in chapters 10 and 11 and other chapters in this book. These methods are described in the following sections.

Use Teacher-Directed Text Comprehension Strategies

Previewing

Before assigning a reading selection, you can use prereading activities to preview new vocabulary and word pronunciation, motivate students, and activate their prior knowledge.

Scanning the selection and discussing the meaning of boldfaced or italicized terms is helpful. New vocabulary words can be placed in a word file of index cards by chapter.

Previews, structured overviews, and prereading organizers can help students understand the purpose of the reading selection, direct their attention to the relevant information in the selection (Dyck & Pemberton, 2002; Fitzharris & Hay, 2001). For example, you can give students a list of important vocabulary with definitions or an outline of the selection's main points and discuss them before reading or have students complete an outline as they read the selection. As students read the assignment, emphasize key points by underlining and highlighting them; repeating, discussing, and summarizing them; and questioning students about graphs, pictures, and diagrams.

You also can use cues to help students identify and understand essential information presented in print (Dyck & Pemberton, 2002). You can prompt students to focus on important content by highlighting it or labeling it as important in the margins. Margin notes, like the ones in this book, can be written on textbook pages that include definitions, statements, questions, notes, and activities that help students understand and interact with the material.

Activating students' prior knowledge before reading the selection also can help them understand the new material (Vacca & Vacca, 2001). This can be done by using brainstorming, discussing and predicting components of the story, building semantic webs, and using a *K-W-L* strategy: *K* (students identify what they KNOW about the reading selection and the topic), *W* (students create questions or statements related to what they WANT to learn from reading about the topic), and *L* (students discuss what they have LEARNED from reading about the topic) (Fitzharris & Hay, 2001).

Resource

Andrews, Winograd, and DeVille (1996) offer prereading activities for use with students who have hearing impairments and students who are second language learners.

You can improve students' comprehension skills by asking them to do a writing activity related to the assignment before they read the selection. Learning logs, study guides, written summaries, and questions related to readings can be used to help students understand the material by allowing them to organize their thoughts.

Questioning

A popular strategy for guiding text comprehension—having students individually or in groups respond to questions about the text before, during, and after reading—can focus attention on the purpose of the assignment (Gauthier, 2001; Pedrotty Bryant, Ugel, Thompson, & Hamff, 1999). Manzo and Manzo (1990) identified five types of questions that you can use:

1. *Predictable questions* about the facts presented in the selection (who, what, where, when, why, and how)
2. *Mind-opening questions* related to the written and oral language components of the selection
3. *Introspective questions*, which cause students to reflect on the material
4. *Ponderable questions*, which present dilemmas or situations that have no right or wrong answer
5. *Elaborative knowledge questions*, which ask students to incorporate their prior knowledge into information presented in the selection

You can help students answer chapter questions correctly by modifying the type and timing of the questions. At first, you can present questions that deal with factual information. Then you can move to those that require inference and more complex skills. Rather than using open-ended questions, you can rephrase them, using simpler language or a multiple-choice format. You can help students gain information from books by using *prequestions* posed before the selection is read and *postquestions* posed afterward. Postquestions are particularly effective in promoting recall by establishing the need for review. Be careful in using prequestions; they can cause students to focus too much on information related to the answers while ignoring other content. You can help students develop text comprehension skills by asking them to generate their own questions and summarize a selection's content in their own words.

Reciprocal Teaching

Text comprehension skills also can be improved by *reciprocal teaching*, which involves a dialogue between you and your students (Lederer, 2000; Palincsar & Klenk, 1991). Here you ask students to read a selection silently, summarize it, discuss and clarify problem areas and unclear vocabulary, use questions to check understanding, and give students the opportunity to predict future content. After you model these strategies, students take the role of the teacher while you provide help through prompting ("What type of question would a teacher ask in this situation?"), instructing ("A summary is a short statement that includes only essential information."), modifying the activity ("If you can't predict what's going to happen, summarize the information again."), praising students ("That was a good prediction."), and offering corrective feedback ("What information could help you make your prediction?").

Story-Mapping

Some students may benefit from *story-mapping*, in which you help them identify the major story grammar elements of a story using a visual representation (Babyak, Koorland, & Mathes, 2000). Give students story maps that contain spaces for them to list the setting (characters, time, and place), the problem, the goal, the action, the outcome, and the characters' reactions. As students read information on the components of the story map, ask them to discuss the information and write the correct response on their story map. As students learn to do this, they can complete the story map independently.

Resource

Boyle and Weishaar (1997) have developed TRAVEL, a learning strategy to help students create cognitive organizers to help them understand text.

Story maps can facilitate students' text comprehension. What strategies do you use to foster your students' reading comprehension?

Teach Student-Directed Text Comprehension Strategies

In addition to using teacher-directed strategies, you can teach students to use a variety of student-directed comprehension strategies, which are described in the following sections. You can foster their use of these strategies by providing them with strategy reference cards such as the ones presented in Figure 8.3.

Finding the Main Idea

Students can learn to identify the main idea of a paragraph, which is usually embedded in the topic sentence. Therefore, you can teach your students how and where to find topic sentences. Students also can be taught how to identify main points by looking for repetition of the same word or words throughout the paragraph, examining headings and subheadings, and delineating major and supporting ideas (Saenz & Fuchs, 2002). They also can be taught to ask who, what, where, when, and how questions to identify the main ideas in paragraphs (Jitendra, Hoppes, & Xin, 2000).

Surveying

Students can be taught to survey reading assignment through use of *SQ3R*, a technique that consists of the following steps:

Survey. Surveying allows students to look for clues to the content of the chapter. In surveying, students can do the following: (a) examine the title of the chapter and try to anticipate what information will be presented; (b) read the first paragraph to try to determine the objectives of the chapter; (c) review the headings and subheadings to identify main points; (d) analyze visual aids to find relevant supporting information and related details; and (c) read the final paragraph to summarize the main points.

Question. Questioning helps students identify important content by formulating questions based on restating headings and subheadings and their own reactions to the material.

Read. Reading enables students to examine sections more closely and answer the questions raised in the questioning phase.

Recite. Reciting helps students recall the information for further use. In this step, students can be encouraged to study the information they have just covered.

Review. Reviewing also helps students remember the content. This can be done by having them prepare an oral or written summary of the main topics.

Multipass. A modified version of SQ3R is *multipass*, in which students review the content of a reading selection three times (Schumaker et al., 1982). In the first pass, or *survey*, students become familiar with the structure and organization of the selection. The second review, the *size-up* pass, helps students identify the main points of the chapter. In the final, or *sort-out* pass, students read the selection again and answer the accompanying questions.

ANSWERING QUESTIONS

How do I do it?

I need to decide what kind of question it is so I will know what strategy to use.

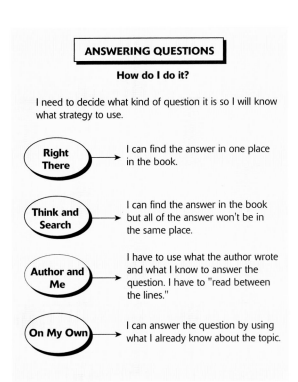

Right There → I can find the answer in one place in the book.

Think and Search → I can find the answer in the book but all of the answer won't be in the same place.

Author and Me → I have to use what the author wrote and what I know to answer the question. I have to "read between the lines."

On My Own → I can answer the question by using what I already know about the topic.

Based on Raphael's QAR (1982)

USING FIX-UP STRATEGIES

What to do when I don't understand

Choose one of these.

- Ignore and read on.

- Guess by context

- Reread to clear up confusion.

- Look back to previous information. See whether it helps me understand the difficult part.

ORGANIZING INFORMATION

I can use designs like these to help me organize the information I read about. I can use these designs as they are, or I can add to them, or I can use others.

COMPARE & CONTRAST

SEQUENCE

MAIN IDEA & SUPPORTING DETAILS

SUMMARIZING

FOR STORY READING	FOR CONTENT READING
To summarize a story I need to:	To summarize content reading I need to:
• Give the setting.	• Give the topic.
• Tell who the main characters were.	• Tell the main idea.
• Tell what the problem was.	• Tell important categories of information about the main idea.
• Briefly tell about the main event(s).	• Tell the purpose of the information. (How can it be helpful to you?)
• Tell how the story ended. (How was the problem solved?)	• Try to summarize in just a few sentences.

FIGURE 8.3   **Strategy reference cards**

Source: From "Creating Confident and Competent Readers," by C. P. Casteel, B. A. Isom, and K. F. Jordan, 2000, *Intervention in School and Clinic, 36*, pp. 67–74. Copyright 2000 by PRO-ED, Inc. Reprinted with permission.

Other similar techniques, such as *SOS* (Schumaker, Deshler, Alley, & Warner, 1983), *OK5R* (Pauk, 1984), *PQST* (Pauk, 1984), *PARTS* (Ellis, 1996), and *SCROL* (Grant, 1993), also can be selected based on the ability levels of students.

Self-Questioning

Students can be taught to use several self-questioning procedures to improve their text comprehension skills (Lebzelter & Nowacek, 1999). In one self-questioning technique, students determine the reasons for studying the passage, identify the passage's main ideas by underlining them, generate a question associated with each main idea and write it in the margin, find the answer to the question and write it in the margin, and review all the questions and answers.

Paraphrasing

Paraphrasing requires students to read text, ask questions about it to determine the main idea and other relevant information, and paraphrase the answers to these questions (Lebzelter & Nowacek, 1999). Paraphrased statements should consist of a complete sentence, be correct and logical, and provide new and useful information. Students can learn to use *RAP*, a learning strategy that involves **R**eading the paragraph, **A**sking yourself what is the main idea and the important supporting details, and **P**utting the main idea and details in words you can understand.

Outlining

Outlining chapters allows students to identify, sequence, and group main and secondary points so that they can better understand what they have read. Students can learn to use a separate outline for each topic, identify essential parts of a topic using Roman numerals, present subtopics by subdividing each main heading using capital letters, and group information within a subdivision in a sequence using numbers.

Summarizing

Another approach to teaching text comprehension skills is *summarization* (Casteel, Isom, & Jordan, 2000; Parker, Hasbrouck, & Denton, 2002b). The five basic rules students can employ in summarizing text: (a) identify and group main points; (b) eliminate information that is repeated or unnecessary; (c) find the topic sentence; (d) devise topic sentences for paragraphs that have none; and (e) delete phrases and sentences that fail to present new or relevant information (Gajria, 1988).

Paragraph Restatements and Paragraph Shrinking

Paragraph restatements help students actively process reading material by encouraging them to create original sentences that summarize the main points of the selection. The sentences should include the fewest possible words. They can be written in the textbook, recorded as notes on a separate sheet, or constructed mentally. In *paragraph shrinking*, students read a paragraph orally and then state its main idea in 10 words or less by identifying the most important information about who or what the paragraph is about (Fuchs, Fuchs, & Kazdan, 1999).

Visual Imagery

Visual imagery requires students to read a section of a book, create an image for every sentence read, contrast each new image with the prior one, and evaluate the images to make sure they are complete. You can teach students to use visual imagery by asking them to create visual images for concrete objects, having them visualize familiar objects and settings, asking them to create images while listening to high-imagery stories, and having them devise images as they read. You also can teach them to use *SCENE*, a learning strategy that involves **S**earching for picture words, **C**reating or changing the scene, **E**ntering details, **N**aming the parts, and **E**valuating your picture.

Verbal Rehearsal

In verbal rehearsal, students pause after reading several sentences to themselves and verbalize to themselves the selection's content. At the beginning, you can cue students to use verbal rehearsal by placing red dots at various points in the selection.

Reflective

Try the various comprehension strategies using material in this textbook or in a textbook for the grade you would like to teach. Which were easiest? Which were most effective?

Enhance the Readability of Materials

Students with reading and learning difficulties must often use commercially produced and teacher-developed print materials whose readability levels are too high for them. You can increase students' understanding of reading matter by modifying the material, making the text less complex, and using instructional technology.

Highlight Essential Information

You can make print materials more readable by highlighting critical information. This will help students identify main points and locate essential information. Cues linking questions

Teachers can use the principles of typographic design to produce highly readable and legible materials for use with students. How successful are you at using these principles?

IDEAS FOR IMPLEMENTATION

Adjusting the Complexity of Text Language

Ms. Mantel's class had several students whose reading abilities varied widely. Sometimes they were able to read the material and understand it. At other times, they struggled. Ms. Mantel noticed that her students' reading abilities appeared to be related to the linguistic complexity of the text. She began to simplify the choice and arrangements of words and sentences in the selections that caused her students the most trouble. First, she examined the length of sentences and shortened them. She broke long sentences into two or three shorter sentences. Second, she highlighted main ideas, concepts, and words, and introduced one idea at a time. Third, she helped her students understand the order of the concepts presented by using signal words such as *first, second,* and *third*. Fourth, because her students had difficulty understanding the relationship between concepts, she used words that show relationships, such as *because, after,* and *since*.

Here are some other strategies you can use to reduce the linguistic complexity of text:

- Eliminate unnecessary words and sections that may distract students.
- Use words with which students are familiar rather than uncommon or unusual words (e.g., *use* rather than *utilize*).

- Refrain from using proper names, irregularly spelled words, ambiguous terms, and use of multiple terms for the same word or concepts.
- Use coordinate and subordinate conjunctions to establish cohesive ties between concepts.
- Use clear pronoun references and word substitution to clarify relationships.
- Rephrase paragraphs so that they begin with a topic sentence followed by supporting details.
- Present a series of events or actions in chronological order, and cluster information that is related.
- Embed definitions and examples of new words and concepts, and avoid using different words that have identical meanings.
- Insert text and examples to clarify main points.
- Present text in the present tense and avoid use of the passive voice.
- Create visual aids that present content and depict processes.

Note: Brown (1999); Thompson, Johnstone, & Thurlow (2002).

with the location of the answers in the selection can help students learn how to find the answers. For example, you can color-code study questions and their answers in the text. Pairing questions with the numbers of pages containing the answers, simplifying vocabulary by paraphrasing questions, defining important and difficult terms, breaking multiple-part questions into separate questions, or recording questions on cassettes and including the pages where the answers occur are other helpful methods.

Use Instructional Technology

You can foster text comprehension by giving students audiocassettes of the text that are commercially produced or made by volunteers. Audiocassettes can be made more effective through the use of variable speech-control recorders that allow users to control the playback speed (Raskind & Higgins, 1998).

Resource

Dyck and Pemberton (2002) offer guidelines for preparing text-based audiocassettes.

Videocassettes of content that is related to or parallels the material presented in textbooks and other print materials also can orient students to content in these materials. Videocassettes also provide direct visual experience with the material that can improve students' understanding and memory of the content to be mastered.

USING TECHNOLOGY TO PROMOTE INCLUSION

Preparing Readable and Legible Materials

An important factor in differentiating instruction for your students is providing them with instructional materials that support their learning. Since the visual look of text also affects its readability, you can use the principles of typographic and visual design to produce materials that promote speed, clarity, and understanding. Computers and word processing offer you access to various dimensions of typographic design that can help you produce printed instructional materials for students that are very readable and legible. These dimensions, which are outlined below, also can be used to prepare teacher-made tests (see chapter 12); overheads and PowerPoint presentations (see chapter 9); content enhancements (see chapter 11); and written communications with families and other professionals (see chapter 4).

Type Size

Type that is too small is difficult to decipher and type that is too large requires excessive eye movements to follow the text and can cause the reader to pause more often while reading a line.

You can make material more readable by using typefaces with simple designs, as well as those familiar to students. In terms of type size, 12- to 14-point type is easier to read than smaller or larger print at typical reading distances. However, larger type of at least 18-point may be more appropriate for young students who are beginning to read and for students who have visual difficulties. Larger type also can reduce eye fatigue.

Case

Lowercase letters provide cues that help readers perceive and remember differences in letters and word shapes. For this reason, text should be printed in lowercase and capital letters where grammatically appropriate. ALL-CAPITAL PRINTING CAN SLOW DOWN THE READING PROCESS and its use should be limited to short, noncontinuous text that needs to be HIGHLIGHTED, such as headings and subheadings, or an essential word in a sentence or paragraph.

Style

Style refers to variants such as *italics* and **boldface.** *The use of italics or boldface variants slows reading of continu-* *ous text* and should be used only to **emphasize** and *highlight* small amounts of text embedded in sentences and paragraphs or to make headings stand out. Italics and boldface are preferable to underlining to highlight important material; underlining can distract the reader and make it harder to discriminate letters. For example, underlining can cause students to perceive *y* as *v* or *u* and *g* as *a.*

Proportional and Monospaced Type

Monospaced or fixed type uses the same horizontal space for all letters, while proportionally spaced type varies the horizontal space of letters, depending on their form. Although proportionally spaced type makes reading easier by providing additional perceptual cues for letter recognition and enhancing the flow of the text, some learners may prefer monospaced type.

Line Length

Line length refers to the number of characters and spaces in a line. Material that is printed in long lines may cause fatigue by making it difficult to find the next line to read, while text that is printed in short lines

demands that students' eyes change lines frequently.

You can use several strategies to design materials that have an appropriate line length of about 4 inches. One method is to count characters and spaces and to maintain a line length and character count of between 40 and 70. Another method is to structure the material by using line lengths of 7 to 12 words. This method adjusts the line length to the linguistic complexity of the material and therefore the reading skill of students.

Spacing

When designing print materials, it is useful to view space as a hierarchy that proceeds from smallest to largest, as follows: (a) space between letters, (b) space between words, (c) space between lines, (d) space between paragraphs, (e) space between columns, (f) space between sections, and (g) space from the text area to the edge of the page. Failure to follow these spatial relationships can confuse and frustrate readers. For example, if the space between letters exceeds the space between words, the words appear to "fall apart," and if the space between words is greater than the space between lines, the lines break up and the eye may be tempted to move down rather than across. Therefore, you should examine the impact of all spaces on a page and make adjustments when necessary. It is also recommended that you provide space between paragraphs and columns to make them more readable.

Leading
The vertical space between lines, referred to as *leading,* can be adjusted to make materials more readable. In general, you can increase the readability of your materials by making the leading 25 percent to 30 percent of the point size. For students with low vision, it is important to increase the leading so that the space between lines of text is greater.

Justification
Justification refers to the alignment of the edges of text. Left-justified or aligned text and staggered right margins are the best choices for readability at all reading levels, as it makes it easier for the reader to see and track the text. Right-justified text results in uneven word and letter spac-

ing of text and can cause students with and without reading difficulties to experience problems tracking the flow of text.

Centered text slows the reading process and is best used for special purposes like titles or lists.

Right-aligned text disturbs the flow of reading because the eye does not know where to go to begin reading the next line.

Background/Contrast
Since students' ability to read and eye strain also can be affected by the color contrast between the text and the background, material should consist of black or blue text on a off-white or matte pastel background. It is also important to avoid gray backgrounds, especially when essential information is presented. When selecting colors, choose those whose lightness differs as much as possible.

Note: Arditi (1999); Hoener, Salend, & Kay, (1997); Thompson, Johnstone, & Thurlow (2002).

How Can I Differentiate Instruction for Students from Diverse Cultural and Language Backgrounds?

In addition to using cooperative learning and the other strategies presented in this book, you can consider the following guidelines when adjusting your curriculum and teaching methods for students from diverse cultural and language backgrounds. Again, these guidelines can be used to enhance instruction for *all students.*

Use a Multicultural Curriculum

As Ms. Taravella and her colleagues did in the chapter-opening vignette, one means of making learning relevant, interdisciplinary, and challenging for *all students* is by using a *multicultural curriculum,* which acknowledges the voices, histories, experiences, and contributions of all ethnic and cultural groups (Taylor & Whittaker, 2003). The goal of a multicultural curriculum is to help *all students* do the following: (a) understand, view, and appreciate events from various cultural perspectives; (b) understand and function in their own and other cultures; (c) take personal actions to promote racial and ethnic harmony and to counter racism and discrimination; (d) understand various cultural and ethnic alternatives; (e) develop their academic skills; and (f) improve their ability to make reflective personal and public decisions and actions that contribute to changing society and culture (Banks, 2003; Sleeter & Grant, 2002).

Multicultural education is often seen as focusing on the needs of students of color and students who speak languages other than English. However, a true multicultural cur-

REFLECTING ON YOUR PRACTICES

Examining the Readability and Legibility of Your Materials

You can examine the readability and legibility of the materials and tests you develop for students by considering the following questions:

- Are the materials too wordy?
- Are key terms and concepts highlighted?
- Do you use words that students can read and understand?
- Are definitions and examples of new and difficult words and concepts embedded in the text?
- Are the lengths of sentences and paragraphs appropriate?
- Do sentences contain no more than one complex idea?
- Do you avoid using double negatives, abbreviations, contractions, acronyms, quotations, and parentheses?
- Do paragraphs begin with a topic sentence and present information and events logically and in chronological order?
- Do you number or letter directions, lists, and steps?
- Are transitions to and connections between concepts clearly established?
- Are the visual aids necessary; are they placed in the right locations; and do they explain, highlight, or summarize the material?
- Are there too many visuals and unnecessary stimuli or text?

- Are the materials grammatically correct and presented in a tense and voice that students can understand?
- Do you use type sizes and typefaces that are appropriate for and simple and familiar to students?
- Do you present text in lowercase and capital letters when grammatically appropriate?
- Do you use brief, highlighted headings?
- Do you use boldface and italics sparingly and only to highlight headings or small amounts of text within sentences or paragraphs?
- Do you use appropriate spaced type, line lengths, spacing, and leading?
- Do you use left-justified margins, staggered right margins, and wider margins at the bottom of the page?
- Is the overall spacing consistent, and does it provide a logical structure for the reader to follow?
- Is the length of the material appropriate, and are pages numbered?
- Is there appropriate contrast between lettering color and background color?

How would you rate the readability and legibility of your materials? ( ) Excellent ( ) Good ( ) Need Improvement ( ) Need Much Improvement

What steps could you adopt to improve the readability and legibility of your materials?

Note: Boone et al. (1999); Hoener et al. (1997).

riculum should teach information about all groups and should be directed at all students (Gay, 2004; Nieto, 2000). Besides including all students, the multicultural curriculum should address all content areas. For example, a science lesson on plants can include a discussion of plants in other countries and in various regions of the United States. The Native American counting technique that uses knots in a rope can be taught as part of a math lesson.

Banks and Banks (2001) identified four hierarchical methods for incorporating multicultural information into the curriculum. In the *contributions* approach, various ethnic heroes, highlights, holidays, and cultural events are added to the curriculum. In the *additive* approach, content, concepts, themes, and issues related to various cultures are added to the curriculum. In both of these approaches, no substantive changes are made in the organization or goals of the curriculum. As a result, while students are introduced to the contributions of various cultural groups, they are often given little information about various cultural groups, and fail to understand the social and political realities behind the experiences of these groups (Taylor & Whittaker, 2003).

Resource

Banks (2003), Irvine and Armento (2001), Sleeter and Grant (2002), and Gollnick and Chinn (2001) offer examples, guidelines, and resources for creating and implementing a multicultural curriculum.

Reflective

How has your cultural background influenced your perspectives? How are your cultural perspectives similar to and different from those of others? How would multicultural education influence your cultural perspectives?

The *transformation* approach to multicultural curriculum reform tries to modify the curriculum by encouraging students to examine and explore content, concepts, themes, issues, problems, and concerns from various cultural perspectives. In this approach, students learn to think critically and reflect on the viewpoints of different cultural, gender, and social class groups. For example, a lesson on the impact of the North American Free Trade Agreement (NAFTA) can compare its impact from the perspectives of groups in all countries of North America.

The *social action* approach, although similar to the transformation approach, encourages and teaches students to identify social problems and take action to solve them. Students are given opportunities to challenge and change practices that they consider unfair. For example, as part of their unit, Ms. Taravella's and Ms. Stoudamire's class might analyze data on the number of people of color and females working as scientists studying the solar system. They can then propose and evaluate actions to address the problems that discourage people of color and females from becoming scientists.

Parallel Lessons

You can make your curriculum multicultural by using *parallel lessons*, which allow students to learn about individuals and content from both the mainstream culture and other cultures. For example, a lesson on Abraham Lincoln could be paired with a lesson on Benito Juarez, a comparable historical figure in his country.

Use Multicultural Teaching Materials

Resource

Corso, Santos, and Roof (2002) offer guidelines for adapting instructional materials for use with students from diverse backgrounds, and Santos et al. (2000) offer guidelines for selecting culturally and linguistically appropriate early childhood materials.

A multicultural curriculum should contain teaching materials that reflect a wide range of experiences and aspirations (Corso, Santos, & Roof, 2002; Sapon-Shevin, 2001). Therefore, materials that reflect cultural, ethnic, linguistic, and gender diversity should be used frequently and should be fully integrated into the curriculum (Montgomery, 2001). Other activities and materials for promoting an acceptance and appreciation of cultural diversity are presented in chapter 5. Guidelines for evaluating multicultural teaching materials are presented in Figure 8.4.

A multicultural curriculum should teach information about *all* groups and should be directed at *all* students. How could you make your curriculum more multicultural?

FIGURE 8.4

Guidelines for evaluating multicultural teaching materials.

To what extent do the materials include the various groups in U.S. society?

How are various groups portrayed in the materials?

Are the viewpoints, attitudes, reactions, experiences, and feelings of various groups accurately presented?

Do the materials present a varied group of credible individuals to whom students can relate in terms of lifestyle, values, speech and language, and actions?

Are individuals from diverse backgrounds depicted in a wide range of social and professional activities?

Do the materials show a variety of situations, conflicts, issues, and problems as experienced by different groups?

Are a wide range of perspectives on situations and issues offered?

Does the material incorporate the history, heritage, experiences, language, and traditions of various groups?

Are the experiences of and issues important to various groups presented in a realistic manner that allows students to recognize and understand their complexities?

Are culturally diverse examples, situations, experiences, and anecdotes included throughout the materials?

Are the materials factually correct?

Are the experiences, contributions, and content of various groups fully integrated into the materials and the curriculum?

Are graphics accurate, inclusive, and ethnically sensitive?

Do the materials avoid stereotypes and generalizations about groups?

Are members of various groups presented as having a range of physical features (e.g., hair texture, skin color, facial features)?

Is the language of the materials inclusive, and does it reflect various groups?

Do the materials include learning activities that help students develop a multicultural perspective?

Note: Santos et al. (2000); Taylor (2000).

Use Culturally Relevant and Responsive Teaching Strategies

Teaching strategies should reflect the students' experiences, cultural perspectives, and developmental ages (Garcia, 2002; Gay, 2000). Your teaching strategies should be aligned with your students' cultural backgrounds and preferred learning styles, which in turn requires you to be aware of your students' cultural values (Kea & Utley, 1998). It also means that you teach in a way that helps your students find relevant connections between themselves and the subject matter, the instructional strategies used, and the tasks they are asked to perform (Bynoe, 1998).

Research has identified effective strategies for teaching students from diverse cultural and language backgrounds, and other groups of students:

Emphasizing verbal interactions.   Use activities that encourage students to respond verbally to the material in creative ways such as group discussions, role plays, storytelling, group recitations, choral and responsive reading, and rap.

Teaching students to use self-talk.   Encourage and teach students to learn new material by verbalizing it to themselves.

Facilitating divergent thinking.   Encourage students to explore and devise unique solutions to issues and problems through activities such as brainstorming, group discussions, debates, and responding to open-ended questions.

Using small-group instruction and cooperative learning.   Allow students to work in small groups, and use cooperative learning arrangements including peer tutoring and cross-age tutoring.

Resource

Montgomery (2001) offers guidelines and strategies for creating culturally responsive, inclusive classrooms.

Resource

Sparks (2000a) and Mathews (2000) offer classroom and curriculum accommodations for use with Native American and Southeast Asian students, respectively.

Set Your Sites

For more information on multicultural curricula, instructional materials, and teaching practices, go to the Web Links module in Chapter 8 of the Companion Website..

Employing verve in the classroom.   Introduce *verve,* a high level of energy, exuberance, and action, into the classroom by displaying enthusiasm for teaching and learning, using choral responding, moving around the classroom, varying your voice quality, snapping your fingers, using facial expressions, and encouraging students to use their bodies to act out and demonstrate content.

Focusing on real-world tasks.   Introduce content, language, and learning by relating them to students' home, school, and community life, and to their cultures and experiences.

Promoting teacher–student interactions.   Use teaching methods based on exchanges between students and teachers. Ask frequent questions, affirm students' responses, give feedback, offer demonstrations and explanations, and rephrase, review, and summarize material (Franklin, 1992; Gay, 2000).

Use Reciprocal Interaction Teaching Approaches

Teaching models using task analysis, structured drills, teacher-directed instruction, and independent seatwork may not be effective with many students, including second language learners, because they fail to provide a language context for students. Therefore, you can supplement teaching activities that emphasize the development of skills with *reciprocal interaction teaching approaches (RITA)* that foster learning through verbal and written dialogues between students and teachers and among students (Echevarria & McDonough, 1995). In using reciprocal interaction, you use students' prior knowledge and experiences to add a context that promotes comprehension and incorporates language development and use. The curriculum and teaching focus on meaningful, authentic activities related to students' lives, and they target higher-level critical thinking skills rather than basic skills.

When implementing RITA, you also use student-centered teaching and dialogues, student–student interactions, problem-solving situations, and guided questioning to help students control their learning. Higher-level thinking is promoted through teacher modeling and thinking aloud, presenting new information as collaborative problems to be solved, posing open-ended questions, asking students to justify their responses and explain their reasoning, helping students explore alternative perspectives, encouraging students to evaluate and monitor their thinking and that of others, and viewing students' miscues as opportunities to discuss new information.

You also can employ *scaffolding,* breaking down comments students don't understand or a task students have difficulty performing into smaller components that promote understanding or mastery. Scaffolding methods include relating the task to students' prior knowledge, using visual and language cues, modeling effective strategies, and highlighting the key parts of the task (Langdon, 2002). As students gain skill or mastery, scaffolding supports are gradually removed so that students function independently to understand, apply, and integrate their new learning.

When using RITA, you also can promote teacher–student interactions through the use of confirmation checks ("Are you saying . . . ?"), comprehension checks ("Do you understand what I just said?" "Tell me in your own words what I'm saying."), clarification requests ("Can you explain that again?" "In a different way?"), repetitions, and expansions. Conversational interactions also can be fostered by you and your students asking who, where, why, when, and what questions.

Use Effective ESL Approaches

Instruction for second language learners can be differentiated by using effective ESL approaches such as total physical response, sheltered English, natural language approaches, and new vocabulary and concept instructional techniques.

Total Physical Response

Total physical response (TPR) improves students' vocabulary through modeling, repeated practice, and movement (Schoen & Schoen, 2003). In TPR, you model the message by emphasizing physical gestures and objects. (You state the message, model, and physically emphasize movements related to the concept of, say, sharpening a pencil.) Next, the class as a group responds to your directions. (You ask the students to sharpen their pencils and the students, as a group, make the appropriate motion.) Finally, individual students respond to verbal commands given by you and their peers. (Individual students are asked by you and their peers to sharpen a pencil.) As students develop skills, the complexity of the language skills taught increases. Adaptations of TPR include having students write statements and comply with written statements.

Sheltered English

Sheltered English, or *content-based instruction*, uses cues, gestures, technology, manipulatives, drama, and visual stimuli and aids to teach new vocabulary and concepts. As part of your use of sheltered English, you need to simplify your vocabulary and grammar. When using a sheltered English approach, present lessons that cover grade-level content and teach students the terminology needed to understand the concepts in specific content areas. Create a context; present information orally and visually; use hands-on activities and media; and help students learn by restating, paraphrasing, simplifying, and expanding the material. It is also important to connect the curriculum to students' culture, experiences, and language and to promote interactions among students.

Lessons using a sheltered English approach typically are organized in the following sequence:

1. Identify, define, and teach terminology that is essential to understanding the lesson and related to the curriculum. Key terms are posted as a visual reference for students and are added to students' word banks.
2. Select and explain the main concepts to students.
3. Help students learn and understand the main concepts by presenting content using visual aids, objects, physical gestures, facial expressions, manipulatives, and technology. Where possible, allow students to experience the concepts.
4. Make instruction meaningful by giving students opportunities to relate the concepts to their experiences.
5. Check students' understanding, encourage them to seek clarification, and offer feedback.
6. Encourage students to work and interact with their peers (Echevarria, 1995).

Natural Language Techniques

You also can help students develop language by using natural language techniques: expansion, expatiation, parallel talk, and self-talk (Lowenthal, 1995). *Expansion* allows you to present a language model by expanding on students' incomplete sentences or

IDEAS FOR IMPLEMENTATION

Differentiating Instruction for Second Language Learners

Ms. Phalen's class included several second language learners. The class was learning about the cycle of the butterfly. First, Ms. Phalen read and discussed a book on this topic with her students. They talked about such terms as *caterpillar, cocoon,* and *butterfly.* Then Ms. Phalen had the students reenact the cycle of the butterfly. She told them to roll themselves into a little ball. Then she asked them to pretend they were caterpillars. They acted like caterpillars, and then became a cocoon and broke out of the cocoon as butterflies. With their arms outstretched like butterflies, the students then "flew" around the room. After this activity, Ms. Phalen had her students work in small groups to draw pictures of the cycle of the butterfly.

Here are some other strategies you can use to differentiate instruction for second language learners:

- Establish a relaxed learning environment that encourages students to take risks and attempt to use both languages, and emphasize communication rather than language form. For example, correct students indirectly by restating their incorrect comments in correct form (If the student says "My notebook home," you say, "I see, your notebook is at home.")
- Begin new lessons with reviews of relevant previously learned concepts, and show the relationships between previously learned concepts and new material.
- Relate material and examples to students' experiences, use cultural referents, and use real-world language and meaningful, functional activities.
- Be consistent in your use of language, and use repetition to help students acquire the rhythm, pitch, volume, and tone of their new language.
- Use gestures, facial expressions, voice changes, pantomimes, demonstrations, rephrasing, visuals,

props, manipulatives, and other cues to provide a context that conveys the meaning of new terms and concepts.

- Introduce new material in context, discussing changes in the context while it is occurring. Talk about what has occurred in context so that ambiguities are reduced.
- Develop students' language competence by using modeling, questioning, art forms, drama, simulations, role plays, storytelling, music, and games.
- Supplement oral instruction and descriptions with demonstrations; hands-on activities; and visual materials such as charts, maps, graphs, pictures, graphic organizers, and chalkboard writing.
- Make it easier for students to understand and respond by articulating clearly; pausing often; limiting the use of idiomatic expressions, slang, and pronouns; highlighting key words through increased volume and slight exaggeration; using rephrasing, simple vocabulary, and shorter sentences; and giving students enough wait time.
- Allow students to express their knowledge, understanding, and intended meaning nonverbally. For example, rather than asking a student to define a word or concept, ask the student to draw a picture depicting it.
- Encourage and show students how to use bilingual dictionaries, pictionaries, and glossaries.
- Offer regular summaries of important content, and check students' understanding frequently.

Note: Brice & Roseberry-McKibbin (2001); Fueyo (1997); Gebhard (2003); Garcia (2002); Gersten (1999); and Watson & Houtz, (2002).

---

thoughts. *Expatiation* occurs when you add new information to the comments of students. *Parallel talk* involves describing an event that students are seeing or doing. *Self-talk* consists of talking about your actions, experiences, or feelings.

New Vocabulary and Concept Teaching Techniques

Effective teaching for second language learners requires you to help them learn new vocabulary and concepts (Brice & Roseberry-McKibbin, 2001). To aid these students, focus on essential vocabulary key words and concepts that students use often, and are related to their lives and the material they are learning (Gersten & Baker, 2000). In addition, teach vocabulary in context rather than in isolation; teach related words and concepts together; and teach using visuals, pictorials, and physical movements to highlight the important features of new vocabulary words when possible (Alber & Foil, 2003). For example, you can teach words like *cold* or *frigid* by pretending to shiver. When introducing new vocabulary and concepts, you can consider the following sequence:

Step 1. Analyze the concept to be taught and identify its key features, including the concept's structure and characteristics. Determine whether the context is important for understanding the concept.

Step 2. Introduce and label the concept in a variety of situations. If possible, present the concept using clear, consistent language, concrete materials, manipulatives, and visuals.

Step 3. Show and discuss examples and nonexamples of the concept, moving from easy to difficult. Present and use the concept in many naturally occurring situations, and elaborate on the characteristics that define the concept and distinguish it from others.

Step 4. Contrast the concept with other related concepts.

Step 5. Allow students to practice using the concept in functional activities related to their interests and learning levels (Martorella & Beal, 2002).

Additional strategies for developing your students' vocabulary are presented in chapters 10 and 11.

Resource

Alber and Foil (2003) offer guidelines for using drama and physical movements to foster students' vocabulary development.

Reflective

Watch a television show or film in a second language. What factors helped you understand the content?

Encourage Students to Respond

You may need to encourage second language learners and students with speech and language difficulties to respond verbally. You can promote student responding by using open-ended questions, allowing students to use gestures until they develop language competence, and praising and expanding on students' contributions and seeking more information when necessary. Give students enough time to interact and discuss material before responding, and encourage students to share their opinions, ask questions, and expand on the comments of others. You also can stimulate the use of language by providing experiences that encourage discussion, such as introducing new objects into the classroom; changing the classroom environment; allowing students to work and play together; sending students on errands; creating situations in which students need to ask for help; asking students to recount events or talk about doing something while doing it; and using visuals that display pictorial absurdities.

Resource

Haver (2002) and Kottler and Kottler (2002) offer guidelines, strategies, and resources for differentiating instruction for second language learners.

How Can I Use Instructional Technology and Assistive Devices to Differentiate Instruction for Students?

As we saw in the chapter-opening vignette, you can use a range of instructional technologies and assistive devices to differentiate instruction. These technologies and devices are presented here.

Instructional Technology

Resource

Gardner et al. (2003) provide guidelines and examples related to the use of technology to plan and deliver a range of learning activities.

Recent technological developments now allow you to use instructional technology and interactive multimedia to create motivating and contextualized learning environments for students (Gardner, Wissick, Schweder & Canter, 2003). Interactive multimedia link text, sound, animation, video, and graphics to present information to students in a non-linear, instantaneous fashion that promotes critical thinking skills and social interactions. These technologies can be integrated across the curriculum to differentiate instruction and allow students to be more actively involved in directing their learning. Several related multimedia teaching technologies are described in the following section, and in other chapters of this book.

Computer-Based Instruction

Resource

Forgan and Weber (2001) provide guidelines for selecting software for students with high incidence disabilities, and Higgins, Boone, and Williams (2000) offer questions for soliciting feedback from students concerning software programs.

As we have seen throughout this book, you can supplement and individualize teaching by using *computer-based instruction*. Computers can help you individualize your instruction and assessment by directing students to items related to their skill levels and allowing students to work at their own pace (See chapter 12 for information on technology-based assessment strategies). Through the use of computers, you can differentiate your instruction by providing your students with access to drill-and-practice, instructional game, tutorial, simulation, and problem-solving programs. However, the effectiveness of computer-based instruction depends on the software program used. Many programs are open to criticism; you should carefully evaluate the ones you use (Baker, 2003). A form for evaluating software programs is presented in Figure 8.5

You also can differentiate instruction by creating *widgets*, a series of individualized computer-based learning activities for students (Miller, Brown, & Robinson, 2002). Students can then work on these activities independently or in small groups.

Set Your Sites

For more information on software evaluation, go to the Web Links module in Chapter 8 of the Companion Website.

Hypertext/Hypermedia

Resource

Miller, Brown, and Robinson (2002) offer guidelines for developing widgets and using them in inclusive classrooms.

Hypertext or *hypermedia* is a computerized teaching system that provides alternative nonsequential and nonlinear formats for mastering content, including additional text, specialized graphics, digital video clips, animated presentations, and computer-produced speech and sound effects. Hypermedia systems offer experiential or direct learning opportunities and are especially helpful for second language learners. Most traditional print materials present content in a linear fashion. Hypermedia, by contrast, allows students to view and link information controlled by a computer into a unified lesson. In hypertext, information presented on one screen is linked to related content on other screens that students access based on their needs and interests. Hypermedia also can be used to create and share portfolios of students' work (see chapter 12).

Resource

Lock and Carlson (2000) offer guidelines for using computer labs to provide students with access to computer-based instruction.

Videocassettes, CDs, and DVDs

You can present information via *videocassettes*, or digitally by using *CDs*, and *DVDs*. High-resolution color video and digital cameras can display images of three-dimensional objects, photographs, slides, and documents, and allow students to record activities that can be included in the learning products they produce in school. The taping, stopping, and starting capabilities of videocassettes and digital materials allow demonstrations, experiments, and other classroom activities to be taped and then played back to highlight or repeat key parts or information. These materials also can facilitate modeling and prompting and can be used in simulation activities or group discussions.

FIGURE 8.5

Computer software evaluation form

COMPONENTS	YES	NO
Student Needs		
◇ communicates relevant features of a task		
◇ does not require teacher monitoring		
◇ high attention level		
◇ provides tutorial for using the software		
◇ requires students to respond before moving on to next task		
◇ manual dexterity not considered an important skill		
◇ simple directions		
Teacher Options		
◇ adjustable reading level		
◇ allows teacher to individualize to learner needs		
◇ content and activities can be modified		
◇ content and activities can be added		
Software Options and Design		
◇ adequate prompts		
◇ allows use of alternate input devices		
◇ minimal keyboarding skills required		
◇ uncluttered screen		
◇ tasks presented in alternate formats		
Screen Design		
◇ includes animation		
◇ includes color-cuing		
◇ underlines important points or concepts		
◇ nondistracting graphics		
◇ double-spaced text		
◇ unambiguous typeface		
◇ on-screen directions		
◇ text that is not complex		
◇ written in active voice		
Appropriate Instructional Options		
◇ built-in learning guidance for complex tasks		
◇ consistent screen design features (student can predict)		
◇ hints		
◇ includes optional game format		
◇ identical navigational elements on every screen		
◇ readability of software corresponds to identified users		

Source: From "Evaluating Educational Software for Special Education," by K. Higgins, R. Boone, and D. L. Williams, 2000, *Intervention in School and Clinic, 36,* pp. 109–115. Copyright 2000 by PRO-ED, Inc. Reprinted with permission.

Figure 8.5 (continued)

COMPONENTS	YES	NO
Sound		
❖ can be disabled		
❖ speech capabilities		
❖ utilizes appropriate sound		
❖ verbal directions have corresponding on-screen text		
Feedback		
❖ consistent		
❖ provides corrective feedback		
❖ immediate		
❖ appropriate duration		
❖ obvious and overt		
❖ relevant to input/task		
Instructional and Screen Design		
❖ errorless learning		
❖ input is not automatic entry		
❖ multiple-choice answers		
❖ opportunity for ample practice to reach mastery		
❖ provides for overlearning		
❖ opportunity to review concepts		
❖ option for competition		
❖ provides for cumulative review		
❖ small instructional sets		
❖ software keeps score		
❖ software records student work		
❖ math problems are in vertical format		
❖ information presented in multiple media (print & spoken)		
❖ content and materials can be modified		
❖ provision for alternative means of expression and control		

Set Your Sites

For videos that you can use in your classroom, go to the Web Links module in Chapter 8 of the Companion Website.

DVD- and *CD-ROM based teaching materials* have many multimedia features that can help you differentiate your instruction. As we saw in the chapter-opening vignette, you can present content via CD/DVDs containing frames of realistic computer graphic displays, video segments, slides, motion pictures, audio information, and sound effects. With remote control, you can quickly access high-quality visual and auditory information randomly or continuously, and you can halt the presentation to highlight critical information or to ask students questions. Thus, digitally based teaching allows students to hear explanations in various languages, and view colorful, animated, and expressive visual displays and demonstrations, computer graphics, and sound effects that accurately depict concepts and material in a gradual and systematic way.

You can use digital materials to differentiate your instruction. They can be presented through the use of music, speech, and dynamic illustrations to motivate students and promote concept and vocabulary development across content areas, as well as reading and listening comprehension (Castellani & Jeffs, 2001). These materials can present text and illustrations using different voices and languages for the various characters, including sign language. Individual words and text can be repeated, defined, presented in sign language, or translated into another language by highlighting the text to be pronounced or pressing a button (Andrews & Jordan, 1998). Digital technology also allows you and your students to adjust the pace of the oral reading, magnify the text, vary the colors of the illustrations, and compare their reading with the oral reading on the CD/DVD. Digital equipment that allows you and your students to develop materials and products also is available. For example, students can use DVD technology to develop, publish, and animate their stories.

DVD and CD-ROM technology is also being used to make teaching and reference materials more accessible and understandable to students. Because this technology integrates graphics, spoken text, video segments, animation, and sound effects, information presented in encyclopedias and dictionaries can become more meaningful and motivating to students.

Digital Cameras

Digital cameras give you and your students access to technology in order to create video-based projects. Users can immediately see the recorded image, store it in memory, delete it, or download it directly to computers so that it can be edited, enlarged, e-mailed, embedded in web pages, added to student products or learning materials, or printed (Lazarus, 1998).

Set Your Sites

For more information on using digital cameras, go to the Web Links module in Chapter 8 of the Companion Website.

Captioned Television and Liquid Crystal Display Computer Projection Panels

Captioned television and *liquid crystal display (LCD) computer projection panels* are other valuable teaching methods, particularly for students with hearing disabilities and second language learners. The dialogue that accompanies closed-caption materials can be presented on the screen in real-time via a device that receives closed-caption signals connected to the screen. Real-time closed-captioning was developed for students with hearing disabilities, but it can be used with a wide variety of students, including those with reading difficulties and those who speak different languages; it provides an auditory and a visual context for learning new vocabulary and information (Gartland, 1994). For example, set-top television translators can convert closed captions from one language into another. As we saw in the chapter-opening vignette, students with visual disabilities like Julia benefit from descriptive video services, a specialized sound track system that enhances television and CD/DVD viewing by providing a running description of the images, events, characters' actions and body language, and scenes.

LCD computer projection panels promote information sharing by interfacing a computer with an overhead projector so that students can view more easily the information displayed on the monitor. With LCD panels, you can display images from multimedia sources with more colors and sharper resolution. You can also teach content in ways that are interesting, multidimensional, motivating, and tailored to students' needs.

Resource

Blubaugh (1999) offers guidelines that increase the effectiveness of videos and television programs used in classrooms.

Virtual Reality

Virtual reality systems allow students to experience what it feels like to see, touch, smell, and move through artificial, three-dimensional, interactive environments with the use of head-mounted goggles, headsets, or specially designed gloves and body suits that present computer-generated images. For example, virtual reality systems allow students to experience Newton's law of gravity first-hand. They also allow students to try newly learned skills in community-based locations (Davies & Hastings, 2003). For example, virtual reality can provide students with significant cognitive disabilities with a safe environment to learn and practice how to cross the street.

Internet

The Internet provides you and your students with access to the information superhighway, as well as many exploratory and discovery-based learning and communication experiences. It allows you to access national, state, and district learning standards, and instructional activities and materials aligned with the standards. It allows students to control the curriculum more effectively, and it offers them options related to what and how they learn. **To view examples of teachers and students using the Internet to support student learning, go to Case 4: Support Participation on the CD-ROM and click on the Multiple Goals, Self-Advocacy, Recognize Efforts, and Involve Students video clips. How does the Internet support the instructional process for students and teachers?**

When using the Internet with students, you need to be aware of the digital divide; make sure that *all* students have access (see chapter 3). You also need to teach them how to evaluate websites, and web-based information (Forcier & Descy, 2002) (See Figure 8.6). You also need to establish and teach students rules and etiquette for using the Internet and protecting their privacy. This involves teaching them about conducting searches, accessing appropriate material, interacting with others, protecting their confidentiality, properly using copyrighted material, and avoiding plagiarism. It also should teach them to refrain from giving out personal information and pictures; how to deal with advertising and avoid offensive sites, mischief and viruses; and proper use of Internet accounts (Lever-Duffy, McDonald, Mizell, 2003). You also can help students by previewing sites, and providing students with links to recommended sites that can help them gather information and complete their assignments.

The Internet allows students to learn and communicate with others. Bulletin board folders, E-mail, and chat groups offer students opportunities to talk to, share information and experiences with, and learn from others (Tao & Boulware, 2002). Internet bulletin boards allow students to locate and meet others with whom they may want to interact. E-mail gives them the chance to send private messages to and receive them from other individuals, as well as to develop social and academic skills. Chat groups or computer conferences offer students a forum to talk with others. Through the Internet, students and classes can have computer pals from other schools in the district, geographic region, country, and world with whom they communicate and learn (McGoogan 2002; Stanford & Siders, 2001). These interactions give students direct opportunities to learn about and with others, to experience different ways of life, and to learn and use a second language.

Technology is available to help *all* of your students communicate via the Internet. For example, RJ Cooper's IcanEmail serves as a talking E-mail program that uses prompts and an augmentative communication device to foster interactions with others electronically. Inter_Comm is a software program that allows students to use picture symbols when E-mailing.

The Internet provides you and your students with access to an enormous electronic library of lesson plans, learning activities, resources, pictorials, and databases containing information about virtually every subject and content area and in every language (Smith & Smith, 2002). Internet connections allow you and your students to examine and browse through these electronic documents. Students can visit and access information from mu-

Resource

Guernsey (2003) offers strategies and resources that can help you teach your students to conduct more effective and efficient Internet searches.

cd-rom

Resource

Teicher (1999) presents activities, resources, and websites that can help you teach students about Internet safety and responsibility.

Set Your Sites

For more information on teaching your students to evaluate websites and web-based information, go to the Web Links module in Chapter 8 of the Companion Website.

Resource

Trollinger and Slavkin (1999) provide guidelines for using E-mail to promote the learning and socialization of students with cognitive and behavioral disabilities.

Resource

Klemm (1998) offers guidelines for involving students in online conferences.

Resource

Smith and Smith (2002) describe Trackstar, an online resource designed to assist educators and students in integrating web-based information into instructional activities and assignments.

FIGURE 8.6

Guidelines for evaluating websites and web-based information

Credibility	
	◇ Who produces the information?
	◇ Is contact information for the creator(s) available?
	◇ Did the creators provide the sources of the information? Are the sources credible?
	◇ Are the credentials of the creators provided?
	◇ Is there evidence of revisions to the site?
Content	
	◇ How current and accurate is the information?
	◇ Are the purposes and objectives for the site clearly stated?
	◇ Does the title of the site reflect the content?
	◇ Is the language used at the site free of biases?
	◇ Is the site readable by the students at the appropriate grade level?
	◇ Is the information at the site properly organized?
	◇ How relevant is the information?
	◇ Were links provided to a variety of sites?
	◇ Are links appropriate and helpful?
Design and Navigability	
	◇ Is the site free of errors?
	◇ Is the site welcoming and user friendly?
	◇ Does the site load quickly and clearly?
	◇ Is navigation of the site logical and clear?
	◇ Are links clearly labeled?
Accessibility for individuals with disabilities	
	◇ Are clear options available for individuals with disabilities?
	◇ Does the site offer a text-only option?
	◇ Does the site offer links to support software designed especially for individuals with disabilities?

Source: From "Using the Internet to Improve Homework Communication and Completion," by S. J. Salend, D. Duhaney, D. J. Anderson and C. Gottschalk, 2004, *Teaching Exceptional Children, 36* (3) pp. 64–73. Copyright 2004 by The Council for Exceptional Children. Reprinted with permission.

seums via the Internet, and use streaming audio and video technology to watch or hear live or prerecorded broadcasts of events occurring throughout the world.

Software programs are available that help individuals with disabilities access the Internet. These programs, which are available in several languages, allow individuals with visual, dexterity-based, cognitive, and reading disabilities to browse and navigate the Internet by using audio prompting and error-minimization strategies, reducing the visuals presented on the screen, presenting computer text and graphics that are read aloud, or displaying text in large type.

You also can use the Internet to create accessible, easy-to-use classroom websites (Otto, 2002). Creating a website or page for your class is a good way to involve students in learning about the Internet and communicating with other students, families, and individuals throughout the world. For example, your class can work as a group to plan, design, and create a classroom web page relating to important aspects of your class. Like Ms. Taravella and Ms. Stoudamire, you also can post students' work on your class's web page, and students can receive and respond to inquiries from others about their web page. You also can use your website to make important learning materials available to students, and to create *weblogs*, online diaries that are easily updated regularly to present information about your class's activities. As we saw in chapter 4, your website can help you communicate with your students' families and involve them in the learning process. A variety of online resources (e.g., www.scholastic.com, www.schoolnotes.com, and www.TeacherWeb.com) offer easy-to-use assistance and services for creating and maintaining websites.

 Set Your Sites

For more on helping students with disabilities access the Internet and on evaluating the accessibility of websites, go to the Web Links module in Chapter 8 of the Companion Website.

Resource

March (2004) and Kelly (2000) offer guidelines, examples, and forms for using WebQuests and making them accessible to students with disabilities.

Set Your Sites

For more information on Web-Quests, go to the Web Links module in Chapter 8 of the Companion Website.

Reflective

What instructional technologies and assistive devices did you use as a student? As a teacher? What were the positive and negative effects of these technologies on your learning and your students' learning?

Resource

Atkinson, Neal, and Grechus (2003) offer a review of strategies built into software programs for addressing computer and Internet accessibility.

Set Your Sites

For more information on helping students with disabilities use computers, go to the Web Links module in Chapter 8 of the Companion Website.

Set Your Sites

For more information on voice-activated software, go to the Web Links module in Chapter 8 of the Companion Website.

Resource

Bauer and Ulrich (2002) offer guidelines and strategies for using PDAs in inclusive classrooms.

WebQuests.   Another type of Internet-based instructional activity that is becoming more common in classrooms is a WebQuest (Kelly, 2000; March, 2004). A WebQuest is an inquiry-oriented, cooperatively structured group activity in which some or all of the information that learners interact with comes from resources on the Internet or video-conferencing. For example, Ms. Taravella and her colleagues had students work in collaborative groups to complete WebQuests that asked them to use the Internet to gather and present information on the early explorations of the solar system and the corresponding cultural beliefs of different groups.

Assistive Devices

Computer technology has been used to develop many assistive devices to promote the learning, independence and communication abilities of students with various disabilities like Julia and Tom. These devices, described below, are an integral part of students' IEPs.

Devices for Students with Physical Disabilities

For students who have difficulty speaking intelligibly, assistive communication devices are invaluable. Low-technology devices, such as communication boards with pictures/words/objects, are nonelectric and tend to be homemade by clinicians.

High-technology assistive communication systems based on computer hardware and software and output devices transform word input into speech. Students can input a phrase or press a key or icon that activates the computer's speech capabilities. Specific vocabulary sets can be programmed based on students' educational and communicative needs, as well as the setting in which they need to communicate. As the technology evolves, these devices are being made more portable and with digitized speech that sounds more natural.

Some students, including those with physical disabilities, also may have problems inputting information into the computer in traditional ways (such as pressing more than one key at a time). To meet their needs, alternative methods have been developed (see Figure 8.7). These students also may benefit from accommodations to the standard keyboard such as ergonomic and alternative keyboards, keyguards, stickers to signify keys, key locks, and word-prediction and speech-recognition programs. They also may need to use built-in systems such as sticky keys, mouse keys, repeat keys, slow keys, bounce keys, and serial keys. Some students also may benefit from other built-in accessibility features including on-screen keyboarding, screen magnification, visual and auditory warnings, text-to-speech recognition, text narration, and mouse visibility and movement (Atkinson, Neal, & Grechus, 2003).

Voice-recogniton and voice-activated systems are allowing students with a range of disabilities to use computers, access and browse the Internet, and interact and share their ideas with others. These systems can convert spoken words into text, or into actions that activate computers and computer menus. For example, students can write papers or complete exams by dictating their ideas into the computer and then edit and spell check their work via use of word processing. Keep in mind that these systems are still being perfected; the programs will need to be taught to recognize a student's voice and students will need training to use them effectively.

Assistive devices also help individuals with disabilities organize and take notes in class. Some students use laptop computers with word processing programs and lightweight, voice-activated microcassette recorders or digital dictation systems for note-

FIGURE 8.7

Alternative methods of inputting information into computers

1. *Voice recognition:* The computer recognizes the user's speech and converts it into action.
2. *Key guard:* A device that modifies the traditional keyboard to change the size and spacing of the keys. It may include a key lock that automatically toggles specialty keys.
3. *Keyboard alteration programs:* Programs that modify the keyboard in terms of key accept time and key repeating.
4. *Graphics tablet:* A small slate that may be covered by templates of words, pictures, numerals, and letters that are input when touched by a special stylus.
5. *Adapted switches:* Switches controlled by pressure or body movements. They can be activated by foot, head, cheek, chin, or eye movements.
6. *Scanning systems:* An array of letters, phrases, and numerals displayed on the screen at a rate that is adjusted to the student's need. The student selects the message from the scanner by using the keyboard or a switch.
7. *Touch screens/light pens:* Devices that allow the student to activate the computer by touching or writing on the screen.
8. *Joystick:* A stick that is moved in different directions, controlling the movement of the cursor.
9. *Mouthstick:* A tool that is placed in the mouth and used to press buttons and activate switches.
10. *Headband:* A headband-like device that is worn by the student to control the computer through head or eye movements.
11. *Sip and puff systems:* A long command tube attached to a computer or wheelchair on which the student sucks.
12. *Skateboard:* A block of wood on rollers attached to the student's arm that is moved in different directions to control cursor movements.
13. *Mouse:* A mouselike object that is moved in different directions to control the computer. Adaptations of the mouse can be controlled by using the numeric pad of the keyboard (keyboard mouse) or by a headsetlike device, such as a headband, that conveys directions to the computer via head movements.
14. *Eye gaze:* Use of eye gazes and scanning to select stimuli that appear on the computer screen.
15. *Sensors:* Sensors are attached to the user and the computer and activated by facial movements or physical gestures.

taking. Personal digital assistants (PDAs) allow students to take notes that include illustrations. PDAs provide access to information and resources available through other technologies such as the Internet. PDAs and paging systems also can help students recall and access information and remember the correct sequence of tasks and routines, as well as organize schedules, information, and events (Bauer & Ulrich, 2002).

Computer technology has also helped increase the range of movements and thus the independence of individuals with physical disabilities (Cook & Cavalier, 1999). The iBOT mobility system employs sensors and gyroscopes which allow users of wheelchairs to go up and down stairs, shift into four-wheel drive, and elevate the chair to reach objects and adjust their eye levels. Robotic devices and computerized systems in the home can be programmed to turn on the oven, shut off lights, lock doors, and adjust the sound of the television so that these individuals can live on their own. Infrared remote control systems also allow individuals to control and operate devices and appliances.

Resource

Cook and Cavalier (1999) offer guidelines and a training sequence for using robotics with students.

Set Your Sites

For more information on robotics, go to the Web Links module in Chapter 8 of the Companion Website.

Devices for Students with Visual and Reading Disabilities

Several assistive devices have been developed to help use print materials (Mull & Sitlington, 2003). Various lightweight, inexpensive text scanners and character-recognition software such as the *Kurzweil 3000* recognize letters, group letters into words, pronounce words, and provide the correct pronunciation of words in a sentence in several languages. Printed materials are scanned and stored in memory. Students can then view the printed page, hear the text being read aloud, look up the meaning of unfamiliar words, highlight important content, and insert bookmarks. When selecting a scanning-based reading adaptive device, you should consider the ability of the scanner to scan accurately and the availability of an automatic document/page feeder.

Computer-based screen-reading programs allow computers to read text letter by letter or by phonetic markers; or convert words, sentences, and paragraphs into fluent speech. These programs, which can be read in different voices and languages, also allow users to search for or highlight words, sentences, and paragraphs that can be read aloud. These programs also can be customized to create pronunciation dictionaries and to control the speed, pitch, and volume of the speech.

Technological accommodations also are being developed to help students with visual and reading disabilities learn and use computers. As we discussed earlier in this chapter, digitized books help students use printed materials, including textbooks. Electronic dictionaries with digitized speech help students define unfamiliar words. Screen magnification programs enlarge computer-generated text and graphics to an appropriate size and adjust the colors on the screen to offer users the best contrast (Griffin et al., 2003). Font enlargement features also allow users to adjust the size of the fonts in which text is presented. Students with visual difficulties can benefit from use of Braille, larger keys, flicker-free monitors that have a higher resolution and contrast, and external magnification devices that are placed over the existing monitor.

Technology also is available to help students like Julia access computer-based information. A descriptive video system like the one Julia used also can provide access by offering a description of visually presented computer images and text (Curry, 2003). Students with visual disabilities also may use a tactile graphics display (TGD), which uses 36,000 tiny pins that adjust their configuration so users can tactilely access electronic images and text.

Technology also is available to assist students and professionals in converting print materials into Braille and to assist students with visual disabilities in taking Braille-based notes (Medina, 2002). Technology allows you and your students and colleagues to scan print materials, and then translate and convert them into Braille materials for use by students. A va-

Instructional technology and assistive devices are helping students succeed in inclusive settings. What technologies and assistive devices help your students?

riety of optical aids including goggles, hand-held magnifiers, magnifiers mounted on a base, and magnifiers attached to eyeglass frames or incorporated in the lenses magnify printed materials for individuals with visual disabilities (Griffin et al., 2003).

Communication systems for individuals with visual disabilities also exist. *Tele-Braille* helps deaf and blind individuals communicate by converting a message typed on a Braille keyboard into print on a video monitor, which is read by a sighted person. The sighted person then types a response, which is converted into a Braille display. Computers with large-print, Braille, and voice output capabilities also allow students with visual disabilities to communicate. These students also may benefit from the use of Braille printers, refreshable Braille displays, and Braille note-takers.

Electronic travel aids can increase the independent movement of students with visual disabilities. The *Mowat Sensor* is a handheld electronic device that uses vibrations to alert students to barriers in their path and to indicate the distance to obstacles. The *Laser Cane* emits three laser beams that provide a sound signaling objects, dropoffs, or low-hanging obstacles in the user's path.

Resource

Griffin et al. (2002) provide a listing of technology to support the learning of students with visual disabilities.

Devices for Students with Hearing Disabilities

Technology is making a profound improvement in assistive devices for individuals with hearing disabilities. New types of hearing aids based on digital technology contain powerful computer chips that filter out background noises, deliver more realistic sound, and tailor the sound to the individual's needs and acoustic setting. Systems that convert verbal statements to print allow individuals with and without hearing disabilities to communicate. The *teletypewriter* translates speech into a visual display on a screen that can be read by individuals with hearing disabilities.

Cell phones with text messaging features allow these individuals to communicate by telephone. As we saw in chapter 7, some students with hearing or attention disabilities may benefit from assistive communication devices that amplify sounds in the classroom.

With computer software and assistive devices, students with hearing disabilities can access oral presentations and material presented on computers. Speech-to-text translation systems allow students with hearing disabilities to view a monitor that presents the speaker's comments within 3 seconds (Elliot, Foster, & Stinson, 2002). At the end of class sessions, text files are edited to provide students with notes. Students with hearing disabilities also can access computer-based information via systems where the text and graphics appear on the video monitor accompanied by a video of a signer who signs the text. For students who have some hearing, a digitized voice can read the text as the signer signs it. Some students who rely on speechreading may benefit from a classroom speechreading technology system that involves a live video transmission of the speaker's lips to a small desktop monitor located on students' desks.

Devices for Students from Diverse Language Backgrounds

The academic performance and language learning of students who are second language learners also can be enhanced through many of the instructional technology and assistive devices previously discussed, which they can access using their preferred language (Curry, 2003). They also may benefit from technology that provides meaningful, active, sensory-based support. They can use a hand-held talking translator that can convert verbal statements or text from one language into another. They can use Quicktionary, a pen-like device that scans text in one language and translates it into another language. CD-ROM technology also is available that allows students to see mouth and tongue

Using Instructional Technology and Assistive Devices to Differentiate Instruction

Mr. Nealon, a social studies teacher, and Ms. Camac, the school's technology specialist, were excited about developing and teaching a unit on the Vietnam War using instructional technology. They started to develop the unit by searching the Internet for content, online lesson plans, and teaching resources about Vietnam and the war. They also participated in a chat room related to teaching and technology, which also provided suggestions for the unit. Then they identified and reviewed interesting and relevant websites and resources and created their unit. They also visited the websites, which provided help in designing various web-based activities.

Since their students' experience with the Internet varied, Mr. Nealon and Ms. Camac began by teaching students about the Internet and how to use it. They provided an overview of how to access and navigate the Internet, and paired experienced users with novices to perform a World Wide Web scavenger hunt that required them to conduct searches for various topics. They had students go online to www.cybersmartcurrriculum.org to access a curriculum that taught them how to use the Internet safely, responsibly, efficiently, and effectively. They brainstormed with students and framed rules for use of the Internet by having students respond to such questions as "What would you do if you were asked for personal information or your password?" "What would you do if someone wanted to meet you or sell you something?" and "What would you do if you received or encountered offensive material?" They also told students not to believe everything they read or heard via the Internet. They gave students guidelines for examining and verifying sites and information, which included identifying the individuals who created the site, the dates on which it was created and updated, the location and organizational affiliation of the site, and the content of the site.

Once they were convinced that students could use the technology appropriately, Mr. Nealon and Ms. Camac assigned students to work in groups. Each group selected a variety of learning activities from a menu that included:

- viewing a DVD that portrayed actual battles and presented interviews with soldiers.
- taking a three-dimensional panoramic tour of the Vietnam Memorial through pictures that Ms. Camac had taken the previous summer with a digital camera and downloaded to a computer.
- watching online videos of news reports from the 1960s and 1970s and documentaries about the Vietnam War and antiwar activities throughout the United States and the world.
- exchanging e-mail messages with military experts and leaders of the antiwar movement.

- using virtual reality to attend rallies for and against the war.
- examining primary-source documents online.
- hearing eyewitness accounts of the war from the viewpoint of soldiers, protestors, and Vietnamese citizens.
- making an online visit to an exhibition on the Vietnam War at the Smithsonian Museum.
- establishing a keypal relationship with Vietnamese and U.S. students and their families.

While the groups worked, Mr. Nealon and Ms. Camac helped them. When computers froze because students tried to download too much information, they helped students reboot them. They also aided students who had difficulty reading information from websites by using Internet screen reading programs and reformatting the text and images so that they were easier for students to read.

Mr. Nealon and Ms. Camac also allowed each group to choose its own final product. Group projects included writing and making a video of a play about the Vietnam War, completing a WebQuest about the war, preparing a presentation about the war using presentation software, conducting an online survey of the community's knowledge of the Vietnam War, and creating a memorial to Vietnam Veterans and the peace movement. All students helped to develop their group's project. Steven, a student with a severe disability, used his assistive communication system to speak lines in his group's play, and Marta, a second language learner, helped her group translate their community survey into Spanish.

Mr. Nealon and Ms. Camac shared the groups' projects by posting them on the class's web page. They were pleased when they received e-mail messages from other teachers and their students' families commenting on the students' products and requesting to use activities from their unit.

- What strategies did Mr. Nealon and Ms. Camac use to differentiate instruction for their students?
- What process and resources did they use to create and implement their technology-based unit?
- What do you think the students and their families thought about this unit?
- What difficulties might you encounter in using instructional technology activities in your classroom?
- How could you attempt to solve these difficulties?

 To answer these questions online and share your responses with others, go to the Reflection module in Chapter 8 of the Companion Website.

movements associated with sounds, hear the pronunciation of words and sentences in their new language, and then record and receive feedback on their own attempts to speak the new language (Biederman, 2002). The *Language Master* is an electronic dictionary, thesaurus, and grammar and spell checker that pronounces words, gives definitions and synonyms, corrects the spelling of phonetic words, and offers educational games involving more than 83,000 words. The *Language Master* allows you and your students to play, record, and erase oral material on stimulus cards and write on the stimulus cards to provide visual cues.

Bilingual word processing programs provide bilingual online assistance with dictionaries, thesauruses, and spell and grammar checkers. Interactive DVDs and CD-ROM programs offer access to bilingual glossaries and many opportunities for students to develop their vocabulary, word recognition, and reading and listening comprehension skills.

Summary

This chapter offered guidelines for differentiating instruction to address the diverse learning strengths and challenges of your students. As you review the questions posed in this chapter, remember the following points:

How Can I Differentiate Instruction for Students?

CEC 2, 3, 4, 5, 7, 9, 10, PRAXIS 3, INTASC 1, 2, 3, 4, 5, 6, 7, 9

You can tailor your curricular goals and teaching strategies to the individual strengths and challenges of your students and your learning environment. It is also important to use individualized curricular, teaching and instructional materials accommodations, and universally designed materials. You also can provide personal support; address students' learning styles, preferences, and sensory abilities.

How Can I Differentiate Instruction for Students Who Have Difficulty Reading and Gaining Information from Print Materials?

CEC 2, 4, 7, 9, PRAXIS 3, INTASC 2, 3, 4, 7, 9

You can use a variety of teacher- and student-directed strategies. In addition, you can make materials more readable by modifying them, reducing their linguistic complexity, incorporating the principles of typographical design, and using instructional technology.

How Can I Differentiate Instruction for Students from Diverse Cultural and Language Backgrounds?

CEC 1, 3, 4, 5, 6, 7, 9, 10, PRAXIS 3, INTASC 1, 2, 3, 4, 5, 6, 7, 8, 9, 10

You can use a multicultural curriculum, multicultural instructional materials, culturally relevant and responsive teaching strategies, reciprocal interaction, and effective ESL techniques. You can also encourage students to respond.

How Can I Use Instructional Technology and Assistive Devices to Differentiate Instruction for Students?

CEC 6, 7, 9, PRAXIS 3, INTASC 4, 6, 7, 9

Recent developments in instructional technology allow you to create differentiated, interactive, motivating, and contextualized learning environments for

Council for Exceptional Children

PRAXIS

inTASC

students by using computer-based instruction, hypertext/hypermedia, videocassettes, CDs, and DVDs, digital cameras, caption television, liquid crystal display projection panels, presentation software, virtual reality, and the Internet. You also can use assistive devices to help students learn, communicate with others, use technology, be organized, take notes, increase their range of movements and mobility, read text, hear sounds, and learn a second language.

What Would You Do in Today's Diverse Classroom?

Your class includes the following students:

★   Alexis is an inconsistent reader. Her reading difficulties are greatest when she is asked to read handouts and tests. She also has trouble understanding text. Alexis likes to work with others, and works hard to please her teachers and her family.

★   Raymond, a student with cerebral palsy, has difficulty walking and limited use of his hands. While he can speak, it is very hard to understand him. Because of his communication difficulties, it is hard to assess his cognitive abilities. However, the professionals who work with him report that he has normal intelligence.

★   Carla, a student with a moderate hearing impairment, has difficulty following orally presented information and directions. She relies heavily on gestures and visual stimuli. Usually she can understand face-to-face communications. Her speech, which is impaired, is intelligible to others. However, she needs to be prodded to speak in class.

★   Malik is an African American student who is in the gifted and talented program. Despite his intellectual abilities, his performance is erratic. Occasionally, he appears to be bored in class and rushes through his work so that he can work with others or use one of the learning centers.

1.   How would you determine the appropriate strategies to differentiate instruction for Alexis, Raymond, Carla, and Malik?

2.   What strategies would you use to differentiate instruction for these students?

3.   How could you use instructional technology and assistive devices to differentiate instruction for Alexis, Raymond, Carla, and Malik?

4.   What difficulties might you encounter in differentiating instruction for these students?

5.   What knowledge, skills, dispositions, and support do you need to differentiate instruction for these students?

 To answer these questions online and share your responses with others, go to the Reflection module in Chapter 8 of the Companion Website.

Chapter 9

Differentiating Large- and Small-Group Instruction

Ms. Anderson

Ms. Anderson begins her lesson by reminding students, "We have been learning about poetic elements and devices." She then tells them, "One of the most popular types of poetry is song. Yes, when each of you listens to the radio or a favorite CD, you're actually attending a poetry reading of sorts. For homework, I asked you to bring the lyrics of your favorite song to class. Who would like to share their favorite song with us? And what you like about it?" Ms. Anderson pauses for several seconds before randomly picking a student to respond. She tells the students that later on they will be working with their songs/poems.

Ms. Anderson tells the students, "We are going to learn about several new poetic devices." She reviews the poetic devices they have learned and then identifies and defines several new ones. She then plays her favorite song and discusses what she likes about it. Using a PowerPoint presentation, she displays the words of her favorite song for students and highlights and discusses the different poetic elements in the song, focusing on the new poetic devices she wants them to learn. She periodically asks students to identify the poetic element depicted, and justify their responses ("Why do you think it is that device?"). Sometimes she asks another student if he or she agrees with a student's response.

Next, Ms. Anderson has students work in think-pair-share groups to identify poetic devices in statements. Students independently think about the statements, discuss their answers with their partners, and then share their responses with the class. She then gives students an independent assignment that involves identifying the various poetic elements they have been learning about. She describes the assignment to students, explains what she wants them to do, and does an example with the students. She differentiates the assignment for students in several ways. Some students respond to true/false statements, while others match poetic devices to their corresponding statements. Some students are asked to identify poetic devices in various statements, while others are given a list of poetic elements and asked to compose statements that reflect them. As students work on the assignment, Ms. Anderson circulates around the room, acknowledging them, providing feedback, and assisting them. She also solicits feedback from students by asking them to identify things that are still confusing and what she can do to help them understand the material better. For homework, she asks students to identify the poetic devices used in their favorite songs. She also tells the students that tomorrow they will be working in cooperative learning groups to analyze their favorite songs and the poetic devices used.

What other ways could Ms. Anderson use to differentiate instruction for her students? After reading this chapter, you should have the knowledge, skills, and dispositions to answer this as well as the following questions:

★ **How can I adapt large-group instruction for students?**
★ **How can I use effective teacher-centered instruction?**
★ **How can I successfully use cooperative learning arrangements with students?**

L ike Ms. Anderson, you teach in many different ways. You use oral presentations, effective teacher-centered instruction, and cooperative learning to help students learn. However, if *all your students* are to benefit from these varied arrangements, you must adapt these arrangements to the unique needs of your students and your curriculum. This chapter offers strategies that you can use to differentiate large- and small-group instruction for *all students*.

How Can I Adapt Large-Group Instruction for Students?

The following section offers information on strategies you can use to foster student learning when you are teaching large groups of students.

Have Students Work Collaboratively

The amount of information students gain from teacher-directed presentations can be increased by using a variety of learning arrangements in which students work collaboratively, such as collaborative discussion teams, Send a Problem, Numbered Heads Together, and Think-Pair-Share.

Collaborative Discussion Teams

Collaborative discussion teams can be used throughout the presentation. After a certain amount of time, usually 10 to 15 minutes, teams can respond to discussion questions, react to material presented, or predict what will happen or be discussed next. Teams can then be called on to share their responses. At the end of the presentations, teams can summarize the main points and check each other's comprehension.

Send a Problem

In the Send a Problem technique, groups make up questions that are answered by other groups. This is done by developing a list of questions related to material being presented in class, recording the answers to each question, and passing the questions from group to group.

Numbered Heads Together

Numbered Heads Together can be used to help students review and check their understanding of orally presented information (Kagan, 1992; Maheady, Michielli-Pendl, Mallette, & Harper, 2002). You can use this method by doing the following:

1. Assign students to mixed-ability groups of three or four.
2. Assign a number (1, 2, 3, or 4) to each student in each group.
3. Break up the oral presentation by periodically asking the class a question and telling each group, "Put your heads together and make sure that everyone in your group knows the answer."
4. Tell the groups to end their discussion, call a number, ask all students with that number to raise their hands, select one of the students with that number to answer, and ask the other students with that number to agree with or expand on the answer.

REFLECTING ON YOUR PRACTICES

Delivering Oral Presentations to Students

You can examine your success in giving oral presentations to students by addressing the following questions:

- Are the objectives, purpose, and relevance of the oral presentation stated at the beginning?
- Are prerequisite information and key terms reviewed and explained so that students understand them?
- Has the relationship between the new material and old material been established?
- Are the pace and sequence of the presentation appropriate?
- Is student interest maintained by using changes in voice level, stories to make a point, jokes, and humorous anecdotes?
- Are students provided with opportunities to participate and ask questions?
- Are ordinal numbers and time cues (*first, second, finally*) used to organize information for students?
- Are important concepts and critical points emphasized by varying voice quality and by using cues (e.g., "It is important that you remember")— speaking them with emphasis, writing them on the blackboard, and repeating them?
- Are examples, illustrations, charts, diagrams, advance organizers, maps, and multimedia used to make the material more concrete and to supplement oral material?
- Are individuals, places, or things referred to by nouns rather than pronouns, and by using specific numerals instead of ambiguous ones (using *two* instead of *a couple*)?
- Are vague terms ("these kinds of things," "somewhere") and phrases ("to make a long story short," "as you all know") avoided?
- Are questions asked that require students to think about the information presented and that assess understanding and recall?
- Do you pause periodically to have students discuss and review new content and their notes, jot down questions, and rehearse important points?
- Do students have opportunities to ask questions during and after the class?
- Do students have time at the end of class to review, discuss, summarize, and organize the main points and their notes?

How would you rate your oral presentations? ( ) Excellent ( ) Good ( ) Need Improvement ( ) Need Much Improvement

What steps could you adopt to improve your oral presentations?

Think-Pair-Share

Think-Pair-Share, another cooperative learning strategy that Ms. Anderson used in the chapter-opening vignette, can help students master content presented orally. The process is as follows:

1. Pair students randomly.
2. Give students a question, problem, or situation.
3. Ask individual students to think about the question.
4. Have students discuss their responses with their partners.
5. Select several pairs to share their thoughts and responses with the class.

Encourage Students to Ask Questions

To benefit from oral instruction and to understand assignments and directions, students can ask questions. However, many students may be reluctant to do so. To help these students overcome their fear of asking questions, you can praise them for asking questions, give them time to write down and ask questions during class, give students the correct answer and ask them to state the corresponding question, and teach students when and how to ask questions.

Help Students Take Notes

The amount of information gained from the teacher's oral presentations also depends on the students' ability to take notes, which can help students stay engaged (Fisher, Frey, & Williams, 2002). A variety of strategies for improving students' note-taking skills are presented below.

Outlines

You can give students a framework for note taking by using a strategic note-taking form (Boyle & Weishaar, 2001), a listening guide or a skeleton/slot/frame outline (Katamaya & Robinson, 2000), or Cornell notes (Fisher, Frey, & Williams, 2002). A *strategic note-taking form* contains teacher-prepared cues that guide students in taking notes and prompts them to use effective note-taking skills during oral presentations (see Figure 9.1).

While a strategic note-taking form can be used repeatedly regardless of the content of the class, listening guides and skeleton/slot/frame outlines are tailored to the unique content of a specific class (Hamilton, Selbert, Gardner, & Talbert-Johnson, 2000). A *listening guide* is a list of important terms and concepts that parallels the order in which they will be presented in class. Students add to this list by writing supplemental information and supportive details. A *skeleton/slot/frame outline* or *guided notes* present a sequential overview of the key terms and main points as an outline made up of incomplete statements with visual cues such as spaces, letters, and labels that can help students determine the amount and type of information to be recorded (Figure 9.2). Students listen to the lecture or read the textbook chapter and fill in the blanks to complete the outline, which then serves as the students' notes. You can encourage students to use outlines by periodically pairing students to check each other's outlines and sometimes collecting them.

If giving students outlines is not feasible, you can teach students to use Cornell notes (Fisher, Frey, & Williams, 2002). Students implement this note-taking system by:

1. placing a vertical line 2 inches from the left side of the page.
2. recording key points and words to the left of the line.
3. writing details related to the key points and words to the right of the line.
4. using the bottom of the page to summarize the critical ideas from the lesson.

You can foster note-taking by listing the major points. You also can structure students' notes at the beginning of class by listing questions on the blackboard relating to the day's work and then discussing answers to them at the end of class.

Highlighting Main Points

To help students determine important points to include in their notes, you can emphasize these points by adjusting your pace and rate of speaking, pausing for attention, using introductory phrases (e.g., *an important point, remember that, it is especially important*), and changing inflection (Boyle, 2001). You also can highlight main points by writing them on the board and reviewing them before you erase them.

Another method that can help students identify important points is *oral quizzing,* in which the teacher allots time at the end of the class to respond to students' questions and to ask questions based on the material presented. End-of-class time can also be devoted to summarizing and reviewing notes and main points and discussing what points should be in the students' notes (Boyle, 2001). Pairing students to check each other's notes after class also ensures that students' notes are in the desired format and include

Resource

Porte (2001) describes a manipulative note-taking process that can be used across content areas, and Yell (2002) offers guidelines for teaching students to use a guide to take notes during video-based presentations.

Resource

Lazarus (1996) offers guidelines for developing and using skeleton guided notes.

FIGURE 9.1

Strategic note-taking form

STRATEGIC NOTE-TAKING FORM

Fill in this portion before the lecture begins.

What is today's topic?

Describe what you know about the topic.

As the instructor lectures, use these pages to take notes on the lecture.

Today's topic?

Name three to seven main points with details of today's topic as they are being discussed.

Summary—Quickly describe how the ideas are related.

New Vocabulary or Terms:

Name three to seven *new* main points with details as they are being discussed.

New Vocabulary or Terms:

Summary—Quickly describe how the ideas are related.

Name three to seven *new* main points with details as they are being discussed.

New Vocabulary or Terms:

Summary—Quickly describe how the ideas are related.

At End of Lecture

Write five main points of the lecture and describe each point.

1.
2.
3.
4.
5.

Source: From "Enhancing the Note-Taking Skills of Students with Mild Disabilities," by J. R. Boyle, 2001, *Intervention in School and Clinic, 36,* pp. 221–224. Copyright 2001 by PRO-ED, Inc. Reprinted with permission.

FIGURE 9.2

Sample listening guide

Civil War

A. The sides
   1. The Union:

   2. The Confederacy:

   3. The Border States:
      a.   c.
      b.   d.

B. Advantages of each side
   1. The Union:
      a.   c.
      b.   d.
   2. The Confederacy:
      a.   c.
      b.   d.

C. The strategy of each side:
   1. The Union:
      a.
      b.
      c.
   2. The Confederacy:
      a.
      b.
      c.

D. Key individuals to know
   1. Abraham Lincoln
   2. Jefferson Davis
   3. Stonewall Jackson
   4. Robert E. Lee
   5. Ulysses S. Grant
   6. Clara Barton

Source: Developed by Peter Goss, social studies teacher, New Paltz Central Schools, New Paltz, New York.

Teachers can use a variety of strategies to help students take notes. What strategies do your teachers use to promote your note-taking in class?

relevant content. In addition, you can check the student notes by regularly collecting and reviewing them.

Peer Note-Takers and Audiocassette Recorders

For students who have difficulty taking notes, peer note-takers can be used (Elliot, Foster, & Stinson, 2002). When selecting peer note-takers, you should consider their mastery of the content, sensitivity to students who need help with note-taking, and ability to take legible and organized notes. Students also can record class sessions and then replay them after class using a variable speech-control tape recorder that allows students to listen to notes at their own pace (Mull & Sitlington, 2003). Whether students are using peer note-takers or audiocassettes, they can be required to take notes during class. This allows them to practice their note-taking skills and keep alert in class. It also helps prevent resentment from other students who may think that students with peer note-takers have to do less work. You also can foster the note-taking process by providing students with time at the end of the class to compare their notes with their peers.

Reflective

What skills and strategies do you use to pay attention and take notes in class? Are they successful? How do they compare with the strategies presented in this book?

Teach Note-Taking Skills and Strategies

You can help students learn to use a variety of note-taking skills and strategies. Students can improve their note-taking skills by using several behaviors before, during, and after the class. These behaviors and note-taking skills are presented in Figure 9.3. Since the note-taking strategy selected depends on the content, students also can be taught to match their strategy to the material. A *chart* is used when the speaker is contrasting information. When information is ordered by the date of occurrence, students can use a *timeline*, which involves making a horizontal line across the page and recording the events and dates in sequence. If the material is presented in steps, then *stepwise*, or numerical, note-taking is best. Examples of these three systems are presented in Figure 9.4.

Resource

Strategies that can help students take notes include CALL UP and "A" NOTES (Czarnecki, Rosko, & Fine, 1998) and LINKS and AWARE (Suritsky & Hughes, 1996).

Foster Students' Listening Skills

Since listening is critical to learning from teacher-directed presentations, you can foster students' listening skills. Periodically, you can ask questions about critical content and have students try to predict what will be discussed next. To increase listening, you can also provide visual aids, vary the pace of the oral presentation to emphasize critical points, move around the room, place the student near the speaker, and minimize unimportant and distracting noises and activities. Additional strategies to help students learn to listen are presented next.

Using Cues

Both nonverbal and verbal cues can help students listen. *Nonverbal* cues, such as eye contact and gestures, as well as awareness of the reactions of their peers, can increase a student's listening skills. For example, if a student observes others in the class looking intently at the teacher, it can indicate the need to listen carefully. Some students may benefit from using a cue card that lists the guidelines for listening.

Students can be taught how to respond to *verbal* cues such as pacing, inflection, and loudness. They can also learn the words and statements that teachers use to highlight and organize key points.

Listening Materials

Many materials that help teach listening skills have been developed for elementary and secondary students (Tilley-Gregory, 2004). These materials teach a variety of listening skills, including identifying and paying attention to auditory stimuli; using memory strategies such as visualization, rehearsal, and grouping; following directions; determining the sequence, main ideas, and details of the information; identifying supporting information; and making inferences and predicting outcomes.

Set Your Sites

For more information on listening skills, go to the Web Links module in Chapter 9 of the Companion Website.

FIGURE 9.3

Recommended student note-taking skills

BEFORE THE CLASS

◇ Try to anticipate what the teacher will cover by reading the assigned material and reviewing notes from previous classes.
◇ Bring writing utensils, notebooks, and an audiocassette recorder if necessary.
◇ Come to class mentally and physically prepared.
◇ Select a seat near the speaker, and take a good listening posture.
◇ List the name of the class, page number, and date on each page to ensure continuity.
◇ Organize notebook pages into two columns, one on the left for checking understanding and the other on the right for recording notes.

DURING THE CLASS

◇ Pay attention, and avoid being distracted by outside stimuli.
◇ Listen to and watch for verbal and nonverbal cues from the speaker and the audience.
◇ Write legibly, and record notes in your own words.
◇ Jot down only critical points and essential details.
◇ Write complete statements rather than unconnected words or phrases.
◇ Record the teacher's examples to clarify information.
◇ Listen for key phrases that indicate important information and transitions from one point to another.
◇ Highlight important ideas through highlighting, underlining, extra spacing, and boxing.
◇ Skip a line to indicate transitions between material.
◇ Draw diagrams and sketches to help you understand key points and concepts.
◇ Use symbols. For example, a ? can indicate missed information, and an = can indicate a relationship between two concepts.
◇ Use shorthand and abbreviations.

NEAR THE END OF CLASS

◇ Add any missing words, incomplete thoughts, related details, or original ideas.
◇ Summarize the main points using a *noteshrink* technique, which involves surveying the notes, identifying and highlighting main points, and listing these points in the quiz column.

AFTER THE CLASS

◇ Review and edit notes.
◇ Identify important points and information that needs further clarification, and then seek additional explanations from teachers and/or peers.
◇ Ask the teacher or a peer to provide missed information.
◇ Indicate an overlap between the textbook and the teacher's comments.
◇ Record the length of time spent on a topic.

Note: Boyle (2001); Suritsky & Hughes (1996).

Gain and Maintain Students' Attention

An important aspect of listening to and following directions is paying attention. However, many students have difficulty focusing their attention. You may have to use several attention-getting strategies, such as

1. directing them to listen carefully ("Listen carefully to what I say.").
2. giving clear, emphatic instructions ("Take out your books and open to page 24.").
3. pausing before speaking to make sure that all students are paying attention.
4. limiting distractions.

Chart Method

	Hamilton	*Jefferson*
Cabinet Position	Secretary of the Treasury	Secretary of State
Political Party	Federalist	Republican
Constitutional	Supported England	Supported France

Timeline Method

Archduke Ferdinand Assassinated	Germany Declares War on France	U.S. Declares War on Germany

1914	1914	1915	1917

Germany Declares War on Russia	Germany Sinks *Lusitania*

Stepwise Method

The three principles underlying Roosevelt's "Good Neighbor" Policy:

1. Noninterference in affairs of independent countries
2. Concern for economic policies of Latin American countries
3. Establishment of inter-American cooperation

FIGURE 9.4   Three methods of note-taking

You also can use age-appropriate cues, such as a verbal statement or physical gesture (raising a hand, blinking the lights), to alert students to the need to pay attention.

Once you have gained students' attention, you can use several methods to maintain it. First, you can present material rapidly and have students respond often. For example, like Ms. Anderson, you can select students randomly to respond, remind students that they may be called on next, ask students to add information to or explain an answer given by a peer, and use repetition. You also can group students with peers who can stay attentive, maintain eye contact with *all students*, create suspense, change activities frequently, and vary the ways of presenting material and asking students to respond.

Give Clear and Detailed Directions

Students will perform better during large- and small-group instruction if you use certain techniques for giving clear and detailed directions (Salend, Elhoweris, & van Garderen, 2003). When explaining assignments, make certain that *all students* are attentive, pausing when they are not. Communicate by speaking slowly and clearly, using a voice that your students can hear and language they can understand (Saunders, 2001). Try to keep your statements as brief as possible, and emphasize key words and statements.

Start by describing the assignment and the reasons for working on it ("This assignment will help us remember the parts and functions of plants, which will be on your test next week."), and highlighting the motivating aspects of the assignment ("You are going to work in groups to compare the different plants we have around our school."). Next, give directions visually and review them orally. When giving directions orally, you can simplify the vocabulary, cut down on unnecessary words and irrelevant information, and use consistent terms from assignment to assignment. Students can copy the directions in their notebooks. For students who have difficulty copying from the blackboard or writing, a teacher-prepared handout can be given, using the writing style to which the students are accustomed. Directions for completing assignments can also be recorded on an audiocassette. **To view an example of a teacher giving directions to students, go to Case 2: Classroom Climate on the CD-ROM and click on the Clear Expectations video clip. What did the teacher do to help the students understand her expectations for completing the assignment?**

cd-rom

In presenting directions that have several steps, you can number and list the steps in order and provide visual prompts via use of pictorials and symbols (Downing & Eichinger, 2003). For example, an assignment using dictionary skills can be presented by listing and using visuals to depict the steps:

1. Use the dictionary guide words.
2. Check the pronunciation of each word.
3. Write the definition.

You can also use software and digital cameras to create computer-based activity directions, which employ combinations of pictures, graphics, symbols, words, sounds, and voices to help students understand and follow sequential directions (Kimball, Kinney, Taylor, & Stromer, 2003).

Students will also understand directions more clearly if you provide a model of the assignment, and describe the qualities you will use in evaluating it (Whittaker, Salend, & Duhaney, 2001). It also helps to encourage students to ask questions about the assignment, and have students paraphrase and explain the directions to the rest of the class (Rademacher, 2000). You may also question students to see how well they understand the:

- instructions ("What am I asking you to do?" "What steps are you required to follow in doing this assignment?" "Can you anticipate any problems in doing this assignment?").
- materials they need to complete the assignment ("What materials do you need?").
- ways they can get help ("If you have a problem, whom should you ask for help?").
- time frame for completing the assignment ("How long do you have to work on the assignment?").
- things they can do if they finish the assignment ("What can you do if you finish early?").
- questions they have about the assignment ("Do you have any questions about the assignment?").

Finally, to ensure understanding, students can complete several problems from the assignment under your supervision before beginning to work independently.

For students who continue to have problems in following directions, you can break directions into shorter, more meaningful statements. When possible, give no more than two instructions at a time. These students can work on one part of the assignment at a time and can check with an adult before advancing to the next part. Long assignments can be divided into several shorter ones, with students completing one part before working on the next.

Another way to help students follow directions is to allow time for students to receive teacher assistance. You can move around the room to monitor students and provide assistance to those who need it. You can also teach them to use a signup sheet to schedule teacher–student meetings. The times when adults are available to provide help can be listed, and students can sign their names next to the desired time. **To view an example of a teacher circulating around the room to check whether students understand their assignments, go to Case 4: Support Participation on the CD-ROM and click on the Empower Students video clip. How does monitoring students' understanding foster the instructional process for students and teachers?**

Motivate Students

Motivation is an important aspect of learning, listening, and following directions. Motivation is often categorized as *extrinsic* or *intrinsic* (Witzel & Mercer, 2003). *Extrinsic motivation* relates to taking actions as a result of external consequences such as tangibles, and approval from others. *Intrinsic motivation* refers to taking actions as a result of internally based consequences (e.g., sense of mastery and accomplishment) and is viewed as a higher level of motivation than extrinsic motivation.

Because of their past history of struggle or failure, some students with special needs may lack the motivation necessary to be successful learners. Since motivation is dependent on a range of factors, you may need to employ a variety of instructional techniques and curriculum accommodations to motivate your students (Brim & Whitaker, 2000). **To hear educators discussing the importance of motivation as well as strategies for motivating students, go to Case 3: Assess Plan on the CD-ROM and click on the Academic Inroads, Social Setting, and Identify Goals video clips. What factors affected the student's motivation and how did the educators use them to motivate the student?**

Create a Supportive and Rewarding Learning Environment

One of the most important motivational strategies for students is providing them with a supportive learning environment that includes positive interactions with their teachers

Teachers may need to modify the ways they give directions to students. How do you modify directions for your students?

that build students' self-efficacy and sense of belonging and usefulness (Margolis & Mc-Cabe, 2003).

You can create a positive learning environment for students by displaying enthusiasm for teaching and learning and building and maintaining rapport with them. Rapport can be established by talking with students about topics that interest them, participating in after-school activities with them, and recognizing their unique talents and important events in their lives. **To view an example of a teacher motivating a student by recognizing the student's unique talents, go to Case 2: Classroom Climate on the CD-ROM and click on the Accept Others video clip. What does the teacher say to motivate the student?** Additional strategies for creating a supportive and rewarding learning environment and building positive relationships with and among students are presented in chapters 5 and 7.

Offer a Meaningful, Interesting, Age-Appropriate, Creative and Challenging Curriculum and Instructional Program

Providing students with access to a meaningful, interesting, and challenging curriculum and an age-appropriate and creative instructional program are also critical factors in establishing a learning environment that motivates students to succeed (Tomlinson, 2002a). Student motivation can be built by using high-interest activities, relevant and integrated content, and culturally relevant topics and instructional materials that relate to students' lives as Ms. Anderson did in linking poetry to students' favorite songs (Kern, Bambara, & Fogt, 2002; Voltz, 2003). You also can share with students why the content, process, and learning activities and products are worthwhile to them.

Use Novelty and Movement

Students also may benefit from learning activities that are enjoyable and pique their curiosity via use of novelty and movement (Prigge, 2002). Novelty can be integrated into lessons by using suspense, fantasy, color, technology, and other innovative ways to arouse student interest, and keep them engaged in the learning process. Novelty also can be fostered by using students' interests and experiences and popular characters, items and trends in classroom examples and assignments. Novelty and movement also can be incorporated through use of active academic games, which we will discuss later in this chapter.

Involve Students in the Instructional Process

Involving students in the instructional process so that they have a greater commitment to and control over their learning also can increase their motivation (Oldfather, 2002). Therefore, you can provide students with numerous opportunities to select personally important goals, participate in instructional planning and evaluation, and respond and make choices during instructional activities (Margolis & McCabe, 2003; Mithaug, 2002) (see chapter 6). At the beginning of a lesson you can work with your students to set learning goals, and make choices about the learning activities that will help them achieve their goals. **To view examples of a teacher giving students instructional choices, go to Case 2: Classroom Climate on the CD-ROM and click on the Increasing Interests and Clear Expectations video clips. How did giving the students choices foster their motivation and learning?** At the end of the lesson, they can self-correct their work to evaluate whether they achieved their goals.

cd-rom

Reflective

How do you help your students become intrinsically motivated?

Resources

Desrochers and Desrochers (2000) offer guides for designing and implementing motivating lessons.

Resource

Jolivette, Stichter, and McCormick (2002) offer guidelines for providing students with opportunities to make choices during instructional activities.

cd-rom

Resource

Stafford et al. (2002) and Smith (2002) provide suggestions for facilitating the choice making of students with significant cognitive and communication disabilities.

Student involvement and motivation also can be promoted by attribution training, which involves teaching them to analyze the events and actions that lead to their success and failure (Kozminsky & Kozminsky, 2002). Thus, at the end of an activity, students can complete an attribution self-report or dialogue page to examine the extent to which their effort and motivation affected their learning (see Figures 6.11 and 6.12; also see chapter 6 for additional strategies for teaching students to make choices and fostering positive attributions in students).

Use Student-Directed Learning

You also can use student-directed learning to help students become involved and participate in instruction and gain a sense of ownership in education, which increases their motivation, self-efficacy, and learning (Brown, 2002). To promote student-directed learning, link instruction to students' real-world experiences and interests, use a thematic approach, understand and adapt instruction to students' cultural and language backgrounds and learning styles, and use a problem-solving approach to learning (Voltz, 2003). In addition, use open-ended learning activities and independent projects that allow students to identify activities, learning products, and areas of interest to be studied.

Solicit Feedback from Students

You can involve and motivate students and build academic relationships with them to support their learning by soliciting feedback from them (Lenz, Graner, & Adams, 2003). Like Ms. Anderson, you can periodically ask your students to provide information on their educational challenges, progress in and questions about learning new material, reactions to instructional activities, situations that are affecting their learning, and strategies for completing a task. For example, according to Lenz, Graner, and Adams (2003), you can ask students to respond to the following prompts: "I don't understand . . . ." "I am not sure how to . . . ." "I would like additional practice with and examples of . . . ." "I would like you to review . . . ." "It would help me learn better if you . . . .". You can incorporate these prompts into learning logs that students maintain or self-evaluation interviews (see chapter 12). You also can provide students with a feedback form such as the one in Figure 9.5, which allows students and teachers to communicate to support teaching and learning.

How Can I Use Effective Teacher-Centered Instruction?

Elements of Effective Teacher-Centered Instruction

What are the elements of effective teacher-centered lessons? These elements, which can be used for both large- and small-group instruction (Alvarado, 2003; Good & Brophy, 2000), are discussed here. When using these techniques with second language learners, teachers should provide contextual cues and should integrate tasks into a meaningful whole.

These elements are effective in helping students to master basic skills. However, you will also need to use other teaching frameworks and formats to promote learning and the development of higher-order thinking and problem-solving abilities. Therefore, you should also use alternative methods such as learning strategy instruction, reciprocal interaction teaching approaches, cooperative learning, hands-on learning activities, technology-based instruction, and individualized learning activities discussed in other sections of this book.

Resource

Rademacher, Cowart, Sparks, and Chism (1997) have developed the Quality Assignment Planning Worksheet and the Assignment Idea Chart to help you plan and use lessons that motivate your students.

Resource

Hertzog (1998a) offers guidelines for using open-ended learning activities that motivate students.

Resource

Margolis (1999) developed *Student Motivation: A Problem Solving Questionnaire* to help analyze and promote student motivation.

Set Your Sites

For more information on motivating students, go to the Web Links module in Chapter 9 of the Companion Website.

Set Your Sites

For more information on using direct instruction, go to the Web Links module in Chapter 9 of the Companion Website.

Class	Eng 10		Name	Jamie Benson	

LEARNING EXPRESS-WAYS FEEDBACK FORM

Date: Feb 14 M T W ⓣ F	Date: Feb 15 M T W T ⓕ
Message from Student	Message from Teacher
Rating · How was learning today? 1----2--③---4----5----6----7 Low . . . . High	
Today, when you were teaching about argumentation and persuasion, I did not understand what you meant by evidence. Could you clear this up?	Thanks for letting me know. I guess I did rush through the information in trying to cover everything. I will review the information again before the test next Friday.

Date: Feb 14 M T W T ⓕ	Date: Feb 15 M ⓣ W T F
Message from Student	Message from Teacher
Rating · How was learning today? ①---2----3----4----5----6----7 Low . . . . High	Beginning next Monday, we will start a group project, so I will be leading and talking a lot less.
Are you going to be lecturing in every class? Will we ever have any group activities?	By the way, your notes from the lectures are pretty good. However, try using the two column format that I described last week.

FIGURE 9.5   Sample learning express-ways feedback form

Source: From "Learning Express-Ways: Building Academic Relationships to Improve Learning," by K. Lenz, P. Graner, and G. Adams, 2003, *Teaching Exceptional Children, 35*(3), pp. 70–73. Copyright 2003 by The Council for Exceptional Children. Reprinted with permission.

Element 1: Establish the Lesson's Purpose by Explaining Its Goals and Objectives

As Ms. Anderson did in the chapter-opening vignette, you can begin lessons by identifying their purpose and emphasizing how the lesson's objectives relate to students' lives. This helps to focus their attention on the new information. When students know the lesson's purpose, they will understand your goals and the importance of the content. Chappuis and Stiggins (2002) suggest that teachers share the goals and objectives of their lessons with students by:

- presenting them to students explicitly ("We are going to learn to . . . .").
- listing them and asking students to read them and ask questions about them.
- telling students why the goals/objectives are important to learn and connecting them to past and future learning.

IDEAS FOR IMPLEMENTATION

Motivating Students

Ms. Wilhem notices that her students are not as enthusiastic as they were earlier in the school year. Some students are not completing their assignments, and fewer students are participating in class. The number of yawns and notes passed in class seems to be increasing.

To reverse this cycle, Ms. Wilhem decides to change the major assignment for her upcoming unit on spreadsheets. Noticing that her students spend a lot of time talking about getting jobs and buying a car and clothes, she decides to have them research a career and develop a spreadsheet that outlines their expenditures during the first year of employment. She also asks them to write a narrative answering the following questions: Why did you choose this career? What education or training do you need? What is the anticipated demand for this career? What is the beginning salary?

She asks students to share their spreadsheets and narratives with the class. All the students complete the assignment and seem to enjoy sharing their findings. Here are some other strategies you can use to motivate students:

* Survey students at the beginning of a unit to determine what they already know about it and what questions they have.

* Give students choices in terms of content and process, including what, when, and how they learn. For example, you can ask students to identify innovative ways to demonstrate mastery, such as role plays, skits, and art projects.
* Use activities, materials, and examples that are interesting, creative, challenging, and relevant to students' lives, academic abilities, learning styles, and cultural perspectives.
* Personalize instruction by using the students' names, interests, and experiences, as well as incorporating popular characters, items, and trends in classroom examples and assignments.
* Display enthusiasm for learning and for the material being presented.
* Use suspense, fantasy, curiosity, games, technology, simulations, experiments, color, uncertainty, novelty, activities, and sensory experiences that arouse students' curiosity.
* Vary the teaching format, grouping arrangements, and student products, and incorporate self-correction and self-reinforcement into learning activities.

Note: Gunter, Coutinho, & Cade (2002); Herschell et al. (2002); Margolis & McCabe (2003).

You also can start the lesson with an *anticipatory set,* a statement or an enjoyable activity that introduces the material and motivates students to learn it by relating the goals of the lesson to their prior knowledge, interests, strengths, and future life events (Armstrong & Savage, 2002). Some teachers use a visual as part of their anticipatory set (Albert & Ammer, 2004). For example, in the chapter-opening vignette, Ms. Anderson used an anticipatory set that asked students to identify and share their favorite songs. **To view an example of a teacher using an anticipatory set, go to Case 2: Classroom Climate on the CD-ROM and click on the Increasing Interest video clip. What makes the activity with the book and the pencils a good anticipatory set?**

 *cd-rom*

Element 2: Review Prerequisite Skills

After clarifying the lesson's purpose, it is important for you to review previously learned relevant skills. For example, before introducing new poetic devices, Ms. Anderson reviewed the ones students had already learned. You can review prerequisite skills by correcting and discussing homework, asking students to define key terms, having them apply concepts, or assigning an activity requiring mastery of prior relevant material.

Element 3: Use Task Analysis and Introduce Content in Separate Steps Followed by Practice

Next, specific points are presented to students in small, sequential steps. Task analysis can help you identify the steps used to master a skill and individualize the lesson matching the level of difficulty of the task to the various skill levels of students (Swanson & Hoskyn, 2001). *Task analysis* is a systematic process of stating and sequencing the parts of a task to determine what subtasks must be performed to master the task. For example, Ms. Anderson used task analysis to sequence the level of difficulty of her assignments to differentiate them for her students so that some students answered true/false statements, some matched poetic devices to their corresponding statements, some identified poetic devices in statements, and others composed statements that reflected the various types of poetic devices.

Element 4: Give Clear Directions, Explanations, and Relevant Examples

Remember the guidelines for giving directions presented earlier in this chapter, and give students detailed explanations and examples of content using clear, explicit statements. Avoid using confusing wording ("you know," "a lot," "these things") and try to use terms that students understand. While the rate of presentation will depend on the students' skills and the complexity of the material, you should maintain a swift pace. However, to ensure understanding, you can repeat key points, terms, and concepts, and adjust the pace of the lesson to allow for reteaching and repetition.

Element 5: Provide Time for Active and Guided Practice

Practice activities provide *all students* with numerous opportunities to respond so that you can ensure that they have mastered the skill. It is often best to structure time for practice after you introduce small amounts of difficult or new material. Since success during practice helps students learn, you should strive for a practice success rate of at least 75 percent to 80 percent and prepare practice activities that require students to respond to both easier and harder items. Good practice activities include responding to the teacher's questions, summarizing major points, and using peer tutoring.

Academic Learning Games.   *Academic learning games* can motivate students to practice skills and concepts learned in lessons (Kellough & Kellough, 2003; Rotter, 2004). Academic games may take several forms including board games, movement-oriented games, simulations, and role plays.

In academic games, the academic component is controlled by the teacher, who can vary the level of the skill, the presentation, and the response modes to match the needs and levels of many different students. Thus, students of varying abilities can interact within the same teaching format, yet use skills that differ in complexity.

Games can stress cooperation rather than competition. One cooperative strategy requires players to strive for a common goal. In this technique, winning occurs when the whole group achieves the goal. Devising game pawns as puzzle pieces also fosters cooperation in an academic game. For example, each player's pawn can be part of a puzzle that is completed when each player reaches a specified goal. Competition with oneself can be built into common-goal games by setting individualized time limits or by increasing the difficulty of the content. The time limits and content levels can be based on a previously established standard or a prior level of performance. You also can help players

Resource

Rotter (2004) and Blum and Yocom (1996) offer guidelines for designing academic learning games to use in inclusive settings.

Reflective

Identify a game you or your students like to play. How can you apply the principles presented here to make this game cooperative?

Academic games should promote the involvement of all participants. How do you structure your academic games to help all your students learn?

cooperate by phrasing questions so that they require the input of more than one player to be answered correctly.

　　Rules too can be designed to optimize cooperation. A rule that requires players to change teams or movers periodically during the game can promote cooperation. A rule that requires one player to move toward the goal, depending on the academic perform-ance of another player, also fosters a coalition of game players. Another cooperative rule allows a player who has reached the goal to aid the other players by helping to answer questions put to them.

Set Your Sites

For more information on learning games, go to the Web Links module in Chapter 9 of the Companion Website.

Element 6: Promote Active Responding and Check for Understanding

It is important that you provide students with numerous opportunities to actively respond and check for understanding after presenting each new point (Sutherland, Alder & Gunter, 2003). When checking for understanding, you can have all students respond ac-tively and identify main points or state agreement or disagreement with the comments and responses of their peers.

Questioning.　　Like Ms. Anderson, you can promote active student responding and check for understanding by asking questions. Questions can be stated clearly, at the lan-guage and ability levels of various students, and distributed fairly so that *all students* must respond openly. Thus, rather than targeting a question to a specific student ("Jack, what is the difference between a metaphor and a simile?"), you can phrase questions using comments such as "Everyone listen and then tell me" or "I want you all to think before you answer." Also, you can randomly select students to respond, give them a sufficient amount of time to formulate their answers, and then ask other students to respond to these answers. Questions also can be directed to students so that they expand on their first answers or those of others. If students fail to respond to the question, you can ask them if they know the answer, ask them about related knowledge, direct the question to another student, or provide the correct answer. When questioning students, avoid pro-moting inattention by repeating questions, answering questions for them, or supple-menting incomplete answers. **To view examples of a teacher using questioning, go**

cd-rom

to Case 2: Classroom Climate on the CD-ROM and click on the Promoting Acceptance and Accept Others video clips. What effective questioning techniques does the teacher use?

Questions can be adjusted to the difficulty of the content and the skill levels of the students (Flanagan, 1998). To check understanding of simple facts or basic rules, you can use product questions that ask students to give the answer or to restate information and procedures, such as "What is alliteration?" To check students' ability to use complex skills, you can ask questions that require them to apply basic rules or generalizations. For example, Ms. Anderson asked her students to apply their knowledge of poetic devices by writing statements depicting them. You also can use process questions that ask students to discuss how they arrived at an answer.

Questioning techniques can be adapted for students who are second language learners. You can encourage these students to answer questions by providing visual supports and clues such as pictures, gestures, and words; initially asking students questions that require only one- or two-word answers; rephrasing questions when necessary; asking complex questions that can be answered in many different ways; probing responses such as "I don't know"; and repeating and elaborating on students' answers. Additional guidelines for using questioning effectively are presented in chapter 11.

Active Student Responding.   To encourage active student responding and the review of content that needs to be overlearned, you can use *choral responding*, in which students answer simultaneously on a cue from the teacher, or have students tell their classmates the answer, or have students write down their answer and then check each student's response.

Response cards also help students respond (Maheady et al., 2002). Heward et al. (1996) define *response cards* as "cards, signs, or items that are simultaneously held up by students in the class to display their responses to questions or problems presented by the teacher" (p. 5). Preprinted response cards are given to students so that they can select the cards that give their responses. These cards are appropriate for content that has a limited number of answers, such as true/false questions or questions that require agreement or disagreement. Write-on response cards allow students to record their answers on blank cards or boards and then erase them. While these cards are typically used when teachers want students to recall information, they also can be used to have students respond to open-ended questions.

Group responses that allow each member of the group to respond with a physical gesture also are desirable. For example, students can respond to a question with a "yes" or "no" answer by placing their thumbs up or down, respectively. It can be motivating for students to plan with teachers different ways to answer using physical gestures.

Resource

Foil and Alber (2002) and Heward et al. (1996) offer guidelines for developing and using preprinted and write-on response cards.

Element 7: Give Prompt, Specific Feedback

Students' responses should be followed by frequent, prompt, clear, and constructive feedback from you or other students and adults in the classroom. In general, feedback should be descriptive and specific so that it tells students why their response is correct or incorrect (Chappuis & Stiggins, 2002).

The type of feedback can be related to the nature of the response (Armstrong & Savage, 2002). Therefore, in determining what type of feedback to use, you can categorize students' responses as *correct and confident, correct but unsure, partly correct,* or *incorrect.* If the answer is correct and confident, you can confirm it with praise and ask additional questions at the same or a more difficult level. If the answer is not correct and confident, another type of feedback can be used.

Process Feedback.   Students who are unsure of their correct responses may need *process feedback,* in which you praise students and reinforce their answer by restating why it was correct. Besides responding to correct answers, it is important to provide feedback to students whose answers are partly correct. You can confirm the part of the answer that is correct and then restate or simplify the question to address the incorrect part.

Corrective Feedback.   *Corrective feedback* shows students how to work more effectively. When using corrective feedback, you identify errors and show students how to correct them. Corrective feedback is more effective in promoting learning than *general feedback,* in which responses are identified simply as correct or incorrect; *right-only feedback,* in which only correct responses are identified; or *wrong-only feedback,* in which only incorrect responses are identified.

Instructive Feedback.   *Instructive feedback* promotes learning by giving students extra information and teaching on the task or content. After students answer, you offer instructive feedback by giving verbal or visual information that:

- expands on the target skills being taught (e.g., defining a sight word or giving a word's antonym).
- parallels the skills being taught (e.g., linking a numeral with its corresponding number word or a mathematical/scientific symbol with its meaning).
- offers new information (e.g., describing the color of something or an additional property) (Werts, Wolery, Gast, & Holcombe, 1996).

To view examples of a teacher providing feedback to students, go to Case 4: Support Participation on the CD-ROM and click on the Multilevel Assessing and Recognize Efforts video clips. What types of feedback does the teacher provide?

cd-rom

Prompting.   You can help correct students' errors by using a variety of visual, auditory, or tactile prompts. Prompts can be categorized from most to least intrusive, including *manual prompts,* in which the student is physically guided through the task; *modeling prompts,* in which the student observes someone else perform the task; *oral prompts* that describe how to perform the task; and *visual prompts* that show the student the correct process or answer in a graphic presentation. Prompts can be used sequentially, depending on the skills of the students and the complexity of the task.

Praising.   Praise coupled with comments about strengths and needs can provide valuable feedback to students and improve their work (Sutherland, Wehby, & Yoder, 2002). Since some studies have shown that frequent praise can reduce students' independence, self-confidence, and creativity (Kohn, 2003), you should distribute praise evenly and examine its effect on students. Rather than just praising on-task behavior and task correctness, use praise to encourage independence, determination, and creativity. Additional guidelines for using praise effectively were presented in chapter 7.

Student-Directed Feedback.   Students also can be a valuable source of feedback. They can be encouraged and taught to use self-monitoring and self-correction techniques to record and analyze their own progress. They can chart their mastery of a specific skill by graphing their percentage or number correct every day. Students can also be given answer keys to correct their own work, or they can exchange papers with peers and offer feedback to peers on their work.

Element 8: Offer Time for Independent Activities

You can end successful lessons by giving students independent activities that allow them to demonstrate mastery of the material. Make sure that the activities fit the students' instructional levels and needs, and try to give them numerous opportunities to make correct responses (Gunter, Coutinho, & Cade, 2002). As they work on the assignment, move around the room to monitor their performance and offer prompt feedback. If completed assignments do not meet your expectations, students can be asked to revise or redo them until the product meets your standards.

You can modify independent assignments by providing help or access to peer tutors. Students can ask for help by placing a help sign or card on their desks, raising their hands, or signing a list. At first, you can provide help by asking questions and making statements that help students assume responsibility for figuring out answers, such as "What things can help you figure out the answer?" and "Have you asked three of your classmates for help before asking me?" (Gibson & Govendo, 1999).

Although it is appropriate to modify the tasks, do not have students work in a different content area from the rest of the class since this might isolate them. Also, when possible, students should complete assignments and work with materials similar to those that other students are using.

Boyer (1998) developed a time-saving system of teacher-created graphic templates, forms, and cues that are stamped on student assignments to individualize and modify them. These templates allow all students to work on the same assignments by using visual prompts that adjust the workload of students, inform students how to complete assignments, adapt the ways in which students respond to items, and vary the time students have to complete the assignment. Sample stamps are presented in Figure 9.6.

Element 9: Summarize Main Points and Evaluate Mastery

At the end of the lesson, summarize the main points and evaluate students' understanding and mastery of the content. You can assess students' mastery of content in a 1- to 5-minute probe or by asking them to complete a learning log indicating what they learned, how they learned it, what they are confused about, and what additional information they would like to learn (Flanagan, 1998). Since maintenance of skills is critical for building a foundation for learning new skills, weekly and monthly maintenance probes also are desirable. The results of these assessments can be recorded, shared with students, and used to make teaching decisions. Additional guidelines for evaluating student mastery and progress are presented in chapter 12.

Homework.   Effective teachers like Ms. Anderson recognize that homework can be useful in fostering and evaluating student mastery of content. While homework has the potential to be a valuable tool for supporting and supplementing in-class instruction (Cooper, 2001), students with disabilities often experience greater difficulty completing their homework assignments (Gajria & Salend, 1995). To address these homework difficulties, there is a variety of practices you can use to make it a process that supports student learning (Cooper, 2001; Patton, Jayanthi, & Polloway, 2001).

Adjust the Amount and Type of Homework.   Assigning a reasonable amount of homework and in smaller units can increase the probability that your students will complete it. You also may need to adjust the amount and type of homework by shortening assignments, extending deadlines, using other evaluation strategies, and modifying the

Assignment can be completed
—— orally with the teacher
—— with an adult
—— as we discussed

Allows the teacher to alter the method of student response. Excellent for students who have difficulty organizing thoughts and ideas in writing or those with handwriting/graphomotor deficits. Teacher can specify that the student complete the assignment a certain way (e.g., dictated to a parent, using a tape recorder, in note form, etc.).

Do the ★ items
orally with the
teacher.

Allows the teacher to alter the method of student response on selected items. Useful on quizzes or tests with students who need more time to complete written work. For example, essay questions could be completed orally with the teacher during class testing time rather than making arrangements for additional time to complete the item(s) in writing.

Complete:
—— independently
—— with a learning buddy
—— in a cooperative group
of ——

This stamp allows the teacher to adjust how students work within the classroom — alone or in some type of cooperative group.

Stamps for Providing Additional Time to Complete Assignments

Do you need additional time to complete this assignment?

YES   NO

If yes, see the teacher to make arrangements.

Allows the student to inform the teacher of the need for additional time in a private and unobtrusive way. Arrangements for additional time can then be made. Excellent for quizzes and tests and other tasks where time is often limited.

Incomplete — Complete by

_____

FIGURE 9.6   Sample stamps to differentiate student assignments

Source: From *Using Stamps to Differentiate Student Assignments,* by M. M. Boyer, 1995, Phoenix, AZ: Author. Reprinted by permission.

Stamps for Adjusting Workload

Complete the following:
_____ All
_____ All Odd
_____ All Even
_____ Every Third
_____ First Five
_____ First Ten

This stamp is effective when an assignment has several of the same type of questions/problems (e.g., math worksheet). The teacher can select all or a portion of the items for the student to complete.

Select
_____ ● items
_____ ▲ items
_____ ★ items
to complete

Teacher codes questions by importance, type, or level using the symbols and then writes down how many of each type the student should complete. The student then self-selects from the questions on the page. This provides the student control in work completion—the teacher sets clear expectations while the student is still allowed some choice.

Complete all circled items.

Allows the teacher to select specific items to be completed by the student.

Stamps for Setting Clear Expectations for Written Assignments

Remember:
_____ . ? !
_____ complete sentences
_____ capital letters

Prompts students to pay attention to certain aspects of writing as they complete a writing assignment.

To be graded for:
_____ content/organization
_____ sentence structure
_____ capitalization/punctuation
_____ spelling
_____ form
_____ neatness
_____ all of the above

Teacher checks off what the student is to focus attention on when completing the written assignment. One or more things can be checked off.

FIGURE 9.6   *Sample stamps to differentiate student assignments (continued)*

IDEAS FOR IMPLEMENTATION

Adapting Independent Assignments

Ms. Maphas's class included a wide range of students. Some students completed independent assignments quickly; others took more time. Concerned about student frustration and the need to avoid isolating students, Ms. Maphas decided to modify her independent assignments. First, rather than having students work on one long assignment, she decided to give several shorter assignments that covered the same content. She also prepared different versions of assignments that modified their content to meet students' skill levels by decreasing the number of items students had to answer, by interspersing items on previously mastered content with items on new material, and by placing the most important items to be completed at the beginning of the assignment. She also built in opportunities for students to receive feedback by asking students to correct their own work or to seek feedback after completing a specific number of items tailored to the students' skill levels.

Here are some other strategies you can use to help students complete independent assignments:

- Give clear and concise directions in a list of steps.
- Have students work on one assignment or worksheet at a time.
- Provide cues to highlight key parts of directions, details of items, and changes in item types.
- Offer examples of correct response formats.
- Divide assignments into sections by folding, drawing lines, cutting off parts of the page, boxing, and blocking out with an index card or a heavy crayon, and give students one section at a time.
- Provide enough space for students to record their answers, and limit the amount of distracting visual stimuli.
- Scan assignments into a computer and allow students to complete the assignment using a computer.
- Limit the types of questions.

Note: Gunter, Coutinho, & Cade (2002); Reichel (1997); Shank & Hooser (1999).

types of assignments and the responses required (Warger, 2001). It is also important to coordinate homework assignments with others—particularly for secondary-level students who have different teachers in each content area.

While you should try to create homework assignments that are interesting and challenging, the type of homework will depend on the instructional purpose (Stewart & Rope, 2001). If the goal of homework is to practice material learned in class, it may be appropriate to assign some type of drill-oriented assignment. When the purpose of homework is to prepare students for upcoming lessons, assignments can be structured to expose them to the information necessary to perform successfully in class. Finally, when you want students to apply and integrate what they have learned, you can use long-term assignments that require the integration of many skills and processes.

Establish and Follow Homework Routines.   You can teach and follow regular routines for assigning, collecting, evaluating, and returning homework. You also should inform your students and their families of your policies for missed or late assignments, extra credit, and homework accommodations. An important part of your homework routine that can motivate students to complete their homework is evaluating it frequently and immediately.

Teach Study and Organizational Skills.   Teaching your students study and organizational skills also can help students complete their homework (Hughes, Ruhl, Schumaker, & Deshler, 2002). Therefore, you can teach your students skills related to goal setting, task planning, and using a homework notebook and a monthly and weekly planner. Your

Effective teachers provide students with opportunities to work independently and request teacher assistance. How do your students ask for assistance from you?

students also may benefit from instruction in how to schedule and budget their time, select an environment conducive to completing their homework (remember this may not be possible for some of your students), and organize their materials. See chapters 6 and 12 for other strategies related to teaching study and organizational skills.

Collaborate with Families.   Because family members play an important role in the homework process, your homework practices should promote collaboration with them (Warger, 2001). Make families an important part of the homework process by asking them to sign homework, contacting them about the purpose of homework and the amount and type of homework given, and offering suggestions on how to help their children complete their homework (see chapter 4 for guidelines for collaborating with families and using the Internet to foster family involvement in the homework process).

Your homework practices also should recognize the unique strengths and challenges of your students' families. It is also important to make sure that your homework practices do not (a) create disharmony in family–child relationships and interactions; (b) deny students and their families access to leisure time; (c) conflict with the families' economic needs and cultural perspectives; and (d) confuse, frustrate, or embarrass students and their families (Kralovec & Buell, 2001; Lackaye and Rublin, 2001).

How Can I Successfully Use Cooperative Learning Arrangements with Students?

In addition to structuring learning so that students work individually, competitively, or in teacher-centered small and large groups, effective teachers like Ms. Anderson differentiate instruction by having their students work together in *cooperative learning arrangements* (Schniedewind & Davidson, 2000). In cooperative learning arrangements, students work with their peers to achieve a shared academic goal rather than competing against or working separately from their classmates. You structure the learning environment so that each class member contributes to the group's goal. When learning is structured cooperatively, students are accountable not only for their own

IDEAS FOR IMPLEMENTATION

Helping Students Complete Homework

Ms. Rios felt strongly about the value of homework and assigned it 4 days a week. She checked her students' assignments regularly and noticed that Matt often failed to complete his homework. When questioned about his homework, Matt said, "It was too hard," "I did not know what to do," or simply "I can't do this." Recognizing Matt's difficulties, Ms. Rios approached Matt's friend, Jamal, who completed his homework, to see whether he would be willing to work with Matt. Jamal agreed and Ms. Rios spoke to Matt, who also was interested in working with Jamal. Both Matt and Jamal were responsible for making sure that their partners had recorded the assignment in their assignment notebooks. Before starting their homework, Matt and Jamal spoke over the phone or worked at each other's home to make sure that they both understood the material presented in class and the homework assignment. As they worked on their homework assignments, they monitored each other's work, offered feedback, and discussed any difficulties.

Here are some other strategies you can use to help students complete homework:

- Individualize assignments for students by using short- and long-term assignments and by relating assignments to students' experiences, interests, career goals, and IEPs.
- Give clear, explicit directions and monitor students' understanding of their assignments and the guidelines for completing them.
- Encourage students who have difficulty with homework to record assignments in their notebooks, to use homework planners, and to use a daily or weekly teacher-prepared homework assignment sheet or checklist. Encourage students to check with a classmate about homework assignments.
- Give students opportunities to begin their homework in class.
- Motivate students to complete their homework by making homework creative and enjoyable, connecting assignments to real-life situations, and displaying exemplary homework assignments.
- Create a homework club to provide afterschool homework assistance and tutoring for students.

Note: Bryan & Sullivan-Burstein (1997); Gajria & Salend, (1995); Glazer & Williams (2001); Patton, Jayanthi, & Polloway (2001); Stormont-Spurgin (1997).

achievement but also for those of other group members. Cooperative learning is especially worthwhile for heterogeneous student populations as it helps students actively participate and stay engaged in the learning process (Jenkins, Antil, Wayne, & Vadasy, 2003). It promotes friendships and encourages mutual respect, self-esteem, and learning among students of various academic abilities and different language, racial, and ethnic backgrounds (Kellough & Kellough, 2003).

Cooperative learning activities have three important components: positive interdependence, individual accountability, and face-to-face interactions (Lotain, 2003). *Positive interdependence* is established when students understand that they must work together to achieve their goal. You can promote positive interdependence by using cooperative learning activities with mutual goals, role interdependence and specialization, resource sharing, and group rewards. *Individual accountability* is understanding that each group member is responsible for contributing to the group and learning the material. This is often established by giving individualized tests or probes, adding group members' scores together, assigning specific parts of an assignment to different group members, randomly selecting group members to respond for the group, asking all members of the group to present part of the project, asking students to keep a journal of their contributions to the group, or tailoring roles to the ability levels of students (Whittaker, 1996). Building individual accountability into cooperative learning groups helps to reduce the *free-rider effect*, in which some members fail to contribute and allow others to do the majority of the

Students benefit academically and socially from working in cooperative learning groups. How has working in cooperative groups affected you academically and socially?

cd-rom

Resource

Schniedewind and Davidson (2000) offer guidelines about differentiating cooperative learning-based instruction, and Lotain (2003) provides suggestions for determining cooperative learning activities.

work. *Face-to-face interactions* occur when students encourage and help each other learn the material. **To view examples of students working collaboratively, go to Case 4: Support Participation on the CD-ROM and click on the Multiple Assignments and Peer Supports video clips. How did the teacher structure the assignments to promote positive interdependence and individual accountability?**

Guidelines for using cooperative learning arrangements are discussed next.

Select an Appropriate Cooperative Learning Format

Cooperative learning begins by selecting an appropriate format. The format you choose will depend on the needs and characteristics of your students, as well as their experiences in working cooperatively. Generally, it is wise to start by having students work in pairs before they work in groups (Armstrong & Savage, 2002).

The cooperative learning format selected also will depend on the content, objectives, and mastery levels of the assignment. According to Maheady, Harper, and Mallette (1991), peer tutoring, and Classwide Peer Tutoring (CWPT), are best for teaching basic skills and factual knowledge in content areas; Jigsaw is appropriate for text mastery; and Learning Together is the desired format for teaching higher-level cognitive material and having students learn how to work together and reach a consensus on controversial material.

Peer Tutoring

In *peer tutoring*, one student tutors and assists another in learning a new skill. Peer tutoring increases student learning and fosters positive attitudes toward school for tutors and tutees (Heron, Welsch, & Goddard, 2003). It also promotes a greater sense of responsibility and an improved self-concept, as well as increased academic skills. When using peer tutoring, you can do the following:

*   Establish specific goals for the sessions.
*   Plan particular learning activities and select appropriate materials to meet the identified goals.

- Select tutors who have mastered the content to be taught.
- Train students to be successful tutors, including how to establish rapport, present the material and tasks, record tutees' responses, use prompts, and offer feedback.
- Train tutees so that they understand the peer tutoring process and are willing to work with a tutor.
- Match tutors and tutees.
- Schedule sessions for no longer than 30 minutes and no more than three times per week.
- Monitor and evaluate the tutoring process periodically and provide feedback to both members of the dyad.
- Allay families' potential concerns by explaining to them the role and value of peer tutoring.

It is important that you use reciprocal peer tutoring so that *all* your students have opportunities to serve as tutors and tutees (Spencer & Balboni, 2003; Tournaki & Criscitiello, 2003). For example, a student who performs well in math could teach math to a student who tutored to him or her in reading. Students who are not proficient at teaching academic skills can teach nonacademic skills related to their hobbies or interests.

It is also important for you to give peer tutors feedback and to have them reflect on their success. For example, following a peer tutoring session, tutors can reflect on the lesson by responding to the following:

- I think the lesson went well because:
- The things I liked about teaching this lesson were:
- During this lesson, my classmate learned:
- My classmate still needs to work on:
- Next time I teach this lesson, I will: (Brewer, Reid, & Rhine, 2003).

Resource

Brewer, Reid, and Rhine (2003) and Tournaki and Criscitiello (2003) provide suggestions and forms for establishing a peer-tutoring program and Longwill and Kleinert (1998) offer guidelines for setting up a high school peer-tutoring program.

Classwide Peer Tutoring

Classwide Peer Tutoring (CWPT) is effective in teaching reading, spelling, vocabulary, math, and social studies to a wide range of students educated in a variety of settings (Fulk & King, 2001; Greenwood, Arreaga-Mayer, Utley, Gavin, & Terry, 2001; Maheady, Harper, & Mallette, 2001). Randomly divide the class into two groups and set up tutoring dyads within both groups. During the first 10 to 15 minutes of the period, one student tutors the other. The members of each dyad then reverse their roles and continue for another equal time period.

You should train students to tutor using a set procedure that involves the following:

1. Tutors present material that requires a response from tutees ("Spell the word," "Answer the question").
2. Tutees say and write their responses. A correct response earns two points. An incorrect response prompts tutors to offer the correct response, ask tutees to write this response three times, and award a point to tutees for correcting their errors.
3. You circulate around the classroom to give bonus points for appropriate tutee and tutor behavior.

After this procedure is repeated throughout the week, students take individual tests and receive points for each correct response. All points earned by the groups are totaled at the end of the week, and the group with the most points is acknowledged through badges, stickers, certificates, public posting of names, or additional free time. You can make this system less competitive by giving all groups a chance to earn rewards and acknowledgment if they achieve their goals or exceed a previously established point total. The Peer-Assisted Learn-

Resource

Fulk and King (2001) offer guidelines for teaching students to participate in a Classwide Peer Tutoring program.

ing Strategies (PALS) system offers variations of these steps to teach reading (see chapter 10) and math (Fuchs et al., 2001; Mathes, Grek, Howard, Babyak, & Allen, 1999).

Jigsaw

The *Jigsaw* format divides students into groups, with each student assigned a task that is essential in reaching the group's goal (Aronson, Blaney, Stephan, Sikes, & Snapp, 1978). Every member makes a contribution that is integrated with the work of others to produce the group's product. When teams work on the same task, expert groups can be formed by having a member of each group meet with peers from other groups who have been assigned the same subtask. The expert group members work together to complete their assignment and then share the results with their original jigsaw groups.

You can structure the students' assignment so that each group member can succeed. For example, a lesson about Martin Luther King Jr. was structured by giving each student one segment of King's life to learn about and teach to others in their group. Students who were assigned the same aspect of King's life met in expert groups to complete their part; then the original group answered questions on all segments of King's life.

Learning Together

A cooperative learning format that places more responsibility on group members is the *Learning Together Approach* (Johnson, Johnson, & Holubec, 2002). In this format, students are assigned to teams, and each team is given an assignment. Teams decide whether to divide the task into its components or approach the task as a whole group. All group members are involved in the team's decisions by offering their knowledge and skills and by seeking help and clarification from others. Every group produces one product, which represents the combined contributions of all group members. You then grade this product, with each student in the group receiving the group grade. For example, you could use Learning Together to teach students about mammals by dividing the class into groups and having each group develop part of a bulletin board display with information and artwork about a particular mammal. The students in each group then would contribute to the group's display by reporting information, doing artwork, or dictating material about mammals.

Establish Guidelines for Working Cooperatively

Set Your Sites

For more information on cooperative learning, go to the Web Links module in Chapter 9 of the Companion Website.

You and your students can establish guidelines for working cooperatively. Some guidelines that can foster cooperation include the following:

- Each group will produce one product.
- Each group member will help other group members understand the material.
- Each group member will seek help from her or his peers.
- Each group member will stay in his or her group.
- No group member will change her or his ideas unless logically persuaded to do so.
- Each group member will indicate acceptance of the group's product by signing his or her name.

Maheady et al. (1991) identified three problems that might occur in cooperative learning arrangements: increased noise, complaints about partners, and cheating. They suggest that noise can be minimized by developing and posting rules, developing signals that make students aware of their noise levels, assigning a student to monitor the group's noise level, providing rewards for groups that follow the rules, and teaching students to use their quiet voices. Complaints can be discussed with the group and students who work collaboratively can be reinforced. Cheating can be lessened by random checks of each group's work.

The issue of equitable contributions of each member to the group can be addressed in a variety of ways. One way is via a Group Project Work Log, a process log or journal of the group's activities, including a description of each student's contribution and effort (Goor & Schwenn, 1993). Individual group members can also keep a journal of their participation and contributions. You can remind students that the standard classroom behaviors will be used during cooperative learning lessons. You can help *all students* participate and share their learning by conducting debriefing, rehearsing, and revoicing sessions that allow individual students to examine their learning and prepare to share it with their classmates (Palincsar, Magnusson, Cutter, & Vincent, 2002).

Form Heterogeneous Cooperative Groups

Assign students to cooperative, heterogeneous groups by considering their sex, race, ethnicity, language ability, disability, and academic and social skill levels (Maxim, 2003). You also can consider characteristics such as motivation, personality, and communication skills. For example, students who sit quietly and do not participate could be assigned to a highly supportive team.

Another factor to consider in forming groups is the students' ability to work together. You can get this information through observation and/or by administering a sociogram (see chapter 5). While groups can be changed for each cooperative lesson, keeping the students in the same group for several weeks provides continuity that is helpful in developing cooperative skills. How long a group remains together can depend on the students' ages, the nature of the task, and the group's interpersonal skills. At the beginning, you can use small groups of two or three students, increasing them to five when students become accustomed to cooperative learning. When forming new groups, start with activities that help students get acquainted.

Arrange the Classroom for Cooperative Learning

To structure your classrooms for cooperative work, arrange the students' desks or tables in clusters, place individual desks in pairs for peer tutoring, or block off a carpeted corner of the room. For larger groups, desks can be placed in circles rather than rows, which prevent eye contact and communication. Since the time needed to complete cooperative projects may vary, you can give groups a safe area to store in-progress projects and other materials.

Another way to promote cooperative work is to post group reminders. For example, you can post a chart with strategies for respecting the individuality of each group member. These strategies include referring to each group member by name, speaking quietly, and encouraging all members to participate (Ammer, 1998).

Develop Students' Cooperative Skills

Cooperative learning depends on the quality of the interactions of group members. Because many students have little experience with this arrangement, you may have to devote some time to helping students learn to work together effectively (Armstrong &

Resource

Wolford, Heward, and Alber (2001) offer strategies for teaching students to seek peer assistance during cooperative learning group activities.

Savage, 2002; Gut, 2000). Interpersonal and group processing skills that students must develop to work well together include getting to know and trust peers, communicating directly and clearly, listening actively, seeking assitance, supporting, encouraging and complementing others, accepting differences, managing resources, balancing personal and group goals, building consensus, making decisions, and resolving conflicts (Prater, Bruhl, & Serna, 1998; Siperstein & Leffert, 1999).

Maxim (2003) suggests that you use a *T-chart* to help students develop cooperative skills. This involves (a) drawing a horizontal line and writing the cooperative skill on the line; (b) drawing a vertical line from the middle of the horizontal line; (c) listing students' responses to the question "What would the skill look like?" on one side of the vertical line; and (d) listing students' responses to the question "What would the skill sound like?" on the other side of the vertical line.

You also can use the *round robin,* the *round table,* and the *paraphrase passport* to promote team-building and communication skills. Round robin gives each student a chance to participate and to share comments and reactions with others. Whereas round robin involves oral sharing, round table involves passing a pencil and paper around so that each student can contribute to the group's response. The paraphrase passport requires students to paraphrase the statements of their teammate who has just spoken and then share their own ideas and perspectives.

Communication and consensus skills can be fostered by such strategies as *Talking Chips* and *Spend-a-Buck* (Karnes, Collins, Maheady, Harper, & Mallette, 1997). Talking Chips helps students participate equally by giving each of them a set number of talking chips, which are placed in the middle of the work area each time a student speaks. Once students use up all their chips, they cannot speak until all group members have used all their chips. Spend-a-Buck helps groups reach a consensus by giving each group member four quarters, which are then spent on the group's options.

Another method of teaching cooperative learning skills is *role delineation,* in which each member of the group is given a specific role (Kellough & Kellough, 2003). For example, to produce a written product, a team might need a reader, a group facilitator to promote brainstorming and decision making, a recorder to record all contributions, a writer to edit the product, a reporter to share information about the group's process and product. Other students might be assigned the roles of keeping the group on task, keeping track of time, explaining word meanings, managing materials, monitoring the group's noise level, operating media, encouraging all group members to participate and help others, and providing positive comments. Periodically, students can complete evaluation sheets that ask them to react to the roles and contributions of group members, as well as suggest what the group could do to improve.

Monitoring groups and providing feedback can build cooperative skills. Therefore, it is important for you to observe groups, model cooperative skills, intervene when necessary, and provide feedback on group processing skills. After students complete a cooperative lesson, they can be encouraged to reflect on their experience by responding to such questions as "What did members do to help your group accomplish its goal?" "What did members do that hindered your group in achieving its goal?" and "What will your group do differently next time?" You also can use sentence completion questions to prompt students to reflect on their group's collaborative efforts (Gut, 2000). For example, after working collaboratively students can be asked to respond to:

- Our group was good at _____.
- The things that surprised me the most about our group were _____.
- Our group needs to work on _____.

Resource

Gut (2000), Goodwin (1999), and Goor and Schwenn (1993) provide guidelines for teaching students how to learn cooperatively, and Vernon, Schumaker, and Deshler (1995) have developed the Cooperative Strategies Series to teach students cooperative and teamwork skills, which includes the Teamwork Strategy.

FIGURE 9.7

Cooperative learning student feedback form

OBSERVATION SHEET

Group Members: **Roles:**

_____   _____

_____   _____

_____   _____

_____   _____

Cooperative Behavior Observed in Our Group:

(Rating: 1–outstanding; 2–good; 3–needs improvement)

We worked and planned together.	1	2	3
We shared ideas and took turns.	1	2	3
We checked with each other for understanding.	1	2	3
We used quiet voices.	1	2	3
We divided roles and responsibilities equally.	1	2	3
We presented information as a group.	1	2	3

GROUP PROCESSING:

Things our group can do to improve next time.

_____

_____

What our group learned from this activity.

_____

_____

Source: From "We Are Social Beings: Learning How to Learn Cooperatively," by D. M. Gut, 2000, *Teaching Exceptional Children,* 32(5), pp. 46–53. Copyright 2000 by The Council for Exceptional Children. Reprinted with permission.

Students also can comment on how well the group is working collaboratively by writing and keeping a journal (Gut, 2000). Finally, students can give feedback on their own collaborative skills by completing a form such as the one presented in Figure 9.7.

Evaluate Cooperative Learning

You can evaluate groups based on their mastery of subject matter, as well as on their ability to work together. To promote peer support and group accountability, students are evaluated as a group, and each student's learning contributes to the group's evaluation. A popular method for evaluating cooperative learning is the *group project/group grade* format. The group submits for evaluation one final product (a report, an oral presentation) that represents all members' contributions. You then evaluate the product and give each group member the same grade.

In another evaluation format, *contract grading*, groups contract for a grade based on the amount of work they agree to do according to a set of criteria. Thus, group members who have different skill levels can perform different parts of the task according to their ability. For example, a cooperative lesson might contain five activities, some more difficult than others, with each activity worth 10 points. The contract between you and the groups might then specify the criteria the groups must meet to achieve an A (50 points),

USING TECHNOLOGY TO PROMOTE INCLUSION

Making Large- and Small-Group Instruction Accessible to All Students

Technology is available to help you differentiate your large- and small-group instruction to make it accessible to all of your students. Technologies such as using presentation software or an overhead projector can support student learning by providing visual support and computer-generated text and graphics. They also allow you to present content and highlight main points and key vocabulary while maintaining eye contact with students, and adjusting the pace of instruction. With these technologies, you can also model and provide students with high-quality notes. Presentation software or transparencies can help you gain and maintain student attention and foster your students' motivation by using color, animation, sound, simple and realistic visuals, photographs rather than line drawings, consistent backgrounds, easy-to-read color combinations, and the principles of graphic design (see chapter 8) (Thoms, 1999).

Here are some other ways you can use technology to create inclusive classrooms that support student learning in large- and small-group instruction:

- Supplement teacher-directed presentations by using multimedia programs and websites that contain video, sound, and animation. Wissick and Gardner (2000) provide multimedia programs and websites that can be used to complement direct instruction and cooperative learning arrangements.
- Provide students, particularly those with hearing disabilities, with access to lectures and notes by using speech-to-text technology-based note-taking systems such as Communication Access Realtime Translation or Computer Assisted Notetaking (CAN) (Elliot, Foster, & Stinson, 2002). In these systems, individuals use a computerized abbreviation system to record comments of teachers and students, which are then displayed as text within 3 seconds for others via a laptop computer or television monitor. At the end of class sessions, text files are edited to provide students with notes.
- Provide students with visual disabilities with access to notes and handouts by scanning these materials and then converting them to Braille. Students with visual disabilities also can use *Braille Lite,* a personal digital assistant that allows students to take and retrieve notes in Braille and store books and other important

documents and files. Similarly, *Braille and Speak,* a handheld note-taker, allows students to record notes in class in Braille and then reads the notes back using a speech synthesizer (Medina, 2002).

- Use the Mimio interactive whiteboard to provide notes for students with visual disabilities or students who have difficulty copying from the board. In this system, handwriting and graphics displayed on the whiteboard are sent to a computer and then printed out in either standard or Braille formats.
- Create a class website that allows students to access teacher- or peer-prepared class notes and outlines, assignments and their directions, cooperative learning groups, and independent and guided practice activities. Course management software is available to assist you in doing this (e.g., *Blackboard, Learning Space, TopClass,* and *WebCT*). You also can access a variety of online resources (e.g., www.schoolnotes.com and www.TeacherWeb.com) that offer easy-to-use assistance and services for creating and maintaining websites.
- Structure in-class and homework assignments so they provide students with the opportunity to use academic game software programs and play Internet-based academically integrated games such as those at www.yahooligans.com/computers__games__and_online/Online_Games and www.homeworkplanet.com/games.
- Create a communication system that allows your students to use PDAs or graphic calculators to beam questions silently to you and allows you to send responses or provide feedback to individuals or groups of students.
- Use a Group Response System to involve students in teacher-directed activities, solicit feedback from them, and assess their comprehension. These systems allow students to respond to teacher-directed questions by using a personal wireless keypad that transfers their responses to a computer, which instantly presents their responses to the teacher.
- Offer multilingual homework hotlines via the telephone, television, fax, or E-mail. For example, some schools use a telephone homework hotline, which allows families and students to access homework assignments by using special codes that

are linked to teachers and their assignments (Glazer & Williams, 2001).

- Provide students with a list of homework assistance websites and other resources (e.g., websites, search tools, virtual trips, books, and articles) that can be used in completing the homework assignments, such as www.homeworkhelp.com, www. homeworkplanet.com, and www.homeworkspot. com. Students and family should also be encouraged to find appropriate information from

other sources (see chapter 4 for information on creating a homework website).

- Use the Internet to provide your students with opportunities to work in online cooperative learning groups with classmates. You also can use the Internet to have your students learn with students from all over the world by contacting such websites as the Global Schoolhouse (www.gsn.org), KIDLINK (www.Kidlink.org) and E-Pals (www.epals. com/projects).

REFLECTING ON PROFESSIONAL PRACTICES

Using Cooperative Learning

After reading about and attending several inservice sessions on cooperative learning, Ms. Johnson decides to try it with her students. She divides the students into groups and gives each group an assignment to work on together. She then circulates throughout the room and observes the groups. In one group, Luis, a second language learner, sits quietly and does not participate in his group's project. Luis does not speak throughout the activity, and no one speaks to him. In another group, students rely on Maria to do the assignment while they talk about an upcoming school event. In still another group, students disagree over who will do what to complete the group's project.

Frustrated but not about to give up, Ms. Johnson realizes that she needs to help her students learn to work collaboratively. She decides to start by having pairs of students study for a quiz together and receive their average grade score. Next, she has students work together in peer tutoring dyads; she arranges it so that all students serve as both tutors and tutees.

She also teaches her students how to develop specific collaborative skills. For example, she has them discuss the need to encourage all group members to participate. They then brainstorm, role-play, and practice ways to encourage others to contribute to the group. Another lesson focuses on the need for and use of developing consensus.

After several lessons on collaborative skills, Ms. Johnson asks students to perform a science experiment and write a report while working in cooperative learning groups. She tells them that they will be working cooperatively and asks, "How will I know if you're cooperating?" The students' responses are listed on the blackboard and discussed.

To ensure the participation of all students, Ms. Johnson assigns shy or quiet students like Luis to groups with supportive peers. To make sure that all students contribute to and understand the group's project, she tells the class that she will randomly select group members to explain parts of the group's report. To help groups work efficiently, she assigns one student in each group to be the group's recorder and another student to make sure that each member of the group participates.

As the groups work on their projects, Ms. Johnson monitors their progress and observes their use of collaborative skills. When students demonstrate such skills, she acknowledges them. Periodically, she asks groups to model various collaborative skills. She also asks each group to keep a record of the skills they use. At the end of the class session, she and the students discuss and reflect on their collaborative skills.

- Why do you think Ms. Johnson wanted her students to use cooperative learning?
- What problems did she encounter?
- How did she attempt to solve these problems?
- What other problems might teachers encounter in using cooperative learning? How can teachers address these problems?
- What have been your experiences in using cooperative learning as a teacher? As a student?

 To answer these questions online and share your responses with others, go to the Reflection module in Chapter 9 of the Companion Website.

Companion Website

a B (40 points), or a C (30 points). Additional guidelines for using contract grading are discussed in chapter 12.

One evaluation system that gives students strong incentives to help others learn the material is the *group average.* Individual grades on a quiz or part of a project are averaged into a group grade. Each group member receives the average grade. For example, each group member could be given an individualized test tailored to his or her abilities in math. During the week, group members help each other master their assignments and prepare for their tests. At first, some students may resist the concept of group grades. You can minimize this resistance by assuring students that group members will be assigned only work that they can complete. Inform students that if all group members do their best and help others, they will all receive high grades. You can modify the group average by using improvement scores. In this system, students are assigned a base score, depending on their prior performance, and earn points for their teams by improving on their base score.

Summary

This chapter offered guidelines for differentiating large- and small-group instruction to meet the unique learning needs of students. As you review the questions posed in this chapter, remember the following points.

How Can I Adapt Large-Group Instruction for Students?
CEC 3, 4, 5, 6, 7, 9, PRAXIS 3, INTASC 2, 3, 4, 5, 6, 7, 9

You can have students work collaboratively, use presentation software or an overhead, encourage students to ask questions, help students take notes, teach note-taking skills and strategies, foster students' listening skills, gain and maintain students' attention, and motivate students.

How Can I Use Effective Teacher-Centered Instruction?
CEC 3, 4, 5, 6, 7, 9, PRAXIS 3, INTASC 2, 3, 4, 5, 6, 7, 9

To teach effectively, you should establish the lesson's purpose; review prerequisite skills; give clear directions, explanations, and relevant examples; provide time for active and guided practice; promote active responding and check for comprehension; give prompt and specific feedback; offer time for independent activities; and summarize main points and evaluate mastery.

How Can I Successfully Use Cooperative Learning Arrangements with Students?
CEC 3, 4, 5, 6, 7, 9, 10, PRAXIS 3, INTASC 2, 3, 4, 5, 6, 7, 9

You can select an appropriate cooperative learning format, establish guidelines for working collaboratively, form heterogeneous cooperative groups, arrange the classroom for cooperative learning, develop students' cooperative skills, and evaluate cooperative learning.

What Would You Do in Today's Diverse Classroom?

As a teacher in an inclusion classroom, you encounter the following situations:

1. Although your students claim that they are studying, they are doing poorly on tests. You ask them how they study for tests. They tell you that they study notes from class. You examine their notes and notice that they are often incomplete and focused on material that you do not consider relevant.

2. You have been using cooperative learning, and several families have started to complain. They think their children did the work for the group and received a poor grade because others did not do their share.

3. Several of your students are not completing their homework. When you ask for an explanation, students say, "You give too much homework; I have other responsibilities." "I forget what the assignment was," and "It's too noisy at home." Since you consider homework as part of their grades, these students are in danger of failing.

★ What problem(s) are you encountering in each situation?

★ What would you do to address each situation?

★ What knowledge, skills, dispositions, resources and support would you need in designing and implementing strategies to address each situation?

 To answer these questions online and share your responses with others, go to the Reflection module in Chapter 9 of the Companion Website.

Chapter 10

Differentiating Reading, Writing, and Spelling Instruction

Mr. Pike

As Mr. Pike's students enter his classroom, they start working on either independent reading or journal writing. Mr. Pike then shares a book with them. He is reading an African folktale, which is part of a theme on understanding people from diverse cultures. Before reading the story, Mr. Pike discusses the African reverence for nature and the use of animals in folktales to represent human traits.

As a follow-up activity to his lesson on folktales, Mr. Pike asks his students to work in groups to write and illustrate a short folktale using animals as the characters in the story, to be read to or performed for the class in a week. Before assigning students to groups, Mr. Pike conducts a lesson and discussion on folktales. While the students work, Mr. Pike circulates around the room to observe and meet with individual students and groups. One group conference focuses on why that group selected a camel to be its main character; another conference deals with creating a story line.

The group activity is followed by individualized reading. Students independently read books about individuals from various cultures that they have selected from a list prepared and previewed by Mr. Pike and the class. When students come across a word they don't know, Mr. Pike prompts them to figure it out by asking what words make sense or encouraging them to sound it out. Students who select the same book to read are grouped together in literature circles, and meet with Mr. Pike to discuss the book and work on group projects. Steven, a student with a severe cognitive disability, chooses a picture book to read with another student. Occasionally, Mr. Pike teaches a mini-lesson to help his students learn sound–symbol correspondence, blending, new vocabulary, spelling, and strategies for reading fluently. While Mr. Pike teaches his mini-lesson, his paraeducator works with Steven and several other students on phonemic awareness, word identification skills, and vocabulary.

The students and Mr. Pike also read these books during sustained silent reading. Students react to what they have read by making entries in their literature-response journals. Mr. Pike periodically collects and reads the journals and responds to students' entries via written comments or individual conferences.

What strategies does Mr. Pike use to promote the literacy skills of his students? After reading this chapter, you should have the knowledge, skills, and dispositions to answer this as well as the following questions.

★ **How can I help students learn to read?**
★ **How can I help students learn to write?**
★ **How can I help students learn to spell?**

I n addition to differentiating instruction for diverse learners and teaching with large and small groups, teachers like Mr. Pike also need to help students develop literacy skills. This chapter offers guidelines for differentiating instruction so that you can help your students learn to read, write, and spell.

How Can I Help Students Learn to Read?

Offer Early Identification and Intervention

Resource

Gersten and Geva (2003) provide guidelines for teaching reading to second language learners.

Resource

Weikle and Hadadian (2003) offer suggestions and resources for using technology to foster early literacy skills.

Set Your Sites

For more information on early reading identification and intervention, go to the Web Links module in Chapter 10 of the Companion Website.

Resource

Lane and Pullen (2004) offer a listing of assessment techniques, teaching techniques, and commercially available instructional and software programs related to phonological awareness.

Early identification and intervention are critical aspects in teaching students who have reading difficulties (Speece, Mills, Ritchey & Hillman, 2003; Torgesen, 2000). Research indicates that students who experience reading difficulties have problems with *fluency*, which refers to the speed and accuracy with which they can identify letter names and sounds and read orally. They also exhibit difficulties in the areas of phonemic awareness, vocabulary development, memory, decoding, word recognition, reading comprehension, and using clues to help them read. These students also are characterized by their failure to respond to instructional strategies that are usually effective in teaching students to read (Al Otaiba & Fuchs, 2002). Because students identified as having reading difficulties are not likely to outgrow them, it is important to recognize their special needs. You also can support their literacy development by using the principles of effective early reading interventions (See Figure 10.1), as well as the following guidelines for developing their phonemic awareness, reading fluency, vocabulary, and text comprehension. As we will discuss, it also is important for you to employ a balanced approach to teaching reading and supplement your instruction with remedial reading programs, strategies, and materials.

Promote Phonological Awareness

Effective early reading intervention programs promote students' *phonological awareness*, the understanding that words are made up of different sounds and that spoken and written language are linked (Abbott, Walton, & Greenwood, 2002). Phonological aware-

---

Principles of effective early reading interventions

FIGURE 10.1

1. Recognize that reading is a developmental process.
2. Use an instructional sequence that gradually moves from easy to more difficult tasks.
3. Promote students' phonetic awareness, print awareness, oral language, alphabetic understanding, and decoding.
4. Offer explicit instruction to help students develop accurate and fluent word-analysis skills.
5. Emphasize use of language and teach vocabulary in a systematic and integrative way.
6. Structure learning activities so that students have numerous opportunities to respond.
7. Activate students' prior knowledge.
8. Incorporate students' experiences, ideas, and referents into instructional activities.
9. Provide students with meaningful interactions with text.
10. Begin to develop students' comprehension skills by exposing them to a variety of texts.

Note: Coyne, Kame'enui & Simmons (2001); Foorman & Torgesen (2001); Gersten & Geva (2003); Pullen & Justice (2003); Spear-Swerling & Sternberg (2001).

ness instruction usually includes activities to develop students' ability to rhyme, identify sounds, blend sounds into words, segment or break words into sounds, and manipulate or delete sounds (Lane, Pullen, Eisele, & Jordan, 2002).

Motivate Students to Read

Since students develop their phonemic awareness and reading proficiency by reading regularly, it is important to motivate *all students* to read (Dreher, 2003; Guthrie & Davis, 2003). You can do this by:

- modeling the enjoyment of reading and demonstrating that reading can be fun.
- using reading materials that are well written, easy to comprehend, challenging, and interesting to students and related to their lives.
- giving students a range of reading choices including stories and information books.
- creating a relaxed learning and reading environment.
- playing recordings of selections and students' favorite stories and songs.
- using the Internet.
- giving students a variety of ways to express their reactions to material they have read.
- acknowledging students' attempts to read as well as their progress (Dreher, 2003; Guthrie & Davis, 2003; Richards, 2003; Sanacore, 2002).

As Mr. Pike did in the chapter-opening vignette, you can motivate students to read by choosing reading selections that relate to students' experiences and cultures. You also can use many of the motivation enhancing strategies we discussed in chapter 9 to encourage your students to read.

Reading Aloud to Students.   Reading aloud to students can motivate them by introducing them to the enjoyment and excitement of reading. Reading aloud to students also allows you to model good oral reading, promote phonological awareness and vocabulary development, and offer background knowledge in such areas as story structure and content (Allor & McCathren, 2003). When reading to students, you can introduce the selection by discussing the title and cover of the book and asking students to make predictions about the book. You also can introduce the author and illustrator and talk with students about other books they have read by the author or on a similar topic or theme.

As you read to students, you can promote their interest and understanding by using animated expressions; displaying illustrations so that all students can see and react to them; relating the book to students' experiences; discussing the book in a lively, inviting, and thought-provoking manner; and offering students a variety of learning activities (i.e., writing, drama, art) to respond to and express their feelings about the selection (Hoffman, Roser, & Battle, 1993).

Picture Books.   You can motivate students to read and write through the use of *picture books*, short books that use pictures and illustrations to enhance the reader's understanding of the meaning and content of the story (Billman, 2002). While they are appropriate for *all students*, they are particularly effective with students with reading difficulties and second language learners. Picture books also can help students learn a wide range of reading strategies, such as prediction and using context and syntactical cues.

Involve Families

The active involvement of families also can motivate students and help them develop their reading and phonemic awareness skills (Baker, 2003). Family members can serve

Resource

Tompkins (2003), Abbott, Walton, and Greenwood (2002), Levy, Coleman, and Alsman (2002), Flett and Conderman (2002), and Kaderavek and Justice (2000) offer activities, resources, and instructional procedures for teaching phonological awareness.

Resource

Dreher (2003) offers resources and strategies for using information books to motivate elementary- and secondary-level students to read.

Resource

Sanacore (1999) offers guidelines for reading aloud to students.

Resource

Billman (2002) offers guidelines for using picture books with elementary and secondary students, and Bligh (1996) and Perry (1997) provide a bibliography of recommended picture books.

Resource

Al Otaiba and Smartt (2003) offer guidelines and activities for helping family members teach phonological awareness to their children.

Set Your Sites

For more information on family literacy, go to the Web Links module in Chapter 10 of the Companion Website.

as role models by reading a variety of materials, showing their children that reading is useful, fun, interesting, and informative (Baker, 2003).

You can support the involvement of families by providing them with copies and lists of age- and reading level-appropriate books, sharing effective reading instructional strategies with them, and communicating regularly with them about their child's reading progress.

Promote Reading Fluency

Reading fluency is an essential skill for you to promote. It is an especially important reading goal for students whose reading difficulties make them reluctant to read in front of others. You can address their reluctance and develop their reading fluency skills in several ways (Chard, Vaughn & Tyler, 2002; Mercer, Campbell, Miller, Mercer & Lane, 2000). You can use choral reading, which involves you and your students reading selections, stories, poems, books, and student-authored materials together (Mariage et al., 2000).

Rather than calling on them, you can solicit their permission to be called on to read aloud. You also can prepare them to read a specific selection fluently in class by preteaching vocabulary and using *repeated reading* and *previewing*. In *repeated reading*, students are given numerous opportunities to practice reading the text they will be asked to read in class. Since repeated reading is most effective when students have a model, you use various previewing techniques to enhance its effectiveness. *Previewing* refers to methods that give students opportunities to read or listen to text prior to reading. The most popular previewing strategies include oral previewing, where the students read the passage aloud prior to the whole-class reading session; silent previewing, where students read the passage silently before the reading session; and listening previewing, in which students listen and follow along as an adult reads the selection aloud.

Family members can promote literacy by showing that reading is fun, interesting, and informative. How do you collaborate with family members to promote literacy?

You can engage in several other teaching practices to foster your students' reading fluency (Levy, Coleman, & Alsman, 2002). You can offer them opportunities to read each day, give them reading materials that allow them to be successful, use speed-based drill-and-practice activities, and have them set goals and record and graph their progress. You can emphasize rate by prompting them to try to make their eyes go faster, combine several words together at the same time, pair words like *a* and *the* with words that follow them, and ask themselves if the word makes sense (Gaffney, Methven, & Bagdasarian, 2002). You also can offer immediate corrective feedback and model reading at an appropriate pace and with expression and encourage students to do the same.

You also can teach them to use a variety of fluency-enhancing reading strategies. These strategies include:

- using root words and affixes to decode unknown words.
- pausing appropriately based on the punctuation.
- using semantic and syntactic cues to read with expression.
- self-correcting errors.
- limiting omissions by using a finger to trace the print (Allinder, Dunse, Brunken, & Obermiller-Krolikowski, 2001).

You also can record students during reading activities and have them analyze and reflect upon their reading.

Foster Word Identification

You can promote reading fluency by fostering your students' word identification skills. One way to do that is to teach your students to use strategies for identifying unfamiliar words. Lovett, Lacerenza, and Borden (2000) propose several word-recognition strategies that can help your students decode unfamiliar words, including the following:

- *Rhyming Strategy:* Students read unfamiliar words by comparing them with rhymes of familiar or keywords that they already know (e.g., using the keyword *time* as a rhyme to read *crime*).
- *Vowel Alert Strategy:* Students read unfamiliar words by identifying the vowel sound after examining the letters that precede and follow the vowels.
- *Seek the Part You Know Strategy:* Students read unfamiliar words by identifying parts of the unfamiliar words they know (e.g. dividing *rainbow* into *rain* and *bow*).
- *Peeling Off Strategy:* Students read unfamiliar words by using affixes at the beginnings and endings of words and then focusing on the root word (e.g. peeling off the affixes *un* and *ing* to facilitate reading of *unlocking*).

Students can also be taught to use an Integrated Processing Strategy to help them read unknown words (Pemberton, 2003). Students implement this strategy by making a line below each part of an unknown word, verbalizing each part of the word without raising their writing instrument, and attempting to quickly reread the word. The student then rereads the sentence, and makes sure that the word makes sense in the context of the sentence.

Word flashcard and computer-presented drills can be used to provide the repetition that some students need to identify words. You can modify these drills by using interspersal of known items, a technique that involves adjusting the percentage of unknown and known words. For example, an interspersed word sequence of 30 percent unknown words and 70 percent known words has been successful in helping students with learning problems recognize words (Knight, Ross, Taylor, & Ramasamy, 2003).

Resource

Bryant, Ugel, Thompson, and Hamff (1999) offer activities for teaching word identification, vocabulary, and comprehension.

Resource

Kaderavek and Justice (2000) offer activities and resources for promoting students' awareness of environmental print.

Environmental Print.   Environmental print—that is, materials that are found in students' natural environments—can help *all your students,* particularly those who are learning English, develop their reading fluency and give meaning to printed symbols. You prompt students to interact with environmental print by providing them with opportunities to read magazines and newspapers written at different levels of difficulty, as well as signs, labels, posters, calendars, advertisements, menus, and wall charts.

Use Prompting Strategies

Resource

Rohena, Jitendra and Browder (2002) offer strategies for teaching word identification reading to second language learners with mental retardation.

Like Mr. Pike, you can use a variety of prompting strategies to help your students read difficult or unfamiliar words (Gipe, 2002). Reading prompts refer to cues and reminders that assist students in reading successfully. They can be divided into two types: teacher prompting and student prompting. Teacher prompting is used by the teacher to help students make the correct response and guide them to use effective cues. Student prompting is used by students to determine the correct response and include configuration and context cues.

Reflective

What strategies do you use to identify unfamiliar words? How did you learn these strategies?

Both teacher and student prompting should be natural and age- and culturally appropriate, and should be faded out as students progress (Ernsbarger, 2002). For example, it is often more appropriate to teach secondary students to use configuration, context, syntactic, semantic, and syntactic cues than delivering language, visual, and physical prompts to them.

Language Prompts.   Language cues use the students' language skills as the basis for triggering the correct response. For example, if a student had difficulty decoding the word *store,* a vocabulary cue such as "You buy things at a . . . " might elicit the correct response. Other language-oriented cues include rhyming ("It rhymes with door"), word associations ("Choo! Choo!" to cue the word *train*), analogies ("Light is to day as dark is to night"), antonyms ("It's the opposite of"), and binary choices ("Is the trip long or short?"). Language cues also include phonemic cues, which entail prompting students to read a word by providing them with the initial sound or syllable (Bellon & Ogletree, 2000).

Visual Prompts.   Visual prompts can help students focus on certain aspects of words. For instance, attention to medial vowels can be fostered visually by color cues (make the medial vowel a different color than the other letters), size cues (enlarge the medial vowel while keeping the other letters constant, such as cAt), or graphic cues (accentuate the medial vowel by underlining or circling it, such as c<u>a</u>t). Visual prompts are valuable in correcting reversals. For example, difficulty discriminating *b* and *d* can be reduced by cuing one of the letters graphically.

Resource

Wauters, Knoors, Vervloed, and Aarnoutse (2001) and Goldin-Meadow and Mayberry (2001) offer guidelines for promoting the word-recognition skills of students with hearing impairments.

Pictorial prompting, in which words and their pictures are linked, is a good strategy for helping students with hearing impairments and students with severe cognitive disabilities read words (Goldin-Meadow & Mayberry, 2001). It is especially helpful in reading nouns and prepositions. These students also may benefit from picture reading, which involves students responding to teachers asking questions about characters, objects, topics, and sequences in wordless books (Alberto & Frederick, 2000).

Resource

Alberto and Frederick (2000) provide guidelines for teaching picture reading.

Pictorial cues can also he helpful to students who reverse words. For example, if a student typically reads the word *saw* as *was,* a drawing of a saw above the word *saw* would help the student make this distinction. Finally, visual cues, such as pointing to an object in the classroom or showing a numeral, can be used to prompt the reading of words that correspond, respectively, to objects in the classroom and number words.

Physical Prompts.   Physical prompts are most effective in communicating words or concepts with perceptually salient features (Bellon & Ogletree, 2000). These words can be cued by miming the distinct qualities or actions associated with them. In addition to miming, you can use finger spelling or pointing as a cue to elicit a correct response.

Configuration Cues.   Configuration cues relate to the outline of the word and can be useful when there are noticeable differences in the shape and length of words. Students use configuration cues when they note the length of the words and the size and graphic characteristics of the letters. While research on the effectiveness of configuration cues is inconclusive, it appears that they are most effective when used with context and other prompting strategies.

Context Cues.   The context in which the word is presented can provide useful cues for determining the pronunciation of unknown words. Potential context cues that students can use include syntactic, semantic, and picture features of the text. Context cues are best suited for words that occur near the middle or the end of the sentence.

Syntactic Cues.   Syntactic cues deal with the grammatical structure of the sentence containing the word. The syntactic structure of English dictates that only certain words can fit into a particular part of a sentence or statement. Thus, students can be taught to use parts of sentences to figure out difficult words.

Semantic Cues.   Semantic cues, available by examining the meanings of the text, can help students improve their word identification skills. Semantic cues can be taught by having students closely examine the sentence containing the unknown word, as well as the entire reading selection in which the word appears. These cues are particularly appropriate when students are learning to read abstract words.

Resource

Salembier and Cheng (1997) have developed SCUBA-DIVE, a learning strategy that helps students use six cues to decode unfamiliar words.

Pictorial Cues.   Many reading passages contain illustrations to promote fluency, comprehension, and motivation. These pictorial cues also can help students recognize new words by helping them establish the context of the story. To maximize the effects of illustrations on word recognition, the students' attention can be directed to the word and the illustration.

Reflective

What types of cues do you use to prompt your students' reading?

Support Older Struggling Readers

You need to understand and be particularly sensitive to older students who struggle with reading (Guthrie & Davis, 2003). In addition to motivating these students to read using the strategies we discussed, you can make reading an integral part of content area instruction (Vacca, 2002). You can do this by selecting appropriate textbooks (see chapter 11), teaching students to use text comprehension strategies (see chapter 8), and using technology and content enhancements to support their learning (see chapters 8 and 11).

It is also important for you to be aware of students' frustration, instructional, and independent instructional levels. You can use this information to plan instruction so that students are working on appropriate learning activities that challenge them and are not asked to perform tasks that cause them to become frustrated and anxious.

You also can offer specialized instruction to address their needs by:

* using high-interest, easy-to-read, age- and curriculum-appropriate materials and young adult novels.
* delivering nonintrusive and age-appropriate prompts and error-correction techniques.

Teachers can promote students' reading skills by helping them select interesting and appropriate reading materials. What types of reading materials do your students find most interesting?

- teaching phonological awareness skills via multisyllable age-appropriate words and lyrics from popular songs and poetry.
- developing word-recognition and phonetic skills and fluency via reading games.
- reading aloud to students and providing them with time for independent reading.
- expanding their vocabulary knowledge.
- acknowledging their progress (Brozo & Simpson, 2003; Brucker & Piazza, 2002; Foil & Alber, 2002; Ivey, 2002; Moats, 2001; Salinger, 2003).

You can support students who struggle with reading by teaching them how to choose reading materials that are appropriate for them (Schirmer & Lockman, 2001). One way to do that is to teach students to use the *Five Finger Test*, which involves students:

- choosing a book that they might want to read.
- reading a page in the middle of the book.
- holding up a finger each time they encounter a word they don't know.
- selecting another book if they hold up at least five fingers before completing the page.

Resource

Bean (2002) offers guidelines and examples to making reading relevant to secondary students.

You also can provide your students with a rubric for self-selecting reading material (see Table 10.1) and teach them how to use it.

Enhance Students' Text Comprehension

In addition to promoting students' phonological awareness and reading fluency, an effective reading program also focuses on developing students' comprehension. In addition to using the text comprehension strategies, teaching techniques, and instructional technology discussed in chapters 8 and 11, you can use the following guidelines to enhance your students' text comprehension.

TABLE 10.1

Rubric for self-selecting appropriate reading material

Book/Story/Chapter/Article Title: _____

Author(s): _____

Readability Factors	Score 1	Score 2	Score 3	Score 4
Vocabulary ❑ Score	❑ There are 10 or more words I do not know.	❑ There are 7–9 words I do not know.	❑ There are 4–6 words I do not know.	❑ There are 3 or fewer words I do not know.
Sentences ❑ Score	❑ Almost all of the sentences are long and complex.	❑ A few sentences are easy but most are long and complex.	❑ A few sentences are long and complex but most are easy.	❑ Almost all of the sentences are short and easy.
Topic and Concepts ❑ Score	❑ I am unfamiliar with the topic and most of the concepts are new to me.	❑ I know a little about the topic and concepts.	❑ I know much about the topic and concepts.	❑ I am highly familiar with the topic and none of the concepts are new to me.
Clarity of Ideas ❑ Score	❑ The ideas are presented unclearly and are difficult to understand.	❑ A few of the ideas are presented clearly enough to understand without difficulty.	❑ Most of the ideas are presented clearly enough to understand easily.	❑ The ideas are presented very clearly and are easy to understand.
Level of Abstraction (includes figurative language, metaphors, similes, slang, symbols, theories) ❑ Score	❑ The author uses language and/or presents ideas that are highly abstract.	❑ The author uses many abstract words and phrases and/or presents more than one abstract idea.	❑ The author uses a few abstract words and phrases and/or presents an abstract idea.	❑ The author uses language and/or presents ideas that are concrete.
Organization ❑ Score	❑ I cannot figure out the organization.	❑ It is difficult to follow the organization.	❑ I can follow the organization but I have to concentrate.	❑ I can follow the organization easily.
Design and Format (includes font, print size, paragraph length, use of columns, use of illustrations and other visuals, and other design issues) ❑ Score	❑ The material is poorly designed and the format impedes reading.	❑ The design and format create some problems for me.	❑ The design and format create no serious problems for me.	❑ The material is well designed and the format facilitates reading.
Genre ❑ Score	❑ I am not familiar with the writing form and style.	❑ I have only read this kind of writing once or twice.	❑ I have read this kind of writing a few times.	❑ I am very familiar with the writing form and style.
Interest and Motivation ❑ Score	❑ I am not interested in the topic and don't have any particular motivation or reason to read this material.	❑ I am slightly interested in the topic and would have difficulty explaining why I want to read this material.	❑ I am somewhat interested in the topic and have a couple of ideas about why I want to read this material.	❑ I am extremely interested in the topic, highly motivated, and have a definite reason to read this material.
Pacing and Fluency ❑ Score	❑ If others watched and heard me read, they would describe me as tense and my reading as choppy.	❑ If others watched and heard me read, they would describe me as uneasy and my reading as frequently hesitant.	❑ If others watched and heard me read, they would describe me as confortable but my reading as sometimes unsure	❑ If others watched and heard me read, they would describe me as relaxed and my reading as fluent.
❑ Total Score				

(continued)

Table 10.1 (continued)

Directions:

1. Read the first page of the book. If the first page is not a full page, read the next page also.

2. Check the box of the score most appropriate for each readability factor.

3. Write the score in the box under each readability factor.

4. Total the scores.

5. Determine if you can read the material independently.

* If the total score is 30–40, the material can be read independently. If the score is 38–40, perhaps this material is too easy for you.

* If the total score is 20–29, the material is challenging. Decide which factors are most important to you. If you scored 3 or 4 on each of these factors, the material can be read independently. If you scored 1 or 2 on the most important factors, the material should be read only with assistance.

* If the total score is < 20, the material is too difficult to read without assistance.

Source: From "How Do I Find a Book to Read? Middle and High School Students Use a Rubric For Self-Selecting Material for Independent Reading," by B. R. Schirmer and A. S. Lockman, 2001, *Teaching Exceptional Children, 34*(1), pp. 36–42. Copyright 2001 by The Council for Exceptional Children. Reprinted with permission.

Develop Students' Vocabulary

Developing your students' vocabulary is a good way to enhance their reading fluency and comprehension (Saenz & Fuchs, 2002). As we discussed in chapter 8, you can identify, preview, and teach new vocabulary in reading selections and use effective ESL approaches and new vocabulary and concept instructional techniques with *all* your students.

Alber and Foil (2003) suggest that teachers use the following instructional sequence to introduce new vocabulary to students:

* Visually display the word, pronounce it, and ask students to say it.
* Discuss the word's meaning and give students multiple examples of the word's usage in context.
* Link the word and its meaning to students' prior knowledge and prompt students to describe their experiences with the word.
* Provide students with multiple opportunities to use the word in context and offer specific feedback.
* Promote generalization by teaching multiple examples of the word, helping students understand slight differences in words that have similar meanings (e.g., integrate and incorporate), prompting and reinforcing students' use of new vocabulary, and having students self-record their use of vocabulary words.

You can introduce new vocabulary by creating a memorable event or physically presenting the important attributes of the words (Alber & Foil, 2003). For example, you can dress up in a memorable way to depict the word *garish*, or spin around to introduce students to the salient features of the word *pirouette*. You also can explain new vocabulary after it is encountered in a reading selection, and have students maintain a file or notebook containing new vocabulary words, their definitions, and drawings depicting them (Fisher, Frey, & Williams, 2002). Other vocabulary development strategies include using repetition, modeling, and drama; teaching students how to use context and root words to determine meanings; discussing the origins of words; explaining idiomatic expressions, synonyms, and antonymns; and teaching students to use dictionaries and thesauruses (Foil & Alber, 2002).

You also can visually present the critical features of new vocabulary words via graphic organizers, concept teaching routines, or semantic webs (see chapter 11). Another visually oriented method of teaching new vocabulary words is *semantic feature analysis (SFA)* (Walker, 2000). SFA involves creating a visual that guides students in comparing vocabulary words to determine the ways they are similar and different. Video clips depicting new vocabulary also can be used to teach vocabulary.

Story Grammars and Frames.   Story grammars and frames can support your students' comprehension of text. *Story grammars* are outlines of the ways stories are organized (Bellon & Ogletree, 2000). They often involve identifying and articulating a reading selection's main characters, story lines, conflicts, and ending.

Frames outline important components of stories and provide cues to help students understand text in a variety of genres. One effective frame is the circle story, which is developed by plotting a story's important components in a clockwise sequence on a circle diagram.

Storytelling and Drama.   Storytelling and drama can help students construct meaning from text, and promote listening comprehension and vocabulary skills. While *all students* benefit from storytelling and drama, they are particularly good teaching techniques for students whose cultures have an oral tradition and for those who are learning a second language (Craig, Hull, Haggart, & Crowder, 2001). Students can act out and retell stories through miming, gestures, role-playing, and the use of props.

Use Peer-Based Instruction

Reading instruction in inclusive settings can be supplemented by using peer-based instruction (Schmidt, Rozendal & Greenman, 2002). Peer tutoring and classwide peer tutoring programs, following the principles presented in chapter 9, can help your students improve their reading fluency, word identification, and reading comprehension.

Peer-Assisted Learning Strategies.   One peer-mediated system that has been effective in promoting elementary and secondary level students' reading fluency and comprehension is Peer-Assisted Learning Strategies (PALS) (Fuchs et al., 2001). Students work with peers in Partner Reading, Paragraph Shrinking, and Prediction Relay. *Partner Reading* involves students taking turns reading aloud for 5 minutes, with the more proficient student reading first. *Paragraph Shrinking* involves students reading orally and then asking each other questions designed to identify the main idea of each paragraph. In the *Prediction Relay*, students work in dyads with one student making a prediction about a half page of text, orally reading the text, and then summarizing the main idea. Other peer-mediated reading interventions include Book Buddies and Sound and Thinking Partners (Vadasy, Sanders, Peyton, & Jenkins, 2002).

Literature Circles and Response Journals.   Like Mr. Pike, you can use literature circles or literature discussion groups, small groups of students who work collaboratively to share their reactions to and discuss various aspects of books that all group members have decided to read (Dreher, 2003). Some teachers adapt literature circles by assigning specific roles to students such as discussion leader (monitors and fosters the discussion), passage reader (reads key passages aloud), connector (links content to students' experiences), definer (looks up and explains key vocabulary), summarizer (reviews key points and the sequence of action), and illustrator (develops corresponding graphics). Students

Resource

Alber and Foil (2003) and Foil and Alber (2002) offer activities and learning strategies for developing students' vocabulary.

Resource

Craig et al. (2001) offer guidelines and activities for using storytelling to promote students' literacy.

Set Your Sites

For more information on storytelling, go to the Web Links module in Chapter 10 of the Companion Website.

Resource

Gaffney, Methven, and Bagdasarian (2002) provide guidelines for teaching students to be effective reading tutors, and Parker, Hasbrouck and Denton (2002a, 2002b) offer strategies for tutoring students and evaluating tutoring programs.

Resource

Tompkins (2003) and Hindin, Morocco, and Aguilar (2001) offer guidelines for using literacy circles to support the literacy skills of secondary level students, and Montgomery (2000) provides strategies for using literature circles to develop students' cross-cultural understanding.

also can work in literature response groups to read different genres and respond to them in various ways.

Literature response journals can be used as a follow-up to sustained silent reading periods or literature circles (Bean, 2002). In these journals, students describe their reactions to and thoughts about the material they have been reading, as well as any questions they have. Students also are encouraged to write about their opinions and emotional responses to the book, relate the book to their own experiences, and make predictions about the book and its characters. You can read students' journals and offer comments that encourage students to redirect, expand, and refocus their reactions and questions.

One type of literature response journal is the character study journal, in which students make entries related to an interesting character (Galda, Cullinan, & Strickland, 1997). While reading the selection, students react to and write about their character, including the character's dilemmas, feelings, and responses.

Shared Book Reading.   You and your students can sit close together and share in reading a variety of materials. You read a new or familiar story; students react to it through arts and crafts, drama, reading, or writing; and students then reread the story on their own. Big books with large print and pictures and storybooks are particularly appropriate for shared book reading for younger students, as they allow you to display the words the students are reading (Allor & McCathren, 2003).

Older students can share their reactions via readers' theater or dinner party (Bean, 2002; Sanacore, 2002). In readers' theater, students give a dramatic reading of key passages, which are then discussed by a group of students. In the dinner party, students role-play characters from the book, who are interviewed by a commentator.

Guided Reading.   Guided reading involves working with students in small groups to explore books and ideas. Guided reading usually starts with you introducing the story and fostering students' interest in reading it. Next, the students read the text to themselves as you observe them and listen to note their reading behaviors. After reading the story, you talk with your students about it to have them make predictions about and personal connections to the story. You also may have them reread parts of the story, and demonstrate reading strategies and help students learn how to use them.

An important component of guided reading is the group reading conference, a time when groups discuss books or selections that they have been reading independently. Structure the conference by asking open-ended questions that require students to think, express an opinion, and relate the selection to their own experiences.

Sustained Silent Reading.   A group-oriented reading technique that teachers like Mr. Pike employ is *sustained silent reading.* During sustained silent reading you, your students, and other members of the class read self-selected materials for an extended period of time (Bean, 2002). Typically, the rules for sustained silent reading are (a) read silently, (b) do not interrupt others, and (c) do not change books.

Resource

Allor and McCathren (2003) offer strategies for using storybooks to foster students' literacy and Bellon and Ogletree (2000) provide guidelines for selecting appropriate storybooks for students to read.

Resource

Alber (1996) offers guidelines for creating interest, holding students accountable, and preventing disruptions during sustained silent reading.

Use a Balanced Approach

Most reading programs are based on a particular teaching philosophy, and therefore they differ in their instructional approach. In planning reading instruction for your students, select approaches that are appropriate to your students' individual learning needs and characteristics. In addition, examine the impact of these approaches on your students' rate of learning and emotional responsiveness. Some students may benefit from one specific reading approach. Most students, however, perform best if you use a balanced approach that combines elements of the various approaches described in the following sections (Tompkins, 2003).

Phonetic-Based Approaches

Phonetic reading approaches teach students to recognize and understand the phonological features of language and of individual words (Tompkins, 2003). These approaches also teach students strategies for decoding or "sounding out" new and unknown words. Therefore, phonics instruction is geared to teaching students the relationship between letters, and it focuses on helping students learn to blend and segment sounds within words (Wanzek & Haager, 2003). The effectiveness of phonics instruction is increased when it is combined with phonemic awareness, fluency, and comprehension instruction (Foorman & Torgesen, 2001).

Phonetic approaches are categorized as synthetic or analytic (Groff, 2001). The synthetic approach develops phonetic skills by teaching students the specific symbol–grapheme (e.g., *g*) to sound–phoneme (e.g., *guh*) correspondence rules. Once students learn the sound and symbol rules, they are taught to synthesize the sounds into words through blending.

In the analytic approach to phonetics instruction, the phoneme–grapheme correspondence is learned by teaching students to analyze words. These word analysis skills help students understand that letters within words sound alike and are written the same way.

Another analytic method uses a linguistic approach to teach reading. Students learn to read and spell words within word families that have the same phonetic patterns. Through repeated presentations of these word families, students learn the rules of sound–symbol correspondence. For example, the *at* family would be introduced together, using words such as *bat*, *cat*, *fat*, *hat*, *rat*, and *sat*.

Phonetic approaches might present some problems for students with disabilities. Students taught using these phonetic approaches tend to not guess words that do not follow phonetic rules; read more regular words than irregular words; and pronounce words based on graphic and phonetic cues rather than semantic and syntactic cues. Students

Resouce

Wanzek and Haager (2003) provide guidelines and activities for teaching letter–sound correspondence and blending and Joseph (2002) offers phonetic-based activities for small- and large-groups

Resource

Chard and Osborn (1999) offer guidelines and activities for using a phonetic approach to teach letter–sound correspondence, regular and irregular words, story reading, and word analysis.

Phonics instruction teaches students the relationship between letters and sound. What difficulties do your students encounter in using a phonetic approach to reading?

may have difficulty in identifying words that do not follow phonetic patterns and in isolating and blending sounds, so you may need to supplement phonetics instruction with other approaches.

Whole Word Approaches

Whole word approaches help students make the link between whole words and their oral counterparts. In the whole word approach, meaning also is emphasized. New words are taught within sentences and passages or in isolation. Students taught through whole word methods tend to attempt to read unfamiliar words, use context cues rather than graphic cues, and substitute familiar words for new words. You can modify whole word approaches by decreasing the number of words to be learned, using flash cards that contain the word and a pictorial of the word, offering spaced practice sessions, providing opportunities for overlearning, and delivering more frequent reinforcement.

Language Experience Approach

A language experience approach is based on the belief that what students think about, they can talk about; what students can say, they can write or have someone write for them; and what students can write, they can read (Tompkins, 2003). Language experience approaches are highly individualized; they use the students' interests, hobbies, and experiences as the basis for creating reading materials that are highly motivating and that foster creativity.

Whole Language Approach

A balanced reading program also can include many of the elements and strategies associated with a whole language approach. A whole language approach uses students' natural language and experiences in and out of school to immerse all students in a supportive, stimulating, natural learning environment that promotes their literacy. In a whole language approach, reading, writing, listening, speaking, and thinking are integrated into each lesson and activity, and learning is viewed as proceeding from the whole to the part rather than the reverse.

The whole language curriculum is developmental, and is often organized around themes and units that increase language and reading skills (Mariage, Englert, & Garmon, 2000). Students are motivated to read and improve their reading by reading authentic, relevant, and functional materials that make sense to them and relate to their experiences (Tucker & Bakken, 2000). At first, students read meaningful, predictable whole texts. Next, they use the familiar words in these texts to learn new words and phrases. While learning to read, students also learn to write. They are encouraged to write about their experiences by composing letters, maintaining journals, making lists, labeling objects in the classroom, and keeping records.

Set Your Sites

For more information on the teaching of reading, go to the Web Links module in Chapter 10 of the Companion Website.

Use Remedial Reading Programs, Strategies, and Materials

Because many students, particularly those with disabilities, have difficulty reading, you may need to supplement your reading instruction with some of the remedial reading programs, strategies, and materials described here.

Multisensory Strategies

Multisensory strategies teach letters and words using combinations of visual, auditory, kinesthetic, and tactile modalities. Several multisensory strategies are available, including writing the word in chalk, spelling the word after saying it, tracing three-dimensional letters with students' eyes shut, and tracing letters on the students' backs.

Fernald Method.   A multisensory, whole word, language experience strategy that was developed for students with learning problems is the Fernald Method, which involves four steps: tracing, writing without tracing, recognition in print, and word analysis (Stahl, 1998).

Orton-Gillingham-Stillman Strategy.   The Orton-Gillingham-Stillman Strategy uses a multisensory synthetic phonics approach to teaching reading (Stahl, 1998). At first, students are taught letter–sound symbol correspondence by viewing the letters, hearing the sounds they make, linking the letters to their sounds, and writing the letters. Once 10 letters (*a, b, f, h, i, j, k, m, p, t*) are mastered, blending of the sounds is taught. Blending is followed by story writing, syllabification, dictionary skills, and instruction in spelling rules.

Set Your Sites

For more information on teaching reading and writing, go to the Web Links module in Chapter 10 of the Companion Website.

Set Your Sites

For more information on the Orton-Gillingham-Stillman Strategy, go to the Web Links module in Chapter 10 of the Companion Website.

Programmed Reading Materials

Some students may benefit from a highly structured approach to the teaching of reading that involves use of programmed materials such as Reading Mastery, Corrective Reading, and Distar (Englemann & Associates, 1999; Gunn, Biglan, Smolkowski, & Ary, 2000). These programs present information in small, discrete steps that follow a planned sequence of skills. Each skill within the sequence is presented so that students can review, practice, overlearn, and apply the skill while receiving feedback. Errors are corrected before students can proceed to the next skill. You follow the presentation sequence by adhering to the directions outlined in the manual.

How Can I Help Students Learn to Write?

Make Writing Meaningful and an Integral Part of the Curriculum

One content area directly related to reading that occurs throughout the school curriculum is written language. However, rather than assume that students are improving their writing skills by writing during reading and content-area assignments, opportunities to write and the teaching of written expression should be an ongoing part of the students' instructional program (Gleason & Isaccson, 2001). For example, writing can be incorporated into content-area instruction and assessment by using the following instructional techniques:

- *Sentence synthesis:* Students are given several key words from a lesson and asked to use them in writing meaningful sentences related to the main points of the lesson ("Write two meaningful sentences about virus, bacteria, and fungus.").
- *Question all-write:* Students respond in writing to questions posed by their teachers ("What is the difference between weathering and erosion?").
- *Outcome sentences:* Students respond in writing to teacher-directed prompts during the lesson ("I learned that _____ " "I am not sure why _____ ").

Reflecting on Your Practices

Creating a Balanced and Literacy-Rich Learning Environment

You can examine your ability to create a balanced and literacy-rich learning environment by considering the following questions:

- Do you select and use reading approaches that are appropriate to your students' individual learning needs and characteristics?
- Do you use a range of activities to develop your students' phonemic awareness?
- Do you maintain a classroom environment that is print-rich through the use of charts, mobiles, logos, signs, flash cards, and posters, as well as the labeling of objects and areas in the classroom?
- Do you help students develop reading fluency and use a variety of strategies to foster their word-identification skills?
- Do you create opportunities for students to interact verbally with their peers, talk about their ideas and reactions, and participate actively in reading and writing activities?
- Do you give students access to a variety of high-quality literature genres?
- Do you give students choices concerning the books they read, the topics they write about, and the projects they complete?
- Do you teach students how to use context and root words, dictionaries, and thesauruses to determine word meanings?
- Do you use visuals, memorable events, physical exaggerations, story grammars, repetition, modeling, and drama to foster students' vocabulary and text comprehension?
- Are reading and writing activities focused on students' experiences, interests, and background knowledge?

- Do you model reading and writing by demonstrating and sharing your ongoing efforts in these areas?
- Are areas for reading, writing, speaking, listening, and content-area learning available to students?
- Do you display work on bulletin boards, blackboards, doors, and walls that has been written and read by students?
- Do you create a comfortable physical environment for learning, and involve families in literacy development?
- Do you maintain a classroom library of books and materials related to students' reading levels, interests, and cultural backgrounds?
- Is your classroom stocked with books that contain repetitive language, an interesting story line, pictures related to the text, and a predictable structure?
- Do you use technology to support your students' reading and writing?
- Do students maintain personal and dialogue journals and logs of books read, and do they make and read invitations, cards, and recipes?
- Do you supplement your reading instruction by using remedial reading programs, strategies, and materials?

How would you rate your ability to create a balanced and literacy-rich learning environment? ( ) Excellent ( ) Good ( ) Needs Improvement ( ) Needs Much Improvement

What steps could you adopt to improve your ability to create a balanced learning environment that supports your students' literacy?

- *Frames:* Students are asked to complete skeletal paragraphs that include important information and ideas and transition words related to the lesson.
- *Short statements:* Students are asked to write short statements describing people, places, and things covered in lessons, comparing concepts, or outlining the process they used to solve a problem or perform an experiment (e.g., "Write a short statement outlining how you solved the problems we discussed in class.") (Yell, 2002).

Instruction in writing should be meaningful and should allow students to write for social, creative, recreational, and occupational purposes, as well as to express opinions and share information. Students also should be allowed to perform meaningful writing tasks that have an authentic audience, are of interest to them, and serve a real purpose.

Use Journals

As we saw in the chapter-opening vignette, journals in which students write about their personal reactions to events and their experiences are a good way to make writing meaningful (Graves, Valles, & Rueda, 2000; Montgomery, 2001b). For example, students can maintain a personal journal or a dialogue journal. In the personal journal, students write about their own lives, including such topics as family members, friends, feelings, hobbies, and personal events. The dialogue journal, in which you and your students write confidential responses to each other, can motivate students to write while promoting a good relationship between you and your students (Regan, 2003). As students become comfortable with writing in their journals, you can probe the meaning of their statements and seek more in-depth responses by using probing questions, making comments, sharing observations, responding to students' questions, and asking for more detail. Students also can be asked to maintain simulated journals in which they take and write about the perspective of another person, or a buddy journal in which they maintain a written conversation with one of their classmates (Montgomery, 2001b).

Students also can be encouraged to write by linking writing to content-area instruction, and their culture and experiences. All students can be given opportunities to write poems, essays, and short stories related to content-area learning that express their ideas and cultural experiences. As they write about their cultural backgrounds, students also learn about and understand the cultural experiences of their classmates.

Use a Process-Oriented Approach to Writing Instruction

Although there is considerable overlap in the stages of writing, many advocate a process-oriented approach in teaching writing (Marchisan & Alber, 2001; Scott & Vitale, 2003). Research indicates that when this approach is combined with writing strategy instruction, computer-supported writing, and ongoing feedback, *all students,* including those with disabilities and other special needs, improve their writing (Baker, Gersten, & Graham, 2003; Graham, Harris & Larsen, 2001; Hallenbeck, 2002).

A process-oriented approach to writing is viewed as consisting of holistic subprocesses: planning/prewriting, drafting, editing, revising and publishing (see Figure 10.2. These subprocesses lead to writing activities that have a real purpose and a real audience. The subprocesses and writing strategies, together with computer-supported writing applications, are presented in the following sections.

Planning/Prewriting

During the planning or prewriting phase, students determine the purpose of the writing task, generate and group ideas, identify the audience, and plan how to present the content to the reader. You can facilitate the planning process by providing students with engaging and varied experiences to write about, helping them generate and organize their ideas, and assisting them in developing a plan. Prewriting activities to help students with the planning process are discussed here.

Idea Generation.   Allowing students to work on topics they themselves have chosen can foster idea generation. When students select their own topics and make decisions about content, they have a personal connection to their work and develop a sense of ownership toward writing. Multimedia, computer software, simulations, trips, interviews,

Resource

Montgomery (2001b) offers guidelines for using journals to foster students' reading and writing.

Resource

Regan (2003) offers guidelines for using dialogue journals, and Kluwin (1996) describes how to use dialogue journals to encourage students working in dyads to write to each other.

Resource

Gregg and Mather (2002) and Isaacson and Gleason (1998) offer strategies for assessing students' written language skills, and McAlister, Nelson, and Bahr (1999) offer strategies for assessing students' understanding of and attitudes toward a writing process approach.

Set Your Sites

For more information on teaching writing, go to the Web Links module in Chapter 10 of the Companion Website.

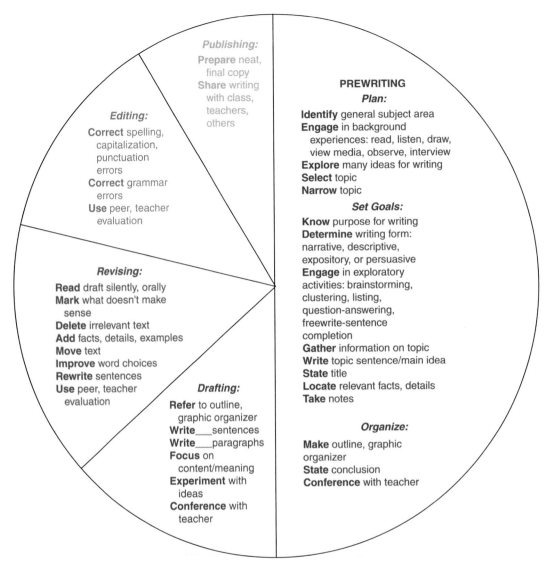

FIGURE 10.2   **Stages of the writing process**

Source: "Teaching the writing process to students with LD," by B. J. Scott and M. R. Vitale, 2003, *Intervention in School and Clinic, 38,* pp. 220–225. Copyright 2003 by The Council for Exceptional Children. Reprinted with permission.

pictorial representations, music, sensory explorations, creative and visual imagery, speakers, demonstrations, interviews, brainstorming, and researching can be used to help students select topics.

Because writing is linked to reading, students can obtain ideas for writing from reading. Reading and discussing passages before writing can help students select topics and add details to their writing. Students can write stories by changing the characters or action in a story they have just listened to or read. Predictable books can stimulate such story writing since they often follow repetitive story lines. Students also can be given books containing pictures that tell a story and asked to write the text that tells the story.

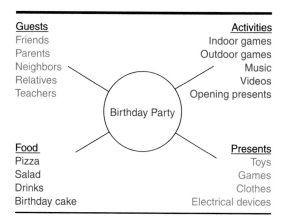

<u>Guests</u>
Friends
Parents
Neighbors
Relatives
Teachers

<u>Activities</u>
Indoor games
Outdoor games
Music
Videos
Opening presents

Birthday Party

<u>Food</u>
Pizza
Salad
Drinks
Birthday cake

<u>Presents</u>
Toys
Games
Clothes
Electrical devices

FIGURE 10.3   A sample writing semantic map

Story Starters/Enders.   Some students may benefit from the use of story starters or story enders, in which they are given the first or last paragraph of a story or the initial or ending sentence of a paragraph, and are asked to complete the story or paragraph. Music, pictures, and videos also can prompt students to write by serving as starters. Similarly, you can use story frames in which students complete blank frames by writing in information related to the frame (Staal, 2001). In addition, you can use paragraph organization worksheets and paragraph draft outlines to help students plan and organize their writing.

Outlines and Semantic Maps.   Ideas generated by students can be organized by helping students to develop an outline, which includes the main topics and supporting ideas grouped together, as well as the order in which the ideas will be presented. Students also can be taught to organize their writing by developing a semantic map—a diagram or map of the key ideas and words that make up the topic (Sturm & Rankin-Erickson, 2002). Mapping allows students to identify main points and to plan the interrelationship between them. In introducing semantic maps, you can ask questions that help students understand their own decision-making processes and learn from others. A sample writing semantic map is presented in Figure 10.3.

Models and Prompts.   Models and prompts also can facilitate the planning process (Marchisan & Alber, 2001). You or your students who write well can serve as models for others by verbalizing the process used to plan writing projects. You also can help students plan their writing by giving them a Planning Think Sheet, which contains a series of questions that prompt them in planning their writing.

Resource

Graham (1992) describes a strategy called PLANS, which helps students establish writing goals.

Resource

Mariage, Englert, and Garmon (2000) offer think sheets for the different subprocesses of the writing process.

Drafting

In the drafting phase, writers transform their ideas and plans into sentences and paragraphs. They attempt to establish a relationship and an order between sentences and paragraphs and make appropriate word choices. While it should not be emphasized in the drafting stage, some attention to the rules of grammar, punctuation, and spelling may be appropriate. In a writing process approach, these skills are taught using the students' own writing through individualized or group lessons. During this step, you encourage students to plan their draft and provide time to revise it.

FIGURE 10.4

Sample writing self-evaluation questions

Does each paragraph start with a topic sentence?
Does each paragraph include relevant supporting information?
Are the paragraphs organized appropriately?
Are the main characters introduced and described?
Is the location of the story presented and described?
Is the time of the story introduced?
Does the story include a starting event?
Does the story include the main characters' reactions to the starting event?
Does the story present actions to resolve conflicts?
Does the story have an ending?
Does the ending include the outcome's effects on the main characters?

Resource

James, Abbott, and Greenwood (2001) and Schirmer and Bailey (2000) offer examples of rubrics for a wide range of writing assignments, and Wansart (2003) offers strategies for helping students evaluate their writing.

You can help students prepare the draft in several ways. These include asking questions to help students explore alternatives, offering suggestions, giving them exemplary models, encouraging them, and focusing attention on the writing task. You also can give students self-evaluation questions and encourage them to use the self-evaluation guidelines throughout the writing process (Gleason & Isaccson, 2001; Wansart, 2003). Sample self-evaluation questions for writing stories are presented in Figure 10.4. Giving your students instructional rubrics can help them in drafting, editing, and revising processes. (We will learn more about how to create instructional rubrics in chapter 12.) Some of your students may benefit from the opportunity to use individualized word banks containing words they often use in writing, and to dictate to an audiocassette or a scribe, which can be gradually reduced as students learn to write independently (Marchisan & Alber, 2001; Scott & Vitale, 2003).

Editing and Revising

In this phase, students edit their drafts by making revisions to ensure that their products achieve their writing goals. You can introduce students to revision by reviewing a sample paper as a group. The class can identify the positive aspects of the paper, as well as the problems a reader would have in reading it. The discussion should focus on the content, organization, and word choices rather than on mechanical errors. The class can then complete the revision by correcting the problems identified in the paper as a group. For example, you and your students can help classmates generate a list of synonyms to replace nondescriptive words (such as *nice, great, fine,* and *good*) that have been used repeatedly. The Find (Search) and Replace functions of many word-processing programs can then be used to locate the nondescriptive word and replace it with the new words.

Resource

Ellis and Covert (1996) provide guidelines for implementing strategies such as DEFENDS, TOWER, PENS, SEARCH, and WRITER to help students monitor the quality of their writing.

Students also can be taught to correct their own papers and to do content, organizational, and mechanical editing by maintaining an editing log (see Figure 10.5). The editing log includes the date, the error, the correction, and the rule being applied.

Proofreading.   Proofreading is an important part of the editing and revising processes. Students can be taught to review their written products to check for misspelled words, sentence fragments, and errors in punctuation, capitalization, and grammar. You can help students proofread their work by giving them a proofreading checklist.

FIGURE 10.5

Sample editing log

Name_____

Date	Error and Correction	Rule
1/25/2005	*Error:* The student suddenly jumped out of his seat, however, the teacher ignored him. *Correction:* The student suddenly jumped out of his seat; however, the teacher ignored him. or The student suddenly jumped out of his seat. However, the teacher ignored him.	This is called a comma splice or run-on sentence. It can be corrected by replacing the first comma with a semicolon or with a period and a capital letter to start a new sentence.
1/25/2005	*Error:* The boys father met them at school. *Correction:* The boys' father met them at school.	The father "belongs" to the boys, so *boys* should be possessive. The apostrophe comes after the *s* because the word *boys* is plural.

Note: Prepared by Catharine Whittaker.

One strategy that trains students to use these proofreading skills in a systematic way is COPS (Schumaker, Nolan, & Deshler, 1985). In this procedure, students learn to proofread their papers by asking the following:

C: Have I capitalized letters that need to be capitalized?
O: What is the overall appearance of my paper?
P: Have I used proper punctuation?
S: Are the words I used spelled correctly?

Students can improve their proofreading skills by using proofreader's marks. You can train students to use these marks by teaching them the system and modeling its use when giving feedback on written assignments. Additionally, you can give students a handout of editing symbols paired with examples of their use, as shown in Figure 10.6.

Models.   You can foster the editing process by giving students writing sample models that show the correct format, writing style, and organization of content. The value of the model can be increased by reviewing it with students and marking it with comments highlighting the qualities that help to make it an excellent product. For example, you can emphasize the topic sentence by circling it and writing "This is a good topic sentence. It introduces the reader to the content in the paragraph." Similarly, the inclusion of specific sections in the written product can be noted to ensure that the student's paper includes all the necessary sections.

In addition to providing students with a model, teachers can promote writing by providing a checklist of items or an instructional rubric they will use in evaluating the paper. The evaluation guidelines or rubric can then guide students in evaluating their papers before handing them in. You also can create an evaluation form that guides students in evaluating the mechanical aspects of their work such as their punctuation, capitalization, grammar, and spelling (Carr, 2002; Marchisan & Alber, 2001).

Editing Symbols

Mark	Explanation	Example
⬭	Circle words that are spelled incorrectly.	My (freind) and I went to the zoo last Sunday.
/	Change a capital letter to a small leter.	Mary and Jim watched /Television for one hour.
≡	Change a small letter to a capital letter.	bob loves the way I play horn.
∧	Add letters, words, or sentences.	My friend lives in the ∧*brick* house next door. ∧
⊙	Add a period.	My dog, Frisky, and I are private detectives⊙
ℓ	Take out letters, words, or punctuation.	Last summer Bob (went and) flew an airplane in Alaska.
⁄\	Add a comma.	Bob visited Alaska⁄\ Ohio⁄\ and Florida.

FIGURE 10.6   Editing symbols

Source: From "Motivate Reluctant Learning Disabled Writers," by J. Whitt, P. V. Paul, and C. J. Reynolds, 1988, *Teaching Exceptional Children, 20,* p. 38. Copyright 1988 by The Council for Exceptional Children. Reprinted with permission.

Collaborative Writing Groups.   Collaborative writing groups can promote a positive environment for writing and improving the writing skills of students from various language and cultural backgrounds (Englert, Berry, & Dunsmore, 2001). Students can work in collaboration by reading their products to the group or to individual group members; editing the products of group members; brainstorming ideas for writing; developing outlines as a group; and producing a group product such as a class newsletter.

Collaborative groups can be particularly helpful in editing and revising written assignments. One collaborative strategy is the author's chair (Graves & Hansen, 1983). In this technique, once their product has been completed, students read it aloud to their peers, who discuss its positive features and ask questions about strategy, meaning, and writing style.

Students can work in groups to offer feedback and to edit drafts (Mariage, 2001). You can establish guidelines for peer writing groups, including focusing on feedback that emphasizes the positive aspects of the product, being specific, directing feedback at the work rather than the author, phrasing negative reactions as questions, giving reactions orally or in writing, and offering writers time to respond to the reactions of their peers (Levy, 1999). You can enhance the value of the peer editing process by providing students with evaluation guidelines such as the one in Figure 10.4 or by giving students forms that can guide the editing and feedback process (See Figure 10.7).

Resource

Marchisan and Alber (2001) offer peer editing forms for revising fiction and nonfiction.

Sample peer editing forms

FIGURE 10.7

SAMPLE PEER EDITOR FEEDBACK FORM

Author:

Editor:

Title of Piece:

1. The things I like about this piece are:

2. The things you need to improve about this piece are:

3. The ways you could improve this piece are:

SAMPLE AUTHOR FORM

Author:

Editor:

Title of Piece:

1. The positive things about my piece are:

2. The things I need to improve about my piece are:

3. The ways I could improve my piece are:

You also can help students receive feedback from others by establishing rules for accepting reactions from others, including the following:

- Listen carefully to all comments from others.
- Ask for feedback from as many people as possible.
- Do not dispute or dismiss feedback from others.
- Seek clarification or examples when you don't understand another person's reaction.
- Check your understanding of another person's reaction by paraphrasing the statements in your own words.

Resource

Marchsin and Alber (2001) offer guidelines and forms for using peer editing partners or groups.

Writers' Workshop.   Another collaborative writing strategy designed to create a community of writers is the Writers' Workshop, where students write and receive feedback from peers and teachers on topics they select (Tompkins, 2002). The Writers' Workshop is divided into four parts: *status of the class, mini-lessons, workshop proper,* and *sharing.* In the status component, you work with individual students to identify the

Collaborative writing groups can foster students' writing. How successful are your collaborative writing groups?

project(s) on which they are working, the help they will need, and the progress they are making. Mini-lessons, approximately 5 minutes long, offer students direct instruction on specific skills such as process skills (e.g., idea generation), grammar and spelling skills, writing skills (e.g., paragraph development), and classroom routines. The majority of the Writers' Workshop consists of the workshop proper, during which you and your students actively write. In addition to writing, you circulate around the room to monitor student progress, help students hear their own voices and solve minor problems, and confer with individual students. In the final component, students share their work with others, receive feedback, and publish their work.

Publishing

Publishing students' written products presents an excellent opportunity for sharing their work with others and for receiving feedback. For example, students can publish their work in books that they design, submit work to magazines and newspapers, and create newsletters. Technology also can be a valuable resource in the fourth stage of the writing process: publishing. For instance, students also can "publish" their work via the Internet.

Provide Feedback

Feedback should facilitate, not frustrate, the writing process (Bradley, 2001). A teacher conference is an excellent means of providing feedback and encouraging students to reflect on their writing. By meeting individually with students you serve as both reader and coach, helping students learn to examine their writing.

Initially, you can focus on the positive aspects of the students' writing, and acknowledge and encourage them to write by praising them, sharing their stories with others by reading them in class, and posting their writing in the room or elsewhere in the school. Because identifying all errors can frustrate students, corrective feedback should focus on no more than two writing problems at a time. You can pinpoint errors that interfere with the writer's ability to make the product understandable to the reader rather than emphasize grammar, punctuation, spelling, and usage errors. Instruction to correct gram-

Reflecting on Professional Practices

Using a Process Approach to Teaching Writing

Ms. Rogers notices that many of her students are having difficulty with writing assignments. A review of their written products reveals that they are extremely short and disorganized, lack important elements, and include irrelevant information. To correct these problems, Ms. Rogers decides to try a different approach to teaching students to write.

Ms. Rogers begins by writing a description of herself, reading it to her students, and asking them to guess who is being described. After the students guess correctly, Ms. Rogers explains how she wrote it. She draws a semantic map on the board and demonstrates how she used it to list the important characteristics she wanted to mention in her description. She then gives the students a semantic map outline and asks them to complete it using the characteristics that best describe themselves.

The next day, Ms. Rogers asks the students to use their semantic maps to write a draft that describes themselves. After the drafts are completed, Ms. Rogers collects them, selects students to read them to the class, and has the class guess who wrote each piece. Ms. Rogers concludes the day's writing lesson by telling students that tomorrow they will work on revising their descriptions.

Ms. Rogers begins the next day's lesson by explaining the purpose of revising a draft. Using her description of herself, Ms. Rogers asks students to identify things they liked about it. After this is done, she asks them to identify ways in which the description could be improved. Following this discussion, Ms. Rogers reviews several guidelines for giving and accepting feedback. She then selects a student's draft and role-plays giving feedback with the student.

Ms. Rogers then places students in dyads, gives each group member a checklist to guide the feedback process, and asks members to read each other's papers and share their reactions. While students work collaboratively, Ms. Rogers monitors their progress and assists them in developing collaborative skills. During the last 15 minutes of the period, Ms. Rogers and the whole class discuss how it feels to give and receive feedback.

The next day's writing period is devoted to revising students' drafts based on the feedback they have received. Ms. Rogers works on her draft, and circulates around the room to monitor student progress and to confer with individual students. After students revise their writing, they type their product on the computer and share their printout with their dyad partner. They then make final revisions, and a copy of each student's description is printed out and compiled into a class book called *Who's Who*, which is shared with students' families, other teachers, and the principal and is posted on the class's web page.

- Why did Ms. Rogers decide to use a process approach to teach writing?
- What procedures and strategies did she use to implement a writing process approach?
- What are the advantages of using a process approach to teach writing?
- What are the potential problems with this approach?

What resources would you need to implement a process approach to teach writing?

To answer these questions online and share your responses with others, go to the Reflection module in Chapter 10 of the Companion Website.

matical and spelling errors can focus on skills that are within the student's repertoire and occur within the context of the student's writing.

Teach Students to Use Learning Strategies

You can help students improve their writing by teaching them to use learning strategies (Troia & Graham, 2002). For example, Harris, Graham, and Mason (2002) used a learning strategy, POW + TREE, to improve students' ability to write opinion essays. The self-instructional strategy involves:

P: Pick my idea.
O: Organize my notes.
W: Write and say more.

Resource

Harris, Graham, and Mason (2002) offer a model for teaching students to use writing learning strategies.

Resource

Lenz, Deshler, and Kissam (2004) offer sentence-writing, paragraph-writing, error-monitoring, and theme-writing learning strategies for use by secondary level students.

Resource

Learning strategies that can be taught to students include TREE (Sexton, Harris, & Graham, 1998), PLAN and WRITE (De La Paz, Owen, Harris, & Graham, 2000), STOP and DARE (De La Paz, 2001), and STOP and LIST (Troia & Graham, 2002).

Reflective

How did you learn to write? When you write a paper for class or a letter to a friend, what processes do you use? How does the use of a computer and a word-processing program affect your writing?

cd - rom

T: Topic sentence. Tell what you believe!
R: Reasons (three or more). Why do I believe this?
E: Explain reasons. Say more about it.
E: Ending. Wrap it up right!

Use Computer-Supported Writing Applications

Students can improve their writing skills and the writing products they produce by using computer-supported writing applications (MacArthur, 1999; Mull & Sitlington, 2003). These technological applications can support communication and collaboration and the subprocesses in the writing process. Several of these applications are described next.

Word Processing

Word processing allows students to store, copy, cut and paste, insert, format, print text, and choose font types and sizes electronically. Word processing has several advantages. It allows students to focus on the writing process; minimizes spelling errors; facilitates publication; eliminates handwriting problems so that all students produce a neat, clean copy; provides students with a novel experience that motivates them to write; makes text revision easy; eliminates the tedious process of copying; and allows students to insert graphics that illustrate and support written text. Word-processing programs also offer students access to electronic thesauruses and dictionaries that can guide them in making appropriate and varied word choices. **To hear educators discussing how computers can support reluctant writers, go to Case 3: Assess Plan on the CD-ROM and click on the Academic Inroads video clip. How did access to a computer support the student's writing?**

Enlarged print systems and talking word processors that "read" the text on the computer screen can enhance the writing capabilities of students with visual and reading disabilities (Williams, 2002). Talking word processors allow students to detect syntax errors, receive feedback on spelling as they enter words, and hear their text read. Word processors that have voice output systems can provide immediate auditory and visual feedback to users concerning keystrokes and various commands as they type, as well as orally reviewing individual letters and words, sentences, paragraphs, highlighted text, and whole documents after the text has been typed. These applications can be combined with text windowing, the simultaneous visual highlighting of text as it is read to help students focus on, monitor, and proofread their writing. Because most talking word processors pronounce words based on phonetic spellings, some word-processing programs include pronunciation editing, which allows students to adjust the speech of the program so that words that are not phonetically based are pronounced correctly. A variety of special monitors and print enlargement programs also are available for students who can benefit from word processing through the use of enlarged print.

Talk-type or voice-activated word-processing programs based on computerized speech recognition can help students improve their writing and overcome their spelling difficulties. They are especially appropriate for students who struggle with written communication but have strong verbal communication skills. In these programs, the individual talks into a headphone-mounted microphone, pausing briefly after each word. The individual's comments then appear as electronic text on a video monitor and may be revised via word processing. While researchers are developing voice-recognition systems

Students can improve their writing skills through the use of computer-supported writing applications, such as word processing. How do you use technology to support your writing and your students' writing?

that are not speaker-dependent, require little pretraining to use, process a large vocabulary accurately, screen background noises, and recognize continuous speech, students need to learn how to use the system. They also need to speak clearly, refrain from making extraneous sounds, articulate punctuation, and correct errors.

Students with disabilities may experience difficulties using word processing such as having difficulty remembering functions that require multiple key presses or syntax codes, using inefficient cursor movements, and using deletion procedures inappropriately. Therefore, some students may need to use word-processing programs that have safeguards to prevent the loss of documents, offer easy-to-read manuals and directions for use, and contain pictures and cues as prompts. Students also may benefit from word-processing programs that use simple keystrokes to delete and insert text and move the cursor; offer prompting and verification to help students save documents and load features; include easy-to-use menus; and use language that students can understand.

To benefit from word processing, students might need instruction in keyboarding skills and the word-processing program. Such training should teach students to enter and save text; return to the menu; print copies; load disks; clear memory; center, justify, add, delete, and move text; skip lines; and move the cursor. Keyboarding skills also can be taught to students through the use of typing programs that accept only correct responses, provide numerous practice activities, introduce skills gradually, contain graphics for finger positions, and offer frequent feedback. Prompt cards that display the keys and their functions help students to remember key functions and patterns of multiple-key pressing. Typing teaching programs that analyze students' typing patterns, including strengths and weaknesses, and plan customized programs tailored to students' unique learning styles also are available.

Resource

Disability Resources (2000) offers information on specially designed programs to teach typing skills to individuals with visual impairments.

Spell Checkers

Word-processing programs come with a spell checker, which can help students with spelling difficulties and aid them in revising their writing (MacArthur, 1999). Spell checkers review written text and identify spelling errors and other words that do not match the program's dictionary. Students then correct the spelling errors by typing in the correct spelling or by choosing from a list of alternatives presented by the spell checker. Students can add words to the spell checker's dictionary to tailor it to their unique spelling needs. Those with reading disabilities may benefit from programs that use talking spell checkers to read word choices to them, while other students may prefer a program that offers a definition of each word presented as an alternative. Spell checkers that present word choices in short lists also may assist students with reading and spelling difficulties.

However, spell checkers have several limitations (MacArthur, Graham, Haynes, & De La Paz, 1996). They often cannot identify words that are spelled correctly but used in the wrong context, such as homonyms. Spell checks often identify correctly spelled words as errors if these words are not available in their dictionaries, such as proper nouns, uncommon words, and specialized vocabulary. Spell checkers also may not be able to provide the correct spelling of every word that has been misspelled. In particular, they cannot suggest the correct spelling of words when the student's version does not resemble the correct spelling. Ashton (1999) developed the CHECK procedure, a mnemonic learning strategy designed to help students use spell checkers.

Word Cueing and Prediction

Word cueing and prediction programs offer students choices of words and phrases as they compose text and are helpful for students who have difficulty recalling words (Williams, 2002). As students type text, a changing list of predicted words and phrases appears on the screen. Students can then decide to select the predicted words and insert them into their written products or to continue typing. The word and phrase banks that are integral parts of these programs can be customized for students based on their needs and the topic and content of their written product.

Whereas word cueing programs offer choices based on the first letters typed by students, word prediction programs offer word and phrase options based on context, word frequency (i.e., how frequently the word is used in English), word recency (i.e., how recently the word has been used by the writer), grammatical correctness, and commonly associated words and phrases. Many word prediction programs also include dictionaries for students who are performing at different levels. Thesaurus programs also can improve students' writing by increasing the variety of words used in writing and limiting word repetition.

Text Organization, Usage, Grammar, and Punctuation Assistance

Programs that help students organize the text and check text for word usage, syntax, punctuation, capitalization, and style can be useful (Glater, 2003; Sturm, Rankin, Beukelman, & Schutz-Muehling, 1997). Some word-processing programs have interactive prompting capabilities that help students write effectively. These programs provide prompts and guidelines that appear on the screen to guide development of the student's product. You can tailor these and create your own prompts to adapt to the different types of writing assignments and needs of students. Some programs offer students assistance in generating ideas to write about, selecting a writing style, and conforming to the writing style selected. Graphics-based writing software programs, which offer story-boarding and framing, pictures, video, sound, animation, and voice recording, can motivate students and assist them in planning, organizing, and composing text (Castellani & Jeffs, 2001).

Word usage and grammar checkers identify inappropriate word choices and grammatical and punctuation errors and present alternatives to address them. Students then examine the alternatives and select the option that they believe best corrects the error.

Resource

McNaughton, Hughes, and Ofiesh (1997) developed INSPECT, a learning strategy to teach students to use a spell checker.

Resource

Sturm et al. (1997) offer guidelines for selecting appropriate software for computer-assisted writing.

Resource

Smith, Boone, and Higgins (1998) offer guidelines for using the Internet as part of the writing process.

Resource

Graham, Harris, and Fink (2000) and Naus (2000) provide guidelines, materials, and activities for teaching handwriting skills and a checklist for evaluating handwriting instruction.

IDEAS FOR IMPLEMENTATION

Teaching Handwriting

Although Ms. Stepanovich had her students write using computers, she also wanted them to develop the legibility and fluency of their handwriting so that they could express themselves in writing. During handwriting activities, she noticed that several students had poor writing posture that interfered with the size, slant, proportion, alignment, and spacing of letters. Therefore, Ms. Stepanovich used modeling to teach her students proper posture and paper positioning. She asked students to watch her as she wrote at her desk and told them, "Look at me when I write. I sit upright, with my back against the back seat of my chair and both of my feet on the floor. As I write, I lean my shoulders and upper back forward in a straight line, place my elbows extended slightly at the edge of my desk, and use my forearms as a pivot for my movements. I hold my pen lightly between the index finger and the middle finger, with the thumb to the side and the index finger on top. My thumb is bent to hold the pen high in the hand and the utensil rests near the knuckle of the index finger, and my pinky and ring fingers touch the paper."

Ms. Stepanovich also created and posted charts that showed students how to position their paper when writing. For manuscript writing, a chart demonstrated how to hold the paper perpendicular to the front of the body, with the left side placed so that it is aligned with the center of the body. For cursive writing, the charts showed right-handers slanting the paper counterclockwise and left-handers slanting it clockwise. As students wrote, Ms. Stepanovich guided them physically, encouraged them to look at the charts, and gave them feedback on their posture and ability to hold the pen correctly.

Here are some other strategies you can use to improve your students' handwriting:

- Focus initial instruction on helping students develop the prerequisite fine motor, visual motor, and visual discrimination skills and wrist stability needed for handwriting by using activities such as cutting, tracing, coloring, fingerpainting, discriminating, and copying shapes.

- Teach the meaning of the directional concepts that guide letter formation instruction such as up, down, top, center, bottom, around, left, right, across, middle, and diagonal.
- Use a combination of procedures that includes modeling, self-instruction, copying, cueing, and teaching the basic strokes.
- Verbalize how to form letters and discuss the similarities and differences among letters.
- Teach students to use proper writing postures and appropriate ways to hold their writing instruments and position their papers when writing. For example, mark students' writing utensils with dots to teach them where to hold them, and tap on students' work areas to teach them how to align their papers.
- Adapt writing paper by emphasizing the base lines and marking the starting and end points with green and red dots, respectively.
- Use paper with colored, solid, and dashed lines to help students learn correct letter heights and paper with perpendicular lines to teach proper spacing.
- Offer left-handed students left-handed models, group them together, teach them to write letters vertically or with a slight backward slant, have them write on the left side of the blackboard, and provide them with left-handed desks.
- Post writing models and place a chart presenting lowercase and uppercase letters, the numerals 1 through 10, and numbered arrow cues indicating the corresponding stroke directions in a location that all students can see.
- Provide students with opportunities to evaluate and self-correct their handwriting
- Monitor students handwriting legibility and fluency and offer them corrective feedback.

Note: Baker, Gersten, & Graham (2003); Edwards, (2003); Graham, Harris, & Fink (2000); Keller (2001); Naus (2000).

Many of these programs guide students in selecting an appropriate alternative by offering prompts, as well as reviews and explanations of the different selections and their corresponding word meanings and grammatical applications. Some programs also help students produce grammatically correct written products by automatically capitalizing proper nouns and the first words of sentences.

How Can I Help Students Learn to Spell?

Use a Combination of Approaches

A skill area that can affect both writing and reading is spelling. Reading is a decoding process; spelling is an encoding process. Consequently, many students who experience difficulties in reading also are likely to have problems with spelling, which hinders their writing (Baker, Gersten, & Graham, 2003). These students may benefit from a spelling program that combines several of the approaches presented in the following sections (Graham, Harris, & Larsen, 2001).

Rule-Governed Approaches

Resource

Graham, Harris, and Fink-Chorzempa (2003) developed the CASL Spelling Program, a series of forty-eight 20-minute lessons to teach spelling.

Rule-governed models promote spelling skills by teaching students to use morphemic and phonemic analysis and basic spelling rules (Baker, Gersten, & Graham, 2003). In using rule-governed approaches, you help students learn spelling rules and patterns by asking them to analyze words that follow the same grapheme–phoneme correspondence, to discuss similarities and differences in words, to identify the rules that apply, to practice the use of the rule with unfamiliar words, and to learn exceptions to the rule.

One rule-governed model for teaching spelling is the linguistic approach, in which spelling instruction focuses on the rules of spelling and patterns related to whole words. Once the students learn a series of words with similar spelling, opportunities to generalize the rule to other words in the family arise. For example, students are taught the *oat* family using the words *boat* and *coat.* Later, they apply the pattern to other words from that family such as *goat, moat,* and *float.*

While the linguistic approach is based on learning spelling patterns within whole words, the phonetic approach is based on learning to apply phoneme–grapheme correspondence within parts of words. Thus, a phonetic approach to spelling involves teaching students the sound–symbol correspondence for individual letters and combinations of letters (such as digraphs and diphthongs). Students then apply these rules by breaking words into syllables, pronouncing each syllable, and writing the letter(s) that correspond to each sound. While phonetic approaches to teaching spelling have been successful, words that represent irregularities in the English language, including multiple-letter sounds, word pronunciations, and unstressed syllables, are deterrents to phonetic spelling.

Whole Word Approaches

Whole word approaches help students focus on the whole word through a variety of multisensory activities. Whole word approaches include test-study-test procedures, corrected-test methods, and word study techniques.

Test-Study-Test Procedures.   Perhaps the most frequently used method of spelling instruction is the test-study-test method. In this method, students take a pretest on a fixed list of words, study the words they misspell, and take a posttest to assess mastery. You also can use a study-test procedure in which students study all the week's spelling words and then take a test. When posttesting students with these procedures, it is recommended that teachers intersperse known and unknown words in the test.

You can adapt test-study-test procedures by decreasing the number of spelling words given to students from five to three to increase their spelling performance. Thus, rather than having students try to master a large list of words each week, you can break down the list so that students study and are tested on three words each day. You also can use a flow word list rather than a fixed list. Flow lists can help you individualize spelling by allowing students who master spelling words to delete those words from the list and replace them with new words. Whether using a fixed or flow list of spelling words, you can give students time to work at their own rate and can require them to demonstrate mastery over a period of time.

Corrected-Test Methods.   The corrected-test method allows you to guide students in correcting their spelling errors by spelling words orally while students correct them; spelling words and accentuating each letter as students simultaneously point to each letter in the word; spelling words while students write the correct letter above the crossed-out, incorrect letter; writing the correct spelling on students' papers near the incorrectly spelled word, which students then correct; and copying students' errors, modeling the correct spelling, and observing students as they write the word correctly.

Word Study Techniques.   Word study techniques include a wide range of activities designed to help students systematically study and remember spelling words (Graham, Harris, & Larsen, 2001). A multistep word study procedure can include verbalizing the word; writing and saying the word; comparing the written word with a model; tracing and saying the word; writing the word from memory and checking it; and repeating prior steps as necessary. You also can use word study methods that encourage students to close their eyes and visualize the spelling word, or verbalize the word while writing it, or finger spell or write words in the air (Graham, Harris, & Fink-Chorzempa, 2003).

Reflective

What approaches were used by your teachers to teach you spelling? What were the strengths of these approaches? What were their weaknesses?

Adapt Spelling Instruction

Many students, including those with disabilities, may exhibit problems in spelling. You can adapt spelling instruction for them in the following ways.

Explain the Importance of Spelling

Explaining the importance and relevance of spelling can motivate students to improve their spelling skills (Fulk & Stormont-Spurgin, 1995). You can emphasize the relevance of spelling by helping students see the connection among spelling, reading, and writing.

Analyze Students' Spelling Errors

You can observe students while they spell and their spelling products to note the progress and the types of errors they make (Gregg & Mather, 2002; Jones, 2001a). For example, many second language learners may engage in cross-linguistically developed spelling, spelling words incorrectly by mixing elements from their first and second languages. Appropriate spelling instruction can be based on the students' error patterns.

Resource

Gregg and Mather (2002) and Jones (2001) offer guidelines and strategies for using formal and informal assessment to monitor students' spelling skills.

Choose Relevant Spelling Words

You can motivate students and improve their spelling by focusing initially on a core of frequently used words, as well as on words that are part of the student's listening and spelling vocabulary. Students' spelling words can be selected by both students and teachers and be those that frequently appear in students' writing products.

IDEAS FOR IMPLEMENTATION

Teaching Spelling

Ms. Sylvestre noticed that Ricardo, a second language learner, was struggling with his spelling. Ms. Sylvestre observed that many of the vocabulary words that Ricardo chose to use in writing assignments were misspelled. She analyzed his errors and noticed several patterns. Ricardo often left off the "ed" when writing words in the past tense. For example, he wrote "encourage" instead of "encouraged." She also noticed that he had difficulty spelling words with a double consonant in the middle such as "putting," "happen," and "pressure."

Ms. Sylvestre used this information to help Ricardo improve his spelling. She started by teaching him to hear and add the "ed" to words in the past tense. First, she explained past tense to him and then articulated words in the past tense and asked Ricardo to repeat them. Then, she presented him with a series of words and asked him to identify those that were in the past tense. When she felt confident that Ricardo understood past tense and could hear the "ed" sound, she introduced a mnemonic device to help him remember to add the "ed" ending to regular verbs that are past tense. She told Ricardo to, "think of a person named Ed who did everything yesterday. Ed will often be at the end of the verb because everything he does has happened already. Remember if the verb ends with a consonant, that consonant is doubled before the "ed" is added." She then had Ricardo practice this skill using regular verbs and verbs that ended in a consonant.

When Ricardo demonstrated mastery on several spelling activities involving "ed" words, Ms. Sylvestre focused instruction on helping him to spell words with the double consonant in the middle. She used a phonetic approach with Ricardo that involved her modeling how to look at the words, sound them out, and break them apart to analyze the spelling. After she modeled doing it, she and Ricardo did it together. Eventually, she had Ricardo do it without her assistance. As Ricardo became successful in spelling these words, Ms. Sylvestre identified a new set of words to teach him to spell.

Here are some other strategies you can use to improve your students' spelling:

- Involve students in the spelling instructional process by having them choose some of their spelling words and assess and monitor their progress.
- Limit the number of spelling words taught each week to between 6 and 12.
- Encourage students to visualize spelling words.
- Have students use spelling words in sentences.
- Teach students to use visual representation to help them remember the spelling of words. For example, students can visually represent the spelling of the word *handle* by drawing a picture of a hand with an L shaped out of the index finger and the thumb and the letter E connected to it.
- Use peer tutoring systems such as Classwide Peer Tutoring to help students improve their spelling.

Note: Baker, Gersten, & Graham (2003); Graham, Harris, & Larsen (2001); Keller (2002); Provost, Rullo, & Buechner (2000).

Provide Time to Review Words Previously Learned

Students with disabilities may experience difficulty remembering words previously mastered. Therefore, you can provide time to review and study previously learned words and use spelling words in other situations (Graham, Harris, & Larsen, 2001).

Teach Students to Use Cues and Learning Strategies

Students can use meaning and sound-alike cues, mnemonic devices, and configuration clues to figure out the correct spellings (Cunningham, 1998). For example, some students may benefit from drawing blocks around the outline of the word to remember its configuration. Students can be encouraged to select cues that make sense to them and relate to their experiences and culture.

You also can use classroom posters to provide students with spelling cues. For example, you can post spelling strategy charts to give students a range of spelling techniques (Beckman, 1999). Students can be taught learning strategies that prompt them to use effective spelling techniques and cues. For example, Keller (2002) created SPELLER Steps, a learning strategy that prompts students to spell words.

Teach Dictionary Skills

Spelling problems can be minimized by encouraging students to use the dictionary to confirm the spelling of unknown or irregular words, spelling demons, confusing rules, and difficult word combinations. Therefore, students need to learn dictionary skills, including alphabetizing, locating words, using guide words, and understanding syllabification and pronunciation. Students in primary grades can use a picture dictionary until they learn the skills needed to use a regular dictionary.

You can have students make personal dictionaries or word banks of the words that are difficult for them to spell (Gipe, 2002). As students write, they consult their personal dictionaries to help them with word choice and spelling. Personal dictionaries also can be developed for math, science, and social studies words. Students, including second language learners, also can create word books that include pages for each letter of the alphabet, with weekly entries of spelling words in sentences and their definitions on the appropriate page (Isaacson & Gleason, 1997).

Teach Students to Proofread and to Correct Spelling Errors

Spelling can be enhanced having students proofread their work and correct their spelling errors (McNaughton, Hughes & Clark, 1997). You can encourage students to proofread for spelling errors by:

*   giving them a list of words and having them identify and correct the misspellings.
*   assigning them to find the spelling errors in the assignments of their peers.
*   listing the number of errors in a student's assignment and having students locate and correct the errors.
*   marking words that may be incorrectly spelled and having students check them.

Students also can be encouraged and taught to correct their own spelling errors. Fulk and Stormont-Spurgin (1995) suggest that students correct their spelling by (a) comparing their spelling of words with a correct spelling model; (b) noting incorrect letter(s) by crossing them out, boxing them, or circling them; (c) writing the correct letters above the incorrect letters; and (d) writing the correct spelling on a line next to the incorrect spelling.

Model Appropriate Spelling Techniques

You can improve the spelling skills of students by giving them oral and written models to imitate (Graham, Larsen, & Harris, 2001). When writing on the blackboard, you can periodically emphasize the spelling of words, and occasionally spell words or have peers spell them for the class. You also can model a positive attitude toward spelling by teaching spelling with enthusiasm and encouraging positive attributions regarding the use of spelling strategies (Fulk, 1997).

Using Technology to Promote Inclusion

Making Literacy Instruction Accessible to All Students

In addition to the hardware resources and software applications already discussed in this chapter, there are other emerging technologies you can integrate into your inclusive classroom to differentiate literacy instruction (Baker, 2003; Weikle & Hadadian, 2003). You can enhance the effectiveness of these technologies by motivating students to use them, teaching students how to use them, and recognizing their limitations.

You can use a variety of hardware and software resources to help your students to develop their reading skills. Some teachers use computer-mediated word-recognition systems to help their students access reading materials and decode unknown words (Mike, 2001). They use an optical scanner to convert print materials to electronic text, which is then converted into speech by the talking word processor. Students then select and highlight sections, sentences, words, or syllables, which are then pronounced by the computer. Students also can use pronunciation dictionaries, and control the speed, pitch, and volume of the speech used to read the text. Different students use the system in different ways. Some students use it to read the whole text, while other students use it only when they encounter an unknown word. The system also can be adapted for second language learners by including a CD-ROM talking dictionary that pronounces and defines highlighted English words in the students' native languages. A CD-ROM American Sign Language dictionary can be used to help students with hearing impairments access the text.

A lightweight and portable computer-mediated word-recognition device that students can use is the Readingpen (www.wiztech.com). Students scan individual words or a line of text by tracing over them with the pen. Controls on the pen then allow the scanned text to be read to students, defined, spelled, or broken into syllables for them, or displayed in various character sizes.

Here are some other ways you can use technology to create inclusive classrooms that support students' literacy development:

- Use a variety of types of software programs to teach phonological awareness and phonics to students, and to promote students' reading fluency and comprehension and their word recognition, decoding and spelling skills (Jimenez et al., 2003; Miller & Felton, 2001). For example, Lane et al.

(2002) present lists of software programs that can support your teaching of phonological awareness and Baker (2003) offers guidelines for evaluating literacy software.

- Use technology-based curriculum materials. For example, Leapfrog and IntelliTools have developed a series of curriculum packages that employ technology to teach literacy skills related to state standards.
- Determine the readability of print materials by using software programs. For example, software programs using Spache, Dale-Chall, and Fry readability formulas are available (Schirmer & Lockman, 2001), and you can access the Flesch-Kinkaid readability formula through use of Microsoft Word (Scott & Weishaar, 2003).
- Provide students with access to reading models and repeated reading via use of audiocassette or computerized-model reading (Chard, Vaughn, & Tyler, 2002).
- Embed pictures and symbols in text to prompt students using word-processing and other software programs.
- Faciliate students' ability to plan and compose written text by using visual and auditory prompts, outlining, semantic mapping, and graphics-based writing programs and multimedia. For example, software programs such as Inspiration, Kidspiration, Semantic Mapper, Claris Works, Timeliner, and Semnet help students develop outlines and semantic maps by allowing them to add, delete, and move text and concepts, highlight relationships and key terms, and check for spelling. Report Writer Interactive offers prompts to assist students in improving their writing (Raskind & Higgins, 1998; May, 2003; Sturm & Rankin-Erickson, 2002).
- Use digital pictures of school- and community-based events and locations to prompt students to write (May, 2003).
- Allow students to provide feedback to each other on writing products via an Electronic Read Around and instant messaging (Strassman & D'Amore, 2002). In an Electronic Read Around, students post their work on a Local Area Network (LAN) computer, and then choose a computer that

contains the work of one of their peers. They then select a font and use it to provide their peers with feedback and suggestions for improving their written product, which also can be discussed via instant messaging.

- Have your students maintain a weblog, a regularly updated written log of their activities.
- Have students collaborate with online peers on writing projects or write to others via the Internet and E-mail (Tao & Boulware, 2002). For example, Stanford and Siders (2001) and Harmston, Strong, and Evans (2001) offer guidelines and websites for having students write to and work with online pen-pals.
- Teach students to use desktop publishing and graphics programs to publish their work. For example, students can publish their work using such programs as Pagemaker, Printshop, SuperPrint, and Newspaper Maker.

- Determine students' spelling skills and errors by using spelling assessment software programs. For example, SPELL (Masterson, Apel, & Wasowicz, 2003) is a software assessment instrument that analyzes students' spelling errors and makes suggestions about instructional strategies.
- Help students hold their writing utensils by using such low technology devices as tape, wrist weights, foam rubber bands, a triangle or grips to slip over the writing utensil, or specialized writing utensils that allow for adapted grips such as large-diameter pencils, crayons, and holders, Wiggle pens, weighted holders, and writing frames.
- Provide students with slantboards, templates, and adapted paper such as Right Line writing paper, which has raised green lines that provide students with visual and tactile handwriting writing cues (Keller, 2001).

Teach Students to Use the Spell Checker

As we discussed earlier in this chapter, you can help students with spelling by teaching them to use spell checkers.

Teach Useful Prefixes, Suffixes, and Root Words

Teaching students useful prefixes, suffixes, and root words can help them spell and define new multisyllabic words (Cunningham, 1998).

Use Computer Programs

Computer programs have been successful in improving students' spelling (Fulk & Stormont-Spurgin, 1995). These programs offer students opportunities to practice their spelling skills within individualized teaching formats and instructional learning games. For example, Simon Spells is a software program that teaches students to spell 1,000 frequently read or written words (Ochoa, Vasquez, & Gerber, 1999).

Use Spelling Games

Spelling games can motivate students and give them the opportunity to practice spelling skills in a nonthreatening environment (Graham, Harris, & Fink-Chorzempa, 2003). Teacher-made games include spelling bingo, hangman, road race, baseball, and lotto. Commercially produced games include Scrabble, Spello, and Boggle.

Have Students Record Their Progress

Self-recording motivates students by giving them a visual representation of their progress. For example, students can keep a cumulative chart or graph of words spelled correctly, maintain weekly graphs that measure performance on pretests and posttests, or self-correct and track their spelling performance on writing tasks. Students also can set spelling goals for themselves based on their prior performance and chart their success in achieving their goals (Goddard & Heron, 1998).

Summary

This chapter presented guidelines and strategies for differentiating reading, writing, and spelling instruction. As you review the questions posed in this chapter, remember the following points.

How Can I Help Students Learn to Read?

CEC 3, 4, 5, 6, 7, 8, 9, PRAXIS 3, INTASC 1, 2, 3, 4, 5, 6, 7, 9

You can support students' reading by using the principles of effective early reading interventions and focusing your instruction on developing and promoting their phonemic awareness, reading fluency, vocabulary, and text comprehension. You can do this by motivating students to read; involving their families; fostering their word identification skills; using prompting strategies; supporting older struggling readers; developing their vocabulary; and using peer-based instruction. It also is important for you to employ a balanced approach to teaching reading and supplement your instruction by using remedial reading programs, strategies, and materials.

How Can I Help Students Learn to Write?

CEC 3, 4, 5, 6, 7, 8, 9, PRAXIS 3, INTASC 1, 2, 3, 4, 5, 6, 7, 9

You can make writing a meaningful, integral part of the curriculum, use a process-oriented approach to writing instruction, teach students to use learning strategies, and employ computer-supported applications.

How Can I Help Students Learn to Spell?

CEC 3, 4, 5, 6, 7, 8, 9, PRAXIS 3, INTASC 2, 3, 4, 5, 6, 7, 9

You can help students learn to spell by employing a combination of approaches and by using a variety of strategies to adapt spelling instruction.

What Would You Do in Today's Diverse Classroom?

Richard is having difficulty with reading, writing, and spelling. He reads haltingly and stiffly and often has to read words several times as he attempts to sound them out. He is reluctant to read aloud and makes excuses to avoid doing it. His writing, which is limited, is disorganized, contains repetitive words and irrelevant information, and is very difficult to follow. As a result, he dislikes writing and see it as a tedious way to communicate. Because of his poor spelling and handwriting, even Richard has difficulty deciphering his writing.

1.   What would you do to help Richard learn to read?

2.   What would you do to help Richard learn to write?

3. What would you do to help Richard learn to spell?

4. What knowledge, skills, dispositions, resources, and support from others would be useful in helping Richard learn to read, write, and spell?

 To answer these questions online and share your responses with others, go to the Reflection module in Chapter 10 of the Companion Website.

Chapter 11

Differentiating Mathematics, Science, and Social Studies Instruction

Ms. Rivlin

Ms. Rivlin and her students are studying geometry, including the perimeter and area of various geometric shapes. To help motivate her students and develop their appreciation of geometry as a factor in their lives, she begins by reading a selection to her students from a book where the characters use geometry. She then asks her students to identify shapes in their environment, and write journal entries describing them. For homework, students are asked to find pictures of two-dimensional figures and write about and orally describe these shapes. Ms. Rivlin uses students' homework in class by having them exchange their geometric shapes so they can describe the figures their classmates have collected.

The students experiment with shapes by performing various geoboard activities. Using tangrams, they investigate the properties of shapes, discuss the similarities and differences among the shapes, and create new shapes. Ms. Rivlin uses computer graphics to create and display various geometry shapes, and to introduce the various concepts related to geometric shapes, area and perimeter. She also has her students electronically construct and experiment with various shapes with Geometer's Sketchpad and perform exercises using online manipulatives, which they access from the National Library of Virtual Manipulatives for Interactive Mathematics (www.matti.usu.edu/nlvm/nav/vlibrary).

Ms. Rivlin also has students work in cooperative learning groups to experiment with, brainstorm about, and solve problems. In their groups, students research and write about the cultural origins and meanings of geometric shapes. One group reports about the Egyptian pyramids, including information about the area and perimeter of these structures, while another group uses the Internet to gather and present information about Mayan ruins and geometric shapes. As a culminating activity, Ms. Rivlin asks each group to design a community-based recreational area. Groups begin by collecting data about the various dimensions of the area and the different types of recreational areas. One group chooses to design a skateboarding area, while other groups design a park, a series of gardens, athletic fields, and an art and music center. They then create and draw their recreational area, and share their designs with the whole class. At the end of the unit, Ms. Rivlin works with her students to create portfolios that demonstrate their knowledge and mastery of geometry.

What additional strategies can Ms. Rivlin use to promote the mathematics skills of her students? After reading this chapter, you should have the knowledge, skills, and dispositions to answer this as well as the following questions.

★ **How can I differentiate mathematics instruction?**
★ **How can I differentiate science and social studies instruction?**

M any strategies for differentiating classroom instruction to enhance learning, motivation, and social development can be used across academic disciplines (see chapters 8 and 9). However, like Ms. Rivlin, you may find that you must make accommodations to a specific content area to promote learning for students. This chapter offers guidelines for differentiating mathematics, science, and social studies instruction. It is important to remember that many of these instructional strategies can be used across the different content areas.

How Can I Differentiate Mathematics Instruction?

Use a Problem-Solving Approach

Set Your Sites

For more information on teaching mathematics and about the NCTM standards, go to the Web Links module in Chapter 11 of the Companion Website.

The National Council of Teachers of Mathematics (NCTM) established guidelines that promote five general mathematical goals for *all students:* (a) learning to value mathematics, (b) developing confidence in one's mathematical ability, (c) becoming mathematical problem solvers, (d) learning to communicate mathematically, and (e) learning to reason mathematically (Gersten & Chard, 1999; Robinson, Menchetti, & Torgesen, 2002). The NCTM endorsed a problem-solving approach to the teaching and assessment of mathematics that gives *all students* opportunities to use mathematics to solve meaningful problems.

Many students, particularly those with disabilities, experience problems in learning mathematics (Cawley, Parmar, Foley, Salmon, & Roy, 2001; Kroesbergen & Van Luit, 2003; Xin & Jitendra, 1999). Figure 11.1 presents some of the common characteristics displayed by students who have difficulties with mathematics. However, these students can improve their computational and mathematics reasoning skills when they are taught using a hands-on, engaging, and interactive problem-solving curriculum that involves them in experiencing, thinking about, and solving meaningful mathematical problems (Bottge, 1999; Cawley & Foley, 2002).

FIGURE 11.1

Common characteristics of students with mathematics difficulties

Students with mathematics problems may have difficulty:

- ◈ writing, copying, and spelling numerals and other mathematics symbols.
- ◈ counting without using fingers.
- ◈ identifying signs and other mathematical symbols.
- ◈ ordering, aligning, and spacing numbers.
- ◈ beginning calculations in the proper place.
- ◈ recalling number facts quickly.
- ◈ understanding mathematics vocabulary.
- ◈ performing proper operations.
- ◈ estimating and checking answers.
- ◈ performing multistep operations.
- ◈ solving word problems.

Note: Bryant, Bryant, & Hammill (2000); Jordan & Hanich (2000).

Because of learning, language, and behavioral difficulties, some students may initially have difficulty with a problem-solving approach (Cawley et al., 2001). You can help these students benefit from and succeed with this approach by planning and organizing instruction according to the following principles, many of which also can be used to structure your teaching of science and social studies.

Present Mathematics Appropriately

Organize Instruction to Follow a Developmental Sequence

You can follow an instructional sequence that involves three stages: concrete, representational, and abstract (Butler, Miller, Crehan, Babbitt, & Pierce, 2003). First, you introduce new concepts by using three-dimensional objects such as concrete aids and manipulatives. Next, you use semiconcrete aids, such as demonstrations or illustrations on overheads, in computers, and in textbooks to represent concepts and develop proficiency (Witzel, Mercer, & Miller, 2003). Finally, you promote understanding, speed and accuracy by using abstract strategies such as mathematical symbols and oral and written language. Following this developmental approach, you can use a graduated word problem sequence in which students first work on word problems without irrelevant information, then progress to word problems with irrelevant information, and finally create their own word problems.

Introduce Concepts and Present Problems Through Everyday Situations

You can promote learning, motivate students, and help them learn to value mathematics by connecting mathematics to situations and problems that are familiar and meaningful to them (Bottge, 2001; Witzel, Smith, & Brownell, 2001). As Ms. Rivlin did in the chapter-opening vignette, you can present math problems related to real-life situations, and discuss the relevance of learning a new skill and the situations in which the skill can be applied. For example, students can investigate problems by gathering data related to employment, social and environmental issues, friends, health, sports, music, and art (Cangelosi, 2003). By linking mathematical problems to other subject areas such as reading and science, you can make mathematical connections to the practical, recreational, and cultural aspects of students' lives.

You also can connect mathematics to students' cultural backgrounds and world cultures, which is referred to as *ethnomathematics* (D'Ambrosio, 2001; Gay, 2004). Materials that explore the different cultural origins of mathematics, discuss mathematical solutions and practices developed and used in all parts of the world, present the achievements of mathematicians from various language and cultural backgrounds, and offer various culturally diverse, practical applications of mathematics can be used to relate students' experiences to mathematics. For example, students can be taught number sense by learning about and comparing our number system with the hieroglyphic numerals of Egypt, Chinese rod numerals, and ancient Mayan numerals (Zaslavsky, 2002). Connections to students' lives and cultures also can be established by using rhythms, songs, raps, and chants that teach mathematics, as well as by employing strategies that were used to teach mathematics in students' native countries. You also can frame word problems using familiar community and multicultural and nonsexist references so that students conduct problem-solving activities focused on problems in the community.

Resource

Karp and Voltz (2000) offer strategies for teaching mathematics in inclusive settings.

Resource

Cawley and Foley (2002) present Activity-Based Mathematics Units that can be used to connect mathematics and science instruction.

Resource

Anderson, Casey, and Kerrigan (2002) created a series that introduces mathematical concepts and problem solving through books and storytelling and Midkiff and Cramer (1993) and Hopkins (1993) provide lists of children's books that relate language arts instruction and students' experiences to mathematics.

Resource

Patton, Cronin, Bassett, and Koppel (1997) offer guidelines and resources for focusing mathematics teaching on the real-life demands of adulthood.

Resource

Gay (2004) and Moses and Cobb (2001) provide multicultural activities for teaching mathematics. De la Cruz, Cage, and Lian (2000) offer examples of multicultural games to teach mathematics.

Set Your Sites

For more information on the relationship between math and culture, go to the Web Links module in Chapter 11 of the Companion Website.

Teach the Language of Mathematics

Resource

Cangelosi (2003) provides guidelines and activities for teaching the language of mathematics and Jones (2001b) offers lists of mathematics vocabulary by grade level and strategies for assessing students' math content-reading levels.

Learning the language of mathematics can promote mathematical literacy and proficiency, communication, and reasoning and give students a framework for solving problems (Cangelosi, 2003; Cawley et al., 2001; Monroe & Orme, 2002). Therefore, it is important for you to identify and teach important mathematics vocabulary (e.g., *numerator, divisor, sum, square root, surface area*, etc.) and symbols (e.g., <, >, %, etc.) (Bryant, Bryant, & Hammill, 2000; Jones, 2001b). You can help students learn math vocabulary by assigning and teaching math terms as vocabulary words and posting math terms and their definitions on bulletin boards and walls in your classroom. In particular, students who are second language learners can learn math more easily by using methods that foster their understanding of English language mathematics vocabulary, such as using concrete activities and developing a picture file or bilingual glossary of frequently used math terms (Scott & Raborn, 1996).

Fisher, Frey, and Williams (2002) and Bley and Thornton (1995) propose that you and your students develop and maintain a math notebook or dictionary that contains definitions, visual explanations, examples, and graphics of mathematical terminology. For example, the dictionary can contain definitions and examples of math terms such as *sums, quotients, proper fractions, prime number, binomial, quadrilateral*, and *reciprocals*. Students having difficulty with the term *denominator*, for example, can locate its definition and view examples ("The denominator is the bottom part of a fraction that indicates the number of parts. In this fraction, the 6 is the denominator."). In addition, students can write in their notebooks definitions for mathematical terms using their own words. They also can create a mathematical operations chart that lists various mathematical symbols, terms, and the words that imply different mathematical operations and terms.

Use Teaching Aids

Teach Students to Use Manipulatives and Concrete Teaching Aids

Like Ms. Rivlin, you can use manipulatives and concrete teaching aids to promote students' understanding of abstract and symbolic concepts by introducing these concepts in a non-threatening way that makes the connection between mathematics and students' lives (Butler et al., 2003; Cass, Cates, Smith, & Jackson, 2003). They also offer students opportunities to explore concepts before learning standard math terms and notation. Manipulatives are particularly valuable in helping students with language difficulties learn math concepts.

Resource

Brosnan (1997) describes a variety of geoboard activities that you can use to teach mathematics.

A range of manipulatives are available to teach a variety of concepts (Cangelosi, 2003; Posamentier & Stepelman, 2002; Tucker, Singleton, & Weaver, 2002). Software programs that allow students to manipulate objects also can be used to foster your students' mathematical problem-solving abilities.

Resource

Butler et al. (2003) present strategies for using manipulatives to teach fractions, and Cass et al. (2003) offer guidelines for employing manipulatives to teach students to solve area and perimeter problems.

When using manipulatives and concrete teaching aids to teach math concepts, the following guidelines are helpful (Cass et al., 2003). At first, introduce them by modeling their use and explaining the concepts illustrated. Next, allow students to experiment with the materials, to solve problems independently and in groups, and to describe their actions. You can structure students' use of the materials by asking questions that guide their experimentation. To promote generalization, give students opportunities to use a variety of manipulatives. When using manipulatives with students who have behavioral difficulties, you may need to remind them of the classroom rules and reinforce them for complying with the procedures for using and handling the materials.

Problem solving can be aided by using manipulatives and other teaching aids. What manipulatives do your students like to use?

Use Visuals to Illustrate Concepts, Problems, Solutions, and Interrelationships

Oral and textbook-based math instruction can be supplemented by the use of visuals (Barton, Heidema, & Jordan, 2002). Drawings and diagrams of new concepts, patterns and interrelationships can help students discuss and visualize mathematical ideas, concepts, and solutions (Woodward, Baxter, & Robinson, 1999). Students gain a visual, concrete framework for understanding the foundations of the process, as well as the steps necessary to solve problems (Allsopp, 1999). Because material used to present mathematics can be difficult to read, misunderstandings related to reading mathematical language can be minimized by using drawings and diagrams that depict difficult content. Graphing calculators and personal digital assistants also can provide students with opportunities to learn mathematics visually (Posamentier & Stepelman, 2002).

When offering depictions of math concepts and problem-solving techniques, you can discuss patterns and relationships, highlight essential information, and focus students' attention by using colored chalk, marking pens, or computer graphics. For example, when introducing students to the definitions of and differences among equilateral, isosceles, and scalene triangles, you can record the definitions and present examples of each type of triangle and then highlight key words in the definition and shade key sides.

You also can encourage students to visualize solutions to math problems, draw pictures, illustrate and translate findings, and record notes to help them solve problems. Students also can learn to solve problems by using graphs. They can be taught how and when to create different types of graphs (e.g., circle, bar, line, histogram) to help them visualize and present solutions to problems.

Resource

Gagnon and Maccini (2001) and Witzel, Mercer and Miller (2003) offer a variety of instructional strategies and examples for teaching algebra.

Set Your Sites

For more information on teaching algebra, go to the Web Links module in Chapter 11 of the Companion Website.

Use Instructional Technology and Teach Students to Use It

Like Ms. Rivlin, you can use instructional technology to enhance and support mathematics instruction. Instructional technology can offer you and your students visual and auditory stimuli and interactive simulations that can make mathematics come alive for students and help them collect real data and explore solutions to problems (Bottge, 2001; Bryant, Bryant, & Hammill, 2000; Woodward, 1999). These stimuli, including software programs, spreadsheets, databases, computer simulations, tutorials, graphics programs, and graphing calculators, also can help students develop number sense and solve math problems (Cangelosi, 2003; Stanger, Symington, Miller and Johns, 2000). The Internet and CD-ROM programs allow students to access real data that can be used in solving meaningful problems.

Instructional technology can provide you with opportunities to differentiate mathematics instruction for a wide range of students. For example, *My Math* is a mathematics software program that contains three components: Computation Problems, Word Problems, and Story Problems (Cawley, Foley, & Doan, 2003). Students and teachers can choose the level of difficulty of the content to be used in each of the three components. For example, the Word Problems Component allows students to choose from word problems that are of varying structures and lengths, and to access questions that prompt students.

Instructional technology can help you structure lessons so that students with different learning abilities can work together to solve problems. For example, the video-based *The Adventures of Jasper Woodbury, Kim's Komet*, and *Bart's Pet Project* present stories and math problems visually. These problems can be used with students who have different reading abilities and serve as springboards or anchors for hands-on projects that have students use their mathematical skills to solve problems of interest to them (Bottge, Heinrichs, Mehta, & Hung, 2002; Bottge & Hasselbring, 1999). The video series *The Wonderful Problems of Fizz and Martina* stimulates students to talk about mathematical solutions and work collaboratively to help the characters solve problems that require mathematical solutions (Dockterman, 1995).

IntelliTools has developed a series of software and accessible hardware curriculum materials that employ electronic manipulatives to teach content related to the NCTM standards (Symington & Stanger, 2000). For example, *Number Concepts 2* is a series of software programs with individualized and cooperative learning formats that use friendly penguins as characters (Stanger et al., 2000). It also allows teachers to tailor instruction for individual students by providing auditory support, repetition, on-screen manipulatives, and error correction. For example, for students who are second language learners and students with reading or visual difficulties, the software can be programmed to read the numbers aloud.

Set Your Sites

For more information on using technology to teach mathematics, go to the Web Links module in Chapter 11 of the Companion Website.

Encourage and Teach Students to Use Calculators

Calculators can help students develop their mathematical literacy and solve problems (Woodward, 1999). Once students know how and why to perform an algorithm, calculators give them the ability to learn, retrieve, and check computation facts, thus promoting their independence and increasing their speed in solving problems (Cangelosi, 2003). For these reasons, the NCTM has called for teachers to provide students with calculators.

Some students who have difficulty computing with calculators, such as those who reverse numbers, may benefit from calculators with special features such as a talking calculator, which states the numerals entered and computed (Raskind & Higgins, 1998). The *Speech Plus Calculator*, developed by Telesensory Systems, has a 24-word vocabulary that can help students perform addition, subtraction, multiplication, division, square root, and percentage calculations by stating the function or name of each key as it is pressed. Calculators that provide a printout or display of all numerals and operations entered may be helpful for students with motor, memory, or attention difficulties because they offer products that can be checked for memory and accuracy (Bley & Thornton, 1995). Some students may need to use calculators with large keys and displays or those that allow on-screen entry of numbers.

Use a Variety of Instructional Approaches

Use Peer-Mediated Instruction

As Ms. Rivlin did in the chapter-opening vignette, you can use peer-mediated instruction such as cooperative learning arrangements (see chapter 9) so that your students work in groups to communicate about and experiment with solutions to mathematical problems (Baxter, Woodward, Voorhies, & Wong, 2002; Calhoon & Fuchs, 2003). Peer-mediated instruction allows students to work in groups to ask questions, share ideas, clarify thoughts, experiment, brainstorm, and present solutions with their classmates. Students can understand many perspectives and solutions to mathematical problems and appreciate that math problems can be approached and solved in a variety of ways. (Guidelines for using cooperative learning were discussed in chapter 9.)

Offer Students Specialized Instruction in Solving Word Problems

While many students have difficulty solving mathematics word problems, students with learning difficulties may experience particular difficulties. Therefore, these students will need specialized instruction in approaching and solving word problems (Cawley et al., 2001; Xin & Jitendra, 1999). Specialized instruction can be tailored to address the individual needs of students by examining students' error patterns when solving word problems with respect to:

- Problem recognition: Does the student recognize a representation of a mathematical question in word problems?
- Problem definition: Does the student know what mathematical processes to use to solve word problems?
- Problem comprehension: Does the student understand the mathematical language in word problems?

Such factors as length, syntactic complexity, vocabulary level, context, amount of nonessential information and irrelevant numbers, sequence and number of ideas presented, and mathematical steps required can make it difficult to solve word problems (Fuchs & Fuchs, 2002). Therefore, you can improve your students' problem-solving abilities by:

- simplifying the syntax.
- using vocabulary students understand.
- deleting irrelevant or ambiguous information.
- limiting the number of ideas presented.
- rearranging the information and presenting it in the order students can follow in solving the problem.
- using word problems that depict situations that relate to students' lives.

Students also can be taught to identify the critical elements of word problems, eliminate irrelevant details, and sequence information in the order in which it will be needed. These skills can be developed by teaching students to underline the question and circle the given parts of the problem, by providing practice items in which students restate the specifics of the problem in their own words, and by having students act out the problem.

You also can teach students to use graphic representations to solve problems by using visuals that organize and facilitate the understanding of information in a problem (Jitendra, 2002; van Garderen & Montague, 2003). Sample graphic representations are presented in Figure 11.2. Initially, you can verbally explain and visually model how to identify the type of problem pattern and visually represent relevant information in word

Resource

Jitendra (2002) offers guidelines and examples for teaching math problem solving using visual representations.

Sample Procedures for Solving (a) Change, (b) Group, and (c) Compare Problems

Change Problem

A balloon man had some balloons. Then 14 balloons blew away and the man now has 29 balloons. How many balloons did the man begin with?

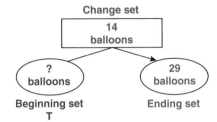

Change set

14 balloons

? balloons

Beginning set
T

29 balloons

Ending set

Total is not known, so add.
29 + 14 = 43
The man began with 43 balloons.

Group Problem

Jenny saw 25 birds on a camping trip. She saw 17 sparrows and some owls. How many owls did Jenny see on the camping trip?

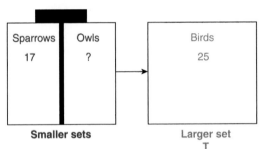

Sparrows
17

Owls
?

Birds
25

Smaller sets

Larger set
T

Total is known, so subtract.
25 − 17 = 8
Jenny saw 8 owls on the camping trip.

Compare Problem

Barbara is 37 years old. Cindy is 7 years older than Barbara. How old is Cindy?

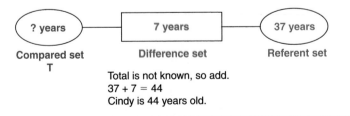

? years

7 years

37 years

Compared set
T

Difference set

Referent set

Total is not known, so add.
37 + 7 = 44
Cindy is 44 years old.

FIGURE 11.2   **Sample graphic representations**

Source: From "Teaching Students Math Problem-Solving Through Graphic Representations," by A. K. Jitendro, 2002, *Teaching Exceptional Children 34*(4), pp. 34–39. Copyright 2002 by The Council for Exceptional Children. Reprinted with permission.

problems. Next, you can teach students to identify and highlight important information in the problem that can be added to teacher-prepared visuals provided for them, and indicate unknown information through use of a question mark. Finally, students can be taught to independently identify essential information, create visuals that depict the essential information presented in the word problems, and solve the problem. This instructional sequence can be used to teach students to visually represent the key features in the different types of word problems they will encounter.

Because many students who find mathematics difficult may often come up with unreasonable answers and settle for their first answer (Bryant, Bryant, & Hammill, 2000), your students' ability to solve word problems also can be enhanced by teaching them to estimate and check their answers (Mittag & Van Reusen, 1999). You can do this by helping them understand the importance of estimation and verification, and the relationship between estimates and answers. You also can model, teach, and prompt students to use the different ways to estimate and check answers (Montague & van Garderen, 2003).

The problem-solving skills of students can be enhanced by incorporating writing tasks into mathematics instruction (Brandenburg, 2002; Cangelosi, 2003). Students can keep a math journal that contains reactions to and notes on mathematics activities and teaching, as well as explanations, clarifications, and applications of math problems (Posamentier & Stepelman, 2002). Students also can write their story problems; write letters to others outlining a mathematical solution, rule, or concept; translate visual representations into text; and describe and reflect on their problem-solving strategies. They also can design, implement, and write up a math project that requires them to collect data, compute results, develop graphs and other pictorials, and share conclusions.

Teach Students to Use Self-Management Techniques and Learning Strategies

Students who struggle with mathematics often have difficulties with multistep tasks and problems (Bryant, Bryant, & Hammill, 2000). Self-management techniques and learning strategies can be taught to help students solve problems involving a variety of mathematical procedures (Fuchs & Fuchs, 2001; Tournaki, 2003). Techniques such as self-monitoring checklists prompt students to remember and engage in the multiple steps necessary to complete a task (Gagnon & Maccini, 2001).

Self-management also can be effective in helping students learn the math facts and computation skills needed to solve problems that require multistep math operations (Maccini & Hughes, 1997; McDougall & Brady, 1998). For example, self-instruction teaches students to perform computations by describing to themselves the steps and questions necessary to identify and perform the calculations.

Several learning strategies have been developed to help students solve mathematical problems (Landi, 2001), including *Solve It!* (Montague, Warger, & Morgan, 2000). In general, the steps in these strategies include the following:

> *Step 1. Read the problem.* First, students read the problem to determine the question and to find any unknown words and clue words. Clue words are those words that indicate the correct operation to be used. For example, the words *all together, both, together, in all, and, plus,* and *sum* suggest that the problem involves addition; words like *left, lost, spend,* and *remain* indicate that the correct operation is subtraction. However, you need to be aware that clue words do not always cue the appropriate operation. When students encounter unknown words, they can ask you to pronounce and define them.

Resource
Montague and van Garderen (2003) offer multiple-choice items and interview questions that can assess students' estimation skills.

Resource
Posamentier and Stepelman (2002) offer a range of ways in which writing can be incorporated into the teaching of mathematics.

Resource
Fuchs, Fuchs, Prentice, Burch, and Paulsen (2002) developed Hot Math, a multistep intervention for teaching word problem solving.

Resource
Successful self-instructional techniques for teaching computation skills include equal additions (Sugai & Smith, 1986), count-bys (Lloyd, Saltzman, & Kauffman, 1981), touch math (Miller, Miller, Wheeler, & Selinger, 1989), count-ons, count-all, maximum and minimum addend, zero facts, doubles, and turn-around (Jones, Thornton, & Toohey, 1985; Tournaki, 2003).

IDEAS FOR IMPLEMENTATION

Developing Students' Word Problem-Solving Skills

Although Ms. Ventnor's students were making progress in developing their computation skills, she was concerned about the difficulties they were having with word problems. To help them, she decided to focus on developing their problem-solving skills. She started by presenting word problems through the use of pictorials, highlighting important words in problems, and having students write or state math problems without computing the answers. She also began to personalize problems by using students' names and relating problems to their interests, cultures, experiences, and classroom or current events. When presenting these problems, she asked students to paraphrase the problems in their own words, and had them work in groups to act out word problems, create drawings of the problems, and compose problems to be solved by their classmates. As her students began to develop their problem-solving skills, she asked them to solve problems and minimized the complexity of the calculations by using easier and smaller numbers. Here are some other strategies you can use to develop your students' word problem-solving skills:

- Teach students how to differentiate between relevant and irrelevant information by presenting problems that have too little or too much information.

- Teach students the unique features of the various problem types.
- Write number cues above specific parts of word problems to show the steps students can follow to solve the problems.
- Encourage students to estimate answers and brainstorm solutions to word problems.
- Teach students to look for patterns in problems, use charts and graphs to organize data, and relate solutions to previous problems.
- Give students diagrams and teach them to draw diagrams to identify the important features of word problems.
- Give students problems that have more than one answer and problems that can be solved in several ways.
- Encourage and recognize multiple solution strategies to solve problems.

Note: Jitendra, DiPipi, & Perron-Jones (2002); Landi (2001); Montague & van Garderen (2003); Parmar, Cawley, & Frazita (1996).

Step 2. Reread and paraphrase the problem. Read the problem a second time to identify and paraphrase relevant information, which can be highlighted by underlining, while deleting irrelevant information and facts. Focus on determining what mathematical process and unit can be used to express the answer.

Step 3. Visualize and draw the problem. Students visualize the problem and draw a representation of the information given.

Step 4. Make a plan and write the problem. Students hypothesize and write the steps in solving the problem in order with the appropriate sign.

Step 5. Estimate the answer. Before solving the problem, students estimate the answer. The estimate provides a framework for determining the reasonableness of their response.

Step 6. Solve the problem. Students solve the problem, as outlined in step 4, by calculating each step in the process, giving attention to the correctness of the calculations and the unit used to express the answer.

Step 7. Check the answer. Students check their work and compare their answer with their estimate. They examine each step in terms of necessity, order, operation selected, and correctness of calculations.

Landi (2001) and Montague, Warger, and Morgan (2000) offer activities and examples for teaching these steps to students.

Resource

Miller, Strawser, and Mercer (1996) offer examples of acronym mnemonics that can be used to help students solve word problems.

Give Students Models, Cues, and Prompts

Students with learning difficulties may understand the processes used to solve problems involving several operations executed in a particular sequence, but they may need models, cues, and prompts to guide them in performing these operations. Problem-solving assignments can be coded so that they include a model for calculating the answer. The model can vary, depending on the skill level and needs of the students. Sample models are presented in Figure 11.3. Flip charts can offer students a model of the correct format and order in approaching a task (Bley & Thornton, 1995). Each page of the flip chart represents a step students must perform to complete the task. A sample flip chart for division of fractions is presented in Figure 11.4.

Charts also can be placed in the room to help students. These charts can present math terms, facts, and symbols (*subtract = take away = −*), as well as the steps to follow for a specific type of problem, such as the steps in dividing fractions. For example, a fraction strip chart presenting strips divided into halves, thirds, fourths, and so on can be posted to help students learn the concepts associated with fractions.

Cues also can be used with students who have difficulty remembering the order in which to solve computation items. Arrows can be drawn to indicate the direction in which

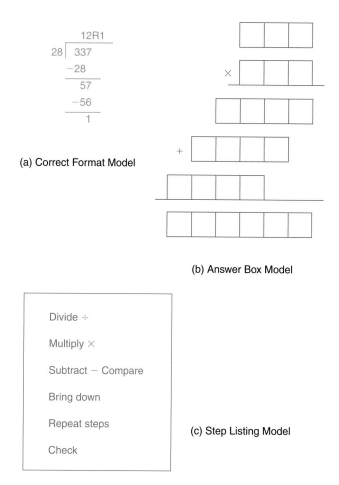

(a) Correct Format Model

(b) Answer Box Model

(c) Step Listing Model

Divide ÷

Multiply ×

Subtract − Compare

Bring down

Repeat steps

Check

FIGURE 11.3 **Algorithm models**

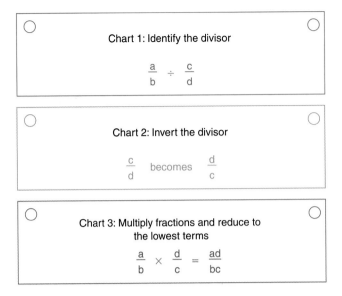

FIGURE 11.4   **Flip chart for dividing fractions**

students should proceed. Cues such as green and red dots, go and stop signs, and answer boxes tell students when to proceed or stop when working on a specific item. Attention to signs $(+, -, \times)$ can be emphasized by color coding, boldfacing, and underlining. It can also be fostered by listing the sign and its operation at the top of each worksheet $(+ = \text{add}: 6 + 3 = 9)$ and teaching students to trace the sign before beginning the computation.

Another type of cue, *boxing*, or placing boxes around items, can focus students' attention on specific problems within a group. When boxing items, you should leave enough space within the box to do the calculations needed to solve the item. As students' skills increase, they can be encouraged to assume responsibility for boxing items. Boxing also can aid students who have problems placing their answer in the correct column. A color-coded, smaller box or broken line can be drawn to delineate columns so that students place their answers appropriately. Problems with aligning answers also can be minimized by having students use centimeter graph paper, on which only one digit can be written in each box, or by turning lined paper so that the lines run vertically. Alignment problems also can be reduced by teaching students to estimate the answer and check its reasonableness. An answer that deviates significantly from the estimate may indicate an alignment problem, and students can check their work accordingly.

You can use visual and verbal prompts to help students solve problems and perform computations (Butler et al., 2003; Joseph, 2000). For example, students can be given a cue card (see Figure 11.5) with steps and examples for performing math tasks successfully.

Help Students Develop Their Math Facts and Computation Skills

You can promote the success of a problem-solving approach to mathematics by offering instruction that helps students develop their math facts and computation skills (Wood & Frank, 2000). A *demonstration plus model* strategy has been successful in helping students with learning problems develop computational skills. The strategy involves these steps:

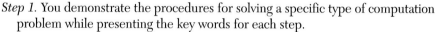

Sample mathematics cue card

1. Are fractions the same on the bottom?

   If not, find Least Common Multiple (LCM)

   Multiply top and bottom number by same number to get both bottom numbers to equal each other.

   Example: $\dfrac{2 \times 4}{3 \times 4}$ $+$ $\dfrac{1 \times 3}{4 \times 3}$

   $=$ $\dfrac{8}{12}$ $+$ $\dfrac{3}{12}$

2. Add or subtract on top only when bottom number is the same.

   Example: $\dfrac{8}{12}$ $+$ $\dfrac{3}{12}$ $=$ $\dfrac{11}{12}$

3. Can it be reduced? Can top number and bottom number be divided by same number?

   Example: $\dfrac{8/4}{12/4}$ $=$ $\dfrac{2}{3}$

Source: From "Student As a Strategic Participant in Collaborative Problem-Solving Teams: An Alternative Model for Middle and Secondary Schools," by L. M. Joseph, 2000, *Teaching Exceptional Children, 36,* pp. 47–53. Copyright by The Council for Exceptional Children. Reprinted with permission.

Step 1. You demonstrate the procedures for solving a specific type of computation problem while presenting the key words for each step.

Step 2. Students view your example and perform the steps in the computation while giving the key words for each step.

Step 3. Students complete additional problems, referring to your example if necessary.

Vary the Instructional Sequence

Some students who are having difficulty learning math facts and computation skills may benefit from modifications in their teaching sequence (Cawley, 2001; Woodward & Baxter, 2001). For example, while the traditional teaching sequence for addition computation skills is based on the numeric value of the sum, some teachers use a teaching sequence that progresses from count-ons (e.g., +1, +2, +3) to zero facts (3 + 0, 7 + 0) to doubles (3 + 3, 8 + 8) to 10 sums (4 + 6, 3 + 7).

Varying the teaching sequence to cluster math facts can make it easier to remember them. Rather than teaching math facts in isolation, you can present related math facts together (Tucker, Singleton, & Weaver, 2002). For example, students can learn the cluster of multiplying by 2 together. As students demonstrate mastery, they can practice mixed groups of math facts. Students also can be taught to use *doubling* (e.g., learning 7×4 by doubling 7×2) and *helping* or *near facts* (e.g., learning 5×6 by adding 5 to 5×5) to multiply.

Promote Mastery and Automaticity

An important goal of math instruction in basic facts is to have students respond quickly and accurately (Cawley et al., 2001). You can offer students a variety of activities that promote mastery and automaticity, such as using student- or peer-directed flash cards, software programs, and having students listen to math facts on a Language Master or an

Resource

Kaufmann, Handl, and Thony (2003) and Kroesbergen, Van Luit, and Naglieri (2003) offer strategies to teach math facts and computation skills.

Resource

Cawley (2001) provides instructional strategies for teaching multiplication and Wood and Frank (2000) offer memory-enhancing strategies for teaching multiplication facts.

audiocassette. Independent assignments and homework also can be used to help students develop automaticity. Rather than giving students a large number of items, Parmar and Cawley (1991) suggest that you give them assignments with two sample computation items, discuss the key features of the items, and ask students to create and answer new items that resemble the sample items.

Match Instruction to Students' Error Types

The instructional strategy selected often will depend on the types of errors that students make. You can use the principle of the *least error correction*, which involves identifying the nature of students' errors by analyzing their performance on items between the last correct item and the first item failed, and then planning instruction to address the dominant errors (Cawley et al., 2001).

Provide Feedback and Use Assessment to Guide Future Teaching

Offer Prompt Feedback

Prompt feedback is an important part of effective mathematics instruction. Allsopp (1999) suggests that you use corrective feedback to tell students that their response is correct or incorrect, identify which part is correct or incorrect, and offer students a strategy to obtain the correct response (see Chapter 9).

Involve Students in the Assessment Process

The NCTM calls for involving students in the assessment process to help them gain insight into their knowledge of math and the ways in which they think about math (Cangelosi, 2003). Therefore, you can consider using student-centered strategies that involve students in setting goals, choosing appropriate assessment techniques, and identifying helpful teaching strategies and materials such as portfolio assessment, learning logs, think-alouds, and student interviews. (These student-centered assessment strategies are discussed in chapter 12.)

As part of the self-assessment process, students can reflect upon, locate, and correct their errors. In addition to giving their answers to problems, students also can be asked to write their explanations of problems. Student reflection also can be fostered by asking them to discuss or write about the following:

*   How they approached the problem(s).
*   Why they approached the problem in that way.
*   Whether their approach was successful or unsuccessful.
*   What was successful about their approach.
*   How they would approach the problem(s) differently (Naglieri & Johnson, 2000).

Resource

Helwig, Anderson, and Tindal (2002) provide guidelines for designing ongoing mathematics probes to assess students' mathematics fluency and conceptual understanding.

You also can provide an error analysis and correction sheet that asks students to list the problem, the steps in solving the problem, the correct answer(s), the errors made, and the reason for the errors. Students also can be taught to evaluate their mastery of concepts by graphing their performance on computer programs, worksheets, and follow-up probes. A checking center equipped with answer keys, teacher's guides, supplementary materials, peer tutors, and recordings of potential solutions can promote self-checking and minimize the demands on your time.

Assess Mastery and Progress Over Time

Maintaining skills is important for students with disabilities, so you can periodically conduct reviews and curriculum-based probes to assess their mastery and retention of previously learned skills (Foegen & Deno, 2001; Helwig, Anderson, & Tindal, 2002). You also can observe your students and ask them questions to identify the strategies they use to perform computations and solve problems (Jordan & Hanich, 2000). You can use this information to give students feedback on their performance and encourage them to record their own progress over time.

How Can I Differentiate Science and Social Studies Instruction?

In addition to the strategies for differentiating instruction presented in this section, many of the suggestions for teaching mathematics outlined in the previous section also apply to teaching science and social studies.

Choose and Use Appropriate Instructional Materials

While the specific content in each area is different, science and social studies share several teaching methods. Both areas are often taught using content-oriented approaches that rely on oral presentations and textbooks. Because some students, including students with disabilities, may sometimes have difficulty learning information from oral presentations and textbooks, science and social studies teaching should be differentiated by using appropriate instructional materials.

Set Your Sites

For more information on teaching and standards for science, go to the Web Links module in Chapter 11 of the Companion Website.

Choose Textbooks Carefully

Much of the content in science and social studies, particularly at the middle and secondary levels, is presented in textbooks that are often difficult for students, particularly those with learning difficulties, to use (Brozo & Hargis, 2003; Daniels & Zemelman, 2004). It is important to determine the readability level of the textbook and to use the teacher- and student-directed text comprehension strategies we reviewed in chapter 8 to help students gain information from textbooks (Allington, 2002). In addition, textbooks for students should be chosen carefully in terms of structure, coherence, content, and audience appropriateness. You also can supplement textbook instruction via use of young adult novels, instructional technology, and the Internet (Brozo & Hargis, 2003).

Textbooks also should relate to students' background knowledge. Unfortunately, many textbooks and instructional materials do not include the accomplishments or perspectives of individuals from diverse cultural and language backgrounds. Many of them ignore other cultures and female students, use stereotyping, offer only one interpretation of issues, avoid important issues, and present information about certain groups in isolation (Zittleman & Sadker, 2003). Because of the bias in many textbooks, many teachers rely on hands-on, activity-based teaching approaches instead.

Choosing appropriate textbooks is a crucial part of successful content area instruction. What guidelines do you use in selecting textbooks?

Teach Students How to Use Textbooks and Instructional Materials

Students can be taught how to use and obtain information from the textbooks and instructional materials used in the general education classroom. You can examine the vocabulary and concept development that students will need to use the book and teach students how to identify and define these terms (Allington, 2002). For example, you and your students can review chapters from the book, selecting key terms and concepts that they can define by using the book's glossary or another resource, such as a dictionary or an encyclopedia. When students become adept at this task, they can be encouraged to perform the steps alone.

Because information is usually presented in a similar way from chapter to chapter in textbooks and instructional materials, reviewing the organization of the materials is also helpful (Kellough & Kellough, 2003). This involves reviewing and explaining the functions of and interrelationships among the material's components (table of contents, text, glossary, index, appendices) and the elements of the book's chapters (titles, objectives, abstract, headings, summary, study guides, follow-up questions, references, alternative learning activities).

You also can help students use learning strategies to access information from textbooks (Katims & Harmon, 2000). For example, they can learn to use text headings to enhance their reading and learning from textbooks through learning strategies such as *SCROL* (Grant, 1993). The SCROL strategy involves the following:

> **S**urvey: Students read the headings and subheadings and ask themselves, "What do I know about this topic?" and "What information is going to be presented?"
> **C**onnect: Students ask, "How do the headings and subheadings relate to each other?" and list key words that provide connections.
> **R**ead: Students read the headings and outline the major ideas and supporting details without looking back at the text.
> **O**utline: Students record the headings and outline the major ideas and supporting details without looking back at the text.
> **L**ook back: Students look back at the heading and subheadings, and check and correct their outlines.

When teaching about textbooks and instructional materials, it may be helpful to teach students the strategies and text structures and styles used by the author(s) to pres-

Resource

Katims and Harmon (2000) offer guidelines for using the Person-Event-Place (PEP) strategy to help students learn to use social studies textbooks.

ent content (Barton et al., 2002). Students can learn to identify five patterns that are typically used by authors: enumeration, time order, compare-contrast, cause-effect, and problem solution. These strategies are often repeated throughout the book, so students can be taught to analyze a book by examining:

- the numbering (*1, 2, 3*), lettering (*a, b, c*), or word (*first, second, third*) system used to show the relative importance of information, as well as the order of ideas.
- the typographic signs (*boldfacing, underlining, color cueing, boxing*) used to highlight critical information.
- the word signals that indicate the equal importance of information (*furthermore, likewise*), elaboration (*moreover*), rebuttal and clarification (*nevertheless, however, but*), summarization (*therefore, consequently*), and termination (*finally, in conclusion*).

You can also also help students by showing them how to gain information from visual displays (Barton et al., 2002). Prompt them to examine illustrations and to preview the graphics to get a general idea of their purpose. You can teach them to read the title, captions, and headings to determine relevant information from the graphic; identify the units of measurement; and discuss, relate, and generalize graphic information to the text.

Many textbooks and instructional materials often come with supplemental materials such as student activity worksheets and overviews. Therefore, students can receive some training in completing the activity worksheets and interpreting information presented in graphic displays. For example, you can help students learn to complete end-of-chapter questions by training them to do the following:

- Read each question to determine what is being asked.
- Identify words in the question that can guide the reader to the correct answer.
- Determine the requirement of the question and the format of the answer.
- Convert appropriate parts of the question into part of the answer.
- Identify the paragraphs of the chapter that relate to the question.
- Locate the answer to the question by reading the chapter.
- Write the answer to the question.
- Check the answer for accuracy and form.

Learning to look for highlighted information that is usually italicized or boldfaced also can help students identify main points that often contain answers to study questions.

Note Taking from Textbooks. Good note-taking skills are invaluable in learning from textbooks (Dyck & Pemberton, 2002). A useful method to teach students involves setting up a margin, about 2 inches from the left side of the paper, where students can jot down questions based on the information presented in the chapter, on chapter subheadings, and on discussion/study questions. Students also can use this column to list vocabulary words and their definitions. They can use the rest of the page to record answers to the questions and other critical information from the chapter.

If the school allows it, highlighting information in a textbook can help students identify parts of a chapter that are critical for class discussions and can assist them in studying for exams. When marking in a textbook, <u>students can be taught to use double lines to delineate text that denotes main ideas</u> and <u>single lines to identify supporting ideas</u>. [When several continuous lines present essential content, students can use a vertical bracket in the margin rather than underlining.]

Symbols in margins and in the text are also helpful. Asterisks in the margins can be used to identify and rate important content, and question marks in the margins can

Reflective

How is this book organized to present information? What strategies are used to highlight information? What aspects of the book help promote your learning?

Resource

Beck and McKeown (2002) provide guidelines and examples for using Question the Author.

Resource

Ellis (1996) developed SNIPS, and Barry, cited in Ellis and Lenz (1987), developed the *Reading Visual Aids Strategy (RVAS)* to help students gain information from visual aids and graphic presentations.

Reflective

Look back at the notes you have taken for this book. What note-taking strategies did you use? How well do you use them? Which strategies do you find to be most efficient?

REFLECTING ON YOUR PRACTICES

Selecting Textbooks

In selecting the textbooks you use, consider the following questions:

- Is the content appropriate, multidimensional, correct, and up-to-date?
- Is the content organized around critical concepts and big ideas?
- Is the language clear and appropriate for students?
- Are there informative headings and subheadings?
- Does the textbook provide signals to highlight main points and key vocabulary (marginal notations, graphic aids, pointer words and phrases)?
- Is information presented in an organized fashion (using preview or introductory statements, topic sentences, summary statements, lists, enumeration words)?
- Does the textbook offer transitions that help the reader adjust to changes in topics?
- Does the textbook come with support materials to help students learn, such as study guides, graphic organizers, concept maps, illustrations, pictorials, supplemental learning activities, a table of contents, an index, a glossary, appendices, and computer programs?
- Are the pictorial and graphic aids easy to read and interpret?
- Do the illustrations provide a visual framework for understanding the material and supplementing the text?
- Are illustrations referred to and explained?

- Are chronological sequences or events presented in order of occurrence?
- Is the content balanced and integrated, as well as sufficiently broad and deep?
- Does the textbook clearly establish and highlight the relationships among important facts, concepts, and roles?
- Does the textbook include information about and the perspectives of individuals from diverse cultural backgrounds, as well as their contributions?
- Is the book free of stereotyping and linguistic bias (e.g., exclusive use of masculine terms)?
- Does the textbook include strategies to check for student understanding, such as interspersed and review questions and activities that help students identify, understand, apply, and assess their mastery of critical information?
- Is the textbook interesting looking, and does it make good use of space and colors?

How would you rate your selection of textbooks?
( ) Excellent
( ) Good
( ) Needs Improvement
( ) Needs Much Improvement

What steps could you take to improve your selection of textbooks?

Note: Dynneson, Gross, & Berson (2003); Kellough & Kellough (2003); Martorella & Beal (2002); Stein, Stuen, Carnine, & Long (2001); Zittleman & Sadker (2002).

prompt students to seek clarification for material that they do not agree with or do not understand. Finally, students can be taught to circle key words and to box words that indicate enumeration and transition.

Use Study Guides

You can prepare *study guides* to help students identify the critical information in assignments and provide activities to help students master it (Boyle & Yeager, 1997; Fernstorm & Goodnite, 2000). Study guides contain a series of statements, questions, and/or activities that help students identify and learn critical information from textbooks and oral presentations. They can be used to teach content-specific vocabulary, structure content-specific readings, practice and review previously learned material, and introduce new material.

While study guides vary, they often include the reading assignment, objectives, rationale, text references, a chapter summary, an outline, study questions, activities, definitions of key terms, and student evaluation probes. Study guides also can take the form of a *framed outline,* an ordered list of the chapter's main points with key words blanked out. The students fill in the blanks while reading the selection or listening to a lecture in class. You also can use hypertext to develop computerized study guides for students.

Wood (1995) identified five types of study guides that can be used to assist students in reading informational text: (a) the point-of-view reading guide, (b) interactive reading guide, (c) learning-from-text guide, (d) textbook activity guide, and (e) reading road map. Samples of a point-of-view reading guide, an interactive reading guide, and a reading road map are presented in Figure 11.6.

The point-of-view reading guide uses an interview format to prompt students to see events and material from multiple viewpoints (see Figure 11.6A). This guide requires students to assume the roles and perspectives of the individuals depicted in the text. For example, when reading about the abolition of slavery, students can be asked to provide text and reader-based information by responding to the question "As an abolitionist, how did you feel about slavery?"

A: Point-of-view reading guide

Chapter 11: The War of 1812

You are about to be interviewed as if you were a person living in the United States in the early 1800s. Describe your reactions to each of the events discussed next.

Planting the Seeds of War (p. 285)

  1. As a merchant in a coastal town, tell why your business is doing poorly.

The War Debate (pp. 285–287)

  2. Explain why you decided to become a war hawk. Who was your leader?
  3. Tell why many of your fellow townspeople lowered their flags to half mast. What else did they do?
  4. What was the reaction of Great Britain to you and your people at that time?
  5. In your opinion, is America ready to fight? Explain why you feel this way.

Perry's Victory (p. 287)

  6. In what ways were your predictions either correct or incorrect about Americans' readiness to fight this war?
  7. Tell about your experiences under Captain Perry's command.

Death of Tecumseh (p. 288)

  8. Mr. Harrison, describe what really happened near the Thames River in Canada.
  9. What was Richard Johnson's role in that battle?
 10. Now, what are your future plans?

Death of the Creek Confederacy (p. 288)

 11. Explain how your people, the Cherokees, actually helped the United States.
 12. Tell about your leader.

British Invasion (pp. 288–290)

 13. As a British soldier, what happened when you got to Washington, D.C.?
 14. You headed to Fort McHenry after D.C.; what was the outcome?
 15. General Jackson, it's your turn. Tell about your army and how you defeated the British in New Orleans.

The Treaty of Ghent (p. 290)

 16. We will end our interview with some final observations from the merchant questioned earlier. We will give you some names and people. Tell how they fare now that the war is over: the British, the Indians, the United States, Harrison, Jackson.

FIGURE 11.6A   Sample study guides

Source: From "Guiding Students Through Informational Text, " by K. D. Wood, May 1988. *The Reading Teacher, 41*(9), pp. 912–920. Reprinted with permission of Karen D. Wood and the International Reading Association. All rights reserved.

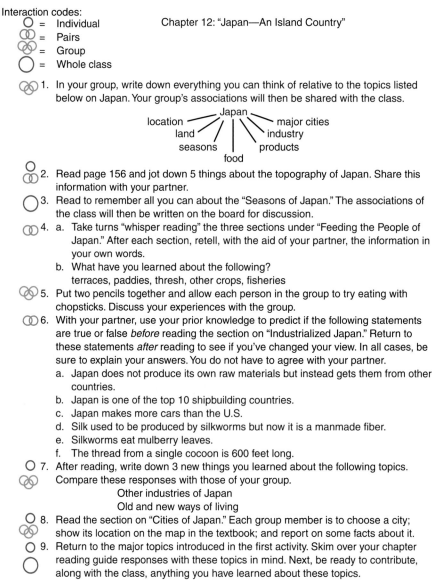

B: Interactive reading guide

Interaction codes:
O   =   Individual
⊕   =   Pairs
⊛   =   Group
◯   =   Whole class

Chapter 12: "Japan—An Island Country"

⊛ 1. In your group, write down everything you can think of relative to the topics listed below on Japan. Your group's associations will then be shared with the class.

location ——— Japan ——— major cities
land ——— / | \ ——— industry
seasons | products
food

O⊕ 2. Read page 156 and jot down 5 things about the topography of Japan. Share this information with your partner.

◯ 3. Read to remember all you can about the "Seasons of Japan." The associations of the class will then be written on the board for discussion.

⊕ 4. a. Take turns "whisper reading" the three sections under "Feeding the People of Japan." After each section, retell, with the aid of your partner, the information in your own words.
    b. What have you learned about the following?
       terraces, paddies, thresh, other crops, fisheries

⊛ 5. Put two pencils together and allow each person in the group to try eating with chopsticks. Discuss your experiences with the group.

⊕ 6. With your partner, use your prior knowledge to predict if the following statements are true or false *before* reading the section on "Industrialized Japan." Return to these statements *after* reading to see if you've changed your view. In all cases, be sure to explain your answers. You do not have to agree with your partner.
    a. Japan does not produce its own raw materials but instead gets them from other countries.
    b. Japan is one of the top 10 shipbuilding countries.
    c. Japan makes more cars than the U.S.
    d. Silk used to be produced by silkworms but now it is a manmade fiber.
    e. Silkworms eat mulberry leaves.
    f. The thread from a single cocoon is 600 feet long.

O 7. After reading, write down 3 new things you learned about the following topics.
⊛   Compare these responses with those of your group.
           Other industries of Japan
           Old and new ways of living

O 8. Read the section on "Cities of Japan." Each group member is to choose a city;
⊛   show its location on the map in the textbook; and report on some facts about it.

O 9. Return to the major topics introduced in the first activity. Skim over your chapter
◯   reading guide responses with these topics in mind. Next, be ready to contribute, along with the class, anything you have learned about these topics.

FIGURE 11.6B   (continued)

The interactive reading guide is designed so that students can collaborate to complete it (see Figure 11.6B). This reading guide asks students "to predict, develop associations, write, chart, outline, or re-tell information in their own words to a partner or a group" (Wood, 1995, p. 138). Once groups or pairs complete the guide, they discuss their responses with the whole class.

The learning-from-text guide is structured so that students progress by answering questions about the textbook that proceed from a literal level ("What is erosion?") to an inferential level ("How does erosion affect people?") to a generalization or evaluative

C: Reading road map

SKIM
1st

Chapter 13: Arthropods

READ
&
WRITE
2nd

Overall mission: You are about to take a tour of the world of the arthropods.

Location	Speed	Mission

START

Read Quickly

p. 205

Characteristics

pp. 206–7

SLOW

READ AND WRITE

Millipedes and Centipedes

pp. 208–9

Crustaceans

pp. 209–11

SLOW ~ TURN AHEAD

Arachnids

p. 211

SKIM

pp. 212–13

SLOW DOWN AND WRITE

Insects

p. 213

pp. 214–15

THINK AND WRITE

STOP

LOOK AHEAD

1. Name three major characteristics of arthropods.
2. a. What does *arthropod* mean? Find at least 2 other words with the root *pod* in them.
   b. Why is the exoskeleton so important?
   c. Briefly describe the molting process. Why does it take place?
   d. How are arthropods grouped?
3. a. Recall three traits of millipedes; of centipedes.
   b. How do millipedes protect themselves?
   c. Why are centipedes called "predators"? What other animals are predators?
4. a. How would you know a crustacean when you saw one? Where would you look for one?
   b. In your own words, tell how barnacles can be harmful.
5. a. How could you recognize an arachnid: (paragraphs 1 & 2)
   b. How and what does a spider eat? (paragraph 3)
   c. Retell the second paragraph on page 213 in your own words.
6. a. In what ways are insects different from the other arthropods?
   b. Fill in the following information:
      I. Insects
      A. Beetles
         1)
         2)
      B.
         1)
         2)
      C.
         1) social
         2)
7. What have you learned from looking at the pictures on pages 214–15?
8. Reflect back on the four types of arthropods. See how much you can remember about each type: millipedes, centipedes, crustaceans, insects.

FIGURE 11.6C   **(continued)**

level ("If you were on a committee to minimize the effects of erosion in your community, what things would you want the committee to do?").

The textbook activity guide provides students with a study guide that prompts them to use self-monitoring and metacognitive strategies as they read the textbook. For example, as students read textbooks, they are guided to assess their understanding of the material by responding to self-monitoring statements such as, "I understand this information," "I don't think I understand this information," and "I don't understand this information and need help." Metacognitive strategy codes also direct students to use various metacognitive strategies to enhance their understanding of the textbook material. For example, metacognitive strategy codes can prompt students to predict information; paraphrase information in their own words; survey material; create a chart; and use self-questioning.

The reading road map gives students a time frame for adjusting their reading rate based on the importance of the textbook material (see Figure 11.6C). A reading road map "includes missions (interspersed questions and activities), road signs (indicating the speed or rate of reading), and location signs (headings and page or paragraph numbers)" (Wood, 1995, p. 141).

In developing and using study guides, consider the following:

- Create separate study guides for each chapter, unit of content, or class presentation.
- Identify the key words, main points, and important concepts to be highlighted.
- Adjust the readability of the study guide, highlight critical vocabulary and points, and give students cues to indicate the pages and paragraphs where answers and relevant information to complete the study guides are located.
- Be creative and use pictures, drawings, and activities that engage students' attention and provide motivation.
- Devise interspersed questions, brief sentences, and multimodality activities focusing on the critical components of the material so that they are consistent with the order of the information presented in the textbook or in class.
- Give students enough space to write their answers on the study guide.
- Distribute the study guides, explain their purpose, and model how to use and complete them.
- Have students complete the study guides individually or in groups.
- Discuss and review the answers and offer students feedback on their performance.

Use Adapted Textbooks and a Parallel Alternative Curriculum

Some of your students may have difficulty reading on-grade science and social studies textbooks. For these students, it may be appropriate to use *adapted textbooks*, which present the same content as the on-grade textbook but at a lower readability level. You can find appropriate adapted textbooks corresponding to on-grade textbooks by contacting representatives from book companies.

In addition to adapted textbooks, *Parallel Alternative Curriculum (PAC)* materials have been developed for students with learning difficulties. These materials supplement the textbook by providing students with alternative ways to master critical information.

Use Content Enhancements

Content enhancements are strategies that help students identify, organize, understand, and remember important content (Lenz, Deshler, & Kissam, 2004). They help students

Resource

Boudah, Lenz, Bulgren, Schumaker, and Deshler (2000) offer guidelines for using a unit organizer, an interactive content enhancement technique.

understand abstract information and see the relationship between different pieces or types of information. A variety of content enhancements are presented next.

Advance and Post Organizers

Advance and *post organizers* are written or oral statements, activities, and/or illustrations that offer students a framework for determining and understanding the essential information in a learning activity (Munk, Bruckert, Call, Stoehrmann, & Radandt, 1998). Advance organizers are used at the beginning of a lesson to orient students to the content to be presented. Post organizers are used at the end of the lesson to help students review and remember the content that has been presented. For example, when assigning a reading selection in a science textbook, you can focus students' reading via an advance organizer such as, "Read pages 65 to 68 on mirrors and find out how a mirror works. Pay careful attention to such terms as *plane mirror, virtual image, parabolic mirror, principal axis, principal focus*, and *focal length*." Similarly, a class-developed outline that summarizes the main points of a presentation on the geography of your state could serve as a post organizer. In addition to social studies and science, advance and post organizers can be used to teach in all content areas. Several types of advance and post organizers are described next.

Graphic Organizers.   One advance or post organizer is a *graphic organizer*, also called a *structured overview,* which explicitly identifies and presents key terms before or after students encounter them in class and textbooks. A graphic organizer is a visual-spatial illustration of the key terms that comprise concepts and their interrelationships (DiCecco & Gleason, 2002). It presents information through the use of webs, matrices, timelines, process chains, cycles, and networks. Graphic organizers help students identify and organize important information so that they can activate prior knowledge and link it to new concepts. They also help students see the big picture and the relationships between main points and supporting details, make comparisons, clarify relationships, develop inferences, and draw conclusions (Gajria, Mullane, Sharp, & Heim, 2003).

There are several types of graphic organizers: central and hierarchical, directional, and comparative (Baxendell, 2003; Gajria et al., 2003). *Central* and *hierarchical* graphic organizers are structured around one central topic (i.e., an idea or a concept) and are typically

Graphic organizers help students make comparisons, clarify relationships, formulate inferences, and draw conclusions. What types of graphic organizers help you learn?

Dehydration Synthesis and Hydrolysis

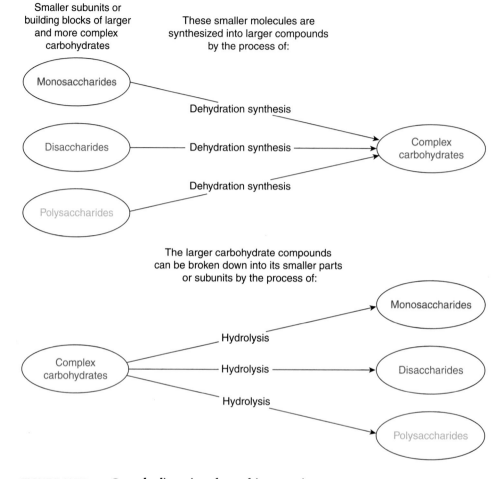

FIGURE 11.7A   Sample directional graphic organizers

Source: From *Concept Mapping: Improving Content Area Comprehension for Secondary Students with Learning Disabilities*, by M. Gajria, T. Mullane, E. R. Sharp, and T. Heim, April 2003, Presentation at the annual meeting of the Council for Exceptional Children, Seattle. Copyright 2003 by The Council for Exceptional Children. Reprinted with permission.

used to depict concepts and the elements that describe them. In a central graphic organizer, important information related to the central topic is depicted visually as radiating outward from the central topic. In a hierarchical graphic organizer, supporting information is presented in order of importance, with items being supraordinate to other items. *Directional* graphic organizers present information in a sequence and are often used to depict cause-effect information or content that can be presented in a timeline or flowchart. Directional organizers are often used to present processes, procedures, sequences of events, and timelines (see Figure 11.7A). *Comparative* graphic organizers are used to compare two or more concepts and typically include information presented in a matrix, Venn Diagram, or chart (see Figure 11.7B).

You can develop graphic organizers by doing the following:

- Preview and analyze the curriculum area or textbook to identify key information, concepts, and terms.

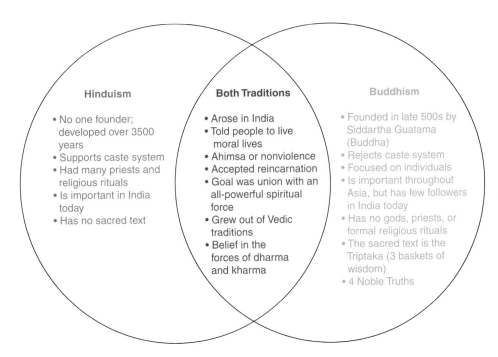

FIGURE 11.7B   Sample comparative graphic organizers (continued)

- Construct an outline of the main information. Arrange the information, concepts, and terms students are to learn based on their interrelationships.
- Select a graphic organizer format that coincides with the organization of the information to be learned.
- Label important ideas and concepts clearly.
- Delete information you want students to contribute, as well as information that is distracting or irrelevant.
- Include additional terms that are important for students to know.
- Add graphics to motivate students and promote mastery of the information.
- Assess the graphic organizer for completeness, clarity, and organization.
- Prepare three versions of the graphic organizer: a completed version, a semicompleted version, and a blank version. Use the blank version with students who write quickly. Use the semicompleted version with students who have some difficulty copying and organizing information. Use the completed version with students who have significant difficulties copying and organizing information.
- Introduce the graphic organizer to the students.
- Include additional information relevant to the overview (Baxendell, 2003; DiCecco & Gleason, 2002; Dye, 2000; Gajria et al. 2003).

As students become accustomed to using graphic organizers, they can be encouraged to develop their own. Scanlon, Deshler, and Schumaker (1996) developed a learning strategy called ORDER to help students develop their own graphic organizers.

Semantic Webs.   *Semantic webs,* also called *semantic maps,* like graphic organizers, provide a visual depiction of important points and concepts, as well as the relationships between these points and concepts, and can be developed by students (Barton et al., 2002).

Resource

Baxendell (2003) and Gajria et al. (2003) offer examples and guidelines for creating graphic organizers

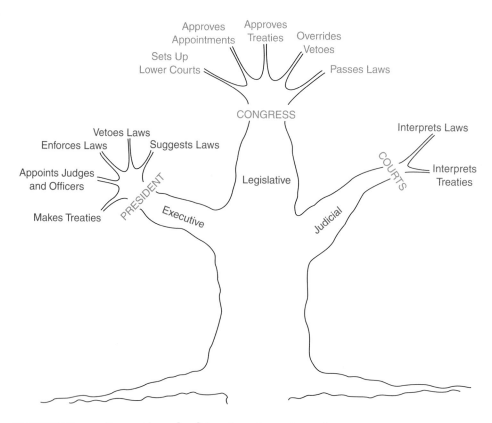

FIGURE 11.8   **Semantic web of the three branches of government**

Resource

Boyle and Yeager (1997) describe TRAVEL, a learning strategy that helps students generate their own semantic webs.

Semantic webs can be used to introduce, review, and clarify new and previously learned material. A semantic web includes a key word or phrase that relates to the main point of the content, which serves as the focal point of the web; web strands, which are subordinate ideas related to the key word; strand supports, which include details and information related to each web strand; and strand ties, which establish the interrelationships between different strands. Semantic webs may take other shapes as well (see Figure 11.8).

Anticipation Guides.   The *anticipation guide* is an advance organizer that introduces students to new content by having them respond to several teacher-generated oral or written statements or questions concerning the material (Barton et al., 2002). For example, an anticipation guide might include a series of true/false statements that the students answer and discuss before reading a chapter in the textbook (see Figure 11.9). The steps in constructing anticipation guides are as follows:

1. Analyze the text and determine the main points.
2. Convert main points into short, declarative, concrete statements that students can understand.
3. Present statements to students in a way that leads to anticipation and prediction.
4. Have students discuss their predictions and responses to the statements.
5. Discuss the students' reading of the text selection, and then compare and evaluate their responses with the information presented in the text.

REFLECTING ON PROFESSIONAL PRACTICES

Using Semantic Webs

Mr. Tejada collects and grades students' notebooks at the end of each unit of instruction. He notices that his students are handing in notebooks that lack many pieces of information from classes and textbook readings that he thinks are important. As a result, many students are having difficulty in class and are doing poorly on tests.

To help his students identify and retain information, Mr. Tejada decides to use semantic webs to help them review and organize material relating to the unit they are studying on the federal government.

After asking students to read about the roles of the three branches of government, Mr. Tejada writes the key words *executive, legislative,* and *judicial* on the board. He asks students what these words mean and then asks them to brainstorm related ideas and concepts. As students present their ideas, Mr. Tejada asks the class to determine whether the ideas are new and relevant and should be listed on the board or whether they are not relevant or overlap with the ideas already on the board. He then asks the students to work in groups to examine the relationships between the concepts listed on the board and group the related concepts together under the key words.

After reviewing their groupings, Mr. Tejada and his students create a tree-like semantic web that contains the

branches of the government and the duties performed by the president, Congress, and the courts (see Figure 11.8). The students then review the web, add new material based on texts and classroom discussions, and copy it in their notebooks. To further reinforce the concept of checks and balances, Mr. Tejada draws a picture of a seesaw balanced by an equal number of checkmarks on both sides. Before the unit ends, Mr. Tejada collects students' notebooks and is pleased to see that they have copied the webs and pictorials. He also is pleased when he sees that students' knowledge of the material has improved.

- Why did Mr. Tejada decide to use semantic webs?
- How do content enhancements like semantic webs benefit students?
- What steps and strategies did Mr. Tejada follow in using semantic webs?
- What other strategies could he use to help his students learn the material?

To answer these questions online and share your responses with others, go to the Reflection module in Chapter 11 of the Companion Website.

FIGURE 11.9

Anticipation guide on energy resources

Working as a group, read the statements and place a *T* next to those that are true and an *F* next to those that are false. Be prepared to explain the reasons for rating a statement as true or false.

- ◇ Ninety-five percent of the energy needs of the United States are provided by fossil fuels.
- ◇ Spacecraft and many homes use solar energy.
- ◇ Hydroelectric power has no negative effects on the environment.
- ◇ Fossil fuels produce more energy per gram than nonfossil fuels.
- ◇ Before the radiation decays, radioactive wastes must be stored for a thousand years.

Concept-Teaching Routines. Many science and social studies concepts can be taught using a *concept-teaching routine,* which is a set of instructional strategies for fostering student learning of content-based information and concepts (Deshler et al., 2001a; Walther-Thomas & Brownell, 2000). The *concept mastery routine* involves presenting new concepts in the form of a concept diagram containing the relevant characteristics of the concept. The concept diagram can also be used to help students review for tests. A sample concept diagram is presented in Figure 11.10. Once concepts are mastered, teachers can use a *concept comparison routine,* or *concept anchoring routine.* In the

Resource

Deshler et al. (2001b) offer guidelines for implementing Concept Anchoring Routines

Concept Name:	Democracy

Definitions:

> A democracy is a form of government in which the people hold the ruling power, citizens are equal, the individual is valued, and compromise is necessary.

Characteristics Present in the Concept:

Always	Sometimes	Never
form of government	direct representation	king rules
people hold power	indirect representation	dictator rules
individual is valued		
citizens equal		
compromise necessary		

Example:

(Germany today)

(Athens (about 500 B.C.))

Nonexample:

(Germany under Hitler)

(Macedonia (under Alexander))

FIGURE 11.10   Sample concept diagram

Source: From "Effectiveness of a Concept Teaching Routine in Enhancing the Performance of LD Students in Secondary-Level Mainstream Classes," by J. Bulgren, J. B. Schumaker, and D. Deshler, 1988, *Learning Disability Quarterly, 11*. Copyright 1988. Reprinted by permission.

Resource

Scanlon (2002) developed the PROVE strategy, a learning strategy that helps students name, verify, and express their knowledge of concepts.

Reflective

Develop a graphic organizer, concept-teaching routine, anticipation guide, or semantic web for the content presented in this chapter.

concept comparison routine, the mastered concept is explored more fully by comparing examples from the same category (e.g., comparing two types of diseases). Mastered concepts are used to teach students new and difficult concepts through use of a *concept anchoring routine*, where characteristics that are shared by the known and new concepts are listed and examined in a table (Deshler et al., 2001b).

Use a Variety of Instructional Approaches and Practices

You can differentiate social studies and science instruction by using a variety of approaches and practices such as the ones described below. Again, it is important to remember that you can use these approaches and practices to teach mathematics and other content areas.

IDEAS FOR IMPLEMENTATION

Ensuring Safety in Laboratory Settings

Ms. Castro's chemistry class included several students with sensory and physical disabilities. She was concerned about their ability to use and learn from the frequent laboratory experiments that students performed. Her principal and several of her colleagues suggested that she purchase specialized equipment such as spoons with sliding covers, glassware with raised letters and numbers, lightweight fire extinguishers, and devices with visual and auditory on/off indicators and warnings. They also recommended that she label important areas, material, and substances in the room and assign students to work with lab partners.

Here are some other strategies you can use to ensure safety in the laboratory:

• Post, discuss, and distribute to students the rules, safety considerations, and evacuation procedures before beginning an experiment.

• Make sure that students wear safety equipment such as splashproof goggles and rubber gloves and aprons.

• Use print and sandpaper labeling for hazardous materials, and make sure that combustible gas supplies contain odorants.

• Provide adapted laboratory stations for students who need them. An adapted station may include a work surface 30 inches from the floor, accessible and modified equipment controls, appropriate space for clearance, and wider-than-usual aisles.

• Equip the laboratory with adjustable-height storage units, pull-out or drop-leaf shelves and countertops, single-action lever controls and blade-type handles, and flexible connections to water, electrical, and gas lines.

Note: Chiappetta & Koballa (2002); Kucera (1993).

Use Activities-Oriented Approaches

Instead of a content-oriented approach to teaching science and social studies, you can use an activities-oriented approach. This approach uses discovery and inquiry to help students develop their knowledge and understanding of science and social studies based on their experiences (Maroney, Finson, Beaver, & Jensen, 2003; Palincsar et al., 2002). When using an activities-oriented approach, offer students a variety of active educational experiences that provide engagement, exploration, development, and extension. The learning cycle begins with the *engagement phase*, in which real-life activities, problems, and questions are used to motivate students to learn about the topic and to assess their prior knowledge. Students explore the content and phenomena by manipulating materials and start to address the questions presented in the engagement phase. For example, as part of a unit on simple machines, you can ask students to identify simple machines that they use and have them take apart broken household appliances. During the *exploration phase*, students formulate new ideas and questions to be developed in the later phases. For example, you can have students explore how the household appliances work, identify their components, and develop hypotheses about how to fix them. In the *development phase*, students investigate and add to their understanding by gathering more information and drawing conclusions about the concepts, the phenomena, and the questions previously generated. Using our example, students can access the Internet to learn more about the appliances and to draw conclusions about how they work. The final stage, *extension*, gives students opportunities to apply their learning to new and different situations as well as to their own experiences. They also often report their learning to others. In our example, students can hypothesize how other machines and household appliances that they use work, and report on their findings to their classmates.

Resources

Maroney et al. (2003) offer guidelines for using an inquiry approach in inclusive science classrooms

cd-rom

Set Your Sites

For more information on teaching mathematics and science, and standards for teaching science, go to the Web Links module in Chapter 11 of the Companion Website.

An effective activities-oriented approach provides students with hands-on and multisensory experiences and materials (Cawley, Foley, & Miller, 2003). Hands-on learning offers students concrete experiences that establish a foundation for learning abstract concepts. Hands-on and multisensory activities also allow students to explore and discover content. In addition, these activities reduce the language and literacy demands that may interfere with the learning of students with disabilities and students who are learning a second language (Westby & Torres-Velazquez, 2000). For example, students can learn about electricity by building electric circuits and can become familiar with the geography of a region by making a topographical map out of papier-mâché. **To view an example of students using hands-on materials to learn about abstract concepts, go to Case 4: Support Participation on the CD-ROM and click on the Involve Students video clip. How does working on hands-on activities foster student motivation and learning?**

Organize Instruction Around Big Ideas and Interdisciplinary Themes

Activities-oriented approaches focus on depth of understanding rather than broad coverage of science and social studies. Kameenui and Carnine (1998) suggest that you organize science and social studies around *big ideas:* critical topics, concepts, issues, problems, experiences, or principles that assist students in organizing, interrelating, and applying information so that meaningful links can be established between the content and students' lives (Voltz, Brazil, & Ford, 2001). Organizing instruction through big ideas also gives students a framework for learning "smaller ideas" such as facts related to the broader concepts and big ideas being studied (Stein et al., 2001).

Student learning can also be promoted by linking instruction to important broad, common, and interdisciplinary themes that can accommodate the diverse learning abilities of students (Findley, 2002; Gardner et al., 2003). Interdisciplinary themes can link the various science and social studies disciplines, as well as relate them to other subject areas. For example, an integrated unit on the Incas of Peru could include a social studies investigation of the geographical area affected by the Incas, Incan cultural traditions, and Incan religious beliefs. In science class, students could study the scientific, medical, and agricultural methods of the Incas. In math, they could learn about the Incan system of record-keeping based on different colored cords and knots. For art, students could learn about cultural symbols associated with the Incas and produce art forms that reflect these traditional symbols. Throughout this unit, students can read and write about the Incas.

Resource

Gardner et al. (2003) provide guidelines and examples related to the use of technology to enhance interdisciplinary thematic units.

Use Problem-Based Learning to Relate Instruction to Students' Lives and General Societal Issues

Relating science and social studies to practical, recreational, and cultural events and problems that are familiar and relevant to students can promote learning, increase motivation, and help students learn to value science and social studies (Chiappetta & Koballa, 2002; Maxim, 2003). In using problem-based learning, you present students with information, issues, and problems related to real-life situations and discuss with students the relevance of these problems to their lives, as well as the situations in which this content can be applied (Appelget, Matthews, Hildreth, & Daniel, 2002; Ferretti, MacArthur, & Okolo, 2002). For example, students can investigate important social problems and issues such as immigration, discrimination, water supply, weather, pollution, nutrition, and solar energy.

Relating science, social studies and mathematics to practical problems that are relevant to students can promote learning and motivation. What are some practical problems that may interest your students in science, social studies, and mathematics?

Science and social studies can also be connected to students' cultural backgrounds and communities (Raborn & Daniel, 1999; Westby & Torres-Velasquez, 2000). Learning activities and instructional materials that explore the different cultural and historical origins of science, discuss scientific solutions and practices developed and used in all parts of the world, highlight the achievements of scientists and historians from various cultural and language backgrounds, and present a range of culturally diverse practical applications of science can be used to help students understand the multicultural aspects of science. Connections to students' lives and cultures also can be established by having students perform activities that address community problems; use artifacts, buildings, geographical sites, museums, and other resources in the students' community; and interview community members to illustrate and reinforce concepts, issues, phenomena, and events (Lee & Fradd, 1998; Smith, 2002).

Instruction also can foster the development of *social responsibility,* an interest in and concern for the well-being of others and the environment (Martorella & Beal, 2002). Social responsibility encourages the development of social consciousness, which helps students explore their hopes for the future and the impact of their actions on others. A curriculum to teach students social responsibility can help them develop an understanding of our social and ecological interdependence, a sense of what it means to be part of a community, a sense of history, and basic social skills including communication, conflict management, and perspective-taking. Social responsibility can be taught throughout the curriculum by examining real-word issues. For example, mathematics classes can explore the impact of math (such as statistics) on the political process; science classes can address the relationship between science, technology, and the world; and social studies classes can examine racism in society.

Use Effective Questioning Techniques

Another way to foster and direct student learning is by using effective questioning strategies that guide learning and promote critical thinking and reflection (Posamentier

Resource

Smith (2002) presents information and resources on learning activities that address community- and school-based needs.

Resource

Appelget et al. (2002) offer guidelines for teaching the history of science.

Set Your Sites

For more information on problem-based learning, go to the Web Links module in Chapter 11 of the Companion Website.

Resource

Martorella and Beal (2002) present guidelines and activities for helping students develop social responsibility.

Set Your Sites

For more information on integrating social responsibility into the curriculum, go to the Web Links module in Chapter 11 of the Companion Website.

& Stepelman, 2002). (See chapter 9 for a discussion of effective questioning techniques.) Effective questioning also can help you assess whether your students are learning the material and identify misconceptions students have that need to be addressed. Maxim (2003) identified three types of questions teachers typically ask: literal, inferential, and critical. *Literal questions* focus on content derived from class presentations and instructional materials and ask students to recall, name, list, or describe information presented. *Inferential questions* require students to provide answers that are not explicitly stated in the presentation and instructional materials and ask students to analyze, compare, and synthesize information presented. *Critical questions* ask students to provide personal judgments and reactions to the content and ask students to apply and evaluate the information presented to other situations. **To view an example of a teacher using questioning, go to Case 2: Classroom Climate on the CD-ROM and click on the Promoting Acceptance video clip. What types of questions does the teacher use to guide student learning?**

You also can use questions to differentiate your instruction and motivate students (Kellough & Kellough, 2003). For example, you can use literal questions to help students who are in the process of learning new material and employ inferential questions to enrich the learning of students who have already demonstrated mastery of the material (Caine, Caine, & McClintic, 2002).

cd-rom

Reflective

Select a content area and create literal, inferential, and critical questions. Share and critique your questions with a partner.

Use Specially Designed Programs and Curricula

Specially designed programs and curricula are available and can be integrated into existing science and social studies instructional programs (Cawley, Foley, & Miller, 2003). Educators have developed activity-based science programs for students with visual disabilities called *Science Activities for the Visually Impaired (SAVI)* and programs for students with physical disabilities called *Science Enrichment Learning for Learners with Physical Handicaps (SELPH)*. These programs use a laboratory approach to teaching science that stresses observations, manipulation of materials, and the development of scientific language. *Project MAVIS (Materials Adaptations for Visually Impaired Students)* has adapted social studies materials for students with visual and physical disabilities, but these materials also can be used with other students. Other laboratory-based curriculum models and materials include *Science for All Children (SAC)* (Cawley, Foley, & Miller, 2003) and *Applications in Biology/Chemistry (ABC)* (Prescott, Rinard, Cockerill, & Baker, 1996).

Set Your Sites

For more information on specially designed programs and curricula, go to the Web Links module in Chapter 11 of the Companion Website.

Improve Students' Memory

Because content-oriented approaches to teaching science and social studies require students to retain large amounts of information and many new terms, training in developing memory skills can help students succeed in inclusive settings (Martorella & Beal, 2002). You can improve your students' memory by providing them with access to:

- visual representations of the words or content to be remembered.
- conceptual representations of what the words or content to be remembered does.
- linguistic representations of the sounds of the words and content to be remembered as well as how they fit into sentences.

You can introduce new words and content by creating a memorable event or physically presenting the important attributes of the material to be remembered (Alber & Foil, 2003).

A variety of methods and mnemonic devices can be used to help students remember content, including pictures, acronyms, acrostics, and rhymes (Bulgren, Deshler, & Schumaker, 1997). Whereas acronyms and first-letter mnemonics foster memory by

IDEAS FOR IMPLEMENTATION

Promoting Students' Memory

Mr. Contreras was very surprised by the difficulty many students had in memorizing information and decided to use a variety of strategies to help his students remember it. During science instruction, he taught students to use a first-letter mnemonic strategy to memorize the colors of the spectrum. By using the first letter of each word in the list, students created a word, name, or sentence that helped them remember and retrieve information. One group of students learned about the mnemonic "Roy G Biv," a name composed of the first letter of each color of the light spectrum. Another time, when students were having trouble memorizing the names of the states in the United States, he taught them to categorize states according to geographic location and then memorize each geographic cluster.

Here are some other strategies you can use to improve students' memory:

- Have students work with partners to rehearse critical information and check each other's memory of the material.

- Give students opportunities to review small amounts of material frequently rather than trying to memorize large amounts of information at once.
- Encourage students to use mnemonics by teaching them to use such learning strategies as the FIRST-Letter Mnemonic Strategy and LISTS (Nagel, Schumaker, & Deshler, 1986) and the Paired Associates Strategy (Bulgren, Schumaker, & Deshler [in Bulgren, Hock, Schumaker, & Deshler, 1995]).
- Teach students to use mental visualization, in which they create a mental picture of the content. For example, to remember the definition of *stalactite*, they can visualize a stalactite mentally.
- Have students create vocabulary picture cards—index cards with a word, its definition and a picture depicting it (Foil & Alber, 2002).

creating a meaningful word or phrase using the first letter of the words or phrases to be remembered, acrostics trigger recall by employing a sentence based on the first letter of the words to be memorized (Kleinheksel & Summy, 2003). For example, your students can learn the acronym HOMES to prompt their memory of the Great Lakes, and use the acrostic **M**y **V**ery **E**ducated **M**om **J**ust **S**olved **U**s **N**ine **P**uzzles to remember the planets in their order from the sun.

You can plan your lessons so that they foster student memory of new content (King-Friedrichs, 2001; Prigge, 2002). You can facilitate your students' memory of new content by linking it to material your students already know, and making it personally relevant to them. You also can use creative repetition to have your students practice their new learning by using a variety of motivating instructional formats (Foil & Alber, 2002). Additionally, structure your lessons so that you present new material at the beginning of your lessons and review it at the end of your lessons.

Key Word Method. An effective strategy for helping students remember science and social studies vocabulary is the *key word* method (Uberti, Scruggs, & Mastropieri, 2003). This mnemonic device associates the new vocabulary word with a word that sounds similar to an easy-to-remember illustration. The steps in the key word method are:

1. *Recoding.* The new vocabulary word is recoded into a key word that sounds similar and is familiar to the student. The key word should be one that students can easily picture. For example, the key word for the word *Sauro* might be a *saw*.
2. *Relating.* An *interactive illustration*—a mental picture or drawing of the key word interacting with the definition of the vocabulary word—is created. A

Resource

Bulgren et al. (1997) have developed a recall enhancement routine that can help you plan and use mnemonic strategies to improve your students' memory.

Resource

Several learning strategies have been developed to help students learn to use the key word method, including LINCS and IT FITS (Foil & Alber, 2002; Hughes, 1996; Lebzelter & Nowacek, 1999).

sentence describing the interaction also is developed. For example, the definition of *Sauro* and the key word *saw* can be depicted using the sentence "A lizard is sawing."

3. *Retrieving.* On hearing the new vocabulary word, students retrieve its definition by thinking of the key word, creating the interactive illustration and/or its corresponding sentence, and stating the definition.

Use Instructional Technology and Multimedia

As we discussed in chapter 8, instructional technology and multimedia can enhance science and social studies instruction and play a key role in activities-based approaches (Dynneson et al., 2003). Instructional technology, virtual reality, and multimedia can be used to introduce, review, and apply science and social studies concepts. Using these devices, students can experience events, places, and phenomena such as scientific experiments, geographic locations around the world, or historical events. For example, multimedia applications allow students to perform complicated scientific experiments, such as those involving chemical reactions, on the computer. In addition to providing an opportunity to obtain and observe unique aspects of the content, these instructional delivery systems can motivate students and stimulate their curiosity. **To view examples of teachers and students using the Internet to provide students with motivating learning experiences, go to Case 4: Support Participation on the CD-ROM and click on the Multiple Goals, Self-Advocacy, Recognize Efforts, and Involve Students video clips. How can the Internet differentiate mathematics, science, and social studies instruction and motivate students?**

cd-rom

Through the Internet and telecommunications, students can learn science and social studies by being linked to data and educational resources, problem-solving experiences, and interactions with students and professionals around the world (Chiappetta & Koballa, 2002). For example, the National Geographic Society and the Technical Education Research Center sponsor the Kids Network (www.nrel.gov), an international telecommunications-based curriculum that teaches science and geography to elementary and middle school students.

Set Your Sites

For more information on teaching social studies, go to the Web Links module in Chapter 11 of the Companion Website.

Set Your Sites

For more information on teaching history, go to the Web Links module in Chapter 11 of the Companion Website.

Take Students on Field Trips

Field trips also can make learning more meaningful and real for students and connect learning to community-based situations. In particular, visits to historical and science museums, as well as ecological and historical sites, allow students to experience what they hear and read about (Maxim, 2003; Tam, Nassivera, Rousseau, & Vreeland, 2000). Many museums and sites offer students hands-on experiences that promote learning and provide information as well as after-school learning opportunities for students (McLeod & Kilpatrick, 2001). Museums also can provide students with access to authentic and primary sources, artifacts, documents, and photos, which can add to the excitement of learning. To help you and your students benefit from field trips, many museums and sites provide teacher training programs, model curricula and teaching strategies, special tours, exhibits, and materials for school groups, as well as traveling exhibits that prepare students for and build upon experiences at the museum. **To view an example of a teacher using a field trip to support student learning, go to Case 4: Support Participation on the CD-ROM and click on the Multiple Goals video clip. How could this field trip motivate students and support their learning?**

Resource

Tanner (2001) provides suggestions for using outdoor environments to foster student learning.

Resource

Maxim (2003) and Martin and Seevers (2003) provide guidelines, resources, and a field trip checklist to assist educators in planning and taking field trips.

cd-rom

USING TECHNOLOGY TO PROMOTE INCLUSION

Making Mathematics, Science, and Social Studies Instruction Accessible to All Students

Technological advances are resulting in the development of hardware and software that can help you differentiate mathematics, science, and social studies instruction. One such technological innovation are digital textbooks or electronic textbooks (e-textbooks), which are electronic versions of textbooks that can be read aloud to students via computers or handheld devices (Boone & Higgins, 2003; Cavanaugh, 2002; Pisha & Coyne, 2001). E-textbooks have several advantages over traditional textbooks: Because digital texts can be read to students via text-to-speech programs, they help students to access textbook content. Other features that help students identify key topics and text structures (e.g., variable text size, highlighting, multicolored headings, bookmarking) also assist them in accessing content and taking notes. E-textbooks also help students understand the material by allowing them to use on-line resources such as abridged editions, graphics, outlines, pictures, audio, video, and strategic learning prompts. For example, e-textbooks can contain prompts that are strategically placed throughout the text to motivate students and encourage them to engage in specific learning behaviors or strategies. E-textbooks also have built-in dictionaries and glossaries, and allow students to conduct word searches to help them understand unfamiliar concepts and vocabulary (see Figure 11.11). E-textbooks also have capabilities that allow students to take notes, and connect to and download information from the Internet and other electronic sources. Additional information about e-books is presented in chapter 8.

You also can obtain digital and analog recordings of textbooks and other published materials for students with visual and reading disabilities by contacting the National Library Service for the Blind and Physically Handicapped (www.lcweb.loc.gov/nls), the American Printing House for the Blind (www.aph.org), or Recordings for the Blind and Dyslexic (www.rfbd.org). When digital recordings are accessed via CD-ROM playback technology, they allow students to use them in much the same manner as they might use printed materials (Boyle et al., 2002). For example, students can bookmark important material, vary the rate at which the text is read, and move easily by chapter, page, heading and subsections. Through Web-Braille, a new service of the National Library Service, digital Braille books can be accessed from home via a computer and a Braille embosser or refreshable Braille

display. Contact these organizations as early as possible so that the recordings are available when needed.

Here are some other ways you can use technology to create inclusive classrooms that support student learning in the areas of mathematics, science, and social studies:

- Take your students on "virtual field trips" to various museums and scientific, mathematical and historical sites via the Internet (Chiappetta & Koballa, 2002; Gardner et al., 2003). For example, the American Museum of Natural History National Center for Science Literacy, Education and Technology offers a website (www.amnh.org/nationalcenter) with a variety of online activities that make scientists and exhibitions available to schools and families.
- Provide students with access to primary sources, electronic libraries, and journals through use of the Internet, DVDs, and CD-ROMs (Boone & Higgins, 2003). For example, the Library of Congress's American Memory Web Site (www.memory.loc.gov) provides teachers and students with access to and tips for using a wide range of primary sources.
- Teach students to use multimedia programs to access references and resources and obtain information about specific topics (Gardner et al., 2003; Kellough & Kellough, 2003).
- Use the Internet to provide students with opportunities to perform learning activities related to mathematics, science, and social studies (Gardner et al., 2003). For example, Try Science (www.tryscience.org) offers students opportunities to perform scientific experiments online, and Interactive Mathematics on the Internet (www.wims.unice.fr) provides interactive mathematics-based online activities for students.
- Use problem-solving and simulation software programs that ask students to respond in varied ways to authentic and multidimensional dilemmas and situations (Armstrong & Savage, 2002; Maxim, 2003). For example, students can perform software simulations of various types of science experiments (Chiappetta & Koballa, 2002) and manipulate objects to solve math problems.

(continued)

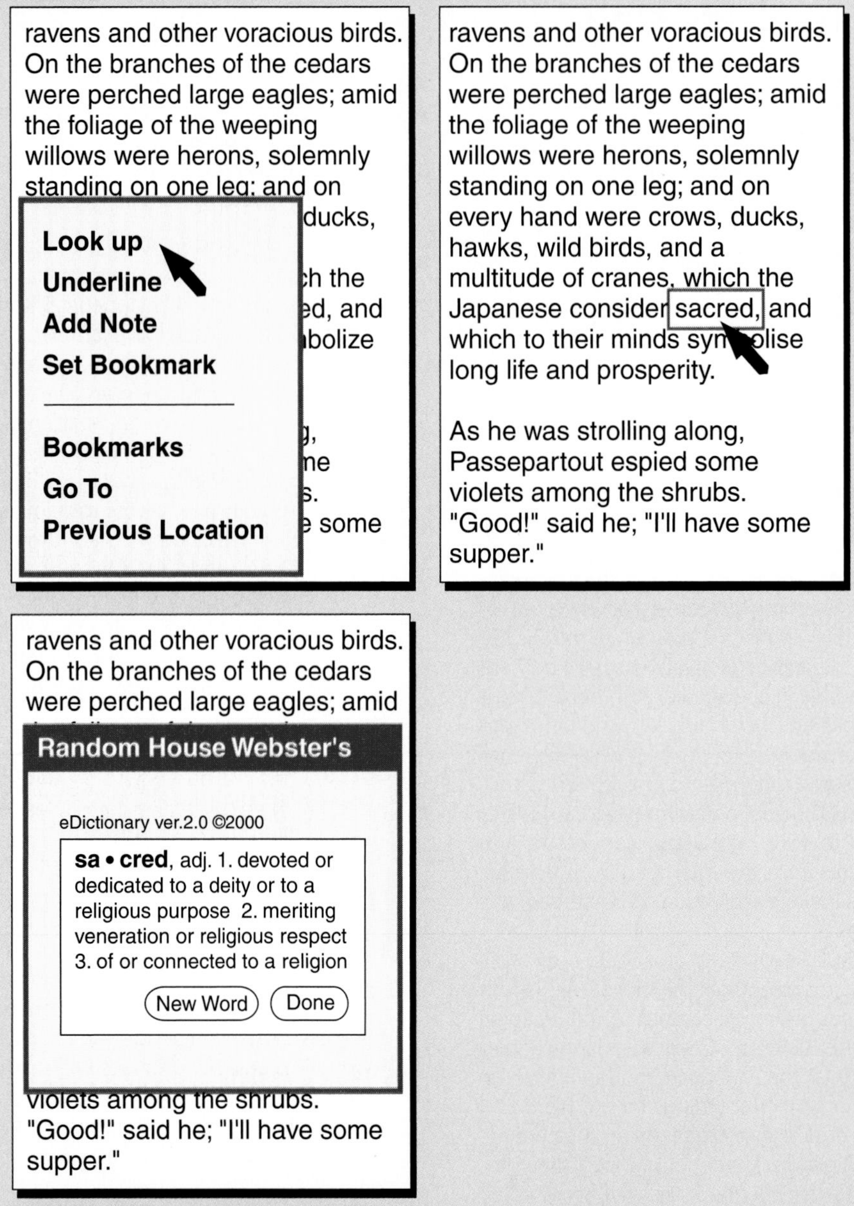

ravens and other voracious birds. On the branches of the cedars were perched large eagles; amid the foliage of the weeping willows were herons, solemnly standing on one leg; and on

Look up
Underline
Add Note
Set Bookmark

Bookmarks
Go To
Previous Location

...ducks,

...h the ...ed, and ...bolize

...ng, ...ne ...s.

...e some

ravens and other voracious birds. On the branches of the cedars were perched large eagles; amid the foliage of the weeping willows were herons, solemnly standing on one leg; and on every hand were crows, ducks, hawks, wild birds, and a multitude of cranes, which the Japanese consider sacred, and which to their minds symbolise long life and prosperity.

As he was strolling along, Passepartout espied some violets among the shrubs. "Good!" said he; "I'll have some supper."

ravens and other voracious birds. On the branches of the cedars were perched large eagles; amid

Random House Webster's

eDictionary ver.2.0 ©2000

sa • cred, adj. 1. devoted or dedicated to a deity or to a religious purpose 2. meriting veneration or religious respect 3. of or connected to a religion

(New Word) (Done)

violets among the shrubs. "Good!" said he; "I'll have some supper."

An online companion dictionary provides quick access to new or difficult vocabulary with immediacy and within a meaningful context. The user chooses the "Look up" function, then clicks on an unfamiliar word. The appropriate entry from a built-in dictionary is shown in a pop-up window. Text is from Jules Verne's *Around the World in Eighty Days*, which is no longer under copyright. Facsimile screens are based on the RCA eBook layout.

FIGURE 11.11   **Online electronic-textbook dictionary**

Source: From "Reading, Writing, and Publishing Digital Text," by R. Boone and K. Higgins, 2003, *Remedial and Special Education, 24,* pp. 132–140. Copyright 2003 by PRO-ED, Inc. Reprinted with permission.

- Integrate into instructional activities websites that offer access to information presented via Web Cameras (Web Cams) that allow students to view live events (Vitek, 2003). For example, you can use Web Cams to have students observe wildlife and weather conditions. You can identify potential Web Cams by visiting Discovery Cams from the Discovery Channel (www.dsc.discovery.com/cams/cams.html), and Web Cam Directory (www.leonardsworlds.com/webcam_directories/webcam_directories.htm). Prior to using WebCam sites, check to make sure that they are appropriate for your students.
- Incorporate streaming video and audio available via the Internet into lessons. For example, you can search for and obtain relevant streaming video by accessing such websites as UnitedStreaming (www.unitedstreaming.com).
- Use the Internet to locate alternate easy-to-read text on various content areas and to supplement textbook information (Brozo & Hargis, 2003).
- Use software such as MathType 5.0 to convert calculations, symbols, and unusual alignments in complex mathematical and scientific text documents into electronic files that can be more easily accessed by students using technology.
- Use software programs for designing a range of graphic organizers such as Inspiration, Semantic Mapper, and Semnet (Gardner et al., 2003; Raskind & Higgins, 1998).
- Provide your students with hypermedia-developed study guides and computer-based study strategies to take notes in class and from textbooks (Anderson-Inman, Knox-Quinn, & Horney 1996; Higgins, Boone, & Lovitt, 1996).
- Use specialized technology to support the learning of students with sensory disabilities, and second language learners. For example, Kapperman and Sticken (2002) developed an interactive software tutorial that employs speech and tactile features to help students with visual impairments learn the Nemeth Code of Braille mathematics. In addition, Andrews and Jordan (2000) created *Meet the Math Wiz*, a series of CD-ROMs that are presented in American Sign Language or Spanish. The series uses multicultural names, themes, and stories to teach word problems of varying levels of difficulty, and includes animated hints and a listing of mathematics terminology that is linked to ASL signs and a dictionary.

It is important for all students to have role models who have been successful in math and science. Do your students have diverse role models?

IDEAS FOR IMPLEMENTATION

Promoting Math and Science Education for All Students

The teachers in the Madison School were shocked and disappointed at the small number of female students who had enrolled in their after-school science and math program. Unsure of the reasons for the low turnout, the teachers spoke to several of their female students, who said that they didn't sign up for the program because "Science is for nerds" "My friends will think I'm weird," and "I'm not good at science and math." Struck by these comments, the teachers decided to revamp their math and science teaching so that it appealed to *all students*. First, they shared studies with students that showed the relationship among gender and math, science, and technology. They also had their students analyze textbooks, instructional materials, and activities that presented females in nonstereotypic science and math roles. They then developed and taught an interdisciplinary unit about scientists and mathematicians who are female, from culturally and linguistically diverse backgrounds, or who have disabilities. They invited several local scientists and mathematicians from these diverse groups to speak about their jobs and training. As a culminating activity, students worked in cooperative learning groups to study why females, individuals from diverse backgrounds, and people with disabilities are underrepresented in science and mathematics.

Here are some other strategies you can use to promote math and science education for *all students:*

- Model and encourage *all students* to have a positive attitude toward math and science and take intellectual risks.
- Establish a learning environment that fosters high expectations for *all students* and allows them to be active, inquiring participants.

- Provide students with a historical and multicultural understanding of math and science, and infuse math and science into other subject areas.
- Present problems and situations so that *all students* are depicted in active, nonstereotypical ways, and avoid using statements, materials, and pictorials that suggest that certain groups of students are not skilled in math and science.
- Emphasize the problem-solving aspects of math and science rather than speed and competition, and encourage students to use a variety of verbal and visual problem-solving techniques.
- Teach math and science using real-life situations, hands-on materials, cooperative learning groups, projects, and games. For example, as part of a unit on pollution, students can work in cooperative learning groups to study water, air, and noise pollution in their own communities.
- Communicate and demonstrate to students, their families, and other teachers the importance of seeking advanced training and pursuing careers in math and science.
- Contact a diverse group of scientists and mathematicians in your community to serve as mentors for your students.
- Assign class and school jobs to *all students* that require them to solve problems and use their math and science skills.

Note: American Association of University Women (2000); Furner & Duffy (2002); Jobe (2003); Nelson & Smith (2001).

Resource

Furner and Duffy (2002) provide guidelines and strategies for identifying and addressing math anxiety that also can extend across content areas.

Address the Needs of Diverse Learners

Female students, students from various cultural and language backgrounds, and students with disabilities are often underrepresented in advanced math and science classes and in careers in these fields. This underrepresentation is often attributed to math/science anxiety, as well as to societal expectations and norms that make it acceptable for these students to ignore or question their abilities in science and math. There also is evidence that teachers treat male and female students differently, encouraging males to achieve in math and science and discouraging females. Therefore, you need to be aware of your behavior, and of societal pressures, so that you can change any such tendencies and create a classroom that encourages math and science competence in *all students*.

Summary

This chapter presented guidelines and strategies for differentiating mathematics, science, and social studies instruction. As you review the questions posed in this chapter, remember the following points.

How Can I Differentiate Mathematics Instruction?

CEC 3, 4, 5, 7, 9, PRAXIS 3, INTASC 1, 2, 3, 4, 5, 6, 7, 9

Use a problem-solving approach that involves students in learning mathematics by experiencing and thinking about meaningful problems related to their lives. In addition, present mathematics appropriately, use teaching aids and a variety of instructional approaches, help students develop their math facts and computation skills, and provide feedback and use assessment to guide future teaching.

How Can I Differentiate Science and Social Studies Instruction?

CEC 3, 4, 5, 7, 9, PRAXIS 3, INTASC 1, 2, 3, 4, 5, 6, 7, 9

Choose textbooks carefully, teach students how to use textbooks and instructional materials, and use study guides, adapted textbooks, a parallel alternative curriculum, and content enhancements. In addition, you can promote students' memory, use activities-oriented approaches, organize instruction around big ideas and interdisciplinary themes, and employ problem-based learning to relate instruction to students' lives and social problems. You also can use effective questioning techniques, instructional technology and multimedia, and specially designed programs and curricula, take students on field trips, and address the needs of diverse learners.

What Would You Do in Today's Diverse Classroom?

Felicia, one of your students, is having difficulty in mathematics, science, and social studies. She is struggling to understand word problems and more abstract concepts. An examination of her science and social studies notebooks indicates that she is not identifying important information from textbooks and lessons.

1. What would you do to help Felicia learn mathematics, science, and social studies?
2. What knowledge, skills, dispositions, resources, and support do you need to help Felicia learn mathematics, science, and social studies?

Using a textbook in a subject area and a grade level you would like to teach, create a point-of-view reading guide, an interactive reading guide, a learning-from-text guide, a textbook activity guide, and a reading road map.

1. Which study guide(s) are easiest for you to develop? Why?
2. Which one(s) would your students like best? Why?
3. Which one(s) would be most effective? Why?
4. What knowledge, skills, dispositions, resources, and support do you need to develop these instructional materials?

To answer these questions online and share your responses with others, go to the Reflection module in Chapter 11 of the Companion Website.

Part IV

Evaluating Individual and Programmatic Progress

You have learned about the fundamentals of inclusion, the need to create a school and classroom environment that supports learning for *all students,* and strategies for differentiating instruction to accommodate *all your students.* With these components in place, it is essential for you to learn how to evaluate the effectiveness of your inclusion program. This evaluation can help you assess the impact of your program on *all* your students, family members, and teachers, including yourself. It also can aid you in documenting the strengths of your inclusion program and pinpointing areas in need of revision.

Part IV, which consists of chapter 12, provides a framework and specific strategies and resources for evaluating inclusion programs. Specifically, it presents guidelines for determining whether your inclusion program is resulting in positive educational, social, behavioral, and self-concept outcomes for *all your students.* It also provides guidelines for grading your students and techniques for examining students', as well as family members' and educators,' perceptions of and experiences with inclusion that can help you assess your students' progress and evaluate various programmatic components of your inclusion program.

Chapter 12

Evaluating Student Progress and the Effectiveness of Your Inclusion Program

The Madison School District

For several years, the Madison School District had implemented inclusion programs in all their schools. Although things seemed to be going well, the district was now faced with the question of whether their inclusion programs were benefiting their students. It first came up at a meeting with the students' families. Some families of students without disabilities expressed concerns about whether the needs of the students with disabilities were interfering with the education of other students. A few of the families of students with disabilities also were worried about their children being ridiculed by others and about losing individualized services. As a result, the school board asked the superintendent of schools to provide data on the program and justify the money being spent on the program.

The superintendent created a committee to evaluate the school district's inclusion programs. The committee included a diverse group of students, family members, educators, administrators, and community members. The committee began by identifying ways to examine the impact of the program on students' academic, social, and behavioral performance by reviewing the results of standardized tests, report card grades, and the findings of alternative assessments. They also discussed other data sources including attendance patterns, participation in after-school programs, behavioral referrals, and observations of student interaction patterns. For secondary-level students, they considered such factors as the types of diplomas students received as well as their success in attending college and finding jobs.

The committee also thought the perceptions and experiences of students, educators, and family members should be an important part of the evaluation process. They created interviews and surveys for these different groups designed to identify successful inclusive educational policies as well as issues that needed to be addressed or revised. For example, both educators and family members expressed some concerns about the school district's report card grading policies and made recommendations for improving them.

How can school districts evaluate the effectiveness of their inclusion programs on an ongoing basis? After reading this chapter, you should have the knowledge, skills, and dispositions to answer this as well as the following questions:

★ **How can I evaluate the academic performance of students?**
★ **How can I grade students in inclusive settings?**
★ **How can I evaluate the social and behavioral performance of students?**
★ **How can I measure perceptions of my inclusion program?**
★ **How can I improve the effectiveness of my inclusion program?**

L ike the Madison School District, it is important for you to evaluate the effectiveness of your inclusion program by examining its impact on *all your students*, on yourself and other teachers, and on students' families (see Table 12.1). An evaluation can assess the impact of your inclusion program on your students' academic, social, and behavioral performance (Rafferty, Picitelli, & Boettcher, 2003). It can also allay the concern that the academic and behavioral needs of students with disabilities will require excessive school resources and teacher attention and therefore jeopardize the education of students without disabilities. Information on the perceptions of students, teachers, and family members regarding your inclusion program is also helpful in examining what these groups think about your inclusion program. This information can validate successful programmatic factors and inclusive educational policies that should be continued, as well as pinpoint procedures that need to be revised.

How Can I Evaluate the Academic Performance of Students?

An important goal of inclusion programs is to enhance the academic performance of *all students*. A variety of strategies for examining your program's impact on your students' academic performance are presented next.

Standardized Testing

As we saw in chapters 1 and 2, *all students*, including those with disabilities, are expected to participate in testing programs. Student performance on these standardized statewide tests also can be used to examine the impact of your inclusion program on your students' academic performance. This is done by comparing the scores of students educated in inclusion classes with the scores of their counterparts who are not taught in inclusion classes (Rea, McLaughlin, & Walther-Thomas, 2002). These test scores also can be used to contrast the performance of students with disabilities taught in inclusion classes with the performance of their classmates without disabilities.

Concerns About Standardized Testing

While standardized testing has been used to document students' academic achievement, and identify general programmatic strengths and needs, these tests are often referred to as *high-stakes testing* because important decisions about students' educational programs are made based on their results, including grade-level promotion and graduation (Nichols, 2003; Wasburn-Moses, 2003). As a result students, educators, and families have raised concerns about high-stakes testing and its reliance on one exam as the measure of student learning (Amrein & Berliner, 2003; Neill, 2003). Many students report that standardized testing puts an enormous amount of pressure on them, hinders their motivation and learning, and minimizes the effort that they have put in throughout the school year. Teachers also report concerns about the quality of the tests and the ways they are used. The pressure to judge student learning and teacher effectiveness based on the results of standardized tests can result in educators teaching to the test at the expense of other im-

Reflective

What has been the effect of high-stakes testing on you, your students and their families, and your school district?

TABLE 12.1	**Evaluating inclusion programs**		
	Students	**Educators**	**Families**
	Evaluation Variables	*Evaluation Variables*	*Evaluation Variables*
	• Student's academic, social and behavioral performance	• Student performance measures	• Child performance measures
	• Student's perceptions and experiences	• Perceptions and experiences	• Perceptions and experiences
	• Programmatic factors	• Programmatic factors	• Programmatic factors
		• Cooperative teaching experiences	
	Data Collection Strategies	*Data Collection Strategies*	*Data Collection Strategies*
	• Test scores and participation rates	• Interviews and questionnaires	• Interviews and questionnaires
	• Classroom-based alternatives to standardized testing (e.g., curriculum-based measurement, portfolio assessment, instructional rubrics, dynamic assessment, observations, teacher-made tests, etc.)	• Observations	• Observations
	• Mastery of IEP goals, promotion and graduation rates, and report card grades		
	• Observational, sociometric, and self-concept measures, participation in extracurricular activities, attendance records, and discipline reports, etc.		
	• Post-school outcomes		
	• Interviews and questionnaires		

portant aspects of the curriculum. Family members report that they often do not understand what the tests measure, how to interpret the results, and why their child's test scores differ from their report card grades. To help minimize this confusion, it is important for schools to help families understand and interpret test results and support their children's learning.

The concerns of students, families, and educators can be addressed by using multiple ways to assess student learning, including classroom-based assessment strategies (Popham, 2003), which we will discuss later in this chapter. The usefulness of standardized testing also can be enhanced by educators analyzing the data to identify the content and skills mastered by students as well as changes to the curriculum and instructional strategies that need to be implemented to support student learning (Guskey, 2003; Thurlow, 2002).

Resource

Bernhardt (2003) offers guidelines and questions for collecting and examining data to improve student learning.

Set Your Sites

For more information on the problems associated with standardized testing and on the use of other forms of assessment, go to the Web Links module in Chapter 12 of the Companion Website.

Types of Standardized Tests

Some states have developed performance assessments (Kearns, Kleinert, Clayton, Burdge, & Williams, 1998). However, most statewide and districtwide tests are either norm-referenced or criterion-referenced.

Norm-Referenced Testing. *Norm-referenced tests* provide measures of performance that allow teachers to compare a student's score with the scores of others. Norms are determined and are then used to compare students in terms of such variables as age and grade level. For example, norm-referenced testing may reveal that your inclusion program has improved a student's performance so that he or she is now reading at a fifth-grade level and doing mathematics at a sixth-grade level.

Criterion-Referenced Testing. In contrast to norm-referenced testing, *criterion-referenced testing* compares a student's performance with a specific level of skill mastery. That is, rather than giving the grade level at which students are functioning, criterion-referenced testing demonstrates specific skills mastered and not mastered by the student. For example, the test may show that a student in your inclusion program can now add and subtract decimals and fractions but still needs to learn how to multiply or divide them.

Testing Accommodations for Diverse Learners

Many diverse learners, including students with disabilities, will need accommodations to take part in statewide and local testing, as well as when they take tests in your classroom. *Testing accommodations*, also referred to as *alternative testing techniques*, are adaptations in testing administration, environment, and procedures that allow students to access testing programs and accurately demonstrate their competence, knowledge, and abilities. For students with disabilities, they should be individually selected and implemented so that tests assess students' abilities rather than their disabilities. Accommodations related to high-stakes testing also should be consistent with statewide policies on approved testing accommodations and should be provided under certain testing situations (Goh, 2004; Thurlow, Elliott, & Ysseldyke, 2003).

The testing accommodations needed, which should appear in students' IEPs or Section 504 accommodation plans, are related to students' individual characteristics, abilities, and needs as well as the instructional modifications used to help them learn content (Shriner & DeStefano, 2003). Because testing accommodations should not alter the constructs or content on which tests are based, they also depend on the purpose of the test, the nature of the items, and the regulations that guide the test's administration. For example, it would not be appropriate to provide a reader for students taking tests designed to assess their reading ability. However, it might to appropriate to use a reader for a math test that requires considerable reading. In addition, the accommodations, if used with general education students, should have little effect on their test performance (Tindal, Heath, Hollenbeck, Almond, & Harniss, 1998). After the testing accommodations are used, their effectiveness, usefulness, and fairness should be assessed (Elliott, Kratochwill, & Schulte, 1998; Goh, 2004).

Accommodations typically relate to presentation and response mode formats, and to timing, scheduling and setting alternatives (Goh, 2004; Wasburn-Moses, 2003). Other accommodations are to train students before they take the test, and to use technology-based testing. A discussion of various alternative testing techniques follows.

Presentation of Items and Directions. Alternative testing techniques may include adaptations in the way test questions and directions are presented to students (Helwig & Tindal, 2003). You can help your students to understand test items and directions by:

- clarifying or simplifying the language used.
- repeating directions as needed.
- masking so that sections of assessment pages are isolated.
- formatting the test so that there is only one complete sentence per line.
- providing models and visuals, and written copies of oral directions.
- listing directions in the order in which they should be followed.
- using cues to help students perform well (Elliott et al., 1998).

Reflective

Many states have policies regarding approved accommodations, and what is allowed in one state may not be allowed in other states (Thurlow, House, Scott, & Ysseldyke, 2000). What testing accommodations have been approved for use with your students? What should happen to scores that are based on use of nonapproved accommodations?

Set Your Sites

For an update on legal issues related to assessing students with special needs and other topics discussed in this chapter, go to the Legal Update module in Chapter 12 of the Companion Website.

Resource

Thurlow, Elliott, and Ysseldyke (2003) offer guidelines for including students in assessment systems and Shriner (2000) provides a review of legal guidelines related to the assessment of students with disabilities.

Resource

Goh (2004) provides policies and practices for determining testing accommodations for individual students and reporting assessment results for these students.

Testing accommodations include changes in the manner in which test questions and directions are presented to students. Do testing accommodations give students with disabilities an advantage over other students or violate the integrity of your tests?

For example, to indicate a change in directions among types of items, you can provide a sample of each type of problem set off in a box with each change in directions or a reminder (e.g., Remember to use common denominators). Similarly, cues such as color coding, underlining, enlarging, or highlighting key words or phrases can alert your students to the specifics of each item. Cues, such as arrows, can be placed at the bottom of the test pages to indicate those pages that are a continuous part of a section of the test; stop signs can be placed to indicate ending pages.

Some students will require the help of school personnel when taking tests. A proctor or computer can read aloud and/or simplify the test directions and questions for these students, or adjust the pace at which items are presented (Hollenbeck, Rozek-Tedesco, Tindal, & Glasgow, 2000; Meloy, Deville, & Frisbie, 2002). They also can monitor students for signs of fatigue and adjust the testing schedule and administration accordingly. Proctors should be careful not to give students cues and additional information that may affect their performance. School personnel also can help students during the test by answering student questions about the test, turning pages for them, helping them maintain their place in a standard exam booklet, providing a copy of the text to avoid having to flip between the text and the items, delivering on-task and focusing prompts, and motivating students to sustain their effort (Elliott et al., 1998). Students with hearing disabilities may benefit from a trained teacher who can sign and interpret oral directions and translate their answers.

Some students may need specialized materials and equipment to gain information about test directions and items. Students with visual impairments may benefit from screen readers, visual magnification aids, readers, verbal descriptions of pictorials, tactile materials, photo-enlarged examinations and answer sheets, and Braille or large-print versions of tests. You also may need to provide them with materials with increased spacing between items or fewer items on a page. Students with hearing impairments may need to use devices that amplify sound and closed-captioning of video materials. Audiocassettes of test directions and items, and markers or masks to focus the students' attention and help them maintain their place during reading, can help students with reading disabilities.

Resource

Elliott et al. (1998) developed the Assessment Accommodation Checklist, and Fuchs and Fuchs (2001b) offer the Dynamic Assessment of Test Accommodations (DATA) system to help teachers select testing accommodations for students with a wide range of disabilities.

Reflective

What testing accommodations do your students receive? How are they determined? What is their impact on your students' test performance?

Responses to Items.   You also may need to make changes in the way students respond to test items or determine their answers. Some students may need to indicate their responses by providing oral responses or pointing, respectively. Some students may benefit from fewer items per page or line, extra space between items, lined or grid paper, and a larger answer block. Students who have difficulty transferring their responses to a separate answer sheet can be allowed to mark their responses on the test protocol, to use enlarged answer bubbles, or to fold test pages and position the answer sheet so that only one page appears (Erickson, Ysseldyke, Thurlow, & Elliott, 1998). School personnel can monitor students during testing to make sure that they record answers in the correct space and follow the correct sequence, check to see that the question numbers correspond to the numbers on the answer sheet, or record or transfer students' answers (Ysseldyke, Thurlow, Bielinski, House, Moody, & Haigh, 2001).

Students who have difficulty with writing or speaking can be helped in several ways. For example, students with hearing disabilities can respond via sign language, and students with physical disabilities can respond through use of eye movements. You also can use multiple-choice items instead of sentence completion and essay questions to minimize the amount of writing necessary to complete the test. When grammar, punctuation, and spelling are not essential aspects of the response, students can record their answers on an audiocassette or take an oral test. If the mechanics of written language are important in evaluating the response, students can dictate their complete response, including spelling, punctuation, paragraphing, and grammar, to a scribe (Kearns et al., 1998). Students can then review their response in written form and direct their recorder to the correct grammar, punctuation, and word choices. Devices such as word processors, Braille writers, speech synthesizers, pointers, spell and grammar checkers, electronic dictionaries and thesauruses, audiocassettes, and communication boards can help students who have difficulty answering orally or in writing to respond.

Because of their unique conditions, some students with disabilities may need to use aids and technology to respond to test items. Computational and memory aids such as calculators, glossaries, software programs, and mathematics tables can be useful for students who have the ability to complete items but lack the memory skills to remember facts or word definitions.

Timing, Scheduling, and Setting Alternatives

> It was my first high school final. I studied more than I ever had and thought I had a good chance of getting an A or B. I . . . took my regular seat at the large table by the window. During the teacher's directions, I forced myself to listen. I was doing good. Then I noticed this squirrel outside in the tree. . . . I watched the squirrel for 20 minutes. My teacher walked over and asked when I was going to start my exam. I looked away from the squirrel, but then I noticed this girl snapping her gum. . . . It was driving me crazy. I couldn't think. . . . She finally spit her gum out, but by that time it was too late. I didn't have enough time to finish now that I didn't even start the exam. . . . I felt sick to my stomach. I knew my mom would be mad. (Yehle & Wambold, 1998, p. 8)

You may need to adjust the timing and scheduling of tests, as well as the location in which the tests are given (Goh, 2004). Therefore, you can consider timing and scheduling alternatives such as:

- giving them more time to complete tests.
- providing them with shorter versions of tests.
- allowing students to take breaks as needed.
- adjusting the order in which the test(s) are administered.

- eliminating portions of tests.
- changing the times of day when the test is given so that the test is administered at the most optimal times for students.
- dividing the testing session into several shorter periods during the day.
- allowing students to complete the test over several days (Erickson et al., 1998).

Students who have difficulty remaining on task and are anxious about taking tests may perform better if they take the test in a small group or individually in a quiet place free of auditory and visual distractions (Herschell et al., 2002). You may need to motivate some students to start and sustain their effort.

Resource

Herschell et al. (2002) offer strategies and examples for minimizing student misbehavior during testing sessions.

Test Accommodations for Second Language Learners.   Since language proficiency can affect students' test performance, you may need to modify tests for second language learners. In addition to the previously discussed test accommodations, consider the following:

- Provide context clues, and present items and directions using graphics and pictures.
- Teach students the language of academic testing, and allow them to use bilingual dictionaries, glossaries, and word lists for content-area tests.
- Provide students with review sheets, lists of vocabulary, and important terms before giving tests.
- Simplify items so they are easy to understand, phrased using familiar language, and appropriate to students' language levels.
- Allow students to demonstrate mastery of test material in alternative ways, such as with projects developed by cooperative learning groups or through the use of drawings, charts, manipulatives, demonstrations, or drama.
- Use a translator to administer the test, and allow students to respond in their native language or dialect.

Some teachers have tried to minimize the bias in English-language tests by translating them into the student's dominant language (Goh, 2004). However, translations do not remove the cultural bias in tests that are related to content, item, picture, and task selection. Some concepts in English, referred to as *empty concepts* (e.g., certain time and color concepts), may not exist in other cultures and languages. In addition, because words may have different levels of difficulty across languages and dialects, test translations may change the psychometric properties of the original test. Additionally, translation does not account for experiences and words that have different or multiple meanings in different cultures. Thus, despite the translation, the constructs underlying the test items still reflect the dominant culture and may not be appropriate for students from other cultures.

Reflective

What studying and test-taking strategies do you use? Are they successful? How did you learn these strategies?

Training Prior to Testing.   An appropriate alternative testing procedure for many students may be training prior to testing to improve their test-taking, preparedness (e.g., experience with the type and content of the questions and the scoring procedures), and approach skills (e.g., eating and sleeping properly) (Elliott et al., 1998; Wasburn-Moses, 2003). Instruction in these skills can reduce some of the anxiety about testing that students experience and can help them feel comfortable with the test format (Berendt & Koski, 1999). Therefore, prior to testing, you can allow your students to practice taking tests, and give them time to work in groups to take and prepare for tests. These small groups can review notes and chapters, predict possible questions, and quiz members on specific facts, terms, and concepts.

Set Your Sites

For more information on test-taking and reducing test anxiety, go to the Web Links module in Chapter 12 of the Companion Website.

Advances in technology and multimedia are providing new ways to assess student learning. How do you use technology to assess your students?

Resource

Thompson et al. (2002) present technology-based accommodations and potential problems associated with their use.

Reflective

Have you taken a technology-based test? How did it affect your performance? What was helpful for you? Difficult for you?

Set Your Sites

For more information on high-stakes testing, testing accommodations, and alternative assessment techniques, go to the Web Links module in Chapter 12 of the Companion Website.

Resource

Kleinert et al. (2002), Browder, Fallin, Davis, and Karvonen (2003), Kelly, Siegel, and Allinder (2001), and Denham and Lahm (2001) offer examples of and guidelines for creating meaningful alternate assessments for students not partici-pating in traditional statewide testing programs.

While students can be taught to use many of the learning strategies discussed in other chapters in this book in testing situations, they also can be taught to use test-taking learning strategies such as *PIRATES* and *ANSWER.* Hughes, Deshler, Ruhl, and Schumaker (1993) improved students' test performance by teaching them to use PIRATES: **P**repare to succeed; **I**nspect the instructions; **R**ead, remember, reduce; **A**nswer or abandon; **T**urn back; **E**stimate; **S**urvey. Hughes (1996) developed ANSWER, an essay test-taking learning strategy: **A**nalyze the situation, **N**otice requirements, **S**et up an outline, **W**ork in details, **E**ngineer your answer, and **R**eview your answer.

You also can teach your students to develop their test-taking skills (Strichart & Mangrum, 2002). Recommended test-taking skills that can be taught to students are presented in Figure 12.1.

Alternatives to Standardized Testing

Most students with disabilities should be able to participate in statewide tests with appropriate testing accommodations. However, some students who are not working on general education goals or standards may not need to take part in these statewide assessments (see your state's guidelines for determining student eligibility for alternate assessments). These students must participate in an alternate assessment system developed by your state and aligned with state standards (Kleinert, Green, Hurte, Clayton, & Oetinger, 2002). In these cases, you and your colleagues may want to use some of the classroom assessment alternatives presented below as part of or to supplement your state's alternative assessment system. In selecting appropriate classroom-based assessment techniques for use with your students, you can consider the following:

- Will the assessment technique measure meaningful skills and content?
- Will the assessment technique help me plan, deliver, and evaluate my instructional program?
- Will the assessment technique take away time from my instructional program? (Popham, 2003).

FIGURE 12.1

Recommended student test-taking skills

PRIOR TO TESTING

◇ Review the content to be studied over a spaced period of time rather than cramming.

◇ Determine the specific objectives of each study session.

◇ Study the most difficult content areas first.

◇ Make sure that the study area is conducive to studying.

◇ Gather all the materials necessary for studying, including notebooks, textbooks, paper, writing utensils, reference books, and calculators.

◇ Review prior tests in terms of format, length, response types, and the completeness of the responses required.

◇ Develop and use study guides, review sheets, vocabulary lists, and outlines of the material to be covered on the test.

◇ Sleep and eat well before the test.

◇ Develop a positive attitude about the test and your effort.

DURING TESTING

◇ Remain calm.

◇ Preview the test to determine the number and nature of test items before beginning the test.

◇ Be aware of the time left to complete the test.

◇ Develop an order and a timeline for working on the test based on the total time allotted to the test, the point values of sections (work on those sections worth the most points in descending order), and the difficulty of the items.

◇ Make three passes through the test. In the first pass, read all questions and respond to the ones you know how to answer, noting those that are somewhat difficult or very difficult. During the second pass, respond to those questions skipped in the first pass that have been identified as somewhat difficult. Answer all unanswered questions during the third pass.

◇ Read the directions to all parts of the test to determine what type of response is required, the aids allowed, the sequence to be followed in completing the test, the point values of items and sections of the test, and the time and space limits.

◇ Underline important parts of test items and directions.

◇ Seek clarification about the specifics of test items and directions.

◇ Identify and analyze critical words, look for word clues, and rephrase questions in language you can understand.

◇ Jot down on the test paper essential facts and formulas that you will use throughout the test.

◇ Check responses to make sure that they are correct, complete, neat, and marked appropriately.

◇ Stay with your first choice when you are unsure of an answer.

◇ Answer all questions. However, when you lose additional points for incorrect responses, answer only those questions that have a high probability of being correct.

WHEN WORKING ON MULTIPLE-CHOICE ITEMS

◇ Read the question and think of the answer before reading and carefully analyzing all the choices.

◇ Examine each response alternative, select the one that is most complete and inclusive, and eliminate choices that are obviously false or incorrect, that are not related to the content covered in class, or that are absurd or deal with nonsense or irrelevant material.

◇ Be aware that the choices *all of the above, none of the above,* and numbers that represent the middle range are often correct, as are alternatives that are unusually long or short.

◇ Be aware that when alternative answers are contradictory, one of them is likely to be correct, and that when two options provide similar information, neither of them should be considered.

◇ Use clues such as subject–verb agreement, verb tense, modifiers such as *a* or *an,* and other information from the stem of the item to determine the correct response.

WHEN WORKING ON MATCHING ITEMS

◇ Survey both lists to get an idea of the choices, to note if each column has an equal number of items, and to determine if an alternative can be used more than once.

◇ Read the initial item in the left-hand column first and then read each choice in the right-hand column before answering.

◇ Work on the easiest items first and skip items that are difficult.

◇ Record the correct answer if you know it immediately, and highlight choices in the right-hand column that have been used.

◇ Avoid guessing until all other items have been answered, as an incorrect match can multiply the number of errors.

(continued)

Figure 12.1 (continued)

WHEN WORKING ON TRUE-FALSE ITEMS

◇ Determine the type of true-false items on the test before beginning.

◇ Examine the questions for *specific determiners,* which are words that modify or limit a statement (e.g., *rarely, usually*). In general, false statements often include a qualifier that suggests that the statement is extreme or true 100 percent of the time (e.g., *no, never, every, always, all*).

◇ Words that moderate a statement (e.g., *sometimes, most, many, generally, usually*) often indicate that a statement is true. If true-false statements lack a specific determiner, the question should be marked *True* only if it is always true.

◇ Read all parts of the statement, and mark the statement *False* if any part of it is not true or correct.

◇ Highlight the negative words or prefixes in true-false statements and identify the meaning of the item while deleting the negatives.

WHEN WORKING ON SENTENCE COMPLETION ITEMS

◇ Answer sentence completion items by converting them into questions.

◇ Use the grammatical structure of the item to help you formulate the answer. If the stem ends in *a* or *an,* the correct answer probably starts with a consonant or a vowel, respectively. The verb form also indicates whether the answer is singular or plural.

◇ Use the number and length of the blanks provided as a clue. Often, two blanks with no words between them indicate that a two-word response, such as an individual's name, is the answer. Two blanks separated by words should be approached as two separate statements. A long blank tends to suggest that the correct answer is a phrase or a sentence.

WHEN WORKING ON ESSAY QUESTIONS

◇ Read the questions and record relevant points to be mentioned or addressed next to each question.

◇ Highlight key words related to directions and important information to be addressed.

◇ Work on the easiest questions first, rereading each question and adding new information or deleting irrelevant statements.

◇ Outline the response before writing, and then use the outline as a guide for composing the answer.

◇ Consider the following when writing the response: rephrase the question as the first sentence of the answer; present the answer in a logical order, with transitions from one paragraph to another; give specifics when necessary; use examples to support statements; and summarize the main points at the end of the essay.

◇ Proofread responses for clarity, organization, legibility, spelling, and grammar.

◇ Write down the outline and key points rather than leaving the question blank.

Note: Hoy (1995); Hudson (1996); Hughes (1996).

Curriculum-Based Measurement

Curriculum-based measurement (CBM) provides individualized, direct, and repeated measures of students' proficiency and progress in the curriculum (Deno, 2003; Stecker & Fuchs, 2000). Because CBM is an ongoing, dynamic process involving content derived directly from students' instructional programs, it provides continuous measurements of your students' progress (Burns, 2002; Jones, Southern, & Brigham, 1998). For instance, teachers in the Madison School District can examine their students' progress in reading by using CBM to record and graph measures of their students' performance on the selections they read every day in class.

Hagan-Burke and Jefferson (2002) and Scott and Weishaar (2003) offer the following guidelines for conducting a CBM:

1. *Identify the content area(s) to be assessed.* CBM begins by examining and determining the content areas to be assessed.

2. *Define the school-related tasks that will constitute the assessment and the sample duration.* For example, you can measure reading by having students read aloud from their readers for a sample duration of 1 minute, and measure writing by the number of words written during a sample duration of 5 minutes.

USING TECHNOLOGY TO PROMOTE INCLUSION

Using Technology-Based Testing

Advances in technology and multimedia offer alternatives to traditional paper-and-pencil tests (Woodfield, 2003). In addition to converting these tests into technology-based formats, these advances allow you to assess students' responses to authentic situations and give students opportunities to use and develop their critical thinking, social, and metacognitive skills (Moore, 2003). For example, your students can be given audio and video clips of academic and social situations, or simulations or virtual reality that depict real experiences and asked to respond to them in a variety of ways. You also can use technology to assess your students via electronic portfolios, online discussions and group projects, and case analyses.

Technology-based testing also allows you to tailor the administration of exams to the skill levels and scheduling needs of your students (Thompson, Thurlow, Quenemoen & Lehr, 2002). For example, an exam administered via the computer can be structured so that the difficulty of each question depends on how the student performed on the prior question. If the student answers a question correctly, the computer can branch to a more difficult item; if he or she answers a question incorrectly, the computer can branch to an easier item. Student performance on these exams is then based on their correct responses and the level of difficulty. The flexibility associated with technology-based testing also can address students' varied scheduling needs by allowing for individualized and group administrations in various locations, extended time, breaks, multiple testing sessions, time of day considerations, and variations in the sequence in which subtests are administered.

Technology-based assessment employs the principles of universal design we learned about in chapter 8 to give students choices concerning a test's presentation and response mode formats and the testing accommodations they want to use (Thompson et al., 2002). For example, your linguistically diverse students can choose to take tests administered in their preferred language, and access bilingual dictionaries/glossaries and pop-up translations. Your students can decide whether they want to have test items presented in verbal or written formats, or via Braille, text/screen readers and enlargers, captioning, or sign language. They also can select whether they want to respond via voice-recognition technology; word processor; Brailler; tape recorder; calculator; touch screens; mouse clicks; or adapted switches, devices, and keyboards (see chapter 8). Students also can make choices to repeat directions; highlight text; and adjust the font, print size, color, spacing, and background of the test, the pace of the test administration, and the number of items that appear on the screen at a time.

It is important to be aware of concerns about computer-based testing. In addition to the digital divide (see chapter 3), these concerns include:

- limiting test takers because it may take longer and be more tiring to read text presented on computer screens.
- making it more difficult to identify errors in material presented this way.
- preventing test-takers from using such test-taking techniques as underlining or highlighting key words, eliminating choices, and scanning materials.
- failing to remove the cultural bias associated with testing.
- placing students who do not have experience with technology at a disadvantage.
- requiring students to use malfunctioning or dated hardware and software (e.g., small screen with low resolution, technology that does not translate graphics into text or speech, and slow Internet connections).

Here are some other ways you can use technology to assess student learning and the effectiveness of your inclusion program:

- Employ web-based software to record, analyze, and share curriculum-based measurement data. For example, you can use Edformation (www.aimsweb.com) or DIBELS (www.dibels.uoregon.edu).
- Use software programs to prepare, administer, and score tests and quizzes electronically (Thompson et al., 2002). Test preparation, administration, and scoring software include eMeasurement services (www.ncspearson.com), Test Pilot (www.clearlearning.com), Exam Manager (www.examanager.com), Perceptions (www.questionmark.com), and Saxon Test Generator (www.saxonpub.com). In preparing legible and appropriate tests, consider the typographic design guidelines presented in chapter 8, and the test development guidelines presented in this chapter.

(continued)

- Allow and encourage students to write responses to essay questions by using word-processing programs.
- Use PDAs and graphing calculators to conduct real-time quizzes.
- Use such sites as Quia.com or Funbrain.com to create online quizzes and games to assess student learning.
- Teach your students the skills they need to take tests online (e.g., scrolling with a mouse, and accessing text on multiple screens), and give them practice in taking tests online. You can do this by creating online practice tests or having students visit the websites of online test-preparation companies such as eduTest (www.eduTest.com) and Homeroom.com (www.Homeroom.com).
- Limit your students' access to outside information during online testing sessions by using software programs such as VANGuard (www.vantage.com).
- Maintain an electronic gradebook by using a web-based system or spreadsheet that stores and computes grades and makes them available to students and their families via password protection. Web-based systems also can be programmed to notify families with information about grades and absences.
- Use software and hardware (e.g., handheld computers) to record and graph information about student behaviors and interactions (Bauer & Ulrich, 2002). Wallace et al. (2002) provide information about using the Ecobehavioral Assessment System Software (EBASS) program to observe and assess student and teacher instructional behaviors in inclusive settings.
- Record and evaluate students' academic and social behaviors via video and audio recordings.
- Create surveys using technology. For example, Sophia (www.assessmentresearch.com) is a web-based tool for designing, administering, and analyzing data from surveys.

3. *Determine whether performance or progress measurement will be used.* Performance measurement involves changes on a specific task that remains constant throughout the CBM. Progress measurement evaluates student progress on sequentially ordered levels/objectives within the curriculum.

4. *Prepare and organize the necessary materials.* Select material from the curriculum related to the assessment tasks in advance.

5. *Administer the CBM.*

6. *Decide how frequently the CBM will be administered.* Depending on your time, the students' skill, and the nature of the task, decide how frequently to administer the CBM.

7. *Record and graph students' performance over time.* A sample graph is presented in Figure 12.2. The vertical axis measures the student's performance on the school-related task (such as the number of words read or spelled). The horizontal axis indicates the days on which the CBM is given. Data points on the graph should provide a measure of the correct and incorrect responses. The diagonal broken line starting at the left and ending on the right side of the graph is called the *aimline;* it establishes the expected rate of student learning and provides a reference point for judging students' progress and making decisions about their instructional program. The vertical broken lines indicate changes in the program. Scott and Weishaar (2003) and Gable, Arllen, Evans, and Whinnery (1997) offer additional guidelines for graphing student performance and interpreting these data.

8. *Analyze the results to determine students' progress in terms of skills mastered and not mastered.* You can use the data to identify the students who have mastered the skills and are ready for new instructional objectives; those who are progressing but need additional teaching to demonstrate mastery of skills; and those who have not progressed and need modifications in their instructional program.

9. *Examine and compare the efficacy of different instructional strategies.* You can examine the data to assess and compare the efficacy of different teaching methods and make decisions about students' educational programs.

Resource

Idol, Nevin, and Paolucci-Whitcomb (1999) offer guidelines and models for using CBM to assess student performance in inclusive classrooms.

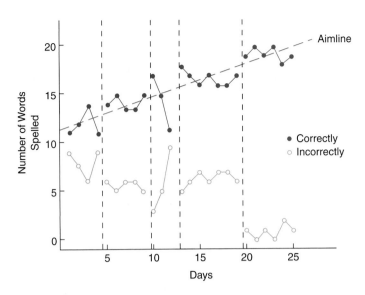

FIGURE 12.2   **Graph of CBM of spelling**

Authentic/Performance Assessment

You also can use *authentic/performance assessment* to measure the impact of your in-structional programs on your students' academic performance (Moulds, 2004; Serafini, 2002). In this type of assessment, students work on meaningful, complex, and relevant learning activities that are incorporated into the assessment process. The results of these activities are authentic products that reveal their ability to apply the knowledge and skills they have learned to contextualized problems and real-life settings. For example, for an authentic assessment at the elementary level related to a unit on the plant life cycle, your students could create a book explaining this topic to others. At the secondary level, your students can develop and disseminate a brochure on election issues as an authentic as-sessment for a unit on the electoral process.

Portfolio Assessment

Authentic/performance assessment is closely related to *portfolio assessment,* which involves teachers, students, and family members working together to create a continuous and pur-poseful collection of various authentic student products across a range of content areas throughout the school year that show the process and products associated with student learn-ing (Boerum, 2000). Portfolios are student-centered and archival in nature and allow students to set goals and have more control over their learning (Ezell & Klein, 2003). They contain samples over time that are periodically reviewed to reflect on and document progress, effort, attitudes, achievement, development, and the strategies students use to learn.

Here are some guidelines for using portfolio assessment that you may want to consider:

1. *Identify the goals of the portfolio.* Typically, the goals of students' portfolios are in-dividualized, broadly stated, related directly to the curriculum, and cover an extended pe-riod of time. For students with disabilities, portfolio goals also can be linked to their IEPs.

2. *Determine the type of portfolio.* Jochum et al. (1998) and Swicegood (1994) iden-tified four types of portfolios: showcase, reflective, cumulative, and goal-based. A

Resource

Moulds (2004) and Martin-Kniep (2000) offer criteria that can guide you in selecting appropriate perfor-mance/authentic assessment tasks.

Reflective

What performance/authentic assess-ment tasks might be appropriate for measuring your understanding of the material presented in this course and book?

Resource

Kearns et al. (1999) offer guidelines for using an alternate portfolio assessment system to involve students with moderate and severe cognitive disabilities in the statewide testing system.

Resource

Gelfer and Perkins (1998) and O'Malley and Valdez Pierce (1996) provide guidelines for developing portfolios with young children, and with students from various cultural and language backgrounds, respectively.

In authentic/performance assessment, students apply the knowledge and skills they have learned to contextualized problems and real-life settings. How can you use authentic assessment with your students?

Resource

Jochum et al. (1998) outline the roles of students, family members, general and special educators, and ancillary support personnel in the portfolio process.

showcase portfolio presents the student's best work and is often used to help students enter a specialized program or school or apply for employment. A *reflective portfolio* helps teachers, students, and family members reflect on students' learning, including attitudes, strategies, and knowledge. A *cumulative portfolio* shows changes in the products and process associated with students' learning throughout the school year. A *goal-based portfolio* has preset goals and items are selected to fit those goals, such as goals from a student's IEP. Another type of portfolio is a *process portfolio,* which documents the steps and processes a student has used to complete a piece of work.

3. *Select a variety of real classroom products that address the goals of the portfolio.* Students and teachers jointly select a range of authentic classroom products related to the goals of the portfolio. You also can use video and audio recordings to document students' accomplishments.

Some teachers schedule a selection day on which students choose items for their portfolios; others encourage students to select items that are in progress or completed. You can help students select portfolio items by offering models, allowing students to learn from each other by sharing their portfolios, and creating and sharing evaluation criteria with students (Wesson & King, 1996).

4. *Establish procedures for collecting, storing, organizing, and noting the significance of students' products.* Portfolio items are usually stored in individualized folders such as file folders, binders, and boxes with dividers organized in a variety of ways: chronologically (e.g., early/intermediate/later works) or according to students' IEPs, academic or content-area subjects, student interests, or thematic units (Reetz, 1995). You can ask your students to personalize their portfolios by covering them with photographs, pictures, and logos.

Technology and multimedia can be used to store items and organize electronic or digital portfolios (Denham & Lahm, 2001). Software programs offer ways to scan student-produced projects and artwork; enter sound and video clips of student presentations;

organize portfolios by subject, theme, or project; and link students' work to national and districtwide standards. A sample hypermedia-based electronic portfolio is presented in Figure 12.3.

5. *Record the significance of items included in students' portfolios and help students reflect on them.* When selecting products for a portfolio, teachers and students write *caption statements*, brief descriptions that identify the document, provide the context in which it was produced, and reflect on why it was selected. For students who have difficulty writing caption statements, peer or adult scribes or audio and video recordings can be used to engage them in the self-reflection process. A sample caption statement is presented in Figure 12.4.

Reetz (1995) and Countryman and Schroeder (1996) identified the following prompts, which can be used to help students compose caption statements:

Improvements
This piece shows my improvement in _____ . I used to _____ but now I

_____ .

Pride
I am proud of this work because _____ . In this piece, notice how I _____ .

Special Efforts
This piece shows something that is hard for me. As you can see, I have worked hard to _____ .

IEP Objectives
This work shows my progress on _____ . I have learned to _____ . I will continue to _____ .

Content Areas
In (content area) I have been working on _____ . My goal is to _____ .

Thematic Units
I have been working on a unit relating to the theme of _____ . As part of this unit, I selected the following pieces: _____ . These pieces show that I _____ .

Projects
I have been working on a project about _____ . I learned _____ . The project shows I can _____ .

Difficulties
This piece shows the trouble I have with _____ .

Strategy Use
This piece shows that I used the following method: _____ . The steps I used were _____ and _____ .

You can help your students reflect on their portfolios by asking them to discuss why they selected a particular piece. Questions also can relate to:

- *learning outcomes* (e.g., "What did you learn from working on this project?" or "What did you do well on this project?")
- *improvement* (e.g., "If you could redo this, how would you improve it?" or "How is this piece different from your other pieces?")

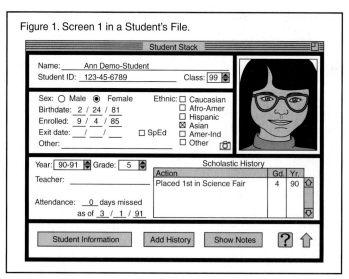

Figure 1. Screen 1 in a Student's File.

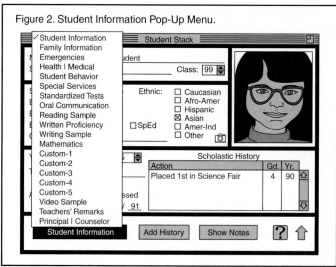

Figure 2. Student Information Pop-Up Menu.

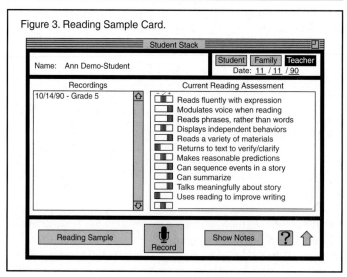

Figure 3. Reading Sample Card.

FIGURE 12.3   **Sample hypermedia-based electronic portfolio**

Source: From "An Equation to Consider: The Portfolio Assessment Knowledge Base + Technology = The Grady Profile," by D. L. Edyburn, 1994, *LD Forum, 19,* 1994, pp. 36, 37. Copyright 1994 by *LD Forum.* Reprinted with permission.

Sample caption statement

FIGURE 12.4

Date: 12/18/2005

Teacher Comments: This piece demonstrates James's ability to engage in the writing process and use story elements. James was given a choice of several themes and selected a theme relating to Thanksgiving. James completed the piece using a checklist that guided him in creating and organizing the elements of the story. When James first discussed the piece with me, I encouraged him to elaborate on his story.

Student Comments: I have been working on a story about Thanksgiving. I feel good about this item because I made up the story. In working on this story, I used a checklist that Ms. Feld gave me. The checklist asked me: What is the title of the story?, Who are the characters?, Where does the story take place?, What happens in the story?, and How does the story end?

- *process* (e.g., "What process did you go through to complete this assignment?")
- *strategy use* (e.g., "What strategies did you use to work on this piece?" "Were they effective?"), as well as other aspects of student learning.

You also can promote reflection by asking students to compare a recently completed item with an earlier work, by having students reflect on each other's work, by asking them to write letters for their portfolios explaining why a specific item was chosen, or by writing a portfolio introduction that compares items, identifies patterns, and interprets the meaning of the whole portfolio.

6. *Review and evaluate portfolios and share them with others.* Portfolios should be reviewed and evaluated periodically by teachers, students, family members, and administrators throughout the school year during conferences. Students can share their portfolios with others. The following questions can guide that process:

- What does the portfolio reveal about the student's IEP and academic, behavioral, language, and social-emotional performance and skills?
- What are the student's strengths and instructional challenges?
- What does the portfolio indicate about the student's learning style, attitudes, motivation, interests, cultural background, and use of learning strategies?
- Do items in the portfolio relate to each other? If so, what patterns do they reveal?
- How can the information presented in the portfolio be used to plan the student's educational program? (Swicegood, 1994).

Near the end of the conference, participants can be asked to write or dictate a note or letter to the portfolio stating what they think is the most meaningful information in the portfolio, as well as what the portfolio indicates about the student's progress and educational program.

Instructional Rubrics

Authentic/performance assessment and portfolio assessment include the use of *instructional rubrics,* statements specifying the criteria associated with different levels of proficiency for evaluating student performance (Whittaker, Salend, & Duhaney, 2001). Educators using instructional rubrics assess process, performance, and progress by delineating the various categories associated with assessment tasks and learning activities, the different levels of performance, and the indicators describing each level and then rating student performance on products that show their learning. A writing rubric

Resource

Graham and Fahey (1999) offer guidelines for conducting a collaborative assessment conference to engage teachers in a discussion of students' work.

Reflective

You applied for a job in a local school district by sending a resumé and a letter of interest. The superintendent's office asks you to come in for an interview and bring a portfolio showing your experiences and training. What items would you include in the portfolio? How would you organize and present them?

Resource

Hall and Salmon (2003) offer guidelines for teaching students to understand and use instructional rubrics including using a learning strategy called RUBRIC.

Reflecting on Professional Practices

Using Student Portfolios

James moved into the school district in November and was placed in Ms. Feld's class. To prepare an educational program for James, Ms. Feld examined his performance on several norm-referenced tests administered while he attended his prior school. The test results indicated that James's reading and writing skills were significantly below grade level. However, they provided little information about his strengths and the teaching strategies that could be used to help him. Therefore, Ms. Feld decided to work with James to develop a reading and writing portfolio.

Throughout the school year, James and Ms. Feld selected a variety of items for his portfolio, including a recording of James reading, a collection of pieces that he wrote based on a single theme using a process approach to writing, written summaries of books he read, and a self-recording graph of James's daily reading. The items were stored in an accordion file folder by date and subject area. When James and Ms. Feld selected an item for the portfolio, they discussed what it revealed about James's progress in reading and writing. After discussing the item's significance, each of them wrote a caption statement that was attached to the item.

During several family–teacher conferences throughout the school year, Ms. Feld and James shared his portfolio with his family. Before these meetings, James and Ms. Feld examined the whole portfolio and summarized what it demonstrated about James's progress in reading and writing. James began the conference by presenting his portfolio. First, he mentioned the goals and purpose of the portfolio and how it was organized. He then spoke about the content and special items in the portfolio, discussing why items were selected and what they showed about his learning. Ms. Feld spoke about James's progress by citing various portfolio items. James's family gave their reactions to his portfolio and asked questions

about it. James, his family, and Ms. Feld discussed how his reading and writing had changed, the patterns that were evident in his reading and writing, the strategies he was using in these areas, and the changes in his attitude and motivation. They also talked about the skills and learning strategies that needed to be developed, as well as goals and plans for future work to address his instructional needs.

At the end of the meetings, Ms. Feld, James, and James's family wrote notes summarizing their reactions to the portfolio, which then were included in the portfolio. James's family was proud of him, and pleased to see real and understandable signs that James was learning. James's notes indicated that he was feeling good about himself and that he liked having some control over his learning. Ms. Feld felt much better knowing that her instructional program was helping James make progress in reading and writing.

- Why did Ms. Feld decide to work with James to develop a portfolio?
- What roles did James perform in the portfolio process?
- What roles did James's family perform?
- How did Ms. Feld involve James and his family in the portfolio process?
- What was the effect of the portfolio on James, his family, and Ms. Feld?
- How could you use portfolios with your students?

 To answer these questions online and share your responses with others, go to the Reflection module in Chapter 12 of the Companion Website.

developed by Ms. Cheryl Ebert, an English teacher at the Johnson City (New York) High School, is presented in Figure 12.5.

Rubrics can help you promote student learning and clarify and communicate your expectations (Andrade, 2000; Jackson & Larkin, 2002). They also make grading and feedback more objective and consistent, which in turn helps students understand the qualities associated with assignments and aids them in monitoring and self-evaluating their own work (Hall & Salmon, 2003; Stanford & Siders, 2001).

Instructional rubrics are most effective when you create them with your students, and teach them to use them.

 Set Your Sites

For more information on instructional rubrics, go to the Web Links module in Chapter 12 of the Companion Website.

Sample writing rubric

FIGURE 12.5

Name: **Assignment:**

Narrative/Descriptive Writing Scoring Guide   **Date:**

Course Outcome: Students will be able to internalize a writing process which includes planning, composing, revising, and self-evaluating.

Criteria Quality	Focus on and Organization of Task	Narrative	Descriptive	Style and Diction	Grammar, Usage, and Mechanics
Excellent 90+ (A)	• Topic is approached in a unique and imaginative way. • Attitude and point of view remain the same for entire paper. • Paragraphs and sentences are organized and make sense.	• Opening situation is clearly established. • Characters are effectively introduced and developed. • Description is original and vivid. • Conflict is clearly developed. • Conflict is logically and completely solved.	• Very descriptive words or phrases are used. • Details are chosen to create a very clear picture or image for the reader throughout the writing.	• Uses well-chosen and appropriate words all of the time. • Expresses ideas in an imaginative and creative way. • Effective paragraphing. • Varies sentence structure.	• Can correctly use certain parts of speech, ending punctuation, and indentation at all times. • Correctly uses comma and quotations at all times. • Uses proper tense throughout. • Few or no spelling errors. • Capitalization correct throughout.
Quality 80+ (B)	• Topic is understood. • Attitude and point of view are clear, but not used throughout the paper. • Paragraphs are not always organized, but sentences are organized in a pattern.	• Opening situation is established. • Characters are adequately introduced and developed. • Includes some description. • A conflict is developed. • Conflict is solved.	• Descriptive words or phrases are used. • Details are chosen to create a good picture or image for the reader throughout the writing.	• Generally chooses appropriate words. • Expresses ideas clearly. • Some sentence structures are repetitious. • Some errors in sentences. • Correct paragraphing.	• Can correctly use certain parts of speech, ending punctuation, and indentation in most cases. • Correctly uses commas and quotations most of the time. • Uses proper tense throughout. • Minor spelling errors. • Capitalization appropriate.
Acceptable 70+ (C)	• Topic is understood, but ideas are not developed enough. • Attitude and point of view change throughout the writing. • Paragraphs are not always organized, and sentence order does not make sense.	• Opening situation is not appropriate or established. • Characters are not well developed. • Conflict is not established or does not make sense. • Conflict is not completely solved.	• Few descriptive words or phrases are used. • There are not enough details to keep the picture or image in the reader's mind.	• Sometimes chooses inappropriate words. • Meaning is clear, but word choice is not varied. • Some sentences are choppy. • Fragments/run-ons. • Errors in paragraphing.	• Word usage is limited. • Errors or omissions in the use of commas or quotations. • Errors in verb tense, but meaning is clear. • Several spelling errors, but meaning is clear.
Below Expectations	• Topic is not understood. • Attitude, point of view are unclear. • Paragraphs are not organized, nor do the sentences make sense.	• Lacking major elements of narrative structure.	• Almost no descriptive words or phrases are used. • Details, if any, do not create a picture for the reader.	• Chooses incorrect or inappropriate words. • Meaning is unclear or confusing, point is not made. • Many fragments and/or run-ons. • Incorrect or no paragraphing.	• Little or no knowledge of use of parts of speech or ending punctuation. • Commas, quotes, capitalization, punctuation errors throughout the paper. • Spelling errors interfere with understanding. • Constant shifting of verb tenses.

Notes:

Source: Developed by Cheryl Ebert, English teacher, Johnson City High School, Johnson City Central School District, Johnson City, NY.

Observations

Although observational techniques are typically used to record students' social behaviors, you also can use them to document students' academic performance and academic-related behaviors (Alexandrin, 2003). You can maintain recorded anecdotal records of students performing various content-area activities, as well as observing students' products and/or the processes or strategies they use. Some teachers structure their observations by using teacher-made rating scales and checklists such as the one in Figure 12.6. **To view an example of a teacher using observation, go to Case 1: Difficult Behavior on the CD-ROM and click on the Monitor and Evaluate video clip. How does the teacher use her observations to support and document student learning?**

cd-rom

Resource

Alexandrin (2003) offers guidelines for conducting observations to evaluate student progress in inclusive classrooms.

Observational techniques can be used to collect data on the amount of time planned for teaching, time actually spent teaching, and time spent by students on teaching activities in class, as well as the rates and sources of interruptions to planned teaching activities (Wallace et al., 2002). These data also can be used to help determine if the presence of students with disabilities in general education classrooms reduces the teacher's attention and instructional time devoted to their classmates without disabilities.

FIGURE 12.6

Observation checklist of students' understanding of narrative text

Student: _____

Teacher: _____

Date(s): _____

Directions: Use the following system to record student behavior:

  N = Student does not engage in the behavior.

  B = Student is beginning to engage in the behavior.

  D = Student is developing the behavior.

  P = Student has proficiency in the behavior.

Support your notations with comments.

Narratives	Behavior	Date(s)	Comments
Names characters			
Describes the setting			
Identifies time/place			
Identifies problems			
Identifies solutions			
Predicts story outcomes			
Identifies mood			
Describes author's view			
States theme of story			

Source: From "Authentic Assessment Strategies," by K. Pike and S. J. Salend, 1995, *Teaching Exceptional Children, 28,* p. 16. Copyright 1995 by The Council for Exceptional Children. Reprinted by permission.

Teacher-Made Tests

Traditional teacher-made tests are often used to evaluate students' performance in general education classrooms. Creating a good test is not easy. Several factors you can consider when developing tests are presented below. When designing tests and using testing accommodations discussed earlier in this chapter, you must be careful not to compromise the integrity of the test, course, or curriculum.

Test Content. The content of the items on your tests should be directly related to the objectives of your instructional program. The tests should reflect not only *what* but also *how* content has been taught. Content taught via analysis, synthesis, or problem-solving techniques is best tested through essay questions, whereas factual and rote memory material may be tested by objective items. Additionally, the language and terminology used in both test directions and items should be consistent with those used in class.

The percentage of test questions related to specific content areas should reflect the amount of time your class spent on these topics. For example, on a test following a unit in which 30 percent of class time was spent on the U.S. Constitution, approximately 30 percent of the test items should focus on material related to the Constitution. Shorter and more frequent tests of specific content rather than fewer, longer, and more comprehensive tests can help your students who have difficulty remembering large amounts of information.

Test Format. Even though many of your students can master the content necessary to perform well on a test, they may have difficulty with the test's format. Tests that cause confusion and distraction because of poor appearance or spatial design can defeat students before they begin. Therefore, items should be clearly and darkly printed on a solid, nondistracting background. Ideally, tests should be typed. If they must be written, the writing should be in the style (manuscript or cursive) familiar to the student.

Confusion can be minimized by proper spacing and sequencing of items. Items and the directions for completing them should appear on the same page so that students do not have to turn back and forth. Presenting items in a fixed, predictable, symmetrical sequence that emphasizes the transition from one item to another can help ensure that your students do not skip lines or fail to complete test items. Allowing students to write on the test itself rather than transferring answers to a separate page can reduce confusion for students with organizational difficulties. Providing enough space for responses allows students to complete an answer without continuing on another page and can structure the length of responses. Some students may benefit from you providing them with space between items so that they can provide a rationale for their responses to short-answer items (Kellough & Kellough, 2003).

Make sure that your directions are presented in language students understand and that you include directions for each section of the test that contains different types of items (Dynneson, Gross, & Berson, 2003). It also is helpful to students if you organize the presentation of items so that they are sequenced from easiest to hardest. In writing items, be careful to avoid clues that can unintentionally guide students to the correct response. Therefore, you should proofread your tests to make sure that they do not include grammatical cues (e.g., the articles *a* and *an*, plurals), word cues (e.g., the same words appear in the question and answer), and similarity cues (e.g., the information in one question leads to the answers in other questions) (Conderman & Koroghlanian, 2002). Additional guidelines you can use in writing test items are discussed here.

Multiple-Choice Items.   Students' performance on multiple-choice items can be improved by composing well-written, grammatically correct items that students can read and understand—using language free of double negatives (Armstrong & Savage, 2002; Kellough & Kellough, 2003). The stem should provide a context for answering the item, contain only one major point and only relevant information, and be longer than the answer alternatives. The choices should be feasible and of the same length, should be presented vertically, and should not contain categorical words such as *always, all, only,* or *never.* Choices can be arranged in a logical sequence such as by alphabetical, numerical, or chronological order (Conderman & Koroghlanian, 2002). Multiple-choice items can be tailored to the needs of students by highlighting keywords, reducing the number of choices, eliminating more difficult choices, such as having to select *all of the above* or *none of the above.* Finally, allowing students to circle the answer they choose can alleviate problems in recording answers. An example of an adapted multiple-choice item is as follows:

> *Directions:* (Circle) the lettered choice that answers the question.
>
> In which court case did the Supreme Court decide that *segregating students by race was unconstitutional?*
>
> (a) Plessy v. Ferguson
> (b) Baker v. Carr
> (c) Newkirk v. Phalen School District
> (d) Brown v. Board of Education of Topeka

Matching Items.   When writing matching items, you should consider several variables that can affect students' performance (Conderman & Koroghlanian, 2002). Use matching items when you can create homogeneous lists of corresponding premises and responses that relate to a single theme or concept. Each matching section of the test should contain a maximum of 10 items. When more than 10 items are needed, group the additional items by topic in a separate matching section. There should be 25 percent more items in one column than in the other and only one correct response for each pair. Because students usually approach matching items by reading an item in the left-hand column and then reading all the available choices in the right-hand column, you can help your students save time and work in a coordinated fashion by listing the longer items in the left-hand column. For example, a matching item designed to assess mastery of vocabulary would have the definitions in the left-hand column and the vocabulary words in the right-hand column.

Place clear, unambiguous directions and both columns on the same page and label the items in one column with numbers and the items in the other column with letters (Brookhart, 2004). This prevents the frustration some students encounter when matching questions are presented on more than one page. To avoid the disorganization that can occur when students respond by drawing lines connecting their choices from both columns, direct students to record the letter or number of their selection in the blank provided. You also can improve student performance on this type of test question by giving choices that are clear and concise, embedding an example in the matching question, informing students whether items from columns can be used more than once, labeling both columns, and organizing columns in a sensible and logical fashion. An adapted matching item is as follows:

Directions: Write the letter from column 2 in the blank next to the best answer in column 1. The first one is done for you as an example.

Column 1		Column 2
__E__ 1.	A small, raised part of the land, lower than a mountain.	A. Peninsula
____ 2.	Land surrounded by water on three sides.	B. Plateau
____ 3.	An area of high, flat land.	C. Reservoir
____ 4.	A lake where a large water supply is stored.	D. Valley
____ 5.	Low land between mountains or hills.	E. Hill
____ 6.	Low and wet land.	F. Swamp
		G. Isthmus
		H. Island

True-False Items.   Many of your students may have difficulty responding to the true-false part of a test. In particular, they may have problems responding to items that require them to correct all false choices. To eliminate problems, phrase questions concisely so they are clearly either true or false, highlighting critical parts of the statements (Conderman & Koroghlanian, 2002). Eliminate items that assess trivial information or values or that mislead students, and avoid stating items negatively. Focus each item on only one point, avoid items that ask students to change false statements into true statements, and limit the number of true-false questions per test. Phrase items so that they do not provide students with cues by avoiding words that indicate a statement is true (e.g., *often, probably*, and *sometimes*) or false (*always, all*, or *none*) (Kellough & Kellough, 2003). Try to make all true-false items of the same length and avoid predictable answer patterns (e.g., TTFF or FTFT) (Brookhart, 2004). Students who fail to discriminate the *T* and the *F*, or who write *T*'s that look like *F*'s and vice versa, should be allowed to record their response by circling either *True* or *False*. An adapted true-false question is as follows:

Directions: Read each statement. If the statement is *true*, circle (True.) If the statement is *false*, circle (False.)

True False 1. The bee that lays eggs in the colony is the *queen*.

Sentence Completion Items.   Sentence completion items can be especially difficult for students who have memory deficits. You can reduce the memory requirements of these items by making sure that they assess critical information and by providing several response choices or a word bank that includes a list of choices from which students select to complete the statement. For example, the sentence completion question *The outer layer of the atmosphere is called the* _____ can be modified by listing the choices of *stratosphere, exosphere,* and *ionosphere* under the blank. Where possible, the words in word banks can be categorized and placed together in the list. Because statements to be completed that come directly from print materials such as textbooks can be too vague when taken out of context, you should clearly phrase sentence completion items so that students can understand them. Additionally, word blanks should be placed near the end of items, be of the same length, kept to a minimum in each sentence, and require a one-word response or a short phrase. You also can modify the scoring of these items by accepting synonyms as correct responses and by not penalizing students for misspelling correct answers.

Essay Questions.   Essay questions present unique problems for many students because of the numerous skills needed to answer them. You can adapt essay questions by making sure that they are focused, appropriate, and understandable in terms of readability and level of difficulty. Key words that guide students in analyzing and writing the essay can be highlighted and defined or students can be allowed to use a word list or dictionary. You also can consider allowing students to use their books and notes to answer essay questions. It is also important to make sure that students, especially those with writing difficulties, have sufficient time to draft and write their answers (Kellough & Kellough, 2003).

You also can help your students interpret essay questions correctly and guide their essays in several ways. You can provide check sheets or outlines listing the components that can help them organize their response. Rather than using a single open-ended essay question, you can direct the organization and ensure the completeness of the response by using subquestions that divide the open-ended question into smaller sequential questions that can elicit all the parts of an accurate, well-structured, detailed answer. Similarly, important concepts that students should include in their essays can be listed, highlighted, and located in a prominent place so that students will read them before writing their essays. For example, an essay question on meteors can be adapted as follows:

Directions: When writing this essay on meteors, some terms you should discuss include *comets, dust, orbits, atmosphere, radiant, velocity, vaporize,* and *composition.*

1. Describe the *occurrence* of meteors and *why* we see them. In writing your answer, discuss the following:
   - What are meteors made of?
   - Why do we see meteors at certain predictable times of the year?
   - Why do predictable meteor showers always seem to begin at the same place?
   - What are we actually seeing when we see a bright meteor streak through the night sky?

Readability of Items.   Another factor to consider when developing a test is the readability of its items. For example, the essay terms requiring students to compare and contrast two concepts can be simplified by asking students to identify how the concepts are alike and different. Additional information on making tests more readable and legible is presented in chapter 8.

In cooperative group testing, students work collaboratively on open-ended tasks that have nonroutine solutions. What are some tasks that you could use to assess your students using cooperative group testing?

Scoring.   The scoring of your tests can be modified to address the unique needs of students. This can be done by omitting certain questions, offering extra-credit opportunities, giving bonus points for specific questions, allowing students to earn back points by correcting incorrect answers using their notes and textbooks, and giving partial credit for showing correct work. When grammar, spelling, and punctuation are not the elements being tested, you can consider not penalizing students for these errors or giving students separate grades for content and mechanics. On essay tests, students initially can be given credit for an outline, web, diagram, or chart in place of a lengthy response.

In addition to grading the test, you can offer students corrective feedback on their test performance. When the test is returned, review it carefully with the class (Brookhart, 2004). You and your students should analyze tests to determine what types of errors were made and how often they occurred. If patterns of errors are noted, preparation for upcoming tests should address these trends. Error trends also can provide information for adapting tests to meet students' skills and preparing students for tests. For example, if students' tests showed problems with true-false items, you could use other types of items or review with the students strategies for handling true-false items.

Cooperative Group Testing.   In *cooperative group testing*, students work collaboratively on open-ended tasks that have nonroutine solutions. You can then evaluate each group's product and cooperative behavior. Students also can be asked to respond individually to questions about their group's project.

Some teachers use a *two-tiered testing system.* In this system, students working in collaborative groups take a test, and each student receives the group grade. After the group test, students work individually on a second test that covers similar material. Students can be given two separate grades, their two grades can be averaged together into one grade, or they can be allowed to select the higher grade.

Student Involvement.   Your tests can be made fairer by involving students in the testing process (Levine, 2003). You can incorporate students' suggestions in writing and scoring tests. Ask them to submit possible test questions. Students also can be allowed to choose the type of test they take. For example, you can create three versions of a test: multiple-choice, essay, and sentence completion. Your students can then select the test that best fits their response style and study habits. Similarly, you can structure your tests to give students some choice in responding to items. For example, a test can consist of 20 items with varying formats, and students can be directed to respond to any 15 of them.

Gathering Additional Information About the Academic Progress of Diverse Learners

In addition to using various types of standardized and nonstandardized assessments, you can gather additional information about your students' academic progress by using a variety of techniques described in the following sections.

Error Analysis

You can increase the amount of information obtained from formal and informal assessment procedures by using *error analysis.* This method is used to examine students' responses to identify areas of difficulty and patterns in the ways students approach a task.

REFLECTING ON YOUR PRACTICES

Evaluating Teacher-Made Tests

You can evaluate your teacher-made tests by addressing the following:

Content

- Do items measure important information related to the objectives taught?
- Does the test require students to apply skills that they have not been specifically taught?
- Are the types of questions consistent with the strategies used to help students learn the content?
- Are the language and terms used in test directions and items consistent with those used in class?
- Does the percentage of items devoted to specific content areas reflect the amount of class time spent on those areas?
- Is the scope of the material being tested too broad? Too narrow?

Format and Readability

- Is the readability of the test appropriate?
- Are directions and items presented in language students can understand and for all sections of the test that contain different types of items?
- Are cues provided to indicate a change in directions? To alert students to the specifics of each item?
- Are items organized within each section based on their level of difficulty?
- Is the length of the test reasonable?
- Is there a reasonable number of items per page?
- Do items on a page have proper spacing, and are they ordered correctly?
- Do students have to transfer their responses to a separate answer sheet?
- Do students have enough space to record their responses?
- Is space provided for students to write justifications for their responses to short-answer items?
- Is the test legible, neat, and free of distracting features?
- Is the test free of clues that can unintentionally guide students to the correct response?

Multiple-Choice Items

- Does the stem provide a context for answering the item, and is it longer than the answer alternatives?

- Does the stem relate to only one point and include only relevant information?
- Are items grammatically correct, and free of double negatives and categorical words?
- Are all the choices feasible, of the same length, and presented in a logical order?
- Is the correct choice clearly the best answer?

Matching Items

- Does the content to be assessed relate to homogeneous lists of corresponding premises and responses that address one concept?
- Does the matching section include no more than 10 items?
- Are there 25 percent more choices in one column than in the other?
- Is an example embedded?
- Is there only one correct response for each pair?
- Are the directions and the columns presented on the same page?
- Are columns labeled and organized in a sensible, logical manner?
- Do students respond by writing the letter or number in a blank rather than drawing lines from column to column?
- Are the longer item statements listed in the left-hand column and the shorter statements in the right-hand column?

True-False Questions

- Are questions phrased clearly, without double negatives?
- Do items relate to relevant information?
- Are critical parts of statements highlighted?
- Are items focused on only one point?
- Do students respond by circling their choice of *True* or *False* rather than writing out their response or changing false statements into true statements?
- Are items unequivocally true or false?

Sentence Completion Items

- Do items relate to meaningful information?
- Are items understandable to students and do they have only one answer?
- Do items provide students with a sufficient context for answering?

- Do word blanks require a one-word response or a short phrase?
- Are word blanks placed at the end of the item, of the same length, and kept to a minimum?
- Are response choices or word banks provided?

Essay Questions

- Are the readability and level of difficulty of the question appropriate?
- Are key words highlighted?

- Are open-ended questions divided into smaller sequential questions?
- Are students provided with a list of important concepts that should be discussed in the essay?

How would you rate your teacher-made tests?

( ) Excellent ( ) Good ( ) Needs Improvement ( ) Needs Much Improvement

What are some goals and steps you could adopt to improve your teacher-made tests?

Error analysis usually focuses on identifying errors related to inappropriate use of rules and concepts, rather than careless random errors or those caused by lack of training.

Think-Aloud Techniques

The ways students approach a task can also be determined by *think-aloud techniques*, in which students state the processes they are using and describe their thoughts while working on a task (Carr, 2002b). You can encourage students to think aloud by modeling the procedure and talking as you work through tasks and situations. You can also prompt students to think aloud by asking probing questions such as "What are you doing now?" "What are you thinking about?" and "How did you come up with that answer?"

Student Journals/Learning Logs

Student learning in inclusive settings also can be assessed through the use of *journals* or *learning logs* (Carr, 2002b). Periodically, you can ask students to write comments in their journals on what they learned, how they learned it, what they do not understand, why they are confused, and what help they would like to receive (Lenz, Graner, & Adams, 2003). Students who have difficulty writing can maintain an audio log or complete sentence prompts (e.g., I learned . . . .). You and the students can then examine the logs to identify instructional goals and modifications.

Students also can make journal entries on specific information covered in classes, attitudes toward a content area, how material covered in class relates to their lives, and additional questions that need to be studied. For example, after learning about decimals, students can be asked to respond to the following questions: (a) What are decimals, and why do we use them? (b) What part of learning about decimals do you find easy? Hard? and (c) Write a story to go with the problem $9.5 + 3.3 = 12.8$.

Resource

Carr (2002b) offers examples and guidelines for using think-alouds, and learning logs and journals.

Self-Evaluation Questionnaires/Interviews

Self-evaluation questionnaires or *interviews* can provide information on students' perceptions of their educational challenges, progress in learning new material, and strategies for completing a task. For example, according to Pike, Compain, and Mumper (1997), a questionnaire or interview might focus on asking students to respond to the following questions: "What are some things you do well when you read?" "What are some areas in reading that cause you difficulty?" "In what ways is your reading improving?" and "What areas of your reading would you like to improve?" Additional strategies

Resource

Lenz, Graner, and Adams (2003) offer guidelines and forms for soliciting feedback from students about their learning.

for soliciting feedback from students about their learning and reactions to your instructional program are presented in chapter 9.

Reporting Information About the Academic Progress of Diverse Learners

IEPs

Students' academic performance in inclusive settings also can be determined by examining their IEPs (Rea et al., 2002). For example, you can assess their progress by examining their success in attaining the goals outlined in their IEPs. If specific goals have not been achieved, the evaluation can attempt to explain why, and whether these goals are still appropriate.

Promotion and Graduation Rates

Promotion and graduation from high school rates are important indicators of success of inclusion programs. However, because many states have adopted promotion and graduation requirements that are tied to students' performance on high-stakes testing (Wasburn-Moses, 2003), many students, particularly students with special needs are not being promoted or graduating (Heubert, 2003).

Some states employ some type of diploma alternatives to acknowledge students' efforts and motivate them to stay in school. These alternative diplomas include use of:

Resource

Langford and Cary (2000) provide legal and practical guidelines regarding graduation requirements for students with disabilities including standards, credit and attendance requirements, ceremonies, testing, diplomas, and termination of services.

- a regular diploma, which is based on alternative assessment data (e.g., portfolios) rather than passage of high-stakes testing.
- an IEP-based diploma, which is awarded to students who have demonstrated mastery of their IEP goals.
- a certificate of completion or attendance, which is awarded to students who have completed a course of study or attended a specific educational program for a specified period of time.

Many states have changed their graduation requirements and the types of diplomas they offer. Has this occurred in your state? What is its impact on your students and their families?

- a work-study diploma, which is awarded to students based on their work in community-based settings.

In using these alternatives, you should be careful that they do not demean students, lessen the availability of services for them or limit their postsecondary options and opportunities. It is particularly important to provide these students with a comprehensive transition plan according to the guidelines we learned about in chapter 6.

How Can I Grade Students in Inclusive Settings?

Mr. Jones, a general educator, and Ms. Gold, a special education teacher, worked as a cooperative teaching team in the Madison School District. While they had worked well together to design and implement a variety of teaching accommodations to support student learning, their different perspectives on grading became evident when they started to work on students' report cards. Mr. Jones considered it his responsibility to grade all the students. He also felt that it was only fair to grade all students in the same way, as their averages and class ranking would determine their eligibility for honors, awards and admission to college. While he recognized the importance of classroom-based assignments, he thought students' grades should be based mostly on tests since all students would ultimately have to pass the statewide assessments. He also thought that some of the students had received special help from Ms. Gold, and that students who did not receive accommodations should receive higher grades. He also was concerned that the students' families get a true picture of their children's learning in relation to others.

Ms. Gold agreed with Mr. Jones about the need to communicate accurate and realistic information about their children's learning to families. However, Ms. Gold believed that she should collaborate with Mr. Jones in grading students, and that grades should be based on multiple assessment measures and not just tests. She thought that students with special needs should not be penalized for receiving accommodations, as these accommodations allowed them to learn and demonstrate their mastery of the class content and did not violate the integrity of the curriculum and standards.

Report Card Grading

Report card grades, which are given periodically, are another indicator of student progress in inclusive classrooms. As the conflict between Mr. Jones and Ms. Gold reveals, major challenges of grading students in inclusive classrooms include:

- considering and communicating the impact of differentiated instruction and the use of instructional accommodations to support student learning.
- determining the roles of different professionals in the grading process.
- fostering equity and fairness.

Guidelines and models for addressing these issues by implementing equitable and legally sound districtwide report card systems that promote communication and support the use of differentiated instruction in inclusive classrooms are presented next.

Resource

Salend and Garrick Duhaney (2002a) present a model that school districts can use for determining inclusive grading policies and practices.

Consider and Address the Legal Guidelines for Grading

Section 504 and Title II of the ADA, which are under the supervision of the Office of Civil Rights (OCR), have led to specific legal interpretations that guide the grading of *all* students in inclusive settings. These OCR guidelines mandate that:

- *all* students must be treated similarly in terms of grades, class ranking, honors, awards, graduation, and diplomas.
- a modified grading system can be employed if it is available to *all* students.
- students who take a general education class for no credit or reasons other than mastery of the curriculum can be provided with grading procedures that are different from the rest of the class.
- guidelines and criteria for ranking *all* students or granting awards cannot arbitrarily lessen or exclude the grades of students with disabilities.
- the weighting of grades and awarding of honors are allowable if they are based on objective criteria and courses that are open and available to *all* students.
- report card or transcript designations, symbols, or terminology that indicate participation in special education or that a student received pedagogical accommodations or a modified curriculum in general education classes are not permissible unless the grades and courses of *all* students are treated in the same manner.

Identify the Purpose of Report Card Grades

The grading of *all* students should be compatible with the district's preferences regarding the purposes of grading. Since the purposes of grading may change as students progress through school, different grading systems may be appropriate for different grades. At the elementary level, an anecdotal grading system can be used to communicate academic gains as well as social and developmental accomplishments. In high schools where grading is used to rank students to determine their eligibility for programs and awards, a grading system that compares students based mostly on their academic performance is often used.

Agree On the Nature and Impact of Differentiated Instruction Techniques

Teachers like Mr. Jones and Ms. Gold can use the instructional accommodations continuum we discussed in chapter 8 to resolve their differences regarding the nature and impact of differentiated instruction. The continuum delineates three levels of accommodations that are based on their impact on the curriculum mastery expected of students: access, low-impact, and high-impact accommodations (Stough, 2002).

Select Grading Systems that Support Differentiated Instruction and Communication

Resource

Guskey (2001) provides guidelines for linking report cards to learning standards.

After agreeing on the nature and impact of the instructional accommodations, educators can select appropriate report card alternatives that support differentiation and communication. For example, educators can use report card instructional and testing accommodations cover sheets for *all students* (see Figure 12.7) to communicate the conditions

FIGURE 12.7

Sample instructional and testing accommodations report card cover sheet

Student's name: _____

Grade: _____

Teacher(s): _____

INSTRUCTIONAL ACCOMMODATIONS RECEIVED

Check all the instructional accommodations delivered

- ☐ Word processor/spell checker
- ☐ Note-taking assistance
- ☐ Use of technology (please specify)
- ☐ Learning strategies instruction
- ☐ Specialized seating arrangements
- ☐ Study skills instruction
- ☐ Memory aids and strategies
- ☐ Additional time to complete tasks
- ☐ Manipulatives
- ☐ Electronic textbooks
- ☐ Frequent comprehension checks
- ☐ Daily/weekly planner
- ☐ Redirection
- ☐ Tiered assignments
- ☐ Adapted directions
- ☐ Shorter assignments
- ☐ Scheduling adaptations
- ☐ Frequent reinforcement
- ☐ Modeling
- ☐ Adapted textbooks
- ☐ Visuals to support instruction

- ☐ Adapted materials
- ☐ Adult assistance
- ☐ Peer-mediated instruction
- ☐ Verbal prompts
- ☐ Curriculum overlapping
- ☐ Self-correcting materials
- ☐ Cues to highlight information
- ☐ Adapted homework
- ☐ Calculators
- ☐ Graphic organizers
- ☐ Frequent communication with families
- ☐ Generalization strategies
- ☐ Listening/note-taking guides
- ☐ Frequent feedback
- ☐ Examples/models of correct response formats
- ☐ Prompting
- ☐ Concrete teaching aids
- ☐ Limited distractions
- ☐ Study guides

☐ Other (please specify) _____

TESTING ACCOMMODATIONS RECEIVED

Check all the testing accommodations delivered

- ☐ Items omitted
- ☐ Extended time
- ☐ Individual administration
- ☐ Directions/items read
- ☐ Adapted directions
- ☐ Word processor/spell check
- ☐ Adapted multiple-choice items
- ☐ Calculator
- ☐ Increased space in between items
- ☐ Fewer items
- ☐ Adapted matching items
- ☐ Adapted true-false items
- ☐ Adapted sentence completion items
- ☐ Adapted essay questions

- ☐ Proctor
- ☐ Scribe
- ☐ Separate location
- ☐ Breaks
- ☐ Alternate response mode
- ☐ Administration over several sessions
- ☐ Cues to highlight information
- ☐ Oral test
- ☐ Cooperative group testing
- ☐ Extra credit options
- ☐ Bonus points
- ☐ Writing mechanics waived
- ☐ Use of technology (please specify)

☐ Other (please specify) _____

associated with their students' grades. As described next, a range of norm-referenced, criterion-referenced, or self-referenced grading systems or a combination of these types of referent grading systems can be used in inclusive settings to support and communicate your use of differentiated instruction (Brookhart, 2004).

Norm-Referenced Grading Systems

Norm-referenced grading alternatives involve giving numeric or letter grades to compare students using the same academic standards. They can be tailored to inclusive classrooms to foster communication and differentiation in a variety of ways.

As in a figure skating competition where a skater's score is based on the quality and level of difficulty of the routine, numerical grades for specific assignments or courses can be computed based on pre-established difficulty levels. For example, you can give *all* your students a list of differentiated assignments, and their corresponding levels of difficulty. They can choose which assignment(s) to complete and receive grades that reflect the quality and level of difficulty of the assignment. For example, a student who completes an assignment of an average level of difficulty with a quality grade of 90 could have that grade multiplied by 1 to compute a final grade (e.g., $90 \times 1.0 = 90$), while a student who completes a more difficult assignment with a grade of quality grade of 90 could have the grade multiplied by a factor of 1.05 to compute a final grade (e.g., $90 \times 1.05 = 94.5$).

You also can use *multiple grading* to adjust your numerical grades by grading students on multiple factors: achievement, effort, and level of curriculum difficulty. Grades for these factors can then be averaged or weighted to produce a composite final grade. For example, a student who was assigned an achievement grade of 95, an effort grade of 90, and a level-of-curriculum-difficulty grade of 85 could have these grades averaged into a final grade of 90. Additionally, based on their importance, you can weight the various factors used to grade your students. For example, a formula that gives a double weighting to students' achievement grade could be used to compute the same student's final grade as follows:

$$\frac{2 \times \text{Achievement grade (95)} + \text{effort grade (90)} + \text{level-of-curriculum-difficulty grade (85)}}{4} = 91.25$$

Level grading can help you individualize your grading by using a numeric or letter subscript to indicate your use of differentiated instruction techniques to help your students achieve a specific level of curriculum mastery. For example, a B_3 grade can indicate that a student is performing in the B range on a third-grade level of curriculum mastery, and a C_{10a} grade can indicate that a student is performing in the C range on a 10th-grade level of curriculum mastery with accommodations.

You also can supplement your use of numeric or letter grades by communicating the accommodations that students received to support their learning. For example, you list the instructional and testing accommodations associated with students' grades as follows:

Grade	Accommodations
89	Peer note-taker, individualized homework, extended time on assignments and tests

Criterion-Referenced Grading Systems

Rather than comparing your students based on their numerical or letter grades, *criterion-referenced grading systems* allow you to report on your students' mastery within the curriculum. You can modify these grading systems to promote communication and differentiation in several ways.

You can report on your students' levels of curriculum mastery and instructional accommodations by completing a series of predetermined, open-ended statements addressing important aspects of your curriculum. Examples of open-ended question prompts across a variety of academic and social domains and grade levels are as follows:

- Pays attention for _____ minutes.
- Recognizes numbers up to _____.
- Solves algebraic equations up to _____.
- Identifies _____ letters of the alphabet.
- Reads _____ words.
- Writes a paragraph of _____ sentences.
- Writes using the following conventions:
- Uses the following learning strategies:
- Understands the following forms of poetry:
- Successfully performs the following experiments:

To help students' families interpret this information, you can share normative data regarding a student's relative standing with them (Tomlinson, 2001). You can do this by giving them a listing of age-appropriate curricular expectations, or embedding this information within each item. For example, the context for judging the report card statement "defines <u>30</u> scientific terms" can be provided by placing the age appropriate expectations for students in terms of numbers recognized in parenthesis (e.g., "defines <u>30</u> (50) scientific terms"). Open-ended sentences also can be phrased so that they provide a list of the accommodations delivered. For example, the sentence completion statement *"solves the following types of word problems:"* can be revised to add accommodations so that it reads, *"solves the following types of word problems, with* _____ *(list accommodations)"*.

You also can use rating scales and checklists to present criterion-referenced grading information and instructional accommodations to others (Tomlinson, 2001). You do this by linking items to benchmarks associated with the curriculum and evaluating your students according to their mastery of these benchmarks. As presented in Figure 12.8, checklist and rating scale items can include information on the nature and degree of the instructional accommodations associated with student mastery.

You also can individualize criterion-referenced grading systems by using mastery level grading and contract grading. *Mastery level grading* involves you and your students dividing course content into a hierarchy of skills and determining appropriate learning activities and instructional accommodations based on an initial assessment of your students' individual needs. After your students complete these learning activities and receive the appropriate instructional accommodations, they demonstrate their mastery of the content by performing an activity or taking a test. This process is repeated until all skills are mastered. Similarly, in *contract grading*, you and your students develop a contract outlining the learning goals/objectives; the amount, nature, and quality of the learning activities and instructional accommodations; and the products your

FIGURE 12.8

Sample checklist and rating scale items addressing the use of instructional accommodations

---

SAMPLE CHECKLIST ITEMS

1. Performs computations with a calculator _____ .
2. Maintains place when reading using a mask or marker _____ .
3. Writes using a teacher-produced word bank _____ .

SAMPLE RATING SCALE ITEMS

1. Writes a complete paragraph:

_____	_____	_____	_____	_____
Performs independently	Performs mostly independently	Performs with some assistance	Performs with some accommodations	Performs with considerable accommodations and assistance

2. Takes notes:

_____	_____	_____
independently	with a teacher-prepared outline	with the aid of peer note-takers

3. Completes assignments and exams:

_____	_____	_____	_____	_____
independently	with step-by-step instructions	with a reduced number of items	with extended time	with peer or adult assistance

4. Spells:

_____	_____	_____	_____
independently	with a spell checker	with a dictionary or pictionary	with a word bank

---

students must complete as well as the procedures for evaluating learning products and assigning grades.

Self-Referenced Grading Systems

Self-referenced grading systems are often used to communicate your students' progress over a period of time. In self-referenced grading systems, *all* your students are graded based on their progress in comparison with their past performance, ability levels, effort, and special needs. One type of self-referenced grading you can use is *descriptive grading*, which involves your writing comments that address your students':

*   academic progress in terms of mastery of the curriculum.
*   learning styles.
*   use of learning strategies.
*   effort, attitudes, behavior, and socialization.
*   special talents and challenges.
*   instructional accomodations.

You also can use *progressive improvement grading* to report student learning and communicate the use and impact of instructional accommodations. *Progressive improvement grading* involves your providing your students with feedback and instructional accommodations as they work on a range of individualized assessment and learning activities throughout the grading period. However, you only use their performance on assessment and learning activities during the final weeks of the grading period to assess their growth and determine grades.

Address the Special Needs and Situations of Students and Teachers

District policies also can offer teachers guidance on the:

*   types of grading systems to be used.
*   the factors to considered in determining students' grades.
*   the weighting of final exams and other grading activities.
*   the level for passing a class.
*   the computation of grades, grade-point averages and class ranks (Brookhart, 2004).

Reflective

Do grading alternatives and accommodations compromise standards and reduce course integrity? Should grades be assigned only by the general education classroom teacher or through collaboration with others?

Issues related to collaborative grading should be addressed to minimize the confusion that teachers like Mr. Jones and Ms. Gold experience by clarifying each team member's role and responsibility in grading students. Christiansen and Vogel (1998) offer a decision model that teachers working in cooperative teaching arrangements can use to resolve conflicts in their grading practices, and make grading students a collaborative process. The district's policies can also cover the assignment of incomplete grades.

The district's policy also should address procedures for determining grading adaptations for *all students* who are not working on general education goals and learning standards and will not participate in statewide assessments. Munk and Bursuck (2001) developed a collaborative model that the multidisciplinary team can use to personalize grading plans that involves selecting, implementing and evaluating grading alternatives that address the individualized needs and grading purposes of students. For example, some students might benefit from use of an *IEP grading system,* in which the individualized goals, instructional accommodations, and performance criteria on students' IEPs serve as the reference point for judging student progress and assigning grades.

Use Effective Practices That Support the Teaching, Learning, and Grading Processes

You will need to use practices that foster the use of differentiated instruction, enhance student learning, and facilitate the grading process (Brookhart, 2004; Tomlinson, 2001). Effective practices that support the teaching, learning, and grading processes include:

*   *Communicating expectations and grading guidelines to your students and their families.*
*   *Informing students and families regarding grading progress on a regular basis.*
*   *Reviewing exemplary models of classroom assignments.*
*   *Using a range of assignments that addresses students' varied learning needs, strengths, and styles.*
*   *Employing classroom-based assessment alternatives to traditional testing.*
*   *Providing feedback on assignments and grading students after they have learned something rather than while they are learning it.*
*   *Involving students in the grading process.*
*   *Avoiding competition and promoting collaboration.*
*   *Giving separate grades for content and style.*
*   *Designing valid tests and providing students with appropriate testing accommodations.*

- *Using extra credit judiciously*. Use extra credit to motivate students to expand their understanding of concepts, and assist those students who need additional points to raise their grades from one level to another (e.g., moving from a 75 to an 80). However, because extra credit should not be used to help students compensate near the end of the grading period for work they failed to do, use it judiciously.
- *Using median scores to compute grades*. Averaging tends to accentuate the effect of a poor score and makes it difficult for students to receive a good grade, which can be discouraging for students. Therefore, consider using the median to determine students' grades.

How Can I Evaluate the Social and Behavioral Performance of Students?

One premise of inclusion programs is that such programs will have a positive effect on students' social and behavioral development. For students with disabilities, desired social and behavioral outcomes include being on task, making friends, increasing their social and behavioral skills, and improving their self-concepts. For students without disabilities, social and behavioral outcomes include becoming more accepting and understanding of individual differences, more aware of and sensitive to the needs of others, and more willing to make friends with students with disabilities.

Observational and Sociometric Techniques

Resource

Voltz, Brazil, and Ford (2001) offer ways to evaluate various aspects of inclusion programs, including student interaction patterns.

cd-rom

As we discussed in chapter 5, you can use observational and sociometric techniques to gain insights into students' interaction and friendship patterns (Hall & Strickett, 2002; Tur-Kaspa, 2002). These techniques also can help you learn about your students' social and behavioral competence. Observations of students' behavioral and social skills also can be recorded on checklists and rating scales (Epstein, Hertzog, & Reid, 2001). These scales provide a list of behavioral and social skills that guide your observations of your students, and help you identify their strengths and challenges. To ensure that the results are accurate and representative of student behavior, you may want to ask several different individuals to rate your students in various settings. A sample rating scale based on the social and behavioral skills that teachers believe are important for success in inclusive classrooms is presented in Figure 12.9. **To hear educators discussing the use of observations to assess student progress, go to Case 3: Assess Plan on the CD-ROM and click on the Observable Outcomes video clip. How did the educators use observation to assess the success of their program?**

Data collected via observation can be supplemented by sociograms (see chapter 5), observations, and interviews with family members, other teachers, and students (Lee, Yoo, & Bak, 2003). Still other information sources are documents revealing the number and types of discipline reports, behavioral incidents, interruptions caused, bullying and teasing behaviors, suspension/expulsions, and referrals to special education (Rea et al., 2002). Changes in students' attendance patterns and friendships also can be examined to assess their social and behavioral development.

FIGURE 12.9

Inclusive setting behavioral and social skills rating scale

Please rate each skill using the following scale:

Always	Usually	Sometimes	Rarely	Never
(1)	(2)	(3)	(4)	(5)

Behavioral and Social Skills	Always (1)	Usually (2)	Sometimes (3)	Rarely (4)	Never (5)
1. Follows directions	1	2	3	4	5
2. Asks for help when it's appropriate	1	2	3	4	5
3. Begins an assignment after teacher gives assignment to class	1	2	3	4	5
4. Obeys class rules	1	2	3	4	5
5. Doesn't speak when others are talking	1	2	3	4	5
6. Works well with others	1	2	3	4	5
7. Interacts cooperatively with others	1	2	3	4	5
8. Shares with others	1	2	3	4	5
9. Attends class regularly	1	2	3	4	5
10. Seeks teacher's permission before speaking	1	2	3	4	5
11. Works independently on assignments	1	2	3	4	5
12. Seeks teacher's permission before leaving seat	1	2	3	4	5
13. Brings necessary materials to class	1	2	3	4	5
14. Participates in class	1	2	3	4	5
15. Makes friends	1	2	3	4	5
16. Has a sense of humor	1	2	3	4	5

Self-Concept Measures

Many strategies have been developed to assess students' self-concepts, which you can use as part of your evaluation of your inclusion program (Elbaum, 2002). You can measure the academic self-concepts of your students and their perceptions of how they learn by asking them to complete instruments such as the *Student Self-Report System* (Meltzer & Roditi, 1994), and the *Student Skills Rating Survey* (Stone & May, 2002). Other instruments used to measure aspects of the self-concept of students in inclusion programs include the *Self-Perception Profile* (Frederickson & Turner, 2003) and the *Children's Loneliness and Social Dissatisfaction Scale* (Pavri & Luftig, 2000).

Resource

Bryan (1997) offers examples of assessment instruments that assess students' affective status, self-efficacy, social status, and social skills.

How Can I Measure Perceptions of My Inclusion Program?

As we saw in chapter 1, students, teachers, and family members have varied perceptions of inclusion that are often related to the effectiveness of the inclusion program. Therefore, as the Madison School District committee realized, any evaluation of inclusion programs must include an examination of the perceptions and experiences of students, teachers, and family members (Bernhardt, 2003). This information can help you analyze the effectiveness of your inclusion program, document changes over time, validate successful inclusive programmatic factors and educational policies that should be continued, and pinpoint procedures that need to be revised.

Students' Perceptions

Your students' perceptions are crucial in evaluating your inclusion program. Interviews and questionnaires can be used to collect information from students on the academic and social benefits of the program, as well as their insights and experiences. When using interviews and questionnaires, items and directions should be clearly stated and phrased using students' language rather than professional jargon. When professional terms like *inclusion* must be used, these terms should be defined so that your students can understand them.

You also need to consider whether it is appropriate to use phrases such as *students with and without disabilities* and to tailor specific items for both types of students. Because interviews and questionnaires may take a long time to complete, you may choose to administer them over several days. Interviews are particularly appropriate for younger students and those who have difficulty reading and writing. A list of potential interview questions is presented in Figure 12.10.

Questionnaires also allow you to investigate your students' feelings about and reactions to various aspects of inclusion programs. It is best to use a closed-form questionnaire that is easy for them to complete. This type of questionnaire has a yes-no or true-false format or asks students to mark a number or a statement that best indicates their response. For students who have reading and/or writing difficulties, you may need to read items for them as well as record their responses. A sample questionnaire is presented in Figure 12.11.

Teachers' Perceptions

Teachers are vital to the success of inclusion programs. Therefore, in evaluating inclusion programs, their perceptions of and experiences with inclusion are very important. This information can help school districts assess the impact of their inclusion programs on students, evaluate various aspects of these programs, and design and implement effective inclusion programs.

Sample student interview

FIGURE 12.10

Others sometimes call your class an inclusion classroom. This means that students who learn, act, look, and speak in different ways are learning together in the same class. It also means that other teachers work with students in this classroom rather than taking them to another classroom.

I am going to ask you some questions about your class.

1. Do you think that all types of students learning in the same class is a good idea? Why or why not?
2. What things do you like about being in this class?
3. What things don't you like about being in this class?
4. What have you learned from being in this class?
5. In what areas are you doing well? Having difficulty?
6. Are you completing all your schoolwork and homework? If so, what things are helping you to complete your work? If not, what things are keeping you from completing your work?
7. What are your teachers doing to help you in your class?
8. How do you get along with other students in this class? How has being in this class affected your friendships and popularity?
9. In what afterschool activities do you participate? If none, why?
10. How do you think your classmates feel about being in this class?
11. What do you think your classmates learned from being in this class?
12. What changes have you observed in your classmates since being in this class?
13. What parts of being in this class have been hard for you? For your classmates? For your teacher(s)? Why?
14. What would you tell other students about being in this class?
15. What ways can you think of to make this class work better?

FIGURE 12.11

Sample student inclusion survey

Please circle the word that best describes your feelings about your class:

1. I like being in a class with different types of students.	Yes	Maybe	No
2. I learned a lot, and so did others.	Yes	Maybe	No
3. I am more likely to help other students.	Yes	Maybe	No
4. I saw other students making fun of their classmates.	Yes	Maybe	No
5. I have improved at teaching others.	Yes	Maybe	No
6. I am more understanding of the behaviors and feelings of others.	Yes	Maybe	No
7. I was made fun of by my classmates.	Yes	Maybe	No
8. I feel better about myself.	Yes	Maybe	No
9. I feel that I belong in this class.	Yes	Maybe	No
10. I improved my schoolwork and grades.	Yes	Maybe	No
11. I am better at making friends.	Yes	Maybe	No
12. I improved at learning from others.	Yes	Maybe	No
13. I am less likely to make fun of others.	Yes	Maybe	No
14. I felt the same as the other students in my class.	Yes	Maybe	No
15. I received help from my teacher(s) when I needed it.	Yes	Maybe	No
16. I did most of my schoolwork without help.	Yes	Maybe	No
17. I liked having several teachers in the classroom.	Yes	Maybe	No
18. I liked working with other students.	Yes	Maybe	No
19. I enjoyed being in this classroom.	Yes	Maybe	No
20. I would like to be in a class like this next year.	Yes	Maybe	No

Note: See Companion Website for additional survey questions.

Questionnaires

Questionnaires and interviews can be used to elicit teachers' feelings about and reactions to inclusion programs, including their beliefs and concerns, as well as their feelings about the impact of the programs (McLeskey et al., 2001). Questionnaires and interviews also can address teachers' satisfaction with (a) their roles in implementing inclusion programs;

All students can benefit from inclusive teaching practices. How do your students benefit from your inclusive teaching practices?

(b) the quality of the resources they have received to implement inclusion; (c) their experiences in collaborating and communicating with others; (d) their skills and training to implement inclusion successfully; and (e) the policies and practices concerning inclusion of the school and the district. A sample questionnaire designed to assess teachers' perceptions of and experiences with inclusive education is presented in Figure 12.12.

Interviews

Interviews give teachers the opportunity to respond to open-ended questions. These responses can provide rich and descriptive examples, insights, and suggestions that can be valuable in evaluating inclusive educational programs (Hollingsworth, 2001). In addition to individual interviews, focus group interviews can be used (Stanovich, 1999). Potential

FIGURE 12.12

Sample teacher's inclusion survey

Please indicate your feelings about and experiences with inclusion using the following scale:

Strongly Disagree (SD)	Disagree (D)	Neutral (N)	Agree (A)	Strongly Agree (SA)
1	2	3	4	5

	SD	D	N	A	SA
1. I feel that inclusion is a good idea.	1	2	3	4	5
2. I feel that I have the time and the training to implement inclusion successfully.	1	2	3	4	5
3. I feel that inclusion helps students develop friendships.	1	2	3	4	5
4. I feel that inclusion is working well in my class.	1	2	3	4	5
5. I feel that I receive the necessary support and assistance to implement inclusion successfully.	1	2	3	4	5
6. I feel that it is difficult to modify instruction and my teaching style to meet the needs of students with disabilities.	1	2	3	4	5
7. I feel that inclusion helps students academically.	1	2	3	4	5
8. I feel that having other adults in the classroom is an asset.	1	2	3	4	5
9. I feel that the demands of the curriculum make it difficult to implement inclusion.	1	2	3	4	5
10. I feel that I have been sufficiently involved in the inclusion process in my school.	1	2	3	4	5
11. I feel that I perform a subordinate role as a result of inclusion.	1	2	3	4	5
12. I feel that I do not have enough time to communicate and collaborate with others.	1	2	3	4	5
13. My students' academic performance has been negatively affected.	1	2	3	4	5
14. My students have become more accepting of individual differences.	1	2	3	4	5
15. My students feel better about themselves.	1	2	3	4	5
16. My students have picked up undesirable behaviors from their classmates.	1	2	3	4	5
17. My students have received less teacher attention.	1	2	3	4	5
18. My students have been teased by their classmates.	1	2	3	4	5
19. My students have grown socially and emotionally.	1	2	3	4	5
20. My students feel that they belong in my class.	1	2	3	4	5
21. My students feel positive about my class.	1	2	3	4	5
22. My students show pride in their work.	1	2	3	4	5

Note: See Companion Website for additional survey questions.

interview questions that can be used to examine teachers' experiences in inclusion programs are presented in Figure 12.13.

Interviews with teachers also can provide valuable information that can pinpoint students' strengths and existing or potential problems in their academic, behavioral, and social-emotional performance by addressing the following questions:

- How is the student performing academically, socially, and behaviorally in your class?
- To what extent has the student achieved the goals listed in the IEP? If the goals have not been achieved, what is an explanation?
- Does the student complete classwork, homework, and other assigned projects?
- What methods, materials, instructional accommodations, and alternative testing techniques have been successful? Unsuccessful?
- What accommodations have been provided to meet the student's cultural and language needs? How effective have these accommodations been?

Sample interview questions to examine the experiences of educators working in inclusive classrooms

1. How is inclusion working in your class? Your school? What is working well? What is not working well?
2. What factors have contributed to the success of inclusion in your class? At your school?
3. What factors have prevented inclusion from working in your class? At your school?
4. What are your biggest concerns about and frustrations with inclusion?
5. What things do you enjoy most about inclusion?
6. Do you have difficulty meeting the needs of students with certain types of disabilities? If so, what types of disabilities do these students have and what problems are you experiencing?
7. Do you feel that you have the support, resources, and time to implement inclusion effectively? If not, what support, resources, and scheduling arrangements would be helpful to you?
8. Do you feel that you have the skills and training to implement inclusion effectively? If not, what skills would you like to develop and what training would you like to receive?
9. Which individuals (give titles, not names) have been most helpful in assisting you to implement inclusion? How have these individuals assisted you? What additional assistance would you like to receive?
10. How has inclusion affected your students with disabilities? Please describe any benefits and/or negative consequences you have observed in these students.
11. What accommodations have been provided to meet the cultural and linguistic needs of your students? How effective have these accommodations been?
12. Have your students participated in the statewide testing program? If yes, what were the results? What, if any, alternative testing techniques were employed? Were they effective? If no, why not and what alternative assessment strategies have been employed?
13. How has inclusion affected your students without disabilities? Please describe any benefits and/or negative consequences you have observed for these students.
14. How has inclusion affected you as a professional and a person? Please describe any benefits and/or any negative consequences for you.
15. In what ways has your role changed as a result of your school's effort to implement inclusion? What do you enjoy about your new roles? What concerns do you have about your new roles?
16. How did it feel to collaborate with another professional? What was most difficult? Most enjoyable? Most surprising?
17. How did the collaboration process change throughout the school year?
18. What did you learn from collaborating with another professional?
19. What suggestions would you have for other professionals who are planning to work collaboratively?
20. If another professional asked you for advice about inclusion, what advice would you give?
21. What things has your school district done to facilitate inclusion in your school? To hinder inclusion in your school?
22. What schoolwide and districtwide inclusion practices would you like to see retained? What practices would you like to see revised?
23. What additional information would you like to have about inclusion?

FIGURE 12.13

Note: Banerji & Dailey (1995); Bennett et al. (1997); Downing et al. (1997); Giangreco et al. (1993); Janney, Snell, Beers, & Raynes (1995); Phillips et al. (1995); York & Tundidor (1995).

Resource

Hollingsworth (2001) offers guidelines for using questionnaires and focus group interviews to evaluate aspects of inclusion programs.

Resource

Hourcade, Parette, and Anderson (2003) and Salend, Gordon, and Lopez-Vona (2002) offer guidelines for using observations, journals, and portfolios to examine the effectiveness of cooperative teaching teams.

- How does the student get along with classmates?
- In what extracurricular activities does the student participate?
- Is the student receiving the necessary supportive services?
- How is the communication system with other personnel and the student's family working?

Teachers also can provide feedback on students' performance by completing a weekly or monthly rating scale such as the one presented in Figure 12.14.

Cooperative Teaching Experiences

Many school districts like the Madison School District employ cooperative teaching arrangements as part of their efforts to implement inclusion programs (Gately & Gately,

---

DATE DISTRIBUTED: _____
DATE COMPLETED: _____
DATE RETURNED: _____
CLASS: _____
How are you feeling about _____'s:
                          (student's name)

	Please Rate				Comments
1. Goals	Not Clear---------------------Very Clear				
	1	2	3	4	
2. Participation in class	Passive------------------------------Active				
	1	2	3	4	
3. Behavior	Unmanageable------------ Manageable				
	1	2	3	4	
4. Progress	Unnoticeable------------------Noticeable				
	1	2	3	4	
5. Impact on classroom atmosphere	Negative------------------------- Positive				
	1	2	3	4	
6. Peer connections	Isolated------------------------Connected				
	1	2	3	4	
7. Request for my time/ attention	Too Demanding-Reasonable Amount				
	1	2	3	4	

Please list three positive comments and three concerns that you may have for _____ .
                                                                              (class)

POSITIVES	CONCERNS	Please list any initial thoughts you may have that address your concerns.
1.	1.	
2.	2.	
3.	3.	

FIGURE 12.14   Sample student progress rating form

Source: From "Measuring Perceptions About Inclusion," by M. Prom, 1999, *Teaching Exceptional Children, 31,* pp. 38–42. Copyright 1999 by The Council for Exceptional Children. Reprinted with permission.

2001). Therefore, an ongoing evaluation of inclusion programs also should include an examination of the experiences and perceptions of cooperative teaching teams (Hourcade, Parette & Anderson, 2003; Noonan et al., 2003). Such information can help validate successful collaborative practices and identify those practices in need of revision. Sample surveys and interviews to solicit feedback from teachers concerning their efforts to work collaboratively are presented in chapter 4.

Family Members' Perceptions

Family members are particularly affected by the impact of inclusion programs on their children. Therefore, they too can provide feedback on the academic, social, and behavioral development of their children (Salend & Garrick Duhaney, 2002b). They can also assess the effectiveness of the school district's inclusion practices and policies, as well as identify and make recommendations about programmatic policies and practices that need revision.

Interviews and Questionnaires

Schools should not assume that families are satisfied with the inclusion program. Their experiences with and perceptions of the program should be assessed as part of the evaluation of the program. A sample interview and a questionnaire on the perceptions and experiences of families concerning inclusion programs are provided in Figures 12.15 and 12.16, respectively.

Resource

Salend and Garrick Duhaney (2002b) offer guidelines for designing and conducting inclusion interviews and surveys with families.

FIGURE 12.15

Sample family interview questions concerning inclusive education programs

1. Do you think that placing students with disabilities in general education classrooms with their peers who do not have disabilities is a good idea? Why or why not?
2. What things do you like about your child being in an inclusion classroom?
3. What concerns do (did) you have about your child being in an inclusion classroom? Do you still have these concerns?
4. How does your child feel about being in an inclusion classroom? What things does your child like about being in an inclusion classroom? What concerns, if any, does your child have about being in an inclusion classroom? How could these concerns be addressed?
5. How do you feel about the educational program your child is receiving in his or her inclusion classroom?
6. How do you feel about the special education and supportive services your child is receiving in his or her inclusion classroom?
7. How has being in an inclusion classroom affected your child academically, socially, and behaviorally? Please describe any benefits and/or negative consequences you have observed in your child. What factors led to these changes?
8. How has your child's placement in an inclusion classroom affected other students? His or her teachers? Other families? Other professionals who work with your child? Please describe any benefits and/or any negative consequences for these individuals.
9. How has your child's placement in an inclusion classroom affected you? Please describe any benefits and/or any negative consequences for you.
10. Have your goals for your child's future changed as a result of your child's being placed in an inclusion classroom? If yes, in what ways?
11. What roles have you performed in the inclusion process? Are you satisfied with your roles in the inclusion process? If so, what roles have been particularly important and satisfying? If not, why not, and what roles would you like to perform?
12. What things seem to make inclusion work well at your child's school? What things seem to prevent inclusion from working well at your child's school? In what ways can inclusion be improved in your child's class and school?
13. What schoolwide and districtwide inclusion practices would you like to see retained? What practices would you like to see revised?
14. What do you think of the access to, timeliness, and coordination of the services your child is receiving?
15. How is the communication system between you and the school working?
16. What additional information would you like to have about inclusion and your child's class?

Note: Gibb et al. (1997); Green & Shinn (1995); Peck et al. (1992); Ryndak et al. (1995); York & Tundidor (1995).

FIGURE 12.16

Sample family inclusion survey

Please indicate your feelings about and experiences with inclusion using the following scale:

Strongly Disagree (SD)	Disagree (D)	Neutral (N)	Agree (A)	Strongly Agree (SA)
1	2	3	4	5

	SD	D	N	A	SA
1. I feel satisfied with the educational and supportive services my child is receiving.	1	2	3	4	5
2. I feel satisfied with the school's communication with families.	1	2	3	4	5
3. I feel that being in an inclusion class has been positive for my child.	1	2	3	4	5
4. I feel that inclusion helps children academically and socially.	1	2	3	4	5
5. I feel that families are adequately involved in the inclusion process.	1	2	3	4	5
6. I feel that the school district did a good job of explaining the inclusion program to me.	1	2	3	4	5
7. My child learned a lot.	1	2	3	4	5
8. My child talks positively about school.	1	2	3	4	5
9. My child feels proud of his/her classwork.	1	2	3	4	5
10. My child has learned to feel comfortable interacting with other students.	1	2	3	4	5
11. My child has grown socially and emotionally.	1	2	3	4	5
12. My child's education has been negatively affected.	1	2	3	4	5
13. My child has received fewer services.	1	2	3	4	5
14. My child has made more friends.	1	2	3	4	5
15. My child has become more confident and outgoing.	1	2	3	4	5
16. My child has become more accepting of individual differences.	1	2	3	4	5
17. My child has picked up undesirable behavior from classmates.	1	2	3	4	5
18. My child has been teased by classmates.	1	2	3	4	5
19. My child has teased classmates.	1	2	3	4	5
20. My child would like to be in an inclusion class next year.	1	2	3	4	5

Note: See Companion Website for additional survey questions.

How Can I Improve the Effectiveness of My Inclusion Program?

After you have collected data on students' progress and on students', teachers', and family members' perceptions of your inclusion program, members of the school or school district's comprehensive planning team or inclusive educational program planning committee can analyze them (Bernhardt, 2003). The data can be used to examine the effect of the program and develop an action plan to improve the program's effectiveness.

Examine the Impact on Student Performance

First, the committee can examine the effect of your inclusion program on the academic, social, and behavioral performance of your students by reviewing the results of standardized tests and the findings of alternative assessments. This information can be supplemented by an examination of other indicators of student progress and program effectiveness. Such indicators include data on graduation rates, participation in statewide tests, attendance patterns, participation in extracurricular activities, behavioral referrals, course failures, and accrual of credits (Rea et al., 2002). For secondary students, data on the types of diplomas students are receiving, as well as their success in attending college, finding a job, living independently, and being socially integrated into their communities can be measures of the ability of the inclusion program to help students make the transition from school to adulthood.

Determine Program Strengths, Concerns, and Possible Solutions

The data on the perceptions of students, teachers, and family members regarding your inclusion program also can be analyzed to determine the strengths of the program and validate aspects of the program that appear to be working well (Bernhardt, 2003). In addition, these data can be used to identify components of the program that need revision, as well as develop an action plan to implement potential solutions (McTighe & Thomas, 2003). Possible concerns associated with inclusion programs and potential solutions to address these concerns are presented in Table 12.2. **To practice evaluating inclusion programs, go to Cases 1, 2, 3, and 4 on the CD-ROM and view all the video clips. What effective practices do the educators use? How could the educators improve their inclusive classroom?**

Resource

McTighe and Thomas (2003) offer guidelines and questions for collecting and examining student performance data and developing action plans.

cd-rom

TABLE 12.2

Possible concerns about inclusion and potential solutions

Possible Concerns	Potential Solutions
Students are not benefitting academically, socially, and behaviorally.	• Collect and examine data on the impact of the program on students (see chapter 12). • Meet with families (see chapter 4). • Revise students' IEPs (see chapter 2). • Use strategies to promote the academic development of students, such as teaching students to use learning strategies, adapting large- and small-group instruction, modifying instructional materials and techniques, employing technology, and using culturally relevant instructional strategies (see chapters 2, 3, 6 and 8–11). • Use strategies to promote acceptance of individual differences and friendships (see chapter 5). • Use strategies to modify classroom behavior (see chapter 7). • Modify the classroom environment to promote students' academic, social, and behavioral development (see chapter 7).
Students with disabilities are having a difficult time adjusting to inclusive classrooms.	• Help students with disabilities make the transition to inclusive settings (see chapter 6). • Learn about the strengths and needs of students with disabilities (see chapter 2).
Students with disabilities are not participating in statewide and districtwide assessments.	• Identify and use appropriate testing accommodations and report card grading practices (see chapter 12). • Differentiate instruction to promote the learning of all students (see chapters 8–11).
Students from various cultural and language backgrounds are having difficulties in inclusive settings and are disproportionately represented.	• Learn more about the unique needs of students from various cultural and language backgrounds (see chapter 3) and about disproportionate representation (see chapter 1). • Promote interactions among students (see chapters 5 and 9). • Use culturally relevant instructional strategies and instructional materials, cooperative learning, and a diversified curriculum (see chapters 8–11). • Communicate and collaborate with families and community organizations (see chapter 4).
Teachers express negative attitudes about working in inclusion programs.	• Give teachers information and research about inclusion programs (see chapter 1). • Identify the sources of teachers' negative attitudes and plan activities to address these concerns (see chapters 1, 4, and 12). • Provide opportunities to talk with teachers, family members, and students who have experience with successful inclusion programs (see chapters 1 and 4). • Involve teachers in planning and evaluating all aspects of inclusion programs (see chapters 1, 4, and 12).
Family and community members have negative attitudes about inclusion programs.	• Give family and community members information and research about inclusion programs (see chapter 1). • Identify the sources of these negative attitudes and plan activities to address these concerns (see chapters 1, 4, and 12). • Invite family members, other professionals, and community members to visit inclusion programs (see chapter 1 and 4). • Offer family and community members data on the impact of the inclusion program (see chapter 1 and 12). • Involve family and community members in planning and evaluating all aspects of the inclusion program (see chapters 1, 4, and 12).

(continued)

Possible Concerns	Potential Solutions
General education teachers report that they are not receiving enough support from others.	• Examine existing arrangements for providing teaching support (see chapter 4). • Provide general education teachers with greater support from special educators, paraeducators, and ancillary support personnel (see chapters 4 and 8).
Teachers report difficulty meeting the requirements of the general education curriculum.	• Give teachers appropriate curriculum materials, technology, and equipment (see chapters 8–11). • Explore ways to diversify and modify the curriculum (see chapters 2, 3, and 7–11).
Teachers indicate that the large class size reduces the success of the program and their ability to meet the needs of students.	• Make sure that the class size is appropriate (see chapters 1 and 4). • Encourage teachers to differentiate instruction, and use cooperative learning arrangements and peer-mediated instructional, instructional technology, and behavior management techniques (see chapters 7–11).
Teachers express concerns about educating students with certain types of disabilities in inclusive settings.	• Identify teachers' specific concerns (see chapters 1 and 12). • Provide teachers with training and information to understand and address the educational, social, medical, physical, cognitive, and behavioral strengths and challenge of students (see chapters 2 and 3). • Make sure that teachers and students are receiving the necessary assistance (see all chapters).
Teachers report that they do not have the expertise and training to implement inclusion effectively.	• Conduct a needs assessment to identify teachers' training needs (see chapter 12). • Offer systematic, ongoing, coordinated, and well-planned staff development activities (see chapter 4). • Encourage teachers to visit model programs and attend professional conferences (see chapter 4). • Provide teachers with access to professional journals and other resources addressing current trends, models, research, and strategies (see all chapters).
Teachers report that there is not enough time for collaboration and communication among staff members.	• Use flexible scheduling to give teachers the time to collaborate and communicate (see chapter 4). • Maintain appropriate caseloads for teachers (see chapters 1 and 4). • Schedule regular meetings (see chapter 4).
Cooperative teaching teams report that they are having problems resolving problems involving teaching style, personality, and philosophical differences.	• Examine the mechanism and variables used for matching teachers in cooperative teaching teams (see chapter 4). • Offer education to help teachers work collaboratively (see chapter 4). • Provide mechanisms for resolving disagreements among teachers working in teaching teams (see chapter 4). • Establish mechanisms for ensuring equal-status, cooperative teaching relationships among teachers, and for sharing accountability for educational outcomes for all students (see chapter 4). • Provide time for teachers to collaborate and coordinate instructional activities and supportive services (see chapter 4).

Summary

This chapter offered a variety of strategies for evaluating the progress of students and the effectiveness of inclusion programs. As you review the questions posed in this chapter, remember the following points.

How Can I Evaluate the Academic Performance of Students?

CEC 5, 7, 8, 9, PRAXIS 3, INTASC 8, 9, 10

You can use standardized tests, testing accommodations, curriculum-based measurement, authentic/performance assessment, portfolio assessment, rubrics, technology-based testing, observation, and teacher-made tests. You also can gather additional information about students' academic progress by using error analysis, think-aloud techniques, student journals/learning logs, and self-evaluation questionnaires/interviews. Students' academic progress can be assessed by examining their IEPs and promotion and graduation rates.

How Can I Grade Students in Inclusive Settings?

CEC 1, 5, 7 8, 9, PRAXIS 3, INTASC 8, 9, 10

You can grade students in your inclusive classroom by considering and addressing legal issues; identifying the purpose of grades; agreeing on the nature and impact of differentiated instruction techniques; selecting grading systems that support differentiated instruction and communication; addressing the special needs and situations of students and teachers; and using effective practices that support the teaching, learning, and grading processes.

How Can I Evaluate the Social and Behavioral Performance of Students?

CEC 5, 7, 8, 9, PRAXIS 3, INTASC 8, 9, 10

You can evaluate the impact of your inclusion program on your students' social and behavioral performance by using observational and sociometric techniques, and self-concept measures.

How Can I Measure Perceptions of My Inclusion Program?

CEC 1, 4, 5, 8, 9, 10, PRAXIS 3, INTASC 8, 9, 10

You can measure students', teachers', and family members' perceptions of your inclusion program by using questionnaires, and interviews.

How Can I Improve the Effectiveness of My Inclusion Program?

CEC 1, 4, 5, 8, 9, 10, PRAXIS 3, INTASC 8, 9, 10

You can work with others to analyze data on the impact of your program on student performance to validate program strengths, identify program components that need revision, and determine strategies for improving the program.

What Would You Do in Today's Diverse Classroom?

1. Your inclusion classroom includes some of the students we met earlier in this book:

★ Mary enjoys social studies, science, and socializing with her friends during lunch. She has difficulty communicating orally and in writing, and difficulty remembering content and applying it to new situations (see chapter 1).

★   Marty knows a lot about a variety of different topics and likes to share his knowledge with others. However, he struggles to complete his assignments and has difficulties with reading and math. Marty likes to interact with others but sometimes gets carried away, which bothers some of his friends (see chapter 2).

★   Halee has had a difficult time adjusting to the culture and language of the United States. She appears to be shy and withdrawn and has had some difficulties completing her assignments. Her difficulties in school appear to be having a negative effect on her self-esteem (see chapter 3).

★   Matthew exhibits a variety of behaviors that interfere with his learning. He has difficulty paying attention and completing assignments because he seeks attention from others and shifts from one activity to another (see chapter 7).

★   Tom's abilities and skills are significantly below those of his peers. He speaks in one-, two-, or three-word sentences and often has difficulty understanding others. It takes him a while to learn things and generalize his new learning to new situations (see chapter 8).

★   Julia, a student with a visual disability, is an effective learner when she receives differentiated instruction (see chapter 8).

1.   What would be the goals of your inclusion program for these students?

2.   How would you evaluate the effectiveness of your inclusion program based on the academic, behavioral, and social performance of these students?

3.   Would you include these students in your school's statewide and districtwide testing programs? If yes, what testing accommodations might they need? If no, what alternative techniques would you use to assess their progress?

4.   What roles would the perceptions of students, other teachers, and family members play in your evaluation of your inclusion program? How would you gather information from these groups about the program?

5.   How would you assess your perceptions of your inclusion program?

6.   What knowledge, skills, dispositions, resources, and supports do you need to evaluate your inclusion program?

7.   What difficulties might arise in educating these students in your inclusion program? How could you address these difficulties to improve the effectiveness of the program?

2.   As a member of your grade-level team, you are asked to prepare questions for a unit your team has been teaching. Using a unit you have developed or a textbook you use in your class, develop one essay, two multiple-choice, one matching, two true-false, and two sentence completion items for inclusion in your team's test.

★   How would you adapt the content and format of the test items for different types of students?

★   What testing accommodations would you use for students with disabilities? For students from various cultural and language backgrounds?

   To answer these questions online and share your responses with others, go to the Reflection module in Chapter 12 of the Companion Website.

References

Abbott, M., Walton, C., & Greenwood, C. R. (2002). Phonemic awareness in kindergarten and first grade. *Teaching Exceptional Children, 34*(4), 20–26.

Abernathy, T. V., & Obenchain, K. M. (2001). Student ownership of service-learning projects: Including ourselves in our community. *Intervention in School and Clinic, 37*, 86–95.

Abrams, J., Ferguson, J., & Laud, L. (2001). Assessing ESOL students. *Educational Leadership, 59*(3), 62–65.

Ada, A. F. (1993). *My name is Maria Isabel.* New York: Atheneum.

Adair, J. (2000). Tackling teens' No. 1 problem. *Educational Leadership, 57*(6), 44–47.

Adger, C. T. (1997). *Issues and implications of English dialects for teaching English as a second language.* Alexandria, VA: Teachers of English to Speakers of Other Languages, Inc.

Adreon, D., & Stella, J. (2001). Transition to middle and high school: Increasing the success of students with Asperger syndrome. *Intervention in School and Clinic, 36*, 266–271.

Agostino v. Felton, 117 S. Ct. (1997).

Agran, M., Alper, S., & Wehmeyer, M. (2002). Access to the general curriculum for students with significant disabilities: What it means to teachers. *Education and Training in Mental Retardation and Developmental Disabilities, 37*, 123–133.

Alber, S. R. (1996). Sustained silent reading: Practical suggestions for successful implementation. *Reading and Writing Quarterly: Overcoming Learning Difficulties, 12*(4), 403–406.

Alber, S. R., & Foil, C. R. (2003). Drama activities that promote and extend your students' vocabulary proficiency. *Intervention in School and Clinic, 39*, 22–29.

Albert, L. R., & Ammer, J. J. (2004). Lesson planning and delivery. In B. K. Lenz, D. D. Deshler, & B. R. Kissam (Eds.), *Teaching content to all: Evidence-based inclusive practices in middle and secondary schools* (pp. 195–220). Boston: Allyn & Bacon.

Alberto, P. A., & Frederick, L. D. (2000). Teaching picture reading as an enabling skill. *Teaching Exceptional Children, 33*(1), 60–64.

Alberto, P. A., & Troutman, A. C. (2003). *Applied behavior analysis for teachers* (6th ed.). Upper Saddle River, NJ: Merrill/Prentice Hall.

Albinger, P. (1995). Stories from the resource room: Piano lessons, imaginary illness, and broken-down cars. *Journal of Learning Disabilities, 28*(10), 615–621.

Alexandrin, J. R., (2003). Using continuous, constructive classroom evaluations. *Teaching Exceptional Children, 36*(1), 52–57.

Al-Hassan, S., & Gardner, R. (2002). Involving immigrant parents of students with disabilities in the educational process. *Teaching Exceptional Children, 34*(5), 52–59.

Allbritten, D., Mainzer, R., & Ziegler, D. (2004). Will students with disabilities be scapegoats for school failures? *Teaching Exceptional Children. 36*(3), 74–75.

Allen, R. (2001, August). Make me laugh: Using humor in the classroom. *Education Update, 43*(5), 1, 3, 7–8.

Allen, R. (2001, November). Passages to learning: Schools find ways to help students make transitions. *Education Update, 43*(7), 1, 3, 6–7.

Allen, R. (2003). The democratic aims of service learning. *Educational Leadership, 60*(6), 51–54.

Allinder, R. M., Dunse, L., Brunken, C. D., & Obermiller-Krolikowski, H. J. (2001). Improving fluency in at-risk students with learning disabilities. *Remedial and Special Education, 22*, 48–54.

Allington, R. L. (2002). You can't learn much from books you can't read. *Educational Leadership, 60*(3), 16–19.

Allor, J. H., & McCathren, R. B. (2003). Developing emergent literacy skills through storybook reading. *Intervention in School and Clinic, 39*, 72–79.

Allsopp, D. H. (1999). Using modeling, manipulatives, and mnemonics with eighth-grade math students. *Teaching Exceptional Children, 32*(2), 46–54.

Al Otaiba, S., & Fuchs, D. (2002). Characteristics of children who are unresponsive to early literacy intervention: A review of the literature. *Remedial and Special Education, 23*, 300–316.

Al Otaiba, S., & Smartt, S. (2003). Summer sound camp: Involving parents in early literacy intervention for children with speech and language delays. *Teaching Exceptional Children, 35*(3), 30–35.

Alper, S., Schloss, P. J., & Schloss, C. N. (1996). Families of children with disabilities in elementary and middle school: Advocacy models and strategies. *Exceptional Children, 62*(3), 261–270.

Alson, A. (2003). The minority student achievement network. *Educational Leadership, 60*(4), 76–78.

Alvarado, J. L. (2003). Teachers' rationale and procedures used during lesson script deviations. *Behavioral Disorders, 28*, 370–385.

Amen, D. G. (2000). *Healing ADD.* New York: G. P. Putnam's Sons.

American Association of University Women. (1998). *Gender gaps: Where schools still fail our children.* Washington, DC: Author.

American Association of University Women. (2000). *Techsavvy: Educating girls in the new computer age.* Washington, DC: Author.

American Federation of Teachers. (1993). *Draft AFT position on inclusion.* Washington, DC: Author.

American Psychiatric Association. (1994). *Diagnostic and statistical manual of mental disorders* (4th ed.). Washington, DC: Author.

Ammer, J. J. (1998). Peer evaluation model for enhancing writing performance of students with learning disabilities. *Reading and Writing Quarterly: Overcoming Learning Difficulties, 14*(3), 263–282.

Amrein, A. L., & Berliner, D. C. (2003). The effects of high-stakes testing on student motivation and learning. *Educational Leadership, 60*(5), 32–38.

Anderegg, M. L., & Vergason, G. A. (1992). Preparing teachers for their legal responsibilities in facing school-age suicide. *Teacher Education and Special Education, 15*(4), 295–299.

Anderson, J. A., Kutash, K., & Duchnowski, A. J. (2001). A comparison of the academic progress of students with EBD and students with LD. *Journal of Emotional and Behavioral Disorders, 9,* 106–115.

Anderson, J. A., & Matthews, B. (2001). We care . . . for students with emotional and behavioral disabilities and their families. *Teaching Exceptional Children, 33*(5), 34–39.

Anderson, K. L. (2001). Voicing concerns about noisy classrooms. *Educational Leadership, 58*(7), 77–79.

Anderson, K. L., Casey, B., & Kerrigan, M. (2002). *Round the rug math: Adventures in problem solving.* New York: Wright Group/McGraw-Hill.

Anderson, P. L. (2000). Using literature to teach social skills to adolescents with LD. *Intervention in School and Clinic, 35*(5), 271–279.

Anderson, P. P., & Fenichel, E. S. (1989). *Serving culturally diverse families of infants and toddlers with disabilities.* Washington, DC: National Center for Clinical Infant Programs.

Anderson-Inman, L., Knox-Quinn, C., & Horney, M. A. (1996). Computer-based study strategies for students with learning disabilities: Individual differences associated with adoption level. *Journal of Learning Disabilities, 29*(5), 461–484.

Andrade, H. G. (2000). Using rubrics to promote thinking and learning. *Educational Leadership, 57*(5), 13–18.

Andrews, J. F., & Jordan, D. (1998). Multimedia stories for deaf children. *Teaching Exceptional Children, 30*(5), 28–33.

Andrews, J. F., & Jordan, D. L. (2000). Lamar professors offer ESL and math CD-ROMs for deaf and hearing students. *Hispanic Outlook, 10*(17), 19–21.

Andrews, J. F., Winograd, P., & DeVille, G. (1996). Using sign language summaries during prereading lessons. *Teaching Exceptional Children, 28*(3), 30–35.

Anti-Defamation League. (2000). *World of difference institute anti-bias study guide.* New York: Author.

Antonak, R. F., & Livneh, H. (1988). *The measurement of attitudes toward people with disabilities: Methods, psychometrics and scales.* Springfield, IL: Charles C. Thomas.

Appelget, J., Matthews, C. E., Hildreth, D. P., & Daniel, M. L. (2002). Teaching the history of science to students with learning disabilities. *Intervention in School and Clinic, 37,* 298–303.

Appl, D. J., Troha, C., & Rowell, J. (2001). Reflections of a first-year team: The growth of a collaborative partnership. *Teaching Exceptional Children, 33*(3), 4–8.

Archer, A. (1988). Strategies for responding to information. *Teaching Exceptional Children, 20,* 55–57.

Archer, A., & Gleason, M. (1996). Advanced skills for school success. *Intervention in School and Clinic, 32*(3), 119–123.

Arditi, A. (1999). *Making print legible.* New York: Lighthouse.

Armstrong, D. G., & Savage, T. V. (2002). *Teaching in the secondary school: An introduction* (5th ed.). Upper Saddle River, NJ: Merrill/Prentice Hall.

Aronson, D. (1997). No laughing matter. *Teaching Tolerance, 6*(2), 20–23.

Aronson, E., Blaney, N., Stephan, C., Sikes, J., & Snapp, M. (1978). *The jigsaw classroom.* Beverly Hills, CA: Sage.

Artiles, A. J., & Zamora-Duran, G. (1997). *Reducing disproportionate representation of culturally and linguistically diverse students in special and gifted education.* Reston, VA: Council for Exceptional Children.

Ashton, T. M. (1999). Spell checking: Making writing meaningful in the inclusive classroom. *Teaching Exceptional Children, 32*(2), 24–27.

Askov, E., & Greff, K. (1975). Handwriting: Copying versus tracing as the most effective type of practice. *Journal of Educational Research, 69,* 96–98.

Atkinson, T., Neal, J., & Grechus, M. (2003). Microsoft Windows XP accessibility features. *Intervention in School and Clinic, 38,* 177–180.

Austin, V. L. (2001). Teachers' beliefs about co-teaching. *Remedial and Special Education, 22,* 245–255.

Austin, V. L. (2003). Pharmacological interventions for students with ADD. *Intervention in School and Clinic, 38,* 289–296.

Babbitt, B. C., & White, C. M. (2002). R U ready?: Helping students assess their readiness for postsecondary education. *Teaching Exceptional Children, 35*(2), 62–67.

Babkie, A. M., & Provost, M. C. (2002). Select, write, and use metacognitive strategies in the classroom. *Intervention in School and Clinic, 37,* 173–177.

Babyak, A. E., Koorland, M., & Mathes, P. G. (2000). The effects of story mapping instruction on the reading comprehension of students with behavioral disorders. *Behavioral Disorders, 25,* 239–258.

Babyak, A. E., Luze, G. J., & Kamps, D. M. (2000). The good behavior game: Behavior management for diverse classrooms. *Intervention in School and Clinic, 35,* 216–223.

Baca, L. M. (1998). Bilingual special education: A judicial perspective. In L. M. Baca & H. T. Cervantes (Eds.), *The bilingual special education interface* (3rd ed., pp. 76–97). Upper Saddle River, NJ: Merrill/Prentice Hall.

Baca, L. M., & Cervantes, H. T. (1998). *The bilingual special education interface* (3rd ed). Upper Saddle River, NJ: Merrill/Prentice Hall.

Baca, L. M., & de Valenzuela, J. S. (1998). Development of the bilingual special education interface. In L. M. Baca & H. T. Cervantes (Eds.), *The bilingual special education interface* (3rd ed., pp. 98–118). Upper Saddle River, NJ: Merrill/Prentice Hall.

Bacon, E., & Bloom, L. (2000). Listening to student voices: How student advisory boards can help. *Teaching Exceptional Children, 32*(6), 38–43.

Bacon, N. A., & Kischner, G. A. (2002). Shaping global classrooms. *Educational Leadership, 60*(2), 48–51.

Bailey, A. B., & Smith, S. W. (2000). Providing effective coping strategies and supports for families with children with disabilities. *Intervention in School and Clinic, 35,* 294–296.

Bailey, D. (1993). *Wings to fly: Bridging theatre arts to students with special needs.* Bethesda, MD: Woodbine House.

Baker, E. A. (2003). Integrating literacy and technology: Making a match between software and classroom. *Reading and Writing Quarterly: Overcoming Learning Difficulties, 19,* 193–197.

Baker, J. M., & Zigmond, N. (1995). The meaning and practice of inclusion for students with learning disabilities: Themes and implications from five cases. *Journal of Special Education, 29*(2), 163–180.

Baker, L. (2003). The role of parents in motivating struggling readers. *Reading and Writing Quarterly: Overcoming Learning Difficulties, 19,* 87–106.

Baker, S., Gersten, R., & Graham, S. (2003). Teaching expressive writing to students with learning disabilities: Research-based applications and examples. *Journal of Learning Disabilities, 36,* 109–123.

Baker, S., Gersten, R., & Scanlon, D. (2002). Procedural facilitators and cognitive strategies: Tools for unraveling the mysteries of comprehension and the writing process, and for providing meaningful access to the general curriculum. *Learning Disabilities Research and Practice, 17,* 65–77.

Balboni, G., & Pedrabissi, L. (2000). Attitudes of Italian teachers and parents toward school inclusion of students with mental retardation: The role of experience. *Education and Training in Mental Retardation and Developmental Disabilities, 35,* 148–159.

Baldwin, B. A. (1989). The cornucopia kids. *US Air Magazine, 11*(10), 30–34.

Banerji, M., & Dailey, R. A. (1995). A study of the effects of an inclusion model on students with specific learning disabilities. *Journal of Learning Disabilities, 28*(8), 511–522.

Banks, J. A. (1991). A curriculum for empowerment, action, and change. In C. E. Sleeter (Ed.), *Empowerment through multicultural education* (pp. 125–141). Albany: State University of New York Press.

Banks, J. A. (2003). *Teaching strategies for ethnic studies* (7th ed.). Boston: Allyn & Bacon.

Banks, J. A., & Banks, C. A. (2001). *Multicultural education: Issues and perspectives* (4th ed.). Boston: Allyn & Bacon.

Barkley, R. A. (1998). *ADHD and the nature of self-control.* New York: Guilford.

Barnes, E., Berrigan, C., & Biklen, D. (1978). *What's the difference? Teaching positive attitudes toward people with disabilities.* Syracuse, NY: Human Policy.

Barnett, W. S., & Hustedt, J. T. (2003). Preschool: The most important grade. *Educational Leadership, 60*(7), 54–57.

Barnhill, G. P. (2001). What is Asperger Syndrome? *Intervention in School and Clinic, 36,* 259–265.

Barrie, W., & McDonald, J. (2002). Administrative support for student-led individualized education programs. *Remedial and Special Education, 23,* 116–121.

Bartlett, L. (2000). Medical services: The disputed related service. *The Journal of Special Education, 33,* 215–233, 247.

Barton, M. L., Heidema, C., & Jordan, D. (2002). Teaching reading in mathematics and science. *Educational Leadership, 60*(3), 24–29.

Bauer, A. M., & Ulrich, M. E. (2002). "I've got a palm in my pocket": Using handheld computers in an inclusive classroom. *Teaching Exceptional Children, 35*(2), 18–22.

Baxendell, B. W. (2003). Consistent, coherent, creative: The 3 C's of graphic organizers. *Teaching Exceptional Children, 35*(3), 46–53.

Baxter, J., Woodward, J., Voorhies, J., & Wong, J. (2002). We talk about it, but do they get it? *Learning Disabilities Research and Practice, 17,* 173–185.

Beakley, B. A., & Yoder, S. L. (1998). Middle schoolers learn community skills. *Teaching Exceptional Children, 30*(3), 16–21.

Bean, T. W. (2002). Making reading relevant for adolescents. *Educational Leadership, 60*(3), 34–38.

Beane, A. L. (1999). *The bully free classroom: Over 100 tips and strategies for teachers K–8.* Minneapolis, MN: Free Spirit Publishing.

Beck, I. L., & McKeown, M. G. (2002). Questioning the author: Making sense of social studies. *Educational Leadership, 60*(3), 24–29.

Beckman, P. (1999). Strategies for independent learning in reading and spelling. *Teaching Exceptional Children, 32*(2), 93.

Belcher, R. N., & Fletcher-Carter, R. (1999). Growing gifted students in the desert: Using alternative, community-based assessment and an enriched curriculum. *Teaching Exceptional Children, 32*(1), 17–24.

Belinger, N. T. (2001, March 6). Siblings of disabled children have own special needs. *The New York Times,* F5.

Bellon, M. L., & Ogletree, B. T. (2000). Repeated storybook reading as an instructional method. *Intervention in School and Clinic, 36,* 75–81.

Belluck, P. (2000, May 18). Indian schools, long failing, press for money and quality. *The New York Times,* A1, A24.

Bender, W. M. (1997). *Understanding ADHD: A practical guide for teachers and parents* Upper Saddle River, NJ: Merrill/Prentice Hall.

Bender, W. N., & McLaughlin, P. J. (1997). Weapons violence in schools: Strategies for teachers confronting violence and hostage situations. *Intervention in School and Clinic, 32*(4), 211–216.

Bender, W. N., Shubert, T. H., & McLaughlin, P. J. (2001). Invisible kids: Preventing school violence by identifying kids in trouble. *Intervention in School and Clinic, 37,* 105–111.

Benner, G. J., Nelson, J. R., & Epstein, M. H. (2002). Language skills of children with EBD: A literature review. *Journal of Emotional and Behavioral Disorders, 10,* 43–59.

Bennett, T., DeLuca, D., & Bruns, D. (1997). Putting inclusion into practice: Perspectives of teachers and parents. *Exceptional Children, 64,* 115–131.

Benz, M. R., Lindstrom, L., & Yovanoff, P. (2000). Improving graduation and employment outcomes of students with disabilities: Predictive factors and student perspectives. *Exceptional Children, 66,* 509–529.

Berendt, P. R., & Koski, B. (1999). No shortcuts to success. *Educational Leadership, 56*(6), 45–47.

Bergert, S. (2000, December). *The warning signs of learning disabilities.* Reston, VA: ERIC Clearinghouse on Disabilities and Gifted Education.

Bernhardt, V. L. (2003). No schools left behind. *Educational Leadership, 60*(5), 26–31.

Bernstein, N. (2000, February 1). Study documents homelessness in American children each year. *The New York Times,* A12.

Bernstein, N. (2002, July 29). Side effect of welfare law: The no-parent family. *The New York Times,* A1, A14.

Bessell, A. G. (2001). Children surviving cancer: Psychological adjustment, quality of life, and school experiences. *Exceptional Children, 67,* 345–360.

Best, S. J. (2001a). Definitions, supports, issues, and services in schools and communities. In J. L. Bigge, S. J. Best, & K. W. Heller (Eds.), *Teaching individuals with physical, health, or multiple disabilities* (4th ed., pp. 3–33.). Upper Saddle River, NJ: Merrill/Prentice Hall.

Best, S. J. (2001b). Physical disabilities. In J. L. Bigge, S. J. Best, & K. W. Heller (Eds.), *Teaching individuals with physical, health, or multiple disabilities* (4th ed., pp. 33–64.). Upper Saddle River, NJ: Merrill/Prentice Hall.

Best, S. J. (2001c). Health impairments and infectious diseases. In J. L. Bigge, S. J. Best, & K. W. Heller (Eds.), *Teaching individuals with physical, health, or multiple disabilities* (4th ed., pp. 65–92). Upper Saddle River, NJ: Merrill/Prentice Hall.

Best, S. J., & Bigge, J. L. (2001). Multiple disabilities. In J. L. Bigge, S. J. Best, & K. W. Heller (Eds.), *Teaching individuals with physical, health, or multiple disabilities* (4th ed., pp. 92–117). Upper Saddle River, NJ: Merrill/Prentice Hall.

Best, S. J., Bigge, J. L., & Reed, P. (2001). Supporting physical and sensory capabilities through assistive technology. In J. L. Bigge, S. J. Best, & K. W. Heller (Eds.), *Teaching individuals with physical, health, or multiple disabilities* (4th ed., pp. 195–228). Upper Saddle River, NJ: Merrill/Prentice Hall.

Biddle, B. J., & Berliner, D. C. (2002). Unequal school funding in the United States. *Educational Leadership, 59(8)*, 48–59.

Biederman, M. (2002, July 4). Learning the king's English (or Columbo's). *The New York Times,* G7.

Bigby, L. M. (2004). Medical and health-related services: More than treating boo-boos and ouchies. *Intervention in School and Clinic, 39,* 233–235.

Biklen, D., Corrigan, C., & Quick, D. (1989). Beyond obligation: Students' relations with each other in integrated classes. In D. Lipsky & A. Gartner (Eds.), *Beyond separate education: Quality education for all* (pp. 207–221). Baltimore: Paul H. Brookes.

Billingsley, F., & Albertson, L. R. (1999). Finding the future for functional skills. Journal of *The Association for Persons with Severe Handicaps, 24,* 298–302.

Billman, L. W. (2002). Aren't these books for little kids? *Educational Leadership, 60(3),* 48–51.

Bisson, J. (1997). *Celebrate! An anti-bias guide to enjoying holidays in early childhood programs.* St. Paul, MN: Redleaf Press.

Blair, C., & Scott, K. G. (2002). Proportion of LD placements associated with low socioeconomic status: Evidence for a gradient? *The Journal of Special Education, 39,* 14–22.

Blanchett, W. J. (2000). Sexual risk behaviors of young adults with LD and the need for HIV/AIDS education. *Remedial and Special Education, 21,* 336–345.

Blazer, B. (1999). Developing 504 classroom accommodation plans: A collaborative, systematic parent-student-teacher approach. *Teaching Exceptional Children, 32(2),* 28–33.

Bley, N. S., & Thornton, C. A. (1995). *Teaching mathematics to students with learning disabilities* (3rd ed.). Austin, TX: PRO-ED.

Bligh, T. (1996). Choosing and using picture books for mini-lessons with middle school students. *Reading and Writing Quarterly: Overcoming Learning Difficulties, 12(4),* 333–349.

Bloom, L. A., Perlmutter, J., & Burrell, L. (1999). The general educator: Applying constructivism to inclusive classrooms. *Intervention in School and Clinic, 34(3),* 132–136.

Blubaugh, D. (1999). Bringing cable into the classroom. *Educational Leadership, 56(5),* 61–65.

Blum, H. T., Lipsett, L. R., & Yocom, D. J. (2002). Literature circles: A tool for self-determination in one middle school inclusive classroom. *Remedial and Special Education, 23,* 99–108.

Blum, H. T., & Yocom, D. J. (1996). Using instructional games to foster student learning. *Teaching Exceptional Children, 29(2),* 60–63.

Board of Education of the Hendrick Hudson Central School District v. *Rowley,* 102 S. Ct. 3034 (1982).

Bock, M. A. (2003). SODA strategy: Enhancing the social interaction skills of youngsters with Asperger syndrome. *Intervention in School and Clinic, 36,* 272–278.

Boersma, F. J., & Chapman, J. W. (1992). *The Perception of Ability Scale for Students.* Los Angeles: Western Psychological Services.

Boerum, L. J. (2000). Developing portfolios with learning disabled stduents. *Reading and Writing Quarterly: Overcoming Learning Difficulties, 16,* 211–238.

Boone, R., & Higgins, K. (2003). Reading, writing, and publishing digital text. *Remedial and Special Education, 24,* 132–140.

Boone, R., Wolfe, P. S., & Schaufler, J. H. (1999). Written communication in special education: Meeting the needs of culturally and linguistically diverse families. *Multiple Voices, 3(1),* 25–36.

Booth, T., & Ainscow, M. (1998). *From them to us: An international study of inclusion in education.* New York: Routledge.

Bostic, J. Q., Rustuccia, C., & Schlozman, S. C. (2001). The suicidal student. *Educational Leadership, 59(2),* 81–82.

Bottge, B. A. (1999). Effects of contextualized math instruction on problem solving of average and below-average achieving students. *The Journal of Special Education, 33(2),* 81–92.

Bottge, B. A. (2001). Building ramps and hovercrafts and improving math skills. *Teaching Exceptional Children, 34(1),* 16–23.

Bottge, B. A., & Hasselbring, T. S. (1999). Teaching mathematics to adolescents with disabilities in a multimedia environment. *Intervention in School and Clinic, 35(2),* 113–116.

Bottge, B. A., Heinrichs, M., Mehta, Z. D., & Hung, Y. (2002). Weighing the benefits of anchored math instruction for students with disabilities in general education classes. *The Journal of Special Education, 35,* 186–200.

Boudah, D. J., Knight, S. L., Kostobryz, C., Welch, N., Laughter, D., & Branch, R. (2000). Collaborative research in inclusive classrooms: An investigation with reflections by teachers and researchers. *Teacher Education and Special Education, 23,* 241–252.

Boudah, D. J., Lenz, B. K., Bulgren, J. A., Schumaker, J. B., & Deshler, D. D. (2000). Don't water down: Enhance content learning through the unit organizer routine. *Teaching Exceptional Children, 32(3),* 48–56.

Boudah, D. J., & O'Neill, K. J. (1999, August). *Learning strategies.* Reston, VA: ERIC Clearinghouse on Disabilities and Gifted Education.

Boudah, D. J., & Weiss, M. P. (2002, January). *Learning disabilities overview: Update 2002.* Arlington, VA: ERIC Clearinghouse on Disabilities and Gifted Education.

Bowers, E. M. (1980). *The handicapped in literature: A psychosocial perspective.* Denver: Love.

Boyer, M. (1998, April). *Using stamps to differentiate student assignments.* Presentation at the annual meeting of the Council for Exceptional Children, Minneapolis, MN.

Boyle, A. R., Washburn, S. G., Rosenberg, M. S., Connelly, V. J., Brinckerhoff, L. C., & Banerjee, M. (2002). Reading SLICK with new audio texts and strategies. *Teaching Exceptional Children, 35(2),* 50–55.

Boyle, J. R. (2001). Enhancing the note-taking skills of students with mild disabilities. *Intervention in School and Clinic, 36,* 221–224.

Boyle, J. R., & Weishaar, M. (1997). The effects of expert-generated versus student-generated cognitive organizers on the reading comprehension of students with learning disabilities. *Learning Disabilities Research and Practice, 12(4),* 228–235.

Boyle, J. R., & Weishaar, M. (2001). The effects of strategic notetaking on the recall and comprehension of lecture information for high school students with learning disabilities. *Learning Disabilities Research and Practice, 16,* 133–141.

Boyle, J. R., & Yeager, N. (1997). Blueprints for learning: Using frameworks for understanding. *Teaching Exceptional Children, 29(4),* 26–31.

Bradley, D. H. (2001). 20 ways to help students who struggle with writing become better writers. *Intervention in School and Clinic, 37*, 118–121.

Bradsher, K. (1995a, April 17). Gap in wealth in U.S. called widest in west. *The New York Times,* A1, D4.

Bradsher, K. (1995b, August 14). Low ranking for poor American children. *The New York Times,* A9.

Brady, M. P., & Rosenberg, H. (2002). Job observation and behavior scale: A supported employment assessment instrument. *Education and Training in Mental Retardation and Developmental Disabilities, 37*, 427–433.

Brandenburg, M. L. (2002). Advanced Math? Write. *Educational Leadership, 60*(3), 67–68.

Brantlinger, E. (1995). Social class in school: Students' perspectives. *Research Bulletin, 14,* 1–4.

Braus, N., & Geidel, M. (2000). *Everyone's kids' books.* Brattleboro, VT: Everyone's Books.

Brewer, R. D., Reid, M. S., & Rhine, B. G. (2003). Peer coaching: Students teaching to learn. *Intervention in School and Clinic, 39*, 113–126.

Brice, A. (2001, November). *Children with communication disorders: Update 2001.* Arlington, VA: ERIC Clearinghouse on Disabilities and Gifted Education.

Brice, A., & Roseberry-McKibbin, C. (2001). Choice of languages in instruction: One language or two? *Teaching Exceptional Children, 33*(4), 10–17.

Brim, S. A., & Whitaker, D. P. (2000). Motivation and students with attention deficit hyperactivity disorder. *Preventing School Failure, 44*(2), 57–60.

Brolin, D. E. (1997). *Life-centered career education: A competency-based approach* (5th ed.). Reston, VA: Council for Exceptional Children.

Bronheim, S. (n.d.). *An educator's guide to Tourette syndrome.* Bayside, NY: Tourette Syndrome Association.

Brookhart, S. M. (2004). *Grading.* Upper Saddle River, NJ: Merrill/ Prentice Hall.

Brooks-Gunn, J., & Duncan, G. J. (1997, Summer/Fall). The effects of poverty on children. *The Future of Children,* 55–71.

Brosnan, P. A. (1997). Visual mathematics. *Teaching Exceptional Children, 29*(3), 18–22.

Browder, D. M., & Bambara, L. M. (2000). Home and community. In M. E. Snell & F. Brown (Eds.), *Instruction of students with severe disabilities* (5th ed., pp. 543–589). Upper Saddle River, NJ: Merrill/Prentice-Hall.

Browder, D. M., Fallin, K., Davis, S., & Karvonen, M. (2003). Consideration of what may influence student outcomes on alternate assessment. *Education and Training in Developmental Disabilities, 38*, 255–270.

Browder, D. M., & Lohrmann-O'Rourke, S. (2001). Promoting self-determination in planning and instruction. In D. Browder (Ed.), *Curriculum and assessment for students with moderate and severe disabilities* (pp. 148–178). New York: Guilford.

Brown v. Board of Education of Topeka, 347 U.S. 483 (1954).

Brown, D. F. (2002). Self-directed learning in an 8th grade classroom. *Educational Leadership, 60*(1), 54–59.

Brown, L. W. (1997). Seizure disorders. In M. L. Batshaw (Ed.), *Children with disabilities* (4th ed., pp. 553–595). Baltimore: Paul H. Brookes.

Brown, M. R., Higgins, K., & Hartley, K. (2001). Teachers and technology equity. *Teaching Exceptional Children, 33*(4), 32–39.

Brown, M. S., Ilderton, P., & Taylor, A. (2001). 20 ways to include a student with an attention problem in the general education classroom. *Intervention in School and Clinic, 37*, 50–52.

Brown, P. J. (1999). *Findings of the 1999 plain language field test.* University of Delaware, Newark, DE: Delaware Education Research and Development Center.

Brown, P. L. (2000, March 10). Sudden wealth syndrome brings new stress. *The New York Times,* 1, 14.

Brownell, M. T., & Walther-Thomas, C. (2000). An interview with Dr. Angelita Felix. *Intervention in School and Clinic, 35*, 290–293.

Brownell, M. T., Yeager, E., Rennells, M. S., & Riley, T. (1997). Teachers working together: What teacher educators and researchers should know. *Teacher Education and Special Education, 20*(4), 340–359.

Brozo, W. G., & Hargis, C. (2003). Using low-stakes reading assessment. *Educational Leadership, 61*(3), 60–64.

Brozo, W. G., & Simpson, M. (2003). *Readers, teachers, learners: Expanding literacy across the content areas* (4th ed.). Upper saddle river, nj: merrill/prentice hall ed.). Upper Saddle River, NJ: Merrill/Prentice-Hall.

Brucker, P. O., & Piazza, R. (2002). Reading instruction for older students. *CEC Today, 9*(3), 12–13.

Bruns, D. A., & Fowler, S. A. (1999). Culturally sensitive transition plans for young children and their families. *Teaching Exceptional Children, 31*(5), 26–30.

Bryan, T. (1997). Assessing the personal and social status of students with learning disabilities. *Learning Disabilities Research and Practice, 12*(1), 63–76.

Bryan, T., & Sullivan-Burstein, K. (1997). Homework how-to's. *Teaching Exceptional Children, 29*(6), 32–37.

Bryant, B. R., & Seay, P. C. (1998). The Technology-Related Assistance to Individuals with Disabilities Act: Relevance to individuals with learning disabilities and their advocates. *Journal of Learning Disabilities, 31*(1), 4–15.

Bryant, D. P., Bryant, B. R., & Hammill, D. D. (2000). Characteristic behaviors of students with LD who have teacher-identified math weaknesses. *Journal of Learning Disabilities, 33*, 168–177, 199.

Bryant, D. P., Bryant, B. R., & Raskind, M. H. (1998). Using assistive technology to enhance the skills of students with learning disabilities. *Intervention in School and Clinic, 34*(1), 53–58.

Bryant, D. P., Ugel, N., Thompson, S., & Hamff, A. (1999). Instructional strategies for content-area reading instruction. *Intervention in School and Clinic, 34*(5), 293–302.

Bryde, S. (1998, April). *Using children's literature to teach about disabilities and other issues.* Presentation at the annual meeting of the Council for Exceptional Children, Minneapolis.

Buck, G. H. (1999). Smoothing the rough edges of classroom transitions. *Intervention in School and Clinic, 34*(4), 224–227, 235.

Buck, G. H., Polloway, E. A., Kirkpatrick, M. A., Patton, J. R., & Fad, K. M. (2000). Developing behavioral intervention plans: A sequential approach. *Intervention in School and Clinic, 36*(1), 3–9.

Buck, G. H., Polloway, E. A., Smith-Thomas, A., & Cook, K. W. (2003). Prereferral intervention processes: A survey of state practices. *Exceptional Children, 69*, 349–360.

Buggey, T. (1999). Look! I'm on TV!: Using videotaped self-modeling to change behavior. *Teaching Exceptional Children, 31*(4), 27–30.

Bui, Y. N., & Turnbull, A. (2003). East meets west: Analysis of person-centered planning in the context of Asian American values. *Education and Training in Developmental Disabilities, 38*, 18–31.

Bulgren, J. A., Deshler, D. D., & Schumaker, J. B. (1997). Use of a recall enhancement routine and strategies in inclusive secondary classes. *Learning Disabilities Research and Practice, 12*(4), 198–208.

Bulgren, J. A., Hock, M. F., Schumaker, J. B., & Deshler, D. D. (1995). The effects of instruction in a paired associates strategy on the information mastery performance of students with learning disabilities. *Learning Disabilities Research and Practice, 10*(1), 22–37.

Bullard, H. R. (2004). 20 ways to ensure the successful inclusion of a child with Asperger syndrome in the general education classroom. *Intervention in School and Clinic, 39,* 176–180.

Bullock, C., & Foegen, A. (2002). Constructive conflict resolution for students with behavioral disorders. *Behavioral Disorders, 27,* 289–295.

Burcham, B. G., & DeMers, S. T. (1995). Comprehensive assessment of children and youth with ADHD. *Intervention in School and Clinic, 30*(4), 211–220.

Burcroff, T. L., Radogna, D. M., & Wright, E. H. (2003). Community forays: Addressing students' functional skills in inclusive settings. *Teaching Exceptional Children, 35*(5), 52–57.

Burnette, J. (2000, December). Assessment of culturally and linguistically diverse students for special education eligibility. *ERIC Digest.*

Burns, M. K. (2002). Comprehensive system of assessment to intervention using curriculum-based assessments. *Intervention in School and Clinic, 38,* 8–13.

Burrell, B., Wood, S. J., Pikes, T., & Holliday, C. (2001). Student mentors and proteges learning together. *Teaching Exceptional Children, 33*(3), 24–29.

Butler, F. M., Miller, S. P., Crehan, K., Babbitt, B., & Pierce, T. (2003). Fraction instruction for students with mathematics disabilities: Comparing two teaching sequences. *Learning Disabilities Research and Practice, 18,* 99–111.

Buysse, V., Goldman, B. D., & Skinner, M. L. (2002). Setting effects on friendship formation among young children with and without disabilities. *Exceptional Children, 68,* 503–518.

Buysse, V., Sparkman, K. L., & Wesley, P. W. (2003). Communities of practice: Connecting what we know with what we do. *Exceptional Children, 69*(3), 263–278.

Bynoe, P. F. (1998). Rethinking and retooling teacher preparation to prevent perpetual failure for our children. *The Journal of Special Education, 32,* 37–40.

Caffrey, J. A. (1997). *First star I see.* Fairport, NY: Verbal Image Press.

Caine, G., Caine, R. N., & McClintic, C. (2002). Guiding the innate constructivist. *Educational Leadership, 60*(1), 70–73.

Calderon, M. E., & Minaya-Rowe, L. (2003). *Designing and implementing two-way bilingual programs: A step-by-step guide for administrators, teachers, and parents.* Thousand Oaks, CA: Corwin Press.

Calhoun, M. B., & Fuchs, L. S. (2003). The effects of peer-assisted learning strategies and curriculum-based measurement on the mathematics performance of secondary students with disabilities. *Remedial and Special Education, 24,* 235–245.

Callahan, C. M. (2001). Beyond the gifted stereotype. *Educational Leadership, 59*(3), 42–46.

Callahan, K., & Rademacher, J. A. (1999). Using self-management strategies to increase the on-task behavior of a student with autism. *Journal of Positive Behavioral Interventions, 1*(2), 117–122.

Calloway, C. (1999). Promote friendship in the inclusive classroom. *Intervention in School and Clinic, 34*(3), 176–177.

Campbell, L. (1997). How teachers interpret MI theory. *Educational Leadership, 55*(1), 14–19.

Campbell, P. C., Campbell, R. C., & Brady, M. P. (1998). Team environmental assessment mapping system: A method for selecting curriculum goals for students with disabilities. *Education and Training in Mental Retardation and Developmental Disabilities, 33*(3), 264–272.

Campbell-Whatley, G. D. (2001). Mentoring students with mild disabilities: The "nuts and bolts" of program development. *Intervention in School and Clinic, 36,* 211–216.

Campbell-Whatley, G. D., Algozinne, B., & Obiakor, F. (1997). Using mentoring to improve academic programming for African American male youths with mild disabilities. *The School Counselor, 44,* 362–367.

Canfield, J., & Wells, H. C. (1976). *100 ways to enhance self-concept in the classroom.* Upper Saddle River, NJ: Prentice Hall.

Cangelosi, J. S. (2003). *Teaching mathematics in secondary and middle school: An interactive approach.* Upper Saddle River, NJ: Merrill/Prentice Hall.

Capper, C. A., & Pickett, R. S. (1994). The relationship between school structure and culture and student views of diversity and inclusive education. *The Special Education Leadership Review, 2*(1), 102–122.

Carbo, M. (1994). *Reading style inventory.* Syosset, NY: National Reading Styles Institute.

Carbone, E. (2001). Arranging the classroom with an eye (and ear) to students with ADHD. *Teaching Exceptional Children, 34*(2), 72–81.

Carger, C. L. (2002). Multicultural literature: Talking with Francisco Jimenez. *Book Links, 11*(3), 14–19.

Carlson, C. L., Booth, J. E., Shin, M., & Canu, W. H. (2002). Parent-, teacher- and self-related motivational styles in ADHD subtypes. *Journal of Learning Disabilities, 35,* 104–113.

Carpenter, C. D., Bloom, L. A., & Boat, M. B. (1999). Guidelines for special educators: Achieving socially valid outcomes. *Intervention in School and Clinic, 34*(3), 143–149.

Carpenter, C. D., Ray, M. S., & Bloom, L. A. (1995). Portfolio assessment: Opportunities and challenges. *Intervention in School and Clinic, 31*(1), 34–41.

Carr, S. C. (2002a). Self-evaluation: Involving students in their own learning. *Reading and Writing: Overcoming Learning Difficulties, 18,* 195–199.

Carr, S. C. (2002b). Assessing learning processes: Useful information for teachers and students. *Intervention in School and Clinic, 37,* 156–162.

Carrington, S., Templeton, E., & Papinczak, T. (2003). Adolescents with Asperger syndrome and perceptions of friendships. *Focus on Autism and Other Developmental Disabilities, 18,* 211–218.

Carroll, C. J. (2001). Teacher-friendly curriculum-based assessment in spelling. *Teaching Exceptional Children, 34*(2), 32–39.

Carroll, D. (2001). Considering paraeducator training, roles, and responsibilities. *Teaching Exceptional Children, 34*(2), 60–64.

Carter, E. W., & Wehby, J. H. (2003). Job performance of transition-age youth with emotional and behavioral disorders. *Exceptional Children, 69,* 449–465.

Cartledge, G. (1999). African-American males and serious emotional disturbance: Some personal perspectives. *Behavioral Disorders, 25,* 76–79.

Cartledge, G., Kea, C. D., & Ida, D. J. (2000). Anticipating differences—Celebrating strengths: Providing culturally competent services for students with serious emotional disturbance. *Teaching Exceptional Children, 32*(3), 30–37.

Cartledge, G., & Kiarie, M. W. (2001). Learning social skill through literature for children and adolescents. *Teaching Exceptional Children, 34*(2), 40–47.

Cartledge, G., Tillman, L. C., & Johnson, C. T. (2001). Professional ethics within the context of student discipline and diversity. *Teacher Education and Special Education, 24,* 25–37.

Cartledge, G., Wang, W., Blake, C., & Lambert, M. C. (2002). Middle school students with behavior disorders acting as social skill trainers for peers. *Beyond Behavior, 11*(3), 14–18.

Cass, M., Cates, D., Smith, M., & Jackson, C. (2003). Effects of manipulative instruction on solving area and perimeter problems by students with learning disabilties. *Learning Disabilities Research and Practice, 18,* 112–120.

Casteel, C. P., Isom, B. A., & Jordan, K. F. (2000). Creating confident and competent readers. *Intervention in School and Clinic, 36,* 67–74.

Castellani, J., & Jeffs, T. (2001). Emerging reading and writing strategies using technology. *Teaching Exceptional Children, 33*(5), 60–67.

Cavanaugh, T. (2002). Ebooks and accommodations. *Teaching Exceptional Children, 35*(2), 56–61.

Cawley, J. F. (2001). Perspectives: Mathematics interventions and students with high-incidence disabilities. *Remedial and Special Education, 23,* 2–6.

Cawley, J. F., Fitzmaurice, A. M., Sedlak, R., & Althaus, V. (1976). *Project math.* Tulsa, OK: Educational Progress.

Cawley, J. F., & Foley, T. E. (2002). Connecting math and science for all students. *Teaching Exceptional Children, 34*(4), 14–19.

Cawley, J. F., Foley, T. E., & Doan, T. (2003). Giving students with disabilities a voice in the selection of arithmetical content. *Teaching Exceptional Children, 36*(1), 8–16.

Cawley, J. F., Foley, T. E., & Miller, J. (2003). Science and students with mild disabilities: Principles of universal design. *Intervention in School and Clinic, 38,* 160–171.

Cawley, J. F., Hayden, S., Cade, E., & Baker-Kroczynski, S. (2002). Including students with disabilities into the general education science classroom. *Exceptional Children, 68,* 423–435.

Cawley, J. F., Parmar, R. S., Foley, T. E., Salmon, S., & Roy, S. (2001). Arithmetic performance of students: Implications for standards and programming. *Exceptional Children, 67,* 311–328.

Cedar Rapids Community School District v. Garret F. 96–1793 S. Ct. (1999).

Center for Special Education Finance. (1995). *Supported education in Oregon: Resource implications of inclusion.* Palo Alto, CA: American Institutes of Research.

Center for Universal Design (1997). *What is universal design?* Center for Universal Design, North Carolina State University. Retrieved July, 2003, from the World Wide Web: www.design.ncsu.edu.

Chalmers, L., Olson, M. R., & Zurkowski, J. K. (1999). Music as a classroom tool. *Intervention in School and Clinic, 35*(1), 43–45, 52.

Chamberlain, S. P. (2003a). An interview with Susan Conners: An educator's observations about living with and educating others about Tourette's Syndrome. *Intervention in School and Clinic, 39,* 99–108.

Chamberlain, S. P. (2003b). An interview with Susan Limber and Sylvia Cedillo: Responding to bullying. *Intervention in School and Clinic, 38,* 236–242.

Chamot, A. U., & O'Malley, J. M. (1996). The Cognitive Academic Language Learning Approach (CALLA): A model for linguistically diverse classrooms. *Elementary School Journal, 96,* 259–274.

Chappuis, S., & Stiggins, R. J. (2002). Classroom assessment for learning. *Educational Leadership, 60*(1), 40–43.

Chard, D. J., & Osborn, J. (1999). Word recognition instruction: Paving the road to successful reading. *Intervention in School and Clinic, 34*(5), 271–277.

Chard, D. J., Vaughn, S., & Tyler, B. (2002). A synthesis of research on effective interventions for building fluency with elementary students with learning disabilities. *Journal of Learning Disabilities, 35,* 386–406.

Charles, R. I. (1984). *Problem solving experiences in mathematics.* Menlo Park, CA: Addison-Wesley.

Chiappetta, E. L., & Koballa, T. R. (2002). *Science instruction in the middle and secondary schools* (5th ed.). Upper Saddle River, NJ: Merrill/Prentice Hall.

Chiong, J. A. (1998). *Racial categorization of multiracial children in schools.* Westport, CT: Bergin & Garvey.

Chira, S. (1995, March 19). Struggling to find stability when divorce is a pattern. *The New York Times,* 1, 42.

Christiansen, J., & Vogel, J. R. (1998). A decision-making model for grading students with disabilities. *Teaching Exceptional Children, 31*(2), 30–35.

Chubb, J. E., & Loveless, T. (2002). *Bridging the achievement gap.* Washington, DC: The Brookings Institution.

Chuoke, M., & Eyman, B. (1997). Play fair—And not just at recess. *Educational Leadership, 54*(8), 53–55.

Church, K., Gottschalk, C. M., & Leddy, J. N. (2003). 20 ways to enhance social and friendship skills. *Intervention in School and Clinic, 38,* 307–310.

Clark, E. (1996). Children and adolescents with traumatic brain injury: Reintegration challenges in educational settings. *Journal of Learning Disabilities, 29*(5), 549–560.

Clark, S. G. (2000). The IEP process as a tool for collaboration. *Teaching Exceptional Children, 33*(2), 56–66.

Clay, M. M. (1985). *The early detection of reading difficulties* (3rd. ed.). Auckland, NZ: Heinemann.

Clemetson, L. (2003a, September). Census shows ranks of poor rose in 2002 by 1.3 million. *The New York Times,* A16.

Clemetson, L. (2003b, January). Hispanics now largest minority, census shows. *The New York Times,* A1, A17.

Cloud, N., & Landurand, P. M. (n.d.). *Multisystem: Training program for special educators.* New York: Teachers College Press.

Clyde K. and Sheila K. v. Puyallup School District, 35 F.3d 1396, 9th Circuit, 1994.

Coffland, J. A., & Baldwin, R. S. (1985). *Wordmath.* St. Louis: Milliken.

Cole v. Greenfield-Central Community Schools, 657 F.Supp. 56 (S.D. Ind. 1986).

Cole, C. M., & McLeskey, J. (1997). Secondary inclusion programs for students with mild disabilities. *Focus on Exceptional Children, 29*(6), 1–15.

Collet-Klingenberg, L. L. (1998). The reality of best practices in transition: A case study. *Exceptional Children, 65*(1), 67–78.

Collicott, J. (1991). Implementing multi-level teaching: Strategies for classroom teachers. In G. L. Porter & D. Richler (Eds.), *Changing Canadian schools: Perspectives on disability and inclusion* (pp. 191–218). Toronto: Roeher Institute.

Collier, C. (1996, January). *Cross cultural assessment: New tools and strategies.* Presentation at the nineteenth annual statewide conference for teachers of linguistically and culturally diverse students, Chicago.

Collier, V. P., & Thomas, W. P. (2002, Winter). Reforming education policies for English learners. *National Association of State Boards of Education*, 31–36.

Collins, B. C., Epstein, A., Reiss, T., & Lowe, V. (2001). Including children with mental retardation in the religious community. *Teaching Exceptional Children, 33*(5), 53–59.

Collins, B. C., Hendricks, T. B., Fetko, K., & Land, L. (2002). Student-2-student learning in inclusive classrooms. *Teaching Exceptional Children, 34*(4), 56–61.

Colvin, G., Ainge, D., & Nelson, R. (1997). How to defuse confrontations. *Teaching Exceptional Children, 29*(6), 47–51.

Communication Briefings. (1989). *Teamwork tips.* Pitman, NJ: Author.

Conderman, G., Ikan, P. A., & Hatcher, R. E. (2000). Student-led conferences in inclusive settings. *Intervention in School and Clinic, 36*, 22–26.

Conderman, G., & Katsiyannis, G. (2002). Instructional issues and practices in secondary special education. *Remedial and Special Education, 23*, 169–179.

Conderman, G., & Koroghlanian, C. (2002). Writing test questions like a pro. *Intervention in School and Clinic, 38*, 67–74.

Conderman, G., & Stephens, J. T. (2000). Voices from the field: Reflections from beginning special educators. *Teaching Exceptional Children, 33*(1), 16–21.

Condon, K. A., & Tobin, T. J. (2001). Using electronic and other new ways to help students improve their behavior: Functional behavioral assessment at work. *Teaching Exceptional Children, 34*(1), 44–51.

Conoley, J. C., & Sheridan, S. (1996). Pediatric traumatic brain injury: Challenges and interventions for families. *Journal of Learning Disabilities, 29*(6), 662–669.

Conroy, M. A., Brown, W. H., & Davis, C. (2001). Applying the IDEA 1997 disciplinary provisions to preschoolers with challenging behaviors. *Beyond Behavior, 11*(1), 23–26.

Conroy, M. A., & Stichter, J. P. (2003). The application of antecedents in the functional assessment process: Existing research, issues and recommendations. *Journal of Special Education, 37*, 15–25.

Cook, A. M., & Cavalier, A. R. (1999). Young children using assistive robotics for discovery and control. *Teaching Exceptional Children, 31*(5), 72–78.

Cook, B. G. (2001). A comparison of teachers' attitudes toward their included students with mild and severe disabilities. *The Journal of Special Education, 34*, 203–213.

Cook, B. G., Semmel, M. I., & Gerber, M. M. (1999). Attitudes of principals and special education teachers toward the inclusion of students with mild disabilities: Critical differences of opinion. *Remedial and Special Education, 20*(4), 199–207, 243.

Cook, B. G., Tankersley, M., Cook, L., & Landrum, T. J. (2000). Teachers' attitudes toward their included students. *Exceptional Children, 67*, 115–135.

Cook, D. (1999). Behavior bucks: A unique motivational program. *Intervention in School and Clinic, 34*(5), 307–308, 316.

Cook-Sather, A. (2003). Listening to students about learning differences. *Teaching Exceptional Children, 35*(4), 22–27.

Cooper, H. (2001). Homework for all—in moderation. *Educational Leadership, 58*(7), 34–38.

Coots, J. J., Bishop, K. D., & Grenot-Scheyer, M. (1998). Supporting elementary age students with significant disabilities in general education classrooms: Personal perspectives on inclusion. *Education and Training in Mental Retardation and Developmental Disabilities, 33*(4), 317–330.

Copeland, S. R., & Hughes, C. (2002). Effects of goal setting on task performance of persons with mental retardation. *Education and Training in Mental Retardation and Developmental Disabilities, 37*, 40–54.

Copeland, S. R., McCall, J., Williams, C. R., Guth, C., Carter, E. W., Presley, J. A., Fowler, S. E., & Hughes, C. (2002). High school peer buddies: A win-win situation. *Teaching Exceptional Children, 35*, 22–29.

Corral, N., & Antia, S. D. (1997). Self-task: Strategies for success in math. *Teaching Exceptional Children, 29*(4), 42–45.

Corso, R. M., Santos, R. M., & Roof, V. (2002). Honoring diversity in early childhood education materials. *Teaching Exceptional Children, 34*(3), 30–38.

Cosden, M. (2001). Risk and resilience for substance abuse among adolescents and adults with LD. *Journal of Learning Disabilities, 34*, 352–358.

Cosmos, C. (2000, October). Promise and peril: A look at charter schools. *Today, 7*(3), 1, 5, 7, 15,

Costa, A. L., & Kallick, B. (2000). Getting into the habit of reflection. *Educational Leadership, 57*(7), 60–62.

Council for Exceptional Children. (2001). Virtual reality, brain imaging, the LD debate and more to impact special education. *CEC Today 8*(3), 1, 9–10, 14–15.

Council for Exceptional Children. (2002). Help students cope with chronic fear. *CEC Today 8*(6), 1, 9, 12, 14.

Council for Exceptional Children. (2003). Exceptional and homeless. *CEC Today 9*(6), 7, 13, 15.

Countryman, L. L., & Schroeder, M. (1996). When students lead parent–teacher conferences. *Educational Leadership, 53*(7), 64–68.

Coutinho, M. J., Oswald, D. P., & Best, A. M. (2002). The influence of sociodemographics and gender on the disproportionate identification of minority students as having learning disabilities. *Remedial and Special Education, 23*, 49–59.

Cox, P. R., & Dykes, M. K. (2001). Effective classroom adaptations for students with visual impairments. *Teaching Exceptional Children, 33*(6), 68–74.

Coyne, M. D., Kame'enui, E. J., & Simmons, D. C. (2001). Prevention and intervention in beginning reading: Two complex systems. *Learning Disabilities Research and Practice, 16*, 62–73.

Craig, S., Hull, K., Haggart, A. G., & Crowder, E. (2001). Storytelling: Addressing the literacy needs of diverse learners. *Teaching Exceptional Children, 33*(5), 46–51.

Craig, S., Hull, K., Haggart, A. G., & Perez-Selles, M. (2000). Promoting cultural competence through teacher assistance teams. *Teaching Exceptional Children, 32*(3), 6–12.

Cramer, S., Erzkus, A., Mayweather, K., Pope, K., Roeder, J., & Tone, T. (1997). Connecting with siblings. *Teaching Exceptional Children, 30*(1), 46–51.

Crockett, J. B. (2002). Special education's role in preparing responsive leaders for inclusive schools. *Remedial and Special Education, 23*, 157–168.

Cronin, M. E., & Patton, J. R. (1993). *Life skills instruction for all students with special needs: A practical guide for integrating real-life content into the curriculum.* Austin, TX: PRO-ED.

Cruz, L., & Cullinan, D. (2001). Awarding points, using levels to help children improve behavior. *Teaching Exceptional Children, 33*(3), 16–23.

Cullinan, D., Evans, C., Epstein, M. H., & Ryser, G. (2003). Characteristics of emotional disturbance of elementary school students. *Behavioral Disorders, 28*, 94–110.

Cummins, J. (1989). *Empowering minority students*. Sacramento, CA: Association for Bilingual Educators.

Cunningham, P. M. (1998). The multisyllabic word dilemma: Helping students build meaning, spell, and read "big" words. *Reading and Writing Quarterly: Overcoming Learning Difficulties, 14*(2), 189–218.

Curry, C. (2003). Universal design accessibility for all learners. *Educational Leadership, 61*(2), 55–60.

Curtiss, V. S., Mathur, S. R., & Rutherford, R. B. (2002). Developing behavioral intervention plans: A step-by-step approach. *Beyond Behavior, 11*(2), 28–31.

Cushing, L. S., & Kennedy, C. H. (1997). Academic effects of providing peer support in general education classrooms on students without disabilities. *Journal of Applied Behavior Analysis, 30*, 139–151.

Czarnecki, E., Rosko, D., & Fine, E. (1998). How to call up notetaking skills. *Teaching Exceptional Children, 30*(6), 14–19.

Dabkowski, D. M. (2004). Encouraging active parent participation in IEP team meetings. *Teaching Exceptional Children, 36*(3), 34–39.

D'Alonzo, B. J., Giordano, G., & Vanleeuwen, D. M. (1997). Perceptions by teachers about the benefits and liabilities of inclusion. *Preventing School Failure, 42*(1), 4–11.

Daly, P. M., & Ranalli, P. (2003). Using countoons to teach self-monitoring skills. *Teaching Exceptional Children, 35*(5), 30–35.

D'Amato, R. C., & Rothlisberg, B. A. (1996). How education should respond to students with traumatic brain injury. *Journal of Learning Disabilities, 29*(6), 670–683.

D'Ambrosio, U. (2001). What is ethnomathematics, and how can it help children in schools? *Teaching Children Mathematics, 7*, 308–310.

Damico, J. S. (1991). Descriptive assessment of communicative ability in limited english proficient students. In E. Hamayan & J. S. Damico (Eds.), *Limiting bias in the assessment of bilingual students* (pp. 157–218). Austin, TX: PRO-ED.

Daniel, R. R. v. State Board of Education, 874 F.2d 1036, 5th Circuit, 1989.

Daniels, H., & Zemelman, S. Out with textbooks, in with learning. *Educational Leadership, 61*(4), 36–40.

Daresh, J. C. (2003). *Teachers mentoring teachers: A practical approach to helping new and experienced staff*. Thousand Oaks, CA: Corwin Press.

Dattilo, J., & Hoge, G. (1999). Effects of leisure education programs on youth with mental retardation. *Education and Training in Mental Retardation and Developmental Disabilities, 34*(1), 20–34.

Daunic, A. P., Smith, S. W., Robinson, T. R., Miller, M. D., & Landry, K. L. (2000). School-wide conflict resolution and peer mediation programs: Experiences in three middle schools. *Intervention in School and Clinic, 36*, 94–100.

Davern, L. (1999). Parents' perspectives on personnel attitudes and characteristics in inclusive school settings: Implications for teacher preparation programs. *Teacher Education and Special Education, 22*(3), 165–182.

Davies, D. K., Stock, S. E., & Wehmeyer, M. L. (2001). Enhancing independent Internet access for individuals with mental retardation through use of a specialized web browser: A pilot study. *Education and Training in Mental Retardation and Developmental Disabilities, 36*, 107–113.

Davies, D. K., Stock, S. E., & Wehmeyer, M. L. (2002). Enhancing independent task performance through use of a handheld self-directed visual and audio prompting system. *Education and Training in Mental Retardation and Developmental Disabilities, 37*, 209–218.

Davies, S., & Hastings, R. P. (2003). Computer technology in clinical psychology services for people with mental retardation: A review. *Education and Training in Developmental Disabilities, 38*, 341–352.

Davis, C., Brown, B., Bantz, J. M., & Manno, C. (2002). African American parents' involvement in their children's special education programs. *Multiple Voices, 5*(1), 13–27.

Davis, S. (1997). *Child labor in agriculture*. Charleston, WV: ERIC Clearinghouse on Rural Education and Small Schools. (ERIC Document Reproduction Service No. ED 405 159).

Day, J. (1998, November). *A program to teach standard American English to African-American English speakers*. Presentation at the Council for Exceptional Children/Division of Diverse Exceptional Learners Symposium on Culturally and Linguistically Diverse Exceptional Learners, Washington, DC.

De Avila, E. A. (1988). *Finding out/Descubrimiento*. Northvale, NJ: Santillana.

DeBettencourt, L. U., (2002). Understanding the differences between IDEA and Section 504. *Teaching Exceptional Children, 34*(3), 16–23.

Deck, M., Scarborough, J. L., Sferrazza, M. S., & Estill, D. M. (1999). Serving students with disabilities: Perspectives of three school counselors. *Intervention in School and Clinic, 34*(3), 150–155.

DeGeorge, K. L. (1998). Friendship and stories: Using children's literature to teach friendship skills to children with learning disabilities. *Intervention in School and Clinic, 33*(3), 157–162.

De la Cruz, R. E., Cage, C. E., & Lian, M. J. (2000). Learning math and social skills through ancient multicultural games. *Teaching Exceptional Children, 32*(3), 38–42.

De La Paz, S. (2001). STOP and DARE: A persuasive writing strategy. *Intervention in School and Clinic, 36*, 234–243.

De La Paz, S., Owen, B., Harris, K. R., & Graham, S. (2000). Riding Elvis's motorcycle: Using self-regulated strategy development to PLAN and WRITE for a state writing exam. *Learning Disabilities Research and Practice, 15*, 101–109.

Demchak, M., & Greenfield, R. G. (2000). A transition portfolio for Jeff, a student with multiple disabilities. *Teaching Exceptional Children, 32*(6), 44–49.

Denham, A., & Lahm, E. A. (2001). Using technology to construct alternate portfolios of students with moderate and severe disabilities. *Teaching Exceptional Children, 33*(5), 10–17.

Dennis, R. E., & Giangreco, M. F. (1996). Creating conversation: Reflections on cultural sensitivity in family interviewing. *Exceptional Children, 63*(1), 103–116.

Deno, E. (1970). Special education as developmental capital. *Exceptional Children, 37*, 229–237.

Deno, S. L. (2003). Developments in curriculum-based measurement. *The Journal of Special Education, 37*, 184–192.

Derman-Sparks, L. (1989). *Anti-bias curriculum*. Washington, DC: National Association for the Education of Young Children.

Derman-Sparks, L., & Phillips, C. B. (1997). *Teaching/learning anti-racism: A developmental approach*. New York: Teachers College Press.

Deshler, D. D., Schumaker, J. B., Lenz, B. K., Bulgren, J. A., Hock, M. F., Knight, J., & Ehren, B. J. (2001a). Ensuring content-area learning by secondary students with learning disabilities. *Learning Disabilities Research and Practice, 16*, 96–108.

Desrochers, C., & Desrochers, M. (2000). Creating lessons designed to motivate students. *Contemporary Education, 71*(2), 51–55.

Dever, M. T., Whitaker, M. L., & Byrnes, D. A. (2001). The 4th R: Teaching about religion in the public schools. *Social Studies, 92,* 220–230.

Diana v. California State Board of Education, No. C-70-37, RFP, (N.D. Cal., 1970).

DiCecco, V., & Gleason, M. M. (2002). Using graphic organizers to attain relational knowledge from expository text. *Journal of Learning Disabilities, 35,* 306–320.

Dickinson, D. L., & Verbeek, R. L. (2002). Wage differentials between college graduates with and without learning disabilities. *Journal of Learning Disabilities, 35,* 175–184.

Disability Resources. (2000, December). Readers ask. *Disability Resources Monthly,* 6.

Disarno, N. J., Schowalter, M., & Grassa, P. (2002). Classroom amplification to enhance student performance. *Teaching Exceptional Children, 34*(6), 20–27.

Dockterman, D. A. (1995). Interactive learning: It's pushing the right buttons. *Educational Leadership, 53*(2), 58–59.

Dodd-Murphy, J., & Mamlin, N. (2002). Minimizing minimal hearing loss in the schools: What every classroom teacher should know. *Preventing School Failure, 46,* 86–92.

Doelling, J. E., & Bryde, S. (1995). School reentry and educational planning for the individual with traumatic brain injury. *Intervention in School and Clinic, 31*(2), 101–107.

Doelling, J. E., Bryde, S., & Parette, H. P. (1997). What are multidisciplinary and ecobehavioral approaches and how can they make a difference for students with traumatic brain injuries? *Teaching Exceptional Children, 30*(1), 56–60.

Donnelly, J. A. (2002). Guidelines for respectful support of individuals on the autism spectrum. *DDD Express, 13*(1), 1, 11.

Dore, R., Dion, E., Wagner, S., & Brunet, J. P. (2002). High school inclusion of adolescents with mental retardation: A multiple case study. *Education and Training in Mental Retardation and Developmental Disabilities, 37,* 253–261.

Dormans, J. P., Pellegrino, L., & Batshaw, M. L. (1998). *Caring for children with cerebral palsy: A team approach.* Baltimore: Brookes.

Douglas, S. L. (2002). Teaching about religion. *Educational Leadership, 60*(2), 32–37.

Dowdy, C. A., Patton, J. R., Smith, T. E. C., & Polloway, E. A. (1998). Attention-deficit/hyperactivity disorder: A practical guide for teachers. Austin, TX:PRO-ED.

Downing, J. A. (2002). Individualized behavior contracts. *Intervention in School and Clinic, 37,* 168–172.

Downing, J. E., & Chen, D. (2003). Using tactile strategies with students who are blind and have severe disabilities. *Teaching Exceptional Children, 36*(2), 56–60.

Downing, J. E., & Eichinger, J. (2003). Creating learning opportunities for students with severe disabilities in inclusive classrooms. *Teaching Exceptional Children, 36*(1), 26–31.

Downing, J. E., Eichinger, J., & Williams, L. J. (1997). Inclusive education for students with severe disabilities. Comparative views of principals and educators at different levels of implementation. *Remedial and Special Education, 18,* 133–142, 165.

Downing, J. E., & Peckham-Hardin, K. D. (2001). Daily schedules: A helpful learning tool. *Teaching Exceptional Children, 33*(3), 62–68.

Doyel, A. W. (2000). *No more job interviews! Self-employment strategies for people with disabilities.* St. Augustine, FL: Training Resource Network.

Doyle, M. B. (2000). Transition plans for students with disabilities. *Educational Leadership, 58*(1), 46–48.

Doyle, M. B. (2002). *The paraprofessional's guide to the inclusive classroom: Working as a team* (2nd ed.). Baltimore: Brookes.

Drasgow, E., Yell, M. L. & Robinson, T. R. (2001). Developing legally correct and educationally appropriate IEPs. *Remedial and Special Education, 22,* 359–373.

Drecktrah, M. E., & Chiang, B. (1997). Instructional strategies used by general educators and teachers of students with learning disabilities. *Remedial and Special Education, 18*(3), 174–181.

Dreher, M. J. (2003). Motivating struggling readers by tapping the potential of information books. *Reading and Writing Quarterly: Overcoming Learning Difficulties, 19,* 25–38.

Drug Strategies. (1999). *Making the grade: A guide to school drug prevention programs.* Washington, DC: Author.

Duchardt, B. A., Deshler, D. D., & Schumaker, J. B. (1995). A strategic intervention for enabling students with learning disabilities to identify and change their ineffective beliefs. *Learning Disability Quarterly, 18*(3), 186–201.

Duckworth, S., Smith-Rex, S., Okey, S., Brookshire, M. A., Rawlinson, D., Rawlinson, R., Castillo, S., & Little, J. (2001). Wraparound services for young schoolchildren with emotional and behavioral disorders. *Teaching Exceptional Children, 33,* 54–60.

Dudley-Marling, C., & Fine, E. (1997). Politics of whole language. *Reading and Writing Quarterly: Overcoming Learning Difficulties, 13,* 247–260.

Duenwald, M. (2002, March 26). 2 portraits of children of divorce: Rosy and dark. *The New York Times,* F6.

Duenwald, M., & Grady, D. (2003, January 8). Young survivors of cancer battle effects of treatment. *The New York Times,* A1, A20.

Duff, C. (2000). Online mentoring. *Educational Leadership, 58*(2), 49–52.

Dunlap, G., & Bunton-Pierce, M. K. (1999, October). *Autism and autism spectrum disorder.* Reston, VA: ERIC Clearinghouse on Disabilities and Gifted Education.

Dunn, L. M. (1968). Special education for the mildly retarded—is much of it justifiable? *Exceptional Children, 35,* 5–22.

Dunn, R. (1996). *How to implement and supervise a learning styles program.* Alexandria, VA: Association for Supervision and Curriculum Development.

Dunn, R., Griggs, S. A., Olson, J., Beasley, M., & Gorman, B. S. (1995). A meta-analytic validation of the Dunn and Dunn model of learning style preferences. *The Journal of Educational Research, 88,* 353–362.

Dunst, C. J., & Bruder, M. B. (2002). Valued outcomes of service coordination, early intervention, and natural environments. *Exceptional Children, 68,* 361–375.

DuPaul, G. J., & Eckert, T. L. (1998). Academic interventions for students with attention-deficit/hyperactivity disorder: A review of the literature. *Reading and Writing Quarterly: Overcoming Learning Difficulties, 14*(1), 59–82.

Dwyer, K., Osher, D., & Hoffman, C. C. (2000). Creating responsive schools: Contextualizing early warning, timely response. *Exceptional Children, 66,* 347–365.

Dyches, T. T., & Burrow, E. (2003). Using children's books with characters with developmental disabilities. *DDD Express, 13*(3), 5.

Dyck, N., & Pemberton, J. (2002). A model for making decisions about text adaptations. *Intervention in School and Clinic, 38,* 28–35.

Dye, G. A. (2000). Graphic organizers to the rescue: Helping students link and remember information. *Teaching Exceptional Children, 32*(3), 72–76.

Dynneson, T. L., Gross, R. E., & Berson, M. J. (2003). *Designing effective instruction for secondary social studies* (3rd ed.). Upper Saddle River, NJ: Merrill/Prentice Hall.

Easterbrooks, S. R., & Baker, S. K. (2001). Enter the matrix: Considering the communication needs of students who are deaf or hard of hearing. *Teaching Exceptional Children, 33*(3), 70–76.

Eber, L., Smith, C., Sugai, G., & Scott, T. M. (2002). Wraparound and positive behavioral interventions and supports in schools. *Journal of Emotional and Behavioral Disorders, 10,* 171–180.

Echevarria, J. (1995). Sheltered instruction for students with learning disabilities who have limited English proficiency. *Intervention in School and Clinic, 30*(5), 302–305.

Echevarria, J., & McDonough, R. (1995). An alternative reading approach: Instructional conversations in a bilingual special education setting. *Learning Disabilities Research and Practice, 10*(2), 108–119.

Eckman, A. (2001). Having faith: Teaching about religion in public schools. *Education Update, 43*(2), 1, 4, 8.

Edens, R. M., Murdick, N. L., & Gartin, B. C. (2003). Preventing infection in the classroom: The use of universal precautions. *Teaching Exceptional Children, 35*(4), 62–66.

Edgar, E., Patton, J. M., & Day-Vines, N. (2002). Democratic dispositions and cultural competency: Ingredients of school renewal. *Remedial and Special Education, 23,* 231–241.

Edmiaston, R. K., & Fitzgerald, L. M. (2000). How Reggio Emilia encourages inclusion. *Educational Leadership, 58*(1), 66–69.

Education Commission of the States. (2000). *Technology: Equitable access in schools.* Denver, CO: Author.

Educational Equity Concepts. (n.d.). *Beginning science equitably.* New York: Author.

Edwards, A. T. (1997). Let's stop ignoring our gay and lesbian youth. *Educational Leadership, 54*(7), 68–70.

Edwards, L. (2003). Writing instruction in kindergarten: Examining an emerging area of research for children with writing and reading difficulties. *Journal of Learning Disabilities, 36,* 136–148.

Egan, J. (2002, March 24). To be young and homeless. *The New York Times Magazine,* 32–37, 58–59.

Ehlenberger, K. R. (2002). The right to search students. *Educational Leadership, 59*(4), 31–35.

Eisenman, L. T., & Tascione, L. (2002). "How come nobody told me?" Fostering self-realization through a high school English curriculum. *Learning Disabilities Research and Practice, 17,* 35–46.

Elbaum, B. (2002). The self-concept of students with learning disabilities: A meta-analysis of comparisons across different placements. *Learning Disabilities Research and Practice, 17,* 216–226.

Elksnin, L. K., & Elksnin, N. (1998). Teaching social skills to students with learning and behavior problems. *Intervention in School and Clinic, 33*(3), 131–140.

Elksnin, L. K., & Elksnin, N. (2000). Teaching parents to teach their children to be prosocial. *Intervention in School and Clinic, 36,* 27–35.

Elliott, L., Foster, S., & Stinson, M. (2002). Student study habits using notes from a speech-to-text support service. *Exceptional Children, 69,* 25–40.

Elliott, S. N., Kratochwill, T. R., & Schulte, T. R. (1998). The assessment accommodation checklist. *Teaching Exceptional Children, 31*(2), 10–14.

Ellis, E. S. (1989). A metacognitive intervention for increasing class participation. *Learning Disabilities Focus, 5*(1), 36–46.

Ellis, E. S. (1994). Integrating writing strategy instruction with content-area instruction: Part 1—Orienting students to organizational strategies. *Intervention in School and Clinic, 29*(3), 169–179.

Ellis, E. S. (1996). Reading strategy instruction. In D. D. Deshler, E. S. Ellis, & B. K. Lenz (Eds.), *Teaching adolescents with learning disabilities: Strategies and methods* (2nd ed., pp. 61–125). Denver: Love.

Ellis, E. S. (1997). Watering up the curriculum for adolescents with learning disabilities. *Remedial and Special Education, 18*(6), 326–346.

Ellis, E. S. (1998). Watering up the curriculum for adolescents with learning disabilities—Part 2. *Remedial and Special Education, 19*(2), 91–105.

Ellis, E. S., & Covert, G. (1996). Writing strategy instruction. In D. D. Deshler, E. S. Ellis, & B. K. Lenz (Eds.), *Teaching adolescents with learning disabilities: Strategies and methods* (2nd ed., pp. 127–207). Denver: Love.

Ellis, E. S., & Lenz, B. K. (1987). A component analysis of effective learning strategies for LD students. *Learning Disabilities Focus, 2,* 94–107.

Ellis, E. S., & Lenz, B. K. (1996). Perspectives on instruction in learning strategies. In D. D. Deshler, E. S. Ellis, & B. K. Lenz (Eds.), *Teaching adolescents with learning disabilities: Strategies and methods* (2nd ed., pp. 9–60). Denver: Love.

Embry, D. D. (1997). Does your school have a peaceful environment? Using an adult to create a climate for change and resiliency. *Intervention in School and Clinic, 32*(4), 217–222.

Emerson, J., & Lovitt, T. (2003). Perspective: The educational plight of foster children in schools and what can be done about it. *Remedial and Special Education, 24,* 199–203.

England, G., Collins, S., & Algozzine, B. (2002). Effects of failure free reading on culturally and linguistically diverse students with learning disabilities. *Multiple Voices, 5*(1), 28–37.

Engleman, M. D., Griffin, H. C., Griffin, L. W., & Maddox, J. I. (1999). A teacher's guide to communicating with students with deaf-blindness. *Teaching Exceptional Children, 31*(5), 64–70.

Englemann, S., & Associates. (1999). *Corrective reading series.* Blacklick, OH: Science Research Associates.

Englemann, S., & Carnine, D. W. (1975). *Distar arithmetic level 1.* Chicago: Science Research Associates.

Englemann, S., & Carnine, D. W. (1976). *Distar arithmetic level 2.* Chicago: Science Research Associates.

Englemann, S., & Carnine, D. W. (1982). *Corrective mathematics program.* Chicago: Science Research Associates.

Englert, C. S., Berry, R., & Dunsmore, K. (2001). A case study of the apprenticeship process: Another perspective on the apprentice and the scaffolding metaphor. *Journal of Learning Disabilities, 34,* 152–171.

Englert, C. S., & Mariage, T. V. (1991). Making students partners in the comprehension process: Send for the reading POSSE. *Learning Disability Quarterly, 14,* 123–138.

English, K., Goldstein, H., Kaczmarek, L., & Shafer, K. (1996). "Buddy skills" for preschoolers. *Teaching Exceptional Children, 28*(3), 62–66.

English, K., Goldstein, H., Shafer, K., & Kaczmarek, L. (1997). Promoting interactions among preschoolers with and without disabilities: Effects of a buddy skills-training program. *Exceptional Children, 63*(2), 229–243.

Enright, B. E., (1987). Enright S.O.L.V.E.: Action problem solving series. N. Billerica, MA: Curriculum Associates.

Epstein, M. H., Hertzog, M. A., & Reid, R. (2001). The behavioral and emotional rating scale: Long term test-retest reliability. *Behavioral Disorders, 26,* 314–320.

ERIC Clearinghouse on Urban Education. (2001, August). *Gender differences in educational achievement within racial and ethnic groups.* New York: Author.

Erickson, R., Ysseldyke, J., Thurlow, M., & Elliott, J. (1998). Inclusive assessments and accountability systems: Tools of the trade in educational reform. *Teaching Exceptional Children, 31*(2), 4–9.

Ernsbarger, S. C. (2002). Simple, affordable, and effective strategies for prompting reading behavior. *Reading and Writing Quarterly: Overcoming Learning Difficulties, 18,* 279–284.

Etscheidt, S. K. (2002). Discipline provisions of IDEA: Misguided policy or tacit reform initiatives? *Behavioral Disorders, 27,* 408–422.

Etscheidt, S. K., & Bartlett, L. (1999). The IDEA amendments: A four-step approach for determining supplementary aids and services. *Exceptional Children, 65*(2), 163–174.

Evans, I. M., Salisbury, C. L., Palombaro, M. M., Berryman, J., & Hollowood, T. M. (1992). Acceptance of elementary-aged children with severe disabilities in an inclusive school. *Journal of the Association for Persons with Severe Handicaps, 17,* 205–212.

Evans, S., Tickle, B., Toppel, C., & Nichols, A. (1997). Here's help for young children exposed to drugs. *Teaching Exceptional Children, 29*(3), 60–62.

Ewing, N. J., & Duhaney, L. G. (1996, April). *Effective behavior management and counseling practices for culturally diverse students.* Presentation at the annual meeting of the Council for Exceptional Children, Orlando, FL.

Ezell, D., & Klein, C. (2003). Impact of portfolio assessment on locus of control of students with and without disabilities. *Education and Training in Developmental Disabilities, 38,* 220–228.

Fabiano, G. A., & Pelham, W. E. (2003). Improving the effectiveness of behavioral classroom interventions for attention-deficit/hyperactivity disorder: A case study. *Journal of Emotional and Behavioral Disorders, 11,* 122–128.

Fallows, J. (2000, March 19). The invisible poor in the shadow of wealth. *The New York Times Magazine,* 68–78, 95, 111–112.

Farmer, T. W. (2000). Misconceptions of peer rejection and problem behavior: Understanding aggression in students with mild disabilities. *Remedial and Special Education, 21,* 194–208.

Favazza, P. C., & Odom, S. L. (1997). Promoting positive attitudes of kindergarten-age children toward people with disabilities. *Exceptional Children, 63*(3), 405–418.

Favazza, P. C., Phillipsen, L., & Kumar, P. (2000). Measuring and promoting acceptance of young children with disabilities. *Exceptional Children, 66,* 491–508.

Feldhusen, J. F. (2001, June). *Talent development in gifted education.* Arlington, VA: ERIC Clearinghouse on Disabilities and Gifted Education.

Fennick, E. (2001). Coteaching: An inclusive curriculum for transition. *Teaching Exceptional Children, 33*(6), 60–67.

Fennick, E., & Liddy, D. (2001). Responsibilities and preparation for collaborative teaching: Co-teaching perspectives. *Teacher Education and Special Education, 24,* 229–240.

Ferguson, P. M. (2002). A place in the family: An historical interpretation of research on parental reactions to having a child with a disability. *The Journal of Special Education, 36,* 124–130.

Fernstrom, P., & Goodnite, B. (2000). Accommodate student diversity in the general education social studies classroom. *Intervention in School and Clinic, 35,* 244–245.

Ferretti, R. P., MacArthur, C. D., & Okolo, C. M. (2002). Teaching effectively about historical things. *Teaching Exceptional Children, 34*(6), 66–69.

Ferri, B. A., Keefe, C. H., & Gregg, N. (2001). Teachers with learning disabilities: A view from both sides of the desk. *Journal of Learning Disabilities, 34,* 22–31.

Fidler, D. J., Hodapp, R. M., & Dykens, E. M. (2002). Behavioral phenotypes and special education: Parent report of educational issues for children with Down Syndrome, Prader-Willi Syndrome, and Williams Syndrome. *The Journal of Special Education, 36,* 80–88.

Fiedler, B. C. (2001). Considering placement and educational approaches for students who are deaf and hard of hearing. *Teaching Exceptional Children, 34*(2), 54–60.

Field, S., & Hoffman, A. (1996). *Steps to self-determination.* Austin, TX: PRO-ED.

Fierro-Cobas, V., & Chan, E. (2001). Language development in bilingual children: A primer for pediatricians. *Contemporary Pediatrics, 18*(7), 79–98.

Findley, N. (2002). In their own ways. *Educational Leadership, 60*(1), 60–63.

Finn, K., Willert, H. J., & Marable, M. A. (2003). Substance use in schools. *Educational Leadership, 60*(6), 80–83.

Firman, K. B., Beare, P., & Loyd, R. (2002). Enhancing self-management in students with mental retardation: Extrinsic versus intrinsic preferences. *Education and Training in Mental Retardation and Developmental Disabilities, 37,* 163–171.

Fisher, D., & Frey, N. (2001). Access to the core curriculum: Critical ingredients for student success. *Remedial and Special Education, 22,* 148–157.

Fisher, D., Frey, N., & Thousand, J. (2003). What do special educators need to know and be prepared to do for inclusive schooling to work? *Teacher Education and Special Education, 26,* 42–50.

Fisher, D., Frey, N., & Williams, D. (2002). Seven literacy strategies that work. *Educational Leadership, 60*(3), 70–74.

Fisher, D., Pumpian, I., & Sax, C. (1998). Parent and caregiver impressions of different educational models. *Remedial and Special Education, 19,* 173–180.

Fitzharris, L. H., & Hay, G. H. (2001). Working collaboratively to support struggling readers in the inclusive classroom. *Reading and Writing Quarterly: Overcoming Learning Difficulties, 17,* 175–180.

Flanagan, B. (1998, April). *Strategies for improving student comprehension of textbook content.* Presentation at the meeting of the Council for Exceptional Children, Minneapolis.

Fleming, J. L., & Monda-Amaya, L. E. (2001). Process variables critical for team effectiveness. *Remedial and Special Education, 22,* 158–171.

Fleming, M. B. (1988). Getting out of the writing vacuum. In J. Golub (Ed.), *Focus on collaborative learning* (pp. 77–84). Urbana, IL: National Council of Teachers of English.

Flett, A., & Conderman, G. (2002). 20 ways to promote phonemic awareness. *Intervention in School and Clinic, 37,* 242–245.

Fleury, M. L. (2000). Confidentiality issues for substitutes and paraeducators. *Teaching Exceptional Children, 33*(1), 44–45.

Flint, L. J. (2001). The challenges of identifying and serving gifted children with ADHD. *Teaching Exceptional Children, 33*(4), 62–69.

Flor Ada, A. (1993). *My name is Maria Isabel.* New York: Atheneum.

Foegen, A., & Deno, S. L. (2001). Identifying growth indicators for low-achieving students in middle school mathematics. *The Journal of Special Education, 35,* 4–16.

Foil, C. R., & Alber, S. R. (2002). Fun and effective ways to build your students' vocabulary. *Intervention in School and Clinic, 37,* 131–139.

Foorman, B. R., & Torgesen, J. (2001). Critical elements of classroom and small-group instruction promote reading success in all children. *Learning Disabilities Research and Practice, 16,* 203–212.

Forcier, R. C., & Descy, D. E., (2002). *The computer as an educational tool: Productivity and problem solving* (3rd ed.). Upper Saddle River, NJ: Merrill/Prentice Hall.

Ford, A., Davern, L., & Schnorr, R. (2001). Learners with significant disabilities. Curricular relevance in an era of standards-based reform. *Remedial and Special Education, 22,* 214–222.

Ford, D. Y. (1998). The underrepresentation of minority students in gifted education: Problems and promises in recruitment and retention. *The Journal of Special Education, 32,* 4–14.

Ford, D. Y. (2000, December). *Infusing multicultural content into the curriculum for gifted students.* Reston, VA: ERIC Clearinghouse on Disabilities and Gifted Education.

Fordham, S., & Ogbu, J. (1986). Black students' school success: Coping with the burden of "acting white." *The Urban Review, 18,* 176–206.

Forgan, J. W. (2002). Using bibliotherapy to teach problem solving. *Intervention in School and Clinic, 38,* 75–82.

Forgan, J. W., & Jones, C. D. (2002). How experiential adventure activities can improve students' social skills. *Teaching Exceptional Children, 34*(3), 52–58.

Forgan, J. W., & Vaughn, S. (2000). Adolescents with and without LD make the transition to middle school. *Journal of Learning Disabilities, 33,* 33–43.

Forgan, J. W., & Weber, R. K. (2001). Selecting software for students with high incidence disabilities. *Intervention in School and Clinic, 37,* 40–47.

Forness, S. R., Walker, H. M., & Kavale, K. A. (2003). Psychiatric disorders and treatments: A primer for teachers. *Teaching Exceptional Children, 36*(2), 42–49.

Foss, J. M. (2001, December). *Nonverbal learning disablity: How to recognize it and minimize its effects.* Arlington, VA: ERIC Clearinghouse on Disabilities and Gifted Education.

Fowler, S. A., Donegan, M., Lueke, B., Hadden, D. S., & Phillips, B. (2000). Evaluating community collaboration in writing interagency agreements on the age 3 transition. *Exceptional Children, 67,* 35–50.

Fox, J., Conroy, M., & Heckaman, K. (1998). Research issues in functional assessment of the challenging behaviors of students with emotional and behavioral disorders. *Behavioral Disorders, 24*(1), 26–33.

Fox, L., & Dunlap, G. (2002). Family-centered practices in positive behavior support. *Beyond Behavior, 11*(2), 24–26.

Fox, L., Dunlap, G., & Cushing, L. (2002). Early intervention, positive behavior support, and transition to school. *Journal of Emotional and Behavioral Disorders, 10,* 149–157.

Fox, L., Vaughn, B. J., Wyatte, M. L., & Dunlap, G. (2002). "We can't expect other people to understand": Family perspectives on problem behavior. *Exceptional Children, 68,* 437–450.

Fradd, S. H., & Weismantel, M. J. (1989). *Meeting the needs of culturally and linguistically different students: A handbook for educators.* Austin, TX: PRO-ED.

Franklin, E. A. (1992). Learning to read and write the natural way. *Teaching Exceptional Children, 24*(3), 45–48.

Frederickson, N., & Turner, J. (2003). Utilizing the classroom peer group to address children's social needs: An evaluation of the circle of friends intervention approach. *The Journal of Special Education, 36,* 234–245.

Frederico, M. A., Herrold, W. G., & Venn, J. (1999). Helpful tips for successful inclusion: A checklist for educators. *Teaching Exceptional Children, 32*(1), 76–82.

Freedman-Harvey, G., & Johnson, W. (1998). How it feels. *Teaching Tolerance, 7*(1), 29.

Freeman, S. F. N., Alkin, M. C., & Kasari, C. L. (1999). Satisfaction and desire for change in educational placement for children with Down syndrome: Perceptions of parents. *Remedial and Special Education, 20*(3), 143–151.

Freeman, S. H., & Alkin, M. C. (2000). Academic and social attainments of children with mental retardation in general education and special education settings. *Remedial and Special Education, 21,* 3–18.

Freeman, Y. S., & Freeman, D. E. (1992). *Whole language for second language learners.* Portsmouth, NH: Heinemann.

Freire, P. (1970). *Pedagogy of the oppressed.* New York: Continuum.

French, N. K. (2002). Maximize paraprofessional services for students with learning disabilities. *Intervention in School and Clinic, 38,* 50–55.

French, N. K. (2003). *Managing paraeducators in your school: How to hire, train, and supervise non-certified staff.* Thousand Oaks, CA: Corwin Press.

French, N. K., & Pickett, A. L. (1997). Paraprofessionals in special education: Issues for teacher educators. *Teacher Education and Special Education, 20*(1), 61–73.

Frey, L. (2003). Abundant beautification: An effective service-learning project for students with emotional or behavioral disorders. *Teaching Exceptional Children, 35*(5), 66–74.

Frieman, B. B. (1997). Two parents—two homes. *Educational Leadership, 54*(7), 23–25.

Friend, M., & Cook, L. (2000). *Interactions: Collaborative skills for school professionals* (3rd ed.). New York: Longman.

Froschl, M., & Gropper, N. (1999). Fostering friendships, curbing bullying. *Educational Leadership, 56*(8), 72–75.

Fuchs, D., Deshler, D., & Zigmond, N. (1994, March). *How expendable is general education? How expendable is special education?* Paper presented at the meeting of the Learning Disabilities Association of America, Washington, DC.

Fuchs, D., Fernstrom, P., Scott, S., Fuchs, L., & Vandermeer, L. (1994). A process for mainstreaming: Classroom ecological inventory. *Teaching Exceptional Children, 26*(3), 11–15.

Fuchs, D., Fuchs, L. S., Mathes, P. G., Lipsey, M. E., & Eaton, S. (2000). A meta-analysis of reading differences with and without the disabilities label: A brief report. *Learning Disabilities: A Multidisciplinary Journal, 10,* 1–3.

Fuchs, D., Fuchs, L. S., Mathes, P. G., & Martinez, E. A. (2002). Preliminary evidence on the social standing of students with learning disabilities in PALS and no-PALS classrooms. *Learning Disabilities Research, 17,* 205–215.

Fuchs, D., Fuchs, L. S., Thompson, A., Svenson, E., Yan, L., Al Otaiba, S., Yang, N. McMater, K. N., Prentice, K., Kazdan, S., & Saenz, L. (2001). Peer-assisted learning strategies in reading: Extensions for kindergarten, first grade, and high school. *Remedial and Special Education, 22,* 15–21.

Fuchs, L. S., & Fuchs, D. (2001a). Principles for the prevention and intervention of mathematics difficulties. *Learning Disabilities Research and Practice, 16,* 85–95.

Fuchs, L. S., & Fuchs, D. (2001b). Helping teachers formulate sound test accommodation decisions for students with learning disabilities. *Learning Disabilities Research and Practice, 16,* 174–181.

Fuchs, L. S., & Fuchs, D. (2002). Mathematical problem-solving profiles of students with mathematical disabilities with and without comorbid reading difficulties. *Journal of Learning Disabilities, 35,* 563–573.

Fuchs, L. S., Fuchs, D., & Kazdan, S. (1999). Effects of peer-assisted learning strategies on high school students with serious reading problems. *Remedial and Special Education, 20*(5), 309–318.

Fuchs, L. S., Fuchs, D., Prentice, K., Burch, M., & Paulsen, K. (2002). Hot Math: Promoting mathematical problem solving among third-grade students with disabilities. *Teaching Exceptional Children, 35*(1), 70–73.

Fuentes, A. (2001, March 13). Clinic casts lifeline to isolated migrant workers. *The New York Times,* F5, F8.

Fueyo, V. (1997). Below the tip of the iceberg: Teaching language-minority students. *Teaching Exceptional Children, 30*(1), 61–65.

Fulk, B. M. (1997). Think while you spell: A cognitive motivational approach to spelling instruction. *Teaching Exceptional Children, 29*(4), 70–71.

Fulk, B. M., & King, K. (2001). Classwide peer tutoring at work. *Teaching Exceptional Children, 34*(2), 48–53.

Fulk, B. M., & Stormount-Spurgin, M. (1995). Fourteen spelling strategies for students with learning disabilities. *Intervention in School and Clinic, 31*(1), 16–20.

Furner, J. M., & Duffy, M. L. (2002). Equity for all students in the new millenium: Disabling math anxiety. *Intervention in School and Clinic, 38,* 67–74.

Gable, R. A., Arllen, N. L., Evans, W. H., & Whinnery, K. M. (1997). Strategies for evaluating collaborative mainstream instruction: "Let the data be our guide." *Preventing School Failure, 41*(4), 153–158.

Gable, R. A., Butler, C. J., Walker-Bolton, I., Tonelson, S. W., Quinn, M. M., & Fox, J. J. (2003). Safe and effective schooling for all students: Putting into practice the disciplinary provisions of the 1997 IDEA. *Preventing School Failure, 47,* 74–78.

Gaffney, J. S., Methven, J. M., & Bagdasarian, S. (2002). Assisting older students to read expository text in a tutorial setting: A case for a high-impact intervention. *Reading and Writing Quarterly: Overcoming Learning Difficulties, 18,* 119–150.

Gagnon, J. C., & Maccini, P. (2001). Preparing students with disabilities for algebra. *Teaching Exceptional Children, 34*(1), 8–15.

Gajria, M. (1988). *Effects of a summarization technique on the text comprehension skills of learning disabled students.* Unpublished doctoral dissertation, Pennsylvania State University.

Gajria, M. (1995, November). *Preparing adolescents with learning disabilities to meet the demands of regular classrooms.* Presentation at the annual meeting of the New York State Federation of Chapters of the Council for Exceptional Children, Niagara Falls, NY.

Gajria, M., Mullane, T., Sharp, E. R., & Heim, T. (2003, April). *Concept mapping: Improving content area comprehension for secondary students with learning disabilities.* Presentation at the annual meeting of the Council for Exceptional Children, Seattle.

Gajria, M., & Salend, S. J. (1995). Increasing the homework completion rates of students with mild disabilities. *Remedial and Special Education, 16*(5), 271–278.

Gajria, M., & Salend, S. J. (1996). Treatment acceptability: A critical dimension for overcoming teacher resistance to implementing adaptations for mainstreamed students. *Reading and Writing Quarterly: Overcoming Learning Difficulties, 12*(1), 91–108.

Galda, L., Cullinan, B. E., & Strickland, D. S. (1997). *Language, literacy and the child* (2nd ed.). New York: Harcourt Brace.

Gallagher, P. A., Floyd, J. H., Stafford, A. M., Taber, T. A., Brozovic, S. A., & Alberto, P.A. (2000). Inclusion of students with moderate or severe disabilities in educational and community settings: Perspectives from parents and siblings. *Education and Training in Mental Retardation and Developmental Disabilities, 35,* 135–147.

Galvin, J. C., & Scherer, M. J. (1996). *Evaluating, selecting, and using appropriate assistive technology.* Gaithersburg, MD: Aspen.

Gantos, J. (2000). *Joey Pigza loses control.* New York: Farrar, Straus & Giroux.

Ganzel, A. K., Peterson, R., & Snyder, M. (2002). Being part of the solution: Learning about special needs adoptions. *Beyond Behavior, 11*(2), 20–23.

Garay, S. V. (2003). Listening to the voices of deaf students: Essential transition issues. *Teaching Exceptional Children, 35*(4), 44–48.

Garbarino, J., & deLara, E. (2003). Words can hurt forever. *Educational Leadership, 60*(6), 18–21.

Garcia, E. (2002). *Student cultural diversity: Understanding and meeting the challenge* (3rd ed.). Boston: Houghton Mifflin.

Garcia, S. B., & Malkin, D. H. (1993). Toward defining programs and services for culturally and linguistically diverse learners in special education. *Teaching Exceptional Children, 26*(1), 52–58.

Garcia, S. B., Mendez Perez, A., & Ortiz, A. A. (2000). Mexican American mothers' beliefs about disabilities: Implications for early childhood intervention. *Remedial and Special Education, 21,* 90–100, 120.

Gardner, H. (1993). *Multiple intelligences: The theory in practice.* New York: Basic Books.

Gardner, J. E., Wissick, C. A., Schweder, W., & Canter, L. S. (2003). Enhancing interdisciplinary instruction in general and special education: Thematic units and technology. *Remedial and Special Education, 24,* 161–172.

Garmston, R., & Wellman, B. (1998). Teacher talk that makes a difference. *Educational Leadership, 55*(7), 30–34.

Garrett, M. T., Bellon-Harn, M. L., Torres-Rivera, E., Garrett, J. T., & Roberts, L. C. (2003). Open hands, open hearts: Working with native youth in the schools. *Intervention in School and Clinic, 38,* 225–235.

Garrick Duhaney, L. M. (2003). A practical approach to managing the behaviors of students with ADD. *Intervention in School and Clinic, 38,* 267–279.

Garrick Duhaney, L. M., & Salend, S. J. (2000). Parental perceptions of inclusive educational placements. *Remedial and Special Education, 21,* 121–128.

Garrick Duhaney, L. M., & Whittington-Couse, M. (1998, April). *Using learning styles and strategies to enhance academic learning for linguistically and culturally diverse students.* Presentation at the Conference on Providing Appropriate Instruction and Services to Culturally and Linguistically Diverse Learners, Fishkill, NY.

Garrity, C., Jens, K., Porter, W., Sager, N., & Short-Camilli, C. (1997). Bully-proofing your school: Creating a positive climate. *Intervention in School and Clinic, 32*(4), 235–243.

Gartin, B.C., Murdick, N. L., Thompson, J. R., & Dyches, T. T. (2002). Issues and challenges facing educators who advocate for students with disabilities. *Education and Training in Mental Retardation and Developmental Disabilities, 37*, 3–13.

Gartland, D. (1994). Content area reading: Lessons from the specialists. *LD Forum, 19*(3), 19–22.

Gately, S. E., & Gately, F. J. (2001). Understanding coteaching components. *Teaching Exceptional Children, 33*(4), 40–47.

Gauthier, L. R. (2001). Coop-Dis-Q: A reading comprehension strategy. *Intervention in School and Clinic, 36*, 217–220.

Gay, G. (2000). *Culturally responsive teaching: Theory, research, and practice.* New York: Teachers College Press.

Gebhard, M. (2003). Getting past "see spot run." *Educational Leadership, 60*(4), 35–39.

Geisthardt, C. L., Brotherson, M. J., & Cook, C. C. (2002). Friendships of children with disabilities in the home environment. *Education and Training in Mental Retardation and Developmental Disabilities, 37*, 223–234.

Gelfer, J. I., & Perkins, P. G. (1998). Portfolios: Focus on young children. *Teaching Exceptional Children, 31*(2), 44–47.

George, H. P., Harrower, J. K., & Knoster, T. (2003). School-wide prevention and early intervention: A process for establishing a system of school-wide behavior support. *Preventing School Failure, 47*, 170–176.

George, M. P., Valore, T., Quinn, M. M., & Varisco, R. (1997). Preparing to go home: A collaborative approach to transition. *Preventing School Failure, 41*(4), 168–172.

George, N. L., & Lewis, T. J. (1991). EASE: Exit assistance for special educators—Helping students make the transition. *Teaching Exceptional Children, 23*(2), 34–39.

Gerber, P. J., & Price, L. A. (2003). Persons with learning disabilities in the workplace: What we know so far in the Americans with Disabilities Act era. *Learning Disabilities Research & Practice, 18*(2), 132.

Gersten, R. (1999). The changing face of bilingual education. *Educational Leadership, 56*(7), 41–45.

Gersten, R., & Baker, S. (2000). What we know about effective instructional practices for English-language learners. *Exceptional Children, 66*, 454–470.

Gersten, R., & Chard, D. (1999). Number sense: Rethinking arithmetic instruction for students with mathematical disabilities. *Journal of Special Education, 33*, 18–28.

Gersten, R., & Geva, E. (2003). Teaching reading to early language learners. *Educational Leadership, 60*(7), 44–49.

Getch, Y. Q., & Neubarth-Pritchett, S. (1999). Children with asthma: Strategies for educators. *Teaching Exceptional Children, 31*(3), 30–36.

Getty, L. A., & Summy, S. E. (2004). The course of due process. *Teaching Exceptional Children, 36*(3), 40–43.

Giangreco, M. F., Baumgart, M. J., & Doyle, M. B. (1995). How inclusion can facilitate teaching and learning. *Intervention in School and Clinic, 30*(5), 273–278.

Giangreco, M. F., Cloninger, C. J., & Iverson, V. S. (1998). *Choosing options and accommodations for children: A guide to educational planning for students with disabilities* (2nd ed.). Baltimore: Paul H. Brookes.

Giangreco, M. F., Dennis, R., Cloninger, C., Edelman, S., & Schattman, R. (1993). "I've counted Jon": Transformational experiences of teachers educating students with disabilities. *Exceptional Children, 59*, 359–372.

Giangreco, M. F., Edelman, S. W., & Broer, S. M. (2001). Respect, appreciation, and acknowledgment of paraprofessionals who support students with disabilities. *Exceptional Children, 67*, 485–498.

Giangreco, M. F., Edelman, S. W., & Broer, S. M. (2003). Schoolwide planning to improve paraeducator supports. *Exceptional Children, 70*, 63–79.

Giangreco, M. F., Edelman, S. W., Luiselli, T. E., & McFarland, S. Z. C. (1997). Helping or hovering? Effects of instructional assistant proximity on student with disabilities. *Exceptional Children, 64*(1), 7–18.

Gibb, G. S., Young, J. R., Allred, K. W., Dyches, T. T., Egan, M. W., & Ingram, C. F. (1997). A team-based junior high inclusion program. Parent perceptions and feedback. *Remedial and Special Education, 18*, 243–249, 256.

Gibb, S. A., Allred, K., Ingram, G. F., Young, J. R., & Egan, W. M. (1999). Lessons learned from the inclusion of students with emotional and behavioral disorders in one junior high school. *Behavioral Disorders, 24*(2), 122–136.

Gibson, B. P., & Govendo, B. L. (1999). Encouraging constructive behavior in middle school classrooms: A multiple-intelligences approach. *Intervention in School and Clinic, 35*(1), 16–21.

Gilbert, S. E., & Gay, G. (1989). Improving the success in school of poor black children. In B. J. Shade (Ed.), *Culture, style and the educative process* (pp. 275–283). Springfield, IL: Charles C. Thomas.

Gipe, J. P. (2002). *Multiple paths to literacy: Classroom techniques for struggling readers* (5th ed.). Upper Saddle River, NJ: Merrill/Prentice Hall.

Glaeser, B. C., Pierson, M. R., & Fritschmann, N. (2003). Comic strip conversation: A positive behavioral support strategy. *Teaching Exceptional Children, 36*(2), 14–21.

Glater, J. D. (2003, June 14). Holy change agent! Consultants edit jargon. *The New York Times*, C1, C14.

Glazer, N. T., & Williams, S. (2001). Averting the homework crisis. *Educational Leadership, 58*(7), 43–45.

Gleason, M. M., & Isaacson, S. (2001). Using the new basals to teach the writing process: Modifications for students with learning problems. *Reading and Writing Quarterly: Overcoming Learning Difficulties, 17*, 75–92.

GLSEN. (2002a). *Curricular inclusion of LGBT content.* New York: Author.

GLSEN. (2002b). *Selected bibliography of books for children and young adults with LGBT characters and themes.* New York: Author.

Goddard, Y. L., & Heron, T. E. (1998). Pleaze, teacher, help me learn to spell better: Teach me self-correction. *Teaching Exceptional Children, 30*(6), 38–43.

Goh, D. S. (2004). *Assessment accommodations for diverse learners.* Boston: Allyn & Bacon.

Goldberg, L., & O'Neill, L. M. (2000, July). Computer technology can empower students with learning disabilities. *Exceptional Parent Magazine*, 72–74.

Goldin-Meadow, S., & Mayberry, R. I. (2001). How do profoundly deaf children learn to read? *Learning Disabilities Research and Practice, 16*, 222–229.

Goldstein, N. (2001). *Zero indifference: A how-to guide for ending name calling in schools.* New York: GLSEN.

Goleman, D. (1995). *Emotional intelligence.* New York: Bantam Books.

Gollnick, D. M., & Chinn, P. C. (2002). *Multicultural education in a pluralistic society* (6th ed.). Upper Saddle River, NJ: Merrill/Prentice Hall.

Good, T. L., & Brophy, J. E. (2000). *Looking in classrooms* (8th ed.). New York: Addison Wesley Longman.

Goode, E. (2003, January 14). Study finds jump in children taking psychiatric drugs. *The New York Times*, 21.

Goodman, G. (1979). From residential treatment to community based education: A model for reintegration. *Education and Training of the Mentally Retarded, 14*(2), 95–100.

Goodwin, M. W. (1999). Cooperative learning and social skills: What skills to teach and how to teach them. *Intervention in School and Clinic, 35*(1), 29–33.

Goor, M. B., & Schwenn, J. O. (1993). Accommodating diversity and disability with cooperative learning. *Intervention in School and Clinic, 29*(1), 6–16.

Gosselin, K. (1996a). *ZooAllergy*. Valley Park, MO: JayJo Books.

Gosselin, K. (1996b). *Taking epilepsy to school*. Valley Park, MO: JayJo Books.

Gosselin, K. (1998a). *Taking asthma to school*. Valley Park, MO: JayJo Books.

Gosselin, K. (1998b). *Taking diabetes to school*. Valley Park, MO: JayJo Books.

Graham, B. I., & Fahey, K. (1999). School leaders look at student work. *Educational Leadership, 56*(6), 25–27.

Graham, S. (1992). Helping students with LD progress as writers. *Intervention in School and Clinic, 27*(3), 134–144.

Graham, S., & Harris, K. R. (1992). Cognitive strategy instruction in written language for learning disabled students. In S. Vogel (Ed.), *Educational alternatives for teaching students with learning disabilities* (pp. 95–115). New York: Springer Verlag.

Graham, S., Harris, K. R., & Fink, B. (2000). Extra handwriting instruction: Prevent writing difficulties right from the start. *Teaching Exceptional Children, 33*(2), 88–91.

Graham, S., Harris, K. R., & Fink-Chorzempa, B. (2003). Extra spelling instruction: Promoting better spelling, writing and reading performance right from the start. *Teaching Exceptional Children, 35*(6), 66–68.

Graham, S., Harris, K. R., & Larsen, L. (2001). Prevention and intervention of writing difficulties for students with learning disabilities. *Learning Disabilities Research and Practice, 16*, 74–84.

Graham, S., Harris, K. R., & Loynachan, C. (1996). The directed spelling thinking activity: Application with high-frequency words. *Learning Disabilities Research and Practice, 11*(1), 34–40.

Grant, R. (1993). Strategic training for using text headings to improve students' processing of content. *Journal of Reading, 36*, 482–488.

Graves, A. W., Valles, E. C., & Rueda, R. (2000). Variations in interactive writing instruction: A study in four bilingual special education settings. *Learning Disabilities Research and Practice, 15*, 1–9.

Graves, D. H. (1994). *A fresh look at writing*. Portsmouth, NH: Heinemann.

Graves, D. H., & Hansen, J. (1983). The author's chair. *Language Arts, 60*, 176–183.

Green, A. L., & Stoneman, Z. (1989). Attitudes of mothers and fathers of nonhandicapped children. *Journal of Early Intervention, 13*, 292–304.

Green, S. K., & Shinn, M. R. (1995). Parent attitudes about special education and reintegration: What is the role of student outcomes? *Exceptional Children, 61*(3), 269–281.

Greenhouse, S. (2000, August 6). Farm work by children tests labor laws. *The New York Times*, 12.

Greenwood, C. R., Arreaga-Mayer, C., Utley, C. A., Gavin, K. M., & Terry, B. J. (2001). Classwide peer tutoring learning

management system: Applications with elementary-level English language learners. *Remedial and Special Education, 22*, 34–47.

Greer v. Rome City School District, 950 f.2d, 699, 11th Circuit, 1991.

Gregg, N., & Mather, N. (2002). School is fun at recess: Informal analyses of written language for students with learning disabilities. *Journal of Learning Disabilities, 35*, 7–22

Gresham, F. M., Sugai, G., & Horner, R. H. (2001). Outcomes of social skills training for students with high-incidence disabilities. *Exceptional Children, 67*, 331–344.

Griffin, H. C., Williams, S. C., Davis, M. L., & Engleman, M. (2002). Using technology to enhance cues for children with low vision. *Teaching Exceptional Children, 35*(2), 36–42.

Grigal, M., Neubert, D. A., & Moon, M. S. (2002). Postsecondary options for students with significant disabilities. *Teaching Exceptional Children, 35*(2), 68–73.

Groff, P. (2001). Teaching phonics: Letter-to-phoneme, phoneme-to-letter, or both? *Reading and Writing Quarterly: Overcoming Learning Disabilities, 17*, 307–322.

Grove, K. A., & Fisher, D. (1999). Entrepreneurs of meaning: Parents and the process of inclusive education. *Remedial and Special Education, 20*(4), 208–215, 256.

Guernsey, L. (2003, September). Fishing for information? Try better bait. *The New York Times*, G8.

Guetzloe, E. (1989). *Youth suicide: What the educator should know*. Reston, VA: Council for Exceptional Children.

Guetzloe, E., Hirschfield, S., Kosciw, J., & Schwartz, S. (2002, April). *Meeting the emotional needs of gay, lesbian, and bisexual youth: What parents, educators and advocates can do*. Presentation at the annual meeting of the Council for Exceptional Children, Indianapolis.

Gullingsrud, M. (1998). I am the immigrant in my classroom. *Voices from the Middle, 6*(1), 30–35.

Gunn, B., Biglan, A., Smolkowski, K., & Ary, D. (2000). The efficacy of supplemental instruction in decoding skills for Hispanic and Non-Hispanic students in early elementary school. *The Journal of Special Education, 34*, 90–103.

Gunter, P. L., Coutinho, M. J., & Cade, T. (2002). Classroom factors linked with academic gains among students with emotional and behavioral problems. *Preventing School Failure, 46*, 126–132.

Gunter, P. L., Miller, K. A., Venn, M. L., Thomas, K., & House, S. (2002). Self-graphing to success: Computerized data management. *Teaching Exceptional Children, 35*(2), 30–35.

Gunter, P. L., Shores, R. E., Jack, S. L., Rasmussen, S. K., & Flowers, J. (1995). On the move: Using teacher/student proximity to improve students' behavior. *Teaching Exceptional Children, 28*(1), 12–14.

Guskey, T. R. (2001). Helping standards make the grade. *Educational Leadership, 59*(1), 20–27.

Guskey, T. R. (2002). Critical friends. *Educational Leadership, 59*(6), 45–51.

Guskey, T. R. (2003). How classroom assessments improve learning. *Educational Leadership, 60*(5), 6–11.

Gut, D. M. (2000). We are social beings: Learning how to learn cooperatively. *Teaching Exceptional Children, 32*(5), 46–53.

Gut, D. M., & Safran, S. P. (2002). Cooperative learning and social stories: Effective social skills strategies for reading teachers. *Reading and Writing Quarterly: Overcoming Learning Difficulties, 18*(1), 87–91.

Guterman, B. R. (1995). The validity of learning disabilities services: The consumer's view. *The Reading Teacher, 62*(2), 111–124.

Guthrie, J. T., & Davis, M. H. (2003). Motivating struggling readers in middle school through an engagement model of classroom practice. *Reading and Writing Quarterly: Overcoming Learning Difficulties, 19,* 59–85.

Habel, J. C., & Bernard, J. A. (1999). School and educational psychologists: Creating new service models. *Intervention in School and Clinic, 34*(3), 156–162.

Hadden, S., & Fowler, S. A. (1997). Preschool: A new beginning for children and parents. *Teaching Exceptional Children, 30*(1), 36–39.

Hagan-Burke, S., & Jefferson, G. L. (2002). Using data to promote academic benefit for included students with mild disabilities. *Preventing School Failure, 46,* 113–117.

Hagiwara, T. (1998). Introduce multiculturalism in your classroom. *Intervention in School and Clinic, 34*(1), 43–44.

Hale-Benson, J. E. (1986). *Black children: Their roots, culture, and learning style* (2nd ed.). Baltimore: Johns Hopkins University Press.

Hall, E. W., & Salmon, S. J. (2003). Chocolate chip cookies and rubrics: Helping students understand rubrics in inclusive settings. *Teaching Exceptional Children, 35*(4), 8–11.

Hall, L. J., & McGregor, J. A. (2000). A follow-up study of the peer relationships of children with disabilities in an inclusive school. *The Journal of Special Education, 34,* 114–126, 153.

Hall, L. J., & Strickett, T. (2002). Peer relationships of preadolescent students with disabilities who attend a separate school. *Education and Training in Mental Retardation and Developmental Disabilities, 37,* 399–409.

Hall, M., Kleinert, H. L., & Kearns, J. F. (2000). Going to college! Postsecondary programs for students with moderate and severe disabilities. *Teaching Exceptional Children, 32*(3), 58–65.

Hall, T. E., Wolfe, P. S., & Bollig, A. A. (2003). The home-to-school notebook: An effective communication strategy for students with severe disabilities. *Teaching Exceptional Children, 36*(2), 68–73.

Hallenbeck, M. J. (2002, November). *Cognitive strategy instruction writing: Teaching essay writing to struggling writers.* Presentation at the annual meeting of the New York Federation of Chapters of Council for Exceptional Children, Albany, New York.

Halpern, A. S., Herr, C. M., Wolf, N. K., Lawson, J. D., Doren, B., & Johnson, M. D. (1997). *Next S.T.E.P.: Student transition and educational planning.* Austin, TX: PRO-ED.

Hamill, L., & Everington, C. (2002). *Teaching students with moderate to severe disabilities: An applied approach for inclusive environments.* Upper Saddle River, NJ: Merrill/Prentice Hall.

Hamilton, S. L., Selbert, M. A., Gardner, R., & Talbert-Johnson, C. (2000). Using guided notes to improve the academic achievement of incarcerated adolescents with learning and behavior problems. *Remedial and Special Education, 21,* 133–140, 170.

Hanson, M. J. (1999, September). *Early transitions for children and families: Transitions from infant/toddler services to preschool education.* Reston, VA: ERIC Clearinghouse on Disabilities and Gifted Education.

Hanson, M. J., Horn, E., Sandall, S., Beckman, P., Morgan, M., Marquart, J., Barnwell, D., & Chou, H. (2001). After preschool inclusion: Children's educational pathways over the early school years. *Exceptional Children, 68,* 65–83.

Hapner, A., & Imel, B. (2002). The students' voices: "Teachers started to listen and show respect." *Remedial and Special Education, 23,* 122–126.

Hardman, E., & Smith, S. W. (1999). Promoting positive interactions in the classroom. *Intervention in School and Clinic, 34*(3), 178–180.

Haring, N. G., & Romer, L. T. (1995). *Welcoming students who are deaf-blind into typical classrooms.* Baltimore: Paul H. Brookes.

Harmston, K. A., Strong, C. J., & Evans, D. D. (2001). Writing to South Africa: International pen-pals for students with language-learning disabilities. *Teaching Exceptional Children, 33*(3), 46–51.

Harn, W. E., Bradshaw, M. L., & Ogletree, B. T. (1999). The speech-language pathologist in the schools: Changing roles. *Intervention in School and Clinic, 34*(3), 163–169.

Harris, C. R. (1991). Identifying and serving the gifted new immigrant. *Teaching Exceptional Children, 23,* 26–30.

Harris, K. R., Graham, S., & Mason, L. (2002). POW plus Tree equals powerful opinion essays. *Teaching Exceptional Children, 34*(5), 74–77.

Harry, B. (1995). African American families. In B. A. Ford, F. E. Obiakor, & J. M. Patton (Eds.), *Effective education of African American exceptional learners* (pp. 211–233). Austin, TX: Pro-ED.

Harry, B. (2002). Trends and issues in serving culturally diverse families of children with disabilities. *The Journal of Special Education, 36,* 131–138.

Harry, B., Allen, N., & McLaughlin, M. (1995). Communication versus compliance: African-American parents' involvement in special education. *Exceptional Children, 61*(4), 364–377.

Harry, B., Kalyanpur, M., & Day, M. (1999). *Building cultural reciprocity with families.* Baltimore, MD: Paul H. Brookes.

Hartwell, R. (2001). Understanding disabilities. *Educational Leadership, 58*(7), 72–75.

Hartwig, E. P., & Ruesch, G. M. (2000). Disciplining students in special education. *The Journal of Special Education, 33,* 240–247.

Harvard Civil Rights Project (2001). *Schools more separate: Consequences of a decade of resegregation.* Cambridge, MA: Author.

Haver, J. J. (2002). *Structured English immerson: A step-by-step guide for K–6 teachers and administrators.* Thousand Oaks, CA: Corwin Press.

Haynes, C. C., Chaltain, S., Ferguson, J. E., Hudson, D. L., & Thomas, O. (2003). *The First Amendment in schools.* Alexandria: VA: ASCD.

Haynes, C. C., & Thomas, O. (2001). *Finding common ground: A guide to religious liberty in public schools.* Nashville, TN: First Amendment Center.

Heal, L. W., Khoju, M., & Rusch, F. R. (1997). Predicting quality of life of youth after they leave special education high school programs. *Journal of Special Education, 31*(3), 279–299.

Healey, B. (1996). Helping parents deal with the fact that their child has a disability. *CEC Today, 3*(5), 12–13.

Heaton, S., & O'Shea, D. J. (1995). Using mnemonics to make mnemonics. *Teaching Exceptional Children, 28*(1), 34–36.

Heckaman, K., Conroy, M., Fox, J., & Chait, A. (2000). Functional assessment-based intervention research on students with or at risk for emotional and behavioral disorders in school settings. *Behavioral Disorders, 25,* 196–210.

Heinrichs, R. R. (2003). A whole-school approach to bullying: Special considerations for children with exceptionalities. *Intervention in School and Clinic, 38,* 195–204.

Heller, K. W., Fredrick, L. D., Best, S., Dykes, M. K., & Cohen, E. T. (2000). Specialized health care procedures in the schools: Training and service delivery. *Exceptional Children, 66*(2), 173–186.

Heller, K. W., Fredrick, L. D., Dykes, M. K., Best, S., & Cohen, E. T. (1999). A national perspective of competencies for teachers of individuals with physical and health disabilities. *Exceptional Children, 65*(2), 219–234.

Helms, R. G. (2000). An exceptional NBPTS certificate for special educators. *Teaching Exceptional Children, 32*(5), 4–11.

Helmstetter, E., Curry, C. A., Brennan, M., & Sampson-Saul, M. (1998). Comparison of general and special education classrooms of students with severe disabilities. *Education and Training in Mental Retardation and Developmental Disabilities, 33*(3), 216–227.

Helmstetter, E., Peck, C. A., & Giangreco, M. F. (1994). Outcomes of interactions with peers with moderate or severe disabilities: A statewide survey of high school students. *Journal of the Association of Persons with Severe Handicaps, 19*(4), 263–276.

Helwig, R., Anderson, L., & Tindal, G. (2002). Using a concept-grounded, curriculum-based measure in mathematics to predict statewide test scores for middle school students with LD. *The Journal of Special Education, 36*, 102–112.

Helwig, R., & Tindal, G. (2003). An experimental analysis of accommodation decisions on large-scale mathematics tests. *Exceptional Children, 69*, 211–226.

Henderson, K. (2001, March). Overview of ADA, IDEA, and Section 504: Update 2001. *ERIC Digest.*

Hendrickson, J. M., Shokoohi-Yekta, M., Hamre-Nietupski, S., & Gable, R. A. (1996). Middle and high school students' perceptions on being friends with peers with severe disabilities. *Exceptional Children, 63*(1), 19–28.

Henker, B., & Whalen, C. K. (1999). The child with attention-deficit/hyperactivity disorder in school and peer settings. In H.C. Quay and A. E. Hogan (Eds.), *Handbook of disruptive behavior disorders* (pp. 157–178). New York: Kluwer/Plenum.

Herner, L. M., & Higgins, K. (2000). Forming and benefitting from educator study groups. *Teaching Exceptional Children, 32*(5), 30–37.

Heron, T. E., Welsch, R. G., & Goddard, Y. L. (2003). Applications of tutoring systems in specialized subject areas. An analysis of skills, methodologies, and results. *Remedial and Special Education, 24*, 288–300.

Herron, B., & Barnes, K. (2001). *Teaching social skills in inclusive classrooms. CEC Today, 7*(7), 12–13.

Herschell, A. D., Greco, L. A., Filcheck, H. A., & McNeil, C. B. (2002). Who is testing whom? Ten suggestions for managing the disruptive behavior of young children during testing. *Intervention in School and Clinic, 37*, 140–148.

Hertzog, N. B. (1998a). Gifted education specialist. *Teaching Exceptional Children, 30*(3), 39–43.

Hertzog, N. B. (1998b). Using open-ended learning activities to empower teachers and students. *Teaching Exceptional Children, 30*(6), 26–31.

Hester, P. (2002). What teachers can do to prevent behavior problems in schools. *Preventing School Failure, 47*, 33–38.

Hetherington, E. M., & Kelly, J. (2000). *For better or for worse: Divorce reconsidered.* New York: Norton.

Heubert, J. P. (2003). First, do no harm. *Educational Leadership, 60*(4), 26–31.

Heumann, J. E., & Hehir, T. (1995). *Policy guidance on educating blind and visually impaired students.* Washington, DC: U.S. Department of Education.

Heuttig, C., & O'Connor, J. (1999). Wellness programming for preschoolers with disabilities. *Teaching Exceptional Children, 31*(3), 12–17.

Heward, W. L., (2003). *Exceptional children: An introduction to special education* (7th ed.). Upper Saddle River, NJ: Merrill/Prentice-Hall.

Heward, W. L., Gardner, R., Cavanaugh, R. A., Courson, F. H., Grossi, T. A., & Barbetta, P. M. (1996). Everyone participates in this class: Using response cards to increase active student response. *Teaching Exceptional Children, 28*(2), 4–10.

Higgins, K., & Boone, R. (2003). Beyond the boundaries of school: Transition considerations in gifted education. *Intervention in School and Clinic, 38*, 138–144.

Higgins, K., Boone, R., & Lovitt, T. C. (1996). Hypertext support for remedial students and students with learning disabilities. *Journal of Learning Disabilities, 29*(4), 402–412.

Higgins, K., Boone, R., & Williams, D. L. (2000). Evaluating educational software for special education. *Intervention in School and Clinic, 36*, 109–115.

Hill, J. L. (1999). *Meeting the needs of students with special physical and health care needs.* Upper Saddle River, NJ: Merrill/Prentice Hall.

Hilliard, A. (2000). Excellence in education versus high stakes standardized testing. *Journal of Teacher Education, 51*, 293–304.

Hindin, A., Morocco, C. C., & Aguilar, C. M. (2001). "This book lives in our school" Teaching middle school students to understand literature. *Remedial and Special Education, 22*, 204–213.

Hines, R. A. (2001, December). *Inclusion in middle schools.* Champaign, IL: ERIC Clearinghouse on Elementary and Early Childhood Education.

Hirsch, I. B. (2000). *12 things you must know about diabetes care right now!* Atlanta, GA: American Diabetes Association.

Hitchcock, C., Dowrick, P. W., & Prater, M. A. (2003). Video self-modeling intervention in school-based settings: A review. *Remedial and Special Education, 24*, 36–45, 56.

Hitchcock, C., Meyer, A., Rose, D., & Jackson, R. (2002). Providing new access to the general curriculum: Universal design for learning. *Teaching Exceptional Children, 35*(2), 8–17.

Hitchings, W. E., Luzzo, D. A., Ristow, R., Horvath, M., Retish, P., & Tanners, A. (2001). The career development needs of college students with learning disabilities: In their own words. *Learning Disabilities Research and Practice, 16*, 8–17.

Hobbs, T., Bruch, L., Sanko, J., & Astolfi, C. (2001). Friendship on the inclusive electronic playground. *Teaching Exceptional Children, 33*(6), 46–51.

Hobson v. Hansen, 269 F. Supp. 401 (1967) (D.C.C., 1967).

Hodgin, K. B., Levin, B., & Matthews, C. (1997). *Gender equity in the elementary school.* CD-ROM. Greensboro: University of North Carolina at Greensboro.

Hodgkinson, H. (2001). Educational demographics: What teachers should know. *Educational Leadership, 58*(4), 6–11.

Hoener, A., Salend, S. J., & Kay, S. (1997). Creating readable handouts, worksheets, overheads, tests, review materials, study guides and homework assignments through effective typographic design. *Teaching Exceptional Children, 29*(3), 32–35.

Hoffman, J. V., Roser, N. L., & Battle, J. (1993). Reading aloud in classrooms: From the modal toward the "model." *The Reading Teacher, 46*(6), 496–503.

Hollenbeck, K., Rozek-Tedesco, M. A., Tindal, G., & Glasgow, A. (2000). An exploratory study of student-paced versus teacher-paced accommodations for large-scale math tests. *Journal of Special Education Technology, 15*(2), 27–38.

Hollingsworth, H. L. (2001). We need to talk: Communication strategies for effective collaboration. *Teaching Exceptional Children, 33*(5), 6–9.

Holloway, J. H. (2003). Addressing the needs of homeless students. *Educational Leadership, 60*(4), 89–90.

Holloway, L. (2000, May 25). Turnover of teachers and pupils deepens troubles of poor schools. *The New York Times*, A1, B15.

Hollowood, T. M., Salisbury, C. L., Rainforth, B., & Palombaro, M. M. (1994). Use of instructional time in classrooms serving students with and without severe disabilities. *Exceptional Children, 61*(3), 242–253.

Holmes, S. A. (1994, July 20). Birthrate for unwed women up 70% since '83, study says. *The New York Times*, A1, A8.

Holmes, S. A. (1998, August 7). Black populace nearly equaled by Hispanic. *The New York Times*, A15.

Hopkins, M. H. (1993). Ideas. *Arithmetic Teacher, 40,* 512–519.

Horne, J. (1998). Rising to the challenge. *Teaching Tolerance, 7*(1), 26–31.

Horney, M. A., & Anderson-Inman, L. (1999). Supported text in electronic reading environments. *Reading and Writing Quarterly: Overcoming Learning Difficulties, 15*(2), 127–168.

Hourcade, J., Parette, P., & Anderson, H. (2003). Accountability in collaboration: A framework for evaluation. *Education and Training in Developmental Disabilities, 38,* 398–404.

House of Representatives Report 103–208. (1993). Washington, DC: Author.

Howard, E. R. (2002). Two-way immersion: A key to global awareness. *Educational Leadership, 60*(2), 62–65.

Howe, K. R., & Welner, K. G. (2002). School choice and the pressure to perform: Déjà vu for children with disabilities? *Remedial and Special Education, 23,* 212–221.

Howell, K. W., Evans, D., & Gardiner, J. (1997). Medications in the classroom: A hard pill to swallow? *Teaching Exceptional Children, 29*(6), 58–61.

Hoy, A. W. (1995). *Educational psychology* (6th ed.). Boston: Allyn & Bacon.

Hoyt, K. B. (2001). Career education and education reform: Time for rebirth. *Phi Delta Kappan, 83,* 327–331.

Hudson, P. (1996). Using a learning set to increase the test performance of students with learning disabilities in social studies classes. *Learning Disabilities Research and Practice, 11*(2), 78–85.

Hudson, R. F., & Smith, S. W. (2001). Effective reading instruction for struggling Spanish-speaking readers: A combination of two literatures. *Intervention in School and Clinic, 37,* 36–39.

Huefner, D. S. (2000). The risks and opportunities of the IEP requirements under IDEA 97. *The Journal of Special Education, 33*(4), 195–204.

Hughes, C., Carter, E. W., Hughes, T., Bradford, E., & Copeland, S. R. (2002). Effects of instructional versus non-instructional roles on the social interactions of high school students. *Education and Training in Mental Retardation and Developmental Disabilities, 37,* 146–162.

Hughes, C., Copeland, S. R., Agran, M., Wehmeyer, M., Rodi, M. S., & Presley, J. A. (2002). Using self-monitoring to improve performance in general education high school classes. *Education and Training in Mental Retardation and Developmental Disabilities, 37,* 262–272.

Hughes, C., Copeland, S. R., Guth, C., Rung, L. L., Hwang, B., Kleeb, G., & Strong, M. (2001). General education students' perspectives on their involvement in a high school peer buddy program. *Education and Training in Mental Retardation and Developmental Disabilities, 36,* 343–356.

Hughes, C., Guth, C., Hall, S., Presley, J., Dye, M., & Byers, C. (1999). "They are my best friends": Peer buddies promote inclusion in high school. *Teaching Exceptional Children, 31*(5), 32–37.

Hughes, C., Pitkin, S. E., & Lorden, S. W. (1998). Assessing preferences and choices of persons with severe and profound mental retardation. *Education and Training in Mental Retardation and Developmental Disabilities, 33*(4), 299–316.

Hughes, C., Rung, L. L., Wehmeyer, M. L., Agran, M., Copeland, S. R., & Hwang, B. (2000). Self-prompted communication book use to increase social interactions among high school students. *The Journal of the Association for Persons with Severe Handicaps, 25,* 153–166.

Hughes, C. A. (1996). Memory and test-taking strategies. In D. D. Deshler, E. S. Ellis, & B. K. Lenz (Eds.), *Teaching adolescents with learning disabilities: Strategies and methods* (2nd ed., pp. 209–266). Denver: Love.

Hughes, C. A., Deshler, D. D., Ruhl, K. L., & Schumaker, J. B. (1993). Test-taking strategy instruction for adolescents with emotional and behavioral disorders. *Journal of Emotional and Behavioral Disorders, 1*(3), 189–198.

Hughes, C. A., Ruhl, K. L., Schumaker, J. B., & Deshler, D. D. (2002). Effects of instruction in an assignment completion strategy on the homework performance of students with learning disabilities in general education classes. *Learning Disabilities Research and Practice, 17,* 1–18.

Humphries, T. (1993). Deaf culture and cultures. In K. M. Chritensen & G. L. Delgado (Eds.), *Multicultural issues in deafness* (pp. 3–13). White Plains, NY: Longman.

Hundt, T. A. (2002). Videotaping young children in the classroom. Parents as partners. *Teaching Exceptional Children, 34*(3), 38–43.

Hunt, P., Alwell, M., Farron-Davis, F., & Goetz, L. (1996). Creating socially supportive environments for fully included students who experience multiple disabilities. *Journal of the Association for Persons with Severe Handicaps, 21,* 53–71.

Hunt, P., Farron-Davis, F., Beckstead, S., Curtis, D., & Goetz, L. (1994). Evaluating the effects of placement of students with severe disabilities in general education versus special class. *Journal of the Association for Persons with Severe Handicaps, 19*(3), 200–214.

Hunt, P., Hirose-Hatae, A., Doering, K., Karasoff, P., & Goetz, L. (2000). "Community" is what I think everyone is talking about. *Remedial and Special Education, 21,* 305–317.

Hunt, P., Soto, G., Maier, J., & Doering, K. (2003). Collaborative teaming to support students at risk and students with severe disabilities in general education classrooms. *Exceptional Children, 69,* 315–332.

Hutchins, M. P., & Renzaglia, A. (1998). Interviewing families for effective transition to employment. *Teaching Exceptional Children, 30*(4), 72–78.

Hutchinson, S. W., Murdock, J. Y., Williamson, R. D., & Cronin, M. E. (2000). Self-recording plus encouragement equals improved behavior. *Teaching Exceptional Children, 32*(5), 54–58.

Hutinger, P. L., & S. Clark, L. (2000). TEChPLACEs: An internet community for young children, their teachers, and their families. *Teaching Exceptional Children, 32*(4), 56–63.

Hyun, J. K., & Fowler, S. A. (1995). Respect, cultural sensitivity, and communication. *Teaching Exceptional Children, 28*(1), 25–28.

Idol, L. (1987). Group story mapping: A comprehension strategy for both skilled and unskilled readers. *Journal of Learning Disabilities, 20,* 196–205.

Idol, L. (1997). Key questions related to building collaborative and inclusive schools. *Journal of Learning Disabilities, 30*(4), 384–394.

Idol, L., Nevin, A., & Paolucci-Whitcomb, P. (1999). *Models for curriculum-based assessment: A blueprint for learning.* Austin, TX: PRO-ED.

Igoa, C. (1995). *The inner world of the immigrant child.* New York: St. Martin's Press.

Imada, D., Doyle, B. A., Brock, B., & Goddard, A. (2002). Developing leadership skills in students with mild disabilities. *Teaching Exceptional Children, 35*(1), 48–55.

Institute on Community Integration. (n.d.). *Integration checklist: A guide to full inclusion of students with disabilities.* Minneapolis: Author.

Irvine, J. J. (1991, May). *Multicultural education: The promises and obstacles.* Paper presented at the Sixth Annual Benjamin Matteson Invitational Conference of the State University of New York at New Paltz, New Paltz, NY.

Irvine, J. J., & Armento, B. J. (2001). *Culturally responsive teaching: Lesson planning for elementary and middle school grades.* Boston: McGraw-Hill.

Irving Independent School District v. Tatro, 104 S. Ct. 3371, 82 L.Ed. 2d 664 (1984).

Isaacson, S., & Gleason, M. M. (1997). Mechanical obstacles to writing: What can teachers do to help students with learning problems? *Learning Disabilities Research and Practice, 12*(3), 188–194.

Isaacson, S., & Gleason, M. M. (1998, April). *Practical writing instruction for students with learning problems.* Presentation at the annual meeting of the Council for Exceptional Children, Minneapolis.

Ivey, G. (2002). Getting started: Manageable literacy practices. *Educational Leadership, 60*(3), 20–23.

Jackson, C. W., & Larkin, M. J. (2002). RUBRIC: Teaching students to use grading rubrics. *Teaching Exceptional Children, 35*(1), 40–47.

Jackson, F. B. (2002). Crossing content: A strategy for students with learning disabilities. *Intervention in School and Clinic, 37,* 279–282.

Jackson, L., Ryndak, D. L., & Billingsley, F. (2000). Useful practices in inclusive education: A preliminary view of what experts in moderate and severe disabilities are saying. *The Journal of the Association for Persons with Severe Handicaps, 25,* 129–141.

Jacobs, A. (2001, June 10). At the gym, grunts, groans and a discrimination suit. *The New York Times,* 48.

Jairrels, V. (1999). Cultural diversity: Implications for collaboration. *Intervention in School and Clinic, 34*(4), 236–238.

Jairrels, V., Brazil, N., & Patton, J. R. (1999). Incorporating popular literature into the curriculum for diverse learners. *Intervention in School and Clinic, 34*(5), 303–306.

James, L. A., Abbott, M., & Greenwood, C. R. (2001). How Adam became a writer. *Teaching Exceptional Children, 33*(3), 30–37.

Janiga, S. J., & Costenbader, V. (2002). A transition from high school to postsecondary education for students with learning disabilities: A survey of college service coordinators. *Journal of Learning Disabilities, 35,* 462–468.

Janney, R. E., Snell, M. E., Beers, M. K., & Raynes, M. (1995). Integrating students with moderate and severe disabilities in general education classes. *Exceptional Children, 61,* 425–439.

Janofsky, M. (2001, September 19). Debate weighs merits of schools for homeless. *The New York Times,* A12.

Janover, C. (1997). *Zipper: The kid with ADHD.* Bethesda, MD: Woodbine House.

Jenkins, J. R., Antil, L. R., Wayne, S. K., & Vadasy, P. F. (2003). How cooperative learning works for special education and remedial students. *Exceptional Children, 69,* 279–292.

Jenson, E. (2001). Fragile brains. *Educational Leadership, 59*(3), 32–37.

Jimenez, J. E., del Rosario Ortiz, M., Rodrigo, M., Hernandez-Valle, I., Ramirez, G., Estevez, A., O'Shanahan, I., & de la Luz Trabue, M. (2003). Do the effects of computer-assisted practice differ for children with reading disabilities with and without IQ-achievement discrepancy? *Journal of Learning Disabilities, 36,* 34–47.

Jitendra, A. K. (2002). Teaching students math problem-solving through graphic representations. *Teaching Exceptional Children, 34*(4), 34–39.

Jitendra, A. K., DiPipi, C. M., & Perron-Jones, N. (2002). An exploratory study of schema-based word-problem-solving instruction for middle school students with learning disabilities: An emphasis on conceptual and procedural understanding. *The Journal of Special Education, 36,* 23–38.

Jitendra, A. K., Edwards, L. L., Choutka, C. M., & Treadway, P. S. (2002). A collaborative approach to planning in the content areas for students with learning disabilities: Accessing the general curriculum. *Learning Disabilities Research and Practice, 17,* 252–267.

Jitendra, A. K., Hoppes, M. K., & Xin, Y. P. (2000). Enhancing the main idea comprehension for students with learning problems: The role of a summarization strategy and self-monitoring instruction. *The Journal of Special Education, 34,* 127–139.

Jobe, D. A. (2003). Helping girls succeed. *Educational Leadership, 60*(4), 64–66.

Jochum, J., Curran, C., & Reetz, L. (1998). Creating individual educational portfolios in written language. *Reading and Writing Quarterly, 14*(3), 283–306.

Johanneson, A. S. (1999, Spring). Follow the stream. *Teaching Tolerance, 15,* 32–39.

Johns, B. H., & Carr, V. G. (1995). *Techniques for managing verbally and physically aggressive students.* Denver: Love.

Johnson, D. E., Bullock, C. C., & Ashton-Shaeffer, C. (1999). Families and leisure: A context for learning. *Teaching Exceptional Children, 30*(2), 30–34.

Johnson, D. R., Stodden, R. A., Emanuel, E. J., Luecking, R., & Mack, M. (2002). Current challenges facing secondary education and transition services: What research tells us. *Exceptional Children, 68,* 519–531.

Johnson, D. T. (2000, April). *Teaching mathematics to gifted students in mixed-ability classrooms.* Reston, VA: ERIC Clearinghouse on Disabilities and Gifted Education.

Johnson, D. W., Johnson, R. T. (1996). Peacemakers: Teaching students to resolve their own and schoolmates' conflicts. In E. L. Meyen, G. A. Vergason, & R. J. Whelan (Eds.), *Strategies for teaching exceptional children in inclusive settings* (pp. 311–329). Denver: Love.

Johnson, D. W., Johnson, R. T., & Holubec, E. (2002). *Circles of learning* (5th ed.). Edina, MN: Interaction Book Company.

Johnson, G., Johnson, R. L., & Jefferson-Aker, C. R. (2001). HIV/AIDS prevention: Effective instructional strategies for adolescents with mild mental retardation. *Teaching Exceptional Children, 33*(6), 28–33.

Johnson, L. J., Zorn, D., Kai Yung Tam, B., Lamontagne, M., & Johnson, S. A. (2003). Stakeholders' views of factors that impact successful interagency collaboration. *Exceptional Children, 69,* 195–209.

Johnson, L. R., & Johnson, C. E. (1999). Teaching students to regulate their own behavior. *Teaching Exceptional Children, 31*(4), 6–10.

Johnston, C. A. (1998). Using the learning combination inventory. *Educational Leadership, 55*(4), 78–82.

Johnston, P., Allington, R., & Afflerbach, P. (1985). The congruence of classroom and remedial reading instruction. *Elementary School Journal, 83,* 465–477.

Jolivette, K., Stichter, J. P., & McCormick, K. M. (2002). Making choices—Improving behavior—Engaging in learning. *Teaching Exceptional Children, 34*(3), 24–29.

Jones, C. J. (2001a). Teacher-friendly curriculum-based assessment in spelling. *Teaching Exceptional Children, 34*(2), 32–39.

Jones, C. J. (2001b). CBAs that work: Assessing students' math content-reading levels. *Teaching Exceptional Children, 34*(1), 24–29.

Jones, E. D., Southern, W. T., & Brigham, F. J. (1998). Curriculum-based assessment: Testing what is taught and teaching what is tested. *Intervention in School and Clinic, 33*(4), 239–249.

Jones, G. A., Thornton, C. A., & Toohey, M. A. (1985). A multioption program for learning basic addition facts: Case studies and an experimental report. *Journal of Learning Disabilities, 18,* 319–325.

Jones, V. (2002). Creating communities of support: The missing link in dealing with student behavior problems and reducing violence in schools. *Beyond Behavior, 11*(2), 16–23.

Jones, V., & Jones, L. (2001). *Comprehensive classroom management* (6th ed.). Boston: Allyn & Bacon.

Jordan, N. C., & Hanich, L. B. (2000). Mathematical thinking in second-grade children with different forms of LD. *Journal of Learning Disabilities, 33,* 567–579.

Joseph, L. M. (2000). Student as a strategic participant in collaborative problem-solving teams: An alternative model for middle and secondary schools. *Intervention in School and Clinic, 36,* 47–53.

Joseph, L. M. (2002). Helping children link sound to print: Phonics procedures for small-group or whole-class settings. *Intervention in School and Clinic, 37,* 217–221.

Kaderavek, J. N., & Justice, L. (2000). Children with LD as emergent readers: Bridging the gap to conventional reading. *Intervention in School and Clinic, 36,* 82–93.

Kaderavek, J. N., & Pakulski, L. A. (2002). Minimal hearing loss is not minimal. *Teaching Exceptional Children, 34*(6), 14–19.

Kagan, S. (1992). *Cooperative learning.* San Juan Capistrano, CA: Resources for Teachers.

Kameenui, E., & Carnine, D. (1998). *Effective teaching strategies that accommodate diverse learners.* Upper Saddle River, NJ: Merrill/Prentice Hall.

Kamps, D., Royer, J., Dugan, E., Kravits, T., Gozalez-Lopez, A., Garcia, L., Carnazzo, K., Kampwirth, T. J. (1999). *Collaborative consultation in the schools: Effective practices for students with learning and behavior problems.* Upper Saddle River, NJ: Prentice Hall.

Kapperman, G., & Stickerman, J. (2002). A software tutorial for learning the Nemeth Code of Braille mathematics. *Journal of Visual Impairment and Blindness, 96,* 855–857.

Karasik, J., & Karasik, P. (2003). *The ride together: A brother and sister's memoir of autism in the family.* New York: Washington Square Press.

Karnes, M., Collins, D., Maheady, L., Harper, G. F., & Mallette, B. (1997). Using cooperative learning strategies to improve literacy skills in social studies. *Reading and Writing Quarterly: Overcoming Learning Difficulties, 13*(1), 37–51.

Karp, K. S., & Voltz, D. L. (2000). Weaving mathematical instructional strategies into inclusive settings. *Intervention in School and Clinic, 35,* 206–215.

Katamaya, A. D., & Robinson, D. H. (2000). Getting students "partially" involved in note-taking using graphic organizers. *The Journal of Experimental Education, 68,* 119.

Katims, D. S., & Harmon, J. M. (2000). Strategic instruction in middle school social studies: Enhancing academic and literacy outcomes for at-risk students. *Intevention in School and Clinic, 35,* 280–289.

Katsiyannis, A., Ellenburg, J. S., Acton, O. M., & Torrey, G. (2001). Addressing the needs of students with Rett syndrome. *Teaching Exceptional Children, 33*(5), 74–78.

Katsiyannis, A., Landrum, T. J., & Reid, R. (2002). Rights and responsibilities under Section 504. *Beyond Behavior, 11*(2), 9–15.

Katsiyannis, A., Landrum, T. J., & Vinton, L. (1997). Practical guidelines for monitoring treatment of attention-deficit/hyperactivity disorder. *Preventing School Failure, 41*(3), 131–136.

Katsiyannis, A., & Maag, J. W. (2001). Manifestation determination as a golden fleece. *Exceptional Children, 68,* 85–96.

Katsiyannis, A., & Yell, M. L. (2000). The supreme court and school health services: (*Cedar Rapids* v. *Garret F.*) *Exceptional Children, 66,* 317–326.

Katsiyannis, A., Yell, M. L., & Bradley, R. (2001). Reflections on the 25th anniversary of the Individuals with Disabilities Education Act. *Remedial and Special Education, 22,* 324–334.

Katsiyannis, A., Zhang, D., & Archwamety, T. (2002). Placement and exit patterns for students with mental retardation: An analysis of national trends. *Education and Training in Mental Retardation and Developmental Disabilities, 37,* 134–145.

Kauffman, J. M. (2001). *Characteristics of emotional and behavioral disorders of children and youth* (7th ed.). Upper Saddle River, NJ: Merrill/Prentice Hall.

Kaufmann, L., Handl, P., & Thony, B. (2003). Evaluation of a numeracy intervention program focusing on basic numerical knowledge and conceptual knowledge: A pilot study. *Journal of Learning Disabilities, 36,* 564–573.

Kavale, K. A., & Forness, S. A. (2000). History, rhetoric, and reality: Analysis of the inclusion debate. *Remedial and Special Education, 21,* 279–296.

Kavale, K. A., Hirshoren, A., & Forness, S. R. (1998). Meta-analytic validation of the Dunn and Dunn model of learning style preferences: A critique of what was Dunn. *Learning Disabilities Research and Practice, 13*(2), 75–80.

Kea, C. D., & Utley, C. A. (1998). To teach me is to know me. *The Journal of Special Education, 32,* 44–47.

Kearns, J. F., Kleinert, H. L., Clayton, J., Brudge, M., & Williams, R. (1998). Principal supports for inclusive assessment: A Kentucky story. *Teaching Exceptional Children, 31*(2), 16–23.

Kearns, J. F., Kleinert, H. L., & Kennedy, S. (1999). We need not exclude anyone. *Educational Leadership, 56*(6), 33–38.

Keefe, C. H., & Spence, C. D. (2003, August). Successful transition into kindergarten. *CEC Today, 10*(2), 12.

Kelker, K., Hecimovic, A., & LeRoy, C. H. (1994). Designing a classroom and school environment for students with AIDS. *Teaching Exceptional Children, 26*(4), 52–55.

Keller, C. L. (2002). A new twist on spelling instruction for elementary school teachers. *Intervention in School and Clinic, 38,* 3–7.

Keller, M. (2001). Handwriting club: Using sensory integration strategies to improve handwriting. *Intervention in School and Clinic, 37,* 9–12.

Kellner, M. H., Bry, B. H., & Colleti, L. (2002). Teaching anger management skills to students with severe emotional or behavioral disorders. *Behavioral Disorders, 27,* 400–407.

Kellough, R. D., & Kellough, N. G. (2003). *Secondary school teaching: A guide to methods and resources* (2nd ed.). Upper Saddle River, NJ: Merrill/Prentice Hall.

Kelly, K. M., Siegel, E. B., & Allinder, R. M. (2001). Personal profile assessment summary: Creating windows into the worlds of children with special needs. *Intervention in School and Clinic, 36,* 202–210.

Kelly, R. (2000). Working with WebQuests: Making the web accessible to students with disabilities. *Teaching Exceptional Children, 32*(6), 4–13.

Kennedy, C. H., Shukla, S., & Fryxell, D. (1997). Comparing the effects of educational placement on the social relationships of intermediate school students with severe disabilities. *Exceptional Children, 64,* 31–47.

Kennedy, K. Y., Higgins, K., & Pierce, T. (2002). Collaborative partnerships among teachers of students who are gifted and have learning disabilities. *Intervention in School and Clinic, 38,* 36–49.

Kern, L., Bambara, L., & Fogt, J. (2002). Class-wide curricular modifications to improve the behavior of students with emotional and behavioral disorders. *Behavioral Disorders, 27,* 317–326.

Kern, L., Dunlap, G., Clarke, S., & Childs, K. E. (1994). Student-assisted functional assessment interview. *Diagnostique, 19*(2–3), 29–39.

Kershaw, S. (2003, January 18). Freud meets Buddha: Therapy for immigrants. *The New York Times,* B1–B2.

Kerwin, C., & Ponterotto, J. G. (1994). Counseling multiracial individuals and their families—don't believe all myths. *Guidepost, 36*(11), 9–11.

Keyes, M. W., & Owens-Johnson, L. (2003). Developing person-centered IEPs. *Intervention in School and Clinic, 38,* 145–152.

Keyser-Marcus, L., Briel, L., Sherron-Targett, P., Yasuda, S., Johnson, S., & Wehman, P. (2002). Enhancing the schooling of students with traumatic brain injury. *Teaching Exceptional Children, 34(4),* 62–67.

Kimball, J. W., Kinney, E. M., Taylor, B. A., & Stromer, R. (2003). Lights, camera, action! *Teaching Exceptional Children, 36*(1), 40–45.

Kindler, A. L. (1995). *Education of migrant children in the United States.* Washington, DC: National Clearinghouse for Bilingual Education at George Washington University.

King-Friedrichs, J. (2001). Brain-friendly techniques for improving memory. *Educational Leadership, 59*(3), 76–79.

King-Sears, M. E. (1999). Teacher and researcher co-design self-management content for an inclusive setting: Research training, intervention, and generalization effects on student performance. *Education and Training in Mental Retardation and Developmental Disabilities 34*(2), 134–156.

King-Sears, M. E. (2001). Three steps for gaining access to the general education curriculum for learners with disabilities. *Intervention in School and Clinic, 37,* 67–76.

King-Sears, M. E., & Bonfils, K. A. (2000). Self-management instruction for middle school students with LD and ED. *Intervention in School and Clinic, 35*(2), 96–107.

King-Sears, M. E., & Carpenter, S. L. (1997). Teaching self-management for elementary students with developmental disabilities. *Innovations.* Washington, DC: American Association on Mental Retardation.

Kinnell, G. (2003, November). *Sticks and stones: What to do about bullying and teasing.* Presentation at annual meeting of the New York State Migrant Education Programs, Syracuse, NY.

Kirby, K. M. (1997). A school counselor's guide to working with children adopted after infancy: Jason's story. *Elementary School Guidance and Counseling, 31*(3), 226–238.

Kleinert, H., Green, P., Hurte, M., Clayton, J., & Oetinger, C. (2002). Creating and using meaningful alternate assessments. *Teaching Exceptional Children, 34*(4), 40–49.

Kleinheksel, K. A., & Summy, S. E. (2003). Enhancing student learning and social behavior through mnemonic strategies. *Teaching Exceptional Children, 36*(2), 30–35.

Klemm, W. R. (1998). Eight ways to get students more engaged in online conferences. *Technological Horizons in Education Journal, 26*(1), 62–64.

Kling, B. (2000). ASSERT yourself: Helping students of all ages develop self-advocacy skills. *Teaching Exceptional Children, 32*(3), 66–70.

Klingner, J. K., Vaughn, S., Hughes, M. T., Schumm, J. S., & Elbaum, B. (1998). Outcomes for students with and without learning disabilities in inclusive classrooms. *Learning Disabilities Research and Practice, 13*(3), 153–161.

Klingner, J. K., Vaughn, S., Schumm, J. S., Cohen, P., & Forgan, J. W. (1998). Inclusion or pull-out: Which do students prefer? *Journal of Learning Disabilities, 31*(2), 148–158.

Kluth, P., (2000). Community-referenced learning in the inclusive classroom. *Remedial and Special Education, 21,* 19–26.

Kluth, P. (2004). Autism, autobiography, and adaptations. *Teaching Exceptional Children, 36* (4), 42–47.

Kluth, P., Villa, R. A., & Thousand, J. S. (2002). Our school doesn't offer inclusion and other legal blunders. *Educational Leadership, 59*(4), 24–27.

Kluwin, T. N. (1996). Getting hearing and deaf students to write to each other through dialogue journals. *Teaching Exceptional Children, 28*(2), 50–53.

Knight, M. G., Ross, D. E., Taylor, R. L., & Ramasamy, R. (2003). Constant time delay and interspersal of known items to teach sight words to students with mental retardation and learning disabilties. *Education and Training in Developmental Disabilities, 38,* 179–191.

Knoster, T. P. (2000). Practical application of functional behavioral assessment in schools. *The Journal of the Assocation for Persons with Severe Handicaps, 25,* 201–211.

Knotek, S. (2003). Bias in problem solving and the social process of student study team: A qualitative investigation of two SSTs. *The Journal of Special Education, 37,* 2–14.

Kohler, P. D., & Field, S. (2003). Transition-focused education: Foundation for the future. *The Journal of Special Education, 37,* 174–183.

Kohn, A. (2003). Almost there, but not quite. *Educational Leadership, 60*(6), 27–29.

Kolar, K. A. (1996). Seating and wheeled mobility aids. In J. C. Galvin & M. J. Scherer (Eds.), *Evaluating, selecting, and using appropriate assistive technology* (pp. 61–76). Gaithersburg, MD: Aspen.

Kolb, S. M., & Hanley-Maxwell, C. (2003). Critical social skills for adolescents with high incidence disabilities: Parental perspectives. *Exceptional Children, 69,* 163–180.

Kollins, S. H., Barkley, R. A., & DuPaul, G. J. (2001). Use and management of medications for children diagnosed with attention deficit hyperactivity disorder (ADHD). *Focus on Exceptional Children, 33*(5), 1–23.

Koppang, A. Curriculum mapping: Building collaboration and communication. *Intervention in School and Clinic, 30,* 154–161.

Kortering, L. J., & Braziel, P. M. (1999). Staying in school: The perspective of ninth-grade students. *Remedial and Special Education, 20*(2), 106–113.

Kottler, E., & Kottler, J. A. (2002). *Children with limited English: Teaching strategies for the regular classroom* (2nd ed.). Thousand Oaks, CA: Corwin Press.

Kozminsky, E., & Kozminsky, L. (2002). The dialogue page: Teacher and student dialogues to improve learning motivation. *Intervention in School and Clinic, 38,* 88–95.

Kozminsky, E., & Kozminsky, L. (2003). Improving motivation through dialogue. *Educational Leadership, 61*(1), 50–53.

Kozol, J. (1991). *Savage inequalities: Children in American schools.* New York: Crown.

Krajewski, J. J., & Hyde, M. S. (2000). Comparison of teen attitudes toward individuals with mental retardation between 1987 and 1998: Has inclusion made a difference? *Education and Training in Mental Retardation and Developmental Disabilities, 35,* 284–293.

Kralovec, E., & Buell, J. (2001). Averting the homework crisis. *Educational Leadership, 58*(7), 39–42.

Kroeger, S. D., Leibold, C. K., & Ryan, B. (1999). Creating a sense of ownership in the IEP process. *Teaching Exceptional Children, 32*(1), 4–9.

Kroesbergen, E. H., & Van Luit, J. E. H. (2003). Mathematics interventions for children with special needs: A meta-analysis. *Remedial and Special Education, 24,* 97–114.

Kroesbergen, E. H., Van Luit, J. E. H., & Naglieri, J. A. (2003). Mathematical learning difficulties and PASS cognitive processes. *Journal of Learning Disabilities, 36,* 574–582.

Kubina, R. M., & Cooper, J. O. (2000). Changing learning channels: An efficient strategy to facilitate instruction and learning. *Intervention in School and Clinic, 35*(3), 161–166.

Kucera, T. J. (1993). *Teaching chemistry to students with disabilities.* Washington, DC: American Chemical Society.

Kuhn, B. R., Allen, K. D., & Shriver, M. D. (1995). Behavioral management of children's seizure activity: Intervention guidelines for primary-care providers. *Clinical Pediatrics, 34,* 570–575.

Kuoch, H., & Mirenda, P. (2003). Social story interventions for young children with autism spectrum disorders. *Focus on Autism and Other Developmental Disabilities, 18,* 219–227.

Lackaye, T., & Rublin, H. (2001). Lots of pain, little gain: Five problems with homework in the elementary school. *New York Exceptional Individuals, 26*(4), 8–9.

Ladd, W. (2002). Children, cancer, and learning. *CEC Today, 8*(8), 12.

Lago-Delello, E. (1998). Classroom dynamics and the development of serious emotional disturbance. *Exceptional Children, 64*(4), 479–492.

Lake, J., & Billingsley, B. S. (2000). An analysis of factors that contribute to parent-school conflict in special education. *Remedial and Special Education, 21,* 240–251.

Lamme, L. L., & Lamme, L. A. (2002). Welcoming children from gay families into our schools. *Educational Leadership, 59*(4), 65–69.

Lamorey, S. (2002). The effects of culture on special education services: Evil eyes, prayer meetings, and IEPs. *Teaching Exceptional Children, 34*(5), 67–71.

Landau, E. D., Epstein, S. E., & Stone, A. P. (1978). *The exceptional child through literature.* Upper Saddle River, NJ: Prentice Hall.

Landau, S., Milich, R., & Diener, M. B. (1998). Peer relations of children with attention-deficit hyperactivity disorder. *Reading and Writing Quarterly: Overcoming Learning Difficulties, 14*(1), 83–105.

Landi, M. A. G. (2001). Helping students with learning disabilities make sense of word problems. *Intervention in School and Clinic, 37,* 13–18, 30.

Lane, H. B., & Pullen, P. C. (2004). *Phonological awareness assessment and instruction.* Needham Heights, MA: Allyn & Bacon.

Lane, H. B., Pullen, P. C., Eisele, M. R., & Jordan, L. (2002). Preventing reading failure: Phonological awareness assessment and instruction. *Preventing School Failure, 46,* 101–111.

Lane, K. L., Mahdavi, J. N., & Borthwick-Duffy, S. (2003). Teacher perceptions of the prereferral intervention process: A call for assistance with school-based interventions. *Preventing School Failure, 47,* 148–155.

Langan, J. (1982). *Reading and study skills* (2nd ed.). New York: McGraw-Hill.

Langdon, H. W. (1989). Language disorder or difference? Assessing the language skills of Hispanic students. *Exceptional Children, 56,* 160–167.

Langdon, H. W. (2002). Factors affecting special education services for English language learners with suspected language learning disbilities. *Multiple Voices, 5*(1), 66–82.

Langerock, N. L. (2000). Collaborative strategies: A passion for action research. *Teaching Exceptional Children, 33*(2), 26–34.

Langford, A. D., & Cary, L. G. (2000). Graduation requirements for students with disabilities: Legal and practice considerations. *Remedial and Special Education, 21,* 152–160.

La Paro, K. M., Pianta, R. C., & Cox, M. J. (2000). Teachers' reported transition practices for children transitioning into kindergarten and first grade. *Exceptional Children, 67,* 7–20.

Larry P. v. Riles, 495 F. Supp. 926 (N.D. Cal. 1979).

Larson, P. J., & Maag, J. W. (1998). Applying functional assessment in general education classrooms: Issues and recommendations. *Remedial and Special Education, 19*(6), 338–349.

Lassman, K. A., Jolivette, K., & Wehby, J. H. (1999). Using collaborative behavioral contracting. *Teaching Exceptional Children, 31*(4), 12–18.

Lau v. Nichols, 414 U.S. 563 (1974).

Lawry, J. R., Storey, K., & Danko, C. D. (1993). Analyzing problem behaviors in the classroom: A case study of functional analysis. *Intervention in School and Clinic, 20,* 96–100.

Lazarus, B. D. (1996). Flexible skeletons: Guided notes for adolescents. *Teaching Exceptional Children, 28*(3), 36–40.

Lazarus, B. D. (1998). Say cheese: Using personal photographs as prompts. *Teaching Exceptional Children, 30*(6), 4–7.

Leachman, G., & Victor, D. (2003). Student-led class meetings. *Educational Leadership, 60*(6), 64–68.

Lebzelter, S., & Nowacek, E. J. (1999). Reading strategies for secondary students with mild disabilities. *Intervention in School and Clinic, 34*(4), 212–219.

Lederer, J. M. (2000). Reciprocal teaching of social studies in inclusive elementary classrooms. *Journal of Learning Disabilities, 33,* 91–106.

LeDuff, C. (2001, May 29). A perilous 4,000-mile passage to work. *The New York Times,* A1, A16.

Lee, O., & Fradd, S. H. (1998). Science for all, including students from non-English language backgrounds. *Educational Researcher, 27*(4), 12–21.

Lee, S., Yoo, S., & Bak, S. (2003). Characteristics of friendships between children with and without disabilities. *Education and Training in Developmental Disabilities, 38,* 157–166.

Leffert, J. S., Siperstein, G. N., & Millikan, E. (2000). Understanding social adaptation in children with mental retardation: A social cognitive perspective. *Exceptional Children, 66,* 530–545.

Lehmann, J. P., Davies, T. G., & Laurin, K. M. (2000). Listening to student voices about postsecondary education. *Teaching Exceptional Children, 32*(5), 60–65.

Lenz, B. K., Bulgren, J. A., Kissam, B. R., & Taymans, J. (2004). Smarter planning for academic diversity. In B. K. Lenz, D. D. Deshler, & B. R. Kissam (Eds.). *Teaching content to all: Evidence-based inclusive practices in middle and secondary schools* (pp. 47–77). Boston: Allyn & Bacon.

Lenz, B. K., Deshler, D. D., & Kissam, B. R. (2004). *Teaching content to all: Evidence-based inclusive practices in middle and secondary schools.* Boston: Allyn & Bacon.

Lenz, K., Graner, P., & Adams, G. (2003). Learning express-ways: Building academic relationships to improve learning. *Teaching Exceptional Children, 35*(3), 70–73.

Let's Face It (2000). *Resources for people with facial differences.* Bellingham, WA: Author.

Levendoski, L. S., & Cartledge, G. (2000). Self-monitoring for elementary school children with serious emotional disturbances: Classroom applications for increased academic responding. *Behavioral Disorders, 25,* 211–224.

Lever-Duffy, J., McDonald, J. B., & Mizell, A. P. (2003). *Teaching and learning with technology.* Boston: Allyn & Bacon.

Levine, M. (2003). Celebrating diverse minds. *Educational Leadership, 61*(2), 12–18.

Levine, P., & Nourse, S. W. (1998). What follow-up studies say about postschool life for young men and women with learning disabilities: A critical look at the literature. *Journal of Learning Disabilities, 31*(3), 212–233.

Levy, S. (1999). The end of the never-ending line. *Educational Leadership, 56*(6), 74–77.

Levy, S., Coleman, M., & Alsman, B. (2002). Reading instruction for elementary students with emotional/behavioral disorders: What's a teacher to do? *Beyond Behavior, 11*(3), 3–10.

Lewin, T. (2000, October 24). Now a majority: Families with 2 parents who work. *The New York Times,* A20.

Lewin, T. (2001, July 19). Child well-being improves, U.S. says. *The New York Times,* 14.

Lewis, S. (2004). Blindness and low vision. In R. Turnbull, A. Turnbull, M. Shank, & S. Smith (Eds.) *Exceptional lives: Special education in today's schools* (4th ed.) (pp. 456–486). Upper Saddle River, NJ: Prentice Hall.

Lewis, S., & Tolla, J. (2003). Creating and using tactile experience books for young children with visual impairments. *Teaching Exceptional Children, 35*(3), 22–28.

Lewis, T. J. (2001). Building infrastructure to enhance schoolwide systems of positive behavioral support: Essential features of technical assistance. *Beyond Behavior, 11*(1), 10–12.

Lewis, T. J., Scott, T. M., & Sugai, G. (1994). The Problem Behavior Questionnaire: A teacher-based instrument to develop functional hypotheses of problem behavior in general education classrooms. *Diagnostique, 19*(2–3), 103–115.

Leyva, C. (1998, November). *Increasing intercultural competence in students while celebrating diversity in the biracial child.* Paper presented at the Council for Exceptional Children/Division of Diverse Exceptional Learners Symposium on Culturally and Linguistically Diverse Exceptional Learners, Washington, D.C.

Lieber, J., Hanson, M. C., Beckman, P. J., Odom, S. L., Sandall, S. R., Schwartz, I. S., Horn, E., & Wolery, R. (2000). Key influences on the initiation and implementation of inclusive preschool programs. *Exceptional Children, 67,* 83–98.

Lingnugaris/Kraft, B., Marchand-Martella, N., & Martella, R. C. (2001). Strategies for writing better goals and short-term objectives or benchmarks. *Teaching Exceptional Children, 34*(1), 52–58.

Litchfield, S., & Lartz, M. N. (2002). Role analysis of teachers certified in teaching students who are deaf/hard of hearing who team-teach in co-enrollment classrooms. *Teacher Education and Special Education, 25,* 145–153.

Lloyd, C., Wilton, K., & Townsend, M. (2000). Children at high-risk for mild intellectual disability in regular classrooms: Six New Zealand case studies. *Education and Training in Mental Retardation and Developmental Disabilities, 35,* 44–54.

Lloyd, J. W., Saltzman, N. J., & Kauffman, J. M. (1981). Predictable generalization in academic learning as a result of preskills and strategy training. *Learning Disability Quarterly, 4,* 203–216.

Lloyd, S. R., Wood, T. A., & Moreno, G. (2000). What's a mentor to do? *Teaching Exceptional Children, 33*(1), 38–42.

Lo, Y., Loe, S. A., & Cartledge, G. (2002). The effects of social skills instruction on the social behaviors of students at risk for emotional or behavioral disorders. *Behavioral Disorders, 27,* 371–385.

Lock, R. H., & Carlson, D. M. (2000). Planning for effective, enjoyable computer lab use. *Teaching Exceptional Children, 32*(4), 4–7.

Lock, R. H., & Layton, C. A. (2001). Succeeding in postsecondary ed through self-advocacy. *Teaching Exceptional Children, 34*(2), 66–71.

Logan, K. R., & Malone, D. M. (1998). Comparing instructional contexts of students with and without severe disabilities in general education classrooms. *Exceptional Children, 64*(3), 343–358.

Logan, K. R., & Stein, S. S. (2001). The research lead teacher model: Helping general education teachers deal with classroom behavior problems. *Teaching Exceptional Children, 33*(3), 10–15.

Lohrmann-O'Rourke, S., Browder, D. M., & Brown, F. (2000). Guidelines for conducting socially valid systematic preference assessments. *Journal of the Association for Persons with Severe Handicaps, 25,* 42–53.

Lombardi, T. P. (1995). Teachers develop their own learning strategies. *Teaching Exceptional Children, 27*(3), 52–55.

Longwill, A. W., & Kleinert, H. L. (1998). The unexpected benefits of high school peer tutoring. *Teaching Exceptional Children, 30*(4), 60–65.

Lopez, G. R., Scribner, J. D., & Mahitivanichcha, K. (2001). Redefining parental involvement: Lessons from high-performing migrant-impacted schools. *American Educational Research Journal, 38,* 253–288.

Lopez-Reyna, N. A. (1996). The importance of meaningful contexts in bilingual special education: Moving to whole language. *Learning Disabilities Research and Practice, 11*(2), 120–131.

Lord, C., & McGee, J. P. (2001). *Educating children with autism.* Washington, DC: National Academy Press.

Losen, D. J., & Orfield, G. (2002). *Racial inequity in special education.* Cambridge, MA: Harvard Education Press.

Lotain, R. A. (2003). Group-worthy tasks. *Educational Leadership, 60*(6), 72–75.

Lovett, M. W., Lacerenza, L., & Borden, S. L. (2000). Putting struggling readers on the PHAST track: A program to integrate phonological and strategy-based remedial reading instruction and maximize outcomes. *Journal of Learning Disabilities, 33,* 409–504.

Lovitt, T. C., & Cushing, S. (1999). Parents of youth with disabilities: Their perceptions of school programs. *Remedial and Special Education, 20*(3), 134–142.

Lovitt, T. C., Plavins, M., & Cushing, S. (1999). What do pupils with disabilities have to say about their experience in high school? *Remedial and Special Education, 20*(2), 67–76, 83.

Lowenthal, B. (1995). Naturalistic language intervention in inclusive environments. *Intervention in School and Clinic, 31*(2), 114–118.

Lowenthal, B. (2001). *Abuse and neglect: The educator's guide to the identification and prevention of child maltreatment.* Baltimore, MD: Brookes.

Luckner, J., Bowen, S., & Carter, K. (2001). Visual teaching strategies for students who are deaf or hard of hearing. *Teaching Exceptional Children, 33*(3), 38–43.

Ludi, D. C., & Martin, L. (1995). Self-determination: The road to personal freedom. *Intervention in School and Clinic, 30*(3), 164–169.

Lue, M. S., & Green, C. E. (2000). No easy walk: African-American educators coping with their own children with special needs. *Multiple Voices, 4*(1), 30–40.

Lustig, D. C. (2002). Family coping in families with a child with a disability. *Education and Training in Mental Retardation and Developmental Disabilities, 37,* 14–22.

Lutkenhoff, M. (1999). *Children with Spina Bifida: A parent's guide.* Bethesda, MD: Woodbine House.

Lytle, R. K., & Bordin, J. (2001). Enhancing the IEP team: Strategies for parents and professionals. *Teaching Exceptional Children, 33*(5), 40–45.

Maag, J. W. (2000). Managing resistance. *Intervention in School and Clinic, 35*(3), 131–140.

Maag, J. W., & Reid, R. (1998). Attention-deficit hyperactivity disorder in schools: Introduction. *Reading and Writing Quarterly: Overcoming Learning Difficulties, 14*(1), 5–7.

MacArthur, C. A. (1999). Overcoming barriers to writing: Computer support for basic writing skills. *Reading and Writing Quarterly: Overcoming Learning Difficulties, 15*(2), 169–192.

MacArthur, C. A., Graham, S., Haynes, J. B., & De La Paz, S. (1996). Spelling checkers and students with learning disabilities: Performance comparisons and impact on spelling. *The Journal of Special Education, 30*(1), 35–37.

MacArthur, C. A., Schwartz, S. S., & Graham, S. (1991). A model for writing instruction: Integrating word processing and strategy instruction into a process approach to writing. *Learning Disabilities Research and Practice, 6*(4), 230–236.

Maccini, P., & Hughes, C. A. (1997). Mathematics interventions for adolescents with learning disabilities. *Learning Disabilities Research and Practice, 12*(3), 168–176.

Macciomei, N. R. (1996). Loss and grief awareness: A "class book" project. *Teaching Exceptional Children, 28*(2), 72–73.

Macmillan, D. L., & Reschly, D. J. (1998). Overrepresentation of minority students: The case for greater specificity or reconsideration of variables examined. *The Journal of Special Education, 32,* 15–24.

Madaus, J. W. (2003). What high school students with learning disabilities need to know about college foreign language requirements. *Teaching Exceptional Children, 36*(2), 62–67.

Madden, J. A. (2000). Managing asthma at school. *Educational Leadership, 57*(6), 50–52.

Madrick, J. (2002, June 13). Economic scene. *The New York Times,* C2.

Maheady, L., Harper, G. F., & Mallette, B. (1991). Peer-mediated instruction: A review of potential applications for special education. *Reading, Writing, and Learning Disabilities International, 7,* 75–103.

Maheady, L., Harper, G. F., & Mallette, B. (2001). Peer-mediated instruction and interventions and students with mild disabilities. *Remedial and Special Education, 22,* 4–14.

Maheady, L., Michielli-Pendl, J., Mallette, B., & Harper, G. (2002). A collaborative research project to improve the academic performance of a diverse sixth grade science class. *Teacher Education and Special Education, 25,* 55–70.

Maldonado-Colon, E. (1991). Development of second language learners' linguistic and cognitive abilities. *The Journal of Educational Issues of Language Minority Students, 9,* 37–48.

Maldonado-Colon, E. (1995, April). *Second language learners in special education: Language framework for inclusive classrooms.* Paper presented at the international meeting of the Council for Exceptional Children, Indianapolis.

Male, M. (2003). *Technology for inclusion: Meeting the special needs of all students* (4th ed). Boston: Allyn & Bacon.

Malian, I. M., & Love, L. (1998). Leaving high school: An ongoing transition study. *Teaching Exceptional Children, 30*(3), 4–10.

Malian, I. M., & Nevin, A. (2002). A review of self-determination literature: Implications for practitioners. *Remedial and Special Education, 23,* 68–74.

Manley, R. S., Rickson, H., & Standeven, B. (2000). Children and adolescents with eating disorders: Strategies for teachers and school counselors. *Intervention in School and Clinic, 35,* 228–231.

Manset, G., & Semmel, M. I. (1997). Are inclusive programs for students with mild disabilities effective? A comparative review of model programs. *The Journal of Special Education, 31,* 155–180.

Manzo, A. (1969). The request procedure. *Journal of Reading, 13,* 123–126.

Manzo, A., & Manzo, U. (1990). *Content area reading: A heuristic approach.* Upper Saddle River, NJ: Merrill/Prentice Hall.

March, T. (2004). The learning power of webquests. *Educational Leadership, 61*(4). 30–35.

Marchisan, M. L., & Alber, S. R. (2001). The write way: Tips for teaching the writing process to resistant writers. *Intervention in School and Clinic, 36,* 154–162.

Marcotte, D., Fortin, L., Potvin, P., & Papillon, M. (2002). Gender differences in depressive symptoms during adolescence: Role of gender-typed characteristics, self-esteem, body image, stressful life events, and pubertal stress. *Journal of Emotional and Behavioral Disorders, 10,* 29–42.

Margolis, H. (1999). Lack of student motivation: A problem solving focus. *Channels, 13,* 18–19.

Margolis, H., & McCabe, P. P. (2003). Self-efficacy: A key to improving the motivation of struggling learners. *Preventing School Failure, 47,* 162–169.

Mariage, T. V. (2001). Features of an interactive writing discourse: Conversational involvement, conventional knowledge, and internalization in "Morning Message." *Journal of Learning Disabilities, 34,* 172–196.

Mariage, T. V., Englert, C. S., & Garmon, M. A. (2000). The teacher as a "more knowledgeable other" in assisting literacy learning with special needs students. *Reading and Writing Quarterly: Overcoming Learning Difficulties, 16,* 299–336.

Marks, S. U., Schrader, C., & Levine, M. (1999). Paraeducator experiences in inclusive settings: Helping, hovering, or holding their own? *Exceptional Children, 65*(3), 315–328.

Marks, S. U., Shaw-Hegwer, J., Schrader, C., Longaker, T., Peters, I., Powers, F., & Levine, M. (2003). Instructional tips for teachers of students with autistic spectrum disorder (ASD). *Teaching Exceptional Children, 35*(4), 50–54.

Marlatt, E. A. (2004). Practical knowledge storage among preservice, novice, and experienced educators of students who are deaf and hard-of-hearing. *Exceptional Children, 70.* 201–214.

Maroney, S. A. (2000). What's good? Suggested resources for beginning special education teachers. *Teaching Exceptional Children, 33*(1), 22–27.

Maroney, S. A., Finson, K. D., Beaver, J. B., & Jensen, M. M. (2003). Preparing for successful inquiry in inclusive science classrooms.*Teaching Exceptional Children, 36*(1), 18–5.

Marshall, L. H., Martin, J. E., Maxson, L., Hughes, W., Miller, T., McGill, T., & Jerman, P. (1999). *Take action: Making goals happen.* Longmont, CO: Sopris West.

Marshall, R. M., Hynd, G. W., Handwerk, M. J., & Hall, J. (1997). Academic underachievement in ADHD subtypes. *Journal of Learning Disabilities, 30*(6), 635–642.

Marston, D. (1996). A comparison of inclusion only, pull-out only, and combined service models for students with mild disabilities. *The Journal of Special Education, 30*(2), 121–132.

Martin, D. (1997, June 1). Disability culture: Eager to bite the hands that would feed them. *The New York Times,* 1, 6.

Martin, E. J., Tobin, T. J., & Sugai, G. M. (2002). Current information on dropout prevention: Ideas from practitioners and the literature. *Preventing School Failure, 47*(1), 10–17.

Martin, J. E., Marshall, L. H., Maxson, L., & Jerman, P. (1996a). *Self-directed IEP: Student workbook* (2nd ed.). Longmont, CO: Sopris West.

Martin, J. E., Marshall, L. H., Maxson, L., & Jerman, P. (1996b). *Self-directed IEP: Teacher's manual* (2nd ed.). Longmont, CO: Sopris West.

Martin, J. E., Mithaug, D. E., Cox, P., Peterson, L. Y., Van Dycke, J. L., & Cash, M. E. (2003). Increasing self-determination: Teaching students to plan, work, evaluate, and adjust. *Exceptional Children, 69,* 431–447.

Martin, S. S., & Seevers, R. L. (2003). A field trip planning guide for early childhood classes. *Preventing School Failure, 47,* 177–180.

Martinez, Y. G., & Velazquez, J. A. (2000, December). *Involving migrant families in education.* Charleston, WV: ERIC Clearinghouse on Rural Education and Small Schools.

Martin-Kniep, G. O. (2000). Standards, feedback, and diversified assessment: Addressing equity issues at the classroom level. *Reading and Writing Quarterly: Overcoming Learning Difficulties, 16,* 239–256.

Martorella, P. H., & Beal, C. (2002). *Social studies for elementary school classrooms: Preparing children to be global citizens* (3rd ed.). Upper Saddle River, NJ: Merrill/Prentice Hall.

Marzano, R. J., & Marzano, J. S. (2003). The key to classroom management. *Educational Leadership, 61*(1), 6–13.

Mason, C. Y., McGahee-Kovac, M., & Johnson, L. (2004). How to help students lead their IEP meetings. *Teaching Exceptional Children, 36*(3), 18–25.

Mason, S. A., & Egel, A. L. (1995). What does Amy like? Using a mini-reinforcer to increase student participation in instructional activities. *Teaching Exceptional Children, 28*(1), 42–45.

Masterson, J. J., Apel, K., & Wasowicz, J. (2003). *SPELL: Spelling performance evaluation for language and literacy.* Winooski, VT: Learning by Design.

Mathes, P. G., Grek, M. L., Howard, J. K., Babyak, A. E., & Allen, S. H. (1999). Peer-assisted learning strategies for first-grade readers: A tool for preventing early reading failure. *Learning Disabilities Research and Practice, 14*(1), 50–60.

Mathur, S., & Smith, R. M. (2003). 20 ways to collaborate with families of children with ADD. *Intervention in School and Clinic, 38,* 311–315.

Mathews, R. (2000). Cultural patterns of south Asian and southeast Asian Americans. *Intervention in School and Clinic, 36,* 101–104.

Matlock, L., Fielder, K., & Walsh, D. (2001). Building the foundation for standards-based instruction for all students. *Teaching Exceptional Children, 33*(5), 68–72.

Maxim, G. W. (2003). *Dynamic social studies for elementary classrooms* (7th ed.). Upper Saddle River, NJ: Merrill/Prentice Hall.

May, S. W. (2003, March). Integrating technology into a reading program. *The Journal: Technological Horizons in Education,* 34–38.

McAdams, C. R., & Lambie, G. W. (2003). A changing profile of aggression in schools: Its impact and implications for school personnel. *Preventing School Failure, 47,* 122–130.

McAlister, K. M., Nelson, N. W., & Bahr, C. M. (1999). Perceptions of students with language and learning disabilities about writing process instruction. *Learning Disabilities Research and Practice, 14*(3), 159–172.

McBrien, J. L. (2003). A second chance for refugee students. *Educational Leadership, 61*(2), 76–79.

McCarty, H., & Chalmers, L. (1997). Bibliotherapy: Intervention and prevention. *Teaching Exceptional Children, 29*(6), 12–17.

McConnell, M. E. (1999). Self-monitoring cueing, recording, and managing: Teaching students to manage their own behavior. *Teaching Exceptional Children, 32*(2), 14–21.

McCormick, L., Noonan, M. J., Ogata, V., & Heck, R. (2001). Co-teacher relationships and program quality: Implications for preparing teachers for inclusive preschool settings. *Education and Training in Mental Retardation and Developmental Disabilities, 36,* 119–132.

McDonnell, J. (2002, August). New insights on special education practice. *CEC Today, 9*(2), 15.

McDonnell, J., Johnson, J. W., Polychronis, S., & Risen, T. (2002). Effects of embedded instruction on students with moderate disabilities enrolled in general education classes. *Education and Training in Mental Retardation and Developmental Disabilities, 37,* 363–377.

McDonnell, J., Thorson, N., & McQuivey, C. (2000). Comparison of the instructional contexts of students with severe disabilities and their peers in general education classes. *The Journal of the Association for Persons with Severe Handicaps, 25,* 54–58.

McDonnell, J., Thorson, N., McQuivey, C., & Kiefer-O'Donnell, R. (1997).The academic engaged time of students with low incidence disabilities in general education classes. *Mental Retardation, 35,* 18–26.

McDougall, D., & Brady, M. P. (1998). Initiating and fading self-management interventions to increase math fluency in general education class. *Exceptional Children, 64*(2), 151–166.

McDowell, K. C. (2002, Winter). Accommodating without endorsing: Recognizing religious diversity in public schools. *The State Education Standard,* 44–46.

McFadyen, G. M. (1996). Aids for hearing impairment and deafness. In J. C. Galvin & M. J. Scherer (Eds.), *Evaluating, selecting, and using appropriate assistive technology* (pp. 144–161). Gaithersburg, MD: Aspen.

McGahee, M., Mason, C., Wallace, T., & Jones, B. (2001). *Student-led IEPs: A guide for student involvement.* Arlington, VA: Council for Exceptional Children.

McGoogan, G. (2002). Around the world in 24 hours. *Educational Leadership, 60*(2), 44–47.

McIntosh, P. I., & Guest, C. L. (2000). Suicidal behavior: Recognition and response for children and adolescents. *Beyond Behavior, 10*(2), 14–17.

McLeod, J., & Kilpatrick, K. M. (2001). Exploring science at the museum. *Educational Leadership, 58*(7), 59–63.

McLeskey, J., Henry, D., & Hodges, D. (1999). Inclusion: What progress is being made across disability categories? *Teaching Exceptional Children, 31*(3), 60–64.

McLeskey, J., & Waldron, N. L. (2002). Inclusion and school change: Teacher perceptions regarding curricular and instructional adaptations. *Teacher Education and Special Education, 25*, 41–54.

McLeskey, J., Waldron, N. L., So, T. H., Swanson, K., & Loveland, T. (2001). Perspectives of teachers toward inclusive school programs. *Teacher Education and Special Education, 24*, 108–115.

McLoughlin, J. A., & Nall, M. (1995). Allergies and learning/behavioral disorders. *Intervention in School and Clinic, 29*, 198–207.

McNally, J. (2003). A ghetto within a ghetto: African-American students are over-represented in special education programs. *Rethinking Schools, 17*(3), 6–7, 25.

McNamara, B. E. (1996, November). *Bullying: Implications for special educators.* Presentation at the annual meeting of the New York Federation of Chapters of the Council for Exceptional Children, Albany, NY.

McNamara, J. K., & Wong, B. (2003). Memory for everyday information in students with learning disabilities. *Journal of Learning Disabilities, 36*, 394–406.

McNaughton, D., Hughes, C. A., & Clark, K. (1997). The effects of five proofreading conditions on the spelling performance of college students with learning disabilities. *Journal of Learning Disabilities, 30*(6), 643–651.

McNaughton, D., Hughes, C. A., & Ofiesh, N. (1997). Proofreading for students with learning disabilities: Integrating computer with strategy use. *Learning Disabilities Research and Practice, 12*(1), 16–28.

McTighe, J., & Thomas, R. S. (2003). Backward design for forward action. *Educational Leadership, 60*(5), 52–55.

Mechling, L. C., & Gast, D. L. (2003). Multi-media instruction to teach grocery word associations and store locations: A study of generalization. *Education and Training in Developmental Disabilities, 38*, 62–76.

Medina, J. (2002, July 3). Technology eases the way for the visually impaired. *The New York Times,* B9.

Meese, R. L. (1997). Student fights: Proactive strategies for preventing and managing student conflicts. *Intervention in School and Clinic, 33*(1), 26–29, 35.

Meese, R. L. (1999). Teaching adopted students with disabilities: What teachers need to know. *Intervention in School and Clinic, 34*(4), 232–235.

Meloy, L. L., Deville, C., & Frisbie, D. A. (2002). The effect of a read aloud accommodation on test scores of students with and without a learning disability in reading. *Remedial and Special Education, 23*, 248–255.

Meltzer, L. J., & Roditi, B. (1994). *The student observation system.* Chelmsford, MA: Research ILD.

Menchaca, V., & Ruiz-Escalante, J. (1995). *Instructional strategies for migrant students.* (ERIC Document Reproduction Service No. 388 491).

Menchetti, B. M., & Garcia, L. A. (2003). Personal and employment outcomes of person-centered career planning. *Education and Training in Developmental Disabilities, 38*, 145–156.

Menkart, D. J. (1999). Deepening the meaning of heritage months. *Educational Leadership, 56*(7), 19–21.

Menlove, R. R., Hudson, P. J., & Suter, D. (2001). A field of IEP dreams: Increasing general education teacher participation in the IEP development process. *Teaching Exceptional Children, 33*(5), 28–33.

Mercer, C. D. (1987). *Students with learning disabilities* (3rd ed.). Upper Saddle River, NJ: Merrill/Prentice Hall.

Mercer, C. D. (1997). *Students with learning disabilities* (5th ed.). Upper Saddle River, NJ: Merrill/Prentice Hall.

Mercer, C. D., Campbell, K. U., Miller, M. D., Mercer, K. D., & Lane H. B. (2000). Effects of a reading fluency intervention for middle schoolers with specific learning disabilities. *Learning Disabilities Research and Practice, 15*, 179–189.

Mercer, C. D., & Miller, S. P. (1992). Teaching students with learning problems in math to acquire, understand, and apply basic math facts. *Remedial and Special Education, 13*(3), 19–35, 61.

Merritt, S. (2001). Clearing the hurdles of inclusion. *Educational Leadership, 59*(3), 67–70.

Merryfield, M. M. (2002). The difference a global educator can make. *Educational Leadership, 60*(2), 18–21.

Met, M. (2001). Why language learning matters. *Educational Leadership, 59*(2), 36–40.

Meyer, D. J., & Vadasy, P. F. (1994). *Sibshops: Workshops for siblings of children with special needs.* Baltimore: Paul H. Brookes.

Meyer, D. J., Vadasy, P. F., & Fewell, R. (1996). *Living with a brother or sister with special needs: A book for sibs* (2nd ed). Seattle: University of Washington Press.

Mhoon, L. (2003). Early beginnings: Transitions to Pre-K. *Beyond Behavior, 12*(2), 17–18.

Michael, R. J. (1992). Seizures: Teacher observations and record keeping. *Intervention in School and Clinic, 27*(4), 211–214.

Michael, R. J. (1995). *The educator's guide to students with epilepsy.* Springfield, IL: Charles C. Thomas.

Midkiff, R. B., & Cramer, M. M. (1993). Stepping stones to mathematical understanding. *Arithmetic Teacher, 40*, 303–305.

Migliore, E. T. (2003). 20 ways to eliminate bullying. *Intervention in School and Clinic, 38*, 172–176.

Mike, D. G. (2001). Computer mediated word recognition: Poised to make a difference? *Reading and Writing Quarterly: Overcoming Learning Difficulties, 17*, 99–102.

Miller, D., Brown, A., & Robinson, L. (2002). Widgets on the web: Using computer-based learning tools. *Teaching Exceptional Children, 35*(2), 24–29.

Miller, L. L., & Felton, R. H. (2001). "It's one of them . . . I don't know": Case study of a student with phonological, rapid naming, and word-finding deficits. *The Journal of Special Education, 35*, 125–133.

Miller, M., Miller, S. R., Wheeler, J., & Selinger, J. (1989). Can a single-classroom treatment approach change academic performance and behavioral characteristics in severely behaviorally disordered adolescents? An experimental inquiry. *Behavioral Disorders, 14*(4), 215–225.

Miller, S. P., Strawser, S., & Mercer, C. D. (1996). Promoting strategic math performance among students with learning disabilities. *LD Forum, 21*(2), 34–40.

Millman, J., & Pauk, W. (1969). *How to take tests.* New York: McGraw-Hill.

Mills v. Board of Education of the District of Columbia, 348 F. Supp. 866 (D.D.C., 1972).

Mills, G. E., & Duff-Mallams, K. (2000). Special education mediation: A formula for success. *Teaching Exceptional Children, 32*(4), 72–78.

Mills, P. E., Cole, K. N., Jenkins, J. R., & Dale, P. S. (1998). Effects of differing levels of inclusion on preschoolers with disabilities. *Exceptional Children, 65*(1), 79–90.

Mills, R. P. (1998). *Least restrictive environment implementation policy paper.* Albany, NY: State Education Department.

Milstein, S. (2002, December 5). Volunteers are virtual, but connections are real. *The New York Times,* G7.

Miranda, A., Presentacion, M. J., & Soriano, M. (2002). Effective school-based multicomponent program for treatment of children with ADHD. *Journal of Learning Disabilities, 35,* 546–562.

Mishna, F. (2003). Learning disabilities and bullying: Double jeopardy. *Journal of Learning Disabilities, 36,* 336–347.

Mitchem, K. J., & Young, K. R. (2001). Adapting self-management programs for classroom use: Acceptability, feasibility, and effectiveness. *Remedial and Special Education, 22,* 75–88.

Mitchem, K. J., Young, K. R., & West, R. P. (2000). Changing student, parent, and faculty perceptions: School is a positive place. *Intervention in School and Clinic, 35,* 248–252.

Mithaug, D. K. (2002). "Yes" means success: Teaching children with multiple disabilities to self-regulate during independent work. *Teaching Exceptional Children, 35*(1), 22–27.

Mittag, K. C., & Van Reusen, A. K. (1999). Learning estimation and other advanced mathematics concepts in an inclusive class. *Teaching Exceptional Children, 31*(6), 66–72.

Moats, L. C. (2001). When older students can't read. *Educational Leadership, 58*(6), 36–40.

Modell, S. J., & Valdez, L. A. (2002). Beyond bowling: Transition planning for students with disabilities. *Teaching Exceptional Children, 34*(6), 46–53.

Monda-Amaya, L. E., Dieker, L., & Reed, F. (1998). Preparing students with learning disabilities to participate in inclusive classrooms. *Learning Disabilities Research and Practice, 13*(3), 171–182.

Monroe, E. E., & Orme, M. P. (2002). Developing mathematical vocabulary. *Preventing School Failure, 46,* 139–142.

Montague, M. (1997). Cognitive strategy instruction in mathematics for students with learning disabilities. *Journal of Learning Disabilities, 30*(2), 164–177.

Montague, M., & van Garderen, D. (2003). A cross-sectional study of mathematics achievement, estimation skills, and academic self-perception in students with varying ability. *Journal of Learning Disabilities, 36,* 437–448.

Montague, M., Warger, C., & Morgan, T. H. (2000). Solve It! Strategy instruction to improve mathematical problem solving. *Learning Disabilities Research and Practice, 15,* 110–116.

Montgomery, W. (2000). Literature discussion in the elementary school classroom: Developing cultural understanding. *Multicultural Education, 8*(1), 33–36.

Montgomery, W. (2001a). Creating culturally responsive, inclusive classrooms. *Teaching Exceptional Children, 33*(4), 4–9.

Montgomery, W. (2001b). Journal writing: Connecting reading and writing in mainstream educational settings. *Reading and Writing Quarterly: Overcoming Learning Difficulties, 17,* 93–98.

Moore, W. (2003). Facts and assumptions of assessment: Technology, the missing link. *The Journal of Technological Horizons in Education, 30*(6), 20–28.

Morgan, J., & Ashbaker, B. Y. (2001). Work more effectively with your paraeducator. *Intervention in School and Clinic, 36,* 230–231.

Morgan, R. L., Ellerd, D. A., Gerity, B. P., & Blair, R. J. (2000). That's the job I want! How technology helps young people in transition. *Teaching Exceptional Children, 32*(4), 44–49.

Morocco, C. C., & Hindin, A. (2002). The role of conversation in a thematic understanding of literature. *Learning Disabilities Research and Practice, 17,* 144–159.

Morris, S. (2002). Promoting social skills among students with nonverbal disabilities. *Teaching Exceptional Children, 34*(3), 66–70.

Morrison, L., & Kane, L. (2002). Peer training to facilitate social interaction for elementary students with autism and their peers. *Exceptional Children, 68,* 173–188.

Morrison, W. F., & Rude, H. A. (2002). Beyond textbooks: A rationale for a more inclusive use of literature in preservice special education teacher programs. *Teacher Education and Special Education, 25,* 114–123.

Moses, R. P., & Cobb, C. E. (2001). *Radical equations: Math literacy and civil rights.* Boston: Beacon Press.

Moulds. P. (2004). Rich tasks. *Educational Leadership, 61*(4), 75–78.

Mu, K., Siegel, E. B., & Allinder, R. M. (2000). Peer interactions and sociometric status of high school students with moderate or severe disabilities in general education classrooms. *The Journal of the Association for Persons with Severe Handicaps, 25,* 142–152.

Mueller, F., Jenson, W. R., Reavis, K., & Andrews, D. (2002). Functional assessment of behavior can be as easy as A-B-C. *Beyond Behavior, 11*(3), 23–27.

Mueller, P. H., & Murphy, F. V. (2001). Determining when a student requires paraeducator support. *Teaching Exceptional Children, 33*(6), 22–27.

Mull, C. A., & Sitlington, P. L. (2003). The role of technology in the transition to postsecondary education of students with learning disabilities: A review of the literature. *The Journal of Special Education, 37,* 26–32.

Mull, C. A., Sitlington, P. L. & Alper, S. (2001). Postsecondary education for students with learning disabilities: A synthesis of the literature. *Exceptional Children, 68,* 97–118.

Mullin-Rindler, N., Froschl, M., Sprung, B., Stein, N., & Gropper, N. (1998). *QUIT IT! A teacher's guide on teasing and bullying for use with students in grades K–3.* Wellesley, MA: Wellesley Centers for Women.

Mullins, F., McKnab, P. A., & Dempsey, S. D. (2002). 20 ways to make the most of a conference experience. *Intervention in School and Clinic, 38,* 113–116.

Munk, D. D., Bruckert, J., Call, D. T., Stoehrmann, T., & Randandt, E. (1998). Strategies for enhancing the performance of students with LD in inclusive science classes. *Intervention in School and Clinic, 34*(2), 73–78.

Munk, D.D., & Bursuck, W.D. (2001). Preliminary findings on personalized grading plans for middle school students with learning disabilities. *Exceptional Children, 67,* 211–234.

Murdick, N. L., Gartin, B. C., & Stockall, N. (2003). Step by step: How to meet the functional assessment of behavior requirements of IDEA. *Beyond Behavior, 12*(2), 25–30.

Murdick, N. L., Gartin, B. C., & Yalowitz, S. J. (1995, April). *Enhancing the effective inclusion of students with violent behaviors in the public schools.* Presentation at the annual meeting of the Council for Exceptional Children, Indianapolis.

Murdick, N. L., & Petch-Hogan, B. (1996). Inclusive classroom management: Using preintervention strategies. *Intervention in School and Clinic, 31*(3), 172–176.

Murray, C. (2003). Risk factors, protective factors, vulnerability, and resilence: A framework for understanding and supporting the adult transitions of youth with high-incidence disabilities. *Remedial and Special Education, 24*, 16–26.

Murray, C., & Wren, C. T. (2003). Cognitive, academic, and attitudinal predictors of the grade point averages of college students with learning disabilities. *Journal of Learning Disabilities, 36*, 407–415.

Muscott, H. (2001). An introduction to service learning for students with emotional and behavioral disorders: Answers to frequently asked questions. *Beyond Behavior, 10*(3), 8–15.

Myers, M. E., & Myers, B. K. (2002). Holidays in the public school kindergarten: An avenue for emerging religious and spiritual literacy. *Childhood Education, 78*(2) 79–83.

Nagel, D. R., Schumaker, J. B., & Deshler, D. D. (1986). *The FIRST-Letter mnemonic strategy.* Lawrence: University of Kansas Institute for Research in Learning Disabilities.

Naglieri, J. A., & Johnson, D. (2000). Effectiveness of a cognitive strategy intervention in improving arithmetic computation based on the PASS theory. *Journal of Learning Disabilities, 33*, 591–597.

Nahme Huang, L. (1989). Southeast Asian refugee children and adolescents. In J. Taylor Gibbs and L. Nahme Huang (Eds.), *Children of color: Psychological interventions with minority youth* (pp. 278–321). San Francisco: Jossey-Bass.

National Academy of Sciences. (2002). Disproportionate representation report.

National Coalition of Advocates for Students. (1991). *New voices: Immigrant students in U.S. public schools.* Boston: Author.

National Coalition of Advocates for Students. (1993). *Achieving the dream: How communities and schools can improve education for immigrant students.* Boston: Author.

National Council for the Accreditation of Teacher Education. (2001). *Professional standards for the accreditation of schools, colleges, and departments of education.* Washington, DC: Author

National Information Center for Children and Youth with Disabilities. (2000). *Resources you can use: Disability awareness.* Washington, D.C.: Author.

Naus, J. M. (2000). Helping hands: A world of manipulatives to boost handwriting skills. *Teaching Exceptional Children, 32*(4), 64–70.

Neal, J., Bigby, L., & Nicholson, R. (2004). Occupational therapy, physical therapy, and orientation and mobility services in public schools. *Intervention in School and Clinic, 39*, 218–222.

Neal, L. I., McCray, A. D., Webb-Johnson, G., & Bridgest, S. T. (2003). The effects of African American students' movement styles on teachers' perceptions and reactions. *Journal of Special Education, 37*, 49–57.

Neill, M. (2003). The dangers of testing. *Educational Leadership, 60*(5), 43–47.

Nelson, J. R., Martella, R. M., & Marchand-Martella, N. (2002). Maximizing student learning: The effects of a comprehensive

school-based program for preventing problem behaviors. *Journal of Emotional and Behavioral Disorders, 10*, 136–148.

Nelson, J. R., & Roberts, M. L. (2000). Ongoing reciprocal teacher-student interactions involving disruptive behaviors in general education classrooms. *Journal of Emotional and Behavioral Disorders, 8*, 27–37.

Nelson, M. A., & Smith, S. (2001). External factors affecting gifted girls' academic and career achievements. *Intervention in School and Clinic, 37*, 19–22.

Neubert, D. A., & Moon, M. S. (2000). How a transition profile helps students prepare for life in the community. *Teaching Exceptional Children, 33*(2), 20–25.

Nevin, A., Malian, I., & Williams, L. (2002). Perspectives on self-determination across the curriculum: Report of a preservice special education teacher preparation program. *Remedial and Special Education, 23*, 75–81.

New York State Education Department. (n.d.). *Guidelines for educational interpreting.* Albany, NY: Author.

New York State Education Department. (n.d.). *The identification and reporting of child abuse and maltreatment.* Albany, NY: Author.

Nichols, J. D. (2003). Prediction indicators for students failing the state of Indiana high school graduation exam. *Preventing School Failure, 47*, 112–120.

Nieto, S. (2000). *Affirming diversity. The sociopolitical context of multicultural education* (3rd ed.). New York: Longman.

Nieto, S. (2003). Profoundly multicultural questions. *Educational Leadership, 60*(4), 6–10.

Noble, L. S. (1997). The face of foster care. *Educational Leadership, 54*(7), 26–28.

Nolan, E. E., Volpe, R. J., Gadow, K. D., & Sprafkin, J. (1999). Developmental, gender, and comorbidity differences in clinically referred children with ADHD. *Journal of Emotional and Behavioral Disorders, 7*(1), 11–20.

Nolet, V., & McLaughlin, M. (2000). *Accessing the general curriculum. Including students with disabilities in standards-based reform.* Thousand Oaks, CA: Corwin Press.

Noonan, M. J., McCormick, L., & Heck, R. H. (2003). The co-teacher relationship scale: Applications for professional development. *Education and Training in Developmental Disabilities, 38*, 113–120.

Nord, W. A., & Haynes, C. C. (1998). *Taking religion seriously across the curriculum.* Alexandria, VA: Association for Supervision and Curriculum Development.

Obenchain, K. M., & Abernathy, T. V. (2003). 20 ways to build community and empower students. *Intervention in School and Clinic, 39*, 55–60.

Oberti v. *Board of Education of the Borough of Clementon School District*, 995 F.2d, 1009, 3rd Circuit, 1993.

Obiakor, F. E. (1999). Teacher expectations of minority exceptional learners: Impact on accuracy of self-concepts. *Exceptional Children, 66*(1), 39–53.

Obiakor, F. E. (2001a). Developing emotional intelligence in learners with behavioral problems: Refocusing special education. *Behavioral Disorders, 26*, 321–331.

Obiakor, F. E. (2001b). Multicultural education: Powerful tool for preparing future general and special educators. *Teacher Education and Special Education, 24*, 241–253.

Obiakor, F. E., & Ford, B. A. (2002). Educational reform and accountability: Implications for African Americans with exceptionalities. *Multiple Voices, 5*(1), 83–93.

Ochoa, S. H., Robles-Pina, R., Garcia, S. B., & Breunig, N. (1999). School psychologists' perspectives on referrals of language minority students. *Multiple Voices, 3*(1), 1–13.

Ochoa, T. A., Vasquez, L. R., & Gerber, M. M. (1999). New generation of computer-assisted learning tools for students with disabilities. *Intervention in School and Clinic, 34*(4), 251–254.

Office of Diversity Concerns. (1999). *Multicultural book reviews for K–12 educators.* Reston, VA: Council for Exceptional Children.

Office of Vocational and Educational Services for Individuals with Disabilities. (2000, January). *Provider guidelines for supported employment.* Albany, NY: Author.

Ogletree, B. T., Bull, J., Drew, R., & Lunnen, K. Y. (2001). Team-based service delivery for students with disabilities: Practice options and guidelines for success. *Intervention in School and Clinic, 36,* 138–145.

Oldfather, P. (2002). Students' experiences when not initially motivated for literacy learning. *Reading and Writing Quarterly: Overcoming Learning Difficulties, 18,* 231–256.

Olweus, D. (2003). A profile of bullying at school. *Educational Leadership, 60*(6), 12–17.

Olweus, D., Limber, S., & Mihalic, S. (1999). *Blueprints for violence prevention: The bullying prevention program.* Boulder, CO: Center for the Study and Prevention of Violence.

O'Malley, J. M., & Valdez Pierce, L. (1996). *Authentic assessment for English language learners: Practical approaches for teachers.* New York: Addison-Wesley.

O'Neill, R. E., Horner, R. H., Albin, R. W., Sprague, J. R., Storey, K., & Newton, J. S. (1997). *Functional assessment and program development for problem behavior* (2nd ed.). Pacific Grove, CA: Brooks/Cole.

Orfield, G., Frankenberg, E. D., & Lee, C. (2003). The resurgence of school segregation. *Educational Leadership, 60*(4), 16–20.

Ormsbee, C. K. (2001). Effective preassessment team procedures: Making the process work for teachers and students. *Intervention in School and Clinic, 36,* 146–153.

Ormsbee, C. K., & Finson, K. D. (2000). Modifying science activities and materials to enhance instruction for students with learning and behavioral problems. *Intervention in School and Clinic, 36,* 10–13.

Ortiz, A. A. (1997). Learning disabilities occurring concomitantly with linguistic differences. *Journal of Learning Disabilities, 30*(3), 321–332.

Ortiz, A. A. (2001, December). *English language learners with special needs: Effective instructional strategies.* Washington, DC: ERIC Clearinghouse on Languages and Linguistics.

Ortiz, A. A., & Wilkinson, C. Y. (1989). Adapting IEPs for limited English proficient students. *Academic Therapy, 24,* 555–568.

Ortiz, A. A., & Wilkinson, C. Y. (1991). Assessment and intervention model for bilingual exceptional student (Aim for the Best). *Teacher Education and Special Education, 14*(1), 35–42.

Osborne, A. G., Russo, C. J., & DiMattia, P. (2000). IDEA 97: Providing special education services to students voluntarily enrolled in private schools. *The Journal of Special Education, 33,* 224–231.

Ostrow, W., & Ostrow, V. (1989). *All about asthma.* Morton Grove, IL: Albert Whitman & Co.

Ottinger, B. (2003). *Tictionary.* Shawnee Mission, KS: Autism Asperger Publishing Company.

Otto, J. C. (2002). Building a great web site. *The Journal of Technological Horizons in Education, 29*(7), 40–41.

Owens, L., & Dieker, L. A. (2003). How to spell success for secondary students labeled EBD: How students define effective teachers. *Beyond Behavior, 12*(2), 19–23.

Owens, R. E. (2001). *Language development: An introduction* (5th ed.). Needham Heights, MA: Allyn & Bacon.

Oxer, T., & Klevit, M. (1995, April). *Cooperative discipline: A positive management approach.* Presentation at the annual meeting of the Council for Exceptional Children, Indianapolis.

Padeliadu, S., & Zigmond, N. (1996). Perspectives of students with learning disabilities about special education placement. *Learning Disabilities Research and Practice, 11*(1), 15–23.

Pakulski, L. A., & Kaderavek, J. N. (2002). Children with minimal hearing loss: Interventions in the classroom. *Intervention in School and Clinic, 38,* 96–103.

Palincsar, A. S., & Klenk, L. J. (1991). Learning dialogues to promote text comprehension. In B. Means & M. S. Knapp (Eds.), *Teaching advanced skills to educationally disadvantaged students—Final report* (pp. 20–34). Washington, DC: U.S. Department of Education.

Palincsar, A. S., Magnusson, S. J., Cutter, J., & Vincent, M. (2002). Supporting guided-inquiry instruction. *Teaching Exceptional Children, 34*(3), 88–91.

Palmer, D. S., Borthwick-Duffy, S. A., & Widaman, K. (1998). Parent perceptions of inclusive practices for their children with significant cognitive disabilities. *Exceptional Children, 64,* 271–282.

Palmer, D. S., Fuller, K, Aurora, T., & Nelson, M. (2001). Taking sides: Parent views on inclusion for their children with severe disabilities. *Exceptional Children, 67,* 467–484.

Palmer, S. B., & Wehmeyer, M. L. (2003). Promoting self-determination in early elementary school: Teaching self-regulated problem-solving and goal-setting skills. *Remedial and Special Education, 24,* 115–126.

Pancheri, C., & Prater, M. A. (1999). What teachers and parents should know about Ritalin. *Teaching Exceptional Children, 31*(4), 20–26.

Panchyshym, R., & Monroe, E. E. (1986). *Developing key concepts for solving word problems.* Baldwin, NY: Barnell Loft.

Parette, H. P., Huer, M. B., & Hourcade, J. J. (2003). Using assistive technology focus groups with families across cultures. *Education and Training in Developmental Disabilities, 38,* 429–440.

Parette, H. P., & McMahan, G. A. (2002). What should we expect of assistive technology? Being sensitive to family goals. *Teaching Exceptional Children, 35*(1), 56–61.

Parette, H. P., & McMahan, G. A. (2002). What should we expect of assistive technology? Being sensitive to family goals. *Teaching Exceptional Children, 35*(1), 56–61.

Parette, H. P., & Petch-Hogan, B. (2000). Approaching families: Facilitating culturally/linguistically diverse family involvement. *Teaching Exceptional Children, 33*(2), 4–11.

Parish, T. S., Ohlsen, R. L., & Parish, J. G. (1978). A look at mainstreaming in light of children's attitudes toward the handicapped. *Perceptual and Motor Skills, 46,* 1019–1021.

Park, J., & Turnbull, A. P. (2001). Cross-cultural competency and special education: Perceptions and experiences of Korean parents of children with special needs. *Education and Training in Mental Retardation, 36,* 133–147.

Park, J., Turnbull, A. P., & Turnbull, H. R. (2002). Impacts of poverty on quality of life in families of children with disabilities. *Exceptional Children, 68,* 151–172.

Parker, J. G., & Asher, S. R. (1993). Friendship and friendship quality in middle childhood: Links with peer group acceptance and feelings of loneliness and social dissatisfaction. *Developmental Psychology, 29,* 611–621.

Parker, R., Hasbrouck, J. E., & Denton, C. (2002a). Tips for teaching. How to tutor students with reading problems. *Preventing School Failure, 47*, 42–44.

Parker, R., Hasbrouck, J. E., & Denton, C. (2002b). How to tutor students with reading comprehension problems. *Preventing School Failure, 47*, 45–47.

Parmar, R. S., & Cawley, J. F. (1991). Challenging the routines and passivity that characterize instruction for children with mild handicaps. *Remedial and Special Education, 12*(5), 23–32, 43.

Parmar, R. S., Cawley, J. F., & Frazita, R. R. (1996). Word problem-solving by students with and without mild disabilities. *Teaching Exceptional Children, 26*(4), 16–21.

Patton, J. M., & Townsend, B. L. (1999). Ethics, power, and privilege: Neglected considerations in the education of African American learners with special needs. *Teacher Education and Special Education, 22*, 276–286.

Patton, J. R., Cronin, M. E., Bassett, D. S., & Koppel, A. E. (1997). A life skills approach to mathematics instruction: Preparing students with learning disabilities for the real-life math demands of adulthood. *Journal of Learning Disabilities, 30*(2), 178–187.

Patton, J. R., Jayanthi, M., & Polloway, E. A. (2001). Home-school collaboration about homework: What do we know and what should we do? *Reading and Writing Quarterly: Overcoming Learning Difficulties, 17*(3), 227–242.

Patton, P. L., de la Garza, B., & Harmon, C. (1997). Successful employment. *Teaching Exceptional Children, 29*(3), 4–10.

Pauk, W. (1984). *How to study in college.* Boston: Houghton Mifflin.

Pavri, S. (2001). Loneliness in children with disabilities: How teachers can help. *Teaching Exceptional Children, 33*(6), 52–58.

Pavri. S., & Luftig, R. (2000). The social face of inclusive education: Are students with learning disabilities really included in the classroom? *Preventing School Failure, 45*(1), 8–14.

Pavri, S., & Monda-Amaya, L. (2000). Loneliness and students with learning disabilities in inclusive classrooms: Self-perceptions, coping strategies, and preferred interventions. *Learning Disabilities Research and Practice, 15*, 22–33.

Pavri, S., & Monda-Amaya, L. (2001). Social support in inclusive schools: Student and teacher perspectives. *Exceptional Children, 67*, 391–411.

Peacock, C. A., & Gregory, K. C. (1998). *Sugar was my best food: Diabetes and me.* Morton Grove, IL: Albert Whitman & Co.

Pearl, C. (2004). Laying the foundation for self-advocacy. *Teaching Exceptional Children, 36*(3), 44–49.

Peck, C. A., Carlson, P., & Helmstetter, E. (1992). Parent and teacher perceptions of outcomes for typically developing children enrolled in integrated early childhood programs: A statewide survey. *Journal of Early Intervention, 16*, 53–63.

Peck, C. A., Donaldson, J., & Pezzoli, M. (1990). Some benefits non-handicapped adolescents perceive for themselves from their social relationships with peers who have severe disabilities. *Journal of the Association for Persons with Severe Handicaps, 15*(4), 241–249.

Peckham, V. C. (1993). Children with cancer in the classroom. *Teaching Exceptional Children, 25*(1), 27–32.

Pedrotty Bryant, D., Ugel, N., Thompson, S., & Hamff, A. (1999). Instructional strategies for content-area reading instruction. *Intervention in School and Clinic, 34*(5), 293–302.

Peetsma, T. (2001). Inclusion in education: Comparing pupils' development in special and regular education. *Educational Review, 53*, 125–136.

Pemberton, J. B. (2003). Integrated processing: A strategy for working on unknown words. *Intervention in School and Clinic, 38*, 247–250.

Pennsylvania Association for Retarded Children v. *Commonwealth of Pennsylvania*, 343 F. Supp. 279 (E.D. Pa., 1972).

Perry, L. A. (1997). Using wordless picture books with beginning readers (of any age). *Teaching Exceptional Children, 29*(3), 68–69.

Phelps, B. R. (1995, April). *Practical solutions for functional problems in transitioning students with traumatic brain injuries.* Paper presented at the annual meeting of the Council for Exceptional Children, Indianapolis.

Phillips, L., Sapona, R. H., & Lubic, B. L. (1995). Developing partnerships in inclusive education: One school's approach. *Intervention in School and Clinic, 30*(5), 262–272.

Pike, K., Compain, R., & Mumper, J. (1997). *New connections: An integrated approach to literacy* (2nd ed.). New York: Longman.

Pisha, B., & Coyne, P. (2001). Smart from the start: The promise of universal design for learning. *Remedial and Special Education, 22*, 197–203.

Pittman, P., & Huefner, D. S. (2001). Will the courts go bi-bi? IDEA 1997, the courts,, and deaf education. *Exceptional Children, 67*, 187–198.

Pivik, J., McComas, J., & Laflamme, M., (2002). Barriers and facilitators to inclusive education. *Exceptional Children, 69*, 97–107.

Pivik, J., McComas, J., Macfarlane, I., & Laflamme, M. (2002). Using virtual reality to teach disability related awareness. *Educational Computing Technology, 26*, 225–240.

Plyler v. *Doe*, 457 U.S. 202 (1982).

Pocock, A., Lambros, S., Karvonen, M., Test, D. W., Algozinne, B., Wood, W., & Martin, J. E. (2002). Successful strategies for promoting self-advocacy among students with LD: The lead group. *Intervention in School and Clinic, 37*, 209–216.

Poland, S. (1995). Suicide intervention. In A. Thomas & J. Grimes (Eds.), *Best practices in school psychology—3* (pp. 459–468). Washington, DC: National Association of School Psychologists.

Polloway, E. A. (2000). Influential persons in the development of the field of special education. *Remedial and Special Education, 21*, 322–324.

Poolaw v. *Bishop*, 23IDELR 406, 9th Circuit, 1995.

Poon-McBrayer, K. F., & Garcia, S. B. (2000). Profiles of Asian American students with LD at initial referral, assessment, and placement in special education. *Journal of Learning Disabilities, 33*, 61–71.

Popham, W. J. (2003). The seductive allure of data. *Educational Leadership, 60*(5), 48–51.

Porte, L. K. (2001). Cut and paste 101: New strategies for note taking and review. *Teaching Exceptional Children, 34*(2), 14–20.

Portes, A. (2002). English-only triumphs, but the costs are high. *Contexts, 1*(1), 10–15.

Posamentier, A. S., & Stepelman, J. (2002). *Teaching secondary mathematics: Techniques and enrichment units* (6th ed.). Upper Saddle River, NJ: Merrill/Prentice Hall.

Post, M., Storey, K., & Karabin, M. (2002). Cool headphones for effective prompts: Supporting students and adults in work and community environments. *Teaching Exceptional Children, 34*(3), 60–65.

Powers, L. (1998). *TAKE CHARGE.* Portland: Oregon Health Sciences University.

Praisner, C. L. (2003). Attitudes of elementary school principals toward the inclusion of students with disabilities. *Exceptional Children, 69*, 135–145.

Prater, M. A. (1998, April). *Using children's literature to teach about disabilities.* Presentation at the annual meeting of the Council for Exceptional Children, Minneapolis.

Prater, M. A. (2000). Using juvenile literature with portrayals of disabilities in your classroom. *Intervention in School and Clinic, 35*(3), 167–176.

Prater, M. A. (2003). She will succeed: Strategies for success in inclusive classrooms. *Teaching Exceptional Children, 35*(5), 58–64.

Prater, M. A., Bruhl, S., & Serna, L. A. (1998). Acquiring social skills through cooperative learning and teacher-directed instruction. *Remedial and Special Education, 19*(3), 160–172.

Prater, M. A., & Sileo, N. M. (2001). Using juvenile literature about HIV/AIDS: Ideas and precautions for the classroom. *Teaching Exceptional Children, 33*(6), 34–45.

Premack, D. (1959). Toward empirical behavior laws. *Psychological Review, 66*(4), 219–233.

Prendergast, D. E. (1995). Preparing for children who are medically fragile in educational programs. *Teaching Exceptional Children, 27*(2), 37–41.

Prescott, C., Rinard, B., Cockerill, J., & Baker, N. (1996). Science through workplace lenses. *Educational Leadership, 53*(8), 10–13.

Presley, J. A., & Hughes, C. (2000). Peers as teachers of anger management to high school students with behavioral disorders. *Behavioral Disorders, 25*, 114–130.

Prestia, K. (2003). Tourette's syndrome: Characteristics and interventions. *Intervention in School and Clinic, 39*, 67–71.

Price, L. A., Wolensky, D., & Mulligan, R. (2002). Self-determination in action in the classroom. *Remedial and Special Education, 23*, 109–115

Prigge, D. J. (2002). 20 ways to promote brain-based teaching and learning. *Intervention in School and Clinic, 37*, 237–241.

Program Development Associates. (1995). *I belong out there.* Syracuse, NY: Author.

Prom, M. (1999). Measuring perceptions about inclusion. *Teaching Exceptional Children, 31*(5), 38–42.

Provost, M. C., Rullo, A., & Buechner, M. (2000). 20 ways to make spelling sizzle. *Intervention in School and Clinic, 36*, 45–46.

Pugach, M. C., & Warger, C. L. (2001). Curriculum matters: Raising expectations for students with disabilities. *Remedial and Special Education, 22*, 194–196, 213.

Pullen, P. C., & Justice, L. M. (2003). Enhancing phonological awareness, print awareness, and oral language skills in preschool children. *Intervention in School and Clinic, 39*, 87–98.

Putnam, M. L. (1992). Characteristics of questions on tests administered by mainstream secondary classroom teachers. *Learning Disabilities Research and Practice, 7*, 129–136.

Quinn, A. E. (2001). Moving marginalized students inside the lines: Cultural differences in classrooms. *English Journal, 90*(4), 44–50.

Raborn, D. T., & Daniel, M. J. (1999). Oobleck: A scientific encounter of the special education kind. *Teaching Exceptional Children, 31*(6), 32–40.

Rademacher, J. A. (2000). Involving students in assignment evaluation. *Intervention in School and Clinic, 35*(3), 151–156.

Rademacher, J. A., Cowart, M., Sparks, J., & Chism, V. (1997). Planning high-quality assignments for diverse learners. *Preventing School Failure, 42*(1), 12–18.

Rafferty, Y. (1998). Meeting the educational needs of homeless children. *Educational Leadership, 55*(4), 48–52.

Rafferty, Y., Piscitelli, V., & Boettcher, C. (2003). The impact of inclusion on language development and social competence among preschoolers with disabilities. *Exceptional Children, 69*, 467–480.

Ramig, P. R., & Shames, G. H. (2002). Stuttering and other disorders of fluency. In G. H. Shames & N. B. Anderson (Eds.), *Human communication disorders: An introduction* (6th ed.) (pp. 258–302). Boston: Allyn & Bacon.

Ramirez, J. D. (1992). Executive summary. *Bilingual Research Journal, 16*(1&2), 1–63.

Rao, S., Hoyer, L. Meehan, K., Young, L., & Guerrera, A. (2003). Using narrative logs—Understanding students' challenging behaviors. *Teaching Exceptional Children, 35*(5), 22–29.

Raschke, D. (1981). Designing reinforcement surveys—Let the student choose the reward. *Teaching Exceptional Children, 14*, 92–96.

Raschke, D., & Dedrick, C. (1986). An experience in frustration: Simulations approximating learning difficulties. *Teaching Exceptional Children, 18*, 266–271.

Raskind, M. H., & Higgins, E. L. (1998). Assistive technology for postsecondary students with learning disabilities: An overview. *Journal of Learning Disabilities, 31*(1), 27–40.

Raymond, E. B. (1997, November). *Accommodating diversity, combating homophobia.* Presentation at the annual meeting of the New York Federation of Chapters of the Council for Exceptional Children, New York.

Rea, P. J., McLaughlin, V. L., & Walter-Thomas, C. (2002). Outcomes for students with learning disabilities in inclusive and pullout programs. *Exceptional Children, 68*, 203–222.

Reese, S. M. (2003, January/February). You can't say no to blood. *Modern Maturity, 56*–59, 61–62.

Reetz, L. J. (1995, April). *Portfolio assessment in inclusion settings: A shared responsibility.* Presentation at the annual meeting of the Council for Exceptional Children, Indianapolis.

Regan, K. S. (2003). Using dialogue journals in the classroom: Forming relationships with students with emotional disturbance. *Teaching Exceptional Children, 36*(2), 34–39.

Reichart, D. C., Lynch, E. C., Anderson, B. C., Svobodny, L. A., Di Cola, J. M., & Mercury, M. G. (1989). Parental perspectives on integrated preschool opportunities for children with handicaps and children without handicaps. *Journal of Early Intervention, 13*, 6–13.

Reichel, H. (1997, November). *Now we can do worksheets on the computer.* Presentation at the meeting of the New York State Federation of Chapters of the Council for Exceptional Children, New York.

Reid, D. K., & Button, L. J. (1995). Anna's story: Narratives of personal experience about being labeled learning disabled. *Journal of Learning Disabilities, 28*(10), 602–614.

Reid, R., & Maag, J. W. (1998). Functional assessment: A method for developing classroom-based accommodations and interventions for children with ADHD. *Reading and Writing Quarterly: Overcoming Learning Difficulties, 14*(1), 9–42.

Reid, R., & Nelson, J. R. (2002). The utility, acceptability, and practically of functional behavioral assessment for students with high-incidence problem behaviors. *Remedial and Special Education, 23*, 15–23.

Reis, S. M., Schader, R., Milne, H., & Stephens, R. (2003). Music and minds: Using a talent development approach for young adults with Williams Syndrome. *Exceptional Children, 69*, 293–313.

Rhodes, R. L. (1996). Beyond our borders: Spanish-dominant migrant parents and the IEP process. *Rural and Special Education Quarterly, 15*(2), 19–22.

Ricci-Balich, J., & Behm, J. A. (1996). Pediatric rehabilitation nursing. In S. P. Hoeman (Ed.), *Rehabilitation nursing: Process and application* (pp. 660–682). St. Louis: Mosby.

Rice, D., & Zigmond, N. (2000). Co-teaching in secondary schools. *Learning Disabilities Research and Practice, 15*, 190–197.

Rice, L. S., & Ortiz, A. A. (1994). Second language difference or learning disability? *LD Forum, 19*(2), 11–13.

Richards, J. C. (2003). Facts and feelings response diaries: Connecting efferently and aesthetically with informational text. *Reading and Writing Quarterly: Overcoming Learning Difficulties, 19*, 107–111.

Richardson, B. G., & Shupe, M. J. (2003). The importance of teacher self-awareness in working with students with emotional and behavioral disorders. *Teaching Exceptional Children, 36*(2), 8–13.

Rigby, K. (2002). *New perspectives on bullying.* London: Jessica Kingsley.

Riggs, C. G. (2001). Work effectively with paraeducators in inclusive settings. *Intervention in School and Clinic, 37*, 114–117.

Riggs, C. G., & Mueller, P. H. (2001). Employment and utilization of paraeducators in inclusive settings. *The Journal of Special Education, 35*, 54–60.

Roach, V., Salisbury, C., & McGregor, G. (2002). Applications of a policy framework to evaluate and promote large-scale change. *Exceptional Children, 68*, 451–464.

Roberts, R. L., & Baumberger, J. P. (1999). T.R.E.A.T.: A model for constructing counseling goals and objectives for students with special needs. *Intervention in School and Clinic, 43*(4), 239–243.

Robertson, H. M., Priest, B., & Fullwood, H. L. (2001). Assist learners who are strategy-inefficient. *Intervention in School and Clinic, 36*, 182–184.

Robinson, C. S., Menchetti, B. M., & Torgesen, J. K. (2002). Toward a two-factor theory of one type of mathematics disabilities. *Learning Disabilities Research and Practice, 17*, 81–89.

Robinson, K., & Toporek, C. (1999). *Hydrocephalus: A guide for patients, families, and friends.* Sebastopol, CA: O'Reilly and Associates.

Robinson, S. M. (1999). Meeting the needs of students who are gifted and have learning disabilities. *Intervention in School and Clinic, 34*(4), 195–204.

Rock, M. L. (2000).Parents as equal partners: Balancing the scales in IEP development. *Teaching Exceptional Children, 32*(6), 30–37.

Rockwell, S. (2001). Service learning: Barriers, benefits, and models of excellence. *Beyond Behavior, 10*(3), 16–21.

Rodis, P., Garrod, A., & Boscardin, M. L. (2001). *Learning disabilities and life stories.* Needham Heights, MA: Allyn & Bacon.

Rogers, E. L., & Rogers, D. C. (2001). Students with E/BD transition to college: Make a plan. *Beyond Behavior, 11*(1), 42–49.

Rohena, E. I., Jitendra, A. K., & Browder, D. M. (2002). Comparison of the effects of Spanish and English constant time delay instruction on sight word reading by Hispanic learners with mental retardation. *The Journal of Special Education, 36*, 169–184.

Rohner, J., & Rosberg, M. (2003). Children with special needs—An update. *Book Links, 12*(4), 40–44,

Roll-Pettersson, L. (2001). Teacher perceptions of supports and resources needed in regard to pupils with special needs in Sweden. *Education and Training in Mental Retardation and Developmental Disabilities, 36*, 42–54.

Rolon, C. A. (2003). Educating Latino students. *Educational Leadership, 60*(4), 40–43.

Romero, M., & Parirno, A. (1994). Planned alternation of languages (PAL): Language use and distribution in bilingual classrooms. *The Journal of Educational Issues of Language Minority Students, 13*, 137–161.

Roney, L. (1999). *Sweet invisible body: Reflections on life with diabetes.* New York: Henry Holt.

Rose, T. D. (1999). Middle school teachers: Using individualized instruction strategies. *Intervention in School and Clinic, 34*(3), 137–142, 162.

Rosenberg, M. S., & Jackman, L. A. (2003). Development, implementation, and sustainability of comprehensive school-wide behavior management systems. *Intervention in School and Clinic, 39*, 10–21.

Rosenthal-Malek, A. L., & Greespan, J. (1999). A student with diabetes is in my class. *Teaching Exceptional Children, 31*(3). 38–43.

Rotter, K. (2004). Modifying "Jeopardy!" games to benefit all students. *Teaching Exceptional Children, 36*(3) 38–43.

Routman, R. (2002). Teacher talk. *Educational Leadership, 59*(6), 32–35.

Rowley-Kelley, F. L., & Reigel, D. H. (1993). *Teaching the student with spina bifida.* Baltimore: Paul H. Brookes.

Ruder, S. (2000). We teach all. *Educational Leadership, 58*(1), 41–52.

Rudolph, S., & Epstein, A. A. (2000). Using strength-based *assessment* in transition planning. *Teaching Exceptional Children, 32*(6), 50–54.

Rueda, R., & Garcia, E. (1997). Do portfolios make a difference for diverse students? The influence of type of data on making instructional decisions. *Learning Disabilities Research and Practice, 12*(2), 114–122.

Ruef, M. B., Higgins, C., Glaeser, B. J. C., & Patnode, M. (1998). Positive behavioral support: Strategies for teachers. *Intervention in School and Clinic, 34*(1), 21–32.

Ryan, A. K., Kay, P. J., Fitzgerald, M., & Paquette, S. (2001). Kyle: A case study in parent–teacher action research. *Teaching Exceptional Children, 33*(3), 56–60.

Ryan, A. L., Halsey, H. N., & Matthews, W. J. (2003). Using functional assessment to promote desirable student behavior in schools. *Teaching Exceptional Children, 35*(5), 8–15.

Ryan, D. J. (2000). *Job search handbook for people with disabilities.* Indianapolis, IN: JIST Publishing.

Ryan, S., Whittaker, C. R., & Pinckey, J. (2002). A school-based elementary mentoring program. *Preventing School Failure, 46*, 133–138.

Ryndak, D. L., Downing, J. E., Jacqueline, L. R., & Morrison, A. P. (1995). Parents' perceptions after inclusion of their child with moderate or severe disabilities in general education settings. *Journal of the Association for Persons with Severe Handicaps, 20*, 147–157.

Sacramento City Unified School District, Board of Education v. *Holland,* 14F.3d, 1398, 9th Circuit, 1994.

Sadao, K. C., & Walker, W. L. (2002). Emancipation for youth with behavior disorders and emotional disturbance: A study of student perceptions. *Preventing School Failure, 46*, 119–125.

Sadker, M. P., & Sadker, D. (1994). *Failing at fairness: How America's schools cheat girls.* New York: Scribner.

Sadler, F. H. (2001). The itinerant teacher hits the road: A map for instruction in young children's social skills. *Teaching Exceptional Children, 34*(1), 60–66.

Saenz, L. M., & Fuchs, L. S. (2002). Examining the reading difficulty of secondary students with learning disabilities: Expository versus narrative text. *Remedial and Special Education, 23*, 31–41.

Safran, J. S. (2002a). Supporting students with Asperger's syndrome in general education. *Teaching Exceptional Children, 34*(5), 60–65.

Safran, J. S. (2002b). A practitioner's guide to resources on Asperger syndrome. *Intervention in School and Clinic, 37*, 283–291.

Safran, S. P. (1998). Disability portrayal in film: Reflecting the past, directing the future. *Exceptional Children, 64*(2), 227–238.

Safran, S. P. (2000). Using movies to teach students about disabilities. *Teaching Exceptional Children, 32*(3), 44–47.

Safran, S. P. (2001). Asperger syndrome: The emerging challenge to special education. *Exceptional Children, 67*, 151–160.

Safran, S. P., & Oswald, K. (2003). Positive behavior supports: Can schools reshape disciplinary practices? *Exceptional Children, 69*, 361–373.

Sailor, W., Gee, K., & Karasoff, P. (2000). Inclusion and school restructuring. In M. E. Snell & F. Brown (Eds.), *Instruction of students with severe disabilities* (5th ed, pp. 1–30).Upper Saddle River, NJ: Merrill/Prentice Hall.

Saint-Laurent, L. (2001). The SIO: An instrument to faciliate inclusion. *Reading and Writing Quarterly: Overcoming Learning Difficulties, 17*, 349–355.

Saint-Laurent, L., Dionne, J., Giasson, J., Royer, E., Simard, C., & Pierard, B. (1998). Academic achievement effects of an in-class service model on students with and without disabilities. *Exceptional Children, 64*, 239–253.

Salembier, G. B., & Cheng, L. C. (1997). SCUBA-DIVE into reading. *Teaching Exceptional Children, 29*(6), 68–70.

Salend, S. J. (2001). Creating your own professional portfolio. *Intervention in School and Clinic, 36*, 195–201.

Salend, S. J., & Allen, E. M. (1985). A comparison of self-managed response-cost systems on learning disabled children. *Journal of School Psychology, 23*, 59–67.

Salend, S. J., Dorney, J. A., & Mazo, M. (1997). The roles of bilingual special educators in creating inclusive classrooms. *Remedial and Special Education, 16*(5), 271–278.

Salend, S. J., & Duhaney, L. G. (1999). The impact of inclusion on students with and without disabilities and their educators. *Remedial and Special Education, 20*(2), 114–126.

Salend, S. J., Elhoweris, H., & van Garderen, D. (2003). Educational interventions for students with ADD. *Intervention in School and Clinic, 38*, 280–288.

Salend, S. J., & Garrick Duhaney, L. M. (2002a). Grading students in inclusive settings. *Teaching Exceptional Children, 34*(3), 8–15.

Salend, S. J., & Garrick Duhaney, L. M. (2002b). What do families have to say about inclusion?: How to pay attention and get results. *Teaching Exceptional Children, 35*(1), 62–66.

Salend, S. J., Garrick Duhaney, L. M., & Montgomery, W. (2002). A comprehensive approach to identifying and addressing issues of disproportionate representation. *Remedial and Special Education, 23*, 289–299.

Salend, S.J., Gordon, J., & Lopez-Vona, K. (2002). Evaluating cooperative teaching teams. *Intervention in School and Clinic, 37*, 195–200.

Salend, S. J., & Lamb, E. M. (1986). The effectiveness of a group-managed interdependent contingency system. *Learning Disability Quarterly, 9*, 268–274.

Salend, S. J., & Rohena, E. (2003). Students with attention deficit disorders: An overview. *Intervention in School and Clinic, 38*, 259–266.

Salend, S. J., & Salinas, A. (2003). Language differences or learning difficulties: The work of the multidisciplinary team. *Teaching Exceptional Children, 35*(4), 36–43.

Salinger, T. (2003). Helping older, struggling readers. *Preventing School Failure, 47*, 79–85.

Salisbury, C. L., Evans, I. M., & Palombaro, M. M. (1997). Collaborative problem solving to promote the inclusion of young children with significant disabilities in primary grades. *Exceptional Children, 63*(2), 195–209.

Salisbury, C. L., & McGregor, G. (2002). The administrative climate and context of inclusive elementary schools. *Exceptional Children, 68*, 259–274.

Sanacore, J. (1999). Encouraging children to make choices about their literacy learning. *Intervention in School and Clinic, 35*(1), 38–42.

Sanacore, J. (2002). Questions often asked about promoting lifetime literacy efforts. *Intervention in School and Clinic, 37*, 163–167.

Sander, N. (1993). *So you have asthma too!* Research Triangle, NC: Allen & Hanburys.

Sandler, A. G. (1998). Grandparents of children with disabilities: A closer look. *Education and Training in Mental Retardation and Developmental Disabilities, 33*(4), 350–356.

Sands, D. J., Adams, L., & Stout, D. M. (1995). A statewide exploration of the nature and use of curriculum in special education. *Exceptional Children, 62*(1), 68–83.

Santos, K. E., & Rettig, M. D. (1999). Going on the block: Meeting the needs of students with disabilities in high schools with block scheduling. *Teaching Exceptional Children, 31*(3), 54–59.

Santos, R. M., Fowler, S. A., Corso, R. M., & Bruns, D. (2000). Acceptance, acknowledgment and adaptability: Selecting culturally and linguistically appropriate early childhood materials. *Teaching Exceptional Children, 32*(3), 30–37.

Santos, R. M., Lee, S., Validivia, R., & Zhang, C. (2001). Translating translations: Selecting and using translated early childhood materials. *Teaching Exceptional Children, 34*(2), 26–31.

Sapon-Shevin, M. (1999). *Because we can change the world: A practical guide to building cooperative, inclusive classroom communities.* Boston: Allyn & Bacon.

Sapon-Shevin, M. (2001). Schools fit for all. *Educational Leadership, 58*(4), 34–39.

Sapon-Shevin, M. (2003). Inclusion: A matter of social justice. *Educational Leadership, 61*(2), 25–28.

Sarouphim, K. M. (1999). Discovering multiple intelligence through a performance based assessment: Consistency with independent ratings. *Exceptional Children, 65*(2), 151–161.

Saunders, M. D. (2001). Who's getting the message? Helping your students understand in a verbal world. *Teaching Exceptional Children, 33*(4), 70–75.

Saunders, W., O'Brien, G., Lennon, D., & McLean, J. (1998). Making the transition to English literacy successful: Effective strategies for studying literature with transition students. In R. Gersten & R. Jimenez (Eds.), *Effective strategies for teaching language minority students* (pp. 99–131). Monterey, CA: Brooks/Cole.

Sax, C. L., & Thoma, C. A. (2002). *Transition assessment: Wise practices for quality lives.* Baltimore, MD: Brookes Publishing.

Scanlon, D. (2002). Proving what they know: Using a learning strategy in an inclusive classroom. *Teaching Exceptional Children, 34*(4), 50–54.

Scanlon, D., & Mellard, D. F. (2002). Academic and participation profiles of school-age dropouts with and without disabilities. *Exceptional Children, 68*, 239–258.

Scanlon, D. J., Deshler, D. D., & Schumaker, J. B. (1996). Can a strategy be taught and learned in secondary inclusive classrooms? *Learning Disabilities Research and Practice, 11*(1), 41–57.

Schaps, E. (2003). Creating a school community. *Educational Leadership, 60*(6), 31–33.

Schemo, D. J. (2001, July 20). U.S. schools turn more segregated, a study shows. *The New York Times,* A14.

Scheuermann, B., & Johns, B. (2002). Advocacy for students with emotional or behavioral disorders in the 21st century. *Behavioral Disorders, 28,* 57–69.

Schiff-Meyers, N. B., Djukic, J., McGovern-Lawler, J., & Perez, J. (1993). Assessment considerations in the evaluation of second-language learners: A case study. *Exceptional Children, 60,* 237–248.

Schirmer, B. R. (2004). Hearing loss. In R. Turnbull, A. Turnbull, M. Shank, & S. Smith (Eds.), *Exceptional lives: Special education in today's schools* (4th ed., pp. 424–454). Upper Saddle River, NJ: Merrill/Prentice Hall.

Schirmer, B. R., & Bailey, J. (2000). Writing assessment rubric: An instructional approach with struggling writers. *Teaching Exceptional Children, 33*(1), 52–58.

Schirmer, B. R., & Lockman, A. S. (2001). How do I find a book to read? Middle and high school students use a rubric for self-selecting material for independent reading. *Teaching Exceptional Children, 34*(1), 36–42.

Schlozman, S. C. (2001). Too sad to learn? *Educational Leadership, 59*(1), 80–81.

Schlozman, S. C. (2002a). An explosive debate: The bipolar child. *Educational Leadership, 60*(3), 89–90.

Schlozman, S. C. (2002b). Feast or famine. *Educational Leadership, 59*(6), 86–87.

Schlozman, S. C. (2002c). The jitters. *Educational Leadership, 59*(4), 82–83.

Schlozman, S. C., & Schlozman, V. R. (2000). Chaos in the classroom: Looking at ADHD. *Educational Leadership, 58*(3), 28–33.

Schmid, R. E. (1998). Three steps to self-discipline. *Teaching Exceptional Children, 30*(4), 36–39.

Schmidt, R. J., Rozendal, M. S., & Greenman, G. G. (2002). Reading instruction in the inclusion classroom: Research-based practices. *Remedial and Special Education, 23,* 130–140.

Schmitt, E. (2001a, March 13). For 7 million people in census, one race category isn't enough. *The New York Times,* A1, A14.

Schmitt, E. (2001b, May 15). For first time, nuclear families drop below 25% of households. *The New York Times,* A1, A20.

Schnapp, L., & Olsen, C. (2003). Teaching self-advocating strategies through drama. *Intervention in School and Clinic, 38,* 211–219.

Schniedewind, N., & Davidson, E. (1998). *Open minds to equality: A sourcebook of learning activities to affirm diversity and promote equity* (2nd ed.). Boston: Allyn & Bacon.

Schniedewind, N., & Davidson, E. (2000). Differentiating cooperative learning. *Educational Leadership, 58*(1), 24–27.

Schnur, B. (1999). A newcomer's high school. *Educational Leadership, 56*(7), 50–52.

Schoen, S. F., & Bullard, M. (2002). Action research during recess: A time for children with autism to play and learn. *Teaching Exceptional Children, 35*(1), 36–39.

Schoen, S. F., & Schoen, A. A. (2003). Action research in the classroom: Assisting a linguistically different learner with special needs. *Teaching Exceptional Children, 35*(3), 16–21.

Schoenbrodt, L., Kumin, L., & Sloan, J. M. (1997). Learning disabilities existing concomitantly with communication disorder. *Journal of Learning Disabilities, 30*(3), 264–281.

Scholastic Press. (2002). *Hip Kid Hop.* New York: Author.

Schon, I. (2000). Recent children's books about Latinos. *Book Links, 9*(1), 37–41.

School Board of Nassau County, Florida et al. v. Arline, 480 U.S. 273 (1987).

Schorr, J. (1997, January 2). Give Oakland's schools a break. *The New York Times,* A19.

Schrumpf, F., Crawford, D. K., & Bodine, R. J. (1997). *Peer mediation: Conflict resolution in schools program guide* (Rev. ed.). Champaign, IL: Research Press.

Schulz, E. G., & Edwards, E. G. (1997). Stimulant medication management of students with attention deficit hyperactivity disorder: What educators need to know. *Teacher Education and Special Education, 20*(2), 170–178.

Schumaker, J. B., Deshler, D. D., Alley, G. R., & Warner, M. M. (1983). Toward the development of an intervention model for learning disabled adolescents: The University of Kansas Institute. *Exceptional Education Quarterly, 4,* 45–74.

Schumaker, J. B., Deshler, D. D., Denton, P. H., Alley, G. R., Clark, F. L., & Warner, M. M. (1982). Multipass: A learning strategy for improving reading comprehension. *Learning Disability Quarterly, 5,* 295–304.

Schumaker, J. B., Deshler, D. D., Nolan, S. M., & Alley, G. R. (1994). *The self-questioning strategy,* Lawrence: University of Kansas.

Schumaker, J. B., Nolan, S. M., & Deshler, D. (1985). *Learning strategies curriculum: The error monitoring strategy.* Lawrence: University of Kansas Press.

Schwartz, A. A., Jacobson, J. W., & Holburn, S. C. (2000). Defining person centeredness: Results of two consensus methods. *Education and Training in Mental Retardation and Developmental Disabilities, 35,* 235–249.

Schwartz, W. (1997, May). *Strategies for identifying the talents of diverse students.* New York: ERIC Clearinghouse on Urban Education.

Schwartz, W. (2001, September). *School practices for equitable discipline of African American students.* New York: ERIC Clearinghouse on Urban Education.

Schwarz, S. P. (1995). *Dressing tips and clothing resources for making life easier.* Madison, WI: Author.

Schweinhart, L., & Weikart, D. (1993). *The High/Scope Perry preschool project.* Ypsilanti, MI: High/Scope Educational Research Foundation.

Scott, B. J., & Vitale, M. R. (2003). Teaching the writing process to students with LD. *Intervention in School and Clinic, 38,* 220–225.

Scott, J. (2002, February 7). Foreign born in U.S. at record high. *The New York Times,* A26.

Scott, P. B., & Raborn, D. T. (1996). Realizing the gifts of diversity among students with learning disabilities. *LD Forum, 21*(2), 10–18.

Scott, S. L. (2002, Winter). Diversity and the structure of public education. *The State Education Standard,* 25–29.

Scott, S. S., McGuire, J. M., & Shaw, S. F. (2003). Universal design for instruction: A new paradigm for adult instruction in postsecondary education. *Remedial and Special Education, 24,* 369–379.

Scott, T. M., Liaupsin, C. J., Nelson, C. M., & Jolivette, K. (2003). Ensuring student success through team-based functional behavioral assessment. *Teaching Exceptional Children, 35*(5), 16–21.

Scott, V. G., & Weishaar, M. K. (2003). Curriculum-based measurement for reading progress. *Intervention in School and Clinic, 38*, 153–159.

Seattle School District No 1 v. B. S., 82 F.3d 1493 (9th Cir. 1996).

Seif, E. (2004). Social studies revived. *Educational Leadership, 61*(4), 54–59.

Serafini, F. W. (2002). Dismantling the factory model of assessment. *Reading and Writing Quarterly: Overcoming Learning Difficulties, 18*, 67–86.

Serna, L. A., & Lau-Smith, J. (1995). Learning with purpose: Self-determination skills for students who are at risk for school and community failure. *Intervention in School and Clinic, 30*(3), 142–146.

Serry, M. E., Davis, P. M., & Johnson, L. J. (2000). Seeing eye-to-eye: Are parents and professionals in agreement about the benefits of preschool inclusion? *Remedial and Special Education, 21*, 268–278, 319.

Sewall, A. M., & Balkman, K. (2002). DNR orders and school responsibility: New legal concerns and questions. *Remedial and Special Education, 23*, 7–14.

Sexton, M., Harris, K. R., & Graham, S. (1998). Self-regulated strategy development and the writing process: Effects on essay writing and attributions. *Exceptional Children, 64*(3), 295–311.

Shafer, G. (2001). Standard English and the migrant community. *English Journal, 90*(4), 37–43.

Shank, K. S., & Hooser, C. M. (1999, April). *Curriculum adaptations in general education settings: Creating effective learning environments for all students.* Presentation at the annual meeting of the Council for Exceptional Children, Charlotte, NC.

Shapiro, A. (1999). *Everyone belongs: Changing negative attitudes toward classmates with disabilities.* New York: RoutledgeFalmer.

Shapiro, D. R., & Sayers, L. K. (2003). Who does what on the interdisciplinary team regarding physical education for students with disabilities? *Teaching Exceptional Children, 35*(6), 32–38.

Sharpe, M. N., York, J. L., & Knight, J. (1994). Effects of inclusion on the academic performance of classmates without disabilities. *Remedial and Special Education, 15*(5), 281–287.

Shelton, C. M. (2000). Portraits in emotional awareness. *Educational Leadership, 58*(1), 30–32.

Sheras, P. L., & Tippins, S. (2002). *Your child: Bully or victim? Understanding and ending schoolyard tyranny.* New York: Fireside.

Shinn, M. R., Powell-Smith, K. A., Good, R. H., & Baker, S. (1997). The effects of reintegration into general education reading instruction for students with mild disabilities. *Exceptional Children, 64*, 59–79.

Shippen, M. E., Simpson, R. G., & Crites, S. A. (2003). A practical guide to functional behavioral assessment. *Teaching Exceptional Children, 35*(5), 36–44.

Shriner, J. G. (2000). Legal perspectives on school outcomes assessment for students with disabilities. *The Journal of Special Education, 33*, 232–239.

Shriner, J. G., & DeStefano, L. (2003). Participation and accommodation in state assessment: The role of individualized education programs. *Exceptional Children, 69*, 147–162.

Shukla-Mehta, S., & Albin, R. W. (2003). Twelve pratical strategies to prevent behavioral escalation in classroom settings. *Preventing School Failure, 47*, 156–161.

Siegel-Causey, E., McMorris, C., McGowen, S., & Sands-Buss, S. (1998). In junior high you take science: Including a student with severe disabilities in an academic class. *Teaching Exceptional Children, 31*(1), 66–72.

Simone, G. (2001). Space to learn. *Educational Leadership, 59*(1), 66–70.

Sinclair, M. F., Christenson, S. L., Evelo, D. L., & Hurley, C. M. (1998). Dropout prevention for youth with disabilities: Efficacy of a sustained school engagement procedure. *Exceptional Children, 65*(1), 7–21.

Singer, G. H. S. (2002). Suggestions for a programatic program of research on families and disability. *The Journal of Special Education, 36*, 148–154.

Singh, G. R. (2001). How character education helps students grow. *Educational Leadership, 59*(2), 46–49.

Siperstein, G. N., & Leffert, J. S. (1999). Managing limited resources: Do children with learning problems share? *Exceptional Children, 65*(2), 187–199.

Skelton, M., Wigford, A., Harper, P., & Reeves, G. (2002). Beyond food, festivals, and flags. *Educational Leadership, 60*(2), 52–55.

Skinner, M. E., & Lindstrom, B. D. (2003). Bridging the gap between high school and college: Strategies for the successful transition of students with learning disabilities. *Preventing School Failure, 47*, 132–137.

Skutch, R. (1995). *Who's in the family?* Berkeley, CA: Tricycle Press.

Slavin, R. E. (1990). *Cooperative learning: Theory, research, and practice.* Upper Saddle River, NJ: Prentice Hall.

Slavin, R. E. (1998). Can education reduce social inequity? *Educational Leadership, 55*(4), 6–10.

Sleeter, C. E., & Grant, C. A., (2002). *Making choices for multicultural education: Five approaches to race, class, and gender* (4th ed.). New York: Wiley.

Smart, J. (2001). *Disability, society and the individual.* Gaithersburg, MD: Aspen.

Smead, V. S. (1999). Personal accounts of exceptionality: An untapped resource for child service professionals. *Intervention in School and Clinic, 35*(2), 79–86, 107.

Smith, A. F. (2002). How global is the curriculum? *Educational Leadership, 60*(2), 38–43.

Smith, C. R. (2000). Behavioral and discipline provisions of IDEA 97: Implicit competencies yet to be confirmed. *Exceptional Children, 66*, 403–412.

Smith, D. D., & Lovitt, T. C. (1982). *The computational arithmetic program.* Austin, TX: PRO-ED.

Smith, D. J. (1997). Mental retardation as an educational construct: Time for a new shared view? *Education and Training in Mental Retardation and Developmental Disabilities, 32*(3), 167–173.

Smith, G. A. (2002). Going local. *Educational Leadership, 60*(1), 30–33.

Smith, J. D. (2000). The power of mental retardation: Reflections on the value of people with disabilities. *Mental Retardation, 38*, 70–72.

Smith, R. M. (2002). Inscrutable or meaningful? Understanding and supporting your inarticulate students. *Teaching Exceptional Children, 34*(4), 28–33.

Smith, R. M., Salend, S. J., & Ryan, S. (2001). Watch your language: Closing or opening the special education curtain. *Teaching Exceptional Children, 33*(4), 18–23.

Smith, S., Boone, R., & Higgins, K. (1998). Expanding the writing process to the Web. *Teaching Exceptional Children, 30*(5), 22–26.

Smith, S. J., & Smith, S. B. (2002). On the right track: Technology for organizing and presenting digital information. *Intervention in School and Clinic, 37*, 304–311.

Smith, S. W., & Gilles, D. L. (2003). Using key instructional elements to systematically promote social skill generalization for students with challenging behaviors. *Intervention in School and Clinic, 39*, 30–37.

Smith, T. E. C. (2002). Section 504: What teachers need to know. *Intervention in School and Clinic, 37*, 259–266.

Smith-Davis, J. (2002). World initiatives for inclusive education. *Teaching Exceptional Children, 35*(1), 77.

Smithson, I. (1990). Introduction: Investigating gender, power, and pedagogy. In S. L. Gabriel & I. Smithson (Eds.), *Gender in the classroom: Power and pedagogy* (pp. 1–27). Chicago: University of Illinois Press.

Snell, M. E., & Brown, F. (2000). *Instruction of students with severe disabilities* (5th ed.). Upper Saddle River, NJ: Merrill/Prentice Hall.

Snell, M. E., & Janney, R. E. (2000). Teachers' problem-solving about children with moderate and severe disabilities in elementary classrooms. *Exceptional Children, 66*, 472–490.

Snider, V. E., Busch, T., & Arrowood, L. (2003). Teacher knowledge of stimulant medication and ADHD. *Remedial and Special Education, 24*, 46–56.

Snyder, E. P. (2002). Teaching students with combined behavioral disorders and mental retardation to lead their own IEP meetings. *Behavioral Disorders, 27*, 340–357.

Snyder, L., Garriott, P., & Aylor, M. W. (2001). Inclusion confusion: Putting the pieces together. *Teacher Education and Special Education, 24*, 198–207.

Soodak, L. C., & Ervin, E. J. (2000). Valued member or tolerated participant: Parents' experiences in inclusive early childhood settings. *The Journal of the Association for Persons with Severe Handicaps, 25*, 29–41.

Soodak, L. C., Podell, D. M., & Lehman, L. R. (1998). Teacher, student, and school attributes as predictors of teachers' responses to inclusion. *The Journal of Special Education, 31*, 480–497.

Sparks, S. (2000a). Classroom and curriculum accommodations for Native American students. *Intervention in School and Clinic, 35*, 259–263.

Sparks, S. (2000b). Utilize native American elders in the classroom and school. *Intervention in School and Clinic, 35*, 306–307.

Spear-Swerling, L. & Sternberg, R. J. (2001). What science offers teachers of reading. *Learning Disabilities Research and Practice, 16*, 51–57.

Speece, D. L., Mills, C., Ritchey, K. D., & Hillman, E. (2003). Initial evidence that letter fluency tasks are valid indicators of early reading skill. *The Journal of Special Education, 36*, 223–233.

Spencer, V. G., & Balboni, G. (2003). Can students with mental retardation teach their peers? *Education and Training in Developmental Disabilities, 38*, 32–61.

Spiegel, G. L., Cutler, S. K., & Yetter, C. E. (1996). What every teacher should know about epilepsy. *Intervention in School and Clinic, 32*(1), 34–38.

Sprague, J., & Walker, H. (2000). Early identification and intervention for youth with antisocial and violent behavior. *Exceptional Children, 66*, 367–379.

SRI International. (1993). *Traversing the mainstream: Regular education and students with disabilities in secondary school.* A report from the National Longitudinal Transition Study of Special Education Students. Menlo Park, CA: SRI International.

Staal, L. A. (2001). Writing models: Strategies for writing composition in inclusive settings. *Reading and Writing Quarterly: Overcoming Learning Difficulties, 17*, 243–248.

Stafford, A. M., Alberto, P. A., Fredrick, L. D., Heflin, L. J., & Heller, K. W. (2002). Preference variability and the instruction of choice making with students with severe intellectual disabilities. *Education and Training in Mental Retardation and Developmental Disabilities, 37*, 70–88.

Stahl, S. A. (1998). Teaching children with reading problems to decode: Phonics and 'not-phonics' instruction. *Reading and Writing Quarterly: Overcoming Learning Difficulties, 14*(2), 165–188.

Stainback, S., Stainback, W., East, K., & Sapon-Shevin, M. (1994). A commentary on inclusion and the development of a positive self-identity by people with disabilities. *Exceptional Children, 60*(6), 486–490.

Stanford, P. (2003). Multiple intelligence for every classroom. *Intervention in School and Clinic, 39*, 80–85.

Stanford, P., & Siders, J. A. (2001). E-pal writing. *Teaching Exceptional Children, 34*(2), 21–25.

Stanger, C., Symington, L., Miller, H., & Johns, S. (2000). Teaching number concepts to all students. *Teaching Exceptional Children, 33*(1), 65–69.

Stanovich, P. J. (1999). Conversations about inclusion. *Teaching Exceptional Children, 31*(6), 54–58.

Staub, D. (1998). *Delicate threads: Friendships between children with and without special needs in inclusive settings.* Bethesda, MD: Woodbine House.

Staub, D., Schwartz, I. S., Galluci, C., & Peck, C. A. (1994). Four portraits of friendship at an inclusive school. *Journal of the Association for Persons with Severe Handicaps, 19*(4), 314–325.

Stecker, P. M., & Fuchs, L. S. (2000). Effecting superior achievement using curriculum-based measurement: The importance of individual progress monitoring. *Learning Disabilities Research and Practice, 15*, 128–134.

Steere, D. E., & Cavaiuolo, D. (2002). Connecting outcomes, goals, and objectives in transition planning. *Teaching Exceptional Children, 34*(6), 54–59.

Stein, M., Stuen, C., Carnine, D., & Long, R. M. (2001). Textbook evaluation and adoption practices. *Reading and Writing Quarterly: Overcoming Learning Difficulties, 17*, 5–23.

Stein, N. D., & Cappello, D. (1999). *Gender violence/gender justice: An interdisciplinary teaching guide for teachers of English, literature, social studies, psychology, health, peer counseling, and family and consumer sciences (grades 7–12).* Wellesley, MA: Wellesley Centers for Women.

Steinberg, J. (1998, March 19). Reading experts suggest teachers mix 2 methods. *The New York Times,* A1, A17.

Stephens, H., & Jairrels, V. (2003). Weekend study buddies: Using portable learning centers. *Teaching Exceptional Children, 35*(3), 36–39.

Stephens, K. R., & Karnes, F. A. (2000). State definitions for the gifted and talented revisited. *Exceptional Children, 66*(2), 219–238.

Sternberg, R. J. (1996). Investing in creativity: Many happy returns. *Educational Leadership, 53*(4), 80–84.

Stewart, L. H., & Rope, J. (2001). Homework: Is it worth the effort? *CEC Today 8*(1), 12.

Stolberg, S. G. (1998, June 29). Eyes shut, black America is being ravaged by AIDS. *The New York Times,* A1, A12.

Stone, C. A., & May, A. L. (2002). The accuracy of academic self-evaluations in adolescents with learning disabilities. *Journal of Learning Disabilities, 35*, 370–383.

Stormont-Spurgin, M. (1997). I lost my homework: Strategies for improving organization in students with ADHD. *Intervention in School and Clinic, 32*(5), 270–274.

Stough, L. M. (2002). Teaching special education in Costa Rica: Using a learning strategy in an inclusive classroom. *Teaching Exceptional Children, 34*(5), 34–39.

Stough, L. M., & Baker, L. (1999). Identifying depression in students with mental retardation. *Teaching Exceptional Children, 31*(4), 62–66.

Strassman, B. K., & D'Amore, M. (2002). The write technology. *Teaching Exceptional Children, 34*(6), 28–31.

Strichart, S., & Mangrum, C. T. (2002). *Teaching learning strategies and study skills to students with learning disabilities, attention deficit disorders or special needs* (3rd ed.). Boston: Allyn & Bacon.

Strong, K., & Sandoval, J. (1999). Mainstreaming children with neuromuscular disease: A map of concerns. *Exceptional Children, 65*(3), 353–366.

Strong, M. F., & Maralani, V. J. (1998). *Farmworkers and disability: Results of a national survey.* Austin, TX: National Center for Farmworkers Health.

Stroud, J. E., Stroud, J. E., & Staley, L. M. (1997). Understanding and supporting adoptive families. *Early Childhood Education Journal, 24*(4), 229–234.

Stuart, J. L., & Goodsitt, J. L. (1996). From hospital to school: How a transition liaison can help. *Teaching Exceptional Children, 28*(2), 58–62.

Stuart, S. K. (2003). Choice or chance: Career development and girls with emotional or behavioral disorders. *Behavioral Disorders, 28*, 150–161.

Students for Social Justice. (n.d.). Being gay at Greeley. *Left Is Right, 2*(1), 1–4.

Sturm, J. M., Rankin, J. L., Beukelman, D. R., & Schutz-Muehling, L. (1997). How to select appropriate software for computer-assisted writing. *Intervention in School and Clinic, 32*(3), 148–161.

Sturm, J. M., & Rankin-Erickson, J. L. (2002). Effects of hand-drawn and computer-generated concept mapping on the expository writing of middle school students with learning disabilities. *Learning Disabilities Research and Practice, 17*, 124–139.

Sugai, G., & Horner, R. H. (1999–2000). Including the functional behavioral assessment technology in schools. *Exceptionality, 8*, 145–148.

Sugai, G., & Horner, R. H. (2001). Features of an effective behavior support at the school district level. *Beyond Behavior, 11*(1), 16–19.

Sugai, G., Horner, R. H., & Sprague, J. R. (1999). Functional-assessment-based behavior support planning: Research to practice to research. *Behavioral Disorders, 24*(3), 253–257.

Sugai, G., Lewis-Palmer, T., & Hagan-Burke, S. (1999–2000). Overview of the functional behavioral process. *Exceptionality, 8*, 149–160.

Sugai, G., & Smith, P. (1986). The equal additions method of subtraction taught with a modeling technique. *Remedial and Special Education, 7*, 40–48.

Summers, L., Mikell, S., Redmond, S., Roberts, D., & Hampton, J. (1997, April). *Educating the student with muscular dystrophy: A collaborative approach.* Presentation at the annual meeting of the Council for Exceptional Children, Salt Lake City, UT.

Suritsky, S. K., & Hughes, C. A. (1996). Notetaking strategy instruction. In D. D. Deshler, E. S. Ellis, & B. K. Lenz (Eds.), *Teaching adolescents with learning disabilities: Strategies and methods* (2nd ed, pp. 267–312). Denver: Love.

Sutherland, K. S., Alder, N., & Gunter, P. L. (2003). The effect of varying rates of opportunities to respond to academic requests on the classroom behavior of students with EBD. *Journal of Emotional and Behavioral Disorders, 11*, 239–248.

Sutherland, K. S., & Wehby, J. A. (2001). Exploring the relationship between increased opportunities to respond to academic requests and the academic and behavioral outcomes of students with EBD: A review. *Remedial and Special Education, 22*, 113–121.

Sutherland, K. S., Wehby, J. A., & Yoder, P. J. (2002). Examination of the relationship between teacher praise and opportunities for students with EBD to respond to academic requests. *Journal of Emotional and Behavioral Disorders, 10*, 5–13.

Swaggart, B. L. (1998). Implementing a cognitive behavior management program. *Intervention in School and Clinic, 33*(4), 235–238.

Swanson, H. L., & Deshler, D. (2003). Instructing adolescents with learning disabilities: Converting a meta-analysis to practice. *Journal of Learning Disabilities, 36*, 124–135.

Swanson, H. L., & Hoskyn, M. (2001). Instructing adolescents with learning disabilities: A component and composite analysis. *Learning Disabilities Research and Practice, 16*, 109–119.

Sweeney, D. P., Forness, S. R., Kavale, K., & Levitt, J. G. (1997). An update on psychopharmacologic medication: What teachers, clinicians, and parents need to know. *Intervention in School and Clinic, 33*(1), 4–21, 25.

Swicegood, P. R. (1994). Portfolio-based assessment practices. *Intervention in School and Clinic, 30*(1), 6–15.

Swisher, K. G., & Tippiconnic, J. W. (1999). *Next steps: Research and practice to advance Indian education.* (ERIC Clearinghouse on Rural Education & Small Schools ED 1.310/:427902).

Symington, L., & Stanger, C. (2000). New inclusionary math software programs add up to a bright future. *Teaching Exceptional Children, 32*(4), 28–32.

Symons, F. J., Clark, R. D., Roberts, J. P., & Bailey, D. B. (2001). Classroom behavior of elementary school-age boys with fragile X syndrome. *The Journal of Special Education, 34*, 194–202.

Szabo, J. L. (2000). Maddie's story: Inclusion through physical and occupational therapy. *Teaching Exceptional Children, 33*(2), 12–19.

Tam, K. Y., Nassivera, J. W., Rousseau, M. K., & Vreeland, P. (2000). More than just a field trip: Using the museum as a resource for inclusive secondary science classrooms. *Teaching Exceptional Children, 33*(1), 70–78.

Tankersley, M. (1995). A group-contingency management program: A review of research on the good behavior game and implications for teachers. *Preventing School Failure, 40*(1), 19–24.

Tanner, C. K. (2001). Into the woods, wetlands, and prairies. *Educational Leadership, 58*(7), 64–66.

Tannock, R., & Martinussen, R. (2001). Reconceptualizing ADHD. *Educational Leadership, 59*(3), 20–25.

Tao, L., & Boulware, B. (2002). E-mail: Instructional potentials and learning opportunities. *Reading and Writing Quarterly: Overcoming Learning Difficulties, 18*, 285–288.

Tatum, B. (2000, May). *Children, race and racism: What concerned adults should know.* Presentation at the Multicultural Education Conference, New Paltz, NY.

Taunt, H. M., & Hastings, R. P. (2002). Positive impact of children with developmental disabilities on their families. *Education and Training in Mental Retardation and Developmental Disabilities, 37,* 399–410.

Taylor, D., & Lorimer, M. (2003). Helping boys succeed. *Educational Leadership, 60*(4), 68–70.

Taylor, J. A., & Baker, R. A. (2002). Discipline and the special education student. *Educational Leadership, 59*(4), 28–30.

Taylor, K. L. (2003). Through the eyes of students. *Educational Leadership, 60*(4), 72–75.

Taylor, L. S. (1992). *Adult remedial mathematics: Diagnostic and teaching strategies.* Manuscript submitted for publication.

Taylor, L. S., & Whittaker, C. R. (2003). *Bridging multiple worlds: Case studies of diverse educational communities.* Boston: Allyn & Bacon.

Taylor, S. (2000). Multicultural is who we are: Literature as a reflection of ourselves. *Teaching Exceptional Children, 32*(3), 24–29.

Taymans, J. M., & West, L. L. (2001, December). *Selecting a college for students with learning disabilities or attention deficit hyperactivity disorder (ADHD).* Arlington, VA: ERIC Clearinghouse on Disabilities and Gifted Education.

Teicher, J. (1999). An action plan for smart Internet use. *Educational Leadership, 56*(5), 70–74.

Teicher, M. H. (2002, March). Scars that won't heal: The neurobiology of child abuse. *Scientific American,* 68–75.

Tekin, E., & Kirgaali-Iftar, G. (2002). Comparison of the effectiveness and efficiency of two response prompting procedures delivered by sibling tutors. *Education and Training in Mental Retardation and Developmental Disabilities, 37,* 283–299.

Telzrow, C. F., & Bonar, A. M. (2002). Responding to students with nonverbal learning disabilities. *Teaching Exceptional Children, 34*(6), 8–13.

Test, D. W., Browder, D. M., Karvonen, M., Wood, W., & Algozzine, B. (2002). Writing lesson plans for promoting self-determination. *Teaching Exceptional Children, 35*(1), 8–15.

Thoma, C. A. (1999). Supporting student voice in transition planning. *Teaching Exceptional Children, 31*(5), 4–9.

Thoma, C. A., Nathanson, R., Baker, S. R., & Tamura, R. (2002). Self-determination: What do special educators know and where do they learn it? *Remedial and Special Education, 23,* 242–247.

Thoma, C. A., Rogan, P., & Baker, S. R. (2001). Student involvement in transition planning: Unheard voices. *Education and Training in Mental Retardation and Developmental Disabilities, 36,* 42–54.

Thomas, C., Correa, V. I., & Morsink, C. V. (2001). *Interactive teaming: Enhancing programs for students with special needs* (3rd ed.). Upper Saddle River, NJ: Merrill/Prentice Hall.

Thomas, S. B. (2000). College students and disability law. *Journal of Special Education, 33*(4), 248–257.

Thomas, S. B., & Hawke, C. (1999). Health-care services for children with disabilities: Emerging standards and implications. *Journal of Special Education, 32*(4), 226–237.

Thomas, S. B., & Rapport, M. J. K. (1998). The least restrictive environment: Understanding the directions of the courts. *The Journal of Special Education, 32*(2), 66–78.

Thomas, W. P., & Collier, V. P. (1997). *School effectiveness for language minority students.* Washington, DC: National Clearinghouse for Bilingual Education.

Thomas, W. P., & Collier, V. P. (2003). The mutual benefits of dual language. *Educational Leadership, 61*(2), 61–64.

Thompson, C. D., & Wiggins, M. F. (2002). *The human cost of food: Farmworkers' lives, labor, and advocacy.* Austin, TX: University of Texas Press.

Thompson, K. L., & Taymans, J. M. (1994). Development of a reading strategies program: Bridging the gaps among decoding, literature, and thinking skills. *Intervention in School and Clinic, 30*(1), 17–27.

Thompson, S. J., Johnstone, C. J., & Thurlow, M. L. (2002) *Universal design applied to large scale assessments (Synthesis Report 44).* Minneapolis, MN: University of Minnesota, National Center on Educational Outcomes.

Thompson, S. J., Thurlow, M. L., Quenemoen, R. F., & Lehr, C. A. (2002). *Access to computer-based testing for students with disabilities (Synthesis Report 45).* Minneapolis, MN: University of Minnesota, National Center on Educational Outcomes.

Thoms, K. J. (1999). Teaching via ITV: Taking instructional design to the next level. *The Journal, 26*(9), 60–66.

Thorp, E. K. (1997). Increasing opportunities for partnership with culturally and linguistically diverse families. *Intervention in School and Clinic, 32*(5), 261–269.

Thousand, J. S., Rosenberg, R. L., Bishop, K. D., & Villa, R. A. (1997). The evolution of secondary inclusion. *Remedial and Special Education, 18*(5), 270–284, 306.

Thurlow, M. L. (2002). Positive educational results for all students: The promise of standards-based reform. *Remedial and Special Education, 23,* 195–202.

Thurlow, M. L., Elliott, J. L., & Ysseldyke, J. E. (2003). *Testing students with disabilities: Practical strategies for complying with district and state requirements.* Thousand Oaks, CA: Corwin Press.

Thurlow, M. L., House, A. L., Scott, D. L., & Ysseldyke, J. E. (2000). Students with disabilities in large-scale assessments: State participation and accommodation policies. *The Journal of Special Education, 34,* 154–163.

Tiedt, P. L., & Tiedt, I. (2002). *Multicultural teaching: A handbook of activities, information, and resources* (6th ed.). Boston: Allyn & Bacon.

Tilley-Gregory, D. (2004). How to improve your students' auditory processing skills. *CEC Today, 10*(5), 16.

Timothy W. v. Rochester, N.H. Sch. Dist., 875 F.2d 954, 1st Circuit, 1989.

Tindal, G., Heath, B., Hollenbeck, K., Almond, P., & Harniss, M. (1998). Accommodating students with disabilities on large-scale tests: An experimental study. *Exceptional Children, 64*(4), 439–450.

Tobias, T. (1977). *Easy or hard? That's a good question.* Chicago: Children's Press.

Tobin, T. J., & Sugai, G. M. (1999). Using sixth-grade school records to predict school violence, chronic discipline problems, and high school outcomes. *Journal of Emotional and Behavioral Disorders, 7*(1), 40–53.

Tolla, J. (2000). Follow the bear: Encouraging mobility in a young child with visual impairment and multiple disabilities. *Teaching Exceptional Children, 32*(5), 72–77.

Tomlinson, C. A. (2000). Reconcilable differences: Standards-based teaching and differentiation. *Educational Leadership, 58*(1), 6–11.

Tomlinson, C.A. (2001). Grading for success. *Educational Leadership, 58*(6), 12–15.

Tomlinson, C. A. (2002). Invitations to learn. *Educational Leadership, 60*(1), 6–10.

Tomlinson, C. A. (2003). Deciding to teach them all. *Educational Leadership, 61*(2), 6–11.

Tomlinson, C. A., & Eidson, C. C. (2003). *Differentiate in practice: A resource guide for differentiating curriculum.* Alexandria, VA: Association for Supervision and Curriculum Development.

Tompkins, G. E. (2002). Struggling readers are struggling writers, too. *Reading and Writing Quarterly: Overcoming Learning Difficulties, 18,* 175–194.

Tompkins, G. E. (2003). *Literacy for the 21st century* (3rd ed.). Upper Saddle River, NJ: Merrill/Prentice-Hall.

Torgesen, J. K. (2000). Individual differences in response to early interventions in reading: The lingering problem of treatment resisters. *Learning Disabilities Research and Practice, 15*(1), 55–64.

Torgerson, C. W., Miner, C. A., & Shen, H. (2004). Developing student competence in self-directed IEPs. *Intervention in School and Clinic, 39,* 162–167.

Tournaki, N. (2003). The differential effects of teaching addition through strategy instruction versus drill and practice to students with and without learning disabilities. *Journal of Learning Disabilities, 36,* 449–458.

Tournaki, N., & Criscitiello, E. (2003). Using peer tutoring as a successful part of behavior management. *Teaching Exceptional Children, 36*(2), 22–29.

Townsend, B. L. (2000). The disproportionate discipline of African American learners: Reducing school suspensions and expulsions. *Exceptional Children, 66,* 381–391.

Townsend, B. L. (2002). "Testing while black": Standards-based school reform and African American learners. *Remedial and Special Education, 23,* 222–230.

Trautman, M. L. (2003). Identify and reduce bullying in your classroom. *Intervention in School and Clinic, 38,* 243–246.

Trautman, M. L. (2004). Preparing and managing paraprofessionals. *Intevention in School and Clinic, 39,* 131–138.

Troia, G. A., & Graham, S. (2002). The effectiveness of a highly explicit, teacher-directed strategy instruction routine: Changing the writing performance of students with learning disabilities. *Journal of Learning Disabilities, 35,* 290–306.

Trollinger, G., & Slavkin, R. (1999). Purposeful e-mail as stage 3 technology: IEP goals online. *Teaching Exceptional Children, 32*(1), 10–15.

Tucker, B. F., Singleton, A. H., & Weaver, T. L. (2002). *Teaching mathematics to all children: Designing and adapting instruction to meet the needs of diverse learners.* Upper Saddle River, NJ: Merrill/Prentice Hall.

Tucker, D. L., & Bakken, J. P. (2000). How do your kids do at reading? And how do you assess them? *Teaching Exceptional Children, 32*(6), 14–19.

Tur-Kaspa, H. (2002). The socioemotional adjustment of adolescents with learning disabilites in the Kibbutz during high school transition periods. *Journal of Learning Disabilities, 35,* 87–96.

Turnbull, A., Edmonson, H., Griggs, P., Wickham, D., Sailor, W., Freeman, R., Guess, D., Lassen, S., McCart, A., Park, J., Riffel, L., Turnbull, R., & Warren, J. (2002). A blueprint for schoolwide positive behavior support: Implementation of three components. *Exceptional Children, 68,* 377–402.

Turnbull, A., Pereira, L., & Blue-Banning, M. (2000). Teachers as friendship facilitator: Respeto and personalismo. *Teaching Exceptional Children, 32*(5), 66–71.

Turnbull, R., Turnbull, A., Shank, M., & Smith, S. (2004). *Exceptional lives: Special education in today's schools* (4th ed.). Upper Saddle River, NJ: Merrill/Prentice Hall.

Turnbull, R., Turnbull, A., Wehmeyer, M. L., & Park, J. (2003). A quality of life framework for special education outcomes. *Remedial and Special Education, 24,* 67–74.

Uberti, H. Z., Scruggs, T. E., & Mastropieri, M. A. (2003). Keywords make the difference! Mnemonic instruction in inclusive classrooms. *Teaching Exceptional Children, 35*(3), 56–61.

Udell, T., Peters, J., & Templeman, T. P. (1998). From philosophy to practice in early childhood programs. *Teaching Exceptional Children, 30*(3), 44–49.

Ulrich, M. E., & Bauer, A. M. (2003). Levels of awareness: A closer look at communication between parents and professionals. *Teaching Exceptional Children, 35*(6), 20–25.

U.S. Department of Education. (1995). *Seventeenth annual report to Congress on the implementation of the Individuals with Disabilities Education Act.* Washington, DC: U.S. Government Printing Office.

U.S. Department of Education. (1996). *Eighteenth annual report to Congress on the implementation of the Individuals with Disabilities Education Act.* Washington, DC: U.S. Government Printing Office.

U.S. Department of Education. (1997). *Nineteenth annual report to Congress on the implementation of the Individuals with Disabilities Education Act.* Washington, DC: U.S. Government Printing Office.

U.S. Department of Education. (1998). *Twentieth annual report to Congress on the implementation of the Individuals with Disabilities Education Act.* Washington, DC: U.S. Government Printing Office.

U.S. Department of Education. (2001). *Twenty-third annual report to Congress on the implementation of the Individuals with Disabilities Education Act.* Washington, DC: U.S. Government Printing Office.

Vacca, D. M. (2001). Confronting the puzzle of nonverbal learning disabilities. *Educational Leadership, 59*(3), 26–31.

Vacca, R. T. (2002). From efficient decoders to strategic readers. *Educational Leadership, 60*(3), 6–11.

Vacca, R. T., & Vacca, J. L. (2001). *Content area reading: Literacy and learning across the curriculum* (7th ed.). Boston: Allyn & Bacon.

Vadasy, P. F., Sanders, E. A., Peyton, J. A., & Jenkins, J. R. (2002). Timing and intensity of tutoring: A closer look at the conditions for effective early literacy training. *Learning Disabilities Research and Practice, 17,* 227–241.

Valle, J. W., & Aponte, E. (2002). IDEA and collaboration: A Bakhtinian perspective on parent and professional discourse. *Journal of Learning Disabilities, 35,* 469–479.

Van Dycke, J. L., & Peterson, L. Y. (2003). Eight steps to help students develop IEP goals. *CEC Today, 10*(4), 13.

Van Garderen, D., & Montague, M. (2003). Visual-spatial representation, mathematical problem solving, and students of varying abilities. *Learning Disabilities Research and Practice, 18,* 246–254.

Van Reusen, A. K., Bos, C. S. (1994). Facilitating student participation in individualized education programs through motivation strategy instruction. *Exceptional Children, 60,* 466–475.

Vargo, S. (1998). Consulting teacher-to-teacher. *Teaching Exceptional Children, 30*(3), 54–55.

Vaughn, S., Bos, C. S., & Lund, K. A. (1986). . . . But they can do it in my room: Strategies for promoting generalization. *Teaching Exceptional Children, 18*, 176–180.

Vaughn, S., Elbaum, B. E., & Schumm, J. S. (1996). The effects of inclusion on the social functioning of students with learning disabilities. *Journal of Learning Disabilities, 29*, 598–608.

Vaughn, S., & Klingner, J. K. (1998). Students' perceptions of inclusion and resource room settings. *The Journal of Special Education, 32*(2), 79–88.

Vernon, D. S., Schumaker, J. B., & Deshler, D. D. (1995). Programs to teach cooperation and teamwork. *Intervention in School and Clinic, 31*(2), 121–125.

Villa, R. A., & Thousand, J. S. (2000). Setting the context: History of and rationales for inclusive schooling. In R. A. Villa & J. S. Thousand (Eds.), *Restructuring for caring and effective education: Piecing the puzzle together* (pp. 7–37). Baltimore: Brookes.

Villa, R. A., Thousand, J. S., Meyers, H., & Nevin, A. (1996). Teacher and administrator perceptions of heterogeneous education. *Exceptional Children, 63*(1), 29–45.

Vitek, K. (November 4, 2003). *Web cameras in the classroom.* Presentation at the State University of New York at New Paltz, New Paltz, NY.

Voltz, D. L. (1998). Cultural diversity and special education teacher preparation: Critical issues confronting the field. *Teacher Education and Special Education, 21*, 63–70.

Voltz, D. L. (2003). Personalized contextual instruction. *Preventing School Failure, 47*, 138–143.

Voltz, D. L., Brazil, N., & Ford, A. (2001). What matters most in inclusive education: A practical guide for moving forward. *Intervention in School and Clinic, 37*, 23–30.

Wadsworth, D. E., & Knight, D. (1999). Preparing the inclusion classroom for students with special physical and health needs. *Intervention in School and Clinic, 34*(3), 170–175.

Waldron, N. L., & McLeskey, J. (1998). The effects of an inclusive school program on students with mild and severe learning disabilities. *Exceptional Children, 64*, 395–405.

Waldron, N. L., McLeskey, J., & Pacchiano, D. (1999). Giving teachers a voice: Teachers' perspectives regarding elementary inclusive school programs (ISP). *Teacher Education and Special Education, 22*(3), 141–153.

Walker, B. J. (2000). *Diagnostic teaching of reading* (4th ed.). Upper Saddle River, NJ: Prentice Hall.

Walker, H. M., & Gresham, F. M. (1997). Making schools safer and violence free. *Intervention in School and Clinic, 32*(4), 199–204.

Wallace, T., Anderson, A. R., Bartholomay, T., & Hupp, S. (2002). An ecobehavioral examination of high school classrooms that include students with disabilities. *Exceptional Children, 68*, 345–359.

Wallerstein, J. S., Lewis, J. A., & Blakeslee, S. (2000). *The unexpected legacy of divorce: A 25-year landmark study.* New York: Hyperion.

Walsh, J. M. (2001). Getting the big picture of IEP goals and state standards. *Teaching Exceptional Children, 33*(5), 18–26.

Walther-Thomas, C., & Brownell, M. (2000). An interview with Dr. Janis Bulgren. *Intervention in School and Clinic, 35*, 232–236.

Walther-Thomas, C., & Brownell, M. (2001). An interview with Bonnie Jones: Using student portfolios effectively. *Intervention in School and Clinic, 36*, 225–229.

Walther-Thomas, C., Korinek, L., McLaughlin, V. L., & Williams, B. T. (2000). *Collaboration for inclusive education: Developing successful programs.* Boston: Allyn & Bacon.

Wansart, W. L. (2003). Co-participation evaluation: Students with writing problems become aware of their writing abilities and progress. *Reading and Writing Quarterly: Overcoming Learning Disabilities, 19*, 329–346.

Wanzek, J., & Haager, D. (2003). Teaching word recognition and blending and analogizing: Two strategies are better than one. *Teaching Exceptional Children, 36*(1), 32–38.

Warger, C. (2001). *Five homework strategies for teaching students with disabilities.* Arlington, VA: Council for Exceptional Children.

Warger, C. (2002). *Full-service schools' potential for special education.* Arlington, VA: Council for Exceptional Children.

Warger, C., & Burnette, J. (2000, March). *Planning student-directed transitions to adult life.* Reston, VA: ERIC Clearinghouse on Disabilities and Gifted Education.

Wasburn-Moses, L. (2003). What every special educator should know about high-stakes testing. *Teaching Exceptional Children, 35*(4), 12–15.

Washington, J. A. (2001). Early literacy skills in African-American children: Research considerations. *Learning Disabilities Research and Practice, 16*, 213–221.

Watanabe, T. (2002). Learning from Japanese lesson study. *Educational Leadership, 59*(6), 36–39.

Waters, J. (2001). Review of the video: We're not stupid: Living with a learning difference. *Intervention in School and Clinic, 36*, 185–186.

Watson, S. M. R., & Houtz, L. E. (2002). Teaching science: Meeting the academic needs of culturally and linguistically diverse students. *Intervention in School and Clinic, 37*, 267–278.

Watson, S. M. R., & Westby, C. E. (2003). Prenatal drug exposure: Implications for personnel preparation. *Remedial and Special Education, 24*, 204–214.

Wauters, L. N., Knoors, H. E. T., Vervloed, M. P. J., & Aarnoutse, C. A. J. (2001). Sign facilitation in word recognition. *The Journal of Special Education, 35*, 31–30.

Webb, J. T. (1995). Nurturing the social-emotional development of gifted children. *Teaching Exceptional Children, 27*(2), 76–77.

Webber, J. (1997) Comprehending youth violence: A practical perspective. *Remedial and Special Education, 18*(2), 94–104.

Wegner, J. R., & Edmister, E. (2004). Communication disorders. In R. Turnbull, A. Turnbull, M. Shank, & S. Smith (Eds.) *Exceptional lives: Special education in today's schools* (4th ed.) (pp. 398–454). Upper Saddle River, NJ: Prentice Hall.

Wehman, P., & Targett, P. (2002). Supported employment: The challenges of new staff requirements, selection and retention. *Education and Training in Mental Retardation and Developmental Disabilities, 37*, 434–446.

Wehmeyer, M. L. (2003). Defining mental retardation and ensuring access to the general curriculum. *Education and Training in Developmental Disabilities, 38*, 271–282.

Wehmeyer, M. L., Lance, G. D., & Bashinski, S. (2002). Promoting access to the general curriculum for students with mental retardation: A multi-level models. *Education and Training in Mental Retardation and Developmental Disabilities, 37*, 223–234

Wehmeyer, M. L., & Lawrence, M. (1997). Whose future is it anyway? Promoting student involvement in transition planning. *Career Development for Exceptional Individuals, 18*, 69–83.

Wehmeyer, M. L., Palmer, S. B., Agran, M., Mithaug, D. E., & Martin, J. E. (2000). Promoting causal agency: The self-determined learning model of instruction. *Exceptional Children, 66,* 439–453.

Weikle, B., & Hadadian, A. (2003). Can assistive technology help us to not leave any child behind? *Preventing School Failure, 47,* 181–186.

Weiss, M. P., & Lloyd, J. W. (2002). Congruence between roles and actions of secondary special educators in co-taught and special education settings. *The Journal of Special Education, 36,* 58–68.

Weiss, M. P., & Lloyd, J. W. (2003). Conditions for co-teaching: Lessons from a case study. *Teacher Education and Special Education, 26,* 27–41.

Welch, A. B. (2000). Responding to student concerns about fairness. *Teaching Exceptional Children, 33*(2), 36–40.

Welch, M. (1994). Ecological assessment: A collaborative approach to planning instructional interventions. *Intervention in School and Clinic, 29*(3), 160–164, 183.

Werts, M. G., Mamlin, N., & Pogoloff, S. M. (2002). Knowing what to expect: Introducing preservice teachers to IEP meetings. *Teacher Education and Special Education, 25,* 413–418.

Werts, M. G., Wolery, M., Gast, D. L., & Holcombe, A. (1996). Sneak in some extra learning by using instructive feedback. *Teaching Exceptional Children, 28*(3), 70–71.

Wessler, S. L. (2001). Sticks and stones. *Educational Leadership, 58*(4), 28–33.

Wesson, C. L., & King, R. P. (1996). Portfolio assessment and special education students. *Teaching Exceptional Children, 28*(2), 44–48.

Wesson, C. L., & Mandell, C. (1989). Simulations promote understanding of handicapping conditions. *Teaching Exceptional Children, 21*(1), 32–35.

West, R. P., Young, K. R., Callahan, K., Fister, S., Kemp, K., Freston, J., & Lovitt, T. C. (1995). The musical clocklight: Encouraging positive classroom behavior. *Teaching Exceptional Children, 27*(2), 46–51.

Westby, C. E., & Torres-Velasquez, D. (2000). Developing scientific literacy: A sociocultural approach. *Remedial and Special Education, 21,* 101–110.

Westling, D. L., & Fox, L. (2000). *Teaching students with severe disabilities* (2nd ed.). Upper Saddle River, NJ: Merrill/Prentice Hall.

Whitaker, S. D. (2000). What do first-year special education teachers need? Implications for induction programs? *Teaching Exceptional Children, 33*(1), 28–36.

White, R., Algozzine, B., Audette, R., Marr, M. B., & Ellis, E. D. (2001). Unified discipline: A school-wide approach for managing problem behavior. *Intervention in School and Clinic, 37,* 3–8.

Whitney-Thomas, J., & Moloney, M. (2001). "Who I am and what I want": Adolescents' self-definition and struggles. *Exceptional Children, 67,* 375–389.

Whittaker, C. R. (1996). Adapting cooperative learning structures for mainstreamed students. *Reading and Writing Quarterly: Overcoming Learning Difficulties, 12*(1), 23–39.

Whittaker, C. R., Salend, S. J., & Duhaney, D. (2001). Creating instructional rubrics for inclusive classrooms. *Teaching Exceptional Children, 34*(2), 8–13.

Whittaker, C. R., Salend, S. J., & Gutierrez, M. (1997). "Voices from the fields": Including migrant workers in the curriculum. *The Reading Teacher, 50*(6), 482–493.

Wigle, S. E., & DeMoulin, D. F. (1999). Inclusion in a general classroom setting and self-concept. *The Journal of At-Risk Issues, 5*(2), 27–32.

Wilkinson, L. A. (2003). Using behavioral consultation to reduce challenging behavior in the classroom. *Preventing School Failure, 47,* 100–105.

Willard-Holt, C. (1999, April). *Dual exceptionalities.* Reston, VA: ERIC Clearinghouse on Disabilities and Gifted Education.

Willard-Holt, C. (2003). Raising expectations for the gifted. *Educational Leadership, 61*(2), 72–75.

Williams, C. B., & Finnegan, M. (2003). From myth to reality: Sound information for teachers about students who are deaf. *Teaching Exceptional Children, 35*(3), 40–45.

Williams, G. J., & Reisberg, L. (2003). Successful inclusion: Teaching social skills through curriculum integration. *Intervention in School and Clinic, 38,* 193–210.

Williams, K. (2001). Understanding the student with Asperger syndrome. *Intervention in School and Clinic, 36,* 287–292.

Williams, S. C. (2002). How speech-feedback and word-prediction software can help students write. *Teaching Exceptional Children, 34*(3), 72–78.

Williams, V. I., & Cartledge, G. (1997). Passing notes—Parents. *Teaching Exceptional Children, 30*(1), 30–34.

Williamson, R. D. (1997). Help me organize. *Intervention in School and Clinic, 33*(1), 36–39.

Winebrenner, S. (2001). *Teaching gifted kids in the regular classroom.* Minneapolis, MN: Free Spirit Publishing.

Winebrenner, S. (2003). Teaching strategies for twice-exceptional students. *Intervention in School and Clinic, 38,* 131–137.

Winsor, P. J. T. (1998). Talking-point: Books about children with learning disabilities. *Teaching Exceptional Children, 30*(3), 34–35.

Winter, E. (2000). School bereavement. *Educational Leadership, 57*(6), 80–85.

Wissick, C. A., & Gardner, J. E. (2000). Multimedia or not to multimedia? That is the question for students with learning disabilities. *Teaching Exceptional Children, 32*(4), 34–43.

Witte, R. (1998). Meet Bob, a student with traumatic brain injury. *Teaching Exceptional Children, 30*(3), 56–60.

Witzel, B., & Mercer, C. D. (2003). Using rewards to teach students with disabilities: Implications for motivation. *Remedial and Special Education, 24,* 88–96.

Witzel, B., Mercer, C. D., & Miller, M. D. (2003). Teaching algebra to students with learning difficulties: An investigation of an explicit instruction model. *Learning Disabilities Research and Practice, 18,* 121–131.

Witzel, B., Smith, S. W., & Brownell, M. T. (2001). How can I help students with learning disabilities learn algebra? *Intervention in School and Clinic, 37,* 101–104.

Wolery, M., & Schuster, J. W. (1997). Instructional methods with students who have significant disabilities. *The Journal of Special Education, 31*(1), 61–79.

Wolfe, P., Burkman, M. A., & Streng, K. (2000). The science of nutrition. *Educational Leadership, 57*(6), 54–59.

Wolfe, P. S., & Hall, T. E. (2003). Making inclusion a reality for students with severe disabilities. *Teaching Exceptional Children, 35*(4), 56–61.

Wolfensberger, W. (1972). *The principle of normalization in human services.* Toronto: National Institute on Mental Retardation.

Wolford, P. L., Heward, W. L., & Alber, S. R. (2001). Teaching middle school students with learning disabilities to recruit peer assistance during cooperative learning group activities. *Learning Disabilities Research and Practice, 16,* 161–173.

Wong, B. Y. L. (1986). A cognitive approach to spelling. *Exceptional Children, 53,* 169–173.

Wood, D. K., & Frank, A. R. (2000). Using memory-enhancing strategies to learn multiplication facts. *Teaching Exceptional Children, 32*(5), 78–82.

Wood, J. (2002). Hostile hallways. *Educational Leadership, 59*(4), 20–23.

Wood, K. D. (1995). Guiding middle school students through expository text. *Reading and Writing Quarterly: Overcoming Learning Difficulties, 11*(2), 137–147.

Wood, W. M., Karvonen, M., Test, D. W., Browder, D., & Algozzine, B. (2004). Promoting student self-determination skills in IEP planning. *Teaching Exceptional Children, 36*(3), 8–17.

Woodfield, K. (2003). Getting on board with online testing. *The Journal Technological Horizons in Education, 30*(6), 32–37.

Woodward, J. (1999). Redoing the numbers: Secondary math for a postsecondary work world. *Teaching Exceptional Children, 31*(4), 74–79.

Woodward, J., & Baxter, J. (2001). Working with numbers. *Teaching Exceptional Children, 33*(5), 80–84.

Woodward, J., Baxter, J., & Robinson, R. (1999). Rules and reasons: Decimal instruction for academically low achieving students. *Remedial and Special Education, 14*(1), 15–24.

Woolsey-Terrazas, W., & Chavez, J. A. (2002, February/March). Strategies to work with students with oppositional defiant disorder. *CEC Today,* 12.

Wright-Strawderman, C., Lindsey, P., Navarette, L., & Flippo, J. R. (1996). Depression in students with disabilities: Recognition and intervention strategies. *Intervention in School and Clinic, 31*(5), 261–275.

Wyatt, E. (2000, April 5). More special education students taking and passing the Regents exam. *The New York Times,* B6.

Xin, Y. P., & Jitendra, A. K. (1999). The effects of instruction on solving mathematical word problems for students with learning problems: A meta-analysis. *Journal of Learning Disabilities, 32*(4), 207–225.

Yasutake, D., Bryan, T., & Dohrn, E. (1996). The effects of combining peer tutoring and attribution training on students' perceived self-competence. *Remedial and Special Education, 17*(2), 83–91.

Yeh, C. J., & Drost, C. (2002, February). *Bridging identities among minority youth in schools.* New York: ERIC Clearinghouse on Urban Education.

Yehle, A. K., & Wambold, C. (1998). An ADHD success story: Strategies for teachers and students. *Teaching Exceptional Children, 30*(6), 8–13.

Yell, M. L.,(1997). Teacher liability for student injury and misconduct. *Beyond Behavior, 8*(1), 4–9.

Yell, M. L. (1998). *The law and special education.* Upper Saddle River, NJ: Merrill/Prentice Hall.

Yell, M. L., & Peterson, R. L. (1995). Disciplining students with disabilities and those at risk of school failure: Legal issues. *Preventing School Failure, 39*(2), 39–44.

Yell, M. L. & Rozalski, M. E. (2000). Searching for safe schools: Legal issues in the prevention of school violence. *Journal of Emotional and Behavioral Disorders, 8,* 187–196.

Yell, M. M. (2002). Putting gel to pen to paper. *Educational Leadership, 60*(3), 63–66.

York, J., & Tundidor, M. (1995). Issues raised in the name of inclusion: Perspectives of educators, parents, and students. *Journal of the Association for Persons with Severe Handicaps, 20,* 31–44.

Ysseldyke, J., Thurlow, M., Bielinski, J., House, A., Moody, M., & Haigh, J. (2001). The relationship between instructional and assessment accommodations in an inclusive state accountability system. *Journal of Learning Disabilities, 34,* 212–220.

Zaslavsky, C. (2002). Exploring world cultures in math class. *Educational Leadership, 60*(2), 66–69.

Zentall, S. S., Moon, S. M., Hall, A. M., & Grskovic, J. A. (2001). Learning and motivational characteristics of boys with AD/HD and or giftedness. *Exceptional Children, 67,* 400–519.

Zhang, D. (2001). Self-determination and inclusion: Are students with mild mental retardation more self-determined in regular classrooms? *Education and Training in Mental Retardation and Developmental Disabilities, 36,* 357–362.

Zhang, D., & Katsiyannis, A. (2002). Minority representation in special education: A persistent challenge. *Remedial and Special Education, 23,* 180–187.

Zickel, J. P., & Arnold, E. (2001). Putting the I in the IEP. *Educational Leadership, 59,* 71–73.

Zigmond, N., Jenkins, J., Fuchs, L. S., Deno, S., Fuchs, D., Baker, J. N., Jenkins, L., & Couthino, M. (1995). Special education in restructured schools. Findings from three multi-year studies. *Phi Delta Kappan, 76,* 531–540.

Zinkil, S. S., & Gilbert, T. S. (2000). Parents' view: What to consider when contemplating inclusion. *Intervention in School and Clinic, 35,* 224–227.

Zionts, L. T., & Callicott, K. (2002). The many faces of children's advocacy. *Beyond Behavior, 11*(3), 33–34.

Zittleman, K., & Sadker, D. (2003). Teacher education textbooks: The unfinished gender revolution. *Educational Leadership, 60*(4), 59–63.

Zylstra, E. (2001). A year with Bobby. *Educational Leadership, 59*(3), 74–75.

Name Index

Page numbers followed by "n" (such as 420n) indicate notes.

Aarnoutse, C. A. J., 420n
Abbott, M., 416, 417n, 434n
Abernathy, T. V., 210, 243, 244n, 272n
Abrams, J., 126
Access Resources, 242n
Acton, O. M., 96, 96n
Ada, A. F., 227
Adair, J., 148, 148n
Adams, G., 391, 392n, 479n, 480, 521, 521n
Adreon, D., 254, 254n
Afflerbach, P., 181
Agran, M., 83, 243, 245, 275, 275n, 310
Aguilar, C. M., 425n
Ainge, D., 307, 318
Ainscow, M., 6n
Alber, S. R., 363, 363n, 396n, 407n, 422, 424, 425n, 426n, 431, 433, 434, 435, 436n, 437n, 484, 485, 486n
Albert, L. R., 393
Alberto, P. A., 41, 41n, 204, 277, 277n, 290, 307, 309, 309n, 390n, 420, 420n
Albertson, L. R., 33
Albin, R. W., 74n, 293n, 318, 318n
Alder, N., 395
Alexandrin, J. R., 514, 514n
Algozzine, B., 59n, 279, 279n, 282, 283n, 288, 288n
Al-Hassan, S., 187, 192n, 193, 196
Alkin, M. C., 32, 32n, 34, 41
Allbritten, D., 23, 24n
Allen, E. M., 314
Allen, K. D., 92
Allen, N., 185
Allen, R., 254, 254n, 272, 272n, 300, 300n
Allen, S. H., 406
Alley, G. R., 350, 352
Allied, K. W., 36, 41, 537n
Allinder, R. M., 35, 167, 419, 503n
Allington, R. L., 181, 467, 468
Allor, J. H., 417, 426, 426n

Allsopp, D. H., 457, 466
Almond, P., 498
Al Otaiba, S., 406, 416, 418n, 425
Alper, S., 83, 245, 274n
Alsman, B., 417n, 419
Alson, A., 121
Alvarado, J. L., 391
Alwell, M., 214n
Amen, D. G., 69
American Association of University Women, 135, 136, 490n
American Federation of Teachers, 61
American Foundation for the Blind, 239
American Psychiatric Association, 77
Ammer, J. J., 393, 407
Amrein, A. L., 496
Anderegg, M. L., 76n
Anderson, A. R., 33, 35, 37, 506, 515
Anderson, B. C., 41, 42
Anderson, D. J., 369n
Anderson, H., 536n, 537
Anderson, J. A., 73, 75, 75n, 158
Anderson, K. L., 327, 455n
Anderson, L. M., 467, 466n
Anderson, P. L., 303n
Anderson-Inman, L., 342, 489
Andrade, H. G., 512
Andrews, D., 293, 293n
Andrews, J. F., 348n, 367, 489
Antia, S. D., 280, 280n
Anti-Defamation League, 236
Antil, L. R., 403
Antonak, R. F., 211
Apel, K., 449
Aponte, E., 189, 192
Appelget, J., 482, 483n
Appl, D. J., 177, 177n, 179n,
Archer, A., 260n
Archwamety, T., 16, 33
Arditi, A., 356n
Arguelles, M. E., 174n
Arllen, N. L., 506
Armento, B. J., 227n, 358n
Armstrong, D. G., 393, 396, 404, 407, 487, 516

Arnold, E., 62n
Aronson, D., 138n, 236n
Aronson, E., 406
Arreaga-Mayer, C., 405
Arrowood, L., 99
Artiles, A. J., 22
Ary, D., 429
Ashbaker, B. Y., 343n
Asher, S. R., 214
Ashton, T. M., 442
Ashton-Shaeffer, C., 273
Astolfi, C., 239
Atkinson, T., 370, 370n
Audette, R., 288, 288n
Aurora, T., 41
Austin, V. L., 38, 40, 78, 99, 99n, 170
Aylor, M. W., 8, 39

Babbitt, B. C., 273, 455, 456, 456n, 464
Babkie, A. M., 254, 255, 255n, 305n
Babyak, A. E., 313, 315n, 349, 406
Baca, L. M., 20, 51n, 117
Bacon, E., 300, 301n
Bacon, N. A., 232
Bagdasarian, S., 419, 425n
Bahr, C. M., 431n
Bailey, A. B., 194
Bailey, D. B., 80
Bailey, J., 434n
Bak, S., 34, 214, 238, 241, 530
Baker, J. M., 32
Baker, J. N., 33
Baker, L., 76n
Baker, N., 484
Baker, R. A., 304, 305
Baker, S. K., 102n
Baker, S. R., 32, 61, 255, 266, 267, 283, 363, 431, 443n, 416, 418
Baker-Kroczynski, S., 33, 35, 37, 40
Bakken, J. P., 428
Balboni, G., 38, 405
Baldwin, B. A., 117
Balkman, K., 92, 93n
Bambara, L., 390
Banbury, M. M., 303n

Banerjee, M., 487

Banerji, M., 34, 535*n*

Banks, C. A., 117, 150, 356, 357

Banks, J. A., 117, 150, 236*n*, 356, 357, 358*n*

Bantz, J. M., 193

Barbetta, P. M., 396, 396*n*

Barkley, R. A., 77, 99*n*

Barnes, E., 213*n*

Barnes, K., 304, 304*n*, 307

Barnett, W. S., 16

Barnhill, G. P., 97

Barnwell, D., 41

Barrie, W., 61

Bartholomay, T., 33, 35, 37, 506, 515

Bartlett, L., 54*n*, 86

Barton, M. L., 457, 469, 477, 478

Bashinski, S., 83, 338*n*, 340

Bassett, D. S., 455*n*

Baton, S., 71

Batshaw, M. L., 87, 87*n*

Battle, D. A., 201*n*

Battle, J., 417

Bauer, A. M., 194, 276, 327, 371, 370*n*, 506

Baumberger, J. P., 54*n*

Baxendell, B. W., 475, 477, 477*n*

Baxter, J., 457, 459, 465

Beal, C., 363, 470*n*, 483, 483*n*, 484

Bean, T. W., 422*n*, 426

Beane, A. L., 322

Beare, P., 310*n*

Beasley, M., 344*n*

Beaver, J. B., 481, 482*n*

Beck, I. L., 469*n*

Beckman, P., 41, 447

Beckstead, S., 34

Beers, M. K., 535*n*

Belcher, R. N., 132

Bellon, M. L., 420, 421, 425, 426*n*

Bellon-Harn, M. L., 116, 116*n*

Belluck, P., 116

Bender, W. M., 77, 78

Bender, W. N., 323*n*

Benner, G. J., 73, 81

Bennett, T., 41, 535*n*

Benz, M. R., 21*n*, 268, 270

Berendt, P. R., 501

Bergert, S., 71, 72

Berliner, D. C., 22, 111, 496

Berlinger, N. T., 204

Bernard, J. A., 161

Bernhardt, V. L., 497*n*, 531, 539, 539

Bernstein, N., 113, 142

Berrigan, C., 213*n*

Berry, R., 436

Berryman, J., 34

Berson, M. J., 470*n*, 485, 515

Bessell, A. G., 91

Best, A. M., 22

Best, S. J., 4, 61, 82, 84, 85, 86, 87*n*, 88, 92, 93, 329, 329*n*, 330*n*

Beukelman, D. R., 442, 442*n*

Biddle, B. J., 22, 111

Biederman, M., 375

Bielinski, J., 500

Bigby, M., 163, 163*n*

Bigge, J. L., 82, 86, 87*n*, 329, 329*n*, 330*n*

Biglan, A., 429

Biklen, D., 37, 213*n*

Billingsley, B. S., 192

Billingsley, F., 6, 8, 33, 41*n*

Billman, L. W., 417, 417*n*

Bishop, K. D., 39, 67*n*, 68, 68*n*

Bisson, J., 233*n*, 234

Biyant, B. R., 17

Biyde, S., 145*n*, 147*n*, 223*n*, 235*n*

Blair, C., 70

Blair, R. J., 276

Blake, C., 266

Blakeslee, S., 142, 143

Blanchett, W. J., 139, 235

Blaney, N., 406

Blazer, B., 30*n*

Bley, N. S., 456, 458, 463

Bligh, T., 417*n*

Bloom, L. A., 6, 7, 245, 300, 301, 301*n*, 306

Blubaugh, D., 367*n*

Blue-Banning, M., 241*n*, 243

Blum, H. T., 228, 394*n*

Boat, M. B., 245

Bock, M. A., 240

Boerum, L. J., 507

Boettcher, C., 32*n*, 496

Bollig, A. A., 199, 199*n*

Bonar, A. M., 71, 72, 72*n*

Bonfils, K. A., 310*n*

Boone, R., 131*n*, 132, 197, 197*n*, 268*n*, 272, 278, 279*n*, 282, 357*n*, 364*n*, 365*n*, 442*n*, 487, 488*n*, 489

Booth, J. E., 78

Booth, T., 6*n*

Borden, S. L., 419

Bordin, J., 65*n*, 167*n*

Borthwick-Duffy, S., 51

Bos, C. S., 261*n*, 279

Boscardin, M. L., 223

Bostic, J. Q., 75, 76, 76*n*

Bottge, B. A., 455, 457, 458

Boudah, D. J., 39, 71, 255, 474*n*

Boulware, B., 368, 449

Bowen, S., 346, 346*n*

Bowers, E. M., 223

Boyer, M. M., 398, 399*n*

Boyle, A. R., 487

Boyle, J. R., 349*n*, 382, 383*n*, 386*n*, 470, 478*n*

Bradford, E., 35

Bradley, D. H., 438

Bradley, R., 20, 26*n*

Brady, M. P., 252, 270, 461

Branch, R., 39

Brandenburg, M. L., 461

Braus, N., 227*n*

Braziel, P. M., 21*n*

Brazil, N., 6, 7, 15, 175, 219, 230, 328, 330, 482, 530*n*

Brennan, M., 32

Breunig, N., 22, 123

Brewer, R. D., 405, 405*n*

Brice, A., 81, 124, 362, 362*n*

Bridgest, S. T., 296

Briel, L., 93, 94, 95, 96*n*, 306*n*

Brigham, F. J., 504

Brim, S. A., 389

Brinckerhoff, L. C., 487

Brock, B., 274, 279*n*

Broden, M., 311*n*

Broer, S. M., 159, 160, 344, 343*n*

Brolin, D. E., 272

Bronheim, S., 90*n*

Brookhart, S. M., 516, 517, 519, 526, 529

Brooks-Gunn, J., 112

Brookshire, M. A., 318

Brophy, J. E., 391

Brosnan, P. A., 456*n*

Brotherson, M. J., 62*n*, 210, 238, 246

Browder, D. M., 59*n*, 61*n*, 275*n*, 278*n*, 283*n*, 420*n*, 503*n*

Brown, A., 364, 364*n*

Brown, B., 193

Brown, F., 98*n*, 278*n*

Brown, L. W., 91

Brown, M. R., 134, 134*n*

Brown, M. S., 79*n*

Brown, P. J., 338*n*

Brown, P. L., 117, 391

Brown, W. H., 297*n*

Brownell, M. T., 116, 170, 455, 479

Brozo, W. G., 422, 467, 489

Brozovic, S. A., 41, 41*n*, 204

Bruch, L., 239
Brucker, P. O., 422
Bruckert, J., 475
Bruder, M. B., 16
Brudge, M., 497
Bruhl, S., 408
Brunet, J. P., 33, 35, 38
Brunken, C. D., 419
Bruns, D. A., 41, 195, 264n, 358n, 359n, 535n
Bry, B. H., 322n
Bryan, T., 280, 403n, 531n
Bryant, B. R., 17, 454n, 456, 457, 461
Bryant, D. P., 17, 419n, 454n, 456, 457, 461
Bryde, S., 94, 94n, 96n, 146n, 264n
Buck, G. H., 50, 297n, 305
Buechner, M., 446n
Buell, J., 402
Buggey, T., 265
Bui, Y. N., 167n, 187, 192, 193, 194, 296
Bulgren, J. A., 339, 474n, 479, 479n, 480, 480n, 484, 485n, 485
Bull, J., 158, 166, 167n
Bullard, H. R., 97, 97n
Bullard, M., 240
Bullock, C. C., 273, 301, 302n
Bunton-Pierce, M. K., 96
Burch, M., 461
Burcroff, T. L., 271, 272n
Burell, B., 282n
Burns, M. K., 504
Burrell, B., 282
Burrell, L., 6, 7, 301, 306
Burrow, E., 204n, 223, 223n
Bursuck, W. D., 529
Busch, T., 99
Butler, C. J., 289
Butler, F. M., 455, 456, 456n, 464
Button, L. J., 35, 210
Buysse, V., 181, 181n, 214, 238
Bynoe, P. F., 359
Byrnes, D. A., 233n, 234

Cade, E., 33, 35, 37, 40
Cade, T., 75, 75n, 316, 393n, 398, 401n
Caffrey, J. A., 79
Cage, C. E., 455n
Caine, G., 484
Caine, R. N., 484
Calderon, M. E., 120, 120n
Calhoun, M. B., 459
Call, D. T., 475

Callahan, C. M., 131, 131n
Callahan, K., 310, 319
Callicott, K., 188, 188n
Campbell, K. U., 418
Campbell, L., 131
Campbell, P. C., 252
Campbell, R. C., 252
Campbell-Whatley, G. D., 282, 282n
Canfield, J., 244
Cangelosi, J. S., 455, 456n, 456, 456, 458, 458, 461, 466
Canter, L. S., 364, 364n, 482, 482n, 487, 489
Canu, W. H., 78
Cappello, D., 322n
Capper, C. A., 38
Carbone, E., 77, 79n, 324, 329, 330n
Carger, C. L., 235
Carlson, C. L., 78
Carlson, D. M., 364n
Carlson, P., 41, 42, 537n
Carnine, D., 470n, 479n, 480, 482
Carpenter, C. D., 245
Carr, S. C., 435, 521, 521n
Carr, V. G., 320
Carrington, S., 97, 214n
Carroll, D., 160n, 344
Carter, E. W., 35, 270n
Carter, K., 346, 346n
Cartledge, G., 193, 197, 199, 228, 265, 266, 295, 296n, 303, 303n, 304, 310n
Casey, B., 455n
Cass, M., 456, 456n
Casteel, C. P., 351n, 352
Castellani, J., 367, 442
Castillo, S., 318
Cavaiuolo, D., 59, 60n, 270, 274
Cavalier, A. R., 371, 371n
Cavanaugh, R. A., 396, 396n
Cavanaugh, T., 342, 342n, 487
Cawley, J. F., 33, 35, 37, 40, 454, 455, 455n, 456, 458, 459, 462n, 465, 465n, 466, 482, 484
CeDIR, 239
Center for Universal Design, 341n
Cervantes, H. T., 117
Chait, A., 297n
Chalmers, L., 146n, 305n
Chaltain, S., 232
Chamberlain, S. P., 89, 89n, 320
Chamot, A. U., 267
Chan, E., 126
Chappuis, S., 392, 396

Chard, D., 454
Chard, D. J., 418, 427n, 448
Chavez, J. A., 74n
Chen, D., 104, 345, 345n
Cheng, L. C., 421n
Chiappetta, E. L., 481n, 482, 487
Childs, K. E., 293n
Chinn, P. C., 22, 358n
Chiong, J. A., 135
Chira, S., 144
Chism, V., 391n
Chou, H., 41
Choutka, C. M., 339
Christenson, S. L., 21n
Christiansen, J., 529
Chubb, J. E., 121
Chuoke, M., 244
Church, K., 240, 240n
Clark, E., 96n
Clark, F. L., 350
Clark, K., 447
Clark, L., 200
Clark, R. D., 80
Clark, S. G., 54n
Clarke, S., 293n
Clayton, J., 497, 503, 503n
Clemetson, L., 111, 118
Cloninger, C. J., 38, 39, 41, 98n, 535n
Cloud, N., 122, 296
Cobb, C. E., 455n
Cockerill, J., 484
Cohen, E. T., 61, 85
Cohen, P., 34
Cohen, S. B., 269n
Cole, C. M., 38
Cole, K. N., 33
Coleman, M., 417n, 419
Colleti, L., 322n
Collet-Klingenberg, L. L., 21
Collicott, J., 340
Collier, C., 118
Collier, V. P., 117, 120, 121n, 125
Collins, B. C., 273n, 343n
Collins, D., 408
Colvin, G., 307, 318
Compain, R., 521
Conderman, G., 61, 159n, 182, 182n, 183n, 270, 417n, 515, 516, 517
Condon, K. A., 327
Connelly, V. J., 487
Conoley, J. C., 96
Conroy, M. A., 293, 297n, 297n, 304, 304n
Cook, A. M., 371, 371n

Cook, B. G., 39, 40
Cook, C. C., 210, 238, 246
Cook, D., 316
Cook, K. W., 50
Cook, L., 39, 168
Cook-Sather, A., 38, 277
Cooper, H., 398
Cooper, J. O., 344
Coots, J. J., 39
Copeland, S. R., 35, 37, 243, 245, 245*n*, 252, 275, 310
Corral, N., 280, 280*n*
Correa, V. I., 164, 166
Corrigan, C., 37
Corso, R. M., 358, 358*n*, 359*n*
Cosden, M., 148
Cosmos, C., 24–25
Costa, A. L., 8
Costenbader, V., 273
Council for Exceptional Children, 113, 276
Countryman, L. L., 509
Courson, F. H., 396, 396*n*
Coutinho, M. J., 22, 33, 75, 75*n*, 316, 393*n*, 398, 401*n*
Covert, G., 434*n*
Cowart, M., 391*n*
Cox, M. J., 16, 260
Cox, P. R., 104, 326, 328, 328*n*, 345
Coyne, M. D., 416*n*
Coyne, P., 341, 487
Craig, S., 51, 51*n*, 296*n*, 425, 425*n*
Cramer, M. M., 455*n*
Cramer, S., 204
Crehan, K., 455, 456, 456*n*, 464
Criscitiello, E., 405, 405*n*
Crites, S. A., 295, 297*n*
Crockett, J. B., 5
Cronin, M. E., 272, 310, 312, 455*n*
Crowder, E., 425, 425*n*
Cruz, L., 316, 317*n*
Cullinan, B. E., 426
Cullinan, D., 75, 316, 317*n*
Cummins, J., 124
Cunningham, P. M., 446, 449
Curran, C., 507, 508*n*
Curry, C., 32, 372, 373
Curtis, D., 34
Curtiss, V. S., 297, 297*n*
Cushing, L. S., 37
Cushing, S., 35, 41
Cutler, S. K., 91, 91*n*, 92*n*
Cutter, J., 266, 407, 481
Czarnecki, E., 385*n*

Dabkowski, D. M., 61*n*
Dailey, R. A., 34, 535*n*
Dale, P. S., 33
D'Alonzo, B. J., 39
Daly, P. M., 311, 311*n*
D'Amato, R. C., 94
D'Ambrosio, U., 455
Damico, J. S., 128
D'Amore, M., 448
Daniel, M. J., 483
Daniel, M. L., 482, 483*n*
Daniels, H., 467
Danko, C. D., 293*n*
Daresh, J. C., 182, 182*n*
Dattilo, J., 273
Daunic, A. P., 302*n*
Davern, L., 6, 8, 25*n*, 41, 85, 186, 216, 338, 339, 339*n*
Davidson, E., 228*n*, 227*n*, 232, 244, 402, 404*n*
Davies, D. K., 276
Davies, S., 276, 368
Davies, T. G., 274
Davis, B., 479*n*, 480, 482*n*
Davis, C., 193, 297*n*
Davis, M. H., 417, 421
Davis, M. L., 104, 326, 327, 345, 372, 373, 373*n*
Davis, P. M., 39
Davis, S., 115, 503*n*
Day, J., 230
Day, M., 187
Day-Vines, N., 121, 121*n*, 226
deBettencourt, L. U., 28, 29*n*, 30
Deck, M., 162
DeGeorge, K. L., 238*n*
De la Cruz, R. E., 455*n*
de la Garza, B., 270*n*
de la Luz Trabue, M., 448
De La Paz, S., 440*n*, 442
deLara, E., 237, 320
del Rosario Ortiz, M., 448
Deluca, D., 41, 535*n*
Demchak, M., 250, 250*n*
DeMoulin, D. F., 34
Dempsey, S. D., 184*n*
Denham, A., 503*n*, 508
Dennis, R. E., 39, 41, 186*n*, 535*n*
Deno, E., 13
Deno, S. L., 33, 467, 504
Denton, C., 352, 425*n*, 429
Denton, P. H., 350
Derman-Sparks, L., 227, 227*n*, 235, 236, 237

Descy, D. E., 368
Deshler, D. D., 32–33, 38, 180*n*, 245, 245*n*, 255, 255*n*, 280*n*, 350, 352, 401, 408*n*, 435, 439*n*, 474, 474*n*, 477, 479, 479*n*, 480, 480*n*, 484, 485*n*, 485, 502
Desrochers, C., 390*n*
Desrochers, M., 390*n*
DeStefano, L., 498
de Valenzuela, J. S., 51*n*
Dever, M. T., 233*n*, 234
Deville, C., 499
DeVille, G., 348*n*
DiCecco, V., 475, 477
Dickens-Wright, L. L., 201*n*
Dicker, L. A., 299
Dickinson, D. L., 30
Di Cola, J. M., 41, 42
Dieker, L., 250, 252, 252*n*, 254
DiMattia, P., 20, 26*n*
Dion, E., 33, 35, 38
Dionne, J., 36
DiPipi, C. M., 462*n*
Disability Resources, 441*n*
Disarno, N. J., 327
Djukic, J., 126
Doan, T., 458
Dockterman, D. A., 458
Dodd-Murphy, J., 326, 327
Doelling, J. E., 94, 94*n*, 96*n*, 264*n*
Doering, K., 6, 8, 32, 34, 37, 38, 82, 84, 151, 168, 338*n*, 343
Dohrn, E., 280
Donegan, M., 260*n*, 262
Donnelly, J. A., 97
Dore, R., 33, 35, 38
Doren, B., 283
Dormans, J. P., 87, 87*n*
Dorney, J. A., 163*n*
Douglas, S. L., 233, 234*n*
Dowdy, C. A., 77
Downing, J. A., 309, 310*n*
Downing, J. E., 39, 40, 104, 258, 305, 305*n*, 340, 345, 345*n*, 388, 535*n*, 537*n*
Dowrick, P. W., 265
Doyel, A. W., 270*n*
Doyle, B. A., 274, 279*n*
Doyle, M. B., 159, 250, 250*n*, 343*n*
Drasgow, E., 51
Drew, R., 158, 166, 167*n*
Drost, C., 121, 135, 227, 235, 264
Drug Strategies, 148*n*
Duchardt, B. A., 280*n*

Duchnowski, A. J., 73, 75
Duckworth, S., 318, 318
Duenwald, M., 91, 143
Duff, C., 276
Duff-Mallams, K., 49
Duffy, M. L., 490n, 490n
Duhaney, D., 369n, 388, 511
Duhaney, L. G., 32n, 297, 304
Duncan, G. J., 112
Dunlap, G., 17n, 96, 260, 288n, 289, 289n, 293n
Dunn, L. M., 21
Dunn, R., 344n
Dunse, L., 419
Dunsmore, K., 436
Dunst, C. J., 16
DuPaul, G. J., 79n, 99n
Dwyer, K., 322
Dyches, T. T., 41, 188, 188n, 204n, 223, 223n, 537n
Dyck, N., 348, 338n, 469
Dye, G. A., 477
Dykens, E. M., 80
Dykes, M. K., 61, 85, 104, 326, 328, 328n, 345
Dynneson, T. L., 470n, 486, 515

East, K., 281, 282n
Easterbrooks, S. R., 102n
Eber, L., 75, 158
Ebert, C., 512, 513n
Echevarria, J., 360, 361
Eckert, T. L., 79n
Eckman, A., 232
Edelman, S. W., 39, 41, 159, 160, 343, 343n, 344, 535n
Edens, R. M., 141n, 141n
Edgar, E., 121, 121n, 226
Edmiaston, R. K., 7, 17n
Edmister, E., 81, 82n
Edmonson, H., 288n
Education Commission of the States, 134n
Edwards, A. T., 138, 140n
Edwards, E. G., 99, 99n
Edwards, L. L., 339, 443n
Edyburn, D. L., 510n
Egan, J., 113, 113
Egan, M. W., 41, 537n
Egan, W. M., 36
Egel, A. L., 309n
Ehlenberger, K. R., 322n
Ehren, B. J., 479
Eichinger, J., 39, 40, 305n, 340, 388, 535n

Eidson, C. C., 337
Eisele, M. R., 417, 448
Eisenman, L. T., 34, 35, 211, 219, 278
Elbaum, B., 33, 34, 37, 72, 531
Elhoweris, H., 79n, 387
Elksnin, L. K., 303, 304n
Elksnin, N., 303, 304n
Ellenburg, J. S., 96, 96n
Ellerd, D. A., 276
Elliott, J. L., 373, 384, 498, 498n, 500, 501
Elliott, L., 410
Elliott, S. N., 498, 499, 499n, 501
Ellis, E. D., 288, 288n
Ellis, E. S., 180n, 257n, 256, 279n, 352, 434n, 469n
Elmquist, D. L., 149n
Emanuel, E. J., 268
Embry, D. D., 323n
Emerson, J., 145, 145n
Englemann, S., 429
Engleman, M., 98n 104, 326, 327, 345, 372, 373, 373n
Englert, C. S., 418, 428, 433n, 436
English, K., 97
Epstein, A., 273n
Epstein, M. H., 73, 75, 81, 530
Epstein, S. E., 223
ERIC Clearinghouse on Urban Education, 121, 135
Erickson, R., 500, 501
Ernsbarger, S. C., 420
Ervin, E. J., 41n
Erzkus, A., 204
Estevez, A., 448
Estill, D. M., 162
Etscheidt, S. K., 54n, 288
Evans, C., 75
Evans, D., 99
Evans, D. E., 449
Evans, I. M., 34, 98, 225
Evans, S., 330
Evans, W. H., 506
Evelo, D. L., 21n
Everington, C., 80, 80n, 83, 84
Ewing, N. J., 297, 304
Eyman, B., 244
Ezell, D., 507

Fabiano, G. A., 327
Fad, K. M., 297n
Fahey, K., 511
Fallin, K., 503n
Fallows, J., 111

Farmer, T. W., 69, 210
Farron-Davis, F., 34, 214n
Favazza, P. C., 210, 211, 212, 223, 246
Feldhusen, J. F., 132
Felton, R. H., 71, 448
Fennick, E., 40, 170, 173, 173n
Ferguson, J. E., 126, 232
Ferguson, P. M., 195
Fernstrom, P., 470
Ferretti, R. P., 482
Ferri, B. A., 34
Fetko, K., 343n
Fewell, R., 204
Fidler, D. J., 80
Fiedler, B. C., 102
Field, S., 267, 279, 283
Fielder, K., 6, 24, 25n, 65, 65n, 66n, 339n
Fierro-Cobas, V., 126
Filcheck, H. A., 304, 318, 318, 319, 393n, 501, 501n
Findley, N., 482
Fine, E., 385n
Fink, B., 443n, 442n
Fink-Chorzempa, B., 416n, 417, 449
Finn, K., 148
Finnegan, M., 101, 102, 239, 326, 346, 347
Finson, K. D., 343n, 481, 482n
Firman, K. B., 310n
Fisher, D., 6, 7, 23, 40, 41, 84, 159, 170, 340, 382, 382, 424, 456
Fister, S., 319
Fitzgerald, L. M., 7, 17n
Fitzgerald, M., 158, 167
Fitzharris, L. H., 348
Flanagan, B., 396, 398
Fleming, J. L., 165n, 166
Fletcher-Carter, R., 132
Flett, A., 417n
Fleury, M. L., 189n, 343n
Flint, L. J., 78, 132
Flippo, J. R., 76n
Flowers, J., 304
Floyd, J. H., 41, 41n, 204
Foegen, A., 301, 302n, 467
Fogt, J., 390
Foil, C. R., 363, 363n, 396n, 422, 424, 425n, 484, 485, 485, 486n
Foley, T. E., 454, 455, 455n, 456, 458, 459, 465, 466, 482, 484
Foorman, B. R., 416n, 427
Forcier, R. C., 368
Ford, A., 6, 7, 8, 15, 25n, 85, 175, 328, 330, 338, 339, 339n, 482, 530n

Ford, B. A., 22
Ford, D. Y., 22, 132, 132*n*
Fordham, S., 296
Forgan, J. W., 34, 228*n*, 244, 303*n*, 364*n*
Forness, S. A., 6*n*
Forness, S. R., 73, 73*n*, 75, 99*n*, 344
Fortin, L., 75, 76*n*
Foss, J. M., 71, 72
Foster, S., 373, 384, 410
Fowler, S. A., 195, 260*n*, 262, 264*n*, 358*n*, 359*n*
Fox, J. J., 289, 293, 297*n*
Fox, L., 17*n*, 83, 96, 98, 98*n*, 260, 288*n*, 289, 289*n*
Fradd, S. H., 123*n*, 483
Frank, A. R., 464, 465*n*
Frankenberg, E. D., 133
Franklin, E. A., 360
Frazita, R. R., 462*n*
Frederick, L. D., 420, 420*n*
Frederickson, N., 243, 243*n*, 531
Frederico, M. A., 170, 171*n*
Fredrick, L. D., 61, 85, 277, 277*n*, 390*n*
Freedman-Harvey, G., 218*n*
Freeman, R., 288*n*
Freeman, S. F. N., 41
Freeman, S. H., 32, 32*n*, 34
Freire, P., 150
French, N. K., 160, 343*n*, 344
Freston, J., 319
Frey, L., 272, 272*n*
Frey, N., 6, 7, 23, 40, 84, 159, 170, 340, 382, 382, 424, 456
Frieman, B. B., 142, 144, 145*n*
Friend, M., 168
Frisbie, D. A., 499
Fritschmann, N., 303*n*
Froschl, M., 238, 322*n*
Fryxell, D., 35, 98, 214*n*
Fuchs, D., 32–33, 33, 70, 71, 72, 244, 252*n*, 352, 406, 416, 425, 459, 461, 461, 499*n*
Fuchs, L. S., 33, 70, 71, 72, 244, 252*n*, 350, 352, 406, 424, 425, 459, 459, 461, 461, 499*n*, 504
Fuentes, A., 115
Fueyo, V., 125, 362*n*
Fulk, B. M., 405, 405*n*, 417, 447, 448
Fuller, K., 41
Fullwood, H. L., 255*n*
Furner, J. M., 490*n*, 490*n*

Gable, R. A., 38, 289, 506
Gaffney, J. S., 419, 425*n*

Gagnon, J. C., 457*n*, 461, 461
Gajria, M., 260*n*, 279, 352, 398, 403*n*, 475, 476*n*, 477, 477*n*
Galda, L., 426
Gallagher, P. A., 41, 41*n*, 204
Galloway, C., 219, 243
Galluci, C., 37
Gantos, J., 79
Ganzel, A. K., 145, 145*n*
Garay, S. V., 268*n*, 279
Garbarino, J., 237, 320
Garcia, E., 359, 362*n*
Garcia, L. A., 268
Garcia, S. B., 22, 61, 123, 194
Gardiner, J., 99
Gardner, H., 131
Gardner, J. E., 364, 364*n*, 410, 482, 482*n*, 487, 489
Gardner, R., 187, 193, 192*n*, 196, 396, 396*n*
Garmon, M. A., 418, 428, 433*n*
Garmston, R., 166
Garrett, J. T., 116, 116*n*
Garrett, M. T., 116, 116*n*
Garrick Duhaney, L. M., 22, 22*n*, 30, 40, 79*n*, 329, 330*n*, 344, 523*n*, 537, 537*n*
Garriott, P., 8, 39
Garrity, C., 322*n*, 322
Garrod, A., 223
Gartin, B. C., 141*n*, 141*n*, 188, 188*n*, 290, 297*n*, 323*n*
Gartland, D., 367
Gary, L. G., 522, 522*n*, 524
Gast, D. L., 277, 397
Gately, F. J., 170, 172, 175, 536–537
Gately, S. E., 170, 172, 175, 536–537
Gates, D., 456, 456*n*
Gauthier, L. R., 348
Gavin, K. M., 405
Gay, G., 122, 227, 357, 359, 360, 455, 455*n*
Gay, Lesbian, and Straight Education Network (GLSEN), 138*n*, 140*n*
Gebhard, M., 362*n*
Gee, K., 83
Geidel, M., 227*n*
Geisthardt, C. L., 210, 238, 246
Gelfer, J. I., 507*n*
George, H. P., 288*n*
George, M. P., 262
George, N. L., 252*n*
Gerber, M. M., 40, 449

Gerity, B. P., 276
German, B. S., 344*n*
Gersten, R., 255, 266, 363, 362*n*, 416*n*, 431, 443*n*, 416, 446*n*, 454
Getch, Y. Q., 88, 88*n*
Getty, L. A., 49, 49*n*
Geva, E., 416*n*
Giangreco, M. F., 38, 39, 41, 98*n*, 159, 160, 186*n*, 343, 344, 343*n*, 535*n*
Giasson, J., 36
Gibb, G. S., 41, 537*n*
Gibb, S. A., 36
Gibson, B. P., 305, 398
Giek, K., 178*n*
Gilbert, S. E., 122
Gilbert, T. S., 41*n*
Gilles, D. L., 259, 265, 302, 304*n*, 304, 312
Giordano, G., 39
Gipe, J. P., 420, 447
Glaeser, B. C., 303*n*
Glaeser, B. J. C., 306*n*
Glasgow, A., 499
Glater, J. D., 442
Glazer, N. T., 403*n*, 411
Gleason, M., 260*n*
Gleason, M. M., 429, 431*n*, 434, 447, 475, 477
GLSEN (Gay, Lesbian, and Straight Education Network), 138*n*, 140*n*
Goddard, A., 274, 279*n*
Goddard, Y. L., 404, 449
Goetz, L., 6, 8, 32, 34, 37, 38, 151, 214*n*
Goh, D. S., 124, 498, 498*n*, 500, 501
Goldberg, L., 17
Goldin-Meadow, S., 101, 102*n*, 420, 420*n*
Goldman, B. D., 214, 238
Goldstein, H., 97
Goldstein, N., 138*n*, 140*n*, 237
Goleman, D., 131
Gollnick, D. M., 22, 358*n*
Good, R. H., 32
Good, T. L., 391
Goode, E., 98
Goodman, G., 262
Goodnite, B., 470
Goodsitt, J. L., 96*n*, 264*n*
Goodwin, M. W., 408*n*
Goor, M. B., 407, 408*n*
Gordon, J., 175, 536*n*
Goss, P., 382*n*
Gosselin, K., 88, 90–91, 92
Gothelf, C., 269*n*

Gottschalk, C. M., 240, 240n, 369n
Govendo, B. L., 305, 398
Grady, D., 91
Graham, B. I., 511
Graham, S., 431, 433n, 439, 439n, 440n, 442, 443n, 416, 442n, 416n, 417, 446n, 446, 447, 449
Graner, P., 391, 392n, 521, 521n
Grant, C. A., 356, 358n
Grant, R., 352, 468
Grassa, P., 327
Graves, A. W., 431
Graves, D. H., 436
Grechus, M., 370, 370n
Greco, L. A., 304, 318, 318, 319, 393n, 501, 501n
Green, A. L., 42
Green, C. E., 193
Green, P., 503, 503n
Green, S. K., 537n
Greenfield, R. G., 250, 250n
Greenhouse, S., 114, 115
Greenman, G. G., 425
Greenspan, J., 89, 90
Greenwood, C. R., 405, 416, 417n, 434n
Gregg, N., 34, 431n, 417, 417n
Gregory, K. C., 91
Grek, M. L., 406
Grenot-Scheyer, M., 39
Gresham, F. M., 265, 323n
Griffin, H. C., 98n, 104, 326, 327, 345, 372, 373, 373n
Griffin, L. W., 98n
Grigal, M., 275n
Griggs, P., 288n
Griggs, S. A., 344n
Groff, P., 427
Gropper, N., 237, 238, 322n
Gross, R. E., 470n, 485, 515
Grossen, B., 479n, 480
Grossi, T. A., 396, 396n
Grove, K. A., 41
Grskovic, J. A., 78, 79n, 390
Guernsey, L., 368
Guerrera, A., 292, 293n
Guess, D., 288n
Guest, C. L., 76, 76n
Guetzloe, E., 76, 76n, 138
Gullingsrud, M., 230n
Gunn, B., 429
Gunter, P. L., 75, 75n, 304, 316, 327, 393n, 395, 398, 401n
Gushing, L., 17n, 260, 288n
Guskey, T. R., 181, 497, 526n

Gut, D. M., 303n, 304, 408, 408n, 409, 409n
Guterman, B. R., 35
Guthrie, J. T., 417, 421
Gutierrez, M., 235

Haager, D., 427, 427n
Habel, J. C., 161
Hadadian, A., 416n, 448
Hadden, D. S., 260n, 262
Hagan-Burke, S., 289, 295, 504
Haggart, A. G., 51, 51n, 297n, 425, 425n
Hagiwara, T., 229, 230n
Haigh, J., 500
Hall, A. M., 78, 79n, 390
Hall, E. W., 511n
Hall, L. J., 34, 212, 214, 530
Hall, M., 275n
Hall, R. V., 311n
Hall, T. E., 98, 98n, 199, 199n, 337, 338n
Hallenbeck, M. J., 431
Halpern, A. S., 283
Halsey, H. N., 290, 297n, 297
Hamff, A., 348, 419n
Hamill, L., 80, 80n, 83, 84
Hammill, D. D., 454n, 456, 457, 461, 461
Hampton, J., 93
Hamre-Nietupski, S., 38
Hams, K. R., 442n, 417, 449
Handl, P., 465n
Hanich, L. B., 454n, 467
Hanley-Maxwell, C., 303
Hansen, J., 436
Hanson, M. J., 41, 260n
Hapner, A., 60, 61, 62n
Hardman, E., 306
Hargis, C., 467, 489
Haring, N. G., 98n
Harmon, C., 270n
Harmon, J. M., 468, 468n
Harmston, K. A., 449
Harniss, M., 498
Harper, G. F., 380, 396, 404, 405, 406, 408
Harper, P., 232
Harris, C. R., 119n
Harris, K. R., 431, 439, 439n, 440n, 442n, 443n, 416, 416n, 417, 446n, 446, 447
Harrower, J. K., 288n
Harry, B., 185, 187, 192, 193, 194, 195, 195n
Hartley, K., 134, 134n

Hartwell, R., 218, 218n, 219
Hartwig, E. P., 288
Harvard Civil Rights Project, 133
Hasbrouck, J. E., 352, 425n
Hasselbring, T. S., 458
Hastings, R. P., 195, 276, 368
Hatcher, R. E., 61
Haver, J. J., 264, 264n, 363n
Hawke, C., 86
Hay, G. H., 348
Hayden, S., 33, 35, 37, 40
Haynes, C. C., 232, 233, 234n
Haynes, J. B., 442
Heal, L. W., 21n
Healey, B., 194
Heath, B., 498
Heaton, S., 255n
Hebert, C. R., 303n
Hecimovic, A., 92, 141n
Heck, R. H., 170, 172
Heckaman, K., 293, 297n
Heflin, L. J., 277, 277n, 390n
Hehir, T., 61
Heidema, C., 457, 469, 477
Heim, T., 475, 476n, 477, 477n
Heinrichs, M., 458
Heinrichs, R. R., 320, 321, 321n, 322
Heller, K. W., 61, 85, 277, 277n, 390n
Helms, R. G., 182
Helmstetter, E., 32, 38, 41, 42, 537n
Helwig, R., 466n, 467, 498
Henderson, K., 29n
Hendricks, T. B., 343n
Hendrickson, J. M., 38
Henker, B., 77
Henry, D., 15
Hernandez-Valle, I., 448
Herner, L. M., 181n
Heron, T. E., 259n, 404, 449
Herr, C. M., 283
Herrold, W. G., 170, 171n
Herron, B., 304, 304n, 307
Herschell, A. D., 304, 318, 318, 319, 393n, 501, 501n
Hertzog, M. A., 530
Hertzog, N. B., 391n
Hester, P., 300, 305, 305, 307, 319
Hetherington, E. M., 143
Heubert, J. P., 21, 522
Heumann, J. E., 61
Heward, W. L., 102, 396, 396n, 407n
Higgins, C., 306n
Higgins, E. L., 279n, 338, 442, 448, 458, 489

Higgins, K., 131*n*, 132, 134, 134*n*, 170,
181*n*, 268*n*, 272, 278, 282, 364*n*,
365*n*, 442*n*, 487, 488*n*, 489
Hildreth, D. P., 482, 483*n*
Hill, J. L., 61, 85, 86, 87*n*, 88, 88*n*, 91,
92, 92*n*, 93*n*, 96
Hilliard, A., 121
Hillman, E., 416
Hindin, A., 228*n*, 425*n*
Hines, R. A., 8
Hirose-Hatae, A., 6, 8, 32, 37, 38, 151
Hirschfield, S., 138
Hirshoren, A., 344
Hitchcock, C., 8, 18, 67, 265, 340
Hitchings, W. E., 278
Hobbs, T., 239
Hock, M. F., 479, 485
Hodapp, R. M., 80
Hodges, D., 15
Hodgin, K. B., 239
Hodgkinson, H., 110, 117, 117,
117*n*, 144
Hoener, A., 356*n*, 357*n*
Hoffinan, A., 283
Hoffinan, J. V., 417
Hoffman, C. C., 322
Hoge, G., 273
Holburn, S. C., 268, 268*n*
Holcombe, A., 397
Hollenbeck, K., 498, 499
Holliday, C., 282, 283*n*
Hollingsworth, H. L., 181, 181*n*, 199,
534, 535*n*, 536
Holloway, J. H., 113, 115*n*
Holloway, L., 111
Hollowood, T. M., 34, 37
Holmes, S. A., 117, 142
Holubec, E., 406
Homey, M. A., 342
Hooser, C. M., 401*n*
Hopkins, M., 455*n*
Hoppes, M. K., 350
Horn, E., 41
Horne, J., 218*n*, 220*n*
Horner, R. H., 265, 288, 288*n*, 289, 293*n*
Horney, M. A., 489
Horvath, M., 278
Hoskyn, M., 394
Hourcade, J. J., 58*n*, 536*n*, 537
House, A., 500
House, A. L., 498*n*
House, S., 327
Houtz, L. E., 51, 67, 129, 338, 362*n*
Howard, J. K., 406

Howe, K. R., 25
Howell, K. W., 99
Hoy, A. W., 328*n*
Hoyer, L., 292, 293*n*
Hoyt, K. B., 271
Hudson, D. L., 232
Hudson, P., 503*n*
Hudson, P. J., 59*n*, 64*n*, 65*n*
Huefner, D. S., 51, 64, 102*n*
Huer, M. B., 58*n*
Hughes, C., 35, 243, 275, 278*n*, 303, 310
Hughes, C. A., 38, 245, 245*n*, 385*n*,
386*n*, 401, 442*n*, 447, 461, 486*n*,
502, 503*n*
Hughes, M. T., 33, 37
Hughes, T., 35
Hughes, W., 283
Hull, K., 51, 51*n*, 297*n*, 425, 425*n*
Humphries, T., 102
Hundt, T. A., 203
Hung, Y., 458
Hunt, P., 6, 8, 32, 34, 37, 38, 82, 84,
151, 168, 214*n*, 338*n*, 343
Hupp, S., 33, 35, 37, 506, 515
Hurley, C. M., 21*n*
Hurte, M., 503, 503*n*
Hustedt, J. T., 16
Hutchins, M. P., 270*n*
Hutchinson, S. W., 310, 312
Hutinger, P. L., 200
Hwang, B., 243
Hyde, M. S., 37, 210

Ida, D. J., 193, 295, 296*n*
Idol, L., 506*n*
Igoa, C., 118
Ikan, P. A., 61
Ilderton, P., 79*n*
Imada, D., 274, 279*n*
Imel, B., 60, 61, 62*n*
Ingram, C. F., 41, 537*n*
Ingram, G. F., 36
Institute on Community
Integration, 252*n*
Irvine, J. J., 122, 227*n*, 358*n*
Isaccson, S., 429, 431*n*, 434, 447
Isom, B. A., 351*n*, 352
Iverson, V. S., 38, 98*n*
Ivey, G., 422

Jack, S. L., 304
Jackman, L. A., 288, 288*n*, 306
Jackson, C. W., 456, 456*n*, 512
Jackson, F. B., 255

Jackson, L., 6, 8, 41*n*
Jackson, R., 8, 18, 67, 340
Jacobs, A., 89
Jacobson, J. W., 268, 268*n*
Jacqueline, L. R., 537*n*
Jairrels, V., 170, 185, 219, 227, 325
James, L. A., 434*n*
Janiga, S. J., 273
Janney, R. E., 84, 535*n*
Janofsky, M., 113
Janover, C., 79
Jantzen, J. E., 479*n*, 480
Jayanthi, M., 398, 403*n*
Jefferson, G. L., 504
Jefferson-Aker, C. R., 141*n*, 235
Jeffs, T., 367, 442
Jenkins, J. R., 33, 403, 425
Jenkins, L., 33
Jens, K., 322*n*, 322
Jensen, E., 74*n*, 76*n*, 148
Jensen, M. M., 481, 482*n*
Jenson, W. R., 293, 293*n*
Jerman, P., 62*n*, 283
Jimenez, J. E., 448
Jitendra, A. K., 339, 339*n*, 350, 420*n*,
454, 459, 459, 459*n*, 460*n*, 462*n*
Jobe, D. A., 135, 136, 136*n*, 227*n*,
232, 490*n*
Jochum, J., 507, 508*n*
Johanneson, A. S., 115, 235
Johns, B., 187, 188*n*
Johns, B. H., 320
Johns, S., 458, 458
Johnson, C. E., 310*n*
Johnson, C. T., 295
Johnson, D., 466
Johnson, D. E., 273
Johnson, D. R., 268
Johnson, D. T., 131, 132
Johnson, D. W., 302*n*, 406
Johnson, G., 141*n*, 235
Johnson, J. W., 33
Johnson, L., 60, 61, 62*n*
Johnson, L. J., 39, 270, 268*n*
Johnson, L. R., 310*n*
Johnson, M. D., 283
Johnson, R. L., 141*n*, 235
Johnson, R. T., 302*n*, 406
Johnson, S., 93, 94, 95, 96*n*, 306*n*
Johnson, S. A., 268, 268*n*
Johnson, W., 218*n*
Johnston, L. R., 344*n*
Johnston, P., 181
Johnstone, C. J., 341*n*, 338*n*, 356*n*

Jolivette, K., 250, 277, 277n, 289n, 299, 309, 390n
Jones, C. D., 244
Jones, C. J., 417, 417n, 456, 456n
Jones, E. D., 504
Jones, G. A., 461n
Jones, L., 244, 301
Jones, V., 244, 288, 288, 299, 301
Jordan, D. L., 367, 457, 469, 477, 489
Jordan, K. F., 351n, 352
Jordan, L., 417, 448
Jordan, N. C., 454n, 467
Joseph, L. M., 427n, 464, 465n
Justice, L. M., 416n, 420n

Kaczmarek, L., 97
Kaderavek, J. N., 101, 102, 326, 327, 346, 417n, 420n
Kagan, S., 380
Kai Yung Tarn, B., 268, 268n
Kallick, B., 8
Kalyanpur, M., 187
Kame'enui, E. J., 416n, 482
Kamps, D. M., 240, 245, 313, 315n
Kampwirth, T. J., 177, 240, 245
Kapperman, G., 489
Karabin, M., 276, 327
Karasoff, P., 6, 8, 32, 37, 38, 83, 151
Karnes, F. A., 129
Karnes, M., 408
Karp, K. S., 455n
Karvonen, M., 59n, 279, 279n, 283n, 503n
Kasari, C. L., 41
Katamaya, A. D., 382
Katims, D. S., 468, 468n
Katsiyannis, A., 16, 20, 22, 26n, 29, 29n, 33, 93n, 96, 96n, 99, 288
Katsiyannis, G., 159n, 270
Kauffman, J. M., 75, 461n
Kaufmann, L., 465n
Kavale, K. A., 6n, 73, 73n, 75, 99n, 344
Kay, P. J., 158, 167
Kay, S., 356n, 357n
Kazdan, S., 352, 406, 425
Kea, C. D., 193, 295, 296n, 359
Kearns, J. F., 275n, 497, 507n
Keefe, C. H., 34, 260n, 262
Kelker, K., 92, 141n
Keller, C. L., 446n, 447
Keller, M., 443n, 449
Kellner, M. H., 322n
Kellough, N. G., 394, 403, 408, 468, 470n, 484, 487, 515, 516, 517, 518

Kellough, R. D., 394, 403, 408, 468, 470n, 484, 487, 515, 516, 517, 518
Kelly, J., 143
Kelly, K. M., 167, 503n
Kelly, R., 370, 370n
Kemp, K., 319
Kennedy, C. H., 35, 37, 98, 214n
Kennedy, K. Y., 170
Kennedy, S., 507n
Kern, L., 293n, 390
Kerrigan, M., 455n
Kershaw, S., 73, 118
Kerwin, C., 135n
Keyes, M. W., 167, 168n
Keyser-Marcus, L., 93, 94, 95, 96n, 306n
Khoju, M., 21n
Kiarie, M. W., 228, 304, 303n
Kiefer-O'Donnell, R., 34
Kilpatrick, K. M., 486
Kimball, J. W., 327, 388
Kindler, A. L., 115
King, K., 405, 405n
King, R. P., 508
King-Friedrichs, J., 485
King-Sears, M. E., 83, 310, 310n
Kinnell, G., 237, 322
Kinney, E. M., 327, 388
Kirby, K. M., 145
Kirgaali-Iftar, G., 204
Kirkpatrick, M. A., 296n
Kischner, G. A., 232
Kissam, B. R., 255, 255n, 339, 439n, 474
Kitsch, I. B., 89
Klein, C., 507
Kleinert, H. L., 275n, 405n, 497, 503, 503n, 507n
Kleinheksel, K. A., 485
Klemm, W. R., 368n
Klenk, L. J., 349
Klevit, M., 299, 300n
Kling, B., 279, 279n
Klingner, J. K., 33, 34, 37
Kluth, P., 7, 12, 15, 223, 271
Kluwin, T. N., 431n
Knackendoffel, E. A., 180n
Knight, D., 85, 86n, 251
Knight, J., 37, 479
Knight, M. G., 419
Knight, S. L., 39
Knoors, H. E. T., 420n
Knoster, T. P., 289, 288n, 293n
Knotek, S., 22, 51
Knox-Quinn, C., 489
Koballa, T. R., 481n, 482, 487

Kohler, P. D., 267, 279
Kohn, A., 308, 397
Kolar, K. A., 329n
Kolb, S. M., 303
Kollins, S. H., 99n
Koorland, M., 349
Koppang, A., 69, 69n
Koppel, A. E., 455n
Korinek, L., 170
Koroghlanian, C., 515, 516, 517
Kortering, L. J., 21n
Kosciw, J., 138
Koski, B., 501
Kostobryz, C., 39
Kottler, E., 363n
Kottler, J. A., 363n
Kozminsky, E., 280, 281n, 391
Kozminsky, L., 280, 281n, 391
Kozol, J., 133
Krajewski, J. J., 37, 210
Kralovec, E., 402
Kratochwill, T. R., 498, 499, 499n, 501
Kroeger, S. D., 61
Kroesbergen, E. H., 454, 465n
Kubina, R. M., 344
Kucera, T. J., 481n
Kuhn, B. R., 92
Kumar, P., 210, 211, 212, 246
Kumin, L., 81
Kuoch, H., 240n
Kutash, K., 73, 75

Lacerenza, L., 419
Lackaye, T., 402
Ladd, W., 91, 92
Laflamme, M., 34, 41, 85, 239, 327, 328, 328n
Lago-Dellelo, E., 75
Lahm, E. A., 503n, 508
Lake, J., 192
Lamb, E. M., 315
Lambert, M. C., 266
Lambie, G. W., 297, 299
Lamme, L. A., 140n, 145, 145n
Lamme, L. L., 140n, 145, 145n
Lamontagne, M., 268, 268n
Lamorey, S., 194, 194n
Lance, G. D., 83, 338n, 340
Land, L., 343n
Landau, E. D., 223
Landi, M. A. G., 461, 462n, 462
Landrum, T. J., 29, 29n, 39, 99
Landry, K. L., 302n

Landurand, P. M., 122, 296
Lane, H. B., 416*n*, 417, 418, 448
Lane, K. L., 51
Langdon, H. W., 126, 127*n*, 264, 266, 360
Langerock, N. L., 173
Langford, A. D., 522*n*
La Paro, K. M., 16, 260
Larkin, M. J., 512
Larsen, L., 431, 416, 417, 442*n*, 446*n*, 446, 447
Larson, P. J., 293
Lartz, M. N., 102
Lassen, S., 288*n*
Lassman, K. A., 250, 309
Laud, L., 126
Laughter, D., 39
Laurin, K. M., 274
Lau-Smith, J., 283
Lawrence, M., 283
Lawry, J. R., 293*n*
Lawson, J. D., 283
Laymen, L., 269*n*
Layton, C. A., 274, 274*n*
Lazarus, B. D., 307, 367, 382*n*
Leachman, G., 299, 301, 301*n*
Lebzelter, S., 255, 255*n*, 352, 486*n*
Leddy, J. N, 240, 240*n*
Lederer, J. M., 349
LeDuff, C., 118
Lee, C., 133
Lee, O., 483
Lee, S., 34, 196, 198, 198*n*, 214, 238, 241, 530
Leffert, J. S., 80, 408
Lehman, L. R., 38
Lehmann, J. P., 274
Lehr, C. A., 505
Leibold, C. K., 61
Lennon, D., 266*n*
Lenz, B. K., 180*n*, 255, 257*n*, 339, 439*n*, 474, 474*n*, 479, 479*n*, 480, 482*n*
Lenz, K., 391, 392*n*, 521, 521*n*
LeRoy, C. H., 92, 141*n*
Let's Face It, 88*n*
Levendoski, L. S., 310*n*
Lever-Duffy, J., 368
Levin, B., 239
Levine, M., 97, 97*n*, 305, 305*n*, 305, 330, 343, 519
Levine, P., 21*n*
Levitt, J. G., 99*n*
Levy, S., 417*n*, 419, 436
Lewin, T., 122, 142
Lewis, J. A., 142, 143

Lewis, S., 103, 345
Lewis, T. J., 252*n*, 288, 293*n*
Lewis-Palmer, T., 289, 295
Leyva, C., 135
Lian, M. J., 455*n*
Liaupsin, C. J., 289*n*
Liddy, D., 40, 170
Lieber, J., 16
Lignugaris/Kraft, B., 65*n*
Limber, S., 322*n*
Lindsey, P., 76*n*
Lindstrom, B. D, 274
Lindstrom, L., 21*n*, 268, 270
Lipsett, L. R., 228
Lipsey, M. E., 71
Litchfield, S., 102
Little, J., 318, 318
Livneh, H., 211
Lloyd, C., 33, 34
Lloyd, J. W., 39, 40, 170, 173*n*, 461*n*
Lloyd, S. R., 182*n*, 183*n*
Lo, Y., 265, 303
Lock, R. H., 274, 274*n*, 364*n*
Lockman, A. S., 422, 424*n*, 448
Loe, S. A., 265, 303
Logan, K. R., 32, 175, 177, 179*n*
Lohrmann-O'Rourke, S., 61*n*, 275*n*, 278*n*
Lombardi, T. P., 255
Long, R. M., 470*n*, 482
Longaker, T., 97, 97*n*, 305, 305*n*, 305, 330
Longwill, A. W., 405*n*
Lopez, G. R., 116, 196, 197, 197*n*, 203, 204
Lopez-Vona, K., 175, 536*n*
Lord, C., 96
Lorden, S. W., 278*n*
Lorimer, M., 136, 136*n*
Losen, D. J., 22
Lotain, R. A., 403, 404*n*
Love, L., 33
Loveland, T., 38, 533
Loveless, T., 121
Lovett, M. W., 419
Lovitt, T. C., 35, 41, 145, 145*n*, 319, 489
Lowe, V., 273*n*
Lowenthal, B., 147, 147*n*, 361
Loyd, R., 310*n*
Lubic, B. L., 170, 535*n*
Luckner, J., 346, 346*n*
Ludi, D. C., 283
Lue, M. S., 193
Luecking, R., 268
Lueke, B., 260*n*, 262

Luftig, R., 34, 531
Luiselli, T. E., 343
Lund, K. A., 261*n*
Lunnen, K. Y., 158, 166, 167*n*
Lustig, D. C., 195
Lutkenhoff, M., 88*n*
Luze, G. J., 313, 315*n*
Luzzo, D. A., 278
Lynch, E. C., 41, 42
Lytle, R. K., 65*n*, 167*n*

Maag, J. W., 288, 293, 293*n*, 319
MacArthur, C. A., 440, 441, 442
MacArthur, C. D., 482
Maccini, P., 457*n*, 461, 461
Macciomei, N. R., 92
Macfarlane, I., 239
Mack, M., 268
Macmillan, D. L., 22
Madaus, J. W., 274*n*
Madden, J. A., 88
Maddox, J. I., 98*n*
Madrick, J., 111, 111
Magnusson, S. J., 266, 407, 481
Mahdavi, J. N., 51
Maheady, L., 380, 396, 404, 405, 406, 408
Mahitivanichcha, K., 116, 196, 197, 197*n*, 203, 204
Maier, J., 8, 32, 34, 82, 84, 168, 338*n*, 343
Mainzer, R., 23, 24*n*
Maldonado-Colon, E., 125*n*
Male, M., 239
Malian, I. M., 33, 60, 278, 283
Malkin, D. H., 61
Mallette, B., 380, 396, 404, 405, 406, 408
Malone, D. M., 32
Mamlin, N., 64, 326, 327
Mandell, C., 222*n*
Mangrum, C. T., 255*n*, 502
Manley, R. S., 137, 137*n*, 138, 138*n*
Manno, C., 193
Manset, G., 33
Manzo, A., 348
Manzo, U., 348
Marable, M. A., 148
Maralani, V. J., 115
March, T., 370, 370*n*
Marchand-Martella, N., 65*n*, 288, 302*n*
Marchisan, M. L., 431, 433, 434, 435, 436*n*, 437*n*
Marcotte, D., 75, 76*n*
Margolis, H., 274, 279, 390, 390, 391*n*, 393*n*, 421
Mariage, T. V., 418, 428, 433*n*, 436

Marks, S. U., 97, 97*n*, 305, 305*n*, 305, 330, 343

Marlatt, E. A., 102, 346

Maroney, S. A., 182*n*, 183*n*, 238, 238*n*, 481, 482*n*

Marquart, J., 41

Marquis, J., 479*n*, 480

Marr, M. B., 288, 288*n*

Marshall, L. H., 62*n*, 283

Marston, D., 33

Martella, R. C., 65*n*

Martella, R. M., 288, 302*n*

Martin, D., 20

Martin, E. J., 21, 21*n*

Martin, J. E., 62*n*, 275, 275*n*, 277*n*, 279, 279*n*, 283

Martin, L., 283

Martin, S. S., 486, 486*n*

Martinez, E. A., 72, 244

Martinez, Y. G., 116, 116*n*

Martin-Kniep, G. O., 507*n*

Martinussen, R., 69, 77

Martorella, P. H., 363, 470*n*, 483, 483*n*, 484

Marzano, J. S., 299

Marzano, R. J., 299

Mason, C. Y., 60, 61, 62*n*

Mason, L., 439, 439*n*

Mason, S. A., 309*n*

Masterson, J. J., 449

Mastropieri, M. A., 485

Mather, N., 431*n*, 417, 417*n*

Mathes, P. G., 71, 72, 244, 349, 406

Mathews, R., 193, 196, 360*n*

Mathur, S. R., 188, 192, 297, 297*n*

Matlock, L., 6, 24, 25*n*, 65, 65*n*, 66*n*, 339*n*

Matthews, B., 75, 75*n*, 158

Matthews, C., 239

Matthews, C. E., 482, 483*n*

Matthews, W. J., 290, 297*n*, 297

Maxim, G. W., 406, 408, 482, 484, 486, 486*n*, 487

Maxson, L., 62*n*, 283

May, A. L., 531

May, S. W., 448

Mayberry, R. I., 101, 102*n*, 420, 420*n*

Mayweather, K., 204

Mazo, M., 163*n*

McAdams, C. R., 297, 299

McAlister, K. M., 431*n*

McBrien, J. L., 118, 118*n*

McCabe, P. P., 274, 279, 390, 390, 393*n*

McCart, A., 288*n*

McCarty, H., 146*n*

McCathren, R. B., 417, 426, 426*n*

McClintic, C., 484

McComas, J., 34, 41, 85, 239, 327, 328, 328*n*

McConnell, M. E., 310*n*

McCormick, K. M., 277, 277*n*, 299, 390*n*

McCormick, L., 170, 172

McCray, A. D., 296

McDonald, J., 61

McDonald, J. B., 368

McDonnell, J., 32, 33, 34, 37

McDonough, R., 360

McDougall, D., 461

McDowell, K. C., 233, 234, 234*n*

McFarland, S. Z. C., 343

McGahee-Kovac, M., 60, 61, 62*n*

McGee, J. P., 96

McGill, T., 283

McGoogan, G., 232, 239, 368

McGovern-Lawler, J., 126

McGowen, S., 39

McGregor, G., 6, 7, 23, 25*n*, 158, 166

McGregor, J. A., 34, 214

McGuire, J. M., 340

McIntosh, P. L., 76, 76*n*

McKeown, M. G., 469*n*

McKnab, P. A., 184*n*

McLaughlin, M., 25*n*, 185

McLaughlin, P. J., 323*n*

McLaughlin, V. L., 33, 35, 170, 496, 522, 530, 539

McLean, J., 266*n*

McLeod, J., 486

McLeskey, J., 15, 32, 38, 158, 170, 533

McLoughlin, J. A., 88, 88*n*

McMahan, G. A., 17, 58, 58*n*

McMater, K. N., 406, 425

McMorris, C., 39

McNally, J., 270

McNamara, B. E., 320

McNamara, J. K., 71

McNaughton, D., 442*n*, 447

McNeil, C. B., 304, 318, 318, 319, 393*n*, 501, 501*n*

McQuivey, C., 32, 34

McTighe, J., 539, 539*n*

Mechling, L. C., 277

Medina, J., 372, 410

Meehan, K., 292, 293*n*

Meese, R. L., 145, 323*n*

Mehta, Z. D., 458

Mellard, D. F., 21

Meloy, L. L., 499

Menchaca, V., 115

Menchetti, B. M., 268, 454

Mendez Perez, A., 194

Menkart, D. J., 227*n*

Menlove, R. R., 59*n*, 64*n*, 65*n*

Mercer, C. D., 70, 123*n*, 308, 308*n*, 389, 418, 455, 457*n*, 462*n*

Mercer, K. D., 418

Mercury, M. G., 41, 42

Merritt, S., 84

Merryfield, M. M., 232

Met, M., 120

Methven, J. M., 419, 425*n*

Meyer, A., 8, 18, 67, 340

Meyer, D. J., 204

Mhoon, L., 262

Michael, R. J., 91, 91*n*, 92

Michielli-Pendl, J., 380, 396

Mid-Hudson Library System, 242*n*

Midkiff, R. B., 455*n*

Migliore, E. T., 322, 322

Mihalic, S., 322*n*

Mike, D. G., 448

Mikell, S., 93

Miller, D., 364, 364*n*

Miller, H., 458, 458

Miller, J., 482, 484

Miller, K. A., 327

Miller, L. L., 71, 448

Miller, M., 461*n*

Miller, M. D., 302*n*, 418, 455, 457*n*

Miller, S. P., 455, 456, 456*n*, 462*n*, 464

Miller, S. R., 461*n*

Miller, T., 283

Millikan, E., 80

Mills, C., 416

Mills, G. E., 49

Mills, P. E., 33

Mills, R. P., 13

Milne, H., 80

Milstein, S., 276

Minaya-Rowe, L., 120, 120*n*

Miner, C. A., 60, 62, 62*n*

Miranda, A., 78, 79*n*

Mirenda, P., 240*n*

Mishna, F., 321

Mitchem, K. J., 301, 301*n*, 313

Mithaug, D. E., 275, 275*n*

Mithaug, D. K., 275, 277, 278*n*, 390

Mittag, K. C., 461

Mitts, B., 311*n*

Mizell, A. I., 368

Moats, L. C., 422

Modell, S. J., 273, 273, 273*n*

Moloney, M., 274, 277, 279
Monda-Amaya, L. E., 72, 165n, 166, 210, 225n, 244, 250, 252, 252n, 254
Monroe, E. E., 456
Montague, M., 255n, 459, 461n, 461, 462n, 461, 462
Montgomery, W., 22, 22n, 226, 227, 227n, 228, 228n, 358, 359n, 425n, 431, 431n
Moody, M., 500
Moon, M. S., 268, 275n
Moon, S. M., 78, 79n, 390
Moore, W., 505
Moreno, G., 182n, 183n
Morgan, J., 343n
Morgan, J. W., 33, 35
Morgan, M., 41
Morgan, R. L., 276
Morgan, T. H., 461, 462
Morocco, C. C., 228n, 425n
Morris, S., 72, 72n, 240, 240n, 303, 304n
Morrison, A. P., 537n
Morrison, W. F., 223
Morsink, C. V., 164, 166
Moses, R. P., 455n
Moulds, P., 507, 507n
Mu, K., 35
Mueller, F., 293, 293n
Mueller, P. H., 160n, 343n
Mull, C. A., 371, 385, 440
Mullane, T., 475, 477, 476n, 477n
Mulligan, R., 275, 277
Mullin-Rindler, N., 322n
Mullins, F., 184n
Mumper, J., 521
Munk, D. D., 475, 529
Murdick, N. L., 141n, 141n, 188, 188n, 290, 297n, 306n, 323n
Murdock, J. Y., 310, 312
Murphy, F. V., 160n, 343n
Murphy, S., 201n
Murray, C., 270, 273, 273, 279
Muscott, H., 272n
Myers, B. K., 233n, 234
Myers, M. E., 233n, 234

Nagel, D. R., 485
Naglieri, J. A., 465n, 466
Nall, M., 88, 88n
Nassivera, J. W., 486
Nathanson, R., 283
National Council for the Accreditation of Teacher Education (NCATE), 6n, 150

National Information Center for Children and Youth with Disabilities, 224, 224n
National Research Council at the Academy of Science, 22
Naus, J. M., 443n, 442n
Navarette, L., 76n
NCATE (National Council for the Accreditation of Teacher Education), 6n, 150
Neal, J., 163n, 370, 370n
Neal, L. L., 296
Neill, M., 496
Nelson, C. M., 289n
Nelson, J. R., 73, 81, 288, 289, 297n, 300, 302n
Nelson, M. A., 41, 135, 490n
Nelson, N. W., 431n
Nelson, R., 307, 318
Neubarth-Pritchett, S., 88, 88n
Neubert, D. A., 268, 275n
Nevin, A., 60, 278, 283, 506n
Newton, J. S., 293n
New York State Education Department, 146n, 347n
Nichols, A., 330
Nichols, J. D., 496
Nicholson, R., 163n
Nieto, S., 133, 150, 151, 227n, 230n, 234
Noble, L. S., 145n
Nolan, S. M., 435
Nolet, V., 25n
Noonan, M. J., 170, 172, 175, 537
Nord, W. A., 233
Nourse, S. W., 21n
Nowacek, E. J., 255, 255n, 352, 486n

Obenchain, K. M., 210, 243, 244n, 272n
Obermiller-Krolikowski, H. J., 419
Obiakor, F. E., 22, 131n, 149, 187, 282
O'Brien, G., 266n
Ochoa, S. H., 22, 123
Ochoa, T. A., 449
Odom, S. L., 223
Oetinger, C., 503, 503n
Office of Diversity Concerns, 227n
Office of Vocational and Educational Services for Individuals with Disabilities (VESID), 270, 271
Ofiesh, N., 442n
Ogata, V., 172
Ogbu, J., 296
Ogletree, B. T., 158, 166, 167n, 420, 421, 425, 426n

Ohlsen, R. L., 211
Okey, S., 318, 318
Okolo, C. M., 482
Oldfather, P., 390
Olsen, C., 279n
Olson, J., 344n
Olson, M. R., 305n
Olweus, D., 320, 320, 322n
O'Malley, J. M., 267, 507n
O'Neill, J., 269n
O'Neill, K. J., 255
O'Neill, L. M., 17
O'Neill, R. E., 293n
Orfield, G., 22, 133
Orme, M. P., 456
Ormsbee, C. K., 50, 51n, 52n, 343n
Ortiz, A. A., 49, 51, 51n, 61, 128, 129, 194
Osborn, J., 427n
Osborne, A. G., 20, 26n
O'Shanahan, I., 448
O'Shea, D. J., 257n
Osher, D., 322
Ostrow, V., 88
Ostrow, W., 88
Oswald, D. P., 22
Oswald, K., 289, 289n
Ottinger, B., 89, 89n, 90n
Otto, J. C., 369
Owen, B., 440n
Owens, L., 299
Owens, R. E., 81
Owens-Johnson, L., 167, 168n
Oxer, T., 299, 300n

Pacchiano, D., 38
Padeliadu, S., 34
Pakulski, L. A., 101, 102, 326, 327, 346
Palincsar, A. S., 266, 349, 407, 481
Palmer, D. S., 41
Palmer, S. B., 274, 275, 275n, 277n
Palombaro, M. M., 34, 37, 98, 225
Pancheri, C., 99n
Paolucci-Whitcomb, P., 506n
Papillon, M., 75, 76n
Papinczak, T., 97, 214n
Paquette, S., 158, 167
Parette, H. P., 17, 58, 58n, 94, 94n, 192n
Parette, P., 58n, 536n, 537
Parish, J. G., 211
Parish, T. S., 211
Park, J., 111, 112n, 112, 115n, 196, 270, 288n
Parker, J. G., 214
Parker, R., 352, 425n

Parmar, R. S., 454, 455, 456, 459, 462n, 465, 466
Parrette, H. P., 62n
Patnode, M., 306n
Pattern, J. M., 121, 121n, 226, 228
Pattern, J. R., 455n
Patton, J. M., 22
Patton, J. P., 227
Patton, J. R., 77, 219, 272, 296n, 398, 403n
Patton, P. L., 270n
Pauk, W., 352
Paul, P. V., 436n
Paulsen, K., 461
Pavri, S., 34, 72, 210, 210n, 225n, 240, 243, 244, 279, 531, 1971
Peacock, C. A., 91
Pearl, C., 218, 218n, 221n
Peck, C. A., 37, 38, 41, 42, 537n
Peckham, V. C., 92, 92n
Peckham-Hardin, K. D., 258, 305, 305n
Pedrabissi, L., 38
Pedrotty Bryant, D., 348
Peetsma, T., 32
Pelham, W. E., 327
Pellegrino, L., 87, 87n
Pemberton, J., 348, 338n, 419, 469
Pereira, L., 241n, 243
Perez, J., 126
Perez-Selles, M., 51, 51n, 296n
Perkins, P. G., 507n
Perlmutter, J., 6, 7, 301, 306
Perron-Jones, N., 462n
Perry, L. A., 417n
Petch-Hogan, B., 192n, 306n
Peters, J., 17n
Peters, L., 97, 97n, 305, 305n, 305, 330
Peterson, L. Y., 60n
Peterson, R., 145, 145n
Peyton, J. A., 425
Phelps, B. R., 61, 96n, 264n, 276
Phillips, B., 260n, 262
Phillips, C. B, 227n, 235, 236
Phillips, L., 170, 535n
Phillipsen, L., 210, 211, 212, 246
Pianta, R. C., 16, 260
Piazza, R., 422
Pickett, R. S., 38
Pierard, B., 36
Pierce, T., 170, 455, 456, 456n, 464
Pierson, M. R., 303n
Pike, K., 514n, 521
Pikes, T., 282, 282n
Pinckey, J., 282, 282n

Piscitelli, V., 32n, 496
Pisha, B., 341, 487
Pitkin, S. E., 278n
Pittman, P., 102n
Pivik, J., 34, 41, 85, 216, 221, 239, 327, 328, 328n
Plavins, M., 35
Pocock, A., 279, 279n
Podell, D. M., 38
Pogoloff, S. M., 64
Poland, S., 76n
Polloway, E. A., 5n, 50, 77, 296n, 398, 403n
Polychronis, S., 33
Ponterotto, J. G., 135n
Poon-McBrayer, K. F., 22
Pope, K., 204
Popham, W. J., 497, 503
Porte, L. K., 382n
Porter, W., 322n, 322
Portes, A., 120, 120
Posamentier, A. S., 456, 461, 461n, 483
Post, M., 276, 327
Potvin, P., 75, 76n
Powell-Smith, K. A., 32
Powers, F., 97, 97n, 305, 305n, 305, 330
Powers, L., 283
Praisner, C. L., 38
Prater, M. A., 99n, 141n, 223, 223n, 235, 235n, 250, 252, 265, 408
Premack, D., 308
Prendergast, D. E., 61, 92–93
Prentice, K., 406, 425, 461
Prescott, C., 484
Presentacion, M. J., 78, 79n
Presley, J. A., 303, 310
Prestia, K., 89, 89n, 90n
Price, L. A., 275, 277
Priest, B., 255n
Prigge, D. J., 390, 485
Program Development Associates, 274
Prom, M., 536n
Provost, M. C., 254, 255, 255n, 305n, 446n
Pugach, M. C., 64
Pullen, P. C., 416n, 417, 448

Quenemoen, R. F., 505
Quick, D., 37
Quinn, A. E., 115, 195, 228, 296
Quinn, M. M., 262, 289

Raborn, D. T., 456, 483
Rademacher, J. A., 310, 388, 391n, 398n

Radogna, D. M., 271, 272n
Rafferty, Y., 32n, 113, 496
Rainforth, B., 37
Ramasamy, R., 419
Ramig, P. R., 81
Ramirez, G., 448
Ramirez, J. D., 120, 296
Ranalli, P., 311, 311n
Randandt, E., 475
Rankin, J. L., 442, 442n
Rankin-Erickson, J. L., 433, 448
Rao, S., 292, 293n
Rapport, M. J. K., 13, 15, 20
Raschke, D., 309n
Raskind, M. H., 17, 338, 442, 448, 458, 489
Rasmussen, S. K., 304
Rawlinson, D., 318, 318
Rawlinson, R., 318, 318
Raymond, E. B., 138, 140n
Raynes, M., 535n
Rea, P. J., 33, 35, 496, 522, 530, 539
Reavis, K., 293, 293n
Redmond, S., 93
Reed, F., 250, 252, 252n, 254
Reed, P., 329, 329n
Reese, S. M., 144
Reetz, L., 507, 508, 508n, 509
Reeves, G., 232
Regan, K. S., 431, 431n
Reichart, D. C., 41, 42
Reichel, H., 401n
Reid, D. K., 35, 210
Reid, M. S., 405, 405n
Reid, R., 29, 29n, 289, 293n, 297n, 530
Reigel, D. H., 88, 88n
Reis, S. M., 80
Reisberg, L., 303, 304, 304n, 322n
Reiss, T., 273n
Rennells, M. S., 170
Renzaglia, A., 270n
Reschly, D. J., 22
Retish, P., 278
Rettig, M. D., 305n
Reward, W. L., 5, 80, 98, 103
Reynolds, C. J., 436n
Rhine, B. G., 405, 405n
Rhodes, R. L., 197
Rice, D., 170, 172, 175n
Rice, L. S., 128
Richards, J. C., 417
Richardson, B. G., 300, 300n
Rickson, H., 137, 137n, 138, 138n
Riffel, L., 288n

Rigby, K., 322n
Riggs, C. G., 160, 160n, 344, 343n
Riley, T., 170
Rinard, B., 484
Risen, T., 33
Ristow, R., 278
Ritchey, K. D., 416
Roach, V., 6, 7, 23, 25n
Roberts, D., 93
Roberts, J. P., 80
Roberts, L. C., 116, 116n
Roberts, M. L., 300
Roberts, R. L., 54n
Robertson, H. M., 255n
Robinson, C. S., 454
Robinson, D. H., 382
Robinson, K., 88n
Robinson, L., 364, 364n
Robinson, R., 457
Robinson, S. M., 132
Robinson, T. R., 51, 302n
Robles-Pina, R., 22, 123
Rock, M. L., 61n, 193
Rockwell, S., 272n
Rodi, M. S., 310
Rodis, P., 223
Rodrigo, M., 448
Roeder, J., 204
Rogan, P., 61, 267
Rogers, D. C., 274, 274n
Rogers, E. L., 274, 274n
Rohena, E. I., 78, 420n
Rohner, J., 223, 223n
Roll-Pettersson, L., 38
Rolon, C. A., 121
Romer, L. T., 98n
Roney, L., 91
Roof, V., 358, 358n
Rope, J., 401
Rosberg, M., 223, 223n
Rose, D., 8, 18, 67, 340
Roseberry-McKibbin, C., 124, 129,
        362, 362n
Rosenberg, H., 270
Rosenberg, M. S., 288, 288n, 306, 487
Rosenberg, R. L., 67n, 68, 68n
Rosenthal-Malek, A. L., 89, 90
Roser, N. L., 417
Rosko, D., 385n
Ross, D. E., 419
Rothlisberg, B. A., 94
Rotter, K., 394, 394n
Rousseau, M. K., 486
Routman, R., 181n

Rowell, J., 177, 179n, 177n
Rowley-Kelley, F. L., 88, 88n
Roy, S., 454, 455, 456, 459, 465, 466
Royer, E., 36
Rozalski, M. E., 322n
Rozek-Tedesco, M. A., 499
Rozendal, M. S., 425
Rublin, H., 402
Rude, H. A., 223
Ruder, S., 8
Rueda, R., 431
Ruef, M. B., 306n
Ruesch, G. M., 288
Ruhl, K. L., 38, 245, 245n, 401, 502
Ruiz-Escalante, J., 115
Rullo, A., 446n
Rung, L. L., 243
Rusch, F. R., 21n
Russo, C. J., 20, 26n
Rustuccia, C., 75, 76, 76n
Rutherford, R. B., 297, 297n
Ryan, A. K., 158, 167
Ryan, A. L., 290, 297n, 297
Ryan, B., 61
Ryan, D. J., 270n
Ryan, S., 84, 217, 282, 282n
Ryndak, D. L., 6, 8, 41n, 537n
Ryser, G., 75

Sadao, K. C., 271
Sadker, D., 135, 136, 230n, 232,
        467, 470n
Sadker, M. P., 135, 136
Sadler, F. H., 14, 304n
Saenz, L. M., 350, 406, 424, 425
Safran, J. S., 96, 97, 97n
Safran, S. P., 96, 222, 289, 289n,
        303n, 304
Sager, N., 322n, 322
Sailor, W., 83, 288n
Saint-Laurent, L., 36, 68
Salembier, G. B., 421n
Salend, S. J., 22, 22n, 30, 32n, 40, 49,
        78, 79n, 81, 84, 123, 126, 163n,
        175, 217, 235, 253, 314, 315,
        315n, 356n, 357n, 369n, 387,
        388, 398, 403n, 511, 514n, 523n,
        536n, 537, 537n
Salinas, A., 49, 81, 123, 126
Salinger, T., 422
Salisbury, C. L., 6, 7, 23, 25n, 34, 37,
        98, 158, 166, 225
Salmon, S., 454, 455, 456, 459, 465,
        466, 511n

Saltzman, N. J., 461n
Sampson-Saul, M., 32
Sanacore, J., 417, 417n, 426
Sandall, S., 41
Sander, N., 88
Sanders, E. A., 425
Sandoval, J., 93
Sands-Buss, S., 39
Sanko, J., 239
Santos, K. E., 305n
Santos, R. M., 196, 198, 198n, 358,
        358n, 359n
Sapona, R. H., 170, 535n
Sapon-Shevin, M., 7, 8, 151, 210, 217,
        230n, 232, 234, 237, 244, 281,
        282n, 358
Sarouphim, K. M., 132
Saunders, M. D., 387
Saunders, W., 266n
Savage, T. V., 393, 396, 404, 408,
        487, 516
Sax, C. L., 268
Sayers, L. K., 163, 163n
Scanlon, D., 21, 255, 477, 480n
Scarborough, J. L., 162
Schader, R., 80
Schaps, E., 244, 297
Schattman, R., 39, 535n
Schaufler, J. H., 197, 197n, 357n
Scheuermann, B., 187, 188n
Schiff-Meyers, N. B., 126
Schirmer, B. R., 100, 102, 346, 422,
        424n, 434n, 448
Schlozman, S. C., 73, 75, 76, 76n, 99,
        137, 138, 138n
Schlozman, V. R., 99
Schmid, R. E., 313
Schmidt, R. J., 425
Schmitt, E., 117, 135, 142
Schnapp, L., 279n
Schniedewind, N., 230n, 232, 244,
        402, 404n
Schnorr, R., 6, 8, 25n, 85, 338, 339, 339n
Schnur, B., 267
Schoen, A. A., 361
Schoen, S. F., 240, 361
Schoenbrodt, L., 81
Scholastic Press, 236
Schon, I., 227n
Schorr, J., 230
Schowalter, M., 327
Schrader, C., 97, 97n, 305, 305n, 305,
        330, 343
Schroeder, M., 509

Schulte, T. R., 498, 499, 499*n*, 501

Schulz, E. G., 99, 99*n*

Schumaker, J. B., 38, 245, 245*n*, 280*n*, 350, 352, 401, 408*n*, 435, 474*n*, 477, 479, 479*n*, 480, 484, 485*n*, 485, 502

Schumm, J. S., 33, 34, 37, 174*n*

Schuster, J. W., 80

Schutz-Muehling, L., 442, 442*n*

Schwartz, A. A., 268, 268*n*

Schwartz, I. S., 37

Schwartz, S. S., 138

Schwartz, W., 132, 295

Schweder, W., 364, 364*n*, 482, 482*n*, 487, 489

Schweinhart, L., 16

Schwenn, J. O., 407, 408*n*

Scott, B. J., 431, 432*n*, 434

Scott, D. L., 498*n*

Scott, J., 118

Scott, K. G., 70

Scott, P. B., 456

Scott, S. L., 150

Scott, S. S., 340

Scott, T. M., 75, 158, 289*n*, 293*n*

Scott, V. G., 448, 504, 506

Scribner, J. D., 116, 196, 197, 197*n*, 203, 204

Scruggs, T. E., 485

Sealey, E., 119*n*

Seay, P. C., 17

Seevers, R. L., 486*n*

Seif, E., 25*n*, 339, 339*n*

Selinger, J., 461*n*

Semmel, M. I., 33, 40

Serafini, F. W., 507

Serna, L. A., 283, 408

Serry, M. E., 39

Sewall, A. M., 92, 93*n*

Sexton, M., 440*n*

Sferrazza, M. S., 162

Shafer, G., 114, 115, 229, 230*n*, 235

Shafer, K., 97

Shames, G. H., 81

Shank, K. S., 401*n*

Shank, M., 25, 80, 98

Shapiro, A., 4, 5*n*, 82*n*, 210, 211, 212, 215, 215*n*, 218*n*, 219, 220*n*, 222, 223, 224, 225*n*, 236, 242*n*, 243, 328

Shapiro, D. R., 163, 163*n*

Sharp, E. R., 475, 477, 476*n*, 477*n*

Sharpe, M. N., 37

Shaw, S. F., 340

Shaw-Hegwer, J., 97, 97*n*, 305, 305*n*, 305, 330

Shelton, C. M., 131, 131*n*, 344

Shen, H., 60, 62, 62*n*

Sheras, P. L., 321

Sheridan, S., 96

Sherron-Targett, P., 93, 94, 95, 96*n*, 305*n*

Shields, J. M., 259*n*

Shin, M., 78

Shinn, M. R., 32, 537*n*

Shippen, M. E., 295, 297*n*

Shoemaker, J., 482*n*

Shoemaker, J. B., 480*n*

Shokoohi-Yekta, M., 38

Shores, R. E., 304

Short-Camilli, C., 322*n*, 322

Shriner, J. G., 498, 498*n*

Shriver, M. D., 92

Shubert, T. H., 323*n*

Shukla, S., 35, 98, 214*n*

Shukla-Mehta, S., 74*n*, 318, 318*n*

Shupe, M. J., 300, 300*n*

Siders, J. A., 232*n*, 239, 449, 512

Siegel, E. B., 35, 167, 503*n*

Siegel-Causey, E., 39

Sikes, J., 406

Sileo, N. M., 141*n*, 235, 235*n*

Simard, C., 36

Simmons, D. C., 416*n*

Simpson, M., 422

Simpson, R. G., 295, 297*n*

Sinclair, M. F., 21*n*

Singer, G. H. S., 194, 205

Singh, G. R., 218

Singleton, A. H., 456, 465

Siperstein, G. N., 80, 408

Sitlington, P. L., 371, 385, 440

Skelton, M., 232

Skinner, M. E., 274

Skinner, M. L., 214, 238

Skutch, R., 147

Slavin, R. E., 111

Slavkin, R., 368*n*

Sleeter, C. E., 356, 358*n*

Sloan, J. M., 81

Smart, J., 218

Smartt, S., 418*n*

Smead, V. S., 223, 223*n*

Smith, C., 75, 158

Smith, M., 456, 456*n*

Smith, P., 461*n*

Smith, R. M., 84, 188, 192, 217

Smith, S., 25, 80, 98, 135, 442*n*, 490*n*

Smith, S. B., 368, 368*n*

Smith, S. J., 368, 368*n*

Smith, S. W., 194, 259, 265, 302*n*, 304, 304*n*, 306, 455

Smith, T. E. C., 77

Smith-Davis, J., 6*n*

Smith-Rex, S., 318, 318

Smithson, I., 136

Smith-Thomas, A., 50

Smolkowski, K., 429

Snapp, M., 406

Snell, M. E., 84, 98*n*, 535*n*

Snider, V. E., 99

Snyder, E. P., 61

Snyder, L., 8, 39

Snyder, M., 145, 145*n*

So, T. H., 38, 533

Soodak, L. C., 38, 41*n*

Soriano, M., 78, 79*n*

Soto, G., 8, 32, 34, 82, 84, 168, 338*n*, 343

Southern, W. T., 504

Sparkman, K. L., 181, 181*n*

Sparks, J., 391*n*

Sparks, S., 116, 116*n*, 194*n*, 296, 360*n*

Spear-Swerling, L., 416*n*

Speece, D. L., 416

Spence, C. D., 260*n*, 262

Spencer, V. G., 405

Spiegel, G. L., 91, 91*n*, 92*n*

Sprague, J., 323*n*

Sprague, J. R., 289, 293*n*

Sprung, B., 322*n*

SRI International, 33

Staal, L. A., 433

Stafford, A. M., 41, 41*n*, 204, 277, 277*n*, 390*n*

Stahl, S. A., 429

Stainback, S., 281, 282*n*

Stainback, W., 281, 282*n*

Staley, L. M., 145, 145*n*

Standeven, B., 137, 137*n*, 138, 138*n*

Stanford, P., 131, 131*n*, 232*n*, 239, 449, 512

Stanger, C., 458, 458

Stanovich, P. J. I, 39, 534

Staub, D., 37, 41, 238*n*, 241, 241*n*

Stecker, P. M., 504

Steere, D. E., 59, 60*n*, 270, 274

Stein, M., 470*n*, 482

Stein, N. D., 322*n*

Stein, S. S., 175, 177, 179*n*

Stella, J., 254, 254*n*

Stepelman, J., 456, 461, 461*n*, 483

Stephan, C., 406

Stephens, H., 185, 325

Stephens, J. T., 182, 182n, 183n
Stephens, K. R., 129
Stephens, R., 80
Sternberg, R. J., 132n, 416n
Stewart, L. H., 401
Stichter, J. P., 277, 277n, 299, 304, 304n, 390n
Stickerman, J., 489
Stiggins, R. J., 392, 396
Stinson, M., 373, 384, 410
Stock, S. E., 276
Stockall, N., 290, 297n
Stodden, R. A., 268
Stoehrmann, T., 475
Stolberg, S. G., 139
Stone, A. P., 223
Stone, C. A., 531
Stoneman, Z., 42
Storey, K., 276, 293n, 327
Stormont-Spurgin, M., 403n, 417, 447, 449
Stough, L. M., 76n, 342, 524
Strassman, B. K., 448
Strawser, S., 462n
Strichart, S., 255n, 502
Strickett, T., 212, 214, 530
Strickland, D. S., 426
Stromer, R., 327, 388
Strong, C. J., 449
Strong, K., 93
Strong, M. F., 115
Stroud, J. E., 145, 145n
Stuart, J. L., 96n, 264n
Stuart, S. K., 270
Students for Social Justice, 138
Stuen, C., 470n, 482
Sturm, J. M., 433, 442, 442n, 448
Sugai, G., 21, 21n 75, 158, 265, 288, 288n, 289, 289, 293n, 295, 461n
Sullivan-Burstein, K., 403n
Summers, L., 93
Summy, S. E., 49, 49n, 485
Suritsky, S. K., 385n, 386n
Suter, D., 59n, 64n, 65n
Sutherland, K. S., 75, 300, 395, 397
Svenson, E., 406, 425
Svobodny, L. A., 41, 42
Swaggart, B. L., 313
Swanson, H. L., 255, 394
Swanson, K., 38, 533
Sweeney, D. P., 99n
Swicegood, P. R., 507, 511
Swisher, K. G., 116, 116n
Symington, L., 458, 458

Symons, F. J., 80
Szabo, J. L., 165n

Taber, T. A., 41, 41n, 204
Tam, K. Y., 486
Tamura, R., 283
Tankersley, M., 39, 315
Tanner, C. K., 486n
Tanners, A., 278
Tannock, R., 69, 77
Tao, L., 368, 449
Targett, P., 270, 271, 271
Tascione, L., 34, 35, 211, 219, 278
Tatum, B., 210, 211
Taunt, H. M., 195
Taylor, A., 79n
Taylor, B. A., 327, 388
Taylor, D., 136, 136n
Taylor, J. A., 304, 305
Taylor, K. L., 133
Taylor, L. S., 356, 357
Taylor, R. L., 419
Taylor, S., 227, 227n, 359n
Taymans, J. M., 274, 339
Teher, M. J., 417, 417n, 425
Teicher, J., 368n
Teicher, M. H., 146
Tekin, E., 204
Telzrow, C. F., 71, 72, 72n
Templeman, T. P., 17n
Templeton, E., 97, 214n
Terry, B. J., 405
Test, D. W., 59n, 279, 279n, 283n
Thoma, C. A., 61, 267, 268, 268n, 283
Thomas, C., 164, 166
Thomas, K., 327
Thomas, O., 232, 234n
Thomas, R. S., 539, 539n
Thomas, S. B., 13, 15, 86, 274n
Thomas, W. P., 117, 120, 121n, 125
Thompson, A., 406, 425
Thompson, C. D., 114
Thompson, J. R., 188, 188n
Thompson, S. J., 341n, 348, 338n, 356n, 419n, 502n, 505
Thoms, K. J., 410
Thony, B., 465n
Thornton, C. A., 456, 458, 461n, 463
Thorp, E. K., 193, 196
Thorson, N., 32, 34
Thousand, J. S., 6n, 7, 12, 15, 40, 67n, 68, 68n, 159, 170, 339
Thurlow, M. L., 24, 341n, 338n, 356n, 497, 498, 498n, 500, 501, 505

Tickle, B., 330
Tiedt, I., 126, 229n, 231, 236n, 300n
Tiedt, P. L., 126, 229n, 231, 236n, 300n
Tilley-Gregory, D., 385
Tillman, L. C., 295
Tindal, G., 467, 466n, 498, 499
Tippiconnic, J. W., 116, 116n
Tippins, S., 321
Tobin, T. J., 21, 21n, 327
Tolla, J., 104, 328, 345
Tomlinson, C. A., 6, 7, 216, 218, 337, 390, 527, 529,
Tompkins, G. E., 417n, 425n, 427, 428, 437
Tom Snyder Productions, 239
Tone, T., 204
Tonelson, S. W., 289
Toohey, M. A., 461n
Toporek, C., 88n
Toppel, C., 330
Torgerson, C. W., 60, 62, 62n
Torgesen, J., 416n, 427
Torgesen, J. K., 416, 454
Torres-Rivera, E., 116, 116n
Torres-Velasquez, D., 482, 483
Torrey, G., 96, 96n
Tournaki, N., 405, 405n, 461, 461n
Townsend, B. L., 22, 25n, 295, 296n
Townsend, M., 33, 34
Trautman, M. L., 82n, 84, 320, 343, 343n
Treadway, P. S., 339
Troha, C., 177, 179n, 177n
Troia, G. A., 440, 440n
Trollinger, G., 368n
Troutman, A. C., 290, 307, 309, 309n
Tucker, B. F., 456, 465
Tucker, D. L., 428
Tundidor, M., 535n, 537n
Tur-Kaspa, H., 214, 530
Turnbull, A. P., 25, 80, 98, 111, 112n, 112, 115n, 167n, 187, 192, 193, 194, 196, 241n, 243, 270, 288n, 296
Turnbull, H. R., 25, 80, 98, 111, 112n, 112, 115n, 270, 288n
Turner, J., 243, 243n, 531
Tyler, B., 418, 448

Uberti, H. Z., 485
Udell, T., 17n
Ugel, N., 348, 419n
Ulrich, M. E., 194, 276, 327, 370, 370n, 506

U.S. Department of Education, 33, 78, 112, 113, 136, 185, 185n, 195n
Utley, C. A., 359, 405

Vacca, D. M., 71, 72n
Vacca, J. L., 348
Vacca, R. T., 348, 421
Vadasy, P. F., 204, 403, 425
Valdez, L. A., 273, 273, 273n
Valdez Pierce, L., 507n
Validivia, R., 196, 198, 198n
Valle, J. W., 189, 192
Valles, E. C., 431
Valore, T., 262
Van Dycke, J. L., 60n
van Garderen, D., 79n, 387, 459, 461n, 461, 462n
Vanleeuwen, D. M., 39
Van Luit, J. E. H., 454, 465n
Van Reusen, A. K., 279, 461
Vargo, S., 177
Varisco, R., 262
Vasquez, L. R., 449
Vaughn, B. J., 289
Vaughn, S., 33, 34, 35, 37, 174n, 261n, 418, 448
Velazquez, J. A., 116, 116n
Venn, J., 170, 171n
Venn, M. L., 327
Verbeek, R. L., 30
Vergason, G. A., 76n
Vernon, D. S., 408n
Vervloed, M. P. J., 420n
VESID (Office of Vocational and Educational Services for Individuals with Disabilities), 270, 271
Victor, D., 299, 301, 301n
Viglianti, D., 253n
Villa, R. A., 6n, 7, 12, 15, 67n, 68, 68n, 339
Vincent, M., 266, 407, 481
Vinton, L., 99
Vitale, M. R., 431, 432n, 434
Vitek, K., 489
Vogel, J. R., 529
Voltz, D. L., 6, 7, 15, 22, 175, 328, 330, 339, 390, 391, 455n, 482, 530n
Voorhies, J., 459
Vreeland, P., 486

Wadsworth, D. E., 85, 86n, 251
Wagner, S., 33, 35, 38
Waldron, N. L., 32, 38, 158, 170, 533

Walker, B. J., 425
Walker, H., 323n
Walker, H. M., 73, 73n, 75, 322n
Walker, W. L., 271
Walker-Bolton, I., 289
Wallace, T., 33, 35, 37, 506, 515
Wallerstein, J. S., 142, 143
Walsh, D., 6, 24, 25n, 65, 65n, 66n, 339n
Walsh, J. M., 24, 65, 65n, 339n
Walther-Thomas, C., 33, 35, 116, 170, 479, 496, 522, 530, 539
Walton, C., 416, 417n
Wambold, C., 500
Wang, W., 266
Wansart, W. L., 434, 434n
Wanzek, J., 427, 427n
Warger, C., 64, 113, 401, 402, 461, 462
Warner, M. M., 350, 352
Warren, E., 18
Warren, J., 288n
Wasburn-Moses, L., 496, 498, 501, 522
Washburn, S. G., 487
Washington, J. A., 230
Wasowicz, J., 449
Waters, J., 279
Watson, S. M. R., 51, 67, 129, 148, 338, 339, 362n
Wauters, L. N., 420n
Wayne, S. K., 403
Weaver, T. L, 456, 465
Webber, J., 323n
Webb-Johnson, G., 296
Weber, R. K., 364n
Wegner, J. R., 81, 82n
Wehby, J., 309
Wehby, J. A., 75, 300, 397
Wehby, J. H., 270n
Wehby, J. P., 250
Wehman, P., 93, 94, 95, 96n, 270, 271, 271, 306n
Wehmeyer, M. L., 78, 83, 243, 245, 270, 274, 275, 275n, 276, 277n, 283, 310, 338n, 340
Weikart, D., 16
Weikle, B., 416n, 448
Weishaar, M. K., 349n, 382, 448, 504, 506
Weismantel, M. J., 123n
Weiss, M. P., 39, 40, 71, 170, 173n
Welch, A. B., 218
Welch, M., 252n
Welch, N., 39
Wellman, B., 166
Wells, H. C., 244

Welner, K. G., 25
Welsch, R. G., 404
Werts, M. G., 64, 397
Wesley, P. W., 181, 181n
Wessler, S. L., 237
Wesson, C. L., 222n, 508
West, L. L., 274
West, R. P., 301, 301n, 319
Westby, C. E., 148, 482, 483
Westling, D. L., 83, 96, 98, 98n
Whalen, C. K., 77
Wheeler, J., 461n
Whinnery, K. M., 506
Whitaker, D. P., 389
Whitaker, M. L., 233n, 235
Whitaker, S. D., 182, 182n, 183n
White, C. M., 273
White, R., 288, 288n
Whitney-Thomas, J., 274, 277, 279
Whitt, J., 436n
Whittaker, C. R., 235, 282, 282n, 356, 357, 388, 403, 435n, 511
Whittington-Couse, M., 344
Wickham, D., 288n
Wigford, A., 232
Wiggins, M. F., 114
Wigle, S. E., 34
Wilkinson, C. Y., 51n
Wilkinson, L. A., 177, 179n
Willard-Holt, C., 84, 131, 132, 132n
Willert, H. J., 148
Williams, B. T., 170
Williams, C. B., 101, 102, 239, 326, 346, 346
Williams, D. L., 364n, 365n, 382, 382, 424, 456
Williams, G. J., 303, 304, 304n, 322n
Williams, K., 96, 97
Williams, L. J., 39, 40, 60, 278, 535n
Williams, S. C., 104, 326, 327, 345, 372, 373, 373n, 403n, 411, 440, 442
Williams, V. I., 197, 199
Williamson, R. D., 257, 260, 260n, 310, 312
Wilton, K., 33, 34
Winebrenner, S., 131, 131n, 132
Winograd, P., 348n
Winsor, P. J. T., 223n
Wissick, C. A., 364, 364n, 410, 482, 482n, 487, 489
Witte, R., 93
Witzel, B., 308, 308n, 389, 455, 457n
Wolensky, D., 275, 277
Wolery, M., 80, 397

Wolf, N. K., 283
Wolfe, P. S., 98, 98n, 197, 197n, 199, 199n, 337, 338n, 357n
Wolfensberger, W., 16
Wolford, P. L., 407n
Wong, B. Y. L., 71
Wong, J., 459
Wood, D. K., 464, 465n
Wood, J., 237, 237n
Wood, K. D., 471, 472, 471n, 474
Wood, S. J., 282, 283n
Wood, T. A., 182n, 183n
Wood, W. M., 59n, 279, 279n, 283n
Woodfield, K., 505
Woodward, J., 457, 459, 465
Woolf, S. B., 269n
Woolsey-Terrazas, W., 74n
Wren, C. T., 273
Wright, E. H., 271, 272n
Wright-Strawderman, C., 76n
Wyatt, E., 33
Wyatte, M. L., 289

Xin, Y. P., 350, 454, 459

Yalowitz, S. J., 323n
Yan, L., 406, 425
Yang, N., 406, 425
Yasuda, S., 93, 94, 95, 96n, 306n
Yasutake, D., 280
Yeager, E., 170
Yeager, N., 470, 478n
Yeh, C. J., 121, 135, 227, 235, 264
Yehle, A. K., 500
Yell, M. L., 15, 20, 26n, 51, 93n, 288, 322n
Yell, M. M., 382n, 430
Yetter, C. E., 91, 91n, 92n
Yocom, D. J., 228, 394n
Yoder, P. J., 300, 397
Yoo, S., 34, 214, 238, 241, 530
York, J. L., 37, 535n, 537n
Young, J. R., 36, 41, 537n
Young, K. R., 301, 301n, 313, 319
Young, L., 292, 293n

Yovanoff, P., 21n, 268, 270
Ysseldyke, J. E., 498, 498n, 500, 501

Zamora-Duran, G., 22
Zaslavsky, C., 455
Zemelman, S., 467
Zentall, S. S., 78, 79n, 390
Zhang, C., 196, 198, 198n
Zhang, D., 16, 22, 33, 35
Zickel, J. P., 62n
Ziegler, D., 23, 24n
Zigmond, N., 32–33, 33, 34, 170, 172, 173n
Zinkil, S. S., 41n
Zionts, L. T., 188, 188n
Zittleman, K., 136, 232, 233n, 467, 470n
Zorn, D., 268, 268n
Zurkowski, J. K., 305n

Subject Index

Page numbers followed by "*n*" (such as 145*n*) indicate notes.

A-B-C (Antecedents-Behavior-Consequences) analysis, 293–294, 295
ABC (Applications in Biology/Chemistry), 484
Ability Magazine, 277
Ability Online Support Network, 277
Absence seizure, 91
Academic difficulties, 71
Academic language development, 267
Academic learning games, 394, 410
Academic performance, impact of inclusion on, 32–33, 36–37
Academic performance evaluation, 496–522
  gathering information, 519–522
  in mathematics, 466–467
  reporting information, 522
  standardized testing, 496–502, 503
  standardized testing alternatives, 502, 503, 504–519
Acceptance, fostering, 239–240
Acceptance Scale, 211
Access accommodations, 342
Accommodations
  access, 342
  curricular, 339–340
  high-impact, 342
  individualized teaching, 342
  instructional, 526–528
  instructional materials, 342–343
  low-impact, 342
  Section 504 plans, 29, 30, 31
  testing, 498–500, 501
Acculturation, 193
Acronym mnemonics, 484–485
Acrostic mnemonics, 484–485
Active student responding, 396
Activities-oriented approaches to science and social studies instruction, 481–482

Activity-Based Mathematics Units, 455*n*
Activity reinforcers, 308
ADA (Americans with Disabilities Act), 28, 30, 524
Adapted switches, 370, 371
Adapted textbooks, 474
ADD (attention deficit disorder), 76–78, 79
Additive approach to multicultural curriculum, 357
Administrators, school, 158
Adopted children, 145
Adulthood, transition from school to, 267–273
Advance organizers, 475–480
Adventures of Jasper Woodbury, The, 458
Advocacy groups, 20
Advocating for students and their families, 187
Affective education techniques, 302
Affinity support groups, 277, 281–282
African American English, 230–231
African Americans
  court cases, 20
  disproportionate representation, 22
  gender bias, 136
  individual *versus* group performance, 296
  learning style, 122
  racial discrimination, 133
  teacher proximity and movement, 304
Aggressive behaviors, 322–323
Agostini v. *Felton* (1997), 20
AIDS (acquired immune deficiency syndrome), 139, 140, 141, 235
Aimline, 506
Alexander Graham Bell Association for the Deaf, 223
Algorithm models, 463
All About Asthma (Ostrow & Ostrow), 88
Allergies, 88
All Kids Can, 239
"All learners/students," as term, 6*n*
Alternative teaching, 168, 169

Alternative testing techniques, 498–500
American Lung Association, 88
American Memory Web Site, 487
American Museum of Natural History, 487
American Printing House for the Blind, 487
American Sign Language (ASL), 489
Americans with Disabilities Act (ADA), 28, 30, 524
Analytic approach to phonetics instruction, 427
Anecdotal records, 292
Anorexia nervosa, 137
"A" NOTES strategy, 385*n*
Answer box models, 463
ANSWER learning strategy, 502
Antecedent-based interventions, 304–307
Antecedents, 293–294
Antecedents-Behavior-Consequences (A-B-C) analysis, 293–294, 295
Antibias curricula, 226
Anticipation guides, 478–479
Anticipatory set, 393
Anxiety disorders, 73
Applications in Biology/Chemistry (ABC), 484
A priori instructional model, 179
Art centers, 325
Articulation disorders, 81
ASD (autism spectrum disorder), 96–97
Asian Americans and Pacific Islanders, 117, 302, 360*n*
AskERIC service, 185
ASL (American Sign Language), 489
Asperger syndrome, 96–97
ASSERT learning strategy, 279*n*
Assessment. *See* Academic performance evaluation
Assessment Accommodation Checklist, 499*n*
Assignment Idea Chart, 391*n*
Assignment logs, 257–258
Assignment notebooks, 257

Assignments
  independent, 257
  stamps for, 399–400
  tiered, 340
Assistive technology
  and IEPs, 54, 58, 62, 63
  and low-incidence disabilities, 84
  for medically fragile students, 93
Assistive Technology Act, 17
Assistive technology devices
  defined, 17
  in differentiated instruction, 370–375
  for hearing disabilities, 373
  information about, 225–226
  for physical disabilities, 370–371
  for reading disabilities, 371–373
  for second language learners, 373, 375
  vignette, 19
  for visual disabilities, 371–373
Assistive technology services, 17–18
Asthma, 88, 89
Ataxia, 86
Athetosis, 86
Attention deficit disorder (ADD), 76–78, 79
Attention-getting strategies, 386–387
Attitude assessment instruments, 211
Attitude change strategies, 214–226
  books, 222–224
  collaborative problem-solving, 225–226
  curriculum guides and instructional materials, 224–225
  disability simulations, 218, 220–221, 222
  fairness issues, 217–218, 219
  films/videos, 222–223
  guest speakers, 219, 221–222
  information about assistive devices, 225
  successful individuals with disabilities, 218–219
  teacher language and interactions, 216–217, 219, 226
Attitudes toward individual differences, 210–214
Attribution training, 279–280, 281, 390–391
Atypical autism, 96
Audiocassette recorders, 385
Audiocassettes, 354
Auditory learners, 445
Aura, 91
Authentic/performance assessment, 507

Author's chair, 436
Autism, 96
Autism spectrum disorder (ASD), 96–97
Awakenings, 223
AWARE strategy, 385*n*

Background/contrast, of printed materials, 356
Balanced approach to reading instruction, 426–428, 430
Bandaids and Blackboards, 239
BARNGA: A Simulation Game on Cultural Clashes, 230
Barriers–The Awareness Challenge, 239
Bart's Pet Project, 458
Basic interpersonal communication skills (BICS), 124, 265–266
Beautiful Mind, A, 222
Behavior, classroom. *See* Classroom behavior
Behavioral/emotional disorders, 54, 72–76, 330
Behavioral intervention plan, 297
Behavioral momentum, 318–319
Behavioral outcomes, 33–36
Behavioral performance evaluation, 530–531
Behavior reduction interventions, 318–320
BELIEF learning strategy, 280*n*
Bell, Alexander Graham, 18*n*
Bias. *See* Discrimination and bias
BICS (basic interpersonal communication skills), 124, 265–266
Big ideas, 482
Bilingual-bicultural communication, 102
Bilingual education, 119–120
Bilingual Education Act, 119
Bilingual educators, 161
Bipolar disorder, 76
Black English, 229–231
Board of Education of the Hendrick Hudson School District v. *Rowley* (1982), 20
Bodily-kinesthetic intelligence, 131
Boldface type, 355
Book Buddies, 425
Books, as attitude change strategy, 222–223
Boxing, in mathematics instruction, 464
Boys, and gender stereotypes, 136–137
Braille, 54, 103, 242, 372–373, 410, 487

Braille and Speak, 410
Braille Bug, 239
Braille Lite, 410
Bridge system, 230
Brown v. Topeka Board of Education (1924), 18
Buddy journals, 431
Bulimia nervosa, 137
Bulletin boards, 324
Bullies, 320–322
Butterfly cycle lesson, 362

Calculators, 458
California State Board of Education, 20
CALLA (Cognitive Academic Language Learning Approach), 267
CALL UP strategy, 385*n*
CALM learning strategy, 322*n*
CALP (cognitive/academic language proficiency), 124–125, 266
CAMP (College Assistance Migrant Program), 116
Cancer, 91–92
CAN (Computer Assisted Notetaking), 410
Captioned television, 367
Caption statements, 509, 511
Career education, 271, 272
Case, in printed materials, 355
Case managers, 159, 164
CBM (curriculum-based measurement), 504–507
CD-ROMs, 276, 364, 366–367, 489
Cedar Rapids Community School District v. *Garret F.* (1999), 20
Center for Children and Technology, 276
Central graphic organizers, 475
CEPI (Classroom Ecological Preparation Inventory), 86*n*
Cerebral palsy, 86–87
Certificates of completion or attendance, 522
Certification, teacher, 182, 183*n*, 184*n*
Change problems, in mathematics instruction, 460
Character study journals, 426
Charts
  Assignment Idea Chart, 391*n*
  in mathematics instruction, 463, 464
  for note-taking, 385, 387
  T-charts, 408
Chat groups, 368
Cheating, 407

Checklists
    Assessment Accommodation
        Checklist, 499n
    attitude change strategy, 215
    cooperative teaching, 171–172
    instructional accommodations, 528
    narrative text understanding, 514
    Social Interaction Checklist, 214n
CHECK procedure, 442
Child abuse, 146–147
Childhood Disintegrative
    Disorder, 96
Child-rearing practices, 194
Children of a Lesser God, 223
Children's Loneliness and Social
    Dissatisfaction Scale, 531
Child study team, 50–51, 52, 53, 130
Choice cards, 275, 278
Choice Magazine Listening, 277
Choices, 277, 390
Choice statements, 318
Choosing Options and Accommodations
    for Children (C.O.A.C.H.), 98n
Choral reading, 418
Choral responding, 396
Circles of friends, 243
Circle story, 425
Civil rights movement, 18
Class jobs, 308
Class meetings, 245, 301
Classroom behavior, 297–320
    antecedent-based interventions,
        304–307
    behavior reduction interventions,
        318–320
    consequence-based interventions,
        307–310
    group-oriented management
        systems, 313–317
    relationship building strategies,
        297–302
    self-management interventions,
        310–313, 314
    social-skills instruction, 302–304
Classroom design, 323–330
    behavior and attention disorders, 330
    cooperative learning arrangements,
        406–407
    diverse cultural and language
        backgrounds, 325
    health and physical disabilities,
        328–330
    hearing impairments, 326
    visual impairments, 326, 328

Classroom Ecological Preparation
    Inventory (CEPI), 86n
Classroom environment, 243–244
Classroom lottery, 308
Classroom management plan, 288
Classroom observations, by families, 203
Classwide Peer Tutoring (CWPT), 405
Clyde K. and Sheila K v. Puyallup
    School District (1994), 15
C.O.A.C.H. (Choosing Options and
    Accommodations for
    Children), 98n
Code switching, 124
Cognitive Academic Language Learning
    Approach (CALLA), 267
Cognitive/academic language proficiency
    (CALP), 124–125, 266
Cognitive behavioral interventions,
    310–313, 314
Cognitive disabilities, 335–336
Collaboration, 8, 83–84, 380–381,
    402–403
Collaborative consultation, 175,
    177–179, 180
Collaborative discussion teams, 380
Collaborative problem-solving, 225
Collaborative writing groups,
    436–438
College Assistance Migrant Program
    (CAMP), 116
Color of Paradise, The, 222
Communication
    with individuals with disabilities,
        240–243
    and language difficulties, 71–72
    systems for individuals with visual
        disabilities, 372–373
Communication Access Realtime
    Translation, 410
Communication books, 242–243
Community agencies staff, 161
Community and collaboration, 8
Community-based activities, 245
Community-based education programs,
    for families, 205
Community-based learning, 271–272
Comparative graphic organizers,
    476, 477
Compare problems, in mathematics
    instruction, 460
Competency-oriented approach, to
    low-incidence disabilities, 84
Competitive employment, 270
Complex partial seizures, 91

Comprehensive planning team, 162–183
    collaborative and interactive
        teaming, 162–167
    collaborative consultation, 175,
        177–179, 180
    congruence, 179–180, 181, 182
    cooperative teaching, 168–175,
        175–177, 176–179
    members, 158–160
    person-centered planning, 167–168
    professional development, 181–185
    special education identification
        process, 49
    for students with cultural and
        language differences, 123
Compromise, 241
Computer Assisted Notetaking (CAN),
    373, 410
Computer-based instruction, 364,
    365–366
Computer-based testing, 505–506
Computer mouse, 370, 371
Computer-presented drills, 419
Computers
    inputting information into, 370, 371
    programs to foster acceptance and
        friendships, 239
    spelling instruction programs, 449
Computer-supported writing
    applications, 440–443
Concept anchoring routines, 479n, 480
Concept comparison routines, 480
Concept diagrams, 480
Concept mastery routines, 479–480
Concept-teaching routines, 362–363,
    479–480, 481
Concrete teaching aids, in mathematics
    instruction, 456
Conferences
    family-educators', 159, 189–190
    group reading, 426
    professional, 184
Confidentiality, 188–189
Configuration cues, 421
Conflict resolution, 192, 302
Congruence, 179–180, 181, 182
Connect/Net/Connectado Campaign, 134
Consensus-based evaluation system, 316
Consequence-based interventions,
    307–310
Consequences, 293–294
Content-based curriculum, 267
Content-based instruction, 361
Context cues, 421

Continuous recording, 292

Continuum of educational placements, 13–15

Contract grading, 409, 527

Contracts, 200, 309–310

Contrast, of printed materials, 356

Contributions approach to multicultural curriculum, 356

Convulsive disorder, 91, 92

Cooperation, 297, 394

Cooperative group testing, 519

Cooperative learning, 402–411
  classroom arrangement, 406–407
  components, 403
  developing students' cooperative skills, 407–409, 412
  in differentiated instruction, 359
  evaluating, 409–412
  formats, 404
  guidelines, 406
  heterogeneous cooperative groups, 407
  in mathematics instruction, 453
  using, 411

Cooperative Strategies Series, 408n

Cooperative teaching, 168–175, 176–179
  checklist, 171–172
  sample interview, 175
  sample survey, 177
  team member perceptions, 536–537

COPS strategy, 435

Cornell notes, 382

Cornucopia kids, 117

Corrected-test methods, 445

Correct format models, in mathematics instruction, 463

Corrective feedback, 397–397

Corrective Reading, 428

Corrective teaching, 318

Counselors, school, 160

Countoon, 311

Course management software, 410

Court cases, 18, 20. *See also specific cases*

Creative thinking questions, 301

Creativity centers, 325

Criterion-referenced grading systems, 527–528

Criterion-referenced testing, 497

Critical questions, 483–484

Cross-cultural differences, 195–196, 295

Cueing cards, 313

Cues
  classroom behavior, 304
  configuration, 421
  context, 421
  as listening skill, 385
  in mathematics instruction, 463–464
  nonverbal, 385
  phonemic, 420
  pictorial, 421
  semantic, 421
  for spelling, 446
  syntactic, 421
  verbal, 385

Cultural awareness, 187

Cultural factors, in family differences, 192–193

Culturally and linguistically diverse backgrounds, students with
  assessment alternatives, 126
  child abuse, 146–147
  classroom design, 325
  comprehensive planning team, 49
  cultural considerations, 121–122
  differentiated instruction for, 356–363
  individualized education program, 61
  versus learning difficulties, 122–129
  learning style, 122
  linguistic considerations, 122, 123
  making transition to inclusive settings, 264–267
  mentors, 282
  prereferral system, 51
  vignette, 109–110

Cultural norms, 264

Cumulative portfolios, 508

Curricular accommodations, 339–340

Curriculum
  content-based, 267
  functional, 272
  individualizing, 337
  Learning with PURPOSE curriculum, 283
  multicultural, 356–358
  Open Airways for Schools curriculum, 88
  Parallel Alternative Curriculum (PAC), 474
  PURPOSE-PLANNING curriculum, 283
  self-determination, 283

Curriculum-based measurement (CBM), 504–507

Curriculum compacting, 132

Curriculum guides, 224–225, 239

Curriculum mapping, 69

Curriculum overlapping, 340

CWPT (Classwide Peer Tutoring), 405

Daily notes, 199

Daniel R. R. v. State Board of Education (1989), 15

Deafness, 100–101. *See also* Hearing impairments, students with

Decorative bulletin boards, 324

DEFENDS strategy, 434n

Defiant behaviors, 73, 74

Defining questions, 301

Deinstitutionalization, 16

Demographic shifts, 117–121

Demonstration plus model strategy, 464–465

Dependent group systems, 316

Depression, 75–76

Descriptive grading, 528

Desks, teacher's, 324

Developmental approach to mathematics instruction, 455

Developmental expectations, of families, 194

Development phase of learning cycle, 481

Diabetes, 89–91

Dialect differences, 229–231

Dialogue journals, 431

Dialoguing, 301

Diana v. California State Board of Education (1940), 20

DIBELS, 505

Dictionaries, online, 488

Dictionary skills, 447

Differences
  cross-cultural, 195–196, 295
  dialect, 229–231
  family, 192–196, 234
  individual, 210–214

Differential reinforcement techniques, 319

Differentiated instruction
  assistive devices, 370–375
  grading, 524, 525
  and IEPs, 66–67
  as inclusion principle, 8
  instructional technology, 364–370, 374
  nature and impact, 524
  practices, 337–347
  solar system lesson vignette, 335–336

Digital cameras, 367

Digital divide, 134

Digital textbooks, 487, 488
Dinner party, 426
Diploma alternatives, 522–523
Directional graphic organizers, 476
Directions, 304–305, 387–389, 394
"Disabilities," as term, 27
Disability Awareness, 239
Disability Radio Worldwide, 277
Disability Resources, 239
Disability simulations, 218, 220–221, 222
Disability World, 277
Discovery Cams, 489
Discovery/enrichment centers, 325
Discrimination and bias
    antibias curricula, 226
    families, 192
    gender bias, 135–137
    responding to, 236–238
    students and schools, 133, 135–141
    teaching about, 235–236
Disparate impact, 22
Disparate treatment, 22
Disproportionate representation,
        21–23, 24
Distar, 429
Divergent thinking, 359
Diversity self-assessment, 227
Divided page method, 266
Divorce, 142–144, 145
Domains of Adulthood, 272
Down syndrome, 80
Drafting phase of writing, 433–434
Drama, 425
Drawings, student, 212, 213
Drills, word, 419
Duration recording, 289, 291
DVDs, 240, 364, 366–367
Dynamic Assessment of Test
        Accommodations (DATA), 499n
Dyskinetic, 86

Early childhood programs, 16
Early intervention, 16
Early production period of second
        language learning, 125
Eating disorders, 137–138
E-buddies, 239
Ecobehavioral Assessment System
        Software (EBASS), 506
Economic barriers to family
        participation, 197
Economic changes, 110–117
Edformation, 505
Editing logs, 434, 435

Editing phase of writing, 434–435
Editing symbols, 436
*Educational Assessment of Social
        Interaction* (Hunt, Alwell,
        Farron-Davis, & Goetz), 214n
Educational interpreters, 347
Educational Resources Information
        Center (ERIC), 185
Education Development Center, 276
Education for All Handicapped
        Children Act, 20, 25, 26, 27
Educators. *See* Teachers
eduTest, 506
Elaborative knowledge questions, 348
Elders, respect for, 296
Electronic mail, 185, 200, 202, 203,
        368, 449
Electronic portfolios, 509, 510
Electronic Read Around, 448–449
Electronic textbooks, 487, 488
Electronic travel aids, 373
Elementary students
        academic performance, 32–33, 36–37
        career education programs, 271
        social, behavioral, and self-concept
                outcomes, 34–35, 37
E-mail, 185, 200, 202, 203, 368, 449
eMeasurement services, 505
Emotional/behavioral disorders, 72–76
Emotional responses, family
        differences in, 194–195
Empathy (game), 224
Employment preparation, 270–272
Empty concepts, 501
Engagement phase of learning cycle, 481
English as a second language (ESL),
        121, 361–363
Enrichment period of second language
        learning, 125
Environmental assessment, 251, 252, 253
Environmental print, 420
E-Pals, 239, 411
Epilepsy, 91, 92
Equity in classroom, 139
ERIC (Educational Resources
        Information Center), 185
Error analysis, 519
ESL (English as a second language),
        121, 361–363
ESL teachers, 161
ESOL (English to Speakers of Other
        Languages), 121, 361–363
Essay test items, 518, 519
Essential Lifestyle Planning strategy, 168n

E-textbooks, 487, 488
Ethnomathematics, 455
Event recording, 290–291
Exam Manager, 505
Expansion, 361
Expatiation, 362
Expectations, 194, 216
Exploration phase of learning cycle, 481
Expressive language, 81, 82
Extended families, 144, 192–193
Extension phase of learning cycle, 481
Extensions and expansions period of
        second language learning, 125
Extinction, 319
Extra credit, 530
Extracurricular activities, 245
Extrinsic motivation, 389, 390
Eye gaze technology, 370, 371

Face-to-face interactions, 404
Fairness, 217–218, 219
Families
        advocating for, 187
        changing definition of, 141–145
        as comprehensive planning team
                members, 158
        and confidentiality, 188–189
        and criterion-referenced grading
                systems, 527
        developmental expectations, 194
        educational programs for, 203–205
        explaining inclusion program to, 42
        extended, 144, 192–193
        foster, 145–146
        gaining trust of, 186–187
        homework collaboration, 402–403
        impact of inclusion on, 40–42
        meeting with, 159, 189–192
        observations by, 200, 203
        online services for, 200, 205
        perceptions of disability, 194
        perceptions of inclusion program,
                537, 538
        reading and phonological awareness,
                417–418
        resolving conflicts with, 192
        single-parent, 142
        structure, 193
        and student friendships, 246
        technology-based
                communications, 200
        written communication with, 197–200
Family and student participation
        principle, 25

Family differences
  cross-cultural communication
     patterns, 195–196
  cultural factors, 192–193
  in emotional responses, 194–195
  linguistic factors, 196
  socioeconomic factors, 196–197
  teaching about, 234
Family Educational Rights and Privacy
     Act (FERPA), 141, 188, 189*n*
Family-educators' conferences, 159,
     189–192
FBA (functional behavioral
     assessment), 289–297
Feedback
  cooperative learning, 409
  corrective, 397
  mathematics instruction, 466
  soliciting from students, 391, 392
  student-directed, 397
  teacher-centered instruction, 217,
     396–397
  writing instruction, 439
Fernald Method, 429
FERPA (Family Educational Rights
     and Privacy Act), 141, 188, 189*n*
Field-independent students, 344
Field-sensitive students, 344
Field trips, 486, 487, 489–490
Films, 222–223, 240. *See also* Videos
Films Involving Disabilities, 240
FIRST-Letter Mnemonic
     Strategy, 485
First Star I See (Caffrey), 79
Five Finger Test, 422
Fix-up strategies, for text
     comprehension, 351
Flagging, 498*n*
Flashcard drills, 419
Flip charts, 463, 464
Flow word lists, 445
Fluency, reading, 416, 418–422, 423–424
Fluency disorders, in speech, 81
Food allergies, 88
Food reinforcers, 308–309
Forms
  assignment log, 258
  author, 437
  behavioral and social skills rating
     scale, 531
  collaborative consultation, 180
  computer software evaluation,
     365–366
  contract outline, 310

  cooperative learning student
     feedback, 409
  cooperative teaching lesson plan, 174
  environmental assessment, 253
  instructional rubric, 511, 513
  learning express-ways feedback, 392
  observational recording, 290
  peer editing, 437
  prereferral planning, 52
  report cards, 199–200, 201
  self-selecting reading material rubric,
     423–424
  strategic note-taking, 381–382, 383
  student progress rating, 536
Forrest Gump, 222
Foster families, 145–146
Foxfire Fund, 187*n*
Fragile X syndrome, 80
Framed outlines, 471
Frames, 425, 430
Free and appropriate education
     principle, 25, 29
Free-rider effect, 403
Friendship Quality Questionnaire
     (Parker & Asher), 214
Friendships, 238–246
Full-service schools, 112
Funbrain.com, 506
Functional behavioral assessment
     (FBA), 289–297
Functional curriculum, 272
Functionally blind students, 103

Games
  academic learning, 394, 410
  BARNGA: A Simulation Game on
     Cultural Clashes, 230
  Empathy, 224
  Good Behavior Game, 315
  In My Shoes, 243
  spelling, 449
Gay parents, 145
Gay students, 138–141
Gender bias, 135–137
Gender equity, 230, 232
General education
  implementing IEP, 64–69
  and low-incidence disabilities, 83
  transition to, 249, 250–260
General educators, 39, 64, 65, 159. *See
     also* Teachers
General feedback, 396
Generalization, 259–260, 261–262, 263
Generalized anxiety disorder, 73

Geometer's Sketchpad, 453
Geometry instruction vignette, 453
Gifted and talented students, 129,
     131–133
Gifted and Talented Students Act,
     129, 131
Girls
  and gender bias, 135–136
  math and science instruction, 490, 490
Global Junior Challenge, 239
Global perspective, 231–232
Global Schoolhouse, 411
Global SchoolNet Foundation, 239
Glossaries, 266
Goal-based portfolios, 508
Goals
  lesson, 392–393
  and problem analysis, clarification
     and identification, 177
  setting and attaining, 274, 275, 278
Good Behavior Game, 315
Grading, 523–530
  criterion-referenced grading systems,
     527–528
  norm-referenced grading systems,
     526, 527
  report card grading, 199–200, 201,
     523–524, 525
  self-referenced grading systems, 528
Graduation rates, 522
Grand mal seizure, 91
Grandparents, 144. *See also* Families
Graphic organizers, 475–477
Graphic representations, in mathematics
     instruction, 459, 460
Graphics tablets, 370, 371
Greer v. *Rome City School District*
     (1991), 15
Group average evaluation system,
     316, 412
Group evaluation, 316
Group free-token response-cost system,
     314–315
Group instruction. *See* Large-group
     instruction; Small-group
     instruction
Group-oriented management systems,
     313–317
Group problems, in mathematics
     instruction, 460
Group projects/group grade format,
     408–409
Group Project Work Log, 407
Group reading conference, 426

Group response-cost system, 314, 315
Group responses, 396
Group Response System, 410
Group timeout ribbon, 315
Group *versus* individual performance, 296
Guest speakers, 219, 221–222
Guided notes, 382, 382
Guided reading, 426

"Handicapped," as term, 27
Handwriting, 443
Harm prevention, 320–323
Headbands, 370, 371
Health needs, 85–86
Health problems. *See* Physical disabilities
Hearing impairments, students with, 100–103
    assistive devices, 373, 410
    classroom design, 326
    communicating with, 242
    differentiated instruction, 346–347
    individualized education program, 54
    mathematics instruction, 489
    testing accommodations, 499, 500
Hearing impairment simulations, 220
HEP (High School Equivalency Programs), 116
Hierarchical graphic organizers, 475
High-impact accommodations, 342
High-incidence disabilities, 69–70. *See also specific disabilities*
High School Equivalency Programs (HEP), 116
High school students, 33, 35–36, 37–38, 271
High-stakes testing, 496–497
High technology assistive devices, 17, 370–371
Hip Kid Hop series, 236
Hispanic Americans
    demographic shifts, 117
    disproportionate representation, 22
    gender bias, 136
    individual *versus* group performance, 296
    racial discrimination, 133
HIV (human immunodeficiency virus), 139, 141, 141, 235
Hobson v. *Hansen* (1967), 20
Home-based education programs, for families, 204
Homebound instruction, 15
Homelessness, 113–114, 115, 234–235

Homeroom.com, 506
Home-school contracts, 200
Home visits, 197
Homework, 202–203, 398, 398–402, 411
Hospitals, 15
Hotlines, homework, 411
Hot Math, 461*n*
Humor, 300
Hyperglycemia, 89–90
Hypermedia-based electronic portfolios, 510
Hypertext/hypermedia, 364
Hypertonia, 86
Hypoglycemia, 89–90
Hypothesis statements, 295–295
Hypotonia, 86

I Belong Out There, 275
iBOT mobility system, 371
iCan, 277
IDEA. *See* Individuals with Disabilities Education Act (IDEA)
IDEA Amendments of 1997, 26, 27
Idea generation, for writing, 431
IEP. *See* Individualized Education Program (IEP)
IFSP (Individualized Family Service Plan), 26, 27
Ignoring, planned, 319
Immigrants, 73–74, 118–121
Inclusion
    defined, 6
    factors contributing to movement, 15–18, 20–25
    impact, 32–43
    implementing, 9–11
    principles, 6–8
    vignette, 3–4
Inclusion programs
    evaluating, 497
    family members' perceptions of, 537, 538
    improving effectiveness of, 539–541
    students' perceptions of, 532, 533
    teachers' perceptions of, 532–537
Independent activities, 398, 399–400, 401
Independent assignments, 257
Independent group systems, 316–317
Independent learning period of second language learning, 125
Independent living arrangements, 272–273
Individual accountability, 403

Individual differences, attitudes toward, 210–214
Individualism *versus* group cooperation, 296
Individualized Education Program (IEP), 51–60
    aligning to general education curriculum, 65–66
    and assessment, 522
    assistive technology, 54, 58, 62, 63
    components, 51–54
    curriculum mapping, 69
    developing, 54, 61
    differentiated instruction, 66–67
    grading system, 529
    and IDEA, 25, 26, 27
    IEP-based diplomas, 522
    implementation plan, 67–68
    implementing in general education settings, 64–69
    individualizing curriculum, 338–339
    meetings, 65, 181, 181
    sample, 55–58
    sample matrix, 67
    sample meeting agenda, 59
    sample program-at-a-glance, 68
    student involvement, 60–64
    teacher involvement, 64–65
    transition services component, 59–60
Individualized Family Service Plan (IFSP), 26, 27
Individualized teaching accommodations, 342
Individualized technology assessment, 63. *See also* Assistive technology
Individualized Transition Plan (ITP), 267–269
Individuals with Disabilities Education Act Amendments of 1997, 26, 27
Individuals with Disabilities Education Act (IDEA), 25–28
    assistive technology, 17
    attention deficit disorder, 77, 78
    confidentiality, 188
    court cases, 20
    disproportionate representation, 24
    students with AIDS, 140–141
    vs. Section 504 of the Rehabilitation Act, 28–30
Individual *versus* group performance, 296
Infants and Toddlers with Disabilities Act, 26, 27
Inferential questions, 484

Information organizing strategies, 351
Informative notices, 199
In My Shoes game, 243
INSPECT learning strategy, 442n
Institute on Independent Living, 277
Institutional placement, 15
Instructional accommodations, 527–528
Instructional bulletin boards, 324
Instructional materials
 for acceptance and friendships, 239
 accommodations, 342–343
 as attitude change strategy, 224–225
 science and social studies instruction,
  467–474
Instructional rubrics, 511, 513
Instructional support team, 50–51, 52,
 53, 130
Instructional technology
 differentiated instruction,
  363–370, 374
 low-incidence disabilities, 84
 for mathematics instruction, 457–458
 medically fragile students, 93
 science and social studies instruction,
  486–486
 text comprehension, 354, 357
Instructive feedback, 397
Integrated Processing Strategy, 419
IntelliTools, 448, 458
Interactive illustrations, 485
Interactive Mathematics on the
 Internet, 487
Interactive Partnership Scale
 (Hunt et al.), 214n
Interactive reading guides, 471–472
Inter_Comm (software program), 368
Interdependent group systems,
 314–316
Interdisciplinary themes, in science and
 social studies instruction, 482
Interlanguage and intermediate fluency
 period of second language
 learning, 125
International Children's Digital
 Library, 228
International Education Resource
 Network, 239
Internet
 academic learning games, 410
 acceptance and friendships, 239–240
 bulletin boards, 368
 communicating with families, 200
 cooperative learning, 411
 differentiated instruction, 368–370

homework websites, 202–203
literacy instruction, 449
mathematics, science, and social
 studies instruction, 487, 488, 489
professional development, 185
science and social studies
 instruction, 486
supporting successful transitions, 277
Interpersonal intelligence, 131
Interpreters, 196, 347
Interspersed requests, 319
Interval recording, 291, 292
Intervention in School and Clinic, 78n, 97
Interviews
 of family members, 537
 sample cooperative teaching, 175
 self-evaluation, 521–522
 of students, 181, 532
 of teachers, 533–536
Intrapersonal intelligence, 131
Intrinsic motivation, 389, 390
Introspective questions, 348
I-PLAN strategy, 279
Irving Independent School District v.
 Tatro (1984), 20
I SOLVE learning strategy, 228n
Italics, 355
IT FITS learning strategy, 486n
Itinerant teachers, 14
ITP (Individualized Transition Plan),
 267–269
It's Elementary, 140

Jigsaw cooperative learning format, 406
Job cards, 257
Job coaches, 271
Joey Pigza Loses Control (Gantos), 79
Journals
 literature response, 425
 student, 521
 for writing instruction, 431
Joysticks, 371
Junior high students, 271
Justification, in printed materials, 356

Kaleidoscope, 277
Keyboard alteration programs, 370, 371
Keyboarding skills, 441
Key guards, 370, 371
Key word memory method, 485–486
KidAbility, 240
KIDLINK, 239, 411
Kids Network, 486
Kids on the Block, 224–225

Kim's Komet, 458
King Gimp, 222
Knowledge of individual differences
 probes, 212, 213
Kurzweil 3000, 371
K-W-L strategy, 348

Laboratory approach to science
 instruction, 481, 484
Language and communication
 difficulties, 71–72
Language and speech disorders,
 80–82, 242
Language clinicians, 159
Language diversity, 229–230. *See also*
 Culturally and linguistically
 diverse backgrounds
Language dominance, 124
Language experience approach to
 reading instruction, 428
Language Master, 375
Language preference, 124
Language proficiency, 124
Language prompts, 420
Large-group instruction, 380–391. *See
 also* Small-group instruction
 attention-getting strategies, 386–387
 directions, 387–389
 encouraging questions, 381
 listening skills, 385
 motivating students, 389–391, 393
 note-taking skills, 382–385, 386, 387
 student collaboration, 380–381
Larry P. v. *Riles* (1949), 20
Laser Cane, 373
Latency recording, 291
Lau v. *Nichols* (1944), 20
Laws, 25–31. *See also specific laws*
LCCE (Life-Centered Career
 Education), 272
LCD computer projection panels, 367
Leadership positions, 217
Leadership skills, 278–279
Leading, in printed materials, 356
Leapfrog, 448
Learning centers, 325–325
Learning disabilities, 35, 70–72, 122–129
*Learning Disabilities and Life
 Stories* (Rodis, Garrod, &
 Boscardin), 223
Learning disabilities simulations, 221
Learning environment, 389–390
Learning-from-text guides, 471–472
Learning logs, 521

Learning strategies
in CALLA, 267
designing, 255, 257
mathematics instruction, 461
spelling instruction, 446
teaching, 254–255, 256
test-taking skills, 502
writing instruction, 439
Learning styles, 122–122, 344, 445
Learning Together Approach, 406
Learning with PURPOSE
curriculum, 283
Least error correction, 466
Least intrusive alternative, 318
Least restrictive alternative, 318
Least restrictive environment (LRE),
12–15, 25
Leisure activities, 273–273, 275
Lesbian parents, 145
Lesbian students, 138–141
Level grading, 526
Library of Congress, 487
Life-Centered Career Education
(LCCE), 272
Light pens, 371
LINCS learning strategy, 486n
Line length, in printed materials, 355
Linguistically diverse backgrounds. See
Culturally and linguistically
diverse backgrounds, students
with
Linguistic approach to spelling
instruction, 444–444
Linguistic diversity, 229–230
Linguistic factors, in family
differences, 196
LINKS strategy, 385n
Liquid crystal display (LCD) computer
projection panels, 367
Listening centers, 325
Listening guides, 381–382
Listening materials, 385
Listening previewing, 418
Listening skills, 385
LISTS learning strategy, 485
Literacy instruction, 417, 430, 448–449.
See also Reading instruction;
Spelling instruction; Writing
instruction
Literal questions, 484
Literature circles, 425
Literature response journals, 425
Litigation, 18, 20. See also specific cases
Lizst, 185n

Logical-mathematical intelligence, 131
Logs
assignment, 257–258
editing, 434, 435
group project, 407
learning, 521
narrative, 292
weblogs, 200, 369
Low-impact accommodations, 342
Low-incidence disabilities, 82–85. See
also specific disabilities
Low technology assistive devices, 17, 370
Low vision, 103
LRE (least restrictive environment),
12–15, 25

Macros, 442
Magazines, disability-related, 277
Main ideas, 350, 382
Mainstream, Magazine of the Able-
Disabled, 277
Mainstreaming, 8, 11–12
Manipulative bulletin boards, 324
Manipulatives, in mathematics
instruction, 456
Manual communication, 101
Manual prompts, 397
Map Action Planning System (MAPS),
167–168
Mastery level grading, 527
Matching test items, 516, 520
Mathematics difficulties, 71, 454–455
Mathematics instruction, 454–467
developing math facts and
computation skills, 464–466
feedback and assessment, 466–467
instructional approaches, 458–464
presenting mathematics
appropriately, 455
problem-solving approach, 454–455
teaching aids, 456–458
vignette, 453
MathType 5.0, 489
McKinney-Vento Homelessness
Assistance Act, 113
Measurement centers, 325
Median scores, 530
Medically fragile students, 92–93
Medical services, 20
Medication monitoring, 98–100
Meetings
class, 245, 301
with families, 159, 189–192
IEP, 59, 65, 181, 181

Meet the Math Wiz series, 489
Memory skills, 484–486
Mental retardation, 32, 34, 35, 78, 80
Mental visualization, 485
Mentors
electronic, 276
for students, 281, 282, 283
for teachers, 182, 183
Mexican Americans, 20. See also
Hispanic Americans
Microsoft Word, 448
Middle school students, 271
Migrant educators, 162
Migrant workers, 114–116, 234–235
Mildly emotionally disturbed, 74–75
Mild retardation, 70, 80
Mills v. Board of Education of the
District of Columbia (1942), 18
Mimio interactive whiteboard, 410
Mind-opening questions, 348
Mini-lessons, 438
Misunderstood Minds, 239
Mobility related disabilities, 34
Mobility skills, 327
Modeling, 265
Modeling prompts, 397
Models
a priori, 179
career education, 272
in mathematics instruction, 463
post hoc, 180
School Based Career Education
Model, 272
transitional, 262–264
for writing, 433, 435
Moderate retardation, 80
Monochronic cultures, 122
Monospaced type, 355
Motivation, 389–391, 393, 417
Motivational bulletin boards, 324
Motor difficulties, 72
Mouse, computer, 370, 371
Mouthsticks, 371
Movement, cross-cultural differences
in, 296
Mowat Sensor, 373
Mrs. Karen Lakes Home Page, 239
Multicultural curriculum, 356–358
Multicultural education, 150–151
Multicultural teaching materials, 358–359
Multilevel teaching, 340
Multimedia, 276–277, 486–486, 487, 509
Multipass, 350
Multiple-choice survey format, 309

Multiple-choice test items, 516, 520
Multiple grading, 526
Multiple intelligences, 131
Multiracial/ethnic students, 135
Multisensory strategies for reading
    instruction, 429
Musical intelligence, 131
Music Educators National Conference
    Publication Sales, 228
Myelomeningocele, 87–88
My Left Foot, 222
My Math, 458
My Name Is Maria Isabel (Ada), 227

Name-calling, 35
Narrative logs, 292
National Board for Professional Teaching
    Standards (NBPTS), 182
National Center for Science Literacy,
    Education and Technology, 487
National Coalition of Auditory
    Processing Disorders, 239
National Council of Teachers of
    Mathematics (NCTM), 454,
    458, 466
National Geographic Society, 486
National Information Center for
    Children and Youth with
    Disabilities, 239
National Library of Virtual
    Manipulatives for Interactive
    Mathematics, 453
National Library Service for the Blind
    and Physically Handicapped,
    104n, 277, 487
National Parent Information Network
    (NPIN), 204
Native Americans, 116
    differentiated instruction, 359, 360n
    disproportionate representation, 22
    groups, 117
    individual *versus* group
        performance, 296
Naturalistic intelligence, 131
Natural language techniques, 361
NBPTS (National Board for
    Professional Teaching
    Standards), 182, 183n, 184n
NCLB (No Child Left Behind) Act,
    23–25
NCTM (National Council of Teachers
    of Mathematics), 454, 458, 466
Neglect, 146. *See also* Child abuse
Nell, 222

Nemeth Code of Braille
    mathematics, 489
Newborns, substance-abused, 148–148
Newcomer programs, 267
Newsletters, 199
Next STEP (Student Transition and
    Educational Planning), 283
No Child Left Behind (NCLB) Act,
    23–25
Noise, 406
Nondiscriminatory evaluation
    principle, 25
Nonverbal communication, 301–302
Nonverbal cues, 385
Normalization, 16
Norm-referenced grading systems, 526
Norm-referenced testing, 497
Notebooks, 199, 257
Note card systems, 181
Notes, daily, 199
Notes, guided, 382, 382
Note taking
    with assistive devices, 371, 410
    and hearing disabilities, 373, 410
    skills and strategies, 382–385, 386, 387
    from textbooks, 469
NPIN (National Parent Information
    Network), 204
Number Concepts 2 series, 458
Numbered Heads Together, 380
Nurses, school, 160

Oberti v. *Board of Education of the
    Borough of Clementon School
    District* (1993), 15
Observational recording strategies,
    290–293
Observations
    of academic performance, 514, 515
    for attitude assessment, 212, 214
    of classroom by families, 200–203
    of social and behavioral
        performance, 530
Obsessive-compulsive disorders
    (OCD), 73
Occupational therapists, 160
O'clock directions, 345
Office of Civil Rights (OCR), 28, 29, 524
Office of Special Education
    Programs, 29
OK5R technique, 352
On a Roll, 277
One teaching/one helping method,
    168, 169

Online dictionaries, 488
Online services, 185, 200–201, 205. *See
    also* Internet
Open Airways for Schools curriculum, 88
Open-ended survey format, 309
Oppositional behaviors, 73, 74
Optical aids, 373
Oral/aural communication, 101
Oral interpreters, 346
Oral presentations, 381
Oral previewing, 418
Oral prompts, 397
Oral quizzing, 384
ORDER learning strategy, 477
Oregon Research Initiative, 327
Organizational skills, 401–402
Organization skills, 257–258, 260
Orientation, school, 264–265
Orthopedic impairments, 85
Orton-Gillingham-Stillman Strategy, 429
Other health impairments, 85
Otherwise qualified principle, 28, 30
Outcome sentences, 429
Outlines
    framed, 470
    for note-taking, 382
    sample contract, 310
    for text comprehension, 352
    for writing, 433
Overweight children, 138

PAC (Parallel Alternative
    Curriculum), 474
PAIC (Personal Attribute Inventory for
    Children), 211
Paired Associates Strategy, 485
PAL (Planned Alternation of
    Languages), 264n
PALS (Peer-Assisted Learning
    Strategies), 405–406, 425
Panic disorders, 73
Paraeducators, 159–158, 343–344
Paragraph restatements, 352
Paragraph shrinking, 352, 425
Parallel Alternative Curriculum
    (PAC), 474
Parallel lessons, 358
Parallel talk, 362
Parallel teaching, 168, 169
Paraphrase passport, 408
Paraphrasing, 352
Parent Teacher Association (PTA), 204
Partial seizures, 91
Partner Reading, 425

Partner systems, 245

PARTS technique, 352

PASS (Portable Assisted Study Sequence), 116

PDAs (personal digital assistants), 276, 327, 370–371, 410

PDD (Pervasive Developmental Disorder), 96

PDD-NOS (Pervasive Developmental Disorder-Not Otherwise Specified), 96

Pediatric Neurology.Com, 239

Peeling Off Strategy, 419

Peer-Assisted Learning Strategies (PALS), 405–406, 425

Peer-based reading instruction, 425–426

Peer buddy systems, 245

Peer harassment, 320–322

Peer interactions, 313

Peer-mediated mathematics instruction, 459

Peer mediation, 302

Peer note-takers, 384–385

Peer support committees, 245

Peer tutoring, 404–405

Pennsylvania Association for Retarded Children v. *Commonwealth of Pennsylvania* (1942), 18

PENS strategy, 434n

PEP (Person-Event-Place) strategy, 468n

Perceived function, of behavior, 293–294

Perceptions (software program), 505

Perceptual difficulties, 72

Personal Attribute Inventory for Children (PAIC), 211

Personal digital assistants (PDAs), 276, 327, 371, 410

Personal FM amplification systems, 327

Personalizing questions, 301

Personal journals, 431

Person-centered planning, 167–168

Person-Event-Place (PEP) strategy, 468n

Pervasive Developmental Disorder-Not Otherwise Specified (PDD-NOS), 96

Pervasive Developmental Disorder (PDD), 96

Petit mal seizure, 91

Philadelphia, 222

Phonemic cues, 420

Phonetic approach to spelling instruction, 444

Phonetic-based approaches to reading instruction, 427–428

Phonological awareness, 416–418

Physical abuse, 146. *See also* Child abuse

Physical and health needs, 85–86

Physical disabilities
    assistive devices, 370–371
    classroom design, 328–330
    communicating with individuals with, 242
    simulations, 220

Physical prompts, 421

Physical therapists, 161

Physicians, school, 160

Pictorial cues, 421

Pictorial prompting, 420

Picture books, 417

PIRATES learning strategy, 502

PL 93–112. *See* Section 504 of the Rehabilitation Act

PL 94–142 (Education for All Handicapped Children Act), 20, 25, 26, 27

PL 99–457 (Infants and Toddlers with Disabilities Act), 26, 27

PL 101–336 (Americans with Disabilities Act), 28, 30, 524

PL 101–476. *See* Individuals with Disabilities Education Act (IDEA)

PL 105–17 (Individuals with Disabilities Education Act Amendments of 1997), 26, 27

PLAN and WRITE learning strategy, 440n

Plan evaluation, 178

Plan implementation, 177

Planned Alternation of Languages (PAL), 264n

Planned ignoring, 319

Planning, person-centered, 167–168

Planning/prewriting phase of writing, 431–433

Planning Think Sheets, 433

PLANS strategy, 433n

Playmates and Friends Questionnaire for Teachers (Buysse, Goldman, & Skinner), 214

Plyler v. *Doe* (1982), 119

Poetry lesson vignette, 379

Point-of-view reading guides, 471, 474

Polychronic cultures, 122

Ponderable questions, 348

Poolaw v. *Bishop* (1995), 15

Portable Assisted Study Sequence (PASS), 116

Portfolio assessment, 507–512

Positive-comment box, 245

Positive interdependence, 403

Positive reductive procedures, 319

Positive reinforcement, 307–308

Post hoc instructional model, 180

Post organizers, 475–480

Postquestions, 348

Postsecondary opportunities, 273–274

Poverty, 111–117

POW + TREE learning strategy, 440

PQST technique, 352

Practice activities, 394–394

Prader-Willi syndrome, 80

Praise, 300–301, 397

Predictable questions, 348

Prediction Relay, 425

Premack Principle, 308

PREP learning strategy, 256

Preproduction period of second language learning, 125

Prequestions, 348

Prereferral system, 50–51, 52, 53, 130

Pretask requests, 319

Preteaching, 254

Previewing, 347–348, 418

Print materials
    access to, 277
    enhancing readability, 353–357
    student-directed text comprehension strategies, 350–353
    teacher-directed text comprehension strategies, 347–350

PROACT learning strategy, 279n

Problem analysis, 177

Problem-based learning, in science and social studies instruction, 487

Problem clarification and identification, 177, 177

Problem-solving approach to mathematics instruction, 454–455, 487

Procedural due process principle, 25, 29

Process feedback, 397

Process-oriented approach to writing instruction, 431–439

Process portfolios, 508

Proctors, 499

Prodrome, 91

Professional development, 181–185

Programmed reading materials, 428

Progressive improvement grading, 528

Project MAVIS (Materials Adaptations for Visually Impaired Students), 484
Project Take Charge, 283
Promotion rates, 522
Prompting, 266, 397, 420, 420
Prompts
    mathematics instruction, 464, 465
    modeling, 397
    reading, 420–421, 423–424
    writing, 433
Proofreading, 434–435, 436, 447–449
Proportional type, 355
PROVE strategy, 480n
Psychologists, school, 159
Psychomotor seizure, 91
PTA (Parent Teacher Association), 204
Publishing phase of writing, 432, 438
Pull-out programs, 14, 32–33, 170
PURPOSE-PLANNING
    curriculum, 283
Push-in programs, 14

Quality Assessment Planning
    Worksheet, 391n
Question all-write, 429
Questioning
    effective, 484
    of second language learners, 396
    self-questioning, 352
    as text comprehension strategy,
        347–348
    as understanding check, 395
Questionnaires
    for family members, 537, 538
    on friendship, 214
    for self-evaluation, 521–522
    on student motivation, 391n
    for students, 532, 533
    for teachers, 533, 534
Questions
    answering, 351
    for class meetings, 301
    encouraging, 381
    information sharing, 251
Quia.com, 506
Quicktionary, 373

Racial discrimination, 133, 135
Radio programs, 277
Ragged Edge Magazine Online, The, 277
Rain Man, 223
Rank order survey format, 309
RAP learning strategy, 352

Rapport with students, 300
Readability, 353–357, 448
Readers' theater, 426
Reading
    choral, 418
    guided, 426
    repeated, 418
    shared book, 426
    and student motivation, 417
    sustained silent, 426
Reading aloud to students, 417
Reading centers, 325
Reading difficulties, 71, 421–422,
    423–424
Reading disabilities
    assistive devices for, 371–373
    mathematics, science, and social
        studies instruction, 487
    word processing, 440
Reading fluency, 416, 418–422, 423–424
Reading instruction, 416–429
    balanced approach, 427–428, 430
    differentiated instruction, 347–357
    early identification and
        intervention, 416
    phonological awareness, 416–418
    reading fluency, 416, 418–422,
        423–424
    remedial programs, strategies, and
        materials, 428
    text comprehension, 422, 424–426
Reading Mastery, 429
Reading material selection rubric,
    423–424
Readingpen, 448
Reading prompts, 420–421, 423–424
Reading road maps, 471–472, 473
Reading Visual Aids Strategy
    (RVAS), 469n
Receptive language, 81
Reciprocal Friendships Nomination, 214
Reciprocal interaction teaching
    approaches (RITA), 360
Reciprocal teaching, 349
Recordings for the Blind and
    Dyslexic, 487
Redirection, 318–319
Reflective portfolios, 508
Reflective practices, 8
Rehabilitation Act. *See* Section 504 of
    the Rehabilitation Act
Reinforcement surveys, 309
Reinforcers, 308–309
Relationship building strategies, 297–302

Religious diversity, 232–234
Religious schools, 20
Remedial and Special Education, 5n
Repeated reading, 418
Report card grading, 199, 201,
    523–526, 525
Report Writer Interactive, 448
Reprimands, 319
Residential schools, 14–15
Resource room teachers, 14
Response cards, 396
Rett Syndrome, 96
Revising phase of writing, 434–435
Rewards, 308–309
Rhyming Strategy, 419
Right-only feedback, 397
RITA (reciprocal interaction teaching
    approaches), 360
RJ Cooper's IcanEmail, 368
Role delineation, 408
Role models, 281–282, 282
Role playing, 265–266
Round robin, 408
Round table, 408
Routines, 305
RUBRIC learning strategy, 511n
Rubrics, 423–424, 511–512, 513
Rule-governed approaches to spelling
    instruction, 444
Rules, 306–308
Rural poverty, 113–116
RVAS (Reading Visual Aids
    Strategy), 469n

*Sacramento City Unified School
    District, Board of Education* v.
    Holland (1994), 15
SAC (Science for All Children), 484
SAVI (Science Activities for the Visually
    Impaired), 484
Saxon Test Generator, 505
Scaffolding, 360
Scanning systems, 371
SCENE learning strategy, 353
Scheduling, 258–259, 305–306
Schizophrenia, 73
School administrators, 158
School Based Career Education
    Model, 272
School-Based Social Network Form
    (Kennedy et al.), 214n
*School Board of Nassau County, Florida
    et al.* v. *Arline* (1987), 140
School choice, 24–25

School counselors, 160
School nurses, 160
School physicians, 160
School psychologists, 159
Science Activities for the Visually
    Impaired (SAVI), 484
Science and social studies instruction,
    467–490
    content enhancements, 474–480
    for diverse learners, 490–490
    instructional approaches and
        practices, 480–490
    instructional materials, 467–474
Science Enrichment Learning for
    Learners with Physical
    Handicaps (SELPH), 484
Science for All Children (SAC), 484
Scripting, 266
SCROL strategy, 352, 468
SCUBA-DIVE learning strategy, 421n
SEARCH strategy, 434n
Seating arrangements, 323
Seattle School District No. 1 v. *B.S.*
    (1996), 15
Secondary students, 33, 35–36,
    37–38, 271
Second language learners
    assessing, 126, 127–128, 130
    assistive devices, 373, 375
    and comprehensive planning team,
        159–162
    differentiated instruction, 360–363
    directions, 389
    individualized education program, 54
    mathematics instruction, 456, 459, 489
    questioning techniques, 395
    second language acquisition, 124–126
    spelling instruction, 446
    versus students with learning
        difficulties, 122–129
    test accommodations, 501
Section 504 of the Rehabilitation Act,
    28–30, 31
    accommodation plan, 29, 30, 31
    attention deficit disorder, 78
    grading, 524
    infectious diseases, including
        AIDS, 140
    promotion and graduation, 522
    vs. IDEA, 28–30
Seek the Part You Know Strategy, 419
Segregation, 21
Seizure disorders, 91, 92
Self-advocacy, 278–279

Self-assessment, 227, 311–312, 466,
    521–522
Self-awareness, 278
Self-concept measures, 33–36, 531
Self-determination, 274–274, 275,
    277–283
Self-Determination (Ludi and
    Martin), 283
Self-efficacy, 390
Self-esteem, 136, 279, 299–301
Self-evaluation, 227, 311–312, 466,
    521–522
Self-instruction, 313
Self-managed free-token response-cost,
    312–313
Self-management, 310–313, 314,
    461–462
Self-monitoring, 310–313
Self-operated auditory prompt
    system, 276
Self-Perception Profile, 532
Self-questioning, 352
Self-recording, 310–311
Self-referenced grading systems, 528
Self-reinforcement, 312
Self-talk, 359, 362
SELPH (Science Enrichment Learning
    for Learners with Physical
    Handicaps), 484
Semantic cues, 421
Semantic feature analysis (SFA), 425
Semantic maps, 433, 477–478
Semantic webs, 433, 477–478, 479
Send a Problem technique, 380
Sensors, for computer input, 371
Sensory disabilities, 61, 100–104. *See
    also specific disabilities*
Sentence completion test items, 517,
    520–521
Sentence synthesis, 429
*SERI—Special Education Resources on
    the Internet*, 185
Service coordinators, 159, 164
Service learning programs, 272
Severe and profound retardation, 80
Sexual abuse, 147. *See also* Child abuse
SFA (semantic feature analysis), 425
Shared book reading, 426
Sheltered English, 361
Shine, 222
Showcase portfolios, 508
Siblings, 204. *See also* Families
Signed system interpreters, 346
Sign language, 241–242, 489

Silent period of second language
    learning, 125
Silent previewing, 418
Simon Spells, 449
Simple partial seizures, 91
Simulated journals, 431
Single-parent families, 142
Sip and puff systems, 371
Size-up pass, 350
Skateboards, 371
Skeleton/slot/frame outline, 382
Skill centers, 325
Small-group instruction, 359. *See also*
    Large-group instruction
SNIPS, 469n
Social action approach to multicultural
    curriculum, 356–358
Social Contact Assessment Form
    (Kennedy et al.), 214n
Social Interaction Checklist (Kennedy
    et al.), 214n
Social outcomes, impact of inclusion
    on, 33–36
Social performance, 37–38, 530–531
Social phobias, 73
Social responsibility, 483
Social skills instruction, 240, 267,
    302–304. *See also* Friendships
Social workers, 161
Sociocultural factors, in behavior,
    295–296
Socioeconomic factors, in family
    differences, 196–197
Sociometric techniques, 214, 530
SODA learning strategy, 240
Solar system lesson vignette, 335–336
Solve It! strategy, 461
Sophia (web-based tool), 506
Sort-out pass, 350
SOS technique, 352
Sound and Thinking Partners, 425
Sound-field amplification systems, 327
"Sources of Braille Reading
    Materials," 104n
Southeast Asian students, 302, 360n
So You Have Asthma Too! (Sander), 88
Spacing, of printed materials,
    355–356
Spanish language materials, for
    mathematics instruction, 489
Spasticity, 86
Special day schools, 14
Special education, defined, 5
Special education classrooms, 14

Special education identification process, 49–64
  comprehensive planning team, 49
  eligibility determination, 51
  flow chart, 50
  prereferral system, 50–51, 52, 53
  student involvement, 60–64
  vignette, 47–48
Special educators, 40, 64, 65, 159. *See also* Teachers
Special Needs—Special Kids, 239
Special Olympics Get Into It, 239
Specific learning disability, 70
Speech and language disorders, 80–82, 242
Speech clinicians, 159
Speech impairment simulations, 221
Speech Plus Calculator, 458
Speech recognition technology, 370, 371, 440–441
Spell checkers, 441–442, 449
SPELLER Steps, 447
Spelling games, 449
Spelling instruction, 444–449, 449
  adapting, 445–449, 449
  rule-governed approaches, 444
  whole word approaches, 444–445
SPELL program, 449
Spend-a-Buck, 408
Spina bifida, 87–88
Spreadsheets lesson, 393
SQ3R technique, 350
Stage-setting behaviors, 122
Stamps, for assignments, 399–400
Standardized testing, 496–503
  alternatives, 126, 502, 503, 504–519
  concerns about, 496–497
  testing accommodations for diverse learners, 498–500, 501
  test-taking skills, 501–502, 503–504
  timing, scheduling, and setting alternatives, 500–502
  types, 497–498
Standards-based reform, 23–25
Station teaching, 168, 169
Step listing models, in mathematics instruction, 463
Steps to Self-Determination (Field & Hoffman), 283
Stepwise note-taking, 385, 387
Stereotyping, 235, 236–238
STOP and DARE learning strategy, 440n
STOP and LIST learning strategy, 440n
Stop It! I Can't, 90

Story grammars, 425
Story-mapping, 349
Story starters/enders, 433
Storytelling, 425
Strategic note-taking form, 382, 383
Strategy reference cards, 351
Structured overview, 475–477
Student collaboration, 380–381
Student-directed feedback, 397
Student-directed learning, 391
Student drawings, 212, 213
Student interviews, 181, 531, 532
Student journals, 521
Student-managed free-token response-cost, 312–313
Student Motivation: A Problem Solving Questionnaire, 391n
Student prompting, 420
Students
  advocating for, 187
  communication among, 241–243
  in grading process, 529
  impact of inclusion on, 32–38
  in instructional process, 390–391
  perceptions of inclusion, 532, 533
  personal interest in, 298–299
  in special education identification process, 60–64
  in testing process, 519
  without disabilities, 36–38
Student Self-Report System, 531
Student Skills Rating Survey, 531
Student study team, 50–51, 52, 53, 130
Study carrels, 330
Study guides, 470–474
Study skills, 401–402
Stuttering, 81, 82
Style, of printed materials, 355
Substance abuse, 148–148
Suburban poverty, 117
Sugar Was My Best Food (Peacock & Gregory), 91
Suicide, 75–76
Summarizing, 351, 352, 398, 401–402
Supported employment, 270–271
Supported employment specialists, 270–271
Support facilitators, 159, 164
Supreme Court, U.S., 15, 20
Surveying, 350–352
Surveys
  on cooperative teaching, 177
  creating using technology, 506
  for family members, 537, 538

reinforcement, 309
  for students, 531, 533
  for teachers, 177, 533, 534
Sustained silent reading, 426
Sweet Invisible Body (Roney), 91
Syntactic cues, 421
Synthetic approach to phonetics instruction, 427

Tactile graphics display (TGD), 372
Take Action, 283
Taking Asthma to School (Gosselin), 88
Taking Diabetes to School (Gosselin), 90
Taking Seizure Disorders to School (Gosselin), 92
Talented students, 129, 131–133
Talking Chips, 408
Talking word processors, 440
Task analysis, 394
TBI (traumatic brain injury), 93–96
T-charts, 408
TDD (Telecommunication Devices for the Deaf), 373
Teacher assistance team, 50–51, 52, 53, 130
Teacher-centered instruction, 391–402
  active responding and understanding, 396
  directions, explanations, and examples, 394
  giving feedback to students, 396–397
  independent activities, 398, 399–400, 401
  lesson goals and objectives, 392–393
  practice activities, 394–394
  prerequisite skills, 393
  summarizing main points and evaluating mastery, 398, 401–402
  task analysis, 394
Teacher-made tests, 515–521
Teachers. *See also* General educators; Special educators
  attitudes toward inclusion, 38–39
  beginning, 183
  certification, 182, 183n, 184n
  desk, 324
  expectations for students, 216
  feedback to students, 217
  and IEP, 64–65
  impact of inclusion on, 38–40
  language and interactions, 216–217, 219, 226

mentoring, 182, 183
perceptions of inclusion program, 532–537
personal interest in students, 298–299
prompting, 420
proximity and movement, 304
Teaching
alternative, 168, 169
cooperative, 168–175, 175–177, 176–179
parallel, 168, 169
station, 168, 169
team-teaching, 168, 169
Teaching aids, for mathematics instruction, 456–458
Teaching Students to Be Peacemakers program, 302n
Teaching walls, 324
Team-teaching, 168, 169
Teamwork Strategy, 408n
Technical Assistance for Parent Programs, 205n
Technical Education Research Center, 486
Technology
advances in, 17–18
communications with families, 200–203
fostering acceptance and friendships, 239–240
for literacy instruction, 448–449
making group instruction accessible, 410–411
for mathematics, science, and social studies instruction, 487–489
portfolio assessment, 509, 511
supporting student learning and behavior, 327
supporting successful transitions, 276–277
Technology-based testing, 505–506
Technology-Related Assistance for Individuals with Disabilities Act, 17
Tele-Braille, 373
Telecommunication Devices for the Deaf (TDD), 373
Teleconferencing, 192
Telegraphic period of second language learning, 125
Telesensory Systems, 458
Teletypewriters, 373
Television, captioned, 367

Ten Commandments of Communicating with People with Disabilities, The, 240
Testing accommodations, 498–500, 501
Test Pilot, 505
Tests
teacher-made, 515–521
technology-based, 505–506
translations of, 501
Test-study-test procedures, 444–445
Test-taking skills, 501–502, 503–504
Textbook activity guides, 474
Textbooks, 467–469, 474, 487, 488
Text comprehension
reading instruction, 422, 424–426
student-directed, 350–353
teacher-directed, 347–349
Text phones, 373
TGD (tactile graphics display), 372
Think-aloud techniques, 521
Thinking
creative, 301
critical, 353
divergent, 359
Think-Pair-Share, 381
3-Steps, 313
Tic Code, The, 222
Tiered assignments, 340
Time, cross-cultural differences in, 296
Timelines, 385, 387
Time sampling, 291, 292–293
Timothy W. v. Rochester, N.H. School District (1989), 20
Token economy system, 316–317
Tonic-clonic seizure, 91
Tonic seizure, 91
Topic sentences, 350
Total communication, 102
Totally blind students, 103
Total physical response (TPR), 361
Touch screens, 371
Tourette syndrome, 89, 90
Tourette Syndrome Plus, 239
TOWER strategy, 434n
TPR (total physical response), 361
Trace R & D Center, 18
Trace trailing, 328
Tracking, 20
Trackstar, 368n
Transenvironmental programming, 251–260
environmental assessment, 251, 252, 253

generalization, 259–260, 261–262, 263
intervention and preparation, 251, 252, 254–259
Transformation approach to multicultural curriculum, 358
Transgendered parents, 145
Transgendered students, 138–141
Transitional models, adapting, 262–264
Transitional program planning, 260, 262
Transitions
to adulthood, 267–273
for culturally and linguistically diverse students, 264–267
to general education, 249, 250–260, 264–267
during school day, 305–306
from specialized schools and preschool programs, 260, 262–264
videos for, 249, 276
Transition services, 59–60
Translations of English-language tests, 501
Translators, 199
Traumatic brain injury (TBI), 93–96
Travel aids, electronic, 373
TRAVEL learning strategy, 349n, 478n
TREE learning strategy, 440n
True-false test items, 517, 520
Trust, of families, 186–187
Try Science, 487
Two-tiered testing system, 519
Two-way bilingual education programs, 120
Two-way notebooks, 199
Type size, of printed materials, 355
Typographic design, of printed materials, 355–356

UADD (undifferentiated attention deficit disorder), 77
UDL (universal design for learning), 340–342, 505
Underlining, 355
Understanding, checking for, 395–396
Undifferentiated attention deficit disorder (UADD), 77
UnitedStreaming, 489
Universal design for learning (UDL), 340–342, 505
University of Wisconsin at Madison, 18
Urban poverty, 112–113

VANGuard, 506
Verbal cues, 385

Verbal-linguistic intelligence, 131
Verbal rehearsal, 353
Verve, 360
Video Guide to (Dis)Ability Awareness, A, 240
Video observations, 203
Videos
　for acceptance and friendships, 240, 240
　as attitude change strategy, 223
　in differentiated instruction, 364, 366–367
　for text comprehension, 357
　for transitions, 249, 276
Vietnam War lesson, 374
Violent behaviors, 322–323
Virtual field trips, 487
Virtual reality, 276, 327, 367–368
Virtual Volunteering Project, 276
Visual design, of printed materials, 355–356
Visual disability, 103
Visual imagery, 353
Visual impairments, students with, 103–104
　assistive devices, 371–373, 410
　classroom design, 326, 328
　communicating with, 242
　differentiated instruction, 335–336, 345
　individualized education program, 54
　mathematics, science, and social studies instruction, 487, 489
　science and social studies instruction, 484
　simulations, 220
　testing accommodations, 499
　word processing, 440
Visual learners, 445
Visual prompts, 397, 420

Visuals, in mathematics instruction, 457
Visual-spatial intelligence, 131
Vocabulary, 362–363, 424, 424–425
Vocabulary picture cards, 485
Vocational educators, 160
Voice disorders, 81
Voice recognition technology, 370, 371, 370, 440–441
Volunteer/Match, 276
Vowel Alert Strategy, 419

Wealthy children, 117
Web-Braille, 487
Web Cam Directory, 489
Web Cams, 489
Weblogs, 200, 369
WebQuests, 240, 336, 370
Website evaluation guidelines, 369
What Do You See When You See a Blind Person?, 240
Wheelchairs
　assistive devices for, 371
　and classroom environment, 328, 329
　communicating with students using, 242
　guidelines for, 88n
　positioning techniques, 329
　transferring students using, 330
　and virtual reality, 327
Whole language approach to reading instruction, 428
Whole word approaches
　to reading instruction, 428
　to spelling instruction, 444–445
Whose Future Is It Anyway? (Wehmeyer & Lawrence), 283
Who's in the Family? (Skutch), 145
Widgets, 364
Williams syndrome, 80

Wonderful Problems of Fizz and Martina, The, 458
Word cueing programs, 442
Word flashcard drills, 419
Word identification skills, 419–420
Word prediction programs, 442
Word problems, in mathematics instruction, 459–462
Word processing, 440–441
Word study techniques, 445
Work-study diplomas, 523
World Volunteer Web, 276
Wraparound planning, 75, 158
WRITER strategy, 434n
Writers' Workshop, 437
Writing
　difficulties in, 71
　drafting phase, 432, 433–434
　editing and revising phase, 432, 434–438
　planning/prewriting phase, 431–433
　publishing phase, 432, 438
　rubric for, 513
Writing instruction, 429–443
　computer-supported writing applications, 440–443
　feedback, 438–439
　integrating into curriculum, 429–430
　journals, 431
　learning strategies, 439
　process-oriented approach, 431–438
Written assignment structure, 257
Written communication with families, 197–200
Wrong-only feedback, 397

Zero reject principle, 25
Zipper (Janover), 79
ZooAllergy (Gosselin), 88